FEMINISM IN LITERATURE

A Gale Critical Companion

FEMINISM IN LITERATURE

A Gale Critical Companion

Volume 5: 20th Century, Authors (A-G)

Foreword by *Amy Hudock, Ph.D.*
University of South Carolina

Jessica Bomarito, Jeffrey W. Hunter, Project Editors

THOMSON
GALE

Detroit • New York • San Francisco • San Diego • New Haven, Conn. • Waterville, Maine • London • Munich

THOMSON

GALE

Feminism in Literature, Vol. 5

Project Editors
Jessica Bomarito, Jeffrey W. Hunter

Editorial
Tom Burns, Jenny Cromie, Kathy D. Darrow, Michelle Kazensky, Jelena O. Krstović, Michael L. LaBlanc, Julie Landelius, Michelle Lee, Allison McClintic Marion, Ellen McGeagh, Joseph Palmisano, Linda Pavlovski, James E. Person Jr., Thomas J. Schoenberg, Marie Toft, Lawrence J. Trudeau, Russel Whitaker

Indexing Services
Synapse, the Knowledge Link Corporation

Permissions
Emma Hull, Lori Hines, Shalice Shah-Caldwell

Imaging and Multimedia
Lezlie Light, Daniel Newell, Kelly A. Quin

Product Design
Michael Logusz, Pamela Galbreath

Composition and Electronic Capture
Carolyn Roney

Manufacturing
Rhonda Williams

Product Manager
Janet Witalec

This publication is a creative work fully protected by all applicable copyright laws, as well as by misappropriation, trade secret, unfair competition, and other applicable laws. The authors and editors of this work have added value to the underlying factual material herein through one or more of the following: unique and original selection, coordination, expression, arrangement, and classification of the information.

For permission to use material from the product, submit your request via the Web at http://www.gale-edit.com/permissions, or you may download our Permissions Request form and submit your request by fax or mail to:

Permisssions Department
Thomson Gale
27500 Drake Rd.
Farmington Hills, MI 48331-3535
Permissions Hotline:
248-699-8006 or 800-877-4253, ext. 8006
Fax 248-699-8074 or 800-762-4058

Cover photograph reproduced by permission of Corbis (portrait of Charlotte Perkins Gilman).

Since this page cannot legibly accommodate all copyright notices, the acknowledgments constitute an extension of the copyright notice.

While every effort has been made to secure permission to reprint material and to ensure the reliability of the information presented in this publication, Thomson Gale neither guarantees the accuracy of the data contained herein nor assumes any responsibility for errors, omissions or discrepancies. Thomson Gale accepts no payment for listing; and inclusion in the publication of any organization, agency, institution, publication, service, or individual does not imply endorsement of the editors or publisher. Errors brought to the attention of the publisher and verified to the satisfaction of the publisher will be corrected in future editions.

LIBRARY OF CONGRESS CATALOGING-IN-PUBLICATION DATA

Feminism in literature : a Gale critical companion / foreword by Amy Hudock ; Jessica Bomarito, project editor, Jeffrey W. Hunter, project editor.
    p. cm. -- (Gale critical companion collection)
Includes bibliographical references and index.
    ISBN 0-7876-7573-3 (set hardcover : alk. paper) -- ISBN 0-7876-7574-1 (vol 1) -- ISBN 0-7876-7575-X (vol 2) -- ISBN 0-7876-7576-8 (vol 3) -- ISBN 0-7876-9115-1 (vol 4) -- ISBN 0-7876-9116-X (vol 5) -- ISBN 0-7876-9065-1 (vol 6)
    1. Literature--Women authors--History and criticism. 2. Women authors--Biography. 3. Women--History. I. Bomarito, Jessica, 1975- II. Hunter, Jeffrey W., 1966- III. Series.
    PN471.F43 2005
    809'.89287--dc22
                                      2004017989

Printed in the United States of America
10 9 8 7 6 5 4 3 2

CONTENTS

VOLUME 2

VOLUME 3

VOLUME 4

VOLUME 5

Anna Akhmatova 1889-1966
Russian poet, essayist, and translator

Isabel Allende 1942-
Chilean novelist, essayist, journalist, short
story writer, memoirist, playwright, and
juvenile fiction writer

Virginia Woolf 1882-1941

English novelist, critic, essayist, short story
writer, diarist, autobiographer, and
biographer

When I was a girl, I would go to the library with my class, and all the girls would run to the Nancy Drew books, while the boys would head toward the Hardy Boys books—each group drawn to heroes that resembled themselves. Yet, when I entered formal literary studies in high school and college, I was told that I should not read so much in the girls' section any more, that the boys' section held books that were more literary, more universal, and more valuable. Teachers and professors told me this in such seemingly objective language that I never questioned it. At the time, the literary canon was built on a model of scarcity that claimed that only a few literary works could attain "greatness"—defined according to a supposed objective set of aesthetic criteria that more often than not excluded women authors. New Criticism, a way of reading texts that focuses on a poem, short story, or novel as an autonomous artistic production without connections to the historical and social conditions out of which it came, ruled my classrooms, making the author's gender ostensibly irrelevant. Masculine experience was coded as universal, while women's experience was particular. Overall, I had no reason to question the values I had been taught, until I encountered feminism.

Feminism, sometimes put in the plural *feminisms*, is a loose confederation of social, political, spiritual, and intellectual movements that places women and gender at the center of inquiry with the goal of social justice. When people in the United States speak of feminism, they are often referring to the mainstream liberal feminism that grew out of the relationship between grassroots civil rights movements of the 1960s and 1970s and these movements' entrance into the academy through the creation of Women's Studies as an interdisciplinary program of study in many colleges and universities. Mainstream liberal feminism helped many women achieve more equity in pay and access to a wider range of careers while it also transformed many academic disciplines to reflect women's achievements. However, liberal feminism quickly came under attack as largely a movement of white, heterosexual, university-educated, middle-class women who were simply trying to gain access to the same privileges that white, middle-class men enjoyed, and who assumed their experiences were the norm for a mythical universal "woman." Liberal feminists have also been critiqued for echoing the patriarchal devaluation of traditional women's nurturing work in their efforts to encourage women to pursue traditional men's work, for creating a false opposition between work and home, and for creating the superwoman stereotype that can cause women to believe they have failed if they do not achieve the perfect balance of work and home lives. Other feminisms developed representing other women and other modes of thought: Marxist, psychoanalytic, social/radical, lesbian, trans- and bi-sexual, black womanist, first nations, chicana, nonwestern, postcolonial, and approaches that even question the use of "woman" as a unifying signifier in the first place. As Women's Studies and these many feminims gained power and credibility in the academy, their presence forced the literary establishment to question its methodology, definitions, structures, philosophies, aesthetics, and visions as well at to alter the curriculum to reflect women's achievements.

Once I learned from Women's Studies that women mattered in the academy, I began exploring women in my own field of literary studies. Since male-authored texts were often the only works taught in my classes, I began to explore the images of women as constructed by male authors. Many other women writers also began their critique of women's place in society studying similar sites of representation. Mary Wollstonecraft's *A Vindication of the Rights of Women* (1792), Margaret Fuller's *Woman in the Nineteenth Century* (1845), Simone de Beauvoir's *The Second Sex* (1949), and Kate Millet's *Sexual Politics* (1969) explored how published images of women can serve as a means of social manipulation and control—a type of gender propaganda.

However, I began to find, as did others, that looking at women largely through male eyes did not do enough to reclaim women's voices and did not recognize women's agency in creating images of themselves. In *Sexual/Textual Politics* (1985), Toril Moi further questioned the limited natures of these early critical readings, even when including both male and female authors. She argued that reading literature for the accuracy of images of women led critics into assuming their own sense of reality as universal: "If the women in the book feel real to me, then the book is good." This kind of criticism never develops or changes, she argued, because it looks for the same elements repetitively, just in new texts. Also, she was disturbed by its focus on content rather than on how the text is written—the form, language, and literary elements. Moi and others argued for the development of new feminist critical methods.

However, examination of images of women over time has been fruitful. It has shown us that representation of women changes as historical forces change, that we must examine the historical influences on the creators of literary texts to understand the images they manufacture, and that we cannot assume that these images of women are universal and somehow separate from political and culture forces. These early explorations of woman as image also led to discussions of

femininity as image, not biologically but culturally defined, thus allowing analysis of the feminine ideal as separate from real women. This separation of biological sex and socially constructed gender laid the foundation for the later work of Judith Butler in *Gender Trouble: Feminism and the Subversion of Identity* (1990) and Marjorie Garber's *Vested Interests: Cross Dressing and Cultural Anxiety* (1992) in questioning what IS this thing we call "woman." These critics argued that gender is a social construct, a performance that can be learned by people who are biologically male, female, or transgendered, and therefore should not be used as the only essential connecting element in feminist studies. The study of woman and gender as image then has contributed much to feminist literary studies.

Tired of reading almost exclusively texts by men and a small emerging canon of women writers, I wanted to expand my understanding of writing by women. As a new Ph. D. student at the University of South Carolina in 1989, I walked up the stairs into the Women's Studies program and asked the first person I saw one question: were there any nineteenth-century American women writers who are worth reading? I had recently been told there were not, but I was no longer satisfied with this answer. And I found I was right to be skeptical. The woman I met at the top of those stairs handed me a thick book and said, "Go home and read this. Then you tell me if there were any nineteenth-century American women writers who are worth reading." So, I did. The book was the *Norton Anthology of Literature by Women* (1985), and once I had read it, I came back to the office at the top of the stairs and asked, "What more do you have?" My search for literary women began here, and this journey into new terrain parallels the development of the relationship between western feminism and literary studies.

In *A Room of Her Own* (1929), Virginia Woolf asks the same questions. She sits, looking at her bookshelves, thinking about the women writers who are there, and the ones who are not, and she calls for a reclaiming and celebrating of lost women artists. Other writers answered her call. Patricia Meyer Spacks's *The Female Imagination: A Literary and Psychological Investigation of Women's Writing* (1972), Ellen Moers's *Literary Women: The Great Writers* (1976), Elaine Showalter's *A Literature of Their Own: British Women Novelists from Brontë to Lessing* (1977), and Sandra Gilbert and Susan Gubar's *The Madwoman in the Attic* (1979) are a few of the early critical studies that explored the possibility of a tradition in women's literature.

While each of these influential and important books has different goals, methods, and theories, they share the attempt to establish a tradition in women's literature, a vital means through which marginalized groups establish a community identity and move from invisibility to visibility. These literary scholars and others worked to republish and reclaim women authors, expanding the number and types of women-authored texts available to readers, students, and scholars.

Yet, I began to notice that tradition formation presented some problems. As Marjorie Stone pointed out in her essay "The Search for a Lost Atlantis" (2003), the search for women's traditions in language and literature has been envisioned as the quest for a lost continent, a mythical motherland, similar to the lost but hopefully recoverable Atlantis. Such a quest tends to search for similarities among writers to attempt to prove the tradition existed, but this can sometimes obscure the differences among women writers. Looking to establish a tradition can also shape what is actually "found": only texts that fit that tradition. Traditions are defined by what is left in and what is left out, and the grand narratives of tradition formation as constructed in the early phases of feminist literary criticism inadvertently mirrored the exclusionary structures of the canon they were revising.

Some critics began discussing a women's tradition, a lost motherland of language, in not only what was written but also how it was written: in a female language or *ecriture feminine*. Feminist thinkers writing in France such as Hélène Cixous, Julia Kristeva, and Luce Irigaray argued that gender shapes language and that language shapes gender. Basing their ideas on those of psychoanalyst Jacques Lacan, they argued that pre-oedipal language—the original mother language—was lost when the law and language of the fathers asserted itself. While each of these writers explored this language differently, they all rewrote and revisioned how we might talk about literature, thus offering us new models for scholarship. However, as Alicia Ostriker argued in her essay, "Notes on 'Listen'" (2003), for the most part, women teach children language at home and at school. So, she questioned, is language really male and the "the language of the father," or is it the formal discourse of the academy that is male? Ostriker and others question the primacy of the father as the main social/language influence in these discussions. Other critics attacked what came to be known as "French Feminism" for its ahistorical, essentializing approach to finding a women's

tradition in language. Despite its problems, it offered much to the general understanding of gender and language and helped us imagine new possible forms for scholarship.

The idea that language might be gendered itself raised questions about how aesthetic judgement, defined in language, might also be gendered. Problems with how to judge what is "good" literature also arose, and feminist literary critics were accused of imposing a limited standard because much of what was being recovered looked the same in form as the traditional male canon, only written by women. Early recovered texts tended to highlight women in opposition to family, holding more modern liberal political views, and living nontraditional lives. If a text was "feminist" enough, it was included. Often times, this approach valued content over form, and the forms that were included did not differ much from the canon they were reacting against. These critics were still using the model of scarcity with a similar set of critical lens through which to judge texts worthy of inclusion. However, because later scholars started creating different critical lenses through which to view texts does not mean we need to perceive difference as inequality. Rather, texts that differ greatly began to be valued equally for different reasons. In order to do this, critics had to forfeit their tendency to place literary forms on a hierarchical model that allows only one at the apex. Instead, they exchanged the structure of value from one pyramid with a few writers at the apex for one with multiple high points, a model which celebrates a diversity of voices, styles, and forms. The model functioning in many past critical dialogues allowed for little diversity, privileging one type of literature—western, male, linear, logical, structured according to an accepted formula—over others—created by women and men who fail to fit the formula, and, thus, are judged not worthy. Creating hierarchies of value which privilege one discourse, predominantly Anglo male, over another, largely female, non-Anglo, and nonwestern undermines the supposed "impartiality" of critical standards. Breaking down the structure of canon formation that looks for the "great men" and "great women" of literature and instead studies what was actually written, then judging it on its own terms, has the potential for less bias. Challenging the existence of the canon itself allows more writers to be read and heard; perhaps we can base our understanding of literature not on a model of scarcity where only a few great ones are allowed at the top of the one peak, but where there are multiple peaks.

Another problem is that the tradition that was being recovered tended to look most like the critics who were establishing it. Barbara Smith's essay "Toward a Black Feminist Criticism" (1977) and bell hooks's *Ain't I a Woman? Black Women and Feminism* (1981) argued that academic feminism focused on the lives, conditions, histories, and texts of white, middle-class, educated women. Such writers revealed how the same methods of canon formation that excluded women were now being used by white feminists to exclude women of color. They also highlighted the silencing of black women by white women through the assumption that white womanhood was the norm. These writers and others changed the quest for one lost Atlantis to a quest for many lost continents as anthologies of African American, Chicana, Native American, Asian, Jewish, lesbian, mothers, and many more women writers grouped together by identity began to emerge. *This Bridge Called My Back: Writings by Radical Women of Color* (1981), edited by Ana Castillo and Cherríe Moraga, is one such collection. Yet, while these and other writers looked for new traditions of women's writing by the identity politics of the 1980s and 1990s, they were still imposing the same structures of tradition formation on new groups of women writers, still looking for the lost Atlantis.

Western feminist critics also began looking for the lost Atlantis on a global scale. Critiques from non-western critics and writers about their exclusion from feminist literary histories that claimed to represent world feminisms is bringing about the same pattern of starting with an exploration of image, moving to recovery of writers and traditions, then a questioning of recovery efforts that we have seen before. Now, however, all these stages are occurring at the once. For example, American feminist critics are still attempting to make global primary texts available in English so they can be studied and included at the same time they are being critiqued for doing so. Chandra Talpade Mohanty in "Under Western Eyes: Feminist Scholarship and Colonial Discourses" (1991) argues that systems of oppression do not affect us all equally, and to isolate gender as the primary source of oppression ignores the differing and complex webs of oppressions non-western women face. Western tendencies to view non-western women as suffering from a totalizing and undifferentiated oppression similar to their own "universal" female oppression cause feminist literary critics to impose structures of meaning onto non-western texts that fail to reflect the actual cultures and experiences of the writers. Therefore, to simply add the women from non-western literary traditions into existing western timelines, categories, and periodizations may not fully reflect the complexity of non-western writing. In fact, critics such as Gayatri Chakravorty Spivak, Ann DuCille, and Teresa Ebert argue post-colonial and transnational critics have created yet another master narrative that must be challenged. Yet, before the westernness of this new, transnational narrative can be addressed, critics need to be able read, discuss, and share the global texts that are now being translated and published before we can do anything else; therefore, this reclaiming and celebration of a global women's tradition is a necessary step in the process of transforming the very foundations of western feminist literary criticism. But it is only an early step in the continual speak, react, revise pattern of feminist scholarship.

Some critics argue that the ultimate goal of feminist literary history should be to move beyond using gender as the central, essential criteria—to give up looking for only a woman's isolated traditions and to examine gender as one of many elements. In that way, we could better examine female-authored texts in relationship with male-authored texts, and, thus, end the tendency to examine texts by women as either in opposition to the dominant discourse or as co-opted by it. As Kathryn R. King argues in her essay "Cowley Among the Women; or, Poetry in the Contact Zone" (2003), women writers, like male writers, did not write in a vacuum or only in relationship to other women writers. King argues for a more complex method of examining literary influence, and she holds up Mary Louise Pratt's discussion of the contact zone in *Imperial Eyes: Travel Writing and Transculturation* (1992) as a potential model for exploring the web of textual relationships that influence women writers. Pratt argues that the relationship between the colonized and the colonizer, though inflected by unequal power, often creates influence that works both ways (the contact zone). Using Pratt's idea of mutual influence and cultural hybridity allows, King argues, women's literary history to be better grounded in social, historical, philosophical, and religious traditions that influenced the texts of women writers.

So, what has feminism taught me about literary studies? That it is not "artistic value" or "universal themes" that keeps authors' works alive. Professors decide which authors and themes are going to "count" by teaching them, writing scholarly books and articles on them, and by making sure they appear in dictionaries of literary biography, bibliographies, and in the grand narratives of literary history. Reviewers decide who gets attention by reviewing them. Editors and publishers decide who gets read by keeping them in print. And librarians decide what books to buy and to keep on the shelves. Like the ancient storytellers who passed on the tribes' history from generation to generation, these groups keep our cultural memory. Therefore, we gatekeepers, who are biased humans living in and shaped by the intellectual, cultural, and aesthetic paradigms of an actual historical period must constantly reassess our methods, theories, and techniques, continually examining how our own ethnicities, classes, genders, nationalities, and sexualities mold our critical judgements.

What has literary studies taught me about feminism? That being gendered is a text that can be read, interpreted, manipulated, and altered. That feminisms themselves are texts written by real people in actual historical situations, and that feminists, too, must always recognize our own biases, and let others recognize them. That feminism is forever growing and changing and reinventing itself in a continual cycle of statement, reaction, and revision. As the definitions and goals of feminisms change before my eyes, I have learned that feminism is a process, its meaning constantly deferred.

—Amy Hudock, Ph.D.
University of South Carolina

The Gale Critical Companion Collection

In response to a growing demand for relevant criticism and interpretation of perennial topics and important literary movements throughout history, the Gale Critical Companion Collection (GCCC) was designed to meet the research needs of upper high school and undergraduate students. Each edition of GCCC focuses on a different literary movement or topic of broad interest to students of literature, history, multicultural studies, humanities, foreign language studies, and other subject areas. Topics covered are based on feedback from a standing advisory board consisting of reference librarians and subject specialists from public, academic, and school library systems.

The GCCC is designed to complement Gale's existing Literary Criticism Series (LCS) , which includes such award-winning and distinguished titles as *Nineteenth-Century Literature Criticism* (*NCLC*), *Twentieth-Century Literary Criticism* (*TCLC*), and *Contemporary Literary Criticism* (*CLC*). Like the LCS titles, the GCCC editions provide selected reprinted essays that offer an inclusive range of critical and scholarly response to authors and topics widely studied in high school and undergraduate classes; however, the GCCC also includes primary source documents, chronologies, sidebars, supplemental photographs, and other material not included in the LCS products. The graphic and supplemental material is designed to extend the usefulness of the critical essays and provide students with historical and cultural context on a topic or author's work. GCCC titles will benefit larger institutions with ongoing subscriptions to Gale's LCS products as well as smaller libraries and school systems with less extensive reference collections. Each edition of the GCCC is created as a stand-alone set providing a wealth of information on the topic or movement. Importantly, the overlap between the GCCC and LCS titles is 15% or less, ensuring that LCS subscribers will not duplicate resources in their collection.

Editions within the GCCC are either single-volume or multi-volume sets, depending on the nature and scope of the topic being covered. Topic entries and author entries are treated separately, with entries on related topics appearing first, followed by author entries in an A-Z arrangement. Each volume is approximately 500 pages in length and includes approximately 50 images and sidebar graphics. These sidebars include summaries of important historical events, newspaper clippings, brief biographies of important figures, complete poems or passages of fiction written by the author, descriptions of events in the related arts (music, visual arts, and dance), and so on.

The reprinted essays in each GCCC edition explicate the major themes and literary techniques of the authors and literary works. It is important to note that approximately 85% of the essays reprinted in GCCC editions are full-text, meaning that they are reprinted in their entirety, including footnotes and lists of abbreviations. Essays are selected based on their coverage of the seminal works and themes of an author, and based on the importance of those essays to an appreciation of the author's contribution to the movement and to literature in general. Gale's editors select those essays of most value to upper high school and undergraduate students, avoiding narrow and highly pedantic interpretations of individual works or of an author's canon.

Scope of Feminism in Literature

Feminism in Literature, the third set in the Gale Critical Companion Collection, consists of six volumes. Each volume includes a detailed table of contents, a foreword on the subject of feminism in literature written by noted scholar Amy Hudock, and a descriptive chronology of key events throughout the history of women's writing. Volume 1 focuses on feminism in literature from antiquity through the 18th century. It consists of three topic entries, including Women and Women's Writings from Classical Antiquity through the Middle Ages, and seven author entries on such women writers from this time period as Christine de Pizan, Sappho, and Mary Wollstonecraft. Volumes 2 and 3 focus on the 19th century. Volume 2 includes such topic entries as United States Women's Suffrage Movement in the 19th Century, as well as author entries on Jane Austen, Charlotte Brontë, and Elizabeth Barrett Browning. Volume 3 contains additional author entries on figures of the 19th century, including such notables as Kate Chopin, Emily Dickinson, and Harriet Beecher Stowe. Volumes 4, 5, and 6 focus on the 20th century to the present day; volume 4 includes coverage of topics relevant to feminism in literature during the 20th century and early 21st century, including the Feminist Movement, and volumes 5 and 6 include author entries on such figures as Margaret Atwood, Charlotte Perkins Gilman, Sylvia Plath, and Virginia Woolf.

Organization of Feminism in Literature

A *Feminism in Literature* topic entry consists of the following elements:

- The **Introduction** defines the subject of the entry and provides social and historical information important to understanding the criticism.
- The list of **Representative Works** identifies writings and works by authors and figures associated with the subject. The list is divided into alphabetical sections by name; works listed under each name appear in chronologi-

cal order. The genre and publication date of each work is given. Unless otherwise indicated, dramas are dated by first performance, not first publication.

- Entries generally begin with a section of **Primary Sources**, which includes essays, speeches, social history, newspaper accounts and other materials that were produced during the time covered.
- Reprinted **Criticism** in topic entries is arranged thematically. Topic entries commonly begin with general surveys of the subject or essays providing historical or background information, followed by essays that develop particular aspects of the topic. Each section has a separate title heading and is identified with a page number in the table of contents. The critic's name and the date of composition or publication of the critical work are given at the beginning of each piece of criticism. Unsigned criticism is preceded by the title of the source in which it appeared. Footnotes are reprinted at the end of each essay or excerpt. In the case of excerpted criticism, only those footnotes that pertain to the excerpted texts are included.
- A complete **Bibliographical Citation** of the original essay or book precedes each piece of criticism.
- Critical essays are prefaced by brief **Annotations** explicating each piece. Unless the descriptor "excerpt" is used in the annotation, the essay is being reprinted in its entirety.
- An annotated bibliography of **Further Reading** appears at the end of each entry and suggests resources for additional study. In some cases, significant essays for which the editors could not obtain reprint rights are included here.

A *Feminism in Literature* author entry consists of the following elements:

- The **Author Heading** cites the name under which the author most commonly wrote, followed by birth and death dates. Also located here are any name variations under which an author wrote. If the author wrote consistently under a pseudonym, the pseudonym will be listed in the author heading and the author's actual name given in parentheses on the first line of the biographical and critical information. Uncertain birth or death dates are indicated by question marks.
- A **Portrait of the Author** is included when available.
- The **Introduction** contains background infor-

mation that introduces the reader to the author that is the subject of the entry.

- The list of **Principal Works** is ordered chronologically by date of first publication and lists the most important works by the author. The genre and publication date of each work is given. Unless otherwise indicated, dramas are dated by first performance, not first publication.

- Author entries are arranged into three sections: **Primary Sources, General Commentary,** and **Title Commentary.** The Primary Sources section includes letters, poems, short stories, journal entries, novel excerpts, and essays written by the featured author. General Commentary includes overviews of the author's career and general studies; Title Commentary includes in-depth analyses of seminal works by the author. Within the Title Commentary section, the reprinted criticism is further organized by title, then by date of publication. The critic's name and the date of composition or publication of the critical work are given at the beginning of each piece of criticism. Unsigned criticism is preceded by the title of the source in which it appeared. All titles by the author featured in the text are printed in boldface type. However, not all boldfaced titles are included in the author and subject indexes; only substantial discussions of works are indexed. Footnotes are reprinted at the end of each essay or excerpt. In the case of excerpted criticism, only those footnotes that pertain to the excerpted texts are included.

- A complete **Bibliographical Citation** of the original essay or book precedes each piece of criticism.

- Critical essays are prefaced by brief **Annotations** explicating each piece. Unless the descriptor "excerpt" is used in the annotation, the essay is being reprinted in its entirety.

- An annotated bibliography of **Further Reading** appears at the end of each entry and suggests resources for additional study. In some cases, significant essays for which the editors could not obtain reprint rights are included here. A list of **Other Sources from Gale** follows the further reading section and provides references to other biographical and critical sources on the author in series published by Gale.

Indexes

The **Author Index** lists all of the authors featured in the *Feminism in Literature* set, with references to the main author entries in volumes 1, 2, 3, 5, and 6 as well as commentary on the featured author in other author entries and in the topic volumes. Page references to substantial discussions of the authors appear in boldface. The Author Index also includes birth and death dates and cross references between pseudonyms and actual names, and cross references to other Gale series in which the authors have appeared. A complete list of these sources is found facing the first page of the Author Index.

The **Title Index** alphabetically lists the titles of works written by the authors featured in volumes 1 through 6 and provides page numbers or page ranges where commentary on these titles can be found. Page references to substantial discussions of the titles appear in boldface. English translations of foreign titles and variations of titles are cross-referenced to the title under which a work was originally published. Titles of novels, dramas, nonfiction books, films, and poetry, short story, or essay collections are printed in italics, while individual poems, short stories, and essays are printed in roman type within quotation marks.

The **Subject Index** includes the authors and titles that appear in the Author Index and the Title Index as well as the names of other authors and figures that are discussed in the set, including those covered in sidebars. The Subject Index also lists hundreds of literary terms and topics covered in the criticism. The index provides page numbers or page ranges where subjects are discussed and is fully cross referenced.

Citing Feminism in Literature

When writing papers, students who quote directly from the *FL* set may use the following general format to footnote reprinted criticism. The first example pertains to material drawn from periodicals, the second to material reprinted from books.

Bloom, Harold. " Feminism as the Love of Reading," *Raritan* 14, no. 2 (fall 1994): 29-42; reprinted in *Feminism in Literature: A Gale Critical Companion,* vol. 6, eds. Jessica Bomarito and Jeffrey W. Hunter (Farmington Hills, Mich: Thomson Gale, 2004), 29-42.

Coole, Diana H. "The Origin of Western Thought and the Birth of Misogyny," in *Women in Political Theory: From Ancient Misogyny to Contemporary Feminism* (Brighton, Sussex: Wheatsheaf Books, 1988), 10-28; reprinted in *Feminism in Literature: A Gale Critical Companion,* vol. 1, eds. Jessica Bomarito and Jeffrey W. Hunter (Farmington Hills, Mich: Thomson Gale, 2004), 15-25.

Feminism in Literature *Advisory Board*

The members of the *Feminism in Literature* Advisory Board—reference librarians and subject specialists from public, academic, and school library systems—offered a variety of informed perspectives on both the presentation and content of the *Feminism in Literature* set. Advisory board members assessed and defined such quality issues as the relevance, currency, and usefulness of the author coverage, critical content, and topics included in our product; evaluated the layout, presentation, and general quality of our product; provided feedback on the criteria used for selecting authors and topics covered in our product; identified any gaps in our coverage of authors or topics, recommending authors or topics for inclusion; and analyzed the appropriateness of our content and presentation for various user audiences, such as high school students, undergraduates, graduate students, librarians, and educators.

We wish to thank the advisors for their advice during the development of *Feminism in Literature*.

Suggestions are Welcome

Readers who wish to suggest new features, topics, or authors to appear in future volumes of the Gale Critical Companion Collection, or who have other suggestions or comments are cordially invited to call, write, or fax the Product Manager.

Product Manager, Gale Critical Companion
    Collection
Thomson Gale
27500 Drake Road
Farmington Hills, MI 48331-3535
1-800-347-4253 (GALE)
Fax: 248-699-8054

The editors wish to thank the copyright holders of the excerpted criticism included in this volume and the permissions managers of many book and magazine publishing companies for assisting us in securing reproduction rights. We are also grateful to the staffs of the Detroit Public Library, the Library of Congress, the University of Detroit Mercy Library, Wayne State University Purdy/Kresge Library Complex, and the University of Michigan Libraries for making their resources available to us. Following is a list of the copyright holders who have granted us permission to reproduce material in this edition of *Feminism in Literature*. Every effort has been made to trace copyright, but if omissions have been made, please let us know.

Copyrighted material in Feminism in Literature *was reproduced from the following periodicals:*

African American Review, v. 35, winter, 2001 for "'The Porch Couldn't Talk for Looking': Voice and Vision in *Their Eyes Were Watching God*" by Deborah Clarke; v. 36, 2002 for "Phillis Wheatley's Construction of Otherness and the Rhetoric of Performed Ideology" by Mary McAleer Balkun. Copyright © 2001, 2002 by the respective authors. Both reproduced by permission of the respective authors.—*Agora: An Online Graduate Journal,* v. 1, fall, 2002 for "Virgin Territory: Murasaki Shikibu's Ôigimi Resists the Male" by Valerie Henitiuk. Copyright © 2001-2002 Maximiliaan van Woudenberg. All rights reserved. Reproduced by permission of the author.—*American Literary History,* v. 1, winter, 1989 for "Bio-Political Resistance in Domestic Ideology and *Uncle Tom's Cabin*" by Lora Romero. Copyright © 1989 by Oxford University Press. Reproduced by permission of the publisher and the author.—*American Literature,* v. 53, January, 1982. Copyright © 1982, by Duke University Press. Reproduced by permission.—*The American Scholar,* v. 44, spring, 1975. Copyright © 1975 by the United Chapters of Phi Beta Kappa. Reproduced by permission of Curtis Brown Ltd.—*The Antioch Review,* v. 32, 1973. Copyright © 1973 by the Antioch Review Inc. Reproduced by permission of the Editors.—*Ariel: A Review of International English Literature,* v. 21, January, 1990 for "Female Sexuality in Willa Cather's *O Pioneers!* and the Era of Scientific Sexology: A Dialogue between Frontiers" by C. Susan Wiesenthal; v. 22, October, 1991 for "Margaret Atwood's *Cat's Eye*: Re-Viewing Women in a Postmodern World" by Earl G. Ingersoll. Copyright © 1990, 1991 The Board of Governors, The University of Calgary. Both reproduced by permission of the publisher and the author.—*Atlantis: A Women's Studies Journal,* v. 9, fall, 1983. Copyright © 1983 by *Atlantis.* Reproduced by permission.—*Black American Literature Forum,* v. 24, summer, 1990 for "Singing the Black Mother: Maya Angelou and Autobiographical Continuity" by Mary Jane Lupton. Copyright © 1990 by the author. Reproduced by permission of the author.—*The Book Collector,* v. 31, spring, 1982. Reproduced by permission.—*The CEA Critic,* v. 56, spring/summer, 1994 for "Feminism and Children's Literature: Fitting *Little Women* into the American Literary Canon" by Jill P. May. Copyright © 1994 by the College English Association, Inc. Reproduced by permission of the publisher and the author.—*The Centennial Review,* v. xxix, spring, 1985 for "'An Order of Constancy': Notes on Brooks and the Feminine" by Hortense J. Spillers. Michigan State University Press. Copyright © 1985 by *The Centennial Review.* Reproduced by permission of the publisher.—*Chaucer Review,* v. 37, 2003. Copyright © 2003 by The Pennsylvania State University. All rights reserved. Reproduced by permission.—*Christianity and Literature,* v. 51, spring, 2002. Copyright © 2002 by the Conference on Christianity and Literature. Reproduced by permission.—*CLA Journal,* v. XXXIX, March, 1996. Copyright © 1966 by The College Language Association. Used by permission of The College Language Association.—*Classical Quarterly,* v. 31, 1981 for "Spartan Wives: Liberation or Licence?" by Paul Cartledge. Copyright © 1981 The Classical Association. Reproduced by permission of Oxford University Press and the author.—*Colby Library Quarterly,* v. 21, March, 1986. Reproduced by permission.—*Colby Quarterly,* v. XXVI, September 1990; v. XXXIV, June, 1998. Both reproduced by permission.—*College English,* v. 36, March, 1975 for "Who Buried H. D.?: A Poet, Her Critics, and Her Place in 'The Literary Tradition'" by Susan Friedman. Copyright © 1975 by the National Council of Teachers of English. Reproduced by permission of the publisher and the author.—*Connotations,* v. 5, 1995-96. Copyright © Waxmann Verlag GmbH, Munster/New York 1996. Reproduced by permission.—*Contemporary Literature,* v. 34, winter, 1993. Copyright © 1993 by University of Wisconsin Press. Reproduced by permission.—*Critical Quarterly,* v. 14, autumn, 1972; v. 27, spring, 1985. Copyright © 1972, 1985 by Manchester University Press. Both reproduced by permission of Blackwell Publishers.—*Critical Survey,* v. 14, January, 2002. Copyright © 2002 Berghahn Books, Inc. Reproduced by permission.—*Critique: Studies in Modern Fiction,* v. XV, 1973. Copyright © by *Critique,* 1973. Copyright © 1973 by Helen Dwight Reid Educational Foundation. Reproduced with permission of the Helen Dwight Reid Educational Foundation, published by Heldref Publications, 1319 18th Street, NW, Washington, DC 20036-1802.—*Cultural Critique,* v. 32, winter, 1995-96. Copyright © 1996 by *Cultural Critique.* All rights reserved. Reproduced by permission.—*Denver Quarterly,* v. 18, winter, 1984 for "Becoming Anne Sexton" by Diane Middlebrook. Copyright © 1994 by Diane Middlebrook. Reproduced by permission of Georges Bou-

chardt, Inc. for the author.—*Dissent,* summer, 1987. Copyright © 1987, by Dissent Publishing Corporation. Reproduced by permission.—*The Eighteenth Century,* v. 43, spring, 2002. Copyright © 2002 by Texas Tech University Press. Reproduced by permission.—*Eighteenth-Century Fiction,* v. 3, July, 1991. Copyright © McMaster University 1991. Reproduced by permission.—*Emily Dickinson Journal,* v. 10, 2000. Copyright © 2000 by The Johns Hopkins University Press for the Emily Dickinson International Society. All rights reserved. Reproduced by permission.—*The Emporia State Research Studies,* v. 24, winter, 1976. Reproduced by permission.—*Essays and Studies,* 2002. Copyright © 2002 Boydell & Brewer Inc. Reproduced by permission.—*Essays in Literature,* v. 12, fall, 1985. Copyright © 1985 Western Illinois University. Reproduced by permission.—*Feminist Studies,* v. 6, summer, 1980; v. 25, fall, 1999. Copyright © 1980, 1999 by *Feminist Studies.* Both reproduced by permission of Feminist Studies, Inc., Department of Women's Studies, University of Maryland, College Park, MD 20724.—*French Studies,* v. XLVIII, April, 1994; v. LII, April, 1998. Copyright © 1994, 1998 by The Society for French Studies. Reproduced by permission.—*Frontiers,* v. IX, 1987; v. XIV, 1994. Copyright © The University of Nebraska Press 1987, 1994. Both reproduced by permission.—*Glamour,* v. 88, November 1990 for "Only Daughter" by Sandra Cisneros. Copyright © 1996 by Wendy Martin. All rights reserved. Reproduced by permission of Susan Bergholz Literary Services, New York.—*Harper's Magazine,* for "Women's Work" by Louise Erdrich. Copyright © 1995 by *Harper's Magazine.* All rights reserved. Reproduced from the May edition by special permission.—*History Today,* v. 50, October, 2000; v. 51, November, 2001. Copyright © 2000, 2001 by The H. W. Wilson Company. All rights reserved. Reproduced by permission.—*The Hudson Review,* v. XXXVI, summer, 1983. Copyright © 1983 by The Hudson Review, Inc. Reproduced by permission.—*Hypatia,* v. 5, summer, 1990 for "Is There a Feminist Aesthetic?" by Marilyn French. Copyright by Marilyn French. Reproduced by permission.—*International Fiction Review,* v. 29, 2002. Copyright © 2002. International Fiction Association. Reproduced by permission.—*Irish Studies Review,* spring, 1996 from "History, Gender and the Colonial Movement: Castle Rackrent" by Colin Graham. Reproduced by permission of Taylor & Francis and the author.—*Journal of Evolutionary Psychology,* v. 7, August, 1986. Reproduced by permission.—*Journal of the Midwest Modern Language Association,* v. 35, 2002 for "The Gospel According to Jane Eyre: The Suttee and the Seraglio" by Maryanne C. Ward. Copyright © 2002 by The Midwest Modern Language Association. Reproduced by permission of the publisher and the author.—*Journal of the Short Story in English,* autumn, 2002. Copyright © Université d'Angers, 2002. Reproduced by permission.—*Keats-Shelley Journal,* v. XLVI, 1997. Reproduced by permission.—*Legacy,* v. 6, fall, 1989. Copyright © The University of Nebraska Press 1989. Reproduced by permission.—*The Massachusetts Review,* v. 27, summer, 1986. Reproduced from The Massachusetts Review, The Massachusetts Review, Inc. by permission.—*Meanjin,* v. 38, 1979 for "The Liberated Heroine: New Varieties of Defeat?" by Amanda Lohrey. Copyright © 1979 by *Meanjin.* Reproduced by permission of the author.—*MELUS,* v. 7, fall, 1980; v. 12, fall, 1985; v.18, fall, 1993. Copyright © MELUS: The Society for the Study of Multi-Ethnic Literature of the United States, 1980, 1985, 1993. Reproduced by permission.—*Modern Drama,* v. 21, September, 1978. Copyright © 1978 by the University of Toronto, Graduate Centre for Study of Drama. Reproduced by permission.—*Modern Language Studies,* v. 24, spring, 1994 for "Jewett's Unspeakable Unspoken: Retracing the Female Body Through *The Country of the Pointed Firs*" by George Smith. Copyright © Northeast Modern Language Association 1990. Reproduced by permission of the publisher and author.—*Mosaic,* v. 23, summer, 1990; v. 35, 2002. Copyright © 1990, 2002 by *Mosaic.* All rights reserved. Acknowledgment of previous publication is herewith made.—*Ms.,* v. II, July, 1973 for "Visionary Anger" by Erica Mann Jong; June 1988 for "Changing My Mind About Andrea Dworkin" by Erica Jong. Copyright © 1973, 1988. Both reproduced by permission of the author.—*New Directions for Women,* September-October, 1987 for "Dworkin Critiques Relations Between the Sexes" by Joanne Glasgow. Copyright © 1987 New Directions for Women, Inc., 25 West Fairview Ave., Dover, NJ 07801-3417. Reproduced by permission of the author.—*The New Yorker,* 1978 for "Girl" by Jamaica Kincaid. Copyright © 1979 by Jamaica Kinkaid. All rights reserved. Reproduced by permission of the Wylie Agency; v. 73, February 17, 1997 for "A Society of One: Zora Neal Hurston, American Contrarian" by Claudia Roth Pierpont. Copyright © 1997 by The New Yorker Magazine, Inc. All rights reserved. Reproduced by permission of the author.—*Nineteenth-Century Feminisms,* v. 2, spring-summer, 2000. Reproduced by permission.—*Nineteenth-Century French Studies,* v. 25, spring-summer, 1997. Copyright © 1977 by *Nineteenth-Century French Studies.* Reproduced by permission.—*Novel,* v. 34, spring, 2001. Copyright © NOVEL Corp. 2001. Reproduced with permission.—*Oxford Literary Review,* v. 13, 1991. Copyright © 1991 the *Oxford Literary Review.* All rights reserved. Reproduced by permission.—*P. N. Review,* v. 18, January/February, 1992. Reproduced by permission of Carcanet Press Ltd.—*Papers on Language & Literature,* v. 5, winter, 1969. Copyright © 1969 by The Board of Trustees, Southern Illinois University at Edwardsville. Reproduced by permission.—*Parnassus,* v. 12, fall-winter, 1985 for "Throwing the Scarecrows from the Garden" by Tess Gallagher; v. 12-13, 1985 for "Adrienne Rich and Lesbian/Feminist Poetry" by Catharine Stimpson. Copyright © 1985, 1986 by Poetry in Review Foundation. Both reproduced by permission of the publisher and the respective authors.—*Philological Papers,* v. 38, 1992. Copyright © 1992 by *Philological Papers.* Reproduced by permission.—*Philological Quarterly,* v. 79, winter, 2000. Copyright © 2001 by the University of Iowa. Reproduced by permission.—*Quadrant,* v. 46, November, 2002 for "The Mirror of Honour and Love: A Woman's View of Chivalry" by Sophie Masson. Copyright © 2002 Quadrant Magazine Company, Inc. Reproduced by permission of the publisher and the author.—*Raritan,* v. 14, fall, 1994. Copyright © 1994 by *Raritan: A Quarterly Review.* Reproduced by permission.—*Resources for American Literary Study,* v. 22, 1996. Copyright © 1996 by The Pennsylvania State University. Reproduced by permission of The Pennsylvania State University Press.—*Revista Hispánica Moderna,* v. 47, June, 1994. Copyright © 1994 by Hispanic Institute, Columbia University. Reproduced by permission.—*Rhetoric Society Quarterly,* v. 32, winter, 2002. Reproduced by permission of the publisher, conveyed through the Copyright Clearance Center.—*Romanic Review,* v. 79, 1988. Copyright © 1988 by The Trustees of Columbia University in the City of New York. Reproduced by permission.—*The Russian Review,* v. 57, April, 1998. Copyright © 1998 *The Russian Review.* Reproduced by permission of Blackwell Publishers.—*San Jose Studies,* v. VIII, spring, 1982 for "Dea, Awakening: A Reading of H. D.'s *Trilogy*" by Joyce Lorraine Beck. Copyright © 1982 by Trustees of the San Jose State University Foundation. Reproduced by permission of the publisher and the author.—*South Atlantic Review,* v. 66, winter, 2001. Copyright © 2001 by the South Atlantic Modern Language Association. Reproduced by permission.—*Southern Humanities Review,* v. xxii, summer, 1988. Copyright © 1988 by Auburn University. Reproduced by permission.—*The Southern Quarterly,* v. 35, spring, 1997; v. 37, spring-summer, 1999. Copyright © 1997, 1999 by the University of Southern Mississippi. Both reproduced by permission.—*Southern Review,* v. 18, for "Hilda in Egypt" by Albert Gelpi. Reproduced by permission of the author.—*Soviet Literature,* v. 6, June, 1989. Reproduced by permission

ACKNOWLEDGMENTS

of FTM Agency Ltd.—*Studies in American Fiction,* v. 9, autumn, 1981. Copyright © 1981 Northeastern University. Reproduced by permission.—*Studies in American Humor,* v. 3, 1994. Copyright © 1994 American Humor Studies Association. Reproduced by permission.—*Studies in the Humanities,* v. 19, December, 1992. Copyright © 1992 by Indiana University Press of Pennsylvania. Reproduced by permission.—*Studies in the Novel,* v. 31, fall 1999; v. 35, spring, 2003. Copyright © 1999, 2003 by North Texas State University. Reproduced by permission.—*Textual Practice,* v. 13, 1999 for "Speaking Un-likeness: The Double Text in Christina Rossetti's 'After Death' and 'Remember'" by Margaret Reynolds. Copyright © 1999 Routledge. Reproduced by permission of the publisher and the author.—*The Threepenny Review,* 1990 for "Mother Tongue" by Amy Tan. Reproduced by permission.—*Transactions of the American Philological Association,* v. 128, 1998. Copyright © 1998 American Philological Association. Reproduced by permission of The Johns Hopkins University Press.—*Tulsa Studies in Women's Literature,* v. 6, fall, 1987 for "Revolutionary Women" by Betsy Erkkila. Copyright © 1987, The University of Tulsa. All rights reserved. Reproduced by permission of the publisher and the author.—*The Victorian Newsletter,* v. 82, fall, 1992 for "Revisionist Mythmaking in Christina Rossetti's 'Goblin Market': Eve's Apple and Other Questions" by Sylvia Bailey Shurbutt; v. 92, fall, 1997 for "The Poet and the Bible: Christina Rossetti's Feminist Hermeneutics" by Lynda Palazzo; spring, 1998 for "'No Sorrow I Have Thought More About': The Tragic Failure of George Eliot's St. Theresa" by June Skye Szirotny. All reproduced by permission of The Victorian Newsletter and the author.—*Victorians Institute Journal,* v. 13, 1985. Copyright © Victorians Institute Journal 1985. Reproduced by permission.—*Women: A Cultural Review,* v. 10, winter, 1999 from "Consorting with Angels: Anne Sexton and the Art of Confession" by Deryn Rees-Jones. Copyright © 1999, by Taylor & Francis Ltd. Reproduced by permission of the publisher and the author. (http://www.tandf.co.uk/journals).—*Women and Language,* v. 13, March 31, 1995; v. 19, fall, 1996. Copyright © 1995, 1996 by Communication Department at George Mason University. Reproduced by permission of the publisher.—*Women's Studies: An Interdisciplinary Journal,* v. 3, 1975; v. 4, 1976; v. 17, 1990; v. 18, 1990; v. 23, September, 1994; v. 30, 2001. Copyright © 1975, 1976, 1990, 1994, 2001 Gordon and Breach Science Publishers S.A. Reproduced by permission.—*Women's Studies in Communication,* v. 24, spring, 2001. Reproduced by permission.—*Women's Writing,* v. 3, June, 1996. Reproduced by permission of the publisher; v. 4, 1997 for "(Female) Philosophy in the Bedroom: Mary Wollstonecraft and Female Sexuality" by Gary Kelly. Copyright © Triangle Journals Ltd, 1997. All rights reserved. Reproduced by permission of the publisher and the author.—*World & I,* v. 18, March, 2003. Copyright © 2003 News World Communications, Inc. Reproduced by permission.—*World Literature Today,* v. 73, spring, 1999. Copyright © 1999 by the University of Oklahoma Press. Reprinted by permission of the publisher.—*World Literature Written in English,* v. 15, November, 1976 for "Doris Lessing's Feminist Plays" by Agate Nesaule Krouse. Copyright © 1976 by WLWE. Reproduced by permission of the publisher and the author.

Copyrighted material in Feminism in Literature *was reproduced from the following books:*

Acocella, Joan. From *Willa Cather and the Politics of Criticism.* University of Nebraska Press, 2000. Copyright © 2000, by Joan Acocella. All rights reserved. Reproduced by permission.—Aimone, Joseph. From "Millay's Big Book, or the Feminist Formalist as Modern," in *Unmanning Modernism: Gendered Re-Readings.* Edited by Elizabeth Jane Harrison and Shirley Peterson. University of Tennessee Press, 1997. Copyright © 1997 by The University of Tennessee Press. All rights reserved. Reproduced by permission of The University of Tennessee Press.—Allende, Isabel. From "Writing as an Act of Hope," in *Paths of Resistance: The Art and Craft of the Political Novel.* Edited by William Zinsser. Houghton Mifflin Company, 1989. Copyright © 1989 Isabel Allende. Reproduced by permission of the author.—Angelou, Maya. From *And Still I Rise.* Random House, 1978. Copyright © 1978 by Maya Angelou. Reproduced by permission of Random House, Inc. and Time Warner Books UK.—Arenal, Electa. From "The Convent as Catalyst for Autonomy: Two Hispanic Nuns of the Seventeenth Century," in *Women in Hispanic Literature.* Edited by Beth Kurti Miller. University of California Press, 1983. Copyright © 1983 by The Regents of the University of California. Reproduced by permission of the publisher and the author.—Arndt, Walter. From "Introduction: I The Akhmatova Phenomenon and II Rendering the Whole Poem," in *Anna Akhmatova: Selected Poems.* Edited and translated by Walter Arndt. Ardis, 1976. Reproduced by permission.—Atwood, Margaret. From *Second Words.* Anansi Press Limited, 1982. Copyright © 1982, by O. W. Toad Limited. All rights reserved. Reproduced by permission of the author.—Baker, Deborah Lesko. From "Memory, Love, and Inaccessibility in *Hiroshima mon amour*," in *Marguerite*

Duras Lives On. Edited by Janine Ricouart. University Press of America, 1998. Copyright © 1998 University Press of America, Inc. All rights reserved. Reproduced by permission.—Barlow, Judith E. From "Into the Foxhole: Feminism, Realism, and Lillian Hellman," in *Realism and the American Dramatic Tradition.* Edited by William W. Demastes. University of Alabama Press, 1996. Copyright © 1996, The University of Alabama Press. Reproduced by permission.—Barratt, Alexandra. From *Women's Writing in Middle English.* Edited by Alexandra Barratt. Longman Group UK Limited, 1992. Copyright © Longman Group UK Limited 1992. Reproduced by permission.—Barrett Browning, Elizabeth. From "A Letter to Mary Russell Mitford, September 18, 1846," in *Women of Letters: Selected Letters of Elizabeth Barrett Browning and Mary Russell Mitford.* Edited by Meredith B. Raymond and Mary Rose Sullivan. Twayne Publishers, 1987. Reproduced by permission of The Gale Group.—Barrett Browning, Elizabeth. From "Glimpses into My Own Life and Literary Character," in *The Brownings' Correspondence,* Vol. 1. Edited by Phillip Kelley and Ronald Hudson. Wedgestone Press, 1984. All rights reserved. Reproduced by permission of Eton College.—Bassard, Katherine Clay. From *Spiritual Interrogations: Culture, Gender, and Community in Early African American Women's Writing.* Princeton University Press, 1999. Copyright © 1999 by Katherine Clay Bassard. Reproduced by permission of Princeton University Press.—Beauvoir, Simone de. From "The Independent Woman," in *The Second Sex.* Translated by H. M. Parshley. Alfred A. Knopf, Inc., 1952. Copyright © 1952, renewed 1980 by Alfred A. Knopf, Inc. All rights reserved. Reproduced by permission of Alfred A. Knopf, Inc., a division of Random House, Inc. and The Random House Group.—Behrendt, Stephen. From "Mary Shelley, Frankenstein, and the Woman Writer's Fate," in *Romantic Women Writers: Voices and Countervoices.* Edited by Paula R. Feldman and Theresa M. Kelley. University Press of New England, 1995. Copyright © 1995 by University Press of New England. All rights reserved. Reproduced by permission.—Bell, Barbara Currier and Carol Ohmann. From "Virginia Woolf's Criticism: A Polemical Preface," in *Feminist Literary Criticism: Explorations in Theory.* Edited by Josephine Donovan. The University Press of Kentucky, 1989. Copyright © 1975, 1989 by The University Press of Kentucky. Reproduced by permission of The University Press of Kentucky.—Berry, Mary Frances. From *Why ERA Failed: Politics, Women's Rights, and the Amending Process of the Constitution.* Indiana University Press, 1986. Copyright © 1986 by Mary Frances Berry. All rights reserved. Reproduced by permission.—Birgitta of Sweden. From *Life and Selected Revelations.* Edited with a preface by Marguerite Tjader Harris, translation and notes by Albert Ryle Kezel, introduction by Tore Nyberg from *The Classics of Western Spirituality.* Paulist Press, 1990. Copyright © 1990 by the Order of St. Birgitte, Rome. Translation, notes and Foreword copyright © 1990 by Albert Ryle Kezel, New York/Mahwah, NJ. Reproduced by permission of Paulist Press. www.paulistpress.com.—Blundell, Sue. From *Women in Ancient Greece.* British Museum Press, 1995. Copyright © 1995 Sue Blundell. Reproduced by permission of the author.—Bogan, Louise. From *The Blue Estuaries: Poems 1923-1968.* Farrar, Straus & Giroux, Inc., 1968. Copyright © 1968 by Louise Bogan. Copyright renewed 1996 by Ruth Limmer. All rights reserved. Reproduced by permission of Farrar, Straus and Giroux, LLC.—Booth, Alison. From "Not All Men Are Selfish and Cruel," in *Greatness Engendered: George Eliot and Virginia Woolf.* Cornell University Press, 1992. Copyright © 1992 by Cornell University Press. Reproduced by permission of the publisher, Cornell University Press.—Brammer, Leila R. From *Excluded from Suffrage History: Matilda Joslyn Gage, Nineteenth-Century American Feminist.* Greenwood Press, 2000. Copyright © by Leila R. Brammer. All rights reserved. Reproduced by permission of Greenwood Publishing Group, Inc., Westport, CT.—Britzolakis, Christina. From *Sylvia Plath and the Theatre of Mourning.* Oxford at the Clarendon Press, 1999. Copyright © 1999 by Christina Britzolakis. All rights reserved. Reproduced by permission of Oxford University Press.—Broe, Mary Lynn. From "Bohemia Bumps into Calvin: The Deception of Passivity in Lillian Hellman's Drama," in *Critical Essays on Lillian Hellman.* Edited by Mark W. Estrin. G. K. Hall, 1989. Copyright © 1989 by Mark W. Estrin. All rights reserved. Reproduced by permission of The Gale Group.—Brontë, Charlotte. From "Caroline Vernon," in *Legends of Angria: Compiled from The Early Writings of Charlotte Brontë.* Edited by Fannie E. Ratchford. Yale University Press, 1933. Copyright © 1933 by Yale University Press. Renewed 1961 by Fannit Ratchford. Reproduced by permission.—Brooks, Gwendolyn. From *Blacks.* The David Company, 1987. Copyright © 1945, 1949, 1953, 1960, 1963, 1968, 1969, 1970, 1971, 1975, 1981, 1986 by Gwendolyn Brooks Blakely. All rights reserved. Reproduced by consent of Brooks Permissions.—Brown-Grant, Rosalind. From "Christine de Pizan: Feminist Linguist Avant la Lettre?," in *Christine de Pizan 2000: Studies on Christine de Pizan in Honour of Angus J. Kennedy.* Edited by John Campbell and Nadia Margolis. Rodopi, 2000. Copyright © Editions Rodopi B. Reproduced by permission.—Brownmiller,

Susan. From *In Our Time: Memoir of a Revolution*. The Dial Press, 1999. Copyright © 1999, by Susan Brownmiller. All rights reserved. Reproduced by permission of The Dial Press/Dell Publishing, a division of Random House, Inc.—Brügmann, Margret. From "Between the Lines: On the Essayistic Experiments of Hélène Cixous in 'The Laugh of the Medusa'," translated by Debbi Long in *The Politics of the Essay: Feminist Perspectives*. Edited by Ruth-Ellen Boetcher Joeres and Elizabeth Mittman. Indiana University Press, 1993. Copyright © 1993 by Indiana University Press. All rights reserved. Reproduced by permission.—Bunch, Charlotte. From "Women's Human Rights: The Challenges of Global Feminism and Diversity," in *Feminist Locations: Global and Local, Theory and Practice*. Edited by Marianne DeKoven. Rutgers University Press, 2001. Copyright © 2001 by Rutgers, the State University. All rights reserved. Reproduced by permission.—Burke, Sally. From *American Feminist Playwrights: A Critical History*. Twayne, 1996. Copyright © 1996 by Twayne Publishers. All rights reserved. Reproduced by permission of The Gale Group.—Butler-Evans, Elliott. From *Race, Gender, and Desire: Narrative Strategies in the Works of Toni Cade Bambara, Toni Morrison, and Alice Walker*. Temple University Press, 1989. Copyright © 1989, by Temple University. All rights reserved. Reproduced by permission.—Byerman, Keith. From "Gender and Justice: Alice Walker and the Sexual Politics of Civil Rights," in *The World is Our Home: Society and Culture in Contemporary Southern Writing*. Edited by Jeffrey J. Folks and Nancy Summers Folks. The University Press of Kentucky, 2000. Copyright © 2000 by The University Press of Kentucky. Reproduced by permission.—Callaghan, Dympna C. From "The Ideology of Romantic Love," in *The Weyward Sisters: Shakespeare and Feminist Politics*. Edited by Dympna C. Callaghan, Lorraine Helms, and Jyotsna Singh. Blackwell Publishers, 1994. Copyright © Dympna C. Callaghan, Lorraine Helms and Jyotsna Singh 1994. Reproduced by permission of Blackwell Publishers.—Carmody, Denise Lardner. From *Biblical Woman: Contemporary Reflections on Scriptural Texts*. Crossroad Publishing Company, 1988. Copyright © 1988 by Denise Lardner Carmody. All rights reserved. Reproduced by permission of the author.—Castro, Ginette. From *American Feminism: A Contemporary History*. Translated by Elizabeth Loverde-Bagwell. New York University Press, 1990. Copyright © Presses de la Foundation Nationale des Sciences Politiques, Paris, 1990. All rights reserved. Reproduced by permission of New Directions Publishing Corporation and in the UK by Pollinger Limited and the proprietor.—Chadwick, Whitney. From *Women, Art, and Society*. Thames and Hudson, 1990. Copyright © 1990 Thames and Hudson Ltd, London. All rights reserved. Reproduced by permission.—Chafe, William H. From "World War II as a Pivotal Experience for American Women," in *Women and War: The Changing Status of American Women from the 1930s to the 1940s*. Edited by Maria Diedrich and Dorothea Fischer-Horning. Berg, 1990. Copyright © 1990, by Maria Diedrich and Dorothea Fischer-Hornung. All rights reserved Reproduced by permission.—Chesler, Ellen. From *Woman of Valor: Margaret Sanger and the Birth Control Movement in America*. Anchor Books, 1992. Copyright © 1992 by Ellen Chesler. All rights reserved. Reproduced by permission of International Creative Management, Inc.—Cholmeley, Katherine. From *Margery Kempe, Genius and Mystic*. Longmans, Green and Co., 1947. Reproduced by permission.—Christian, Barbara T. From an introduction to *"Everyday Use": Alice Walker*. Edited by Barbara T. Christian. Rutgers University Press, 1994. Copyright © 1994 by Rutgers, The State University. Reproduced by permission of Rutgers, The State University.—Christine de Pizan. From *The Writings of Christine de Pizan*. Translated by Charity Cannon Willard. Persea Books, 1994. Copyright © 1994 by Persea Books, Inc. Reproduced by permission.—Cixous, Hélène. From "The Laugh of the Medusa," in *New French Feminisms: An Anthology*. Edited by Elaine Marks and Isabelle de Courtivron. Essay translated by Keith and Paula Cohen. *Signs*, 1975. All rights reserved. Reproduced by permission of University of Chicago Press and the author.—Conley, Verana Andermatt. From *Hélène Cixous: Writing the Feminine*. University of Nebraska Press, 1984. Copyright © 1984 by University of Nebraska Press. All rights reserved. Reproduced by permission.—Coole, Diana H. From *Women in Political Theory: From Ancient Misogyny to Contemporary Feminism*. Wheatsheaf Books Ltd, 1988. Copyright © Diana Coole, 1988. All rights reserved. Reproduced by permission of the author.—Cooper, Michaela Bruckner. From "Textual Wandering and Anxiety in Margaret Fuller's *Summer on the Lakes*," in *Margaret Fuller's Cultural Critique: Her Age and Legacy*. Edited by Fritz Fleischmann. Peter Lang, 2000. Copyright © 2000 Peter Lang Publishing. All rights reserved. Reproduced by permission.—Cott, Nancy. From "Historical Perspectives: The Equal Rights Amendment Conflict in 1920s," in *Conflicts in Feminism*. Edited by Marianne Hirsch and Evelyn Fox Keller. Routledge, 1990. Copyright © 1990 by Routledge, Chapman and Hall, Inc. All rights reserved. Reproduced by permission of Routledge/Taylor & Francis Books and the author.—Cotton, Nancy. From "Women Playwrights in England," in *Readings in *Renaissance Women's Drama: Criticism, History, and Performance 1594-1998.* Edited by S. P. Cerasano and Marion Wynee-Davies. Bucknell University Press 1981. Reproduced by permission of Associated University Presses and the author.—Coultrap-McQuin, Susan. From *Doing Literary Business: American Women Writers in the Nineteenth Century.* The University of North Carolina Press, 1990. Copyright © 1990 Susan Coultrap-McQuin. All rights reserved. Used by permission of the University of North Carolina Press.—Daly, Brenda. From *Lavish Self-Divisions: The Novels of Joyce Carol Oates.* University Press of Mississippi, 1996. Copyright © 1996 by the University Press of Mississippi. All rights reserved. Reproduced by permission.—Davis, Cynthia J. "What 'Speaks in Us': Margaret Fuller, Woman's Rights, and Human Nature," in *Margaret Fuller's Cultural Critique: Her Age and Legacy.* Edited by Fritz Fleischmann. Peter Lang, 2000. Copyright © 2000 Peter Lang Publishing. All rights reserved. Reproduced by permission.—de Gouges, Olympe. From "The Rights of Women," in *Women in Revolutionary Paris 1789-1795: Selected Documents.* Edited and translated by Daline Gay Levy, Harriet Branson Applewhite, and Mary Durham Johnson. University of Illinois, 1979. Reproduced by permission.—Depla, Annette. From "Women in Ancient Egyptian Wisdom Literature," in *Women in Ancient Societies: An Illusion of the Night.* Edited by Léonie J. Archer, Susan Fischler, and Maria Wyke. Macmillan Press Ltd, 1994. Copyright © The Macmillan Press Ltd 1994. Reproduced with permission of Palgrave Macmillan and Routledge/Taylor & Francis Books, Inc.—Deutsch, Sarah Jane. From "From Ballots to Breadlines: 1920-1940," in *No Small Courage: A History of Women in the United States.* Edited by Nancy F. Cott. Oxford University Press, 2000. Copyright © 2000, by Sarah Jane Deutsch. All rights reserved. Used by permission of Oxford University Press.—Dever, Carolyn. From "Obstructive Behavior: Dykes in the Mainstream of Feminist Theory," in *Cross-Purposes: Lesbians, Feminists, and the Limits of Alliance.* Indiana University Press, 1997. Copyright © 1997, by Indiana University Press. All rights reserved. Reproduced by permission.—Donawerth, Jane. From "Women's Poetry and the Tudor-Stuart System of Gift Exchange," in *Women, Writing, and the Reproduction of Culture in Tudor and Stuart Britain.* Edited by Mary E. Burke, Jane Donawerth, Linda L. Dove, and Karen Nelson. Syracuse University Press, 2002. Reproduced by permission.—Doolittle, Hilda. From *HERmione.* New Directions Publishing, 1981. Copyright © 1981 by the Estate of Hilda Doolittle. Reproduced by permission of New Directions Publishing

Corp.—Douglas, Ann. From *The Feminization of American Culture.* Anchor Press/Doubleday, 1988. Copyright © 1977 by Ann Douglas. Used by permission of Alfred A. Knopf, a division of Random House, Inc.—Driver, Dorothy. From "Reconstructing the Past, Shaping the Future: Bessie Head and the Question of Feminism in a New South Africa," in *Black Women's Writings.* Edited by Gina Wisker. St. Martin's Press, 1993. Copyright © 1993, by Editorial Board, Lumière (Co-operative) Press Ltd. All rights reserved. Reprinted by permission of Palgrave Macmillan.—DuBois, Ellen Carol. From *Remembering Seneca Falls: Honoring the Women Who Paved the Way: An Essay.* Reproduced by permission of the author.—DuBois, Ellen Carol. From "Taking the Law Into Our Own Hands: Bradwell, Minor and Suffrage Militance in the 1870s," in *One Woman, One Vote: Rediscovering the Woman Suffrage Movement.* Edited by Marjorie Spruill Wheeler. NewSage Press, 1995. Copyright © 1995 by NewSage Press and Educational Film Company. All rights reserved. Reproduced by permission.—DuBois, Ellen Carol. From the introduction to *Feminism and Suffrage: The Emergence of An Independent Women's Movement in America.* Cornell University Press, 1978. Copyright © 1978 by Cornell University. All rights reserved. Used by permission of Cornell University Press.—DuBois, Ellen Carol. From "The Limitations of Sisterhood: Elizabeth Cady Stanton and the Division of the American Suffrage Movement, 1875-1902" in *Women and the Structure of Society.* Duke University Press, 1984. Copyright © 1984 by Duke University Press, Durham, NC. All rights reserved. Used by permission.—DuBois, Ellen Carol. From *Woman Suffrage and Women's Rights.* New York University Press, 1998. Copyright © 1998 by New York University. All rights reserved. Reproduced by permission of the publisher and the author.—DuBois, Ellen Carol. From "Woman Suffrage Around the World: Three Phases of Suffragist Internationalism," in *Suffrage and Beyond: International Feminist Perspectives.* Edited by Caroline Daley and Melanie Nolan. Auckland University Press, 1994. Copyright © by Auckland University Press 1994. All rights reserved. Reproduced by permission of the publisher and the author.—Ducrest, Stéphanie-Félicité. From "The Influence of Women on French Literature," in *Women Critics: 1660-1820: An Anthology.* Indiana University Press, 1995. Copyright © 1995 by Indiana University Press. All rights reserved. Reproduced by permission.—Dworkin, Andrea. From *Letters from a War Zone: Writings 1976-1989.* E. P. Dutton, 1988. Copyright © 1988 by Andrea Dworkin. Reproduced by permission of Elaine Markson Literary Agency.—Echols, Alice.

From *The Sixties: From Memory to History.* Edited by David R. Farber. University of North Carolina Press, 1994. Copyright © 1994 by the University of North Carolina Press. Used by permission of the Publisher.—Ehrenreich, Barbara and Deirdre English. From *For Her Own Good: 150 Years of the Experts' Advice to Women.* Anchor Books/Doubleday, 1978. Copyright © 1978 by Barbara Ehrenreich and Deirdre English. All rights reserved. Used by permission of Doubleday, a division of Random House.—Elbert, Sarah. From *A Hunger for Home: Louisa May Alcott and Little Women.* Temple University Press, 1984. Copyright © 1984 by Temple University. All rights reserved. Reproduced by permission of the author.—Emecheta, Buchi. From "Feminism with a Small 'f'!," in *Criticism and Ideology: Second African Writers' Conference.* Edited by Kirsten Holst Petersen. Scandinavian Institute of African Studies, 1988. Copyright © 1988 by Scandinavian Institute of African Studies. All rights reserved. Reproduced by permission of Nordic Africa Institute.—Ensler, Eve. From *The Vagina Monologues: The V-Day Edition.* Villard, 2001. Copyright © 1998, 2001 by Eve Ensler. All rights reserved. Reproduced by permission of Villard Books, a division of Random House, Inc.—Enstad, Nan. From *Ladies of Labor, Girls of Adventure: Working Women, Popular Culture, and Labor Politics at the Turn of the Twentieth Century.* Columbia University Press, 1999. Copyright © 1999 Columbia University Press, New York. All rights reserved. Republished with permission of the Columbia University Press, 61 W. 62nd St., New York, NY 10023.—Ezell, Margaret J. M. From "Women and Writing," in *A Companion to Early Modern Women's Writing.* Edited by Anita Pacheco. Blackwell Publishing Ltd, 2002. Copyright © 2002 by Blackwell Publishers Ltd. Reproduced by permission of Blackwell Publishers.—Fallaize, Elizabeth. From "Resisting Romance: Simone de Beauvoir, *The Woman Destroyed* and the Romance Script," in *Contemporary French Fiction by Women: Feminist Perspectives.* Edited by Margaret Atack and Phil Powrie. Manchester University Press, 1990. Reproduced by permission of the author.—Feng, Pin-chia. From *The Female Bildungsroman* by Toni Morrison and Maxine Hong Kingston: A Postmodern Reading. Peter Lang, 1998. Copyright © 1988 Peter Lang Publishing, Inc. All rights reserved. Reproduced by permission.—Ferree, Myra Marx and Beth B. Hess. From *Controversy and Coalition: The New Feminist Movement across Three Decades of Change.* Twayne Publishers, 1994. Copyright © 1994 by Twayne Publishers. All rights reserved. Reproduced by permission of The Gale Group.—Fishkin, Shelley Fisher. From an interview with Maxine Hong Kingston, in *Con-*

versations with Maxine Hong Kingston. Edited by Paul Skenazy and Tera Martin. University Press of Mississippi, 1998. Copyright © 1998 by University Press of Mississippi. All rights reserved. Reproduced by permission of the author.—Fishkin, Shelley Fisher. From "Reading Gilman in the Twenty-First Century," in *The Mixed Legacy of Charlotte Perkins Gilman.* Edited by Catherine J. Golden and Joanna Schneider Zangrando. University of Delaware Press, 2000. Copyright © 2000 by Associated University Press. Reproduced by permission.—Fleischmann, Fritz. From "Margaret Fuller, the Eternal Feminine, and the 'Liberties of the Republic'," in *Women's Studies and Literature.* Edited by Fritz Fleischmann and Deborah Lucas Schneider. Palm & Enke, 1987. Reproduced by permission.—Foster, M. Marie Booth. From "Voice, Mind, Self: Mother-Daughter Relationships in Amy Tan's *The Joy Luck Club* and *The Kitchen God's Wife,*" in *Women of Color: Mother-Daughter Relationships in 20th-Century Literature.* Edited by Elizabeth Brown-Guillory. University of Texas Press, 1996. Copyright © 1996 by the University of Texas Press. All rights reserved. Reproduced by permission.—Fowler, Robert Booth. From *Carrie Catt: Feminist Politician.* Northeastern University Press, 1986. Copyright © 1986 by R. B. Fowler. All rights reserved. Reproduced by permission.—Fraiman, Susan. From "The Humiliation of Elizabeth Bennett," in *Refiguring the Father: New Feminist Readings of Patriarchy.* Edited by Patricia Yaeger and Beth Kowaleski-Wallace. Southern Illinois University Press, 1989. Copyright © 1989 by the Board of Trustees, Southern Illinois University. All rights reserved. Reproduced by permission.—Francis, Emma. From "Is Emily Brontë a Woman?: Femininity, Feminism, and the Paranoid Critical Subject," in *Subjectivity and Literature from the Romantics to the Present Day.* Edited by Philip Shaw and Peter Stockwell. Pinter, 1991. Copyright © Emma Francis. All rights reserved. Reproduced by permission of the author.—Freedman, Estelle B. and Erna Olafson Hellerstein. From an introduction to *Victorian Women: A Documentary Account of Women's Lives in Nineteenth-Century England, France, and the United States.* Edited by Erna Olafson Hellerstein, Leslie Parker Hume, and Karen M. Offen. Stanford University Press, 1981. Copyright © 1981 by the Board of Trustees of Leland Stanford Junior University. Reproduced with permission of Stanford University Press, www.sup.org.—Frenk, Susan. From "The Wandering Text: Situating the Narratives of Isabel Allende," in *Latin American Women's Writing: Feminist Readings in Theory and Crisis.* Edited by Anny Brooksbank Jones and Catherine Davies. Oxford at the Clarendon Press, 1996. Copyright © 1996 by Anny Brooksbank Jones and Catherine Davies. All rights reserved. Reproduced by permission of Oxford University Press.—From *Victorian Women: A Documentary Account of Women's Lives in Nineteenth-Century England, France, and the United States.* Edited by Erna Olafson Hellerstein, Leslie Parker Hume, and Karen M. Offen. Stanford University Press, 1981. Copyright © 1981 by the Board of Trustees of Leland Stanford Junior University. Reproduced with permission of Stanford University Press, www.sup.org.—Galvin, Mary E. From *Queer Poetics: Five Modernist Women Writers.* Praeger, 1999. Copyright © 1999 by Mary E. Galvin. All rights reserved. Reproduced by permission.—Garner, Shirley Nelson. From "Constructing the Mother: Contemporary Psychoanalytic Theorists and Women Autobiographers," in *Narrating Mother: Theorizing Maternal Subjectivities.* Edited by Brenda O. Daly and Maureen T. Reddy. University of Tennessee Press, 1991. Copyright © 1991 by The University of Tennessee Press. Reproduced by permission of the publisher.—Ghymn, Esther Mikyung. From an introduction to *Images of Asian American Women by Asian American Women Writers.* Peter Lang, 1995. Copyright © 1995, by Esther Mikyung Ghymn. All rights reserved. Reproduced by permission.—Gilbert, Sandra M. and Gubar, Susan. From "Charred Skirts and Deathmask: World War II and the Blitz on Women," in *No Man's Land: The Place of the Woman Writer in the Twentieth Century, Volume 3: Letters from the Front.* Yale University Press, 1994. Copyright © 1994, by Sandra M. Gilbert and Susan Gubar. All rights reserved. Reproduced by permission.—Gilbert, Sandra M. and Susan Gubar. From "The Battle of the Sexes: The Men's Case," in *No Man's Land: The Place of the Woman Writer in the Twentieth Century, Volume 1: The War of the Words.* Yale University Press, 1988. Copyright © 1988, by Yale University Press, All rights reserved. Reproduced by permission.—Gilbert, Sandra M., and Susan Gubar. From "The Second Coming of Aphrodite: Kate Chopin's Fantasy of Desire," in *No Man's Land: The Place of the Woman Writer in the Twentieth Century.* Yale University Press, 1989. Copyright © 1989 by Yale University. Copyright © 1984 by Sandra M. Gilbert and Susan Gubar. All rights reserved. Reproduced by permission.—Gilbert, Susan M., and Susan Gubar. From *The Madwoman in the Attic: The Woman Writer and the Nineteenth-Century Literary Imagination.* Yale University Press, 1979. Copyright © 1979 by Yale University. All rights reserved. Reproduced by permission.—Gleadle, Kathryn. From an introduction to *The Early Feminists: Radical Unitarians and the Emergence of The Women's Rights Movement, 1831-51.* Macmillan Press Ltd., 1995.

Copyright © Kathryn Gleadle 1995. All rights reserved. Reproduced by permission of Palgrave Macmillan.—Golden, Catherine. From "One Hundred Years of Reading 'The Yellow Wallpaper'," in *The Captive Imagination: A Casebook on "The Yellow Wallpaper."* Edited by Catherine Golden. The Feminist Press at the City University of New York, 1992. Copyright © 1992 by Catherine Golden. All rights reserved. Reproduced by permission.—Gorsky, Susan Rubinow. From *Femininity to Feminism: Women and Literature in the Nineteenth Century.* Twayne Publishers, 1992. Copyright © 1992 by Twayne Publishers. All rights reserved. Reproduced by permission of The Gale Group.—Greer, Germaine. From *The Madwoman's Underclothes: Essays and Occasional Writings.* The Atlantic Monthly Press, 1986. Copyright © 1970, 1986, by Germaine Greer. All rights reserved. Reproduced by permission.—Grewal, Gurleen. From *Circles of Sorrow, Lines of Struggle: The Novels of Toni Morrison.* Louisiana State University Press, 1998. Copyright © 1998 by Louisiana State University Press. All rights reserved. Reproduced by permission.—Griffin, Alice and Geraldine Thorsten. From *Understanding Lillian Hellman.* University of South Carolina Press, 1999. Copyright © 1999 University of South Carolina. Reproduced by permission.—Griffin, Susan E. From "Resistance and Reinvention in Sandra Cisneros' *Woman Hollering Creek*," in *Ethnicity and the American Short Story.* Edited by Julie Brown. Garland Publishing, Inc., 1997. Copyright © 1997 by Julie Brown. All rights reserved. Reproduced by permission of the publisher and the author.—Grogan, Susan K. From an introduction to *French Socialism and Sexual Difference: Women and the New Society, 1803-44.* St. Martin's Press, 1992. Copyright © Susan K. Grogan 1992. All rights reserved. Reprinted by permission of Palgrave Macmillan.—Grössinger, Christa. From *Picturing Women in Late Medieval and Renaissance Art.* Manchester University Press, 1997. Copyright © Christa Grössinger 1997. Reproduced by permission.—Grubbs, Judith Evans. From *Women and the Law in the Roman Empire: A Sourcebook on Marriage, Divorce and Widowhood.* Routledge, 2002. Reproduced by permission of the publisher.—Grundy, Isobel. From "(Re)discovering Women's Texts," in *Women and Literature in Britain 1700-1800.* Edited by Vivien Jones. Cambridge University Press, 2000. Copyright © 2000 by Cambridge University Press. Reproduced by permission of Cambridge University Press.—Gubar, Susan. From "Feminist Misogyny: Mary Wollstonecraft and the Paradox of 'It Takes One to Know One'," in *Feminism Beside Itself.* Edited by Diane Elam and Robyn Wiegman. Routledge, 1995. Copyright © 1995 by Routledge.

Gubar, Susan. From "Sapphistries," in *Re-reading
Sappho: Reception and Transmission.* Edited by
Ellen Greene. University of California Press, 1996.
Copyright © 1996 by The Regents of The Univer-
sity of California. Reproduced by permission of
the publisher and the author.—Gunther-Canada,
Wendy. From *Rebel Writer: Mary Wollstonecraft
and Enlightenment Politics.* Northern Illinois
University Press, 2001. Copyright © 2001 by
Northern Illinois University Press. All rights
reserved. Reproduced by permission.—Hagen, Ly-
man B. From *Heart of a Woman, Mind of a
Writer, and Soul of a Poet: A Critical Analysis of
the Writings of Maya Angelou.* University Press of
America, 1997. Copyright © 1997 by University
Press of America. All rights reserved. Reproduced
by permission.—Hallett, Judith From "The Role of
Women in Roman Elegy: Counter-Cultural Femi-
nism," in *Women in the Ancient World: The
Arethusa Papers.* Edited by John Peradotto and J.
Sullivan. State University of New York Press, 1984.
Reproduced by permission of the State University
of New York Press.—Hansberry, Lorraine. From *A
Raisin in the Sun.* Modern Library, 1995. Copy-
right © 1958, 1986 by Robert Nemiroff, as an
unpublished work. Copyright © 1959, 1966, 1984,
1987, 1988 by Robert Nemiroff. All rights reserved.
Reproduced by permission of Random House, Inc.,
Jewell Gresham-Nemiroff and Methuen Publish-
ing Ltd.—Harris, Susan K. From "'But is it any
good?' Evaluating Nineteenth-Century American
Women's Fiction," in *The (Other) American
Traditions: Nineteenth-Century Women Writers.*
Edited by Joyce W. Warren. Rutgers University
Press, 1993. Copyright © 1993 by Rutgers Univer-
sity Press. All rights reserved. Reproduced by
permission of the author.—Head, Bessie. From
"Despite Broken Bondage, Botswana Women Are
Still Unloved," in *A Woman Alone: Autobio-
graphical Writings.* Selected and edited by Craig
MacKenzie. Heinemann, 1990. Copyright © 1990,
by The Estate of Bessie Head. Reproduced by
permission of Johnson & Alcock.—Head, Bessie.
From "The Woman from America," in *A Woman
Alone: Autobiographical Writings.* Selected and
edited by Craig MacKenzie. Heinemann, 1990.
Copyright © 1990, by The Estate of Bessie Head.
Reproduced by permission of Johnson & Alcock.—
Hellerstein, Erna, Leslie Parker Hume and Karen
M. Offen from an introduction to *Victorian
Women: A Documentary Account of Women's
Lives in Nineteenth-Century England, France,
and the United States.* Edited by Erna Olafson
Hellerstein, Leslie Parker Hume, and Karen M. Of-
fen. Stanford University Press, 1981. Copyright ©
1981 by the Board of Trustees of the Leland Stan-
ford Junior University. Reproduced with permis-
sion of Stanford University Press, www.sup.org.—
Henderson, Bruce. From *Images of the Self as
Female: The Achievement of Women Artists in
Re-envisioning Feminine Identity.* Edited by Kath-
ryn N. Benzel and Lauren Pringle De La Vars. The
Edwin Mellen Press, 1992. Copyright © 1992 by
Kathryn N. Benzel and Lauren Pringle De La Vars.
All rights reserved. Reproduced by permission.—
Hill, Mary A. From "Charlotte Perkins Gilman: A
Feminist's Struggle with Womanhood," in *Char-
lotte Perkins Gilman: The Woman and Her Work.*
Edited by Sheryl L. Meyering. UMI Research Press,
1989. Copyright © 1989 by Sheryl L. Meyering.
All rights reserved. Reproduced by permission of
Boydell & Brewer, Inc.—Hobby, Elaine. From *Vir-
tue of Necessity: English Women's Writing 1649-
88.* The University of Michigan Press, 1989.
Copyright © 1988 by Elaine Hobby. All rights
reserved. Reproduced by permission of the author.—Hoffert, Sylvia D. From an introduction to
*When Hens Crow: The Woman's Rights Move-
ment in Antebellum America.* Indiana University
Press, 1995. Copyright © 1995 by Sylvia D. Hof-
fert. All rights reserved. Reproduced by permis-
sion.—Hurston, Zora Neale. From *Their Eyes Were
Watching God.* Perennial Library, 1990. Copyright
© 1937 by Harper & Row, Publishers, Inc. Renewed
1965 by John C. Hurston and Joel Hurston.
Reproduced by permission of Time Warner Books
UK. In North America by HarperCollins Publishers
Inc.—James, Adeola. From "Bessie Head's Perspec-
tives on Women," in *Black Women Writers across
Cultures.* Edited by Valentine Udoh James, James
S. Etim, Melanie Marshall James, and Ambe J.
Njoh. International Scholars Publications, 2000.
Copyright © 2000, by International Scholars
Publications. All rights reserved. Reproduced by
permission.—Jardine, Alice A. From an interview
with Marguerite Duras, translated by Katherine
Ann Jensen, in *Shifting Scenes: Interviews on
Women, Writing, and Politics in Post-68 France.*
Edited by Alice A. Jardine and Anne M. Menke.
Columbia University Press, 1991. Copyright ©
1991 Columbia University Press, New York. All
rights reserved. Reprinted with the permission of
the publisher.—Jelinek, Estelle C. From "The
Paradox and Success of Elizabeth Cady Stanton,"
in *Women's Autobiography: Essays in Criticism.*
Edited by Estelle C. Jelinek. Indiana University
Press, 1980. Copyright © Estelle C. Jelinek. Repro-
duced by permission of the author.—Juhasz, Su-
zanne. From "Maxine Hong Kingston: Narrative
Technique & Female Identity," in *Contemporary
American Women Writers: Narrative Strategies.*
Edited by Catherine Rainwater and William J.
Scheik. The University Press of Kentucky, 1985.
Copyright © 1985 by The University Press of

Kentucky. Reproduced by permission.—Kaminer, Wendy. From "Feminism's Identity Crisis," in *Public Women, Public Words: A Documentary History of American Feminism.* Edited by Dawn Keetley and John Pettegrew. First published in *The Atlantic.* Reproduced by permission of the author.—Kaplan, Cora. From "Pandora's Box: Subjectivity, Class and Sexuality in Socialist Feminist Criticism," in *Making a Difference: Feminist Literary Criticism.* Edited by Gayle Greene and Coppélia Kahn. Methuen & Co., 1985. Copyright © 1985 Gayle Greene and Coppélia Kahn. All rights reserved. Reproduced by permission of Routledge and the author.—Keetley, Dawn and John Pettegrew. From "Identities through Adversity," in *Public Women, Public Words: A Documentary History of American Feminism.* Edited by Dawn Keetley and John Pettegrew. Madison House Publishers, Inc., 1997. Copyright © 1997 by Madison House Publisher, Inc. All rights reserved. Reproduced by permission.—Kelly, Gary. From *Revolutionary Feminism: The Mind and Career of Mary Wollstonecraft.* St. Martin's Press, 1996. Copyright © 1996 by Gary Kelly. All rights reserved. Reproduced by permission of Palgrave Macmillan.—Kempe, Margery. From "Margery Kempe's Visit to Julian of Norwich," in *The Shewings of Julian Norwich.* Edited by Georgia Ronan Crampton. Medieval Publishing Institute, 1994. Reproduced by permission.—Kempe, Margery. From *The Book of Margery Kempe.* Translated by B. A. Windeatt. Penguin, 1985. Copyright © B. A. Windeatt, 1985. All rights reserved. Reproduced by permission.—Kirkham, Margaret. From *Jane Austen, Feminism, and Fiction.* Harvester Press Limited, 1983. Copyright © Margaret Kirkham, 1983. All rights reserved. Reproduced by permission.—Klemans, Patricia A. From "'Being Born a Woman': A New Look at Edna St. Vincent Millay," in *Critical Essays on Edna St. Vincent Millay.* Edited by William B. Thesing. G. K. Hall, 1993. Copyright © by 1993 by William B. Thesing. All rights reserved. Reproduced by permission of The Gale Group.—Knapp, Bettina L. From *Gertrude Stein.* Continuum, 1990. Copyright © 1990 by Bettina L. Knapp. All rights reserved. Reproduced by permission.—Kolodny, Annette. From "Dancing Through the Minefield: Some Observations on the Theory, Practice, and Politics of a Feminist Literary Criticism," originally published in *Feminist Studies,* 1980. Copyright © 1980 by Annette Kolodny. All rights reserved. Reproduced by permission of the author.—Kumin, Maxine. From "How It Was," in *The Complete Poems: Anne Sexton.* Houghton Mifflin Company, 1981. Copyright © 1981, by Maxine Kumin. All rights reserved. Reproduced by permission of Houghton Mifflin and The Anderson Literary Agency.—Lam-

onica, Drew. From *We Are Three Sisters: Self and Family in the Writing of the Brontës.* University of Missouri Press, 2003. Copyright © 2003 by The Curators of the University of Missouri. All rights reserved. Reproduced by permission.—Larsen, Jeanne. From "Lowell, Teasdale, Wylie, Millay, and Bogan," in *The Columbia History of American Poetry.* Edited by Jay Parini. Columbia University Press, 1993. Copyright © 1993 Columbia University Press, New York. All rights reserved. Reprinted with permission of the publisher.—Lascelles, Mary. From *Jane Austen and Her Art.* Oxford University Press, 1939. Reproduced by permission of Oxford University Press.—Lavezzo, Kathy. From "Sobs and Sighs Between Women: The Homoerotics of Compassion in *The Book of Margery Kempe,*" in *Premodern Sexualities.* Edited by Louise Fradenburg and Carla Freccero. Routledge, 1996. Copyright © 1996 by Routledge. All rights reserved. Reproduced by permission of Routledge/Taylor & Francis and the author.—Lessing, Doris. From a preface to *The Golden Notebook* in *A Small Personal Voice.* Edited by Paul Schleuter. Alfred A. Knopf, Inc., 1974. Copyright © 1974 by Doris Lessing. All rights reserved. Reproduced by permission of Jonathan Clowes, Ltd.—Levertov, Denise. From *Poems, 1960-67.* New Directions, 1966. Copyright © 1967, by Denise Levertov. All rights reserved. Reproduced by permission of New Directions Publishing Corporation and in the UK by Pollinger Limited and the proprietor.—Logan, Shirley Wilson. From *"We are Coming": The Persuasive Discourse of Nineteenth-Century Black Women.* Southern Illinois University Press, 1999. Copyright © 1999 by the Board of Trustees, Southern Illinois University. All rights reserved. Reproduced by permission of Southern Illinois University Press and the University of South Carolina Press.—Lorde, Audre. From *The Black Unicorn.* Norton, 1978. Copyright © 1978, by Audre Lorde. All rights reserved. Reproduced by permission of W. W. Norton & Company and Charlotte Sheedy Literary Agency.—Lumsden, Linda J. From *Rampant Women: Suffragists and the Right of Assembly.* The University of Tennessee Press, 1997. Copyright © 1997 by The University of Tennessee Press. Reproduced by permission of The University of Tennessee Press.—Lunardini, Christine A. *From Equal Suffrage to Equal Rights: Alice Paul and the National Women's Party, 1910-1928.* New York University Press, 1986. Copyright © 1986 by New York University. All rights reserved. Reproduced by permission of the author.—Madsen, Deborah L. From "Sandra Cisneros," in *Understanding Contemporary Chicana Literature.* Edited by Matthew J. Bruccoli. University of South Carolina Press, 2000. Copyright © 2000 by University of South Carolina. Reproduced by permission.—Marder, Herbert. From *Feminism & Art: A Study of Virginia Woolf.* University of Chicago Press, 1968. Copyright © 1968 by the University of Chicago. All rights reserved. Reproduced by permission of the publisher and the author.—Marilley, Suzanne M. From *Woman Suffrage and the Origins of Liberal Feminism in the United States.* Harvard University Press, 1996. Copyright © 1996 by the President and Fellows of Harvard College. All rights reserved. Reproduced by permission Harvard University Press.—Marsh-Lockett, Carol P. From "What Ever Happened to Jochebed? Motherhood as Marginality in Zora Neale Hurston's *Seraph on the Suwanee,*" in *Southern Mothers: Facts and Fictions in Southern Women's Writing.* Edited by Nagueyalti Warren and Sally Wolff. Louisiana State University, 1999. Reproduced by permission.—Mason, Nicholas. From "Class, Gender, and Domesticity in Maria Edgeworth's *Belinda,*" in *The Eighteenth-Century Novel,* Vol. 1. Edited by Susan Spencer. AMS Press, 2001. Reproduced by permission.—Massardier-Kenney, Françoise. From *Gender in the Fiction of George Sand.* Rodopi, 1985. Copyright © Editions Rodopi B. V. Reproduced by permission.—McCracken, Ellen. From "Sandra Cisneros' *The House on Mango Street*: Community-Oriented Introspection and the Demystification of Patriarchal Violence," in *Breaking Boundaries: Latina Writing and Critical Readings.* Edited by Asunción Horno-Delgado, Eliana Ortega, Nina M. Scott, and Nancy Saporta Sternbach. University of Massachusetts Press, 1989. Copyright © 1989 by The University of Massachusetts Press. All rights reserved. Reproduced by permission.—McNamara, Jo Ann. From "Women and Power through the Family Revisited," in *Gendering the Master Narrative: Women and Power in the Middle Ages.* Edited by Mary C. Erler and Maryanne Kowaleski. Cornell University Press, 2003. Copyright © 2003 by Cornell University Press. Used by permission of Cornell University Press.—Meisenhelder, Susan. From "Ethnic and Gender Identity in Zora Neale Hurston's *Their Eyes Were Watching God,*" in *Teaching American Ethnic Literatures: Nineteen Essays.* Edited by John R. Maitino and David R. Peck. University of New Mexico Press, 1996. Copyright © 1996, by the University of New Mexico Press. All rights reserved. Reproduced by permission.—Mellor, Anne K. From "Possessing Nature: The Female in Frankenstein," in *Romanticism and Feminism.* Edited by Anne K. Mellor. Indiana University Press, 1988. Copyright © 1988 by Indiana University Press. All rights reserved. Reproduced by permission.—Mermin, Dorothy. From *Godiva's Ride: Women of Letters in England, 1830-1880.* Indiana University Press, 1993. Copyright © 1993 by Dorothy Mermin. All rights reserved. Repro-

duced by permission.—Millay, Edna St. Vincent. From "Sonnet III of Fatal Interview," in *Collected Sonnets of Edna St. Vincent Millay.* HarperCollins, 1952. Copyright © 1931, 1958 by Edna St. Vincent Millay and Norma Millay Ellis. All rights reserved. Reproduced by permission of Elizabeth Barnett, Literary Executor.—Millay, Edna St. Vincent. From "First Fig," in *Collected Poems of Edna St. Vincent Millay.* HarperCollins, 1952. Copyright © 1922, 1950 by Edna St. Vincent Millay. Reproduced by permission of Elizabeth Barnett, Literary Executor.—Millay, Edna St. Vincent. From "I, Being Born a Woman and Distressed," in *Collected Poems of Edna St. Vincent Millay.* HarperCollins, 1952. Copyright © 1923, 1951 by Edna St.Vincent Millay and Norma Millay Ellis. All rights reserved. Reproduced by permission of Elizabeth Barnett, Literary Executor.—Millett, Kate. From "How Many Lives Are Here...," in *The Feminist Memoir Project.* Edited by Rachel DuPlessis and Ann Snitow. Three Rivers Press, 1998. Copyright © 1998 by Rachel DuPlessis and Ann Snitow. All rights reserved. Used by permission of Crown Publishers, a division of Random House, Inc. and Sanford J. Greenburger Associates.—Moi, Toril. From "Who's Afraid of Virginia Woolf? Feminist Readings of Woolf," in *New Casebooks: 'Mrs. Dalloway' and 'To the Lighthouse.'* Edited by Su Reid. St. Martin's Press, 1993. Copyright © Su Reid 1993. All rights reserved. Reproduced by permission of Palgrave Macmillan.—Moore, Marianne. From *The Selected Letters of Marianne Moore.* Edited by Bonnie Costello. Alfred A. Knopf, 1997. Copyright © 1997 by the Estate of Marianne Moore. Introduction, annotations and additional editorial material copyright 1997 by Bonnie Costello. All rights reserved. Reproduced by permission of Alfred A. Knopf, Inc., a division of Random House, Inc.—Morgan, Winifred. From "Alice Walker: *The Color Purple* as Allegory," in *Southern Writers at Century's End.* Edited by Jeffrey J. Folks and James A. Perkins. The University Press of Kentucky, 1997. Copyright © 1997 by The University Press of Kentucky. All rights reserved. Reproduced by permission.—Morrison, Toni. From *Race-ing Justice, En-Gendering Power.* Pantheon Books, 1992. Copyright © 1992 by Toni Morrison. All rights reserved. Used by permission International Creative Management, Inc.—Morrison, Toni. From "What the Black Woman Thinks About Women's Lib," in *Public Women, Public Words: A Documentary History of American Feminism.* Edited by Dawn Keetley and John Pettegrew. Madison House, 1997. Copyright © 1997 by Toni Morrison. Reproduced by permission of International Creative Management, Inc.—Mortimer, Armine Kotin. From "Male and Female Plots in Staël's *Corinne,*" in *Correspondences:*

Studies in Literature, History, and the Arts in Nineteenth-Century France: Selected Proceedings of the Sixteenth Colloquium in Nineteenth-Century French Studies, The University of Oklahoma-Norman, October 11th-13th, 1990. Edited by Keith Busby. Rodopi, 1992. Copyright © Editions Rodopi B. V. Reproduced by permission.—Motard-Noar, Martine. From "From Persephone to Demeter: A Feminist Experience in Cixous's Fiction," in *Images of Persephone: Feminist Readings in Western Literature.* Edited by Elizabeth T. Hayes. University Press of Florida, 1994. Copyright © 1994 by Board of Regents of the State of Florida. All rights reserved. Reproduced with the permission of the University Press of Florida.—Mukherjee, Bharati. From *The Middleman and Other Stories.* Viking, 1988. Copyright © 1988, by Bharati Mukherjee. All rights reserved. Reprinted by permission of Penguin Group Canada and the author.—Mumford, Marilyn R. From "A Feminist Prolegomenon for the Study of Hildegard of Bingen," in *Gender, Culture, and the Arts: Women, the Arts, and Society.* Edited by Ronald Dotterer and Susan Bowers. Associated University Presses, 1993. Copyright © 1993 by Associated University Presses.—Oates, Joyce Carol. From *Where I've Been, and Where I'm Going.* Plume, 1999. Copyright © The Ontario Review, 1999. All rights reserved. Reproduced by permission of Plume, an imprint of Penguin Putnam Inc. In the United Kingdom by John Hawkins & Associates, Inc.—Okely, Judith. From "Re-reading The Second Sex," in *Simone de Beauvoir: A Re-Reading.* Virago, 1986. Reproduced by permission of the author.—Ovid. From "Sappho to Phaon," in *The Sappho Companion.* Edited by Margaret Reynolds. Chatto and Windus, 2000. Copyright © Margaret Reynolds 2000. Reproduced by permission of the editor.—Pan Chao. From *Pan Chao: Foremost Woman Scholar of China.* Edited by Nancy Lee Swann. University of Michigan Center for Chinese Studies, 1932. Copyright © The East Asian Library and the Gest Collection, Princeton University. Reproduced by permission.—Parks, Sheri. From "In My Mother's House: Black Feminist Aesthetics, Television, and *A Raisin in the Sun,*" in *Theatre and Feminist Aesthetics.* Edited by Karen Laughlin and Catherine Schuler. Farleigh Dickinson University Press, 1995. Copyright © 1995 by Associated University Presses. All rights reserved. Reproduced by permission.—Paul, Alice. From *Party Papers: 1913-1974.* Microfilming Corporation of America, 1978. Reproduced by permission of Sewall-Belmont House and Museum.—Paz, Octavio. From "The Response," in *Sor Juana or, The Traps of Faith.* Translated by Margaret Sayers Peden. Cambridge, Mass.: The Belknap Press of Harvard University Press, 1988. Copyright © 1988 by the President and Fellows of Harvard College. All rights reserved. Reproduced by permission.—Perkins, Annie. From "The Poetry of Gwendolyn Brooks (1970s-1980s)," in *Women Making Art: Women in the Visual, Literary, and Performing Arts Since 1960.* Edited by Deborah Johnson and Wendy Oliver. Peter Lang, 2001. Copyright © 2001 Peter Lang Publishing, Inc., New York. Reproduced by permission.—Pierpont, Claudia Roth. From *Passionate Minds: Women Rewriting the World.* Alfred A. Knopf, 2000. Copyright © 2000 by Claudia Roth Piepont. All rights reserved. Reproduced by permission of Alfred A. Knopf, Inc., a division of Random House, Inc.—Plath, Sylvia. From *The Bell Jar.* Faber & Faber, 1966; Harper & Row, 1971. Copyright © 1971 by Harper & Row, Publishers, Inc. Reproduced by permission Faber & Faber Ltd. In the United States by HarperCollins Publishers Inc.—Pryse, Marjorie. From "Origins of American Literary Regionalism: Gender in Irving, Stowe, and Longstreet," in *Breaking Boundaries: New Perspectives on Women's Regional Writing.* Edited by Sherrie A. Inness and Diana Royer. University of Iowa Press, 1997. Copyright © 1997 by the University of Iowa Press. All rights reserved. Reproduced by permission.—Radice, Betty. From an introduction to *The Letters of Abelard and Heloise.* Translated by Betty Radice. Penguin Books, 1974. Copyright © Betty Radice, 1974. Reproduced by permission of Penguin Books, a division of Penguin Putnam Inc.—Rendall, Jane. From an introduction to *The Origins of Modern Feminism: Women in Britain, France and the United States 1780-1860.* Macmillan, 1985. Copyright © Jane Rendall 1985. All rights reserved. Reproduced by permission of Palgrave Macmillan.—Rich, Adrienne. From "Vesuvius at Home: The Power of Emily Dickinson," in *On Lies, Secrets, and Silence: Selected Prose 1966-1978.* W. W. Norton & Company, Inc., 1979. Copyright © 1979 by W. W. Norton & Company, Inc. Reproduced by permission of the author and W. W. Norton & Company, Inc.—Rich, Adrienne. From "When We Dead Awaken: Writing as Re-Vision," in *Arts of the Possible: Essays and Conversations.* W. W. Norton & Company, Inc., 2001. Copyright © 2001 by Adrienne Rich. Reproduced by permission of the publisher and the author.—Richmond, M. A. From *Bid the Vassal Soar: Essays on the Life and Poetry of Phillis Wheatley and George Moses Horton.* Howard University Press, 1974. All rights reserved. Copyright © 1974 by Merle A. Richmond. Reproduced by permission.—Risjord, Norman K. From *Representative Americans: The Colonists.* Second Edition. Rowman & Littlefield Publishers, Inc., 2001. Copyright © 2001 by Rowman & Littlefield Publishers, Inc. All rights reserved. Reproduced by permission.—Robbins,

Johanna M. From "'Cooped Up': Feminine Domesticity in *Frankenstein*," in *Case Studies in Contemporary Criticism: Mary Shelley's* Frankenstein. Edited by Johanna M. Smith. St. Martin's Press, 1992. Copyright © 1992 by Bedford Books of St. Martin's Press. All rights reserved. Reproduced by permission.—Smith, Sidonie. From "Resisting the Gaze of Embodiment: Women's Autobiography in the Nineteenth Century," in *American Women's Autobiography: Fea(s)ts of Memory.* Edited by Margo Culley. University of Wisconsin University Press, 1992. Copyright © 1992 The Board of Regents of the University of Wisconsin System. All rights reserved. Reproduced by permission.—Smith, Sidonie. From *Where I'm Bound: Patterns of Slavery and Freedom in Black American Autobiography.* Greenwood Press, 1974. Copyright © 1974 by Sidonie Smith. All rights reserved. Reproduced by permission of Greenwood Publishing Group, Inc., Westport, CT.—Snyder, Jane McIntosh. From *The Woman and the Lyre: Women Writers in Classical Greece and Rome.* Southern Illinois University Press, 1989. Copyright © 1989 by the Board of Trustees, Southern Illinois University. All rights reserved. Reproduced by permission.—Sor Juana Ines de la Cruz. From *The Answer = La respuesta.* Edited by Electa Arenal and Amanda Powell. The Feminist Press, 1994. Copyright © 1994 by Electa Arenal and Amanda Powell. All rights reserved. Reproduced by permission of The Feminist Press at the City University of New York. www.feministpress.org.—Spender, Dale. From "Introduction: A Vindication of the Writing Woman," in *Living by the Pen: Early British Women Writers.* Edited by Dale Spender. Teachers College Press, 1992. Copyright © 1992 by Teachers College. All rights reserved. Reproduced by permission.—Staley, Lynn. From *Margery Kempe's Dissenting Fictions.* Pennsylvania State University Press, 1994. Copyright © 1994 The Pennsylvania State University. All rights reserved. Reproduced by permission.—Stehle, Eva. From *Performance and Gender in Ancient Greece: Nondramatic Poetry in Its Setting.* Princeton University Press, 1997. Copyright © 1997 by Princeton University Press. All rights reserved. Reproduced by permission of Princeton University Press.—Stein, Gertrude. From "Degeneration in American Women," in *Sister Brother: Gertrude and Leo Stein.* Edited by Brenda Wineapple. G. Putnam's Sons, 1996. Copyright © 1996 by Brenda Wineapple. All rights reserved. Used by permission of G. Putnam's Sons, a division of Penguin Group (USA) Inc. and Bloomsbury Publishing Plc.—Stott, Rebecca. From *Elizabeth Barrett Browning.* Pearson Education Limited, 2003. Copyright © Pearson Educated Limited 2003. All rights reserved. Reproduced by permission.—Straub, Kristina. From *Divided Fic-tions: Fanny Burney and Feminine Strategy.* University Press of Kentucky, 1987. Copyright © 1987 by the University Press of Kentucky. Reproduced by permission.—Swann, Nancy Lee. From *Pan Chao: Foremost Woman Scholar of China.* Russell & Russell, 1968. Copyright © The East Asian Library and the Gest Collection, Princeton University. Reproduced by permission.—Tanner, Laura E. From *Intimate Violence: Reading Rape and Torture in Twentieth-Century Fiction.* Indiana University Press, 1994. Copyright © 1994, by Laura E. Tanner. All rights reserved. Reproduced by permission.—Terborg-Penn, Rosalyn. From *African American Women in the Struggle for the Vote, 1850-1920.* Indiana University Press, 1998. Reproduced by permission.—Tharp, Julie. From "Women's Community and Survival in the Novels of Louise Erdrich," in *Communication and Women's Friendships: Parallels and Intersections in Literature and Life.* Edited by Janet Doubler Ward and JoAnna Stephens Mink. Bowling Green State University Popular Press, 1993. Copyright © 1993 by Bowling Green State University Popular Press. Reproduced by permission of the University of Wisconsin Press.—Trilling, Lionel. From "Emma and the Legend of Jane Austen," in *Beyond Culture: Essays on Literature and Learning.* Harcourt Brace Jovanovich, 1965. Copyright © 1965 by Lionel Trilling. All rights reserved. Reproduced by permission of the Wylie Agency, Inc.—Turner, Katherine S. H. From "From Classical to Imperial: Changing Visions of Turkey in the Eighteenth Century," in *Travel Writing and Empire: Postcolonial Theory in Transit.* Edited by Steve Clark. Zed Books, 1999. Copyright © Katherine S. H. Turner. Reproduced by permission.—Van Dyke, Annette. From "Of Vision Quests and Spirit Guardians: Female Power in the Novels of Louise Erdrich," in *The Chippewa Landscape of Louise Erdrich.* Edited by Allan Chavkin. The University of Alabama Press, 1999. Copyright © 1999, by The University of Alabama Press. Copyright © 1999. All rights reserved. Reproduced by permission.—Waelti-Waters, Jennifer and Steven C. Hause. From an introduction to *Feminisms of the Belle Époque: A Historical and Literary Anthology.* Edited by Jennifer Waelti-Waters and Steven C. Hause. University of Nebraska Press, 1994. Copyright © The University of Nebraska Press, 1994. All rights reserved. Reproduced by permission.—Wagner-Martin, Linda. From "Panoramic, Unpredictable, and Human: Joyce Carol Oates' Recent Novels," in *Traditions, Voices, and Dreams: The American Novel since the 1960s.* Edited by Melvin J. Friedman and Ben Siegel. University of Delaware Press, 1995. Copyright © 1995 by Associated University Presses, Inc. Reproduced by permission.—Wagner-Martin, Linda. From *Sylvia Plath: A Literary Life.*

St. Martin's Press, 1999. Copyright © 1999 by Linda Wagner-Martin. All rights reserved. Reproduced by permission of Palgrave Macmillan.—Walker, Alice. From *Revolutionary Petunias & Other Poems.* Harcourt Brace Jovanovich, 1971. Copyright © 1970, 1971, 1972, 1973, renewed 1998 by Alice Walker. All right reserved. Reproduced by permission of Harcourt Inc. In the British Commonwealth by David Higham Associates.—Watts, Linda S. From *Rapture Untold: Gender, Mysticism, and the 'Moment of Recognition' in Works by Gertrude Stein.* Peter Lang, 1996. Copyright © 1996 Peter Lang Publishing, Inc., New York. All rights reserved. Reproduced by permission.—Weatherford, Doris. From *A History of the American Suffragist Movement.* ABC-CLIO, 1998. Copyright © 1998 by The Moschovitis Group, Inc. Reproduced by permission of Moschovitis Group, Inc.—Weeton, Nellie. From "The Trials of an English Governess: Nelly Weeton Stock," originally published in *Miss Weeton: Journal of a Governess.* Edited by Edward Hall. Oxford University Press (London), H. Milford, 1936-39. Reproduced by permission of Oxford University Press.—Weston, Ruth D. From "Who Touches This Touches a Woman," in *Critical Essays on Alice Walker.* Edited by Ikenna Dieke. Greenwood Press 1999. Reproduced by permission of Greenwood Publishing Group, Inc., Westport, CT.—Wheeler, Marjorie Spruill. From an introduction to *One Woman, One Vote: Rediscovering the Woman Suffrage Movement.* Edited by Marjorie Spruill Wheeler. NewSage Press, 1995. Copyright © 1995 by NewSage Press and Educational Film Company. All rights reserved. Reproduced by permission.—Willard, Charity Cannon. From *Christine de Pizan: Her Life and Works.* Persea Books, 1984. Copyright © 1984 by Charity Cannon Willard. Reproduced by permission.—Willis, Sharon A. From "Staging Sexual Difference: Reading, Recitation, and Repetition in Duras' *Malady of Death,*" in *Feminine Focus: The New Women Playwrights.* Edited by Enoch Brater. Oxford University Press, 1989. Copyright © 1989 by Oxford University Press, Inc. Reproduced by permission of Oxford University Press.—Winter, Kate H. From *Marietta Holley: Life with "Josiah Allen's Wife."* Syracuse University Press, 1984. Copyright © 1984 by Syracuse University Press. All rights reserved. Reproduced by permission.—Woolf, Virginia. From "George Eliot," in *The Common Reader,* Harcourt, Brace & Company, 1925, L. & V. Woolf, 1925. Copyright 1925 by Harcourt Brace & Company. Renewed 1953 by Leonard Woolf. Reprinted by permission of Harcourt, Brace & Company and The Society of Authors.—Wynne-Davies, Marion. From an introduction to *Women Poets of the Renaissance.* Edited by Marion Wynne-Davies.

Routledge, 1999. Reprint. Copyright © 1998 by J. M. Dent. All rights reserved. Reproduced by permission of Routledge/Taylor & Francis and the author—Yalom, Marilyn. From "Toward a History of Female Adolescence: The Contribution of George Sand," in *George Sand: Collected Essays.* Edited by Janis Glasgow. The Whitson Publishing Company, 1985. Reproduced by permission of the author.—Yu Xuanji. From "Joining Somebody's Mourning and Three Beautiful Sisters, Orphaned Young," in *The Clouds Float North: The Complete Poems of Yu Xuanji.* Translated by David Young and Jiann I. Lin. Wesleyan University Press, 1998. Copyright © 1998 by David Young and Jiann I. Lin. All rights reserved. Reproduced by permission.

Photographs and Illustrations in Feminism in Literature *were received from the following sources:*

16th century men and women wearing fashionable clothing, ca. 1565 engraving. Hulton/Archive.—A lay sister preparing medicine as shown on the cover of *The Book of Margery Kempe,* photograph. MS. Royal 15 D 1, British Library, London.—Akhmatova, Anna, photograph. Archive Photos, Inc./Express Newspaper.—Alcott, Louisa May, drawing. The Granger Collection, New York.—Alcott, Louisa May, photograph. Archive Photos, Inc.—Allen, Joan, Joanne Camp, Anne Lange, and Cynthia Nixon, in a scene from the play "The Heidi Chronicles," photograph. Time Life Pictures/Getty Images.—Allende, Isabelle, photograph. Getty Images.—An estimated 5,000 people march outside the Minnesota Capitol Building in protest to the January 22, 1973 Supreme Court ruling on abortion as a result of the "Roe vs. Wade" case, photograph. AP/Wide World Photos.—Angelou, Maya, photograph. AP/Wide World Photos.—Anthony, Susan B., Frances Willard, and other members of the International Council of Women, photograph. Copyright © Corbis.—Atwood, Margaret, photograph by Jerry Bauer. Copyright © Jerry Bauer.—Autographed manuscript of Phillis Weatley's poem "To the University of Cambridge." The Granger Collection, New York.—Beller, Kathleen as Kate in the 1980 film version of Margaret Atwood's novel, *Surfacing,* photograph. Kobal Collection/Surfacing Film.—Blackshear, Thomas, illustrator. From a cover of *The Bluest Eye,* written by Toni Morrison. Plume, 1994. Reproduced by permission of Plume, a division of Penguin USA.—Broadside published by the National American Woman Suffrage Association, featuring "Why Women Want to Vote." The Library of Congress.—Brontë, Anne, Emily and Charlotte, painting by Patrick Branwell Brontë, located at the National Portrait Gallery,

1939, photograph. Copyright © Corbis-Bettmann.—Brontë, Charlotte, painting. Archive Photos.—Brooks, Gwendolyn, holding a copy of *The World of Gwendolyn Brooks,* photograph. AP/Wide World Photos.—Brown, John Mason (right) talking to National Book Award winners Marianne Moore, James Jones, and Rachel Carson, in New York City, NY, 1952, photograph. AP/Wide World Photos.—Brown, Rita Mae, photograph. AP/Wide World Photos.—Browning, Elizabeth Barret, 1848, illustration. Copyright © Corbis-Bettmann.—Burney, Fanny, engraving. Archive Photos, Inc.—Carter, Angela, photograph by Jerry Bauer. Copyright © Jerry Bauer.—Cather, Willa, photograph. AP/Wide World Photos.—Catherine the Great, illustration. Copyright © Archivo Iconografico, S.A./Corbis.—Catt, Carrie Chapman, photograph. The Library of Congress.—Cavendish, Margaret Lucas, engraving. Mary Evans Picture Library.—Child, Lydia Maria, photograph. The Library of Congress.—Childress, Alice, photograph by Jerry Bauer. Copyright © Jerry Bauer.—Chin, Tsai and Tamlyn Tomita in the 1993 film production of Amy Tan's *The Joy Luck Club.* Buena Vista/Hollywood/The Kobal Collection.—Chopin, Kate, photograph. The Library of Congress.—Cisneros, Sandra, 1991, photograph by Dana Tynan. AP/Wide World Photos.—Cixous, Hélène, photograph. Copyright © Bassouls Sophie/Corbis Sygma.—Class on a field trip to Library of Congress, photograph by Frances Benjamin Johnston. Copyright © Corbis.—Cleopatra VII, illustration. The Library of Congress.—Cyanotype by Frances Benjamin Johnson, ca. 1899, of girls and a teacher in a high school cooking class, photograph. Copyright © Corbis.—de la Cruz, Juana Inez, painting. Copyright © Philadelphia Museum of Art/Corbis-Bettmann.—de Pizan, Christine, writing in her study, photograph. MS. Harley 4431, f.4R. British Library, London.—Dickinson, Emily, photograph of a painting. The Library of Congress.—Doolittle, Hilda, 1949, photograph. AP/Wide World Photos.—Duras, Marguerite, photograph. AP/Wide World Photos.—Dworkin, Andrea, 1986, photograph. AP/Wide World Photos.—Edgeworth, Maria, engraving. The Library of Congress.—Eliot, George, photograph. Copyright © The Bettman Archive.—Emecheta, Buchi, photograph by Jerry Bauer. Copyright © Jerry Bauer.—Emily Dickinson Homestead in Amherst, Massachusetts, photograph. Copyright © James Marshall/Corbis.—Erdrich, Louise, photograph by Eric Miller. AP/Wide World Photos.—French, Marilyn, photograph by Jerry Bauer. Copyright © Jerry Bauer.—Friedan, Betty, president of the National Organization for Women, and other feminists march in New York City, photograph. Copyright © JP Laffont/Sygma/Corbis.—Friedan, Betty, with

Yoko Ono, photograph. Copyright © Bettmann/Corbis.—Frontpiece and title page from *Poems on Various Subjects, Religious and Moral,* written by Phillis Wheatley. Copyright © The Pierpont Morgan Library/Art Resource, NY.—Fuller, Margaret, painting by John Plumbe. The Library of Congress.—Gandhi, Indira, photograph. Copyright © Corbis-Bettmann.—Garrison, William Lloyd, (bottom right), with the Pennsylvania Abolition Society, photograph. National Portrait Gallery.—Gilman, Charlotte Perkins, cover photograph. Copyright © Corbis.—Gilman, Charlotte P., photograph. Copyright © Corbis-Bettmann.—Godwin, Mary Wollstonecraft, illustration. Copyright © Corbis-Bettmann.—Hansberry, Lorraine, photograph by David Attie. AP/Wide World Photos.—Head, Bessie, photograph. Reproduced by the kind permission of the Estate of Bessie Head.—"Head of Medusa," marble sculpture by Gianlorenzo Bernini. Copyright © Araldo de Luca/Corbis.—Hellman, Lillian, photograph. AP/Wide World Photos.—Hurston, Zora Neale looking at "American Stuff," at the *New York Times* book fair, photograph. The Library of Congress.—Hurston, Zora Neale, photograph by Carl Van Vechten. The Carl Van Vechten Trust.—Hypatia, conte crayon drawing. Copyright © Corbis-Bettmann.—Illustration depicting a woman's body being the subject of political and social conflict, photograph. Barbara Kruger/Mary Boone Gallery.—Jolie, Angelina (right), and unidentified person, in the film *Foxfire,* photograph by Jane O'Neal. The Kobal Collection/O'Neal, Jane.—Karloff, Boris, in movie *Frankenstein;* 1935, photograph. The Kobal Collection.—Kingston, Maxine Hong, photograph by Jerry Bauer. Copyright © Jerry Bauer.—"La Temptation," depicting Adam and Eve in the Garden of Paradise. The Library of Congress.—Lessing, Doris, photograph by Jerry Bauer. Copyright © Jerry Bauer.—Luce, Clare Booth, portrait. Copyright © UPI/Bettmann Archive.—Manuscript page from *The Book of Ladies,* by Christine de Pizan. Bibliotheque Nationale de France.—Manuscript page of *Vieyra Impugnado,* written by Sor Margarita Ignacia and translated to Spanish by Inigo Rosende. Madrid: Antonio Sanz, 1731. The Special Collections Library, University of Michigan.—Martineau, Harriet, engraving. The Library of Congress.—Migrant mother with child huddled on either shoulder, Nipomo, California, 1936, photograph by Dorothea Lange. The Library of Congress.—Millay, Edna St. Vincent, photograph. AP/Wide World Photos.—Montagu, Lady Mary Wortley, engraving. Archive Photos, Inc.—Moore, Marianne, photograph by Jerry Bauer. Copyright © Jerry Bauer.—Morrison, Toni, 1993, photograph. AP/Wide World Photos.—Murasaki, Lady, looking out from the veranda of a monastery, illustration

ACKNOWLEDGMENTS

from *Tale of Genji*. Copyright © Asian Art Archaeology, Inc./Corbis.—National League of Women Voters' Headquarters, photograph. Copyright © Corbis-Bettmann.—National Women's Suffrage Association (NWSA), during a political convention in Chicago, Illinois, photograph. Copyright © Bettmann/Corbis.—Naylor, Gloria, photograph. Marion Ettlinger/AP/Wide World Photos.—Oates, Joyce Carol, 1991, photograph. AP/Wide World Photos.—October 15, 1913 publication of the early feminist periodical, *The New Freewoman*, photograph. McFarlin Library, Department of Special Collections, The University of Tulsa.—Paul, Alice (second from right), standing with five other suffragettes, photograph. AP/Wide World Photos.—Pfeiffer, Michelle, and Daniel Day-Lewis, in the film *The Age of Innocence*, 1993, photograph by Phillip Caruso. The Kobal Collection.—Plath, Sylvia, photograph. AP/Wide World Photos.—Poster advertising *Uncle Tom's Cabin*, by Harriet Beecher Stowe, "The Greatest Book of the Age," photograph. Copyright © Bettmann/Corbis.—Rich, Adrienne, holding certificate of poetry award, Chicago, Illinois, 1986, photograph. AP/Wide World Photos.—Rossetti, Christina, 1863, photograph by Lewis Carroll. Copyright © UPI/Bettmann.—Russell, Rosalind and Joan Crawford in the 1939 movie *The Women*, written by Clare Boothe Luce, photograph. MGM/The Kobal Collection.—Salem Witch Trial, lithograph by George H. Walker. Copyright © Bettmann/Corbis.—Sand, George, illustration. Copyright © Leonard de Selva/Corbis.—Sand, George, photograph. The Library of Congress.—Sanger, Margaret, Miss Clara Louise Rowe, and Mrs. Anne Kennedy, arranging the first American Birth Control Conference, photograph. Copyright © Underwood and Underwood/Corbis.—Sappho, bronze sculpture. The Library of Congress.—Sappho, illustration. The Library of Congress.—Sappho performing outdoors, illustration. The Library of Congress.—"Sara in a Green Bonnet," painting by Mary Cassatt, c. 1901. National Museum of American Art, Smithsonian Institution, Washington, DC, U.S.A.—Scene from the film *Mill on the Floss*, by George Eliot, engraving. Hulton Archive/Getty Images.—Segwick, Catherine Maria, slide. Archive Photos, Inc.—Sexton, Anne, photograph. Copyright © Bettmann/Corbis.—Sexton, Anne, with her daughters Joy and Linda, photograph. Time Life Pictures/Getty Images.—Shelley, Mary Wollstonecraft, painting by Samuel John Stump. Copyright © Corbis-Bettmann.—Stael, Madame de, color lithograph. Archive Photos, Inc.—Stanton, Elizabeth Cady, illustration. Copyright © Bettmann/Corbis.—Stanton, Elizabeth Cady, photograph. AP/Wide World Photos.—Stein, Gertrude (left), arriving in New York aboard the S. S. Champlain with her secretary and companion Alice B. Toklas, photograph. AP/Wide World Photos.—Stein, Gertrude, photograph by Carl Van Vechten. The Estate of Carl Van Vechten.—Steinem, Gloria, photograph. AP/Wide World Photos.—Stowe, Harriet Beecher, photograph. Copyright © Bettmann/Corbis.—Suffrage parade in New York, New York, October 15, 1915, photograph. The Library of Congress.—Supporters of the Equal Rights Amendment carry a banner down Pennsylvania Avenue, Washington, DC, photograph. AP/Wide World Photos.—Sur la Falaise aux Petites Dalles, 1873. Painting by Berthe Morisot. Copyright © Francis G. Mayer/Corbis.—Tan, Amy, 1993, photograph. AP/Wide World Photos.—*Time*, cover of Kate Millett, from August 31, 1970. Time Life Pictures/Stringer/Getty Images.—Title page of *A Vindication of the Rights of Woman: With Strictures on Political and Moral Subjects*, written by Mary Wollstonecraft. William L. Clements Library, University of Michigan.—Title page of *Adam Bede*, written by George Eliot. Edinburgh & London: Blackwood, 1859, Volume 1, New York: Harper, 1859. The Graduate Library, University of Michigan.—Title page from *De L'influence des Passions sur le Bonheur des Individus et des Nations*, (A Treatise on the Influence of the Passions upon the Happiness of Individuals and of Nations), written by Stael de Holstein, photograph. The Special Collections Library, University of Michigan.—Title page from *Evelina*, written by Fanny Burney, photograph. The Special Collections Library, University of Michigan.—Title page from *Mansfield Park*, written by Jane Austen. The Special Collections Library, University of Michigan.—Title page of *Mary, A Fiction*, written by Mary Wollstonecraft.—Title page from *Youth and the Bright Medusa*, written by Willa Cather. New York, Alfred A Knopf. The Special Collections Library, University of Michigan.—Title page of *A New-England Tale*, written by Catharine Maria Sedgewick. New York: E. Bliss and E. White, 1822. The Special Collections Library, University of Michigan.—Title page of *Aurora Leigh*, written by Elizabeth Barrett Browning. New York, Boston: C. S. Francis and Co., 1857. The Special Collections Library, University of Michigan.—Title page of *Mrs. Dalloway*, written by Virginia Woolf. London: Hogarth Press, 1925. The Special Collections Library, University of Michigan.—Title page of *The Dial: A Magazine for Literature, Philosophy, and Religion*. Boston. Weeks, Jordan and Company (etc.); London, Wiley and Putnam (etc.). Volume 1. The Special Collections Library, University of Michigan.—Title page of *The House of Mirth*, written by Edith Wharton. New York: C. Scribner's Sons, 1905. The Special Collections Library, University of Michigan.—Title page of *The Little Review*,

March 1916. The Purdy/Kresge Library, Wayne State University.—Title page of *Woman in the Nineteenth Century,* written by Sarah Margaret Fuller. New York, Greeley and McElrath. 1845. The Special Collections Library, University of Michigan.—Title page of *Wuthering Heights,* written by Emily Brontë. New York: Harper and Brothers. 1848. The Special Collections Library, University of Michigan.—Truth, Sojourner, photograph. Archive Photos, Inc.—Tubman, Harriet, photograph. The Library of Congress.—Victoria, Queen of England, illustration. The Library of Congress.—Walker, Alice, 1989, photograph. AP/Wide World Photos.—Welles, Orson, as Edward Rochester, with Joan Fontaine as Jane Eyre, in the film *Jane Eyre,* photograph. The Kobal Collection.—Wharton, Edith, photograph. AP/Wide World Photos.—Wheatley, Phillis, photograph. Copyright © The Bettman Archive.—Winfrey, Oprah, as Celie and Danny Glover as Albert with baby in scene from the film *The Color Purple,* written by Alice Walker, directed by Steven Spielberg, photograph. The Kobal Collection.—Women in French Revolution, invade assembly, demanding death penalty for members of the aristocracy, Woodcut. Copyright © Bettmann/Corbis.—Women workers in a shoe factory in Lynn, Massachusetts, photograph. Copyright © Corbis.—Woodhull, Victoria, reading statement before House Committee, drawing. The Library of Congress.—Woolf, Virginia, photograph. AP/Wide World Photos.—Woolson, Constance Fenimore, engraving. Archive Photos.

● = historical event

■ = literary event

1570 B.C.

● Queen Ahmose Nefertari, sister and principal wife of King Ahmose, rules as "god's wife," in a new position created by a law enacted by the King.

C. 1490 B.C.

● Queen Hatshepsut rules as pharaoh, several years after the death of her husband, King Thutmose II.

C. 1360 B.C.

● Queen Nefertiti rules Egypt alongside her husband, pharaoh Akhenaten.

C. 620 B.C.

● Sappho is born on the Isle of Lesbos, Greece.

C. 600 B.C.

■ Sappho organizes and operates a *thiasos*, an academy for young, unmarried Greek women.

● Spartan women are the most independent women in the world, and are able to own property, pursue an education, and participate in athletics.

C. 550 B.C.

● Sappho dies on the Isle of Lesbos.

C. 100 B.C.

● Roman laws allow a husband: to kill his wife if she is found in the act of adultery, to determine the amount of money his wife is owed in the event of divorce, and to claim his children as property.

69 B.C.

● Cleopatra VII Philopator is born in Egypt.

36 B.C.

● Marriage of Antony and Cleopatra.

C. 30 B.C.

● Cleopatra VII Philopator commits suicide in Egypt.

18

● Emperor Augustus decrees the *Lex Julia,* which penalizes childless Roman citizens, adulterers, and those who marry outside of their social rank or status.

C. 370

- Hypatia is born in Alexandria, Egypt.

415

- Hypatia is murdered in Alexandria, Egypt.

C. 500

- Salians (Germanic Franks living in Gaul) issue a code of laws which prohibit women from inheriting land; the law is used for centuries to prevent women from ruling in France.

592

- Empress Suiko (554-628) becomes the first woman sovereign of Japan.

C. 690

- Wu Zetian (624-705) becomes the only female emperor of Imperial China.

C. 700

- Japanese legal code specifies that in law, ceremony, and practice, Japanese men can be polygamous—having first wives and an unlimited number of "second wives" or concubines—, but women cannot.

877

- Lady Ise, Japanese court lady, is born. She is considered one of the most accomplished poets of her time and her poems are widely anthologized.

935

- Hrotsvitha (also Hrotsvit or Roswitha), considered the first German woman poet, is born.

940

- Lady Ise dies.

950

- Publication of the *Kagero Nikki* (*The Gossamer Years*), a diary written by an anonymous Japanese courtesan. The realism and confessional quality of the work influence the works of later court diarists.

C. 960

- Japanese poet Izumi Shikibu, known for her expression of erotic and Buddhist themes, is born. Her body of work includes more than 1,500 *waka* (31-syllable poems).

C. 1002

- Sei Shonagon, Japanese court lady, writes *Makura no Soshi* (*The Pillow Book*), considered a classic of Japanese literature and the originator of the genre known as *zuihitsu* ("to follow the brush") that employs a stream-of-consciousness literary style.

C. 1008

- Murasaki Shikibu writes *Genji Monogatari* (*The Tale of Genji*), considered a masterpiece of classical prose literature in Japan.

C. 1030

- Izumi Shikibu dies.

1098

- Hildegard von Bingen is born in Bermersheim, Germany.

C. 1100

- Twenty women troubadours—aristocratic poet-composers who write songs dealing with love—write popular love songs in France. About twenty-four of their songs survive, including four written by the famous female troubadour known as the Countess of Dia, or Beatrix.

1122

- Eleanor of Aquitaine is born in Aquitaine, France. Her unconventional life is chronicled for centuries in books and dramatic works.

C. 1150

- Sometime in the twelfth century (some sources say 1122), Marie de France, the earliest known female French writer and author of *lais*, a collection of twelve verse tales written in octosyllabic rhyming couplets, flourished. She is thought to be the originator of the *lay* as a poetic form.

C. 1170

- Marie of Champagne (1145-1198), daughter of King Louis VII of France and Eleanor of Aquitaine, cosponsors "courts of love" to debate points on the proper conduct of knights toward their ladies. Marie encourages Chrétien de Troyes to write *Lancelot,* and Andreas Capellanus to write *The Art of Courtly Love.*

1179

- Hildegard von Bingen dies in Disibodenberg, Germany.

C. 1200

- Women shirabyoshi performances are a part of Japanese court and Buddhist temple festivities. In their songs and dances, women performers dress in white, male attire which includes fans, court caps, and swords. This form of traditional dance plays an important role in the development of classical Japanese noh drama.

1204

- Eleanor of Aquitaine dies on 1 April.

C. 1275

- Japanese poet and court lady Abutsu Ni (1222?-1283) writes her poetic travel diary, *Izayoi Nikki (Diary of the Waning Moon)* on the occasion of her travel to Kyoto to seek inheritance rights for herself and her children.

C. 1328

- The French cite the Salic Law, which was promulgated in the early medieval period and prohibits women from inheriting land, as the authority for denying the crown of France to anyone—man or woman—whose descent from a French king can be traced only through the female line.

1346

- Famous mystic St. Birgitta of Sweden (c.1303-1373) founds the Roman Catholic Order of St. Saviour, whose members are called the Brigittines. She authors *Revelations,* an account of her supernatural visions.

1347

- Caterina Benincasa (later St. Catherine of Siena) is born on 25 March in Siena, Italy.

C. 1365

- Christine de Pizan is born in Venice, Italy.

C. 1373

- Margery Kempe is born in King's Lynn (now known as Lynn), in Norfolk, England.

1380

- St. Catherine of Siena dies on 29 April in Rome, Italy.

C. 1393

- Julian of Norwich (1342?-1416?), the most famous of all the medieval recluses in England, writes *Revelations of Divine Love,* expounding on the idea of Christ as mother.

1399

- Christine de Pizan writes the long poem "Letter to the God of Love," which marks the beginning of the *querelle des femmes* (debate on women). This attack on misogyny in medieval literature triggers a lively exchange of letters among the foremost French scholars of the day, and the *querelle* is continued by various European literary scholars for centuries.

1429

- Joan of Arc (1412-1431)—in support of Charles I, who is prevented by the English from assuming his rightful place as King of France—leads liberation forces to victory in Orléans.

1431

- Joan of Arc is burned at the stake as a heretic by the English on 30 May. She is acquitted of heresy by another church court in 1456 and proclaimed a saint in 1920.

C. 1431

- Christine de Pizan dies in France.

C. 1440

- Margery Kempe dies in England.

1451

- Isabella of Castile, future Queen of Spain, is born. She succeeds her brother in 1474 and rules jointly with her husband, Ferdinand of Aragon, from 1479.

1465

- Cassandra Fedele, who becomes the most famous woman scholar in Italy, is born in Venice.

1469

- Laura Cereta, outspoken feminist and humanist scholar, is born in Brescia, Italy.

1485

- Veronica Gambara is born in Italy. Her court becomes an important center of the Italian Renaissance, and Gambara earns distinction as an author of Petrarchan sonnets as well as for her patronage of the artist Corregio.

1486

- *Malleus Maleficarum* (*The Hammer of Witches*), an encyclopedia of contemporary knowledge about witches and methods of investigating the crime of witchcraft, is published in Europe. The volume details numerous justifications for women's greater susceptibility to evil, and contributes to the almost universal European persecution of women as witches that reaches its height between 1580 and 1660 and makes its way to Salem, Massachusetts in 1692.

1492

- Marguerite de Navarre is born on 11 April in France.

1499

- Laura Cereta dies in Brescia, Italy.

C. 1512

- Catherine Parr is born in England.

1515

- Teresa de Alhumadawas (later St. Teresa de Ávila) is born on 28 March in Gotarrendura, Spain.

1524

- Courtesan Gaspara Stampa, widely regarded as the greatest woman poet of the Renaissance, is born in Padua, Italy.

1533

- Queen Elizabeth I is born on 7 September in Greenwich, England, the daughter of King Henry VIII and his second wife, Anne Boleyn.

1536

- King Henry VIII of England beheads his second wife, Anne Boleyn, on 19 May. Boleyn is convicted of infidelity and treason after she fails to produce the desired male heir.

1538

- Vittoria Colonna (1492-1547), an influential woman in Renaissance Italy, achieves distinction as a poet with the publication of her first book of poetry.

1548

- Catherine Parr dies in England.

1549

- Marguerite de Navarre dies in France.

1550

- Veronica Gambara dies in Italy.

1554

- Gaspara Stampa dies on 23 April in Venice, Italy.

1555

- Moderata Fonte (pseudonym of Modesta Pozzo) is born in Venice, Italy.

1558

- Elizabeth I assumes the throne of England and presides over a period of peace and prosperity known as the Elizabethan Age.

Cassadra Fedele dies in Venice. She is honored with a state funeral.

1559

■ Marguerite de Navarre completes her *L'Heptaméron des Nouvelles* (the *Heptameron*), a series of stories primarily concerned with the themes of love and spirituality.

1561

● Mary Sidney, noted English literary patron, is born in England. She is the sister of poet Sir Philip Sidney, whose poems she edits and publishes after his death in 1586, and whose English translation of the Psalms she completes.

1565

● French scholar Marie de Gournay is born on 6 October in Paris. Known as the French "Minerva" (a woman of great wisdom or learning), she is a financial success as a writer of treatises on various subjects, including *Equality of Men and Women* (1622) and *Complaint of Ladies* (1626), which demand better education for women.

1582

● St. Teresa de Avila dies on 4 October in Alba.

1592

● Moderata Fonte (pseudonym of Modesta Pozzo) dies in Venice, Italy.

C. 1600

■ Catherine de Vivonne (c. 1588-1665), Madame de Rambouillet, inaugurates and then presides over salon society in Paris, in which hostesses hold receptions in their salons or drawing rooms for the purpose of intellectual conversation. Salon society flourishes in the seventeenth and eighteenth centuries, and stimulates scholarly and literary development in France and England.

● Geisha (female artists and entertainers) and prostitutes are licensed by the Japanese government to work in the pleasure quarters of major cities in Japan.

1603

● Queen Elizabeth I dies on 24 March in Surrey, England.

■ Izumo no Okuni is believed to originate kabuki, the combination of dance, drama, and music which dominates Japanese theater throughout the Tokugawa period (1600-1868).

1607

● Madeleine de Scudéry, one of the best-known and most influential writers of romance tales in seventeeth-century Europe, is born on 15 November in Le Havre, France.

C. 1612

● American poet Anne Bradstreet is born in Northampton, England.

1614

● Margaret Askew Fell, who helps establish the Society of Friends, or Quakers, and becomes known as the "mother of Quakerism," is born in Lancashire, England. Quakers give women unusual freedom in religious life. An impassioned advocate of the right of women to preach, Fell publishes the tract *Women's Speaking Justified, Proved and Allowed of by the Scriptures* in 1666.

1621

● Mary Sidney dies in England.

C. 1623

● Margaret Lucas Cavendish, later Duchess of Newcastle, is born in England. She authors fourteen volumes of works, including scientific treatises, poems, and plays, and her autobiography *The True Relation of My Birth, Breeding and Life* (1656).

1631

● Katherine Phillips (1631-1664), who writes poetry under the pseudonym "Orinda," is born. She is the founder of a London literary salon called the Society of Friendship that includes such luminaries as Jeremy Taylor and Henry Vaughn.

CHRONOLOGY OF KEY EVENTS

C. 1640

● Aphra Behn is born.

C. 1645

● Deborah Moody (c. 1580-c. 1659) becomes the first woman to receive a land grant in colonial America when she is given the title to land in Kings County (now Brooklyn), New York. She is also the first colonial woman to vote.

C. 1646

● Glückel of Hameln, who records her life as a Jewish merchant in Germany in her memoirs, is born in Hamburg.

1651

● Juana Ramírez de Asbaje (later known as Sor Juana Inés de la Cruz) is born on 12 November on a small farm called San Miguel de Nepantla in New Spain (now Mexico).

1670

■ Aphra Behn becomes the first professional woman writer in England when her first play *The Forced Marriage; or, The Jealous Bridegroom,* is performed in London.

1672

● Anne Bradstreet dies on 16 September in Andover, Massachusetts.

C. 1673

■ Francois Poulain de la Barre publishes *The Equality of the Sexes,* in which he supports the idea that women have intellectual powers equal to those of men. His work stimulates the betterment of women's education in succeeding centuries.

1673

● Margaret Lucas Cavendish, Duchess of Newcastle, dies in England.

1676

■ After being captured and then released by Wampanaoag Indians, Puritan settler Mary White Rowlandson (1636-1678) writes what becomes a famous account of her captivity.

1689

● Mary Pierrpont (later Lady Mary Wortley Montagu) is born on 26 May in London, England.

● Aphra Behn dies on 16 April and is buried in the cloisters at Westminster Abbey.

1692

● The Salem, Massachusetts, witch hysteria begins in February, and eventually leads to the execution of eighteen women convicted of witchcraft in the infamous Salem Witchcraft Trials (1692-1693).

C. 1694

■ Mary Astell (1666-1731) publishes the treatise *A Serious Proposal to the Ladies* in two volumes (1694-1697). In the work, Astell calls for the establishment of private institutions where single women live together for a time and receive quality education.

1695

● Sor Juana Inés de la Cruz dies on 17 April at the Convent of St. Jerome in Mexico.

1701

● Madeleine de Scudéry dies on 2 June in Paris, France.

C. 1704

■ Sarah Kemble Knight (1666-1727), a Puritan author, records her arduous journey from Boston to New York to settle the estate of her cousin.

C. 1713

■ Anne Kingsmill Finch (1661-1720) writes many poems dealing with the injustices suffered by women of the aristocratic class to which she belonged. As Countess of Winchilsea, she becomes the center of a literary circle at her husband's estate in Eastwell, England.

1728

● Mercy Otis Warren is born on 14 September in Barnstable, Massachusetts.

1729

- Catherine the Great is born on 2 May in Germany as Sophia Friederica Augusta.

1744

- Abigail Adams is born Abigail Smith on 11 November in Weymouth, Massachusetts.

1748

- Olympe de Gouges, French Revolutionary feminist, is born Olympe Gouze in Montauban, France. She plays an active role in the French Revolution, demanding equal rights for women in the new French Republic.

1752

- Frances "Fanny" Burney is born on 13 June in England.

C. 1753

- Phillis Wheatley is born in Africa.

1759

- Mary Wollstonecraft is born on 27 April in England.

1762

- Lady Mary Wortley Montagu dies on 21 August in London, England.
- Catherine the Great becomes Empress of Russia.

1766

- Germaine Necker (later Madame de Staël) is born on 22 April in Paris, France.

1768

- Maria Edgeworth is born on 1 January at Black Bourton in Oxfordshire, England.

1774

- Clementina Rind (1740-1774) is appointed publisher of the *Virginia Gazette* by the House of Burgesses in Virginia.

1775

- Jane Austen is born on 16 December at Steventon Rectory, Hampshire, England.

1776

- Men and women who hold property worth over 50 pounds are granted suffrage in New Jersey.

C. 1780

- Madame Roland (1754-1793), formerly Marie Philppon, hosts an important salon where revolutionary politicians and thinkers debate during the French Revolution. An outspoken feminist, she presses for women's political and social rights.

1784

- Hannah Adams (1758-1831) becomes the first American woman author to support herself with money earned from writing, with the publication of her first book, *View of Religions* (later *Dictionary of Religions*).
- Phillis Wheatley dies on 5 December in Boston, Massachusetts.

1787

- Catherine Sawbridge Macaulay publishes *Letters on Education,* an appeal for better education of women.
- Mary Wollstonecraft's *Thoughts on the Education of Daughters: With Reflections on Female Conduct, in the More Important Duties of Life* is published by J. Johnson.

1789

- Catharine Maria Sedgwick is born on 28 December in Stockbridge, Massachusetts.
- Olympe de Gouges writes *The Declaration of the Rights of Women and Citizen,* a 17-point document demanding the recognition of women as political, civil, and legal equals of men, and including a sample marriage contract that emphasizes free will and equality in marriage.

1792

- Sarah Moore Grimké is born on 26 November in Charleston, South Carolina.

■ Mary Wollstonecraft's *A Vindication of the Rights of Woman, with Strictures on Political and Moral Subjects* is published by J. Johnson.

1793

● Lucretia Coffin Mott is born on 3 January in Nantucket, Massachusetts.

● Olympe de Gouges is executed by guillotine for treason on 3 November.

● Madame Roland is executed in November, ostensibly for treason, but actually because the Jacobins want to suppress feminist elements in the French Revolution.

1796

● Catherine the Great dies following a stroke on 6 November in Russia.

1797

● Mary Wollstonecraft Shelley is born on 30 August, in London, England.

● Mary Wollstonecraft dies on 10 September in London, England, from complications following childbirth.

● Sojourner Truth is born Isabella Bomefree in Ulster County, New York.

1799

■ Mary Wollstonecraft's *Maria; or, The Wrongs of Woman: A Posthumous Fragment* is published by James Carey.

1801

● Caroline M. (Stansbury) Kirkland is born on 11 January in New York City.

1802

● Lydia Maria Child is born on 11 February in Medford, Massachusetts.

1804

● George Sand (pseudonym of Armandine Aurore Lucille Dupin) is born on 1 July in Paris, France.

● The Napoleonic Code is established in France under Napoleon I, and makes women legally subordinate to men. The code requires women to be obedient to their husbands, bars women from voting, sitting on juries, serving as legal witnesses, or sitting on chambers of commerce or boards of trade.

1805

● Angelina Emily Grimké is born on 20 February in Charleston, South Carolina.

1806

● Elizabeth Barrett Browning is born on 6 March in Coxhoe Hall, Durham, England.

1807

■ Germaine de Staël's *Corinne, ou l'Italie* (*Corinne, or Italy*) is published by Nicolle.

● Suffrage in New Jersey is limited to "white male citizens."

1808

● Caroline Sheridan Norton is born on 22 March in England.

1810

● (Sarah) Margaret Fuller is born on 23 May in Cambridgeport, Massachusetts.

● Elizabeth Cleghorn Gaskell is born on 29 September in London, England.

1811

● Harriet Beecher Stowe is born on 14 June in Litchfield, Connecticut.

■ Jane Austen's *Sense and Sensibility* is published by T. Egerton.

1813

● Harriet A. Jacobs is born in North Carolina.

■ Jane Austen's *Pride and Prejudice* is published by T. Egerton.

1814

● Mercy Otis Warren dies on 19 October in Plymouth, Massachusetts.

1815

- Elizabeth Cady Stanton is born on 12 November in Johnstown, New York.

- King Louis XVIII of France outlaws divorce.

1816

- Charlotte Brontë is born on 21 April in Thornton, Yorkshire, England.

- Jane Austen's *Emma* is published by M. Carey.

1817

- Madame Germaine de Staël dies on 14 July in Paris, France.

- Jane Austen dies on 18 July in Winchester, Hampshire, England.

1818

- Emily Brontë is born on 30 July in Thornton, Yorkshire, England.

- Lucy Stone is born on 13 August near West Brookfield, Massachusetts.

- Abigail Adams dies on 28 October in Quincy, Massachusetts.

- Jane Austen's *Northanger Abbey and Persuasion* is published by John Murray.

- Educator Emma Hart Willard's *A Plan for Improving Female Education* is published by Middlebury College.

- Mary Wollstonecraft Shelley's *Frankenstein; or, The Modern Prometheus* is published by Lackington, Hughes, Harding, Mavor & Jones.

1819

- Julia Ward Howe is born on 27 May in New York City.

- George Eliot (pseudonym of Mary Ann Evans) is born on 22 November in Arbury, Warwickshire, England.

1820

- Susan B. Anthony is born on 15 February in Adams, Massachusetts.

1821

- Emma Hart Willard establishes the Troy Female Seminary in Troy, New York.

1822

- Frances Power Cobbe is born on 4 December in Dublin, Ireland.

1823

- Charlotte Yonge is born 11 August in Otterbourne, Hampshire, England.

1825

- Frances Ellen Watkins Harper is born on 24 September in Baltimore, Maryland.

1826

- Matilda Joslyn Gage is born on 24 March in Cicero, New York.

1830

- Christina Rossetti is born on 5 December in London, England.

- Emily Dickinson is born on 10 December in Amherst, Massachusetts.

- *Godey's Lady's Book*—the first American women's magazine—is founded by Louis Antoine Godey and edited by Sarah Josepha Hale (1788-1879).

1832

- Louisa May Alcott is born on 29 November in Germantown, Pennsylvania.

- George Sand's *Indiana* is published by Roret et Dupuy.

1833

- Oberlin Collegiate Institute—the first coeducational institution of higher learning— is established in Oberlin, Ohio.

1836

- Marietta Holley is born on 16 July near Adams, New York.

1837

- Mt. Holyoke College—the first college for women—is founded by Mary Lyon in South Hadley, Massachusetts.

Alexandria Victoria (1819-1901) becomes Queen Victoria at the age of eighteen. Her reign lasts for 63 years, the longest reign of any British monarch.

1838

Victoria Woodhull is born on 23 September in Homer, Ohio.

Sarah Moore Grimké's *Letters on the Equality of the Sexes, and the Condition of Woman* is published by I. Knapp.

1840

Frances "Fanny" Burney dies on 6 January in London, England.

Ernestine Rose (1810-1892) writes the petition for what will become the Married Woman's Property Law (1848).

C. 1844

Sarah Winnemucca is born on Paiute land near Humboldt Lake in what is now Nevada.

1845

Margaret Fuller's *Woman in the Nineteenth Century* is published by Greeley & McElrath.

1847

Charlotte Brontë's *Jane Eyre* is published by Smith, Elder.

Emily Brontë's *Wuthering Heights* is published by T. C. Newby.

1848

The first women's rights convention is called by Lucretia Coffin Mott and Elizabeth Cady Stanton on 19 July and is held in Seneca Falls, New York on 20 July.

Emily Brontë dies on 19 December in Haworth, Yorkshire, England.

New York State Legislature passes the Married Woman's Property Law, granting women the right to retain possession of property they owned prior to marriage.

1849

Maria Edgeworth dies on 22 May in Edgeworthstown, her family's estate in Ireland.

Sarah Orne Jewett is born on 3 September in South Berwick, Maine.

Amelia Bloomer publishes the first issue of her Seneca Falls newspaper *The Lily,* which provides a forum for both temperance and women's rights reformers.

The first state constitution of California extends property rights to women in their own name.

1850

Margaret Fuller drowns—along with her husband and son—on 19 July in a shipwreck off of Fire Island, New York.

The first National Woman's Rights Convention, planned by Lucy Stone and Lucretia Mott, is attended by over one thousand women on 23 and 24 October in Worcester, Massachusetts.

Elizabeth Barrett Browning's *Poems,* containing her *Sonnets from the Portuguese,* is published by Chapman & Hall.

The Narrative of Sojourner Truth, transcribed by Olive Gilbert, is published in the Boston periodical, the *Liberator.*

1851

Mary Wollstonecraft Shelley dies on 1 February in Bournemouth, England.

Kate Chopin is born on 8 February in St. Louis, Missouri.

Sojourner Truth delivers her "A'n't I a Woman?" speech at the Women's Rights Convention on 29 May in Akron, Ohio.

1852

Harriet Beecher Stowe's *Uncle Tom's Cabin; or, Life among the Lowly* is published by Jewett, Proctor & Worthington.

Susan B. Anthony founds The Women's Temperance Society, the first temperance organization in the United States.

1853

Charlotte Brontë's *Villette* is published by Smith, Elder.

Paulina Kellogg Wright Davis (1813-1876) edits and publishes *Una,* the first newspaper of the women's rights movement.

1854

■ Margaret Oliphant's *A Brief Summary in Plain Language of the Most Important Laws Concerning Women*, a pamphlet explaining the unfair laws concerning women and exposing the need for reform, is published in London.

1855

● Charlotte Brontë dies on 31 March in Haworth, Yorkshire, England.

● Elizabeth Cady Stanton, speaking in favor of expanding the Married Woman's Property Law, becomes the first woman to appear before the New York State Legislature.

1856

● Harriot Eaton Stanton Blatch is born on 20 January in Seneca Falls, New York.

1857

■ Elizabeth Barrett Browning's *Aurora Leigh* is published by Chapman & Hall.

1858

● Emmeline Pankhurst is born on 4 July in Manchester, England.

● Anna Julia Haywood Cooper is born on 10 August in Raleigh, North Carolina.

1859

● Carrie Chapman Catt is born on 9 January in Ripon, Wisconsin.

1860

● Charlotte Perkins Gilman is born on 3 July in Hartford, Connecticut.

● Jane Addams is born on 6 September in Cedarville, Illinois.

1861

● Victoria Earle Matthews is born on 27 May in Fort Valley, Georgia.

● Elizabeth Barrett Browning dies on 29 June in Florence, Italy.

■ Harriet Jacobs's *Incidents in the Life of a Slave Girl, Written by Herself,* edited by Lydia Maria Child, is published in Boston.

1862

● Edith Wharton is born on 24 January in New York City.

● Ida B. Wells-Barnett is born on 16 July in Holly Springs, Mississippi.

■ Julia Ward Howe's "The Battle Hymn of the Republic" is published in the *Atlantic Monthly.*

1864

● Caroline M. (Stansbury) Kirkland dies of a stroke on 6 April in New York City.

1865

● Elizabeth Cleghorn Gaskell dies on 12 November in Holybourne, Hampshire, England.

1866

● The American Equal Rights Association—dedicated to winning suffrage for African American men and for women of all colors—is founded by Susan B. Anthony and Elizabeth Cady Stanton on 1 May. Lucretia Coffin Mott is elected as the group's president.

● Elizabeth Cady Stanton runs for Congress as an independent; she receives 24 of 12,000 votes cast.

1867

● Catharine Maria Sedgwick dies on 31 July in Boston, Massachusetts.

1868

■ Susan B. Anthony and Elizabeth Cady Stanton found the New York-based weekly newspaper, *The Revolution,* with the motto: "The true republic—men, their rights and nothing more; women, their rights and nothing less," in January.

● Julia Ward Howe founds the New England Woman Suffrage Association and the New England Women's Club.

■ Louisa May Alcott's *Little Women; or, Meg, Jo, Beth, and Amy* (2 vols., 1868-69) is published by Roberts Brothers.

1869

■ John Stuart Mill's treatise in support of women's suffrage, *The Subjection of Women,* is published in London.

- Emma Goldman is born on 27 June in Kovno, Lithuania.

- Louisa May Alcott's *Hospital Sketches and Camp and Fireside Stories* is published by Roberts Brothers.

- Women are granted full and equal suffrage and are permitted to hold office within the territory of Wyoming.

- The National Woman Suffrage Association is founded by Elizabeth Cady Stanton and Susan B. Anthony in May in New York City.

- The American Woman Suffrage Association is founded by Lucy Stone, Julia Ward Howe, and others in November in Boston, Massachusetts.

1870

- *The Woman's Journal,* edited by Lucy Stone, Henry Blackwell, and Mary Livermore, begins publication on 8 January.

- Victoria Woodhull and Tennessee Claflin publish the first issue of their controversial New York weekly newspaper, *Woodhull and Claflin's Weekly.*

1871

- Women are granted full and equal suffrage in the territory of Utah. Their rights are revoked in 1887 and restored in 1896.

- Victoria Woodhull presents her views on women's rights in a passionate speech to the House Judiciary Committee, marking the first personal appearance before such a high congressional committee by a woman.

- Wives of many prominent U. S. politicians, military officers, and businessmen found the Anti-Suffrage party to fight against women's suffrage.

1872

- Victoria Woodhull, as a member of the Equal Rights Party (or National Radical Reform Party), becomes the first woman candidate for the office of U.S. President. Her running mate is Frederick Douglass.

- Susan B. Anthony and 15 other women attempt to cast their votes in Rochester, New York, in the presidential election. Anthony is arrested and fined $100, which she refuses to pay.

- Sojourner Truth attempts to cast her vote in Grand Rapids, Michigan in the presidential election but is denied a ballot.

1873

- Colette is born on 28 January in Burgundy, France.

- Maria Mitchell (1818-1889), astronomer and faculty member at Vassar College, establishes the Association of the Advancement of Women.

- Willa Cather is born on 7 December in Back Creek Valley, Virginia.

- Sarah Moore Grimké dies on 23 December in Hyde Park, Massachusetts.

- Louisa May Alcott's *Work: A Story of Experience* is published by Roberts Brothers.

1874

- Gertrude Stein is born on 3 February in Allegheny, Pennsylvania.

- Amy Lowell is born on 9 February in Brookline, Massachusetts.

1876

- George Sand dies on 9 June in Nohant, France.

- Susan Glaspell is born on 1 July (some sources say 1882) in Davenport, Iowa.

1877

- Caroline Sheridan Norton dies on 15 June in England.

1878

- Passage of the Matrimonial Causes Act in England enables abused wives to obtain separation orders to keep their husbands away from them.

- The "Susan B. Anthony Amendment," which will extend suffrage to women in the United States, is first proposed in Congress by Senator A. A. Sargent.

1879

- Margaret Sanger is born on 14 September in Corning, New York.

- Angelina Emily Grimké dies on 26 October in Hyde Park, Massachusetts.

1880

- Christabel Pankhurst is born on 22 September in Manchester, England.

- Lydia Maria Child dies on 20 October in Wayland, Massachusetts.

- Lucretia Coffin Mott dies on 11 November in Philadelphia, Pennsylvania.

- George Eliot (pseudonym of Mary Ann Evans) dies on 22 December in London, England.

1881

- Hubertine Auclert founds *La Citoyenne* (*The Citizen*), a newspaper dedicated to female suffrage.

- The first volume of *A History of Woman Suffrage* (Vols. 1-3, 1881-1888; Vol. 4, 1903), edited and compiled by Susan B. Anthony, Elizabeth Cady Stanton, Ida Harper Husted, and Matilda Joslyn Gage, is published by Fowler & Welles.

1882

- Virginia Woolf is born on 25 January in London, England.

- Sylvia Pankhurst is born on 5 May in Manchester, England.

- Aletta Jacobs (1854-1929), the first woman doctor in Holland, opens the first birth control clinic in Europe.

1883

- Sojourner Truth dies on 26 November in Battle Creek, Michigan.

- Olive Schreiner's *The Story of an African Farm* is published by Chapman & Hall.

1884

- Eleanor Roosevelt is born on 11 October in New York City.

1885

- Alice Paul is born on 11 January in Moorestown, New Jersey.

- Isak Dinesen is born Karen Christentze Dinesen on 17 April in Rungsted, Denmark.

1886

- Emily Dickinson dies on 15 May in Amherst, Massachusetts.

- H. D. (Hilda Doolittle) is born on 10 September in Bethlehem, Pennsylvania.

1887

- Marianne Moore is born on 15 November in Kirkwood, Missouri.

- Article five of the Peace Preservation Law in Japan prohibits women and minors from joining political organizations and attending meetings where political speeches are given, and from engaging in academic studies of political subjects.

1888

- Louisa May Alcott dies on 6 March in Boston, Massachusetts, and is buried in Sleepy Hollow Cemetery in Concord, Massachusetts.

- Susan B. Anthony organizes the International Council of Women with representatives from 48 countries.

- Louisa Lawson (1848-1920) founds Australia's first feminist newspaper, *The Dawn*.

- The National Council of Women in the United States is formed to promote the advancement of women in society. The group also serves as a clearinghouse for various women's organizations.

1889

- Anna Akhmatova is born Anna Adreyevna Gorenko on 23 June in Bolshoy Fontan, Russia.

1890

- The National American Woman Suffrage Association (NAWSA) is formed by the merging of the American Woman Suffrage Assocation and the National Woman Suffrage Association. Elizabeth Cady Stanton is the NAWSA's first president; she is succeeded by Susan B. Anthony in 1892.

1891

- Zora Neale Hurston is born on 15 (some sources say 7) January in Nostasulga, Alabama. (Some sources cite birth year as c. 1901 or 1903, and birth place as Eatonville, Florida).

- Sarah Winnemucca dies on 16 October in Monida, Montana.

1892

- Edna St. Vincent Millay is born on 22 February in Rockland, Maine.
- Djuna Barnes is born on 12 June in Cornwall on Hudson, New York.
- Rebecca West (pseudonym of Cicily Isabel Fairfield) is born on 21 December in County Kerry, Ireland.
- Charlotte Perkins Gilman's *The Yellow Wallpaper* is published in *New England Magazine*.
- Frances E. W. Harper's *Iola Leroy; or, Shadows Uplifted* is published by Garrigues Bros.
- Olympia Brown (1835-1926), first woman ordained minister in the United States, founds the Federal Suffrage Association to campaign for women's suffrage.
- Ida Wells-Barnett's *Southern Horrors. Lynch Law in All its Phases* is published by Donohue and Henneberry.

1893

- Lucy Stone dies on 18 October in Dorchester, Massachusetts.
- The National Council of Women of Canada is founded by Lady Aberdeen.
- Suffrage is granted to women in Colorado.
- New Zealand becomes the first nation to grant women the vote.

1894

- Christina Rossetti dies on 29 December in London, England.

1895

- The first volume of Elizabeth Cady Stanton's *The Woman's Bible* (3 vols., 1895-1898) is published by European Publishing Company.

1896

- Harriet Beecher Stowe dies on 1 July in Hartford, Connecticut.
- Idaho grants women the right to vote.
- The National Association of Colored Women's Clubs is founded in Washington, D.C.

1897

- Harriet A. Jacobs dies on 7 March in Cambridge, Massachusetts.

1898

- Matilda Joslyn Gage dies on 18 March in Chicago, Illinois.
- Charlotte Perkins Gilman's *Women and Economics* is published by Small Maynard.
- The Meiji Civil Law Code, the law of the Japanese nation state, makes the patriarchal family, rather than the individual, the legally recognized entity.

1899

- Elizabeth Bowen is born on 7 June in Dublin, Ireland.
- Kate Chopin's *The Awakening* is published by Herbert S. Stone.

1900

- Colette's *Claudine a l'ecole* (*Claudine at School*, 1930) is published by Ollendorf.
- Carrie Chapman Catt succeeds Susan B. Anthony as president of the NAWSA.

1901

- Charlotte Yonge dies of bronchitis and pneumonia on 24 March in Elderfield, England.

1902

- Elizabeth Cady Stanton dies on 26 October in New York City.
- Women of European descent gain suffrage in Australia.

1903

- The Women's Social and Political Union, led by suffragists Emmeline and Christabel Pankhurst, stage demonstrations in Hyde Park in London, England.

1904

- Frances Power Cobbe dies on 5 April.
- Kate Chopin dies following a cerebral hemorrhage on 22 August in St. Louis, Missouri.

- Susan B. Anthony establishes the International Woman Suffrage Alliance in Berlin, Germany.

C. 1905

- Lillian Hellman is born on 20 June in New Orleans, Louisiana.

1905

- Austrian activist and novelist Bertha von Suttner (1843-1914) receives the Nobel Peace Prize.

1906

- Susan B. Anthony dies on 13 March in Rochester, New York.

- Finnish women gain suffrage and the right to be elected to public office.

1907

- Victoria Earle Matthews dies of tuberculosis on 10 March in New York City.

- Mary Edwards Walker, M.D.'s pamphlet on women's suffrage, "Crowning Constitutional Argument," is published.

- Harriot Stanton Blatch founds the Equality League of Self-Supporting Women, later called the Women's Political Union.

1908

- Simone de Beauvoir is born on 9 January in Paris, France.

- Julia Ward Howe becomes the first woman to be elected to the American Academy of Arts and Letters.

1909

- Sarah Orne Jewett dies on 24 June in South Berwick, Maine.

- Swedish author Selma Lagerlöf (1858-1940) becomes the first woman to receive the Nobel Prize for Literature.

- "The Uprising of the 20,000" grows from one local to a general strike against several shirtwaist factories in New York City. Over 700 women and girls are arrested, and 19 receive workhouse sentences. The strike is called off on 15 February 1910. Over 300 shops settle with the union, and workers achieve the terms demanded.

- Jeanne-Elisabeth Archer Schmahl (1846-1915) founds the French Union for Woman Suffrage.

1910

- Julia Ward Howe dies of pneumonia on 17 October in Newport, Rhode Island.

- The Women' Political Union holds the first large suffrage parade in New York City.

- Suffrage is granted to women in Washington State.

- Jane Addams's *Twenty Years at Hull House* is published by Macmillan.

1911

- Frances Ellen Watkins Harper dies on 22 February in Philadelphia, Pennsylvania.

- A fire at the Triangle Shirtwaist Factory in New York City on 25 March claims the lives of 146 factory workers, 133 of them women. Public outrage over the fire leads to reforms in labor laws and improvement in working conditions.

- Suffrage is granted to women in California.

- Edith Wharton's *Ethan Frome* is published by Scribner.

1912

- Suffrage is granted to women in Arizona, Kansas, and Oregon.

- A parade in support of women's suffrage is held in New York City and draws 20,000 participants and half a million onlookers.

1913

- Muriel Rukeyser is born on 15 December in New York City.

- Willa Cather's *O Pioneers!* is published by Houghton.

- Ida Wells-Barnett founds the Alpha Suffrage Club in Chicago.

- Suffrage is granted to women in Alaska.

- The Congressional Union is founded by Alice Paul and Lucy Burns.

1914

- Marguerite Duras is born on 4 April in Gia Dinh, Indochina (now Vietnam).

- The National Federation of Women's Clubs, which includes over two million white women and women of color, formally endorses the campaign for women's suffrage.

- Suffrage is granted to women in Montana and Nevada.

- Margaret Sanger begins publication of her controversial monthly newsletter *The Woman Rebel*, which is banned as obscene literature.

1915

- Charlotte Perkins Gilman's *Herland* is published in the journal *Forerunner*.

- *Woman's Work in Municipalities*, by American suffragist and historian Mary Ritter Beard (1876-1958), is published by Appleton.

- Icelandic women who are age 40 or older gain suffrage.

- Members of the NAWSA from across the United States hold a large parade in New York city.

- Most Danish women over age 25 gain suffrage.

1916

- Ardent suffragist and pacifist Jeannette Pickering Rankin (1880-1973) of Montana becomes the first woman elected to the U. S. House of Representatives. She later votes against U. S. involvement in both World Wars.

- The Congressional Union becomes the National Women's Party, led by Alice Paul and Lucy Burns.

- NAWSA president Carrie Chapman Catt unveils her "Winning Plan" for American women's suffrage at a convention held in Atlantic City, New Jersey.

- Suffrage is granted to women in Alberta, Manitoba, and Saskatchewan, Canada.

- Margaret Sanger opens the first U. S. birth-control clinic in Brooklyn, New York. The clinic is shut down 10 days after it opens and Sanger is arrested.

- Margaret Sanger's *What Every Mother Should Know; or, How Six Little Children were Taught the Truth* is published by M. N. Maisel.

1917

- Gwendolyn Brooks is born on 7 June in Topeka, Kansas.

- The National Women's Party becomes the first group in U.S. history to picket in front of the White House. Picketers are arrested and incarcerated; during their incarceration, Alice Paul leads them in a hunger strike. Many of the imprisoned suffragists are brutally force-fed, including Paul. The suffragettes' mistreatment is published in newspapers, the White House bows to public pressure, and they are released.

- White women in Arkansas are granted partial suffrage; they are able to vote in primary, but not general, elections.

- Suffrage is granted to women in New York.

- Suffrage is granted to women in Estonia, Latvia, and Lithuania.

- Women in Ontario and British Columbia, Canada, gain suffrage.

- Suffragists and members of the NAWSA, led by president Carrie Chapman Catt, march in a parade in New York City.

- Margaret Sanger founds and edits *The Birth Control Review*, the first scientific journal devoted to the subject of birth control.

1918

- Willa Cather's *My Antonia* is published by Houghton.

- Suffrage is granted to women in Michigan, Oklahoma, and South Dakota; women in Texas gain suffrage for primary elections only.

- President Woodrow Wilson issues a statement in support of a federal constitutional amendment granting full suffrage to American women.

- A resolution to amend the U.S. constitution to ensure that the voting rights of U.S. citizens cannot "be denied or abridged by the United States or any state on account of sex" passes in the House of Representatives.

- President Wilson urges the Senate to support the 19th amendment, but fails to win the two-thirds majority necessary for passage.

- Women in the United Kingdom who are married, own property, or are college graduates over the age of 30, are granted suffrage.

- Women in Austria, Czechoslovakia, Germany, Luxembourg, and Poland gain suffrage.

- Women in New Brunswick and Nova Scotia, Canada, gain suffrage. Canadian women of British or French heritage gain voting rights in Federal elections.

- Marie Stopes's *Married Love* and *Wise Parenthood* are published by A. C. Fifield.

- Harriot Stanton Blatch's *Mobilizing Woman-Power,* with a foreword by Theodore Roosevelt, is published by The Womans Press.

1919

- Women in the Netherlands, Rhodesia, and Sweden gain suffrage.

- Doris Lessing is born on 22 October in Kermanshah, Persia (now Iran).

- The "Susan B. Anthony Amendment," also known as the 19th Amendment to the U. S. Constitution, after it is defeated twice in the Senate, passes in both houses of Congress. The amendment is sent to states for ratification.

1920

- The 19th Amendment to the U.S. Constitution is ratified by the necessary two-thirds of states and American women are guaranteed suffrage on 26 August when Secretary of State Bainbridge Colby signs the amendment into law.

- The NAWSA is reorganized as the National League of Women Voters and elects Maud Wood Park as its first president.

- Bella Abzug is born on 24 July in New York City.

- Icelandic women gain full suffrage.

- Edith Wharton's *The Age of Innocence* is published by Meredith.

- Colette's *Cheri* is published by Fayard.

1921

- Betty Friedan is born on 4 February in Peoria, Illinois.

- Edith Wharton receives the Pulitzer Prize for fiction for *The Age of Innocence.*

- Margaret Sanger organizes the first American Conference on Birth Control in New York City.

1922

- Irish women gain full suffrage.

- Grace Paley is born on 11 December in New York City.

- Edna St. Vincent Millay's *The Ballad of the Harp-Weaver* is published by F. Shay.

1923

- Edna St. Vincent Millay receives the Pulitzer Prize for Poetry for *The Ballad of the Harp-Weaver.*

- Margaret Sanger opens the Birth Control Clinical Research Bureau in New York to dispense contraceptives to women under the supervision of a licensed physician and to study the effect of contraception upon women's health.

- Margaret Sanger founds the American Birth Control League.

- The Equal Rights Amendment (ERA), written by Alice Paul, is introduced in Congress for the first time in December.

1924

- Phyllis Schlafly is born on 15 August in St. Louis, Missouri.

- Shirley Chisolm is born on 30 November in Brooklyn, New York.

1925

- Amy Lowell dies on 12 May in Brookline, Massachusetts.

- *Collected Poems of H.D.* is published by Boni & Liveright.

- Virginia Woolf's *Mrs. Dalloway* is published by Harcourt.

1926

- Marietta Holley dies on 1 March near Adams, New York.

- Marianne Moore becomes the first woman editor of *The Dial* in New York City, a post she holds until 1929.

- Carrie Chapman Catt and Nettie Rogers Schuler's *Woman Suffrage and Politics; the Inner Story of the Suffrage Movement* is published by Charles Scribner's Sons.

- Grazia Deledda receives the Nobel Prize in Literature.

1927

- Victoria Woodhull dies on 10 June in Norton Park, England.

- Virginia Woolf's *To the Lighthouse* is published by Harcourt.

1928

- Maya Angelou is born Marguerite Johnson on 4 April in St. Louis, Missouri.

- Emmeline Pankhurst dies on 14 June in London, England.

- Anne Sexton is born on 9 November in Newton, Massachusetts.

- Virginia Woolf's *Orlando* is published by Crosby Gaige.

- Women are granted full suffrage in Great Britain.

- Gertrude Stein's *Useful Knowledge* is published by Payson & Clarke.

- Sigrid Undset receives the Nobel Prize in Literature.

1929

- Adrienne Rich is born on 16 May in Baltimore, Maryland.

- Marilyn French is born on 21 November in New York City.

- While Arthur M. Schlesinger Sr. reads her speech for her, Margaret Sanger appears in a gag on a stage in Boston where she has been prevented from speaking.

- Virginia Woolf's *A Room of One's Own* is published by Harcourt.

1930

- Lorraine Hansberry is born on 19 May in Chicago, Illinois.

- Cairine Wilson is appointed the first woman senator in Canada.

1931

- Jane Addams receives the Nobel Peace Prize.

- Toni Morrison is born Chloe Anthony Wofford on 18 February in Lorain, Ohio.

- Ida B. Wells-Barnett dies on 25 March in Chicago, Illinois.

1932

- Sylvia Plath is born on 27 October in Boston, Massachusetts.

1933

- Gertrude Stein's *The Autobiography of Alice B. Toklas* is published by Harcourt.

- Frances Perkins (1882-1965) is appointed Secretary of Labor by President Franklin D. Roosevelt, and becomes the first female cabinet member in the United States.

1934

- Gloria Steinem is born on 25 March in Toledo, Ohio.

- Kate Millett is born on 14 September in St. Paul, Minnesota.

- Lillian Hellman's *The Children's Hour* debuts on 20 November at Maxine Elliot's Theatre in New York City.

1935

- Jane Addams dies of cancer on 21 May in Chicago, Illinois.

- Charlotte Perkins Gilman commits suicide on 17 August in Pasadena, California.

- The National Council of Negro Women is founded by Mary McLeod Bethune (1875-1955).

1936

- First lady Eleanor Roosevelt begins writing a daily syndicated newspaper column, "My Day."

- Margaret Mitchell's *Gone with the Wind* is published by Macmillan.

1937

- Hélène Cixous is born on 5 June in Oran, Algeria.

- Bessie Head is born on 6 July in Pietermaritzburg, South Africa.

- Edith Wharton dies on 11 August in St. Brice-sous-Foret, France.

- Zora Neale Hurston's *Their Eyes Were Watching God* is published by Lippincott.

Margaret Mitchell (1900-1949) receives the Pulitzer Prize in Letters & Drama for novel for *Gone with the Wind*.

Anne O'Hare McCormick becomes the first woman to receive the Pulitzer Prize in Journalism, which she is given for distinguished correspondence for her international reporting on the rise of Italian Fascism in the *New York Times*.

1938

Joyce Carol Oates is born on 16 June in Lockport, New York.

Pearl Buck receives the Nobel Prize in Literature.

1939

Germaine Greer is born on 29 January near Melbourne, Australia.

Lillian Hellman's *The Little Foxes* debuts on 15 February at National Theatre in New York City.

Margaret Atwood is born on 18 November in Ottawa, Ontario, Canada.

Paula Gunn Allen is born in Cubero, New Mexico.

French physician Madeleine Pelletier (1874-1939) is arrested for performing abortions in Paris, France; she dies later the same year. Throughout her medical career, Pelletier advocated women's rights to birth control and abortion, and founded her own journal, *La Suffragist*.

1940

Emma Goldman dies on 14 May in Toronto, Ontario, Canada.

Maxine Hong Kingston is born on 27 October in Stockton, California.

Harriot Eaton Stanton Blatch dies on 20 November in Greenwich, Connecticut.

1941

Virginia Woolf commits suicide on 28 March in Lewes, Sussex, England.

1942

Erica Jong is born on 26 March in New York City.

Isabel Allende is born on 2 August in Lima, Peru.

Ellen Glasgow (1873-1945) receives the Pulitzer Prize for her novel *In This Our Life*.

Margaret Walker (1915-1998) becomes the first African American to receive the Yale Series of Young Poets Award for her collection *For My People*.

1944

Alice Walker is born on 9 February in Eatonton, Georgia.

Martha Gellhorn (1908-1998) is the only woman journalist to go ashore with Allied troops during the D-Day invasion of Normandy, France in June.

Buchi Emecheta is born on 21 July in Yaba, Lagos, Nigeria.

Rita Mae Brown is born on 28 November in Hanover, Pennsylvania.

Women are granted suffrage in France and Jamaica.

1945

Eleanor Roosevelt becomes the first person to represent the U. S. at the United Nations. She serves until 1951, is reappointed in 1961, and serves until her death in 1962.

Gabriela Mistral receives the Nobel Prize in Literature.

Louise Bogan is named U. S. Poet Laureate.

1946

Gertrude Stein dies of cancer on 27 July in Neuilly-sur-Seine, France.

Andrea Dworkin is born on 26 September in Camden, New Jersey.

Mary Ritter Beard's *Woman as a Force in History: A Study in Traditions and Realities* is published by Macmillan.

Eleanor Roosevelt becomes chair of the United Nations Human Rights Commission. She remains chair until 1951.

1947

Carrie Chapman Catt dies on 9 March in New Rochelle, New York.

- Willa Cather dies on 24 April in New York City.
- Dorothy Fuldheim, a newscaster in Cleveland, Ohio, becomes the first female television news anchor at WEWS-TV.

1948

- Susan Glaspell dies on 27 July in Provincetown, Massachusetts.
- Ntozake Shange is born Paulette Linda Williams on 18 October in Trenton, New Jersey.
- Leonie Adams is named U. S. Poet Laureate.

1949

- Simone de Beauvoir's *Le deuxième sexe* (*The Second Sex,* H. M. Parshley, translator: Knopf, 1953) is published by Gallimard.
- Elizabeth Bishop is named U. S. Poet Laureate.
- Gwendolyn Brooks's *Annie Allen* is published by Harper.

1950

- Gloria Naylor is born on 25 January in New York City.
- Edna St. Vincent Millay dies of a heart attack on 19 October at Steepletop, Austerlitz, New York.
- Gwendolyn Brooks receives the Pulitzer Prize for poetry for *Annie Allen.*

1951

- Marianne Moore's *Collected Poems* is published by Macmillan.
- Marguerite Higgins (1920-1960) receives the Pulitzer Prize for Journalism in overseas reporting for her account of the battle at Inchon, Korea in September, 1950.

1952

- Amy Tan is born on 19 February in Oakland, California.
- Rita Dove is born on 28 August in Akron, Ohio.
- bell hooks is born Gloria Jean Watkins on 25 September in Hopkinsville, Kentucky.
- Marianne Moore receives the National Book Critics Circle award for poetry and the Pulitzer Prize for poetry for *Collected Poems.*

1953

- *A Writer's Diary: Being Extracts from the Diary of Virigina Woolf,* edited by Leonard Woolf, is published by Hogarth.
- The International Planned Parenthood Federation is founded by Margaret Sanger, who serves as the organization's first president.
- Women are granted suffrage in Mexico.

1954

- Louise Erdrich is born on 7 June in Little Falls, Minnesota.
- Colette dies on 3 August in Paris, France.
- Sandra Cisneros is born on 20 December in Chicago, Illinois.

1955

- On 1 December American civil rights activist Rosa Parks (1913-) refuses to move from her seat for a white passenger on a Montgomery, Alabama bus and is arrested.

1956

- The Anti-Prostitution Act, written and campaigned for by Kamichika Ichiko, makes prostitution illegal in Japan.

1958

- Christabel Pankhurst dies on 13 February in Los Angeles, California.

1959

- Susan Faludi is born on 18 April in New York City.
- Lorraine Hansberry's *A Raisin in the Sun* debuts in March at the Ethel Barrymore Theatre in New York City.
- Lorraine Hansberry becomes the youngest woman and first black artist to receive a New York Drama Critics Circle Award for best American play for *A Raisin in the Sun.*

1960

- Zora Neale Hurston dies on 28 January in Fort Pierce, Florida.
- Sylvia Pankhurst dies on 27 September in Addis Ababa, Ethiopia.

- The U.S. Food and Drug Administration approves the first oral contraceptive for distribution to consumers in May.

- Harper Lee's *To Kill a Mockingbird* is published by Lippincott.

1961

- H. D. (Hilda Doolittle) dies on 27 September in Zurich, Switzerland.

- Harper Lee receives the Pulitzer Prize for the novel for *To Kill a Mockingbird.*

- President John F. Kennedy establishes the President's Commission on the Status of Women on 14 December and appoints Eleanor Roosevelt as head of the commission.

1962

- Isak Dinesen dies on 7 September in Rungsted Kyst, Denmark.

- Eleanor Roosevelt dies on 7 November in New York City.

- Naomi Wolf is born on 12 November in San Francisco, California.

- Doris Lessing's *The Golden Notebook* is published by Simon & Schuster.

1963

- Betty Friedan's *The Feminine Mystique* is published by Norton and becomes a bestseller.

- Sylvia Plath's *The Bell Jar* is published under the pseudonym Victoria Lucas by Heinemann.

- Sylvia Plath commits suicide on 11 February in London, England.

- Barbara Wertheim Tuchman (1912-1989) becomes the first woman to receive the Pulitzer Prize for general nonfiction for *The Guns of August.*

- The Equal Pay Act is passed by the U.S. Congress on 28 May. It is the first federal law requiring equal compensation for men and women in federal jobs.

- Entitled *American Women,* the report issued by the President's Commission on the Status of Women documents sex discrimination in nearly all corners of American society, and urges the U.S. Supreme Court to clarify legal status of women under the U.S. Constitution.

1964

- Anna Julia Haywood Cooper dies on 27 February in Washington, DC.

1965

- Lorraine Hansberry dies of cancer on 12 January in New York City.

- Women are granted suffrage in Afghanistan.

1966

- Anna Akhmatova dies on 6 March in Russia.

- Margaret Sanger dies on 6 September in Tucson, Arizona.

- National Organization for Women (NOW) is founded on 29 June by Betty Friedan and 27 other founding members. NOW is dedicated to promoting full participation in society for women and advocates for adequate child care for working mothers, reproductive rights, and the Equal Rights Amendment to the U.S. Constitution.

- Anne Sexton's *Live or Die* is published by Houghton.

- Nelly Sachs (1891-1970) receives the Nobel Prize in Literature, which she shares with Shmuel Yosef Agnon.

1967

- Anne Sexton receives the Pulitzer Prize for poetry for *Live or Die.*

- Senator Eugene McCarthy, with 37 cosponsors, introduces the Equal Rights Amendment in the U.S. Senate.

1968

- Audre Lorde's *The First Cities* is published by Poets Press.

1969

- Joyce Carol Oates's *them* is published by Vanguard Press.

- Shirley Chisolm becomes the first African American woman elected to Congress when she takes her seat in the U.S. House of Representatives on 3 January.

- Golda Meir (1898-1978) becomes the fourth Prime Minister of Israel on 17 March.

California adopts the nation's first "no fault" divorce law, allowing divorce by mutual consent.

1970

Toni Morrison's *The Bluest Eye* is published by Holt.

Germaine Greer's *The Female Eunuch* is published by MacGibbon & Kee.

Maya Angelou's *I Know Why the Caged Bird Sings* is published by Random House.

Kate Millett's *Sexual Politics* is published by Doubleday and becomes a bestseller.

Joyce Carol Oates receives the National Book Award for fiction for *them*.

The Equal Rights Amendment passes in the U.S. House of Representatives by a vote of 350 to 15 on 10 August.

Bella Abzug is elected to the U.S. House of Representatives on 3 November.

The Feminist Press is founded at the City University of New York.

Off Our Backs: A Women's News Journal is founded in Washington, D.C.

The Women's Rights Law Reporter is founded in Newark, New Jersey.

1971

Josephine Jacobsen is named U. S. Poet Laureate.

1972

Marianne Moore dies on 5 February in New York City.

Ms. magazine is founded; Gloria Steinem serves as editor of *Ms.* until 1987. The 300,000 copy print run of the first issue of *Ms.* magazine sells out within a week of its release in January.

Shirley Chisolm becomes the first African American woman to seek the presidential nomination of a major political party, although her bid for the Democratic Party nomination is unsuccessful.

The Equal Rights Amendment is passed by both houses of the U.S. Congress and is signed by President Richard M. Nixon. The amendment expires in 1982, without being ratified by the required two-thirds of the states; it is three states short of full ratification.

President Nixon signs into law Title IX of the Higher Education Act banning sex bias in athletics and other activities at all educational institutions receiving federal assistance.

Women's Press is established in Canada.

1973

The U.S. Supreme Court, in their decision handed down on 21 January in *Roe v. Wade,* decides that in the first trimester of pregnancy women have the right to choose an abortion.

Elizabeth Bowen dies of lung cancer on 22 February in London, England.

Rita Mae Brown's *Rubyfruit Jungle* is published by Daughters, Inc.

Erica Jong's *Fear of Flying* is published by Holt and becomes a bestseller.

Alice Walker's *In Love and Trouble: Stories of Black Women* is published by Harcourt.

The Boston Women's Health Book Collective's *Our Bodies, Ourselves: A Book By and For Women* is published by Simon and Schuster.

1974

Andrea Dworkin's *Women Hating* is published by Dutton.

Adrienne Rich receives the National Book Award for *Diving into the Wreck: Poems, 1971-1972.*

Anne Sexton commits suicide on 4 October in Weston, Massachusetts.

Katharine Graham (1917-2001), publisher of the *Washington Post,* becomes the first woman member of the board of the Associated Press.

1975

Paula Gunn Allen' essay "The Sacred Hoop: A Contemporary Indian Perspective on American Indian Literature" appears in *Literature of the American Indian: Views and Interpretations,* edited by Abraham Chapman and published by New American Library.

Hélène Cixous and Catherine Clement's *La Jeune nee (The Newly Born Woman,* University of Minnesota Press, 1986) is published by Union Generale.

- Margaret Thatcher is elected leader of the Conservative Party and becomes the first woman to head a major party in Great Britain.

- Susan Brownmiller's *Against our Will: Men, Women, and Rape* is published by Simon and Schuster.

1976

- Andrea Dworkin's *Our Blood: Prophecies and Discourses on Sexual Politics* is published by Harper.

- Maxine Hong Kingston's *The Woman Warrior: Memoirs of a Girlhood among Ghosts* is published by Knopf.

- Maxine Hong Kingston's receives the National Book Critics Circle award for general nonfiction for *The Woman Warrior.*

- Barbara Walters (1931-) becomes the first female network television news anchorwoman when she joins Harry Reasoner as coanchor of the *ABC Evening News.*

- Shere Hite's *The Hite Report: A Nationwide Study of Female Sexuality* is published by Macmillan.

1977

- Alice Paul dies on 9 July in Moorestown, New Jersey.

- Marilyn French's *The Women's Room* is published by Summit.

- Toni Morrison's *Song of Solomon* is published by Knopf.

- Toni Morrison receives the National Book Critics Circle Award for fiction for *Song of Solomon.*

- Labor organizer Barbara Mayer Wertheimer's *We Were There: The Story of Working Women in America* is published by Pantheon.

- Women's Press is established in Great Britain.

1978

- The Pregnancy Discrimination Act bans employment discrimination against pregnant women.

- Tillie Olsen's *Silences* is published by Delcorte Press/Seymour Lawrence.

1979

- Margaret Thatcher becomes the first woman prime minister of Great Britain. She serves until her resignation in 1990, marking the longest term of any twentieth-century prime minister.

- Barbara Wertheim Tuchman becomes the first woman elected president of the American Academy and Institute of Arts and Letters.

- Mother Teresa (1910-1997) receives the Nobel Peace Prize.

- Sandra M. Gilbert and Susan Gubar's *The Madwoman in the Attic: The Woman Writer and the Nineteenth-Century Imagination* is published by Yale University Press.

1980

- Muriel Rukeyser dies on 12 February in New York City.

- Adrienne Rich's essay "Compulsory Heterosexuality and Lesbian Experience" is published in *Signs: Journal of Women in Culture and Society.*

1981

- bell hooks's *Ain't I a Woman: Black Women and Feminism* is published by South End Press.

- Sylvia Plath's *Collected Poems,* edited by Ted Hughes, is published by Harper.

- Sandra Day O'Connor (1930-) becomes the first woman Justice of the U.S. Supreme Court, after being nominated by President Ronald Reagan and sworn in on 25 September.

- Women of Color Press is founded in Albany, New York by Barbara Smith.

- Cleis Press is established in Pittsburgh, Pennsylvania, and San Francisco, California.

- *This Bridge Called My Back: Writings by Radical Women of Color,* edited by Cherríe Moraga and Gloria Anzaldúa, is published by Persephone Press.

- Maxine Kumin is named U. S. Poet Laureate.

1982

- Djuna Barnes dies on 19 June in New York City.

- Sylvia Plath is posthumously awarded the Pulitzer Prize in poetry for *Collected Poems.*

- Alice Walker's *The Color Purple* is published by Harcourt.

- Carol Gilligan's *In a Different Voice: Psychological Theory and Women's Development* is published by Harvard University Press.

1983

- Rebecca West dies on 15 March in London, England.

- Gloria Steinem's *Outrageous Acts and Everyday Rebellions* is published by Holt.

1984

- Sandra Cisneros's *The House on Mango Street* is published by Arte Publico.

- Lillian Hellman dies on 30 June in Martha's Vineyard, Massachusetts.

- Geraldine Ferraro (1935-) becomes the first woman to win the Vice-Presidential nomination and runs unsuccessfully for office with Democratic Presidential candidate Walter Mondale.

- Firebrand Books, publisher of feminist and lesbian literature, is established in Ann Arbor, Michigan.

- bell hooks's *Feminist Theory: From Margin to Center* is published by South End Press.

1985

- Margaret Atwood's *The Handmaid's Tale* is published by McClelland & Stewart.

- Wilma P. Mankiller is sworn in as the first woman tribal chief of the Cherokee nation. She serves until 1994.

- Gwendolyn Brooks is named U. S. Poet Laureate.

1986

- Simone de Beauvoir dies on 14 April in Paris, France.

- Bessie Head dies on 17 April in Botswana.

- Rita Dove's *Thomas and Beulah* is published by Carnegie-Mellon University Press.

- Sylvia Ann Hewlett's *A Lesser Life: The Myth of Women's Liberation in America* is published by Morrow.

1987

- Toni Morrison's *Beloved* is published by Knopf.

- Rita Dove receives the Pulitzer Prize for poetry for *Thomas and Beulah*.

1988

- Toni Morrison receives the Pulitzer Prize for fiction for *Beloved*.

- *The War of the Words,* Volume 1 of Sandra M. Gilbert and Susan Gubar's *No Man's Land: The Place of the Woman Writer in the Twentieth Century,* is published by Yale University Press.

1989

- Amy Tan's *The Joy Luck Club* is published by Putnam.

1990

- Naomi Wolf's *The Beauty Myth: How Images of Beauty Are Used against Women* is published by Chatto & Windus.

- The Norplant contraceptive is approved by the FDA on 10 December.

- Camille Paglia's *Sexual Personae: Art and Decadence from Nefertiti to Emily Dickinson* is published by Yale University Press.

- Wendy Kaminer's *A Fearful Freedom: Women's Flight from Equality* is published by Addison-Wesley.

- Laurel Thatcher Ulrich's *A Midwife's Tale: The Life of Martha Ballard, Based on Her Diary, 1785-1812* is published by Knopf.

- Judith Butler's *Gender Trouble: Feminism and the Subversion of Identity* is published by Routledge.

1991

- Susan Faludi's *Backlash: The Undeclared War Against American Women* is published by Crown.

- Antonia Novello (1944-) is appointed by President George H.W. Bush and becomes the first woman and first person of Hispanic descent to serve as U. S. Surgeon General.

- Bernadine Healy, M.D. (1944-) is appointed by President George H.W. Bush and becomes the first woman to head the National Institutes of Health.

- Suzanne Gordon's *Prisoners of Men's Dreams: Striking Out for a New Feminine Future* is published by Little, Brown.

- Laurel Thatcher Ulrich receives the Pulitzer Prize for history for *A Midwife's Tale: The Life of Martha Ballard, Based on Her Diary, 1785-1812.*

1992

- Carol Elizabeth Moseley Braun (1947-) becomes the first African American woman elected to the U. S. Senate on 3 November.

- Carolyne Larrington's *The Feminist Companion to Mythology* is published by Pandora.

- Marilyn French's *The War against Women* is published by Summit.

- Clarissa Pinkola Estes's *Women Who Run with the Wolves: Myths and Stories of the Wild Woman Archetype* is published by Ballantine.

- Naomi Wolf's *Fire with Fire: The New Female Power and How It Will Change the Twenty-first Century* is published by Random House.

- Mona Van Duyn is named U. S. Poet Laureate.

1993

- Appointed by President Bill Clinton, Janet Reno (1938-) becomes the first woman U.S. Attorney General when she is sworn in on 12 March.

- Toni Morrison receives the Nobel Prize in Literature.

- Toni Morrison receives the Elizabeth Cady Stanton Award from the National Organization for Women.

- Canada's Progressive Conservative party votes on 13 June to make Defense Minister Kim Campbell the nation's first woman prime minister. Canadian voters oust the Conservative party in elections on 25 October as recession continues; Liberal leader Jean Chrétien becomes prime minister.

- On 1 October Rita Dove becomes the youngest person and the first African American to be named U. S. Poet Laureate.

- Faye Myenne Ng's *Bone* is published by Hyperion.

1994

- The Violence Against Women Act tightens federal penalties for sex offenders, funds services for victims of rape and domestic violence, and provides funds for special training for police officers in domestic violence and rape cases.

- Mary Pipher's *Reviving Ophelia: Saving the Selves of Adolescent Girls* is published by Putnam.

1995

- Ireland's electorate votes by a narrow margin in November to end the nation's ban on divorce (no other European country has such a ban), but only after 4 years' legal separation.

1996

- Marguerite Duras dies on 3 March in Paris, France.

- Hillary Rodham Clinton's *It Takes a Village, and Other Lessons Children Teach Us* is published by Simon and Schuster.

1998

- Bella Abzug dies on 31 March in New York City.

- Drucilla Cornell's *At the Heart of Freedom: Feminism, Sex, and Equality* is published by Princeton University Press.

1999

- Susan Brownmiller's *In Our Time: Memoir of a Revolution* is published by Dial Press.

- Gwendolyn Mink's *Welfare's End* is published by Cornell University Press.

- Martha C. Nussbaum's *Sex and Social Justice* is published by Oxford University Press.

2000

- Gwendolyn Brooks dies on 3 December in Chicago, Illinois.

- Patricia Hill Collins's *Black Feminist Thought: Knowledge, Consciousness, and the Politics of Empowerment* is published by Routledge.

- Jennifer Baumgardner and Amy Richards's *Manifesta: Young Women, Feminism, and the Future* is published by Farrar, Straus, and Giroux.

2002

- Estelle B. Freedman's *No Turning Back: The History of Feminism and the Future of Women* is published by Ballantine.

- *Colonize This! Young Women of Color on Today's Feminism,* edited by Daisy Hernandez and Bushra Rehman, is published by Seal Press.

2003

- Iranian feminist and human rights activist Shirin Ebadi (1947-) receives the Nobel Peace Prize.

- Louise Glück is named U. S. Poet Laureate.

- *Catching a Wave: Reclaiming Feminism for the 21st Century,* edited by Rory Cooke Dicker and Alison Piepmeier, is published by Northeastern University Press.

2004

- The FDA approves the contraceptive mifepristone, following a 16-year struggle by reproductive rights activists to have the abortion drug approved. Opponents made repeated efforts to prevent approval and distribution of mifepristone.

- *The Fire This Time: Young Activists and the New Feminism,* edited by Vivien Labaton and Dawn Lundy Martin, is published by Anchor Books.

- *The Future of Women's Rights: Global Visions and Strategies,* edited by Joanna Kerr, Ellen Sprenger, and Alison Symington, is published by ZED Books and Palgrave Macmillan.

ANNA AKHMATOVA

(1889 - 1966)

(Born Anna Andreevna Gorenko) Russian poet, essayist, and translator.

Considered Russia's finest female poet, Akhmatova is known for her accessible style and concrete images. Her poems deal with personal issues of love and suffering, but are often interpreted as metaphors for the plight of the Russian people as a whole. Her work, considered subversive during the Stalinist era, was banned for many years. After Stalin's death in 1953, her reputation was gradually restored and she was able to resume publishing original verse.

BIOGRAPHICAL INFORMATION

Akhmatova was born Anna Andreevna Gorenko on June 11, 1889, near Odessa, on the coast of the Black Sea. Her father was a retired maritime engineer who moved his family to Tsarskoye Selo near St. Petersburg the year after Akhmatova was born. There she attended the classical school for girls where she was, by her own account, a less-than-dedicated student. She began writing poetry at the age of eleven after recovering from a mysterious illness that nearly proved fatal. In 1905, Akhmatova's parents separated and her mother took the children south to Evpatoria where Akhmatova continued her education with a tutor; the following year, she attended the Fundukleyev school in Kiev. Although she entered Law School at the University of Kiev, she found the subject of literature more interesting, and transferred to St. Petersburg, attending Rayev's Higher Historico-Literary Courses. On April 25, 1910, Akhmatova married the poet Nikolai Gumilyov, whom she had met as a student and who had published her first poem in his literary journal *Sirius* in 1907. The couple honeymooned in Paris and took up residence in Tsarskoe Selo, spending their summers in Slepnyovo. Their son, Lev, was born in 1912, the same year Akhmatova published her first volume of poetry, *Vecher* (*Evening*). The pair had little in common except their love of poetry, and the marriage was further strained by Gumilyov's frequent trips abroad and Akhmatova's increasing fame and success. In 1913, Gumilyov enlisted in the cavalry and the couple was separated for almost six years. They divorced in 1918 and both remarried soon afterward, Akhmatova to Vladimir Kazimirovich Shileyko, another poet to whom she remained married for only a short time.

After the October Revolution in 1917, Akhmatova withdrew from literary society and began working in the library of the Agronomy Institute. At this time, her poetry began attracting unfavorable attention from the government and the Communist Party. Gumilyov was executed for treason in 1921, and Akhmatova's work was unofficially banned in 1925. She published no original poetry for many years although she continued to write, translate verse, and research her literary hero, Alexander Pushkin, a subject that occupied her attention for twenty years. She produced several critical essays on Pushkin, but the book-length study she planned never materialized. The Stalin years were a period of isolation and silence for Akhmatova; she lost many literary friends and associates to the purges, and her son, Lev, was arrested and imprisoned several times. By 1941, Akhmatova was living in Leningrad, but managed to escape to Moscow during the siege. She spent most of the war in Tashkent, returning to Moscow and then to Leningrad in 1944. After Stalin's death in 1953, Akhmatova's standing as a major poet was reevaluated and restored over a period of several years. She was readmitted to the Union of Soviet Writers, from which she had earlier been expelled, and she resumed publication of her poetry, some of which she had committed to memory rather than risk producing a written record during the Stalin years. Two of her most acclaimed works, *Poema Bez Geroya: Triptykh* (1960; *Poem without a Hero*) and *Rekviem: Tsikl Stikhotvorenii* (1963; *Requiem*), were published during this second, very productive period of her career. Akhmatova lived to the age of 78. She died on March 5, 1966, and is buried in a small village near Leningrad.

MAJOR WORKS

Akhmatova's work is generally divided into two periods: the first associated with the love lyrics she produced in her youth, from the beginning of her publishing career until 1922, and the second associated with poems composed during and after her long period of silence. Her early work, published in the collections *Evening, Chetki* (1914; *Rosary*), and *Belaya Staya* (1917; *The White Flock*) were enormously popular among her contemporaries. She developed a cult following in St. Petersburg where young lovers committed her verse to memory and recited it to each other. The religious imagery that characterized her later work began to appear in these early volumes. Her reputation today is based on the two major works of her later period. The first, *Requiem,* is a collection of short poems that loosely form a narrative related to the Crucifixion, but more literally related to her personal suffering and, by extension, the suffering of her fellow citizens in the Soviet Union. The second, *Poem without a Hero,*

was composed and revised over a twenty-year period and deals with the brutality of war and revolution.

CRITICAL RECEPTION

Akhmatova's work is often considered part of the Acmeist movement, a reaction to the late-nineteenth-century Symbolist poetry that preceded it. Her work is praised for its concrete images and a style that is far more straightforward and accessible than that of the Symbolists. Scholars also consider the political nature of some of her work, which reflects the tumultuous events she experienced throughout her long life; they maintain that she acted as spokesperson for the Russian people during those years of war and civil unrest. Recently, feminist scholars have suggested that she was particularly able to articulate the suffering of the women of Russia and to serve as their leader during the most intense periods of hardship, such as the siege of Leningrad in 1941. Often cited is Akhmatova's radio address praising the women of Leningrad for their work in civil defense and care of the wounded and assuring the citizens that "a city which has bred women like these cannot be defeated."

PRINCIPAL WORKS

Vecher [*Evening*] (poetry) 1912

Chetki [*Rosary*] (poetry) 1914

Belaya Staya [*The White Flock*] (poetry) 1917

Anno Domini MCMXXI (poetry) 1921

Podorozhnik [*Plantain*] (poetry) 1921

U Samovo Morya (poetry) 1921

Anno Domini (poetry) 1923

Forty-Seven Love Songs (poetry) 1927

Iz Shesti Knig (poetry) 1940

Izbrannie Stikhi (poetry) 1943

Tashkentskie Stikhi (poetry) 1944

Stikhotvoreniia, 1909-1957 (poetry) 1958

Poema Bez Geroya: Triptykh [*Poem without a Hero*] (poetry) 1960

Stikhi, 1909-1960 (poetry) 1961

Collected Poems: 1912-1963 (poetry) 1963

Rekviem: Tsikl Stikhotvorenii [*Requiem*] (poetry) 1963

Poeziya (poetry) 1964

Beg Vremeni (poetry) 1965

Stikhotvoreniia, 1909-1965 (poetry) 1965

Sochineniia. 2 vols. (poetry) 1965, 1968

Selected Poems (poetry) 1969

Way of All the Earth (poetry) 1979

Anna Akhmatova: Poems (poetry) 1983

Sochineniia v dvukh tomakh. 2 vols. (poetry) 1986

Poems (poetry) 1988

Severnye elegii: stikhotvoreniia, poety, o poetakh (poetry) 1989

The Complete Poems of Anna Akhmatova. 2 vols. (poetry) 1990

PRIMARY SOURCES

ANNA AKHMATOVA (RADIO ADDRESS DATE SEPTEMBER 1941)

SOURCE: Akhmatova, Anna. "A Talk on Leningrad Radio in Late September 1941." *Soviet Literature*, no. 6 (June 1989): 25.

In the following transcript of her radio address to the women of Leningrad, broadcast in September 1941, Akhmatova praises the mothers, wives, and sisters of the city for their strength and courage during the German siege.

Dear fellow-citizens, mothers, wives and sisters of Leningrad:

For more than a month now the enemy has been threatening to overrun our city and inflict upon it mortal wounds. The enemy threatens the city of Peter the Great, the city of Lenin, the city of Pushkin, Dostoevsky and Blok—our city, with its great tradition of culture and labour—with death and disgrace. Like all Leningraders, I am horror-struck at the thought that our city, my city, may be trampled into the dirt. My entire life has been linked with Leningrad—it was in Leningrad that I became a poet, Leningrad is the very air that my verses breathe . . .

At this moment, like all of you, I cling to the unshakeable faith that Leningrad shall never belong to the fascists. And I feel my faith strengthened when I see the women of Leningrad defending their city with simple courage and maintaining its normal human life . . .

Our descendants will pay honour to every mother who lived during this Patriotic War, but their gaze will be drawn as by a magnet to the women of Leningrad, who stood on the roofs as the bombs fell, holding their hooks and tongs, ready to defend the city against the threat of fire; the women of the Leningrad civil-defence corps, who went to the help of the wounded while the ruined buildings blazed around them . . .

No, a city which has bred women like these cannot be defeated. We Leningraders may be suffering hardship and danger, but we know that the entire country and everyone in it is with us. We sense their alarm at our plight, their love, their efforts to help and support us. We thank them and we promise always to stand firm and never to lose heart . . .

September 1941

GENERAL COMMENTARY

VASA D. MIHAILOVICH (ESSAY DATE WINTER 1969)

SOURCE: Mihailovich, Vasa D. "The Critical Reception of Anna Akhmatova." *Papers on Language & Literature* 5, no. 1 (winter 1969): 95-111.

In the following essay, Mihailovich provides an overview of criticism of Akhmatova's work, both within and outside of Russia.

The death of the Russian poet Anna Akhmatova in March 1966 marked the end of a long, illustrious, and eventful career. She appeared in the decade before the Russian Revolution and quickly became one of the leading poets of the time. The events after the Revolution forced her to silence for many years; she reappeared as a voice of Russian poetry during World War II, only to be silenced again at the end of the war. After Stalin's death, she spent the last decade of her life in full creativity, enjoying wide recognition. Now that her opus is finished, the study of her work will hopefully be freed from the shackles of a nonliterary, though understandably human concern. For the truth is that, perhaps because of the vagaries of her personal life, her work has received inadequate critical attention. There is no doubt that in the course of time the Akhmatoviana will be enriched with serious studies of various aspects of her delicate and at times complex poetic world. Until that is done, the existing scholarship on Akhmatova will serve as a guide and illumination. Meanwhile the need exists for a survey that constitutes an account of her publication, of the basic features of her life and work, and of the secondary literature, with some suggestions for future research.[1]

Anna Akhmatova—the pen name of Anna Andreevna Gorenko—was born near Odessa in 1889, the daughter of a naval officer. She began to write poetry when she was eleven, and her first poem was published in 1907. With her inaugural collection of poems, *Evening* (1912), she acquired a sudden and widespread fame, which was subsequently reenforced with every new book of verse. In the course of her long career she published fifteen books of poetry. Her publication can conveniently, though arbitrarily, be divided into three distinct periods: 1912-23, 1940-46, 1956-66 (with a few poems published in 1950). The interim periods are those of enforced silence. The first, 1923-40, came more or less as a result of a tacit admission on Akhmatova's part that the changed way of life in Russia was not compatible with her views. The second, 1946-56, was a direct result of a premeditated attack on her by the authorities with their policy of tightening the reins on artists and intellectuals after the war. Akhmatova kept busy all the time, however, writing more essays than poetry, and translating. Indeed, her overall achievement is a testimony to the human mind and spirit creating under the most adverse conditions.

With her first books—*Evening* (1912) and *Rosary* (1914)—Akhmatova became very popular, especially among women, intellectuals, and younger readers. Her popularity can be perhaps best explained by the remark of a Soviet critic that "The masterly chiseled poetry of Akhmatova is very poor in ideological content and in social problems raised therein." What struck the reader was a fresh note of a young woman's personal concern and of a genuine feeling of love. Coming on the heels of the Symbolist poets, who indulged in complex, mystical, overwrought ambiguities and self-adulation, Akhmatova's poetry was refreshing by its genuineness, simplicity, and clarity—all stemming from the newly formed literary movement of Acmeism. Together with Gumilyov, Mandelshtam, and other poets, Akhmatova endeavored to bring poetry from the lofty clouds of the symbolist Parnassus down to earth. Her unerring poetic touch, her ear for language and rhythm, and a boldness in revealing her innermost sentiments established her quickly as one of the leading poets of the younger generation. The first World War did not diminish her forcefulness and appeal; on the contrary, it lent to her overly private concerns a touch of maturity and a wider scope, as evidenced by her collection *The White Flock*. Never politically inclined, she saw in the war an evil that might eventually destroy the world in which she had been able to address herself to her own problems exclusively. When the end indeed came, she refused to accept it, in the belief that she would be able to continue her relatively sequestered life. But she also refused to emigrate, saying that it takes greater courage to stay behind and accept the blows of the fate than to flee into exile.

The effect of the Revolution on her life and creativity was not immediately evident. She published two more collections of poetry, *Plantain* (1921) and *Anno Domini MCMXXI* (1921), in which there was less of her intimate sentiments of love and more of a concern for the fate of her country. When her former husband, Gumilyov, was shot for alleged counterrevolutionary activities, Akhmatova as it were saw the writing on the wall. After an expanded edition of *Anno Domini* in 1923, she fell silent and ceased to exist for the public. She wrote some poetry but occupied herself mostly with literary studies, especially of Pushkin, and with translations from many languages—a career almost identical to that of Pasternak. This silence may have saved her life during the purges in the 1930's, for, like so many of her compatriots, she endured a veritable purgatory while trying to ascertain the fate of her only son, a highly promising scholar of Asian history, who was arrested on undisclosed charges and later sentenced to fifteen years of exile and slave labor.

Only the second World War brought a change to Akhmatova's dreary and dangerous life. Sensing the perils threatening her people, she, like many Soviet writers, contributed to the struggle against the foreign invader. An edition of her poems, *From Six Books* (1940), composed of her previous five collections and her latest poems, was published on the eve of the attack on Russia. As she had done during and after the Revolution, she once again sided with her people, silencing within herself her complaints and reservations. She spent the first several months of the war in besieged Leningrad and then was evacuated to Tashkent, where she stayed almost to the end of the war. In Tashkent, she was brought in contact with the other part of her ancestry, for her grandmother was a Tartar. Creatively, she used this occasion to declare the whole of Russia, indeed the whole world, her homeland, and to write some of her most beautiful descriptive poems. Also during this time, in 1943, a volume of her selected poetry was published in Moscow, an event leading readers to the natural conclusion that she had made peace with the regime she had been forced to tolerate for seventeen years.

As soon as the war was over, however, and the authorities found it necessary to resort to the old methods—totalitarian and repressive, though not so bloody as before—Akhmatova was among the first to be victimized. In his famous attack upon herself and upon the humorist Zoshchenko, the cultural tsar of the time, Zhdanov, rejected out of hand Akhmatova's poetry as un-Soviet and unsavory, calling her a half-harlot and half-nun (a reference to her verses in an early love poem). Ostensibly Zhdanov professed to be fearful of the "bad" influence of her poetry on Soviet youth; in reality, he needed scapegoats for the restoration of the repressive methods of the earlier era. Akhmatova fell silent once again, this time involuntarily, for a silence of a decade (1946-56) that lasted until after Stalin's death. There are indications that she tried to make amends by publishing a few accommodating poems in 1950; however, this kind of poetry was clearly not her métier. Only after the demise of Stalin and during a relatively more liberal atmosphere in the second half of the 1950's were her rights restored. In 1958 a slender selection of her poetry was published as a sign of rehabilitation, with an afterword by Surkov, one of the leading poets of the regime. Another small collection was published in 1961, and a rather extensive one, prepared by the poet herself, appeared in 1965, *The Course of Time.* Still another edition, including her prose works, was announced for late 1968. In the meantime, several editions of her works were published abroad: *Selected Poems* (New York, 1952), *The Poem without a Hero* (New York, 1960 and 1962), *Requiem* (Munich, 1963), and the first volume of a compendious, two-volume edition of her collected works (1965).

Shortly before her death in 1966, Akhmatova finally received two richly deserved accolades for her work. Ironically, the recognition came from abroad in the forms of the prestigious Italian Etna Taormina Prize in 1964 and an honorary doctor's degree from Oxford University in 1965. On these two festive occasions she left Russia for the first time in half a century. More important, however, during the last decade of her life she wrote the most mature, sophisticated, complex, and, in the opinion of some critics, the best poetry of her career. Her venerable age and the trying experiences of her past brought her not only wisdom and maturity, but also peace with herself and with the world. At the end, she was at long last accepted officially as a Soviet poet. She died ravaged by long illness, yet preserving her dignity and independence to the very end, asking for (and be-

ing granted) a church funeral according to the Russian Orthodox rites. After her death she was eulogized as the last of the four great Russian poets after Blok, in addition to Pasternak, Mandelshtam, Tsvetaeva, and acclaimed by many as the finest woman poet in all Russian literature.

The problems, both scholarly and literary, of Akhmatova's poetry become more difficult as her *oeuvre* achieves completion. Her relatively "simple" poetry of her early days matured into a much more complex and meaning-laden poetry in her last two decades. The circumstances surrounding her creativity after the Revolution and during her silence of seventeen years make it difficult to find out the complete truth, admittedly. While the first of these difficulties can be solved simply by comparing her early and later poems, the second will most likely remain shrouded in mystery for some time Consequently it is helpful to treat the two major periods of her creativity separately.

Her early poetry is distinguished by several easily discernible characteristics. It is above all a love poetry. In many poems having love as their focal point Akhmatova presents love from a woman's point of view. The beloved is never fully revealed, and at times he seems to be almost secondary—only a stimulus or catalyst of woman's feelings. The poet expresses the whole spectrum of love. Her fervent passion is coupled with fidelity to her partner, but as her loyalty is professed time and again, a note of frustration and a fear of incompatibility and rejection become noticeable. The prospect of unrequited love is confirmed by betrayal and parting. The ensuing feeling of loneliness leads to despair and withdrawal. The feminine "I" of the poems seeks refuge, release, and salvation in religion, nature, and poetry. The refuge in religion is especially evident in Akhmatova's second collection of poetry, *Rosary.* It is a peculiar religious feeling at that, pervaded, like her sentiments of love, with a mood of melancholy and inexplicable sadness. In her third collection, *The White Flock,* a new theme joins those of love and religion: a presentiment of doom. Nourished by the horrors of war and revolution, this presentiment grows into a full-blown "tragical intonation," as one critic characterizes the nature of Akhmatova's poetry at that time. As the Revolution drags on, her mood turns bleaker and more hopeless. She seeks rapport with the events by writing poetry with political motifs, to no avail. The poems in *Anno Domini* clearly reveal Akhmatova's state of mind and emotions at this difficult time, as well as her awareness that an era had come to an end.

The basic features of Akhmatova's poetry expressed in her early poems have remained relatively the same throughout her career. She later added other characteristics and themes, but it is by those early features that she is best known. To be sure, there were other themes in addition to that of love, such as the themes of a poet and his muse, the intrinsic splendor of Russia, and the war. But they gained prominence only after Akhmatova's reappearance shortly before World War II. In many poems written during the second World War she extols the beauty of her land and the magnitude of the martyrdom and sacrifice of her people in throes of a ruthless enemy. Especially Leningrad, the city of her life and her dreams, receives her full attention. In addition, Asia, where she spent most of the war years, becomes the subject of her poetry at this time. Nevertheless she could not close her eyes before the Soviet reality, in which she was personally caught in a most tragic way. In a composite poem that is still unpublished in Russia, *Requiem,* she expresses her deep sorrow not only about her personal loss but also about the suffering to which her entire people was being subjected. This work is as close as she came to castigating publicly the regime in her country.

Akhmatova's poetry in the last decade of her life shows a far greater maturity and the wisdom of old age. Her approach to her poetic themes is more epic and historical, with a vaster perspective. This mature poetry is also more psychological and philosophical. The best example perhaps is the long *Poem Without a Hero,* a panoramic view of the previous century as it pertains to the present. It is a subtle and at times a complex poem, which is very difficult to fathom without a proper key.

The stylistic aspect of Akhmatova's poetry is just as important as the thematic, if not even more so. She shows several peculiarly Akhmatovian features. Above all, there is the narrative tone that points to a definite affinity with prose. Connected with this is a dramatic quality, expressed either through inner monologue or dialogue, usually between love partners, but sometimes between the poet and her invisible conversant. The second striking feature is the brief lyric form, consisting mostly of three to four stanzas, rarely five to seven, and never over seven. Parallel to this brevity of form is a pronounced laconism: a few carefully selected details suffice to convey the entire picture. Akhmatova's economy of words, spare almost to the point of frugality, led her to the epigrammatic form and to fragmentation, understatement, and

improvisation. As a result, her sentences are sometimes verbless and even without a subject. Another peculiarity is the concreteness of her word-images, especially with reference to space and time. She tells the reader exactly where and when, almost to the minute, the events in her poems take place. The colors are vividly and exactly given. She avoids metaphors; instead, she uses pointed, explanatory epithets. Finally, her intonation, never scrupulously measured or regulated, is that of a syncopated rhythm, approaching the rhythm of some forms of folk poetry.

Of the poets who have influenced her, Akhmatova herself admits indebtedness to Derzhavin, Pushkin, and Annenskii. The latter two can be said to have exerted the greatest influence on her, although traces of other poets' influence—Nekrasov, Blok, Kuzmin—can also be found.

In addition to poetry, Akhmatova wrote an unfinished play and many essays, these latter especially on Pushkin, her favorite poet. She also translated copiously poems from the Old Egyptian, Hindu, Armenian, Lithuanian, Yiddish, Chinese, Korean, French, Italian, Rumanian, Serbian, and perhaps other languages (most of these in collaboration with various native speakers, one assumes). Her two long absences from the public view, of seventeen and ten years, obviously were not inactive.

Although Akhmatova died only recently, the main body of her poetry has existed for nearly half a century. Yet to this day there is no definite study in depth of her work. To be sure, there are books using her poetry as a point of departure; there are also several scholarly articles, many reviews, and numberless references in various forms to her and her work. But most of these are unsystematic and sketchy. A few years ago there appeared a short, heavily slanted study of Akhmatova by a Soviet critic, A. Pavlovskii, and a second monograph by another Soviet critic, Efim Dobin, has been announced.

The attitude of the prerevolutionary critics toward Akhmatova's poetry differs from that of the critics after the Revolution. Similarly, in the Soviet period the critics looked upon the poet differently before and after Stalin's death. Outside the Soviet Union the critics, both Russian and foreign, differed sharply with Soviet critics in their evaluation of Akhmatova's contribution to Russian literature. All these differences and changes were brought about not so much by changes in Akhmatova's poetry, of which to be sure there were some, as by the different vantage points of, and changes in, the critics themselves. As is often the case with Soviet writers, their purely literary achievements were accepted or rejected for nonliterary reasons.

The prerevolutionary Russian critics—Akhmatova was hardly known outside Russia before the first World War—tended to look at her poetry primarily from a literary or purely formalist point of view. Of the many reviews of her poems, few are mentioned today or are worth reprinting. Nikolai Gumilyov, Akhmatova's husband and a leading poet himself, looked down on his wife's creations and both praised and criticized her poems: she was herself in them, yet she left much unsaid. He found the outstanding feature of her poetry in her style, singling out her unusual and delicate use of color—mostly yellow and gray. Another critic N. Nedobrogo, stressed the first word in "woman-poet," finding in Akhmatova's pronounced femininity the true charm of her poetry: "Throughout this man-made civilization of ours, love in poetry has spoken so much from the point of view of a man and so little from the point of view of a woman." The remarks of other critics follow more or less the same pattern, with fleeting references to her poems stressing the strong emotional appeal of her love lyrics but without any deeper analysis. Such an analysis was attempted by the critic Viktor Zhirmunskii, later a leading Formalist, in his essay on the Acmeist poets. Limiting himself almost exclusively to the stylistic aspects of Akhmatova's poetry, Zhirmunskii publicly recognized its formal traits for the first time: the incomplete rhyming and enjambment; the syncopated rhythm; the conversational and prose character of her poems (the "novel in verse"); the epigrammatic form; the frequent changes of mood; the preponderance of observed detail; the "objectivization"; the expression of the simple beauty of earthly happiness; and an inclination toward a classic discipline. Needless to say, Zhirmunskii thought highly of Akhmatova's first books of verse as a refreshing, genuine, and already accomplished contribution to contemporary Russian poetry suffering from the rigor mortis of Symbolism. Since Akhmatova's early poems are numbered by many among the best poetry she has ever written, Zhirmunskii's detailed albeit brief analysis of their stylistic qualities placed the scholarly consideration of her poetry on the right track.

The Revolution brought about not only a decisive split among Russian writers but also profound changes in the evaluation of the established writers. Akhmatova was tolerated in the first few years of the new era, although she was immediately attacked by inimical critics and even totally rejected by some. It was not until her disappearance from the literary scene that a settled verdict of the undesirability of her work was reached. Her prolonged silence made it unnecessary even to mention her in critical writings and literary polemics. For a while the émigré writers kept referring to her, obviously remembering nostalgically their shared prerevolutionary days, but they, too, soon ceased. An impressionistic critic, Iulii Aikhenval'd, described Akhmatova as a worldly nun living in a sinful capital, surrounded by outstanding persons. Thus her all too personal tone paradoxically becomes social, and her subjective approach turns into an objective one. The poet is "the latest flower of the noble Russian culture, . . . such an embodiment of the past as is capable of consoling the present and of providing hope for the future." Aikhenval'd concludes prophetically that she belongs to the spiritual Russia of all times.

Other scholars who wrote about Akhmatova's poetry were the Formalists Boris Eikhenbaum and Viktor Vinogradov. Eikhenbaum, the leader of the Formalist school of critics, advanced many fine points, most of which are too technical to be dwelled upon here. Like Zhermunskii, for example, he pointed out the affinity of Akhmatova's poetry with the contemporary Russian realistic prose, noting that in her "lyrical novel" one could discern a story, composition, even characterization. Vinogradov, a peripheral Formalist, approached her poetry from a purely linguistic point of view, perceiving in it "semantic clusters"—a selection and grouping of words that give the best clue to Akhmatova's secluded poetic world. Zhirmunskii, Eikhenbaum, and Vinogradov were the first to treat Akhmatova's poetry systematically and expertly; and even though their approach is somewhat exclusive, many of their findings are still valid today and are often repeated.

Akhmatova's reappearance shortly before the second World War provoked no flurry of literary critiques: her long silence, caused by her basically un-Soviet attitude, was all too readily recalled. Her contribution to the body of war poetry was only a part of the common effort and as such deserved no special praise. And when Zhdanov roundly excoriated the poet in 1946, there ensued another period of silence on the part of both herself and the critics. Zhdanov's judgment of Akhmatova's poetry is typically insensitive: a nonliterary, strictly political, totalitarian approach. The greatest fault in her poetry he finds is its individualism.

"The range of her poetry is limited to squalor—it is the poetry of a frenzied lady, dreaming between the boudoir and the chapel. Basic with her are amorous-erotic motifs, intertwined with motifs of sorrow, yearning, death, mysticism, a sense of doom. The feeling of being doomed—an understandable feeling for the social consciousness of a dying group; gloomy tones of a death-bed hopelessness, mystical experiences, coupled with eroticism. . . . Not exactly a nun, not exactly a harlot, but rather nun and harlot, with whom harlotry is mixed with prayer." Her poetry is remote from the people, reflecting as it does "the good old days" of the nobility. As such, she is totally alien to modern Soviet actuality and even dangerous for the upbringing of Soviet youth. This is so much cant, the stock fulminations of many a political hack. The real reason for Zhdanov's attack—a need for a scapegoat—I have already noted.

Only Stalin's death and a relative liberalization of the literary life afterwards brought Akhmatova back to public life and made feasible the publication of a number of writings about her. This second phase of the Soviet critical evaluation of her work was ushered in by the appearance of anthologies of her poetry in 1958 and 1961. In his afterword to the first anthology, A. Surkov, one of the leading "apparatus" men in the literary field, set the tone for a new policy toward Akhmatova when he declared she had entered the ranks of Soviet poets "as a mature writer, made wise by many years of hard living and hard thinking." This she had achieved "without stooping to any moral or artistic compromise." While praising the esthetic quality of her poetry, however, Surkov laments her unawareness of social problems before and after the Revolution: for many years she was unable to understand or accept the new Russia. This is the reason, Surkov explains with a straight-face, why she busied herself with literary essays and translations between two World Wars, while at the same time leading a "complicated, even tragic" life.

The tragic fate of her country in the second World War thus brought Anna Akhmatova back into the mainstream of Soviet poetry. The 1960's have seen several articles and one book on her. A sympathetic view of her poetry was recently expressed by Lev Ozerov in his article "The Secrets of the Trade." After touching upon some of the commonplace aspects of her poetry, such as its laconic and conversational character as well as the influence of Pushkin and Annenskii, Ozerov turns his attention to a transformation he perceives in the mature Akhmatova. He calls the last two decades of her creativity "the most intensive and profound period," while the years between her first silence and reappearance in 1940 were "the years of the lull." The poet found her way out of isolation through her loyalty to the Russian land and people. Her later poetry is philosophically tinged, and her main interest is in the world and man in it. Her strikingly personal poems are now imbued with a generally human concern. Similarly, while she was earlier personally affected by the outside world, she now finds rapport with that world through her spiritual peace. This view of Ozerov, sincere though it may be, is typical of the efforts on the part of some Soviet critics to make amends and to change Akhmatova into a good Soviet poet, whose main concern came to be the welfare of society and the dream of a better future. The early Akhmatova is well-nigh forgotten, the purely literary quality of her poetry is secondary to her social posture. Her terrible ordeal under the Stalinist terror is glossed over in one short paragraph. And **Requiem** is not mentioned at all.

By far the most serious evaluation of Akhmatova has been undertaken by A. I. Pavlovskii. In his book and an article on the poetess he, too, enumerates the well-known qualities of her work, the framework of her poetry, the influences on her, and her stand before and after the Revolution. Interestingly, he divides her creativity into three periods: 1910-17, 1917-41, and 1941-66. In the first period she wrote poems of personal love, as an Acmeist and under the influence of Pushkin and Annenskii. Her reserve and reticence disclose discord and instability, forcing her to seek salvation in religion, nature, and poetry. The second period is one of inner transformation and adjustment to the new society. She comes closer to the people and to her country; she has made peace with the world and thus has entered into Soviet poetry. Admittedly, the price she has had to pay is a "certain uniformity of her poems." From an extrovert "chamber" love poetry she turns inward seeking refuge in dreams and Freudian psychological interpretations. In the third period Akhmatova becomes truly a Soviet poet. She not only accepts the new reality, she views the distant past in retrospect and rejects much that had been near and dear to her. She turns to patriotic and political poetry. "I" becomes "We." She moves toward the epic, acquiring a much profounder sense of history than ever before. Her Pushkinian radiance, harmony, and wisdom are the tangible results of this beneficial transformation.

Such evaluation by Pavlovskii is very much in line with that of Ozerov and other Soviet critics. It is schematic, tendentious, and incomplete. His division into periods exemplifies these strictures. By choosing 1917 and 1941 as dividing points he wants to show how important these years were for Akhmatova. As a matter of truth, her poetry during and after the Revolution, until her silence in 1923, is little different from that before the Revolution. And she reappeared a year before the second World War began in Russia. Furthermore, the period of silence from 1923 to 1940 was simply a matter of involuntary passivity. *Requiem,* the proof of her inability to accept the Stalinist reality, was described by Pavlovskii only as a personal tragedy, "the confession of a suffering mother's heart." That Akhmatova finally made a truce with the Soviet reality is true, but nowhere did she extol the Soviet state; instead, she spoke only of Russia. Pavlovskii also gives too much weight to Akhmatova's "political" poems; they are considered by many to be her weakest. His book nevertheless makes a number of telling points. These concern primarily the literary aspects of Akhmatova's poetry, especially when it is considered within the context of Russian literature in general. Pavlovskii writes of these aspects in more detail than anyone after the Formalist critics and before Dobin. His extensive discussion of the complex *Poem without a Hero* is of special merit. In it he sees the synthesis of Akhmatova's most important themes and forms; he calls it a "poem of conscience." He also points out some omissions in the scholarship dealing with Akhmatova. Until a new study appears, Pavlovskii's book has to be considered the major work in Akhmatoviana, its many serious shortcomings notwithstanding.

Among other writings by Soviet critics and poets, short articles by Kornei Chukovskii, Andrei Siniavskii, Aleksei Surkov, and Aleksandr Tvardovskii should be mentioned. Chukovskii speaks mainly about the *Poem without a Hero,* finding its author "the master of historical painting," which is the essence of her entire poetry. Siniavskii complains about the entrenched fallacy that Akhmatova should be treated primarily as the author of her prerevolutionary poetry. There is a new Akhmatova (Siniavskii pointedly cites *Requiem*), not only thematically but even in structure and tonality. Unlike other poets, she changes while striving toward the perfection of classic Russian poetry. What is needed is a revision of this and other clichés about Akhmatova. Siniavskii cites the example of her miniatures which, seemingly narrow and autobiographical, display a powerful art of the exalted, heroic, and tragic word and gesture. It is indeed unfortunate that Siniavskii has not written, thus far, more about Akhmatova, because he would probably be able to give a very competent and impartial assessment of her poetic art.

Both Surkov and Tvardovskii, in their necrologies after Akhmatova's death, in addition to repeating some well-known facts about her poetry, speak about her attitude toward the Soviet regime. Surkov repeats his argument that she became a Soviet poet shortly before and during World War II. Her ordeal of 1946, the year of Zhdanov's attack, Surkov dismisses lightly as "new trials." Tvardovskii recognizes Akhmatova's increasing popularity, although it has not reached the level of Maiakovskii's or even Blok's. He defends the limited scope of her poetry by evoking Chernishevskii's saying that people do not commit suicide because of world problems but because of problems in their hearts. Tvardovskii then touches upon a very sensitive nerve—the not-so-gallant treatment of the poet "at the well-known time." It is wrong to keep silent about those unjust and crude attacks on the poet, if for no other reason than because she withstood those attacks "with firmness and dignity that could not fail to earn respect for her." As for the attackers and their arguments, life has long since swept them away.

A more ambitious approach to Akhmatova's poetry was undertaken by another Soviet critic, Efim Dobin. In his articles he limits himself to the literary merits of her poetry, thus avoiding tendentiousness and the untenability of politically colored interpretations. There is not much new in his presentation, but he attempts a systematic study of Akhmatova's first decade and of *Poem without a Hero* and, moreover, illustrates his points with copious quotations from the poems; the only two such articles Dobin has published to date, they are undoubtedly chapters from a forthcoming book. If his announced book is based on the kind of examination displayed in his two articles, it should be the outstanding evaluation of her work, especially of its purely literary aspects.

The Akhmatova scholarship outside Russia has been limited to a few articles, and even they have been mostly of an informative character. The critics shortly after the Revolution were mostly Russian émigrés, who did not deal extensively with Akhmatova, probably because she, though never a sympathizer of the Bolsheviks, had nevertheless decided to remain in Russia. It was not until many years later that the critics abroad wrote about her, spurred by Zhdanov's merciless attack. Even then the critics were again mostly émigrés. Leonid Strakhovsky wrote several articles and devoted a chapter to Akhmatova in his book on three Acmeist poets. In all of them he speaks of her as a "poetess of tragic love." He notes her unexpected but convincing, illogical but fine psychological transitions from emotion to description, from the soul to nature, from feeling to fact. While recollecting the past, Akhmatova compares it with the present. She is essentially an urban poet, a poet of St. Petersburg and later of Leningrad. As the first Word War progressed, the poet developed a stronger religious feeling, although she had always possessed a religion of a strong, simple, almost primitive faith. For Strakhovsky, *The White Flock* reflects the war and the Revolution; *The Plantain* represents a turning point, when love begins to acquire a tragic note and the first political themes appear; and *Anno Domini* is Akhmatova's swan song, in which her love has turned to hate and has become "full of evil." Akhmatova reappeared in 1940 with greater wisdom, mellowed by years of want and suffering. It is unfortunate that Strakhovsky's articles are of necessity sketchy and that they are written before Akhmatova's latest works were fully known. Otherwise he might have been able to provide a more rounded picture of the poet as a needed balance to the one-sided Soviet presentation. Even so, Strakhovsky's writings are among the most serious, albeit incomplete, essays on Akhmatova.

Ihor Levitsky, in a brief article in *Books Abroad*, repeats many of Strakhovsky's arguments, adding a few of his own. He sees Akhmatova's entire opus as an epistolary novel about the love of a girl, who becomes a woman before our eyes, for an ever-present but usually silent partner. Akhmatova's best poems are the ones dealing with the poet's craft and with Leningrad, while the *Poem Without a Hero* is "an act of purgation prompted by a desperate inner need." One must take exception to Levitsky's views that the poet does not describe great achievements or heroic deeds, that hers is a limited subject matter, and that she almost never speaks directly of her feelings.

The two articles accompanying the two-volume edition of Akhmatova's works are of necessity informative and explanatory, especially Gleb Struve's introductory piece. He gives the main biographical details, lists her works, discusses her Acmeist past, and enlarges upon her enmity to Soviet authorities and theirs to her, as expressed especially in *Requiem.* Struve also laments the fact that there is no full-length study of her work,

while listing briefly the existing ones. Boris Filippov somewhat impressionistically reflects upon Akhmatova's origin (Petrograd; it could *not* be Moscow!), her kinship with Pushkin and Dostoevsky, some features (all well known) of her poetry, her attractiveness for the reader of today, even in the Soviet Union, and her anti-Soviet poetry, in which he perceives the mood of the Judgment Day. Filippov considers one of her greatest contributions to be her musing upon the Russian idea of love, upon a new life that is not only birth but also resurrection, and upon immortality.

Of the few non-Russian critics abroad, Renato Poggioli sees as the main feature of her poetry love and passion, expressed from a feminine point of view as "fidelity to her man and her passion as well as to nature and life; above all, fidelity to the glories and miseries of her sex." In this respect she recalls Emily Dickinson. Akhmatova never describes her lovers, only hints at them through senses other than sight. And, despite of dreams of happiness, the sense of imminent misfortune is very much evident in the mood of her poems. Poggioli's brief but pertinent remarks, despite some factual inaccuracies (Akhmatova's birth place, the fate of her son), give a vivid picture of the poetess. Frank Thomas speaks of four great Russian poets of the last half century (Akhmatova, Pasternak, Mandelshtam, and Tsvetaeva) and their relationships. Thomas sees the three main characteristics of Akhmatova's poetry as classic austerity, lyrical intensity, and precise and concrete language. He also discerns the poet's search for the truth and her preoccupation with the basic facts of the human condition: bereavement, old age, separation, exile, poetic inspiration, death, and communion with her Muse. Like many other writings of similar scope, this article suffers from sketchiness and the habit of rephrasing the familiar statements and conclusions.

In general, the evaluation of Akhmatova in different periods and by different camps bears the partisan stamp of the periods or camps. While pre-revolutionary references to her are mainly concerned with her new, strong talent and have a relatively easy task because of the single theme of her poetry, later critiques differ sharply in their basic approach. The opponents of the regime tend to see in Akhmatova a victim and a martyr; the proponents of the regime at first reject her, then condescend to accept her into the family. But no matter how all these critics differ in their evaluation of Akhmatova's views or themes, they agree that she is a master of her craft and of the language and that she has decisively contributed to Russian literature. The prerevolutionary critics and those immediately following the Revolution (especially the Formalists) pay much more attention to her purely artistic qualities, while the later critics, both Soviets and émigrés, allow political considerations to govern their judgment and to overshadow their examination and presentation of her works as literary art. More recently, there are signs that such a politically oriented approach may be overcome, both in the Soviet Union and abroad; however, a much more substantial body of scholarship on Akhmatova must come into being to erase the prevalent bias toward the poet and her work.

It has become evident, I hope, that much fertile ground remains to be tilled by the critic and scholar of Akhmatova and her work. What is needed above all is a study in depth. The announced book by the Soviet critic Dobin may fill this gap. Even so, one view of the poet, even if complete, cannot help but be somewhat one-sided, especially when the widely disparate views on literary matters in the Soviet Union and abroad are taken into consideration. There is also a need for a detailed, and disciplined, study of specific aspects of Akhmatova's works: her prosody; the variety and unity of her themes; her world-view, especially in the late period; the nature of her love lyrics; her patriotic poetry; and her relationship to both the Tsarist and the Communist regimes. A scrupulously documented biography is also badly needed. Her prose works have been largely ignored, to be sure because most of those works have not been readily available so far. But once they become available, a study of her prose, especially of her spirited essays about Pushkin, should be undertaken. Her prolific translations from various languages should be indexed and commented upon. The problem of the influence of other poets on Akhmatova has been thus far limited to the mentioning of names. There exist very few studies of influences either on Akhmatova or by her on other poets. Even when there is no discernible influence, the relationships between herself and such writers as Gumilyov, Mandelshtam, and Maiakovskii, can be examined profitably.

Now that Akhmatova's life's journey has ended, the time has come to abandon the writing of cursory, general, merely informative articles about her and to embark upon more ambitious undertakings worthy of her stature. Admittedly, there are still many problems involved, particularly the problem of free access to the poet's manuscripts left behind. The Soviet critics have a decisive advantage in this respect, and it is they who must, and probably will, provide the most important future scholarship. The compulsion to discuss literary matters in a tendentious manner is diminishing among Soviet critics, especially among the younger ones. But even if they continue as in the past, the critics outside Russia will occupy themselves increasingly with Akhmatova's work as it becomes better known to the world and as she more securely gains her place in world literature, where she indeed belongs among a distinguished company.

Note

1. Akhmatova's works have been published both in Russia and abroad. In Russia, her early poems comprise five volumes: *Vecher* [Evening] (St. Petersburg, 1912), *Chetki* [*Rosary*] (St. Petersburg, 1914), *Belaia staia* [*White Flock*] (Petrograd, 1917), *Podorozhnik* [*Plantain*] (Petrograd, 1921), *Anno Domini MCMXXI* (Petrograd, 1921; another edition, without the year number, was published in 1923). *Iz shesti knig* [*From Six Books*] (Leningrad, 1940), the first book after her seventeen-year absence, consists of five previous collections plus the sixth, *Iva* (*Willow Tree*), later entitled *Trostnik* (*Reed*). Several volumes, most of them of a slender size, of selected or collected poems were published subsequently, in 1943, 1958, 1961, and 1965, this last bearing the title *Beg vremeni* (*The Course of Time*). Her poetry is now republished in increasing volume, in anthologies, periodicals, and even newspapers. New editions of her works have been announced. Abroad, there have been two collections of poetry: *Izbrannye stikhotvoreniia* (New York, 1952) and *Sochineniia* in two volumes, of which only the first has appeared so far (Washington, D.C., 1965). In addition, *Poema bez geroia* [*Poem without a Hero*] (New York, 1960) appeared in the United States before it did in the Soviet Union, and *Requiem* (Munich, 1963) has yet to be published in Russia. At the time of going to press, there is no volume of Akhmatova's verse in English, but one has been announced by Washington Square Press for the near future.

   The publication of secondary literature can be divided into three groups: as published in prerevolutionary Russia, in the Soviet Union, and abroad. Before the Revolution, there were relatively few critical studies of Akhmatova. Among the more important are Valerian Chudovskii, "Po povodu stikhov Anny Akhmatovoi," *Apollon*, No. 5 (1912); Nikolai Nedobrovo, "Anna Akhmatova," *Russkaia mysl'* (July 1915), pp. 59-60; Viktor Zhirmunskii, "Preodolevshie simvolizm," *Russkaia mysl'* (Dec. 1916), pp. 25-57. Of these, Zhirmunskii's study is by far the most important. Other references are either brief reviews or remarks within essays on Russian literature. After the Revolution, there were relatively few critical works before Akhmatova's silence in 1923: Iulii Aikhenval'd, "Anna Akhmatova," *Siluety russkikh pisatelei* (Berlin, 1922), pp. 279-93; Boris Eikhenbaum, "Anna Akhmatova," *Opyt analiza* (Petrograd, 1923), pp. 121-32; Viktor Vinogradov, "O simvolike Anny Akhmatovoi," *Literaturnaia mysl'*, I (Petrograd, 1922-23), 91-138; Leonid Grossman, "Anna Akhmatova," *Bor'ba Za Stil'* (Moskva, 1927), pp. 227-39. After this, there are no significant studies or references to Akhmatova until Zhdanov's "analysis" of her work in his speech, published (in English) as

Andrei Zhdanov, "On the Errors of the Soviet Literary Journals *Zvezda* and *Leningrad*," *Essays on Literature, Philosophy, and Music* (New York, 1950), pp. 22-25. After the republication of Akhmatova's poetry there is a steadily increasing number of studies about her: Aleksei Surkov's afterword to her collection of poems (Moskva, 1958); Lev Ozerov, "Tainy remesla," *Rabota poeta* (Moskva, 1963), pp. 174-97; Kornei Chukovskii, "Chitaia Akhmatovu," *Moskva*, VII (1964), 200-03; Andrei Siniavskii, "Raskovannyi golos," *Novyi mir*, XL (1964), 174-76; A. Pavlovskii, *Anna Akhmatova* (Leningrad, 1966); Efim Dobin, "'Poema bez geroia' Anny Akhmatovoi," *Voprosy literatury*, X, 9 (1966), 63-79; Aleksei Surkov, "Poety ne umiraiut," *Novyi mir*, XLII (1966), 283-84; Aleksandr Tvardovskii, "Dostoin-stvo talanta," *Novyi mir*, XLII, (1966), 285-88; Efim Dobin, "Poeziia Anny Akmatovoi," *Russkaia literatura*, IX (1966), 154-74; A. Pavlovskii, "Anna Akhmatova," *Poety-savremenniki* (Moskva, 1966), pp. 103-40. A book on Akhmatova by Efim Dobin has been announced as well as a chapter in the second edition of the official *Istoriia russkoi sovetskoi literatury*. The first edition (1958-61) of this multivolumed history of Soviet literature does not contain any significant reference to Akhmatova.

Of the writings on Akhmatova abroad, the following articles are worth mentioning: Konstantin Mochul-skii, "Poeticheskoe tvorchestvo Anny Akhmatovoi," *Russkaia mysl'* (March-April 1921), 185-201; three articles by Leonid Strakhovsky: "Anna Akhmatova: The Sappho of Russia," *The Russian Student*, VI, 3 (1929); "Anna Akhmatova—Poetess of Tragic Love," *American Slavic and East European Review*, VI (1947), 1-18 (this article can also be found in his book *Three Poets of Modern Russia: Craftsmen of the Word* [Cambridge, 1949], pp. 53-82); and "Fet i Akhmatova," *Novyi zhurnal*, No. 49 (1957), 261-64. Further articles: Renato Poggioli, "Anna Akhmatova," *The Poets of Russia* (Cambridge, 1960), pp. 229-34; N. Tarasova, "Zhivaia sovest'," *Grani*, No. 56 (1964), 5-10; Georgii Adamovich, "Na poliakh 'Requiema' Anny Akhmatovoi," *Mosty*, XI (1964), 206-10; Ihor Levitsky, "The Poetry of Anna Akhmatova," *Books Abroad*, XXXIX (1965), 5-9; Gleb Struve, "Anna Akhmatova," *Sochineniia*, I (Washington, D.C., 1965), 5-15; Boris Filippov, "Anna Akhmatova," *Sochineniia*, I (1965), 17-31; Victor Frank, "Anna Akhmatova 1889-1966," *Survey*, No. 60 (1966), 93-101; Aleksandr Shmeman, "Anna Akhmatova," *Novyi zhurnal*, No. 83 (1966), 84-92; Anne Haight, "Anna Akhmatova's 'Poema bez geroia'," *Slavonic and East European Review*, XLV (1967), 474-96; and Helen Muchnic, "Three Inner Emigrés: Anna Akhmatova, Osip Mandelshtam, Nikolai Zabolotsky," *Russian Review*, XXVI (1967), 13-25. All these articles, except those by Poggioli, Frank, and Haight, were written by Russian émigrés.

Finally, of interest are also several interviews and visits with Anna Akhmatova: E. Osetrov, "Griadushchee, sozrevshee v proshedshem," *Voprosy literatury*, IX (1965), 183-89; Ruth Zernova, "A Visit to Anna Akhmatova," *Soviet Literature*, (Mar. 1965), pp. 148-50; Rita Rait-Kovaleva, "Vospominaniia ob Anne Akhmatove," *Literaturnaia Armeniia*, X (1966), and Alexander Werth, "Akhmatova: Tragic Queen Anna," *Nation* (Aug. 22, 1966), pp. 157-60.

WALTER ARNDT (ESSAY DATE 1976)

SOURCE: Arndt, Walter. "Introduction: I The Akhma-tova Phenomenon and II Rendering the Whole Poem." In *Anna Akhmatova: Selected Poems*, edited and translated by Walter Arndt, pp. xiii-xxxii. Ann Arbor, Mich.: Ardis, 1976.

In the following introduction to Akhmatova's poetry, Arndt discusses the public reception of her work and her role in the Acmeist poetry movement.

I. The Akhmatova Phenomenon

Among the remaining witnesses of the 20th century's "remarkable decade" in Russian poetry, 1912-1922[1], many still speak with animation and awe of the change of air in poetry which was heralded by *Evening*, Anna Akhmatova's first volume of verse. It was placed beyond doubt two years later by her second, *Rosary* (or *Beads*, 1914): a delicate but decisive discharge of lyric direct-ness, authenticity of feeling, palpability of image and phrase, for which "Acmeism" was from the start as poor a tag as any.

This phenomenon ionized, as it were, the stale poetic medium left by Symbolism as it waned prematurely; and the qualities suggested above, if "Acmeist" they are, were evidently more patent in her work then, and more infectious, than was true for years of the other members of the brother-hood. They were temptation enough now—sixty years later—for trying to bring Akhmatova into English for the first time in the fullness of her form and feeling; for a dozen of her poems read in the original or in such largely form-true transla-tions should demonstrate these properties more palpably than is ever contrived by circumlocutory forms of literary criticism practiced upon prosy travesties. As had happened in "her" city of Petersburg with the banished Pushkin's *Ruslan and Liudmila* in 1820, and in Poland two years later when Mickiewicz published his astonishing first collection and was exiled to Russia, the public sensed a change in the literary climate; the critics "pointed" and sniffed the air which had a new bite and sparkle to it.

Public response to Akhmatova, from the start until well into the Soviet era (cultural blight and official rancor smother the evidence), reached beyond the mutual admiration clubs of artists and the crushes of the black-taffeta-hairbow contin-gent from the high-schools—although both of these elements were strongly in evidence. In its intensity, its time profile, and its kinship with an earlier, simpler poetic tradition, her impact recalls

Rilke's; for Rilke's songlike clarity about this same time was quietly ruining the cult of the sacerdotal symbolist-aesthete, Stefan George (neoromanticism with a Wagnerite streak in which infinite preciosity replaced Wagner's *poshlost'*). His poetry went on, of course, to attain an unexampled and irreversible transforming effect in the twenties and beyond, intoxicating each new generation through intervening lapses of taste and sundry fads of "free form." One is also reminded of the triumphal spread, in an outbreak of *samizdat* seemingly defying all technical given data, of the young Pushkin's wrathful odes and epigrams, and his brilliant ribaldry, among the literate of all ages and walks of life in the years between 1819 and 1824. At that, Akhmatova's appeal was not abetted by any of that spice of ideological mutiny and moral freethinking which had seasoned her idol Pushkin's shockers, including even the triply camouflaged *Ruslan and Liudmila*. Not only the older Symbolists, but even those poets of high distinction who were unconnected with or remote from the mode by this time, like Innokenty Annensky (†1909) and Alexander Blok (†1921), both revered by Akhmatova, were eclipsed before their time by the Acmeist constellation. Gumilev himself, Akhmatova's erstwhile schoolmate at Tsarskoe Selo *gimnazija* (where Annensky taught Greek), and first husband (1910-18), who had lent definition to the Acmeist label by distilling often highly perceptive aesthetic manifestos, lost custom. The exotic *chic* in verse he was then mining—generations after Flaubert, Baudelaire, and Sienkiewicz, but with a he-mannerism which just scooped Hemingway—in a stylized East Africa, shocking-pink-in-tooth-and-claw, wilted all too soon. By the beginning of the War, although not unproductive as a poet, he was sliding into a sterile possessiveness toward the Acmeist movement as the other protagonists outgrew his definitions for it and, worse still, threatened to eclipse him for good. By 1920 he appears to have set himself up as a would-be Svengali of poetry for young girls of credulity and looks in the "sounding shell," his absurd studio workshop in the House of Arts for the teaching of verse-writing in four to six months.

Nor were any of the other poets of the Remarkable Decade who were Akhmatova's close co-evals—Khlebnikov, Khodasevich, and her three cherished intimates in sensibility, Mandelstam, Pasternak, and Tsvetaeva[2]—taken to the public's heart with such a personal, almost romantic emotion, or recited and imitated with quite such devotional fervor between a cult and a crush. After *Rosary* was published, adding half a hundred "beads" to the similar-sized first collection, Marc Slonim and other contemporaries recollect that the young who read poetry knew hers by heart, her readings were mobbed, lovers used her verses as letters and to set the mood of their meetings and partings. Later, long after the faddish component of this outpouring had worn away, we hear—with an optional twinge of skepticism—that she was one of the very few poets truly read by factory workers and laboring women. Also, hard though this may be to credit at first, Akhmatova had virtually started a genre which had existed in the West since the high Middle Ages: she was the first Russian poet to create strings and cycles of love lyrics. Personal, unsymbolical, non-allegorical, these truly probed and obliquely reflected, almost without external detail, the whole emotional course of a relationship neither esoteric nor trite. The literary critic Leonid Grossman noted in his article "Struggle for Style" (1927) that Akhmatova had become the favorite poet of the generation whose youth fell into the turbulent second decade of our century.

Akhmatova's original and severe beauty—a contemporary aesthete's dream—and her subfuse *art nouveau* get-ups which, when seen against the foil of Gumilev, suggest a novice furloughed by a rather liberal College of Vestals into the charge of a cross-eyed ogre-professor, were at least a small element in her magic. There is one account, in particular, far from sinfully idolatrous by intent, drawn from the memory of a then fourteen-year-old eyewitness, of a program of benefit performances in 1915. After some singing and a suitably avantgardist stage happening by Meyerhold, Akhmatova followed Sologub and Blok in authors' readings of verse. Perhaps it is not fanciful to say that between the quizzical lines of description below one catches (as in the mental space between those extant pre-revolutionary snapshots, oils, sketches, and doodles by Altman, Kardovskaya, Modigliani, Annenkov which the bloated mask of her seventies cannot blot out) the strange look that can still alert the heart, as it were, touch a node of sensibility: Young Roland on his way to the dark tower, crossed with a Beardsley Salome; a young Tatar soothsayer; and an angular school-girl, surely not over thirteen, with her shyness turned inside out:

> Akhmatova, in a white dress with a then fashion-able Stuart collar, was slender, beautiful, black-haired, exquisite. She was then getting on for

thirty[3], her fame in full flower; the fame of her *pauznik*[4], her bangs, her profile, her allure. "He will not be sending you any more letters,"[5] she recited, arms crossed over her breast, slowly and tenderly, with that musical gravity which was so captivating in her.[6]

Over half a century later, a year after her death, the veteran writer, critic, and translator, Korney Chukovsky, a close contemporary of Akhmatova's, begins his long commemorative essay on Akhmatova as follows:

> I had known Anna Andreevna Akhmatova since 1912, when at some literary evening she was brought up to me by her husband, the young poet Nikolai Stepanovich Gumilev. Thin as could be and gracefully built, resembling a shy fifteen-year-old, she took not a step away from her husband, who right there, upon our first acquaintance, called her his "pupil."
>
> This was the time of her first verse and those unusual, unexpectedly clamorous triumphs. Two or three years passed, and in her eyes, her bearing, her manner with people there had come to the fore that chief mark of her personality—sublimity. Not hauteur, not self-importance, not arrogance, but precisely sublimity: a regal gait of superb dignity, an inviolable sense of respect toward herself and her high mission as a writer.
>
> With every passing year this quality of sublimity became stronger in Akhmatova. She did not strain for this in any way, it emanated from her spontaneously. Over the entire half-century we knew each other I don't remember seeing on her face a single pleading, ingratiating, mean, or lachrymose smile. Gazing at her, one could not help recalling Nekrasov's lines: "There are women in Russian villages / With a quiet dignity of face, / With a fine strength in their movements, / With the gait, with the gaze of queens."
>
> Even queuing up for petroleum or bread, even on a hard bench in a train, even in a tram-car in Tashkent, strangers sensed her "quiet dignity" and showed her special deference, although she conducted herself very simply and warmly toward everyone, without any condescension.
>
> There was another trait in her which was remarkable. She was totally devoid of the acquisitive urge. She did not like to own things and did not try to, and parted with them with amazing ease. Like Gogol, Coleridge, and her close friend Mandelstam, she was a homeless rover and valued possessions so little that she was glad to free herself of them as of a weight. Even in her youth, the years of her brief "blossoming," she lived without cumbersome wardrobes and chests, at times even without a desk . . .
>
> She did, of course, greatly treasure things of beauty and appreciated what they stood for. Antique candlesticks, oriental fabrics, engravings, ikons of old workmanship and the like now and then made their appearance in her modest life, only to vanish again after a few weeks . . . Even books, save for her greatest favorites, she would pass on to others after reading. Only Pushkin, the Bible, Shakespeare, and Dostoevsky were her perennial companions . . .[7]

Before Akhmatova was thirty, leading poets and critics such as Briusov, Blok, Zhirmunsky had examined her work. They sought to account for some elements of her impact largely in terms of prosodic and thematic innovations, perhaps without full awareness as yet of the peculiar interaction between her set of gifts and a sea change in poetic imagination and taste that was taking place in much of Europe. And there was every excuse for this neglect of context. Not only was the European scene in poetry and the visual arts pervaded by several disparate yet overlapping and interacting trends, but each of these tended to assume different forms and names in different sections of a cosmopolitan system of so many imperfectly inter-communicating national vessels. There was bound to exist a confusing, often misleading differential, especially among individual Russian poets, and between Russian poets and their critics, as to what particular blend of foreign traditions—avant-garde, current, and earlier, German, English, French, Italian, Polish—any one of them responded to and thought the other familiar with. Moreover, large poetic trends, schools, even fads, become clearly evident as such only in retrospect; in the contemporary view the personal poetic signature is as a rule writ larger.

The versatile prosody which Akhmatova developed, now stately, not lightfooted in ambiguous anapestic-dactylic beats, but seeming not just to simulate waves of natural speech, but to orchestrate emotion,[8] came from a matrix which included Blok, Vyacheslav Ivanov, Annensky, and Gumilev. The repeated anapestic onrun or ascent which is Akhmatova's favorite line-launcher is hardly encountered outside of Russia in modern metrics and is rare even elsewhere in Russian prosody before the new century. It is startling particularly when the preceding line ends in a feminine rhyme, changing the listener's interlinear metric impression, his rhythmic "intake," to a "⎯⎯⎯" tattoo like the opening of Beethoven's Fifth Symphony; see, e.g., the end of line 1 with the start of line 2 in "When first my dark braids. . . ." After this flying run at the start of each line the meter often brakes intermittently, grippingly, to a pensive, brooding, or baleful iamb as halting by contrast as a spondee; an analogous design blends dactyls with trochees. These devices simulate intermittent bursts of hurried resumption, rejoinder, addition, or afterthought: "oh, and then . . ."; "not to mention . . ."; "let me add . . ."; "and what's more", with an unusual suggestion of rich emotional energy and rhetorical invention in reserve. With each onrun the poem, as it were, begins afresh, statements are amplified and amended, the bearings change. The non-sequiturs between observed environs and an emotion not "produced" by them but coincident and subliminally harmonizing, with which Akhmatova so often operates, harmonize perfectly with the rushing spontaneity, the aptitude for associative short-circuits, of the springboard anapests of the first foot.

Such metric novelty was much enhanced in its effect and removed from its origins by elements of tone and taste all Akhmatova's own, or most distinctively blended. These included a lightness and targetry of diction which owe much to Pushkin, who is often lovingly invoked: a fastidious economy, yet graceful languor of line learnt perhaps from the freshly rediscovered brushwork and lyric of Japan. In terms of feeling, the present collection contains touching examples of a tart girlish frivolity overlying, and suddenly giving way to, a brittle grace of emotion, exultant or desolate; notes, or better, verbal gestures of peasant piety and of an asceticism which in another might be suspect of neoromantic posturing à la early Rilke. But her austere mode of living and feeling imbued it with an authenticity which made critics call her the last poet of Orthodoxy and prompted the just-cited Chukovsky in the early twenties, with a thin sneer all too consonant with the vulgar official line of atheism, to affect surprise that she hadn't taken the veil yet. A further pervasive feature, which will perhaps be found exemplified in this anthology more strikingly than any other, is the offering of abrupt, brief, but evocative glimpses of nature or landscape, alternating with, and made subliminally relevant to, states of emotion.[9]

The flavor of young Akhmatova's initial appeal, both to the milieu of her first public and, one daresay, to some who first sample her early "songs" today, is distinctively Art Nouveau; but Art Nouveau, to say it at once, in the original sense of a revitalizing urge in aesthetics brought by the new century. Her economy of poetic line, the true ingenuousness of feeling, those clairvoyant moods of languor, grief, or caprice of a young poet were symptomatic of the great dismissal of rich, beautiful tushery (poetic Symbolism included) that was all around her. The term Art Nouveau must be understood in its contemporary connotations to do with liberation from the

ornamental, lush, grossly literal which had long dominated the arts, impressionism and its triumph notwithstanding. In terms of this drive, early Art Nouveau and Akhmatova were of a kind. But Art Nouveau as painting and décor quickly calcified into *Jugendstil,* an arsenal of stale motifs, and became in a way part of what it had rebelled against, while most of the Acmeist poets remained consistent and creative. To feel the edge of the change they brought, I spend some little time below surveying the scene preceding them, choosing for illustration that domain of aesthetics which is most easily seen in the aggregate—the visual arts, and especially painting.

Whatever the differences in the timetables and itineraries of artistic trends between the Russian reader of 1912 and his present cultural heirs (who must be sought in the West, not the USSR), they share a long and continuing contact with the stuffy fluidum of epigonism, of stylization rather than style, decoration rather than creation, which smogged the second half of the nineteenth century. By way of the dry air roots of late Art Nouveau, this is enjoying a minor revival among the art-less young of all ages in Anglosaxony now. This was the Morris-down-to-Makart era, so valiantly launched, strange to think, by the high-minded back-to-Botticelli-and-home-weaving brigade, the apostles of "Thoughts towards Nature in Poetry, Literature, and the Arts"—thus the subtitle of the Pre-Raphaelite journal, *The Germ* (1850). Its tastes and manners, which one may roughly sum up as ultra-naturalist neo-romanticism, inevitably had a good deal to do also with the impulses behind literary Symbolism; whence the rapid alienation from the latter on the part of the Acmeists, especially the clearest and simplest among their talents, Akhmatova.

What happened to that powerful artistic urge of the 1840s toward the genuine and natural, comparable in a way to the noble revulsion from plastic foods and fittings and predatory industrialism in our day? A remarkable galaxy of talents in craft work, design, painting, and literature somehow found itself beshrewed by a *Zeitgeist* close to Ivan Karamazov's clammy devil of genial mediocrity, and well exemplified, say, by the flax-topped flab of ululating Rhine maidens or the nervous innocence of the sub-deb of "September Morn." This middle-class dyspepsia of spirit and taste somehow contrived to turn revival, gifted imagination, innovation, renovation, and allusive decadence all into the same thing—Kitsch. It shows how "camp" speaks to "camp" that one of the art fads in the Campbell soup-tin years (the Novecento, so to speak) consisted in admiring "Tiffany" lamps and grandma gowns, and in imitating the artifacts of a previous morass of taste in all arts but music, where the change would have been for the better. There, surrounding Akhmatova's adolescence, was the insistent fluent mediocrity of decaying Morrisdom, the accomplished mimesis of *Jugendstil* art work with its perennial limp creepers, rambling roses, hyperthyroid maidens of tile or stained glass, draped in mysteriously agitated bedsheets and labeled Spring, Summer, Autumn, Winter, which is still to be found in Vanderbilt lodges, some Canadian railway temples, and ex-Armenian cafés in the Levant. There, in fairylands forlorn, framed by unmistakable legends in uncial script, were colorful marvels for the Russian artists to see and translate into Scythian mish-mash and Church Slavonic calligraphy. There lolled, stalked, and pouted those beige innocents of the Pre-Raphaelites with their moot stares. There glossily emoted the self-conscious think and shudder pieces of neo-romantic painters of stark histrionic and decorative gifts, from Delacroix and Boecklin all the way past Ingres and the brilliant interlude of Impressionism, to such latterday story painters as J. W. Waterhouse and J. M. Strudwick (†1935!), Maurice Denis and Puvis de Chavannes; and in Germany the much more ambiguous Hans von Marees. The bottom is reached with Maxfield Parrish, that never missing link between Lord Leighton and N. C. Wyeth, whose epicene greenish couples, spending furloughs from the morgue on triple-glazed moonlit terraces, nicely combine the infantile with the degenerate and lead directly to Disney's Snow-White and the dominant mode of North-American fairy-tale illustrations (green jerklets in jerkins), Christian novelties, and garden dwarfery. In most "gift-stores" and pop posteries today the eye lights with a sour shock of recognition upon billowy cumuli, a ghostly peak over a lake, somber bosks, and one or two liverish nymphlings, not naked but "undraped," which means elaborately unconscious of their displaced, but presumably equally greenish genitalia. Poor Morris . . .

We are dealing, then, with a movement imitative in its conception—imitative of nature and, even more, of literature—which took thirty years to decline thoroughly (ca. 1870-1900) and then contaminated some strains of the Art Nouveau which undertook to bury it. The latter has since then been selectively stylized (ca. 1900-1920) and later dusted off during interludes of necrophilia. But searching for common elements one may find, first, a weakness for neo-romantic, that is

thrice-decocted, chivalry; a cult of a synthetic naiveté of feeling; feigned espousal of a boyish vision of the female, combining innocence with fatality: it is over a late, further vulgarized exemplar of this type of would-be sophisticated infantilism, by the way, that we were invited by H. Humbert to shake our heads in titillated revulsion in an auto-erotic grudge-thriller of the fifties. Next, perhaps, one should note a gradual movement of taste toward the epicene, tentative, elusive (but not allusive) in human figures, a late reaction against the rosy flab of Guido Reni, Tintoretto, and Rubens, and a preparation for a new nakedness where the child-like and asthenic would usurp the privileges of innocence—decadence, in a word. Thus taste is bred down from the virile if decorative angelfolk of Botticelli by and via the Burne-Joneses, Millais', and Rossettis to grovefuls of interchangeably willowy and violet-eyed princelings aged twelve and yet eighteen, too raspberry and swollen of lip quite to fit their dewy stares or the spindly grace of their fawnlike retreats. Besides these, or Maxfield Parrish, or even a less decadent epigone like Kay Nielsen, one should in fairness look also to an honest and technically accomplished piece of Nouveau Art contemporary to the young Akhmatova. Brilliant talents, as we noted, spent themselves in this magic maze of mannerisms—the last of them perhaps being the Arthur Rackham of the illustrations to *Ondine* or *A Midsummer Night's Dream*.

In terms and themes analogous to those of the later Pre-Raphaelites, the Russian painters and illustrators revived the legendary "Scythian," Varangian, and Kievan past; and the visual imagination of the Russian public may be presumed to have been very similarly conditioned by that neo-romantic and, by 1910, Art Nouveau and Mannerist habitat. One may pick one of Rackham's angular gracile maidens, haze Rackham's elaborations of detail—eyelash and grace-lock, tendril and rosebud, dew and rue—with a dash of the Slavic earthiness and self-irony, and arrive at a visual artifact very like one of Akhmatova's lyric mood sketches at 22, as these evidently struck some of her public: "outer and inner landscape with girl," as it were. The interdisciplinary resemblance in the case of Akhmatova is superficial and misleading, as has been suggested. It spreads by association from the girl-poet's personal image to the reception of her poetry. But the portrayal of Akhmatova in those pre-War years, pictorial and memoiristic, suggests forcibly that she herself was widely seen in terms of, first, Art Nouveau, later, briefly, expressionistic or cubist fancy. It was forty years since stricken damsels first came yearning forth from Morris's saga medley, *The Earthly Paradise,* since Swinburne sang those tainted beauties for Burne-Jones and Rossetti to paint, since the Gudruns, Genovefas or Iseults out of every child's book of legends and ballads had in Russia been replaced by similar Olgas, Yaroslavnas, Svetlanas, even Liudmillas—tragic-eyed penitents prodding their sheer damask hairshirts in two places from within as they stride some desert shore. They were presciently twitted by Pushkin in his *Gabriiliada*[10], but a hundred years later they contain the clues to that early Akhmatova image—blending the morbidly vulnerable, sensuous, and austere—which precipitated out of paintings, poetry, and gossip.

The various pat sobriquets for Akhmatova as a woman and a poet which originated then, like the "passionate nun," "the lithe gypsy," curiously miss her point. They seem less redolent of their elusive target than of those allegorical water-lily maidens of the emporium lobbies of 1912. But the 1915 portrait by O. della Voss-Kardovskaya of a seated young vestal, severely but elegantly gowned and posed, startlingly beautiful, calm, and fragile in full profile, does convey an inkling of the magnetism which helped to romanticize both her poems and her relations to them as a woman. Mandelstam in his contemporary collection *Stone* saw now Phaedra, now Rachel in that gracefully portentous feminine emblem. It may now be becoming clearer why a certain amount of oversimplified art history had to percolate into these scene-setting remarks; at the risk of some sense of strain or distortion when read in either the context of Russian poetry alone, or only in the context of European painting as usually treated. It has been my intuitive conviction that both the quality of Akhmatova's visual imagination and the quality of the response to her are best approached not through antecedent poetry—despite prosodic insights available there—but through the spirit of *fin de siècle* ornate and rhetorical painting. The innovations of the *Jugendstil* period in the arts, including Acmeism, were revolts against this accomplished but meretricious theater. Its emotional force of gesture and paysage is taken into Akhmatova's verse, but she purges it of sentimentality and pose; all *intérieurs,* with their fussy preciosity of feature, fabric, and furnishing, are swept away. She goes farther than that—toward a pure dialectic of the sentient intelligence, or eloquent emotion, in poetry. Unlike other creators of the new austerity and elegance (in the modern mathematical sense), she is rarely tempted to enter

any of the premier fields of honor of older poetry—the sensual-functional beauty of man and woman, animal, carved stone, any and all of nature—for its own sake, in the way of, say, Rilke with his stunning "Panther," or "Roman Fountain." Akhmatova's **"Statue in Tsarskoe Selo"** along with all other apparent examples of such noble snapshooting are revealed to derive their *raison d'être* wholly from the self's independent emotion waiting in the wings—often until the last stanza or line. Her abruptness, in fact, her plain gaunt phrase of the later years and often obscure transitions, were consonant with the quasi-Japanese cult of the elliptic and oblique, *poésie pure,* which was a facet of the Art Nouveau sensibility. Aleksis Rannit has much to say about this in his fine introductory article to Volume II of the canonical Struve-Filippov edition of Akhmatova's works.

"Delusion I," one of her charming young-girl-in-hammock poems, may serve to show both her affinity (or initial palatability) to Art Nouveau aesthetics, and some marked differences. Something in its mood, blended of effusiveness and languor, and in the hints of decorative sensual detail (dazzling dark-blue faience, limp morocco leather) makes manifest the nature of Akhmatova's unsought appeal to *Jugendstil* taste. But there is little posing or empty stylization in the whole of *Evening,* of which the four **"Delusion"** poems are part, and less in the later collections. This is single-stroke *aquarelle* sketching, fresh and swift, of delicate moods, especially vagrant states of mind drifting from small events of nature and environment to concurrent and subjectively related small events of the inner life, and back. The exact connection as a rule is logically obscure but emotionally convincing, in that it is precisely the concurrence of inner and outer events (both often in flux and the first frequently involving more than one persona) which give dual or multiple crescendos of tension to the poetic experience. In **"Delusion"** there is hardly any gap between perception and emotion, although it is somehow far in flavor from the simple exultation of Browning's "All's right with the world." In "As if through a straw," as often in that species of Akhmatova lyric that I would call "soul in landscape" poems, the stay-at-home emotion or thought takes a walk, as it were; an unhappy, one-sided relation of moral exploitation—"as through a straw you are drinking my soul, which tastes bitter yet goes to your head, I have no resistance left and have stopped valuing myself"—is suddenly aired. In the second stanza and the third, a step is taken into "normal" human milieu and unconcerned nature, for the sake of poetic foil, or respite perhaps, but not for a restoration of self, or pathetic fallacy; or its mirror image, a theatrical demonstration that there is no refuge in nature or the ordinary. The initial mood of dull despair persists, the poem has merely gained in empathetic force through an outdoors dimension. A different, less characteristic, inward-outward-inward turn of the poetic screen occurs in "All abject, these eyes . . ." There, in the "outward" stanza, the thematic association between the vernally fresh and unsteady breeze and the faraway gentleman who has the audacity to be other than sad is obtrusive; elsewhere such links are rare.

> What kind of criticism, of commentary on the arts, is desirable today? For I am not saying that works of art are ineffable, that they cannot be described or paraphrased. They can be. What would criticism look like that would serve the work of art, not usurp its place? . . . The best criticism, and it is uncommon, is of this sort that dissolves considerations of content into those of form . . . Equally valuable would be acts of criticism that would supply a really accurate, sharp, loving description of the appearance of a work of art.[11]

II. Rendering the Whole Poem

A paradox has it that poetry seems to have a direct, incontrovertible, triumphantly convincing access to a truth which, when so reached, has been commonly called aesthetic. But it is a truth which poetry itself establishes by its mesmerism, and it is discernible and verifiable in no other way. A practical corollary, if paradoxes can have them, is that one is apt to accept in a successful stanza of verse elements of sentiment and modes of statement which one might not accept in prose. Why? Is it because one is more indulgent to verse ("poetry, God help us, must be a little daft," said Pushkin), pleading the restrictions placed on it by the "form" (there aren't any, since it comes about in and through its form), or because one simply takes it to be somehow less "serious," a performance which signifies nothing beyond itself? Or is it rather because the specific gravity of any utterance is higher in verse; provided the verse qualifies as such by having formal identity, even some degree of formal rigor? Its semantic charge is what it seems to "say" and then some: it says what it seems to "mean" in such a manner—elliptic, lucid, dim, portentous, memorable—that what seems manner declares itself directly as part of the semantic burden. What may be mistakenly thought of separately, as "the aesthetic effect," is of one body with whatever cognitive message the utterance might partially share with a prose statement; and the aggregate is more powerful than prose. Prose rhetoric operates in a kindred way, of course; its transitions toward poetry are probably gradual. But cumulatively they integrate into a quantum leap.

The poetic statement, then, is not just "more" moving, dense, striking, terse, beautiful, or whatever, but it is different in kind from any attempted cognitive reduction to prose. (Hence, by the way, the chilling absurdity of V. Nabokov's vivisection of *Eugene Onegin*—"yet each man kills the thing he loves"—with the scalpel of a lexicomaniacal literalism.) It is true in a sense that is both abstract and sensual; it may have truth even when what is misrepresented as its cognitive "base" in prose is perceived as untrue or trite. It convinces in its own aesthetic terms without having appeal to rational plausibility or proof. If, intellectually, the reader is irked, bored, or puzzled by an episode of the *Divine Comedy* or a passage in *Faust II,* he can be so on one level without detriment to their contextual rightness or their subliminal effect on him. The poet—naively speaking—may bore or puzzle in irrationally important, graceful, or gripping ways; and if a translation gravely fails to do the same it is useless. This is why prose texts which call themselves translations or even paraphrases of works of poetry are worse than useless; they are in effect hoaxes or swindles even when they, as is often the case, take in their own perpetrators.

Readers of Russian poetry, and sometimes the poets, have been embarrassed lately by a spate of imitation and *Nachfühlerei* by hopelessly monoglot bards of high or low estate, who were lured by a vague freemasonry of (mutually unintelligible) letters and an aura of intellectual *chic* that has been wafted about such as Voznesensky and Talleyrand-Evtushenko and, more regrettably, Brodsky and (posthumously) all the Acmeists. In our era this sort of humbug started, very mildly indeed, at the time of Louis MacNeice's BBC *Faust* and, via Auden perhaps, infected Lowell, Kunitz, and Bly, as well as some others with neither the language *nor* talent to sustain them. For the little matter of gaining access to the original verse, these poets have recourse to native Pythias or Cassandras of either sex who, all too often, their admonitions scorned, are thrown by the English Pegasus at the first ditch and depart to rend their garments in discreet seclusion. Nothing of value and kinship with the original (except perhaps to the imitator) has yet come out of such heteromorphous imitation. The case is worse with those nonchalant apostasies from rhymed metric art in favor of shapeless strings of gawky verbiage, unrelated to anything but that "contemporary idiom" which by opacity and "privacy" qualifies for the exequatur of the meterless fraternity.

A French structuralist critic some years ago in informal conversation mused about the function of literary criticism. Essentially it was, he submitted, to remove the barriers, linguistic and referential, between the writer and his audience; to add the necessary elucidating and equating discourse as economically as possible, and in a medium so congeneric and qualitatively equivalent to the work as to form in effect a true addition to it, part of its new extended substance . . . Then he interrupted himself and added, apparently somewhat to his own surprise, what may be reported as follows: "Of course, the sparest, most seamless, directly self-applying mode of criticism is translation—comprehensive translation. By which one means, translation of all salient aspects of form which of course embrace or constitute 'substance' or 'content,' along with all salient aspects of content, which of course include so-called 'form.' This species of criticism involves the least intermediacy, neglect, or accretion. It requires a Janus-like sensibility."

Even taking one's stand on somewhat narrower ground, one must insist that there is no other way, certainly no better way, of thoroughly knowing and decoding a poet foreign to others than by that taxing commitment to both tonal and verse-technical assimilation which is metric translation.

One longs to do this, I suspect, not so much in order to make the poet accessible as in order to test and taste him in more than one linguistic medium. In order to move him over one first has to know him rather intimately in his native medium. Exploring the poet's work at large, beyond the range of a particular translating assignment in hand, would seem to be an important preliminary.

What are the distinguishing marks of Akhmatova's handwriting in poetry—of the effective sweep of her pen and the graphics of her versification? These are intricate questions in themselves in relation to any poet of originality, but they take on a desperate edge only if one tries to verbalize them. The sensitive native soon takes these marks in; and the translator, if he has done his job, is thereby relieved of the supererogatory task of attempting the second best—generalizing and classifying by "critical" circumscription. His impulse is to naturalize the "foreign" verse. I insert this

term despite its affected ring because "translate" in its colloquial blandness suppresses both the lure and the magicking labor of what some bring themselves to call "englishing," *Verdeutschen, spolszczenie,* etc. Akhmatova's register of emotions and moods, her rhythms and rhymes, and the interaction between these (which of course only exist with and by virtue of one another) have to be absorbed in the mediator's aesthetic matrix before the need for any actual lexical matching intrudes. There is no intention to suggest that the would-be recreator of Akhmatova's verse by an act of mystic absorption in her *oeuvre* attains a state of communication with her spirit and diction, whence he will speak with her tongue in another tongue. It is merely submitted that reading like this, with occasional pilot translation of tempting lines, is the best road short of metempsychosis to learning to say in English, in a given case later, what Akhmatova is saying, while also speaking as she does. It becomes easier to diagnose (or in Psychspeak, "intuit") the blend and the course of her emotions in a given passage or poem when one knows what she is able and apt to do, how cognate situations develop elsewhere; what her key words and her verbal mimicry are; how, for instance, she uses nature like a half-learnt idiom partially to encode her otherwise inexpressible inner processes; how she may later decode them by some new cipher and obtain an altered semantic freight with equivalent affective changes. One will then have encountered her generosities and engaging gaucheries, harshnesses and offhand surrenders, her hurt cynicism and proud flippancy, her numb withdrawals and arrogant flounces, her rare but terrible curses and guffaws. Only then does the single poem acquire the perspective of her entire personality as a poet.

For examples of the curious state of a poetic sensibility's being connected in parallel, living in a shunt circuit as it were, with the phenomenal world (with at best rare ironic innuendos at the pathetic fallacy), one may point to "Up the bare sky slim willowsprigs climb. / Fanning abreast, / My not becoming your wife that time / Maybe was best." In "It is fine here . . .", nature's apparent reminder of the past is cited wryly as a condition contrary to fact in two throw-away final lines, yet it taps a poignant emotion with admirable parsimony. In "All promised him to me . . .", it is not an anthropopathic sky, dream, wind, waterfalls, willow shoots, or dragonflies that promise fulfillment, but the keen feeling soul that delighted in them and divines the promises of another sensibility that may comprehend all these and complement the first. The "pathos" that embraces the disparate phenomena is the poet's, not nature's.

Lastly, in order to "carry her across" with understanding, one must "learn" Akhmatova as a human being, though that status is inseparable from that of the poet as "content" is from "form." One must, I suspect, fall in love with her, a thing I have found not just easy but unavoidable. That subspecies of the Eternally Feminine that is marked by absolute integrity, an all-or-nothing temperament, a fiercely exacting, slightly outré concept of love and loyalty, found one of its purest and most enchanting specimens in the young Akhmatova. Not a great deal of dependable detail is available of the chain of tempests, teapot ones and others, that must have been her *carrière de coeur* in that first adult decade from 1909 to 1919, if her verse is any guide. Nor do we have more than disjointed and often dubious testimony to the inwardness of her relationship with her intimates among people and places. Partial exceptions are those parts of her life as a poet and friend which were lived with the Mandelstams, and which are reflected in the electrostatic pages of Nadezhda Mandelstam's recent memoirs. But from her poems, in the most extraordinary way, we know it all: no dates, almost no names, yet, in a magic-lantern show of luminous mood sketches, exactly how it all was, and how if felt, and what is now left of it.

Poem after poem hints at how she was hurt and worn by her ever-eager, ever-rebounding perfectionism. Many may be classed as discharges between two poles, one—her cool, inviolable sense of her value as a poet, which contains, if not alone constitutes, her sense of self; the other—a romantic urge for surrender of personality which dwells in her non-poetic self as formed by the epoch's decadent-exalté, Wagner-Schmagner *liebestödlich* concept of Love. The latter may well be reinforced by this artist's urge to make the best, or most tragic, of anything offered by life in its bounty. The boundless expectations, the portentous semantic charge placed on Love, on the confused, vulnerable, now runically unfathomable, now repellently trivial twosomeness, is one of the few things that nature and Art Nouveau seem to have in common.

If the long historical sine curve of literary values and modes between emotionalism and quietism, between ornate and sober forms, which my Istanbul neighbor Erich Auerbach used to

pursue was duly undulating in 1909, we can make out a long, flat wave of the histrionic-declamatory ridden by Gericault, David, and Delacroix, by Wagner and the Pre-Raphaelites and many others, which crested with the Symbolists and subsided in the mannered parsimony and wan eclecticism of Art Nouveau. It is perhaps somewhere on the downslope of this subsiding wave that the young Akhmatova is located, with her emotional make-up still on the melodramatizing *Backfisch* Isolde side, her lean Acmeist technique much farther down toward what one may call the Trough of the Future. Rilke's angelic solemnity about Love, purveyed with a truly angelic gift, is very much in the air, Stefan George, the French and Russian Symbolists are still rampant; Blok, who must have read all of these (while Akhmatova read *him* but also Proust, Eliot, and Joyce), until well into the new century cultivated the poetic vision of his multiform divinity, the Holy Wisdom conjured up by Solovyov, but turning now into a Helen or Aphrodite, now into a chastely shameless Artemis. In each garb it was Love all-significant, polymorphous, wild, wooly, and as overripe as anything by the Rossettis. One may suspect that in poetic forms, in the heat content of emotions, in the swing between exoticism and sobriety, the curves were changing direction between 1903, when Blok forsook poor Sophia, and 1909, when Akhmatova began to write. But for a long while—luckily perhaps—the tense readiness for consuming emotion persisted in Anna Andreevna; and like Eugene Onegin in V. 31, her partners do not seem to have been up to it. "Girls' tragico-hysteric vapors, their swoons and tears . . ." are unnerving enough when not cast into powerful poems. The betrayers retreat, abashed. The sacrificial exaltations, the frozen calms (Anna Andreevna in this mood reminds one a little of a Dying Swan who is very, very angry) spend themselves more and more in a fine irony, chill or ruefully tender. And strength takes the form of a devil-may-care pride, now solemn, now *gamine*, in her real self and in her habitat: the garden where the Muse walks.

Notes

1. When Osip Mandelstam claimed for "Acmeism" in 1922 that it had returned moral power to Russian poetry, Akhmatova had published *Evening* (1912), *Beads* (1914), *White Flock* (1917), *Wayside Herb* (1921), and *Anno Domini* (1922); Nikolai Gumilev (who in retrospect may seem Acmeism's impresario and drummer rather than indispensable contributor) had published *Pearls* (1910), *The Pyre* (1918), and *Pillar of*

Fire (1921); Osip Mandelstam, *Stone* (1913) and *Tristia* (1922); and Pasternak (somewhat more remote in this period from the preceding than later) was known in poetry mainly for *A Twin in the Clouds* (1914) and *My Sister, Life* (1922).

2. In November 1961, Anna Akhmatova paid these the famous brief tribute, *Nas chetvero,* "We are four."

3. Actually, 26 or 27. *W.A.*

4. A current term for the metric line more often called *dol'nik,* a line of generally trisyllabic feet with three stress slots and variable anacrusis and coda. A variant of this, rhythmically suggesting two anapests combined now with an amphibrach (—/—), now an iambus, was so characteristic of Anna Akhmatova (especially in *Poem without a Hero*) as to be called the Akhmatova line by Kornei Chukovsky.

5. See the poem "Consolation" of 1914, S-P I, 135.

6. Berberova, Nina. *Kursiv moi* (München: Wilhelm Fink, 1972), 84. In the index of personages attached to this invaluable book, Anna Akhmatova's biographical note consists of *five* lines, mentioning her three marriages but not one of her works; followed by *fifteen* lines devoted to her third husband, Punin. Berberova's own entry lists thirteen of her works.

7. Kornei Chukovsky, "Anna Akhmatova," in *Sobranie soch. v 6 tomakh* (M. 1967), 725-26 *passim.* Translated by Walter Arndt.

8. N. V. Nedobrovo begins his sensitive essay of April 1914 (endorsed by Anna Akhmatova years later as the piece of criticism she considered closest to the mark), by analyzing the eight lines of "True tenderness there's no aping": "The language is simple and colloquial—perhaps nearly to the point where it ceases being poetry? But on rereading we notice that if people were to converse like this, it would be enough to exchange two or three quatrains to have exhausted the common run of human relationships and be left in a realm of silence . . ." After demonstrating interaction of metric and lexical values for a page or two, Nedobrovo continues: "Turning our attention to the poem's structure, we are inevitably persuaded again of the freedom and potency of Akhmatova's poetic language. An eight-line poem of two differently rhymed quatrains here falls into three syntactic structures, the first taking up two lines, the second four, the third again two. Thus the second syntactic structure, closely linked by rhyme with the first and third, links the two (stanzaic quatrains) by its own (syntactic, not prosodic) unity, and this link is flexible, though strong. I remarked earlier, by way of the dramatic effect of introducing the second "No use," that the change of rhyme scheme and elsewhere is perceived by the reader and has powerful effect. . . . The device described, i.e., a complete syntactic structure bridging two rhyme schemes, so that sentences bend stanzas in the middle and finally round them off as stanzas do sentences, is extremely characteristic of Akhmatova; by this means she achieves a peculiar flexibility and subtlety of line, for lines so made take on a serpentine quality. At times Anna Akhmatova uses this device with the consummate ease of a virtuoso."

9. In the fourth section of his article quoted above Nedobrovo makes some analytic remarks apposite here: "In

the poems examined, the highly-strung intensity of the feelings and the unerring precision and clarity of their expression are overwhelming and need no laboring. Here lies Akhmatova's strength. What pleasure to find that, far from being irked by alleged inexpressibility in the poet's work, one reads turns of phrases which seem to have been taken straight from folk tradition.

For ages man has worn himself out struggling with the difficulty of expressing his inner life in words; yoked by silence, the spirit's growth is sluggish. There are poets who, like Hermes of old, teach man to speak, to release his inner force to work its will freely, and those who have hearts to feel will cherish their memory.

The emotional intensity in Akhmatova's diction at times generates such light and heat as to fuse man's inner world with the outer. Only when this happens do we find the outer world depicted in Akhmatova's verse; hence her pictures of that world are not soberly naturalistic, but stabbed with shafts of feeling as if seen with the eyes of a drowning man:

> It grows light. And over the smithy
> Rises smoke
> Oh, you couldn't once more be with me
> Sad in my yoke.

Or the continuation of the poem about the pleading eyes:

> I walk down the path—on its margin
> Lie timbers in stacks of grey—
> To fields a breeze is at large in
> Like the spiring, uneven and gay.

Sometimes her lyrical intensity constrains Akhmatova to do no more than hint at the suffering which is seeking expression in nature; and yet through her description one senses the heartbeat of feeling:

> In servitude you know I languish,
> For leave to die I plead with God,
> But always, to the edge of anguish,
> I see the Tver-land's grudging sod.
>
> A weathered well with hauling-crane,
> Above it clouds, like vapor leaking,
> Out in the fields the stile-gate creaking,
> And heartache—in the fragrant grain.
>
> Those unspectacular expanses
> Where even winds dare not alarm,
> And those evaluating glances
> Of countrywomen tanned and calm.

That low-voiced wind, though, brings tears to one's eyes."

10. Lines 13-16: "Sixteen of age, pliant of soul and modest, / Raven her brow, the maiden mounds below / Asway against the tautened linen bodice, / A lovesome foot, her teeth a pearly row . . ."

11. Susan Sontag, *Against Interpretation and Other Essays* (New York: 1969).

TITLE COMMENTARY

Poem without a Hero

WENDY ROSSLYN (ESSAY DATE 1992)

SOURCE: Rosslyn, Wendy. "Don Juan Feminised." In *Symbolism and after: Essays on Russian Poetry in Honour of Georgette Donchin*, edited by Arnold McMillin, pp. 102-21. London: Bristol Classical Press, 1992.

In the following excerpt, Rosslyn suggests that Akhmatova's Poem without a Hero *is a reworking of the Don Juan legend with a female protagonist.*

Traditionally the Don Juan legend focuses on a man who claims many female victims of his desires, and who is finally brought to justice by supernatural powers, usually in the form of a statue of a male rival. The legend is not at first sight open to re-telling with a female protagonist, but I wish to suggest that this is indeed what is done by Akhmatova in her *Poema bez geroia* ('Poem without a Hero', 1940-62).

It has become customary to think of *Poema bez geroia* as a reflection on wrongdoing, conscience, and retribution (in the context of the 1917 Revolution and its aftermath) and these are three concepts which also, of course, lie at the heart of the Don Juan legend: Don Juan's misspent life meets with retribution from the Commendatore's statue, and he is dragged down to hell. The purpose of this paper is, therefore, to look at Akhmatova's poem in the light of this legend and to suggest that one reading of the poem is as a narrative about 'love, unfaithfulness and passion'[1] and their moral implications. It will also be necessary to consider the gender changes which Akhmatova's re-telling involves. Akhmatova brings the Don Juan legend to mind by incorporating into her poem allusions to several previous tellings of the myth, and does so from the very outset. The title of the poem, '**Poem without a Hero**', echoes the opening of Byron's *Don Juan* (1819-1824), where the narrator asserts:

I want a hero: an uncommon want,
  When every year and month sends forth a
  new one,
Till, after cloying the gazettes with cant,
  The age discovers he is not the true one:
Of such as these I should not care to vaunt,
  I'll therefore take our ancient friend Don
  Juan—
We all have seen him, in the pantomime,
  Sent to the devil somewhat ere his time.[2]

(Akhmatova let it be known, perhaps with a touch of braggadocio, that she had read Byron's

poem, in English moreover, forty times.)[3] The epigraph to the poem as a whole, 'Di rider finirai / Pria dell'aurora', is taken from Da Ponte's libretto for Mozart's *Don Giovanni* (1787) and serves to pinpoint the core of the myth as far as the *Poema* is concerned, namely imminent retribution for frivolity and mockery before the dawn of a new day in which these attitudes have no place. Part 1 of the poem carries an epigraph, 'In my hot youth—when George the Third was king . . .', also taken from Byron's *Don Juan*. And in Part 2, 'Reshka', Akhmatova adds a note on the omitted stanzas which calls attention to Byron's *Don Juan* via a note of Pushkin's. Molière's *Dom Juan ou Le Festin de Pierre* (1665) is alluded to in the *Poema* in the reference to 'Meierkhol'd's little arabs' (*meierkhol'dovye arapchata*), the proscenium servants used by Meierkhol'd in his production of the play staged in Leningrad in 1910.[4] And Hoffmann's story *Don Juan* of 1813 has also left echoes in the text.[5] Pushkin's play based on the Don Juan legend, *Kamennyi gost'* ('The Stone Guest', 1830), is neither named nor quoted, but lies behind much of Akhmatova's reshaping of the myth in the *Poema*, as I hope to show. As is well known, Akhmatova was writing her essay on Pushkin's little tragedy at the same time as working on her own poem.[6] The poem also contains many allusions to Blok's poem 'Shagi Komandora' ('The Commendatore's Footsteps', 1910-12),[7] which Akhmatova felt to be particularly close to her own work when she was in Tashkent and writing the *Poema*.[8]

In the period round about 1913 which the *Poema* depicts, the Don Juan legend was alive and productive. Not only was Blok writing 'Shagi Komandora'. 1906 saw the 150th anniversary of Mozart's birth, and scenes from *Don Giovanni* were performed at the Mariinskii Theatre in Petersburg as part of the celebrations. It has also been suggested that the epigraph from *Don Giovanni* is connected with Akhmatova's contemporary and friend, the composer Artur Lur'e, who picked out these lines from the libretto in his article on Mozart's opera.[9] Pushkin's text also had a contemporary resonance inasmuch as Dargomyzhskii's *Kamennyi gost'*, the libretto of which was based on Pushkin, was on the Petersburg stage in 1915 at the Teatr muzykal'noi dramy and in 1917 at the Mariinskii, the latter production being by Meierkhol'd.[10] Shaliapin, who, like Meierkhol'd, also figures in the *Poema*, was to have sung Leporello, but withdrew after irreconcilable differences with Meierkhol'd. Not for nothing, therefore, does Akhmatova dress one of the masked figures who visit the author in 1913 at the beginning of the poem as Don Juan.

Don Juan's character is, of course, analysed and presented in very different ways in the texts alluded to in the *Poema,* and the details of the plot vary accordingly. However, the protagonist in each is male. When Hoffmann turned the presentation of Don Juan in a new direction, showing him as a man with a god-like nature who strives towards the sublime, pursuing perfect beauty in the form of the ideal woman who will give him paradise on earth, a new emphasis was given to the last of Don Juan's victims, Donna Anna, who thus became the embodiment of female perfection and the potential saviour of Don Juan. This conception of female beauty was followed by Pushkin, and to a still greater degree by Blok. Akhmatova, however, firstly feminises Don Juan, and secondly rejects the idea of the saving power of female beauty.

Akhmatova's poem by no means constitutes a retelling of the legend with the traditional characters and plot; the foundation for her Don Juan scenario is the theme of wrongdoing followed by retribution. The wrongdoing is partly defined as 'sin' to be punished with 'holy revenge' (consonant with the theological interpretations of the legend)[11] and partly as shamelessness. The important passage is the one from the interlude 'Cherez ploshchadku' which, according to the poem, hovered around the lines

No bespechna, priana, besstydna
Maskaradnaia boltovnia . . .[12]

The passage begins by relating 'the chatter at the masquerade':

'Uveriaiu, eto ne novo . . .
　Vy ditia, sin'or Kazanova . . .'
　'Na Isaak'evskoi rovno v shest' . . .'
'Kak-nibud' pobredem po mraku,
　My otsiuda eshche v "Sobaku".
　'Vy otsiuda kuda?'—
　　　'Bog vest'!'
Sancho Pansy i don Kikhoty
　I, uvy, sodomskie Loty
　　　Smertonosnyi probuiut sok,
Afrodity voznikli iz peny,
　Shevel'nulis' v stekle Eleny,
　I bezum'ia blizitsia srok.
I opiat' iz Fontannogo Grota,
　Gde liubovnaia stonet dremota,
　　Cherez prizrachnye vorota
　I mokhnatyi i ryzhii kto-to
　　　Kozlonoguiu privolok.
Vsekh nariadnee i vsekh vyshe,
　Khot' ne vidit ona i ne slyshit—
　　Ne klianet, ne molit, ne dyshit,
　　　Golova Madame de Lamballe.

ABOUT THE AUTHOR

HAIGHT ON AKHMATOVA'S IMPORTANCE FOR RUSSIAN WOMEN

From the start, Akhmatova was concerned with the necessity of giving voice to the woman's point of view in a culture where women's voices, although beginning to be heard, were few and far between and where women were still suffering from the illusion that to be equal with men, they must be like them. A deeply religious and at the same time passionate woman, with close ties to nature, Akhmatova was forced to examine and reject the false doctrine that placed physical desire so often in opposition to God's purpose. She re-examined and rejected the attitude to her sex which had caused so much suffering over the past century, which had divided women into those who were 'pure' and those who were 'fallen'. When in her poetry she tried to heal this split, she was taunted for years with being 'half nun, half harlot'.

Haight, Amanda. Excerpt from "Instead of a Foreword" in her *Anna Akhmatova: A Poetic Pilgrimage.* New York: Oxford University Press, 1976.

A smirennitsa i krasotka,
　Ty, chto koz'iu pliashesh' chechetku,
　　Snova gulish' tomno i krotko:
　　　'Que me veut mon Prince Carnaval?'

These stanzas are saturated with allusions to sexual promiscuity. Casanova, who requires no further amplification, is here partnered by a woman whose sexual experience allows her to consider him 'a child'. The righteous Lot is tempted. Aphrodite, the goddess of sensual love, is born; Helen, whose beauty was the cause of violence on a cataclysmic scale, looks at herself in the glass—or to be more precise, since Aphrodite and Helen appear in the plural, modern women begin acting out these roles. The grotto in the garden of the House on the Fontanka (the Sheremet'ev palace, where Akhmatova lived for many years) where love is said to lie sleeping, symbolises, on the contrary, the relationship between the actress Parasha Zhemchugova and her husband Count D. N. Sheremet'ev, whose devotion lasted even beyond her death in 1803, as his many inscriptions to her in the house and garden show. A plaque on a marble pedestal in the garden, for instance, reads:

> Je crois son ombre attendrie
> Errer autour de ce séjour,
> J'approche—mais bientôt cette image chérie
> Me rend à ma douleur en fuyant sans retour . . .
>   13

Akhmatova notes in her essay on Pushkin's *Kamennyi gost'* that betrayal of the virtuous spouse after his or her death was in Pushkin's view an unforgivable sin (p. 163) and Sheremet'ev is in this respect a shining example of virtue. But in Akhmatova's poem love, as distinct from sex (*liubov'*, as distinct from *izmena* and *strast'*), 'sleeps', and a contrast is established between this faithful couple and another—the *ryzhii* and *kozlonogaia*, who in the Romanov-Sats ballet *Kozlonogie* (The Fauns, 1912) participate in a triangle of relationships in a plot which, according to one opinion of the time, put *L'Après-midi d'un faune* in the shade as far as pornography was concerned.[14] At the end of the passage one of the heroines of the poem, a beautiful woman who is both the Petersburg actress who plays the faun and the author's double, asks languorously and submissively what her partner wants of her. Akhmatova implies that a prime factor in the wrong-doing for which retribution is to be exacted is sexual licence.

However, although the faults of a society in which Don Juan can flourish are far more narrowly identified than, for example, by Byron in his *Don Juan,* the poem is not merely a puritanical tirade against sexual promiscuity. The fault or sin diagnosed here is self-indulgent behaviour which has no accompanying sense of shame ('No bespechna, priana, besstydna / Maskaradnaia boltovnia . . .'). The author questions her double about her unfaithfulness, and, as is made apparent by the question which follows immediately after, receives no answer:

> Zolotogo l' veka viden'e
>   Ili chernoe prestuplen'e
>   V groznom khaose davnikh dnei?
> Mne otvet' khot' teper':
>   neuzheli
> Ty kogda-to zhila v samom dele?

The actress, who plays the faun and is to be contrasted to Zhemchugova, is unable to say whether her behaviour is innocent or criminal because her conscience is atrophied. Satan is similarly defined as one 'who does not know what conscience means and why it exists', and it is lack of conscience which is the prime ground for condemnation in the poem.[15]

A second allegation made against the culture of 1913 is its predilection for assuming masks and playing roles; these signs of a shallow sophistication lead to a diminished sense of the integrity and uniqueness of the self:

> I vse shepchut svoim dianam
>   Tverdo vyuchennyi urok . . .

and thus again to an inactive conscience. The contrast between play and conscience is established in Part 2 of the poem, '**Reshka**', where the carnival atmosphere of 1913 does not survive the catastrophes brought by the True Twentieth Century (which for Akhmatova began in 1914), but religious anthems do:

> Karnaval'noi polnoch'iu rimskoi
> I ne pakhnet. Napev Kheruvimskoi
> U zakrytykh dverei drozhit . . .

Akhmatova makes the same diagnosis as Nadezhda Mandel'shtam, who wrote that 'the legacy of the pre-revolutionary years was self-indulgence, loss of criteria, an incessant craving for happiness'.[16]

As in the legend, Akhmatova shows in her poem the retribution which this wrong-doing calls down upon itself. And she associates it with an almost apocalyptic event which will happen before dawn:

> Zvuk orkestra, kak s togo sveta,
>   (Ten' chego-to mel'knula gde-to),
>   Ne predchuvstviem li rassveta
>   Po riadam probezhal oznob?

and

> Ved' segodnia takaia noch',
> Kogda nuzhno platit' po schetu . . .

Retribution will be brought about by a quasi-human power which is hardly susceptible to description in advance, but which is variously envisaged as *gost' zazerkal'nyi* and *kto-to* (Part 1, Chapter 1) or *ten'* (Part 1, Chapter 3). All these denote some humanoid phenomenon not unlike the statue in the legend. Akhmatova also shows the decisive moment which symbolises that wrong-doing as a crisis point in the interrelationships of three people, two of whom are rivals for the favours of the third.

However, having incorporated the Don Juan legend into her text, Akhmatova re-formulates it very radically. Firstly, the attributes which traditionally belong to Don Juan are not only given to the rival figure in this triangle, but are distributed more widely. The passage just quoted suggests, in fact, that sexual licence is a rather general mode of behaviour, the loose morality of the times

against which the actress's infidelity to her admirer, the cornet of dragoons, must be seen. One
hypostasis of Don Juan is the cornet's rival:

Na stene ego tverdyi profil'.
   Gavriil ili Mefistofel'
     Tvoi, krasavitsa, paladin?
Demon sam s ulybkoi Tamary,
   No takie taiatsia chary
     V etom strashnom dymnom litse:
Plot', pochti chto stavshaia dukhom,
   I antichnyi lokon nad ukhom—
     Vse—tainstvenno v prishletse.
Eto on v perepolnennom zale
   Slal tu chernuiu rozu v bokale
     Ili vse eto bylo snom?
S mertvym serdtsem i s mertvym vzorom
   On li vstretilsia s Komandorom,
     V tot probravshis' prokliatyi dom?

Like Pushkin's Don Guan, this figure hovers
on the boundary between utter damnation and
salvation and it is unclear whether at heart he is
Gabriel or Mephistopheles. Much in this passage
suggests that the prototype is Blok, who reads
himself into the Don Juan role in his 'Shagi
Komandora'. Indeed, Anna Lisa Crone argues that
Akhmatova resorts to the Don Juan theme as an
allegory for the events in Blok's life.[17] But Blok
was for Akhmatova 'a monument to the beginning of the century', and elsewhere she said, 'Blok
turned up in my poem "Triptych" [ie the three-
part *Poema*] as *an epoch-person*'.[18] There is thus no
need to restrict the identification of Don Juan
exclusively to Blok, especially since when Akhmatova asks whether the cornet's rival is to be identified with Don Juan, she concludes with a question mark and provides no answer.

We therefore have grounds for considering
other possible hypostases of Don Juan, and one of
these is, I suggest, the author of the poem, who
'descends under the dark vaults', prepares supper
for a guest, senses that her end is at hand,[19] and
seems to see a mysterious and horrifying visitor
who emerges from the grave, through the grave-
stone, knocks at the door, comes in, and beckons
her, apparently to the place whence he has come.
All this happens, moreover, at the moment when
the author is challenging the supernatural powers
(God, or fate) with a denial of their control over
her, like the over-confident Don Juan:

Smerti net—eto vsem izvestno,
   Povtoriat' eto stalo presno,
     A chto est'—pust' rasskazhut mne.
Kto stuchitsia?
     Ved' vsekh vpustili.
Eto gost' zazerkal'nyi? Ili
     To, chto vdrug mel'knulo v okne . . .
Shutki l' mesiatsa molodogo,
   Ili vpravdu tam kto-to snova

     Mezhdu pechkoi i shkafom stoit?
Bleden lob, i glaza otkryty . . .
   Znachit, khrupki mogil'nye plity,
     Znachit, miagche voska granit . . .
Vzdor, vzdor, vzdor! Ot takogo vzdora
   Ia sedoiu sdelaius' skoro
     Ili stanu sovsem drugoi.
Chto ty manish' menia rukoiu?!
   Za odnu minutu pokoia
     Ia posmertnyi otdam pokoi.

In her discussion of Pushkin's *Kamennyi gost'*
Akhmatova sets out the evidence for viewing Don
Guan as Pushkin's self-portrait.[20] In this same passage she also observes that Pushkin gradually lost
his readers, and the fact that she made the same
observation of herself allows us to consider Akhmatova's assertion that Don Guan is Pushkin's
self-portrait as an oblique indication that the
equivalence of author and Don Juan applies
equally to her own poem. We may see a parallel
between Pushkin's Don Guan, who is within a
hair's breadth of salvation, and the author's awareness of her own sinfulness and her fear and rejection of her past self:

S toi, kakoiu byla kogda-to
   V ozherel'e chernykh agatov
     Do doliny Iosafata,
       Snova vstretit'sia ne khochu . . .

The author refers ironically in '**Reshka**' to her
earlier books of poems:

Nu, a kak zhe moglo sluchit'sia,
Chto vo vsem vinovata ia?
Ia—tishaishaia, ia—prostaia,
'Podorozhnik', 'Belaia staia' . . .
Opravdat'sia . . . no kak, druz'ia?

And in these books too we find her presenting
herself as a Don Juan figure. The most direct statement is made in a poem of 1913, the year evoked
in *Poema bez geroia*. As in the *Poema*, the setting
for Don Juan-like behaviour in this poem is the
Stray Dog cabaret in prerevolutionary Petersburg:

Vse my brazhniki zdes', bludnitsy,
Kak neveselo vmeste nam!
Na stenakh tsvety i ptitsy
Tomiatsia po oblakam.

Ty kurish' chernuiu trubku,
Tak stranen dymok nad nei.
Ia nadela uzkuiu iubku,
Chtob kazat'sia eshche stroinei.

Navsegda zabity okoshki.
Chto tam—izmoroz' ili groza?
Na glaza ostorozhnoi koshki
Pokhozhi tvoi glaza.

O, kak serdtse moe toskuet!
Ne smertnogo l' chasa zhdu?

A ta, chto seichas tantsuet,
Nepremenno budet v adu.

The seductive heroine exercises her sexual attraction in a relationship which is cold and calculating on both sides, and foresees that the fate of women like herself (*vse my* . . .) who are already spiritually dead is undoubtedly to go to hell. The revelry before the anticipated retribution is a direct reflection of the lines from *Don Giovanni,* 'Di rider finirai / Pria dell'aurora'. Moreover, the heroine of Akhmatova's early poems, who, fearing the intimacy of loving relationships, consistently subverts them and extricates herself from them, going on from one lover to the next in search of utterly elusive happiness, is also the victim of the psychology of a Don Juan.[21]

In the **Poema** the author has a double, and the latter, the actress, is also endowed with the characteristics of Don Juan. We see her at her marriage ceremony thinking of a past affair, and we see her scorn the feelings of her devoted admirer the cornet in favour of a rival. She is compared to Botticelli's Spring—which suggests that she is the embodiment of instinctive sexuality—and to a magnet, which attracts lovers inevitably and indiscriminately. She is thus presented as a symbol of sexuality acting almost on an animal level, as the comparison to a faun (*kozlonogaia*), half-goat and half-human confirms.

It can therefore be argued that in **Poema bez geroia** Akhmatova shows that the sins of Don Juan are the sins of a whole generation, in which women sin in the same ways and to no less an extent than men. This is to say that when Akhmatova feminises the Don Juan figure she does not allot Don Juan's attributes to women alone, but points out that they are, in potential at least, part of human nature in general, and are thus as often to be found in women as in men. This point had, of course, already been made by Byron, whose Don Juan is the seduced rather than the seducer. The prototype of this female Don Juan is to be found in Pushkin's *Kamennyi gost',* where Laura, an actress like the Columbine figure, lives for the sensual pleasures of the moment, has no moral principles, and transfers her affections effortlessly from one man to another; Don Karlos describes her way of life:

Ty moloda . . . i budesh' moloda
Eshche let piat' il' shest'. Vokrug tebia
Eshche let shest' oni tolpit'sia budut,
Tebia laskat', leleiat', i darit',
I serenadami nochnymi teshit',
I za tebia drug druga ubivat'
Na perekrestkakh noch'iu . . .

The recasting of Don Juan as a woman has radical repercussions on other aspects of the legend, as used in the **Poema.** Since women are reinterpreted in this way, there can be, and is, no Hoffmannesque female figure of saving virtue in this poem. Nor is any figure the equivalent of the Commendatore, the animated statue, who is the other embodiment of honour and fidelity in the legend.

At this point reference should be made to V. N. Toporov's discussion of the Don Juan legend in the poem, since Toporov discerns both a Donna Anna and a Commendatore in it. He identifies lines 130-60 of Chapter 1 in Part 1 of the poem as the 'carcass' of the legend, and sees this scene as an inverted imitation of the scene of the destruction of Don Juan:

> . . . the criminal rendez-vous is interrupted by the arrival of the man who considers himself the husband . . . but the death of Don Juan at the hand of the Commendatore is transformed into the death of the man who takes on (even if only in part) the role of the Commendatore, thus turning the woman into his window. But Don Juan remains alive . . .[22]

It is, however, over narrow to restrict the reworking of the Don Juan legend in the poem to a mere thirty lines—passages reflecting the legend which fall outside this section have been mentioned above—and some other objections must also be made.

To Toporov's qualified assertion that the cornet plays the role of the Commendatore one may firstly point out that there is a real husband in the text, though the cornet would certainly like to supplant him. Secondly, that Akhmatova discarded the variant lines about the cornet which refer to him as 'honour's friend'. Thirdly, that Akhmatova sets up a parallel between the cornet and Evgenii from Pushkin's *Mednyi vsadnik*. Both hear the ringing of horses' hooves at their moment of crisis:

Veter, polnyi baltiiskoi soli,
Bal metelei na Marsovom Pole,
I nevidimykh zvon kopyt . . .
I bezmernaia v tom trevoga,
Komu zhit' ostalos' nemnogo
Kto lish' smerti prosit u boga
I kto budet navek zabyt.

Both lose their beloveds. Both are forgotten as soon as they die, except inasmuch as they figure in a poem recounting their fate. The fact that Evgenii is the victim of the animated statue suggests, therefore, that his correlative in Akhmatova's poem, the cornet, is not the equivalent of the

Commendatore. Finally, the cornet is not presented as a character so virtuous that he can act as the means of vengeance for supernatural powers of good. The cornet's fidelity to the actress is viewed in the poem as a fault rather than a virtue. It is alleged that it would have been more worthy to weather the blow to his pride constituted by her unfaithfulness, and to live on to devote himself to other goals. This is to say that fidelity to the beloved is not conceived of as a good sufficient in itself—conscience, discrimination and responsibility are also required. In terms of the legend, the cornet fits better into the role of one of the helpless victims of Don Juan, since he is a victim of the actress whom I construe as one of the Don Juan equivalents. Just as Don Juan claims many female victims, their lives wrecked by seduction, she is likewise the cause of the cornet's suicide. Virtue is the property, as I have already suggested, of Zhemchugova, Sheremet'ev and bygone days; in the twentieth century it is characteristic only of The Poet:

> I ni v chem ne povinen: ni v etom,
> Ni v drugom i ni v tret'em . . .
>   Poetam
> Voobshche ne pristali grekhi.
> Propliasat' pred Kovchegom Zaveta
> Ili sginut'! . . .

Noting Akhmatova's observation that Pushkin's Don Guan is a poet, and bearing in mind the lines about The Poet in the **Poema** which have just been quoted here, Toporov turns to Akhmatova's poem **'Cherez 23 goda'**, which echoes these lines, and finds 'a correspondence (in this case no significance other than a formal-referential one should be given to this word) between Donna Anna in the Don Juan tragedy and the author, who bears the same name' (p. 38). He also adduces evidence for Blok's conception of Akhmatova as a Donna Anna figure.

Akhmatova's constant awareness of the associations surrounding her name make this a weighty argument. However, the question here is not what subtexts attach to the name 'Anna' but whether any person in Akhmatova's poem carries out the function played by Donna Anna. Hoffmann considers her to be:

> . . . a divine woman, against whose pure soul the Devil has been powerless. All the machinations of hell could ruin her only on earth [. . .] Suppose Anna had been destined by heaven to make Don Juan recognise the divine nature within him through love (which Satan skilfully used to ruin him) and to rescue him from the despair of his own striving.[23]

Pushkin views his Donna Anna in a similar light, causing Akhmatova to observe in her discussion of *Kamennyi gost'* that Donna Anna is the instrument of Don Guan's regeneration (p. 100). However, Akhmatova comments in a later revision of this article that while for Don Guan Dona Anna is an angel and his salvation, for Pushkin she is 'a very coquettish, curious and fainthearted woman, and a sanctimonious hypocrite'. Pushkin finds her unfaithfulness to her dead husband unforgivable (p. 163).

Toporov writes that Akhmatova follows Hoffmann in her conception of this figure in **Poema bez geroia**: 'before Akhmatova only Hoffmann in his *Don Juan* saw in the image of Anna in the traditional scheme the hypostasis of the potential saviour of Don Juan who comes (albeit too late) to save him with her love' (p. 175). But he does not explain this statement by reference to the poem and it is difficult to discern a female saviour in it. Although Blok's Donna Anna from 'Shagi Komandora' is mentioned in the poem, it is not asserted unequivocally that this is a characterisation of the lady of the house (the author's double) and thus of the author:

> Over the bed there are three portraits of the lady of the house in some of her roles. On the right she is the Faun, in the centre Lady Confusion, on the left the portrait is in shadow. Some think it is Columbine, others that it is Donna Anna (from 'Shagi Komandora').[24]

However, if the essence of Donna Anna's function in the legend is to attempt to save Don Juan, and if Don Juan can be identified as the author of the poem, then it can be said that the latter looks for salvation to the poem itself, which does have something in common with Donna Anna, in both her Pushkinesque forms. In its personified form, the 'stoletniaia charovnitsa', the *Poema* is certainly coquettish:

> Kruzhevnoi roniaet platochek,
> Tomno zhmuritsia iz-za strochek
> I briullovskim manit plechom.

and it offers the author a kiss, just as Dona Anna kisses Don Guan:

> My s toboi eshche popiruem,
> I ia tsarskim moim potseluem
> Zluiu polnoch' tvoiu nagrazhu.

Moreover, Akhmatova points out in her essay that when his death is at hand, Pushkin's Don Guan turns to Dona Anna, who occupies all his thoughts at this terrible moment (p. 100):

> Ia gibnu—koncheno—o Dona Anna!

Similarly, in Chapter 3 of Part 1 of the **Poema,** when retribution in the form of the True Twentieth Century is approaching, the author too cries out:

A po naberezhnoi legendarnoi
　　Priblizhalsia ne kalendarnyi—
　　　　Nastoiashchii Dvadtsatyi Vek.
A teper' by domoi skoree
Kameronovoi galereei
[. . .]
Razve my ne vstretimsia vzgliadom
Nashikh prezhnikh iasnykh ochei?
Razve ty mne ne skazhesh' snova
　　Pobedivshee
　　　　smert'
　　　　　　slovo
I razgadku zhizni moei?

The fact that the passage is connected with N. V. Nedobrovo, and that the call is thus to a former love and not a present one, suggests that there is no character in the poem who functions as Donna Anna; but the fact that the appeal is for 'the word which conquers death' suggests that the poem itself is, potentially at least, able to save,[25] though we should not ignore the poem's demonic aspects, as described in **'Reshka'.** We may, however, view the poem as a substitute for Donna Anna.

Akhmatova rejects Hoffmann's romantic conception of the saving power of woman, pure in soul and beautiful of face. Her poem illustrates the old truth first symbolised by Helen of Troy that female beauty can be the cause of catastrophe, no less than male Don Juanism, and shows that purity of soul, male or female, is not to be found in the world of the **Poema**—unless it be in The Poet. She is thus spared the necessity which befalls Hoffmann of making out a special case for Donna Anna's exceptional status to explain why she has fallen victim to Don Juan just like multitudes of purportedly lesser women before her. Hoffmann is obliged to divide Donna Anna into flesh and spirit and assert that hell has power only over the former, heaven avenging this corruption of her body by dragging Don Juan off to hell. In succumbing to Don Juan, Hoffmann argues, she succumbs to a supernatural power—the devil—which she cannot be expected to resist successfully, and though she loves Don Juan she does not hope for earthly happiness. The women in Akhmatova's poem both avoid this flesh-spirit divide and are morally responsible agents in control of their own fates, rather than the ground on which supernatural powers vie for superiority.

It may seem that, if there is no character in the poem who represents Donna Anna or the Commendatore, rather little is left of the Don Juan myth: all that remains is Don Juan himself or, as I interpret the poem, herself. However, just as Donna Anna has a substitute in the personified **Poema,** the Commendatore also has a substitute.[26] Akhmatova abandons the animated statue motif[27] but retains the function carried out by the traditional statue: punishment of sin in hell. The poem speaks of the retribution which comes to the Don Juan heroine in terms of going through hell:

Ty sprosi u moikh sovremennits:
　　Katorzhanok, stopiatnits, plennits—
　　　　I tebe porasskazhem my,
Kak v bespamiatnom zhili strakhe,
　　Kak rastili detei dlia plakhi,
　　　　Dlia zastenka i dlia tiur'my.

Posinelye stisnuv guby,
　　Obezumevshie Gekuby
　　　　I Kassandry iz Chukhlomy,
Zagremim my bezmolvnym khorom:
　　(My uvenchannye pozorom)
　　　　'Po tu storonu ada my'.

The substitute for the Commendatore is the history of the True Twentieth Century, which in Part 3 of the poem condemns the author (and by extension all the Don Juans in the poem) to lose her home, to see her city destroyed, to be disgraced and to be kept under tight political control. A double of hers perishes in a camp. It is because of the fact that in Akhmatova's reworking of the legend retribution comes in this world, and not in the next, that Don Juan remains alive: in the twentieth century he (or she) has no need to die in order to go through hell, and to pay the price of wrong-doing.

What then remains of the Don Juan legend in the **Poema**? The Commendatore and Dona Anna disappear as characters, their functions taken over by powers in the poem which are not of a human order. Don Juan's other victims, never amongst the chief protagonists, are likewise subsidiary characters here. Don Juan is virtually all that remains. But this is a more psychologically complex figure than previous Don Juans.

The 'I' of the **Poema** is, as I have argued, a Don Juan figure who pays for wrongdoing by being visited by a supernatural presence and who is punished in hell. But this Don Juan remains alive and is regenerated by this harrowing experience, so that the voice of the author looking back on her sinful youth is no longer that of the conscience-less Don Juan. It is no accident that the lines chosen for the epigraph from Byron's *Don Juan* ('In my hot youth—when George the

Third was king') lead on to a passage which asserts the difference in viewpoint made by the passing of time:

> 'Non ego hoc ferrem calida juventa
>   Consule Planco', Horace said, and so
> Say I; by which quotation there is meant a
>   Hint that some six or seven good years ago
> (Long ere I dreamt of dating from the Brenta)
>   I was most ready to return a blow,
> And would not brook at all this sort of thing
> In my hot youth—when George the Third was
>   King.
>
> But now at thirty years my hair is gray—
>   (I wonder what it will be like at forty?
> I thought of a peruke the other day—)
>   My heart is not much greener; and, in short, I
> Have squander'd my whole summer while 'twas
>   May.
>   And feel no more the spirit to retort; I
> Have spent my life, both interest and principal,
> And deem not, what I deemed, my soul
>   invincible . . .
>
> . . . No more—no more—Oh! never more, my
>   heart,
>   Canst thou be my sole world, my universe!
> Once all in all, but now a thing apart,
>   Thou canst not be my blessing or my curse:
> The illusion's gone for ever, and thou art
>   Insensible, I trust, but none the worse,
> And in thy stead I've got a deal of judgment,
> Though heaven knows how it ever found a lodg-
>   ment.[28]

There are reminiscences of several of these lines in **Poema bez geroia.** The money metaphor is echoed in Akhmatova's 'nuzhno platit' po schetu'. 'My blessing or my curse' has its parallel in 'Gavriil ili Mefistofel'. But most important of all is the contrast between heart, the preserve of youth, and the judgment which comes with maturity. This is also the contrast which holds in the **Poema** between the author's sinful younger self and the judgmental older self who looks back on 1913 from the viewpoint of 1940. To use the imagery of the epigraph from *Don Giovanni*, dawn brings sobriety after the night before and enables one to see more clearly than during the hours of darkness. Akhmatova's comment that in *Kamennyi gost'* 'Pushkin punishes himself, young, carefree and sinful as he was' (p. 108) is equally applicable to her stance in her own poem. One result of the identification of Don Juan with the author's 'I' is that we perceive Don Juan presented by him/ herself and from the inside: we do not observe him from the outside as we do the character in Pushkin's play, or Byron's narrative poem, in which he is spoken of in the third person; we are thus made privy to the workings of his/her conscience.

If we return to the dramatis personae of the legend, we can perhaps call this older self-critical self the internal Commendatore, for it is the self which punishes the Don-Juanish impulses. As the author says, 'sebia kazniu'.[29] Punishment in the forms inflicted by twentieth-century history is willingly suffered, since the self has already acknowledged its justification and necessity, and has sentenced itself to purgative penance. Just as Akhmatova saw *Kamennyi gost'* as exposing the wounds of Pushkin's conscience (p. 104), her own poem is the salving of similar wounds. Finally, we should also bear in mind that the author of the **Poema** is one of those Poets who are described in it as the embodiment of innocence. In this sense the author's personality also embraces an internal Donna Anna: just as Donna Anna is a figure chosen 'by heaven' (in Hoffmann's phrase), Akhmatova likens the Poet to King David, chosen by God.[30] It is precisely because of the complexity of the authorial persona with its three aspects—Don Juan, Commendatore and Donna Anna—that the poem Akhmatova writes is both demonic and potentially a source of salvation.[31] And it is also because of the complexity of her persona that her double in the poem, the Petersburg actress, takes on the very assorted roles of the faun, Lady Confusion, and Columbine or Donna Anna.

The feminisation of the Don Juan image is of course one of the inversions which one would expect to find in a work pervaded by the notion of carnival. Commenting on **Poema bez geroia** as one of the manifestations of the carnival tradition, not only in respect of its imagery, V. V. Ivanov writes:

> . . . it is impossible not to see in it that archetypal sense which Akhmatova herself attributed to these carnival symbols, when she emphasised in another of her poems that the impression of masquerade arises from the author's distancing in time [. . .] The layering of various strata of carnival, which are directly connected with the atmosphere of the 1910s and arise from the point of view of the 'estranged' author distanced in time, makes the analysis of the role of the masks and of the 'chatter at the masquerade' particularly promising: behind the symbol being deciphered another mask may come to light which it will be possible to read only by contrasting the various time dimensions of the poem.[32]

That mask would seem to be Don Juan.

Poema bez geroia replays the Don Juan legend, but though the essence of the plot is retained, two of the central characters, Donna Anna and the Commendatore, are abandoned, substitutes of a nonhuman order being found for them. Of the original characters, only Don Juan remains, and he is translated into the feminine. But the characterisation of this Don Juan is very complex. He is neither the negative hero of most tellings of the myth, nor Hoffmann's exculpated positive hero. Not only is (s)he corrupted flesh and moral vacuity; (s)he is also moral principle and hence self-condemnation, and thereafter self-punishment too. The traditional characters of the Don Juan myth are internalised and, within one single character,[33] play out a drama in which the unthinking immorality of youth is severely condemned by maturity, which consciously accepts the retribution meted out to it, as a means of purgation and atonement. The author is thus a female Don Juan reformed.[34]

Notes

1. *Poema bez geroia*, Part 3

2. Canto I, stanza I. Byron's observations about regiments of heroes with feet of clay hymned by a duplicitous press apply neatly to Stalin's Soviet Union.

3. L. K. Chukovskaia records her as saying in 1955: 'I have read the original 40 times—it is a bad, even ugly piece [. . .] Byron was out to shock his readers and deliberately made the piece sound unharmonious. Moreover there are disgusting bedroom scenes in abundance [. . .] The only good thing Byron has in it is one lyric digression.' See *Zapiski o Anne Akhmatovoi* (Paris, YMCA-Press, 1976-80), Vol. II, pp. 61-2.

4. See my 'Theatre, theatricality and Akhmatova's *Poema bez geroya*', *Essays in Poetics*, Vol. XIII, 1988, No. 1, pp. 100-1.

5. V. N. Toporov, *Akhmatova i Blok*, (Berkeley, Berkeley Slavic Specialties, 1981), p. 176.

6. 'Kamennyi gost' Pushkina', in Anna Akhmatova, *O Pushkine. Stat'i i zametki*, compiled by E. G. Gershtein, (Leningrad, 1977), pp. 89-109 and 161-71.

7. See Toporov, pp. 36-40.

8. V. V. Ivanov, 'Struktura stikhotvoreniia Bloka "Shagi Komandora"', in Z. G. Mints (ed.), *Tezisy I Vsesoiuznoi (III) konferentsii 'Tvorchestvo A. A. Bloka i russkaia kul'tura XX veka'* (Tartu, 1975), p. 38.

9. B. Kats and R. Timenchik, *Anna Akhmatova i muzyka. Issledovatel'skie ocherki* (Leningrad, 1989), p. 199.

10. K. Rudnitskii (*Rezhisser Meierkhol'd* [Moscow, 1969], p. 196) notes the connection between this production of *Kamennyi gost'* and Meierkhol'd's *Maskarad*. Both conceive of life as a masquerade. It was possibly after

the dress rehearsal of the latter that, Akhmatova says, the *Poema* first began 'to sound' within her (Anna Akhmatova, *Sochineniia*, Moscow, 1986, Vol. II, p. 221).

11. Benois' Moscow production of 1915 saw the play as the struggle of the human soul with God and with other souls, which it conquers until at the last it is itself destroyed (see A. Gozenpud, *Russkii opernyi teatr mezhdu dvukh revoliutsii 1905-1917*, (Leningrad, 1975), p. 346.

12. Compare Akhmatova's description of Pushkin's Don Guan as combining coldness and cruelty with 'detskaia bespechnost' ('Kamennyi gost' Pushkina', p. 95).

13. See P. Bezsonov, *Praskov'ia Ivanovna, grafinia Sheremet'eva. Eia narodnaia pesnia i rodnoe eia Kuskovo (Biograficheskii ocherk, s portretom)* (Moscow, 1872), pp. 80-85.

14. F. Lopukhov, *Shest'desiat let v balete* (Moscow, 1966), p. 182. On the ballet in connection with *Poema bez geroia*, see my 'Akhmatova's *Poema bez geroia*: ballet and poem' in *The Speech of Unknown Eyes: Akhmatova's Readers on her Poetry*, edited by Wendy Rosslyn, (Nottingham, Astra Press, 1990), pp. 55-72.

15. See the monk's description of the hero: 'Razvratnym, bessovestnym, bezbozhnym Don Guanom', reinforced by Leporello's 'Bessovestnyi!' in Scene 1 of Pushkin's *Kamennyi gost'*.

16. N. Mandelstam, *Hope Abandoned*, translated by Max Hayward, (New York, Atheneum, 1974), p. 437.

17. Anna Lisa Crone, 'Blok as Don Juan in Axmatova's *Poema bez geroja*', *Russian Language Journal*, XXXV, Nos. 121-2, 1981, pp. 145-62.

18. Quoted by Toporov, p. 20.

19. Compare the lines 'Gibel' gde-to zdes', ochevindo' and 'Ne poslednie l' blizki sroki', the latter identified by Toporov as a quotation from Hoffmann's *Don Juan*, where it is addressed to Donna Anna (p. 176).

20. On the autobiographical nature of Pushkin's *Kamennyi gost'* see also Henry Kucera, 'Puskin and Don Juan', in Morris Halle *et al*. (comp.), *For Roman Jakobson* (The Hague, Mouton, 1956), pp. 281-4.

21. For a discussion of Akhmatova's early poems in this light, see my *The Prince, the Fool and the Nunnery: the Religious Theme in the Early Poetry of Anna Akhmatova*, (Amersham, Avebury, 1984).

22. Toporov, p. 37.

23. Quoted by Toporov, p. 175.

24. Stage directions to Chapter 2 of Part 1. Italics added.

25. See 'Nadpis' na poeme "Triptikh"', which refers to, and addresses, *Poema bez geroia*:

Spasi zh menia, kak ia tebia spasala,
I ne puskai v klokochushchuiu t'mu.

26. Byron also contemplated a substitute for hell: 'I had not quite fixed whether to make him end in Hell, or in an unhappy marriage, not knowing which would

be the severest. The Spanish tradition says Hell; but it is probably only an Allegory of the other state.' (Letter to his editor, quoted in Leo Weinstein, *The Metamorphoses of Don Juan* (Stanford, Stanford University Press, 1959), p. 81.

27. On statues in Akhmatova's poetry see my paper 'Remodelling the statues at Tsarskoe Selo: Akhmatova's approach to the poetic tradition', read at the conference entitled 'A Sense of Place: Tsarskoe Selo and its Poets' held at Dartmouth College in October 1989 and to be published in the conference proceedings.

28. *Don Juan*, Canto 1, stanzas 212-13, 215. Isaiah Berlin (*Personal Impressions* [London, Hogarth Press, 1980], pp. 193-4) writes of his visit to Akhmatova in 1945: '. . . she asked me whether I would like to hear her poetry: but before doing this, she said that she wished to recite two cantos from Byron's *Don Juan* to me, for they were relevant to what would follow. Even if I had known the poem well, I could not have told which cantos she had chosen, for although she read English, her pronunciation of it made it impossible to understand more than a word or two. She closed her eyes and spoke the lines from memory, with intense emotion [. . .] Then she spoke her own poems from *Anno Domini, White Flock, From Six Books* [. . .] She then recited the (at that time) still unfinished *Poem without a Hero* . . . [. . .] Then she read the *Requiem*'. It seems unlikely that Akhmatova recited two cantos—rather, two stanzas. If so, these may be the first two quoted here.

29. Compare Don Guan's 'Polno vam menia kaznit', / Khot' kazn' ia zasluzhil, byt' mozhet' (*Kamennyi gost'*, Scene 4). Don Guan, though less self-critical, is prepared to admit his guilt, a sign of his gradual regeneration.

30. Pushkin's Don Guan, also a poet, hovers on the threshold of regeneration in this life before damnation overtakes him.

31. Goethe observed of *Don Giovanni*: 'Wie kann man sagen, Mozart habe seinen Don Juan komponiert! Komposition—als ob es ein Stück Kuchen oder Biskuit wäre, das man aus Eiern, Mehl und Zucker zusammenrührt!—Eine geistige Schöpfung ist es, das Einzelne wie das Ganze aus einem Geiste und Guss und von dem Hauche eines Lebens durchdrungen, wobei der Produzierende keineswegs versuchte und stückelte und nach Willkür verfuhr, sondern wobei der dämonische Geist seines Genies ihn in der Gewalt hatte, so dass er ausführen musste, was jener gebot.' (Quoted with minor corrections from Egon Wellesz, '"Don Giovanni" and the "dramma giocoso"', *The Music Review*, Vol. IV, 1943, p. 125). This could also be said of *Poema bez geroia*. See also T. V. Tsiv'ian, 'Two Hypostases of *Poema bez geroia*', in *The Speech of Unknown Eyes: Akhmatova's Readers on her Poetry*, pp. 113-20.

32. Viach. Vs. Ivanov, 'K semioticheskoi teorii karnavala kak inversii dvoichnykh protivopostavlenii', in *Trudy po znakovym sistemam*, VIII (*Uchenye zapiski Tartu. gos. universiteta, vyp.* 411), 1977, 63-4.

33. In her discussion of *Kamennyi gost'* Akhmatova writes: 'Pushkin's lyric richness allowed him to avoid the error which he noted in the dramas of Byron, who hands out "one of the constituent parts" of his personality to each of the characters, and thus fractures his creation into "a few shallow and insignificant people"' (p. 109). Akhmatova also avoids this error and, having divided the author's self into various doubles, invites the reader to gather the constituent parts together again to reconstitute the person of the author.

34. I am grateful to Anatolii Naiman for his observations on an earlier draft of this paper, read at the Akhmatova Centenary Conference in Turin in December 1989.

Requiem

BORIS KATZ (ESSAY DATE APRIL 1998)

SOURCE: Katz, Boris. "To What Extent Is *Requiem* a Requiem? Unheard Female Voices in Anna Akhmatova's *Requiem*." *Russian Review* 57 (April 1998): 253-63.

In the following essay, Katz maintains that Akhmatova's poem Requiem *is not a true requiem but should more properly be considered a Russian version of the medieval poem* Stabat Mater.

Some cry up Haydn, some Mozart,
Just as the whim bites. For my part,
I do not care a farthing candle
For either of them, nor for Handel.
Cannot a man live free and easy,
Without admiring Pergolesi?
    —Charles Lamb, "Free Thoughts on Several
        Eminent Composers" (1830)

It is obvious that not every poet would share Charles Lamb's attitude toward music in general, and toward "several eminent composers" in particular. Anna Akhmatova certainly would not. There is no need to cite a great deal of evidence; it is sufficient to recall one passage from the memoirs of Anatoly Naiman, a Russian poet who was close to Akhmatova in her later years. The passage presents a good picture of Akhmatova's diverse and selective preferences in the world of music:

At the head of the truckle-bed was a low table with an electric record player: either I had hired it locally or someone had brought it from town. She listened to music frequently and for long periods; she listened to various kinds of music, but sometimes she would be especially interested in a particular piece or pieces for a certain time. In the summer of 1963 it was the Beethoven's sonatas, in the autumn—Vivaldi; in the summer of 1964— Shostakovich's *Eighth Quartet*, in the spring of 1963—Pergolesi's *Stabat Mater*, and in the summer and autumn—Monteverdi's *L'incoronazione di Poppea* and, especially often, Purcell's *Dido and Aeneas*, the British recording with Schwartzkopf. She liked listening to Beethoven's *Bagatelles*, much of Chopin (played by Sofronitskii), *The Four Seasons* and other Vivaldi's concertos, and also Bach, Mozart, Haydn, and Handel. As we know, Vivaldi's *Adagio* appears in *Midnight Verses*: "We shall meet again in music, in Vivaldi's bold *Adagio*." One day she asked me to find some music on the radio for a change. I began moving the needle along the dial and observed aloud that it was all light music. Akhmatova replied, "Who needs that?" "Ah, here's some opera." "Operas aren't always bad." "When aren't they bad?" "When they're *Khovanshchina*, or *Kitezh Town*."[1]

But since some require evidence to be convinced, one interesting bit of it belongs to Akhmatova herself and is expressed in her poetry—specifically, in the poem with the significant title *A Poet*:

> Подумаешь, тоже работа,—
> Беспечное это житье:
> Подслушать у музыки что-то
> И выдать шутя за свое.
>
> И чье-то веселое скерцо
> В какие-то строки вложив,
> Поклясться, что бедное сердце
> Так стонет средь блещущих нив.[2]

Here we have an authorial confession of a great importance, for one of the distinctive features of Akhmatova's poetry (especially that of the late period) is the abundance of so-called subtexts.[3] Akhmatova's poetry of the late period is literally woven from threads connecting a poem with numerous other texts, often of a very different nature. Such texts may be facts of biography, history, art, and so forth. Literary subtexts, of course, play the most essential part. "In the later period," Susan Amert noted, "the role of literary quotations and references takes on pivotal importance: the identification and interpretation of literary references becomes crucial to an understanding of Akhmatova's poetry, which speaks through such echoes and allusions."[4] That is why intertextual approaches to Akhmatova's poetry have been so widely adopted. Immersion into what Akhmatova herself called "the subtextual depth" seems to be one of the most adequate methods for analyzing her works.

In this regard, at least two points should be emphasized. The first is Akhmatova's well-known, frequent use of the device of concealment. The line from the *Poem without a Hero*, «У шкатулки ж тройное дно», could serve as a motto for studies on Akhmatova's way of referring to different subtexts. One of them may conceal another, the latter may conceal yet another, and so on. A different motto for the same kind of research could be borrowed from the early Akhmatova poem *Pesnia poslednei vstrechi*, «Я на правую руку надела /

Перчатку с левой руки», for Akhmatova rarely uses any sources directly.[5] Usually, she intentionally fuses and transforms them into something new and—quite often—hardly commensurate to the original. That is why it is not easy to recognize Akhmatova's subtexts.

The second point to be emphasized is the most important for these considerations. "The box with a triple bottom" of Akhmatova's poetry conceals not only different literary sources but also musical ones. Akhmatova scholars often neglect these musical sources (especially if they are inclined to share Charles Lamb's attitude toward music). But the stanzas from *A Poet* cited above point to the existence of musical subtexts in Akhmatova's verse, at the same time that they underline their transformation and complex encoding. This being the case, Akhmatova's musical subtexts may be divided into two categories: "heard" and "unheard" melodies. My terms are taken from John Keats' lines from the *Ode on a Grecian Urn* (1820): "Heard melodies are sweet, / But those unheard are sweeter."[6] By "heard melodies" I mean those musical subtexts which are disclosed to the reader by the author herself; by "unheard melodies," those which the author either vaguely hints at or entirely conceals. Three examples will make my division clear. In the first "Dedication" from the *Poem without a Hero* we read:

> Не море ли?
> Нет, это только хвоя
>
> Могильная, и в накипанье пен
> Все ближе, ближе . . .
> *Marche funèbre* . . .
> шопен . . .[7]

Undoubtedly, the piece by Chopin serves as an audible (as though heard by inner ear) musical accompaniment to these lines. Here we have, so to speak, the heard melody.

The poem *The Call* (*Zov*, from the cycle *Polnochnye stikhi*), meanwhile, places us in quite another situation: «В которую-то из сонат / Тебя я спрячу осторожно . . .»[8] To whose sonata did Akhmatova refer? The answer may be found in the previous variants of the poem, and in Akhmatova's drafts. In an early variant of *The Call*, the first line reads: «И в предпоследней из сонат». This version does not make the reference absolutely clear, but it tells us that the poem deals with a certain musical piece. The reader does not know which piece it is, but the author does. Fortunately, in Akhmatova's drafts one can find the discarded motto to this poem, "Arioso Dolente. Beethoven.

Op. 110," so we now know that Akhmatova had in mind the lamenting melody from the finale of Beethoven's *Piano Sonata No. 31,* which is indeed the composer's penultimate sonata.

In this way, Akhmatova transformed the "heard melody" into an "unheard" one. Without touching upon all the reasons for this transformation, let us remember that "unheard melodies are sweeter."[9]

The third example presents the first lines from a poem written in 1914: «Вечерний звон у стен монастыря / Как некий благовест самой природы».[10] Here we have a telling example of a combination of both types of musical subtexts within one line, or, to put it another way, a combination of heard and unheard melodies. The heard one is the melody of the ringing church bells directly mentioned in the text.

At the same time, the first two words refer to the famous Russian romance which eventually became a folk song. The initial words of the song (as well as its title) are the same: "Vechernii zvon." Incidentally, the text of the song is a translation of a poem by Thomas Moore (1779-1852) entitled *Those Evening Bells,* made by the Russian poet Ivan Kozlov, who wrote in the beginning of the nineteenth century. This translation had been set to music several times during the nineteenth century, although the most popular melody belongs to an unknown composer. This melody is well known in Russia and, beyond any doubt, it was known to Akhmatova. Thus her poem imperceptibly evokes two "melodies" at one and the same time: the "heard" sounding of the church bells and the "unheard melody" of the old Russian song.

Turning to the problem of musical subtexts in Akhmatova's *Requiem,* one might suppose that the very title of the poem points to the musical setting of the Latin text that is used in Roman Catholic liturgy. The first composer to come to mind as a potential reference is, of course, Mozart, for it is his *Requiem* that became one of the most famous examples of the genre. Considering Akhmatova's lifelong admiration for Mozart's music one could easily conclude that the identity of the main musical subtext for her *Requiem* is established. The problem cannot be solved so easily, however, because "the box has a triple bottom." First of all let us note that the only explicit statement by Akhmatova on musical subtexts in her *Requiem* is found among her notes on *Poem without a Hero*: "Next to it [this poem] . . . so motley and saturated with music, went [my] funereal *Requiem,* which can only be accompa-

nied by Silence and occasional, distant strokes of funeral bells."[11] If these words refer in any way to musical compositions, it may be to those of one of the greatest Russian composers—Modest Mussorgsky, for the funeral bells sounding behind the stage are among the distinctive features of his best-known operas, *Boris Godunov* and *Khovanshchina.*

In the first, funeral bells resound in one of the opera's most impressive scenes, when the dying Tsar Boris exclaims, «Звон! Погребальный звон!» But the use of the funeral bells in *Khovanshchina* is perhaps even more striking, for here we have precisely the combination of Silence and the distant, sparse tolling of funeral bells. I have in mind the scene from Act 4, when the stroke of a bell breaks a terrifying silence and announces the beginning of the mass execution.

As many readers know, *Khovanshchina* deals with certain historical events at the end of the seventeenth century in Russia. The climax of Act 4 represents the tragic result of the Strel'tsy mutiny of 1698, which Peter I severely suppressed. Many rebels were executed on Red Square in Moscow just at the Kremlin walls. In his opera Mussorgsky presents (not without some deviations from history) the beginning of the execution, and—what is of special importance for our subject—he includes in this scene a choir of female voices. This choir is one of the most impressive musical episodes of the opera. The wives of the doomed victims are crying and wailing. According to Mussorgsky's realistic principles, this musical fragment is more akin to the real wailing of womenfolk than to traditional operatic female choirs.

Remembering that just before this choir the funeral bells ring out in the silence, it is not so difficult to discover the unheard music implied in the last lines of the first poem from Akhmatova's *Requiem*: «Буду я, как стрелецкие женки, / Под кремлевскими башнями выть».[12] And this "unheard melody" is quite definite: it is the abundantly chromatic music of the Choir of Strel'tsy Wives.

It seems that *Khovanshchina* (incidentally, one of Akhmatova's favorite operas) provided more than one melody as musical subtext for *Requiem.* The only heroine of the opera, Marfa, stands on the stage in silence listening to the funeral bells. Marfa is a strong, determined woman, extremely (almost fanatically) religious, yet also a passionate lover. She is absolutely fearless, scorns any danger, and in the end burns herself for the sake of the true faith. Moreover, she has the gift of prophesy and is able to predict the future.

This character had a historical prototype in seventeenth-century Russia. The resistance to the innovations being introduced by Peter the Great and his predecessors was supported to a great degree by the Old Believers. There was one woman among their leaders—the noblewoman Morozova, who was sentenced to exile, imprisonment, and eventually to death. In several poems Akhmatova explicitly identified herself with Morozova.[13] So it comes as no surprise that Akhmatova may well have identified herself with the character of Mussorgsky's opera—with the Morozova-type character Marfa.

One of the most striking episodes involving Marfa is the scene in Act 2 where she foretells the sad destiny that is awaiting the hero in spite of his current prosperity:

> Тебя ожидают опала и ссылка и заточенье в
>   дальнем краю.
> Отнимется власть, и богатство и знатность навек
>   от тебя.
> Ни слава в минувшем, ни доблесть, ни знанья,
>   ничто не спасет . . .
> Узнаешь великую страду, печаль и лишенья . . .
> в той страде, горючих слезах познаешь всю
>   правду земли . . .[14]

The echoes of this aria, *Gadanie Marfy,* may be heard at the beginning of the Epilogue in Akhmatova's **Requiem**:

> Узнала я, как опадают лица,
> Как из-под век выглядывает страх,
> Как клинописи жесткие страницы
> Страдание выводит на щеках.[15]

But Marfa's aria seems to be even closer to the **Requiem**'s Poem 4, which also deals with the prophesy, with the foretelling of a prosperous life turned disastrous:

> Показать бы тебе, насмешнице
> И любимице всех друзей,
> Царскосельской веселой грешнице,
> Что случится с жизнью твоей -
> Как трехсотая с передачею
> Под Крестами будешь стоять
> И своею слезою горячею
> Новогодний лед прожигать.[16]

Besides the obvious similarities («горючих слезах» and «слезою горячею») it is remarkable that Akhmatova uses «показать» (to show) instead of the seemingly more suitable «рассказать» (to tell). The point is, Mussorgsky's Marfa does not merely foretell the future in her aria, she shows it, because this future became visible to her in water. *Gadanie Marfy,* then, might well serve as the musi-

cal subtext to Poem 4, and if this is the case, the sad and gloomy melody sung by a low female voice constitutes its "unheard counterpoint."

This poem also offers one of the most telling examples of Akhmatova's subtextual technique, for in it we see how the different subtexts are combined and how they intersected in her verse. The phrases «царскосельской веселой грешнице» and «под Крестами будешь стоять» deserve special attention. "Kresty" is the name of the Petersburg prison where many victims of Stalin's terror, including the poet's son, were held. The word "kresty" means "the crosses," hence the expression «стоять под Крестами» means more than "to stand near a prison." It has the second meaning of "to stand by the cross." Here it is not difficult to recall the Gospel according to St. John (19:25): "Now there stood by the cross of Jesus his mother, and his mother's sister, Mary the wife of Cleophas, and Mary Magdalene." Mary Magdalene is traditionally identified with the woman characterized in the Gospel according to St. Luke (7:37) as "a woman in the city, who was a sinner."

It seems, then, that the female sinner of Tsarskoe selo who stands by the Crosses in Akhmatova's **Requiem,** and the female sinner of the city who stood by the cross of Jesus, have much in common. She who stood by Jesus was forgiven by Him, as is mentioned in the Latin text of the Requiem service (in *Recordare*): "Qui Mariam absolvisti [It was You to Mary pardon gave]."

Hence, in Poem 4 from Akhmatova's **Requiem** cycle one may see at least two "hidden" faces belonging to one and the same heroine: she is Marfa from Mussorgsky's opera and she is Mary Magdalene from the New Testament and from the canonical text of the Roman Catholic Requiem. Having established this, it is easy to see why precisely these two very different characters became united: there are two sisters in the New Testament who knew Jesus—Mary and Martha (or Marfa in Russian). However, it seems that our heroine has one more "hidden" face, and perhaps this is the most important one.

Before uncovering this third face, let us note that Akhmatova's text does not contain very many references to the text of the Latin Requiem. In addition to the "sinner of the city" one could point to only one more detail: «Это было, когда улыбался / Только мертвый, спокойствию рад».[17] The words «мертвый» and «спокойствию» in these initial lines of *Vstuplenie* obviously echo the initial words of the Latin prayer: "Requiem aeternam dona eis, Domine! [Eternal rest grant to them [the dead], O Lord]!" This complicates matters, however. The Requiem Mass prays for peace for the dead. Akhmatova's **Requiem** asserts that the dead are happy because they already have been granted peace. They are even smiling, in contrast to those still among the living. Indeed, Akhmatova's poem begins as something like an Anti-Requiem, and it continues in the same direction, contradicting the traditional contents of the Requiem Mass.

Many readers noticed the contradiction between the real biographical events reflected in Akhmatova's poem, on the one hand, and its title on the other. Let us briefly recall these events. In 1935, Akhmatova's husband, Nikolai Punin, and Akhmatova's son by her first marriage, Lev Gumilev, were arrested. Akhmatova did her best to save them: she appealed to Stalin personally («Кидалась в ноги палачу»), as a result of which both Punin and Gumilev were soon released. These events inspired Akhmatova's writing some short poems which were eventually turned into the **Requiem** cycle. In 1938, Gumilev was re-arrested and imprisoned in Leningrad. He was sentenced to death, but in August 1939 his sentence was commuted and he was deported from Leningrad, first to a camp, and then into exile. Later he was released, again re-arrested, and finally freed in 1956. Punin was re-arrested in 1949 and died in prison camp in 1953. It is worth stressing that **Requiem** as a cycle of poems was completed in a first version in 1940, while both Gumilev and Punin were alive, though the former was still in prison.

The traditional Requiem, however, is a Mass for the Dead (*Missa pro defunctis*). The implication, therefore, seems to be that when Akhmatova was crafting her **Requiem** she bore in mind not only her own loved ones, but all the victims of Stalin's terror. Still, there are only two more lines (in Poem 4) actually dealing with the dead, or, strictly speaking, with those who are almost dead, or dying: «И ни звука—а сколько там / Неповинных жизней кончается . . .»[18] Are there too few lines about the dead for the genre, then? Is it not strange, in a cycle of poems entitled **Requiem,** to speak about living (albeit doomed) persons, rather than dead ones?

In view of the numerous discrepancies between Akhmatova's text and that of the Catholic Mass for the Dead (there also are no equivalents to, say, the *Dies Irae, Tuba mirum, Rex tremendae, Sanctus, Benedictus, Agnus Dei, Lux aeterna,* and to other important parts of the Requiem Mass), let us put the crucial question: Is Akhmatova's **Requiem** a requiem at all? Did the Requiem Mass serve as both a verbal and musical subtext for Akhmatova's poem?

It seems to me that the answer must be no. The title **Requiem,** in my opinion, illustrates Akhmatova's typical manner of hiding one source under the name of another one, for it was another Catholic prayer that served as verbal and musical subtext for Akhmatova's **Requiem.** We can easily disclose this subtext, for Akhmatova explicitly points to it in the second part of Poem 10, *Raspiatie* (*Crucifixion*):

> Магдалина билась и рыдала,
> Ученик любимый каменел,
> А туда, где молча М   с о л,
> Так взглянуть никто и не посмел.[19]

The italicized words reproduce almost exactly the initial words of the famous medieval devotional poem about the Virgin Mary's vigil by Christ's Cross—*Stabat Mater* ("Stabat Mater dolorosa [A grief-striken Mother was standing]"). This text goes back to the thirteenth century and is still sung in the Roman Catholic rites at the Feast of the Seven Sorrows of the Virgin Mary. It was also set to music by many composers (Palestrina, Pergolesi, Haydn, Rossini, Verdi, and Dvorzak, among others) in numerous oratories with the same title.

Indeed, it was not only Mary Magdalene, who stood by the Cross: Mary, the mother of Christ, stood there as well. Her suffering is the main subject of *Stabat Mater,* and it is a mother's suffering that is the main subject of Akhmatova's **Requiem.** Let us add to this, that the traditional Requiem does not include a description of the Crucifixion, while *Stabat Mater* does, and with many touching details.

Comparing Akhmatova's **Requiem** with *Stabat Mater,* several parallelisms of different kinds become apparent. Touching upon the lexical ones, let us note the key words common to both texts: "mother," "son," "to stand," "death," "tears," "suffering," and "to weep." The word "cross" may be found in Akhmatova's text not only as the name of the prison: the cross appears to be a symbolic instrument of execution of the son. Without quoting from **Raspiatie** again, let us note the last two lines from Poem 6, addressed directly to the son: «О твоем кресте высоком / И о смерти говорят».[20] Some of Akhmatova's metaphors may be understood as transformed metaphors from *Stabat Mater.* For example, the sword that pierced the Virgin Mary's grieving, anguished, and lamenting heart ("Cujus animam gementem / Contristatam et dolentem / Pertransivit gladius") seems to be turned into the "stone word" that fell upon the "still-living breast" in Akhmatova's **Requiem**: «И упало каменное слово / На мою еще живую грудь».[21]

The suffering of the afflicted Mother of an only Son ("O quam tristis et afflicta / Fuit illa benedicta / Mater Unigeneti") as well as the appeal for compassion to the loving mother grieving for her Son ("Quis non posset contristari / Piam matrem contemplari / Dolentem cum Filio?") appear to be condensed in Akhmatova's lines dealing with the ill and lonely woman:

> Эта женщина больна,
> Эта женщина одна
> Муж в могиле, сын в тюрьме
> Помолитесь обо мне.[22]

The motif of "Mater Unigeneti" may well have been especially moving for Akhmatova. Certainly in some poems which are close to **Requiem,** but not included in the cycle, the motif of "an only Son" occurs rather often: «Разлучили с единственным сыном», ("Vse ushli, i nikto ne vernulsia"),[23] «Разлученной с единственным сыном», «Мне он— единственный сын» ("Cherepki").[24]

One more example of Akhmatova's compressing several images of *Stabat Mater* in her own poems may be shown by comparing the words "Inflammatus at accensus" ("Inflamed and burning") and "Cruce hac inebriari" ("intoxicated by his Cross") with the words from Poem 9: «И поит огненным вином». The notion of "inflamation," "intoxication," and "burning" are condensed here in one line.

It is, of course, inappropriate to claim direct structural and metrical influence exerted by the medieval verses of *Stabat Mater,* with its three-line stanzas (trochaic tetrameter with the dactylic foot to conclude the third line) upon Akhmatova's cycle, with its diverse and changeable meters and stanzas. Nonetheless, it is noteworthy that three consecutive poems from **Requiem** (4, 5, and 6) provide us with examples of parallelisms. Thus the lines from Poem 4, «Там тюремный тополь качается» and «Неповинных жизней кончается», are the only two lines in the whole cycle to have a dactylic foot in their ends. Poem 5 gives the only example of three-line structures united in one six-line stanza:

> И только пышные цветы,
> И звон кадильный, и следы
> Куда-то в никуда.
> И прямо мне в глаза глядит
> И скорой гибелью грозит
> Огромная звезда.[25]

Finally, Poem 6 is the only one written in trochaic tetrameter. The sequence of two rhyming lines coincides almost exactly with a similar pattern in *Stabat Mater.*

Ястребиным жарким оком,   Stabat Mater dolorosa
О твоем кресте высоком . . .   Juxta crucem lacrymosa . . .

Perhaps all this is not pure coincidence. In any case, the juxtaposition of the concluding sections of Akhmatova's **Requiem** with *Stabat Mater* is certainly fruitful. The last stanza of *Stabat Mater* reads: "Quando corpus morietur, / Fac ut animae donetur / Paradisi gloria [When my body dies / Let my soul be granted the glory of Heaven]." The end of **Requiem** is also strongly marked by references to a time when the author of **Requiem** will be no more: «И если когда-нибудь в этой стране / Воздвигнуть задумают памятник мне . . .»[26]

Yet **Requiem**—in contrast to *Stabat Mater*—deals with the dream of glory on Earth, not heavenly glory. It is a dream of a posthumous monument which would represent not only the poet's magnificence but first of all the mother's suffering. This monument of the poet's dreams must be erected on the same place where the mother from Akhmatova's **Requiem** "was standing for three hundred hours" («Здесь, где стояла я триста часов»), namely, "by the Crosses"—(«под Крестами»). Thus Akhmatova once more identified herself with the Mother of God while at the same time stressing the special aspect of such an identification: a destiny of a mother who is doomed to see her only son being unjustly imprisoned, sentenced, tormented, and executed.

Thus, ultimately, it is not a requiem that Akhmatova wrote, in spite of the title **Requiem**. Rather, it is a very Russian, even very Soviet, and, of course, very Akhmatovian version of *Stabat Mater.*

In Akhmatova's opinion, Solzhenitsyn was wrong when in a conversation with the poet (as recorded by one of her friends), he said: "It was a national tragedy, but you made it only the tragedy of a mother and son." According to the same source, Akhmatova "repeated these words with her usual shrug of the shoulders, and a slight grimace."[27]

Indeed, another writer (an émigré who belonged to Akhmatova's generation) seems to have had a better understanding of **Requiem** when he called it a "lament, a female, motherly, lament, not only for herself but also for all those who are suffering, for all wives, mothers, brides, and in general for all those who are being crucified."[28] Nevertheless, Solzhenitsyn's judgment contains a grain of truth. Akhmatova's **Requiem**, although it presents, of course, the tragedy of the entire nation, does so through the prism of her personal tragedy, of a mother watching her tormented and dying son.

This fact explains why precisely *Stabat Mater*—the best exemplification of such a Mother-Son tragedy in European literature—may be considered the hidden subtext of Akhmatova's **Requiem.** Akhmatova's knowledge of Latin is beyond any doubt. Her acquaintance with medieval Catholic prayers might have its origin in her close contacts (in the mid-1910s and early twenties) with Arthur Lourie (1892-1966), the avant-garde composer who, after his conversion to Catholicism, wrote several liturgical compositions on the texts of medieval Latin prayers. One of them—*Salve Regina*—is mentioned (rather enigmatically) in Akhmatova's long poem *Putem vseia zemli,* written the same year in which Akhmatova completed her **Requiem,** 1940.[29]

Akhmatova may have had several reasons for hiding the subtext *Stabat Mater* in "the box with a triple bottom" (and the very deepest one at that). For one thing, we know that Akhmatova, for both political and personal reasons, would carefully conceal everything that could shed light on her relationship with Arthur Lourie. For another, *Stabat Mater* was too closely connected with Catholic liturgy and had no equivalents among the Orthodox prayers. Moreover, "requiem" was a term that (at least in Russian culture) had lost, to a certain degree, both its religious and Catholic flavor and turned into something neutral enough to be applied to secular memorial works of art. Finally, if I may say it again, "unheard melodies are sweeter."

With respect to the melodies which Akhmatova's **Requiem** may have secretly implied, this issue is fairly easy to resolve. One of the most famous musical settings of *Stabat Mater* is the oratorio composed by Giovanni Batista Pergolesi (probably in 1739). Anatoly Naiman, as we remember, mentions this oratorio among Akhmatova's favorite musical pieces. It seems to be particularly important that Pergolesi's *Stabat Mater* (in contrast to Mozart's **Requiem,** which usually is performed by a mixed choir with orchestra) is to be sung only by female voices—by two female singers (Soprano and Alto) accompanied by strings and harpsichord. This feminine-sounding image, so to speak, strengthens, in my opinion, the resemblance between Pergolesi's oratorio and Akhmatova's poem.

So, Lamb's ironic question, "Cannot a man live free and easy, / Without admiring Pergolesi?"

may be answered: Perhaps men can, but women cannot. At least one of them could not.

Notes

1. Anatoly Naiman, *Remembering Anna Akhmatova,* trans. Wendy Rosslyn (New York, 1991), 147. Both operas mentioned by Akhmatova were written by Russian composers—*Khovanshchina* by Modest Mussorgsky, and *The Legend of the Invisible City of Kitezh and the Maiden Fevronia* by Nikolai Rimsky-Korsakov.

2. Anna Akhmatova, *Posle vsego* (Moscow, 1989), 145. Unless otherwise noted, all further citations of Akhmatova's texts are from this excellent edition, which combines Akhmatova's works with numerous valuable materials for Akhmatova studies and comprises five books published simultaneously by the Moscow Pedagogical Institute in 1989 (compilers and commentators R. Timenchik, K. Polivanov, and V. Morderer). Unfortunately, the edition lacks any general title and none of the books (*Desiatye gody, Poema bez geroia, Rekviem, Posle vsego,* and *Fotobiografiia*) has a number. Therefore, all further references mention the title of each book and the page number.

3. By "subtext" I mean, following Kirill Taranovskii and Omry Ronen, the source of a literary citation or allusion.

4. Susan Amert, *In a Shattered Mirror: The Later Poetry of Anna Akhmatova* (Stanford, 1992), 14.

5. *Desiatye gody,* 57.

6. These lines were used as the motto to the only (posthumous) collection of the poems by Vsevolod Kniazev (*Stikhi* [St. Petersburg, 1914]) who was to become the prototype for "dragunskii kornet" in Akhmatova's *Poem without a Hero.* For more details see Roman Timenchik, "Zametki o 'Poeme bez geroja,'" in Akhmatova, *Poema bez geroia,* 4-9.

7. *Poema bez geroia,* 33.

8. *Posle vsego,* 188.

9. For elucidation of links between Beethoven's Sonata, op. 110 and Akhmatova's poem *The Call* see B. Kats and R. Timenchik, *Anna Akhmatova i muzyka* (Leningrad, 1989), 148-52.

10. Anna Akhmatova, *Stikhotvoreniia i poemy* (Leningrad, 1977), 280.

11. *Poema bez geroia,* 62.

12. *Rekviem,* 304.

13. «Мне с Морозовою класть поклоны . . .» (*Posledniaia roza,* 1962), «О, если бы вдруг откинуться / В какой-то семнадцатый век . . . С боярынею Морозовой / Сладимый медок попивать . . . Какой сумасшедший Суриков / Мой последний напишет путь?» (*Ia znaiu, s mesta ne sdvinut' sia . . .,* 1939 [?]). Judith Hemschemeyer comments on the last lines: "A picture of the Boyarynya Morozova by Vasily Surikov (1848-1916) depicts her on a sleigh, in chains, being taken into exile. According to Nadezhda Mandelstam in *Hope against Hope . . .* the last two lines of this poem originated in a remark made by Punin to Akhmatova in the Tretyakov Gallery: 'Now let's go and see how they'll take you to your execution.'" See *The Complete Poems of Anna Akhmatova,* trans. Judith Hemschem-

eyer, vol. 2 (Somerville, MA, 1990), 784. Perhaps it is worth adding that another famous picture by V. I. Surikov depicts the execution of Strel'tsy (*Utro Streletskoi kazni*).

14. M. Mussorgskii, *Khovanshchina: Narodnaia muzykal' naia drama* (Moscow, 1932), 140-42.

15. *Rekviem*, 311.

16. Ibid., 306.

17. Ibid., 304.

18. Ibid., 306.

19. Ibid., 310 (emphasis added).

20. Ibid., 307.

21. Ibid.

22. Ibid., 304.

23. Ibid., 293.

24. Ibid., 282.

25. Ibid., 306.

26. Ibid., 312.

27. Natalia Roskina, "Good-by Again," in *Anna Akhmatova and Her Circle*, comp. Konstantin Polivanov, trans. Patricia Beriozkina (Fayetteville, AR, 1994), 193.

28. Boris Zaitsev, "Dni," *Russkaia mysl'* (Paris), 7 January 1964, cited in Akhmatova, *Rekviem*, 299.

29. *Posle vsego*, 120. For more details about this reference to Lourie's *Salve Regina*, as well as about Lourie himself (he emigrated in 1922) and his influence upon Akhmatova's life and works, see Kats and Timenchik, *Anna Akhmatova i muzyka*, 147, 31-36, 170-72; and *Poema bez geroia*, 338-51.

FURTHER READING

Bibliographies

Driver, Sam N. "Akhmatova: A Selected, Annotated Bibliography." *Russian Literature Triquarterly* 1 (1971): 432-34.

Brief annotated listing of criticism on Akhmatova's works.

Terry, Garth M. *Anna Akhmatova in English: A Bibliography 1889-1966-1989.* Nottingham, Eng.: Astra Press, 1989.

Comprehensive bibliography of Akhmatova's works, both literary and non-literary, and criticism on her writings.

Criticism

"Anna Akhmatova 1889-1989: For Akhmatova's Birth Centenary." *Soviet Literature*, no. 6 (1989).

Entire issue devoted to Akhmatova, including selections from her writings, reminiscences on her life, and essays on her work.

Amert, Susan. *In a Shattered Mirror: The Later Poetry of Anna Akhmatova.* Stanford, Calif.: Stanford University Press, 1992.

Discussion of Akhmatova's post-1935 poetry and the political, philosophical, and religious concerns it reflects.

Dalos, György Andrea Dunai. *The Guest from the Future: Anna Akhmatova and Isaiah Berlin*, translated by Antony Wood. London: John Murray, 1998.

Account of the relationship between Akhmatova and Berlin and its effect on her writing.

Driver, Sam N. *Anna Akhmatova.* Boston: Twayne, 1972.

Comprehensive study of Akhmatova's life and works.

Feinstein, Elaine. "Poetry and Conscience: Russian Women Poets of the Twentieth Century." In *Women Writing and Writing about Women,* edited by Mary Jacobus, pp. 133-58. London: Croom Helm, 1979.

Comparative treatment of the poetry of Akhmatova, Tsvetayeva, and their contemporaries.

Gamburg, Haim. "The Biblical Protagonists in the Verse of Anna Axmatova: An Expression of Feminine Identification." *Russian Language Journal* 31, no. 109 (spring 1977): 125-34.

Examines Akhmatova's sympathetic treatment of Biblical heroines in her poetry.

Gasparov, M. L. "The Evolution of Akhmatova's Verse." In *Anna Akhmatova 1889-1989,* edited by Sonia I. Ketchian, pp. 68-74. Oakland, Calif.: Berkeley Slavic Specialties, 1993.

Comparison of Akhmatova's early verse from the period 1909 to 1922 to her poetry written after 1923.

Ozerov, Lev. "Touches to Akhmatova's Portrait." *Soviet Literature,* no. 6 (June 1989): 155-63.

Provides discussion of thematic and stylistic features of Akhmatova's poetry.

Pratt, Sarah. "The Obverse of Self: Gender Shifts in Poems by Tjutcev and Axmatova." In *Russian Literature and Psychoanalysis,* edited by Daniel Rancour-Laferriere, pp. 225-44. Amsterdam: John Benjamins, 1989.

Compares shifts in gender in Akhmatova's "Distant Voice" cycle with a poetic cycle by Tjutcev.

Rosslyn, Wendy. "Gender in Translation: Lowell and Cixous Rewriting Akhmatova." In *Gender and Sexuality in Russian Civilisation,* edited by Peter I. Barta, pp. 71-86. London: Routledge, 2001.

Examination of the gendered differences in two translations of Akhmatova's Requiem, *one by Robert Lowell, the other by Hélène Cixous.*

Tomei, Christine D. "Mirra Loxvickaja and Anna Axmatova: Influence in the Evolution of the Modern Female Lyric Voice." In *Critical Essays on the Prose and Poetry of Modern Slavic Women,* edited by Nina A. Efimov, Christine D. Tomei, and Richard L. Chapple, pp. 135-60. Lewiston, N.Y.: Edwin Mellen Press, 1998.

Traces the sudden emergence, at the beginning of the twentieth century, of two major female poets, Akhmatova and Mirra Loxvickaja.

OTHER SOURCES FROM GALE:

Additional coverage of Akhmatova's life and career is contained in the following sources published by the Gale Group: *Contemporary Authors,* Vols. 19-20, 25-28R; *Contemporary Authors New Revision Series,* Vol. 35; *Contemporary Literary Criticism,* Vols. 11, 25, 64, 126; *DISCovering Authors 3.0; DISCovering Authors Modules: Poets; Encyclopedia of World Literature in the 20th Century,* Ed. 3; *European Writers,* Vol. 10; *Literature Resource Center; Major 20th-Century Writers,* Eds. 1, 2; *Poetry Criticism,* Vols. 2, 55; *Poetry for Students,* Vol. 18; and *Reference Guide to World Literature,* Eds. 2, 3.

ISABEL ALLENDE

(1942 -)

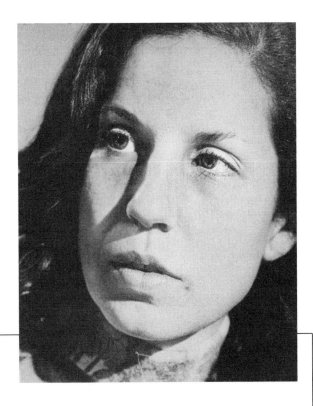

Chilean novelist, essayist, journalist, short story writer, memoirist, playwright, and juvenile fiction writer.

Respected as one of the foremost writers of contemporary Latin-American literature, Allende documents the tumultuous social, political, and gender-based issues particular to South America. She frequently draws upon her own experiences as well as those of family members to examine the violence and repression historically experienced by South Americans. Allende often blends graphic realism with elements of magic realism, illuminating injustices perpetrated against women and to address women's struggles to obtain equality. Widely translated, Allende's fiction has received international popular and critical acclaim, particularly among feminist scholars.

BIOGRAPHICAL INFORMATION

Allende was born in Lima, Peru, where her father served as a Chilean diplomat. Although Allende's contact with her father ceased following her parents' divorce, she remained close to his side of the family—particularly with Salvador Allende, her uncle and godfather, who was president of Chile from 1970 until 1973. In 1973 Salvador Allende was murdered during August Pinochet's right-wing military coup. As a young girl, Allende lived with her maternal grandparents in Santiago, Chile. Her grandparents would later serve as models for Esteban and Clara Trueba, whose family history Allende chronicles in her first novel, *La casa de los espíritus* (1982; *The House of the Spirits*). After spending her adolescence in Bolivia, Europe, and the Middle East with her mother and stepfather, Allende became a television journalist as well as a writer for *Paula*, a radical feminist magazine. In 1973, when Pinochet seized power, Allende went into exile with her husband and children in Caracas, Venezuela. She had difficulty finding work in Venezuela, but eventually began writing satirical essays for the newspaper *El nacional*. In the mid- to late-1980s, she held teaching positions at the University of Virginia, Montclair College, and the University of California, Berkeley. She divorced her husband in 1987 and began a lecture tour in the United States. There she met William Gordon, an attorney from California. The two married in 1988 and settled north of San Francisco. In late 1991, while preparing for the publication of her fourth novel, *El plan infinito* (1991; *The Infinite Plan*) Allende was notified that her daughter Paula had suddenly developed medical complications due to porphyria, a genetic disorder. Paula lingered in a coma for a year, during which Allende rarely left her bedside, until she succumbed to the illness and died in 1992. Allende later documented this period in her memoir *Paula* (1994).

MAJOR WORKS

The House of the Spirits began as a letter written while in exile to Allende's dying grandfather in Chile. She recorded her remembrances of her grandfather to reassure him that although he was dying, he would continue on in her memory. *The House of the Spirits* is set in an unnamed South American country that is recognizable as Allende's home country, Chile. The plot recounts the experiences of four generations of the del Valle-Trueba family, set against the backdrop of Chilean politics from the turn of the century through the military coup of 1973. Although the characters struggle with new political regimes, the larger battle concerns the female protagonist's efforts to gain independence and control of her life in a patriarchal society. *De amor y de sombra* (1984; *Of Love and Shadows*) focuses on journalist Irene Beltrán and photographer Francisco Leal, who uncover evidence of atrocities committed by military personnel and risk great personal harm in their pursuit of justice. They are eventually exiled but have fallen in love and leave their homeland together. Set in a country that resembles Venezuela, *Eva Luna* (1987) relates the story of an illegitimate young girl, Eva, whose mother dies when Eva is only six years old. The narrative focuses on Eva's survival throughout her difficult childhood and adolescence, and progresses to her discovery of success and fulfillment as a television scriptwriter. Eva's claiming of language empowers her to choose her own destiny and eschew dependence on a male character to speak and provide for her. *Cuentos de Eva Luna* (1989; *The Stories of Eva Luna*) again focuses on Eva's character, and transforms several of the biographical sketches in *Eva Luna* into more detailed short stories. *The Infinite Plan* follows Gregory Reeves, a young man raised in a poor Chicano neighborhood in Los Angeles. His father is an ex-preacher who subscribes to his own personal philosophy of salvation, called the "Infinite Plan." When the patriarch becomes ill, Gregory must help support his family before attending law school and then serving in Vietnam. After the war he returns to the United States and seeks happiness through the attainment of material goods, power, and sex. Only when he ends his quest for monetary riches and begins to find emotional fulfillment through other means is he finally able to achieve happiness and peace. *Paula* was written as a family memoir that Allende planned to give to her daughter Paula once she recovered from her coma. The work traces Allende's family history through several generations, recounting her own privileged upbringing, the terror of her uncle's assassination, and the subsequent military coup. *Hija de la fortuna* (1999; *Daughter of Fortune*) is a multigenerational novel involving characters at the fringes of "proper society." The novel traces the life of Eliza Sommers, an orphan who was unknowingly reared by her biological aunt in Chile. Eliza falls in love and becomes pregnant, but the child's father leaves during the California gold rush. Eliza follows him to the United States, but miscarries while a stowaway on the ship to California. She becomes deathly ill and is saved by Tao Chi'en, the ship's cook. While searching America for her lover, Eliza keeps in touch with Tao Chi'en by exchanging letters. She finally realizes that what she feels for her missing lover is more like a dream than the real bond she shares with Tao Chi'en, and she returns to California to marry the man who truly loves her. *Retrato en sepia* (2000; *Portrait in Sepia*) is a continuation of *The House of the Spirits* and *Daughter of Fortune*. Due to severe trauma, Aurora del Valle—the granddaughter of Eliza Sommers—is unable to remember her childhood years. She decides to piece together her fragmented past and, using photographs and language, explores her family history. As she reclaims each memory, she is "reunited" with the strong women from her family history whose spirits have lent their strength to her. By learning their stories, Aurora is able to remember her own life story and write her future in a manner of her choosing.

CRITICAL RECEPTION

Often described as one of the first women to enter the male-dominated Latin-American literary scene, Allende is widely credited with launching the post-"Boom" era in South and Central America with the publication of *The House of the Spirits*. Much of the critical analysis of Allende's work has been devoted to studying her feminist perspective and her focus on marginalized people in society: women, homosexuals, blacks, and Hispanics. Her illumination of female roles in a patriarchal society has been applauded, though some critics charge that Allende's portrayals of Latin males are stereotypical and that she at times resorts to clichés concerning Hispanics. Allende has been noted as a valued commentator on the turbulent nature of Latin American society and also as an author of powerful, humanistic fiction. Although some scholars have faulted her use of magic realism and picturesque language, many reviewers have viewed these embellishments as inherent elements in stories employing a feminine perspective. Such critics have asserted that these methods are natural in fiction written by and for women.

PRINCIPAL WORKS

El embajador (play) 1972

*Civilice a su troglodita: Los impertinentes de Isabel Allende (essays) 1974

La casa de los espíritus [*The House of the Spirits*] (novel) 1982

De amor y de sombra [*Of Love and Shadows*] (novel) 1984

La gorda de porcelana (juvenilia) 1984

Eva Luna (novel) 1987

Cuentos de Eva Luna [*The Stories of Eva Luna*] (short stories) 1989

El plan infinito [*The Infinite Plan*] (novel) 1991

Paula (memoir) 1994

Afrodita: Cuentos, recetas y otros afrodisiacos [*Aphrodite: A Memoir of the Senses*] (essays, folklore, and short stories) 1997

Hija de la fortuna [*Daughter of Fortune*] (novel) 1999

Retrato en sepia [*Portrait in Sepia*] (novel) 2000

La ciudad de las bestias [*City of the Beasts*] (juvenilia) 2002

Mi pas inventado: Un paseo nostalgico por Chile [*My Invented Country: A Nostalgic Journey through Chile*] (memoirs and prose) 2003

El reino del dragon oro [*The Kingdom of the Golden Dragon*] (juvenilia) 2003

---

*   This work is a compilation of Allende's "Los impertinentes" columns for *Paula* magazine.

PRIMARY SOURCES

ISABEL ALLENDE (ESSAY DATE 1989)

SOURCE: Allende, Isabel. "Writing as an Act of Hope." In *Paths of Resistance: The Art and Craft of the Political Novel,* edited by William Zinsser, pp. 39-63. Boston: Houghton Mifflin, 1989.

In the following essay, Allende discusses her reasons for writing, the lessons she hopes her novels teach, and the marginality that women writers face.

In every interview during the last few years I encountered two questions that forced me to define myself as a writer and as a human being: Why do I write? And who do I write for? Tonight I will try to answer those questions.

In 1981, in Caracas, I put a sheet of paper in my typewriter and wrote the first sentence of **The House of the Spirits**: "Barabbas came to us by sea." At that moment I didn't know why I was doing it, or for whom. In fact, I assumed that no one would ever read it except my mother, who reads everything I write. I was not even conscious that I was writing a novel. I thought I was writing a letter—a spiritual letter to my grandfather, a formidable old patriarch, whom I loved dearly. He had reached almost one hundred years of age and decided that he was too tired to go on living, so he sat in his armchair and refused to drink or eat, calling for Death, who was kind enough to take him very soon.

I wanted to bid him farewell, but I couldn't go back to Chile, and I knew that calling him on the telephone was useless, so I began this letter. I wanted to tell him that he could go in peace because all his memories were with me. I had forgotten nothing. I had all his anecdotes, all the characters of the family, and to prove it I began writing the story of Rose, the fiancée my grandfather had had, who is called Rose the Beautiful in the book. She really existed; she's not a copy from García Márquez, as some people have said.

For a year I wrote every night with no hesitation or plan. Words came out like a violent torrent. I had thousands of untold words stuck in my chest, threatening to choke me. The long silence of exile was turning me to stone; I needed to open a valve and let the river of secret words find a way out. At the end of that year there were five hundred pages on my table; it didn't look like a letter anymore. On the other hand, my grandfather had died long before, so the spiritual message had already reached him. So I thought, "Well, maybe in this way I can tell some other people about him, and about my country, and about my family and myself." So I just organized it a little bit, tied the manuscript with a pink ribbon for luck, and took it to some publishers.

The spirit of my grandmother was protecting the book from the very beginning, so it was refused everywhere in Venezuela. Nobody wanted it—it was too long; I was a woman; nobody knew me. So I sent it by mail to Spain, and the book was published there. It had reviews, and it was translated and distributed in other countries.

In the process of writing the anecdotes of the past, and recalling the emotions and pains of my fate, and telling part of the history of my country, I found that life became more comprehensible and the world more tolerable. I felt that my roots had been recovered and that during that patient exercise of daily writing I had also recovered my own soul. I felt at that time that writing was unavoidable—that I couldn't keep away from it. Writing is such a pleasure; it is always a private orgy, creating and recreating the world according to my own laws, fulfilling in those pages all my dreams and exorcising some of my demons.

But that is a rather simple explanation. There are other reasons for writing.

Six years and three books have passed since *The House of the Spirits.* Many things have changed for me in that time. I can no longer pretend to be naïve, or elude questions, or find refuge in irony. Now I am constantly confronted by my readers, and they can be very tough. It's not enough to write in a state of trance, overwhelmed by the desire to tell a story. One has to be responsible for each word, each idea. Be very careful: the written word cannot be erased.

I began to receive academic papers from American universities about the symbols in my books, or the metaphors, or the colors, or the names. I'm always very scared by them. I just received three different papers on Barabbas, the dog. One of them says that he symbolizes the innocence of Clara because he accompanies her during her youth, and when she falls in love, symbolically, the dog dies in a pool of blood. That means the sexual act, it seems. The second paper says that the dog represents repression—the militarists—and the third paper says that he is the male part of Clara, the hidden, dark, big beast in her. Well, really, Barabbas was just the dog I had at home. And he was killed as it was told in the book. But of course it sounds much better to answer that Barabbas symbolizes the innocence of Clara, so that's the explanation I give when somebody asks.

Maybe the most important reason for writing is to prevent the erosion of time, so that memories will not be blown away by the wind. Write to register history, and name each thing. Write what should not be forgotten. But then, why write novels? Probably because I come from Latin America, a land of crazy, illuminated people, of geological and political cataclysms—a land so large and profound, so beautiful and frightening, that only novels can describe its fascinating complexity.

A novel is like a window, open to an infinite landscape. In a novel we can put all the interrogations, we can register the most extravagant, evil, obscene, incredible or magnificent facts—which, in Latin America, are not hyperbole, because that is the dimension of our reality. In a novel we can give an illusory order to chaos. We can find the key to the labyrinth of history. We can make excursions into the past, to try to understand the present and dream the future. In a novel we can use everything: testimony, chronicle, essay, fantasy, legend, poetry and other devices that might help us to decode the mysteries of our world and discover our true identity.

For a writer who nourishes himself or herself on images and passions, to be born in a fabulous continent is a privilege. In Latin America we don't have to stretch our imaginations. Critics in Europe and the United States often stare in disbelief at Latin American books, asking how the authors dare to invent those incredible lies of young women who fly to heaven wrapped in linen sheets; of black emperors who build fortresses with cement and the blood of emasculated bulls; of outlaws who die of hunger in the Amazon with bags full of emeralds on their backs; of ancient tyrants who order their mothers to be flogged naked in front of the troops and modern tyrants who order children to be tortured in front of their parents; of hurricanes and earthquakes that turn the world upside down; of revolutions made with machetes, bullets, poems and kisses; of hallucinating landscapes where reason is lost.

It is very hard to explain to critics that these things are not a product of our pathological imaginations. They are written in our history; we can find them every day in our newspapers. We hear them in the streets; we suffer them frequently in our own lives. It is impossible to speak of Latin America without mentioning violence. We inhabit a land of terrible contrasts and we have to survive in times of great violence.

Contrast and violence, two excellent ingredients for literature, although for us, citizens of that reality, life is always suspended from a very fragile thread.

The first, the most naked and visible form of violence is the extreme poverty of the majority, in contrast with the extreme wealth of the very few. In my continent two opposite realities coexist. One is a legal face, more or less comprehensible and with a certain pretension to dignity and civilization. The other is a dark and tragic face, which we do not like to show but which is always threatening us. There is an apparent world and a real world—nice neighborhoods where blond children play on their bicycles and servants walk elegant dogs, and other neighborhoods, of slums and garbage, where dark children play naked with hungry mutts. There are offices of marble and steel where young executives discuss the stock market, and forgotten villages where people still live and die as they did in the Middle Ages. There is a world of fiction created by the official discourse, and another world of blood and pain and love, where we have struggled for centuries.

In Latin America we all survive on the border-line of those two realities. Our fragile democracies exist as long as they don't interfere with imperialist interests. Most of our republics are dependent on submissiveness. Our institutions and laws are inefficient. Our armed forces often act as mercenaries for a privileged social group that pays tribute to transnational enterprises. We are living in the worst economic, political and social crisis since the conquest of America by the Spaniards. There are hardly two or three leaders in the whole continent. Social inequality is greater every day, and to avoid an outburst of public rancor, repression also rises day by day. Crime, drugs, misery and ignorance are present in every Latin American country, and the military is an immediate threat to society and civil governments. We try to keep straight faces while our feet are stuck in a swamp of violence, exploitation, corruption, the terror of the state and the terrorism of those who take arms against the status quo.

But Latin America is also a land of hope and friendship and love. Writers navigate in these agitated waters. They don't live in ivory towers; they cannot remove themselves from this brutal reality. In such circumstances there is no time and no wish for narcissistic literature. Very few of our writers contemplate their navel in self-centered monologue. The majority want desperately to communicate.

I feel that writing is an act of hope, a sort of communion with our fellow men. The writer of good will carries a lamp to illuminate the dark corners. Only that, nothing more—a tiny beam of light to show some hidden aspect of reality, to help decipher and understand it and thus to initiate, if possible, a change in the conscience of some readers. This kind of writer is not seduced by the mermaid's voice of celebrity or tempted by exclusive literary circles. He has both feet planted firmly on the ground and walks hand in hand with the people in the streets. He knows that the lamp is very small and the shadows are immense. This makes him humble.

But just as we should not believe that literature gives us any sort of power, neither should we be paralyzed by false modesty. We should continue to write in spite of the bruises and the vast silence that frequently surrounds us. A book is not an end in itself; it is only a way to touch someone—a bridge extended across a space of loneliness and obscurity—and sometimes it is a way of winning other people to our causes.

I believe in certain principles and values: love, generosity, justice. I know that sounds old-fashioned. However, I believe in those values so firmly that I'm willing to provoke some scornful smiles. I'm sure we have the capacity to build a more gentle world—that doing so is our only alternative, because our present equilibrium is very fragile. In literature, we have been told, optimism is dangerous; it flirts with simplicity and is an insurrection against the sacred laws of reason and good taste. But I don't belong to that group of desperate intellectuals. Despair is a paralyzing feeling. It only benefits our enemies.

My second novel, *Of Love and Shadows,* tells about the *desaparecidos,* "the disappeared ones." It's based on a political massacre that took place in Chile in 1973 during the military coup that put an end to 150 years of democracy. The novel denounces repression and the impunity of the murderers, and it had a warm reception from most readers and critics. But it also drew some strong attacks. Some said it was too political and sentimental and not very objective, as if one could be objective about the crimes of a dictatorship. Maybe these critics would have forgiven me, as other writers have been forgiven, if the book had only been a story of horror and bitterness. They didn't like the fact that in the novel solidarity and hope prevail over death and torture. If the main characters, Irene and Francisco, had died in a torture chamber, or at least if the violent experiences they endured had drowned them in despair and destroyed forever their capacity to love and to dream, these critics might have been more tolerant. Evidently it's hard to accept in literature that love can be stronger than hatred, although it frequently is in life.

If my books are going to be classified as political, I hope readers will find out that they are not political for ideological reasons only, but for other, more subtle considerations. They are political precisely because Alba Trueba, in *The House of the Spirits,* who has been raped, tortured and mutilated, is able to reconcile herself with life; because Irene and Francisco, in *Of Love and Shadows,* make love in spite of terror; because in my third novel, *Eva Luna,* Eva defeats the odds of her fate with generosity and candor; because these characters search for truth and have the courage to risk their lives.

I suppose I have the secret ambition to become a great writer, to be able to create stories that will resist the passage of time and the judgment of history. Yes, I know, it's terribly pretentious! But I'm more interested in touching my readers—as many of them as possible—on a spiritual and emotional level. To do this from a feminine point of view is a beautiful challenge in the society I live in. The political literature that some women writers have begun to create is so revolutionary that no wonder many critics are scared. Women are questioning the set of values that have sustained human society since the first apes stood on their feet and raised their eyes to the sky. After centuries of silence, women are taking by assault the exclusive male club of literature. Some women have done it before, of course, struggling against formidable obstacles. But now half of the novels published in Europe and the United States are written by women. Our sisters are using the cutting edge of words to change the rules we have always had to obey. Until now, humankind has organized itself according to certain principles that are considered part of nature: we are all born (it has been said) with some original sin; we are basically evil, and without the strict control of religion and laws we would devour each other like cannibals; authority, repression and punishment are necessary to keep us in line. According to these theories, the best proof of our perverse nature is that the world is what it is—a round rock lost in the cosmic nightmare, where abuse, war, inequality and hatred prevail.

But a small group of women and young men are now making the most astonishing statements. Fortunately, most of them work in the best universities, so even if they are only a few, their voices have great impact. These people are questioning everything, starting with our own image as human beings. Until now, men have decided the destiny of this suffering planet, imposing ambition, power and individualism as virtues. (They don't admit this, of course; it is more eloquent to speak of peace and cooperation.) These values are also present in literature. Critics, most of them men, as you probably can guess, have determined what is good in literature—what is valuable or artistic, according to our aesthetic, intellectual and moral patterns—leaving aside the feminine half of the human race, whose opinions on this or any other matter don't interest them.

I think it's time to revise this situation. But it is not the Old Guard who will do it. It will be done by women and by young men who have nothing to lose and therefore have no fear.

In the process of analyzing books, critics have exalted all kinds of literary experiments, some of them quite unbearable. How many books have you tried to read lately and haven't gotten past page fifteen because they were simply boring? Flamboyant literary techniques win awards even though the subject is deplorable. The worst vices are glorified if the writing is elegant. Lies, bitterness and arrogance are forgiven if the language is original and the author already has his laurels. Pessimism is in fashion.

But many novels that don't fit that pattern are now being written by women and by some brave men, not all of them young—for example, García Márquez, who wrote that incredible and sentimental book *Love in the Time of Cholera,* which is a sort of magnificent soap opera about two old people who fall in love, and they love each other for eighty years. It's wonderful.

Those writers are shaking the literary world nowadays because they propose a completely new set of values. They don't accept the old rules anymore. They are willing to examine everything—to invent all over again and to express other ethical and aesthetic values; not always to replace the prevailing ones, but to complement them. It's not a question of changing male chauvinism for militant feminism, but of giving both women and men a chance to become better people and to share the heavy burden of this planet. I believe that this is the true political literature of our time.

All political systems, even revolutions, have been created and directed by men, always within the patriarchal regime. Important philosophical movements have tried to change man and society, but without touching the basis of human relations—that is, inequality of the sexes. Men writers of all periods have written political literature, from *Utopia* to parody, but feminine values have been scorned and women have been denied a voice to express them.

Now, finally, women are breaking the rule of silence and raising a strong voice to question the world. This is a cataclysm. It is a new literature that dares to be optimistic—to speak of love in opposition to pornography, of compassion against cruelty. It is a literature that's not afraid of colloquial language, of being sentimental if necessary; a literature that searches the spiritual dimension of reality, that accepts the unknown and the unexplainable, confusion and terror; a literature that has no answers, only questions; a literature that doesn't invent history or try to explain the world solely with reason, but also seeks knowledge through feelings and imagination. Maybe, this literature says, it's not true that we are perverse and evil. Maybe the idea of original sin is just a terrible mistake. Maybe we are not here to be punished, because the gods love us and are willing to give us a chance to decipher the clues and trace new paths.

The effect of these books is hard to measure, because the old instruments are no longer useful. Probably the strongest literature being written nowadays is by those who stand unsheltered by the system: blacks, Indians, homosexuals, exiles and, especially, women—the crazy people of the world, who dare to believe in their own force. We dare to think that humanity is not going to destroy itself, that we have the capacity to reach an agreement, not only for survival but also to achieve happiness. That is why we write—as an act of human solidarity and commitment to the future. We want to change the rules, even if we won't live long enough to see the results. We have to make real revolutions of the spirit, of values, of life. And to do so we have to begin dreaming them.

So I will continue to write: about two lovers embracing in the moonlight, near an abandoned mine where they have found the bodies of fifteen peasants, murdered by the military. Or about raped women and tortured men and families who sell themselves as slaves because they are starving. And also—why not?—about golden sunsets and loving mothers and poets who die of love. I want to tell stories and say, for example, that I care more for the free man than the free enterprise, more for solidarity than charity. I want to say that it's more important for me to share than to compete. And I want to write about the necessary changes in Latin America that will enable us to rise from our knees after five centuries of humiliations.

Much skill will be needed to write about these things eloquently. But with patience and hard work I hope to acquire that skill. I suppose I'm being very ambitious. Well, most writers are, even women writers.

Now, for whom do I write?

When I face a clean sheet of paper, I don't think of a large audience or of the people who would raise their knives to cut me in pieces. If I did, terror would paralyze me. Instead, when I write, a benevolent image comes to my mind— that of Alexandra Jorquera, a young woman who lives in Chile whom I scarcely know. She has read my books so many times that she can repeat paragraphs by heart. In fact, she knows them better than I do. She quotes me and I don't know she's quoting me. Once she told me that she had discovered in my books the history of Chile that is denied by the official textbooks of the dictatorship—the forbidden and secret history that nevertheless is still alive in the memories of most Chileans.

This is the best compliment my work has ever received. For the sake of this girl I am very demanding with my writing. Sometimes, tempted by the beauty of a sentence, I am about to betray the truth, and then Alexandra comes to my mind and I remember that she, and others like her, don't deserve that. At other times I'm too explicit, too near the pamphlet. But then I step back, thinking she doesn't deserve that either—to be underestimated. And when I feel helpless against brutality and suffering, her candid face brings back my strength. All writers should have a reader like her, waiting for their words. They would never feel lonely, and their work would have a new and shining dimension.

In Latin America today, 50 percent of the population is illiterate. Among those who can read and write, only very few can buy books, and among those who can buy books, very few have the habit of reading. What, then, is the importance of a book in Latin America? None, would be the reasonable answer. But it's not exactly that way. For some strange reason, the written word has a tremendous impact in that illiterate continent. The totalitarian regimes have persecuted, tortured, sent into exile and murdered many writers. This is not an accident; dictators don't make mistakes in these details. They know that a book can be dangerous for them. In our countries most of the press is controlled by private enterprises or by inefficient governments. Eduardo Galeano, the great writer from Uruguay, puts it bluntly: "Almost all mass media promote a colonialistic culture, which justifies the unjust organization of the world as a result of the legitimate victory of the best—that is, the strongest. They lie about the past and about reality. They propose a lifestyle which postulates consumerism as an alternative to communism, which exalts crime as achievement, lack of scruples as virtue, and selfishness as a natural requirement."

What can writers do against this persistent and powerful message? The first thing we should try to do is write clearly. Not simply—that only works with soap advertising; we don't have to sacrifice aesthetics for the sake of ethics. On the contrary, only if we are able to say it beautifully can we be convincing. Most readers are perfectly able to appreciate subtleties and poetic twists and symbols and metaphors. We should not write with a paternalistic attitude, as if readers were simple-minded, but we should also beware of elaborate and unnecessary ornamentation, which frequently hides a lack of ideas. It has been said that we Spanish-speaking people have the vice of empty words, that we need six hundred pages to say what would be better told in fifty.

The opportunity to reach a large number of readers is a great responsibility. Unfortunately, it is hard for a book to stand against the message of the mass media; it's an unfair battle. Writers should therefore look for other forms of expressing their thoughts, avoiding the prejudice that only in books can they make literature. All means are legitimate, not only the cultivated language of academia but also the direct language of journalism, the mass language of radio, television and the movies, the poetic language of popular songs and the passionate language of talking face to face with an audience. These are all forms of literature. Let us be clever and use every opportunity to introduce ourselves in the mass media and try to change them from within.

In Venezuela, José Ignacio Cabrujas, a playwright and novelist, one of the most brilliant intellectuals of the country, writes soap operas. These shows are the most important cultural phenomenon in Latin America. Some people watch three or four a day, so you can imagine how important that kind of writing is. Cabrujas doesn't elude reality. His soap operas show a world of contrasts. He presents problems such as abortion, divorce, machismo, poverty and crime. The result is quite different from "Dynasty." But it's also very successful.

I tried to put some of that soap opera stuff in **Eva Luna,** because I'm fascinated by that version of reality. The ladies on TV wear false eyelashes at eleven in the morning. The difference between rich and poor is that the rich wear cocktail gowns all the time and the poor have their faces painted black. They all go blind or become invalids and then they recover. Just like real life!

Many of the most important Latin American writers have been journalists, and they go back to it frequently because they are aware that their words in a newspaper or on the radio reach an audience that their books can never touch. Others write for the theater or the movies, or write lyrics for popular songs. All means are valid if we want to communicate and don't presume to be writing only for an educated elite or for literary prizes.

In Latin America a book is almost a luxury. My hairdresser calls me Dr. Allende because I usually carry a book, and she probably thinks that a doctorate is the minimum prerequisite for such an extravagance. In Chile a novel of three hundred pages can cost the equivalent of a laborer's monthly wages. In some other countries—like Haiti, for example—85 percent of the population is illiterate. Elsewhere in Latin America, nothing is published in the Indian languages of the majority. Many publishers have been ruined by the economic crisis, and the price of books imported from Spain is very high.

However, we should not despair. There is some hope for the spirit. Literature has survived even in the worst conditions. Political prisoners have written stories on cigarette paper. In the wars of Central America, little soldiers, fourteen years old, write poetry in their school notebooks. The Pieroa Indians, those who haven't yet been exterminated by the genocide being carried out against the aborigines of the Amazon, have published some legends in their language.

In my continent, writers often have more prestige than they do in any other part of the world. Some writers are considered witch doctors, or prophets, as if they were illuminated by a sort of natural wisdom. Jorge Amado has to spend part of the year away from Brazil in order to write, because people crowd into his house seeking advice. Mario Vargas-Llosa directs the opposition to Alan Garcia's government in Peru. García Márquez is a frequent middleman for Central American presidents. In Venezuela, Arturo Uslar Pietri is consulted on issues like corruption and oil. These writers have interpreted their reality and told it to the world. Some of them even have the gift of foretelling the future and put in words the hidden thoughts of their people, which of course include social and political problems, because it is impossible to write in a crystal bubble, disregarding the conditions of their continent.

No wonder Latin American novels are so often accused of being political.

For whom do I write, finally? Certainly for myself. But mainly for others, even if there are only a few. For those who have no voice and for those who are kept in silence. For my children and my future grandchildren. For Alexandra Jorquera and others like her. I write for you.

And why do I write? García Márquez once said that he writes so that his friends will love him more. I think I write so that people will love each other more. Working with words is a beautiful craft, and in my continent, where we still have to name all things one by one, it has a rich and profound meaning.

FROM THE AUTHOR

ALLENDE ON HER STYLE OF WRITING
In the best of cases, literature attempts to give voice to those who are not granted it, or to those who have been silenced, but when I write, I do not assume the task of representing anyone, of transcending, of preaching a message or explaining the mysteries of the universe. I simply try to tell a story in the tone of an intimate conversation.

Allende, Isabel. Excerpt from *Isabel Allende: Life and Spirits*. Houston, Tex.: Arte Público Press, 2002, p. xv.

GENERAL COMMENTARY

SUSAN FRENK (ESSAY DATE 1996)

SOURCE: Frenk, Susan. "The Wandering Text: Situating the Narratives of Isabel Allende." In *Latin American Women's Writing: Feminist Readings in Theory and Crisis*, edited by Anny Brooksbank Jones and Catherine Davies, pp. 66-84. Oxford, Eng.: Clarendon, 1996.

In the following essay, Frenk considers the gender-based, socioeconomic, and political motivations for feminism in Allende's fiction.

Negotiating a path through the critical geographies which have mapped the academic reception of the narratives and public personae of Isabel Allende is a disorienting experience indeed. For all their differences, however, most of these geographies participate in a general deterritorialization as they steer her texts down unmarked roads. This essay offers a reading of the faded signposts and diversion signs along the way, with a tentative sketch for an alternative journey.

Texts are produced and exchanged in a global market-place. In the process a woman, some women, come to represent 'women's writing'—as Jean Franco notes, a commodity that currently sells well in pluralist regimes (Franco 1992). Allende's texts, which engage from exile with Chilean society, are marketed additionally through a dehistoricized 'magical realism' (Martin 1989) and through an academic 'teaching machine' which markets cultures to students while simultaneously feeding the media profiles of trends and superstars (Spivak 1993). It is from within this machine that I write, an outsider to Chile trying not to fall into too many of the potholes excavated by critics working on post-colonial terrain. As they wander from Chile to North American and UK academe and through different fields of discursive struggle Allende's texts generate many readings. The readings produced here are motivated in part by a need to celebrate the achievements of a woman writer in institutions and societies where (despite recent market successes) writing by women and the work of women who teach and research it remain devalued. This essay starts, however, from the assumption that we risk compounding these women's difficulties if we fail to contextualize the voices we gather, or to tease out the threads of 'woman' into the women who speak through these texts, those who do not, and those who are spoken by them inadequately.

What follows is a first stage in this process. It starts with the women's movements which, in different ways, have challenged the linguistic regime of *lo no dicho* (the unsaid) and the attempted abolition of the interlocutor, risking gendered, 'private' bodies in order to assert a broader integrity of the body. Allende's first novel, **La casa de los espíritus,** appeared only in 1982 and cannot be read as part of the literature of immediate resistance (Boyle 1992) nor assimilated to the different forms of *testimonio* (testimonial) generated by women inside Chile.[1] Nor is **La casa de los espíritus** as radically disjunctive in formal terms or as wide-ranging in its representation of subaltern relations as the writing of, for example, Diamela Eltit. Instead, I would argue, it is precisely the familiarity of Allende's narrative modes which empowers women readers, enabling them to respond through different forms of resistance and rebellion. This involves the reappropriation of their bodies, not as the liberation of a natural body, but through the reinscription of bodies in new discourses, including the expansion of political rights to a similarly de- and reconstructed pleasure. What is at stake here is not pleasure as a libidinal escape route from the social but an investigation of the politics of romance. Unlike Wolfgang Karrer—who has claimed that in *Eva Luna* 'Mimí and Eva submit gender structure to change, but ultimately preserve it' (Karrer 1991: 161)—I would argue that the politics of romance in Allende's narratives preserve the specificity of different bodies while troubling the dominant sex-gender naturalizations of them.

A reading of the integrity of sexually differentiated bodies, and of the discursive empowerment of gendered subjects as a strategic response to the situation of Chilean women, can take us beyond the theoretical impasse of 'feminist misogyny'. In her recent exploration of this phenomenon Susan Gubar notes that, since both feminists and misogynists must exploit and expropriate words from a common linguistic store, 'their discourses necessarily intersect in numerous ways, undercutting or supplementing each other over time [in] a cultural "heteroglossia" of gender ideologies and power asymmetries' (Gubar 1994: 465). This is helpful in reassessing the articulation of two pivotal elements in the seemingly polarized critical reception of Allende's writing, and in writing on Latin American women generally: femininity and motherhood. Anxious to escape the straitjacket of motherhood as naturalized self-abnegation, critical writings as diverse as Jean Franco's illuminating but ultimately negative analysis of motherhood in Rosario Castellanos (Franco 1992) and Debra Castillo's lament at the prominent role of marriage in Allende's narratives (Castillo 1992) seem to want to abolish positive representations of motherhood. However, such writing can be revised in a matrix which recognizes the systemic positioning/construction of women while at the same time enabling their agency—in negotiating, resisting, and transforming systemic relations and generating new identities—to be appraised.

If we relate *La casa de los espíritus* to the power of motherhood in the mobilization of Chilean women's groups, and to the rearticulation in the novel of this power in opposition to the discourse of the Pinochet regime, motherhood emerges as historically variable. Mother-daughter relations in particular do not replicate a natural femininity but accommodate new versions: they do not reinforce the patriarchal power of the father but instead provide a mode of empowerment of women's bodies and psyches which the patriarch cannot control. The later novel, *Eva Luna* (1988), expands this type of intergenerational relation between women beyond the biologically grounded narrative of motherhood. It also removes female-male relations almost completely from marriage. This, I would suggest, is related both to a more developed concern with subaltern experience and to the growing autonomy of women's movements (in Chile and elsewhere) through the 1980s, as a consciousness took shape of the need to negotiate political alliances with and within mixed, but still masculinist, opposition groups from a separate sphere of female identification and empowerment.

Allende's narratives can also be read as confronting the oppressive regime through a discursive experience of pleasure and desire which can seem scandalously inappropriate to the scale of suffering under Pinochet. Yet if we read Allende in the light of Patricia Chuchryk's study of women's organizations in the Chilean transition to Democracy (Chuchryk 1989) we can trace a process in which survival and resistance lead to a questioning of patriarchal relations, and in which pleasure and desire are no longer perceived as luxuries but identified as the very substance of those relations. These pleasures are produced in relations of denial and internalized self-denial, prohibited by external and self-imposed surveillance, and mobilized in the service of powerful others. They are harnessed within a specific phallic order which must be reappropriated and redirected according to a different imaginary economy, as a vital part of political projects to alter other relations. These relations include the socio-economic, which was until relatively recently the only sphere recognized as political by the Left.

In this analysis, the question of the integrity of the body expands from the bodies of the disappeared to include the discursive relations in which the bodies of the protesting women are imprisoned. It links domestic violence and state violence through the deconstruction of relations of gender and sexuality. There is a growing corpus of critical work which argues convincingly that Allende does more than 'put "quality" writing . . . at the service of the formulas that have always acted as female pacifiers—heterosexual romance combined with seigneurial goodwill toward the subaltern classes' (Franco 1992: 73). Franco goes on in the same piece to include Allende among a number of women writers who unsettle 'the stance that supports gender power/knowledge as masculine . . . displacing the male-centred national allegory and exposes the dubious stereotyping that was always inherent in the epics of nationhood that constitute the Latin American canon' (Franco 1992: 75). Yet her earlier comment implicitly excludes Allende from the confrontation of the middle-class woman's specific social positioning and the 'ambiguous overlapping of privilege and the aesthetic' (1992: 75) in women writers, a confrontation which she analyses in the writing of Clarice Lispector, Carmen Ollé, and Tununa Mercado. The analysis of post-colonial gender politics here must therefore integrate the representation of subaltern relations.

In *Eva Luna* and *La casa de los espíritus* these relations are associated with appropriations of bodily and discursive pleasure,

> [Consuelo] sacó la cuenta de que en sus treinta y tantos años no había conocido el placer y no lo buscó, convencida de que era un asunto reservado a los protagonistas del cine. Resolvió darse este gusto y de paso ofrecérselo también al enfermo a ver si partía más contento al otro mundo.
>
> (Allende 1988: 22)

> [Consuelo] looked back over her thirty-odd years and realized that she had not experienced pleasure, nor sought it, convinced that that sort of thing only happened in films. She resolved to have a taste of it herself and to offer some in passing to the sick man, to see if he would depart this world in a happier state.

In *Eva Luna*, Consuelo's appropriation of the pleasure which has been unavailable to her as marginalized *sirvienta* (maid) comes about through a process of rebellion. This process is linked to the issue of discursive power, which initiates a series of actions that affirm her as an agent, gradually transforming her from the mirror image of her master's desires. When she decides to try to save the life of the indian gardener (who has been bitten by a poisonous snake) we are told that 'por primera vez en su silenciosa existencia, Consuelo desobedeció una orden y tomó una iniciativa' (for the first time in her silent existence Consuelo disobeyed an order and took the initiative) (Allende 1988: 21).[2]

Consuelo reappropriates her body in a ritual undressing which culminates in loosening her hair: 'deshizo el rodete que llevaba enrollado en la nuca como exigía su patrón' (she unfastened the hair which, at her master's insistence, she wore coiled at the nape of neck) (Allende 1988: 22). Then, as she begins to make love for the first time, she initiates a dialogue with the stricken indian/

subaltern/male other in a language produced by her own desire: 'Susurrándole palabras recién inventadas' (murmuring newly invented words) (1988: 23). The love she offers the indian is accepted, he is restored to agency, and in the mutual pleasure and exchange of their lovemaking Eva is conceived.

A second ritual of reappropriation and inscription marks Eva's birth, celebrating it as 'el momento más importante' (the most important moment) of Consuelo's life and deromanticizing the birth process by foregrounding the 'labour' involved (1988: 23-4). Consuelo's apparent self-sufficiency becomes mutual dependency with the woman who helps her to cut the cord and to whom she eventually entrusts her daughter before dying. This relation is the first of a series of encounters between women which challenge their internalization of patriarchal discourses of the feminine body. It is the godmother who says 'Mala cosa, es hembra' (What bad luck, it's a girl) (1988: 24) and insists on baptizing Eva and giving her a surname, the traditional marker of women as the property of men. Consuelo counters with positive reinscriptions and compromises based on respecting the beliefs of the other. By choosing the tribal name of the father as the child's surname Consuelo simultaneously endows it with a different collective meaning. She identifies Eva with the marginalized indians rather than the *criollista* patriarchal order and reinscribes her in a feminine lineage, since the tribe's name means 'children of the moon' (1988: 24).

Eva's birth brings further release from Consuelo's long education in self-silencing. Consuelo is represented as generating a rich store of counter-stories about herself and the dominant order. Because that order refuses a dialogical relation with her, however, these stories can only be told when Eva becomes first a listener and then their mediator/narrator: 'Aprendió a permanecer quieta y guardó su desmesurado caudal de fábulas como un tesoro discreto hasta que yo le di la oportunidad de desatar ese torrente de palabras que llevaba consigo' (She learned to remain silent, treasuring her boundless stock of stories discreetly until I gave her the opportunity to unleash the torrent of words within her) (1988: 13). Consuelo's discursive transformations are confined to *la intimidad,* the private sphere: in public she maintains a silence that renders her invisible to the powerful, 'como si no existiera' (as if she didn't exist) (1988: 5).

Consuelo's empowerment and double legacy of *rebelión* (rebelliousness) and storytelling are central to her daughter's eventual transformation,

> De mi padre heredé la sangre firme, porque ese indio debió ser muy fuerte para resistir tantos días el veneno de la serpiente y en pleno estado de agonía darle gusto a una mujer. A mi madre le debo todo lo demás . . . Las palabras son gratis, decía y se las apropiaba, todas eran suyas.
>
> (1988: 25-6)

> I inherited my strong blood from my father, because that indian must have been pretty tough to hold out against the snake venom all those days and make love to a woman when he was on the point of death. Everything else I owe to my mother . . . words are free, she would say, and she appropriated them, they were all hers.

As *Eva Luna* progresses, Eva saves her own life by appropriating language and storytelling, sometimes adapting to the desires and discourses of others, eventually constructing alternative her/ histories. Despite economic and social disempowerment, her belief in the integrity of her healthy woman's body and the possibilities of discursive exchange as a counter to capitalist relations enables Eva both to survive and to participate in the process of social transformation and public discourse.

Eva is the sole, albeit extraordinarily complex, narrator of *Eva Luna.* In *La casa de los espíritus,* bodily integrity and discursive power are explored through counterposed female and male narrative voices. Trueba embodies the monologic regime of authoritarian patriarchy, which encompasses censorship, disempowerment through discourses which demean the other (*campesinos,* women, or communists), and physical violence (raping *campesina* women or hitting Clara). His granddaughter Alba is eventually revealed as the female narrator who restores the interlocutor, both by directly contradicting Trueba and by writing down a counter-herstory of the forms of resistance offered by other women and *campesino* men, socialist politics, and protest songs. Gabriela Mora's concern about what she sees as Alba's 'passivity', too-ready desire to forgive past injustice, and her 'limiting' of political activity to writing can thus be rethought through a new understanding of politics in the novel (Mora 1987: 58-9). The centrality of discursive relations to regimes of power, the establishment of a solidarity between women which is not contained within a single party politics, and the dimensions of sexual politics in Alba's relationship with Manuel are all part of this rearticulated politics. Furthermore, as Ronie-Richele García Johnson has shown, Alba's

situation at the end of the novel represents the apex of a gradual 'conquest of space' in the house (García Johnson 1994). We can read this as the democratization of the private which the Chilean women's movements came to see as indivisible in the struggle to democratize the public sphere in the 1980s. The difficult issue of Alba's discourse of forgiveness needs to be reread in the light of Susan de Carvalho's interesting study of male narrative voice in *La casa de los espíritus* and *El plan infinito* (Carvalho 1993-4). Carvalho argues that,

> Allende's male narrators in the novels both reach a nadir at which they are forced to admit their impotence; but the narrative perspective allows also a portrait of the 'post-masculine' male, the man emerging from that nadir, who then reviews his past in segments intercalated throughout the novels. Thus the narrative structure involves various externalized images of the male character, each followed immediately by the repentant male narrator's enlightened commentary on the man he had once been, his recognition of lost opportunities—in most cases opportunities to express love.
>
> (1993-4: 271)

It is in this context of self-analysis, repentance, and reconstruction by authoritarian figures that Alba's projection of a future forgiveness is situated.

The integrity of the (gendered) body is restored, then, through the dismantling of an authoritarian regime which exchanges bodies as commodities, the property of the patriarch, in the different but interrelated economies of desire, discourse, and money. Women and other subaltern groups reappropriate their bodies through acts of resistance that simultaneously rewrite the political discourse of the Chilean Left. The strategic foundationalism of bodies can play a multiplicity of roles in this process. First it celebrates—without idealizing—the female body which has traditionally been discursively deployed to sublimate the male body, while male bodies are *desublimated,* brought under scrutiny in a deconstruction of their phantom identification with the phallus of power (Gimbernat de González 1991). It also reasserts the integrity of the body against physical and discursive violations, while separating the body into bodies which have historically been gendered differently. Finally, it provides a point of identification across the specific struggles of different women which acts as a mooring post in a journey of collective transformation.

By representing desires that cannot be reduced to the specularisms of desire for the phallus— whose rejection in *Eva Luna* is linked to Eva's reassertion of an autonomous gender difference—Allende undermines the monologic system of patriarchal difference. Instead of Lacan's descriptive/prescriptive family romance, *Eva Luna,* for example, starts from a refigured family in which the maternal and feminine are privileged. Eva first reaches out to the male other not in psychic rejection of her dead mother, nor even in substitution of that mother('s lack). She reaches out in desire and, in part, in response to the economic positioning of women and to the problematic models of femininity internalized by her other 'mothers' (Madrina and Elvira).

Eva undergoes a learning process which begins with love for the father, Riad Halabi. As she later realizes, his paternalist form of patriarchy permits her to appropriate the positive aspects of his discourse of femininity, to survive through his protection, and to be encouraged by him to depart on a journey towards an equal subject status which transcends paternalism. Nostalgia for the 'protection' afforded by a paternalist patriarchy was a common feature of the early years of the Pinochet regime, not only in the regime's own refiguration of the ideal family but amongst many women obliged to take on sole responsibility for family income in harsh economic conditions (Chuchryk 1989; Boyle 1992). In the novel, Eva's nostalgia is dissipated in a double movement. On the one hand, there is her realization that a paternalist regime infantilizes women. On the other, there is Riad Halabi's failure to recognize her as an independent woman who seeks equal subject status. She is thus outside the specularisms of paternalism, desirable neither as daughter nor as daughter/lover.

This experience is related to the reader in the critical self-commentary which characterizes key moments in the complex time shifts of the narrative voice (Aguirre Rehbein 1991). Another mode of critical appraisal is dialogue between characters of equal status united by bonds of affect and shared experience, as in Eva and Melecio-Mimí's discussions of bodies, genders, and relationships. Contested positions are set out in terms of both feelings and possible outcomes. Although, when Melecio-Mimí chooses not to have the operation, the narrative ultimately reinforces Eva's position, the different discourses have nonetheless illuminated their relationship and brought into play a range of evaluation systems. The final selection of one rather than another refers once again to the possibility of rejecting the violation of the body required to normalize Mimí in patriarchal gender terms. Having found a male lover who is not rigidly bound to the patriarchal order, Mimí goes on to make his/her gender troublingly public in Eva's *telenovela.*

Eva's journey takes her through a series of relationships with seductive patriarchal masculinities. However she finally chooses not the Romantic hero Huberto—whose performance of machismo continues in the gendered politics of the guerrilla group—but the contrasting male character Rolf Carlé. Despite their different histories Eva and Rolf are able to construct a common, hybrid, narrative together. Or rather Eva constructs one for them both. It is significant that, despite their equal socio-economic status, shared politics, companionship, and erotic compatibility, as in the basic pattern of romance literature there is still a difference to address—in this case Rolf's emotional difficulties: 'Ese hombre tan veloz cuando se trata de captar una imagen con la cámara, resulta bastante torpe ante sus propias emociones' (That man is quick to catch an image on film but pretty sluggish when it comes to his own emotions) (1988: 279).

Their relationship rejects configurations of unequal complementarity, absolute incommunication, or domination/submission. Instead it proposes an equality that works not through the abolition of difference (which would mean the death of the subject) or through the subsuming of one difference into the realm of the other (the logic of specularity) but through respect for what Jacques Derrida terms 'the trace of the other'. Here the reassertion of gender difference functions to preserve the integrity of ethnic and other differences in a rearticulation of hybrid micro and macro identities. So, where Karrer reads the metaphors of fusion in Allende's writing as part of a homogeneous post-war *mestizaje,* I would argue a need to differentiate between specific ideologies of *mestizaje* in the context of emergent articulations of hybridity and transculturation.[3]

Yet we do need to look at the effects of the heterosexual focus in Allende's work, both locally and more broadly: in relation to the regime of *lo no dicho* (the unsaid) and the growing audibility of lesbian voices in Chilean women's groups, but also in relation to the global reception of Allende's work in contexts where the politics of sexuality have played a more crucial role in the 1980s. These other reterritorializations of her texts need to consider whether their magic realism resists or risks reinforcing the exoticism and hierarchical otherness of Latin America, and the tendency to represent machismo as a 'Latin' problem. I will argue that the discourse of magical realism in *La casa de los espíritus* challenges the capitalist destruction of nature and people not merely with a picture of suffering victims but with alternative knowledges and economic relations, forcing the Western reader to engage with them. Through the family of Rolf Carlé, *Eva Luna* can in some ways be seen to take this process further, placing authoritarian regimes and patriarchal relations in Latin America in juxtaposition with Fascist European regimes of the 1930s. This pre-empts the discourse of Latin America as a continent predisposed to authoritarian politics. At the same time it explores the colonial and postcolonial relationships between the two continents through Rolf's wanderings (including his period in the determinedly isolationist enclave of his aunt and uncle) and through the figure of Professor Jones, while problematizing masculinities in Europe as well as Latin America.

The question remains whether, given the situation of a double censorship—that of the regime's compulsory heterosexuality, and the women's movement's initial inability to move beyond the association of lesbianism with an imperialist, man-hating version of Western feminism—we can nonetheless mobilize lesbian and/or homoerotic desire in Allende's texts. And whether, even in this highly coded form, it can still disrupt the compulsory heterosexuality that may be pivotal to authoritarian masculinity and social relations. If we accept Adrienne Rich's theorization of a lesbian continuum, rivalry for any kind of male attention can be resituated along this continuum as forms of appreciation, affect, and solidarity. In this way, the self-love of women can resist patriarchy without recourse to representations of physical lovemaking. The view that the containment of women's erotic desire and pleasure within heterosexual relations requires a form of self-rejection, even self-hatred, would be displaced by a concept of self-love which can include a fully erotic lesbianism but does not depend on it. In this picture erotic desire is displaced from the central position it commanded—at least in Western politics—in the 1970s and 1980s and placed on a continuum, or field, of positively valued relations between women and between women and men. Relations between men are not reconstructed to the same extent in Allende's work. The sole instance of an openly homoerotic relation—Melecio-Mimí and Aravena—is caught up in Melecio's hatred of his own male body, although this becomes a partial self-acceptance as transvestite when he turns down the opportunity to have his body surgically remodelled as female. This seems

to suggest that the patriarchal regime is less amenable to micro resistance and modification by men than by women.

If, as Mario Rojas has suggested, the relationship between Férula and Clara in *La casa de los espíritus* may be read as oneway lesbian desire it is hardly a positive representation (Rojas 1986). In its possessiveness it is a specularism of her brother's authoritarian, controlling desire, in which woman is once again object or private property. Yet, as Rojas goes on to argue, Férula is part of the textual opposition between the 'amor/cadena' (chained love) of the Trueba dynasty and the 'amor libre' (free love) of the Del Valle women (1986: 73). Nonetheless, as the clearest coded representation of lesbian desire it remains problematic.

The concept of a 'lesbian continuum' still allows us to read the all-female households, the friendships, sisterhood, and even the political consciousness-raising and alliance between the women in the concentration camp and between Ana Díaz and Alba at the end of the novel as instances of the self-love that empowers women and makes it possible to resist the system of misogyny. Like Férula and Clara in *La casa de los espíritus* or Eva and Rolf's cousins in *Eva Luna,* all transform their rivalry for male attention into friendship. However, it remains the case that the fulfilment of erotic pleasure in mutual love between equals is exclusively located in the (future) heterosexual relationship between Alba and Manuel in the former novel and between Rolf and Eva in the latter. Similarly, Melecio-Mimí's homosexual relationship with Aravena is represented as an attenuated version of dominant-submissive relations between a purely performative femininity and a powerful masculinity. Although set in political opposition to the authoritarian regime this masculinity still represents the name of the father for Rolf, whom Aravena addresses as *hijo* (son). Literally and metaphorically miles from Rolf's tyrannical biological father, he is none the less in power.

Here too, however, the text projects a dynamic of potential change. The possibility of the guerrillas entering the sphere of democratic political power and Rolf's defiance of his 'father's' injunction not to do anything too risky both point to the emergence of new relationships between men. Within such a relationship Melecio-Mimí, for example, would no longer need to deny the male body as the embodiment of the phallic order. In the novel, this need is positioned in terms of Melecio's brutal experiences and therefore figures as a historically produced desire, rather than the genetically imprinted imperative of the discourse first mobilized to explain his/her sense of self. However, there is nothing comparable for male readers to the spectrum of female to female relationships in Allende's writing: the mother-daughter relationships which permit change without requiring absolute separation or alienation; the sisterhood which moves from a biological representation, which acquires political and historical dimensions in *La casa de los espíritus*, to the metaphorical mother and sister relationships in *Eva Luna*. Even the male guerrillas—that potential site of homoeroticism and non-biological brotherhood and, perhaps, misogynist homosociality—remain locked in the mode of charismatic leadership.

This returns us to the issue of the mobilizing potential of texts which represent problems as well as solutions. Eva adopts a fraternal, friendly relationship with Huberto that is imbued with its own erotic history and posited as a temporary political alliance. However, it is rejected as a model for ideal relations between women and men within a narrative that ends in transition—political transition in the state, transitional relations between women and men—as the Utopian discourse of a reworked romance is both relativized and reiterated.

The representation of bodies in Allende's work is inseparable from the issue of her magical realism. Critics have broadly tended either to focus on Allende's debt to García Márquez or to read it as technique. Philip Swanson (1994) gives both of these tendencies a political twist in his analysis of *La casa de los espíritus,* and concludes that the magical eventually retreats as the women become more politically active. However, his assimilation of the magical to happy times now departed and his reduction of magical discourses to the status of anachronisms seem rather schematic. The early part of the novel has its share of horror after all, and the loss of the house identified with Clara is part of 'la época del estropicio' (the destructive era) in which the Pinochet coup takes place (Swanson 1994: 232). Moreover, the novel does not seem to support the parallel between Clara's magic and Trueba's fantasies asserted by Swanson. Rather, Clara's magic is recuperated by Alba in her (collective) narrative while Trueba finally comes to view his own law as part of a ninety-year history of lies.

A more productive line of enquiry is opened up by William Rowe's rearticulation of magical-realism, which he equates broadly with 'the

suspension of Enlightenment rationalism with its emotion of superstition' (Rowe and Schelling 1991: 214). He traces its development to 'the imposition of the label "idolatry" upon native cultures [which] both foregrounded magic and denied it any cognitive dimension' (1991: 214). Magic thus became a marginal, syncretic,

> alternative knowledge . . . shared by different social classes [and] primarily the province of women . . . In a second sense, insofar as the term has been used say of Arguedas' work, it involves native ritual practices which include not only the idea of magic as action produced by 'irrational' agencies but also a network of shared meanings which the practitioner engages with and reproduces.
>
> (Rowe and Schelling 1991: 214)

In neither case is it reducible to the fantasy projections of individual desire.

Rowe goes on to note that magical belief is not treated exclusively as positive, but that its legitimation 'can be a vindication of pre-capitalist culture, against the logic of capitalist accumulation and positivist social engineering' (Rowe and Schelling 1991: 214). To this extent Allende's refashioning of the national allegory in *La casa de los espíritus* can be seen as a representation of a hybrid culture which differs from both the authoritarian capitalist modernization discourse of the regime and from the proletarianized vision of the Unidad Popular. Rather than an uncritical romanticization of *campesino* and female magical discourses, it is an evaluation of their power/knowledge relationships from the perspective of an outsider discourse—a discourse which proposes an ethics and politics of equality which does not threaten the integrity of equal embodied subjects. Where either the magical or the scientific are analysed as constructing subjects unequally, perpetuating inequality and/or violating the integrity of bodies, they are critiqued or abandoned. This is a postmodern relativization of discourses which confronts the politico-ethical dilemma of addressing conflict *between* discursive regimes. It also effects the troubling of the discursive boundaries between magical and non-magical to which Rowe refers.

In *La casa de los espíritus*, for example, *campesino* knowledge is represented as more efficacious than Western scientific knowledge in dealing with the plague of ants. This is a particularly richly layered scene in which the son who is modernizing distances himself from the discourse of his father yet has to recognize its validity. At the same time, the Western capitalist system is savaged for its 'black magic', for its reduction of people, the land, and knowledge to commodities, and for the large-scale destruction of peoples and territories set in train by these economic and discursive relations. Furthermore, the *campesino* resists this system with a narrative which symbolizes an alternative discursive relation to Nature, that of a conversation which places humans on an equal, not superior, level with the other inhabitants of the earth in relations of ecological negotiation. At first the son and the capitalist can only read this narrative literally, from the perspective of discourses which are constructed in the devaluation of the other. However, in the alliances between the different generations of *campesino* men and the Del Valle women the narrative proposes a place for both groups in an alternative narrative of the nation, presenting *campesino* patriarchy as different from the landowner's yet still in need of transformation.

The scene which ties these issues most closely to the integrity of bodies in *La casa de los espíritus* is the much commented-upon autopsy/rape of Rosa which leads to the symbolic silencing of Clara. Debra Castillo has written persuasively of the productive potential of analysing silence in writing by women. In this case it is a form of internal resistance to the regime which continues in Clara's spiritualist activities. As Swanson has noted, her second silence is part of an outward-looking rebellion which takes various public forms (Swanson 1994: 228).

Like silence, the discourse of love has made some critics uncomfortable and needs to be analysed in its specific (re)articulations. This is not the domain of the isolated couple of heterosexual romance, in which the dominant male and submissive female supplement one another's lack. Instead it offers a spectrum of affective relations which construct subjects respectful of the trace of the other, a will to relationship, perhaps, which can construct an equality in difference.

Towards the end of *Eva Luna*, Eva's bodily integrity is restored when she realizes that she has started menstruating again. She inscribes this in a discourse of love as an openness to a relation of mutual desire with the other, in this case with Rolf. This begins in companionship, in shared dreams and fears in the jungle, taking on an erotic dimension. It does not exhaust their relations, however. Eva is embedded in multiple relationships with others, across a spectrum of affect which sometimes includes sex but in which non-eroticized relations are highly valued. The dual ending may reintroduce a particularly valued *gran amor* (great love) but it effectively relativizes

Romantic versions of it: unlike Zulema, Eva will not die for or in love. She seeks not to annihilate Rolf's difference or her own, but to weave a collective story in which each participates equally, a conversation in which divergent histories are brought together. The Utopia inscribed here can thus be read in terms of the Chile of the transition to democracy. Suspicion of the authoritarian regime's motivation is coupled with hope for the possibilities of a better future. This hope emerges in the privileging of gender difference in the empowerment of women readers, the continuing struggle in both authoritarian and pluralist regimes, the representation of political alliances with Left men.[4]

The deconstruction of the Liberal Enlightenment subject has tended to rearticulate an ideal postmodern subject as infinitely mobile, while the deconstruction of oppressive sex/gender configurations in Western societies has tended to reduce the body to pure libidinality. As Spivak (1993) has reiterated, if the subject 'effect' is 'useful'—and in the case of the disappearances it is fundamental—then it can be deployed strategically (1993: 5). In *La casa de los espíritus,* economically privileged subjects are transformed through respect for the other, while Eva Luna's self at the end of her narration is indelibly marked with the traces of the others who have peopled her life in different kinds of relationships. The vision of subjectivity which emerges is kaleidoscopic, and memory mobilizes history not in the real time of events but in the simultaneity of each successive present,

> Yo escribía cada día un nuevo episodio, inmersa por completo en el mundo que creaba con el poder omnímodo de las palabras, transformada en un ser disperso, producida hasta el infinito, viendo mi propio reflejo en múltiples espejos, viviendo innumerables vidas, hablando con muchas voces.
>
> (Allende 1988: 273)

> Every day I would write a new episode, completely immersed in the world I was creating with the all-encompassing power of words, transformed into a scattered self, repeated to infinity, glimpsing my own image in multiple mirrors, living innumerable lives, talking with many voices.

In this narrative various subaltern figures undergo fables of transformation, yet Allende's texts do not explore 'the heterogeneity of the subaltern' (Spivak 1993: 5) to the same degree in all cases. Broadly speaking *La casa de los espíritus* recognizes the subaltern *nana* but situates her entirely in the borrowed discourses of the dominant order. In *Eva Luna,* by contrast, Consuelo is the author of counter-discourses and Eva becomes an author of publicly circulated (televized) stories. Kavita Panjabi has argued persuasively that the figure of Tránsito Soto moves from the margins of Trueba's world to a central role which illustrates the interdependency of prostitute and wife in patriarchy and the need for the struggle of the women's movements to encompass *all* women (Panjabi 1991). She is nonetheless a sketchy figure in comparison with the narrative space occupied by the privileged female characters, and to this extent contributes to the long history of writing in Latin America which effectively silences subaltern women.

So while the integrity of bodies in Allende's work represents a powerful counter-discourse to both authoritarian and pluralist regimes, these texts cannot be said to harness the empirical 'thickness of description' (Geertz 1983) which testimonial pursues with varying degrees of success. They do, however, reposition different subaltern groups and legitimate subaltern discourses, while, in **Eva Luna,** subaltern women move from the textual margins of Allende's writing to the foreground.

Both locally and globally, then, Allende's writing constructs readings which are intimately bound to the political struggles of women. In the seminar room, absences and problematic issues can be productively mobilized to discuss the sex/gender/sexuality systems of different cultural contexts. The readability of these texts and their critical engagement with familiar narratives—family romance, the *telenovela*—enables political, ethical, and discursive dilemmas to be worked through in relation to theory which is otherwise often intractable in its performativity, universalism, and abstraction. This is a space where it is also possible to bring together other texts whose availability is often limited. The question remains, however, as to how work carried out in the 'teaching machine' can play a wider role in the transformation of postcolonial relations, in different discursive spaces and political movements.

Notes

1. All references will be to the following editions of Allende's novels: *La casa de los espíritus,* 18th edn. (Barcelona, 1985), *De amor y de sombra,* 3rd edn. (Barcelona, 1984), *Eva Luna,* 3rd edn. (Mexico, DF). Unless otherwise indicated, all translations are my own.

2. Consuelo's employer, Professor Jones, has no interest in trying to save the indian's life and, indeed, is eager to add an indian mummy to his 'museo de estatuas humanas' (museum of human statues), in true colonialist fashion.

3. *Mestizaje* is affirmed uncritically in Karrer's article as it has been in much academic writing on Latin America. For a more critical discussion of recent Latin American theorizations of hybridity, see *Travesía,* 1/2 (1992), and Rowe and Schelling (1991).

4. These alliances assume a clear consciousness of the machismo that has to be resisted, not least as a construction of desire in some forms of romance. Carlos Monsiváis is one of the few contemporary male cultural critics in Latin America to analyse machismo in both its historical and contemporary modes. For an introduction to his work which includes articles by a range of male critics, see *Fem's* special issue, 'Hombres', 18 (Apr.-May 1981).

List of Works Cited

Aguirre Rehbein, Edna (1991), 'Isabel Allende's *Eva Luna* and the Act/Art of Narrating', in Riquelme Rojas and Aguirre Rehbein (1991), 179-88.

Allende, Isabel (1984), *De amor y de sombra,* 3rd edn. (Barcelona).

——. (1985), *La casa de los espíritus,* 18th edn. (Barcelona).

——. (1988), *Eva Luna,* 3rd edn. (Mexico, DF).

Boyle, Catherine (1992), *Chilean Theatre 1973-1985* (Rutherford, NJ).

Carvalho, Susan de (1993-4), 'The Male Narrative Perspective in the Fiction of Isabel Allende', *Journal of Hispanic Research, 2.*

Castillo, Debra (1992), *Talking Back: Toward a Latin American Feminist Literary Criticism* (Ithaca, NY).

Chuchryk, Patricia (1989), in Jane S. Jaquette (ed.), *The Women's Movement in Latin America: Feminism and the Transition to Democracy* (Boston, 1989), 149-84.

Franco, Jean (1992), 'Going Public: Reinhabiting the Private', in George Yudice, Jean Franco, and Juan Flores (eds.), *On Edge: The Crisis of Contemporary Latin American Culture* (Minneapolis, 1992).

——. (1990), *Plotting Women: Gender and Representation in Mexico* (London).

García Johnson, Ronie-Richele (1994), 'The Struggle for Space: Feminism and Freedom in *The House of the Spirits*', *Revista Hispánica Moderna,* 47/1 (June).

Geertz, Clifford (1983), *Local Knowledge: Further Essays in Interpretive Anthropology* (New York).

Gimbernat de González, Ester (1991), 'Entre principio y final: la madre/materia de la escritura en *Eva Luna*', in Riquelme Rojas and Aguirre Rehbein (1991).

Gubar, Susan (1994), 'Feminist Misogyny: Mary Wollstonecraft and the Paradox of "It Takes One To Know One"', *Feminist Studies,* 20/3 (Fall), 453-73.

Karrer, Wolfgang (1991), 'Transformation and Transvestism in *Eva Luna,*' in Riquelme Rojas and Aguirre Rehbein (1991), 151-63.

Martin, Gerald (1989), *Journeys Through the Labyrinth* (London).

Mora, Gabriela (1987), 'Las novelas de Isabel Allende y el papel de la mujer como ciudadana', *Ideologies and Literature* (Spring).

Panjabi, Kavita (1991), 'Tránsito Soto: From Periphery to Power', in Riquelme Rojas and Aguirre Rehbein (1991), 11-19.

Riquelme Rojas, Sonia, and Aguirre Rehbein, Edna (1991) (eds.), *Critical Approaches to Isabel Allende's Novels* (New York).

Rojas, Mario (1986), 'Aproximación socio-lingüística a la narrativa de Isabel Allende', in Marcello Coddou, *Los libros tienen sus propios espíritus* (Xalapa).

Rowe, William, and Schelling, Vivienne (1991), *Memory and Modernity: Popular Culture in Latin America* (London).

Spivak, Gayatri Chakravorty (1993), *Outside in the Teaching Machine* (London).

Swanson, Philip (1994), 'Tyrants and Trash: Sex, Class and Culture in *La casa de los espíritus*', *Bulletin of Hispanic Studies*, 71: 217-37.

Zurita, Raúl (1993), 'Chile: Literature, Language and Society (1973-1983)', *Travesía*, 2/2.

TITLE COMMENTARY

The House of the Spirits

RONIE-RICHELE GARCIA-JOHNSON (ESSAY DATE 1 MARCH 1991)

SOURCE: Garcia-Johnson, Ronie-Richele. "The Struggle for Space: Feminism and Freedom in *The House of the Spirits*." *Revista Hispanica Moderna* 47, no. 1 (June 1994): 184-93.

In the following essay, originally delivered as a thesis presentation on March 1, 1991, Garcia-Johnson examines the subtle feminist assertion in The House of the Spirits, *noting that the women in the novel gain empowerment by first controlling their bodies and their living spaces.*

Ayúdame a subir, Lucrecia, por estas paredes, veré mi dolor; si no hundiré con alaridos la casa de mi padre.

Melibea, *La Celestina*, Auto XIX

The temporal setting of the action in *The House of the Spirits*[1] spans fifty years[2]—from the early twenties to about 1974. Historically, and fictionally, within the novel, these were the years in which the women's movement began to gather strength, and then gain progress. While it is apparent that Allende has traced the development of women's struggle for freedom in her novel, some critics have suggested that Nivea, Clara, Blanca, and Alba are allegorical characters which epitomize women at various phases of Chilean social and political history. Michael Handelsman has proposed that Nivea symbolized the early suffragist movement, Clara, more personal statements of liberty, Blanca, the movement towards free and healthy passion, and Alba, the consolida-

tion of these distinct forms of protest and their most recent successes (57-62). Marjorie Agosín asserts that the novel is "*feminocéntrica*" (455). Patricia Hart argues that Clara and Blanca "indulge in passive behavior" (50). Gabriela Mora has insisted that, while both male and female characters broke some stereotypes, Allende's female characters were not feminists (53-61). While the insightful arguments of Handelsman, Hart, Agosín and Mora lead to various conclusions, a spatial interpretation of the novel contributes to the idea that the Trueba women were proponents of their own independence.

A thorough and complex understanding of *The House of the Spirits* demands spatial interpretation, and thus a spatial examination of the treatment of women in the novel is imperative as well. There are treasures hidden in the spaces and rooms of Allende's novel, where the idea that bodies and structures are both houses, and that they are inseparable and essential, is fundamental. Careful examination reveals that, besides the bloody political battle between the military and the liberals, there is another war in the work. The battle of the sexes is cleverly manifested in the continuous struggle for space in the house; the main house in *The House of the Spirits* is a divided one. Allende's magnificent representation of the fight for dominance between men and women, the discordant coexistence of the male and female, is a prime example of the author's perception and presentation of a universal theme.

Allende utilized spatial symbolism to emphasize and parallel the actions of female characters as they sought to overcome the tyranny of patriarchy. In her novel, structures, and the spaces they contain, serve as metaphors for or symbols of social and political barriers. Rather than allowing these metaphorical or symbolic obstacles to determine their lives, the women of the Trueba family overcame them. Clara, Blanca, and Alba managed to defeat Esteban Trueba, who, with traditional notions of honor, of a woman's "place," and of sexuality, attempted to possess and confine these women. The Trueba women confronted Esteban in his own space, usurped his control of that area, expanded their lives into alternative spaces, or left Trueba's property altogether. Trueba and "his" women were contenders struggling to dominate the space they should have shared; by the end of the novel, Trueba found that he had lost the battle and the war.

Trueba's attitude towards women, "possessing" them, and keeping them within his own structures became apparent spatially in the beginning of the novel. After he learned of Rosa the Beautiful's death, he regretted not having married her sooner and he thought that, if he had known that she was to die, he would have "built her a palace studded with treasures from the ocean floor," "kidnapped her and locked her up," and only he "would have had the key" (36).[3] According to Trueba, his betrothed would have never been "stolen" from him by "death" (34) if he had kept her to himself. Like many traditional fathers and husbands, Trueba regarded his women jealously and attempted to confine them as treasure in a chest to maintain their loyalty. So intense was Trueba's determination to keep his women with him that he prepared a tomb with a place for not only himself, but for his wife and his long-dead Rosa. No one, or thing, was going to "steal" his women from him again.

No structure, however, could keep Clara isolated and protected from the outside world. Clara had inherited her mother Nivea's determination to have her own way; she was a strong, willful woman. While Nivea enthusiastically promoted feminist causes, Clara quietly continued her own fight for freedom within her own home, the home that Trueba had built for her. Clara did not have to physically and permanently leave the structure of the house to escape the domination of her husband. She found freedom and battled Trueba with various spatial maneuvers. She existed, spiritually, in another space or dimension, and brought the outside world inside the space of the house to her. She manipulated the space within the house as she pleased and, when all other techniques failed, she locked herself up, in her own secluded space, out of Trueba's reach. This spatial analysis agrees with Agosín's interpretation; according to Agosín, Clara "inhabited her own space and her own imagination" (452)[4] and thus "evaded the presence of her spouse" (452)[5]

Clara had developed the habit of seeking alternative mental spaces in which to dwell as a child in her father's home.[6] She would escape her immediate reality as she read a book, or imagined herself in far-away places. Her "magic" and her attempts to move articles about with the power of her mind distanced her from the "real" world.[7] Once she was married, Clara maintained her secret, interior universe. As she prepared to give birth to her first child, she announced: "I think I'm going to levitate" (113). Clara "meant that she wanted to rise to a level that would allow her to leave behind the discomfort and heaviness of pregnancy and the deep fatigue that had begun to seep into her bones. She entered one of her long

periods of silence . . ." (113). This last sentence is a key to Allende's use of pregnancy as a metaphor. Allende has said: "I need long periods of silence . . . because the books build up inside of me little by little. It's like expecting a baby for some time" (Foster 45). Clara was pregnant with more than a physical child, she was pregnant with love, creativity, and what would later be born as a text. This confirms Agosín's idea that Clara's silence was far from passive, it was a kind of writing (450). Whether Clara's silence is interpreted as a retreat, a refuge, as Agosín has termed it (453), or as a clever victory over the mundane, it is clear that she entered an alternative space, a "closed world free from any masculine insertion" (Handelsman 59)[8] as she "levitated" in silence.

Although, at the moment when Clara was preparing to give birth Trueba understood that this silence was a "last refuge," (113) he later became distressed. He "wanted control over that undefined and luminous material that lay within her and that escaped him even in those moments when she appeared to be dying of pleasure" (96). The patriarch "realized that Clara did not belong to him and that if she continued living in a world of apparitions . . . she probably never would" (96).[9] Trueba could build a house to contain [his] wife, and he could enter the space within her body, but he would never be allowed to enter the home she had built for herself inside her own head. Clara had defeated male domination.[10]

Clara's magic and the happiness she found as she practiced it was attractive to artists, poets, and spiritualists. The "big house on the corner" became a gathering place for these marginal people as Clara invited them into the space of her home. Clara also opened her home to the unfortunates who needed food and shelter.[11] By encouraging these people to enter the exterior world that represented her interior self, Clara let them into the space that was forbidden to Trueba. Not surprisingly, Trueba objected to the carnivalization[12] of his home and the daily parade that marched through it. He insisted that the "big house on the corner" was not a thoroughfare and coldly ordered that the celebration of the everyday be stopped. Clara and her children, especially Nicolás, continued to live as they pleased, and to fill the space as they desired, while Trueba was out of town. Upon his return, the atmosphere of the house changed, and the party was over—temporarily. Trueba continually struggled to dominate the space of the house in the city and his family fought back with determined consistency.

As she found herself trapped in a particular space and time, and could not divorce Trueba (Agosín 452), Clara had to manipulate her immediate area. She attempted to move objects with the power of her mind, and she redefined the limits of the structure Trueba had built for her in the "big house on the corner."

> In response to Clara's imagination and the requirements of the moment, the noble, seignorial architecture began sprouting all sorts of extra little rooms, staircases, turrets, and terraces. Each time a new guest arrived, the bricklayers would arrive and build another addition to the house. The big house on the corner soon came to resemble a labyrinth.
>
> (224)

The use of the word "labyrinth" is telling, for it suggests a space that, rather than possessing a masculine, linear order, is as complex as the intuition of a woman.[13] Trueba's perfect, logical space was transformed by a woman. Instead of allowing his space to enclose her, she opened it and recreated it to suit her.

The struggle for space came to a climax while Clara was still alive and surrounded by her eccentric friends[14] and Trueba campaigned for the office of Senator of the Republic. Clara needed space for her continuous spiritual celebrations, and Trueba needed space for the operations of his political party.

> The house filled with political propaganda and with the members of his party, who practically took it by storm, blending in with the hallway ghosts, the Rosicrucians, and the three Mora sisters. Clara's retinue was gradually pushed into the back rooms of the house . . .
>
> (224)

The house became a house divided as "an invisible border arose between the parts of the house occupied by Esteban Trueba and those occupied by his wife" (225). As the house has traditionally represented the unification of its occupants, the "invisible" spatial division within the house is a symbol, not only of the Truebas's spliced relationship, but of the separation of the sexes.[15]

Trueba believed that the spirituality that captivated his wife and her friends was for women only.[16] Before Nicolás departed to India, he told him "I hope you return a man, because I'm fed up with all your eccentricities" (271). He considered his other son, Jaime, to be eccentric as well, because he cared for the underprivileged and didn't want to join his father in business. Jaime, therefore, was not a "well-adjusted man" (229).

Other readers have noticed that with some special exceptions, such as Jaime, Pedro Tercero García, and the prostitute Tránsito Soto, the men in the novel operate with logical thinking while the women depend on their spiritual and emotional strength[17] to survive.[18] This presentation of men and women is based on beliefs which are prevalent in Latin America.[19] The author of **The House of the Spirits** herself has stated that "at times science is less efficient than magic."[20] As the "big house on the corner" in Allende's novel is a symbol for the family, the house naturally reflects the fact that the family, and the world, exists only because of the differences between two groups: women and men. It is not surprising that Allende chose to represent the schism spatially; as she spoke of her childhood, she noted that men and women were "segregated" (Allende, Address), and this implies a spatial understanding of the problem.

In the arena of the house in the city, Clara was victorious as she defended her independence.[21] While the "façade of the house underwent no alterations" (225) the most intimate interior of the house belonged to, was dominated by, and represented Clara. Even "the rear garden," once a perfect, strict emulation of "a French garden" became hers, "a tangled jungle in which every type of plant and flower had proliferated and where Clara's birds kept up a steady din, along with many generations of cats and dogs" (225). The house belonged to Clara.

Campos discusses this conversion of space and, combining her ideas with those of Gastón Bachelard, concludes that the house "is Clara" . . . the space of the "unconsciousness, of the Imagination, of the mother" (24).[22] Agosín states that Clara is the "soul" of the house on the corner (454).[23] The validity of these ideas is confirmed with Allende's statement that the basement of the house was a womb (Allende, Personal). By manipulating the space of the house, it began to represent Clara, instead of Trueba. Gone was the house that Trueba had desired, planned, and built. His house was not a reflection of himself, as he had wanted, but of Clara, the family, and his relationship to them. One might venture as far [as] to say that the house was female. With spatial symbols, Allende communicates the message that, although the patriarchy may seem to be in control, women and traditionally feminine spirits prevail behind the façade.[24]

After Trueba slapped her and knocked her teeth out as she tried to defend her daughter, Clara's response to his physical violence was twofold. First, she refused to speak [to] him and then, she locked herself in her room. Clara's denial of access to the space of her room, of her body—the spaces which Trueba had violated—was a powerful weapon. Even more potent was her refusal to allow Trueba to enter her mental space; she would never verbally communicate with him again. Clara had once again defeated Trueba with his own space; he was the one who had built and decorated her room. While some have mistaken both of these manuevers for passivity, spatial analysis demonstrates that Clara's actions were far from passive, and thus provides evidence to support Agosín's assertions regarding feminine silence in the novel. Clara had refused the masculine body access to her feminine world, and she swore not to enter masculine verbal space. Trueba was, more than frustrated, defeated; he could not touch Clara's soul, let alone control it.

Blanca, Trueba's only daughter, continued the tradition of independence begun by her grandmother. Although she did not rally for women's suffrage, or practice magic like her mother to assert her freedom, Blanca defied her father. Trueba would have never sanctioned the love that Blanca had for the peasant leader Pedro Tercero García. The house that divided Blanca and Pedro Tercero García was the elaborate symbol of elite wealth and social grace; her home at The Three Marias sharply contrasted with the little hut in which her peasant lover lived. It would have been absurd for Pedro to cross into Trueba's space, to visit the big house, and it would have been scandalous for Blanca to debase herself by setting foot in the peasant's quarters. Nevertheless, Blanca asserted her freedom with her actions and by symbolically passing through space.

Instead of opening her window and waiting for her lover to climb over a wall and into her father's space, Blanca crossed the barriers of her father's home herself. She waited until her father was asleep, until the landscape was hidden in the darkness, to lock her bedroom door and leave her father's house and domination. She would slip out the window, climb down a trellis covered with flowers, and run in the darkness. She did not go to the peasant quarters to meet her lover—that space, technically, belonged to her father.[25] Instead, she and Pedro Tercero García met far from the structures, the houses and the huts, which symbolized the tyranny[26] imposed over both of them and found each other by the banks of the stream, which for them, represented the flow of life, freedom, and passion.

Trueba's characteristic reaction to Blanca's defiance was to violently regain his powerful authority over her. He beat her and forced her to marry the Count. When Blanca arrived at the big house the morning after her wedding to visit her mother, Trueba ordered her to return quickly to her husband. By leaving the hotel to go to her mother's house and space, Blanca was symbolically negating her marriage. Trueba sent Blanca away, out of his space. He could not tolerate the fact that his daughter had willfully negated his position by leaving his house in order to meet Pedro Tercero García. Trueba knew that, by leaving the protective space of his house, Blanca had escaped his masculine domination, and that she aspired to sexual freedom by inviting a man of her own choice to penetrate her physical space. While Blanca did obey her father and marry the Count, she did manage to keep a sacred space within her womb for the product of her union with Pedro: Alba.[27] Later in the novel, Blanca subverted her father's dominion with the brazenly defiant act of bringing Pedro into Trueba's home.

While Clara didn't care to concern herself with the daily up-keep of the house, Blanca, and later, Alba, became devoted to its maintenance. They would feed the members of the household, keep the birds singing, the plants green, and do the gardening. During Trueba's absence, these women effectively ran the household. Bachelard discussed the idea that, while men build the external house, its is the women who, immersed in the day-to-day project of maintenance, make the house livable, or better—make it a home. "In the intimate harmony of walls and furniture, it may be said that we become conscious of a house that is built by women, since men only know how to build a house from the outside" (68). In fact, as time passed, the women of the "big house on the corner" were responsible for the renovation and rebirth of the house. Bachelard is helpful with the concept of the renewal of the house as well: "housewifely care weaves the ties that unite a very ancient past to the new epoch" (68). At the end of the novel it is Alba who convinces her father to renew the house and resurrect the garden, the symbol of freedom. Allende's message seems to be that with love and patience, women maintain their nations as well as their homes.

Alba's youth coincided with the late sixties and the early seventies, a time of sexual revolution. Despite the ideas of the youths, those of the older, empowered generations did not look favorably upon these developments. Trueba would never have consented to Alba having a pre-marital sexual relationship with anyone. He wouldn't have tolerated mere courtship if her suitor were

FROM THE AUTHOR

ALLENDE ON CLARA'S SUBTLE RESISTANCE TO PATRIARCHY IN *THE HOUSE OF THE SPIRITS*

All the women in my book are feminists in their fashion; that is, they ask to be free and complete human beings, to be able to fulfill themselves, not to be dependent on men. Each one battles according to her own character and within the possibilities of the epoch in which she happens to be living. Clara lived at the beginning of the century, when divorce was unthinkable, as was working outside the home. She was subject to a despotic husband whom she did not love, but she freed herself from him by the only path possible for her: the path of her spiritual life and her preoccupation for the poor, the helpless. She was naturally outraged by every form of injustice, but she did not have sufficient information, and possessed neither the power nor the tools necessary to bring about a "women's liberation," as we understand the term now, a half century later.

Allende, Isabel. Excerpt from *Conversations with Isabel Allende.* Austin, Tex: University of Austin Press, 1999, p. 41.

someone like Miguel, a radical leftist. Like her mother, however, Alba did not let her grandfather's attitude stop her from loving the man of her choice. For, in Agosín's words, Alba was "the one destined to leave the benevolent space of the house on the corner"[28] to join the struggle for social justice (456).

Alba did not run away from her home to live as she desired. Although at first she and Miguel would meet in his apartment, she found that the most comfortable solution was to bring Miguel into Trueba's home, where "in the labyrinth of the rear rooms, where no one ever went, they could make love undisturbed." The use of the word "labyrinth" reminds the reader that the house was still Clara's house, even though, after her death, it deteriorated for lack of her laughter. "One by one the lovers tried out all the abandoned rooms, and finally chose an improvised nest in the depths of the basement" (329). Alba would

lead Miguel in through the garden (the symbol of freedom) into the basement. It is spatially significant that the lovers went to the basement because their love, like the basement was "underground"—a secret.[29]

The basement is, as the reader will remember, also a metaphor for the womb.[30] Alba was leading Miguel to the most intimate of spaces, the space where life, (and text, in the cases of Clara and Alba,) is created. Their entrance into the basement was symbolic of sexual intercourse as well as of a more profound act of love. Alba and Miguel rearranged the space Trueba had created, as had her grandmother Clara, although they transformed the basement into a love nest.[31] Alba and Miguel utilized the long-forgotten artifacts they found to turn their underground "nest" into an "nuptial chamber" (329). Although they occupied the same space that Alba's grandparents had, Alba and Miguel shared a more fruitful love, and they did so by transforming the vestiges of an old world into a new "home."

Of all the actions of the women who had gone before her, Alba's spatial statement was by far the most assertive.[32] Instead of preserving her intimate space with silence and magic, as Clara had, or leaving her "father's" home as Blanca had, Alba lived as she pleased in the space where she had grown up. This spatial relationship represents a confrontation with the patriarchy. Alba and Miguel's complicity as they recreated the basement, the history of the Truebas, to suit themselves, suggests that a new generation, women and men alike, would overcome that patriarchy. In Campos's words, they were the "salvation of the future" (25).[33]

The patriarchy, however, manipulated more than the freedom of the Trueba women.[34] Just as Trueba attempted to control "his" women within the structures he had built for them, those with power in the country of which Allende wrote dominated the lives of workers, farmers, and every underprivileged citizen within the political structure. As Alba, and all the women of *The House of the Spirits* battled for their freedom as women, they struggled for political justice. The struggle for independence was not just a feminine one; it was a fight for the rights of all classes, creeds, and sexes. Clara had always been interested in the welfare of the poor. Blanca not only loved a leftist peasant, she hid this wanted man in her father's home after the Coup. Alba hid weapons for the resistance forces and her radical, guerrilla lover in her grandfather's home. She took food from the cupboards and sold furniture, including the portrait of her grandmother Clara, to feed the poor who were starving as a result of the Military's policies. Alba directly defied the government, and her grandfather, the symbol of conservatism, as she utilized Trueba's space and that which it contained. In **The House of the Spirits,** feminism and leftist liberalism were united in the struggle to preserve the Chilean home; feminine auras and the forces of freedom alike dwelt in the "house of the spirits".

Notes

This article originally appeared as one chapter of a senior honors thesis presented to the Department of History and Literature at Harvard College on March 1, 1991. The complete thesis may be found in the Harvard Archives under the name of Ronie-Richele Garcia. I wish to express my gratitude to Ellen Lokos, my thesis advisor and mentor, for her excellent guidance and support as this work progressed. I am also indebted to the Ford Foundation for the fellowship grant which allowed me to revise this thesis.

1. The edition referred to is *The House of the Spirits*. Trans. Magda Bogin. New York: Bantam, 1986. All cited page numbers will refer to this edition.

2. For an example, see Marcelo Coddou ("Historia" 170). Also see Coddou (Leer 82), where he argues that, in Allende's novel, women have access to more than their immediate spaces.

3. Readers of Cervantes's *Novelas Ejemplares* will remember the Estremaduran's paranoid determination to keep his wife imprisoned in the space of his house, and the disastrous results of this obsession in "El celoso extremeño."

4. This is my translation. Clara "habitaba por su propio espacio y su propia imaginación."

5. This is my translation of "evade la presencia de su marido."

6. Agosín supports this idea. She argues that Clara found refuge from "poder autoritario" within herself (451) and also notes that Clara's space was one of magic (449).

7. I disagree with Hart's conclusion that clairvoyance in the novel is a metaphor for passivity (53). Agosín's assertion that Clara's silence was not passive (449-450) supports the notion that Clara's preoccupation with the spiritual was not submissive—Trueba could not restrain Clara in the world to which she transcended.

8. This is my translation of "mundo cerrado y libre de cualquier intromisión masculina."

9. At this point, it is interesting to note the work of Jane S. Jaquette, who states that "The image of the female as mysterious, unfathomable, somehow beyond men's rules, is the second significant archetype in Latin American literature" (20).

10. Handelsman reminds his readers that despite Trueba's facile violation of the peasants, he could not penetrate Clara's interior; Clara had found a "personal state of

feminine autonomy and liberty in a patriarchal and *machista* world that was represented by Esteban" (59-60, my translation). The actual quote is "estado personal de autonomía y libertad femeninas en un mundo patriarcal y machista represando por Esteban."

11. Agosín speaks of Clara's social work "Clara brinda tenura y alimentos a todos los seres indigentes que deambulan por su inmensa casa de la esquina y, por extensión, en el país" (449). My translation: Clara invites tenderness and food to all indigent beings that walked through her immense house on the corner, and by extention, in the country."

12. The use of this word implies that Trueba's home was not static; it was unpredictable, like the streets described by Da Matta (208).

13. Women and men, of course, share logic as well as intuition. Allende's novel, however, seems to suggest that the differences between some men and women are found in the disparity between logic and intuition.

14. Handelsman suggests that these "eccentrics" represent Clara's court, and this metaphor implies Claras matriarchy and the "*poder que la mujer ejerce en*" (power that the woman exerts in Latin America (60).

15. In this discussion of the house and street in Brazil during carnival, Da Matta notes that "The street implies movement, novelty, and action, while the house implies harmony, warmth, and calm" (208). Clearly, the Trueba house seems to fit Da Matta's description of the street. This inversion of the street/house relationship reflects the idea that something was amiss in the "big house on the corner."

16. Muñoz notes that Esteban Trueba thought that the home, the kitchen, magic, and religion, were for women. He also refers to the power of the system of patriarchy. (442).

17. Talmor, for one, notes that with the exception of Jaime, women in the novel "grasp . . . what is good, true, and beautiful" while "men grasp properties, capital" and "jobs" (310).

18. See Earle. He believes that Clara's testimony allowed her to survive, and that "the true heart of literature is neither pleasure nor knowledge, but survival" (551).

19. According to Evelyn P. Stevens, "*Marianismo,*" (not to be confused with a Catholic movement,) the "cult of feminine spiritual superiority, which teaches that women are semi-divine, morally superior to and spiritually stronger than men," is "just as prevalent as *machismo*" (91) in Latin America.

20. This was Allende's reply to a question about the episode of Mr. Brown and the ants: "a veces la ciencia es menos eficiente que la magia" (Moody, "Conversación" 58).

21. Rojas discusses the idea that the patriarch loses control of his home and he links the idea of Clara's importance to the house in Bachelard's work. Rojas's interpretation, however, leads him towards his concept of the "*imagen caleidoscópica*" ("Caleidoscopio" 84).

22. This is my translation. "es Clara" . . . "inconsciente, del Imaginario, de la madre."

23. This is my translation of "alma."

24. This suggestion is supported by the fact that, after her death, the house "changed into a ruin" and the garden "became a thick underbrush" (296). Clara's room, like

her ghost, "remained intact" (297). Handelsman notes that the Truebas's world decayed after Clara's death and comments on her importance (60). Rojas also notes this opening of the house ("Aproximación" 96).

25. Campos agrees that Trueba's home in the city is representative of the patriarch (24).

26. Handelsman states that Blanca "*derrumba las barreras sociales entre la clase pobre y la burguesía chilena*" ("collapsed the social barriers between the poor class and the Chilean bourgeiose") (61), as she made love to García; Blanca and her lover thus escaped more than tyranny, but the social system as they left Trueba's structured property.

27. Here it should be noted that the fruit of the prohibited union was a cross between the rich and the poor, the elites and the peasants, the city and the country, as Cánovas has explained (122).

28. This is my translation of "la destinada a salir del espacio benevolente de su casa de la esquina."

29. René Campos cites Bachelard's discussion of the significance of the basement and notes that the family treasures were located there (24).

30. Campos states that the basement is the womb. Her interpretation of the consequences of this idea differs from mine. Paraphrasing her argument, the womb is the most intimate space of the mother, and the space of the past, of Imagination, and of myth (25).

31. See Bachelard's chapter entitled "Nests" (90-104).

32. Most critics agree on this point. Hart goes as far [as] to say that Alba represents a "new generation" which broke "the chain of passivity" (54). (I have already argued that Alba's mother and grandmother were not passive.)

33. This is my interpretation of "salvación del futuro".

34. Mora agrees with this statement. She writes that Allende's novels "demonstrate the oppression and the dependence in the woman of the oligarchy as well as in the poor peasant woman." (54). This is my translation of "muestran la opresión y la dependencia tanto en la mujer del oligarca como en la campesina pobre".

Works Cited

Agosín, Marjorie. "Isabel Allende: *La casa de los espíritus*" *Revista Interamericana de Bibliografia* 35 (1985): 448-458.

Allende, Isabel. *La casa de los espíritus.* Barcelona: Plaza y Janes, 1982.

——. *The House of the Spirits.* Trans. Magda Bogin. New York: Bantam, 1986.

——. Address. 31 January 1991.

——. Personal Conversation. 31 January 1991.

Bachelard, Gaston. *The Poetics of Space.* Trans. Maria Jolas. Boston: Beacon Press, 1969.

Campos, Rene. "*La casa de los espíritus*: mirada, espacio, discurso de la otra historia." *Los libros tienen sus propios espíritus.* Ed. Marcelo Coddou. Veracruz: Universidad Veracruzana, 1986, 21-28.

Cervantes Saavedra, Miguel. *Novelas Ejemplares.* Zaragoza: Libreria Bosch, 1974.

Coddou, Marcelo. "*La casa de los espíritus*: De la historia a la historia." *Texto Critico* 11 (1985): 165-172.

——. *Para leer a Isabel Allende: Introduccion a La casa de los espíritus* Concepcion, Chile: Ediciones Literatura Americana Reunida, 1988.

Da Matta, Roberto. "Carnival in Multiple Planes." *Rite, Drama, Festival, Spectacle: Rehearsals Toward a Theory of Cultural Performance.* Ed. John J. MacAloon. Philadelphia: ISHI, 1984.

Earle, Peter G. "Literature as survival: Allende's *The House of the Spirits.*" *Contemporary Literature* 28 (1987): 543-554.

Foster, Douglas. "Isabel Allende unveiled." *Mother Jones* 13 1988: 42-46.

Glickman, Nora. "Los personajes femeninos en *La casa de los espíritus* "*Los libros tienen sus propios espíritus.* Ed. Marcelo Coddou. Veracruz: Universidad Veracruzana, 1986, 54-60.

Handelsman, Michael H. "*La casa de los espíritus* y la evolucion de la mujer moderna." *Letras Femeninas* 14 (1988): 51-63.

Hart, Patricia. *Narrative Magic in the Fiction of Isabel Allende.* Rutherford, N.J.: Fairleigh Dickenson UP, 1989.

Jacquette, Jane S. "Literary Archetypes and Female Role Alternatives: The Woman and the Novel in Latin America." *Female and Male in Latin America.* Ed. Ann Pescatello. Pittsburgh: Pittsburgh UP, 1973, 89-101.

Moody, Michael. "Una conversacion con Isabel Allende. *Chasqui: Revista de literatura latinoamericana* 16 (1987): 51-59.

Mora, Gabriela. "Las novelas de Isabel Allende y el papel de la mujer como ciudadana." *Ideologies and Literature* 2 (1987): 53-61.

Munoz, Willy O. "Las re escrituras de *La casa de los espiritus.*" *Discurso Literario* 5 (1988): 433-454.

Rojas, Fernando de. *La Celestina.* Madrid: Alianza Editorial, 1989.

Rojas, Mario A. "*La casa de los espíritus*, de Isabel Allende: Un caleidoscopio de espejos desordenados." *Los libros tienen sus propios espíritus.* Ed. Marcelo Coddou. Veracruz: Universidad Veracruzana, 1986, 83-90.

Stevens, Evelyn P. "Marianismo: The Other Face of Machismo in Latin America." *Female and Male in Latin America.* Ed. Ann Pescatello. Pittsburgh: Pittsburgh UP, 1973, 89-101.

Talmor, Sascha. "The House of the Truebas." *Durham University Journal* 18(2) (1989): 309-312.

FURTHER READING

Biographies

Allende, Isabel, Jennifer Benjamin, and Sally Engelfried. "Magical Feminist." In *Conversations with Isabel Allende,* edited by John Roden, pp. 383-97. Austin, Tex.: University of Texas Press, 1999.

Interview in which Allende discusses sexuality, death, racism in both South and North America, and the importance of dreams.

Allende, Isabel, and Celia Correas Zapata. "Eva Luna." In *Isabel Allende: Life and Spirits*, translated by Margaret Sayers Peden, pp. 63-70. Houston, Tex.: Arte Publico Press, 2002.

Interview in which Allende shares her views about feminism, analyzes her first marriage, and explores the themes of Eva Luna.

Levine, Linda Gould. "Weaving Life into Fiction." *Latin American Literary Review* 30, no. 60 (July-December 2002): 1-25.

Studies the parallels between Allende's life and her works. Levine centers on the autobiographical elements in Allende's works, analyzes events that have shaped Allende's stories, and evaluates Allende's standing as a female writer and as an exiled Latin American writer.

———. "Chronology." *Latin American Literary Review* 30, no. 60 (July-December 2002): 26-28.

Chronology of major events in Allende's life and career.

Criticism

André, María Claudia. "Breaking through the Maze: Feminist Configurations of the Heroic Quest in Isabel Allende's *Daughter of Fortune* and *Portrait in Sepia*." *Latin American Literary Review* 30, no. 60 (July-December 2002): 74-90.

Exploration of the strategies that the women in Daughter of Fortune *and* Portrait in Sepia *employ to gain control of their bodies, minds, and futures, and the techniques they use to subvert patriarchal power.*

Carvalho, Susan. "Transgressions of Space and Gender in Allende's *Hija de la fortuna*." *Letras Femeninas* 27, no. 2 (fall 2001): 24-41.

Studies the female quest for identity, sexual liberation, and the spatial and emotional journey that Eliza undergoes in Daughter of Fortune.

Hart, Patricia. "Magic Feminism in Isabel Allende's *The Stories of Eva Luna*." In *Multicultural Literatures through Feminist/Poststructuralist Lenses*, edited by Barbara Frey Waxman, pp. 103-36. Knoxville, Tenn.: University of Tennessee Press, 1993.

Outlines the recurring themes of abuse, the use of sex to leverage power, and women's quest to gain control of their bodies and destinies in The Stories of Eva Luna.

Jorgensen, Beth. "'Un punado de críticos': Navigating the Critical Readings of Isabel Allende's Work." *Latin American Literary Review* 30, no. 60 (July-December 2002): 128-46.

Highlights elements of Allende's works that have received little critical analysis. Included are opinions on the parallels between The House of the Spirits *and Gabriel García-Márquez's* One Hundred Years of Solitude; *judgments about Allende's use of stylized language and magic realism, and insights into the autobiographical aspects of Allende's works.*

Karrer, Wolfgang. "Transformation and Transvestism in *Eva Luna*." In *Critical Approaches to Isabel Allende's Novels*, edited by Sonia Riquelme Rojas and Edna Aguirre Rehbein, pp. 151-64. New York: Peter Lang, 1991.

Examines the role of sexuality in gender-based relationships and analyzes the balance of power between machismo men and women and the effeminate.

Lagos, Maria Ines. "Female Voices from the Borderlands: Isabel Allende's *Paula* and *Retrato en sepia*." *Latin American Literary Review* 30, no. 60 (July-December 2002): 112-27.

Examines the disconnectedness of exile, gender-based repression, and the strength of the bonds between mothers and daughters.

Laurila, Marketta. "Isabel Allende and the Discourse of Exile." In *International Women's Writing: New Landscapes of Identity*, edited by Anne E. Brown and Marjanne E. Gooze, pp. 177-86. Westport, Conn.: Greenwood Press, 1995.

Examines feminist strategies that the women in The House of the Spirits *use to survive and succeed in a violent, male-dominated society.*

Panjabi, Kavita. "Tránsito Soto: From Periphery to Power." In *Critical Approaches to Isabel Allende's Novels*, edited by Sonia Riquelme Rojas and Edna Aguirre Rehbein, pp. 11-20. New York: Peter Lang, 1991.

Provides analysis of the character Tránsito Soto's self-reliance and independence in The House of the Spirits *and examines her use of prostitution to gain financial security and influence in a patriarchal society.*

Rivero, Eliana S. "Scheherazade Liberated: *Eva Luna* and Women Storytellers." In *Splintering Darkness: Latin American Writers in Search of Themselves*, edited by Lucia Guerra Cunningham, pp. 143-56. Pittsburgh, Penn.: Latin American Literary Review Press, 1990.

Asserts that mastery of language leads Eva, the protagonist in Eva Luna, *to self-determination and personal control of "her/story."*

Swanson, Philip. "Tyrants and Trash: Sex, Class and Culture in *La casa de los espíritus*." *Bulletin of Hispanic Studies* 71, no. 2 (April 1994): 217-37.

Examines traditional interpretations of feminism in The House of the Spirits, *demonstrating the ways the female characters embrace the populace rather than the elite as a means of challenging political and social structures.*

OTHER SOURCES FROM GALE:

Additional coverage of Allende's life and career is contained in the following sources published by the Gale Group: *Authors and Artists for Young Adults*, Vol. 18; *Concise Dictionary of World Literary Biography*, Vol. 3; *Contemporary Authors*, Vol. 130; *Contemporary Authors*, Brief Entry, Vol. 125; *Contemporary Authors New Revision Series*, Vols. 51, 74; *Contemporary Literary Criticism*, Vols. 39, 57, 97, 170; *Contemporary World Writers*, Ed. 2; *Dictionary of Literary Biography*, Vol. 145; *DISCovering Authors Modules: Multicultural* and *Novelists; DISCovering Authors 3.0; Encyclopedia of World Literature in the 20th Century*, Ed. 3; *Feminist Writers; Hispanic Literature Criticism*, Ed. 1; *Hispanic Writers*, Eds. 1, 2; *Latin American Writers Supplement*, Ed. 1; *Literary Movements for Students*, Vol. 2; *Literature and Its Times*, Vol. 5; *Literature of Developing Nations for Students*, Vol. 1; *Literature Resource Center; Major 20th-Century Writers*, Eds. 1, 2; *Nonfiction Classics for Students*, Vol. 1; *Novels for Students*, Vols. 6, 18; *Reference Guide to Short Fiction*, Ed. 2; *Reference Guide to World Literature*, Ed. 3; *Short Stories for Students*, Vols. 11, 16; *World Literature and Its Times*, Vol. 1; and *World Literature Criticism Supplement*.

MAYA ANGELOU

(1928 -)

(Born Marguerite Johnson) American novelist, memoirist, poet, short story writer, playwright, screenwriter, nonfiction writer, and author of children's books.

Hailed as one of the great voices of contemporary African American literature, Angelou is best known for *I Know Why the Caged Bird Sings* (1970), the first of several autobiographical books. Angelou's literary works have generated critical and popular interest in part because they depict her triumph over formidable social obstacles and her struggle to achieve a sense of identity and self-acceptance. Such themes tie Angelou's writings closely to the concerns of the feminist literary movement. Angelou has also been noted for her vivid portrayals of the strong women in her life—notably Annie Henderson, the paternal grandmother who helped raise her, Mrs. Bertha Flowers, a genteel black woman who helped Angelou recover her speech, and her mother, Vivian Baxter. Critics have praised Angelou's dynamic prose style, poignant humor, and illumination of African American history and consciousness through her portrayal of personal experiences. Angelou has stated, "I speak to the black experience but I am always talking about the human condition—about what we can endure, dream, fail at and still survive."

BIOGRAPHICAL INFORMATION

Angelou was born Marguerite Johnson on April 4, 1928, in St. Louis, Missouri. Her father, Bailey, was a doorkeeper and naval dietician; her mother, Vivian, was a nurse and realtor. Angelou's family lived in Missouri, Arkansas, and California during her childhood. Angelou attended public schools and studied music, dance, and drama privately. From 1954 to 1955, she appeared in a twenty-two-nation tour of the musical *Porgy and Bess* that was sponsored by the U.S. Department of State. Angelou moved to New York to pursue her acting career and performed in several off-Broadway plays including *Calypso Heatwave* in 1957 and *The Blacks* in 1960. Also in 1960, she accepted a position as an assistant administrator in the School of Music and Drama at the University of Ghana in Africa. Angelou taught and performed in several plays at the university before returning to the U.S. in 1966. In 1970, Angelou published her first book, the autobiography *I Know Why the Caged Bird Sings,* which focuses on her struggles throughout her formative years and concludes with the birth of her son, Guy, in 1945. In addition to publishing, Angelou continued to produce, direct, and act in stage productions. In 1974 she directed the film *All Day Long* and, in 1988, directed the film *Down in the Delta.* Angelou has held teaching positions at several universities, including the University of California and the

University of Kansas. She holds honorary degrees from Smith College, Mills College, Lawrence University, and Wake Forest University. Angelou also received a Pulitzer Prize nomination for *Just Give Me a Cool Drink of Water 'fore I Diiie* (1971), a Tony Award nomination for best supporting actress in a 1977 production of *Roots,* and the North Carolina Award in Literature in 1992. In 1993 Angelou performed a reading of her poem "On the Pulse of Morning" at the inauguration of U.S. President Bill Clinton.

MAJOR WORKS

After *I Know Why the Caged Bird Sings,* Angelou published five subsequent volumes in her autobiographical series: *Gather Together in My Name* (1974), *Singin' and Swingin' and Gettin' Merry Like Christmas* (1976), *The Heart of a Woman* (1981), *All God's Children Need Traveling Shoes* (1986), and *A Song Flung up to Heaven* (2002). These works trace her psychological, spiritual, and political odyssey as she emerged from a disturbing and oppressive childhood to become a prominent figure in contemporary American literature. Angelou's quest for self-identity and emotional fulfillment resulted in a number of extraordinary experiences, among them encounters with Dr. Martin Luther King Jr. and Malcolm X. Angelou also describes her involvement with the civil rights and feminist movements in the United States and in Africa, her developing relationship with her son, and the hardships associated with lower-class American life. *All God's Children Need Traveling Shoes* is distinctive in its examination of black America's intellectual and emotional connections with post-colonial Africa. In this work, Angelou describes her four-year stay in Ghana where she worked as a freelance writer and editor. Angelou finds much to venerate about Africa, but gradually realizes that although she has cultural ties to the land of her ancestors, she is nevertheless distinctly American and in many ways isolated from traditional African society. *A Song Flung up to Heaven* begins in 1964 when Angelou returns from Africa to the United States. The book covers her plans to assist Malcolm X and Martin Luther King Jr. with various civil rights activities, and her feelings of loss when both are assassinated. The narrative also recounts her experiences as a performer and writer in African American theatre, her friendships with James Baldwin and other writers, and personal anecdotes including details of a painful love affair. The story ends with Angelou putting pen to paper to begin writing *I Know Why the Caged Bird Sings.* Angelou's poetry, in which she combines terse lyr-

ics with jazz rhythms, addresses social and political issues relevant to African Americans and challenges the validity of traditional American values and myths. In "America," for example, she rejects the notion that justice is available to all Americans, citing such deep-rooted problems as racism and poverty. Angelou directed national attention to humanitarian concerns with her poem "On the Pulse of Morning." In this poem, Angelou calls for recognition of the human failings pervading American history and a renewed national commitment to unity and social improvement.

CRITICAL RECEPTION

Some critics have faulted Angelou's poetry as superficial, citing its dependence on alliteration, heavy use of short lines, and conventional vocabulary. Others have praised the honest and candid nature of her poetry, lauding the strength and personal pride within her verse. Scholars have asserted that Angelou's struggle to create a sense of identity and self-acceptance in both her poetry and prose aligns her firmly within the feminist literary tradition. R. B. Stepto has noted the strong female presence in poems such as "And Still I Rise," commenting that "the 'I' of Angelou's refrain is obviously female and . . . a woman forthright about the sexual nuances of personal and social struggle."

Although some critics fault Angelou's autobiographies as lacking in moral complexity and universality, others praise her narrative skills and impassioned responses to the challenges in her life. Many reviewers have acknowledged *The Heart of a Woman* as sharply focused on women's struggles and issues, and as a self-examination of a mature writer and mother. In a review of this volume, Adam David Miller (see Further Reading) stated, "What she keeps constant throughout the book is that it is the account of a black W-O-M-A-N's life." Overall, while critical response to Angelou's autobiographies has been more favorable than reactions to her poetry, critics generally agree that her writing is an important contribution not only to the autobiography genre, but to American literature as well.

PRINCIPAL WORKS

The Least of These (play) 1966

I Know Why the Caged Bird Sings (autobiography) 1970

Just Give Me a Cool Drink of Water 'fore I Diiie (poetry) 1971

Georgia, Georgia (screenplay) 1972

All Day Long (screenplay) 1974

Gather Together in My Name (autobiography) 1974

Oh Pray My Wings Are Gonna Fit Me Well (poetry) 1975

Singin' and Swingin' and Gettin' Merry Like Christmas (autobiography) 1976

And Still I Rise (poetry) 1978

The Heart of a Woman (autobiography) 1981

Shaker, Why Don't You Sing? (poetry) 1983

All God's Children Need Traveling Shoes (autobiography) 1986

Now Sheba Sings the Song (poetry) 1987

I Shall Not Be Moved (poetry) 1990

Life Doesn't Frighten Me (poetry) 1993

On the Pulse of Morning (poetry) 1993

Wouldn't Take Nothing for My Journey Now (essays) 1993

The Complete Collected Poems of Maya Angelou (poetry) 1994

My Painted House, My Friendly Chicken, and Me (juvenilia) 1994

Phenomenal Woman: Four Poems Celebrating Women (poetry) 1994

Soul Looks back in Wonder (poetry) 1994

Even the Stars Look Lonesome (essays) 1997

A Song Flung up to Heaven (autobiography) 2002

PRIMARY SOURCES

MAYA ANGELOU (POEM DATE 1978)

SOURCE: Angelou, Maya. "Woman Work." In *And Still I Rise*, pp. 31-2. New York: Random House, 1978.

In the following poem, the narrator enumerates her many daily chores, juxtaposing them against pleas to Nature as her source of relief from the domestic burdens.

I've got the children to tend
The clothes to mend
The floor to mop
The food to shop
Then the chicken to fry
The baby to dry
I got company to feed
The garden to weed
I've got the shirts to press
The tots to dress

The cane to be cut
I gotta clean up this hut
Then see about the sick
And the cotton to pick.

Shine on me, sunshine
Rain on me, rain
Fall softly, dewdrops
And cool my brow again.

Storm, blow me from here
With your fiercest wind
Let me float across the sky
Till I can rest again.

Fall gently, snowflakes
Cover me with white
Cold icy kisses and
Let me rest tonight.

Sun, rain, curving sky
Mountain, oceans, leaf and stone
Star shine, moon glow
You're all that I can call my own.

GENERAL COMMENTARY

MARY JANE LUPTON (ESSAY DATE SUMMER 1990)

SOURCE: Lupton, Mary Jane. "Singing the Black Mother: Maya Angelou and Autobiographical Continuity." *Black American Literature Forum* 24, no. 2 (summer 1990): 257-76.

In the following essay, Lupton analyzes the plot, characters, and structure of Angelou's first five autobiographies, noting the themes of hope and renewal at the conclusion of each work.

Now my problem I have is I love life, I love living life and I love the art of living, so I try to live my life as a poetic adventure, everything I do from the way I keep my house, cook, make my husband happy, or welcome my friends, raise my son; everything is part of a large canvas I am creating, I am living beneath.

(Chrisman interview 46)

This energetic statement from a 1977 interview with Maya Angelou merely hints at the variety of roles and experiences which sweep through what is presently her five-volume autobiographical series: *I Know Why the Caged Bird Sings* (1970), *Gather Together in My Name* (1974), *Singin' and Swingin' and Gettin' Merry Like Christmas* (1976), *The Heart of a Woman* (1981), and *All God's Children Need Traveling Shoes* (1986).[1] It is fitting that Angelou, so adept at metaphor, should compare her "poetic adventure" to the act of painting: ". . . everything is part of a large canvas I am creating, I am living beneath." Like an unfinished painting, the autobiographical series is an ongoing creation, in a form that rejects the finality of a restricting frame. Its continuity is achieved through characters who enter the picture, leave, and reappear, and through certain interlaced themes—self-acceptance, race, men, work, separation, sexuality, motherhood. All the while Angelou lives "beneath," recording the minutest of details in a constantly shifting environment and giving attention to the "mundane, though essential, ordinary moments of life" (O'Neale 34).

I Know Why the Caged Bird Sings is the first and most highly praised volume in the series. It begins with the humiliations of childhood and ends with the birth of a child. At its publication, critics, not anticipating a series, readily appreciated the clearly developed narrative form. In 1973, for example, Sidonie Smith discussed the "sense of an ending" in *Caged Bird* as it relates to Angelou's acceptance of Black womanhood: "With the birth of her child Maya is herself born into a mature engagement with the forces of life" (374). But with the introduction in 1974 of Angelou's second autobiographical volume, *Gather Together in My Name*, the tight structure appeared to crumble; childhood experiences were replaced by episodes which a number of critics consider disjointed or bizarre. Selwyn Cudjoe, for instance, noted the shift from the "intense solidity and moral center" in *Caged Bird* to the "conditions of *alienation* and *fragmentation*" in *Gather Together*, conditions which affect its organization and its quality, making it "conspicuously weak" (17, 20). Lynn Z. Bloom found the sequel "less satisfactory" because the narrator "abandons or jeopardizes the maturity, honesty, and intuitive good judgment toward which she had been moving in *Caged Bird*" (5). Crucial to Bloom's judgment is her concept of movement *toward*, which insinuates the achievement of an ending.

The narrator, as authentic recorder of the life, indeed changes during the second volume, as does the book's structure; the later volumes abandon the tighter form of *Caged Bird* for an episodic series of adventures whose so-called "fragments" are reflections of the kind of chaos found in actual living. In altering the narrative structure, Angelou shifts the emphasis from herself as an isolated consciousness to herself as a Black woman participating in diverse experiences among a diverse class of peoples. As the world of experience widens, so does the canvas.

What distinguishes, then, Angelou's autobiographical method from more conventional autobiographical forms is her very denial of closure. The reader of autobiography expects a beginning, a middle, and an end—as occurs in *Caged Bird*. She or he also expects a central experience, as we indeed are given in the extraordinary rape sequence of *Caged Bird*. But Angelou, by continuing her narrative, denies the form and its history, creating from each ending a new beginning, relocating the center to some luminous place in a volume yet to be. Stretching the autobiographical canvas, she moves forward: from being a child; to being a mother; to leaving the child; to having the child, in the fifth volume, achieve his independence. Nor would I be so unwise as to call the fifth volume the end. For Maya Angelou, now a grandmother, has already published a moving, first-person account in *Woman's Day* of the four years of anguish surrounding the maternal kidnapping of her grandson Colin.

Throughout the more episodic volumes, the theme of motherhood remains a unifying element, with Momma Henderson being Angelou's link with the Black folk tradition—as George Kent, Elizabeth Schultz, and other critics have mentioned. Since traditional solidity of development is absent, one must sometimes search through three or four books to trace Vivian Baxter's changing lovers, Maya Angelou's ambivalence towards motherhood, or her son Guy's various reactions to his non-traditional upbringing. Nonetheless, the volumes are intricately related through a number of essential elements: the ambivalent autobiographical voice, the flexibility of structure to echo the life process, the intertextual commentary on character and theme, and the use of certain recurring patterns to establish both continuity and continuation. I have isolated the mother-child pattern as a way of approaching the complexity of Angelou's methods. One could as well select other kinds of interconnected themes: the absent and/or substitute father, the use of food as a psycho-sexual symbol, the dramatic/symbolic use of images of staring or gazing, and other motifs which establish continuity within and among the volumes.

Stephen Butterfield says of *Caged Bird*: "Continuity is achieved by the contact of mother and child, the sense of life begetting life that happens automatically in spite of all confusion—perhaps also because of it" (213). The consistent yet changing connection for Maya Angelou through the four subsequent narratives is that same contact of mother and child—with herself and her son Guy; with herself and her own mother, Vivian Baxter; with herself and her paternal grandmother; and, finally, with the child-mother in herself.

Moreover, in extending the traditional one-volume form, Angelou has metaphorically mothered another book. The "sense of life begetting life" at the end of *Caged Bird* can no longer signal the conclusion of the narrative. The autobiographical moment has been reopened and expanded; Guy's birth can now be seen symbolically as the birth of another text. In a 1975 interview with Carol Benson, Angelou uses such a birthing metaphor in describing the writing of *Gather Together*: "If you have a child, it takes nine months. It took me three-and-a-half years to write *Gather Together,* so I couldn't just drop it" (19). This statement makes emphatic what in the autobiographies are much more elusive comparisons between creative work and motherhood; after a three-and-a-half-year pregnancy she gives birth to *Gather Together,* indicating that she must have planned the conception of the second volume shortly after the 1970 delivery of *Caged Bird.*

Each of the five volumes explores, both literally and metaphorically, the significance of motherhood. I will examine this theme from two specific perspectives: first, Angelou's relationship to her mother and to mother substitutes, especially to Momma Henderson; second, Angelou's relationship to her son as she struggles to define her own role as mother/artist. Throughout the volumes Angelou moves backwards and forwards, from connection to conflict. This dialectic of Black mother-daughterhood, introduced in the childhood narrative, enlarges and contracts during the series, finding its fullest expression in *Singin' and Swingin' and Gettin' Merry Like Christmas.*

In flux, in defiance of chronological time, the mother-child configuration forms the basic pattern against which other relationships are measured and around which episodes and volumes begin or end. Motherhood also provides the series with a literary unity, as Angelou shifts positions—from mother to granddaughter to child—in a nonending text that, through its repetitions of maternal motifs, provides an ironic comment on her own sense of identity. For Angelou, despite her insistence on mother love, is trapped in the conflicts between working and mothering, independence and nurturing—conflicts that echo her ambivalence towards her mother, Vivian Baxter, and her apparent sanctification of Grandmother Henderson, the major adult figure in *Caged Bird.*

Annie Henderson is a solid, God-fearing, economically independent woman whose general store in Stamps, Arkansas, is the "lay center of activities in town" (*Caged Bird* 5), much as Annie is the moral center of the family. According to

Mildred A. Hill-Lubin, the grandmother, both in Africa and in America, "has been a significant force in the stability and the continuity of the Black family and the community" (257). Hill-Lubin selects Annie Henderson as her primary example of the strong grandmother in African-American literature—the traditional preserver of the family, the source of folk wisdom, and the instiller of values within the Black community. Throughout *Caged Bird* Maya has ambivalent feelings for this awesome woman, whose values of self-determination and personal dignity gradually chip away at Maya's dreadful sense of being "shit color" (17). As a self-made woman, Annie Henderson has the economic power to lend money to whites; as a practical Black woman, however, she is convinced that whites cannot be directly confronted: "If she had been asked and had chosen to answer the question of whether she was cowardly or not, she would have said that she was a realist" (39). To survive in a racist society, Momma Henderson has had to develop a realistic strategy of submission that Maya finds unacceptable. Maya, in her need to re-image her grandmother, creates a metaphor that places Momma's power above any apparent submissiveness: Momma "did an excellent job of sagging from her waist down, but from the waist up she seemed to be pulling for the top of the oak tree across the road" (24).

There are numerous episodes, both in *Caged Bird* and *Gather Together,* which involve the conflict between Maya and her grandmother over how to deal with racism. When taunted by three "powhitetrash" girls, Momma quietly sings a hymn; Maya, enraged, would like to have a rifle (*Caged Bird* 23-27). Or, when humiliated by a white dentist who'd rather put his "hand in a dog's mouth than in a nigger's" (160), Annie is passive; Maya subsequently invents a fantasy in which Momma runs the dentist out of town. In the italicized dream text (161-62), Maya endows her grandmother with superhuman powers; Momma magically changes the dentist's nurse into a bag of chicken seed. In reality the grandmother has been defeated and humiliated, her only reward a mere ten dollars in interest for a loan she had made to the dentist (164). In Maya's fantasy Momma's *"eyes were blazing like live coals and her arms had doubled themselves in length"*; in actuality she "looked tired" (162).

This richly textured passage is rendered from the perspective of an imaginative child who re-creates her grandmother—but in a language that ironically transforms Annie Henderson from a Southern Black storekeeper into an eloquent heroine from a romantic novel: *"Her tongue had thinned and the words rolled off well enunciated."* Instead of the silent "nigra" (159) of the actual experience, Momma Henderson is now the articulate defender of her granddaughter against the stuttering dentist. Momma Henderson orders the *"contemptuous scoundrel"* to leave Stamps *"now and herewith."* The narrator eventually lets Momma speak normally, then comments: *"(She could afford to slip into the vernacular because she had such eloquent command of English.)"*

This fantasy is the narrator's way of dealing with her ambivalence towards Momma Henderson—a woman who throughout **Caged Bird** represents to Maya both strength and weakness, both generosity and punishment, both affection and the denial of affection. Here her defender is *"ten feet tall with eight-foot arms,"* quite capable, to recall the former tree image, of reaching the top of an oak from across the road. Momma's physical transformation in the dream text also recalls an earlier description: "I saw only her power and strength. She was taller than any woman in my personal world, and her hands were so large they could span my head from ear to ear" (38). In the dentist fantasy, Maya eliminates all of Momma Henderson's "negative" traits—submissiveness, severity, religiosity, sternness, down-home speech. It would seem that Maya is so shattered by her grandmother's reaction to Dentist Lincoln, so destroyed by her illusions of Annie Henderson's power in relationship to white people, that she compensates by reversing the true situation and having the salivating dentist be the target of Momma's wrath. Significantly, this transformation occurs immediately before Momma Henderson tells Maya and Bailey that they are going to California. Its position in the text gives it the impression of finality. Any negative attitudes become submerged, only to surface later, in **Gather Together,** as aspects of Angelou's own ambiguity towards race, power, and identity.

In **Caged Bird** Momma Henderson had hit Maya with a switch for unknowingly taking the Lord's name in vain, "like whitefolks do" (87). Similarly, in **Gather Together** Annie slaps her granddaughter after Maya, on a visit to Stamps, verbally assaults two white saleswomen. In a clash with Momma Henderson that is both painful and final, Maya argues for "the principle of the thing," and Momma slaps her.[2] Surely, Momma's slap is well intended; she wishes to protect Maya from "lunatic cracker boys" and men in white sheets, from all of the insanity of racial prejudice (78-79). The "new" Maya, who has been to the city and

found a sense of independence, is caught in the clash between her recently acquired "principles" and Momma's fixed ideology. Thus the slap—but also the intention behind it—will remain in Maya's memory long after the mature Angelou has been separated from Annie Henderson's supervision. Momma makes Maya and the baby leave Stamps, again as a precaution: "Momma's intent to protect me had caused her to hit me in the face, a thing she had never done, and to send me away to where she thought I'd be safe" (79). Maya departs on the train, never to see her grandmother again.

In the third volume Angelou, her marriage falling apart, is recuperating from a difficult appendectomy. When she tells her husband Tosh that she wants to go to Stamps until she is well, he breaks the news that Annie Henderson died the day after Angelou's operation. In recording her reaction to her grandmother's death, Angelou's style shifts from its generally more conversational tone and becomes intense, religious, emotional:

> Ah, Momma. I had never looked at death before, peered into its yawning chasm for the face of the beloved. For days my mind staggered out of balance. I reeled on a precipice of knowledge that even if I were rich enough to travel all over the world, I would never find Momma. If I were as good as God's angels and as pure as the Mother of Christ, I could never have Momma's rough slow hands pat my cheek or braid my hair.
>
> Death to the young is more than that undiscovered country; despite its inevitability, it is a place having reality only in song or in other people's grief.
>
> (***Singin' and Swingin'*** 41)

This moving farewell, so atypical of Angelou's more worldly autobiographical style, emerges directly from a suppressed religious experience which Angelou narrates earlier in the same text—a "secret crawl through neighborhood churches" (28). These visits, done without her white husband's knowledge, culminate in Angelou's being saved at the Evening Star Baptist Church. During her purification, Angelou cries for her family: "For my fatherless son, who was growing up with a man who would never, could never, understand his need for manhood; for my mother, whom I admired but didn't understand; for my brother, whose disappointment with life was drawing him relentlessly into the clutches of death; and, finally, I cried for myself, long and loudly" (33). Annie Henderson is strangely absent from this list of family for whom Angelou cries during the short-lived conversion. But only a few pages later, Angelou remembers her grandmother's profound importance, in the elegiac passage on Momma's death.

In this passage Angelou creates a funeral song which relies on the Black gospel tradition, on the language of Bible stories, and on certain formative literary texts.[3] Words like *chasm, precipice, angels,* and *beloved* have Sunday School overtones, a kind of vocabulary Angelou more typically employs for humorous effects, as in the well-known portrait of Sister Monroe (*Caged Bird* 32-37).[4] The gospel motif, so dominant in the passage, seems directly related to Angelou's rediscovery of the Black spiritual: "The spirituals and gospel songs were sweeter than sugar. I wanted to keep my mouth full of them and the sounds of my people singing fell like sweet oil in my ears" (*Singin' and Swingin'* 28). During her conversion experience Angelou lies on the floor while four women march round her singing, "Soon one morning when death comes walking in my room" (33); in another spiritual the singers prepare for the "walk to Jerusalem" (31). These and similar hymns about death had been significant elements of the "folk religious tradition" of Momma Henderson (Kent 76). Now, for a brief time, they become part of the mature Angelou's experience. That their revival is almost immediately followed by the death of Momma Henderson accounts, to a large extent, for Angelou's intensely religious narrative.

Angelou's singing of the Black grandmother in this passage contains other refrains from the past, most notably her desire to have "Momma's rough slow hands pat my cheek." These are the same hands that slapped Maya for having talked back to the white saleswomen—an event that was physically to separate grandmother and granddaughter (*Gather Together* 86-88). That final slap, softened here, becomes a loving pat on the cheek akin to a moment in *Caged Bird* in which Maya describes her grandmother's love as a touch of the hand: "Just the gentle pressure of her rough hand conveyed her own concern and assurance to me" (96). Angelou's tone throughout the elegy is an attempt, through religion, to reconcile her ambivalence towards Momma Henderson by sharing her traditions. Angelou wishes to be "as good as God's angels" and as "pure as the Mother of Christ," metaphors which seem to represent Angelou's effort to close off the chasm between herself and Momma Henderson through the use of a common language, the language of the church-going grandmother.

As Momma Henderson, the revered grandmother, recedes from the narrative, Angelou's natural mother gains prominence. By the third volume Maya Angelou and Vivian Baxter have established a closeness that somewhat compensates for Maya's having been sent off to Stamps as a child, a situation so painful that Maya had imagined her mother dead:

> I could cry anytime I wanted by picturing my mother (I didn't quite know what she looked like) lying in her coffin. . . . The face was brown, like a big O, and since I couldn't fill in the features I printed M O T H E R across the O, and tears would fall down my cheeks like warm milk.
>
> (*Caged Bird* 42-43)

Like Maya's fantasy of her grandmother and Dentist Lincoln, the above passage is an imaginative revision of reality, Maya's way to control the frustrations produced by Vivian's rejection. The images of the dream text invoke romance fiction and Amazonian strength. Here the images concern, first, the artist who fills in the empty canvas (the O) with print; second, the mother-like child who cries tears of "warm milk" in sympathy for her imagined dead mother. These interlaced metaphors of writing and nurturance appear frequently in the continuing text, as Angelou explores her relationships with mothers and children.

When Maya is eight years old, she and Bailey visit their mother in St. Louis, where Maya discovers her exquisite beauty: "To describe my mother would be to write about a hurricane in its perfect power. Or the climbing, falling colors of a rainbow. . . . She was too beautiful to have children" (*Caged Bird* 49-50). Ironically, this mother "too beautiful to have children" is to a large degree responsible for her own child's brutal rape. Vivian's beauty attracts a lover, Mr. Freeman, who is constantly in the house waiting for a woman who is not there, and he "uses Angelou as an extension of her mother" to satisfy his sexual urges (Demetrakopoulos 198). It could also be suggested that Vivian uses Maya, somehow knowing that in her own absence Maya will keep her lover amused. When Maya becomes ill, Vivian responds in a motherly manner: making broth, cooking Cream of Wheat, taking Maya's temperature, calling a doctor. After she discovers the rape, Vivian sends Maya to a hospital, bringing her flowers and candy (*Caged Bird* 69).

It is Grandmother Baxter, however, who sees to it that the rapist is punished; after the trial a policeman comes to the house and informs an unsurprised Mrs. Baxter that Freeman has been kicked to death. Mrs. Baxter is a political figure in St. Louis, a precinct captain and gambler whose light skin and "six mean children" bring her both power and respect (51). Like Momma Henderson, Grandmother Baxter is a source of strength for Maya. Both grandmothers are "strong, independent[,] skillful women who are able to manage their families and to insure their survival in a segregated and hostile society" (Hill-Lubin 260).

Despite their positive influence, however, Maya has ambivalent feelings towards her powerful grandmothers. Maya feels guilty for having lied at the trial, a guilt compounded when she learns of Grandmother Baxter's part in Freeman's murder. To stop the "poison" in her breath, Maya retreats into a "perfect personal silence" which neither of the Baxter women can penetrate, and which Maya breaks only for Bailey (73). The disastrous St. Louis sequence stops abruptly, without transition: "We were on the train going back to Stamps . . ." (74). Thus, the end of the visit to Grandmother Baxter parallels chapter one of *Caged Bird*; a train moves from an urban center to rural Arkansas and to the protection of Annie Henderson.

Back at her grandmother's general store, Maya meets Mrs. Bertha Flowers, "the aristocrat of Black Stamps" (77). This unambivalently positive mother figure helps Maya to recover her oral language through the written text—reading *A Tale of Two Cities*. In a series of sharp contrasts, the narrator conveys Maya's divided feelings between the sophisticated mother figure, Mrs. Flowers, and her more provincial grandmother. Mrs. Flowers wears gloves, whereas Mrs. Henderson has rough hands. Mrs. Flowers admires white male writers, whereas Annie Henderson will not tolerate them. And in a set of contrasts that occurs almost simultaneously in the text, the literary Mrs. Flowers rewards Maya's language with sweets, whereas the religious grandmother punishes Maya's spoken words ("by the way") without making any effort to explain her anger. In an earlier passage, however, the narrator merges these basic oppositions into a dynamic interaction between two Black women: "I heard the soft-voiced Mrs. Flowers and the textured voice of my grandmother merging and melting. They were interrupted from time to time by giggles that must have come from Mrs. Flowers (Momma never giggled in her life). Then she was gone" (79). These contrasts appear following Maya's failed relationship with Vivian Baxter. They are indications of the split mother—the absent natural mother, the gentle Mrs. Flowers, the forceful Annie Henderson—whose divisions Angelou must articulate if she is to find her own autobiographical voice.

Although most critics have seen a wholeness in Maya's personality at the conclusion of *Caged Bird,* a few have observed this division of self, which Demetrakopoulos relates to Maya's conflicts about the mother: She "splits the feminine archetype of her mother's cold Venus and her grandmother's primal warm sheltering Demeter aspects" (198). The Jungian metaphors may jar in this African-American context, but I agree with Demetrakopoulos that at the end of *Caged Bird* the narrator is split. She is a mother who is herself a child; a daughter torn by her notions of mother love; an uncertain Black teenager hardly capable of the heavy burden of closure placed on her by Sidonie Smith, Stephen Butterfield, Selwyn Cudjoe, and other critics.

Nor is this split mended when Angelou gives birth to *Gather Together.* Here she introduces herself by way of contradictions: "I was seventeen, very old, embarrassingly young, with a son of two months, and I still lived with my mother and stepfather" (3). Vivian Baxter intermittently takes care of Guy while his young mother works as a cook or shopkeeper. When Momma Henderson forces Maya and her son to leave Stamps, they go immediately to the security of Vivian's fourteen-room house in San Francisco. One gets a strong sense throughout *Gather Together* of Maya's dependence on her mother. Angelou admires her mother for her self-reliance, her encouragement, and her casual approach to sexuality. She also continues to be captivated by Vivian's beauty, by her "snappy-fingered, head-tossing elegance" (*Singin' and Swingin'* 70). On the other hand, she recognizes Vivian Baxter's flaws: "Her own mind was misted by the knowledge of a failing marriage, and the slipping away of the huge sums of money which she had enjoyed and thought her due" (*Gather Together* 24).

As for her son, Angelou reveals similar contradictory feelings. After quitting a job to be with Guy, Angelou writes: "A baby's love for his mother is probably the sweetest emotion we can savor" (*Gather Together* 90). In a more depressed mood, however, she comments that her child's disposition had "lost its magic to make me happy" (174). What Angelou does in these instances is to articulate her feelings as they convey the reality of her experiences, even though some of these negative emotions might not represent her best side.

The most dramatic mother-child episode in *Gather Together* occurs while Angelou is working as a prostitute. She leaves Guy with her sitter, Big Mary. Returning for Guy after several days, she learns that her son has been kidnapped. Angelou finally recovers her child, unharmed; at that moment she realizes that they are both separate individuals and that Guy is not merely a "beautiful appendage of myself" (163). Angelou's awareness of the inevitable separation of mother and child, expressed here for the first time, is a theme that she will continue to explore through the remaining autobiographical volumes.

Gather Together closes with Angelou's and Guy's returning to the protection of Vivian Baxter, following Angelou's glimpse at the horrors of heroin addiction: "I had no idea what I was going to make of my life, but I had given a promise and found my innocence. I swore I'd never lose it again" (181). In its tableau of mother, child, and grandmother, this concluding paragraph directly parallels the ending of *Caged Bird.*

In the next volume, *Singin' and Swingin',* the closeness between mother and daughter continues. As she matures, Angelou becomes more in control of her feelings and more objective in her assessment of Vivian Baxter's personality. Additionally, the separation of egos that Angelou perceived after locating her kidnapped son would extend to the mother-daughter and grandmother-granddaughter relationships as well. But *Singin' and Swingin' and Gettin' Merry Like Christmas* is, despite its joyful title, a mesh of conflicts—many of them existing within the autobiographical self; many of them involving separations which, although consciously chosen, become unbearable. A number of ambiguities appear throughout the book, especially as they concern the mother-child pattern which is to dominate this and the subsequent texts.

The underlying drama in *Singin' and Swingin'* is played out between Angelou, the single parent of a young son, and Angelou, the actress who chooses to leave that son with Vivian Baxter in order to tour Europe with the company of *Porgy and Bess.* Angelou is keenly aware that putting Guy in the care of his grandmother is an echo of her own child-mother experience:

> The past revisited. My mother had left me with my grandmother for years and I knew the pain of parting. My mother, like me, had had her motivations, her needs. I did not relish visiting the same anguish on my son, and she, years later, told me how painful our separation was to her. But I had to work and I had to be good. I would make it up to my son and one day would take him to all the places I was going to see.
>
> (129)

Angelou's feelings are compounded by the fact that, as a young, Black, single mother, she alone is finally responsible for giving her child a sense of stability.[5] In identifying the conflict between working and mothering, Angelou offers a universalized representation of the turmoil which may arise when a woman attempts to fulfill both roles.

Angelou suffers considerably on the European tour. In some instances her longings for Guy make her sleep fitfully (147) or make her distracted—as when she sees some young Italian boys with "pale-gold complexions" who remind her of her son (148). When she is paged at a Paris train station, Angelou fears that something dreadful has happened to Guy, and she blames herself: "I knew I shouldn't have left my son. There was a telegram waiting for me to say he had been hurt somehow. Or had run away from home. Or had caught an awful disease" (151-52). On other occasions she speaks quite directly of her guilt: "I sent my dollars home to pay for Clyde's [Guy's] keep and to assuage my guilt at being away from him" (153).[6]

Of the many examples in *Singin' and Swingin'* which address this conflict, I have selected one particular passage to illustrate the ways in which Angelou articulates her ambivalence about mothering. While she is in Paris, Angelou earns extra money by singing in a nightclub and decides to send the money home rather than spend it on a room with a private bath: "Mom could buy something wonderful for Clyde every other week and tell him I'd sent it. Then perhaps he would forgive my absence" (157). The narrator shows no qualms about lying to her son; Vivian could "tell him I'd sent it." Additionally, she makes no connection between her efforts to buy forgiveness and the anger she felt as a child when her absent mother, the same "Mom" of the above passage, sent Maya a tea set and a doll with yellow hair for Christmas: "Bailey and I tore the stuffing out of the doll the day after Christmas, but he warned me that I had to keep the tea set in good condition because any day or night she might come riding up" (*Caged Bird* 43). Liliane K. Arensberg interprets the tea cups as "symbols of a white world beyond Maya's reach of everyday experience," whereas the torn doll "serves as an effigy of her mother by virtue of being female and a gift" (281). Although I agree with Arensberg's interpretation, I tend to read the gifts as metaphors for Maya's divided self. The preserved tea set, the torn doll—what better signifiers could there be for the split feelings of the abandoned child, who destroys one gift to show anger but saves the other in anticipation of the mother's return? I would also suggest that the seemingly inappropriate title *Singin' and Swingin' and Gettin' Merry Like Christ-*

mas may be intended to signal the reader back to the very unmerry Christmas of *Caged Bird.*

In the Paris sequence the narrator seems to have suppressed, in her role as *mother,* some of the anguish she had experienced during childhood—although in the passage previously cited (*Singin' and Swingin'* 129), she recognizes the similarities between her own "pains of parting" and her son's. Angelou refers to this separation from her son so frequently in the text that he becomes a substantial part of the narrative, the source of Angelou's guilt but also the major factor in the development of dramatic tension. Angelou, in this most complex of the autobiographies, is richly and honestly rendering the split in her own psyche between being a "good" mother (being at home) and being a "bad" mother (selfishly staying in Europe). The narrator pretends to herself that her son wants a gift, thus prolonging the admission that he really wants his mother—as Maya had wanted hers.

To arrive at this interpretation the reader must move back and forth among the texts, perceiving parallels in order to decipher the narrator's motivations. The frequent references in *Singin' and Swingin'* to separation and to guilt give one considerable access to the narrator's complex personality; at the same time, these references demand to be read against and with the entire series—intertextuality in its strictest sense.

Angelou returns from Europe to find her son suffering from a skin disease that is an overt expression of his loneliness. In a promise that recalls the last lines of *Gather Together* (never again to lose her innocence), Angelou vows to Guy: "I swear to you, I'll never leave you again. If I go, you'll go with me or I won't go" (*Singin' and Swingin'* 232). She takes Guy with her to Hawaii, where she has a singing engagement. *Singin' and Swingin'* closes in a sentence which highlights, through its three nouns, the underlying tensions of the book: "Although I was not a great *singer* I was his *mother,* and he was my wonderful, dependently independent *son*" (242, emphasis added). Dialectical in phrasing, this statement not only functions to close the first three books but also opens itself to the mother-son patterns of the future volumes: fluctuations between dependence and independence.

In *The Heart of a Woman* the tension between mothering and working continues, but to a lesser extent. Guy is now living with his mother and not with Vivian Baxter. But Angelou, despite her earlier vow, does occasionally leave her son. During a night club engagement in Chicago, An-

gelou trusts Guy to the care of her friend John Killens. One night Killens phones from Brooklyn and informs her that "there's been some trouble" (75). In a moment of panic that recalls her fears at the Paris train station (*Gather Together* 151-52), Angelou again imagines that Guy has been injured, stolen, "struck by an errant bus, hit by a car out of control" (75).[7]

Angelou confronts these fears in the Brooklyn adventure, the most dramatic episode of *The Heart of a Woman.* Unlike the internal conflicts of *Gather Together,* this one operates outside of the narrator, showing Maya Angelou as a strong, aggressive Black mother rather than a mother torn by self-doubt. While Angelou was in Chicago, Guy had gotten in trouble with a Brooklyn street gang. In order to protect her son, she confronts Jerry, the gang leader, and threatens to shoot his entire family if Guy is harmed. Jerry's response is an ironic comment on the motherhood theme of the autobiographies: "O.K., I understand. But for a mother, I must say you're a mean motherfucker" (84). Powerful, protective of her son, Angelou has become in this episode a reincarnation of Momma Henderson.

Unfortunately, no mother or grandmother or guardian angel, no matter how strong, can keep children forever from danger. Near the end of *The Heart of a Woman,* Guy is seriously injured in a car accident. In a condensed, tormented autobiographical passage, Angelou gazes at the face of her unconscious son and summarizes their life together:

> He was born to me when I was seventeen. I had taken him away from my mother's house when he was two years old, and except for a year I spent in Europe without him, and a month when he was stolen by a deranged woman, we had spent our lives together. My grown life lay stretched before me, stiff as a pine board, in a strange country, blood caked on his face and clotted on his clothes.
>
> (263)[8]

Guy gradually recovers, moving, during the process of physical healing, toward a position of greater independence from his mother.

But Angelou, too, moves towards a separateness, much as she had predicted in *Gather Together* (163). In *The Heart of a Woman* the texture of Angelou's life changes significantly. She travels a lot, seeing far less of Vivian—although she does write to her mother from Ghana asking for financial help after Guy's accident (268). She strengthens her public identity, becoming a coordinator in the Civil Rights Movement and a professionally recognized dancer and actress. She also, for the first time in the autobiographies, begins her account of self as writer. Angelou attends a writer's workshop; publishes a short story; becomes friends with John Killens, Rosa Guy, Paule Marshall, and other Black novelists. Most important, writing forces her into a conscious maturity: "If I wanted to write, I had to be willing to develop a kind of concentration found mostly in people awaiting execution. I had to learn technique and surrender my ignorance" (41). By extension, the rich ambivalence of *Singin' and Swingin'* could only have been achieved by a writer who had abandoned "ignorance" for a conscious self-exploration.

Paradoxically, the independent writer/mother establishes this "kind of concentration" in maternal solitude. *Singin' and Swingin'* had ended with mother and son reunited, both dependent and independent. *The Heart of a Woman* ends in separation. Guy, now a student at the University of Ghana, is moving to a dormitory. In the last two paragraphs we find Angelou alone:

> I closed the door and held my breath. Waiting for the wave of emotion to surge over me, knock me down, take my breath away. Nothing happened. I didn't feel bereft or desolate. I didn't feel lonely or abandoned.
>
> I sat down, still waiting. The first thought that came to me, perfectly formed and promising, was "At last, I'll be able to eat the whole breast of a roast chicken by myself."
>
> (272)

Angelou's reaction to having "closed the door" on her son is, like so many of her feelings in this complicated relationship, ambivalent. The language of the passage is initially charged with negativity: "Nothing happened. I didn't feel. . . . I didn't feel. . . ." The son she had loved through all of "our lives together" (263) is gone. Angelou sits waiting for something dreadful to happen to herself—as she had earlier imagined Guy's being stolen or being hit by a bus. But the narrator counters this negative attitude with a note of irony in which she reverses the biological assumption of the mother as she-who-nourishes: She can now have the "whole breast" to herself.

The family chicken dinner is a recurring motif in the autobiographical series. Recall the marvelous scene from *Caged Bird* in which Maya and Bailey watch Reverend Howard Thomas gobble down Momma Henderson's chicken dinner: "He ate the biggest, brownest and best parts of the chicken at every Sunday meal" (28). Now there is no competition. Angelou has the best part, the

breast, to herself. On the negative side, Angelou is left, at the end of the fourth volume, in isolation; the last word of *The Heart of a Woman* is "myself." But the negativity is outweighed by the more "promising" aspects of being alone, the word *promising* an echo of the resolutions of *Gather Together* and *Singin' and Swingin'*, which end in vows of innocence and of commitment. The "perfectly formed" thought at the end of *The Heart of a Woman* is Angelou's realization of a new "myself," of a woman no longer primarily defined as granddaughter or daughter or mother—a woman free to choose herself.

All God's Children Need Traveling Shoes opens by going back in time to Angelou the mother, who anxiously waits at the hospital following Guy's car accident. In an image that parodies the well-fed mother of *The Heart of a Woman,* Angelou compares her anxiety over Guy to being eaten up:

> July and August of 1962 stretched out like fat men yawning after a sumptuous dinner. They had every right to gloat, for they had eaten me up. Gobbled me down. Consumed my spirit, not in a wild rush, but slowly, with the obscene patience of certain victors. I became a shadow walking in the white hot streets, and a dark spectre in the hospital.
>
> (4)

The months of helplessly waiting for Guy to heal are like fat, stuffed men, a description that evokes memories of Reverend Thomas, who ate Momma Henderson's chicken, and of Mr. Freeman, who ate in Vivian Baxter's kitchen and raped her daughter. Guy's accident has an effect similar to the rape; Angelou retreats into silence. She is a "shadow," a "dark spectre," a Black mother silenced by the fear of her son's possible death.

Guy does recover. Their relationship, which like the autobiographical form itself is constantly in flux, moves once again from dependence to independence, climaxing in a scene in which Angelou learns that her son is having an affair with an American woman a year older than herself. Angelou at first threatens to strike him, but Guy merely pats her head and says: "Yes, little mother. I'm sure you will" (149). Shortly afterwards Angelou travels to Germany to perform in Genet's *The Blacks.* Guy meets her return flight and takes her home to a dinner of fried chicken he has cooked for her. Then, asserting his independence, he announces that he has "plans for dinner" (186).

Reading between the texts, we see Angelou alone again before a plate of chicken, as she was at the conclusion of *The Heart of a Woman.* In the *Traveling Shoes* episode, however, the conflicting feelings of love and resentment are more directly stated:

> He's gone. My lovely little boy is gone and will never return. That big confident strange man has done away with my little boy, and he has the gall to say he loves me. How can he love me? He doesn't know me, and I sure as hell don't know him.
>
> (186)

In this passage Angelou authentically faces and records the confusions of seeing one's child achieve selfhood, universalizing the pain a mother experiences when her "boy" is transformed into a "big confident strange man" who refuses to be his mother's "beautiful appendage" (*Gather Together* 162).

Yet through much of the fifth volume, Angelou continues to separate herself from Guy and to form new relationships. She shares experiences with other women, including her two roommates; she befriends an African boy named Koko; she enjoys her contacts with the colony of Black American writers and artists living in Ghana; and she continues her sexual involvements with men. The love affair which seems most vital in *Traveling Shoes,* however, is with Africa herself. In her travels through West Africa Angelou discovers certain connections between her own traditions and those of her African ancestors. She takes great satisfaction in her heritage when she is mistaken for a Bambara woman. Among African women she discovers strong mother figures, most notably Patience Aduah, whose custom of giving away food by the campfire evokes memories of Momma Henderson's having shared her table with Black American travelers denied rooms in hotels or seats in restaurants during the era of segregation in much of America (*Traveling Shoes* 102). Through her identification with Africa, Angelou reaffirms the meaning of motherhood.[9]

Although captivated by the oral traditions of Mother Africa, Angelou chooses to leave, at the conclusion of *Traveling Shoes,* in order to return to the rhythms of Southern Black churches, the rhythms of her grandmother. In so doing, however, she must also leave her son. The final scene in the book is at the Accra airport. Angelou is saying farewell to her friends and, most specifically, to Guy, who "stood, looking like a young lord of summer, straight, sure among his Ghanaian companions" (208). Through this suggestion of Guy as an African prince, Angelou roots him in the culture of West Africa.

If we look at the closure of *Traveling Shoes* on a literal level, then Angelou's son is a college student, staying on to complete his degree. But if we accept a grander interpretation, Guy has become, through his interaction with the Ghanaians, a "young lord" of Africa, given back to the Mother Continent freely, not lost, like so many other children, in mid-passage or in slavery. Angelou lovingly accepts the separation, knowing that "someone like me and certainly related to me" will be forming new bonds between himself and Mother Africa (209). Guy is making an essentially free choice that centuries of Black creativity in America have helped make possible: "Through the centuries of despair and dislocation we had been creative, because we faced down death by daring to hope" (208).

As in the four earlier autobiographies, this one closes with the mother-son configuration. But in the final, puzzling line of *Traveling Shoes* Angelou swings the focus away from Guy and towards the edge of the canvas: "I could nearly hear the old ones chuckling" (209). In this spiritual call to her ancestors Angelou imaginatively connects herself to the Ketans and the Ghanaians, to the people placed in chains, to all of God's children who had "never completely left Africa" (209). Ironically, the narrator herself has not completely left Africa either. The rhythmic prose that concludes the fifth volume is an anticipated departure to a new world, with the narrator still at the airport. As in the other volumes, the closure is thus another opening into the next narrative journey.

Notes

1. I use the name *Maya* in discussing the protagonist either as child or as the young woman of *Gather Together.* When I refer to the mature woman or to the narrator, I use *Angelou* or *Maya Angelou.*

2. In Fielder Cook's 1978 Learning Corporation of America teleplay of *Caged Bird,* the slap occurs following Annie Henderson's confrontation with the "powhitetrash" girls. Maya, played by Constance Good, says: "I would tell them to go to Hell. I would spit on their faces." Momma, played by Esther Rolle, soundly slaps Maya. The corrective slap is of course not unique in Black drama; the same actress, Esther Rolle, slaps her daughter for blaspheming in the 1988 production of Lorraine Hansberry's *A Raisin in the Sun* directed by Harold Scott at the Morris A. Mechanic Theatre in Baltimore.

3. I wish to thank Nellie McKay and Julia Lupton, respectively, for pointing out to me the echoes of James Weldon Johnson and William Shakespeare in this passage. In Johnson's "Go Down Death—A Funeral Sermon," Jesus "smoothed the furrows" from Sister Caroline's face while angels sing to her. Angelou incorporates these images into her own funeral sermon. Angelou's comparison of death to "that

undiscovered country" is a direct allusion to *Hamlet* (3.1.79-80): "The undiscover'd country from whose bourn / No traveller returns." These references, then, are further articulations of the conflicts in language and culture which Angelou introduces in *Caged Bird* (11); to please their grandmother, Maya and Bailey would recite from Johnson's "The Creation" and not from Shakespeare's *The Merchant of Venice*.

4. See Stephen Butterfield, who discusses Angelou's sense of humor in the church scenes of *Caged Bird* and compares it to humorous techniques used by Langston Hughes and James Weldon Johnson (209).

5. According to Carol E. Neubauer, Angelou "identifies her own situation and the threat of displacement as a common condition among black families in America and acknowledges the special responsibilities of the black mother" (124).

6. *Guy* is the name Angelou's son chooses for himself (*Singin' and Swingin'* 237-38) instead of *Clyde,* the name he was given at birth.

7. In her study of style and displacement in *The Heart of a Woman,* Carol E. Neubauer discusses the Killens phone call and other episodes as aspects of a "pattern of fantasy" through which Angelou reveals "the vulnerability she feels as a mother trying to protect her child from any form of danger" (128).

8. The "strange country" of this passage recalls the "undiscovered country" of the elegy to Annie Henderson.

9. Like David Diop, Léopold Senghor, and other contemporary African writers included in *The African Assertion,* Angelou adopts the image of Africa as mother, expressing this image through the African oral tradition rather than through her own written reflections. Thus Angelou has Ghanaian chief Nana Nketsia extol Mother Africa in "a rhythm reminiscent of preachers in Southern Black churches" (*Traveling Shoes* 112).

Works Cited

Angelou, Maya. *All God's Children Need Traveling Shoes.* 1986. New York: Random House, 1987.

———. *Gather Together in My Name.* 1974. New York: Bantam, 1975.

———. *The Heart of a Woman.* 1981. New York: Bantam, 1982.

———. *I Know Why the Caged Bird Sings.* 1970. New York: Bantam, 1971.

———. "My Grandson, Home at Last." *Woman's Day* Aug. 1986: 46-55.

———. *Singin' and Swingin' and Gettin' Merry Like Christmas.* 1976. New York: Bantam, 1977.

Arensberg, Liliane K. "Death as Metaphor of Self in *I Know Why the Caged Bird Sings.*" *CLA Journal* 20 (1976): 273-96.

Benson, Carol. "Out of the Cage and Still Singing." *Writer's Digest* Jan. 1975: 18-20.

Bloom, Lynn Z. "Maya Angelou." *Dictionary of Literary Biography.* 38. Detroit: Gale, 1985. 3-12.

Butterfield, Stephen. *Black Autobiography in America.* Amherst: U of Massachusetts P, 1974.

Chrisman, Robert. "*The Black Scholar* Interviews Maya Angelou." *Black Scholar* Jan.-Feb. 1977: 44-52.

Cudjoe, Selwyn. "Maya Angelou and the Autobiographical Statement." *Black Women Writers (1950-1980): A Critical Evaluation.* Ed. Mari Evans. Garden City: Doubleday, 1984. 6-24.

Demetrakopoulos, Stephanie A. "The Metaphysics of Matrilinearism in Women's Autobiography: Studies of Mead's *Blackberry Winter,* Hellman's *Pentimento,* Angelou's *I Know Why the Caged Bird Sings,* and Kingston's *The Woman Warrior.*" *Women's Autobiography: Essays in Criticism.* Ed. Estelle Jelinek. Bloomington: Indiana UP, 1980. 180-205.

Hill-Lubin, Mildred A. "The Grandmother in African and African-American Literature: A Survivor of the Extended Family." *Ngambika: Studies of Women in African Literature.* Ed. Carole B. Davies and Anne A. Graves. Trenton: Africa World, 1986. 257-70.

Kent, George E. "*I Know Why the Caged Bird Sings* and Black Autobiographical Tradition." *Kansas Quarterly* 7.3 (1975): 72-78.

Neubauer, Carol E. "Displacement and Autobiographical Style in Maya Angelou's *The Heart of a Woman.*" *Black American Literature Forum* 17 (1983): 123-29.

O'Neale, Sondra. "Reconstruction of the Composite Self: New Images of Black Women in Maya Angelou's Continuing Autobiography." *Black Women Writers (1950-1980): A Critical Evaluation.* Ed. Mari Evans. Garden City: Doubleday, 1984. 25-36.

Schultz, Elizabeth. "To Be Black and Blue: The Blues Genre in Black American Autobiography." *Kansas Quarterly* 7.3 (1975): 81-96.

Shelton, Austin J., ed. *The African Assertion: A Critical Anthology of African Literature.* Indianapolis: Odyssey, 1968.

Smith, Sidonie. "The Song of a Caged Bird: Maya Angelou's Quest after Self-Acceptance." *Southern Humanities Review* 7 (1973): 365-75.

TITLE COMMENTARY

I Know Why the Caged Bird Sings

SIDONIE SMITH (ESSAY DATE 1974)

SOURCE: Smith, Sidonie. "Black Womanhood." In *Where I'm Bound: Patterns of Slavery and Freedom in Black American Autobiography,* pp. 121-36. Westport, Conn.: Greenwood Press, 1974.

In the following essay, Smith analyzes the plot and characters in I Know Why the Caged Bird Sings, *while also examining the themes of quests for self-acceptance, love, and identity in the book.*

But put on your crown, my queen.

Eldridge Cleaver, *Soul On Ice*

Eldridge Cleaver concludes his spiritual journey when he is prepared to greet the black queen in the voice of the new "Eldridge," the black man who is secure in both his physical and intellectual masculinity. But the black woman has also to make her own spiritual journey, for the Amazon, as Cleaver labels her,

> *is in a peculiar position. Just as her man has been deprived of his manhood, so she has been deprived of her full womanhood. Society has decreed that the Ultrafeminine, the woman of the elite, is the goddess on the pedestal. The Amazon is the personification of the rejected domestic component, the woman on whom "dishpan hands" seems not out of character. The worship and respect which both the Omnipotent Administrator and the Supermasculine Menial lavish upon the image of the Ultrafeminine is a source of deep vexation to the Amazon. She envies the pampered, powderpuff existence of the Ultrafeminine and longs to incorporate these elements into her own life. Alienated from the feminine component of her nature, her reinforced domestic component is an awesome burden and shame of which she longs to be free.*
>
> *(188)*

The oppression of natural forces, of physical appearance and processes, foists a self-consciousness on all young girls who must grow from children into women. But in the black girl child's experience these natural forces are reinforced by the social forces of racial subordination and impotence. Being born black is itself a liability in a world ruled by white standards of beauty which imprison the black girl in a cage of ugliness at birth. "Caught in the crossfire of masculine prejudice, white illogical hate, and Black lack of power," the black and blue bruises of her soul multiply and compound as she flings herself against the bars of her cage.[1]

I

Maya Angelou's autobiography, ***I Know Why the Caged Bird Sings***, like Wright's *Black Boy*, opens with a primal childhood scene that brings into focus the nature of the imprisoning environment from which the black girl child seeks to escape. The young, awkward Maya, dressed in a cut-down, faded purple, too-long taffeta gown, stands nervously before an Easter congregation in Stamps, Arkansas, reciting a poem, asking "What you looking at me for?" She cannot remember the next lines, and so this question imprints itself indelibly on the shame-filled silence. Finally, the minister's wife offers her the forgotten lines. She grabs them, spills them into the congregation and then stumbles out of the watching church, "a green persimmon caught between [her] legs." Unable to control the pressure of her physical re-

sponse, she urinates, then laughs "from the knowledge that [she] wouldn't die from a busted head."

But the cathartic laughter never even begins to mute, much less transcend, the real pain that is this experience, the palpable pain that pulses through her long trip down the aisle of that singing church as urine flows down her grotesquely skinny, heavily dusted legs. "What you looking at *me* for?"—over and over until it becomes, "Is something *wrong* with me?" For this child, too much is wrong.

The whole way she looks is wrong, and she knows it. That is why they are all looking at her. Earlier, as she watches her grandmother make over the white woman's faded dress, she revels for one infinitely delicious moment in fantasies of stardom. In a beautiful dress, she would be transformed into a beautiful movie star: "I was going to look like one of the sweet little white girls who were everybody's dream of what was right with the world" (4). But between the taffeta insubstantiality of her ideal vision of herself and the raw (fleshy) edges of her substantiality stands the one-way mirror:

> Easter's early morning sun had shown the dress to be a plain ugly cut-down from a white woman's once-was-purple throwaway. It was old-lady-long too, but it didn't hide my skinny legs, which had been greased with Blue Seal Vaseline and powdered with the Arkansas red clay. The age-faded color made my skin look dirty like mud, and everyone in church was looking at my skinny legs.
>
> (4)

Wrong dress. Wrong legs. Wrong hair. Wrong face. Wrong color. The child lives a "black ugly dream," a nightmare. But since this life is only a dream, the child knows she will awaken soon into a rightened, a whitened reality:

> Wouldn't they be surprised when one day I woke out of my black ugly dream, and my real hair, which was long and blond, would take the place of the kinky mass that Momma wouldn't let me straighten? My light-blue eyes were going to hypnotize them, after all the things they said about "my daddy must of been a Chinaman" (I thought they meant made out of china, like a cup) because my eyes were so small and squinty. Then they would understand why I had never picked up a Southern accent, or spoke the common slang, and why I had to be forced to eat pigs' tails and snouts. Because I was really white and because a cruel fairy stepmother, who was understandably jealous of my beauty, had turned me into a too-big Negro girl, with nappy black hair, broad feet and a space between her teeth that would hold a number two pencil.
>
> (4-5)

In a society attuned to white standards of physical beauty, the black girl child cries herself to sleep at night to the tune of her own inadequacy. At least she can gain temporary respite in the impossible dreams of whiteness. Here in the darkened nights of the imagination, that refuge from society and the mirror, blossoms an ideal self. Yet even the imagination is sometimes not so much a refuge as it is a prison in which the dreamer becomes even more inescapably possessed by the nightmare, since the very self he fantasizes conforms perfectly to society's prerequisites. The cage door jangles shut around the child's question: "What you looking at me for?"

This opening to Maya Angelou's autobiography recreates vividly the dynamics of the black girl child's imprisonment in American society. Grier and Cobbs summarize this predicament of the black woman in *Black Rage*:

> If the society says that to be attractive is to be white, she finds herself unwittingly striving to be something she cannot possibly be; and if femininity is rooted in feeling oneself eminently lovable, then a society which views her as unattractive and repellent has also denied her this fundamental wellspring of femininity.[2]

Maya is a black ugly reality, not a whitened dream. And the attendant self-consciousness and diminished self-image throb through her bodily prison until the bladder can do nothing but explode in a parody of release. Such momentary freedom from the physical pressure of her displacement becomes a kind of metaphor for the freedom from the psychological pressure of her displacement after which she will quest.

II

After establishing the psychic environment out of which the black girl child must achieve maturity, against which she must struggle for selfhood, Angelou returns to the beginning of her quest. Two children, sent away to a strange place by estranging parents, cling to each other as they travel by train across the southwestern United States—and cling to their tag: "'To Whom It May Concern'—that we were Marguerite and Bailey Johnson, Jr., from Long Beach, California, en route to Stamps, Arkansas, c/o Mrs. Annie Henderson" (6). The autobiography of black America is haunted by these orphans, descendants of the orphaned slave narrators, who travel through life desperately in search of a home where they can escape the shadow of lonely displacement. Although Maya and Bailey are traveling toward the home of their grandmother, it is more significant that they are traveling away from the home of their parents. A child may internalize and translate such rejection into rejection of self; thus, the loss of home ultimately occasions the loss of self-worth. For this reason, the quest for a new home is tantamount to the quest for acceptance, for love, and for the resultant feeling of self-worth. Like that of any orphan's, such a quest is intensely solitary, making it all the more desperate, immediate, and demanding, and, making it, above all, an even more estranging process. So long as the "place" is conceived as a function of others' (society's) acceptance, it always recedes into the distance, moving with the horizon, as the "North" receded for the escaped slave and later for the free black American.

Stamps, Arkansas, does not offer a sense of place to Maya:

> The town reacted to us as its inhabitants had reacted to all things new before our coming. It regarded us a while without curiosity but with caution, and after we were seen to be harmless (and children) it closed in around us, as a real mother embraces a stranger's child. Warmly, but not too familiarly.
>
> (7)

The aura of personal displacement is counterpointed by the ambience of displacement within the larger black community of Stamps, which is itself caged in the social reality of racial subordination and impotence. The cotton pickers must face an empty bag every morning, an empty will every night, knowing all along that they would end the season as they had begun it—with no money and no credit. This undercurrent of social displacement, this fragility of the sense of belonging, are evidenced in the intrusion of white reality. Poor white trash humiliate Momma as she stands erect before them singing a hymn. Uncle Willie hides deep in the potato barrel the night the sheriff warns them that white men ride after black, any black. The white apparition haunts the life of Stamps, Arkansas, always present though not always visible.

Against this apparition, the community shores itself up with a subdued hominess, a fundamental faith in a fundamental religion, and resignation. The warmth mitigates the need to resist, or, rather, the impossibility of resistance is sublimated in the bond of community. The people of Stamps, including Momma Henderson, adapt in the best way they know—"realistically": Momma "didn't cotton to the idea that white-folks could be talked to at all without risking one's life. And certainly they couldn't be spoken to insolently" (46). If the young girl stands before the church congregation asking, "What you looking at me for?" the whole black community might just as well be standing before the larger white community and asking that same question. High physical visibility means self-consciousness within the white community. To insure his own survival, the black tries not to be looked at, tries to become invisible. Such a necessary response breeds an overriding self-criticism and self-depreciation into the black experience. Maya Angelou's diminished self-image reflects at the same time that it is reinforced by the entire black community's diminished self-image.

Nevertheless, there is a containedness in this environment called Stamps, just as there was in the black community surrounding young Richard Wright, a containedness which in this case mitigates rather than intensifies the child's sense of displacement. Here is a safe way of life, certainly a hard way of life, but finally a known way of life. Maya, like Richard, does not really want to fit here, but the town shapes her to it. And although she is lonely and suffers from her feelings of ugliness and abandonment, the strength of Momma's arms contains some of that loneliness.

Then suddenly Stamps is left behind as Maya moves to another promise of place, to her mother, aunts, uncles, grandparents, and St. Louis. But even here there is displacement since St. Louis remains a foreign country to the child, with its strange sounds, its packaged foods, its modern conveniences:

> In my mind I only stayed in St. Louis for a few weeks. As quickly as I understood that I had not reached my home, I sneaked away to Robin Hood's forest and the caves of Alley Oop where all reality was unreal and even that changed every day. I carried the same shield that I had used in Stamps: "I didn't come to stay."
>
> (68)

For one moment only, the illusion of being in place overwhelms the child. For that moment Mr. Freeman, her mother's boyfriend, holds her pressed to him:

> He held me so softly that I wished he wouldn't ever let me go. I felt at home. From the way he was holding me I knew he'd never let me go or let anything bad ever happen to me. This was probably my real father and we had found each other at last. But then he rolled over, leaving me in a wet place and stood up.
>
> (71)

The orphan hopes, for that infinite moment, that she has been taken back home to her father;

she feels loved, wanted, special, lovely. Ultimately Mr. Freeman's arms are not succor, but seduction: the second time he holds Maya to him it is to rape her. In short minutes, Maya becomes even more displaced: she becomes a child-woman. Moreover, she is doubly victimized by the experience. As a female child, she is subject to the physical superiority of the male. Then later, when she denies the first incident in court and Mr. Freeman is afterwards found dead, she connects his death with her lie and is psychologically victimized. Her only recourse is to stop talking: "Just my breath, carrying my words out, might poison people and they'd curl up and die like the black fat slugs that only pretended. I had to stop talking" (85).

In total solitude, total self-condemnation, total silence, Maya retreats to Stamps, to gray barren nothingness:

> The resignation of its inhabitants encouraged me to relax. They showed me a contentment based on the belief that nothing more was coming to them, although a great deal more was due. Their decision to be satisfied with life's inequities was a lesson for me. Entering Stamps, I had the feeling that I was stepping over the border lines of the map and would fall, without fear, right off the end of the world. Nothing more could happen, for in Stamps nothing happened.
>
> (86)

Her psychological and emotional devastation find a mirror in Stamps' social devastation. Stamps returns Maya to the familiarity and security of a well-known cage. This imprisoning physical environment, like the prisons holding both Malcolm X and Eldridge Cleaver, becomes a literal metaphor for her spiritual imprisonment. At the nadir of her quest for selfhood, she climbs readily back in, losing herself in her silent world, surrendering herself to her own ugliness and worthlessness: "The barrenness of Stamps was exactly what I wanted, without will or consciousness" (86).

III

Maya lives in solitude for one year until the lovely Mrs. Flowers walks into her grandmother's store and comes to play the role for Maya that Beverly Axelrod plays for Cleaver. It is Mrs. Flowers who opens the door to the caged bird's silence with the key of loving acceptance. For the first time, Maya is accepted as an individual rather than as a relation to someone else. Her identity is self-generated rather than derivative: "I was liked, and what a difference it made. I was respected not as Mrs. Henderson's grandchild or Bailey's sister but for just being Marguerite Johnson" (98). Such unqualified acceptance allows her to experience the incipient power of her own self-worth.

But while a consciousness of her own self-worth germinates inside her, outside, in the life that revolves around her, hovers the stagnant air of impotence and frustration. And precisely because she has always remained an outsider to the way of life in Stamps and precisely because she is beginning to feel the power of her own self-hood, Maya gradually becomes conscious of such powerlessness. The older autobiographer recalls vividly specific moments illustrative of such powerlessness: the evening Bailey comes home later than usual and Maya watches her grandmother worry, "her heartstrings tied to a hanging noose"; the church meeting during which she comes to realize that her neighbors used religion as a way of "bask[ing] in the righteousness of the poor and the exclusiveness of the downtrodden." Even the Joe Louis fight, which sends a thrill of pride through a black community vicariously winning victory over a white man (the white community), becomes a grotesque counterpoint to the normal way of life. Then at the graduation ceremony, during the exciting expectations of the young graduates and their families and friends are exploded casually by the words of an oblivious and insensitive white speaker, who praises the youths for being promising athletes and indirectly reminds them all that they are destined to be "maids and farmers, handymen and washer-women," the young girl comes to understand fully the desperation of impotence: "It was awful to be Negro and have no control over my life. It was brutal to be young and already trained to sit quietly and listen to charges brought against my color with no chance of defense. We should all be dead" (176). Finally, when Maya and her grandmother make an humiliating attempt to see a white dentist who refuses them, informing them cursorily that he would "rather stick [his] hand in a dog's mouth than in a nigger's," the child finds compensation for her impotence the only way she can—by fantasizing that her grandmother has ordered the white dentist to leave town and that he actually obeys her.

One gesture, however, foreshadows Maya's eventual inability to sit quietly and is very much an expression of her growing acceptance of her own self-worth. For a short time, she works in the house of Mrs. Viola Cullinan, but for a short time only, for Mrs. Cullinan, with an easiness that comes from long tradition, assaults her ego by calling her Mary rather than Maya. This oversight, offered so casually, is a most devastating sign of the black girl's invisibility in white society. In failing to call her by her name, the symbol of her uniqueness, Mrs. Cullinan fails to respect her humanity. Maya understands this perfectly and rebels by breaking Mrs. Cullinan's most cherished dish. The black girl is assuming the consciousness of the rebel as the stance necessary for preserving her individuality and affirming her self-worth.

But now there is yet another move, to wartime San Francisco. Here in this big city everything seems out of place: "The air of collective displacement, the impermanence of life in wartime and the gauche personalities of the more recent arrivals tended to dissipate my own sense of not belonging. In San Francisco, for the first time, I perceived myself as part of something" (205). Maya had been on the move when she entered Stamps and thus could not settle into its rigid way of life. She chose to remain an outsider and, in so doing, chose not to allow her personality to become rigidified. The fluidity of her new environment, however, matches the fluidity of her physical, psychological, and intellectual life. She feels in place in an environment where everyone and everything seem out of place.

Even more significant than the total displacement of San Francisco is Maya's trip to Mexico with her father. The older autobiographer, in giving form to her past experience, discovers that this moment was a turning point in her quest after authentic selfhood. Maya accompanies her father to a small Mexican town where he proceeds to get obliviously drunk, leaving her with the responsibility of getting them back to Los Angeles by car, although she had never driven one. For the first time, Maya finds herself totally in control of her situation. Her new sense of power contrasts vividly with her former despair that as a Negro she has no control over her fate.

Then, when Maya and her father return home, an argument between Maya and her stepmother Dolores ensues: Dolores calls Maya's mother a whore; Maya slaps her; Dolores cuts her severely with a knife; Maya's father rushes Maya to a friend's house and leaves her. Because she fears a scene of violence if she returns to her mother, who would certainly discover the wounds, Maya runs away and finds a new home in a wrecked car in a junkyard. Here among a community of homeless youths, "the silt of war frenzy," she lives for a month and discovers warmth, acceptance, security, brotherhood.

These experiences provide Maya with a knowledge of self-mastery and a confirmation of self-worth. With the assumption of this power, she is ready to challenge the unwritten, restrictive social codes of San Francisco. Mrs. Cullinan's broken dish prefigures the struggle for her job on the streetcar as the first black money collector. Stamps' acquiescence is left far behind as Maya assumes control over her own social destiny and engages in the struggle with life's forces. She has broken through the rusted bars of her social cage.

But Maya must still break open the bars of her female sexuality. Although she now feels power over her social identity, she feels insecurity about her sexual identity. She remains the embarrassed child who stands before the Easter congregation asking, "What you looking at me for?" The bars of her physical being close in on her, threatening her peace of mind. The lack of femininity in her small-breasted, straight-lined, hairless physique and the heaviness of her voice become, in her imagination, symptomatic of latent lesbian tendencies. A gnawing self-consciousness plagues her. Even after her mother's amused knowledge disperses her fears, the mere fact of her attraction to a classmate's breasts undermines any confidence that reassurance had provided: it was only brief respite against her fears. The only remedy available to her seems to be a heterosexual liaison. But even making love with a casual male acquaintance fails to quell her suspicions; the whole affair is an unenjoyable experience.

Only her pregnancy provides a climactic reassurance that she is indeed a heterosexual woman: if she can become pregnant, she certainly cannot be a lesbian (a specious argument in terms of logic but a compelling one in terms of the emotions and psychology of a young girl). The birth of the baby brings Maya something totally her own. More important, it brings her to a recognition and acceptance of her full, instinctual womanhood. The child, father to the woman, opens the caged door and allows the fully developed woman to fly out. Now she feels the control of her sexual identity as well as her social identity. The girl child no longer need ask, embarrassed, "What you looking at me for?" No longer need she fantasize any other reality than her own. Like Cleaver, the black man, she has gained physical, intellectual, and spiritual self-mastery.

Maya Angelou's autobiography comes to a sense of an ending: the black American girl child has succeeded in freeing herself from the natural and social bars imprisoning her in the cage of her own diminished self-image by assuming control of her life and fully accepting her black womanhood. The displaced child has found a "place."

With the birth of her child, Maya is herself born into a mature engagement with the forces of life. In welcoming that struggle, she refuses to live a death of quiet acquiescence: "Few, if any, survive their teens. Most surrender to the vague but murderous pressure of adult conformity. It becomes easier to die and avoid conflicts than to maintain a constant battle with the superior forces of maturity" (231).

IV

One way of dying to life's struggle is to suppress its inevitable pain by forgetting the past. Maya Angelou successfully banished the memories of past years to the unconscious where they lay dormant while she continued on to her years of dance and drama, of writing in Africa and in New York. She specifically alludes to this loss when in the acknowledgments she thanks her editor at Random House, "who gently prodded me back into the lost years." To the extent that these years were lost, a part of herself was lost. Once she accepted the challenge of recovering them, she accepted the challenge of rediscovering and thus reaffirming her own selfhood. Maya Angelou, like Richard Wright, comes to understand more fully who she is by remembering who she has been and how she came to be who she is. Unlike a large number of black autobiographers who have achieved a sense of freedom in the achievement of fame, Maya Angelou chooses not to focus on the traditional success story of her life but rather on the adolescence that shaped her and prepared her for those later achievements.

Moreover, she makes the journey back into her past in its own terms by immersing herself once again in the medium of her making. Stamps, Arkansas, imprinted its way of life on the child during her formative years: the lasting evidence of this imprint is the sound of it. Maya Angelou's vitality and genius as a writer lies in her acute sensitivity to the sound of the life around her, in her ability to recapture the texture of the way of life in the texture of its rhythms, its idioms, its idiosyncratic vocabulary, and especially its process of image making. This ability is a product of several factors in her past experience. First of all, she entered Stamps as an outsider, which gave her a conscious ear for all that was said and done around her. She was not born into the life; she adopted it, and to do so most effectively involved learning and then adopting its language. Then, when her experience with Mr. Freeman sent her into a hibernation of silence, she read even more avidly than before and always continued to do so.

Her desire to read was by and large a need to fantasize a more ideal existence, a more ideal self.

> To be allowed, no, invited, into the private lives of strangers, and to share their joys and fears, was a chance to exchange the Southern bitter wormwood for a cup of mead with Beowulf or a hot cup of tea and milk with Oliver Twist. When I said aloud, "It is a far, far better thing that I do, than I have ever done . . ." tears of love filled my eyes at my selflessness.
>
> (97)

And also Mrs. Flowers, her surrogate mother, taught her certain "lessons of living," one of which had directly to do with Maya's sensitivity to the language of Stamps:

> She said I must always be intolerant of ignorance but understanding of illiteracy. That some people, unable to go to school, were more educated and even more intelligent than college professors. She encouraged me to listen carefully to what country people called mother wit. That in those homely sayings was couched the collective wisdom of generations.
>
> (97)

The "collective wisdom of generations" is part of what shaped Maya Angelou's identity. That she chooses to recreate the past in its own sounds suggests that she accepts the past and recognizes its beauty and its ugliness, its strengths and its weaknesses. In **I Know Why the Caged Bird Sings,** not only does the black girl child struggle successfully for the freedom of self-worth; the black self also returns to and accepts the past in the return to and full acceptance of its language, a symbolic construct of a way of life. The liabilities inherent in the way of life are transformed through the agency of art into a positive force.

Notes

1. Maya Angelou, *I Know Why the Caged Bird Sings,* p. 5. Further citations will appear in the text.

2. William H. Grier and Price M. Cobbs, *Black Rage,* p. 40.

The Heart of a Woman

SHIRLEY NELSON GARNER (ESSAY DATE 1991)

SOURCE: Garner, Shirley Nelson. "Constructing the Mother: Contemporary Psychoanalytic Theorists and Women Autobiographers." In *Narrating Mothers: Theorizing Maternal Subjectivities,* edited by Brenda O. Daly and Maureen T. Reddy, pp. 86-93. Knoxville: University of Tennessee Press, 1991.

In the following excerpt, Garner focuses on The Heart of a Woman *as a work that places mothers in a social and cultural context.*

Setting women autobiographers beside these therapists and theorists [D. W. Winnicott, Nancy Chodorow, and others], I think of several who deal with mothers: Maxine Hong Kingston, Maya Angelou, Audre Lorde, and Kim Chernin. Published between 1975 and 1983, *The Woman Warrior,* **The Heart of a Woman,** *Zami,* and *In My Mother's House,* like the more recent theoretical works I have been describing, show the influence of the Women's Movement in their focus on mothers or mothers and daughters, who tend to be less prominent in earlier autobiographies by women. Another feature these autobiographers have in common is that their mothers—and sometimes their fathers—are immigrants. This is not true, of course, of Maya Angelou's mother; coming from a poor, southern black family, however, she, like the immigrant mothers, is outside the dominant culture.

Though mother-daughter relationships are not so central in **The Heart of a Woman** or *Zami,* all of these stories attest to the power of the mother over her children. They are also stories about growing up and leaving home. For all of these writers, leaving home is both literal and metaphorical. In its metaphorical sense, it means separating from one's family, which tends to be only or mainly the mother. To the extent that psychoanalysis highlights the separation and individuation process, it provides a perspective on these texts. Each writer reveals her efforts to establish her difference from her mother, sometimes at a moment of painful confrontation; at the same time, we see each of them consciously or unconsciously incorporating or recognizing aspects of their mothers in themselves.

In most of these works, we see the mother, as we have so often seen her in psychoanalytic theory, through the eyes of her child. Though all of these writers had children when they wrote their autobiographies, only two of them—Kim Chernin and Maya Angelou—write about themselves as mothers. For Chernin, this is a secondary and often submerged theme. There are some obvious reasons for these writers to exclude this part of their lives. To the extent that they have chosen to write a "growing up" story, their reaching maturity seems not to have anything to do with having children. Growing up has more to do with their coming to terms with their families, particularly their mothers. Another apparent motive for Kingston, Chernin, and to some extent Lorde, is to give voice and meaning to their mother's stories, which none of their mothers could write. Quite wonderfully, Chernin's mother asks her daughter to write her story. Chernin's response recalls what the psychoanalysts tell us: "I am torn by contradiction. I love this woman. She was my first great aching love. All my life I have wanted to do whatever she asked of me, in spite of our quarreling." "I'm afraid. I fear, as any daughter would, losing myself back into the mother." (12) Of course, it is probably easier to write about your mother than your children in autobiography, because it is easier to assume—even if it is not true—that your mother is less vulnerable than your children to anything hurtful you might say.

But more significantly, I think, it is harder to see yourself as a parent than to see someone else as a parent, especially if she is *your* parent. Finally, literature has not provided us with enough stories written from the mother's point of view to encourage us to write from this perspective. The absence of these stories leaves us with the special burden of creating our own forms and language for telling them, as well as suggests that they are not interesting or not the proper subject of literature. Literature, psychoanalysis, and even life have conspired to keep us from knowing our own feelings as mothers, much less telling our own stories. It is perhaps here that Muriel Rukeyser's notion—that if one woman told the truth of her life, the world would split open—awakens some of our greatest fears.

All of these writers in some sense make their mothers' cases, even while coming to terms with their own ambivalences toward their mothers. They do not write in the vein of Nancy Friday's *My Mother My Self,* a mother-blaming book. While confronting their mothers and their difficulties with these mothers, they also want to put those difficulties in a context such that they are understandable, to delineate the hardships of their mothers' lives as they see them. They also want to affirm their mothers' strengths, to validate their mothers' lives in a way the world at large does not. They are often making clear why their mothers are not nurturing, even valuing the sides of them that are not nurturing, even though as children they were hurt or puzzled by their mothers' responses to them and their actions.

The most important way these stories suggest the limitations of psychoanalytic theory in their portrayal of mothers is the way they place them in a social and cultural context. I want to look at Maya Angelou's *Heart of a Woman* to illustrate my point because she is the one of these writers who has written mainly from the point of view of a mother. Her position as a daughter and her depiction of her own mother are only secondary.

Having already written autobiographies about her younger life, *I Know Why the Caged Bird Sings* (1970), *Gather Together in My Name* (1974), and *Singin' and Swingin' and Gettin' Merry Like Christmas* (1976), Angelou is present in *The Heart of a Woman* when she is in her thirties and is the mother of a fourteen-year-old son, who in the course of the book turns seventeen.

To begin with, she is an unmarried mother, made pregnant by a shockingly deliberate and almost arbitrary encounter on her part, described in *I Know Why the Caged Bird Sings.*[1] She depicts herself as having an "immaculate pregnancy" without a man around, and she is proud of her independence. There are men who are significant for Angelou in the course of *The Heart of a Woman,* particularly the charismatic African Vus Make, whom she marries without legal ceremony, follows to Egypt to foster their mutual political aims, and finally leaves. But in her family of origin and in the family she makes with her son, she does not count on fathers or men as mates in child-rearing. Her reference to her mother's husbands is casual and dismissive: "My mother had married a few times, but she loved her maiden name. Married or not, she often identified herself as Vivian Baxter" (25). Angelou merely alludes to her own first marriage (which was not to her child's father) to explain something else.

When Angelou describes her mother, she, like Chernin, attests to the strength of the bond between them: "She smiled and I saw again that she was the most beautiful woman I had ever seen" (25). In her depiction of her mother, she makes her larger than life and retains a certain romanticism and idealization, but also draws her vulnerable and with frailties. As nurturer writ large, she is admirably tough. When they meet in Fresno in 1959 to spend the night at the Desert Hotel, where desegregation is a legal requirement but only that, the drama is very powerful. As Angelou walks through the lobby to the bar to meet her mother, she describes the scene: "The crowd made an aisle and I walked through the silence, knowing that before I reached the lounge door, a knife could be slipped in my back or a rope lassoed around my neck" (24). Sensing Angelou's fear, her mother tells her:

> Animals can sense fear. They feel it. Well, you know that human beings are animals, too. Never, never let a person know you're frightened. And a group of them . . . absolutely never. Fear brings out the worst thing in everybody. Now, in that lobby you were as scared as a rabbit. I knew it and all those white folks knew it. If I hadn't been there, they might have turned into a mob. But some-

thing about me told them, if they mess with either of us, they'd better start looking for some new asses, 'cause I'd blow away what their mammas gave them.

(26)

Laughing, according to Angelou, "like a young girl," the mother tells her daughter to open her purse, where half-hidden under her wallet lies a German luger.

Yet, when this gun-wielding woman bids good-bye to her daughter, she reveals her vulnerability as she says to Angelou, "I hate to see the back of someone I love" (29). Later we see Vivian Baxter struggling to shore up her own marriage to an alcoholic man and to cope with loneliness, calling upon Angelou to be "the shrewd authority, the judicious one, the mother" to her (210). Angelou's mother is always there for financial support in an emergency, someone from whom Angelou can gather strength. In a crisis, when Angelou goes to visit her mother, she tells us, "I needed to see my mother. I needed to be told just one more time that life was what you make it, and that every tub ought to sit on its own bottom. I had to hear her say, 'They spell my name W-O-M-A-N, 'cause the difference between a female and a woman is the difference between shit and shinola'" (210). At the same time, this romanticism is undercut by the stark, harsh memory that Angelou's mother deserted her when she was a child. She recounts being sent with her brother, unescorted, when he was four and she was three, with wrist tags for identification, from Long Beach, California, to Stamps, Arkansas, the home of her grandmother.

As the story surrounding Angelou and her mother suggests, a mother in the world of this book cannot simply negotiate the domestic realm. She must be of the world and in it. As the Fresno episode reveals, Angelou's mother is continually showing her how to survive in a racist society and also as a woman alone. As Angelou goes into a Brooklyn bar for the first time, she follows her mother's advice and example in ordering a large drink, offering her largest bill, and inviting the bartender to take out enough for a drink for himself. "Vivian Baxter told me when I was seventeen and on my own that a strange woman alone in a bar could always count on protection if she had treated the bartender right" (98).

When Guy, through no fault of his own, runs into difficulties with the Savages, a gang at school, Angelou follows her mother's example. Borrowing a gun from a friend, she confronts the head of the gang and his girlfriend at the home of his girl-

friend: "If the Savages so much as touch my son, I will then find your house and kill everything that moves, including the rats and cockroaches." After she shows the gang leader the borrowed pistol, he recovers his voice to reply: "O.K., I understand. But for a mother, I must say you're a mean motherfucker" (83-84). Angelou suggests that she is probably up to doing what she needs to do to survive, as is her son. While one could say that this is an example of woman as mother in her caretaking and protective role, since her interests and her son's are, after all, the same, I do not think this kind of action is contemplated by psychoanalytic descriptions of mother-child relationships or the mother as nurturer.

But let me turn to Angelou's actions that are not in her son's behalf or which may be, but may not be felt by him to be. Because Angelou recognizes her and her mother's ambivalences about each other, she understands the complexities of Guy's feelings toward her as well as her own toward him. At the heart of their relationship are three significant factors: their positions as members of a black minority in a predominantly white culture; their economic status, which fluctuates but often is very low; and the fact that Angelou is a single parent. Both Guy and Angelou are sensitive about the extent to which they have had to move around. Angelou recounts: "I followed the jobs, and against the advice of a pompous school psychologist, I had taken Guy along. The psychologist had been white, obviously educated and with those assets I know he was also well to do. How could he know what a young Negro boy needed in a racist world?" (29). By the time Guy is fourteen, he has developed a cynical response to Angelou's announcements that they are going to move yet once again: "Again? Okay. I can pack in twenty minutes. I've timed myself" (29).

This moving continues throughout the autobiography and is a source of Guy's hostility and weary resignation and a cause of Angelou's considerable maternal guilt. Yet she faces their situation head on and doesn't dwell on the guilt:

> My son expected warmth, food, housing, clothes and stability. He could be certain that no matter which way my fortune turned he would receive most of the things he desired. Stability, however, was not possible in my world; consequently it couldn't be possible in Guy's. Too often I had had to decline unplayable hands dealt to me by a capricious life, and take fresh cards just to remain in the game. My son could rely on my love, but never expect our lives to be unchanging.
>
> (123)

Angelou is talking here in part about economic necessity, but she is also talking about making a life for herself rather than having merely an existence. As her life proceeds, we see her finding work that is meaningful to her and important apart from the necessary income it provides; and some of her choices and her moves have to do with taking advantage of good opportunities.

She outlines some of the particular anxieties she feels as a black and single mother:

> The black mother perceives destruction at every door, ruination at each window, and even she herself is not beyond her own suspicion. She questions whether she loves her children enough—or more terribly, does she love them too much? Do her looks cause embarrassment—or even more terrifying, is she so attractive her sons begin to desire her and her daughters begin to hate her. If she is unmarried, the challenges are increased. Her singleness indicates she has rejected, or has been rejected by her mates. Beyond her door, all authority is in the hands of people who do not look or think or act like her and her children. Teachers, doctors, sales clerks, librarians, policemen, welfare workers are white and exert control over her family's moods, conditions and personality; yet within the home, she must display a right to rule which at any moment, by a knock at the door, or a ring of the telephone can be exposed as false. In the faces of these contradictions, she must be a blanket of stability, which warms but does not suffocate, and she must tell her children the truth about the power of white power without suggesting that it cannot be challenged.
>
> (37)

Apart from the circumstances Angelou cannot escape, she makes choices as a single woman that affect her relationship with her son. Because she chooses to fulfill her sexual desires rather than deny them, she brings men and even "fathers" into Guy's life, inevitably causing emotional tumult for both of them. When Angelou settles down with a man, partly because she imagines he will be a good father to Guy and a good role model, the experience, though interesting, is a disaster in emotional terms. An African who is involved in politics and works for black rights internationally, Vus is a caricature of a sexist male. Angelou finds herself in conflict: "I wanted to be a wife and to create a beautiful home to make my man happy, but there was more to life than being a diligent maid with a permanent pussy" (143).

Vus begins to have affairs, which he justifies as his "right," spends money he doesn't have, and brings collectors and disgrace to Angelou and her son. He exerts or tries to exert control over Angelou and prevent her from working, even when they can't pay their bills. Enraged when he learns that she has taken a job as associate editor of the *Arab Observer,* he rages at her, "You took a job without consulting me? Are you a man?" (226). For a time, Guy, coming into adulthood, turns away from Angelou and begins to follow Vus's cues; to see her, in her words, as a "kind and competent family retainer." He begins to incorporate Vus's machismo more surely than his politics. Thus the experiment of marriage and the family fails for Angelou and finally for Guy.

The last image that Angelou evokes of herself as mother may seem contradictory. After Guy is in a very serious car accident, he lies before her unconscious:

> I looked at my son, my real life. He was born to me when I was seventeen. I had taken him away from my mother's house when he was two months old, and except for a year I spent in Europe without him, and a month when he was stolen by a deranged woman, we had spent our lives together. My grown life lay stretched before me, stiff as a pine board, in a strange country, blood caked on his face and clotted on his clothes.
>
> (263)

When he recovers and leaves for college, she comments, "My reaction was in direct contrast with his excitement. I was going to be alone, also, for the first time. I was in my mother's house at his birth, and we had been together ever since. Sometimes we lived with others or they lived with us, but he had always been the powerful axle of my life" (271). Yet, when he walks out the door, she describes something different from what we have been led to expect:

> I closed the door and held my breath. Waiting for the wave of emotion to surge over me, knock me down, take my breath away. Nothing happened. I didn't feel bereft or desolate. I didn't feel lonely or abandoned.
>
> I sat down, still waiting. The first thought that came to me, perfectly formed and promising, was "At last, I'll be able to eat the whole breast of a roast chicken by myself."
>
> (272)

This move from sadness to contemplated pleasure strikes me not as contradiction or ambivalence. It rather suggests the balance and complexity of feeling that exists where love and life are full, as both are when presented in Angelou's story. Angelou clearly struggled with maternal guilt as her son was growing up.[2] This feeling at times must have masked the kind of maternal rage that Adrienne Rich describes so powerfully in *Of Woman Born*. The close of the novel suggests further the way Angelou tends to sublimate that feeling in humor.

Angelou's image of herself as daughter and mother within a kind of matriarchal structure, an image that shows her chafing when she is brought within patriarchal bounds, simply falls outside Winnicott's system. While Chodorow's analysis of the relationships of mothers and daughters may not be entirely irrelevant, it is hard to squeeze this story into psychoanalytic theories. When Angelou and her mother have needed to or wanted to, they have been able to give up their roles as nurturers without disabling and overwhelming guilt or sadness. As for Chodorow's solution to what she views as an unfortunate entanglement of mothers and children, there are no men drawn in this story who are willing and capable participants as child-rearers. The conflicts between autonomy and dependence that Dorothy Litwin describes seem for the most part a luxury in terms of this story. Autonomy is survival and is not something to be chosen or rejected. Susan Spieler's analysis is more to the point, for Angelou's portrait of herself and her mother subverts the categories of masculine and feminine. Because Angelou and her mother are heterosexual, the analysis in *Lesbian Psychologies* introduces issues that do not pertain to them. Yet the attention to class, race, and difference that those essays incorporate may alert us to the perspective we must bring to reading the mother in this autobiography.

To understand the roles, feelings, conflicts, and possibilities of mothers, we must turn to the fiction and autobiography of women writers, and to women's individual essays, and to collections of their writing. Psychoanalysts must learn to listen to mothers as well as to children and recollections of childhood. They must consider the limits of psychoanalytic understanding of class and race and reach for a broader perspective. They must sharpen the analysis of gender issues that some psychoanalysts have begun to elaborate. At this time, stories of mothers may enrich psychoanalytic theories more than these theories may aid us in interpreting mother's stories.

Notes

1. Quotations from *The Heart of a Woman,* by Maya Angelou. Copyright 1981 by Maya Angelou. Reprinted by permission of Random House, Inc.

2. In "Singing the Black Mother: Maya Angelou and Autobiographical Continuity," Mary Jane Lupton discusses Angelou's expression of maternal guilt in autobiographical works written before *The Heart of a Woman.*

LYMAN B. HAGEN (ESSAY DATE 1997)

SOURCE: Hagen, Lyman B. "The Autobiographies: *The Heart of a Woman.*" In *Heart of a Woman, Mind of a Writer, and Soul of a Poet: A Critical Analysis of the Writings of Maya Angelou,* pp. 96-117. Lanham, Md.: University Press of America, 1997.

In the following essay, Hagen examines such themes within The Heart of a Woman *as motherhood, responsibility, family, self-identity, and independence.*

The title of Angelou's fourth autobiography, while less striking or oblique than titles of her preceding books, is taken from a poem by Georgia Douglas Johnson, a Harlem Renaissance writer. This poem is marvelously appropriate as it refers to a *Caged Bird,* thus providing linkage with Angelou's initial series volume. This addition to the ongoing story of Maya Angelou looks into the heart of the maturing woman and focuses on relationships. The relationships with her son, with men, with her racial responsibilities, and with her writing are the thrust of the narrative. These are the normal, everyday concerns, less venturesome and startling. Racial confrontations such as that of Angelou with white school authorities and that of the renowned Billie Holiday versus a nondescript white woman fulfill elements of the black canon of autobiography and therefore discount any drift from the interest of her people. Thus *The Heart of a Woman* (1981) is truly a story of an African-American female. It does not depart much from the factual happenings except for dramatic effect. It is a far more sober assessment of her wide ranging activities.

The Heart of a Woman does not disappoint the Angelou readers who are accustomed to crisp, poetic prose interspersed with "down home" homilies. It is another professionally written work, exhibiting increasing literary competence. The appellation "poetic temperament" holds as true here as in her other books. The prose is captivating; it maintains the richness and texture of her style. The metaphors are still striking: "Time wrapped itself around every word."[1] Angelou continues to use scatology to capture individual speech practices. The essence of Billie Holiday cannot be captured without quoting her colorful, uncensored responses. Angelou is proud of Billie Holiday's friendship and would never demean it by scrubbing street-smart Billie's less than sanitary language. What you hear is what she is.

Angelou fictionalizes dialogue to re-create a sense of place and a sense of history. She incorporates fantasy to reveal her illusions and unfulfilled desires and to acknowledge her lack of control over the future. A degree of fatalism is woven throughout this and other Angelou works. There is a consistent acquiesence to fate. These rhetorical devices are commonly employed by autobiographers for realism and conviction, according to Carol E. Neubauer.[2] Angelou does not stray far from traditional structure.

Critics responded favorably to the professional quality of *The Heart of a Woman.* Janet B. Blundell calls it "lively, revealing, and worth the reading"; however, she saw a weakness in that it is at times "too chatty and anecdotal."[3] But this is the very crux of Angelou's narratives. They are generally a mosaic of episodes—anecdotes—linked by theme and character. Sheree Crute seems to appreciate this approach and says Angelou "makes the most of her wonderfully unaffected story telling skills."[4] *Choice* writes that "while (Angelou's) first book remains her best . . . every book since has been very much worth the reading and pondering."[5] *Caged Bird* gains much of its strength from an extensive use of folklore, a significant omission in *The Heart of a Woman.* However, this and other books since *Caged Bird* are less general in scope. The reviews of all Angelou's books are marked by a uniformity of light praise but great admiration. No critic suggests that any of the works in the series is less than a delight to read. The courage of the author's revelations is always applauded.

The Heart of a Woman, as *Singin' and Swingin',* entails constant movement. Angelou is still seeking to find an appropriate home for herself and her son. This is made more difficult by her ongoing efforts to define herself. This is another volume covering a lot of geography and growth. Angelou moves from San Francisco to a Sausalito houseboat commune trying out the beatnik life style; thence to ultra conservative Laurel Canyon in Los Angeles. Lack of acceptance and racial attacks send her off to the Harlem Writers Guild in New York. She restlessly followed her fate to London to Egypt to Ghana, where the book ends. Whenever the opportunity presents itself, Angelou inserts her rich descriptive passages about these places visited. These descriptions enhance the specific experiences recalled as well as the general credibility of the narrative and also show an appreciation of the diversity of the world. This reflects Angelou's growing familiarity with an enlarging sphere and her comfort within it.

The Heart of a Woman picks up Angelou's story after she has left the cast of the European traveling company of *Porgy and Bess* and returned from Hawaii to the night club circuit in America. The book begins at the precise end of its predecessor. Angelou is still the unmarried African-American female with a rapidly growing now adolescent son to support. She is principally concerned during the seven years covered by *The Heart of a Woman* with her relationship with her son—her love of him and her pride in his developing personality and character. Uppermost in her mind is his welfare and helping him cope as a black young man-child trying to mature in a generally unsympathetic white world. He has been taken care of on occasion by others, but Angelou continuously accepts motherhood and its attendant responsibility to monitor his development. This sense of duty incorporates a family relationship, and Angelou is concerned with establishing a complete family, which includes a father figure for Guy.

This quest for family brings Angelou to describe her encounters with a number of lovers and potential fathers. In the time-frame of the book, she reports on relationships with several men, the last of which is her ill-fated common law marriage to her second "husband," Vusumzi Make, a colorful African radical. This is the liaison that carried her to London, Egypt and Ghana. She eventually finds Make to be a less than desirable role model for Guy and a trying mate for herself. They part after a few years.

A large portion of the book concerns involvement with the Civil Rights movement of the late 1950s and 1960s. Here, she seizes the opportunity to express her pride in her race and in its struggle for equality and acceptance. Like Norman Mailer in his *Armies in the Night,* Angelou serves as an informed personal historian of the moral crisis of the period—racial injustice—that was of popular concern. She is an enthusiastic participant in the movement and not just an outside observer. Daisy Aldan's previously quoted concern regarding the book's ". . . hostility . . . toward all white people"[6] is an outgrowth of the barrage of negative racial experiences Angelou relates. Every possible slur, slight, and affront is visited upon Angelou and her son solely because of their color. This emphasis also seems to be a justification of the motivations of the black activists who people the book. The more moderate views of Martin Luther King are reported too, and with great admiration. When Angelou chooses to work with an organized group, it is the Southern Leadership followers of Doctor King.

In the early books, Angelou's mother and grandmother command a considerable amount of attention. Grandmother Henderson has died and is now rarely mentioned, but Angelou still calls on her mother when she needs reinforcement. Vivian provides her with pragmatic advice in the form of proverbs derived from Mother Wit: "Ask for what you want and be prepared to pay for what you get" (*HW* [*The Heart of a Woman*] 29), a statement that encourages Angelou to be self-reliant and not to expect handouts. This and a lengthy Br'er Rabbit story are the few touches of folklore in *The Heart of a Woman.* This type of imbedded preachment covertly conveys its message.

Angelou accepts the demands of womanhood and is fiercely independent, but is grateful for her mother's support, be it financial or moral. This does not diminish her strength or independence, but rather increases them by knowing that there is a safety net in the person of Vivian Baxter. Angelou does take her son and move away from Vivian's immediate vigilance. Overcoming racial discrimination, she seeks greater independence and middle-class respectability in Laurel Canyon, Los Angeles.

Angelou's love of her son and involvement in his upbringing cause her to realize the special problems faced by African-American mothers when raising their children. Authority, she notes, is "in the hands of people who do not look or think like the (black mother) and her children. Teachers, doctors, sales clerks, librarians, policemen, welfare workers are white and exert control over her family's moods, conditions and personality" (*HW* 37). The African-American parent of that time is obliged to adhere to the existing and white societal coda. The red tape and restrictions may chafe as reported by Angelou, but they maintain order of sorts for all persons.

In spite of the problems articulated in *The Heart of a Woman,* Angelou succeeds in raising a son who turns out well. She does not fail him, and others in her position can thus hope for the same. One particular problem faced by single parent Angelou is that Guy has been hurt by the brief but frequent family separations. Having endured her own feelings of betrayal when passed to different relatives, Angelou knows she must compensate so Guy does not harbor resentment to her and turn to outsiders for guidance. She realizes how much Guy feels the need of a father. It was

also painful for him to be a young man "who had lived with the certainty of white insolence and the unsureness of moving from school to school, coast to coast, and . . . made to find his way through another continent and new cultures" (*HW* 267). Therefore the determined search for family and father is so much a part of *The Heart of a Woman* that it cannot be isolated from the situational responses.

This search allows the introduction of a variety of male characters and allows Angelou to express normal sexual interests. This is an accepted topic of the culture of the time. Angelou reports on a series of lovers associated with her search for a suitable husband and father. Most fall short of her requirements. Angelou does try throughout the book to balance an honest appreciation of ordinary sexual adventures with the wholesome and desirable goal of stability. This is another message of hope for those young women disturbed by their sexuality and unable to come to terms with desires and expectations.

Angelou writes in this book much more graphically about her own sexual activities than in any of the preceding volumes. She is at an age and stage where this is natural and acceptable. One may tend to wonder how much of this detailed interest is real or romanticized. Her admission of shouting in the bedroom and such personal pleasure seems to be atypical material. In previous books, Angelou appears to contradict any extreme preoccupation with base pleasures. For example, in *Gather Together in My Name,* she imagines that the ideal husband made desultory love a few times and never asked for more and this was acceptable. In another instance, she said physical sex only once a month was satisfactory. Her stance was quite Victorian. This expectation may be closer to her real feelings than her "liberated" statements. Each of the contradictory positions may, however, merely reflect thinking of a particular time or circumstance. At the time of her writing *The Heart of a Woman,* more liberal and open talk of human interactions was developing. African-American female writers were not only taking pride in their race but also in themselves as women.[7] The "liberated" modern woman was free to proclaim that she too had sexual urges. Sometimes women seemed inclined to outdo each other for sheer shock value. Frank talk about sex seemed to be almost requisite for a commercially successful book of that era. Despite relating various affairs, Angelou always advocates monogamy and stresses fidelity in relationships. She honors commitment.

Angelou and Guy move from Los Angeles to New York. It was here that she met many of the men she discusses. Several friends had encouraged Angelou to pursue a writing career. She was accepted by the Harlem Writers Guild which was composed of black writers both neophyte and established. Angelou's work was roundly criticized, but the tough lessons provided needed direction. Her night club background supplied a living. Being in the cauldron of New York allows much of *The Heart of a Woman* to be devoted to the major and minor players of the Civil Rights movement and political activism of that period. Angelou's role as personal historian covers both the Civil Rights movement and the black literary movement. She meets and writes about such national figures as Bayard Rustin, Malcolm X, Martin Luther King, and other prominent African Americans caught up in the push for equal treatment for their race. The inclusion of these prominent familiar figures allows for their lessons and messages to be passed along unobtrusively. When Angelou is a coordinator of the SCLC, she is totally involved in the cause. She is an excellent organizer and coordinates volunteer efforts, raises funds, keeps the office running, and attends innumerable functions with groups of various names. All this is for the purpose of furthering the advancement and recognition of black people throughout the world. She has been faulted by some for not being sufficiently involved in the "cause." This is not true; she just chose to be less strident. Her efforts were eminently successful, and her contributions to civil rights causes were effective. Together with Godfrey Cambridge she wrote and directed a well-received musical revue, *Cabaret for Freedom,* which was intended to raise funds and consciousness.

Angelou's sure ear allows her to re-create fictionally scenes of encounters with people with an uncanny touch of reality. She mimics dialogues with notable personages with ease. According to several informed friends, her descriptions of exchanges with Martin Luther King or Malcolm X capture the very essence of the responses they would give, although they are not quoted directly. Angelou is attuned to the intent of a message as well as its delivery.

Many Civil Rights advocates were not shy about acknowledging their African heritage. It is quite natural for them to mingle with and offer their support to Cuban and African Freedom Fighters. These foreign activists solicited assistance and appeared at many related functions. It is therefore not surprising that Maya Angelou aligns herself emotionally as a helpmate to one of these, Vusumzi Make, and fantasizes that together they can free all of Africa from white oppression. This is an unusual lapse from reality for Angelou. She is quite taken with Make and he steps into the role of the strong male she has been seeking. He relates well with Guy, relieving Angelou of sole concern. This largely influences her acceptance of him.

Throughout *The Heart of a Woman,* Angelou continues her indictment of the white power structure and her protests against racial injustice. She again re-creates scenes wherein the dialogue allows comment about shoddy white behavior. She sometimes utilizes flashbacks to youthful indignities endured and sometimes she relates experiences of friends and colleagues. The sketch of a scene involving Mother Vivian at the Desert Hotel in Fresno, California, is a classic. Vivian's every move and word is calculated to instruct Maya and deflate the ignorant whites they encounter. Vivian Baxter displays the ultimate in panache and carries off a put-down of her antagonists with dignity and distinction. Public negative treatment of African-American people validates their sometimes radical responses. The references to earlier affronts and reactions serve to provide continuity to the series.

Not all attitudes expressed regarding whites are negative. Angelou learns from Martin Luther King that he feels that there are many "white people who love right" (*HW* 94). Dr. King was optimistic. He had travelled to and from jails across the south and marched and preached throughout the United States, frequently with whites at his side or in his audience. He felt both white and black people were changing. Angelou herself was surprised by the white volunteers at the SCLC New York office. Although Angelou harbored a suspicion of white liberals, she was impressed by the honesty of actress Shelley Winters who ardently wanted only a peaceful future for her daughter in a mixed society. This idealism was somewhat misplaced; inequality and turmoil are extant today.

In relating experiences with whites, Angelou never offers solutions to the problems exposed. She simply reports, reacts, or dramatizes events. The closest she comes to an analysis or solution for racial problems is the time when she repeats Vivian Baxter's statement that "Black folks can't change because white folks won't change" (*HW* 29). Nevertheless the times were exciting and hopes ran high for progress toward equality.

Angelou's continuing role as a literary historian for the time of the book provides an opportunity to report on some African-American literature that is being published, despite her observation that it is difficult to get black literature accepted and printed. This is a somewhat inaccurate assessment, as many African-American writers were beginning to be published and publicized. Actually it was a time when book sales were in decline and all writers were encountering difficulties. There was a vast amount of publishable material and competition was keen. Talent, like seeping water, found someplace to go, and various movements enjoyed the efforts of the best and the brightest.

Vusumzi Make is called to London to present his cause and Angelou decides she will accompany him. She is committed to freedom for Africa and mixes with black women from many nations. The women did not actively participate in the conference but many exchanged ideas and objectives for their nation-states and people.

Make tells Angelou to find a New York apartment for himself, herself, and Guy. A family of sorts is born. They live well as befits a country's representative. Angelou keeps up her Harlem Writers Guild contacts and takes a leading role in Genet's *The Blacks*. Disturbing phone calls and events intrude upon the solidarity of the marriage, but Angelou was pleased with Guy's progress. This outweighed all other things. They are suddenly evicted from their New York apartment. Angelou and Guy make a quick visit to Vivian in San Francisco while Make arranges to pack them off to Cairo.

For a time, the excitement of the exotic and the foreign mask the realities for Angelou. She soon finds, however, that Make is not faithful or truthful or capable of supporting them.

Initially in Cairo, Angelou is exposed to an increasingly sumptuous life style. But again, reality imposes, and mounting debts become burdensome. Work, to Angelou, becomes a necessity. A meeting with the president of a news service leads to employment for Angelou as an assistant editor for a new magazine, the *Arab Observer*. She avidly pursues knowledge of her new career and accepts her disillusionment with Make. Angelou took on additional work writing commentary for Radio Egypt. An inevitable breakup with Make left her heading to Ghana to enroll Guy in the university in Accra. She shakes off another betrayal by a man and is prepared to accept a job offer in Liberia and to loosen the ties with Guy and let each move along independently. Fate, in the form of an auto accident, intervened. Guy was seriously injured while with friends. Angelou was needed at his side and for a long recuperative period. Friends managed to get her a job at the University as an administrative assistant. She tends to Guy until he once again can function on his own. He moves into a university dormitory to finally begin his independent life. Angelou stays near to quietly launch this venture toward full manhood for her son. She is, however, contemplating following her own single personhood.

The Heart of a Woman follows Angelou's established pattern of ending on a strong note of hope. Angelou and her son Guy have advanced to the point where each of them can move toward divergent, independent paths. Angelou can relish a sense of achievement as Guy looks forward eagerly to his future. She can anticipate a future for herself centered on herself. Again closure brings the cycle to a place that portends a new life for both Guy and Maya, a re-birth: a closing door and an opening door. Both characters are now citizens of a large world. Faithful to the ongoing themes of survival, sense of self, and continuing education, *The Heart of a Woman* moves its central figures to a point of full personhood. Its light humor and bantering carries a message of achievement.

Notes

1. Maya Angelou, *The Heart of a Woman* (New York: Bantam Books, 1982), 9. Hereafter cited in the text as *HW*.

2. Carol E. Neubauer, "Displacement and Autobiographical Style in Maya Angelou's *The Heart of a Woman*," *Black American Literature Forum* 17 (1983): 123-129.

3. Janet B. Blundell, *Library Journal* 106, October 1981, 1919.

4. Sheree Crute, *MS* 10, July 1981, 27.

5. *Choice* 19, January 1982, 621.

6. Daisy Aldan, *World Literature Today* 56, 4 (Autumn, 1982): 697.

7. Estelle C. Jelinek, *The Tradition of Women's Autobiography* (Boston: Twayne Publishers, 1986), 149.

FURTHER READING

Bibliography

Gerry, Thomas M. F. *Contemporary Canadian and U.S. Women of Letters: An Annotated Bibliography.* New York: Garland, 1993, 287 p.

Bibliography of North American women writers.

Biography

Lisandrelli, Elaine Slivinski. *Maya Angelou: More Than a Poet.* Springfield, N.J.: Enslow Publishers, 1996, 128 p.

Biography of Angelou with lengthy bibliographical index.

Criticism

Braxton, Joanne M., ed. *Maya Angelou's I Know Why the Caged Bird Sings: A Casebook.* New York: Oxford University Press, 1999, 162 p.

Collection of critical essays on I Know Why the Caged Bird Sings.

Burr, Zofia. "Maya Angelou on the Inaugural Stage." In *Of Women, Poetry, and Power: Strategies of Address in Dickinson, Miles, Brooks, Lorde, and Angelou,* pp. 180-94, 219-21. Chicago, Ill.: University of Illinois Press, 2002.

Comparison of Robert Frost's reading of his poem "The Gift Outright" at President Kennedy's 1961 inauguration to Angelou's reading of "On the Pulse of Morning" at Bill Clinton's 1993 inauguration.

Kent, George E. "Maya Angelou's *I Know Why the Caged Bird Sings* and Black Autobiographical Tradition." *Kansas Quarterly* 7, no. 3 (summer 1975): 72-8.

Argues that I Know Why the Caged Bird Sings *occupies a unique place within the African American autobiographical tradition.*

Lupton, Mary Jane. "*I Know Why the Caged Bird Sings.*" In *Maya Angelou: A Critical Companion,* pp. 51-73. Westport, Conn.: Greenwood, 1998.

Explores the thematic and stylistic aspects of I Know Why the Caged Bird Sings.

McPherson, Dolly A. *Order out of Chaos: The Autobiographical Works of Maya Angelou.* New York: Peter Lang, 1990, 176 p.

Examines the major thematic concerns in Angelou's autobiographical novels.

Megna-Wallace, Joanne. *Understanding I Know Why the Caged Bird Sings: A Student Casebook to Issues, Sources, and Historical Documents.* Westport, Conn.: Greenwood Press, 1998, 189 p.

Collection of essays placing Angelou's I Know Why the Caged Bird Sings *within political, historical, and literary contexts.*

Miller, Adam David. Review of *The Heart of a Woman. Black Scholar* 13, nos. 4/5 (summer 1982): 48-9.

Positive review praising Angelou's storytelling abilities, characterizations, insights, and conclusions in The Heart of a Woman.

O'Neale, Sondra. "Reconstruction of the Composite Self: New Images of Black Women in Maya Angelou's Continuing Autobiography." In *Black Women Writers (1950-1980): A Critical Evaluation,* edited by Mari Evans, pp. 25-36. Garden City, N.Y.: Anchor Press/Doubleday, 1984.

Provides examination of black American female stereotypes and Angelou's development of new images for black women in her autobiographies.

Vermillion, Mary. "Reembodying the Self: Representations of Rape in *Incidents in the Life of a Slave Girl* and *I Know Why the Caged Bird Sings.*" In *Maya Angelou's* I Know Why the Caged Bird Sings*: A Casebook,* edited by Joanne M. Braxton, pp. 51-73. New York: Oxford University Press, 1999.

Explores the parallels between Harriet Jacobs's Incidents in the Life of a Slave Girl *and* I Know Why the Caged Bird Sings.

OTHER SOURCES FROM GALE:

Additional coverage of Angelou's life and career is contained in the following sources published by the Gale Group: *American Writers Supplement,* Vol. 4; *Authors and Artists for Young Adults,* Vols. 7, 20; *Beacham's Encyclopedia of Popular Fiction: Biography & Resources,* Vol. 1; *Beacham's Guide to Literature for Young Adults,* Vol. 2; *Black Literature Criticism; Black Writers,* Ed. 2; *Children's Literature Review,* Vol. 53; *Concise Dictionary of American Literary Biography Supplement; Contemporary Authors,* Vols. 65-68; *Contemporary Authors New Revision Series,* Vols. 19, 42, 65; *Contemporary Poets; Contemporary Popular Writers; Contemporary Southern Writers; Contemporary Women Poets; Dictionary of Literary Biography,* Vol. 38; *DISCovering Authors; DISCovering Authors: British Edition; DISCovering Authors: Canadian Edition; DISCovering Authors Modules: Most-Studied Authors, Multicultural, Poets,* and *Popular Fiction and Genre Authors; DISCovering Authors 3.0; Exploring Novels; Exploring Poetry; Literature and Its Times,* Vol. 4; *Literature Resource Center; Major Authors and Illustrators for Children and Young Adults Supplement; Major 20th-Century Writers,* Eds. 1, 2; *Modern American Women Writers; Nonfiction Classics for Students; Novels for Students,* Vol. 2; *Poetry Criticism,* Vol. 32; *Poetry for Students,* Vols. 2, 3; *Reference Guide to American Literature; Reference Guide to Short Fiction; St. James Guide to Young Adult Writers; Something About the Author,* Vol. 49; *World Literature Criticism Supplement;* and *Writers for Young Adults.*

MARGARET ATWOOD

(1939 -)

Canadian novelist, poet, short story writer, essayist, critic, and author of children's books.

Internationally acclaimed as a novelist, poet, and short story writer, Atwood has emerged as a major figure in contemporary feminist writing. Through female protagonists and narrators who often journey from victimization to self-actualization, Atwood explores women's issues using elements of science fiction, historical fact, fairy tale, and dystopian vision.

BIOGRAPHICAL INFORMATION

Atwood was born in Ottawa and grew up in suburban Toronto. As a child she spent her summers at her family's cottage in the wilderness of northern Quebec, where her father, a forest entomologist, conducted research. She began to write while in high school, contributing poetry, short stories, and cartoons to the school newspaper. As an undergraduate at the University of Toronto, Atwood was influenced by critic Northrop Frye, who introduced her to the poetry of William Blake. Impressed with Blake's use of mythological imagery, Atwood wrote her first volume of poetry, *Double Persephone,* which was published in 1961. The following year Atwood completed her A.M. degree at Radcliffe College, Harvard University.

She returned to Toronto in 1963, where she began collaborating with artist Charles Pachter, who designed and illustrated several volumes of her poetry. In 1964 Atwood moved to Vancouver, where she taught English for a year at the University of British Columbia and completed her first novel, *The Edible Woman* (1969). After a year of teaching literature at Sir George Williams University in Montreal, Atwood moved to Alberta to teach creative writing at the University of Alberta. Her poetry collection *The Circle Game* (1966) won the 1967 Governor General's Award, Canada's highest literary honor. Atwood's public visibility increased significantly with the publication of the poetry collection *Power Politics* in 1971. Seeking an escape from increasing media attention, Atwood left her teaching position at the University of Toronto to move to a farm in Ontario with her husband. In 1986 she again received the Governor General's Award for her novel *The Handmaid's Tale.*

MAJOR WORKS

Most of Atwood's fiction and poetry concerns women's issues on some level, but her novel *The Handmaid's Tale* has generated the most feminist commentary. The story is set in Cambridge, Massachusetts, in the early twenty-first century, after Christian fundamentalists have transformed the United States into a fascistic theocracy called

Gilead. Birth rates are down in the post-nuclear age of Gilead, so Handmaids—women who are fertile—are designated as sexual slaves to produce offspring for childless couples considered morally fit to raise children. Women in Gilead are not allowed to read, hold jobs, or have money. Narrated by a young Handmaid named Offred—or Of Fred, the man to whom she belongs—the novel is considered a powerful dystopian vision of anti-feminist totalitarianism. The protagonist of Atwood's next novel, *Cat's Eye* (1990), Elaine Risley, is a controversial middle-aged painter who returns to her hometown of Toronto for a retrospective exhibition of her work. The trip triggers unexpected memories and emotions for Elaine, particularly thoughts of Cordelia, a childhood friend to whom Elaine was attracted despite the girl's extreme cruelty. The story is a nonlinear telling of Elaine's confrontation of her past, specifically her complex and difficult friendship with Cordelia, and the ways in which women routinely betray one another. In *The Robber Bride* (1993) Atwood transforms the grisly Brothers Grimm fairy tale "The Robber Bridegroom," about a demonic groom who lures three innocent maidens into his lair and then devours them, into another statement about women's treatment of each other. Three middle-aged friends are relieved to reunite at the funeral of the woman who tormented them in college, stealing from them money, time, and men, and threatening their careers and lives. But the villainous Zenia turns up alive, forcing them to relive painful memories and come to terms with the connection between love and destruction. In earlier novels such as *The Edible Woman* and *Lady Oracle* (1976), Atwood used sarcastic wit and irony to explore the masks women wear to impress men. In her essays and criticism she often discusses the difficulties of being a woman writer and the challenge of developing meaningful female and male characters.

CRITICAL RECEPTION

Atwood's works have achieved both wide popular readership and much critical attention. Criticism has tended to focus on her political and social views as they are represented in her works, most notably her feminism, of which she has spoken frequently in interviews. Because her works often portray physical and psychological violence in relationships between men and women, some commentators have labeled Atwood pessimistic and dismissed her as little more than an ideologue, but other critics have hailed her as a visionary interpreter of contemporary feminist thought.

PRINCIPAL WORKS

Double Persephone (poetry) 1961

The Circle Game (poetry) 1966

The Animals in That Country (poetry) 1968

The Edible Woman (novel) 1969

The Journals of Susanna Moodie (poetry) 1970

Procedures for Underground (poetry) 1970

Power Politics (poetry) 1971

Surfacing (novel) 1972

Survival: A Thematic Guide to Canadian Literature (criticism) 1972

You Are Happy (poetry) 1974

Lady Oracle (novel) 1976

Selected Poems (poetry) 1976

Dancing Girls, and Other Stories (short stories) 1977

Two-Headed Poems (poetry) 1978

Up in the Tree (juvenilia) 1978

Life before Man (novel) 1979

True Stories (poetry) 1981

Bodily Harm (novel) 1982

Second Words: Selected Critical Prose (criticism) 1982

Bluebeard's Egg (short stories) 1983

Murder in the Dark: Short Fictions and Prose Poems (short stories and poetry) 1983

Interlunar (poetry) 1984

The Handmaid's Tale (novel) 1986

Selected Poems II: Poems Selected and New, 1976-1986 (poetry) 1987

Cat's Eye (novel) 1990

Wilderness Tips (short stories) 1991

Good Bones (short stories) 1992

The Robber Bride (novel) 1993

The Blind Assassin (novel) 2001

Negotiating with the Dead: A Writer on Writing (essays) 2002

Oryx and Crake (novel) 2003

PRIMARY SOURCES

MARGARET ATWOOD (ESSAY DATE 1982)

SOURCE: Atwood, Margaret. "On Being a 'Woman Writer': Paradoxes and Dilemmas." In *Second Words*, pp. 190-204. Toronto, Can.: Anansi Press Limited, 1982.

In the following essay, Atwood explores the difficulties of being considered a "woman writer."

I approach this article with a good deal of reluctance. Once having promised to do it, in fact, I've been procrastinating to such an extent that my own aversion is probably the first subject I should attempt to deal with. Some of my reservations have to do with the questionable value of writers, male or female, becoming directly involved in political movements of any sort: their involvement may be good for the movement, but it has yet to be demonstrated that it's good for the writer. The rest concern my sense of the enormous complexity not only of the relationships between Man and Woman, but also of those between those other abstract intangibles, Art and Life, Form and Content, Writer and Critic, etcetera.

Judging from conversations I've had with many other woman writers in this country, my qualms are not unique. I can think of only one writer I know who has any formal connection with any of the diverse organizations usually lumped together under the titles of Women's Liberation or the Women's Movement. There are several who have gone out of their way to disavow even any fellow-feeling; but the usual attitude is one of grudging admiration, tempered with envy: the younger generation, they feel, has it a hell of a lot better than they did. Most writers old enough to have a career of any length behind them grew up when it was still assumed that a woman's place was in the home and nowhere else, and that anyone who took time off for an individual self-ish activity like writing was either neurotic or wicked or both, derelict in her duties to a man, child, aged relatives or whoever else was supposed to justify her existence on earth. I've heard stories of writers so consumed by guilt over what they had been taught to feel was their abnormality that they did their writing at night, secretly, so no one would accuse them of failing as housewives, as "women." These writers accomplished what they did by themselves, often at great personal expense; in order to write at all, they had to defy other women's as well as men's ideas of what was proper, and it's not finally all that comforting to have a phalanx of women—some younger and

relatively unscathed, others from their own generation, the bunch that was collecting china, changing diapers and sneering at any female with intellectual pretensions twenty or even ten years ago—come breezing up now to tell them they were right all along. It's like being judged innocent after you've been hanged: the satisfaction, if any, is grim. There's a great temptation to say to Womens' Lib, "Where were you when I really needed you?" or "It's too late for me now." And you can see, too, that it would be fairly galling for these writers, if they have any respect for historical accuracy, which most do, to be hailed as products, spokeswomen, or advocates of the Women's Movement. When they were undergoing their often drastic formative years there *was* no Women's Movement. No matter that a lot of what they say can be taken by the theorists of the Movement as supporting evidence, useful analysis, and so forth: their own inspiration was not theoretical, it came from wherever all writing comes from. Call it experience and imagination. These writers, if they are honest, don't want to be wrongly identified as the children of a movement that did not give birth to them. Being adopted is not the same as being born.

A third area of reservation is undoubtedly a fear of the development of a one-dimensional Feminist Criticism, a way of approaching literature produced by women that would award points according to conformity or non-conformity to an ideological position. A feminist criticism is, in fact, already emerging. I've read at least one review, and I'm sure there have been and will be more, in which a novelist was criticized for not having made her heroine's life different, even though that life was more typical of the average woman's life in this society than the reviewer's "liberated" version would have been. Perhaps Women's Lib reviewers will start demanding that heroines resolve their difficulties with husband, kids, or themselves by stomping out to join a consciousness raising group, which will be no more satisfactory from the point of view of literature than the legendary Socialist Realist romance with one's tractor. However, a feminist criticism need not necessarily be one-dimensional. And—small comfort—no matter how narrow, purblind and stupid such a criticism in its lowest manifestations may be, it cannot possibly be *more* narrow, purblind and stupid than some of the non-feminist critical attitudes and styles that have preceded it.

There's a fourth possible factor, a less noble one: the often observed phenomenon of the member of a despised social group who manages to transcend the limitations imposed on the group, at least enough to become "successful." For such a person the impulse—whether obeyed or not—is to disassociate him/herself from the group and to side with its implicit opponents. Thus the Black millionaire who deplores the Panthers, the rich *Québecois* who is anti-Separatist, the North American immigrant who changes his name to an "English" one; thus, alas, the Canadian writer who makes it, sort of, in New York, and spends many magazine pages decrying provincial dull Canadian writers; and thus the women with successful careers who say "*I've* never had any problems, I don't know what they're talking about." Such a woman tends to regard herself, and to be treated by her male colleagues, as a sort of honorary man. It's the rest of them who are inept, brainless, tearful self-defeating: not her. "You think like a man," she is told, with admiration and unconscious put-down. For both men and women, it's just too much of a strain to fit together the traditionally incompatible notions of "woman" and "good at something." And if you *are* good at something, why carry with you the stigma attached to that dismal category you've gone to such lengths to escape from? The only reason for rocking the boat is if you're still chained to the oars. Not everyone reacts like this, but this factor may explain some of the more hysterical opposition to Women's Lib on the part of a few woman writers, even though they may have benefitted from the Movement in the form of increased sales and more serious attention.

A couple of ironies remain; perhaps they are even paradoxes. One is that, in the development of modern Western civilization, writing was the first of the arts, before painting, music, composing, and sculpting, which it was possible for women to practice; and it was the fourth of the job categories, after prostitution, domestic service and the stage, and before wide-scale factory work, nursing, secretarial work, telephone operating and school teaching, at which it was possible for them to make any money. The reason for both is the same: writing as a physical activity is private. You do it by yourself, on your own time; no teachers or employers are involved, you don't have to apprentice in a studio or work with musicians. Your only business arrangements are with your publisher, and these can be conducted through the mails; your real "employers" can be deceived, if you choose, by the adoption of an assumed (male) name; witness the Brontës and George Eliot. But the private and individual nature of writing may also account for the low incidence of direct involvement by woman writers in the Movement now. If you are a writer, prejudice against women will affect you *as a writer* not directly but indirectly. You won't suffer from wage discrimination, because you aren't paid any wages; you won't be hired last and fired first, because you aren't hired or fired anyway. You have relatively little to complain of, and, absorbed in your own work as you are likely to be, you will find it quite easy to shut your eyes to what goes on at the spool factory, or even at the university. *Paradox:* reason for involvement then equals reason for non-involvement now.

Another paradox goes like this. As writers, woman writers are like other writers. They have the same professional concerns, they have to deal with the same contracts and publishing procedures, they have the same need for solitude to work and the same concern that their work be accurately evaluated by reviewers. There is nothing "male" or "female" about these conditions; they are just attributes of the activity known as writing. As biological specimens and as citizens, however, women are like other women: subject to the same discriminatory laws, encountering the same demeaning attitudes, burdened with the same good reasons for not walking through the park alone after dark. They too have bodies, the capacity to bear children; they eat, sleep and bleed, just like everyone else. In bookstores and publishers' offices and among groups of other writers, a woman writer may get the impression that she is "special;" but in the eyes of the law, in the loan office or bank, in the hospital and on the street she's just another woman. She doesn't get to wear a sign to the grocery store saying "Respect me, I'm a Woman Writer." No matter how good she may feel about herself, strangers who aren't aware of her shelf-full of nifty volumes with cover blurbs saying how gifted she is will still regard her as a nit.

We all have ways of filtering out aspects of our experience we would rather not think about. Woman writers can keep as much as possible to the "writing" end of their life, avoiding the less desirable aspects of the "woman" end. Or they can divide themselves in two, thinking of themselves as two different people: a "writer" and a "woman." Time after time, I've had interviewers talk to me about my writing for a while, then ask me, "As a woman, what do you think about—for instance—the Women's Movement," as if I could think two sets of thoughts about the same thing, one set as a writer or person, the other as a woman. But no one comes apart this easily; categories like Woman, White, Canadian, Writer are only ways of looking at a thing, and the thing itself is whole, entire and indivisible. *Paradox:* Woman and Writer are separate categories; but in any individual woman writer, they are inseparable.

One of the results of the paradox is that there are certain attitudes, some overt, some concealed, which women writers encounter *as* writers, but *because* they are women. I shall try to deal with a few of these, as objectively as I can. After that, I'll attempt a limited personal statement.

A. Reviewing and the Absence of an Adequate Critical Vocabulary

Cynthia Ozick, in the American magazine *Ms.,* says, "For many years, I had noticed that no book of poetry by a woman was ever reviewed without reference to the poet's sex. The curious thing was that, in the two decades of my scrutiny, there were *no* exceptions whatever. It did not matter whether the reviewer was a man or a woman; in every case, the question of the 'feminine sensibility' of the poet was at the centre of the reviewer's response. The maleness of male poets, on the other hand, hardly ever seemed to matter."

Things aren't this bad in Canada, possibly because we were never fully indoctrinated with the Holy Gospel according to the distorters of Freud. Many reviewers manage to get through a review without displaying the kind of bias Ozick is talking about. But that it does occur was demonstrated to me by a project I was involved with at York University in 1971-72.

One of my groups was attempting to study what we called "sexual bias in reviewing," by which we meant not unfavourable reviews, but points being added or subtracted by the reviewer on the basis of the author's sex and supposedly associated characteristics rather than on the basis of the work itself. Our study fell into two parts: i) a survey of writers, half male, half female, conducted by letter: had they ever experienced sexual bias directed against them in a review? ii) the reading of a large number of reviews from a wide range of periodicals and newspapers.

The results of the writers' survey were perhaps predictable. Of the men, none said Yes, a quarter said Maybe, and three quarters said No. Half of the women said Yes, a quarter said Maybe and a quarter said No. The women replying Yes often wrote long, detailed letters, giving instances and discussing their own attitudes. All the men's letters were short.

This proved only that women were more likely to *feel* they had been discriminated against on the basis of sex. When we got around to the reviews, we discovered that they were sometimes justified. Here are the kinds of things we found.

I) ASSIGNMENT OF REVIEWS

Several of our letter writers mentioned this. Some felt books by women tended to be passed over by book-page editors assigning books for review; others that books by women tended to get assigned to women reviewers. When we started totting up reviews we found that most books in this society are written by men, and so are most reviews. Disproportionately often, books by women were assigned to women reviewers, indicating that books by women fell in the minds of those dishing out the reviews into some kind of "special" category. Likewise, woman reviewers tended to be reviewing books by women rather than by men (though because of the preponderance of male reviewers, there were quite a few male-written reviews of books by women).

II) THE QUILLER-COUCH SYNDROME

The heading of this one refers to the turn-of-the-century essay by Quiller-Couch, defining "masculine" and "feminine" styles in writing. The "masculine" style is, of course, bold, forceful, clear, vigorous, etc.; the "feminine" style is vague, weak, tremulous, pastel, etc. In the list of pairs you can include "objective" and "subjective," "universal" or "accurate depiction of society" versus "confessional," "personal," or even "narcissistic" and "neurotic." It's roughly seventy years since Quiller-Couch's essay, but the "masculine" group of adjectives is still much more likely to be applied to the work of male writers; female writers are much more likely to get hit with some version of "the feminine style" or "feminine sensibility," whether their work merits it or not.

III) THE LADY PAINTER, OR SHE WRITES LIKE A MAN

This is a pattern in which good equals male, and bad equals female. I call it the Lady Painter Syndrome because of a conversation I had about female painters with a male painter in 1960. "When she's good," he said, "we call her a painter; when she's bad, we call her a lady painter." "She writes like a man" is part of the same pattern; it's usually used by a male reviewer who is impressed by a female writer. It's meant as a compliment. See also "She thinks like a man," which means the author thinks, unlike most women, who are held to be incapable of objective thought (their province is "feeling"). Adjectives which often have similar connotations are ones such as "strong," "gutsy," "hard," "mean," etc. A hard-hitting piece of writing by a man is liable to be thought of as merely realistic; an equivalent piece by a woman is much more likely to be labelled "cruel" or "tough." The assumption is that women are by nature soft, weak and not very good, and that if a woman writer happens to be good, she should be deprived of her identity as a female and provided with higher (male) status. Thus the woman writer has, in the minds of such reviewers, two choices. She can be bad but female, a carrier of the "feminine sensibility" virus; or she can be "good" in male-adjective terms, but sexless. Badness seems to be ascribed then to a surplus of female hormones, whereas badness in a male writer is usually ascribed to nothing but badness (though a "bad" male writer is sometimes held, by adjectives implying sterility or impotence, to be deficient in maleness). "Maleness" is exemplified by the "good" male writer; "femaleness," since it is seen by such reviewers as a handicap or deficiency, is held to be transcended or discarded by the "good" female one. In other words, there is no critical vocabulary for expressing the concept "good/female." Work by a male writer is often spoken of by critics admiring it as having "balls;" ever hear anyone speak admiringly of work by a woman as having "tits?"

Possible antidotes: Development of a "good/female" vocabulary ("Wow, has that ever got Womb . . ."); or, preferably, the development of a vocabulary that can treat structures made of words as though they are exactly that, not biological entities possessed of sexual organs.

IV) DOMESTICITY

One of our writers noted a (usually male) habit of concentrating on domestic themes in the work of a female writer, ignoring any other topic she might have dealt with, then patronizing her for an excessive interest in domestic themes. We found several instances of reviewers identifying an author as a "housewife" and consequently dismissing anything she has produced (since, in our society, a "housewife" is viewed as a relatively brainless and talentless creature). We even found one instance in which the author was called a "housewife" and put down for writing like one when in fact she was no such thing.

For such reviewers, when a man writes about things like doing the dishes, it's realism; when a woman does, it's an unfortunate feminine genetic limitation.

V) SEXUAL COMPLIMENT-PUT-DOWN

This syndrome can be summed up as follows;

She: "How do you like my (design for an airplane/mathematical formula/medical miracle)?"

He: "You sure have a nice ass."

In reviewing it usually takes the form of commenting on the cute picture of the (female) author on the cover, coupled with dismissal of her as a writer.

VI) PANIC REACTION

When something the author writes hits too close to home, panic reaction may set in. One of our correspondents noticed this phenomenon in connection with one of her books: she felt that the content of the book threatened male reviewers, who gave it much worse reviews than did any female reviewer. Their reaction seemed to be that if a character such as she'd depicted did exist, they didn't want to know about it. In panic reaction, a reviewer is reacting to content, not to technique or craftsmanship or a book's internal coherence or faithfulness to its own assumptions. (Panic reaction can be touched off in any area, not just male-female relationships.)

B. Interviewers and Media Stereotypes

Associated with the reviewing problem, but distinct from it, is the problem of the interview. Reviewers are supposed to concentrate on books, interviewers on the writer as a person, human being, or, in the case of women, woman. This means that an interviewer is ostensibly trying to find out what sort of person you are. In reality, he or she may merely be trying to match you up with a stereotype of "Woman Author" that pre-exists in her/his mind; doing it that way is both easier for the interviewer, since it limits the range and slant of questions, and shorter, since the interview can be practically written in advance. It isn't just women who get this treatment: all writers get it. But the range for male authors is somewhat wider, and usually comes from the literary tradition itself, whereas stereotypes for female authors are often borrowed from other media, since the ones provided by the tradition are limited in number.

In a bourgeois, industrial society, so the theory goes, the creative artist is supposed to act out suppressed desires and prohibited activities for the audience; thus we get certain Post-romantic male-author stereotypes, such as Potted Poe, Bleeding Byron, Doomed Dylan, Lustful Layton, Crucified Cohen, etc. Until recently the only personality stereotype of this kind was Elusive Emily, otherwise known as Recluse Rossetti: the woman writer as aberration, neurotically denying herself the delights of sex, kiddies and other fun. The Twentieth Century has added Suicidal Sylvia, a somewhat more dire version of the same thing. The point about these stereotypes is that attention is focused not on the actual achievements of the authors, but on their lives, which are distorted and romanticized; their work is then interpreted in the light of the distorted version. Stereotypes like these, even when the author cooperates in their formation and especially when the author becomes a cult object, do no service to anyone or anything, least of all the author's work. Behind all of them is the notion that authors must be more special, peculiar or weird than other people, and that their lives are more interesting than their work.

The following examples are taken from personal experience (mine, of interviewers); they indicate the range of possibilities. There are a few others, such as Earth Mother, but for those you have to be older.

I) HAPPY HOUSEWIFE

This one is almost obsolete: it used to be for Woman's Page or programme. Questions were about what you liked to fix for dinner; attitude was, "Gosh, all the housework and you're a writer too!" Writing was viewed as a hobby, like knitting, one did in one's spare time.

II) OPHELIA

The writer as crazy freak. Female version of Doomed Dylan, with more than a little hope on the part of the interviewer that you'll turn into Suicidal Sylvia and give them something to *really* write about. Questions like "Do you think you're in danger of going insane?" or "Are writers closer to insanity than other people?" No need to point out that most mental institutions are crammed with people who have never written a word in their life. "Say something interesting," one interviewer said to me. "Say you write all your poems on drugs."

III) MISS MARTYR; OR, MOVIE MAG

Read any movie mag on Liz Taylor and translate into writing terms and you've got the picture. The writer as someone who *suffers* more than others. Why does the writer suffer more? Because she's successful, and you all know Success Must Be Paid For. In blood and tears, if possible. If you say you're happy and enjoy your life and work, you'll be ignored.

IV) MISS MESSAGE

Interviewer incapable of treating your work as what it is, i.e. poetry and/or fiction. Great attempt to get you to say something about an Issue and then make you into an exponent, spokeswoman or theorist. (The two Messages I'm most frequently saddled with are Women's Lib and Canadian Nationalism, though I belong to no formal organization devoted to either.) Interviewer unable to see that putting, for instance, a nationalist into a novel doesn't make it a nationalistic novel, any more than putting in a preacher makes it a religious novel. Interviewer incapable of handling more than one dimension at a time.

What is Hard to Find is an interviewer who regards writing as a respectable profession, not as some kind of magic, madness, trickery or evasive disguise for a Message; and who regards an author as someone engaged in a professional activity.

C. Other Writers and Rivalry

Regarding yourself as an "exception," part of an unspoken quota system, can have interesting results. If there are only so many available slots for your minority in the medical school/law school/literary world, of course you will feel rivalry, not only with members of the majority for whom no quota operates, but especially for members of your minority who are competing with you for the few coveted places. And you will have to be better than the average Majority member to get in at all. But we're familiar with that.

Woman-woman rivalry does occur, though it is surprisingly less severe than you'd expect; it's likely to take the form of *wanting* another woman writer to be better than she is, expecting more of her than you would of a male writer, and being exasperated with certain kinds of traditional "female" writing. One of our correspondents discussed these biases and expectations very thoroughly and with great intelligence: her letter didn't solve any problems but it did emphasize the complexities of the situation. Male-male rivalry is more extreme; we've all been treated to media-exploited examples of it.

What a woman writer is often unprepared for is the unexpected personal attack on her by a jealous male writer. The motivation is envy and competitiveness, but the form is often sexual put-down. "You may be a good writer," one older man said to a young woman writer who had just had a publishing success, "but I wouldn't want to fuck you." Another version goes more like the compliment-put-down noted under Reviewing. In either case, the ploy diverts attention from the woman's achievement as a writer—the area where the man feels threatened—to her sexuality, where either way he can score a verbal point.

Personal Statement

I've been trying to give you a picture of the arena, or that part of it where being a "woman" and "writer," as concepts, overlap. But, of course, the arena I've been talking about has to do largely with externals: reviewing, the media, relationships with other writers. This, for the writer, may affect the tangibles of her career: how she is received, how viewed, how much money she makes. But in relationship to the writing itself, this is a false arena. The real one is in her head, her real struggle the daily battle with words, the language itself. The false arena becomes valid for writing itself only insofar as it becomes part of her material and is transformed into one of the verbal and imaginative structures she is constantly engaged in making. Writers, as writers, are not propagandists or examples of social trends or preachers or politicians. They are makers of books, and unless they can make books well they will be bad writers, no matter what the social validity of their views.

At the beginning of this article, I suggested a few reasons for the infrequent participation in the Movement of woman writers. Maybe these reasons were the wrong ones, and this is the real one: no good writer wants to be merely a transmitter of someone else's ideology, no matter how fine that ideology may be. The aim of propaganda is to convince, and to spur people to action; the aim of writing is to create a plausible and moving imaginative world, and to create it from words. Or, to put it another way, the aim of a political movement is to improve the quality of people's lives on all levels, spiritual and imaginative as well as material (and any political movement that doesn't have this aim is worth nothing). Writing, however, tends to concentrate more on life, not as it ought to be, but as it is, as the writer feels it, experiences it. Writers are eye-witnesses, I-witnesses. Political movements, once successful, have historically been intolerant of writers, even those writers who initially aided them; in any revolution, writers have been among the first to be lined up against the wall, perhaps for their intransigence, their insistence on saying what they perceive, not what, according to the ideology, ought to exist. Politicians, even revolutionary politicians, have traditionally had no more respect for writing as an activity valuable in itself, quite apart from any

message or content, than has the rest of the society. And writers, even revolutionary writers, have traditionally been suspicious of anyone who tells them what they ought to write.

The woman writer, then, exists in a society that, though it may turn certain individual writers into revered cult objects, has little respect for writing as a profession, and not much respect for women either. If there were more of both, articles like this would be obsolete. I hope they become so. In the meantime, it seems to me that the proper path for a woman writer is not an all-out manning (or womaning) of the barricades, however much she may agree with the aims of the Movement. The proper path is to become better as a writer. Insofar as writers are lenses, condensers of their society, her work may include the Movement, since it is so palpably among the things that exist. The picture that she gives of it is altogether another thing, and will depend, at least partly, on the course of the Movement itself.

GENERAL COMMENTARY

PATRICIA F. GOLDBLATT (ESSAY DATE SPRING 1999)

SOURCE: Goldblatt, Patricia F. "Reconstructing Margaret Atwood's Protagonists." *World Literature Today* 73, no. 2 (spring 1999): 275-82.

In the following essay, Goldblatt discusses the transformation of Atwood's female protagonists "from ingenues to insightful women."

A weaver employs fragments from life, silk, raw yarns, wool, straw, perhaps even a few twigs, stones, or feathers, and transforms them into a tapestry of color, shape, and form. An author's work is similar, for she selects individuals, locations, images, and ideas, rearranging them to create a believable picture. Each smacks of reality, but is not. This is the artist's art: to reconstruct the familiar into new, fascinating, but often disturbing tableaux from which stories can unfold.

Margaret Atwood weaves stories from her own life in the bush and cities of Canada. Intensely conscious of her political and social context, Atwood dispels the notion that caribou-clad Canadians remain perpetually locked in blizzards while simultaneously seeming to be a polite mass of gray faces, often indistinguishable from their American neighbors. Atwood has continually pondered the lack of an identifiable Canadian culture. For over thirty years her work has aided in fashioning a distinct Canadian literary identity. Her critical catalogue and analysis of Canadian Literature, *Survival* [*Sv*], offered "a political manifesto telling Canadians . . . [to] value their own" (Sullivan, 265). In an attempt to focus on *Canadian experiences,* Atwood has populated her stories with Canadian cities, conflicts, and contemporary people, conscious of a landscape whose borders have been permeated by the frost of Nature, her colonizers and her neighbors. Her examination of how an individual interacts, succeeds, or stagnates within her world speaks to an emerging sense of self and often parallels the battles fought to establish self-determination.

In her novels, Margaret Atwood creates situations in which women, burdened by the rules and inequalities of their societies, discover that they must reconstruct braver, self-reliant personae in order to survive. Not too far from the Canadian blueprint of the *voyageur* faced with an inclement, hostile environment, these women struggle to overcome and to change systems that block and inhibit their security. Atwood's pragmatic women are drawn from women in the 1950s and 1960s: young women blissfully building their trousseaus and imagining a paradise of silver bells and picket fences.

Yet the author herself was neither encumbered nor restricted by the definition of *contemporary female* in her life as a child. Having grown up in the Canadian North, outside of societal propaganda, she could critically observe the behaviors that were indoctrinated into her urban peers who lacked diverse role models. As Atwood has noted, "Not even the artistic community offered you a viable choice as a woman" (Sullivan, 103). Her stories deal with the transformation of female characters from ingenues to insightful women. By examining her heroes, their predators, and how they cope in society, we will discover where Atwood believes the ability to reconstruct our lives lies.

Who are the victims?

"But pathos as a literary mode simply demands that an innocent victim suffer" (*Sv*, 75). Unlike Shakespeare's hubris-laden kings or Jane Austen's pert and private aristocratic landowning families, Margaret Atwood relies on a collection of ordinary people to carry her tales: university students, museum workers, market researchers, writers, illustrators, and even housemaids. In her novels, almost all dwell on their childhood years in flashback or in the chronological telling of their stories. Many of her protagonists' early days are situated in a virtual Garden of Eden setting, replete with untamed natural environments. Exploring shorelines, gazing at stars, gathering rocks, and listening to waves, they are solitary souls, but not lonely individuals: innocent, curious, and affable creatures. Elaine Risley in *Cat's Eye* and an unnamed narrator in *Surfacing* are two women who recall idyllic days unfolded in a land of lakes, berries, and animals. Offred in *The Handmaid's Tale,* in her city landscape, also relates a tale of a happy childhood. She is a complacent and assured child, her mother a constant loving companion. In their comfortable milieus, these girls intuit no danger.

However, other Atwood protagonists are not as fortunate. Their backgrounds suggest an unhealthy, weedy soil that causes their young plants to twist and permutate. *Lady Oracle's* [*LO*] Joan is overweight. Her domineering, impatient mother and her weak father propel her to seek emotional satisfaction away from them. Lesje in *Life before Man* is the offspring of dueling immigrant grandmothers who cannot agree on the child's proper upbringing. Not allowed to frequent the Ukrainian "golden church with its fairytale onion" (*LBM,* 93) of the one, or the synagogue of the other, Lesje is unable to develop self-confidence and focuses instead on the inanimate, the solid traditions of rocks and dinosaurs as her progenitors. Similarly, the females in *The Robber Bride* reveal miserable childhoods united by parental abuse, absence, and disregard: Roz must perform as her mother's helper, a landlady cum cleaning woman; her father is absent, involved in shady dealings in "the old country." Charis, a second character in *The Robber Bride,* abandoned by her mother and deposited with Aunt Vi and Uncle Vern, is sexually violated by those who should have offered love and trust. Toni, the third of the trio, admits to loneliness and alienation in a well-educated, wealthy family. Marked by birth and poverty, Grace Marks, an Irish immigrant in the early 1800s in *Alias Grace,* loses her mother en route to Canada. Grace is almost drowned by the demands of her drunken father and clinging, needy siblings. These exiled little girls, from weak, absent, or cruel families, made vulnerable by their early situations, cling to the notion that their lives will be improved by the arrival of a kind stranger, most likely a handsome suitor. Rather than becoming recalcitrant and cynical, all sustain the golden illusion of the fairy-tale ending. In short, they hold to the belief, the myth perpetrated by society: marriage.

FROM THE AUTHOR

ATWOOD ON STEREOTYPICAL MALE CHARACTERS AND SOCIAL ROLES

It's true that the male sexual role model had a lot of drawbacks, even for men—not everybody could be Superman, many were stuck with Clark Kent—but there were certain positive and, at that time, useful features. What have we replaced this package with? We know that women have been in a state of upheaval and ferment for some time now, and movement generates energy; many things can be said by women now that were once not possible, many things can be thought that were once unthinkable. But what are we offering men? Their territory, though still large, is shrinking. The confusion and desperation and anger and conflicts that we find in male characters in novels don't exist only in novels. They're out there in the real world. "Be a person, my son," doesn't yet have the same ring to it as "Be a man," though it is indeed a worthy goal. The novelist *qua* novelist, as opposed to the utopian romancer, takes *what is there* as a point of departure. What is there, when we're talking about men, is a state of change, new attitudes overlapping with old ones, no simple rules any more. Some exciting form of life may emerge from all this.

Meanwhile, I think women have to take the concerns of men as seriously as they expect men to take theirs, both as novelists and as inhabitants of this earth. One encounters, too often, the attitude that only the pain felt by persons of the female sex is real pain, that only female fears are real fears. That for me is the equivalent of the notion that only working-class people are real, that middle-class people are not, and so forth. Of course there's a distinction between earned pain and mere childish self-pity, and yes, women's fear of being killed by men is grounded in authenticity, not to mention statistics, to a greater extent than men's fear of being laughed at. Damage to one's self-image is not quite the same as damage to one's neck, though not to be underestimated: men have been known to murder and kill themselves because of it.

Atwood, Margaret. Excerpt from "Writing the Male Character." In *Second Words*, pp. 427-28. Toronto: Anansi Press, 1982.

Atwood's women are cognizant of the nurturing omissions in their environments. They attempt to cultivate and cope. Charis in **The Robber Bride** decides to reinvent herself. She changes her name and focuses on what she considers her healing powers inherited from her chicken-raising grandmother. She, Roz, and Toni turn their faith to the power of friendship, a solid ring that lessens the painful lack of supportive families. In **Alias Grace** Grace's burden of an absent family is briefly alleviated by her friendship with another housemaid, Mary Whitney. Mary takes an adoring Grace under her wing and creates for Grace a fleeting vision of sisterly support. Unfortunately for Grace, Mary herself, another trusting young woman, is deceived by her employer's son and dies in a botched abortion, leaving Grace once again abandoned and friendless.

In an attempt to reestablish stable, satisfying homes, these women pursue a path, as have women throughout history, to marriage. They search for a male figure, imagining a refuge. Caught up in the romantic stereotypes that assign and perpetuate gender roles, each girl does not doubt that a man is the solution to her problems.

In **The Edible Woman** Marian and her co-workers at Seymour Surveys, "the office virgins," certainly do not question that marriage will provide fulfillment. In spite of the fact that Marian is suspended between two unappealing men, she does not deviate from *the proper behavior*. Marian's suitor, Peter, with his well-chosen clothes and suave friends, his perfectly decorated apartment, and even Marian as the appropriate marriage choice, is rendered as no more than the wedding cake's blankly smiling ornament. If appearance is all, he should suffice. Peter is juxtaposed to the slovenly, self-centered graduate student, Duncan, whose main pleasure is watching his laundry whirl in the washing machine. Marian is merely a blank slate upon which each man can write or erase his concept of female.

The narrator and her friend Anna, in **Surfacing**, are also plagued by moody men who are not supportive of women's dreams. In one particularly horrifying scene, Anna's husband Dave orders her to strip off her clothes for the movie camera. Anna, humiliated by the request, nevertheless complies. She admits to nightly rapes but rationalizes his behavior: "He likes to make me cry because he can't do it himself" (*Sf*, 80). Similarly, when Joe, the narrator's boyfriend, proposes, "We should get married . . . we might as well" (56), he is dumbfounded and furious at her refusal. Men aware of the role they play accept their desirability as "catches." They believe that women desire lives of "babies and sewing" (*LO,* 159). These thoughts are parroted by Peter in *The Edible Woman* when he proclaims, "People who aren't married get funny in middle age" (*EW,* 102). Men uphold the values of the patriarchy and women conform, few trespassing into gardens of their own design.

In *Alias Grace* Grace's aspirations for a brighter future also dwell on finding the right man: "It was the custom for young girls in this country to hire themselves out, in order to earn the money for their dowries, and then they would marry . . . and one day . . . be mistress of a tidy farmhouse" (*AG,* 157-58). In the employment of Mr. Thomas Kinnear in Richmond Hill, Grace quickly ascertains that the handsome, dark-haired housekeeper, Nancy Montgomery, enjoys many privileges as the reward for being her master's mistress. Yet, although men may be the only way to elevate status, Grace learns that they cannot be trusted when their advances are rejected. Grace, on trial for the murders of Kinnear and Montgomery, is incredulous when she hears a former friend, Jamie Welsh, testify against her.

> Then I was hoping for some token of sympathy from him; but he gave me a stare filled with such reproach and sorrowful anger. He felt betrayed in love. . . . I was transformed to a demon and he would do all in his power to destroy me. I had been counting on him to say a good word for me . . . for I valued his good opinion of me, and it was a grief to lose it.
>
> (*AG,* 360)

Women, it seems, must be made malleable to men's desires, accepting their proposals, their advances. They must submit to their socially determined roles or be seen as "demons."

However, it is not only men but also women as agents of society who betray. In *The Robber Bride* Charis, Roz, and Toni are tricked in their friendship by Zenia, an acquaintance from their university days. Each succumbs to Zenia's web of deceit. Playing the part of a confidante and thoughtful listener, Zenia encourages the three women to divest themselves of their tales of their traumatic childhoods. She learns their tortured secrets and uses their confidences to spirit away the men each woman believes to be the cornerstone in her life.

From little girls to sophisticated women, Atwood's protagonists have not yet discerned that trust can be perverted, that they can be reeled in, taken advantage of, constantly abused, if they are not careful of lurking predators in their landscapes. Joan in *Lady Oracle,* longing for friendship, endures the inventive torments of her Brownie friends: deadly ploys that tie little girls to trees with skipping ropes, exposing them to strange leering men under cavernous bridges. Her assassins jeer, "How do ya' like the club?" (*LO,* 59). Elaine Risley in *Cat's Eye,* like Joan, is a young girl when she discovers the power of betrayal by members of her own sex. For years she passively succumbs to their games. Perhaps, because she has grown up alone in the Canadian North with her parents and brother, Elaine seeks the warming society of girls. Only when Elaine is deserted, left to freeze in a disintegrating creek, does she recognize her peers' malevolence that almost leads to her death. Elaine knows that she is a defeated human, but rather than confronting her tormentors, she increases her own punishment nightly: she peels the skin off her feet and bites her lips.

Unable to turn outward in a society that perpetuates the ideal of a submissive female, these women turn inward to their bodies as shields or ploys. Each has learned that a woman is a commodity, valued only for her appearance. Therefore it comes as no surprise that Atwood's protagonists measure their worth in terms of body. Joan in *Lady Oracle* sees herself as "a huge shapeless cloud" (*LO,* 65); she drifts. However, her soft edges do not keep her from the bruising accusations of society. Although she loves to dance, Joan's bulging body is an affront to her mother and ballet teacher's sensibilities, and so at her ballet recital she is forced to perform as a mothball, not as a butterfly in tulle and spangles.

Joan certainly does not fit her mother's definition of femininity. Because her ungainly shape is rejected, Joan decides to hide her form in a mountain of fat, food serving as a constant to her mother's reproaches: "I was eating steadily, doggedly, stubbornly, anything I could get. The war between myself and my mother was on in earnest: the disputed territory was my body" (*LO,* 67). Interestingly, Joan's loving, supportive, and also fat aunt Louisa bequeaths to Joan an inheritance with the stipulation that she lose one hundred pounds. Atwood herself was fascinated by transformations in fairy stories: a person could not become a swan and depart the dreaded scene that mocked the tender aspirations of an awkward ingenue in real life; she could, however, don a new mask and trick those people who had previously proffered harm.

In *The Edible Woman* Marian's body is also a battlefield. Unable to cope with her impending marriage to Peter, Marian finds herself unable to ingest any food that was once alive. Repulsed by her society's attitude of consumerism, Marian concludes that her refusal to eat is ethical. However, her mind and body have split away from each other. Her mind's revulsion at a dog-eat-dog world holds her body hostage: captive territory when a woman disagrees with her world. Marian "tri[es] to reason with [her body], accus[ing] it of having frivolous whims." She coaxes and tempts, "but it was adamant" (*EW,* 177). Marian's mind expresses her disapproval on the only level on which she possesses control: ironically, herself. Her punishment is circular: first, as a victim susceptible because she is a woman subject to her society's values; and second, as a woman only able to command other women, namely herself. Her sphere is so small she becomes both victim and victimizer.

This view of a woman who connects and projects her image of self onto her body also extends to the functions of a female body: the ability to control life by giving birth. Sarah in the story **"The Resplendent Quetzal"** (1977) is drained of all vitality and desire when her baby dies at birth. Her concept of identity is entangled with her ability to produce a child. When this biological function fails, Sarah's being ebbs. Lesje in *Life before Man* also observes that, without children, "officially she is nothing" (*LBM,* 267). Offred's identity and value as a childbearer as well, in *The Handmaid's Tale,* are proclaimed by her clothes in her totalitarian city of Gilead. She is "two viable ovaries" (*HT,* 135). She no longer owns a name; she is "Of Fred," the concubine named for the man who will impregnate her. Every step, every mouthful of food, every move is observed, reported, circumvented, or approved for the sake of the child she might carry to term. Her only worth resides in her biological function. Her dreams and desires are unimportant. Her goal is survival.

The women described here do not lash out openly. Each who once trusted in family, marriage, and friendship discovers that treading societal paths does not result in happiness. These disillusioned women, with aborted expectations, turn their misery inward, accepting responsibility that *not* society and its expectations but they themselves are weak, unworthy, and have therefore failed.

Who has laid prey and why?
"Sometimes fear of these obstacles becomes itself the obstacle" (*Sv,* 33). Atwood's girls are a vulnerable lot, manipulated, packaged, and devastated by the familiar faces in uncaring, dictatorial circles

that reinforce societal imperatives. Those once free to roam and explore as children as well as those repressed from an early age are subject to the *civilizing forces* that customize young girls to the fate of females. Ironically, this process, for the most part, is performed by mothers.

Mothers, rather than alleviating their girls' distress, increase their children's alienation. When Elaine's mother in *Cat's Eye* ventures to discuss the cruelty of Elaine's friends, her words do not fortify Elaine; they admonish her: "Don't let them push you around. Don't be spineless. You have to have more backbone" (*CE,* 156). Fearing her weakness is comparable to the tiny crumbling bones of sardines, Elaine maligns herself: "What is happening is my own fault, for not having more backbone" (156). Joan's mother in *Lady Oracle* doesn't mince words: "You were stupid to let the other girls fool you like that" (*LO,* 61). Instead of offering support, the mothers blame their daughters, aligning themselves with the girls' accusers.

Mothers who themselves have not found acceptance, success, or ease in society persist in transmitting the old messages of conformity. Joan's mother in *Lady Oracle* is dumbfounded that "even though she'd done the right thing, . . . devoted her life to us, . . . made her family her career as she had been told to do," she had been burdened with "a sulky fat slob of a daughter and a husband who wouldn't talk to her" (*LO,* 179). Joan echoes her mother's complaints when she murmurs, "How destructive to me were the attitudes of society" (102).

Even the work women do conspires to maintain the subjection of their own kind. In her job, in *The Edible Woman,* Marian investigates what soups, laxatives, or drinks will please and be purchased. Sanctioned female activities also reinforce the imposition of correct values. In *Surfacing* and *Cat's Eye* little girls are engrossed in cutting up pictures from Eaton's catalogues that offer labor-saving devices along with fashionable clothes: children piece together a utopia of dollhouse dreams. So brainwashed are these girls that when asked to indicate a possible job or profession, they answer, "A lady" or "A mother" (*CE,* 91).

In *Cat's Eye* Elaine Risley's mother does not fit the stereotype. She wears pants, she ice skates, she "does not give a hoot" (*CE,* 214) about the rules that women are supposed to obey. Rendered impotent as a role model in her daughter's eyes because she does not abide by the Establishment's code of correct deportment, Elaine's mother is an outsider to a woman's world that captivates Elaine.

Instead of her own nonconforming mother, Elaine is most deeply affected by the indictments from her friend Grace Smeath's mother. Mrs. Smeath, spread out on the sofa and covered with afghans every afternoon to rest her bad heart, damns Elaine for being a heathen: there is something very wrong with Elaine's family, who ignore the protocol of proper women's wear, summer city vacations, and regular church attendance. Worse yet, Mrs. Smeath, aware of the cruel games inflicted on Elaine, does not intervene. Instead she invokes deserved suffering when she decrees, "It's God's punishment for the way the other children treat her [Elaine]. It serves her right" (*CE,* 180). With God on her side, Mrs. Smeath relies on the Bible as the oldest and surest way of prescribing a female identity—and instilling fear.

In *The Handmaid's Tale* the Bible is likewise the chief source of female repression. Words are corrupted, perverted, or presented out of context to establish a man's holy vision of women: Sarah's use of her handmaid, Hagar, as a surrogate womb for an heir for Abraham becomes the legalizing basis for fornication with the handmaids. Acts of love are reduced to institutionalized rapes, and random acts of violence, banishment to slag heaps, public hangings, endorsed public killings, bribery, deceit, and pornography all persist under other names in order to maintain a pious hold on women endorsed by the Gilead Fathers.

In spite of the fact that Gilead is praised by its creators as a place where women need not fear, carefully chosen "aunts" persist in treachery that robs women of trust. To perpetuate the status quo, women are kept vulnerable and treated as children: girls must ask permission, dress in silly frocks, are allowed no money, play no part in their own self-determination. Yet Atwood's girls tire of their rigidly enforced placement that would preserve some outdated notion of female acceptability.

The escape.

"*She feels the need for escape*" (*Sv,* 131). After enduring, accepting, regurgitating, denying, and attempting to please and cope, Atwood's protagonists begin to take action and change their lives. Atwood herself, raised on *Grimms' Fairy Tales,* knew that "by using intelligence, cleverness and perseverance" (Sullivan, 36), magical powers could transform a forest into a garden. However, before realizing their possibilities, many of Atwood's protagonists hit rock bottom, some even contemplating death as an escape. In *Surfacing* the narrator, fed up with the superficiality of her companions, banishes them and submits to paranoia.

> Everything I can't break . . . I throw on the floor. . . . I take off my clothes . . . I dip my head beneath the water . . . I leave my dung, droppings on the ground . . . I hollow a lair near the woodpile . . . I scramble on hands and knees . . . I could be anything, a tree, a deer skeleton, a rock.
> (*Sf,* 177-87)

She descends to madness, stripping herself of all the trappings of civilized society.

Although often consumed with thoughts of suicide in *Cat's Eye* and *The Handmaid's Tale,* Atwood's heroines never succumb. Instead they consciously assassinate their former identities through ritual deaths by water. Joan in *Lady Oracle* orchestrates a baptism in Lake Ontario. Pretending to drown, she relinquishes her former life. With sunglasses and scarf, she believes herself reborn, free to begin anew in Italy. Elaine Risley, after her bone-chilling encounter in the icy ravine in *Cat's Eye,* is finally able to ignore the taunts of her friends. Resurrected after two days in bed, a stronger Elaine affirms that "she is happy as a clam, hard-shelled and firmly closed" (*CE,* 201) against those who would sabotage her; she announces, "I'm ready" (203). Fortified by a new body image with a tougher veneer and a protective mask, Elaine no longer heeds her former tormentors. She has sealed herself from further outrage and invasion.

Marian's revelation in *The Edible Woman* is experienced at the precipice of a ravine, where she comments, "In the snow you're as near as possible to nothing" (*EW,* 263). Perhaps the fear of becoming one with the ubiquitous whiteness of the landscape and forever losing herself motivates a stand. Similarly, Sarah in "**The Resplendent Quetzal**" forges a more determined persona after her trial by water. Instead of throwing herself into the sacrificial well in Mexico as her husband Edward fears, she hurls a plaster Christ child stolen from a crèche into the water. Believing the tribal folklore that young children take messages to the rain god and live forever in paradise at the bottom of the well, Sarah pins her hopes on a representative facsimile that she hopes will bring her peace for her lost child in the next world as well as rebirth, freeing herself from anxiety and guilt regarding the child's death.

Rather than resorting to the cool, cleansing agent of water, Grace Marks, the convicted mur-

Kathleen Beller, as Kate, in the 1980 film adaptation of Margaret Atwood's *Surfacing.*

deress in *Alias Grace,* reconstructs her life through stories of her own invention. She fashions a creature always beyond the pale of her listeners' complete comprehension. As told to Dr. Simon Jordan, who has come to study Grace as a possible madwoman, her story ensnares him in a piteous romance. Grace appears outwardly as a humble servant girl always at peril from salacious employers; however, when Grace ruminates in her private thoughts, she reveals that she is wordly wise, knowing how to avoid bad impressions and the advances of salesmen. She is knowledgeable, stringing along Dr. Jordan: "I say something just to keep him happy. . . . I do not give him a straight answer" (*AG,* 66, 98). After rambling from employ to employ in search of security, Grace constructs a home for herself in her stories. Her words, gossamer thin, have the power to erect a façade, a frame that holds her illusions together.

In an attempt to discover the missing parts and prove the veracity of Grace's story, her supporters encourage her to undergo a seance. Although she recognizes Dr. Jerome Dupont, the man who will orchestrate the event, as a former button peddler, she does not speak out. When a voice emerges from the hypnotized Grace, it proclaims, "I am not Grace" (403). As listeners, we ponder the speaker's authenticity. Just who our

narrator might be, madwoman or manipulator, is cast into doubt. We can only be sure that the young innocent who arrived on Canada's shores penniless and motherless has been altered by the necessity to cope with a destructive hierarchical society unsympathetic to an immigrant girl. Rather than persist and be tossed forever at the whim of a wizened world, each saddened young girl moves to reconstruct her tarnished image of her self.

How?

"*One way of coming to terms, making sense of one's roots, is to become a creator*" (*Sv,* 181). Atwood's victims who take control of their lives discover the need to displace societal values, and they replace them with their own. In *Lady Oracle* Joan ponders the film *The Red Shoes,* in which the moral warns that if a woman chooses both family and career, tragedy ensues. Reflecting on childbirth, the narrator in "**Giving Birth**" (1977) hopes for some vision: "After all she is risking her life. . . . *As for the vision, there wasn't one*" (**GB,** 252; italics mine). Toni in *The Robber Bride* and Grace Marks in *Alias Grace* acknowledge that it is not necessary to procreate. Each is more than her body. A grown-up Elaine Risley in *Cat's Eye* and the narrator in *Surfacing* accept motherhood, but not as an outcome of their gender that will foreclose the possibilities of a creative job. In fact, Roz in *The Robber Bride* is quite able to combine motherhood and a successful career. Dissatisfied with traditional knowledge, Atwood's women again turn inward, now avoiding masochistic traps, fully able to deviate from society's dicta. Freed from constraining fears, they locate talents, wings that free them.

Rather than becoming cynical and devastated by society's visions and its perpetrators, Atwood's women forge on. Roz, Toni, and Charis in *The Robber Bride,* who have been betrayed by Zenia, put their faith back into friendship, allowing mutual support to sustain them. It is solid; it has been tested. They have turned to one another, cried and laughed, shared painful experiences, knowing that their friendship has endured in a labyrinth of twisted paths.

Offred in *The Handmaid's Tale* also begins to reshape her world. She envisions a better place in her thoughts, recording her words on tape. She has hope. Consciously, she reconstructs her present reality, knowing she is making an effort to project an optimistic picture. She says, "Here is a different story, a better one. . . . This is what I'd like to tell" (*HT,* 234). She relates that her tryst with Nick the chauffeur, arranged by her commander's wife, is caring and loving, enhanced by memories from her earlier life in order to conjure an outcome of happiness. In the short story "Hair Jewellery" (1977) Atwood's narrator is an academic, a writer who warns, "Be careful. . . . There is a future" (113). With the possibility of a new beginning, there is a chance that life can improve. In *Alias Grace* Grace's fabrications in her stories provide an escape hatch, a version of reality tailored to fit her needs. For both Offred and Grace, stories are ways of rebelling, of avoiding the tentacles of a society that would demean and remold them. Their stories are outward masks, behind which they frantically repair their damaged spirits. Each alters her world through language. Each woman *speaks* a reconstructed world into existence, herself the engineering god of her own fate. Offred confides that handmaids live in the spaces and the gaps between their stories, in their private silences: only alone in their imaginations are they free to control their own destinies.

However, Atwood's protagonists inhabit not only their minds in secret, but also their bodies in the outside world. Joan, after her disappearance from Toronto in *Lady Oracle,* decides that she must return home and support the friends who have aided her disguise. In the past, just as she had wielded her bulk as a weapon, so she has used her writing in order to resolve relationships. She has indulged in Gothic romances, positing scenarios; she has even played out roles with lovers in capes. In the end, she rejects her former craft of subterfuge: "I won't write any more Costume Gothics." Yet we must ponder her choice to "try some science fiction" (*LO,* 345).

Although it is difficult to extirpate behavior, women trust the methods that have helped them cope in the past in order to alter the future. In *The Edible Woman* the womanly art of baking provides Marian with a way to free herself: she bakes a cake that resembles herself. Offering a piece to Peter, she is controlling the tasty image of a woman, allowing him and, more importantly, herself to ingest and destroy it. "It gave me a peculiar sense of satisfaction to see him eat," she says, adding, "I smiled comfortably at him" (*EW,* 281). Her pleasure in their consumption of her former self is symbolic of the death of the old Marian.

One might say that Marian's ingestion of her own image, Joan's adoption of science fiction, and both Offred's and Grace's stories "in the head" do not promise new fulfilling lives, only tactics of escape. However, their personal growth through conscious effort represents a means to wrest control of their lives from society and transform their destinies. These women become manipulators rather than allowing themselves to be manipulated.

In *Cat's Eye* Elaine Risley deals with the torment of her early life in her art by moving to Vancouver and exerting power in paint over the people who had condemned her. She creates surreal studies of Mrs. Smeath: "I paint Mrs. Smeath . . . like a dead fish. . . . One picture of Mrs. Smeath leads to another. She multiplies on the walls like bacteria, standing, sitting, with clothes, without clothes" (*CE,* 338). Empowered by her success as an artist, Elaine returns to Toronto for a showing of her work, able to resist the pleas of her former tormentor, Cordelia, now a pitiful patient in a psychiatric facility. In a dream, Elaine surpasses her desire for revenge and offers Cordelia Christian charity: "I'm the stronger. . . . I reach out my arms to her, bend down. . . . *It's all right,* I say to her. *You can go home*" (*CE,* 419). Elaine is reinforced by the very words spoken to her in the vision that saved her life years before. Her work fosters her liberation. By projecting her rage outside of herself, she confronts her demons and exalts herself as a divine redeemer.

Conclusion.

"*You don't even have to concentrate on rejecting the role of victim because the role is no longer a temptation for you*" (*Sv,* 39). The creative aspect that fortifies each woman enables her to control her life: it is the triumphant tool that resurrects each one. As artists, writers, friends, each ameliorates her situation and her world, positively metamorphosing reality in the process. In societies tailored to the submission of females, Atwood's protagonists refuse to be pinned down to the measurements of the perfect woman. Instead, they reconstruct their lives, imprinting their own designs in worlds of patterned fabric. Atwood has observed that all writing is political: "The writer simply by examining how the forces of society interact with the individual . . . seek[s] to change social structure" (Sullivan, 129).

Literature has always been the place where journeys have been sought, battles fought, insights gleaned. And authors have always dallied with the plight of women in society: young or old, body or mind, mother or worker, traveler or settler. *The woman* has been the divided or fragmented icon who, broken and downcast, has gazed back forlornly at us from the pages of her telling tale. Margaret Atwood has reconstructed this victim, proving to her and to us that we all possess the talent and the strength to revitalize our lives and reject society's well-trodden paths that suppress the human spirit. She has shown us that we can be vicariously empowered by our surrogate, who not only now smiles but winks back at us, daring us to reclaim our own female identities.

Works Cited

Atwood, Margaret. *Alias Grace*. Toronto. McClelland & Stewart. 1996. (*AG*)

———. *Cat's Eye*. Toronto. McClelland & Stewart. 1988. (*CE*)

———. "Giving Birth." In *Dancing Girls*. Toronto. McClelland & Stewart. 1977. (GB)

———. "Hair Jewellery." In *Dancing Girls*. Toronto. McClelland & Stewart. 1977. (HJ)

———. *Lady Oracle*. Toronto. McClelland & Stewart. 1976. (*LO*)

———. *Life before Man*. Toronto. McClelland & Stewart. 1979. (*LBM*)

———. *Surfacing*. Toronto. McClelland & Stewart. 1972. (*Sf*)

———. *Survival: A Thematic Guide to Canadian Literature*. Toronto. Anansi. 1972. (*Sv*)

———. *The Edible Woman*. Toronto. McClelland & Stewart. 1969. (*EW*)

———. *The Handmaid's Tale*. Toronto. McClelland & Stewart. 1985. (*HT*)

———. "The Resplendent Quetzal." In *Dancing Girls*. Toronto. McClelland & Stewart. 1977. (RQ)

———. *The Robber Bride*. Toronto. McClelland & Stewart. 1993. (*RB*)

Sullivan, Rosemary. *The Red Shoes: Margaret Atwood Starting Out*. Toronto. HarperCollins. 1998.

TITLE COMMENTARY

Cat's Eye

EARL G. INGERSOLL (ESSAY DATE OCTOBER 1991)

SOURCE: Ingersoll, Earl G. "Margaret Atwood's *Cat's Eye*: Re-Viewing Women in a Postmodern World." *ARIEL* 22, no. 4 (October 1991): 17-27.

In the following essay, Ingersoll explores the postmodern implications of the autobiographical elements in Cat's Eye.

Although one finds evidence of postmodernism in the manipulation of popular forms such as the Gothic in *Lady Oracle* and science fiction in *The Handmaid's Tale*, *Cat's Eye* is Margaret At-

wood's first full-fledged "postmodern" work. Always the wily evader of critics' pigeonholes, Atwood, in a recent interview,[1] has denied the classification of her work as "postmodern." She expresses her own amused disdain towards the critical-academic world for its attraction to "isms"[2] in the discourse of *Cat's Eye* when Elaine Risley visits the gallery where her retrospective show is to be mounted. Risley dismisses the paintings still on display: "I don't give a glance to what's still on the walls, I hate those neo-expressionist dirty greens and putrid oranges, post this, post that. Everything is post these days, as if we're just a footnote to something earlier that was real enough to have a name of its own" (90). At the same time, this novel is clearly Atwood's most postmodern in its play with form—the fictional autobiography—and in its continual self-referentiality as a text.

At the centre of this postmodern text is Atwood's complex use of her own past. Few writers have spoken out so vehemently against readings of their work as autobiography. As her interviews indicate, she is very aware that her audience is bent upon biographical readings of her fiction.[3] With obvious amusement she tells how in question-and-answer sessions following her public readings she has often just finished disclaiming autobiographical roots for her characters when someone in her audience asks if she was overweight as a child like Joan in *Lady Oracle* or anorexic as a young woman like the unnamed narrator of *The Edible Woman*. For Atwood, there are clearly gender implications here since, as she has argued, women have traditionally been thought so imaginatively impoverished that all they could write about was themselves.

At the same time, although there is no Atwood biography—and she would be one of the last writers to authorize one—she is among the most interviewed contemporary writers. Thus, as she herself must know, serious readers of her work are familiar enough with the outlines of her family and her early life[4] to be enticed into seeing the painter Elaine Risley—that stereotyped persona of modernist fiction—as at least partly her own reflection. Obviously she is not; and yet she *is*, despite the curious warning on the copyright page which reads in part as follows:

> This is a work of fiction. Although its form is that of an autobiography, it is not one . . . with the exception of public figures, any resemblance to persons living or dead is purely coincidental. The opinions expressed are those of the characters and should not be confused with the author's.

It is easy enough to see that Atwood is attempting to protect herself from potential legal action generated by former friends or associates who might choose to see themselves as models for the less appealing characters in *Cat's Eye*. However, the attempt to deny *any* connection with Elaine Risley must encourage the reader to suspect that the lady doth protest too much. In this way, part of the enjoyment of this text involves a shifting back and forth between invention and the facts of the inventor's past.

Atwood has provided her audience with so many of those facts of her early life that it is next to impossible for the informed reader to dismiss as coincidental the roots of Elaine's childhood in Atwood's. She has told her interviewers, for example, about the summers she spent as a child living in tents and motels while the family accompanied her father, an entomologist, doing research in the Canadian north. On more than one occasion she has described to her interviewers how she and her brother would help their father collect insects he shook from trees. In this context, given the writer's having gone on record as frustrated with her audience's misguided autobiographical readings of her earlier work, it is difficult not to conclude that *Cat's Eye* is, among many things, a highly sophisticated expression of play with her audience's expectations. Atwood may plead ignorance of contemporary critical theory, but she is undercutting the conventional notion that autobiography privileges an autobiographical fiction as more truthful than other forms of fiction. She shows us in Elaine Risley, a painter/writer who may seem in a conventional sense to be exploring the truth of her past but who in a truer sense is creating, or writing, a past as she chooses now to see it, rather than as it might have once existed.

The novel begins with a definition of time, justified perhaps by Risley's having returned to Toronto, her home, for a retrospective exhibition of her art. She dismisses linear time in favor of "time as having a shape . . . , like a series of liquid transparencies. . . . You don't look back along time but down through it, like water. Sometimes this comes to the surface, sometimes that, sometimes nothing. Nothing goes away" (3). In the story she tells of her youth, Elaine offers a retrospective of the woman she has been and the women who have been important to her as she now sees herself and them. That past is very much seen through the cat's eye marble into which Elaine looked at eight and saw her future as an artist. The image of the cat's eye is central, since it

represents a world into which she has been allowed access; at the same time, it is a world of inevitably distorted vision. Thus, the truth is not an entity to which we struggle to gain access so much as a way of looking and, in the process, creating the text of that truth.

Elaine Risley's retrospective allows her to review the people and relationships that have been important to the first fifty years of her life. In reconstructing her past—or the critical years from age eight to young womanhood—Elaine Risley is in large part deconstructing that past. The consequences of that deconstruction—what turns out to be the novel itself—is a complicated series of transformations through which the persona discovers that the past is only what we continue to reconstruct for the purposes of the present. And perhaps beyond that, Elaine Risley discovers that of all her relationships—with the opposite sex and with her own—the most important may have been the strange friendship with her tormentor/double Cordelia. By the end of the narrative, the persona will have finally exorcised the spirit of an alter ego who was perhaps primarily *that*, another self whom she no longer needs to fear, hate, or even love.

The focus of the early chapters is the very young Elaine Risley's struggle to find models in the two women who are crucial to her formative years. She begins her retrospective with her eighth birthday, a not surprising age for the onset of consciousness. For Risley, like Atwood, this was the time of her move to Toronto, and for Risley at least the end of happiness. Through the move to Toronto, a backwater of civilization in the 1940s, but still civilization, Elaine as a child is suddenly forced to confront "femininity." Having lived in tents and motels, she and her mother must don the costumes and the roles appropriate to their gender and put away their unfeminine clothes and ungendered roles until the warm weather when they return to the North. Overnight Elaine feels like an alien from another planet. The future of painful socialization is represented by the doorway in her new school marked "GIRLS," the doorway which makes her wonder what the other one marked "BOYS" has behind it from which she has been shut out (49).

We might expect Elaine to cherish the memory of a paradise lost of relatively ungendered life as a child in nature. Instead, she feels guilty for being unprepared to operate in a world of mothers who are housekeepers preoccupied with clothes and labour-saving devices. Although the mature Elaine mutes the resentment, the child

Elaine suspects that her mother has failed her as the role model needed to help her find her way in a world of "twin sets" (54) and wearing hats to church. The young Elaine's inability to fault the mother she loves forces her to internalize as guilt her sense of inadequacy. If she is suffering the pain of being out of place, it must be something that is wrong with *her;* certainly it cannot be anything wrong with the definition of womanhood embodied in the mothers of her friends, Cordelia, Carol, but especially Grace Smeath.

Clearly Mrs. Smeath is the Bad Mother that Elaine suspects her own mother of being for not having prepared her for socialization. In the Smeath household, Elaine and her friends are involved in that socialization; they study to be future housewives by cutting out pictures of "frying pans and washing machines" to paste into scrapbooks for their "ladies" (71). A more important aspect of that socialization is represented by regular attendance at church. When the Smeaths invite Elaine to join them for the first of what eventually seems an endless series of Sundays, Atwood describes the interior of the church through the eyes of the young Elaine who might as well be a creature from Mars. One feature that becomes crucially important to Elaine are the inscriptions under the stained-glass pictures of Jesus— "SUFFER•THE•LITTLE•CHILDREN" (102)—and of Mary— "THE•GREATEST•OF•THESE•IS•CHARITY" (103).

Because she feels radically incapable of fitting into the world outside her home, Elaine becomes the victim of Cordelia's sadistic punishments for her incompetence as a student of womanhood. These punishments, which range from reprimands and shunnings to being buried alive, culminate in the scene of Elaine's almost freezing to death in a nearby ravine where Cordelia has thrown her hat. This is a ravine where "*men*" (51) lurk to molest careless little girls. It is Elaine's victimization at the hands of other little girls, not those mysteriously dangerous men, which leads her to the nervous reaction of peeling the skin off her feet and hands, almost as though she is studying to become a child martyr by flaying herself alive. She is saved, she convinces herself, not so much by her own mother as by the apparition of the ultimate Good Mother, the Virgin Mary.

Mrs. Risley and Mrs. Smeath function then as variants of the Good Mother and the Bad Mother. Elaine's mother suspects that Cordelia and the other girls are tormenting her daughter, but she assumes that Elaine can tell her the truth and she never notices the marks of Elaine's flaying herself.

Mrs. Smeath, on the other hand, *knows* that Elaine is being tormented but does nothing. In fact, Mrs. Smeath even *knows* that Elaine has overheard her saying that Elaine *deserves* to be punished for being at heart a graceless heathen. It is not until Elaine almost dies that Mrs. Risley acts. Somewhere down in the pool of the past lurks the monster of resentment against this Good Mother who should have known and acted sooner. Mrs. Risley becomes the representation, like her husband, of the well-intentioned, virtuous, but not terribly effective liberal humanists who *sense* that evil exists but refuse to acknowledge it, since a knowledge of evil would force them to find a place for it in their world.

Mrs. Smeath, on the other hand, is much easier for Elaine to deal with. Even as a child, Elaine can clearly see Mrs. Smeath's evil in the transparent world of that cat's eye which will be the emblem of her insight as an artist. She comes to see the crucial difference *within* Mrs. Smeath as a woman who professes to being a Christian— "SUFFER•THE•LITTLE•CHILDREN" and "THE• GREATEST•OF•THESE•IS•CHARITY"—yet believes that the greatest charity to little children who happen to be "heathens" is to make them indeed suffer. And, it is very much to the point that the individual who functions as Elaine's Muse is Mrs. Smeath, *not* Mrs. Risley. This variety of the Bad Mother, more in line with Freud's reality principle, generates a whole series of paintings through which Elaine vents her anger, hatred, and malice. Mrs. Smeath as the bad mother may very well represent much of what she finds most despicable in the conventional notion of Woman. At the same time, it is an evil which generates art and it is that art which liberates her from a self enslaved in anger towards and hatred of that image of "Woman."

That same indeterminacy is evident in Elaine's bizarre relationship with Cordelia. When she declares her independence, following Cordelia's move to another school, Elaine becomes powerful, assertive, verbally aggressive, and Cordelia fades into powerlessness, into the kind of silence which was Elaine's position early on in this power struggle veiled as a friendship. Elaine's enjoyment of a new facility with words, as though her tongue has been empowered by her earlier victimization, makes it clear how important the element of the retrospective is in this text. Told in a traditionally chronological fashion, Elaine's empowerment through language would have led the reader to anticipate that she would become a writer, rather than a painter.

In this symbiotic relationship, Elaine's friend/persecutor is given the name Cordelia. Most readers sense the irony in Atwood's borrowing the name of one of Shakespeare's innocent tragic heroines, but there are also implications of a transfer being transacted here. In the years following the Second World War, *King Lear* became one of our most attractive cultural myths in part because Cordelia reminds us how the innocent are swept up in the destruction of war and civil disorder and perhaps also that the innocent embody the redemptive power of love. At the same time, it is the refusal of Lear's single faithful daughter to speak, just as much as her sisters' hypocritical flattery, which sets in motion the machinery of conflict and destruction by which she and her family are overwhelmed. In this sense, Elaine, perhaps following her mother's example, is somewhat like Cordelia, choosing silence and martyrdom rather than risk the anxiety and guilt of self-assertion. Eventually, anger and resentment find their sublimated or socialized modes of expression, first in her verbal assaults on the imperfections of others and finally in her art, so often a visualization of her anguish at the hands of her tormentors.

More than anyone else, Cordelia is the one from whom she must free herself by acknowledging not only difference but kinship. Cordelia *is* a "secret sharer." Like her readers, Elaine keeps expecting her former tormentor to show up at the gallery, the most appropriate ghost to appear in this retrospective. Cordelia, however, does not need to appear: Elaine has already exorcized much of the guilt, hatred, and anger generated in her relationships with Mrs. Smeath and Cordelia through her art, conveniently brought together so that the artist, like her audience, can read this retrospective as a testimony to the transformative power of art. When Elaine returns to the bridge, the power of her creative consciousness calls up an apparition of Cordelia from the deeps of that pool of time with which we began. She tells us:

> I know she's looking at me, the lopsided mouth smiling a little, the face closed and defiant. There is the same shame, the sick feeling in my body, the same knowledge of my own wrongness, awkwardness, weakness; the same wish to be loved; the same loneliness; the same fear. But these are not my own emotions any more. They are Cordelia's; as they always were.

> I am the older now, I'm the stronger. If she stays here any longer she will freeze to death; she will be left behind, in the wrong time. It's almost too late.

> I reach out my arms to her, bend down, hands open to show I have no weapon. *It's all right,* I say to her. *You can go home now.*

> (443)

In a strange and unexpected sense, Cordelia has become her name. Just as Elaine earlier was rescued from physical death in the icy stream below this bridge, this time she acknowledges another variety of rescue. She confirms what this retrospective has been moving toward all along—the recognition that her art has rescued her from the spiritual death of a lifetime wasted in anger and resentment. Having recognized the power of Cordelia within herself, Elaine can at last release the Cordelia she has made to appear in the final hours before she prepares to leave home again. Perhaps she recognizes also that she and Cordelia had identities less distinct from each other than it seemed in childhood, that each had been fashioning the other in the image of a self she could not otherwise confront. Now Elaine herself can be a variety of the "Good Mother" and simply send Cordelia home before she freezes to death in "the wrong time" (443).

In the end, **Cat's Eye** is postmodern in several interrelated ways. Atwood offers the informed reader the lure of a few well-known features of her own childhood and then proceeds to invent an autobiography which is the experience of Elaine Risley, a character who may bear only the most superficial similarities. Autobiography, even when intended, is obviously enough only another form of fiction. By offering us, in the words of the novel's preliminary note, a work of fiction whose form is that of an autobiography, she gives us a text which confirms that truth by showing how Elaine Risley has invented herself, constructed an autobiography, through her art. Elaine is even allowed to be amused by her critics' (mis)readings of her painting, one of whom writes of Risley's "disconcerting deconstruction of perceived gender and its relationship to perceived power, especially in respect to numinous imagery" (406).

In addition, this text raises questions about the representation of women, about writing as a woman, about autobiography, and about mothers and daughters. As Barbara Johnson has argued, autobiography and its reflection in autobiographical fiction are a supplanting of the mother, a kind of giving birth to oneself through the creation of the text. Using the classic text of Mary Shelley's *Frankenstein*, Johnson argues that what a woman writer (the very term "woman writer" has traditionally been conceived of as a "freak of nature") creates has conventionally seemed a "monster."

Johnson asks: "Is autobiography somehow always in the process of symbolically killing the mother off by telling her the lie that we have given birth to ourselves?" (147). In telling us the story of her life, Elaine Risley foregrounds Cordelia as a monster only to show how she freed herself from Cordelia to become as a young woman monstrous in her own way, and appropriately through *language,* with her "mean mouth" (247). She offers us in Mrs. Smeath, the Bad Mother, whom she subsumes psychologically in her art, a kind of monstrosity which exorcizes the monstrous complicity of Mrs. Smeath in her persecution by Cordelia and the other girls. And she offers us in Mrs. Risley, the Good Mother, a failed guide to the intricacies of femininity in the outside world and, therefore, a mother who must be killed off before Elaine can achieve selfhood at fifty.

Why, we might ask, has it taken Elaine so long to give birth to herself, the sort of act managed by the Paul Morels and the Stephen Dedaluses of modernist fiction by their twenty-fifth birthdays? Part of the answer is obvious in the question. Elaine Risley is a female rather than a male character. In this context, a good analogue is Virginia Woolf who was well aware that she could not begin work on *To the Lighthouse,* dealing in part with the loss of her mother, until she was in her forties. As we have learned from sociologists like Nancy Chodorow, women must struggle to achieve a sense of self separate from others, in part because they are "mothered" or nurtured primarily by women (93). In this vein, Chodorow argues, mothers see themselves as continuous with their daughters:

> Because they are the same gender as their daughters and have been girls, mothers of daughters tend not to experience these infant daughters as separate from them in the same way as mothers of infant sons. In both cases, a mother is likely to experience a sense of oneness and continuity with her infant. However, this sense is stronger, and lasts longer, vis-à-vis daughters.
>
> (109)

In these ways, the retrospective of her art is partly an invention to allow Elaine to achieve a sense of self, distinct from both Mrs. Risley and Mrs. Smeath. It is also a belated recognition of her mothering herself as the child and the young woman Elaine as well as her mothering of Cordelia whom she now can release from her hatred and her love. Having completed this retrospective of her life and given birth to herself, Elaine can acknowledge the separateness of her "daughters"—both the girl she was and Cordelia as her "other." At the risk of increasing Atwood's anxiety

with yet another autobiographical reading of her fiction, it might be recalled that *Cat's Eye* is the revision and completion of a manuscript she began in her mid-twenties (Hubbard 205) and finished as she approached her fiftieth birthday. Despite Margaret Atwood's disclaimer that the novel is not autobiographical, it is a text performing itself as a text, a text of the author's own struggle to achieve selfhood as a woman and as an artist.[5]

Notes

1. Unpublished interview with Deborah Weiner and Cristina Bacchilega, 1987.

2. Atwood indicates her disdain of deconstruction: "What it also means is that the text is of no importance. What is of interest is what the critic makes of the text. Alas, alack, pretty soon we'll be getting to pure critical readings with no text at all" (Interview, Hancock 208).

3. Atwood says: "I am very tired of people making autobiographical constructions about my novels, all of which until that time [*Life before Man*] had been first-person-singular novels. And I just get really tired of answering those questions: Are you the person in *Surfacing*? Are your parents dead? Did your father drown? Have you ever been anorexic? Have you ever been crazy? All those autobiographical questions" (Interview, Draine 376).

4. Atwood tells Joyce Carol Oates the story of her family following her father into the Northern bush (Interview, Oates 70). She tells Elizabeth Meese about rebelling against her parents and going to church with her friends (Interview, Meese 182). In the Bonnie Lyons interview, she talks about the culture shock of moving to Toronto as a girl and suddenly being forced to wear dresses (Interview, Lyons 221).

5. This article is based upon a paper presented in the Margaret Atwood Society session at the Modern Language Association Convention, Washington, D.C., December 1989.

Works Cited

Atwood, Margaret. *Cat's Eye.* New York: Doubleday, 1989.

——. Interview. With Betsy Draine. *Interviews With Contemporary Writers: Second Series 1972-1982.* Ed. L. S. Dembo. Madison: U of Wisconsin P, 1983. 366-81.

——. Interview. With Geoff Hancock. Ingersoll 191-220.

——. Interview. With Bonnie Lyons. Ingersoll 221-33.

——. Interview. With Elizabeth Meese. Ingersoll 177-90.

——. Interview. With Joyce Carol Oates. Ingersoll 69-73.

Chodorow, Nancy. *The Reproduction of Mothering: Psychoanalysis and the Sociology of Gender.* Berkeley and Los Angeles: U of California P, 1978.

Hubbard, Kim. "Reflected in Margaret Atwood's *Cat's Eye.*" *People Weekly* 6 Mar. 1989: 205-06.

Ingersoll, Earl G., ed. *Margaret Atwood: Conversations.* Princeton: Ontario Review Press, 1990.

Johnson, Barbara. *A World of Difference.* Baltimore and London: Johns Hopkins UP, 1987.

ATWOOD

CAROL OSBORNE (ESSAY DATE 1994)

SOURCE: Osborne, Carol. "Constructing the Self through Memory: *Cat's Eye* as a Novel of Female Development." *Frontiers* 14, no. 3 (1994): 95-112.

In the following essay, Osborne analyzes Atwood's use of the circular return to past events to allow her protagonist in Cat's Eye *develop and establish an identity.*

The memory is a living thing—it too is in transit. But during its moment, all that is remembered joins, and lives—the old and the young, the past and the present, the living and the dead.

—Eudora Welty, *One Writer's Beginnings*, 114

But I began then to think of time as having a shape, something you could see, like a series of liquid transparencies, one laid on top of another. You don't look back along time but down through it, like water. Sometimes this comes to the surface, sometimes that, sometimes nothing. Nothing goes away.

—Margaret Atwood, *Cat's Eye*, 3

It is against blockage between ourselves and others—those who are alive and those who are dead—that we must work. In blocking off what hurts us, we think we are walling ourselves off from pain. But in the long run the wall, which prevents growth, hurts us more than the pain, which, if we will only bear it, soon passes over us. Washes over us and is gone. Long will we remember pain, but the pain itself, as it was at that point of intensity that made us feel as if we must die of it, eventually vanishes. Our memory of it becomes its only trace. Walls remain. They grow moss. They are difficult barriers to cross, to get to others, to get to closed-down parts of ourselves.

—Alice Walker, *The Temple of My Familiar*, 353

Recovering memories of the past leads Margaret Atwood's protagonist in *Cat's Eye* to her own recovery. In having Elaine create a complete sense of herself through art, dream, and memory, Atwood revises the structure of the traditional bildungsroman and kunstlerroman, privileging what feminist psychoanalytic theorists have posited as a feminine way of achieving self-knowledge. Instead of following a linear plot that emphasizes separation from the past as the mark of maturity, Atwood creates a circular structure emphasizing the protagonist's return to the scenes of her childhood and her reunion, if only in her imagination, with key figures from her past.

In her exploration of memory and the importance of the past for her protagonist, Atwood is part of a trend in contemporary fiction, represented particularly in the works of African-American women writers. Such a parallel is noteworthy, for Elaine identifies with members of minority groups in Canada as she faces the pressures of conforming to white, protestant, middle-class standards. Atwood's alternate plot structure, emphasis on memory, and attention to the pressures placed on minorities link her project in many ways with the concerns of such writers as Toni Morrison, Alice Walker, and Gayl Jones.

The traditional bildungsroman traces the development of the male protagonist in a linear fashion to the end of adolescence when he declares himself free and independent. In Joyce's *A Portrait of the Artist as a Young Man,* for example, Stephen first appears as a young boy being initiated into language as his father tells him stories of the moo-cow and baby tuckoo. The plot progresses chronologically, with a wave-like pattern of epiphanies ending each chapter, until Stephen is able to turn his back on family, nation, and religion "to forge in the smithy of [his] soul the uncreated conscience of [his] race."[1] His gestures are of renunciation; he severs all ties so that he can "fly by those nets" of "nationality, language, religion"[2] to become the independent artist who "remains within or behind or beyond or above his handiwork, invisible, refined out of existence, indifferent."[3] Such a structure emphasizes the male's Oedipal phase in which the boy defines himself in contrast to the mother and in alliance with the father. Stephen rejects his mother and Ireland, "the old sow who eats her farrow," in favor of his symbolic father, Daedalus, the artificer he addresses in the last lines of the novel.[4]

In contrast to this model, many contemporary women writers are adopting structures of circular return.[5] These plots, in emphasizing a woman's need to define herself relationally, reflect the differences in male and female identity formation noted by such feminist scholars as Nancy Chodorow, Carol Gilligan, and Margaret Homans.[6]

In structuring *Cat's Eye,* Atwood mimics the wave-like motion of Joyce's *Portrait,* but in a much more complex way. The book begins with Elaine's return to Toronto on the occasion of a retrospective art show. The return to her childhood home, along with the review of her art, causes her to reconstruct the past, assembling the fragments, as she has subconsciously assembled fragments of her past in her paintings, only this time making sense of them by confronting the memories directly and arranging them in some kind of order. In each section, the reader travels along the same path. Beginning each part of the book in the present tense with Elaine in Toronto, Atwood then switches to the past tense when the surroundings spark a particular memory of Elaine's childhood.

ON THE SUBJECT OF...

ATWOOD'S USE OF FOOD IMAGERY IN HER WORKS

For all Atwoodian heroines the search for self-hood is symbolized by the search for something satisfying to eat. Initially, although Marion eats, she eats poorly. She lives on snack food, frozen meals, and TV dinners. Marion is hungry throughout *The Edible Woman* but cannot find anything to satiate her. Whatever she eats makes her sick. In *Surfacing* the narrator's search for physical sustenance in the natural world becomes symbolic of her lack of spiritual sustenance in the social world. At the end of *Lady Oracle* Joan has nothing to eat except some biscuits which are "hard as plaster and tasted of shelf" and "some cooked pasta, drying out already, and a yellowing bunch of parsley." She has failed to escape her old life and her old self, and the absence of proper, nourishing food indicates that, at the end of the novel, Joan is still trapped in the role of victim. In *Bodily Harm* Rennie seems to spend the entire novel searching for something decent to eat. All her food is awful. In hospital the food is "unbelievable. Green Jello salad and a choice of peas or peas"; on the plane the butter is rancid and the beef leaves a taste of rotting flesh in her mouth; in the hotel there is no choice and all the food is unappetizing and unnourishing. . . In prison, the guards put salt in the tea. Throughout *Cat's Eye* Elaine never eats substantial or nutritious food. The sections of the novel set in modern-day Toronto trace her search for something to eat. When she wakes up in Jon's flat she finds the kitchen devoid of food. She decides she needs "to go shopping and get some decent food, organize. . . . I will buy oranges, yogurt without jam. I will have a positive attitude, take care of myself, I'll feed myself enzymes and friendly bacteria." Her intention to eat health food signals her desire for a positive sense of self. Nevertheless, she is never able to provide herself with the food she knows she needs. She wanders around Toronto moving from one location of food to another without eating. . . She eats leftovers and eggs mashed up in teacups. She eats "haphazardly now, snack[s] on junk food and take-outs without worrying about balanced meals." Because of her poor self-image, she is unable to nourish herself. She abuses herself with a poor diet. When she arrives at the gallery or the opening of her exhibition nobody is there because they have gone out to eat. Elaine stands alone and unnourished. After the party, Charna invites her to dinner but she declines. By the close of the novel Elaine has not rediscovered Cordelia and so has not been able to redefine her relationship with her old tormentor by breaking the strong bond between victim and persecutor. It is possible to interpret the scene in which Elaine returns to the ravine and conjures up a vision of Cordelia as a child as the point of reconciliation, the point at which Elaine finally forgives her old foe and the interdependent positions of victim and victor are transcended. However, the moment of epiphany is equivocal, and at the end of the novel Elaine is still eating mashed-up eggs in teacups.

All the heroines interpret the world in terms of food and negotiate their way through life using food. For women, eating and non-eating articulate that which is ideologically unspeakable. Food functions as a muted form of female self-expression but, more than that, it also becomes a medium of experience. Food imagery saturates the novels and becomes the dominant metaphor the heroines use to describe people, landscape, and emotion. As Sally Cline has pointed out, women appropriate food as a language because traditionally they have always been associated with food. In addition, food is one of the few resources available to women. As a consumer surveyor, Marion is constantly submerged in a food environment, and the other heroines have the major responsibility for cooking and shopping. Women control food, Cline insists, because they cannot control their lives. Given the patriarchal nature of language and its inability to accommodate female experience, it is unsurprising that women choose an alternative, non-verbal form of communication. The failure of language, the inadequacy of words as a mode of communication, is a recurrent theme in Atwood's work.

Parker, Emma. Excerpt from "You Are What You Eat: The Politics of Eating in the Novels of Margaret Atwood." *Twentieth Century Literature* 41, no. 3 (fall 1995): 349-68.

Then the reader becomes completely submerged in the past event when Atwood begins narrating this episode in present tense. These moments from the past progress chronologically, following Elaine's development from age eight to the point of her mother's death a few years before the art show.

With this alternate structure, Atwood explores the nature of memory, showing that "nothing goes away"[7] and that "there is never only one, of anyone."[8] Unlike the male protagonists of bildungsromans who separate themselves from earlier experiences, Elaine finds her identity through consciously going back to and accepting her past and the people in it, and embracing herself as she was and is. In this way, Atwood privileges the relational needs of a female protagonist; although Elaine's childhood makes it difficult for her to form actual relationships with other women, her inner concerns reflect a desire for connection rather than separation from others.

Atwood also departs from the traditional structure of female bildungsromans such as *Jane Eyre* and *The Awakening*. By making her protagonist middle-aged, secure professionally as a minor artist, and already a wife and a mother, Atwood avoids the traditional pattern in which the point of maturation is marked by the heroine's marrying, giving birth, or finding a career. Her protagonist will not have to surrender her newly found sense of self at the end in exchange for security in marriage or society. The reader trained to expect a man to enter the plot, providing a fountain of wisdom through which the woman discovers herself, will be disappointed. No man in *Cat's Eye* is given such power; husbands, lovers, and even a male psychologist do not provide the insight that Elaine must achieve on her own. By making Elaine already secure in job and family, Atwood shows that these aspects of a woman's life do not necessarily lead her to a better understanding of herself. While Atwood does follow the female tradition in making Elaine's development internal, that withdrawal into the inner life is a healing one and does not lead to madness or death as was true with earlier protagonists.[9]

In an interview with Geoff Hancock in December of 1986, Atwood speaks of how intriguing it is for a writer to make changes in traditional forms. Once a writer understands a form and how it works, she says, she can "move beyond the conventions to include things not considered includable. [Therefore] the kind of material thought to be suitable for novels is constantly changing."[10] In an interview conducted in November of 1989, she speaks specifically of *Cat's Eye,* saying that she is dealing with an area of life, the world of girls age eight through twelve, that is not "regarded as serious 'literary' material."[11] Atwood becomes interested in stories because she notices a blank, an area that has not been written about, or because she thinks of a narrative form that could be approached from a different angle.

Because Atwood is consciously altering the traditional structure of the bildungsroman in *Cat's Eye,* she accentuates notions of male and female difference within the text. Elaine communicates with images, finds herself often without words, and is able to use language to her benefit only later in her development. On the other hand, her brother, Stephen, has the power to control the narrative when they play war and to write in the snow with his pee while she stands idly by. (Atwood here seems to be playing with Freud's association of penis and pen.) Stephen becomes more abstract and theoretical as he develops, moving "away from the imprecision of words"[12] to a reliance on numbers, while she is grounded in concrete images.[13] Even Elaine's art differs from the abstract paintings of her first husband, Jon, not serving to dismember, as his statues do, but to re-form, using memories from her past. Most importantly, Elaine, during her prepubescent period, shows the longing for relations, friendships, and mother-daughter bonds, that marks female development as different from male.

It is important to note what triggers Elaine's retrospection in terms of female development before tracing her maturation process. Elaine has reached middle age, her children have grown up, and she is having trouble accepting herself as being as old as the women that used to seem so foreign to her and Cordelia, her childhood friend. She reveals her discomfort with her mid-life status by saying that she feels everyone else her age is an adult and she is in disguise. When passing the cosmetics counter in Simpsons during her stay in Toronto, she wishes she could mummify herself, "stop the drip-drip of time, stay" the way she is, but she is forced to see herself through the eyes of the young saleslady as a middle-aged woman, and she thinks of Macbeth's lines, "My way of life / Is fall'n into the sere and yellow leaf."[14]

Her retrospective is a way for her to deal with this new stage of her life, a way of filling the void, overcoming the inertia, and allaying the threat of madness. As she has done earlier in her life, Elaine projects her own concerns onto the image of Cordelia. When she pictures Cordelia, it is as a woman who is fighting against the deterioration of the body or trapped in an iron lung, in a state of inertia. This projection mirrors the emptiness

Elaine feels during her stay in Toronto, especially when she tries to call her husband, Ben, in British Columbia. He is not at home, and she hears her own disembodied voice on the answering machine. The nothingness that has threatened at two other key moments in her life seems to be approaching. At this time, Elaine does not walk away from the sources of her discomfort as she has in the past. Such movements toward separation fit the male model of maturation. Instead, she works to reintegrate, to re-member the various projections of herself so that she can feel that she has a full identity. She recognizes, through her picture on the art show poster, that she has reached a point where she has an identity, a face that can be defaced, but internally she must realize this identity by filling the void with memories she has blocked out earlier in her life.

Atwood's depiction of Elaine's development agrees with the theories of aging discussed in Kathleen Woodward and Murray Schwartz's *Memory and Desire*. Apparently, aging "generates a multiplicity of self-images," and through "varieties of playing" and "uses of illusion," we can connect past experiences into a continuous narrative that helps us deal with old age.[15] According to Schwartz, "The space of illusion can fail to achieve its integrating aims and yield instead to a regressive search for imaginary unities of youth. Or we may be confronted with a violent return of the repressed, a rupture of all sense of continuity."[16]

In the same volume, Kathleen Woodward suggests that as we age, "we separate what we take to be our real selves from our bodies."[17] She believes "the recognition of our own old age comes to us from the other, that is, from society. We study our own reflection in the body of the others, and as we reflect upon that reflection—reflection is of course a metaphor for thought—we ultimately are compelled to acknowledge the point of view of the Other which has, as it were, installed itself in our body."[18] This recognition makes us experience what Freud called the uncanny, as we recognize our possible future absence, our nothingness, our death. As a result, we react against the images in mirrors and the images we see of ourselves in others.[19]

Carol Gilligan also speaks of mid-life as being "a time of return to the unfinished business of adolescence."[20] When facing the "issues of separation that arise at mid-life," women are vulnerable due to the confusion of identity and intimacy at the crucial stage of adolescence when they formed a notion of themselves as they related with others.[21]

These theories explain why Elaine, when encountering middle age, needs to re-establish her own identity, to integrate past experience into her present sense of self. At first she seems to be looking for the imaginary unities of her youth as she searches for Cordelia in Toronto. As she stays there, scenes she has repressed surface. She sees herself in mirrors and is surprised by the sight; she sees herself in the figures of ladies begging on the streets and answers to their needs; and she plays with illusion, in seeing herself through the eyes of others, even those who seemed so oppressive to her as a child. She is able, through her play with images and with memory, to find continuity, a continuity seen in the narrative that structures the novel and that determines the arrangement of paintings in the art show. But she must work through the unfinished business of her adolescence, and that involves dredging up memories of a very difficult time in her development.

In her concern with memory, with the need for her protagonist to confront the past in coming to know herself, Atwood most resembles contemporary African-American novelists. In *Corregidora*, Gayl Jones portrays Ursa repeatedly recalling her grandmother's words until she understands their meaning; in *The Temple of My Familiar*, Alice Walker stresses how vital recapturing the past is for the personal growth of her protagonists, particularly Suwelo; and in *Beloved*, Toni Morrison depicts Sethe working through the memories of her traumatic escape from slavery and the murder of her daughter so that she can let go of the past. Likewise, Atwood presents Elaine undergoing her own form of psychotherapy in gradually uncovering, for the reader and for herself, the scenes of her childhood.

Atwood, Walker, Morrison and Jones all portray their protagonists' encounters with parental figures, particularly the mother, but the African-American writers place more importance on the interactions between the generations. Storytelling, within the texts, becomes not only a tribute to a cultural tradition, but also an act of community building as characters strive to keep the cultural past alive. While the African-American writers use oral narrative in their works as a tool for uncovering what has been repressed in a character's consciousness, Atwood depends more on Elaine's paintings and her visit to the scenes of her youth to trigger her memory. Few words are spoken, for Atwood is more concerned with Elaine's personal understanding gained through private reflection and is perhaps more skeptical of finding a common cultural past within the metropolis of Toronto, even among individuals who are of the same race, class, and gender.

Cat's Eye differs from the work of contemporary African-American women writers in another significant way: Elaine's memories are restricted to her personal past, and her encounters with the figures of her past are presented in a realistic manner. While Elaine may think she sees the characters from her past as she walks around Toronto, her interactions with these figures are always explained as occurring in her mind. Encounters with the dead come only in her dreams, in her invented narratives, in her reviewing of her art, and in the memories sparked by her return to the scenes of her past.[22]

In commenting on Walker's *The Temple of My Familiar,* Ikenna Dieke writes, "Recollective art is a rhetorical strategy of relocating the lost self, of seeking and uncovering an inner tapestry of identity, not mere psychological identity, but the exterior contexts—social, political, and personal—that make up the human self in all its complexity."[23] He could easily be speaking of Atwood's project in *Cat's Eye.* Atwood may restrict herself to the personal recollections of her protagonist in this work, but the forces that have shaped Elaine reflect much about social and cultural conditions in Canada, particularly in the coercive nature of the white middle class, so dominant in the 1940s and 1950s.

Throughout the novel, the middle-aged Elaine expresses her hatred for Toronto. Even though it may now proclaim itself a multicultural mecca, a "world-class city," offering diversified restaurants, boutiques, and renovated districts, underneath she recognizes the same old city, with "street after street of thick red brick houses, with their front porch pillars like the off-white stems of toadstools and their watchful, calculating windows. Malicious, greedy, vindictive, implacable."[24] Elaine always feels lost in Toronto, even in 1989, because to her it still represents middle-class conformity and intolerance.

During her first eight years while her father is a forest-insect field researcher and the family leads an unconventional, nomadic life in northern Canada, Elaine longs for real girl friends, for a relationship with someone like herself. Then her father takes a position as a professor in Toronto, and Elaine is able to become friends with other girls her age. She finds herself an outsider. Despite being the same race, class, and gender as the girls who befriend her, Elaine painfully discovers how different she is from the rest of middle-class society. She has no religious training since her father, a scientist, does not believe in organized religion. She knows nothing about the material trappings of middle-class culture: pageboy haircuts, Eaton catalogues, chintz curtains, and twin sets. By comparing her home to the homes of her friends, she recognizes that her family is not as well-off financially. Finally, the customs and rituals of little girls seem strange to her because she has grown up playing with and freely emulating her closest companion, her brother, without worrying about society's gender restrictions.

When Elaine first moves to Toronto, Carol Campbell befriends her. Besides offering companionship, Elaine, as an exotic oddity, serves as a means of enhancing Carol's own status. Carol treats Elaine as she would a member of a primitive tribe, marveling at Elaine's ignorance of the objects, rituals, and ways of life of the Toronto middle class. But the differences that amaze Carol at first soon become the targets for attack when other girls join the group.

Elaine begins playing a part so that she can fit in with her girlfriends. Caught between her own tendencies to express herself as her brother would and her society's expectations for her to be delicate, modest, and conforming, she loses her own voice and identity, copying the behavior of her friends and remaining silent when her views do not agree with theirs.

During the summer following her introduction to the society of little girls through Carol Campbell and Grace Smeath, Elaine stands outside her parents' window, imagining that they do not exist. She becomes critical of her parents and begins searching for replacement figures for them. Chodorow explains that as an adolescent girl begins to reject her parents, she longs for a best friend "whom she loves, with whom she is identified, with whom she shares everything. . . . Her friendship permits her to continue to experience merging, while at the same time denying feelings of merging with her mother."[25] The mother substitute Elaine takes is Cordelia, who has joined the group by the time Elaine returns. Attracted by Cordelia's wildness and her potential to be subversive in defying the conventions of society, Elaine soon finds that Cordelia can get away with being different because she is older and wealthier. Instead of providing an outlet for Elaine, Cordelia becomes the embodiment of the culture's intolerance, directing the other girls in their persecution of Elaine.

Cordelia is an abusive mother figure who reinforces Elaine's sense of difference at every turn, making her constantly feel that she is not normal, not like other girls. We learn later that Cordelia feels alienated in her home environment because she is not as gifted as her two sisters are. Cordelia's treatment of Elaine, then, mirrors her own family's treatment of her. In tormenting Elaine, Cordelia is simply acting out of the loneliness and rejection she feels within her own family, even echoing her parents' words in her reprimands of Elaine.

Despite the ill treatment, Elaine doesn't betray her "friend," so strong is her need for relationship. Elaine fears being cast out forever from her circle of friends. Her only defense becomes her silence, and she grows mute even to herself. Even though she tries her best to fit into this new social group, attending church with Grace Smeath, submitting herself to the harsh treatment of Cordelia, and even reaching the point of negating herself, Elaine never feels comfortable conforming in this manner. Elaine shows her continued sense of alienation when she states that she likes cat's eye marbles best because they are "the eyes of something that isn't known but exists anyway . . . like the eyes of aliens from a distant planet."[26] Symbolically, Elaine removes the cat's eye marble, a sign of her secret difference, from her purse when she goes to church.

In church, Elaine feels perhaps the greatest pressure to conform under the watchful eyes of Grace. At first when Elaine notices the pictures of Jesus surrounded by children of all different colors who look at Him with the same worshipful gaze Elaine has directed toward Grace, she feels included, taken in. Yet she also senses a problem with society's desire to privilege what is white over that which is colored. As the Sunday school class watches slides in which knights with very white skin battle evil, Elaine sees through this illusion, so to speak, noticing the light switches and the wainscoting beneath the projected image. And on White Gift Sunday, Elaine is disturbed because the gifts are "made uniform, bleached of their identity and colors. . . . They look dead."[27] The color white in both circumstances is important, for it introduces a racial element that is reinforced not only by Elaine's identification with ethnic and racial minority figures, but by the association of Elaine with the color black throughout the novel, an association that will be discussed in more detail later. As Toni Morrison notes in *Playing in the Dark*, characters of color are often used to define, through their difference, the implications of whiteness.[28]

The individuals portrayed in Elaine's painting "Three Muses" all share with Elaine an outsider status in Toronto. She includes these figures in her portrait because as a child, not only is she treated kindly by each one, but she identifies with all of them in their alienation from the dominant culture. First, she sees in her father's associate from India, Mr. Banerji, a creature like herself, "alien and apprehensive."[29] She notices his chewed nails, the misery underneath his smile, the pressure he feels living in a society so foreign to him. Like Elaine, Mr. Banerji is never totally accepted in Toronto. After suffering through years of racial discrimination in the university's promotional system, he finally returns to India.

The second muse is Mrs. Finestein. Elaine enjoys baby-sitting for her son, Brian, since he is uncritical, unlike her friends. But when Grace and Carol point out that Brian is a Jew, revealing their prejudice against the people they call the killers of Jesus, Elaine fears her own ability to protect the child and stops baby-sitting. Still, she feels there is "something extra and a little heroic" about Brian because he is a member of a group that has suffered under Hitler's rule.[30] She later feels the same dimension of heroism added to her own character when her painting "White Gift" is attacked at the art show by a conservative middle-class woman outraged by its blasphemy.

The third figure with whom Elaine identifies is her teacher, Mrs. Stuart. Elaine enjoys Mrs. Stuart's class much more than Mrs. Lumley's. Instead of indoctrinating the students about the superiority of British culture over the culture of the colonies, Mrs. Stuart, a Scot, stresses the positive aspects of foreign lands. Mrs. Stuart, an exile herself, gives Elaine hope, for she offers her images of wonderful foreign places where she may be able to escape the stifling atmosphere of Toronto.

While Elaine is a white Canadian, not ostensibly a member of a minority in Toronto, Atwood encodes racial difference within the text to accentuate Elaine's feelings of oppression. As Elaine surrenders power over her own self-definition, Atwood associates her more and more with the color black while her oppressors, Cordelia, Carol and Grace, are aligned with white images. For example, Elaine derives her strategy for surviving the taunts of her friends through two sources, both associated with blackness. When she discovers a dead raven one summer, she notices that no matter how she pokes it, it does not feel a thing. She notes its color, black like a hole, and reflects that no one can get at it, no matter what they do. When she subsequently blocks her own feelings, she becomes like the dead raven. After fainting at the Conversat, she discovers an even better way of escaping from her tormentors. By holding her breath until she faints, a sensation she describes as blackness closing in around the edges of her eyes, she is able to avoid Cordelia's reprimands.

When Cordelia and the other girls bury her, Elaine has no image of herself in the dark hole, just a square of blackness, because at this point, she essentially loses her identity. Elaine learns to protect herself by not being, not feeling, not talking. In picturing Cordelia pushing her off a cliff, drawing a self-portrait that shows her figure as a small speck of light in the middle of blackness, and finally finding some type of escape through fainting, losing consciousness, and going into a state of nothingness, Elaine works harder and harder to negate herself.

This negation continues until Elaine is able to find a mother figure who can replace the harmful Cordelia and thus fulfill Elaine's pre-Oedipal need to form an attachment with someone like herself. Her need for a mother substitute becomes exacerbated when her own mother's miscarriage and depression distance her from Elaine. At this point, by dreaming that Mrs. Finestein and Mr. Banerji are her parents, Elaine reveals her perception that these characters, as members of ethnic minorities, have more in common with her and thus promise more support as parents than her own family is able to provide. In the same dream, Elaine pictures her mother giving birth to twins, one gray and the other missing. She sees herself as one twin, gray and without identity, and the double, the role Cordelia serves, is missing. At this point, Elaine realizes, through her dreams, the need for a new figure to whom she can become attached.

The figure that replaces Cordelia is an imaginary one that Elaine chooses in deliberate opposition to the society responsible for the erasure of her identity. When Elaine overhears Grace's mother and aunt discussing her, she realizes that despite her efforts to conform, they still view her as a heathen, and more importantly, that the adult society sanctions the abuse she receives from her peers for being different. At this point, in rebellion against the God Mrs. Smeath and her society seem to control, she chooses her own private icon, the Virgin Mary, a figure always in the background in Grace's religion. Elaine rebels against the rules of the "onion church" by aligning herself with an opposed minority, the Catholics, and kneeling as she prays to this alternate mother figure.

In the scene in which these prayers are answered and Elaine finds the strength to break with Cordelia, black and white imagery again plays a crucial role. Cordelia makes an angel in the white snow and her face appears as a white oval right before she throws Elaine's hat into the ravine. These images of whiteness contain a sinister aspect, however, for the imprint of Cordelia's fingers in the snow makes the angel appear to have claws, and the chilling ice of the ravine

threatens death for Elaine. What comes to her rescue, in contrast to the whiteness, is not the traditional image of Mary, with blue dress and crown, but the figure of Mary dressed in black. Elaine, then, aligns herself with minorities, both literally and figuratively, in order to overcome the oppression of white, middle-class Canadian society.

Once Elaine is able to create a mother substitute, Mary, with her imagination, she can break free of Cordelia's domination. Elaine, released from her silence, begins to seize control through language, becoming the mean mouth that can frighten Cordelia through her stories. Earlier, Cordelia had seized narrative control by telling of her family, the dead people in the ravine, and witches in eggshells, but now Elaine relishes her power over Cordelia by telling her she is a vampire. The figures associated with her power over Cordelia, Mary and a vampire, come again to Elaine's mind as she returns to Toronto. Regretting wearing her powder-blue jogging suit to the interview at the gallery, she wishes for a Nun black or Dracula black outfit to make her feel more powerful. Before reunion with the images of her past, she is still daunted by the judgmental atmosphere she encounters in the gallery, and she looks to black disguises to aid her.

While the imaginary mother substitute, Mary, allows Elaine to escape Cordelia's domination, this vision does not offer a permanent resolution to her relational needs. In the next stage of her development, Elaine avoids others who resemble her, for she still fears facing herself. Not until she can make a connection with her double, with the image of Cordelia, will she feel comfortable with herself or with those who reflect what she is.

In art school, then, Elaine stays away from other girls and looks for acceptance from male students. Securely dressed in black, living in a neighborhood of immigrants, she fits into the art school crowd. Elaine seems to follow traditional lines of development at this point, finding in her art teacher, Joseph, a father figure who promises that although he is beginning with nothing, he can "finish" her. Joseph, called D. P. (Displaced Person) by the other art students because he is an Eastern European refugee, needs Elaine's support as much as she needs his. Once again, Elaine aligns herself with someone else who feels alienated from the culture. Even her intimate life with Joseph is associated with a foreign world, for they always have sex on his Mexican blanket.

The need in Joseph, and later in Jon, does not frighten Elaine the way that need in other women does, for it is the need of someone different from herself. With Cordelia and with her fellow art student, Susie, who parallels Cordelia and is conflated with her in Elaine's dream, Elaine is more frightened, for she sees herself mirrored in both. Susie and Elaine are both dating Joseph and thus parallel. When Elaine meets Cordelia again, her image is mirrored in Cordelia's sunglasses, and Elaine realizes that she is acting her role in relationships with men in her life just as much as Cordelia is acting on stage. Elaine refuses to help either of these women, to form bonds with them, for that would mean confronting herself. She does not become friends with Susie, and she later refuses to aid Cordelia in leaving the mental institution.

Once again, as Elaine had negated herself to fit into the female world of the little girls, she negates herself in fitting into the roles defined by the men in her life. By first allowing Joseph to mold her, and then later in conforming to Jon's expectations when she moves in with and then marries him, she loses a sense of her own identity. She becomes silent, feels vacant, and upon discovering that she is pregnant, feels once again that she is a black square that is totally empty. Indeed, neither Joseph nor Jon sees Elaine; instead, they project onto her the image of their need. Elaine's understanding of how each man views her becomes obvious in her painting of them. In this painting, Elaine, with a cat's eye marble head, appears as the model for Joseph and Jon, yet their portraits are not of her. The symbolism in this piece of art shows that Elaine is capable of seeing, but not of being seen.

Elaine's unresolved problems with her past lead her eventually, in considering her life a ruin, to attempt suicide, longing for death as she did in the ravine. The voice that pushes her in this scene is Cordelia's, for Cordelia is the first to make Elaine feel as though she is nothing. Once Elaine realizes that Cordelia's voice will not go away as long as she stays in Toronto, that the echoes of the past will continue to haunt her, she finds the strength to leave. Within the childhood world of young girls and within the structures of marriage and motherhood, Elaine fails to find her own identity because of the pressure middle-class society places on her to conform. She flees to British Columbia, she says, not only to mark the end of her marriage, but also to escape the city of Toronto.

In her new locale, through her painting, Elaine once again regains control of her life, and she is even able to remarry, but she is unable to find connections with women because her relations with the women earlier in her life have not been resolved. The act of separating oneself from the past, the act that culminates the male bildungsroman, does not lead to resolution in Atwood's novel. Elaine claims that she is good at leaving and not looking back, but while such a separation may allow her to heal some of her wounds, her complete self-knowledge occurs only when she is able to look back, to return and confront the past.

It seems important that Atwood does not portray Elaine as finding herself through feminist collectives or motherhood. Perhaps Atwood is rebelling against the myths that maintain that a woman can get a better sense of herself through organized groups of women who share the same experiences of oppression, or through becoming a mother and thus satisfying her longing, according to Freud, for a penis. Repeatedly, Atwood emphasizes Elaine's alienation from other women—those in her art group, in her consciousness-raising group, and in the gallery holding her retrospective show—for all these women seem as judgmental to her as her first female friends, Cordelia, Grace, and Carol.[31]

The third stage of Elaine's development parallels patterns Diana George notes in the work of female poets. Using Kathleen Woodward's theories on female aging, George concludes that "an encounter with one's parents (and in the case of aging women poets, especially the mother) may permit the poetic self to move toward wholeness, even if not to achieve it."[32] In Atwood's portrayal of Elaine's return to her mother, she also parallels trends in the work of African-American authors. Joyce Pettis, in discussing works by Paule Marshall, Gloria Naylor, and Toni Morrison, notes that often in black women's texts, "Characters travel back to their cultural origins or to the origin of their maternal ancestors in search of bringing coherence to fragmented lives."[33] In the last episode of the chronological narrative that structures *Cat's Eye*, Elaine returns to Toronto to be with her dying mother. Together, they uncover layer upon layer of the past in an old trunk, eventually coming to the red purse, associated in Elaine's mind with the saving figure of Mary.

Earlier in the narrative after Elaine describes the figure of Mary rescuing her from the ravine, she tells of visiting churches wherever she goes, searching for statues of the Virgin Mary. Though she approaches each with hope, she is always disappointed—until she and Ben travel to Mexico. There, in a foreign environment far away from Toronto, she sees a statue of Mary, dressed in black, the only statue of Mary that seems real to her. Recognizing Mary as "a Virgin of lost things, one who restored what was lost," Elaine wants to pray to her but does not because she does not "know what to pray for."[34] At this point in her life, when she has escaped from her past and is beginning a life with Ben, she recognizes the importance of the symbol of Mary, but she does not yet realize what the finder of lost things can restore to her. Once she and her mother begin uncovering the past by going through the trunk, however, Elaine realizes that what was lost were the memories of her past, the sense of self of which Cordelia and others had robbed her.

As the items in the trunk and her mother's recollections help Elaine recover repressed memories, she is able to look into the last item she finds, the cat's eye marble, and see her life entire. Even though her mother is unaware of the importance of these artifacts, they enable Elaine to confront the events of the past and herself. Elaine, now that she is a mother, can understand and forgive her own mother for not protecting her against Cordelia. She realizes that her mother was concerned but powerless, unable to control the social pressure that had been so traumatic for her daughter. Elaine's growth, it seems, depends not so much on her mother's actions, then or now, but on Elaine's efforts to deal with her past during her final trip to Toronto.

Elaine, throughout her life, has resisted being a spectacle, being the subject of either her own gaze or the gaze of others. She does not like Joseph to stand behind her; that reminds her of Cordelia walking behind and judging her. She avoids mirrors, declaring that women do not want to see themselves. Indeed, she resists the whole idea of returning to Toronto for the art show and of staying at Jon's because it is "a silly thing to do, too retrospective," but the *retrospective* art show forces Elaine to look again not only at her painting as it reflects her life, but also at herself and her past.[35] The cat's eye marble once gave her power to see without feeling so that she could separate herself from others; now that this separation has prepared her for a new kind of bonding, she is granted the ability to see with feeling, through her painting and her dredging up of old memories. In looking again at her portraits of Mrs. Smeath, Elaine notices that what she always believed were self-righteous eyes were actually the eyes of a displaced person who shared her own fear and loneliness.

As Elaine imagines seeing herself as a child through the eyes of Mrs. Smeath, she changes her opinion of this woman. Rather than reacting to her with the accustomed hatred, wishing to exact an eye for an eye, she reacts with sympathy and empathy. By imaginatively placing herself in the position of another, Elaine creates the bonds that had been impossible to form earlier in her life. After reviewing the paintings that depict her unconscious grappling with the past, Elaine,

drunk and disappointed with the show, cries, making what she feels is a "spectacle" of herself, even though no one is watching. She has become a spectacle for herself, a means of seeing and the object being seen.

Finally, Elaine is able to overcome the haunting figure of Cordelia by recognizing that the fear and loneliness and pain she felt as a child were the emotions Cordelia experienced as well. When she returns to the ravine, she no longer has to depend on imaginary figures of Mary to help her, for she has become the older figure now, capable of seeing Cordelia from a different perspective. Atwood dispenses with the traditional symbol of maternal care and artistic inspiration by having Elaine dismiss the vision of Mary as being "nobody and nothing."[36] Memory makes the vision return in absolute clarity, but a mature Elaine recognizes that she directs the images of Mary and Cordelia; they no longer control her. By reaching out to comfort the imaginary figure of Cordelia, Elaine shows that she has reached an acceptance, not only of her past and the figures in it, but of herself.[37] That is the reason that, as she turns to look down the path, the image of Cordelia is no longer there. In her place is a middle-aged woman. Elaine has come to accept herself, her present position in life, by taking the inner journey through her past and renewing the relationships from which she had previously run away.

The ending of *Cat's Eye* is not entirely positive, for Elaine still feels the loss from failed relationships. But as she flies home, Elaine realizes that she has regained a sense of herself and that the echoes of her past, like the stars above her, provide her with enough light to see by. Atwood's heroine, unlike the protagonists of earlier bildungsromans, completes her growth in self-knowledge. She does not go mad, she does not commit suicide, and she corrects her earlier actions of separating from others. She achieves full maturity by reforming the pre-Oedipal bonds in accepting, if only in her imagination, the other who is like herself.

In *Cat's Eye*, Atwood shows that Elaine, in search of self-definition, is hampered by the pressure middle-class society places on her to conform to established roles. By establishing her kinship with minority figures, Elaine becomes empowered enough to break away from the coercive influence first of Cordelia and then of Jon and Joseph. But not until Elaine is able to reconnect with these figures in her past does she feel whole. In returning to Toronto, Elaine first makes peace with Jon. Then, through looking again at her art, reviving old memories, and summoning visions of Cordelia and Mrs. Smeath, Elaine is also able to reconnect with the abusive figures of her childhood, recognizing that they felt the same alienation and loneliness as she did. Atwood shows that growth for individuals and for societies comes when people are able to empathize and connect with those who differ from them while also embracing themselves.

In having Elaine return to her childhood home to participate in a retrospective art show, Atwood, like many of her contemporaries, stresses the importance of memory in the maturation process. The bildungsroman evolves, as a result of this change in emphasis, from a linear structure to a circular one that illustrates even in its form the interaction of past and present in a protagonist's psyche. Earlier in her life, when Elaine severed her ties with Cordelia and Jon, she used the imagined mother substitute, Mary, and her painting to help her escape from her past. But such avoidance left her development incomplete so that at middle age, she must overcome her depression by returning to Toronto. There, she fully develops her identity by playing with images of herself as seen in the bodies of others and by embracing those images both as they appeared in her childhood and as they appear now. While growing up under the pressures of white, middle class conformity made Elaine's childhood traumatic, she is able to find emotional release by returning to the scene of this trauma and learning, in her imagination, to identify not only with those who shared her sense of alienation, but also with those who were her oppressors.

Notes

1. James Joyce, *A Portrait of the Artist as a Young Man,* in *The Portable James Joyce,* ed. Harry Levin (New York: Viking Press, 1946), 526.

2. Joyce, *Portrait,* 469.

3. Joyce, *Portrait,* 483.

4. Joyce, *Portrait,* 470.

5. Gayle Greene, *Changing the Story: Feminist Fiction and the Tradition* (Bloomington: Indiana University Press, 1991), 15-16.

6. While I am aware of the objections made to Chodorow's work as universalizing the experience of white women, I find her theories useful in discussing Elaine's development since Elaine fits the model on which Chodorow's observations are based. I do not wish to suggest by my use of Chodorow, however, that all women, regardless of socio-economic, ethnic or racial difference, follow this model exactly. Nor do I believe that this plot structure is restricted only to female authors and female protagonists. Pat Conroy's *The Prince of Tides* proves otherwise. I simply believe that women raised within the family structure Chodorow describes tend to have greater relational needs than men and that contemporary women authors often adopt the circular plot structure as a means of writing against the earlier tradition of the bildungsroman.

7. Margaret Atwood, *Cat's Eye* (New York: Bantam Books, 1989), 3.

8. Atwood, *Cat's Eye,* 6.

9. Elizabeth Abel, Elizabeth Hirsch and Langland, *The Voyage In: Fictions of Female Development* (Hanover, N.H.: University Press of New England, 1983), 9-13.

10. Earl G. Ingersoll, *Margaret Atwood: Conversations* (Princeton: Ontario Review Press, 1990), 194-195.

11. Ingersoll, *Margaret Atwood: Conversations,* 236.

12. Atwood, *Cat's Eye,* 3.

13. Claudine Hermann's observations of differences between male and female conceptions of space and time come to mind here. She links women's being cut off from space and subjected to time without any means of recuperating it through action to an absence of grammar, an inclination toward poetry. She quotes Professor Anastasi of Fordham University: "On the whole, girls are better than boys in subjects that rely primarily on verbal activity, memory, and perceptual speed. Boys are better in subjects involving numerical reasoning, spatial aptitudes, and in certain informational subjects like history, geography, or the sciences in general." Claudine Hermann, "Women in Space and Time," *New French Feminisms,* ed. Elaine Marks and Isabelle de Courtivron (New York: Schocken Books, 1981), 173.

14. Atwood, *Cat's Eye,* 119-120.

15. Murray M. Schwartz, "Introduction," *Memory and Desire: Aging—Literature—Psychoanalysis,* ed. Kathleen Woodward and Murray M. Schwartz (Bloomington: Indiana University Press, 1986), 3-5.

16. Schwartz, "Introduction," 3-5.

17. Kathleen Woodward, "The Mirror Stage of Old Age," *Memory and Desire: Aging—Literature—Psychoanalysis,* ed. Kathleen Woodward and Murray M. Schwartz (Bloomington: Indiana University Press, 1986), 104.

18. Woodward, "The Mirror Stage," 104-105.

19. Woodward, "The Mirror Stage," 109-110.

20. Carol Gilligan, *In a Different Voice* (Cambridge, Mass.: Harvard University Press, 1982), 170.

21. Gilligan, *In a Different Voice,* 170.

22. In *Surfacing,* Atwood uses more of the techniques common to Walker and Morrison, for in this novel, Atwood deals with the way in which one culture, from the United States, threatens to obliterate another culture, that of the Canadians, especially the native Indian population of the North. As Lissie's memory, in extending through many generations in her various incarnations as animal and human, connects Walker's characters with their cultural past, Atwood's protagonist in *Surfacing* goes beyond her own personal past in using Indian cave painting as clues to her father's disappearance and in following Indian ritual to revert to a more animalistic state in which she has visions of her dead parents. In her protagonist's interaction with the dead, Atwood uses a similar technique to the one Morrison employs in *Beloved.*

23. Ikenna Dieke, "Toward a Monistic Idealism: The Thematics of Alice Walker's *The Temple of My Familiar,*" *African American Review* 26/3 (Fall 1992); 509.

24. Atwood, *Cat's Eye,* 14.

25. Nancy Chodorow, *The Reproduction of Mothering: Psychoanalysis and the Sociology of Gender* (Berkeley and Los Angeles: University of California Press, 1978), 138.

26. Atwood, *Cat's Eye*, 67.

27. Atwood, *Cat's Eye*, 132.

28. Toni Morrison, *Playing in the Dark* (Cambridge, Mass.: Harvard University Press, 1992).

29. Atwood, *Cat's Eye*, 138.

30. Atwood, *Cat's Eye*, 143.

31. Gayle Greene argues in *Changing the Story* that *Cat's Eye* is a misogynist text reflecting the current backlash against feminism. I disagree. I feel Atwood is merely attacking the assumption that women readily connect because of their common experience.

32. Diana Hume George, "'Who Is the Double Ghost Whose Head Is Smoke?' Women Poets on Aging," *Memory and Desire: Aging—Literature—Psychoanalysis,* ed. Kathleen Woodward and Murray M. Schwartz (Bloomington: Indiana University Press, 1986), 143.

33. Joyce Pettis, "'She Sung Back in Return': Literary (Re)vision and Transformation in Gayl Jones's *Corregidora*," *College English* 52/7 (November 1990): 787-799.

34. Atwood, *Cat's Eye*, 212.

35. Atwood, *Cat's Eye*, 16.

36. Atwood, *Cat's Eye*, 422.

37. Note the difference between this image and the image at the end of *Portrait* when Stephen becomes the "spiritual-heroic refrigerating apparatus," turning away from Emma, his mother, and his friends to embrace "the white arms of roads" and to be alone. Joyce, *Portrait*, 525.

FURTHER READING

Criticism

Blakely, Barbara. "The Pronunciation of the Flesh: A Feminist Reading of Margaret Atwood's Poetry." In *Margaret Atwood: Language, Text, and System,* edited by Sherrill E. Grace and Lorraine Weir, pp. 33-51. Vancouver, Can.: University of British Columbia Press, 1983.

Examines the notion of identity in Atwood's poetry.

Bouson, J. Brooks. *Brutal Choreographies: Oppositional Strategies and Narrative Design in the Novels of Margaret Atwood.* Amherst, Mass.: University of Massachusetts Press, 1993.

Draws on feminist and psychoanalytic theory to examine political and psychological links among Atwood's novels.

Coad, David. "Hymens, Lips, and Masks: The Veil in Margaret Atwood's *The Handmaid's Tale*." *Literature and Psychology* 47, nos. 1-2 (2001): 54-67.

Analyzes the political symbolism of veils in The Handmaid's Tale.

Cooper, Pamela. "Sexual Surveillance and Medical Authority in Two Versions of *The Handmaid's Tale*." *Journal of Popular Culture* 28, no. 4 (spring 1995): 49-66.

Examines the surveillance of women in The Handmaid's Tale, *arguing that the film version of the novel forces the audience to be complicit in the surveillance.*

Davey, Frank. *Margaret Atwood: A Feminist Poetics.* Vancouver, Can.: Talonbooks Ltd., 1998.

Discusses Atwood's development of a formal feminist poetics throughout her canon.

Deery, June. "Science for Feminists: Margaret Atwood's Body of Knowledge." *Twentieth Century Literature* 43, no. 4 (winter 1997): 470-86.

Contends that Atwood's representation of women's experience draws heavily from the principles of modern physics.

Klarer, Mario. "Orality and Literacy as Gender-Supporting Structures in Margaret Atwood's *The Handmaid's Tale*." *Mosaic* 28, no. 4 (December 1995): 129-42.

Examination of Atwood's portrayal of the oral tradition in The Handmaid's Tale *as a political tactic in which orality is used to uphold gender roles and stereotypes.*

Nicolson, Colin, ed. *Margaret Atwood: Writing and Subjectivity: New Critical Essays.* New York: Palgrave Macmillan, 1994.

Thirteen essays examining Atwood as a woman writing about women.

Nischik, Reingard M., ed. *Margaret Atwood: Works and Impact.* Rochester, NY: Camden House, 2000.

Collection of essays on a wide variety of topics in Atwood's works as well as her influence on literature and culture. Contains an interview with Atwood, examples of her artwork and photographs, and a bibliography.

VanSpanckeren, Kathryn, and Jan Garden Castro, eds. *Margaret Atwood: Vision and Forms.* Carbondale and Edwardsville, Ill.: Southern Illinois University Press, 1988.

Collection of essays with a primarily feminist grounding. Includes an autobiographical foreword by Atwood, an interview, and a moderated discussion with students.

Wilson, Sharon Rose. *Margaret Atwood's Fairy-Tale Sexual Politics.* Jackson, Miss.: University Press of Mississippi, 1993.

Examines Atwood's interpretive use of fairy tales as transformative for women.

OTHER SOURCES FROM GALE:

Additional coverage of Atwood's life and career is contained in the following sources published by the Gale Group: *American Writers Supplement*, Vol. 13; *Authors and Artists for Young Adults*, Vols. 12, 47; *Beacham's Encyclopedia of Popular Fiction: Biography & Resources*, Vol. 1; *Bestsellers*, Vol. 89:2; *Contemporary Authors*, Vols. 49-52; *Contemporary Authors New Revision Series*, Vols. 3, 24, 33, 59, 95; *Contemporary Literary Criticism*, Vols. 2, 3, 4, 8, 13, 15, 25, 44, 84, 135; *Contemporary Novelists*, Ed. 7; *Contemporary Poets*, Ed. 7; *Contemporary Popular Writers; Contemporary Women Poets; Dictionary of Literary Biography*, Vols. 53, 251; *DISCovering Authors; DISCovering Authors: British Edition; DISCovering Authors: Canadian Edition; DISCovering Authors Modules: Most-studied, Novelists* and *Poets; DISCovering Authors 3.0; Encyclopedia of World Literature in the 20th Century*, Ed. 3; *Exploring Novels; Feminist Writers; Literature and Its Times*, Vol. 5; *Literature Resource Center; Major 20th-Century Writers*, Eds. 1, 2; *Novels for Students*, Vols. 4, 12, 13, 14; *Poetry Criticism*, Vol. 8; *Poetry for Students*, Vol. 7; *Reference Guide to Short Fiction*, Ed. 2; *St. James Guide to Young Adult Writers; Short Stories for Students*, Vols. 3, 13; *Short Story Criticism*, Vols. 2, 46; *Something about the Author*, Vol. 50; *Twayne's World Authors; World Literature Criticism;* and *World Writers in English*, Vol. 1.

SIMONE DE BEAUVOIR

(1908 - 1986)

(Full name Simone Lucie Ernestine Marie Bertrand de Beauvoir) French philosopher, novelist, nonfiction writer, short story writer, and playwright.

One of the most prominent writers of her generation, Beauvoir was a member of the French left-wing intellectual circle associated with existentialist Jean-Paul Sartre. She became identified as a leading feminist theorist with the publication of *Le deuxième sexe* (1949; *The Second Sex*), her comprehensive study of the secondary status of women throughout history. Additionally, in her autobiographies, fiction, and criticism, she addressed women's social, economic, and political status as well as the existential meaning of womanhood.

BIOGRAPHICAL INFORMATION

Born in Paris to middle-class parents, Beauvoir was raised a Roman Catholic. In early adolescence, however, she perceived hypocrisies and fallacies in bourgeois morality and rebelled against her class, privately disavowing her belief in God. Following her undergraduate studies at the Institut Catholique and the Institut Sainte-Marie, Beauvoir attended the Sorbonne in 1928, where she specialized in literature and philosophy, and later audited classes at the prestigious Ecole Normale Supérieure. In 1929 she met fellow student Jean-Paul Sartre, and together they prepared for the *agrégation* examination in philosophy. Finding that they were intellectual equals, each of whom desired a lasting relationship free of conventional restraints, Beauvoir and Sartre agreed to a shared life outside the institution of marriage and also mutually consented to "contingent relationships." After graduating from the Sorbonne, Beauvoir taught in Marseilles, Rouen, and Paris. She and Sartre settled in Paris in the late 1930s and became prominent figures amid the intellectual society of the Left Bank, associating with such writers and thinkers as Albert Camus, André Malraux, Raymond Queneau, and Michel Leiris. During World War II, Beauvoir and Sartre organized a resistance group to oppose Nazi occupation of France. Beauvoir spent most of her time during the war years writing. In 1944 she resigned from teaching and, together with Sartre, founded the leftist journal *Les temps modernes.* During the 1950s Beauvoir engaged in numerous social causes and attempted to live out the committed existence that she espoused in her writings by protesting the French-Algerian War, documenting French military atrocities in *Les temps modernes,* and signing a public manifesto against the war. Beauvoir maintained her involvement in social issues during the 1960s and, in particular, supported the radical student uprisings of 1968. Although she joined the Mouvement de la Libération des Femmes (MLF) in

1970 to participate in demonstrations supporting legalized abortion, Beauvoir did not declare herself a feminist until 1972, after which she began writing a column on sexism in *Les temps modernes* and became president of the French League for Women's Rights. Beauvoir continued to promote various social movements, especially those concerning women, until her death in 1986.

MAJOR WORKS

Beauvoir's major theoretical study, *The Second Sex,* is often said to be the first full-length sociophilosophical examination of the status of women in society. In this work Beauvoir incorporated existentialist concepts concerning personal freedom, or individual guidance by choice alone; responsibility, or accepting the consequences of one's choices; bad faith, or denying one's freedom by shifting responsibility to an outside source; and the role of the other, or the relation of an inessential being to an essential being. Positing that men have achieved the favorable status of transcendence while women have assumed that of immanence, Beauvoir proposed assimilation into the male universe as a means of achieving gender equality. Further, she called the existence of essentially feminine and maternal traits a myth and presented the female body in extremely negative terms, highlighting ways in which a woman's freedom is inhibited by her sexuality and fertility. *Mémoires d'une jeune fille rangée* (1958; *Memoirs of a Dutiful Daughter*), is Beauvoir's account of her early years, particularly her intellectual development as a young woman in bourgeois Paris. In this work Beauvoir applied many of the theories she had set forth in *The Second Sex* to her personal experiences, namely her realization that the myths of her childhood did not apply to her burgeoning adult life. In her fiction Beauvoir often portrayed women who depended on the men in their lives for happiness and were disappointed with the results. Her collection of novellas, *La femme rompue* (1967; *The Woman Destroyed*), characterized women whose dependencies on men have crippled their abilities to create positive identities and construct autonomous lives.

CRITICAL RECEPTION

From the time of its publication, when it provoked the ire of both conservative and liberal critics, *The Second Sex* has dominated discussion of Beauvoir's theoretical position. Despite the initially negative reaction of critics to the work, it has attained widespread recognition and has proved vastly influential. Today *The Second Sex* is generally regarded as fundamental to the development of the women's movement of the 1960s as well as to the discipline of feminist studies. With the rise in the 1970s of new French feminists extolling feminine physical and psychological differences, *The Second Sex* was dismissed as out of date, and many feminists disparaged Beauvoir as a Sartrean revisionist, condemning her adoption of a masculine identity. More recently, critics have begun to reassess her importance as a pioneering thinker who established the groundwork for the study and liberation of women in modern Western society. Representing this position, Ellen Willis (see Further Reading) wrote: "Nearly four decades after it was first published in France, despite all the commentary the feminist movement has produced in the meantime, dated and parochial as it is in many respects, *The Second Sex* remains the most cogent and thorough book of feminist theory yet written."

PRINCIPAL WORKS

L'invitée [*She Came to Stay*] (novel) 1943

Pyrrhus et Cinéas (philosophy) 1944

Les bouches inutiles [*Who Shall Die?*] (drama) 1945

Le sang des autres [*The Blood of Others*] (novel) 1946

Tous les hommes sont mortel [*All Men Are Mortal*] (novel) 1946

Pour une morale de l'ambiguité [*The Ethics of Ambiguity*] (philosophy) 1947

L'Amérique au jour le jour [*America Day by Day*] (nonfiction) 1948

L'existentialisme et la sagesse des nations (philosophy) 1948

Le deuxième sexe [*The Second Sex*] 2 vols. (nonfiction) 1949

Les mandarins (novel) 1954

Fait-il bruler Sade? [*Must We Burn de Sade?*] (criticism) 1955

La longue marche: Essai sur la Chine [*The Long March*] (nonfiction) 1957

Mémoires d'une jeune fille rangée [*Memoirs of a Dutiful Daughter*] (autobiography) 1958

La force de l'âge [*The Prime of Life*] (autobiography) 1960

Tout compte fait (autobiography) 1960

La force des choses (autobiography) 1963

Une mort très douce [*A Very Easy Death*] (memoir) 1964

Les belles images (novel) 1966

L'âge de discrétion (novel) 1967

La femme rompue [*The Woman Destroyed*] (novellas) 1967

La vieillesse [*The Coming of Age*; also published as *Old Age*] (nonfiction) 1970

Tout compte fait [*All Said and Done*; also published as *All Accounting Made*] (autobiography) 1972

Quand prime le spirituel [*When Things of the Spirit Come First: Five Early Tales*] (short stories) 1979

Le cérémonie des adieux: Suivi de entretiens avec Jean-Paul Sartre [*Adieux: A Farewell to Sartre*] (memoir) 1981

A Transatlantic Love Affair: Letters to Nelson Algren (letters) 1998

PRIMARY SOURCES

SIMONE DE BEAUVOIR (ESSAY DATE 1952)

SOURCE: Beauvoir, Simone de. "The Independent Woman." In *The Second Sex*, translated by H. M. Parshley, pp. 713-32. New York: Alfred A. Knopf, 1993.

In the following excerpt from The Second Sex, *originally published in 1952, Beauvoir discusses the difficulties of achieving independence for modern women.*

According to French law, obedience is no longer included among the duties of a wife, and each woman citizen has the right to vote; but these civil liberties remain theoretical as long as they are unaccompanied by economic freedom. A woman supported by a man—wife or courtesan—is not emancipated from the male because she has a ballot in her hand; if custom imposes less constraint upon her than formerly, the negative freedom implied has not profoundly modified her situation; she remains bound in her condition of vassalage. It is through gainful employment that woman has traversed most of the distance that separated her from the male; and nothing else can guarantee her liberty in practice. Once she ceases to be a parasite, the system based on her dependence crumbles; between her and the universe there is no longer any need for a masculine mediator.

The curse that is upon woman as vassal consists, as we have seen, in the fact that she is not permitted to do anything; so she persists in the vain pursuit of her true being through narcissism, love, or religion. When she is productive, active, she regains her transcendence; in her projects she concretely affirms her status as subject; in connection with the aims she pursues, with the money and the rights she takes possession of, she makes trial of and senses her responsibility. Many women are aware of these advantages, even among those in very modest positions. I heard a charwoman declare, while scrubbing the stone floor of a hotel lobby: 'I never asked anybody for anything; I succeeded all by myself.' She was as proud of her self-sufficiency as a Rockefeller. It is not to be supposed, however, that the mere combination of the right to vote and a job constitutes a complete emancipation: working, today, is not liberty. Only in a socialist world would woman by the one attain the other. The majority of workers are exploited today. On the other hand, the social structure has not been much modified by the changes in woman's condition; this world, always belonging to men, still retains the form they have given it.

We must not lose sight of those facts which make the question of woman's labor a complex one. An important and thoughtful woman recently made a study of the women in the Renault factories; she states that they would prefer to stay in the home rather than work in the factory. There is no doubt that they get economic independence only as members of a class which is economically oppressed; and, on the other hand, their jobs at the factory do not relieve them of housekeeping burdens.[1] If they had been asked to choose between forty hours of work a week in the factory and forty hours of work a week in the home, they would doubtless have furnished quite different answers. And perhaps they would cheerfully accept both jobs, if as factory workers they were to be integrated in a world that would be theirs, in the development of which they would joyfully and proudly share. At the present time, peasants apart,[2] the majority of women do not escape from the traditional feminine world; they get from neither society nor their husbands the assistance they would need to become in concrete fact the equals of the men. Only those women who have a political faith, who take militant action in the unions, who have confidence in their future, can give ethical meaning to thankless daily labor. But lacking leisure, inheriting a traditional submissiveness, women are naturally just beginning to develop a political and social sense. And not getting in exchange for their work the moral and social benefits they might rightfully count on, they naturally submit to its constraints without enthusiasm.

It is quite understandable, also, that the milliner's apprentice, the shopgirl, the secretary, will not care to renounce the advantages of masculine support. I have already pointed out that the existence of a privileged caste, which she can join by merely surrendering her body, is an almost irresistible temptation to the young woman; she is fated for gallantry by the fact that her wages are minimal while the standard of living expected of her by society is very high. If she is content to get along on her wages, she is only a pariah: ill lodged, ill dressed, she will be denied all amusement and even love. Virtuous people preach asceticism to her, and, indeed, her dietary regime is often as austere as that of a Carmelite. Unfortunately, not everyone can take God as a lover: she has to please men if she is to succeed in her life as a woman. She will therefore accept assistance, and this is what her employer cynically counts on in giving her starvation wages. This aid will sometimes allow her to improve her situation and achieve a real independence; in other cases, however, she will give up her work and become a kept woman. She often retains both sources of income and each serves more or less as an escape from the other; but she is really in double servitude: to job and to protector. For the married woman her wages represent only pin money as a rule; for the girl who 'makes something on the side' it is the masculine contribution that seems extra; but neither of them gains complete independence through her own efforts.

There are, however, a fairly large number of privileged women who find in their professions a means of economic and social autonomy. These come to mind when one considers woman's possibilities and her future. This is the reason why it is especially interesting to make a close study of their situation, even though they constitute as yet only a minority; they continue to be a subject of debate between feminists and antifeminists. The latter assert that the emancipated women of today succeed in doing nothing of importance in the world and that furthermore they have difficulty in achieving their own inner equilibrium. The former exaggerate the results obtained by professional women and are blind to their inner confusion. There is no good reason, as a matter of fact, to say they are on the wrong road; and still it is certain that they are not tranquilly installed in

their new realm: as yet they are only halfway there. The woman who is economically emancipated from man is not for all that in a moral, social, and psychological situation identical with that of man. The way she carries on her profession and her devotion to it depend on the context supplied by the total pattern of her life. For when she begins her adult life she does not have behind her the same past as does a boy; she is not viewed by society in the same way; the universe presents itself to her in a different perspective. The fact of being a woman today poses peculiar problems for an independent human individual.

The advantage man enjoys, which makes itself felt from his childhood, is that his vocation as a human being in no way runs counter to his destiny as a male. Through the identification of phallus and transcendence, it turns out that his social and spiritual successes endow him with a virile prestige. He is not divided. Whereas it is required of woman that in order to realize her femininity she must make herself object and prey, which is to say that she must renounce her claims as sovereign subject. It is this conflict that especially marks the situation of the emancipated woman. She refuses to confine herself to her role as female, because she will not accept mutilation; but it would also be a mutilation to repudiate her sex. Man is a human being with sexuality; woman is a complete individual, equal to the male, only if she too is a human being with sexuality. To renounce her femininity is to renounce a part of her humanity. Misogynists have often reproached intellectual women for 'neglecting themselves'; but they have also preached this doctrine to them: if you wish to be our equals, stop using make-up and nail-polish.

This piece of advice is nonsensical. Precisely because the concept of femininity is artificially shaped by custom and fashion, it is imposed upon each woman from without; she can be transformed gradually so that her canons of propriety approach those adopted by the males: at the seashore—and often elsewhere—trousers have become feminine.[3] That changes nothing fundamental in the matter: the individual is still not free to do as she pleases in shaping the concept of femininity. The woman who does not conform devaluates herself sexually and hence socially, since sexual values are an integral feature of society. One does not acquire virile attributes by rejecting feminine attributes; even the transvestite fails to make a man of herself—she is a travesty. As we have seen, homosexuality constitutes a specific attitude: neutrality is impossible. There is no negative attitude that does not imply a positive counterpart. The adolescent girl often thinks that she can simply scorn convention; but even there she is engaged in public agitation; she is creating a new situation entailing consequences she must assume. When one fails to adhere to an accepted code, one becomes an insurgent. A woman who dresses in an outlandish manner lies when she affirms with an air of simplicity that she dresses to suit herself, nothing more. She knows perfectly well that to suit herself is to be outlandish.

Inversely, a woman who does not wish to appear eccentric will conform to the usual rules. It is injudicious to take a defiant attitude unless it is connected with positively effective action: it consumes more time and energy than it saves. A woman who has no wish to shock or to devaluate herself socially should live out her feminine situation in a feminine manner; and very often, for that matter, her professional success demands it. But whereas conformity is quite natural for a man—custom being based on his needs as an independent and active individual—it will be necessary for the woman who also is subject, activity, to insinuate herself into a world that has doomed her to passivity. This is made more burdensome because women confined to the feminine sphere have grossly magnified its importance: they have made dressing and housekeeping difficult arts. Man hardly has to take thought of his clothes, for they are convenient, suitable to his active life, not necessarily elegant; they are scarcely a part of his personality. More, nobody expects him to take care of them himself: some kindly disposed or hired female relieves him of this bother.

Woman, on the contrary, knows that when she is looked at she is not considered apart from her appearance: she is judged, respected, desired, by and through her toilette. Her clothes were originally intended to consign her to impotence, and they have remained unserviceable, easily ruined: stockings get runs, shoes get down at the heel, light-colored blouses and frocks get soiled, pleats get unpleated. But she will have to make most of the repairs herself; other women will not come benevolently to her assistance and she will hesitate to add to her budget for work she could do herself: permanents, setting hair, make-up materials, new dresses, cost enough already. When they come in after the day's work, students and secretaries always have a stocking with a run to be fixed, a blouse to wash, a skirt to press. A woman who makes a good income will spare herself this drudgery, but she will have to maintain a more complicated elegance; she will lose time in shopping, in having fittings, and the rest. Tradition also requires even the single woman to give some attention to her lodgings. An official assigned to a new city will easily find accommodations at a hotel; but a woman in the same position will want to settle down in a place of her own. She will have to keep it scrupulously neat, for people would not excuse a negligence on her part which they would find quite natural in a man.

It is not regard for the opinion of others alone that leads her to give time and care to her appearance and her housekeeping. She wants to retain her womanliness for her own satisfaction. She can regard herself with approval throughout her present and past only in combining the life she has made for herself with the destiny that her mother, her childhood games, and her adolescent fantasies prepared for her. She has entertained narcissistic dreams; to the male's phallic pride she still opposes her cult of self; she wants to be seen, to be attractive. Her mother and her older sisters have inculcated the liking for a nest: a home, an 'interior,' of her own! That has always been basic in her dreams of independence; she has no intention of discarding them when she has found liberty by other roads. And to the degree in which she still feels insecure in the masculine universe, she tends to retain the need for a retreat, symbolical of that interior refuge she has been accustomed to seeking within herself. Obedient to the feminine tradition, she will wax her floors, and she will do her own cooking instead of going to eat at a restaurant as a man would in her place. She wants to live at once like a man and like a woman, and in that way she multiplies her tasks and adds to her fatigue.

If she intends to remain fully feminine, it is implied that she also intends to meet the other sex with the odds as favorable as possible. Her most difficult problems are going to be posed in the field of sex. In order to be a complete individual, on an equality with man, woman must have access to the masculine world as does the male to the feminine world, she must have access to the *other;* but the demands of the *other* are not symmetrical in the two symmetrical cases. Once attained, fame and fortune, appearing like immanent qualities, may increase woman's sexual attractiveness; but the fact that she is a being of independent activity wars against her femininity, and this she is aware of. The independent woman—and above all the intellectual, who thinks about her situation—will suffer, as a female, from an inferiority complex; she lacks leisure for such minute beauty care as that of the coquette whose sole aim in life is to be seductive; follow the specialists' advice as she may, she will never be more than an amateur in the domain of elegance. Feminine charm demands that transcendence, degraded into immanence, appear no longer as anything more than a subtle quivering of the flesh; it is necessary to be spontaneously offered prey.

But the intellectual knows that she is offering herself, she knows that she is a conscious being, a subject; one can hardly dull one's glance and change one's eyes into sky-blue pools at will; one does not infallibly stop the surge of a body that is straining toward the world and change it into a statue animated by vague tremors. The intellectual woman will try all the more zealously because she fears failure; but her conscious zeal is still an activity and it misses its goal. She makes mistakes like those induced by the menopause: she tries to deny her brain just as the woman who is growing older tries to deny her age; she dresses like a girl, she overloads herself with flowers, furbelows, fancy materials; she affects childish tricks of surprised amazement. She romps, she babbles, she pretends flippancy, heedlessness, sprightliness.

But in all this she resembles those actors who fail to feel the emotion that would relax certain muscles and so by an effort of will contract the opposing ones, forcing down their eyes or the corners of their mouths instead of letting them fall. Thus in imitating abandon the intellectual woman becomes tense. She realizes this, and it irritates her; over her blankly naïve face, there suddenly passes a flash of all too sharp intelligence; lips soft with promise suddenly tighten. If she has trouble in pleasing, it is because she is not, like her slavish little sisters, pure will to please; the desire to seduce, lively as it may be, has not penetrated to the marrow of her bones. As soon as she feels awkward, she becomes vexed at her abjectness; she wants to take her revenge by playing the game with masculine weapons: she talks instead of listening, she displays subtle thoughts, strange emotions; she contradicts the man instead of agreeing with him, she tries to get the best of him. Mme de Staël won some resounding victories: she was almost irresistible. But the challenging attitude, very common among American women, for example, irritates men more often than it conquers them; and there are some men, besides, who bring it upon themselves by their own defiant air. If they would be willing to love an equal instead of a slave—as, it must be added,

do those among them who are at once free from arrogance and without an inferiority complex—women would not be as haunted as they are by concern for their femininity; they would gain in naturalness, in simplicity, and they would find themselves women again without taking so much pains, since, after all, that is what they are.

The fact is that men are beginning to resign themselves to the new status of woman; and she, not feeling condemned in advance, has begun to feel more at ease. Today the woman who works is less neglectful of her femininity than formerly, and she does not lose her sexual attractiveness. This success, though already indicating progress toward equilibrium, is not yet complete; it continues to be more difficult for a woman than for a man to establish the relations with the other sex that she desires. Her erotic and affectional life encounters numerous difficulties. In this matter the unemancipated woman is in no way privileged: sexually and affectionally most wives and courtesans are deeply frustrated. If the difficulties are more evident in the case of the independent woman, it is because she has chosen battle rather than resignation. All the problems of life find a silent solution in death; a woman who is busy with living is therefore more at variance with herself than is she who buries her will and her desires; but the former will not take the latter as a standard. She considers herself at a disadvantage only in comparison with man.

A woman who expends her energy, who has responsibilities, who knows how harsh is the struggle against the world's opposition, needs—like the male—not only to satisfy her physical desires but also to enjoy the relaxation and diversion provided by agreeable sexual adventures. Now, there are still many social circles in which her freedom in this matter is not concretely recognized; if she exercises it, she risks compromising her reputation, her career; at the least a burdensome hypocrisy is demanded of her. The more solidly she establishes her position in society, the more ready people will be to close their eyes; but in provincial districts especially, she is watched with narrow severity, as a rule. Even under the most favorable circumstances—where fear of public opinion is negligible—her situation in this respect is not equivalent to man's. The differences depend both on traditional attitudes and on the special nature of feminine eroticism.

Man has easy access to fugitive embraces that are at the worst sufficient to calm his flesh and keep him in good spirits. There have been women—not many—prepared to demand that brothels for females be provided; in a novel entitled *Le Numéro 17* a woman proposed the establishment of houses where women could resort for 'sexual appeasement' through the services of 'taxi-boys.'[4] It appears that an establishment of this kind formerly existed in San Francisco; the customers were prostitutes, who were highly amused to pay instead of being paid. Their pimps had the place closed. Apart from the fact that this solution is chimerical and hardly desirable, it would doubtless meet with small success, for, as we have seen, woman does not obtain 'appeasement' as mechanically as does the male; most women consider the arrangement hardly conducive to voluptuous abandon. At any rate, this resource is unavailable today.

Another possible solution is to pick up in the street a partner for a night or an hour—supposing that the woman, being of passionate temperament and having overcome all her inhibitions, can contemplate it without disgust—but this solution is much more dangerous for her than for the male. The risk of venereal disease is graver, because it is the man who is responsible for taking precautions against infection; and, however careful she may be, the woman is never wholly protected against the danger of conception. But what is important above all in such relations between strangers—relations that are on a plane of brutality—is the difference in physical strength. A man has not much to fear from the woman he takes home with him; he merely needs to be reasonably on his guard. It is not the same with a woman who takes a man in. I was told of two young women, just arrived in Paris and eager to 'see life,' who, after a look around at night, invited two attractive Montmartre characters to supper. In the morning they found themselves robbed, beaten up, and threatened with blackmail. A more significant case is that of a woman of forty, divorced, who worked hard all day to support three children and her old parents. Still attractive, she had absolutely no time for social life, or for playing the coquette and going through the customary motions involved in getting an affair under way, which, besides, would have caused her too much bother. She had strong feelings, however, and she believed in her right to satisfy them. So she would occasionally roam the streets at night and manage to scare up a man. But one night, after spending an hour or two in a thicket in the Bois de Boulogne, her lover of the moment refused to let her go: he demanded her name and address, he wanted to see her again, to arrange to live together. When she refused, he gave her a severe beating and finally left her covered with bruises and almost frightened to death.

As for taking a permanent lover, as a man often takes a mistress, and supporting or helping him financially, this is possible only for women of means. There are some who find this arrangement agreeable; by paying the man they make him a mere instrument and can use him with contemptuous unconstraint. But as a rule, they must be old to be able to dissociate sex and sentiment so crudely, since in feminine adolescence the two are most profoundly associated, as we have seen. There are many men, for that matter, who never accept the separation of flesh and spirit; and, with more reason, a majority of women will refuse to consider it. Moreover, it involves fraudulence, to which they are more sensitive than is man; for the paying client is also an instrument herself, since her partner uses her as means of subsistence. Masculine pride conceals the ambiguities of the erotic drama from the male: he lies to himself unconsciously. More easily humiliated, more vulnerable, woman is also more clear-sighted; she will succeed in blinding herself only at the cost of entertaining a more calculated bad faith. Even granted the means, woman will never find the purchase of a male a satisfactory solution.

For most women—and men too—it is not a mere matter of satisfying erotic desire, but of maintaining their dignity as human beings while obtaining satisfaction. When a male enjoys a woman, when he gives her enjoyment, he takes the position of sole subject: he is imperious conqueror, or lavish donor—sometimes both at once. Woman, for her part, also wishes to make it clear that she subdues her partner to her pleasure and overwhelms him with her gifts. Thus, when she imposes herself on a man, be it through promised benefits, or in staking on his courtesy, or by artfully arousing his desire in its pure generality, she readily persuades herself that she is overwhelming him with her bounty. Thanks to this advantageous conviction, she can make advances without humiliating herself, because she feels she is doing so out of generosity. Thus in the novel *Blé en herbe* the 'woman in white,' who covets Phil's caresses, says haughtily to him: 'I love only beggars and starved people.' As a matter of fact, she cleverly sees to it that he does take a suppliant attitude. Then, writes Colette, 'she made haste toward that obscure and narrow region where her pride could believe that the plaint is an avowal of distress and where beggars of her kind drink the illusion of liberality.' Mme de Warens is the type of those women who choose young or unfortunate lovers, or those of inferior status, to lend their appetites the appearance of generosity. But there are also intrepid ones who tackle the most sturdy men and who take delight in satisfying them in spite of the fact that they have yielded only through politeness or fright.

Inversely, if the woman who entraps a man likes to imagine that she is giving herself, she who does give herself wants it understood that she also takes. 'As for me, I am a woman who takes,' a young journalist told me one day. The truth of the matter is that, except in the case of rape, neither one really takes the other; but here woman doubly deceives herself. For in fact a man often does seduce through his fiery aggressiveness, actively winning the consent of his partner. Save exceptionally—Mme de Staël has already been mentioned as one instance—it is otherwise with woman: she can hardly do more than offer herself; for most men are very jealous of their role. What they want is to arouse a specific excitement in the woman, not to be chosen as the means for satisfying her need in its generality: so chosen, they feel exploited.[5] A very young man once said to me: 'A woman who is not afraid of men frightens them.' And I have often heard older men declare: 'It horrifies me to have a woman take the initiative.' If a woman offers herself too boldly, the man departs, for he is intent on conquering. Woman, therefore, can take only when she makes herself prey: she must become a passive thing, a promise of submission. If she succeeds, she will think that she performed this magic conjuration intentionally, she will be subject again. But she risks remaining in the status of unnecessary object if the male disdains her. This is why she is deeply humiliated when he rejects her advances. A man is sometimes angered when he feels that he has lost; however, he has only failed in an enterprise, nothing more. Whereas the woman has consented to make herself flesh in her agitation, her waiting, and her promises; she could win only in losing herself: she remains lost. One would have to be very blind or exceptionally clear-sighted to reconcile oneself to such a defeat.

And even when her effort at seduction succeeds, the victory is still ambiguous; the fact is that in common opinion it is the man who conquers, who *has* the woman. It is not admitted that she, like a man, can have desires of her own: she is the prey of desire. It is understood that man has made the specific forces a part of his personality, whereas woman is the slave of the species.[6] She is represented, at one time, as pure passivity, available, open, a utensil; she yields gently to the spell of sex feeling, she is fascinated by the male, who picks her like a fruit. At another time she is regarded as if possessed by alien forces: there is a devil raging in her womb, a serpent lurks in her vagina, eager to devour the male's sperm.

In any case, there is a general refusal to think of her as simply free. Especially in France the free woman and the light woman are obstinately confused, the term *light* implying an absence of resistance and control, a lack, the very negation of liberty. Feminine literature endeavors to combat this prejudice: in *Grisélidis,* for example, Clara Malraux insists on the fact that her heroine does not yield to allurement but accomplishes an act of her own volition. In America a certain liberty is recognized in woman's sexual activity, an attitude that tends to favor it. But the disdain for women who 'go to bed' affected in France by even the men who enjoy their favors paralyzes a great many women who do not. They are horrified by the protests they would arouse, the comment they would cause, if they should.

Even if a woman regards anonymous rumors with contempt, she finds concrete difficulties in her relations with her partner, for common opinion is embodied in him. Very often he views the bed as the proper terrain for asserting his aggressive superiority. He is eager to take and not to receive, not to exchange but to rob. He seeks to possess the woman to an extent over and above what she gives him; he demands that her consent be a defeat and that the words she murmurs be avowals he tears from her—demands that she confess her pleasure and recognize her subjection. When Claudine challenges Renard by her prompt submission, he anticipates her: he hastens to violate her when she was going to offer herself; he obliges her to keep her eyes open so he may contemplate his triumph in their movements. Similarly in *Man's Fate* the overbearing Ferral insists on lighting the lamp that Valerie wants to put out.

If she is proud and demanding, woman meets the male as an adversary, and she is much less well armed than he is. In the first place, he has physical strength, and it is easy for him to impose his will; we have seen, also, that tension and activity suit his erotic nature, whereas when woman departs from passivity, she breaks the spell that brings on her enjoyment; if she mimics dominance in her postures and movements, she fails to reach the climax of pleasure: most women who cling to their pride become frigid. Lovers are rare who allow their mistresses to satisfy dominative or sadistic tendencies; and rarer still are women who gain full erotic satisfaction even from their docility.

There is a road which seems much less thorny for women: that of masochism. When one works all day, struggles, takes responsibilities and risks, it is a welcome relaxation to abandon oneself at night to vigorous caprices. Whether schooled in love or a tyro, woman does in fact very often enjoy annihilating herself for the benefit of a masterful will. But it is still necessary for her to feel really dominated. It is not easy for one who lives her daily life among men to believe in the unconditional supremacy of the male. I have been told of the case of a woman who was not really masochistic but very 'feminine'—that is, who found deep submissive pleasure in masculine arms. She had been married several times since she was seventeen and had had several lovers, always with much satisfaction. After having successfully managed an enterprise in the course of which she had men under her direction, she complained of having become frigid. There was formerly a blissful submission that she no longer felt, because she had become accustomed to dominating over males, and so their prestige had vanished.

When a woman begins to doubt men's superiority, their pretensions serve only to decrease her esteem for them. In bed, at the time when man would like to be most savagely male, he seems puerile from the very fact that he pretends virility, and woman averts her eyes; for he only conjures up the old complex of castration, the shadow of his father, or some such phantasm. It is not always from pride that a mistress refuses to yield to the caprices of her lover: she would fain have to do with an adult who is living out a real moment of his life, not with a little boy telling himself stories. The masochist is especially disappointed: a maternal compliance, annoyed or indulgent, is not the abdication she dreams of. She, too, will have to content herself with ridiculous games, pretending to believe herself dominated and enslaved, or she will pursue men supposed to be 'superior' in the hope of finding a master, or she will become frigid.

We have seen that it is possible to avoid the temptations of sadism and masochism when the two partners recognize each other as equals; if both the man and the woman have a little modesty and some generosity, ideas of victory and defeat are abolished: the act of love becomes a free exchange. But, paradoxically, it is much more difficult for the woman than for the man to recognize an individual of the other sex as an equal. Precisely because the male caste has superiority of status, there are a great many individual women whom a man can hold in affectionate esteem: it is an easy matter to love a woman. In the first place, a woman can introduce her lover into a world that is different from his own and that he enjoys exploring in her company; she fascinates and amuses him, at least for a time. For another thing, on account of her restricted and subordinate situation, all her qualities seem like high achievements, conquests, whereas her mistakes are excusable; Stendhal admires Mme de Rênal and Mme de Chasteller in spite of their detestable prejudices. If a woman has false ideas, if she is not very intelligent, clear-sighted, or courageous, a man does not hold her responsible: she is the victim, he thinks—and often with reason—of her situation. He dreams of what she might have been, of what she perhaps will be: she can be credited with any possibilities, because she *is* nothing in particular. This vacancy is what makes the lover weary of her quickly; but it is the source of the mystery, the charm, that seduces him and makes him inclined to feel an easy affection in the first place.

It is much less easy for a woman to feel affectionate friendship for a man, for he *is* what he has made himself, irrevocably. He must be loved as he is, not with reference to his promise and his uncertain possibilities; he is responsible for his behavior and ideas; for him there are no excuses. Fellowship with him is impossible unless she approves his acts, his aims, his opinions. Julien can love a legitimist, as we have seen; a Lamiel could not cherish a man whose ideas she despised. Even though prepared to compromise, woman will hardly be able to take an attitude of indulgence. For man opens to her no verdant paradise of childhood. She meets him in this world which is their world in common: he comes bearing the gift of himself only. Self-enclosed, definite, decided, he is not conducive to daydreaming; when he speaks, one must listen. He takes himself seriously: if he is not interesting, he bores her, his presence weighs heavily on her. Only very young men can be endued with facile marvels; one can seek mystery and promise in them, find excuses for them, take them lightly: which is one reason why mature women find them most seductive. The difficulty is that, for their part, they usually prefer young women. The woman of thirty is thrown back on adult males. And doubtless she will encounter among them some who will not discourage her esteem and friendship; but she will be lucky if they make no show of arrogance in the matter.

When she contemplates an affair or an adventure involving her heart as well as her body, the problem is to find a man whom she can regard as an equal without his considering himself superior.

I will be told that in general women make no such fuss; they seize the occasion without asking themselves too many questions, and they manage somehow with their pride and their sensuality. True enough. But it is also true that they bury in their secret hearts many disappointments, humiliations, regrets, resentments, not commonly matched in men. From a more or less unsatisfactory affair a man is almost sure of obtaining at least the benefit of sex pleasure; a woman can very well obtain no benefit at all. Even when indifferent, she lends herself politely to the embrace at the decisive moment, sometimes only to find her lover impotent and herself compromised in a ridiculous mockery. If all goes well except that she fails to attain satisfaction, then she feels 'used,' 'worked.' If she finds full enjoyment, she will want to prolong the affair. She is rarely quite sincere when she claims to envisage no more than an isolated adventure undertaken merely for pleasure, because her pleasure, far from bringing deliverance, binds her to the man; separation wounds her even when supposedly a friendly parting. It is much more unusual to hear a woman speak amicably of a former lover than a man of his past mistresses.

The peculiar nature of her eroticism and the difficulties that beset a life of freedom urge woman toward monogamy. Liaison or marriage, however, can be reconciled with a career much less easily for her than for man. Sometimes her lover or husband asks her to renounce it: she hesitates, like Colette's Vagabonde, who ardently desires the warm presence of a man at her side but dreads the fetters of marriage. If she yields, she is once more a vassal; if she refuses, she condemns herself to a withering solitude. Today a man is usually willing to have his companion continue her work; the novels of Colette Yver, showing young women driven to sacrifice their professions for the sake of peace and the family, are rather outdated; living together is an enrichment for two free beings, and each finds security for his or her own independence in the occupation of the mate. The self-supporting wife emancipates her husband from the conjugal slavery that was the price of hers. If the man is scrupulously well-intentioned, such lovers and married couples attain in undemanding generosity a condition of perfect equality.[7] It may even be the man that acts as devoted servant; thus, for George Eliot, Lewes created the favorable

atmosphere that the wife usually creates around the husband-overlord. But for the most part it is still the woman who bears the cost of domestic harmony.

To a man it seems natural that it should be the wife who does the housework and assumes alone the care and bringing up of the children. The independent woman herself considers that in marrying she has assumed duties from which her personal life does not exempt her. She does not want to feel that her husband is deprived of advantages he would have obtained if he had married a 'true woman'; she wants to be presentable, a good housekeeper, a devoted mother, such as wives traditionally are. This is a task that easily becomes overwhelming. She assumes it through regard for her partner and out of fidelity to herself also, for she intends, as we have already seen, to be in no way unfaithful to her destiny as woman. She will be a double for her husband and at the same time she will be herself; she will assume his cares and participate in his successes as much as she will be concerned with her own fate—and sometimes even more. Reared in an atmosphere of respect for male superiority, she may still feel that it is for man to occupy the first place; sometimes she fears that in claiming it she would ruin her home; between the desire to assert herself and the desire for self-effacement she is torn and divided.

There is, however, an advantage that woman can gain from her very inferiority. Since she is from the start less favored by fortune than man, she does not feel that she is to blame *a priori* for what befalls him; it is not her duty to make amends for social injustice, and she is not asked to do so. A man of good will owes it to himself to treat women with consideration, since he is more favored by fate than they are; he will let himself be bound by scruples, by pity, and so runs the risk of becoming the prey of clinging, vampirish women from the very fact of their disarmed condition. The woman who achieves virile independence has the great privilege of carrying on her sexual life with individuals who are themselves autonomous and effective in action, who—as a rule—will not play a parasitic role in her life, who will not enchain her through their weakness and the exigency of their needs. But in truth the woman is rare who can create a free relation with her partner; she herself usually forges the chains with which he has no wish to load her: she takes toward him the attitude of the *amoureuse*, the woman in love.

Through twenty years of waiting, dreaming, hoping, the young girl has cherished the myth of the liberating savior-hero, and hence the independence she has won through work is not enough to abolish her desire for a glorious abdication. She would have had to be raised exactly[8] like a boy to be able easily to overcome her adolescent narcissism; but as it is, she continues into adult life this cult of the ego toward which her whole youth has tended. She uses her professional successes as merits for the enrichment of her image; she feels the need for a witness from on high to reveal and consecrate her worth. Even if she is a severe judge of the men she evaluates in daily life, she none the less reveres Man, and if she encounters him, she is ready to fall on her knees.

To be justified by a god is easier than to justify herself by her own efforts; the world encourages her to believe it possible for salvation to be *given,* and she prefers to believe it. Sometimes she gives up her independence entirely and becomes no more than an *amoureuse;* more often she essays a compromise; but idolatrous love, the love that means abdication, is devastating; it occupies every thought, every moment, it is obsessing, tyrannical. If she meets with professional disappointments, the woman passionately seeks refuge in her love; then her frustrations are expressed in scenes and demands at her lover's expense. But her amatory troubles have by no means the effect of redoubling her professional zeal; she is, on the contrary, more likely to be impatient with a mode of life that keeps her from the royal road of a great love. A woman who worked ten years ago on a political magazine run by women told me that in the office they seldom talked about politics but incessantly about love: this one complained that she was loved only for her body to the neglect of her splendid intelligence; that one moaned that only her mind was appreciated, to the neglect of her physical charms. Here again, for woman to love as man does—that is to say, in liberty, without putting her very *being* in question—she must believe herself his equal and be so in concrete fact; she must engage in her enterprises with the same decisiveness. But this is still uncommon, as we shall see.

There is one feminine function that it is actually almost impossible to perform in complete liberty. It is maternity. In England and America and some other countries a woman can at least decline maternity at will, thanks to contraceptive techniques. We have seen that in France she is often driven to painful and costly abortion; or she frequently finds herself responsible for an un-wanted child that can ruin her professional life. If this is a heavy charge, it is because, inversely, custom does not allow a woman to procreate when she pleases. The unwed mother is a scandal to the community, and illegitimate birth is a stain on the child; only rarely is it possible to become a mother without accepting the chains of marriage or losing caste. If the idea of artificial insemination interests many women, it is not because they wish to avoid intercourse with a male; it is because they hope that freedom of maternity is going to be accepted by society at last. It must be said in addition that in spite of convenient day nurseries and kindergartens, having a child is enough to paralyze a woman's activity entirely; she can go on working only if she abandons it to relatives, friends, or servants. She is forced to choose between sterility, which is often felt as a painful frustration, and burdens hardly compatible with a career.

Thus the independent woman of today is torn between her professional interests and the problems of her sexual life; it is difficult for her to strike a balance between the two; if she does, it is at the price of concessions, sacrifices, acrobatics, which require her to be in a constant state of tension. Here, rather than in physiological data, must be sought the reason for the nervousness and the frailty often observed in her. It is difficult to determine to what extent woman's physical constitution handicaps her. Inquiry is often made, for example, about the obstacle presented by menstruation. Women who have made a reputation through their publications or other activities seem to attach little importance to it. Is this because, as a matter of fact, they owe their success to their relatively slight monthly indisposition? One may ask whether it is not because, on the contrary, their choice of an active and ambitious life has been responsible for this advantage; the interest woman takes in her maladies tends to aggravate them. Women in sports and other active careers suffer less from them than others, because they take little notice of them. There are certainly organic factors also, and I have seen the most energetic women spend twenty-four hours in bed each month, a prey to pitiless tortures; but this difficulty never prevented their enterprises from succeeding.

I am convinced that the greater part of the discomforts and maladies that overburden women are due to psychic causes, as gynecologists, indeed, have told me. Women are constantly harassed to the limit of their strength because of the moral tension I have referred to, because of all the tasks they assume, because of the contradictions among which they struggle. This does not mean that their ills are imaginary: they are as real and destructive as the situation to which they give expression. But the situation does not depend on the body; the reverse is true. Thus woman's health will not affect her work unfavorably when the woman worker comes to have the place she should; on the contrary, work will improve her physical condition by preventing her from being ceaselessly preoccupied with it.

Notes

1. I have indicated in Book I, p. 142, how heavy these are for women who work outside.

2. We have examined their situation in Book I, pp. 115, 141.

3. If that is the word.—Tr.

4. The author—whose name I have forgotten, a slip that I see no urgent need of repairing—explains at length how they could be prepared to satisfy all kinds of clients, what regimen they should follow, and so on.

5. This feeling is the male counterpart of that which we have noted in the young girl. She, however, resigns herself to her destiny in the end.

6. We have seen in Book I, ch. i, that there is a certain amount of truth in this opinion. But it is not precisely at the moment of desire that the true asymmetry appears: it is in procreation. In desire man and woman assume their natural functions identically.

7. It would appear that the life of Clara and Robert Schumann attained a success of this kind for a time.

8. That is to say, not only by the same methods but in the same climate, which is impossible today, in spite of all the efforts of educators.

GENERAL COMMENTARY

ELAINE HOFFMAN BARUCH (ESSAY DATE SUMMER 1987)

SOURCE: Baruch, Elaine Hoffman. "The Female Body and the Male Mind: Reconsidering Simone de Beauvoir." *Dissent,* no. 1 (summer 1987): 351-58.

In the following essay, Baruch analyzes Beauvoir's feminist philosophy in the context of contemporary feminist theory, much of which opposes many of Beauvoir's suppositions.

Forty years ago Simone de Beauvoir sat in front of a blank sheet of paper at the Café des Deux Magots, on the Boulevard St. Germain in Paris, wanting to write about herself:

I realized that the first question to come up was: What has it meant to me to be a woman. At first I thought I could dispose of that pretty quickly. I

had never had any feeling of inferiority, no one had ever said to me: "You think that way because you're a woman"; my femininity had never been irksome to me in any way. "For me," I said to Sartre, "you might almost say it just hasn't counted." "All the same, you weren't brought up in the same way as a boy would have been; you should look into it further!"

And so her book *The Second Sex* was born. It was, in a sense, Jean-Paul Sartre's baby. But when published in France, it was viewed as illegitimate. The public was not pleased by Beauvoir's discovery that "this world was a masculine world," and that her "childhood had been nourished by myths forged by men." She was labeled "unsatisfied, frigid, priapic, nymphomaniac, lesbian, a hundred times aborted," as she tells us in her autobiographical *Force of Circumstance.*

I was a poor, neurotic girl, repressed, frustrated, and cheated by life, a virago, a woman who'd never been made love to properly, envious, embittered, and bursting with inferiority complexes with regard to men, while with regard to women I was eaten to the bone by resentment.

Her friend Albert Camus threw the book across the floor, saying it made men look ridiculous. Not surprisingly, considering its attack on religion and the traditional family, the Pope banned it.

The American edition of *The Second Sex* is not quite the whole story. The translator, H. M. Parshley, omitted large chunks—mainly those having to do with women in history, the drudgery of housework, and the nineteenth-century feminist movement. Still, there is enough. In English the paperback runs to some seven hundred pages, a marvelous source of literary criticism, analysis of myth, physiological, psychological, economic, and social commentary on women.

Nonetheless, *The Second Sex* is a child of its times. It is pervaded by the hierarchical dualism that has marked most of the thinking of Western male culture, which has placed mind above body, man above woman, and culture above nature, a dualism that current feminists are attacking. It's not just the hierarchy of the terms that they are questioning but the concept of dualism itself. Still, *The Second Sex* remains an extraordinary achievement for that necessary phase of feminism which holds that women can—and should—do everything that men do. Beauvoir's life too revealed a dramatic fissure—between the theory of sexual equality and the practice of an eroticized subordination in her relation with Sartre. It is some of the complexities in her work and her life that I would like to explore here.

As a member of the existentialist movement that grew up around Sartre in the 1940s, Beauvoir was nurtured on such heady concepts as engagement, freedom, transcendence. Existentialism posits a philosophical division between Subject and Other, similar in some ways to Hegel's paradigm of master-slave. Whereas Sartre felt that all people could be the Other in relation to others, Beauvoir's brilliance lay in showing that these were divisions that actually marked relations between the two sexes. In relation to men, she said, all women are the Other. Unlike men, who represent consciousness and activity in the world (what Beauvoir calls transcendence or the *pour-soi,* for-itself), women represent being (immanence or the *en-soi,* in-itself) and are therefore aligned with nature.

Yet there is nothing natural in this opposition, according to Beauvoir. "One is not born but rather one becomes a woman. . . . It is civilization as a whole that produces this creature, intermediate between male and eunuch." A problem that Beauvoir did not confront, given her dualistic system, is who will be the Other once women have equality. Will the relation between men and women then be reversed, or will the Other be drawn from a category other than sex? What she does do in *The Second Sex* is try to account for women's position as Other through theories of biology, psychoanalysis, and economics. Despite her weighty evidence, it is comforting that she finds none of these sufficient.

Discerning "Truth" Through Biology

Her first and arguably most prominent chapter is "The Data of Biology." It appears in volume one, entitled "Facts and Myths": significantly, Beauvoir places biology in the category of facts, unlike some feminist scientists today who see traditional biology itself, at least the branch that treats of sexual differences, as part of patriarchal mythology. Although science has been remarkably successful in discovering empirical "truths" that do not threaten the power structure, such as the presence of abnormal cells, it has been far less so in dealing with those parts of the body that have symbolic value. "Truth," Michel Foucault has argued, "is produced through discourse, and its production is imbued with relations of power." In a sense Beauvoir's recognition that this is "a masculine world" exposes a similar "truth."

Beauvoir's historical overview of the respective functions of the two sexes in reproduction notes many of the follies of the past, such as the Aristotelian notion that the fetus is produced by the union of sperm and menstrual blood. One might think that her awareness of such past distortions would make her skeptical of male-oriented descriptions of biology[1]; but as with her male contemporaries, echoes of Victorian courtship sound in Beauvoir's description of the romance between the "wholly alive" sperm and the "stationary" egg which "passively awaits fertilization." Beauvoir argues that the ways of a society cannot be deduced from biology, but what she doesn't recognize sufficiently is that biological "facts" can be deduced from the ways of a society.

Unlike feminists of the 1970s who would seek to minimize biological differences, Beauvoir sees them as crucial. Perhaps because *The Second Sex* was written before the legalization of contraception and abortion in France (brought about in large measure through her efforts in such organizations as *Choisir*—Choice), she sees women's "enslavement by reproduction" as the main sexual differentiator: "the individuality of the female is opposed by the interest of the species; it is as if she were possessed by foreign forces—alienated." In contrast, the male body does not impede movement towards transcendence, for it does not have to be "sacrificed" to the species in pregnancy and childbirth. But man is not happy with his body either, according to Beauvoir, since it too is subject to change and death.

Nonetheless, it is the female body, particularly the mother's body, that Beauvoir (and dualists, in general) sees as particularly loathsome. Beauvoir's description (in a later chapter) of how pregnancy transforms—indeed distorts—the body could scarcely be outdone by the most virulent misogynist and is one reason why the current generation of feminists does not always find her sympathetic:

> Ensnared by nature, the pregnant woman is plant and animal, a stock-pile of colloids, an incubator, an egg; she scares children proud of their young, straight bodies and makes young people titter contemptuously because she is a human being, a conscious and free individual, who has become life's passive instrument.

Notwithstanding Beauvoir's male-identified biology and value system—what is human is male—we must still call her conclusions feminist, an ascription she did not accept until decades later. For despite what she sees as the hindrances of female biology, she urges women to struggle for transcendence, for a place in the public world. The frailties of biology are handicaps that must be overcome—like congenital asthma, I suppose (or perhaps like what Sartre calls the facticity of situation). They cannot be used in "bad faith" as excuses to avoid freedom.[2]

Toward a Feminist Psychoanalysis

Many critics claim that in **The Second Sex** Beauvoir rejects psychoanalysis in her treatment of the woman as Other. Even though she herself might agree, I do not think this is true. What she does reject is the traditional reading of Freud; but she also points ahead in some startling ways to a revisionist psychoanalysis that might be called feminist.

Within a few pages, she forcibly illustrates the distinctions between the penis as vulnerable biological organ and what Jacques Lacan and his disciples would refer to as the phallus, the always erect symbol of male privilege within the patriarchal order. It is the latter that women envy. Not anatomy but culture confers privilege—or denies it. So Beauvoir insists despite her negative view of female biology.

Unlike Freud but rather like Melanie Klein, Beauvoir recognizes the strength of the pre-Oedipal period, which is only now receiving widespread attention. She describes lucidly the difficulties that little boys face in having to turn away from the mother as the first object of identification. But unlike contemporary theorists, she does not go on to connect this forced separation with the masculine formation of a dualistic worldview that reduces women to objects. She does, however, anticipate the new geography of female sexuality that dismisses Freud's phallocentric view of the little girl as an *homme manqué* with a stunted penis, and that grants her organs of her own.[3]

Still, Beauvoir does deny one of the central credos of psychoanalysis, whether traditional or revisionist—the importance of the unconscious—because she feels that such a concept limits choice. Here she sounds very much like the American feminists of the 1970s. In contrast, some feminist theorists are now turning to psychoanalysis to show how the body influences the mind and how what appears to be rational is in fact fueled by desire that is often repressed. But Beauvoir is not interested in this mediation. It is not feeling or body but mind and intellect that she exalts.

Also, her denial of the unconscious sometimes causes Beauvoir to see the myths of women, for example, those of the Virgin Mary and the temptress, as mere mystifications and devices for control. But such myths reveal the place of woman in the imagination even more than in social reality.

They will not go away unless attention is paid to their invisible dwelling place. They may not go away even then, but we will understand them better. We can agree with Beauvoir that there is no fixed human nature—actually what she believes is that there is no fixed woman's nature—and still question her conclusion that "perhaps the myth of woman will some day be extinguished." The myths may change or diminish in force as men share in child-rearing tasks and as women enter the public world. They might conceivably even disappear if reproduction is ever taken out of the body. But as long as women bear children and there is an incest barrier, women will remain objects of mystery for men and to some extent for women as well.

Despite her dislike, Beauvoir's picture of myth is so rich, so subtle compared with later ideological attacks on sexual "stereotypes," that one wonders if her conscious denial of unconscious sources should be taken seriously. As a professed socialist, Beauvoir perhaps saw an emphasis on fantasy and feeling as bourgeois or regressive, "a way of returning women to their subordinate ideological place within the dominant culture," as Cora Kaplan puts it in another context. Part of the new feminism, however, would like a merger of social and psychoanalytic theory to explain women's placement—or displacement—in the world.

Supply and Demand

Given Beauvoir's socialist ideals, her account of economic explanations for women as Other is probably the weakest section in **The Second Sex.** "As for the content," she later wrote in **Force of Circumstance,** "I should take a more materialist position today in the first volume. I should base the notion of woman as *other* and the Manichean argument it entails not on an idealistic and *a priori* struggle of consciences, but on the facts of supply and demand. . . ."

Current feminist theoreticians believe that the examination of women's lives, with their invisible and unpaid labor, both in the household and as reproducers of the work force, brings one to deeper insights into materiality than Marx's analysis of the (male) proletariat. Beauvoir does not consider these aspects in either **The Second Sex** or her later work. In the materialism section, however, she does temper her negativism on women's biology: if a woman "procreates voluntarily and if society comes to her aid during pregnancy and is concerned with child welfare, the burdens of maternity are light and can be easily offset by suitable adjustments in working conditions." These are ideas that some Scandinavian countries have tried to introduce into policy, with varying degrees of success.

When she wrote *The Second Sex*, Beauvoir believed that socialism would end the inequality of women. She later gave up her hopes for worldwide revolution, urging women to fight for their rights independently. Only in the early 1970s did she proclaim herself a feminist, a quarter of a century after writing *The Second Sex.*

It was in the 1970s also that Beauvoir would argue that she was less fearful of maternity than of marriage and the family as enslaving institutions. For this reason, she was opposed to Betty Friedan's idea of wages for housework. Unlike the so-called material feminists early in this century and Dolores Hayden today, whose architectural plans seek to eliminate the split between home and work, Beauvoir wanted women out of the house altogether and in public life. She does not consider domestic labor to be work, nor does she recognize the fact that most men work—outside the home—in alienating jobs, which indeed is the case today with most women.

Brilliant as *The Second Sex* is in its description of women's position in a phallocratic world, it may now also be seen as bound by the ropes of white, Western, middle-class culture. We might go further and say that Beauvoir is a prisoner of gender also—masculine gender. For her, culture is unrelievedly male. And although *The Second Sex* is doubtless the germinal book for what is called liberal feminism, Beauvoir never accepted any other form. One strong current of feminism that Beauvoir dismisses is sometimes called cultural feminism. This feminism stresses sexual difference but transvaluates it, attributing positive values to traditionally female feelings and behavior (what had been disparaged by the general culture before). In France writers such as Hélène Cixous advocate an *écriture féminine,* a style of writing that cultivates difference, as if to capture the fluidity of the female body, with its experience of blood, milk, and cycles. The journal *Questions Féministes,* founded in the late 1970s under the general editorship of Beauvoir, has condemned this approach, seeing it as a tool for patriarchy rather than liberation.

There is a third and perhaps major direction in feminism that Beauvoir was also unsympathetic to at the end of her life, one which seeks to transcend dualist oppositions altogether. Many feminists now see as liberating what Beauvoir saw as oppressive: motherhood, for example, the nurturing of life as a conscious act that involves risk and choice—and growth. Precisely what Beauvoir saw as the major barrier keeping women from full participation in humanity, this third group of feminists sees as a bridge to a greater humanity. They feel that bearing and nurturing a child can help to eliminate the split between nature and culture, body and mind, feeling and action, change and stasis. In this last sense, men can mother also, and are doing so increasingly.

". . . [I]t is not in giving life but in risking life that man is raised above the animal; that is why superiority has been accorded in humanity not to the sex that brings forth but to that which kills," wrote Beauvoir in the 1940s, expressing a worldview that she never substantially changed. It is significant that she doesn't see the risk of life in childbirth as a transcendent act. Nor does she question the male valorization of hunting and war. But by now it is not only women who reject this view.

The Second Sex, never seeing relatedness, community, and cooperation as positive values, presents individual achievement as the supreme goal of human existence. Beauvoir's contribution to humanism and feminism was to urge upon women such achievement rather than self-sacrifice. What contemporary feminism wants is achievement and intersubjectivity—a blend Beauvoir tried to have in her own life.

The problem that forerunners, the *avant-garde,* face is that they are always criticized later for not having been *avant* enough. Because they go so far, we are angry that they are not gods. Beauvoir presents a clearly defined world of supposed reason, truth, and objectivity as one side of her polarized view and insists that women engage in it and gain all the rewards that men have had previously. She is eons away from the current attempt to transcend binary polarization. It remains for a new theorist of Beauvoir's stature to explore the place of women in this new world, and to point the way to further crossings of the gender line into new landscapes of the human.

Although it is primarily for *The Second Sex* that Beauvoir will be remembered, her accomplishments as a novelist are also noteworthy. Her dualism appears there as well. In 1954, Beauvoir received the Prix Goncourt for her novel *The Mandarins,* an extraordinary evocation of the life of postwar intellectuals of the left in France and to some extent a *roman à clef.* The book received highly mixed reviews in this country, in part for its anti-Americanism, also revealed in Beauvoir's travel journal *Day by Day.* (In any conflict between the United States and the Soviet Union, Beauvoir opted for the latter, even after she became aware of and denounced the Stalinist labor camps. This is one of her major blind spots.) Yet *The Mandarins* is remarkably powerful with intensely alive if humorless characters, a lyrical rendering of nature, and a fascinating experiment with point of view. Most of the book is written in the third person, except for the treatment of Anne, in some ways the character closest to Beauvoir. Anne speaks in the first person, and is, perhaps revealingly, a psychoanalyst. Despite these surprises, the novel remains rooted in the bourgeois rather than an avant-garde tradition. The politicized figures are all men, the apolitical ones—women. Should we fault Beauvoir for this split? Perhaps, considering the engagement of her own life, at least after World War II. But the choice was deliberate. Beauvoir saw the novel as a public, rather than as an experimental, genre that aims at credibility, unlike autobiography, where one can be singular, eccentric. As a theoretician, Beauvoir took great risks. As a novelist, she didn't. In her life, she took (or thought she took) the greatest risks of all.

Life with Sartre

Even people who have not read Beauvoir know of her involvement with Sartre. Like Héloïse and Abelard, theirs was one of the great academic romances. Books brought them together at the Sorbonne, where they both took advanced degrees in philosophy. Sartre, who fantasized himself as the "writer-knight" in his autobiography, *Les Mots,* became Beauvoir's rescuer. In *Memoirs of a Dutiful Daughter,* her autobiographical *Bildungsroman,* she describes him as fulfilling her adolescent fantasy: "Sartre corresponded exactly to the dream-companion I had longed for since I was fifteen: he was the double in whom I found all my burning aspiration raised to the pitch of incandescence." Sartre, only a little less than Abelard, was the tutor/lover. And like Héloïse and Abelard in the Middle Ages, Beauvoir and Sartre epitomize our own age's ambivalent attitudes toward sex and love.

Bourgeois as much as bohemian, soulmates who lived apart, they speak to the modern desire for primacy of the couple *and* multiple sexual experience at the same time. It was Sartre who set the terms of their nonmarriage pact, which included "perfect honesty about everything," an honesty that he perhaps desired as much for exhibitionistic gratification as for a means of control. In what may be the most intellectual euphemism for infidelity on record, the two pledged an "essential love" to each other but allowed for "contingent" loves with others. Did Beauvoir accept these conditions because she was the essential one? Perhaps. But they hardly fit the romantic or even existential definition of love, which posits an absolute love that allows room for no other. (In all fairness to Sartre, he did not think such a love could exist.) Interestingly enough, in *The Second Sex,* Beauvoir claimed that an authentic love should assume "the contingence of the other," should recognize his lacks and limitations, and not be idolatrous. Neither could practice what they theorized.

Beauvoir had refused Sartre's early offer of marriage: "I chose what was the hardest course for me at that moment in order to safeguard the future. . . . I knew Sartre did not want marriage. I could not want it all by myself." It is doubtful that she wanted it either. Yet she suffers all kinds of somatic ailments over his affairs and laments the signs of age in her mirror more than the most despondent *hausfrau*—although it is perhaps unfair to attribute this disgust to sexual vulnerability alone: "I loathe my appearance now: the eyebrows slipping down toward the eyes, the bags underneath, the excessive fullness of the cheeks, and that air of sadness around the mouth that wrinkles always bring." Because of her university training and her great gifts, however, she is able to transform her hurts into metaphysical despair over death, political outrage—or into fiction. Perhaps because of her rejection of the unconscious, she never fully recognizes that her obsession with death might stem from her anger turned inwards on the self.

She too had other lovers, chosen perhaps more in retaliation than in freedom: Nelson Algren, the author of *The Man With the Golden Arm,* who figures in *The Mandarins,* and the journalist Claude Lanzmann.

> For myself, I needed some sort of distance if I were to give my heart sincerely, for there could be no question of trying to duplicate the understanding I had with Sartre. Algren belonged to another continent, Lanzmann to another generation; this too was a foreignness that kept a balance in our relationship.

It does not seem that Sartre was so careful about his balancing act. In the end, he adopted a young woman, Arlette Elkahim. Beauvoir too had adopted Sylvie le Bon in what she described as a freely chosen relationship. But Sartre had wanted to marry Arlette, one of his mistresses; here Beauvoir prevailed. Still it was the incestuous daughter who inherited all of Sartre's unpublished papers while Beauvoir, Sartre's "one special reader" for whom he wrote, had no access to them.

Ambiguity may be the one clear mark of Beauvoir's thought and feeling at the end. Her picture of Sartre's last years in *Adieux: A Farewell to Sartre* is problematic at best. Though some critics have praised the book for its truthfulness, it is less a depiction of the vulnerabilities of a great man in old age than a quiet revenge. The conversations and particularly the commentary present the male in all *his* Otherness (a theme taken up in a different way in her book *The Coming of Age*). No longer the transcendent being, he is man crumbling.

Divested of all his strength and even shame, the philosopher has mental lapses, he overturns his soup, fouls his clothes. One wonders why all the painful details are necessary. Beauvoir would probably plead honesty. One suspects that it is more her sense of betrayal that he is no longer a hero. "A fallen god is not a man; he is a fraud," she had written in *The Second Sex*. Actually Sartre seems to bear all his physical limitations with a stoic's calm, but Beauvoir does not admire him for this. At one time he could make her feel as secure as the idea of God did when she was a child, but at the end of his life he suffers a de-idealization and de-idolization at Beauvoir's pen, in part at least because the body has taken over the mind. Still, she writes with some unconscious irony: "It is in itself splendid that we were able to live our lives in harmony for so long."

Like Sartre, Beauvoir sought to create herself. She succeeded in making her life an exemplum but not always in the way she would have liked. She is as much an illustration of the "woman in love" described in *The Second Sex* as a representative of freedom. In that sense she bears some similarity to Mary Wollstonecraft, the eighteenth-century author of *A Vindication of the Rights of Woman*. Wollstonecraft too had argued that women were constructed by the social order, but in relation to her lover Gilbert Imlay if not to her later husband, William Godwin, Wollstonecraft was a romantic victim, subject to betrayal by her feelings. Perhaps Beauvoir writes so well about this subject because in some sense she was betrayed too. Autobiography objectified becomes theory.

But if Beauvoir in *The Second Sex* asked in effect, "Why can't a woman be more like a man?",

Sartre, at least at the end of his life, was asking, "Why can't a man be more like a woman?" There is an extraordinary statement by Sartre in the *Adieux* on his sexuality. I treat it here because I think it affected his philosophy and in turn that of Beauvoir. Sartre confesses that he didn't attach a great deal of importance to intercourse—he simply engaged in it because it was expected. (He too was a prisoner of gender.) "I was more a masturbator of women than a copulator. . . . I should have been quite happy naked in bed with a naked woman, caressing and kissing her, but without going as far as the sexual act." This admission, which implies a fear of women's sexual demands or at least of female sexuality, throws new light on Sartre's emphasis on holes and viscosity in his descriptions of the female sex organ in his earlier work, descriptions that Beauvoir often echoes. "The amorous act is the castration of the man; but this is above all because sex is a hole," he had written. In existential psychoanalysis, unlike Freud's, things possess objective qualities of being. Holes are bad; viscosity is bad. Ironically, considering Beauvoir's criticism, it is Freud's theory that is more emancipating for women than Sartre's. For what Sartre sees as literal truth, Freud sees as metaphor. And metaphor can perhaps be changed whereas fact cannot. It is for Sartre, at least in his earlier work, that anatomy is destiny.

"In herself woman appeals to a flesh which is to transform her into a fullness of being by penetration and dissolution," writes Sartre in *Being and Nothingness*, a statement which assumes that a man is complete in himself and that he has no envy of the specifically feminine *jouissance* or orgasm. Yet in the *Adieux* he reveals that he dislikes the term "adult male" because it distinguishes between the sexes in an odious, comic fashion. "The male is the one with a little tube between his legs." It is the experience of the total body that Sartre now seeks—that which women are supposed to experience. While some of these passages might bear witness that Sartre lacked mature genitality, they also reveal a desire for androgyny—a desire for transcendence of dualism perhaps.

In *The Second Sex*, Beauvoir spoke at length of women as economic parasites, forced to live vicariously. What Sartre reveals in *Adieux* is men's emotional parasitism. Because of their overvaluation of intellect, he says, men constantly look to different women to replenish their emotional resources. This is not, he implies, a good division. Had Sartre come to these conclusions sooner, his (and Beauvoir's) existential psychoanalysis might have been quite different.

But I don't think that it is simply Sartre's influence that causes Beauvoir in **The Second Sex** to describe the female sex organ as "carnivorous plant," "bog," "suction, humus, pitch and glue . . . insinuating and viscous." Nor is it merely centuries of Catholic repulsion for things of the flesh. The reasons are complex and overdetermined, and I can only suggest some of them. Perhaps because of her anti-psychoanalytical bias, Beauvoir doesn't refer to a major reason for female as well as male disgust at the female body that is now being treated at length by such French women analysts as Julia Kristeva: the fear of being engulfed, swallowed up by the "primitive" mother, that dangerous, powerful, overwhelming figure of our infancy. The fear, of course, is also a wish even less acknowledged.

Beauvoir's relation to her mother was particularly ambivalent. (Her great guilt is revealed in her account of her mother's last days, **A Very Easy Death.**) She loved her for her nurturing, but hated her repression of Simone the child. She was constantly watched, as was Sartre, though he with greater indulgence. For Beauvoir in her early emancipation from her family, when she went off to the university, happiness meant a closed door. Like Sartre, she always wanted another's gaze on her—neither ever escaped the need for a mirror.

The need for others to mirror one's activity in order to give it meaning is a principle of existentialist thought. But Beauvoir and Sartre never connect the roots of this idea to the psychoanalytical account of the mirror stage of development, in which the infant starts responding to the mother's face. What Beauvoir and Sartre refuse to acknowledge is the value of the body. The mind, for them, is paramount. For all her professed atheism, Beauvoir's early Catholic teaching survives. It's simply that in her writings soul has been transformed into mind.

Yet in examining Sartre and Beauvoir's dualisms, one is struck by the primacy in their metaphors of things and ultimately of bodies. John Donne in the seventeenth century said, "The body makes the mind." In large part, Sartre and Beauvoir's physical experiences influenced their philosophy. In bondage to the mother, it is her body they both reject. Confined by their body in childhood, they seek to escape it through thought. They reject the body in general, but the mother's above all.

The primacy of the physical is something that transcends sex. In the physical deterioration of both Sartre and Beauvoir at the end of their lives, they reveal what Donne also implies: That far more important than sexual difference are the vulnerabilities that all of us share as part of the human condition.

But if sexual difference isn't all-determining for women, there is another category that is—or has been. Though she doesn't use the term, Beauvoir might have said, "Gender is destiny." By *gender,* I mean here what society does with sexual difference. "You girls will never marry. You have no dowries," Beauvoir's father kept saying to his daughters. "You'll have to work for a living." Though proud of her intellect, he viewed Beauvoir's life of hard study as a punishment, necessary because she was doomed to be alone. Sartre's sisterlike mother, in contrast, promised her son that his reward for the same activity would be the adulation of women. No wonder he needed so many of them. In some way he turned Beauvoir into the mother—and the sister. They did not need children. They were so busy shaping themselves—and others.

Their lives seized the imagination of an age, whether as role models for modernism or as unofficial political and intellectual ambassadors in their travels around the world. Seeking utopia in such countries as Russia, Cuba, China, they were repeatedly disillusioned. But however naïve their expectations, they always supported the downtrodden, whether in colonies far away or the working classes at home.

Beauvoir's greatness as a theorist was to show us the anatomy of sexism, to expose with relentless precision the oppression of women in a "masculine world," thereby implying that with equality women could do whatever men could. Despite her talk of autonomy, she does not escape her dependence on the patriarchal order, and never suggests a system to replace it. She made herself a satellite, not because she was a woman, she said, but because of Sartre's philosophical and political superiority.

If the symbolic nature of funerals is any evidence, the public agreed. Sartre's was a huge affair. Thousands upon thousands attended. It was so crowded, people were pushed onto the grave site. In contrast, Beauvoir's was a quiet affair, so quiet, I've been told, that her loyal feminist following was at one point locked outside the cemetery gates. But it may well be that Simone de Beauvoir made the greater contribution. Those who cannot imagine this do not comprehend feminism as a philosophical and political movement. Yet it is—perhaps the greatest of our time.

Notes

1. As skeptical as Ruth Herschberger was in this country, in a delightful book called *Adam's Rib* (New York: Pellegrini and Cudahy, 1948).

2. Recent scientific developments cast ironic light on Beauvoir's idea of reproduction as forced labor. The new reproductive technology with its use of *in vitro* fertilization (fertilization in a petri dish) and surrogate mothers (women who contribute their ova and/or their uterine environment for the creation and gestation of fetuses meant to be reared by others after birth) would seem to offer women greater choice and control over having children. Such technology even points ahead to the possibility of removing reproduction from the body altogether, a prospect that would no doubt have been welcomed by Beauvoir. Not only would reproduction *ex utero* release women from their "enslavement" to the species, it would also modify if not eliminate the entire mythology of women to which Beauvoir is so opposed. (It is primarily because they are biological mothers that women are alternately exalted and degraded.) But while Beauvoir viewed science and technology as potential liberators of women, these new techniques may lead to some new "enslavements," such as the exploitation of poor, minority, and Third-World women for surrogacy. Many feminist scientists today, such as Ruth Hubbard, fear that male-dominated technology will soon deprive women of the right to conceive in the natural way at all. Should reproduction *ex utero* ever become a reality, it would be potentially liberating only in a nonpatriarchal society.

3. Perhaps *new* is the wrong word since debates about this issue had been going on in the 1920s and 1930s, but certainly Beauvoir is in the vanguard of current thinking on it.

NIZA YANAY (ESSAY DATE 1990)

SOURCE: Yanay, Niza. "Authenticity of Self-Expression: Reinterpretation of Female Independence through the Writings of Simone de Beauvoir." *Women's Studies* 17 (1990): 219-33.

In the following essay, Yanay uses the work of Beauvoir to examine the psychological notions of dependence and independence in women.

This paper aims to reopen discussion of the meaning of "dependence" and "independence" as they reflect the experiences of women. This desire to reexamine and revise accepted concepts and terms in light of principles of female experience is prompted by the work of feminist scholars, who have suggested the adoption of a new language with which to conceptualize accepted values.

Psychology treats the concept of "dependency" as a tendency to rely on and seek attention, care, or help from close others. Thus, dependence is often equated with affiliation (McClain, 1978) or with the need for affection, reassurance and approval (Heathers, 1955). Along these same lines, the concept of "autonomy" or "independence" is often associated with self-reliance and needing no one else—accomplishing things on the basis of one's own efforts in response to one's own interests and in an attempt to reach self-fulfillment.

This conception of autonomy has only recently been challenged by feminist scholars who explore the masculine attributes of the very nature of scientific thought (Keller, 1985). Miller (1976), Gilligan (1982), Keller (1985) and others have pointed out that the prevailing meaning of autonomy is alienating to women because it excludes passion, love, and desire, the very dynamics of interpersonal relations, which, as Kerenberg (1974) argued, require the crossing of ego boundaries. Miller (1976), for example, claims that the concept "autonomy" derives from male development, as it bears the implication that "one should be able to give up affiliations in order to become a separate and self-directed individual" (p. 94). Similarly, Gilligan (1982) believes that the word "autonomy" has become so closely associated with separation that "separation itself becomes the model and the measure of growth" (p. 98). Keller (1985) points to the correlation between the accepted meaning of autonomy and masculinity in Western culture, which she attributes to certain paradigmatic changes in the nature of scientific thinking. She claims that the transition from hermetic science, characterized by metaphors of sexual unity with nature, to a mechanical science, characterized by masculine metaphors of power and domination of nature, has shaped a concept of autonomy separate from desire and dominated by images of impersonality. At the same time, feminist scholarship in psychology (Miller, 1976; Gilligan, 1982) has demonstrated the different values around which women's selves emerge and the importance of inclusiveness and affiliation to their self-concept and identity.

My own contribution to this argument is to explore the concepts of dependency and independence as they are reflected in the autobiographical writings of Simone de Beauvoir.[1] Not only are these works of recognized literary and intellectual merit, but they deal with "a relatively large number of lines of experience, giving a picture of variety, roundness and inter-relatedness in the life from which the structure of life as a whole emerges" (Allport, 1951, p. 77). Moreover—and perhaps most importantly—they mirror a substantial portion of the author's experiences of emotional dependency, and these stand in sharp contrast to the woman herself, who has become a symbol of independence and strength in her own lifetime: "She is a woman who refuses to accept her role passively, who has taken a stand, flouting all convention and opposition" (Schwarzer, 1985, p. 22). While accepting her femininity, de Beauvoir has never used her womanhood as an alibi and, moreover, she recognizes emotional dependency on men as "a curse that weighs upon most women" and a condition she has had to struggle with and to defend herself against through most of her youth and adult life. Her autobiographical works are a testimony to an unresolved struggle to reconcile her longing for independence with the love that drove her "impetuously toward another person."

However, though de Beauvoir perceives her struggle as a conflict between unity with another and separateness—a perception based on the conventional interpretation of "dependence"—it seems that in actuality it revolved around the need to maintain a very close relationship without being false to her innermost needs and feelings.[2] Thus, by drawing out the themes of dependency and independence of de Beauvoir's writings and interpreting them in terms of the development of the feminine self-identity, feminine values, and feminine conceptions of relationships, we challenge accepted definitions of independence and dependency in Western society, particularly the culturally perceived contradiction between love and independence. In this new light, the accepted distinction between emotional "symbiosis" or unity and individual autonomy appears conceptual and culture-bound rather than onthological and absolute. The reflexive reading of de Beauvoir's autobiographical writings through the prism of feminist conceptualizations of autonomy, with the aim of uncovering the author's most inner feelings as a woman, lends new meaning to the concepts of dependency and independence.

Setting the Stage for Reinterpretation

Simone de Beauvoir perceives the struggle for independence as the core experience in a woman's life. In her four-volume autobiography—*Memoirs of A Dutiful Daughter* (*MDD*) (1958), *The Prime of Life* (*PL*) (1960), *Force of Circumstance* (*FC*) (1963), and *All Said and Done* (*ASD*) (1972)—and her first autobiographical novel, *She Came to Stay* (1943), she consciously and subconsciously reveals an ongoing struggle to escape "women's doomed destiny of dependent existence" and to

reconcile independence and intimacy, a struggle which is also characteristic of her fictional characters (Ann in *The Mandarins*, Francoise in *She Came to Stay*, and the heroine of her short story *The Woman Destroyed*).

The earliest signs of this inner conflict appear in her childhood memories. Even as a little girl, de Beauvoir rejected traditional feminine values (but not her own womanhood[3]): "When we played games, I accepted the role of the mother only if I were allowed to disregard its nursing aspects. Despising other girls who played with their dolls in what seemed to us a silly way, my sister and I had our own particular way of treating our dolls" (*MDD*, p. 56). The young de Beauvoir felt that femininity limited a woman's existence, establishing her position as "other," while masculinity offered endless possibilities of intellectual excitement and freedom. Her male teachers were, in her opinion, clever, even brilliant, but the women who taught her were "comical old church hens." Even though the majority of boys she knew seemed of limited intelligence, she recognized intuitively that "they belonged to a privileged category." The world of men appeared to her as free, imaginative, and full of adventure. As an adolescent, de Beauvoir believed that men were the great writers, the finest thinkers, and that women were tied to family conventions, salon smiles, and to small talk. "My education, my culture, and the present state of society all conspired to convince me that women belonged to an inferior cast" (*MDD*, p. 145).

De Beauvoir's adolescent years were marked by the contradictory expectations of her father, who projected onto his first-born daughter (he had hoped for a son) not only his pride and bourgeoise aspirations, but also his economic and social failure:

> The war had ruined him, sweeping away all his dreams, destroying his myths, his self-justifications, and his hopes. I was wrong to think he had resigned himself to the situation: he never stopped protesting against his condition . . . he was trying to show, by his aggressive exhibitionism, that he belonged to a superior class . . . I was not just another burden to be borne: I was growing up to be the living incarnation of his own failure.
>
> (*MDD*, pp. 176-177)

At the same time, though he "liked intelligent and witty women and . . . was of the opinion that a woman should be well read and a good conversationalist," and though he was pleased by de Beauvoir's early scholastic success, he also believed in the myth of femininity and the cult of the family: "When I entered the 'difficult age,' he was disappointed in me: he appreciated elegance and beauty in women. Not only did he fail to conceal his disillusionment from me but he began showing more interest than before in my sister, who was still a pretty girl" (*MDD*, p. 107). So while praising his daughter for her academic achievements, he was exasperated by what he considered her childish scribblings.

Notwithstanding her father's ambivalence toward her, the adolescent de Beauvoir adored and idolized him. "I could not imagine a more intelligent man than my father . . . As long as he approved of me, I could be sure of myself". At times her love for him seems incestuous: "But my real rival was my mother. I dreamed of having a more intimate relationship with my father. But even on the rare occasions when we found ourselves alone together we talked as if she was there with us" (*MDD*, p. 107).

De Beauvoir's mother was a traditional woman; religious, with a strong sense of duty, she remained in the background, moderating her desires, making no demands on life, and teaching her children austerity and unselfishness. She treated her daughter with tenderness, care and understanding and gave her the acceptance that she sought and needed. "I wanted to be noticed: but fundamentally I needed to be accepted for what I was, with all the deficiencies of my age; my mother's tenderness assured me that this wish was a justifiable one . . . Without striving to imitate her, I was conditioned by her" (*MDD*, p. 41).

Exposed to her father's "individualism and pagan ethical standards" on the one hand, and her mother's "rigid moral conventionalism" on the other, and torn between dependency on her mother and admiration for her father, the young de Beauvoir struggled to reconcile her intellectual life with her growing female sensibility. In this imbalanced atmosphere "I grew accustomed to the idea that my intellectual life—embodied by my father—and my spiritual life—expressed by my mother—were two radically heterogeneous fields of experience which had absolutely nothing in common" (*MDD*, p. 41).

De Beauvoir's high esteem for the independent masculine mind and her disparagement of femininity were rooted thus in rebellion, as well as submission, to the image she had of her parents. She internalized their contradictory expectations of herself, particularly her father's ambivalent attitude: "I was obeying his wishes to the letter, and

that seemed to anger him: he had destined me to a life of study, and yet I was being reproached with having my nose in a book all the time . . . I kept wondering what I have done wrong" (*MDD*, p. 179). It was by her father's rules—and against them—that de Beauvoir the child seems to have set her ideals and developed her aspirations for freedom. It was also from those early contradictory experiences of affection, idealization and unexpressed inner resentment towards her parents that her conflict between dependency and independence emerged.

Although she idealized her father and was influenced by his literary preferences and intellectual aspirations, she was deeply wounded by his attitude towards the "fair sex" in general and toward her own femininity in particular. Similarly, although needful of her mother's acceptance, she disparaged her religiosity and traditional femininity. As an adolescent de Beauvoir was caught between the world of her parents and that of herself, and though she was developing her own sense of self and identity, she was unable to express it. She therefore remained the "dutiful daughter," being false to her true self:

> I accepted their verdict while at the same time I looked upon myself with other eyes than theirs. My essential self still belonged to them as much as to me: but paradoxically the self they knew could only be a decoy now; it could be false. There was only one way of preventing this strange confusion: I would have to cover up superficial appearances, which were deceptive.
>
> (*MDD*, p. 108)

Even while preparing herself for graduation from school, a few years later, her outward behavior did not change: "I still didn't dare disobey or tell any outright lies. I still used to tell my mother what my plans were for the day; in the evening I had to give her a full account of how I had passed my time. I gave in. But I was choking with fury and vexation" (*MDD*, p. 211). Hence, de Beauvoir silenced her inner fury and suppressed her true needs. The gap between her real feelings, needs and wishes, on the one hand, and the de Beauvoir she showed to the outside world on the other, seems to signify a pattern of dependency on others, a pattern which continued into her adult life.

By outward appearances the adult de Beauvoir was strong-willed and independent, determined to establish her place in the world: "My own particular enterprise was the development of my life, which I believed lay in my own hands" (*PL*, p. 286). Throughout her adult life she was economically independent and never suffered the constraints of marriage or of motherhood (McCall,

1979). She often took long trips by herself to places "no living soul would ever pass through." She was also daring and unconventional in her teaching, standing unsupported against the values and beliefs of the provincial middle-class community in which she worked. Risking her position, she sacrificed neither her freedom of ideas nor her ideals.

Yet, despite this outward appearance of autonomy, it seems that de Beauvoir was continuously striving for emotional independence, struggling against her imperious need for others: "The existence of otherness maintained a danger for me, one which I could not bring myself to face openly" (**PL,** p. 105). Describing Francoise, the heroine of **She Came to Stay,** she writes: "Now another danger threatened her, one which I myself had been endeavouring to exorcise ever since my adolescence. Other people could not only steal the world from her, but also invade her personality and bewitch it" (**PL,** p. 270). This threat is particularly salient in de Beauvoir's desire and need for absolute emotional and physical unity with her friend and lover, Jean-Paul Sartre.

Ascher (1981), following the normative assumption that separateness, individualism, self-contentment and self-reliance constitute the essence of independence, sees this relation as evidence of an unresolved dependency. In this spirit she has claimed that de Beauvoir's usage of the pronoun "we" in her memoire indicates an unsettled tension between her developing individuated self and developing intimate relationships: "With a relationship to God ended absolutely, a major theme in **The Prime of Life** is the tension between de Beauvoir's sense of herself as an 'I' and as part of a 'we,' that is, the working out of her autonomy and aloneness within the context of her strong ties to Sartre" (Ascher, 1981, p. 22).

It seems, however, that these "we relations" (which she had not only with Sartre, but also with others, male and female alike, whom she loved dearly) did not necessarily threaten her self-identity and autonomy. The story of her relation with Zaza is a case in point.

At the age of ten, de Beauvoir experienced the emotion of love for the first time. Elizabeth Mabille, or Zaza as she called her, was a small, dark, thin-faced girl, who was seated next to the young de Beauvoir in their fourth grade. With Zaza she talked about books, schoolwork, their teachers, and their friends. "She at once seemed to me a very finished person" and "everything she had to say was either interesting or amusing." Zaza ap-

peared to her a fascinating person and de Beauvoir's attitude toward her, as later to Sartre, was one of admiration and total devotion. De Beauvoir was drawn to Zaza's courage and spirit of independence, as well as to her originality and talent, characteristics which attracted her also to Sartre. A simple word of praise from Zaza overwhelmed her with joy and a sarcastic smile would cause her terrible torment; her happiness, indeed her very existence, lay in Zaza's power. "Zaza didn't suspect how much I idolized her, nor that I had adjusted my pride in her favor," reflects de Beauvoir (**MDD,** p. 119). Nonetheless, her all-encompassing feeling toward Zaza did not prevent her from recognizing their individual places in the world, and her sense of "we" in this case did not compromise her recognition and acceptance of their differences. "If it had been suggested that I should be Zaza, I would have refused" (**MDD,** p. 114).

With Sartre, the "we identity" was somewhat different. De Beauvoir, like Sartre, perceived their relationship as a single unity: "I settled the anomaly of Sartre by telling myself that we formed a single entity placed together at the world's center" (**PL,** p. 105). Indeed, feeling one with Sartre was most essential to her inner harmony. However, this oneness of identity represented a value and an ideal to de Beauvoir, not a "problem" as is often suggested by her critics.

The strong feelings of closeness and affiliation that de Beauvoir shared with Zaza and later with Sartre should not be confused with dependence upon them. It is true that the accepted definition of dependency includes affiliation with another—as opposed to separateness—as a major component, and indeed psychology as yet lacks the terminology to distinguish between connectedness and purely negative aspects of dependence, such as experience of inequality (Miller, 1976). Yet the positive and negative aspects of dependency need to be separated. Miller (1976), Stiver (1984) and others have pointed to the positive elements of dependency, such as its providing conditions for growth and enrichment. Along similar lines, Memmi (1984) considers dependency an onthological need: "On the whole, dependence is one of the basic elements of the bond that ties one member of a society to another" (p. 154), and the fear of dependency is a fear of others.

In an attempt to focus only on the negative aspects of dependency, the present paper pursues a new interpretation of the concept which isolates those components that reflect inequality and that have been inhibiting to women's expression of self. Underlying this quest is the assumption that women are governed by different rules of psychological development than men (Gilligan, 1983).

Authenticity of Expressed Feelings as Reflecting Independence

Simone de Beauvoir's admitted need to hide her true feelings in order to be a dutiful daughter has already been discussed, this need seems to have persisted into her adult life and to have been highly salient in her relationship with Sartre. Indeed, her tendency to mask her actual feelings is even apparent in her autobiographical works, where an inner voice seems to express feelings which are quite different from, and even contradictory to, her explicit statements. It is around this striving for authentic expression of her feelings and beliefs—rather than for separateness from others—that the true struggle for independence seems to revolve.

One clue in her autobiographical works to this struggle for authenticity of expression is the sharp contrast between the stated conception of freedom and autonomy proferred by de Beauvoir the philosopher and the intellectual and that which may be inferred from the voice of de Beauvoir the woman. The first voice advocates a conception of freedom in keeping with Sartre's existentialism. Like him, she believes that autonomy has to be attained through one's own actions, and, going further, that any woman can escape her destiny of dependence through her own efforts. Shifting one's responsibilities onto another, she feels, is immoral, and, what is more, in the absence of a God, it is a flight from freedom. According to this existential moral ontology, one transcends animal nature by a continuous affirmation of self. The voice of de Beauvoir the woman, however, suggests a different interpretation of independence, one which is closely linked to authenticity of feelings and needs.

The nature of de Beauvoir's struggle for independence is gleaned from a specific example of the way in which she coped with a triadic love arrangement involving herself, Sartre, and Olga, a young student of hers with whom she became intimate friends. Early on in their relationship, Sartre had explained to de Beauvoir his "philosophy" of attachments: "What we have is an essential love, but it is a good idea for us also to experience contingent love affairs . . . We reflected on this problem a good deal [says de Beauvoir] during our walks together" (*PL*, p. 24). Despite her ostensibly neutral intellectual tone, de Beauvoir's inner voice seems to project jealousy of the lovers and doubts as to her own worth. At the same time "the need to agree with Sartre on all subjects outweighed the desire to see Olga through eyes other than his" (*PL*, p. 195). Unable to bear the anxiety, but worse, unable to even consider diverging from Sartre's ideals, de Beauvoir chooses to glorify the trio and foster its well-being: "From now on we could be a trio rather than a couple. We believed that human relationships are a matter of constant fresh discovery" (*PL*, p. 195). Nevertheless, she admits to feelings of anger: "I was vexed with Sartre for having created this situation and with Olga for taking advantage of it."

Eventually, as is clear from her remarks in **The Prime of Life,** de Beauvoir deals with this love triangle by giving indirect expression to her feelings of jealousy and anger in her first autobiographical novel, **She Came to Stay**: "I exposed myself so dangerously [in that novel] that at times the gap between my emotions and the words to express them seemed insurmountable" (*PL*, p. 271). The novel portrays a love triangle between Francoise the heroine "whom I endowed with my own experiences" (*PL*, p. 269), her lover Pierre and a young woman Xavierre. Slowly, before the reader's eyes, Francoise is transformed from "a position of absolute and all-embracing authority" to "an utterly transparent creature without features of individuality" who betrays her own truth. With no more than a faded image of herself, Francoise becomes obsessively involved in Xavierre's affections, hatreds, and caprices, and with Pierre's desire for Xavierre. She conceals her true feelings and allows Pierre to dictate her desires because she feels lonely experiencing needs different from his. Hence, she permits herself to express only sympathy for Pierre and understanding of the triangular relationship. Even when she clearly sees Pierre as "a man fighting desperately for his masculine triumph" (p. 203), she sacrifices her emotional harmony for the sake of his freedom. Hurting herself is less threatening, easier, clearer, more acceptable. But her support is equivocal and not without conflict; she despises her role of benevolence. In times of "weakness" she challenges her own behavior: "She had always disregarded her dreams and her desire . . . why would she not make up her mind to will what she hoped for?" (p. 364). After all, "she need only say one word to herself, she need only say 'it is I.' But she would have to believe in that word; she would have to know to choose herself" (p. 293). Yet, Francoise continues to attribute her (unexpressed) anger, anxiety, and confusion to her own mistrust, and to her inability to transcend human pettiness. She is incapable of validating her feelings of jealousy and anger in the face of Pierre's higher, more noble emotions.

In the final analysis, however, Francoise chooses to be true to her own feelings and so to achieve the "ultimate" freedom: "Her own image became so loathsome to Francoise that she was faced with two alternatives: A lifetime of self-disgust, or to shatter the spell by destroying her who cast it. This latter course she took, and thus remained, triumphantly, true to herself" (**PL**, p. 270). And it is this fictional murder of Xavierre that gains de Beauvoir her freedom; killing Olga on paper "purged every twinge of irritation and resentment I had previously felt toward her and cleansed our relationship . . ." (**PL**, p. 271). Moreover, destroying Olga in a projected literary act was more than a cathartic experience. It was also a means of extracting and displaying her innermost feelings "By releasing Francoise, through the agency of crime, from the dependent position in which her love for Pierre kept her, I gained my own personal autonomy" (**PL**, p. 271).

The act of crime represents in de Beauvoir's writing the epitome of both individualism and immersing oneself into the whole of society. It is one means albeit an admittedly extreme one, of achieving independence. Indeed, in discussing her feelings of dependence upon Sartre, de Beauvoir makes an explicit connection between crime and personal autonomy:

> The only solution would have been to accomplish some deed for which I alone, and no one else, must bear the consequences. But this would have meant society as a whole taking charge of the matter, since otherwise Sartre would have shared the responsibility with me. Nothing, in fact, short of an aggravated crime could bring me true independence. I often amused myself by a more or less close interweaving of these related themes.
>
> (**PL**, p. 252)

Perhaps that is why the metaphysical aspects of crime have always fascinated de Beauvoir and captured her imagination: ". . . crime figured regularly as an element in my dreams and fantasies. I saw myself in the dock, facing judge, prosecutor, jury, and a crowd of spectators, bearing the consequences of an act which I recognized as my handiwork, and bearing it alone" (**PL**, p. 252). As de Beauvoir could not actually commit a crime—"Francoise, as I have depicted her, is just as incapable of murder as I am" (**PL**, p. 27)—she gained her freedom through a literary projection. The philosophical and ontological ties between the primordial state of "being true to oneself" and

the act of murder has long historical roots. The connotative meaning of the Greek "authento" simultaneously reflects the virtue of power over someone or something and the act of committing a murder (Trilling, 1972). Similarly, "Miller (1973) traces the 'politics of the true self' back to the poet William Blake and shows that violence is conceived of as the ultimate form of self-expression and self-discovery in the writings of Fanon and Sartre" (in Turner, 1976, p. 998).

Much like Raskolikov's murder of the old woman in *Crime and Punishment*, which was a psychological assertion of his freedom and authenticity, even if momentary, so was de Beauvoir's literary solution of killing Xavierre. This was not merely a philosophical stand, but rather a means of recovering her autonomy and reaching a very deep emotional and psychological resolution. Francoise's real crime, then, was having refused to accept responsibility for her inner needs. Indeed, by justifying, rationalizing and suppressing her emotions, and thereby relinquishing her independence, she had been untrue to herself. Ironically, she purges herself of this sin with an act of extreme violence:

> Francoise has given up looking for an ethical solution to the problem of coexistence. She endures the Other as an inevitable burden and then defends herself against this invasion by accomplishing an equally brutal and irrational act herself: murder. The rights and wrongs of her individual case do not concern me.
>
> (**PL**, p. 270)

This should not be construed to mean that any expression of needs and emotions short of crime lacks authenticity. On the contrary, the ultimate solution of murdering Xavierre is employed by de Beauvoir to depict an act of psychological inversion, to indicate how unnecessary the act would have been if only Francoise had accepted and expressed her true emotions and needs. Authentic expression of needs and emotions through language is, according to de Beauvoir, a viable substitute for violence directed toward the self or the other. "The paradoxical thing is that [gaining my autonomy] did not require an unpardonable action on my part, but merely the description of such an action in a book" (**PL**, p. 271).

Interesting enough, the more accepted solution (by social standards) of having Francoise leave Pierre does not seem adequate to de Beauvoir, although it would have relieved her of an "awkward" ending, which has been frequently criticized by her readers, and which she herself recognized to be "beyond any doubt the weakest aspect of the book" (*PL*, p. 270). Yet she insists on this conclusion, as it conveys a personal truth which she desperately needed to express.

In de Beauvoir's autobiographical writings the need for another person (excessive as it may be) is distinct from dependency. Her ardent need for unity with Sartre is congruent with her desire for an absolute and essential existence. Similarly, it was not Francoise's need for unity with Pierre which condemned her to a life of servitude. What drove Francoise from her independent self was the lack of spontaneity and authenticity of her emotions and needs.

In summary, the re-reading of de Beauvoir's autobiography in a new light of feminist criticism, reveals a concept of dependency different from the need to rely on, receive help from, and be influenced by another. When one examines the meanings of dependency and independence through the female language of connectedness and women's values of care and involvement, the essential meaning of dependency shifts from lack of self-reliance to suppression of self-expression, and from struggles with separation to struggles with one's own truth and authenticity with respect to relations with others.

It may not be surprising, within de Beauvoir's philosophical framework of the onthological opposition between self and other, that spontaneity of desire and authenticity of expression are the intrinsic values of a dignified human existence, as well as those qualities which distinguish otherness and alterity from autonomous existence. This is not to say that de Beauvoir did not attach an utter importance to the economic and material condition of women. She continuously argued that a woman can achieve true autonomy only through the practice of an independent profession. However, authentic expression of needs is a necessary mediation between love and autonomy.

With all its philosophical connotations, the connection between authentic self-expression and independence ring intimate and psychologically close. It reveals an unspoken dimension of human experience which needs to be further explored and understood.

Whether inhibited self-expression indeed captures the core of women's inner experience of dependency in our society is an empirical question for another study. Nonetheless, de Beauvoir's autobiography does demand our reconsideration of the concept of independence defined as self-reliance and dependency defined as its lack, and

calls our attention to the themes of spontaneity and authenticity of expression both in our interpersonal relations and in our sense of independence.

Notes

1. I shall not enter here into the discussion of whether autobiography is or is not a genre of introspective text. However, there are a number of good works which discuss the issue of self in autobiography. For example, see Estelle, J. (ed.), *Women's Autobiography: Essays in Criticism,* (London: Indiana University Press, 1980). Weintraub, K. J., *The Value of the Individual: Self and Circumstance in Autobiography,* (Chicago: Chicago University Press, 1978). Olney, J., *Autobiography: Essays Theoretical and Critical.* (Princeton, N.J.: Princeton University Press, 1980). Gunn, V. J., *Autobiography: Toward a Poetic of Experience,* (Philadelphia: University of Pennsylvania Press, 1982). In this paper I adopt Gunn's claims that modern autobiography is a text exposing a displayed self, temporal, historical, and within language. The legitimacy of reading de Beauvoir's autobiography for purposes of learning about women's experiences of dependency and independence is based upon the following reasons: (a) autobiography is an activity within life; (b) autobiography refers to a world which it claims to express; (c) this world is at least partially available to another; and (d) autobiography is an effort of discourse and a system of exchange between the autobiographer and the reader.

2. Even de Beauvoir herself indicates an awareness of the importance of unrepressed feelings. In an interview which took place in Rome in 1978, she told Alice Schwarzer (1984) that "Brecht's 'undignified old lady' was a woman who repressed her desire all her life and really let it rip." In contrast, testifying about herself, de Beauvoir said: "I have always spoken my mind as far as I have been able. I have always followed my desire and my impulses; in other words, I didn't suppress anything" (p. 84).

3. De Beauvoir distinguishes between femininity, which is a "condition brought about by society, on the basis of certain physiological characteristics," and womanhood, which is an existential condition (*PL*, p. 291).

References

Allport, C., The Use of Personal Documents in Psychological Science, prepared for the Committee on Appraisal of Research, Social Science Research Council, 1951.

Ascher, C., *Simone de Beauvoir: A Life of Freedom,* (Boston: Beacon Press, 1981).

De Beauvoir, S., *She Came to Stay,* (New York: Harper and Row, 1943).

———, *Memoirs of a Dutiful Daughter,* (New York: Harper and Row, 1958).

———, *The Prime of Life,* (New York: Harper and Row, 1960).

———, *Force of Circumstance,* (New York: Harper and Row, 1963).

———, *All Said and Done,* (New York: Harper and Row, 1972).

Gilligan, C., *In a Different Voice,* (Cambridge: Harvard University Press, 1982).

Hochschild, A., *The Managed Heart*, (Berkeley: University of California Press, 1983).

Heathers, G., "Acquiring Dependence and Independence: A Theoretical Orientation." *J. of Genetic Psychology*, 87 (1955) 277-291.

Keller, E. F., *Reflections on Gender and Science*, (New Haven: Yale University Press, 1985).

Kerenberg, O., "Mature Love: Prerequisites and Characteristics." *J. of American Psychoanalytic Association*, 22 (1974) 486-511.

McCall, D. K., "Simone de Beauvoir: The Second Sex, and Jean-Paul Sartre." *Signs: Journal of Women in Culture and Society*, 15 (1979) 209-223.

McClain, E., "Feminists and Nonfeminists: Contrasting Profiles in Independence and Affiliation." *Psychological Reports*, 43 (1978) 435-441.

Memmi, A., *Dependence: A Sketch for a Portrait of the Dependent*, (Boston: Beacon Press, 1984).

Miller, J. B., *Toward a New Psychology of Women*, (Boston: Beacon Press, 1976).

Miller, S., "The Politics of the true self." *Dissent*, 20 (1973) 93-98.

Schwartzer, A., *Simone de Beauvoir Today*, (London: Chatto and Windus, Hogarth Press, 1984).

Stiver, I., *The Meanings of 'Dependency' in Female-Male Relationships*, work in progress, No. 83-01, Wellesley College, 1984.

Trilling, L., *Sincerity and Authenticity*, (Cambridge, Mass.: Harvard University Press, 1972).

Turner, R., "The Real Self: From Institution to Impulse." *American J. of Sociology*, 81 (1976) 989-1016.

TITLE COMMENTARY

The Second Sex

JO-ANN P. FUCHS (ESSAY DATE SUMMER 1980)

SOURCE: Fuchs, Jo-Ann P. "Female Eroticism in *The Second Sex*." *Feminist Studies* 6, no. 2 (summer 1980): 304-13.

In the following essay, Fuchs finds Beauvoir's notions about female eroticism in The Second Sex *self-contradictory and sets out to correct the contradiction for contemporary feminists.*

In *The Second Sex*, Simone de Beauvoir presents in scattered form her own analysis of eroticism. It is an analysis which is at base existentialist and phenomenological, making use of the work of other contemporary French thinkers, and adding to this her own unique vision and sensitivity about woman's condition. The analysis was necessary, as she said more than once,[1] yet it

remained unfinished. My contention is that de Beauvoir's analysis unfortunately turned upon an internal contradiction that she did not see and that we need to understand so that our own thinking can transcend the contradiction we inherit from her, when we read *The Second Sex.*

Eroticism

For de Beauvoir, eroticism is that dimension of human existence that has to do with the sexual, but always insofar as it denotes a situation and a lived experience, not a collection of genital facts. "The body is not a thing, it is a situation," she says, acknowledging a debt to Heidegger, Sartre, and Merleau-Ponty (p. 30). Eroticism cannot be reduced to mere energy, or reflex, but should be understood as a form of *desire*, which is, in its turn, the choice of a human consciousness.[2] The essential character of eroticism, for de Beauvoir, is a movement toward the other (p. 420). What will be discovered in this movement is not only that I am flesh, but that I am an active consciousness as well—in short, I discover the "ambiguity" of the human condition.[3]

The erotic may include, but certainly need not include, love. A lesson that de Beauvoir teaches well—particularly in her novels—is the evil of the dependency of woman and, relatedly, how perfect a medium the emotion of love is for this. She finds the woman in love a necessarily conflicted human being, first because of the nature of love itself, and second because of the ease with which love becomes a real trap for a woman, to the extent that it provides her with a reason for being satisfied with less than freedom. So ". . . love represents in its most touching form the curse that lies heavily upon woman confined in the feminine universe, woman mutilated, insufficient unto herself" (p. 629).

Eroticism in The Second Sex

In *The Second Sex*, there are extensive comments on female eroticism, occurring primarily in the chapters on psychoanalysis (chapter 2) and sexual initiation (chapter 14). De Beauvoir relies heavily on the existentialist categories of transcendence and immanence to define the relationship of female to male sexuality. Also, her analysis focuses largely on heterosexuality, except in the chapter on lesbianism.

Transcendence, the forward-movement into the future of a willing subject, struggles with the urge toward immanence that also tempts the subject. This struggle de Beauvoir had analyzed in *The Ethics of Ambiguity.* In *The Second Sex,* she puts it this way:

> Every subject plays his part as such specifically through exploits or projects that serve as a mode of transcendence; he achieves liberty only through a continual reaching out toward other liberties. . . . Every time transcendence falls back into immanence, stagnation, there is a degradation of existence. . . .
>
> [P. xxviii]

Her description of woman carries out the existentialist approach mentioned earlier in regard to her notion of eroticism. Woman is defined as "a human being in quest of values in a world of values, a world of which it is indispensable to know the economic and social structure" (p. 47). The body itself is described as a situation, the particular one which makes possible our grasp on the world (p. 29). A person is a sexual body, better, a "sexuate" body because sexuality is not a part of the person, "appended" to a human being, but the human being is a totality, and sexuality is one dimension of this totality.

In the chapter on psychoanalysis, de Beauvoir asserts that psychoanalysis lacks this understanding of the human being as totality. She claims that for psychoanalysis, sexuality is an irreducible datum, and human existence is mistakenly understood always in terms of this irreducible datum, rather than in terms of the transcendence that can be accomplished by a human being which is always a totality.

But de Beauvoir's rejection of Freudianism is itself hardly complete. In order to retain some of its notions concerning sexuality in women, she uses the idea of "constant," that is, "certain factors of undeniable generality and repetition" (p. 42), which can be found in every individual case. But these "constants" are not "eternals"; they last as long as any particular epoch, according to de Beauvoir; we might call them "epochal," not eternal, truths; thus within the patriarchal epoch, it is a "truth" that the phallus is a symbol of transcendence (p. 43). It is in keeping with the power of men within a patriarchal society that the male sexual organ "means" liberty, and symbolizes the flight from facticity, from immanence, which is the human enterprise. Within patriarchal society, men are not unique in engaging in transcendence, but because they are the sex in power, they become the sex in which the properly human—transcendence—and the genital symbolically merge. Woman, a transcendent being also in that she is human, is continually denied access to

ABOUT THE AUTHOR

BEAUVOIR'S CONCEPT OF LIBERATION

In her early writings, de Beauvoir believed the decision for freedom could be a matter of individual choice—"a radical conversion." One needed only to come to the understanding of the falseness of one's life and make the leap. After World War II, and in the years of the Cold War, de Beauvoir modified her vision to include a more concrete notion of social forces. In *The Ethics of Ambiguity,* and again in *The Second Sex,* she developed the ideas of oppression, on the one hand, and of liberation, on the other. Transcendence is the move of the individual projecting him or herself toward freedom. But when "transcendence is condemned to fall uselessly back upon itself because it is cut off from its goals," this "is what defines a situation of oppression." For the oppressed, no act of radical conversion is possible, since *others* cut them off from their freedom. Thus the oppressed has "only one solution: to deny the harmony of that mankind from which an attempt is made to exclude him, to prove that he is a man and that he is free by revolting against the tyrants." This social act toward freedom is liberation.

Ascher, Carol. An excerpt from *Simone de Beauvoir . . . A Life of Freedom.* Boston: Beacon Press, 1981.

subjecthood through her life situation in general. For woman then, transcendence will be seen as a personal *and* cultural triumph.

Further, for de Beauvoir this sexist oppression has turned woman into an "imperfect being," to use Thomas Aquinas's phrase, and this means sexual as well as intellectual, metaphysical, and psychological imperfection. Woman within patriarchal society is a creature "intermediate between male and eunuch" she says (p. 249), not a fully but only a partially sexed being, because she is not a phallic creature.

De Beauvoir claims that it is to Freud's credit that he maintains that for woman, unlike man, there are two distinct erotic systems at work: the clitoral and the vaginal. With this fact, woman's erotic history as well as her erotic problems commence. Before woman reaches sexual maturity, she must not only pass through the narcissistic phase (at puberty), but she must also go through a second transition, from the clitoral to the vaginal. De Beauvoir's notion of "constant" is at work here again, in her acceptance of the Freudian analysis of a general path of psychogenital development for women—for all women.

The phallocentrism of Freudian thinking is destructive to a thorough analysis of women, but not simply because it is modeled on male sexuality. It has, according to de Beauvoir, prevented the study of female eroticism in its own right. The male libido has become not only the model of sexuality, but it has also acted as the *mask* over the female libido.

Within the pages of **The Second Sex,** de Beauvoir indeed attempts a description of female eroticism. The starting point for her analysis, an existentialist-via-Hegel one,[4] is the idea that eroticism is, in its essential character, "a movement toward the Other" (p. 420). But this creates a problem for woman because she is continually made, or making herself, object, not subject (p. 381). In a striking statement of this fact, de Beauvoir tells us: "Woman, like man, is her body; but her body is something other than herself" (p. 26). Yet as an erotic creature she will have to extend herself to the Other. This amounts to a kind of "aggressiveness"—a will to be more than passive flesh, more than immanence. Woman does still have an ability to be aggressive erotically because she is never reduced finally and forever to the status of object, yet her eroticism becomes, and can remain, a source of ontological confusion to her, due to her being-made-object and not being-made-subject. She is required to *be* passively, but must at the same time *be* actively, in an erotic experience. Carnality and subjectivity simultaneously will be no easy task for woman. The hardest fight, clearly, involves her subjectivity.

Woman's erotic experience, de Beauvoir maintains, is nearly always the experience of passivity. The strength of her assertion of woman's passivity cannot be underestimated. It is extreme. Woman feels the "shame of her flesh," when gazed at, more than man, and she "feels trespassed upon in her flesh" (pp. 357, 366). "She always feels passive; she *is* caressed, penetrated; she undergoes coition, whereas the man exerts himself actively" (p. 361). Woman requires a man to reveal to woman her own body; she is therefore more reliant on him than he on her. She is from the begin-

ning not her own sexual being, but becomes her own through being his—to the extent that she ever becomes her own.

We can easily enough understand the source of de Beauvoir's assertion that the phallus is a symbolic organ of transcendence, and, for woman, of domination as well, but she is not careful enough so that occasionally it seems that she wants to claim that the phallus is both a symbolic and *real* organ of domination, both a symbolic and *real* organ of transcendence.

The contrast continues. We can read in another place: "The sex organ of a man is simple and neat as a finger; it is readily visible . . . but the feminine sex organ is mysterious even to the woman herself, concealed, mucous, and humid as it is. . . . Woman does not recognize herself in it . . ."(p. 362).

De Beauvoir provides a striking metaphor to carry her theory. "Feminine sex desire is the soft throbbing of a mollusk" (p. 362), thus it is similar to an animal that lacks a backbone, and with a soft and unsegmented body. I discovered that Sartre had said, six years earlier in *Being and Nothingness*: "I desire a human being, not an insect or a mollusk. . . ."[5] De Beauvoir seems to be replying: "What one receives, however, is a mollusk!" Woman's erotic experience is thus characterized by de Beauvoir as primarily vaginal—for the "soft throbbing of a mollusk" is a clear reference to the vulva, and it is from this that all female eroticism is claimed to emanate.

The Blood of Others, a novel de Beauvoir published earlier, in 1945, contains a fascinating and similar description of one woman's erotic experience, a gradual metamorphosis from woman, to plant, to spongy moss, to jellyfish, enveloped always in darkness and vapors, becoming less and less capable of voluntary movement.[6] The female erotic subject she describes becomes more uncomfortable as she finds herself becoming like an object in the natural world, a status particularly threatening to woman, and, consequently, she fights against this "naturizing/objectifying" process. To continue her metaphors, we could say the woman "seeks to retain the stark light of subjectivity against the dark and spongy forest world of the female flesh."

It is disappointing that de Beauvoir never acknowledges, to any extent, the other erotic areas of a woman's body. The dependence on the "mollusk" metaphor is what leads her to the cliché that woman's sexuality is inward, mysterious, and unlocalized. By calling attention to the more inward and invisible nature of woman's genitalia, she claims therefore that, sexually, woman is something she can neither see nor understand. Her "wetness" and her bleeding—both signs of her sexuality, erotic and nonerotic (or reproductive)—are dismissed as alienations from, not realizations of, her sexuality.

> Woman lies in wait like the carnivorous plant, the bog, in which insects and children are swallowed up. She is absorption, suction, humus, pitch and glue, a passive influx, insinuating and viscous; thus, at least, she vaguely feels herself to be. Hence it is that there is in her not only resistance to the subjugating intentions of the male, but also conflict within herself.
>
> [P. 362]

And this conflict within herself will bring about on more than one occasion considerable disgust, even physical disgust, both for her own erotic being and for sex in general.

But we need to call de Beauvoir's descriptions into question. If woman's eroticism is "unsegmented" in quality, like a mollusk, it is because it has not been "segmented" intellectually, and verbally, by a culture that treats female sexuality as, precisely, mystery. And this is precisely the way de Beauvoir herself treats it.[7] Because she fails to go beyond cultural stereotypes of woman's eroticism, she leaves us no richer on this topic than we were prior to reading *The Second Sex.* Stopping at the wall of mystery that has been built around woman's sexuality, she articulates for us only the message of a patriarchal culture: passivity, immanence, oppression lived in the erotic night, as well as in the day.

The generalized, unlocalized sexuality and consequent passivity that woman is forced into leads de Beauvoir, dialectically, to assert that woman's general erotic experience is characterized by its stronger intensity than man's; she says that, in lovemaking, woman "loses her mind." Because the very goal of eroticism for woman is itself uncertain according to de Beauvoir, so too her enjoyment as it occurs "radiates throughout her whole body" (p. 371), that is, again, her enjoyment is not localized, nor is woman conscious that her genital organs are the center of this experience.

It is because female eroticism is distinctively a general, totalized body state, unlike man's, that she says women are often repulsed by the too obvious attempts to help them achieve orgasm. Due to her own special form of eroticism, woman wants the achievement of a spell. "She would abolish all surroundings, abolish the singularity of the moment, of herself, and of her lover, she would fain be lost in a carnal night . . ." (p. 372). In de Beauvoir's novel, *The Mandarins,* one can find described such a generalized, unlocalized female eroticism, and the corresponding desire for the creation and maintaining of a "spell."[8] Sexuality becomes a form of mindlessness.

Although de Beauvoir denies early in *The Second Sex* that anything human is totally innate, or totally "natural," she comes dangerously close, in her descriptions of female eroticism, to affirming what she should be denying, by her own standards. At a point where we would expect de Beauvoir to suggest social, historical, or cultural explanations for behavior, we find she avoids them.

Clearly, there are a variety of ways in which the individual may *actively* object to societal oppression—whether it is the oppression of a particular system of morality, as de Beauvoir brilliantly shows in her essay, *Must We Burn Sade?*, or the political oppression felt by a proletariat that eventually revolts, or the oppression of women, whose oppression/situation is unique within human history. We need to understand if woman's erotic passivity, suitable behavior for a patriarchal culture, is not also a protest—a political action, similar to the actions American slaves took, through their listless movements and pretended incompetencies. Is woman's erotic passivity a dimension of woman's political rebellion? De Beauvoir doesn't ask the question in *The Second Sex,* understandably, because the question itself is a product of *The Second Sex.* Further, one might place the body and sexuality in a cultural context, taking account of historical changes and political movements, like feminism, which have had tremendous effects on how woman lives her body, and consequently, her sexuality.

According to de Beauvoir, woman may overcome the erotic passivity that man and culture require of her in two ways. The first way would be by rejecting men permanently, to live out her erotic life with women, thus satisfying her sexuality as well as her ontological need to exercise her subjectivity, for she will be engaging her eroticism within an experience in which the roles are not always, already, determined according to gender. De Beauvoir claims that all women are *naturally* homosexual anyway. Women experience the female body as desirable largely because it was the locus of their first experience of sensuality—the mother—and because the culture has made of it the erotic object par excellence (p. 382). In addition, lesbianism is the form which an active eroticism may take because:

> Woman is an existent who is called upon to make herself object; as subject she has an aggressive element in her sensuality which is not satisfied on the male body: hence the conflicts that her eroticism must somehow overcome. . . . Woman's homosexuality is one attempt among others to reconcile her autonomy with the passivity of her flesh.
>
> [P. 381]

The second way woman may overcome the erotic passivity she experiences within patriarchal culture is through the creation, within heterosexual couples, of a *reciprocal* relationship between female and male, in order that woman's subjectivity be permitted and acknowledged, as her body is desired (p. 377). De Beauvoir displays too cavalier an attitude about the ease of achieving this state. Its content is also unclear. She provides a simplistic answer through her evocation of existentialist categories, which seem to operate merely as rhetoric. We must ask: how can one become an erotic subject if one is not a genuine subject already, that is, within the culture? And how does one escape the fear of cultural male domination even, in order to allow for the production of generosity and reciprocity in sexual intercourse?

Nonetheless, de Beauvoir has provided for the possibility of our thinking through human sexuality as one species differentiated into two "subsets"—female and male—rather than into two separate species. She asserts:

> As a matter of fact, man, like woman, is flesh, therefore passive, the plaything of his hormones and of the species, the restless prey of his desires. And she, like him, in the midst of the carnal fever, is a consenting, a voluntary gift, an activity; they live out in their several fashions the strange ambiguity of existence made body.
>
> [P. 685]

Focusing as it does on the mutuality of the difficulties and pleasures of human sexuality, this passage beautifully and succinctly demystifies sexuality. But it is, of course, only comprehensible as a utopian description of heterosexuality because it requires a state of equality between the sexes which doesn't yet exist, though among "verbal" political acts, no work has done more than *The Second Sex* to bring about such a state.

Beyond The Second Sex

The spectacular achievement of an eroticism not founded in domination will not be easy. It presupposes societal changes, as well as changes made directly by woman upon her own eroticism. In *Brigitte Bardot and the Lolita Syndrome,* published in 1960, de Beauvoir claimed that the real basis for Bardot's appeal lay in the new quality of female eroticism she displayed: an aggressiveness.[10] Bardot, in film after film, was every bit as much the erotic hunter as the male—a self-conscious being, innocent of tricks and in fact oblivious to the opinions of others. Her eroticism was intimidating to men, particularly French men because it was so unconventionally aggressive. Bardot: the ingenue with a woman's body and a sexual appetite we supposedly normally find only in men. The result of Bardot's presence on the screen in this role of erotic hunter has been a "debunking of love and eroticism," according to de Beauvoir, which has had tremendous implications for the demystification and humanization of woman's eroticism.

The age of Bardot has passed, and de Beauvoir's analysis seems problematic. What the sixties brought was a sexual revolution via the increased practice of free love. The availability of sex outside the strictures of marriage certainly increased for women; whether the quality of woman's sexual experience also increased, and her erotic "passivity" decreased, is questionable. In any case, if there were a lessening of female erotic "passivity," the women's movement of the late sixties and seventies would, I think, be largely responsible.

In the Conclusion to *The Second Sex,* de Beauvoir tells us that:

> there will always be certain differences between man and woman; her eroticism, and therefore her sexual world, have a special form of their own and therefore cannot fail to engender a sensuality, a sensitivity, of a special nature. This means that her relations to her own body, to that of the male, to the child, will never be identical with those (of) the male. . . .
>
> [P. 688]

It is at this point (the last full page of the book) that she was on the verge of concretely connecting for us woman's body/form and woman's eroticism.

Thus we need to begin at the point to which de Beauvoir led us, and where she unfortunately left off: with the description of a female erotic, a description of woman's "special sensuality," and with a comprehension of the relationship of human consciousness and human history to all of this. The specific task confronting feminist thinkers here is a comprehension of woman's lived-body which would include[11]: 1) the sensory systems of both the clitoral and vaginal areas, 2) the breasts, for woman, both as zones of erotic pleasure in themselves and as instruments within an erotic drama in which men participate, and are manipulated, 3) the female experience of the male body, 4) the female experience of the female body, and 5) the nature of woman's "unlimited" sexuality, as well as whether and how this is diminished through the controls and regularization of marriage, as de Beauvoir claimed (pp. 410, 418). Some of this has been addressed already in feminist poetry and novels. But more needs to be done.

Woman's victimization within a patriarchal society includes an elaborate intellectual system of silences constructed against the simple facts of her existence, to ignore her manner of being and invalidate her experience. We need to create (and it is a political act to do so) precise/essential/fundamental descriptions to "inform" the silences surrounding all aspects of female human existence. In particular, discovering what, in woman's eroticism, derives directly from the situation of oppression, what is derived from and determined by her bodily structure, and what dimensions woman's eroticism can hope to take on in a nonsexist world, become the basic issues of a feminist theory of eroticism.

Notes

The first version of this paper was presented to the Society for Phenomenology and Existential Philosophy at its 1978 meeting at Duquesne University, Pittsburgh, Pennsylvania. A second version was presented at The Second Sex Conference, sponsored by the New York Institute for the Humanities, at New York University, in September 1979. For this third version, I am grateful to the editors of *Feminist Studies* for their suggestions.

1. Simone de Beauvoir, *The Second Sex,* trans. H. M. Parshley (New York: Alfred A. Knopf, Bantam, 1952), pp. 44-45, 133. All references are to this edition, and page numbers will be supplied in parentheses in the text.

2. Jean-Paul Sartre, *Being and Nothingness,* trans. Hazel Barnes (New York: Philosophical Library, 1956), pp. 379-412.

3. In some cases, de Beauvoir uses "sexuality" to refer simply to the reproductive function, as in the chapter, "The Data of Biology," but in most cases, "sexuality" is used interchangeably with "eroticism." I will make use of this same interchange.

4. An important discussion of the Hegel-via-Kojève influence on de Beauvoir's thinking in *The Second Sex* was presented in Carol Craig's excellent paper at the workshop on "The Philosophical Writings of Simone de Beauvoir" at The Second Sex Conference, sponsored by the New York Institute for the Humanities, September 1979.

5. Sartre, *Being and Nothingness,* p. 384.

6. Simone de Beauvoir, *The Blood of Others,* trans. Roger Senhouse and Yvonne Moyse (New York: Alfred Knopf, Bantam, 1974), p. 86: "She felt enveloped in some pale, sickly vapor: she closed her eyes. She abandoned herself unresistingly to the charm that was slowly metamorphosing her into a plant; now she was a tree, a great silver poplar whose downy leaves were shaken by the summer breeze. A warm mouth clung to her mouth; under her blouse a hand caressed her shoulder, her breasts; warm vapors increased about her; she felt her bones and muscles melt, her flesh became a human and spongy moss . . . fingers wove a burning tunic about her belly; her breath came in quick gasps; . . . paralyzed by that net of burning silk . . . enclosed in that viscid darkness, forever an obscure and flabby jellyfish lying on a bed of magic sea-anemones. She pushed Paul away with both hands and sat up."

7. De Beauvoir had little to go on; the Kinsey Report (on female sexuality) was not published until 1953, and it in fact footnotes *The Second Sex* a number of times.

8. Simone de Beauvoir, *The Mandarins,* trans. Leonard M. Friedman (Cleveland: The World Publishing Co., Meridian Books, 1960), pp. 81-82: "I closed my eyes and stepped into a dream as lifelike as reality itself, a dream from which I felt I would awaken at dawn, carefree and lighthearted . . . I abandoned myself to the black swell of desire. Carried away, tossed about, submerged, aroused, dashed headlong; there were moments when I felt as if I were plummeting through empty space, were about to be stranded in oblivion, in the blackness of night. . . . Becoming aware of my flesh, seeing his unfamiliar face, and under his gaze losing myself within myself—I looked at him and was halted midway in my inner turmoil, in a region without light and without darkness, where I was neither body nor spirit . . . I delivered to his curiosity a slough which was neither cold nor warm."

9. Simone de Beauvoir, "Must We Burn Sade?", trans. Annette Michelson, *The Marquis de Sade: An Essay by Simone de Beauvoir, with Selections from His Writings Chosen by Paul Dinnage* (New York: Grove Press, Inc., Evergreen, 1954), p. 40.

10. Simone de Beauvoir, *Brigitte Bardot and the Lolita Syndrome,* trans. Bernard Frechtman (New York: Arno Press and The New York Times, 1972), p. 37.

11. The descriptive task I mention here, a feminist phenomenology of eroticism as I see it, needs to be clearly differentiated from pornography—the subject of another paper.

JUDITH OKELY (ESSAY DATE 1986)

SOURCE: Okely, Judith. "Rereading *The Second Sex*." In *Simone de Beauvoir: A Critical Reader,* edited by Elizabeth Fallaize, pp. 20-28. New York: Routledge, 1998.

In the following essay, originally published in 1986, Okely considers how elements of The Second Sex *have withstood the passage of time and how the book furthers development of feminist thought.*

Though de Beauvoir's study now reads differently both for her past and her new readers, the earlier reading cannot be easily jettisoned. The book is part of some women's personal history and part of the history of feminism. This double reading, then and now, is the rationale for my selection of certain themes for a critical discussion.

De Beauvoir's central section on mythology proved startling and evocative to a young woman like myself in the early 1960s. Today, thanks partly to anthropology and to feminists' interrogation of the subject and greater awareness of race and class, it is easier to recognise that de Beauvoir's generalisations fit neither all cultures nor all women. Women readers whose experience in no way approximated that of de Beauvoir were undoubtedly sceptical long ago. From the myths, I have selected for critical discussion those concerned with the female body and sexuality: matters which women now feel freer to talk and write about. De Beauvoir's examination of five male authors stands better the test of time. She initiated a way of looking at 'great' literature from a woman's perspective and there is now a serious body of work in feminist literary criticism. I have also recreated some of my past enthusiasm and mixed response to her text.

In the last decade, a number of women have been concerned to consolidate a theoretical approach to feminism. While the attempt to find the 'origins' or 'first cause' of women's subordination has been largely abandoned, greater emphasis is now placed on explanations for women's continuing subordination and the conditions that could change it. As part of this enterprise, feminists have re-examined Marx and Freud. De Beauvoir's interpretation of these two theorists therefore requires comment. Her extensive debate with biological explanations is of continuing and crucial relevance since the resurgence of sociobiologism in the last decade. The implications of the biological difference between males and females have provoked debates both within feminism and outside it. Considerable space is therefore devoted to various biological explanations and a closer reading of de Beauvoir's text.

My general comments on Volume II of **The Second Sex** invite the reader to place her detailed ethnography of women's lives in a specific context. From this volume, I have selected de Beauvoir's discussion of early childhood which contrasts with her more generalised comments on psychoanalysis and social influences in Volume I. Inevitably the record here of a re-reading has to be selective and cannot do justice to de Beauvoir's enterprise of encyclopaedic proportions.[1]

In Volume II de Beauvoir does not make use of statistical or in-depth social science studies of women; the latter appeared in strength only from the late 1960s. Instead she draws on the representation of women's experience in psychoanalysts' case studies and literature, especially those written by women. Parshley [the American translator] has tended to retain the evidence from the former and cut the latter. The other major source is personal observation and experience. Insights into the young girl were drawn both from her own past and from many years of teaching in girls' lycées. De Beauvoir sometimes gives examples of friends and acquaintances to back up her argument, making use of the 'continual interest' which she and Sartre had had for many years in 'all sorts of people; my memory provided me with an abundance of material' (**FC**, p. 196). Her autobiographies in fact reveal how restricted her acquaintance was with people outside café society and the bourgeoisie.

De Beauvoir has in part done an anthropological village study of specific women, but without the anthropological theory and focus. Her village is largely mid-century Paris and the women studied, including herself, are mainly middle class. There are almost no references to working-class urban women and only rare glimpses of the rural, peasant women who still made up the majority of French women at that time. There is just one striking discussion of the burden of the peasant woman in post-war France in the history section (**SS**, p. 165). Despite this hidden subjectivity, her observations and her recourse to historical, literary and psychoanalytical documentation raise questions beyond the local study. A paradoxical strength is the hidden use of herself as a case study, and it was one to which many of her women readers intuitively responded. Although in the text she never uses the word 'I' in a personal example, we can, when we examine her autobiography written nearly ten years later, see the link between her own experience and some of her generalised statements about the girl and woman.

Myths and Ideology

The discussion of the myths which surround 'woman' is the core to Volume I. As with her treatment of other aspects, its strength lies in its focused *description* rather than in any convincing *explanation* or first cause of women's subordination. Some later feminists have read the section only for an explanation of women's subordination and thus missed its cumulative impact.[2]

Whether or not she has been misread and simplified, ideas from this section are frequently referred to by feminists and others. De Beauvoir's words hold the imagination by pointing to powerful symbols of 'the feminine' and either explicitly or implicitly challenge their truth. Her description is not neutral, but accompanied by a mocking value judgement. Certain repetitive themes in different ideologies about women are systematically collected together, but de Beauvoir is most convincing in the treatment of western culture. Her description reminds the reader of a long tradition of the 'earth mother' and the 'eternal feminine' which, she argues, while purporting to be laudatory towards woman, is thoroughly dehumanising. The myths which present woman as a powerful symbol mask her effective powerlessness. De Beauvoir's women readers could learn that western myths which were so often said to be complimentary to themselves were only mystifications; that is, they served to mask the truth of women's objective subordination and oppression.

The opening pages try to link the myths of the feminine to existentialist concepts which de Beauvoir has refined by introducing a gender difference. 'Man' needs 'Others' to affirm his existence and to break away from immanence. He engages in projects to achieve transcendence. The female is used by the male as this 'Other' and she remains the object; she never becomes the subject. De Beauvoir does not convincingly explain why woman never becomes the subject, she merely asserts this, yet she described a painful truth of her time.

There are oblique references to Hegel's 'master-slave dialectic', although she does not always bother to name him. She develops Hegel's ideas by contrasting the position of the slave with that of woman. Whereas in Hegel's view the slave is able also to see himself as subject or 'essential' in his struggle with the master, de Beauvoir asserts that woman is in a worse position because she does not see herself as subject and cannot, like the slave, ever see the master (man) as inessential. Whereas the slave can supersede the master, apparently woman cannot supersede man by the same means. In de Beauvoir's view, woman cannot reach the necessary consciousness for emancipation. It is this use of Hegel which later feminist theorists have teased out of de Beauvoir's text in their analysis of her underlying theoretical position.[3] If woman is deprived even of the potential victory attained by a slave, then it seems that de Beauvoir's message is that woman can never win freedom for herself, except perhaps by some independent change in society and the 'master' male.

If indeed de Beauvoir's Hegelian theory is taken as the major if not sole message of *The Second Sex*, then it would seem that all she is saying is that woman's subordinate state is fixed. But few of de Beauvoir's readers were aware of such embedded theoretical implications. Today it is certainly important to make explicit de Beauvoir's theoretical underpinnings; however, it should not be concluded that these were the key contributions to a past feminist reading of *The Second Sex*.

In contrast to de Beauvoir's preceding examination of biology, psychology, economics and history, the section on myths explores a process whereby women's subordination is continually reaffirmed or 'overdetermined' through ideology. Whether or not de Beauvoir is offering these ideas about women as causes or consequences of women's subordination, she should be credited for pointing to recurrent aspects of the myth of woman, especially in European culture. De Beauvoir sharpened scepticism in her reader.

That woman is the 'Other' is devastatingly stated:

> Since women do not present themselves as subject, they have no virile myth in which their prospects are reflected; they have neither religion nor poetry which belongs to themselves in their own right. It is still through the dreams of men that they dream. It is the gods fabricated by males which they adore.
>
> (*DS* I, p. 235)

The representation of the world, like the world itself, is the work of men; they describe it from the point of view which is theirs and which they confuse with the absolute truth (*DS* I, p. 236).

Whereas de Beauvoir's comments on much of European Christian ideology are fairly systematic, her tendency towards generalisations is very misleading when she strays into cultures in another time and space. De Beauvoir selects from social anthropology cross-cultural examples which confirm her argument and avoids reference to the many available counter-examples. To be fair, she does attempt some broad distinctions between Islam, Graeco-Roman culture and Christianity. But otherwise, random cases are plucked from India, Egypt and Oceania, with only occasional counter-examples.

Indeed, the text oscillates between a defiant angry declaration that woman is always 'Other' and a subdued acknowledgement that this view of women may be eclipsed by the presence of some non-female idols in the course of history (*DS* I, p. 234). For example, under dictatorships, oman may no longer be a privileged object, and in the 'authentic democratic society' advocated by Marx, de Beauvoir observes there is no place for 'the Other'. This recognition of broad differences is modified when she notes that Nazi soldiers held to the cult of female virginity and that communist writers like Aragon created a special place for woman. De Beauvoir hopes that the myth of woman will one day be extinguished: 'the more that women affirm themselves as human beings, the more the wondrous quality of the Other will die in them. But today it still exists in the heart of *all* men' (*DS* I, p. 235; my emphasis). This last sentence reveals her continuing need to conclude with a pan-cultural generalisation.

While she is ambivalent as to whether woman as 'Other' is a universal, she states that 'the Other' is itself ambiguous. It is evil, but 'being necessary for good' it returns to good. Woman embodies 'no fixed concept' (*DS* I, p. 236). In this way, de Beauvoir can explain the apparently conflicting fantasies which women are believed to embody for men. One of these myths is the association of woman with nature. There is a double aspect to this. Nature can be seen as mind, will and transcendence as well as matter, passivity and immanence. On the one hand nature is mind, on the other it is flesh. As evidence for the latter view of nature de Beauvoir looks back to the classical Greek scholars (for example Aristotle), who asserted that only the male is the true creator, while female fertility is merely passive; that is, that woman is the passive earth while man is the seed.

De Beauvoir's examination of classical European writers was helpful to both western and non-western women in exposing the mystification of 'woman' in a long-standing tradition. It was harder for de Beauvoir to look beyond the traditions of her own culture, especially when she had to rely on less accessible sources for a view of nature elsewhere. She offered some examples from India which compare the earth to a mother, but random selections do not prove the universality of any such principle; moreover, her example from Islamic texts where woman is called a field or grapevine (*DS* I, p. 238) is an image from *agriculture* not wild nature. The two are certainly not the same.

Despite these errors, de Beauvoir systematically outlines a dominant European tradition which, since the eighteenth-century Enlightenment, sees nature as inferior to culture.[4] Her suggestions about women and nature have stimulated anthropologists to think about the association.[5]

De Beauvoir's link between women and nature is not as absolute as some of her successors have tried to make it.[6] More recently, anthropologists have given examples from other cultures which challenge any pan-cultural generalisation.[7] For example, Olivia Harris has argued that Indians of the Bolivian Highlands equate the married couple with 'culture' and unmarried persons with 'nature'; the nature-culture opposition is thus not linked simplistically to a gender opposition.[8]

As elsewhere, de Beauvoir proceeds through the stages of a woman's life. Here, they are examined in the light of external ideology rather than of a woman's concrete experience. Women as a group may comply with and internalise these beliefs as if they were 'natural'. Whereas de Beauvoir tries to suggest that much of the ideology is universal, it was in fact her revelation that this was mere belief, mere myth, which was so powerful to her early readers. Insofar as western women were indoctrinated to believe that they might represent 'mother earth', the 'eternal feminine', erotic temptress or virgin purity, de Beauvoir dismantled these images. Some of us could recognise apparently individual fantasies about ourselves as part of an overarching tradition made outside us, not born with us; the fantasies were historical, not fixed. The problem for us was how to throw them off. Non-western women, by contrast, gained a novel critical perspective on western ideology which was seen even more as one to reject.

In searching for the basis for certain ideas and myths of woman, de Beauvoir seizes upon woman's capacity to gestate. Her approach is rooted in the European Cartesian tradition which separates mind from body. Man apparently would like to be a pure Idea, absolute Spirit, but his fate is to be trapped in the 'chaotic shadows of the maternal belly . . . it is woman who imprisons him in the mud of the earth' (*DS* I, p. 239). De Beauvoir compares the womb to 'quivering jelly which evokes the soft viscosity of carrion' (*DS* I, p. 239). 'Wherever life is in the making—germination, fermentation—it arouses disgust . . . the slimy embryo begins the cycle that is completed in the putrefaction of death' (*SS*, p. 178). These extraordinary references to viscosity and slime echo Sartre's extensive discussion of viscous substance both in *Nausea* (1938) and in *Being and Nothingness* (1943) and some of his own personal disgust with aspects of the sexual body (see *Adieux*, 1981).

In aiming to deconstruct the myth of the feminine, de Beauvoir thus naively reproduces her male partner's and lover's ideas about the female body, while possibly deceiving herself that these are objective and fixed philosophical truths. As in her discussion of biology, she is on dubious ground in suggesting that bodily parts inevitably arouse the same feelings (of disgust) in all individuals and all cultures. She is implying it is 'natural' to look at 'nature' in a specific way. In fact she reveals the extent to which she has internalised both the views of her own culture and the extreme reactions of Sartre.

Her problematic assertions are compounded when she makes unsubstantiated generalisations about primitive people's attitudes to childbirth. In her text such people are an undifferentiated lump and she repeats a clichéd belief that their attitudes to childbirth are always surrounded by the most severe taboos. It is interesting to be informed that childbirth in a number of different societies is subject to elaborate ritual; the danger comes when de Beauvoir implies either that taboos vary according to an evolutionary 'progress' or that attitudes to birth are unvaried. De Beauvoir asserts that all the ancient codes demand purification rites from women in confinement, and that gestation always inspires a 'spontaneous repulsion' (*DS* I, p. 240).

De Beauvoir thus falls into the trap of suggesting that gestation is *naturally* and universally disgusting. Her evidence about so-called primitives is suspect, first because even 'taboos' do not necessarily reflect disgust, and second because a people's cultural treatment of childbirth is linked to differences in descent, marriage and kinship systems and control over offspring. De Beauvoir's assertion that disgust at gestation is spontaneous speaks more of herself and her own time. Today I can criticise de Beauvoir for her suspect generalisation about humanity's spontaneous psychological reactions to the physicality of childbirth, but some twenty years ago I underlined it.

De Beauvoir makes similar sweeping statements about menstruation. She maintains that in all civilisations woman inspires in man the horror of his own carnal 'contingence'—she reminds him of his mortality. This, according to de Beauvoir, is confirmed by an assertion that everywhere before puberty the young girl is without taboo. It is only after her first menstruation that she becomes impure and is then surrounded by taboos. De Beauvoir then offers a random collection of menstrual 'taboos' from Leviticus, Egypt, India,

nineteenth-century Britain and France to support this suspect generalisation.

In the 1950s and 1960s this made interesting reading, but it is perilously close to an old-fashioned type of anthropology, exemplified in Frazer's *The Golden Bough,* in which customs are lumped together for their superficial similarity, although in fact they are meaningless when torn from their different contexts. By contrast, a few detailed examples of menstrual taboos in specific cultures are more informative for placing them in context. De Beauvoir does indeed give three such extended examples, but these are excluded by Parshley (*DS* I, pp. 243-6).

In de Beauvoir's view, the taboos associated with menstruation 'express the horror which man feels for feminine fertility' (*DS* I, p. 247). This emphasis on 'horror' is little different from the now discredited view that primitive people's rituals are merely a response to 'fear'. Today, after a wider anthropological reading on these menstrual 'issues' across cultures, I can criticise de Beauvoir's explanation, but I have also to recognise that in 1961 I underlined that single sentence above. Both female writer and reader identified with a myth that woman's body and blood inspired horror and believed it as fact, not fiction. Thus neither de Beauvoir nor the female reader escaped the myths of her own culture.

The myths associated with virginity and the drama of defloration are also discussed by de Beauvoir in terms of psychological fear. Sometimes, de Beauvoir vaguely suggests that customs surrounding defloration have 'mystical' causes, as if this were sufficient explanation. De Beauvoir is at the mercy of outdated European explanations for ritual, partly because any systematic study of rituals associated with women had to await a feminist anthropology.

In recent decades, anthropologists have looked at rituals associated with menstruation, virginity, defloration, pregnancy and childbirth and the connections between a group's specific control over women's sexuality or fertility and the material context. In some societies menstruation will be merely a private event and without ritual taboo. In some cases childbirth and the arrival of a new member to the group will be publicly significant and so marked by ritual elaboration or specific taboos.[9]

De Beauvoir's discussion of the control of women's sexuality and reproduction cross-culturally is in places thoroughly misleading, but in its time it told us about some of the strongest taboos in a specific Judaeo-Christian culture, if not class. In 1961 I underlined in painful recognition her psychological explanation as to the relative importance of virginity:

> Depending whether man feels crushed by the forces which encircle him or whether he proudly believes himself capable of annexing them, he either refuses or demands that his wife be handed over as a virgin.
>
> (*DS* I, p. 250)

In the 1980s the western bourgeois demand for a virgin wife has all but disintegrated, and *not* because the male has miraculously overcome some innate mystical fear. Changes in attitudes towards female virginity coincide with changes in attitudes to sexuality and marriage and even advances in the technology of birth control. In the early 1960s, as a virgin, I could not see that the bourgeois cult of virginity depended only on the social and historical context. In those days, de Beauvoir's critical discussion of virginity had maximum impact precisely because she mistakenly argued that it was widely valued in a variety of cultures. Today, we may be more concerned to point to the many counter-examples in order to argue, as she intended, for alternative freedoms. There is a demand for specific case studies rather than broad and inaccurate generalisations.

Inevitably the author's own culture was the most closely observed. It is therefore not surprising that de Beauvoir should suggest that the most disturbing image of woman as 'the Other' is found in Christianity: 'It is in her that are embodied the temptations of the earth, sex and the devil' (*DS* I, p. 270). In the margin I exclaimed 'et on m'a fait Chrétienne!' ('And they made me a Christian woman!'). De Beauvoir, the former Catholic, suggests that all Christian literature intensifies 'the disgust which man can feel for woman' (*DS* I, p. 270), and her examples from modern male writers show the continuing tradition. Again, as elsewhere, she presumed this disgust to be universal and innate. Thus she had not fully freed herself of her own indoctrination into Christianity when she asserted that its ingredients were general to all societies. But for the reader of the 1950s and early 1960s, de Beauvoir's selection of western traditions, when juxtaposed with a splatter of historical and cross-cultural examples, had a powerful effect. Dominant western beliefs were exposed as of no greater truth than other beliefs and customs.

References and notes

FC Force of Circumstance, Harmondsworth, Penguin, 1965.

SS The Second Sex, Harmondsworth, Penguin, 1972.

DS I/DS II Le Deuxième Sexe, vol. I/vol. II, Paris, Gallimard, 1949 (Okely's translations).

1. See also Okely, 'Sexuality and Biology in *The Second Sex*', paper given to the Social Anthropology Inter-Collegiate Seminar, London University, 1984.

2. See for example M. Barrett, *Women's Oppression Today*, London, Verso, 1980.

3. For example C. Craig, 'Simone de Beauvoir's *The Second Sex* in the light of the Hegelian Master-Slave Dialectic and Sartrean Existentialism', PhD, University of Edinburgh, 1979.

4. See J. and M. Bloch, 'Women and the Dialectics of Nature in Eighteenth-century Thought' in C. McCormack and M. Strathern (eds), *Nature, Culture and Gender*, Cambridge, Cambridge University Press, 1980.

5. See E. Ardener, 'Belief and the Problem of Women', in E. Ardener (ed.), *Perceiving Women*, London, Dent, 1975.

6. For example S. Ortener, 'Is Female to Male as Nature is to Culture?', in M. Rosaldo and L. Lamphere (eds), *Woman, Culture and Society*, Stanford, Stanford University Press, 1974.

7. McCormack and Strathern, *Nature, Culture and Gender*.

8. O. Harris, 'Complementarity and Conflict: An Andean View of Women and Men', in J. La Fontaine (ed.), *Sex and Age as Principles of Social Differentiation*, London, Academic Press, 1978; and 'The Power of Signs: Gender, Culture and the Wild in the Bolivian Andes', in McCormack and Strathern, *Nature, Culture and Gender*.

9. See J. La Fontaine, 'Ritualisation of Women's Life Crises in Bugisu', in *The Interpretation of Ritual*, London, Tavistock, 1972. See also J. Okely, *The Traveller Gypsies*, Cambridge, Cambridge University Press, 1983.

Memoirs of a Dutiful Daughter

ALEX HUGHES (ESSAY DATE APRIL 1994)

SOURCE: Hughes, Alex. "Murdering the Mother: Simone de Beauvoir's *Mémoires d'une jeune fille rangée*." *French Studies* 48, no. 2 (April 1994): 174-83.

In the following essay, Hughes discusses the theme of matricide in Memoirs of a Dutiful Daughter.

In her provocative essay 'Death Sentences: Writing Couples and Ideology', Alice Jardine suggests that Beauvoir's *Une mort très douce* and her *Cérémonie des adieux* emblematize 'the poetics of an ideology that insists upon killing the mother'.[1] Jardine's argument is that in these texts, the maternal body is dissected, exorcized and purified through language, so that Beauvoir may continue to write and may simultaneously preserve the integrity of a disembodied textual realm in which she is definitively shielded from the snares of the maternal/material. It is easy to see how Jardine's thesis is applicable to *Une mort très douce,* since this text charts the (shocking) physical disintegration of Beauvoir's mother Françoise; however, Jardine's perception of *La Cérémonie des adieux,* Beauvoir's farewell to Sartre, as a 'matricidal' work is unexpected, to say the least. Jardine justifies her reading of Beauvoir's last autobiographical volume as an assault upon the maternal body by positing its key player, the moribund Sartre, as a 'maternal' entity—as a 'phallic', rather than biological, mother. The concept of the phallic mother, to which I shall return in the course of my discussion, is Freudian in origin,[2] but is more developed in the work of Julia Kristeva who, as Jardine indicates, theorizes maternal phallicity as 'an organizing fantasy for the denial of sexual difference'.[3] Broadly speaking, the phallic mother, in Freudian terms, constitutes, as Jane Gallop explains, 'the pre-Oedipal mother, apparently omniscient and omnipotent, until the "discovery of her castration", the discovery that she is not a "whole" but a "hole"'.[4]

Jardine's foregrounding of Sartre's phallic/maternal status (the basis for which will be indicated below) permits her to interpret *La Cérémonie des adieux,* as much as *Une mort très douce,* as a vehicle for Beauvoir's matricidal impulses, and to take both texts as evidence that Beauvoir represents a classic example of a woman author operating within a 'masculine' writing economy which necessitates a rejection of the Mother and an identification with the Father. Jardine concludes her discussion with a series of questions. These are destined to encourage her readers to reflect upon whether, in a culture predicated upon the Oedipal Family Romance and the act of symbolic matricide that subtends it, it is possible (for Beauvoir? for any woman? for anyone at all?) to write 'without dismembering the female body; without killing other women in the name of epistemological purity; without killing our mothers, the mother in us?'.[5] This article represents an effort to respond to Jardine's inquiry. In it I focus on the treatment meted out to the mother, and to her substitutes/doubles, in Beauvoir's first autobiographical work, and endeavour

to establish whether the *Mémoires d'une jeune fille rangée* constitute, in the last analysis, a 'matricidal' opus. A focal point of my discussion will be the significance of the stories to which Beauvoir was exposed in childhood and adolescence and which she retells as she weaves the narrative of her youth; stories which attest to her deepest and most secret preoccupations.

In the opening section of Beauvoir's *récit,* it becomes quickly apparent that the relationship between the young Simone and her mother was characterized, in its early stages, by intersubjective interpenetration, continuity and entanglement. That the two women shared a 'mirror-bond' of peculiar intensity should come, perhaps, as no surprise, particularly to readers familiar with the work of Luce Irigaray and Nancy Chodorow, both of whom claim—albeit for different reasons—that the dynamics of the mother/daughter relation are predicated upon specularity, symbiotic identity and boundary merging, and fusionality.[6] It seems at first that Beauvoir merely offers us a detached account of the symbiotic tie that bound her to her maternal parent during her childhood; an account in which her infantile dependency upon her mother—and the response her mother's 'ascendant' (*Mémoires,* Folio, p. 55) aroused in her—are lucidly analysed:

> Tout reproche de ma mère, le moindre de ses froncements de sourcils, mettait en jeu ma sécurité; privée de son approbation, je ne me sentais plus le droit d'exister. [. . .] Certainement, la première raison de ma timidité, c'était le souci d'éviter son mépris. Mais aussi, quand ses yeux brillaient d'un éclat orageux, ou quand simplement sa bouche se fronçait, je crois que je craignais, autant que ma propre déchéance, les remous que je provoquais dans son cœur. [. . .] Ma responsabilité redoublait ma dépendance. Ainsi vivions-nous, elle et moi, dans une sorte de symbiose, et sans m'appliquer à l'imiter, je fus modelée par elle.
>
> (pp. 56-57)

Yes, the adult Beauvoir appears to be saying, I did share a powerful, identificatory relationship ('une sorte de symbiose') with my mother, which complicated my sense of my own autonomous, individual selfhood, but my resultant feeling of insecurity was neither unusual nor especially significant. However, other elements of the first part of the *Mémoires* tell a rather different story. In part one, Beauvoir articulates an anxiety focused upon the maternal/filial bond, whose intensity is discernible and yet is never properly acknowledged. This anxiety is first hinted at, obliquely, at the very start of Beauvoir's autobiography, when she evokes her infantile eating difficulties and her mother's efforts to feed her in a way which, arguably, is indicative of a sense on her part of unwelcome intrusion/engulfment:[7]

> La principale fonction de Louise et de maman, c'était de me nourrir; leur tâche n'était pas toujours facile. [. . .] La fadeur des crèmes de blé vert, des bouillies d'avoine, des panades m'arrachait des larmes; l'onctuosité des graisses, le mystère gluant des coquillages me révoltaient.
>
> (p. 11)

The fear implied by this extract is comparable to that which, in **Le Deuxième Sexe,** Beauvoir analyses in terms of the *male* subject's disgust at his own 'contingence charnelle', which he projects onto/into the mother, who comes to embody the threat of *engloutissement* and *viscosité*.[8] However, the mother-related anguish that permeates part one of the **Mémoires**—a daughter's story, not a son's—is a function rather of issues of invasion and absorption which are commonly associated with the mother/daughter dynamic. It is considerably more apparent in Beauvoir's accounts of fictional or cinematic narratives encountered by her childhood self which, once re-narrated, form *micro-récits* within the main body of the text. From these *micro-récits,* which Beauvoir remembers and which, with elaborate casualness, she reproduces in her narrative—the tale of the child Charlotte who eats an egg which is both 'ventre' and 'berceau' and whose ingestion reduces her to a foetal state (p. 13); the story of Bob, 'le coureur des jungles', who is 'englouti' in a 'corridor souterrain' by a python (p. 72); and that of the heroine of a silent film (watched by the young Simone with her mother and grandmother), who is swallowed up in a *marécage* (pp. 74-75)—there emerges a disquieting vision of the mother as a subjugatory, invasive entity, whose engulfing potential must be conjured at all costs. What, then, is actually at stake in these narratives-within-the-narrative, with whose protagonists Beauvoir clearly identified in childhood, and which, as an adult, she feels compelled to disinter and insert into part one of her **Mémoires**?

The opening section of Beauvoir's autobiography contains a message which is ultimately not dissimilar to that offered by Luce Irigaray's poetic, distressing exploration of mother/daughter bonding, *Et l'une ne bouge pas sans l'autre* (1979). Through her personal recollections of the tales that 'appealed' to the child she was, the mature Beauvoir fearfully and instinctually evokes a mère/miroir/marécage perceived as capable (still?) of absorbing her. Irigaray, on the other hand, creates a complex, focused account of the impossibility

in our culture of mediated relationships between women, and of the absence of processes whereby daughters may achieve an identity distinct from that of the mother. Leaving these differences aside, both women are essentially addressing the anguish of the daughter who senses herself to be filled/fed by her mother so excessively that she is deprived of autonomy and threatened with extinction. What is at issue, in other words, in the early stages of the **Mémoires** as much as in Irigaray's short text, is the inscription of resentful dread—a daughter's dread of a maternal figure who menaces her with obliteration.

At the same time that Beauvoir's autobiographical *récit* chronicles—however implicitly—extreme daughterly anxiety, it also points to strategies adopted by its narrator/heroine in an effort to undermine maternal authority and to emancipate herself from the maternal orbit, via a process of differentiation and liberation. In Parts I and II of the **Mémoires** Simone seeks out doubles or companions whose reassuring presence combats the terror of *engloutissement* and annihilation the mother incarnates. Her account of her dealings with these individuals confirms the point made by Freud in 'The Uncanny' that the 'invention of doubling [is] a preservation against extinction', and that the double constitutes 'an insurance against the destruction of the ego' (*Standard Edition,* XVII, 235). In the first section of the text, the 'homme lige [. . .], second, [. . .], double' (p. 60) in question is Poupette, Beauvoir's sister; in Part II, Poupette is replaced by God. Sister and divine Father (Beauvoir's biological father has curiously little to do with the trajectory I am outlining) are initially represented as capable of shoring up Simone's sense of identity and uniqueness, and of relieving her unconscious fear of being (re)absorbed into the maternal:

> Ce que j'appréciais le plus dans nos rapports, c'est que j'avais sur [ma sœur] une prise réelle. [. . .] Elle seule me reconnaissait de l'autorité; les adultes parfois me cédaient; elle m'obéissait. [. . .] Grâce à ma sœur—ma complice, ma sujette, ma créature—j'affirmais mon autonomie.
>
> (pp. 63-64)

> [La] souveraineté [de Dieu] ne m'ôtait pas la mienne. Il connaissait toutes les choses à sa façon, c'est-à-dire absolument; mais il me semblait que, d'une certaine manière, il avait besoin de mes yeux pour que les arbres aient des couleurs. [. . .] Loin qu'il me détrônât, il assurait mon règne.
>
> (p. 175)

Unfortunately for the young Simone, neither her sister—the first acknowledged object of an intense desire for a double which resurfaces later in the *Mémoires*—nor God proves to be satisfactory partners in her quest for freedom and individuation. The latter is too reliant upon her ('Il avait besoin de mes yeux') to hold out a genuine possibility of liberation. Poupette, as Catherine Portuges argues in her discussion of attachment and separation in Beauvoir's autobiography, does at first appear to 'enable her elder sister, simply by virtue of her existence, to pursue the single-minded search for self-realization that is one of the subjects of the *Memoirs*'.[9] Ultimately, however, she is too close to the mother and too involved in the mother/daughter symbiotic paradigm to offer a means of escape from it. This is why, as Portuges points out, Simone's encounter with Zaza Mabille, her first and only schoolfriend, seems so decisive. In Zaza, it appears, she finds at last the emancipatory companion she has been seeking; a companion whose non-familial status and admirable independence will ensure that 'symbiotic and enmeshed relationships with m/others [are] first challenged and then rapidly replaced'.[10] A brief examination of the terms in which Zaza, and Simone's reaction to her, are described in Parts I and II of the *Mémoires* helps us quickly to see why the other girl is, initially at least, so attractive to Simone:

[E]n Zaza j'entrevoyais une présence, jaillissante comme une source, robuste comme un bloc de marbre, aussi fermement dessinée qu'un portrait de Dürer.

(pp. 156-57)

A la séance récréative qui avait lieu chaque année, aux environs de Noël, on nous fit jouer ensemble une saynète. En robe rose, le visage encadré d'anglaises, j'incarnais Mme de Sévigné enfant! Élisabeth tenait le rôle d'un jeune cousin turbulent; son costume garçonnier lui seyait et elle charma l'auditoire par sa vivacité et son aisance.

(p. 126)

Pendant dix à quinze jours, je me traînai d'heure en heure, du jour au lendemain, les jambes molles. Un après-midi, je me déshabillais dans le vestiaire de l'institut, quand Zaza apparut. [. . .] Si radicale était mon ignorance des vraies aventures du cœur que je n'avais pas songé à me dire: 'Je souffre de son absence.' Il me fallait sa présence pour réaliser le besoin que j'avais d'elle. [. . .] Je me laissai soulever par cette joie qui déferlait en moi, violente et fraîche comme l'eau des cascades, nue comme un beau granit.

(p. 130)

The attributes which Simone associates, explicitly or implicitly, with her friend—whose captivating personality transforms an early reunion, evoked in the last of the extracts cited, into 'a fete, a celebration, a moment of almost mystical revelation'[11]—emerge forcefully from the passages I have selected. Zaza embodies (pseudo-) maleness, hardness and firmly contoured distinctness—characteristics that are the antithesis of those imputed to the mother in the *micro-récits* of Part I of the *Mémoires*. It is precisely because Zaza seems to Simone to have the (masculine) qualities of 'un bloc de marbre' that she promises to constitute the perfect, liberatory love-object Portuges considers her to be. If the female, engulfing mère/marécage that is Françoise de Beauvoir must be spurned by Simone, because she threatens *engloutissement*, Zaza can be loved wholeheartedly, because she in no way embodies the risk of absorption or invasion. If Simone rediscovers Zaza with a quasi-erotic joy after a two-week separation, it is because she perceives her as offering the possibility of 'a satisfactory integration of [the] desire for closeness and differentiation, for attachment and separation'[12] and, more importantly, the means by which Simone may begin to escape her mother and all she represents. As long as Zaza exists, the mother can (apparently, at least) be cast aside.

In the light of the above, it becomes clear why Zaza's role in Simone's development has been interpreted as more or less emancipatory.[13] However, the Zaza/Simone relation is a good deal more complex than critics have generally allowed. Beauvoir's narrator certainly invites us to read her adolescent bond with her friend positively, i.e. as the vehicle for a necessary break with mother and milieu; indeed, she directs us towards just such a reading, by emphasizing at the end of Part I of her *récit* her great good fortune in meeting Zaza.[14] However, there are a number of indications in the *Mémoires* that what Simone discovers in her dealings with Zaza is an interpersonal dynamic which is identical to that linking her to her mother, and which is consequently far from liberatory. If Simone eludes invasion and absorption in the presence of her 'lointaine', granite-hard schoolfriend (p. 201), she none the less finds herself involved in a bond in which she is once again mirror-image, subordinate and vassal:

Et de nouveau une évidence me foudroya: 'Je ne peux plus vivre sans elle.' C'était un peu effrayant: elle allait, venait, loin de moi, et tout mon bonheur, mon existence même reposaient entre ses mains. [. . .] J'avais été jusqu'à avouer la dépendance où me mettait mon attachement pour elle: je n'osai pas en affronter toutes les conséquences.

(p. 131)

[J]'aimais tant Zaza qu'elle me semblait plus réelle que moi-même: j'étais son négatif; au lieu de revendiquer mes propres particularités, je les subis avec dépit.

(p. 158)

Since Zaza effectively affords Simone renewed dependency, and reinforces rather than eliminates problems already encountered vis-à-vis the mother—compare, for example, the first of the above extracts with the narrator's earlier comment, in Section I of the *Mémoires,* that 'privée de [l']approbation [de ma mère], je ne me sentais plus le droit d'exister' (p. 56)—what is her actual function in the *récit*? What, regardless of her apparent status as adored, exemplary classmate, does she really represent? Clearly, she cannot be viewed simply as an extension of the absorbing mère/marécage whose threatening aspect emerges so intensely from Beauvoir's *micro-récits.* None the less, within the psyche of the narrator/heroine of the *Mémoires,* Zaza evidently stands in a relation of some kind to the figure of the mother. Arguably, therefore, what Zaza signifies for Simone is not a *replacement* for the mother but rather a different *sort* of mother; one who, to use Jane Gallop's terminology, is not a 'hole', likely to engulf and obliterate, but a 'whole'. Is Zaza, with her hardness and 'maleness', the pre-oedipal mother, the mother who precedes the discovery of castration, who is possessed of the phallus; the mother who, to quote Gallop, 'is more phallic [than the Primitive Father] precisely by being less obvious'?[15] If this is the case—and it is extremely tempting to 'read' her in this way—why does she attract Beauvoir's narrator/heroine? Conceivably, Simone is drawn to and seeks out in Zaza this archaic mother-figure precisely because, for all her fear of maternal *engloutissement,* absolute *loss* of the mother is also terrifying. Turning to Zaza, the phallic mother, is the one means by which Simone hopes (erroneously) to elude the mother-related anguish evoked in Part I whilst avoiding the 'exil' to which she knows definitive mother/daughter separation condemns her.[16]

All of the above suggests that what the reader is offered in Parts I and II of the *Mémoires* is the same binary, oppositional configuration of phallic/non-phallic mothers that Jardine discerns in **Une mort très douce** and **La Cérémonie des adieux.** There is however—apparently—a distinction between the latter text and the *Mémoires.* In **La Cérémonie des adieux,** according to Jardine, the phallic mother, in this instance the incontinent, ailing Sartre, is immolated, cut up by the violence of Beauvoir's razor-edged discourse. In the *Mémoires,* on the other hand, his equivalent, Zaza—the beloved confidante, the vivacious tomboy who succumbs to the manipulations of family and class and finally takes on the role of 'jeune fille rangée' her friend refuses—seems to emerge as the

object of Simone's enduring love and gratitude. Or does she? As we saw earlier, interaction with Zaza actually involves Simone in a subjugation she has already experienced—and resented—in her dealings with her biological mother, and consequently menaces her with (re)exposure to feelings of *néantisation.* What is her reaction to the renewal of the threat of obliteration? In order to gauge this, we need to look further at the account we are given of the Simone/Zaza relation, and at what happens to Zaza in the course of the *Mémoires.*

Simone's dependency upon Zaza is articulated for the first time at the end of Part I, in the declamatory passage where Beauvoir recalls the epiphanic moment during which she became aware of her love for her friend. In the same section of the text, Zaza's (imagined) death is evoked, also for the first time:

> J'imaginai que Mlle Gontran allait entrer, balayant le sol de sa longue jupe, et elle nous dirait: 'Priez, mes enfants; votre petite compagne, Elisabeth Mabille, a été rappelée par Dieu la nuit dernière,' Eh bien, me dis-je, je mourrais sur l'heure!
>
> (p. 131)

The possibility of Zaza's disappearance resurfaces in Part II of the *Mémoires,* shortly after Beauvoir's narrator petulantly describes herself as the 'négatif' of her cherished companion (p. 158). In the passage in question, Beauvoir evokes another narrative that captivated her youthful imagination, *L'Écolier d'Athènes,* by André Laurie. In the course of the re-narration of this *micro-récit,* Zaza is linked to Euphorion, an extraordinarily gifted youth who none the less dies prematurely, leaving his more pedestrian friend, Théagène, to tell his story, and to become in so doing 'la mémoire et la conscience, le Sujet essentiel' (p. 158)—a position which Simone clearly claims as her own by the end of the *Mémoires.* The *Mémoires* close with the account of Zaza's actual demise, and with the following, passionate tribute from Beauvoir:

> Souvent la nuit elle m'est apparue toute jaune sous une capeline rose, et elle me regardait avec reproche. Ensemble nous avions lutté contre le destin fangeux qui nous guettait et j'ai pensé longtemps que j'avais payé ma liberté de sa mort.
>
> (p. 503)

The final words of the *Mémoires* have engendered speculation about the moral debt Beauvoir felt she owed to the companion whose 'fall' paralleled her own conquest of freedom,[17] and have led to comment regarding the 'reparative function'[18] of her text—which, on one level, can indeed be read as a tribute to the girl who offered

Beauvoir a model of exemplary independence and unconventionality and then died in her stead. Critics who have analysed Beauvoir's account of Zaza's death have interpreted it moreover as the source of her life-long revolt against the bourgeoisie (to whose restrictive moral codes she attributed blame for her friend's tragic end),[19] and have located in this revolt the stimulus for her highly successful literary endeavours.[20] Emphasis has been placed therefore both on the intensity of Beauvoir's grief and (guilty, loving) gratitude and on the positive consequences of these sentiments. It is possible, however, to read Beauvoir's narration of Zaza's fate (m)otherwise, in a way which places the conclusion of her *Mémoires* in the context of the seemingly premonitory visions that assail Simone in Parts I and II in connection with her friend's death. Arguably, for all her idealization of Zaza, Beauvoir's narrator/heroine is manifesting through these visions and their textual reproduction an implicit but powerful need to remove a resented obstacle to her own autonomy. This need, which is already discernible at the end of Part I (when Zaza's death is first evoked) and palpably informs the Euphorion/Théagène *micro-récit,* is murderous and, given that Zaza functions as the phallic mother, is above all matricidal. Once we recognize its nature and force, we can no longer interpret Zaza's demise simply as the unexpected, ironic realization of what was, in Part I, an 'improbable hypothesis'.[21] Inevitably, her 'fall' takes on the appearance of an actualization—however fantastic—of an unconscious, mother-related death wish born out of Simone's (daughterly) rage and sense of subjugation. The *Mémoires,* in other words, offer a confirmation of the point made by Irigaray's narrator in *Et l'une ne bouge pas sans l'autre* that for a daughter (Simone) to achieve subjectivity and identity, the mother (Zaza) has somehow to cede her place and disappear.[22] Obviously, it would be overstating the case to argue that Zaza's death is willed, on a conscious level, or that the closing sentences of Beauvoir's first autobiographical volume are in any way overtly triumphalist. However, the 'maternal' interpretation I am offering makes it impossible to read the end of the *Mémoires* as exclusively loving or reparative, or even simply as the acknowledgement of a moral debt. In addition, my reading situates Beauvoir's *Mémoires* as the first element within an autobiographical sequence whose end point is the matricidal 'Tomb-Books' Jardine discusses, *La Cérémonie des adieux* and *Une mort très douce.*[23]

Apparently, then, for Beauvoir, discursive matricide and the textual decomposition of the maternal body—in death, Zaza's hands are 'friables comme celles d'une très vieille momie' (p. 502)—have the value of an imperative. At the end of the *Mémoires,* Zaza, the archaic phallic mother who displaces/liquidates the biological mère/marécage, is not only dead but has been displaced, as love-object, in her turn—by Sartre, the male lover/father dreamed of by Simone in adolescence ('Sartre répondait exactement au vœu de mes quinze ans: il était le double en qui je retrouvais, portées à l'incandescence, toutes mes manies' (p. 482)). The Oedipal family romance has evidently prevailed. Or has it? Are things so simple? Sartre, after all, corresponds to an ideal incarnated in the first place by a woman, Zaza herself ('Il faudrait que l'élu s'imposât à moi, comme s'était imposée Zaza, par une sorte d'évidence; sinon je me demanderais: pourquoi lui et pas un autre?' (p. 201)). He is a 'double', consequently a partner in a mirror-relationship—and Simone's primordial specular tie was clearly that which bound her to her biological mother ('sans m'appliquer à l'imiter je fus modelée par elle' (p. 57)), even though it is Poupette, hapless sister-vassal rather than mother or mother-substitute, whom Beauvoir presents as her first double. So perhaps the 'matricidal' work of the *Mémoires* is not as complete as all that, and the mother is still present as primary object, in the person of Sartre? Sartre's phallic/maternal status is even made belatedly explicit by Beauvoir, in *Une mort très douce,* when she refers to dreams she has after her biological mother dies: 'Dans mon sommeil—alors que mon père apparaissait très rarement et d'une manière anodine—[ma mère] jouait souvent le rôle essentiel: elle se confondait avec Sartre et nous étions heureuses ensemble' (*Une mort très douce,* Folio, p. 147)—which explains *inter alia* why Jardine reads in the way that she does Beauvoir's positioning of Sartre in her last autobiographical *récit.* It seems therefore that neither the death of Zaza, in the *Mémoires,* nor that of Françoise, in *Une mort très douce,* actually kills off the mother—the one with the phallus, at least—permanently and definitively. As Jardine demonstrates, it is not until *La Cérémonie des adieux,* with its visions of Sartre's putrefying body, that Beauvoir succeeds in liquidating the most phallic mother of all.

Notes

1. Alice Jardine, 'Death Sentences: Writing Couples and Ideology', *Poetics Today,* 6 (1985), 119-31 (p. 121).

2. The notion of the maternal phallus—and of the recognition/non-recognition of its absence—is central

to Freud's work on fetishism (see *Standard Edition*, XXI, 152-53). Laplanche and Pontalis present the figure of the phallic mother as an integral element of the Freudian account of infantile psychosexuality, as well as a common feature of dreams and phantasms, and argue that 'la mise en évidence progressive d'une "théorie sexuelle infantile" puis d'une phase libidinale proprement dite, dans lesquelles il n'y aurait pour l'un et pour l'autre sexe qu'un seul organe sexuel, le phallus, vient donner son fondement à l'image de la femme phallique'. Jean Laplanche and J-B Pontalis, *Vocabulaire de la psychanalyse* (Paris, PUF, 1967), p. 310. Henceforth references to the *Standard Edition* will be given in the text.

3. Jardine, 'Death Sentences', p. 128.

4. Jane Gallop, *The Daughter's Seduction: Feminism and Psychoanalysis* (Basingstoke-London, Macmillan, 1982), p. 22.

5. Jardine, 'Death Sentences', p. 130. Jardine's perception of the Oedipal Family Romance as intrinsically 'matricidal' relates to the fact that the breaking of the (incestuous, pre-oedipal) mother/child dyad which both sexes must effect in order to gain access to the Symbolic order (i.e. the order of language, culture and society) involves a repudiation of the mother that may be read as somehow 'murderous'. Luce Irigaray's remarks concerning the nature of the sociocultural/linguistic order into which the subject is inserted at the Oedipal moment bear Jardine's contention out: 'Freud says our culture is built on a parricide. More fundamentally, our culture is built on a matricide: the matricide of the mother/lover'. Luce Irigaray, 'Interview', in *Women Writers Talking*, ed. by Janet Todd (New York, Holmes and Meier, 1983), pp. 232-45 (p. 238).

6. Irigaray and Chodorow come to similar conclusions about the fusional nature of the mother/daughter bond, but their conceptual contexts are very different. In *The Reproduction of Mothering: Psychoanalysis and the Sociology of Gender* (Berkeley-Los Angeles, University of California Press, 1978), Nancy Chodorow explores at length, from the standpoint of Object Relations theory, the problems of self/other differentiation women experience in their dealings with their mothers, and links identity/boundary blurring between mothers and daughters to the different treatment sociocultural norms lead mothers to offer their male and female offspring. Hers is, therefore, essentially an empirical, psychosociological analysis. Irigaray's approach, on the other hand, is related to her extensive, speculative and philosophical exploration of the place of the female subject in the current social, cultural and linguistic order, and its imaginary. As Margaret Whitford explains, Irigaray's argument is that in the Symbolic order as it stands, there is no recognized space for women outside the place of the mother. The mother/daughter relationship remains unsymbolized, i.e. 'there is an absence of linguistic, social, cultural, iconic, theoretical, mythical, religious, or any other representations of that relationship', and non-symbolization 'hinders women from having an identity in the symbolic order that is distinct from the maternal function'. Consequently, 'women's ontological status in this culture is *déréliction*, the state of abandonment', and 'women have difficulty in separating from their mothers'. What is required, between mothers and daughters and women in general, is an 'interval of *exchange*', permitting differentiation and

individual subjectivity. Margaret Whitford, 'Rereading Irigaray', in *Between Feminism and Psychoanalysis*, ed. by Teresa Brennan (London-New York, Routledge, 1989), pp. 106-26 (pp. 108-12).

7. A similar, eating-related unease is conveyed by the daughter/narrator of Irigaray's *Et l'une ne bouge pas sans l'autre*. In the section of this short text which focuses on maternal nurturing, Irigaray's manipulation of pronouns foregrounds clearly the theme of mother/daughter identity-merging: 'Tu as préparé à manger. Tu m'apportes à manger. Tu me/te donnes à manger. Mais tu me/te donnes trop, comme si tu voulais me remplir toute entière avec ce que tu m'apportes. Tu te mets dans ma bouche et j'étouffe. [. . .] Ne t'engloutis pas, ne m'engloutis pas, dans ce qui passe de toi en moi'. Luce Irigaray, *Et l'une ne bouge pas sans l'autre* (Paris, Éditions de Minuit, 1979), pp. 9-10.

8. For Beauvoir's exploration of the way in which the mother is perceived and represented in the patriarchal imaginary as the source of menacing engulfment, absorption and contingent materiality, see the section entitled 'Mythes' in *Le Deuxième Sexe I* (Paris, Gallimard, 1949).

9. Catherine Portuges, 'Attachment and Separation in *Memoirs of a Dutiful Daughter*', *Yale French Studies*, 72 (1986), 107-18 (p. 113).

10. Ibid., p. 117.

11. Elaine Marks, *Simone de Beauvoir: Encounters with Death* (New Brunswick, NJ, Rutgers University Press, 1973), p. 50.

12. Portuges, 'Attachment and Separation', p. 114.

13. This is the view adopted by Marks and Portuges, and also by Deborah MacKeefe, in a further discussion of the Beauvoir/Zaza relationship entitled 'Mission and Motive in Simone de Beauvoir's *Mémoires*', *Contemporary Literature*, 24 (1983), 204-21.

14. 'J'avais eu la chance de rencontrer l'amitié' (*Mémoires*, p. 125). Elaine Marks notes the presence of almost identical phraseology in Beauvoir's accounts of her encounters with two other key figures in her life, Sartre and Sylvie Le Bon, and comments that it is used to evoke 'privileged relationships [that] have the effect of breaking routines associated with [. . .] stagnation'. Elaine Marks, 'Transgressing the (In)cont(in)ent Boundaries: The Body in Decline', *Yale French Studies*, 72 (1986), 186.

15. Gallop, *The Daughter's Seduction*, p. 118.

16. 'Je continuais à grandir et je me savais condamnée à l'exil' (*Mémoires*, p. 13).

17. See Elaine Marks, *Encounters with Death*, pp. 54-55, and Leah Hewitt, *Autobiographical Tightropes* (Lincoln-London, Nebraska University Press, 1990), pp. 34-39.

18. Portuges, 'Attachment and Separation', p. 114.

19. Marks, Hewitt and Portuges endorse this view.

20. 'Had Zaza not died, it is possible to imagine that Simone de Beauvoir would not have carried with her, after her adolescent liberation, such strong feelings of revolt. Nor would she perhaps have felt so deeply the need to bear witness, through literature, to her own life and that of her generation. Zaza's death was the social evil that no triumph could erase.' Marks, *Encounters with Death*, p. 51.

21. Ibid.

22. 'Quand l'une vient au monde, l'autre retombe sous la terre. Quand l'une porte la vie, l'autre meurt.' Irigaray, *Et l'une ne bouge pas sans l'autre,* p. 22.

23. Jardine, 'Death Sentences', p. 128.

The Woman Destroyed

ELIZABETH FALLAIZE (ESSAY DATE 1990)

SOURCE: Fallaize, Elizabeth. "Resisting Romance: Simone de Beauvoir, *The Woman Destroyed* and the Romance Script." In *Contemporary French Fiction by Women: Feminist Perspectives,* edited by Margaret Atack and Phil Powrie, pp. 15-25. Manchester, Eng.: Manchester University Press, 1990.

In the following essay, Fallaize examines elements of popular romantic fiction in The Woman Destroyed *and the possibility of demythologizing romantic ritualism for Beauvoir.*

The feminist credentials of Simone de Beauvoir's fictional texts are sometimes assumed to be guaranteed by the fact that their author also produced *The Second Sex,* and indeed Beauvoir's fiction is most usually read against her essays (or Sartre's). However, more recently, there has been a tendency to judge the fiction—and to find it wanting in some respects—against the conventions of the romance plot.[1] It is indeed difficult to deny that elements of the romance plot are easily discernible in Beauvoir's early fiction: heterosexual couple formation plays a large part in the narrative, and within this couple the woman tends to be in what Rachel Blau Duplessis has called romantic thraldom (by which she means a totally defining love between apparent unequals—the lover has the power of conferring a sense of identity and purpose upon the loved one) to the often strongly gendered man.[2]

In the early fictional texts, published in the forties and fifties, the central women characters are on the whole rewarded by getting their man when they take the right turning after an initial period of bad faith—thus Françoise of *She Came to Stay* (1943) destroys the rival woman and is rewarded with the love and attention of both the central male characters; Hélène of *The Blood of Others* (1945) valorises love above all else and comes to merit the hero's love when she adopts his quest as her own; the central preoccupation of Anne of *The Mandarins* (1954) is her choice between two men. In more general terms it is quite clear that, despite the strong warnings she gives in *The Second Sex* about the dangers of love

for women, Beauvoir herself valued love and the couple very highly. In the first volume of her autobiography, *Memoirs of a Dutiful Daughter,* she describes her anguish and fury as an adolescent at reading a novel in which a man and a woman 'made for each other' decide to sacrifice the possibility of a relationship in the interests of a cause: 'True love, from the moment it burst into passionate life, was irreplaceable (. . .). Daniel's career, the cause, and so on were all abstract things. I found it absurd and criminal that they should put them before love, happiness, life'.[3] Forty years later, in *Force of Circumstance,* she begins her summing-up of her life: 'There has been one undoubted success in my life: my relationship with Sartre'.[4] It is of course important to distinguish between placing a high value on love within the heterosexual couple on the one hand, and all the baggage of the romance ritual on the other, but maintaining the distinction between the two can be a slippery route.

However, the kind of observation which can be made of the extent to which the ideology of romance permeates Beauvoir's earlier fictional texts appears more difficult to make when we turn to her last two fictional texts, *Les Belles Images* (1966) and *The Woman Destroyed* (1968), written more than a decade after her earlier fiction and in a period of rapid transformation of the social roles of women. The thrust of both these texts is essentially a demystifying one, and though in *Les Belles Images,* Beauvoir's main attack is centred on the ideology of the technocratic bourgeoisie, the text also carries out a brutal dismantling of the ideology of the couple: the heroine finds that her husband and her lover are interchangeable and a whole series of romantic gestures and images—such as the sending of flowers, the gift of an expensive necklace, the romantic image of the handsome and elegant couple driving away in their Ferrari—are shown to be not just conventional and ritualistic but to conceal a materialism, a self-interest and even a violence sufficient to deter the most determined romantic heroine. The deconstruction of the romantic and the technocratic go hand in hand when the richest and most powerful male character of the text announces that he is to marry the daughter of his ex-mistress: 'No-one can rule their heart', he explains in self-satisfied justification.[5]

Nevertheless it is possible to ask whether this attack is really mounted on romantic ideology itself, or whether, on the contrary, it is not the characters' failure to meaningfully enact the amorous ritual which may be intended to signal

FROM THE AUTHOR

BEAUVOIR ON HER EXPECTATIONS OF SEXUAL EQUALITY AS A YOUNG WOMAN

My behavior conformed to the morality implicit in my environment; but with one important exception; I insisted that men should be subject to the same laws as women. Aunt Germaine had complained to my parents, in veiled terms, that Jacques knew too much about life. My father, the majority of writers, and the universal concensus of opinion encouraged young men to sow their wild oats. When the time came, they would marry a young woman of their own social class; but meanwhile it was quite in order for them to amuse themselves with girls from the lowest ranks of society—women of easy virtue, young milliners' assistants, sewing maids, shop girls. This custom made me feel sick. It had been driven into me that the lower classes have no morals: the misconduct of a laundrywoman or a flower girl therefore seemed to me to be so natural that it didn't even shock me; I felt a certain sympathy for those poor young women whom novelists endowed with such touching virtues. Yet their love was always doomed from the start; one day or another, according to his whim or convenience, their lover would throw them over for a well-bred young lady. I was a democrat and a romantic; I found it revolting that, just because he was a man and had money, he should be authorized to play around with a girl's heart. On the other hand, I was up in arms in defense of the pure-hearted fiancée with whom I identified myself. I saw no reason why my future partner in life should permit himself liberties which I wouldn't allow myself. Our love would only be inevitable and complete if he saved himself for me as I had saved myself for him. Moreover, our sexual life, and that of the whole world, should be in its very essence a serious affair; otherwise I should be forced to change my own attitude, and as I was at the moment unable to do so, I should have been thrown into the greatest confusion. Therefore, despite public opinion, I persisted in my view that both sexes should observe the same rules of chastity and continence.

Beauvoir, Simone de. An excerpt from *Memoirs of a Dutiful Daughter.* Translated by James Kirkup, p. 176. Cleveland: World Publishing Co., 1959.

the aridity and inhumanity of the bourgeoisie.[6] And this kind of doubt persists with **"The Woman Destroyed"**, the final story in the cycle of three short stories also entitled *The Woman Destroyed,* in which the problem of the romance plot becomes particularly acute. Before turning to the story itself, however, it is worth examining more closely the nature of the romance against which I propose to read the story. Blau Duplessis defines the romance plot as one which 'muffles the female character, represses female quest, valorises heterosexual ties, puts individuals into couples as a sign of their success. It evokes an aura around the couple itself and constructs couples based on an extreme of sexual difference'. Blau Duplessis accepts that 'narrative is a version of, or a special expression of, ideology: representations by which we construct and accept values and institutions'. But it does not appear that she gives an overwhelming force to this ideology since she assumes that women writers critical of androcentric culture can revise and restructure the romance plot, thus signalling 'a dissent from social norms as well as narrative forms'.[7]

In contrast to this position, Michelle Coquillat in her recent study of the *roman de gare* (popular romance) in France stresses heavily the ideological function of the romance plot, emphasising the way in which it renders 'natural' values which are actually socially determined and describing the *roman de gare* and its central code, romantic love, as a 'prodigious instrument' in our culture's persuasion process that to be real women we must seek our lives in love of our hero and in domesticity.[8] And Coquillat does not confine her conclusions to the more popular versions of literature: though the code can be perceived to be operating in its grossest form in the *roman de gare,* it is also to be discovered, she argues, albeit in more sophisticated wrappings, in the more elite reaches of literature.

The code that Coquillat discovers at work in the Harlequin series, in the novels of Guy des Cars, of Delly and other popular romance writers does in fact have much in common with Blau Duplessis's definition of the romance plot, despite the fact that Coquillat's model is based on reading 'popular' literature and Blau Duplessis's on 'higher' forms. However, both these studies focus on the separately published novel, and in the case of **"The Woman Destroyed"**, an even more relevant intertext is that of women's magazine fiction, since the first publication of **"The Woman Destroyed"** was as serialised extracts in the prestigious French women's magazine *Elle.* Serialised over five issues, from 19 October to 16 November

1967, the text was accompanied by a series of illustrations of the story by Simone de Beauvoir's sister, Hélène de Beauvoir, and by large photographs of the author herself.[9] Both are important in making the story conform to the genre of women's magazine fiction since a series of illustrations of the heroine of the story are virtually *de rigueur.*

Jean Emelina has analysed other conventions of the women's magazine short story in France: like the *roman de gare,* the point of view of the narrative is that of a central female protagonist with whom the reader is encouraged to identify, and is usually a first-person account. There are various sub-genres, but in the 'true confession' type the tone is highly personal and intimate, revealing the connection between the story and the problems page of which the story is in some ways the prolongation. The setting is usually contemporary, the experience recounted always revolves around love and its problems, and there may be a considerable emphasis on the family (noticeably more so than in the English equivalent). The problems raised are always dealt with strictly on an individual level, as in most popular fiction, and not viewed as being related to any social, class or gender base—again, a feature of the *roman de gare* strongly emphasised by Coquillat.[10]

Turning now then to the story of **"The Woman Destroyed"**, we can begin by identifying the features it shares with the women's magazine story in particular, and with romantic fiction in general. One of the most basic features of the women's magazine story is that it must be seen to be about women and for women, and this is much more true of all three stories of **The Woman Destroyed** than of any other of Simone de Beauvoir's fictional texts. In the case of the particular story with which we are concerned here, the central figure is Monique, a woman in her forties whose total energies in life are devoted to her husband and her children. Her diary constitutes the narrative and provides the woman-centred focus and confessional tone of the romance script. The central focus on the complications of love, also essential to the genre, is revealed as early as the sixth entry of the diary, where we find recorded the event which is to form the central crisis of the story: Monique's husband Maurice reveals that he is having an affair with another woman. The presence of the rival woman, virtually a *sine qua non* in Delly,[11] is used here as the stimulus to provoke Monique into examining her life with Maurice, past and present, and into trying out a number of

remedies designed to win back her husband. Most of the remedies are more or less explicitly culled from reading agony and advice columns—after all, Monique's situation of being abandoned by her husband at forty when the children have left home constitutes a stock situation of such pages.

'This evening [writes Monique in her diary] I am going out with Maurice. The advice of Isabelle and of Miss Lonelihearts column—to get your husband back, be cheerful and elegant and go out with him, just the two of you.'[12] Advice also emerges from the female community, since Monique discusses her situation with a number of other women acquaintances. These other women are kept very shadowy, in keeping with another convention of the romance script, which is that the woman is always basically *alone;* other women are understood to be potential rivals rather than sources of support. From the women emerges a body of generalisations about men, of the kind: 'In Maurice, like most men, just beneath the surface slumbers an adolescent lacking in self-assurance'[13] and 'Men choose the easiest solution: it's easier to stay with your wife than to launch out into a new life'.[14] What these infantilising generalisations do is to compensate for the women's actual lack of power over men, and to construct in their attempts to guess at Maurice's likely motivations and behaviour a Maurice who is above all a *man,* above all, in other words, a member of another species. Maurice becomes the unknowable 'other' whose behaviour and remarks Monique must spend hours trying to decode. Here we have an almost pathological—and highly unexistential—construction of sexual difference, again an element crucial to the romantic code.[15]

On the basis of these suppositions about men and about the ground rules of the battle for men, Monique adopts what she calls the 'smile tactic'. Faced for example with the request that Maurice be allowed to spend the whole night out when he sees the other woman, Monique swallows hard and writes in her diary: 'No confrontations. If I ruin this affair for him it will look even more attractive to him from a distance, he'll feel he's missed out on something. If I let him go through with it properly he'll soon get tired of it. That's what Isabelle says'.[16] Bolstering herself with her tactic, Monique increasingly positions herself as a women's magazine reader, feeling optimistic the day that her stars tell her Sagittarians will be lucky in love this week and sending off examples of the handwriting of all three of them to be analysed—interestingly the results are made to be accurate, so that the text supports a belief in graphology, though Monique then has to lose her faith in it at this point in order to be able to avoid facing up to what the results tell her.

Monique's tactic, however, is not allowed to succeed, and in a reversal of the happy end of the genre, she is left alone at the end of the story without her husband. As she writes her diary, she begins to see that she has spent years constructing a mythology of the perfect couple, the perfect wife and mother, the perfect husband, and has refused all other perceptions. She comes, in a half-conscious kind of way, to blame herself for engineering a pregnancy in order to press Maurice into marriage and in order to give up a career in medicine which she found too demanding. She blames herself for having been too stifling as a mother, and Maurice accuses her of moulding one daughter into an exact replica of herself and forcing the other daughter to flee to the US to escape her attentions. In one sense the message of the text is clear and uncompromising—by making a career out of marriage and motherhood, Monique has made a mess of her life and possibly that of others.

So far so good—it is clear that Beauvoir's intention is to exploit the conventions of the romance to make them express different meanings, and to offer a salutary warning to the woman reader. However, as Beauvoir writes in the last volume of her autobiography **All Said and Done**, it is dangerous to ask the reader to read between the lines.[17] We have already seen how closely the story mimics the genre. The ending does leave Monique on her own, but it also leaves her still in thraldom to the handsome Maurice, despite the lies he has told and the way in which he has used Monique as a domestic support (and in fact he has to be left looking like a nice sort of chap in order to allow the reader to focus on Monique's mistakes). Monique is thus left at the end of the story as the loser of the eternal female battle for the man. She does not feel that this particular man was not worth having. On the contrary, what she has learned is that her weapons in the battle were the wrong ones, and that her rival—who is a successful lawyer and takes care to follow Maurice's own career with eager interest—is using the right ones. Monique loses and her rival wins—the man remains the prize.

Even more problematically, perhaps, the use of the diary form and the individual confessional style of the narrative means that the text echoes the assumption of all romantic fiction, which is that Monique's situation is an individual matter. It is not absolutely impossible to squeeze out some

social elements from the story, but we are a long way here from **Les Belles Images,** in which Simone de Beauvoir so strongly stresses the social forces contributing to the creation of the subject. In **Les Belles Images** the characters are seen to be constituted by the discourse of their group; in **"The Woman Destroyed"** Monique is clearly held responsible for her refusal to go beyond the vocabulary of the romantic cliché, her insistence that phrases such as 'Two and two make four' and 'I love you, I love only you' have the same status.

The rules of romantic fiction, which Beauvoir tried to bend to her own purposes, turn out then to be insidiously recuperative. But the structures of the story are not the only thing working against Beauvoir's subversive enterprise. There is also the question of the readers. In **All Said and Done** Beauvoir describes how 'writers, students and teachers' wrote to her 'having fully appreciated my meaning', but after the serialisation in *Elle* she received shoals of a different kind of letter:

> I was overwhelmed with letters from women destroyed, half-destroyed or in the act of being destroyed. They identified themselves with the heroine; they attributed all possible virtues to her and they were astonished that she should remain attached to a man so unworthy of her. Their partiality made it evident that as far as their husbands, their rivals and they themselves were concerned, they shared Monique's blindness. Their reactions were based upon an immense incomprehension.[18]

But to be surprised by the reaction of the *Elle* readers is to fail to recognise the elements which the story has in common with the conventions of romance fiction, and to dismiss the implications of publishing in *Elle*. It is of course true that to publish in *Elle* was not at all the same thing as to publish in the more populist *presse du coeur* type of women's magazine like *Confidences* and *Intimité*. Evelyne Sullerot, in her study of French women's magazines carried out in the early 1960s, identifies *Elle* readers as having a level of education well above average, coming overwhelmingly from the middle classes and living almost exclusively in Paris or large towns. As a consequence, *Elle* readers of the sixties were far less conservative than the less well-educated, more rural and Catholic readers of the populist press, and *Elle*, which knew its readership well, was far more able to overstep limits and question conventions. It was the first French women's magazine to deal with issues of sexuality and contraception before even the advent of the sixties, and it had a highly distinctive agony column, reigned over by Marcelle Ségal. Her style was not the sympathetic, rather saccharine tone adopted by many of her peers in this period but was frequently abrasive and ironic, designed to shake her readers out of the somewhat narcissistic torpor into which many of her correspondents seemed sunk.[19]

However, despite this relatively energetic tone and the encouragement which *Elle* gave its readers to extend their interests outside the home, the *Elle* readership could not read Beauvoir's texts in the way that the 'writers, students and teachers' to whom Simone de Beauvoir refers in **All Said and Done** read it. Publishing in *Elle* meant entering the mass market—Sullerot estimates *Elle*'s readership in the 1960s as in the order of three million women, the majority of whom were unlikely to have read any of Beauvoir's earlier fiction. What they would have had experience of, however, was the magazine fiction genre in which she appeared to be writing, and they clearly read it according to the conventions of the genre, identifying with the heroine whose comfortable middle-class Parisian lifestyle reflected the readers' own, and recognising the how-to-win-a-husband-back vocabulary which Monique clings to. This reading is encouraged by *Elle*'s presentation of the text as 'an analysis of what happens in the mind, in the heart of a woman when the man she loves, and whom she trusts, deceives her'. The adultery of Maurice, understandable or even desirable perhaps in St Germain circles, was likely to be perceived primarily as a threat to domestic stability by the readers of a magazine which, for all its avant-garde reputation, devoted a considerable number of its pages to the domestic arts. The 1975 new law on divorce, replacing the 1889 Naquet law, was still more than six years in the future, and even the realist Marcelle Ségal advised her readers to stick with domestic fidelity and avoid breaking up the home.[20] The reaction of the *Elle* readers demonstrates that reading habits and expectations are not to be changed by a single text. When taken together with the other doubts about the text expressed by readers perfectly aware of Beauvoir's intentions, the difficulties of subverting a highly established and ideological script become evident.[21] However, the reaction of the *Elle* readership was not the only consequence for Beauvoir of the serialisation. In discussing the quality or rather lack of quality of the fiction published in magazines like *Elle* and *Marie-Claire*, relative to the quality of their other articles, Evelyne Sullerot points to the extreme reluctance of writers to sign work appearing in women's magazines, because of the damage to the author's literary reputation likely to ensue.[22] The reception of

'The Woman Destroyed' was heavily marked by its appearance in *Elle*. Bernard Pivot, at that time still a humble columnist for the *Figaro Littéraire*, wrote the book off as a 'shop-girls' romance with pink bows on it' on the strength of a single installment.[23] Jacqueline Piatier in *Le Monde* was equally exultant to be able to damn the story as women's romance. Her review ends with the following line, in which she underlines the gulf between what she takes to be the philosophical pretensions of Simone de Beauvoir and the concerns of the story: 'Can it be that when philosophers start solving problems instead of posing them that they begin producing agony columns?'[24] No other fictional text by Beauvoir met with such a dismissive response on publication as **The Woman Destroyed**, despite the fact that the book quickly became a best-seller. It seems that Beauvoir may have underestimated the dangers of writing between the lines, especially when the lines are those of the romance script.

Most analysts of romantic fiction point to its ideological force, though opinions vary about the actual impact of this force on readers, just as, to look at the issue in a wider scope, commentators on ideology generally are divided about the extent to which it can be resisted. Janice Radway, for example, argues that despite its constant reworking of structures which confine women, romantic fiction can have an integrative and enabling effect on women's lives. Lennard Davis equally urges us to become resisting readers but is more inclined to the view that the novel is a form which 'by and large, is one that fundamentally resists change'.[25] Thus, even if we posit resisting readers, we are still left with the problem of the extent to which it is possible for the writer to subvert the conventions of such a strongly established genre.

To what extent can the writer carry out a demystifying task and become a critic of ideology, while attempting to work within the formal structures of that ideology? Is Beauvoir herself not bound by the very values which she perceives as destroying women? The demands of Beauvoir's own deeply-seated attachment to the value of the couple, the formal and ideological constraints of the genre and the habits of the readership seem, in the case of **"The Woman Destroyed"**, to have all weighed in the balance against this particular attempt to resist romance. Optimism about the scope for revising the romance plot and criticism of a writer on the grounds that she has apparently failed to rewrite the script have to be viewed in the context of these formidable odds.

Notes

1. See for example the chapter on relations between male and female characters in Mary Evans, *Simone de Beauvoir: A Feminist Mandarin* (London: Tavistock, 1985).

2. Rachel Blau Duplessis, *Writing Beyond the Ending. Narrative Strategies of Twentieth-Century Women Writers* (Bloomington: Indiana University Press, 1985), p. 5.

3. *Memoirs of a Dutiful Daughter,* trans. James Kirkup (Harmondsworth: Penguin, 1987), pp. 142-3.

4. *Force of Circumstance,* trans. Richard Howard (Harmondsworth: Penguin, 1985), p. 659.

5. *Les Belles Images,* trans. Patrick O'Brian (Harmondsworth: Penguin, 1983), p. 81; translation adapted.

6. In an article entitled 'What Love Is and Isn't' published in English in the American magazine *McCalls* only the year before the publication of *Les Belles Images,* Beauvoir stressed what she describes as the revolutionary and liberating force of love and suggests that it is doubtful whether a person too much in harmony with society could experience love. From this perspective, the characters of *Les Belles Images* are clearly too other-directed and too anxious to conform to social pressures to allow themselves to experience a potentially revolutionary force. The article is reprinted in Claude Francis and Fernande Gontier, *Les Ecrits de Simone de Beauvoir* (Paris: Gallimard, 1979), pp. 413-21.

7. Blau Duplessis, *Writing Beyond,* p. 20.

8. Michelle Coquillat, *Romans d'amour* (Paris: Odile Jacob, 1989), pp. 10-12.

9. The photographs of Simone de Beauvoir are in fact much more prominent than the illustrations, an indication of the extent to which *Elle* was keen to promote the fact that it was publishing 'the greatest French woman writer of our day'. During the latter part of the sixties, circulation figures for women's magazines fell rapidly; Bonvoisin and Maignien attribute this fall in part to the radical changes taking place in French society affecting women's roles which magazines were unable to keep pace with. Perhaps *Elle* saw the publication of Beauvoir in its pages as a useful tactic at this stage, despite the conservative reaction of readers to earlier extracts from *The Prime of Life.* See Evelyne Sullerot, *La Presse féminine* (Paris: Armand Colin, 1963), p. 138; S-M. Bonvoisin and M. Maignien, *La Presse féminine* (Paris: Armand Colin, 1986), pp. 26-7.

10. Jean Emelina, 'La Nouvelle dans la presse du cœur: étude à partir d'un exemple', in *Hommage à Pierre Nardin* (Paris: Les Belles Lettres, 1977), pp. 291-303. I am grateful to Béatrice Damamme-Gilbert for drawing this article to my attention.

11. Coquillat, *Romans d'amour,* p. 34.

12. *The Woman Destroyed,* trans. Patrick O'Brian (Harmondsworth: Penguin, 1987), p. 117. All subsequent references are to this edition.

13. Ibid., p. 118; translation adapted.

14. Ibid., p. 165; translation adapted.

15. See Anne Barr Snitow, 'Mass Market Romance: Pornography for Women is Different' in Anne Snitow, Christine Stansell, Sharon Thompson (eds.), *Powers of Desire: The Politics of Sexuality* (New York: Monthly Review Press, 1983).

16. *Woman Destroyed,* pp. 121-2; translation adapted.

17. Beauvoir goes on in this paragraph to construct her imaginary reader as a detective: 'I hoped that people would read the books as a detective-story; here and there I scattered clues that would allow the reader to find the key to the mystery—but only if he tracked Monique down as one tracks down the guilty character', *All Said and Done,* trans. Patrick O'Brian (Harmondsworth: Penguin, 1987), p. 140. Subsequent references are to this edition. However, as Toril Moi points out, it is in fact Monique who actually becomes the detective in her frenzied quest for reliable knowledge. See Toril Moi, *Feminist Theory and Simone de Beauvoir* (Oxford: Blackwell, 1990), p. 80.

18. Ibid., p. 142.

19. See Sullerot, *Presse féminine,* pp. 193-5, and Bonvoisin and Maignien, *Presse féminine,* pp. 28-9.

20. A letter from 'Jacky' in the issue of 19 October in which serialisation of 'The Woman Destroyed' was begun, urges the reader to enjoy her lover on a temporary basis while hanging on to her husband. Marcelle Ségal replies: 'No, Jacky, this is not possible. My profession has its obligations, so does marriage, begging your pardon'.

21. See Toril Moi's excellent analysis of the rhetorical effects undermining authorial intentions in the story in *Feminist Theory and Simone de Beauvoir,* cited above.

22. Sullerot, *Presse féminine,* p. 129.

23. See Beauvoir, *All Said and Done,* p. 142.

24. Jacqueline Piatier, *Le Monde (des livres),* 24 janvier 1968, pp. I-II.

25. See Lennard J. Davis, *Resisting Novels: Ideology and Fiction* (London: Methuen, 1987), p. 227. Davis is particularly sceptical about the possibility of subverting romance fiction: 'It is unlikely that this major genre can have any radical political effect, crippled as it is by the weight of tradition and the demands of the audience' (p. 234).

FURTHER READING

Bibliography

Bennett, Joy Gabriella Hochmann. *Simone de Beauvoir: An Annotated Bibliography.* New York: Garland, 1988, 474 p.

Comprehensive annotated bibliography of secondary sources published between 1940 and 1986 in English, French, German, Italian, and Spanish.

Biographies

Appignanesi, Lisa. *Simone de Beauvoir* New York: Penguin Books, 1988, 169 p.

Traces Beauvoir's life and development as a writer.

Ascher, Carol. *Simone de Beauvoir: A Life of Freedom.* Boston, Mass.: Beacon, 1981, 254 p.

Biographical and critical study of Beauvoir's life and works, intended as "a mixture of the personal and the analytical."

Bair, Deirdre. *Simone de Beauvoir: A Biography* New York: Summit Books, 1990, 718 p.

Authorized biography.

Fullbrook, Kate and Edward Fullbrook. *Simone de Beauvoir and Jean-Paul Sartre: The Remaking of a Twentieth-Century Legend.* Hemel Hempstead, Hertfordshire: Harvester-Wheatsheaf, 1993, 214 p.

Biographical account focusing on Beauvoir's experiences with Sartre.

Okely, Judith. *Simone de Beauvoir.* New York: Pantheon Books, 1986, 176 p.

Biography of Beauvoir.

Criticism

Arp, Kristana. *The Bonds of Freedom: Simone de Beauvoir's Existential Ethics.* Peru, Ill.: Carus Publishing, 2001, 256 p.

Explores Beauvoir's existential philosophy before the publication of The Second Sex.

Ascher, Carol. "Simone de Beauvoir—Mother of Us All." *Social Text* 6, no. 2 (fall 1987): 107-09.

Brief discussion of Beauvoir's lasting impact on feminism.

———. "Women and Choice—A New Look at Simone de Beauvoir and *The Second Sex.*" *Faith of a (Woman) Writer,* edited by Alice Kessler-Harris and William McBrien, pp. 173-78. Westport, Conn.: Greenwood Press, 1988.

Examines Beauvoir's views concerning freedom, morality, and oppression as delineated in The Second Sex *and* The Ethics of Ambiguity.

Bauer, Nancy. *Simone de Beauvoir, Philosophy, and Feminism.* New York: Columbia University Press, 2001, 288 p.

Argues for a return to the principles promoted in The Second Sex *for a thorough understanding of contemporary feminism.*

Bieber, Konrad. *Simone de Beauvoir.* Boston, Mass.: Twayne Publishers, 1979, 198 p.

Monograph focusing on the originality of Beauvoir's writings.

Butler, Judith. "Sex and Gender in Simone de Beauvoir's *Second Sex.*" In *Simone de Beauvoir: A Critical Reader,* edited by Elizabeth Fallaize, pp. 30-42. London, Eng., and New York, NY: Routledge, 1998.

An essay originally published in 1986 examining Beauvoir's distinction between sex and gender in The Second Sex.

Cottrell, Robert D. *Simone de Beauvoir.* New York: Frederick Ungar, 1975, 168 p.

Overview of Beauvoir's life and works.

Davis, Mary G. "Introduction: Debating Simone de Beauvoir." *Signs: Journal of Women in Culture and Society* 18, no. 1 (autumn 1992): 74-88.

Provides an overview of contemporary feminist response to The Second Sex *and the significance of Beauvoir's theories for feminist scholars.*

Francis, Claude Fernande Gontier. *Simone de Beauvoir: A Life . . . A Love Story,* translated by Lisa Nesselson. New York: St. Martin's Press, 1987, 412 p.

Incorporates information gleaned from Beauvoir's unpublished letters and numerous interviews with the author.

Fishwick, Sarah. *The Body in the Work of Simone de Beauvoir.* New York: Peter Lang, 2002, 284 p.

Examines Beauvoir's ambivalence about the human body in her work.

Hatcher, Donald L. *Understanding* The Second Sex. New York: Peter Lang, 1984, 281 p.

Introduction to the study of The Second Sex.

Hughes, Alex. "Murdering the Mother: Simone de Beauvoir's *Mémoires d'une jeune fille rangée.*" *French Studies* 48, no. 2 (April 1994): 174-83.

Provides a psychoanalytic reading of Mémoires d'une jeune fille rangée *focusing on Beauvoir's relationship with her mother, Zaza, and Jean-Paul Sartre.*

Keefe, Terry. *Simone de Beauvoir: A Study of Her Writings.* London, Eng.: Harrap, 1983, 247 p.

Overview of Beauvoir's writings.

Kuykendall, Eléanor H. "Simone de Beauvoir and Two Kinds of Ambivalence in Action." *The Thinking Muse: Feminism and Modern French Philosophy,* edited by Jeffner Allen and Iris Marion Young, pp. 35-50. Bloomington: Indiana University Press, 1989.

Offers linguistic analysis of Beauvoir's existentialist ethics and feminist vocabulary in The Second Sex.

McCall, Dorothy Kaufmann. "Simone de Beauvoir, *The Second Sex,* and Jean-Paul Sartre." *Signs: Journal of Women in Culture and Society* 5, no. 2 (winter 1979): 209-23.

Offers reevaluation of Beauvoir's feminist perspective through examination of her complex relationship with Sartre and the influence of Sartre's existentialism in The Second Sex.

Moi, Toril. "Ambiguity and Alienation in *The Second Sex.*" *Boundary 2* 19, no. 2 (summer 1992): 96-112.

Discusses Beauvoir's philosophical analysis of female oppression in The Second Sex.

———. "Beauvoir's Utopia: The Politics of *The Second Sex.*" *South Atlantic Quarterly* 92, no. 2 (spring 1993): 311-60.

Provides an overview of Beauvoir's feminist perspective and philosophical ideals in The Second Sex.

Pilardi, Jo-Ann. "The Changing Critical Fortunes of *The Second Sex.*" *History and Theory* 32, no. 1 (1993): 51-73.

Examines the critical reception and publishing history of The Second Sex *and the lasting significance of Beauvoir's ideas for feminist scholarship.*

Powrie, Phil. "Rereading Between the Lines: A Postscript on *La Femme rompue.*" *Modern Language Review* 87, no. 2 (April 1992): 320-29.

Discusses Beauvoir's presentation of unstable female characters in Le Femme rompue *as a reflection of the difficulty women authors encounter when creating their own fictions within male literary tradition.*

Sargeant, Winthrop. "Growing Pains." *New Yorker* 35, no. 32 (26 September 1959): 186, 189-90.

Review of Memoirs of a Dutiful Daughter, *finding it curiously lacking in psychological depth and awareness.*

Simons, Margaret A. "Simone de Beauvoir: An Interview." *Feminist Studies* 5, no. 2 (summer 1979): 330-45.

Beauvoir discusses her role in the feminist movement and the influence of psychoanalytic theory and literature on her own writings and ideas about women.

———. "Sexism and the Philosophical Canon: On Reading Beauvoir's *The Second Sex.*" *Journal of the History of Ideas* 51, no. 3 (July-September 1990): 487-504.

Discusses Beauvoir's important contributions to existentialism and her problematic status as a woman philosopher in the male-dominated canon of Western philosophical literature.

———. "Lesbian Connections: Simone de Beauvoir and Feminism." *Signs: Journal of Women in Culture and Society* 18, no. 1 (autumn 1992): 136-61.

Examines Beauvoir's romantic attachments to women and the significance of her bisexuality for feminist interpretation of her gender identity and writing.

———. "*The Second Sex*: From Marxism to Radical Feminism." In her *Feminist Interpretations of Simone de Beauvoir*, pp. 243-62. University Park: Pennsylvania State University Press, 1995.

Simons maintains that The Second Sex *is rooted in the principles of radical feminism, noting that Beauvoir used this work and others to draw connections between various forms of oppression.*

Suleiman, Susan Rubin. "Simone de Beauvoir and the Writing Self." *L'Esprit Créateur* 29, no. 4 (winter 1989): 42-51.

Explores issues surrounding sexual identity and authorship in The Second Sex, *Beauvoir's autobiographical writings, and fiction.*

Ward, Julie K. "Beauvoir's Two Senses of 'Body' in *The Second Sex.*" *Feminist Interpretations of Simone de Beauvoir*, edited by Margaret A. Simons, pp. 223-42. University Park: Pennsylvania State University Press, 1995.

Examines Beauvoir's views concerning the nature of the female body and gender roles, and rejects the idea that Beauvoir's feminism is guided by principles of biological determinism.

Westbrook, Perry D. Review of *The Woman Destroyed. Studies in Short Fiction* 7, no. 2 (spring 1970): 337-39.

Provides discussion of the theme of female existential failure in The Woman Destroyed.

OTHER SOURCES FROM GALE:

Additional coverage of Beauvoir's life and career is contained in the following sources published by the Gale Group: *Beacham's Encyclopedia of Popular Fiction: Biography & Resources*, Vol. 1; *Contemporary Authors*, Vols. 9-12R, 118; *Contemporary Authors New Revision Series*, Vols. 28, 61; *Contemporary Literary Criticism*, Vols. 1, 2, 4, 8, 14, 31, 44, 50, 71, 124; *Dictionary of Literary Biography*, Vol. 72; *Dictionary of Literary Biography Yearbook*, 1986; *DISCovering Authors*; *DISCovering Authors: British Edition*; *DISCovering Authors: Canadian Edition*; *DISCovering Authors Modules: Most-studied* and *Novelists*; *DISCovering Authors 3.0*; *Encyclopedia of World Literature in the 20th Century*, Ed. 3; *European Writers*, Vol. 12; *Feminist Writers*; *Guide to French Literature, 1789 to Present*; *Literary Movements for Students*, Vol. 2; *Literature Resource Center*; *Major 20th-Century Writers*, Eds. 1, 2; *Reference Guide to Short Fiction*, Ed. 2; *Reference Guide to World Literature*, Eds. 2, 3; *Short Story Criticism*, Vol. 35; *Twayne's World Authors*; and *World Literature Criticism*.

GWENDOLYN BROOKS

(1917 - 2000)

(Full name Gwendolyn Elizabeth Brooks) American poet, novelist, editor, autobiographer, and author of children's books.

T he first African American to win a Pulitzer Prize, Brooks is considered a major poet of the twentieth century. She is known for her sensitive representations of black urban life and for combining African American vernacular speech with the poetic conventions of traditional verse.

BIOGRAPHICAL INFORMATION

Brooks was born in Topeka, Kansas, on June 7, 1917, to Keziah Wims Brooks, a schoolteacher, and David Anderson Brooks, a janitor who had once hoped to become a doctor. She was raised on Chicago's South Side where, although she encountered racial prejudice in her neighborhood and in her school, her home life was stable and loving. Her enthusiasm for reading and writing was encouraged by her parents, and she published her first poem in a children's magazine at the age of thirteen. Her early work was influenced by Emily Dickinson, William Cullen Bryant, and the English Romantic poets—William Wordsworth, Percy Bysshe Shelley, and John Keats. She was later steered toward the work of more modern poetry through her correspondence with the poet James

Weldon Johnson. Brooks made regular contributions to the *Chicago Defender*, which had published seventy-five of her poems by the time she graduated from Englewood High School in 1934. She attended Wilson Junior College, graduating in 1936, and worked briefly as a maid and then as a secretary for a "spiritual advisor" who sold worthless potions and charms to the residents of a slum tenement known as "The Mecca." Both of these employment experiences were later recounted in her poetry. In 1939 Brooks married Henry Lowington Blakely II, and a year later gave birth to a son, Henry Lowington III; their daughter Nora was born in 1951.

In 1944 and again in 1945, Brooks won the Midwestern Writers Conference Prize for individual poems. She published her first poetry collection, *A Street in Bronzeville*, in 1945. Over the next several years, she received numerous awards, among them the American Academy of Arts and Letters Award, the Eunice Tietjens Memorial Prize, and the Robert F. Ferguson Memorial Award. She was awarded a grant from the National Institute of Arts and Letters, as well as two Guggenheim fellowships, and in 1950 won the Pulitzer Prize. In the 1960s Brooks began teaching at a variety of institutions of higher learning in her home state of Illinois, and served as the Rennebohm Professor of English at the University of Wisconsin at Madison and Distinguished Professor of Arts at New York's City College. She mentored several young poets and established numerous poetry prizes and workshops, including one for the members of the Blackstone Rangers street gang on Chicago's South Side. In 1968, Brooks succeeded Carl Sandburg as poet laureate of the state of Illinois.

Brooks was greatly influenced by her introduction, at the 1967 Writers' Conference at Fisk University, to the black activist poets Amiri Baraka and Haki R. Madhubuti. Her verse after this period took a more militant turn and she began producing work more specifically aimed at a black reading audience and publishing her work with black-owned presses. She eventually founded her own press, the David Company, in 1980. Brooks continued to write and garner awards and honors throughout the 1980s and 1990s. She was appointed poetry consultant for the Library of Congress in 1985 and received the Frost Medal from the Poetry Society of America, a Lifetime Achievement Award from the National Endowment for the Arts in 1989, and a National Book Foundation medal for lifetime achievement in 1994. Brooks died of cancer at the age of eighty-three on December 3, 2000.

MAJOR WORKS

Brooks's first poetry collection, *A Street in Bronzeville,* presents readers with characters from Chicago's South Side as well as tributes to the many black soldiers who served with courage and honor in World War II, despite the racism they encountered both at home and within the armed forces abroad. Her second collection, *Annie Allen* (1949), for which she won the Pulitzer Prize in 1950, is considered by many critics to be her finest achievement. Although the work more than demonstrates Brooks's ability to master conventional literary forms, its content is devoted to exposing and denouncing American racism and injustice. One of the individual poems, "To Those of My Sisters Who Kept Their Naturals," praises those black women who refuse to subscribe to white standards of female beauty by straightening their hair. This same theme, encompassing color prejudice within the black community that also favored straight hair and light skin, was again explored in Brooks's only novel, *Maud Martha* (1953).

In 1956, Brooks published *Bronzeville Boys and Girls,* a volume of poems featuring the experiences of children and intended for young readers. Four years later, she produced a far more political collection, *The Bean Eaters* (1960), which includes "We Real Cool," a frequently anthologized poem describing the short lives of urban black males. Brooks left behind the humor and irony that characterized much of her earlier work with *In the Mecca* (1968), about the inhabitants of a slum tenement Brooks worked in when she first graduated from college. The title poem is a grim account of a mother's search for her missing child who has been brutally raped and murdered by another resident of the housing complex. The volume also contains tributes to Medgar Evers and Malcolm X, two slain heroes of the 1960s civil rights movement.

In her later work, Brooks made a conscious decision to abandon the poetic standards of the Western literary tradition in favor of formal features that would resonate with most African American readers. Collections from this period include *Riot* (1969), *Beckonings* (1975), and *Primer for Blacks* (1980). Her subject matter, still devoted to representations of the lives of blacks in urban America, also eventually included international issues and heroes including the South Africans Steve Biko and Winnie Mandela. Her collections *The Near-Johannesburg Boy, and Other Poems* (1986) and *Winnie* (1988) link the oppression of Africans with that of African Americans. In addition to her novel and her many volumes of poetry, Brooks also produced two autobiographies, *Report from Part One* (1972), and *Report from Part Two* (1996).

CRITICAL RECEPTION

Despite the many honors, awards, and critical accolades Brooks has received, contemporary scholars have asserted that Brook's work as a whole has not received the recognition it deserves. In recent years her writings have been analyzed by feminist scholars, who have rekindled interest in her novel *Maud Martha.* However, critics disagree on whether Brooks herself can be considered a feminist, since she refused to see her treatment of gender as separate from her treatment of race and class issues. Nonetheless, the female characters in her fiction and her poetry are for the most part strong women who challenge the confines of their proper roles both within the black community and within the larger American culture. In discussing Brooks's critique of the accepted standards of feminine beauty in *Maud Martha,* Harry B. Shaw observed, "Maud is clearly less concerned with being thought inferior than she is with being perceived as ugly. This concern is filtered through the point of view of an insecure, self-disparaging black woman who feels that she is homely and, therefore, uncherished because she is black and has nappy hair and 'Negro features.'" Through the character of Maud, Brooks denounced not only the aesthetic standards of white America but the apparent acceptance of those standards by blacks themselves. Brooks's appropriation of the traditional sonnet form—typically associated with a privileged, white, male speaker addressing or imploring a silent female—to give voice to the black female subject was assessed by Stacy Carson Hubbard (see Further Reading) as a transformation of the sonnet into "a vehicle for her own form of complaint, a poetry of power trespassing on the restricted ground of the traditionally male, and white, sonnet." Annie Perkins contended that Brooks always displayed sensitivity to women's issues, citing in particular the poem "Gang Girls," which offers a critique of female submission to male gang members' domination. Perkins concluded that "although Brooks has not aligned herself with feminist movements to challenge white male patriarchy, she nonetheless shares the aim of achieving social equality and economic parity for women while displaying and celebrating the full range of their capabilities and achievements."

PRINCIPAL WORKS

A Street in Bronzeville (poetry) 1945

Annie Allen (poetry) 1949

Maud Martha (novel) 1953

Bronzeville Boys and Girls (juvenilia) 1956

The Bean Eaters (poetry) 1960

Selected Poems (poetry) 1963

In the Mecca (poetry) 1968

Riot (poetry) 1969

Family Pictures (poetry) 1970

Aloneness (poetry) 1971

A Broadside Treasury [editor] (poetry) 1971

Jump Bad: A New Chicago Anthology [editor] (poetry) 1971

The World of Gwendolyn Brooks (poetry and novel) 1971

Aurora (poetry) 1972

Report from Part One (autobiography) 1972

The Tiger Who Wore White Gloves; Or, What You Are You Are (juvenilia) 1974

Beckonings (poetry) 1975

Primer for Blacks (poetry) 1980

Young Poet's Primer (nonfiction) 1980

To Disembark (poetry) 1981

Mayor Harold Washington and Chicago, the "I Will" City (poetry) 1983

Very Young Poets (nonfiction) 1983

The Near-Johannesburg Boy, and Other Poems (poetry) 1986

Blacks (poetry and novel) 1987

Gottschalk and the Grande Tarantelle (poetry) 1988

Winnie (poetry) 1988

Children Coming Home (poetry) 1991

Report from Part Two (autobiography) 1996

PRIMARY SOURCES

GWENDOLYN BROOKS (POEM DATE 1987)

SOURCE: Brooks, Gwendolyn. "To Black Women." In *Blacks*, p. 502. Chicago, Ill.: The David Company, 1987.

In the following poem, Brooks addresses her African American sisters, praising their ability to prevail despite hardship and lack of recognition.

"TO BLACK WOMEN"

Sisters,
where there is cold silence—
no hallelujahs, no hurrahs at all, no handshakes,
no neon red or blue, no smiling faces—
prevail.
Prevail across the editors of the world¡
who are obsessed, self-honeying and self-
    crowned
in the seduced arena.

      It has been a
hard trudge, with fainting, bandaging and death.
There have been startling confrontations.
There have been tramplings. Tramplings
of monarchs and of other men.

But there remain large countries in your eyes.
Shrewd sun.
The civil balance.
The listening secrets.

And you create and train your flowers still.

GENERAL COMMENTARY

HORTENSE J. SPILLERS (ESSAY DATE SPRING 1985)

SOURCE: Spillers, Hortense J. "'An Order of Constancy': Notes on Brooks and the Feminine." In *Reading Black, Reading Feminist: A Critical Anthology*, edited by Henry Louis Gates Jr., pp. 244-71. New York: Meridian, 1990.

In the following essay, the original version of which was published in the spring 1985 issue of the Centennial Review, *Spillers discusses feminist elements in Brooks's work, maintaining that the worlds Brooks represents always include men.*

The adopted procedure for this essay is neither fish nor fowl and, as such, breathes in the impure air of literary interpretation, verging on social theory. It assumes for the moment a sort of critically illegitimate stance—the literary text *does* point outside itself—in the primary interest of leading the reader back inside the universe of the apparently self-contained artifact. With some luck, we hope to negotiate between two different kinds of related critical inquiry: What does the writer teach us, or illuminate in us, concerning situations for which we need a name,[1] in this case, the "feminine," whose very conjuring broaches more confusion than we can comfortably settle in the course of a workday? What does the writer take with her from "experience" to the transmuting work itself?

I

The stage of interaction that arises between an audience and the visible aspects of a public performance sketches a paradigm for understanding the social dimensions of an aesthetic act, but it also brings into focus the most acute aspects of consciousness—to perceive, to be perceived. On the one hand the subject is acting; on the other, acted upon. The distance between these related grammatical properties, mobilized by a single term, is precisely the difference and overlap between subjects and objects of interrogation, neither of which can be split off from the other with integrity. To the extent that the writer and the artistic process that she or he engages are neither wholly autonomous nor dependent, but, rather, interdependent, suspended between opposing yet mutually coexistent means, both writer and process approach the "feminine," whose elusive claims escape not only precise definition but also decided terrain. Gwendolyn Brooks's "feminine" across the poet's writing career is a nominative of many facets. About this still center, modifiers shift, lose and gain emphases alternately, but there is an "order of constancy" here whose active paradoxes throw light on the paradox of the "feminine."

There are few things riskier at the moment than defining the "feminine" in a way that does not offend what, until yesterday, we thought of as its primary subject—"woman herself." Is this complex of traits gender related and, therefore, a locus of attributions culturally conferred, biologically sustained? Can we count on its disappearance when the "revolution" comes? Is the "feminine" yet one other heterosexist hoax whose genuinely fraudulent character will be revealed as such in the figurative "new world" of widened sexualities presently upon us?[2] According to the editors of a fairly recent work on feminist theory,[3] feminine consciousness is only a single aspect of woman-consciousness (whatever we decide that is), but it seems difficult to specify the boundaries of either, except insofar as "woman-consciousness" and "feminine" inscribe the absence of "male" and "masculine." *Feminist Theory: A Critique of Ideology* attempts to correct and revise our negative perspective on ideas regarding the "feminine." For feminist theoreticians, the "feminine" is often, ironically enough, an "object of analysis rather than a source of insight."[4] Insofar as the subject is the "object of attention of another," we might have anticipated that the "feminine" arises "from the sensation of being looked at,"[5] and involves, relatedly, the dialectical tensions at work in the "double consciousness."[6] Simone de Beauvoir in *The Second Sex* describes an existential correspondence between "feminine" and "other" so that both might be seen as a negation of ego (read "male"). We would intrude on this accumulated calculus of power a point of view too often short-shrifted: I would say that the "feminine" and "other" are subjectivities who experience their being from a posture of affirmation. We would regard the exception as aberrance. A theory that maintains the aberrant at the center of its interests might answer the needs of public policy, or unwittingly serve the requirements of the dominant myth, but its responsive capacity to the living situations of the social subject is, at times, embarrassingly limited.

Trapped between the Scylla of feminist mandates on the one hand and the Charybdis of dominative and patriarchal modes of power on the other, the subject of "feminine attributes" is apparently abandoned to a useless set of traits, not unlike a sixth toe or finger in some phase of human evolution. Exactly what it is that women in history are asked to abdicate in order to achieve authentic consciousness has the elusive subtleties of a Steuben glass or a cymbidium orchid and is invested with about as much actively negotiable and comparative power, except we know when we have seen either and that it is difficult for us to say now *why* we'd *prefer* not to be without access, real or imagined, to either. The "feminine" evades definition, perhaps, because it is both ubiquitous and shadowy on the world's body:

> The nuances of sensitivity to appearances, the fine distinctions in the observance of one's behavior and that of others, the silent exploration of the consciousness in which one functions as an "other" deserve our attention as means toward understanding human motivation and psychology as well as our condemnations as the product of asymmetrical power.[7]

For Keohane and the other editors of *A Critique of Ideology,* the "feminine" locates a disposition in the eyes of a gazer, female and male, but if the angle of seeing is obverted, how does the gazed upon see itself, see out?

For Julia Kristeva, the female body, specifically, the "maternal body" takes us to the limen of "nature/culture": The "not-sayable," the body of the mother escapes signification, meaning, sense because the "mother-woman"

> is rather a strange "fold" (*pli*) which turns nature into culture, and the "speaking subject" (*le parlant*) into biology. Although it affects each woman's body, this heterogeneity, which cannot be subsumed by the signifier, literally explodes with pregnancy—the dividing line between nature and culture—and with the arrival of the child—which frees a woman from uniqueness and gives her a chance, albeit not a certainty, of access to the other, to the ethical. These peculiarities of the maternal body make a woman a creature of folds, a catastrophe of being that cannot be subsumed by the dialectic of the trinity or its supplements.[8]

I am not entirely certain that the "feminine" and "female body" may be taken as synonymous constructs, but it does appear that the space of overlap between them is so broad that we cannot imagine one without deploying the other. For theorists of an "écriture feminine," of which Kristeva is said to be one, the "feminine" has little to do with women in history. In fact Alice Jardine's *Gynesis* ("woman-process")[9] concentrates on male writers in "modernity" and their reinstitution of the female body at a fundamental level of writing: 1) the subversion of the idea of a unified speaking subject; 2) the undermining of all authority; and 3) the figurative use of the female genitalia as a mode of decentering and deconstructing the text. The "fold," or "pli," the "hole," the "gap," or "interstice" become items of a revised critical lexis that is designed—we are led to believe—to engender a radically different ideology and practice of writing, focusing "feminine" and "female body" at the center of altered positions and dispositions.

In Jardine's view, these changes on the textual surface of male-writing (Derrida, Lacan, Deleuze, Guattari, of *Anti Oedipus,* specifically) invite a direct response from feminist investigation/theory, lest the latter find itself isolated from the contemporary intellectual scene. What seems to me a fairly complete breach between matters of feminist social theory and feminist metatheory appears beyond repair. If Susan Suleiman is correct, then "the cultural significance of the female body is not only (not even first and foremost) that of a flesh-and-blood entity, but that of a *symbolic* con*struct.*"[10] [Emphasis Suleiman's.] To see the issue otherwise, Suleiman thinks, is to pursue the anachronistic. The "programmatic and polemical aspect" of *The Female Body in Western Culture* is to claim for the "feminine," more pointedly, the "female body," a status of contemporaneity: "Not everything we see and hear today deserves to be called contemporary . . . it is not enough to be *of* our time in order to be *with* our time."[11]

Risking an anachronism, with no hope at all of doing "my bit" here to rejoin "theory and practice," I would offer that the "flesh-and-blood entity" of the female body lends itself to historical enactment—I cannot imagine a more forceful example than the "mother-woman"—whose dimensions are *symbolic* at those points of contact where communities of women *live out* the symbolicities. If we concede that *discursivity* manifests a worrisome element of translation, then I see no reason why we might feel compelled to jettison the terrible flesh and blood. Though I am primarily concerned here with the specific uses of a cultural construct we would designate "feminine" in the case of a particular writer/poet, it is not beyond me to imagine what practical turn a theory *might* take.

The stipulative definition that I would offer for the "feminine" trait of human personality takes us back to Keohane's "Introduction" and an inquiry into the connotations of "everywhereness" and shadow. To the degree that "body" in reference to the "feminine" might be analogously read with Blake's Tharmas,[12] the principle that contains the rational will, the creative powers, the affective dispositions, the erotic centers, I mean "body" alongside the preceding terms—ubiquity, shadow. We might think of all three terms under the head of "surface" and "extensivity," meaning by both the definition that Schiller offers in "Letters on the Aesthetic Education of Man"[13] (sic). If "maximum changeability" and "maximum extensivity" stand here for the "feminine," then we would urge a sense of its application along more than a single line of stress, since neither the "feminine" nor receptivity to phenomena is alien to the masculine potential. Though Brooks's "feminine" refers primarily to the female, the resonance of the former is not at all unlike Woolf's "incandescence,"[14] which is not gender-rigid in its artistic practice and inspiration. My aim in trying to free up the "feminine" from its wonted vocation is not to generate an hermaphroditic wonder and lose women/woman in a figurative replication of naive liberalist gestures, but to suggest that we replace our weapon in our holsters until an enemy has clearly shown itself: The idea (if it ever was) is not to be rid of the "feminine," whose details have yet to be fully elaborated, say nothing of exhausted, but, rather, to purge the world for a wider display of its powers. According to Jardine, at least *some* "men" might agree. More precisely, we wish to know what the "feminine" can do from its own vantage point, and such inquiry is "gynocritical" in its profoundest impulses.[15]

II

Gwendolyn Brooks's feminine landscape is clearly demarcated as heterosexual territory. Males are never far away from its female centers of attention, even when the male presence is overwhelmingly implicit and memorial, as it is in **"The Anniad"** and various other poems in the volume, **Annie Allen**.[16] The poet's particular address to communities of women in her audience is persistent in the canon across four decades of work, reflecting the storm and stress of this period of African-American women's political consciousness with the 1981 publication, **Primer for Blacks: Three Preachments,** **"To Those of My Sisters Who Kept Their Naturals."**[17] Brooks's work interweaves the female and her distinctive feelings into a delicate tissue of poetic response to the human situation, defined by a particular historical order—the African-American personality among the urban poor in the city of Chicago between World War II and the present of the poem.[18] Within this body of work, the female voice, for all its poignant insistence, is a modified noun of vocality, danced through a range of appetite and desire that does not stand isolated from a masculine complement. If poetry is our teacher in this instance, not entirely estranged from theory, but subsuming it, then the "feminine" is manifest as

an emphasis, neither hostile to "masculine" nor silenced by it. We are rather reminded now of an image of Jungian resolution with the circumferences of double circles overlapping to form an altered distance through the diameters of both.[19] It is only by virtue of a perversion in the seeing that the overlapping circles can declare any independence whatsoever. They relinquish their imagined uniqueness to an enlarged order of circularity, as the peripheries of both now involve us at the center of each. Getting the point does not necessarily require that we embrace the idea, or the "man," but that we acknowledge it as a viable figure in the universe of female and "feminine" representability. This involved image of circularity renders a geometry for poets, and those are the depths and surfaces that claim our attention at the moment.

In Brooks's poetic order of things, the "feminine" is neither cause for particular celebration nor certain despair, but near to the "incandescent," it is analogous to that "wedged-shaped core of darkness,"[20] through which vision we see things in their fluid passage between dream and waking reality, as multiple meanings impinge on a central event. The poet's novelette *Maud Martha* does not exhaust Brooks's contemplation of the "feminine," but provides a point of illumination and departure concerning an important phase of her long and distinguished career as an American poet. If not chronologically central to the canon, **Maud Martha,** beside **"The Anniad,"** is experienced by the reader as an "impression point."[21] In the Harper and Row edition of her poetry, **Maud Martha** brings to closure the poems in **A Street in Bronzeville** and **Annie Allen,** while it prepares the way for **The Bean Eaters** and, from the sixties, the stunning poetry of **In the Mecca.**

Maud Martha was published in 1953.[22] The leading subject and sole consciousness of the narrative, Maud Martha Brown, comes of age during the Depression era. As the work is broadly reflective of the social issues of two American decades, it might be read as the poet's version of a cultural synthesis. By the end of World War II, Maud Martha is expecting her second child; her brother Harry returns home in one piece from combat, and her first child Paulette grows up. Paulette is old enough to recognize that the white "Santa Claus" of a large department store in the city of Chicago does not like little black girls. Somehow, the jolly creature cannot even bring himself to *look* at the child, having hugged all the blond ones, Paulette observes, to her mother's chagrin.

The instances that disclose racist sentiment in the text are so muted and understated that they are rendered elements of background in which ambience the primary issues of the narrative unfold: the extent to which the female can articulate her own values of sanctity and ritual, of aspiration and desire, of order and beauty in a hierarchically male-centered world, limited by the idioms of the literal.

Insofar as Maud Martha sustains heterosexual mating, she is "male-identified," but such identification is much less compelling than the imaginative integrity that keeps her alive and well. The woman reader of this text might well wonder how successfully Maud Martha would negotiate a sphere of influence broader than the domestic and the connubial. It is true that her talents are constrained by what we would now consider four narrow walls that provide her with neither a room of her own nor the time to miss it.[23] She is not a culture heroine, is not a woman's warrior, and the big bumbling immensities of the romantic and epic imagination—Rebellion, Bravery, Courage, Triumph, among them, those capitalized terms that Northrop Frye describes as "aureate"[24] and which Brooks's own **"Strong Men Riding Horses"** humorously debunks[25]—do not touch her identity in any remote way. And so we wind down into an arena of choices that take us to the heart of dailiness, of the mundane and the unglamorous, or the carefully circumscribed ambition. We protest—but isn't *this* the customary woman's place?

That the distaff is, from the point of view of the narrative and the world surrounding it, the peculiar custodial property of the female is not a conclusion. It is a beginning. Maud Martha commences with the raw elaborations of realism (read also "reality") and transforms them into a habitable space. This talent for the clean and well-lighted, however, is not only the central and embattled miracle of Maud Martha's world, but also a preeminent social value because it represents an actual living of what has been imagined, imagining what is known. We might think of Maud Martha's "miracle" as a gifted kind of "making" that turns the inner to the outer and redeems the room as an elaboration of the human and social body.[26]

If we look at the structurations of Maud Martha's character from her own place in the order of things, then we accord her special attention because of her highly developed powers *to play* and to play well within the framework of possibilities to which she has access. We can very well wish for her, imagine empathetically, a richer field of play; but the limitations imposed on her in no way mitigate her own considerable abilities to shape and define the world as she encounters it. In contrast to her husband, Paul Phillips, who occupies and rents space in his world, without an angle on it, or a critique of it, Maud Martha engages their common circumstance with an eye for the occasion. This looking through, for want of a better term, might be called a kind of displaced fable making so that Maud Martha might be seen as the "true poet" of the narrative and the writer herself the "imitator" of it. These functions come together under the guise of a central narrator, who speaks Maud Martha's script through a ventriloquized medium—the poet, assigning to the leading agent the primary powers of ordering.

The central thematics of the work are made explicit in the twenty-first and twenty-second episodes:

> Could be nature, which had a seed, or root, or an element (what do you call it) of constancy, under all that system of change. Of course, to say "system" at all implied arrangement, and therefore some order of constancy.
>
> (227)

> What she had wanted was a solid. She had wanted shimmering form; warm, but hard as stone and as difficult to break. She wanted to found—tradition. She had wanted to shape, for their use, for hers, for his, for little Paulette's, a set of falterless customs. She had wanted stone.
>
> (228)

A "stone," a "solid," as isolated lexical features, convey notions of the concrete and abstract at once. We can contemplate them on their own terms, apart from context to modify their function, but in relationship to "shimmering form," to "tradition," their meaning enriches to insinuate an indefinite specificity—a community of notions that range in weight and appeal from the architectural to the ingeniously diminutive object of decoration; from issues concerning values and aspirations to the specific questions and longings of desire. That the terms overlap on "falterless customs" and, by inference, the whole enterprise of shaping and preserving, foreshortened in the enumerated signs, renders Maud Martha a social "conservative," as "order of constancy" implies. But the wealth of connotative markers that the narrator achieves by mixing the metaphorical referents would suggest that Maud Martha's "conservatism" locates not only the preeminent force of intelligence at work in the narrative, but also the intelligence that tries things. I am assuming that Brooks's narrator does not intend irony or mockery when Maud Martha's consciousness speaks a desire for "stone," for "solid," or that she intends to say that Maud Martha is naive in wishing to establish "falterless customs." I would want to see the central figure's essentially experential character and lust for form as a necessary fable of paradox for living a life—in "literature," or "the streets"—that is sane and rewarding. For Maud Martha, "tradition" is not a dead letter, or a reliquary of ancestral ghosts. "Tradition" here would be "founded" the hard way, on the living, on a sort of frontier of immediacy, whose ready-to-hand objects might be invested with the only force for magic that there is—that which the imagination attributes to the event of neutral or indifferent meaning.

None of the items in Maud Martha's catalog of transmuted domestic objects can be regarded as esoteric: coffees, fruitcakes, plain shortbread, black walnut candy in "little flat white sheets," a dinner table spread with "white, white cloth . . . china . . . in cheerful dignity, firmly arranged, upon it" (232). Despite the availability of the scene at hand, we are compelled to consider it in a new light, seeing the details as "the plenitude of plan."[27] Maud Martha's "plan," however, is not so much a reflection of the arbitrary as it is a retrieving from chaos or oblivion the ordinary domestic object, much like poems cut "Out of air, / Night color, wind soprano, and such stuff."[28] If we perceive that the narrator is involving us in a romance of the diurnal, there is much to support the conclusion—the central artistic purpose of **Maud Martha** expresses the essentially "heroic" character of the "unheroic" by altering our opinion of "heroism" in the first place. Furthermore, "art" loses its remoteness and its claim to exclusion as Brooks imposes upon it a radically democratic context and purpose.

This capacity to draw the outer into oneself, retranslating it into an altered exterior, as though fields of force magnetized by an abiding centrality, locates the process that I would stipulate as the "feminine," finding in it the maximum exposure of surface to change. We will see shortly how the particular "epistemic habit of meaning"[29] in this narrative reenforces both the artistic energies of the piece and the function of the narrative itself as suggestive "equipment for living."[30]

In steady contrast to Maud Martha, there is a "husband," both a "real" one and the idea of "husband" in its limited masculine composition: "This man was not a lover of tablecloths, he could eat from a splintery board, he could eat from the earth" (232-233). The often sardonic quality of the writing and its persistently ironical force save the narrative from pathos as it challenges our sympathies to focus on specific detail in whimsical combinations. "Tablecloths" acquires metonymic value, as it defines the whole of Paul Phillips's inadequacies of imagination by humorously remarking a partial instance of it. Laughter here is usually ironically pointed so that antagonism to laughter falls into perspective rather than exaggeration or prominence. In that sense, the work evinces a tough-minded balance of tensions between the impinging extremes of Maud and Paul's "reality."

Maud Martha is herself as much an observer of her own scene as she is a participant in it, a maker of it. Alongside her dreamwork, she maintains the prerogatives of detachment so that at no point in the narrative—even when Maud Martha thinks the most harshly truthful things about herself and those around her—does the reader "feel sorry" for her. She will thrive not simply because she can bear to suffer—as traditional African-American female iconography valorizes beyond any practical use, beyond any probable endurance in the life of female progeny. Maud Martha thrives because she wills it through diverse acts of form, woven from the stuff of everyday life. Quite simply, she is smarter than Paul, who is not without desire, but rather, oppressed by the wrong ones.

Paul is not an adequate husband and lover precisely because he is lacking in "capable imagination." To use Alice Walker's terms for the particular etiology that blocks imaginative expansiveness in the man, Paul is a "racialist," with an overwhelming wish to have a liaison with a "light-skinned" female; the prize of "light-skin" would release in him the fruition of a range of fantasies so elusive to his grasp that they would thrill the analyst's heart and pocket. It is not an exaggeration to say that even now, at some years' remove from the passions, intensities, and commitments of the sixties' Black Nationalist movement in the United States, African-American men's community has yet, it seems, to come to terms with its profoundest impulses concerning African-American women and their "Africanity." The failure would appear ongoing, disquieting, repetitive, and disappointing. So close to the new century, this failure to grasp seems threatening in its political, cultural, and possibly genetic implications for an entire American community. From the vantage of the 1950s—since the tangle of issues to which I allude is not dated—the poet is not unaware of these charged and searching questions in their immediate impact on the ontological dimensions of her characters. Maud Martha is black skinned and, there but by the grace of a keen intelligence and generous affection, might have been undone by her world's sporadically obscene response to the color of her skin.

Paul's limitations are not solely determined by his interest in the "light-skinned" female. We can grant him whatever wishing his heart can stand, but that he sees no farther than the pointed recurrence of an imagistic symptom makes him ripe for a class of psychological subjects that we recognize as the obsessive-neurotic. That this heterosexual male would potentially love many women is not a serious crime, we finally decide, but Paul wants a figure of adoration to fill up his mind; he wants to fall into gyneolatrous[31] madness at the foot of a marvelous deception, male-engendered. There is more: Having no direct route of access to the originating inspiration of the European tradition of courtly love, embodied in "the female body in the West" (and "they" never mean "us,") Paul substitutes the fantasy's *next* best thing—the "high yaller" female hybrid of his community's peculiar American nightmare.

Two observations: First, Paul's low-order, low-key madness is decided not by the fictional context of his dreams but rather by their particular historical context. Traditionally, we are reminded that a lynching rope awaits the neck of the African-American male so bold as to approach his "it"—"the female body in the West." But we are reminded not by the local narrative before us but by the one that *haunts* it—his fate in approaching the woman/woman-body that is not "black."[32] This terroristic imagery is muted in the contemporary period but not at all forgotten. Therefore, the "white" female acquires in Paul's eyes an altogether exaggerated status as object of mimetic desire. Second, the amorous figures that surround the characterizations of "black" are *historically* determined as ideas and icons of "not freedom," of bindings and couplings, of bondage and manipulation so complete that we can barely imagine, for example, just what Paul and Maud Martha would look like in a different universe of figuration. The liberation project would release the character from the diseased "fix" of static iconography just as surely as it would the African-American community from the planned obsolescence of national policy and economic practice. While we must ultimately encounter Maud and Paul on the terms that the story offers and *for themselves,* we understand, unmistakably, that an aspect of "extra-territorial" narrative so decisively shadows their tale that the genuinely agonized

pairing here is not simply "male" and "female," "feminine" and "masculine" (as though they were simple), but these binary oppositions as they have been orchestrated by the loudest and most persistent teleology, "good" and "bad," and finally mediated, through the very force of the language, by the most fateful of culturally ascribed antinomies—"black" and "white." To that extent, Paul is victim. We dislike him because, contrary to Maud Martha, he doesn't *resist;* obeys no individual imperatives or tested arrogance that would push through the accumulated slime of a national history.

III

Chapter 19 of the narrative, "If You're Light and Have Long Hair," brings home the particular social dynamics to which I refer. Married for a time, Paul gets his first invitation to the Foxy Cats' Annual Foxy Cats Dawn Ball. Though we recognize a persistent element of parody in the descriptive apparatus adapted to these scenes, we also acknowledge their quite accurate conformity to a certain configuration of African-American middle-class upward mobility. The Foxy Cats (who resemble the undergraduate fraternity in its earnest and ingenuous allegiance to fixed notions of proper behavior, sartorial style, and brainless imitation of what its members *think* "class" is) bears the brunt of a well-deserved satirical commentary. The wording of the invitation to the "Dawn Ball" is humorously, nervously redundant:

> He was to be present, in formal dress . . . No chances were taken. 'Top hat, white tie and tails,' hastily followed the 'Formal Dress,' and that elucidation was in bold type.
>
> (205)

For Paul, the invitation represents "an honor of the first water, and . . . sufficient indication that he was, at last, a social somebody." This ironical vein is underscored and nourished in Maud Martha's thoughts by a brazen stroke of self-admission:

> My type is not a Foxy Cat favorite. But he can't avoid taking me—since he hasn't yet thought of words or ways strong enough, and at the same time soft enough—for he's kind: he doesn't like to injure—to carry across to me the news that he is not to be held permanently by my type, and that he can go on with this marriage only if I put no ropes or questions around him. Also, he'll want to humor me, now that I'm pregnant.
>
> (207)

Days later, in the "main room of the Club 99," Maud and Paul join the other Foxy Cats and their "foxes" at the "Dawn Ball" itself. Paul, in effect, abandons Maud Martha shortly after their arrival, having escorted her to a bench by the wall, leaving her (211). Who he's left her for—"Maella"—is "red-haired and curved," of the "gold-spangled" bosomness. Rhetorically kin to a "sleek slit-eyed gypsy moan" of **"The Anniad"** and a "lemon-hued lynx / with sandwaves loving her brow" of the **"Ballad of Chocolate Mabbie,"**[33] "Maella" is not so much an embodied representation as she is a structure of emblematic traits that we recognize from other textual sources. The narrator needn't "explain." "Maella" need not speak, does not, nor can, since an entire secondary text speaks around her. In the maelstrom of emotions released by the appearance of this Idea, to whose bosom Paul salutes, we think of "gold-spangled" as a resonance of "star-spangled" and of Paul as locked in a veritable state of adoration. Maud Martha watches, thinking

> not that they love each other. It oughta be that simple. Then I could lick it. It oughta be that easy. But it's my color that makes him mad. I try to shut my eyes to that, but it's no good. What I am inside, what is really me, he likes okay. But he keeps looking at my color, which is like a wall. He has to jump over it in order to meet and touch what I've got for him. He has to jump away up high in order to see it. He gets awful tired of all that jumping.
>
> (214)

The narrator does not dwell on this aspect of the scene as we will see, in time, a cluster of intricately differentiated motives involved in it, nor is the painful resonance elaborated here repeated. We understand its perspective against the whole. My isolating it is intended to point an emphasis in suggesting the nature of schismatic tendencies that divide Paul from himself and those around him and to convey a sense of what it is that Maud Martha strives to overcome as her own imagination projects it, as others impose it.

In psychological terms, we might say that Maud Martha symbolizes a far more successfully "integrated" character than Paul, and this fluency of response is primarily captivated by narrative strategies that blend the advantages and benefits of stream-of-consciousness and concealed narration in bringing to light a character whom we know in the interstices of her thought. The stage of action in **Maud Martha** is embedded in none other than the landscape of its central consciousness, and from this focal point—replete with particular biases and allegiances—we come to know the "world" of the narrative.

What we discover through Maud Martha's perceptions unfolds in a rolling chronology. In other words, the narrator is so selective in the detailing "spots of time" in reference to the character that the work may be described as episodic, paratactic, and notational, or structured from peak points, of which the Foxy Cats' Dawn Ball is a single example. This imitative "autobiography" starts almost in the beginning, as we find out that the subject liked "candy buttons, and books, and painted music (deep blue, or delicate silver) and the west sky, so altering, viewed from the steps of the back porch, and dandelions" (127). The sentences are simple, tending toward the fragmentary, and swift on the surface of the visual, tactile world. We imagine not so much a structure of physical and physiological traits called "Maud Martha" as we do a profoundly active poetic sensibility, happily unbound in a world of marvelous color, of infinite allure.

Metaphors of painting seem especially apposite to narrative strategies here since the content of the opening episodes, in particular, is composed primarily of sensual imagery perceived through the brilliant color and texture often associated with impressionism.[34] To say that the "brush strokes" are light and decidedly whimsical is to insinuate the paratactic character of the writing: episodes, if not individual sentences, are self-contained units of perceptual activity. To speak of writing as painting (and somehow, the figure never goes the other way) metaphorizes either activity, but the narrator appears deliberately involved in the apparent crossing of arbitrary artistic boundaries in order to delineate character and movement in their initial urgency. To do so, the narrator adopts loose connections between things, weak or fairly discontinuous transitions from point to point. The agent is not a studied, or deliberative body, and the narrative, consequently, inscribes a deft movement of "symbol-making," as it starts up, we imagine, from the threshold of immediate feeling, of unchecked sensual response.

The painting metaphor further suggests the poet's attempt to invest the diurnal with vibrant color. Even the "grays" of this "universe" invite lyrical play, as Maud Martha roams her kitchenette for our benefit, building with a passionate eye for the unique angle in human and object relations. As a result of these self-conscious stylistic moves, the narrator intimates a confluence of thematic and strategic modes so thoroughgoing that Maud Martha stands in synecdochic relationship to the surround. Merging into an untrammeled equality of means, agent and scenic device are reversible.

Though the episodes are arbitrarily connected, they are logically sequential: Narrative traces lead from childhood and early years at school through adolescence, to young womanhood and the adult years that follow. Maud Martha's first beaux, the death of her paternal grandmother, the quality of her dream life, the special nature of her relationship to her father and brother, the affective ambivalence that prevails among the women of the immediate family, for instance, become discrete moments of perception that take on even weight and intensity. Significant elements of the tale are, therefore, dispersed and accumulative, rather than dense and elaborated. In fact, the weakened copulatives create an aesthetic surface without "bulges"—the "peaks" and "valleys" of a schematic plot structure—or syntactic elements that do not adhere in a relationship of subordination and coordination. To that extent, the narrative voice speaks in the concise rhythms of the contemporary poem. I have in mind symptoms of alignment rather than particular instances.

It doesn't matter, for instance, that the seeds of Maud Martha's troubled "femininity" are planted early on in her own awareness and, consequently, the reader's, because such information assumes no unusual or immediate focus: Two years older than Maud, sister Helen is "almost her own height and weight and thickness. But oh, the long lashes, the grace, the little ways with the hands and feet" (128-129). We will know more in time about Helen, the beautiful sister, but this clue, closing the inaugural scene, so casually intrudes itself that we register it only later as crucial. Even though the bulk of the narrative concerns Maud Martha's marriage and maternal career, these emphases fall into solid perspective with the whole. Relatedly, the narrative is unplotted (or not obviously plotted), pursues no climactic surprises, and resolves in syntactic and dramatic rhythms that evade rigid closure: "And in the meantime, she was going to have another baby. The weather was bidding her bon voyage" (306). The agreeable sense of an ending here could just as easily mark the beginnings of the next excursive phase of "autobiography," since pregnancy announces new life as well as the anticipation of one kind of finish; "bon voyage," analogously, situates a valedictory and salutatory marker. This strategic ambiguity, with its teasing abeyance of resolution, brings us back to questions concerning the "feminine."

IV

Virginia Woolf conjectured that the woman-text adapted to the rules of interruption—by the female writer's children, lovers, and general imperatives of caretaking; it was, then, of necessity, *short*. An "écriture feminine," apparently hinting the functions of the female body—with its fluidities, secret passageways and escape routes, or those convoluted folds along the uterus and vaginal vault—releases the "feminine," as a corporeality turned trope, onto a wider human path, not blocked by the specificities of female reproductive process. Once upon a time, in a cackle of rage, a Boston-not-so-lady declared to me what might well serve as a point of overlap between Woolf and latter-day theoreticians on the body writing: "Anything that takes more than nine months to bear is a joke!" She was talking about *novels*. But is it true that the vital, concentrated intensities of the pregnant body place on urgent notice the artist everywhere—"study long, study wrong"?

I would exercise the greatest caution in supporting a "feminine writing" as *practice,* if not as *theory,* however, since we presently have no acceptable name for the same individual writer— female or male—when she or he does *not* write in the suspension of authority, in the subversion of the hierarchical, in the shameless assertion of the vibrant mood. Is "Gwendolyn Brooks," for example, of **"In the Mecca,"** the similar body that produced ***Maud Martha***? No outer markings, or facings of the surface suggest it. And it is precisely this protocol of radically divergent aims that comes home in the singularity of an artist's career (or even *a* writing) that would challenge a rigorous notion of trophic determinism. There is in my reading of this novelette, however, symptoms of a program that I would designate "feminine," and it is embedded in the work's insistence on *self-involvement;* if this constant reference and return to the "inner" surrenders to figurative movement, then we might offer that female person's having to "listen" to her body and its cyclical rhythms dictates "stillness" as a redoubtable human and cultural value. This "serenity," replete with its own active turbulences through the whole being, recovers "invisibility," or the mental "calibrations," as a supremely *active* domain of the human. "Mrs. Ramsey" provides an insight:

> To be silent; to be alone. All the being and the doing, expansive, glittering, vocal, evaporated; and one shrunk, with a sense of solemnity, to being oneself, *a wedge-shaped core of darkness, something invisible to others.*[35]
>
> [Emphasis mine.]

I emphasize the latter half of the sentence in order to suggest that the "active"/"passive" split is as culpable in any discussion of the "feminine" as the other patriarchal/patriarchist oppositions that we already know too well to repeat. In a remarkable episode from **Maud Martha,** the narrator provides another example of what I would call a paradoxical nesting of being-impulses—the personality drawn into the pluralities of a self, "shrunk," as it were, opens, capably, outward: As a young woman, Maud Martha essentially preserves her sense of childhood wonder. Walking down a Chicago street, taking in the rich scenes of store windows, she experiences so palpably the objects that she confronts that the reader is not completely sure (and no longer cares to be) if her body remains in Chicago or actually goes off to New York:

> When she was out walking, and with grated iron swish a train whipped by, off, above, its passengers were always, for her comfort, New York bound. She sat inside with them. She leaned back in the plush. She sped, past farms, through tiny towns, where people slept, kissed, quarreled, ate midnight snacks; unfortunate folk who were not New York bound and never would be.
>
> (174)

This complex of desire, through which the encounters of the subject are refracted, measured, considered, consumed, is poised in brazen contrast to the "actual" world of Maud Martha; that the "imagined" and the "real" abrade unrelentingly is intended, because we gauge Maud Martha's internal resources in even bolder relief against the brute "facts." We could go so far as to say that the poet's insistence on the narrative strategies of the piece and its rhetorical energies that plumb the interior world of the character spares Maud Martha the peculiar burdens of the "naturalistic" agent. In other words, if **Maud Martha** were read through eyes not the character's own, as would an omniscient voice, bent on imposing a content from the "outside," already made to order, then we would not only lose Maud Martha's complexity, but would also conclude that victimage alone determines her. By forcing the reader, or inducing her, to confront Maud Martha as the primary and central consciousness of the work, its subject *and* object of gazing, speaking through the redoubled enunciations of her own stream-of-thought and a translation of it, the poet reclaims the territorial rights of an internal self and strikes for our mutual benefit a figure of autonomy. Despite her "blackness," her "femaleness," her poverty-line income, and perhaps *because* of these unalterable "facts" of

mensuration, Maud Martha is allowed access to her own "moment of being," and the narrative renders its record.

It is beside the point that Maud Martha speaks few quoted or dramatic lines in the narrative, or that her private ways are quiet and unspectacular, or that she tolerates more of Paul than we think she ought; she is not a feminist, fifties' style. The demonstration, I believe, of woman-freedom is the text itself that has no centrality, no force, no sticking point other than the imaginative nuances of the subject's consciousness. Maud Martha's drama remains internal, and that interiority engenders the crucial aesthetic address of the work. We might want to alter drastically her "environment," change her clothes, where she lives, grant her a broader sphere of contact, but such is *our* fiction. In spite of it, we suspect that the character already has the capacity to disclose larger and even more refined versions of a fictional self *on her own terms.* Perhaps we could argue that the most impassioned attention to the drama of the interior self exposes the "feminine."

When young Maud Martha looks at magazines that say "New York," describing

> good objects there, wonderful people, recalled fine talk, the bristling or the creamy or the tactfully shimmering . . . her whole body become a hunger, she would pore over its pages.
>
> (174)

That "looking" is governed here by "hunger" in the young Maud Martha reinforces the severe privacy of the perceptual act and provides a remarkable stroke of synaesthesia in the conflating tactile and visual sensation. The subject is not a mere looker, but looks with the entire ingestive range. Maud Martha's "good objects" are placed alongside objects of melancholy or objects of the nakedly furnished within a range of semantic valences that gain distinction solely by her capacity to imbue them with polyvalent meaning. We gather this stylistic trait on the basis of lexical items apparently chosen from two widely divergent arrays of things that operate in a kind of binary adhesion—those "good objects" of the above-quoted passage and those that belong with her kitchen sink, or the radiators in her parents' house, "high and hideous. And underneath the low sink-coiled unlovely pipes, that Helen said made her think of a careless woman's underwear, peeping out" (164). But then there are also natural objects that show the humble in special atmosphere and that persist as the contrapuntal assertion against the ravages of time. From two excerpts of the narrative: The house the Browns fear they might lose to the Home Owner's Loan Association, the one in which Maud Martha and her siblings have grown up, materializes an enamored object of the entire family, but for Maud Martha, "house" abstracts into an object of lyricism—of "writing":

> with the snake plant in the jardiniere in the southwest corner, and the obstinate slip from Aunt Eppie's magnificent Michigan fern at the left side of the friendly door . . . and the emphatic iron of the fence and . . . the poplar tree . . . Those shafts and pools of light, the tree, the graceful iron might soon be viewed possessively by different eyes.
>
> (154-155)

From the ending:

> But the sun was shining, and some of the people in the world had been left alive, and it was doubtful whether the ridiculousness of man would ever completely succeed in destroying the world—or, in fact, the basic equanimity of the least and commonest flower: for would its kind not come up again in the spring? come up, if necessary, among, between, or out of—beastly inconvenient!—the smashed corpses lying in strict composure, in that hush infallible and sincere.
>
> (305)

In the first instance, the vocabulary of natural objects so overwhelms the house of the living that the latter takes on a spirit of timelessness, enters a domain of the immutable. It is noteworthy that Maud Martha believes that the western sky acquires a certain unique aspect only from the back of this house: "the little line of white, somewhat ridged with smoked purple, and all that creamshot saffron". (156). In the second instance, the natural objects—sun and earth—submerge the human deed in a grandly absurd and irresistible carnival of folly. In its concise reverberations of the strangely ridiculous and rhetorical questions of the disembodied voice from *The Waste Land*,[36] Brooks joins Eliot in adopting closural images from the iconic grotesquery of war—World War I for Eliot, World War II for Brooks. For both poets, the corpse loses its gothic and horrible magnificence as it is brought low, so to speak, into the stream of diachronous, even vegetal, being. This collapse of hierarchy in the poetic status of objects is entirely consonant with the principles of writing that order the whole of **Maud Martha.**

Whether or not the objects in Brooks's binary array are human contrivances or aspects of the natural order, both articulate and embody an impression of eternal forms. Their varied aspects and illuminations of the immanent would suggest not only the indeterminacy of their occurrence,

but also the fluent nature of Maud Martha's stunning perceptual powers in the combinations, recombinations, and juxtapositions that the objects achieve on her site. A suggestion from the linguists as an insight into "making": If the objects that claim our attention are to the senses what words are to the vertical columns of the dictionary, then the stuff of seeing is the *lexis* of "experience"; their various combinations and laws of revision and recombination, its "syntax"; and the meanings and their arrangements, its "semantics." By calling the "feminine" a power that operates under concealment, I mean primarily the ability it grants us to stand still and see, or in one's perceptual place, await a content, arrange a consequence.

V

Returning momentarily to the scene of the Foxy Cats Ball will provide us, in a final example, with several crucial and interlocking points concerning the subject's consciousness and the study in subtleties that the "feminine" reveals as a theme of convergence between the beholder and the beheld. The rapidly alternating currents through which the reader watches the simultaneity of opposing rhetorical, aesthetic, and dramatic functions in this scene are translatable into the "feminine" beyond this text inasmuch as they express the intricacies of the "double consciousness." If Maud Martha cannot escape the implications of her mirror, or the pretexts that impinge on her, then she is fully capable of exploiting such captivity to the degree that the scene itself, the other agents on it, its purposes and motivations are reflected in her looking glass, whose thaumaturgic properties can bless or damn the occasion as the subject sees fit. Intent on neither, the voice of the interior monologue mobilizes a plenitude of terms that evoke the fundamental ambivalence at the core of consciousness itself.

We have already examined one of the decisive psychological components of this scene as Maud Martha, suddenly not unaware of her dark skin and its dubious social uses, fixes herself as subject and object of deeply embedded public and private motives. In other words, the extra-text that speaks loudly, even when none of the agents "mouth" it dramatically, and the text of Maud Martha's consciousness are interlarded threads cut cross the same bias. The "extra-text" to which I refer, examined at greater length in a progressive work, traces the historical implications of African-American women's community as a special instance of the "ungendered" female, as a vestibular subject of culture, and as an instance of the "flesh"

ABOUT THE AUTHOR

MULLANEY COMMENTS ON BROOKS'S RELATIONSHIP TO FEMINISM

Today's renewed interest in the writing of black women, Brooks feels, has brought attention once again to her novel, *Maud Martha*, but she does not believe that her works have been sought out as primarily "women's writing." She has never seen her woman's vision as a separate one. As she says, "I've never belonged to that Ms. group of black, or white, women writers." Yet, although Brooks may not write with feminist intent, her female voices speak with a conviction that enables them to rise above the rigid confines of what is often deemed, even in the black experience, a woman's place. Her women are assertive, conscious people who battle "isms" in ways that are consistent with their experience. Like Brooks herself, they defy subordination and reconstruct their own aesthetic in an often hostile, ugly world.

Mullaney, Janet Palmer. An excerpt from "Gwendolyn Brooks." In her *Truthtellers of the Times: Interviews with Contemporary Women Poets*. Ann Arbor: University of Michigan Press, 1998.

as a primary, or first-level "body."[37] Because African-American women in their historic status represent the *only* community of American women *legally* denied the mother's access to her child, their relationship to the prerogatives of "gender" must be reexamined as the select stratagem of an ethnic solidarity; of the dominant community's strict exploitation of the gender rule as an instrument of a "supremacist" program. This systematic unfolding of iconic and epistemic violence embattles Maud Martha, *without naming itself,* and discloses the central impoverishment of a public naming and imagining that have not yet discovered appropriate terms for this community of social subjects. In that sense, the "mulatta"—and we might assume that "Maella" is either proximate to, or appropriates, such status, figures into this calculus as the historic "alibi" that "shields" the African-American female from sight. The weight of *this* textuality, or a "symbolic construct" that *lives* itself out, or of a corporeality-turned-trope-returned "corporeality," *falls* on the historical and fictive subject with the convictions of steel. But the interconnections between "given" and "discovered" become the inseparable discretions of the tailor's herringbone. Or, to shift metaphors, an entire central nervous system is at work so that consciousness is perceived as the stunning poise in a dual and complicated awareness.

The paragraphs that inform us that Maud Martha is escorted to a bench and left—"she sat, trying not to show the inferiority she did not feel"—descries a single pattern in the fabric, intersecting others in an arrangement that the eye takes in at once. We are aware of an emphasis of weight, color, texture, mode of design. Just so, Maud Martha wholly experiences the rich implications of her "objectivity" and "subjectivity" in their yoked occurrence. If she is seen, she also sees, as the scene before us is rendered precisely demonstrative of perceptual activity as an occasion of mutually indulged gazing.

Despite the sharp satirical underpinnings of the scene, Maud Martha acknowledges that the "ball stirred her . . . made toys of her emotions." "The beautiful women in gorgeous attire, bustling and supercilious"; the overgallant young men; the drowsy lights and smell of food and flowers; the body perfumes and "sensuous heaviness of the wine-colored draperies at the many windows" conjure up notions of the sybaritic. The draped and gorgeous flesh, divided between female and male, suggests the tease of sexuality: We call it "glamour" and recognize in the scene the ritual of mating behind whose masks the actualities of lust are arrested. The scene's drama relies on the tensions set in motion between the arrested and the enacted. We are drawn to this moment (and moments like it in "real life") because it configures the vertical suspension of love-making as it leads, eventually, toward the bedroom, either *actively* or *fantastically.* But if "to die," to play a moment on the range of conventional literary meanings released in the infinitive, marks the final move of the love game as well, then the narrator cunningly exploits the ambiguities of intention by bringing together objects of decoration and gaiety that evoke shades of the mortal flesh, of death.

"Wine-colored drapery" also belongs to the funeral procession, as does the terrible satiety of flowers. Even the music of the ball runs a chordal progression that describes over the course of the evening the convoluted objectives of the moment: "now steamy and slow, now as clear and fragile as glass, now raging, passionate, now moaning and thickly gray" (210). The gallant young men, "who at other times unpleasantly blew their noses," master the required social proprieties of the occasion, but they are also the imagined subjects of promising toilet humor, darting "surreptitiously into alleys to relieve themselves" and the comedy of the private, unguarded self that sweats and swears at work and scratches its "more intimate parts." Maud Martha's dancing partner, another male, dispatched to entertain her while Paul celebrates the red arms of Maella, "*reeked* excitedly of tobacco, liquor, pinesoap, toilet water, and Sen, Sen." [Emphasis mine.] This aggregation of disparate olfactory sensations reinforces disparity in the mild tongue-twisting assonance of the second five-syllable grouping of the line—"tobacco" / "liquor." A deeper structural point obtains. The body, disguising from itself the deep knowledge of its own mortality, claims this scene for the grave as well as the bed. We could say that a careful consideration of the weave of the passage might suggest that their shared imagery of the horizontal posture collapses distinction. Just as the flesh is seen here in its various lights, **Maud Martha** dances the range of feeling in its complicated twists and turns.

VI

That the fictional subject disperses across an "inner" and "outer"—differing angles on a mutually concurrent process—fits well with coeval theories of reading that posit "division" at the center of knowing; *je est un autre*—there is no subject, only a "barred subject," in a constant oscillation of deferments. But reading counter to the current, we would claim for Maud Martha a subject's singularity that *contains* "division," in fact, generates it, through a female body, who, among social bodies, is the only one who can reproduce sameness and difference at once: The child resembles the begetters, "borrows" their tendencies, yet describes its own features of uniqueness. If we regard the "feminine," in the artistic instance, as a trope of the reproductive process, we might argue that it, like the female body, locates the convergence of antithetically destined properties—"female," "male," "mind," "body," "same," "other," "past," "future," "gazer," "gazed upon." Inscribing a notion of containment—in rooms, in the serene and vibrant spaces of the interior, in the intimacies that pass from lovers to enemies and back—the narrator suggests that the "feminine" constitutes the particular gifts of a *materialized* interior. Treating the text as a "strategy for encompassing a situation,"[38] we

think of it—in its brevity, in its fluent movement among textures of feeling—as a figure of the "feminine," writing itself into articulate motion.

Notes

1. In discussing the social uses to which literature may be put, Kenneth Burke identifies the art work as a strategy for naming situations for which we need a name, "for selecting enemies and allies, for socializing losses, for warding off evil eye, for purification, propitiation, and desanctification, consolation and vengeance, admonition and exhortation, implicit commands or instructions of one sort or another." In "Literature as Equipment for Living," *The Philosophy of Literary Form: Studies in Symbolic Action* (Berkeley: University of California Press, 1973), 304. The "feminine" as an embattled idea offers a single example of a mandate for strategy.

2. Adrienne Rich, "Compulsory Heterosexuality and Lesbian Experience," Catharine R. Stimpson and Ethel Spector Person, eds., *Women: Sex and Sexuality* (Chicago: University of Chicago Press, 1980). 62-92. Rich's article is addressed primarily to the experiences of lesbian women as they are refracted through the dominant cultural patterns of heterosexuality; implicit in her argument is the idea that the heterosexual synthesis represents an aspect of the oppression of women.

3. Nannerl O. Keohane, Michelle Z. Rosaldo, and Barbara C. Gelpi, eds., *Feminist Theory: A Critique of Ideology* (Chicago: University of Chicago Press, 1982).

4. *Ibid.*, ix.

5. *Ibid.*

6. For an American audience, Du Bois's concept of the "double consciousness" (*Souls of Black Folk*) in reference to African-American cultural apprenticeship remains the preeminent concept and icon for explicating the dual and conflicting character of the misplaced person "at home" in an alien context. Originally published three years after the turn of the century, this collection of essays has undergone a number of editions. (New York: Fawcett Publications, 1963).

7. Keohane *et al, Critique of Ideology,* ix.

8. Susan Rubin Suleiman, ed., *The Female Body in Western Culture: Contemporary Perspectives* (Cambridge: Harvard University Press, 1986); "Stabat Mater," 115.

9. Alice Jardine, *Gynesis* (Ithaca: Cornell University Press, 1985).

10. Suleiman, *The Female Body,* 2.

11. *Ibid.*

12. One of the poet's "prophetic books," *Vala, or the Four Zoas* offers a preromantic view of the "fall" of human society. "Tharmas," or the human body, represents one of four characters in Blake's work, suggesting the various ordering principles of the human personality. David V. Erdman, ed., *The Complete Poetry and Prose of William Blake* (Berkeley: University of California Press, 1982).

13. The excerpts from Schiller to which I refer are taken from his "Letters" in *Critical Theory Since Plato,* ed. Hazard Adams (New York: Harcourt Brace Jovanovich,

1972). The distinction that Schiller draws between sensuality (the sensations) and form (the reason) in "Letter 13" and their mutual reconciliation and repose in the play-drive has been considerably influential on my own thinking about this topic.

Not wishing to confine "sensual/sensuality" to the "feminine" (since I believe that the "feminine" engenders its own forms and formalities), I have, nonetheless, been struck by the evidence of the "common sense" in speculating that the woman's intimate proximity to the theme of human continuance and nurture offers prime material for her cultural apprenticeship in the feelings and notions of receptivity. While I would agree with Dorothy Dinnerstein's position in *The Mermaid and the Minotaur* (New York: Harper Colophon Books, 1976) that the responsibility of human nurture must be shared by female and male, I shudder to think what might happen if the contest for "equal time" leads to women's abandonment of the site of the child, as has men's renunciation too often, and with absolutely fatal results.

14. Virginia Woolf, *A Room of One's Own* (New York: Harcourt, Brace and World, Inc., 1957). "Perhaps a mind that is purely masculine cannot create, any more than a mind that is purely feminine . . . Coleridge . . . meant, perhaps, that the androgynous mind is resonant and porous; that it transmits emotion without impediment;' that it is naturally creative, incandescent and undivided" (102).

15. Elaine Showalter, "Feminist Criticism in the Wilderness," in Elizabeth Abel, ed., *Writing and Sexual Difference* (Chicago: University of Chicago Press, 1982), 9-37. The displacing of male bias by various evidence of female experience generates the gynocritical enterprise that Showalter elaborates in this essay.

16. Gwendolyn Brooks, *The World of Gwendolyn Brooks* (New York: Harper & Row, 1971). During the 1970s, Brooks switched her publishing allegiance from the New York house to Detroit's Broadsides Press and, later on, to the Third World Press of Chicago as testimony to her commitment to the political ideas of the Black Nationalist movement. *Riot, Family Pictures,* and *Beckonings* were all volumes published under the Broadsides logo.

17. Gwendolyn Brooks, *Primer for Blacks: Three Preachments* (Chicago: Brooks Press, 1981). "Black Love," first published in *Ebony*, (August 1981), appeared in 1982 under the auspices of the Brooks Press.

18. Brooks, *The World of GB*, 125-307.

19. Showalter, "Feminist Criticism in the Wilderness," 30-31. Showalter's discussion and diagram of the work of British anthropologist Edwin Ardener poses a useful paradigm for perceiving the relationship between dominant and muted groups. The Ardener diagram is also a circle, reminiscent of a penumbra, in which case the *y* circle (muted) falls within the dominant circle *x*. The crescent of the *y* circle outside the dominant boundary might be called "wild." Showalter proposes that we can think of the "wild zone" of women's culture spatially, experientially, or metaphysically. Spatially, it stands for an area that is literally no-man's land.

In this imagined relationship between Brooks's "feminine" and "masculine," both circles bear crescents on their periphery. These equally "wild zones"

are mutually exclusive, by inference, and we have no idea what the characters who live there utter. My guess is that their "wild" is a spiralling crescent to Ardener/Showalter's so that we would have to draw a far more elaborate configuration in order to address the realities of "color."

20. Woolf's central consciousness in *To the Lighthouse*, Mrs. Ramsay, provides an astonishing association for what I later explore here as a "severe privacy."

21. Frank Kermode, *The Genesis of Secrecy: On the Interpretation of Narrative* (Cambridge: Harvard University Press, 1979). From Dilthey, Kermode adopts this formulation to explain the hermeneutical relationship between interpreter and work. I borrow it here to offer that *Maud Martha* punctuates a significant period of work in the poet's career and that after it Brooks seems to turn increasingly toward the meditative poetry that we associate with *In the Mecca* and *After the Mecca*.

22. Brooks, The World of GB. (All references to *Maud Martha* come from this edition, page numbers noted in the text.)

23. For a full discussion of Brooks's projected sequel to *Maud Martha*, the reader should consult "Update on 'Part One': An Interview with Gwendolyn Brooks," by Gloria T. Hull and Posey Gallagher, *College Language Association Journal*, XXI, No. 1 (September 1977), 26-28. Brooks points out that the extant *Maud Martha* "has much autobiography though I've twisted things" (27).

For a complete autobiographical sketch, Brooks's *Report From Part One* (Detroit: Broadsides Press, 1973) is indispensable. The poet explains to Claudia Tate in a series of recent interviews that she is at work on a second volume of autobiography. Cf. *Black Women Writers at Work* (New York: Continuum, 1983), 39-48.

24. Northrop Frye, in a description of Emily Dickinson's poetic diction, takes the term "aureate" from medieval poetics: "big soft bumbling abstract words that absorb images into categories and ideas." *Fables of Identity: Studies in Poetic Mythology* (New York: Harcourt, Brace and World, 1963) 202.

25. Brooks, *The World of GB*, from "The Bean Eaters," 313.

26. A remarkable study of the human and social body as a site of *contracted* or *expanded* ground, Elaine Scarry's *Body in Pain* (New York: Oxford University Press, 1985) offers an unusual reading of aspects of Holy Scripture and excerpts from the Marxian canon as speculative inquiry into the principles of "making" and "unmaking."

27. From Gwendolyn Brooks, "The Womanhood: The Children of the Poor," *Selected Poems* (New York: Harper & Row, 1963), 53.

28. Brooks, "The Egg Boiler," *The World of GB*, 366.

29. Richard Ohmann's discussion of narrative/prose style as the writer's "epistemic choice" offers a richly suggestive study in the behavior of the rhetoric of fiction, in "Prolegomena to the Analysis of Prose Style," in *Essays in Stylistic Analysis*, ed. Howard S. Babb (New York: Harcourt Brace Jovanovich, 1972), 35-50.

30. Burke, "Literature as Equipment for Living," in *Philosophy of Literary Form*, 293-305.

31. The term is taken from W. J. Cash's classic study of the mythic operations of the "white male mind" of the South: *The Mind of the South* (New York: Alfred A.

Knopf, 1941). It is not altogether surprising that "mind" in this case is confined to the male, while the female becomes the object of investigation.

32. I have placed these typically descriptive words for two American races in quotation marks here because the terms are often inadequate for what we actually mean. As we know, "color" in American is "washable" since "black" registers along a range of genetic traits, and so does "white," or the notion of "passing" would have no value whatsoever, either as an actual deed, or a trophic possibility. "Race" should be an anachronism, or dead, but it is neither. We await, in the meantime, a vocabulary that gets us through the complexities that we sometime observe.

33. Brooks, *The World of GB*.

34. Mary Helen Washington's "Plain, Black, and Decently Wild: The Heroic Possibilities of *Maud Martha*" in Elizabeth Abel, Marianne Hirsch, and Elizabeth Langland, eds. *The Voyage In: Fictions of Female Development*, (Hanover, New Hampshire: University Press of New England, 1983), 270-286 gives a good account of the coeval critical opinions of the work.

35. Compare with note 20.

36. "Stetson! / You who were with me in the ships at My-lae! / That corpse you planted last year in your garden, / Has it begun to sprout? Will it bloom this year? / Or has the sudden frost disturbed its bed?" from Valerie Eliot, ed., *A Facsimile and Transcript of the Original Drafts including the Annotations of Ezra Pound* (New York: Harcourt Brace Jovanovich, 1971), 136.

37. In two separate studies, I examine these historical/terministic issues with an eye to locating African-American women's community in relationship to questions of feminist investigation: "Mama's Baby, Papa's Maybe: An American Grammar Book" and "'The Tragic Mulatta': Notes on an Alternative Model—Neither/Nor." These pieces anticipate a longer work that examines the rift between "the body" and "the flesh" as means of social and cultural production.

38. Burke, "Literature as Equipment for Living," in *Philosophy of Literary Form*.

ANNIE PERKINS (ESSAY DATE 2001)

SOURCE: Perkins, Annie. "The Poetry of Gwendolyn Brooks (1970s-1980s)." In *Women Making Art: Women in the Visual, Literary, and Performing Arts since 1960*, edited by Deborah Johnson and Wendy Oliver, pp. 43-63. New York: Peter Lang Publishing, 2001.

In the following essay, Perkins offers an in-depth analysis of Brooks's life and works.

Gwendolyn Brooks (b. 1917) was born in Topeka, Kansas, and was reared in Chicago, her lifelong home. With the support and nurture of her parents, Brooks began writing poetry at age seven. She was first published at age thirteen, and by the time of her graduation from Englewood High School, had published seventy-five poems in the Chicago Defender.

In 1936, Brooks graduated from Wilson Junior College. In 1939, she married and settled happily into domesticity with her husband, Henry Lowington Blakely II, and later Henry III, their baby son. During this period, Brooks continued to write, first winning the 1943 Midwestern Writers' Conference Award and then publishing her first volume, **A Street in Bronzeville** *(1945). Her second volume,* **Annie Allen** *(1949), earned the 1950 Pulitzer Prize for Poetry, the first to be awarded to a Black writer. A year later, Brooks's daughter, Nora, was born.*

Balancing home, family, and writing, Brooks published within a decade **Maud Martha** *(1953), a novel;* **Bronzeville Boys and Girls** *(1956), a book of children's poetry; and* **The Bean Eaters** *(1960). In 1968, she received a National Book Award nomination for* **In the Mecca,** *written in the aftermath of the Martin Luther King assassination.*

In honor of her distinguished body of work, Brooks has received many awards, including the Frost Medal from the Poetry Society of America, the American Academy of Arts and Letters Award, the National Book Awards Medal for Distinguished Contribution to American Letters, the Sewanee Review's *Aiken-Taylor Award, and the National Medal of Arts from the President of the United States.*

From 1985 to 1986, Brooks served as the twenty-ninth (and final) Consultant in Poetry to the Library of Congress. In 1988, she was inducted into the National Women's Hall of Fame. More recently, in 1994, she was a Jefferson Lecturer. Brooks holds seventy honorary doctorates and has taught at several institutions.

A poetry promoter, Brooks has sponsored poetry prizes throughout the country and has mentored and influenced scores of writers. Two tributes, To Gwen with Love *(1971) and* Say that the River Turns: The Impact of Gwendolyn Brooks *(1987), attest to the devotion and admiration she has inspired among younger writers. Her reminiscences and observations appear in two autobiographies,* **Report from Part One** *(1972) and* **Report from Part Two** *(1996). Among her recent poetry is* **Children Coming Home** *(1991).*

* * *

Gwendolyn Brooks—Pulitzer Prize winner, Illinois Poet Laureate, and poetry ambassador—has earned popular and critical acclaim for a body of work that spans more than five decades. Rich in ideas, complex in form, and centered in the Black experience, Brooks's poetry celebrates human aspiration and the push for empowerment nourished and sustained by respect for self, community and heritage. Through striking poetical sketches, Brooks offers an inspiriting and expansive vision which affirms the necessity for Black unity. However, readers of any race, class, gender, or nationality can identify with her gallery of women, men and children who reflect attitudes and aspirations common to humankind, and who experience life's ordinary—and extraordinary—triumphs and trials.

Critic Dan Jaffe maintains that "the purpose of art is always to communicate to the uninitiated, to make contact across seemingly insurmountable barriers" (54-55). Indeed, Brooks's family pictures do speak across boundaries, for as James N. Johnson observes, "The excellence of Gwendolyn Brooks is that she is able to tell it like it is while speaking to the basic humanness in us" (48). That she sparks this human connection is evident in her sustained popularity among diverse audiences. Brooks enjoys enthusiastic receptions at colleges and universities, at prisons and public schools, at churches and community festivals, at conferences and conventions, wherever she travels—reading, lecturing, mentoring, teaching, and always promoting poetry.

During her distinguished career, Brooks has written prose pieces, including a novel, *Maud Martha* (1953), and a two-volume autobiography—*Report from Part One* (1972) and *Report from Part Two* (1996). But her literary reputation rests principally upon some twenty volumes of poetry, beginning with her debut collection, *A Street in Bronzeville* (1945), and including other volumes such as her 1950 Pulitzer Prize winner, *Annie Allen* (1949). Much of Brooks's poetry is collected in *The World of Gwendolyn Brooks* (1971), *To Disembark* (1981), and *Blacks* (1987).

In her early years, Brooks was primarily an art-for-art's sake poet, who appealed to her largely white audience for equal treatment of Blacks by depicting their lives with dignity and pathos. Like most Black people of that era, Brooks shared the hope that racial equality and equal opportunity could be achieved, but as the civil rights struggles grew more confrontational, her poetry began to reflect the racial tensions of the times. Noting the overly political nature of Brooks's work, a reviewer of *The Bean Eaters* (1960) posed this rhetorical question: "In times as troubled as ours, what sensitive writer can avoid a certain obsession with contemporary ills that may be temporary? . . . Of course she writes of Emmett Till, of Little Rock, of Dorie Miller, of a white [woman] disgusted to see her child embrace the Negro maid. . . . Increasingly, in each of her books, [social poems] have appeared" (Webster 19).

Brooks might have continued writing about social problems had she not attended a writers' conference at Fisk University in Nashville in 1967, where she met a group of Black poets, including Imiri Baraka (then LeRoi Jones). This encounter transformed Brooks's perception of her art and her audience. She was amazed by this group of young, self-affirming writers who were declaring in their poetry what James Brown was commanding in his music: "Say it loud: 'I'm Black and I'm proud.'" This talented group—nurtured in the turbulent decade of civil rights struggle and antiwar sentiment; of marches, demonstrations, and assassinations; of political upheaval, social protest and national trauma—had clarified themselves as BLACK and were shouting it from the ghettoes of the inner-city and from the halls of academia. Feeling as if she were "in some inscrutable and uncomfortable wonderland," Brooks experienced an incipient sea change: "I didn't know what to make of what surrounded me, of what hot sureness began almost immediately to invade me. I had never been, before, in the general presence of such insouciance, such live firmness, such confident vigor, such determination to mold or carve something DEFINITE [capitalization hers]" (*Report from Part One* 85). These young, mostly college-educated Blacks, who combined a Black Power 'Black-is-beautiful' aesthetic with a Black Panther self-help activism, were looking at themselves through their own eyes and celebrating the view. They had rejected totally the integrationist stance of their parents. Presented with this different perspective, Brooks, then in her early fifties, began to reevaluate her own views:

What I saw and heard . . . was of a new nature to me . . . I had been asleep. If I had been asleep. If I had been reading even the newspaper intelligently, I too would have seen that [the integration effort] simply was not working, that there was too much against it, that blacks kept exposing themselves to it only to get their faces smacked. The thing to stress was black solidarity and pride in one's brothers and sisters. People didn't instruct me [in this idea] . . . I just picked it up by osmosis, listening to [the young poets] and watching what they did. I went around with them sometimes and heard them giving readings. Listening to them was wonderful.

(*Report from Part One* 176)

While "apprenticing" with these young artists, Brooks also became involved in her community at the grassroots level, conducting writing workshops for a youth gang (the Blackstone Rangers) and participating in neighborhood and cultural events. These experiences eventually transformed her conception of her artistic role and of her audience. In 1972, she wrote, "Today I am conscious of the fact that—my people are Black people; it is to them that I appeal for understanding" (*Report from Part One* 177). She announced that her intention would be

> to write poems that would somehow successfully "call" . . . all black people: black people in taverns, black people in gutters, schools, offices, factories, prisons, the consulate; I wish to reach black people in pulpits, black people in mines, on farms, on thrones; *not* [italics hers] always to "teach"—I shall wish to entertain, to illumine. My newish voice, which I so admire, but an extending adaptation of today's [Gwendolyn Brooks] voice.
>
> (*Report from Part One* 183)

The contemporary voice of Gwendolyn Brooks is populist, realistic, and celebratory, often hortatory, but always grounded in and attuned to the conditions and sensibilities in Black people. Blackness is what I know very well," she explains. "I want to talk about it, with definitive illustration, in this time, in this time when hostility between races intensifies and swirls." "I go on believing," Brooks observes, "that [Blacks who have little allegiance to Blackness] will, finally, perceive the impressiveness of our numbers, perceive the quality and legitimacy of our essence, and take sufficient, indicated steps toward definition, clarification, connection" (*Report from Part Two* 143). Thus, Brooks's post-1967 poetry became a vehicle for declaring and disseminating a new Gospel— the affirmation of Blackness, group solidarity, self-respect, and a sense of cultural heritage among an "entire range of categories: South Africa, South State Street, the little babe just born in the South Bronx" (Melham, *Heroism* 26).

But in spite of its new impulse, intent, and message, Brooks's poetry remained rooted in the tradition of well-wrought, polished verse. It continued to manifest what Jaffe calls a "dedication to craft, to the business of making" (50). Having studied Black poets like Paul Laurence Dunbar, Langston Hughes, and Countee Cullen at an early age, Brooks had developed an appreciation for craftsmanship. Furthermore, after completing high school, she had received training in the techniques of modern poets—T. S. Eliot, Ezra Pound, and Robert Frost—during classes at the Chicago Southside Community Art Center conducted by Inez Stark Boulton, a wealthy Chicagoan and reader for *Poetry Magazine* (Melham 7-9). With excellent training and natural talent, Brooks developed and cultivated a masterful technique that fuses exquisite diction with allusion, ironic contrasts, juxtaposition, repetition, alliteration,

and other devices to create poems in which language, form, and idea happily coalesce. Poems selected from Brooks's collected works will enable readers to experience the artistry of a remarkable poet to apprehend the values informing her art, and to revisit issues of race and gender through her eyes.

As a female poet, a wife, and a mother, Brooks has been sensitive to issues affecting women and families throughout her career. As a matter of fact, her first published volume, *A Street in Bronzeville*, included "The Mother," a monologue exploring the psychological effects of abortion. And although Brooks has not aligned herself with feminist movements to challenge white male patriarchy, she nonetheless shares the aim of achieving social equality and economic parity for women while displaying and celebrating the full range of their capabilities and achievements. As Brooks has stated, "Black women, like all women, certainly want and are entitled to equal pay and 'privileges,'" but, in her view, the issue of female equality is complicated by a "twoness" that Black women feel, relating to race and gender. Therefore, she continues, "Today's black men, increasingly assertive and proud, need their black women beside them, not organizing against them" (*Report From Part One* 199). Womanist[1] critic Chikweye Okonjo Ogunyemi elaborates upon this view: "The black woman instinctively recoils from mere equality because . . . she has to aim much higher than that to knit the world's black family together to achieve black, not just female transcendence" (69). Or as scholar Barbara Omolade explains, "Black women have united with black men to struggle for national liberation from white male rule" (253). However, espousing racial unity to achieve liberation does not mean accepting Black male rule, for as Alice Walker avers in this context, "Silent, uncritical loyalty is something you don't usually inflict on your child" (353). Brooks herself speaks plainly on the matter of male domination:

> Black women must remember, through all the prattle about walking three or twelve steps behind or ahead of "her" male, that her personhood precedes her femalehood . . . She is a person *in* [emphasis hers] the world with wrongs to right, stupidities to outwit, *with* [emphasis hers] her man when possible, on her own when not. And she is also here to enjoy. She will be here, like any other, once only.
>
> (*Report from Part One* 213)

One can understand, then, Brooks's subtle critique of male domination and female submission in the poem "Gang Girls" from *In the Mecca* (1968). In her poetry workshops, Brooks had interacted with the Blackstone Rangers, a male gang, and although her portraits of the group are mostly sympathetic, she does not romanticize the lifestyle and its effects upon young women. In the poem, the narrator describes gang girls as "sweet exotics," suggesting that they are alien to their tough, male-circumscribed neighborhood. Although Mary Ann, a typical gang girl, "sometimes sighs for Cities of blue and jewel / beyond [the] Ranger rim of Cottage Grove," her longings will not be fulfilled because male rivalries curb her mobility. Excursions beyond the neighborhood are dangerous, the poem states; therefore, Mary Ann, a sensitive, imaginative girl, is restricted by male-imposed boundaries to a stifling, unstimulating environment. The narrator aptly describes her as "a rose in a whiskey glass." This image strikingly reveals the disadvantaged position of gang girls in their relationships with gang members. To escape the deadening effects and frustrations of her confinement, Mary Ann turns to the few diversions her neighborhood offers: "bugle-love," "the bleat of not-obese devotion," and "Somebody Terribly Dying, / under the philanthropy of robins."

In a male-controlled Cottage Grove, gang girls acquiesce to their boyfriends' sexual demands. The narrator describes a passionless encounter in which Mary Ann simply responds as if following a script:

> . . . swallow, straight, the spirals of his flask
> and assist him at your zipper, pet his lips
> and help him clutch you.
> Mary, the Shakedancer's child
> from the rooming-flat, pants carefully, peers at
> her laboring lover . . .
>
> (*In The Mecca* 48)

The phrases "pants carefully" and "peers at her laboring lover" illustrate Mary Ann's lack of interest and involvement during this intimate encounter. Much like Langston Hughes's Harlem dancer, the real Mary Ann is not in that place. The shift in the mood from declarative to imperative lends a coercive quality to the "love-making," thereby implying that Mary Ann is not a consenting partner but a sexually exploited servant. Traditional notions of male authority along with peer influence, negative self-images, and non-affirming family dynamics can condition young women to act against their interests. The narrator warns that the result of female submission will most likely be a blighted future:

> Settle for sandwiches! Settle for stocking caps!
> For sudden blood, aborted carnival
> the props and niceties of non-loneliness—
> the rhymes of Leaning.

This poem suggests that thwarted female potential, arising in this instance from a system of male domination and female submission (complicated by race and social class) is antithetical to Brooks's goal of racial unity and solidarity. Mutual respect and trust, the cornerstones of unity, cannot flourish within a climate of oppression. In this climate, females are unlikely to reach "Cities of blue and jewel," and, ultimately, the creative potential of the human family is diminished.

Gang girls like Mary Ann are not likely to blossom into self-respecting women, but in her gallery, Brooks provides models of self-empowered females worthy of emulation. *Blacks* includes the poem "**To Those of My Sisters Who Kept Their Naturals**," which praises Black women like Brooks herself, who did not abandon the natural hairstyle once it had become unfashionable. The "natural," or Afro, as it was called in the 1960s, symbolized racial solidarity and Black pride, but because it was worn by outspoken activists like Angela Davis and Rap Brown, it represented to the mainstream a threatening militancy, an unsettling statement of willfulness, self-affirmation, and political radicalism, which many were unprepared to accept. Within this context, Brooks salutes those Afro-wearing women who faced social ostracism and economic disadvantage within and beyond their communities. The speaker begins dramatically, announcing,

> Sisters!
> I love you.
> Because you love you.
> Because you are erect.
> Because you are also bent.
> In season, stern, kind.
> Crisp, soft—in season.
>
> (*Blacks* 459)

The opening words trumpet forth like a musical flourish, with the exclamation point in the first line signaling a stentorian call and indicating excited anticipation. To imitate this effusiveness, Brooks lengthens each line so that the first boasts a single word; the second, three; the third, four. The speaker appears to love her "sisters" because, even in their literal difference or their varying postures, they accept and appreciate themselves. Brooks reinforces their heterogeneity by employing metrical diversity—iambs, spondees, and anapests—and she emphasizes their shared qualities through repetition (Because you; in season) and antithesis (stern, kind; Crisp, soft).

The speaker commends the actions of these self-respecting women:

And you withhold.
And you extend.
And you Step out.
And you go back.
And you extend again.

      . . . . .

You reach, in season.
You subside, in season.
And All
below the richrough righttime of your hair.

                       (459)

The lilting regularity of the "And you" lines—mostly iambic diameter except for the final line in iambic trimeter—highlights the common quality of radical pride these women exhibit. Furthermore, the rhythm of the lines suggests the literal and metaphorical acts described in the poem, namely, withholding and extending, stepping out and going back. In addition, the luxuriant alliterative compounds "richrough" and "righttime" mirror the dense texture of the women's natural hair.

Brooks employs a series of negative statements, featuring repetition and rhythm, to convey the speaker's admiration and delight at the "'sisters'" acceptance of Blackness:

You have not bought Blondine.
You have not hailed the hot-comb recently.
You have never worshiped Marilyn Monroe.
You say: Farrah's hair is hers.
You have not wanted to be white.

                       (460)

Recognizing that Caucasian looks are ethnically incorrect for most Black women (although many women classified as Black because of the "one drop" rule look European), the speaker is pleased that her "sisters" accept what is natural for them. Women's studies scholar Rita Dandridge explains that for Brooks, "having a natural . . . is emblematic of being true to one's nature" (294). Therefore, she disdains efforts to "wriggle out of the race" (Melham, *Heroism* 26). It disturbs her that "hordes of Black men and women straighten their hair and bleach their complexions and narrow their noses and spell their eyes light grey or green or cerulean—thereby announcing: What nature afforded is poor, is substandard, is inferior to Caucasian glory" (**Report from Part One** 127). To the contrary, Brooks asserts in her poem that Black hair is "the rough dark Other music!" is "the Real / the Right. / The natural Respect of Self and Seal!" She assures her "sisters" that their natural hair is a "Celebration in the world!" (460).

The self-affirmation lauded in Brooks's poem originates in the sassy, self-assertive attitude many Black girls begin to display in adolescence. Alice Walker characterizes their "audacious, courageous,

and willful behavior" as "womanist" (xi). Scholar Tuzylane Jita Allan observes that this attitude "is a rich, self-affirming psychological resource that facilitates survival advantage in the social pecking order." Indeed, this "womanist audacity," she continues, "becomes in the wider social context an unbidden demolisher of arrogant authority" (10-11). In the seventies and eighties, as Blacks entered the marketplace to assume positions opened as a result the civil rights struggles, the natural hairstyles mentioned earlier were unacceptable in some quarters. Many Black women resisted the dress codes banning natural hairstyles. Until their resistance (coupled with court challenges) changed the workplace culture, many Black women risked reprimand, censure, or even termination because of their womanist determination to be themselves. These Black women, psychologically empowered and sustained by their courage and boldness, demolished the status quo and at the same time, exemplified the authentic Black womanhood that Brooks praises in her poem.

Other poems among Brooks's family pictures depict Black manhood as Brooks has observed it among her family, friends, and national figures. Like other Black female writers, Brooks honors exemplary Black manhood as a corrective to and a shield against the steady assaults the Black male often faces in the wider society. Ogunyemi observes that "the intelligent black woman writer, conscious of black impotence in the context of white patriarchal culture, empowers the black man. She believes in him" (68). Brooks strongly supports the figures she includes in her gallery, beginning with her late brother-in-law, Edgar William Blakely, whom she tenderly praised in his elegy **"In Memoriam: Edgar William Blakely,"** the dedicatory poem in **To Disembark**. The two-line opening stanza affirms, "A friend is one / to whom you *can* [italics mine] say too much." The formal elegiac mood, indicated by "to whom," is sustained in the second stanza by the sermonic opening line: "That was the title and the text of Edgar Blakely" (v).

Shifting to colloquial language, Brooks describes Blakely as "our / rich-humored, raw and ready, / righteous and radiant running-buddy." These alliterative phrases, which appeal to the ear, eye, and intellect, are neatly juxtaposed to the more formal line, "responsible to / community and heart," which conveys both the earthiness and virtue of the late Blakely. Colorful folk and slang expressions like "raw and ready" and "running-buddy" combine with the sedate adjectival-phrase construction "responsible to / community and heart" (linked by the alliterated *r*) to show a vigorous, fun-loving man who had substance, wit, and community spirit. Jaffe says that Brooks "can stir the grits or stroke the rococo" (*To Disembark* 56). Actually, she is at her best when she blends both—the colloquial and the formal—as she does in this poem. Brooks's choice of the word "heart" where one might expect "family" or "friends" conveys not only the compassion of the deceased but also the warmth of the in-laws' relationship. The elegy closes with a summing up of Blakely's virtues:

> The document of his living is
> out and plain,
> level and direct. "Be sane. Be
> neighbor to all the people in the world."
>
> (v)

The word "document" recalls "text and title" in the second stanza just as "neighbor" relates to "friend" in the opening lines. Brooks's effective use of diction and juxtaposition combine with the theme to create a unified impression of an admired and dearly loved brother-in-law and friend.

Another family picture introduces Walter Bradford, whom Brooks scholar D. H. Melhem describes as "a man of solid merits, pragmatic, dedicated, a worker in the social field of the young, specifically the Blackstone Rangers" (*Poetry and the Heroic Voice* 204). Having worked closely with Bradford on several community projects, Brooks grew to admire and respect him because of his talent, his dedication, and his effectiveness with young people. Speaking in supportive voice of the experienced elder, Brooks advises, encourages, and commends Bradford:

> Just As You Think You're "Better Now"
> Something Comes To The Door.
> It's a Wilderness, Walter.
> It's a Whirlpool or Whipper.
>
> THEN you have to revise the messages
> and, pushing through roars
> of the Last Trombones of seduction,
> the deft orchestration,
> settle the sick ears to hear and to heed and to
> hold:
> the sick ears a-plenty.
>
> It's Walter-work, Walter.
> Not overmuch for
> brick-fitter, brick-MAKER, and wave-
> outwitter;
> whip-stopper.

> Not overmuch for a
> Tree-planting Man.
>
> Stay.
>
> (33)

First, Brooks speaks of the never-ending challenges facing Bradford and, by extension, others who try to steer young people in constructive directions. Reflecting the activism and energy of Bradford himself, Brooks chooses motion-charged images. Wilderness, Whirlpool, and Whipper—evoking predators, Charybdis, and slavery, respectively—symbolize the new problems that occur **"Just As You Think You Are Better Now."** Bradford as "brick-fitter, brick-MAKER, wave- / outwitter" and "whip-stopper"—shrewd master craftsman, maker of men and women—is equal to the task, Brooks asserts. He can handle the delicate and difficult problems of "[settling] sick ears to hear and to heed and to hold." Brooks reinforces this fact through typography. The capital letters of the first stanza indicate the looming threats to progress and stability, while the lower-case letters of the third stanza indicate Brooks's confidence that Bradford, like the biblical David, can slay any Goliaths. Further, by identifying Bradford as a "Tree-planting Man," Brooks calls forth literal and metaphorical associations of Johnny Appleseed, the nineteenth-century American tree planter, along with the unknown composer of these lyrics: "Just like a tree planted by the water, I shall not be moved." Brooks appeals to Bradford, the cultivator of young men and women, not to be moved but to stand steadfast, to "Stay." Scholar William Hansell states that Black heroes have always figured prominently in Brooks's poetry (79). Whether these heroes are friends like Walter Bradford, relatives like Edgar Blakely, or national figures like Martin Luther King, Medgar Evers, and Malcolm X, Brooks honors those who demonstrate integrity and an unwavering commitment to Black people around the globe. In the section "To the Diaspora" from *To Disembark,* she includes **"Music for Martyrs,"** a tribute to Steve Biko, the slain South African anti-apartheid activist. Its epigraph declares that Biko was slain "for loving his people." The poem itself contrasts the person's sincere personal grief with orchestrated public memorials. Deeply affected by Biko's martyrdom, the poet mourns:

> I feel a regret, Steve Biko.
> I am sorry, Steve Biko.
>   Biko the Emerger
> laid low.
>
> (42)

Brooks employs repetition, rhyme and sound devices to establish a funereal tone; Biko's name repeated, the assonantal o rhymed, and the *I* alliterated combine to create a lugubrious chant. The anguished "I feel a regret" and "I am sorry" convey turmoil, indicating perhaps the poet's guilt feelings about not having been active enough against apartheid. Alluding to Biko's unfulfilled potential, the title "Biko the Emerger" invests the slain leader with dignity and stature; the mournful euphemism "laid low" implies that the word "murdered" is too inelegant to refer to one so noble.

A catalogue of meaningless tributes contrasts with the poet's heartfelt sorrow:

> Now for the shapely American memorials.
> The polished tears.
> The timed tempest.
> The one-penny poems.
> The hollow guitars.
> The joke oh jaunty.
> The vigorous veal-stuffed voices.
> The singings, the white lean lasses with stream-
> ing yellow hair.
> Now for the organized nothings,
> Now for the weep-words.
>
> Now for the rigid recountings
> Of your tracts, your triumphs, your tribulations.
>   (42)

Brooks very effectively conveys the hollowness of the tributes through damning images— "polished tears," "timed tempests," "vigorous veal-stuffed voices," and "organized nothings"—all of which the poet views as sacrilegious. The bitter tone in this section of the poem extends to the conclusion, which identifies Biko's legacy—his "tracts," his "triumphs," and his "tribulations"— and suggests that the "shapely" memorials dishonor the young hero's memory.

Along with the men and women who comprise Brooks's gallery are children, whose varying situations exhort families and communities to commit themselves to the young and vulnerable. Like William Blake's "Infant Joy," the first poem. **"A Welcome Song for Laini Nzinga"** from *To Disembark,* celebrates the arrival of new life. Laini, the child of Brooks's spiritual son, poet Haki Madhubuti, and his wife, enters "through the rim of the world" to parents and friends eagerly awaiting her arrival: "We are here!" they exclaim, "To meet you and to mold and to maintain you." The word "we" appears five times in this eight-line lyric to signify the unity of this extended family and the necessity for its crucial supportive role. "With excited eyes we see you," the personae say.

This baby, bringing "the sound of new language," ushers in renewal and hope. The poem ends, "We love and we receive you as our own."

Brooks insists that her picture of a stable, joyous, and united Black family can be multiplied by the thousands, yet the media choose to present images of fragmented Black families in crisis. Brooks thinks that the scores of "firm families" among Blacks . . . must be announced, featured and credited" (*Report from Part Two* 134). The successful Black family of the newborn Laini serves as a prototype of the nurturing circle of family and friends that produces "durable, effective, and forward youngsters" (*Report from Part Two* 134). That some children are not born into warm and welcoming families or communities is demonstrated in **"The Life of Lincoln West,"** which Brooks describes as "a poem presenting a small Black boy coming to terms with outdoor and indoor opinions of his identity" (*Report from Part Two* 129).

The child pictured in this popular poem is unattractive by societal standards of handsomeness. The narrator pronounces this general consensus in the opening lines: "Ugliest little boy / that everyone ever saw. / That is what everyone said." The pronoun "everyone" in the second line rather than "someone" makes the baby's ugliness an indisputable fact, which the details support:

> Even to his mother it was apparent—
> when the blue aproned nurse came into the
> northeast end of the maternity ward
> bearing his squeals and plump bottom
> looped up in a scant receiving blanket,
> bending, to pass the bundle carefully
> into the waiting mother-hands—that this
> was no cute little ugliness, no sly baby wayward-
>   ness
> that was going to inch away
> as would baby fat, baby curl, and
> baby spot-rash. The pendulous lip, the
> branching ears, the eyes so wide and wild,
> the vague unvibrant brown of the skin, and
> most disturbing, the great head.
> These components of That Look bespoke
> the sun fibre. The deep grain.
>   (22)

The details of Lincoln's appearance unfold slowly: A "blue-aproned nurse came . . . bearing . . . bending." She bore "squeals and a plump bottom," "a bundle." Synecdoche and metonymy, in this description, heighten the reader's expectation. Likewise, negation intensifies the reader's curiosity about the unfortunate baby's appearance. There is "no cute little ugliness, no sly baby waywardness / that was going to inch away." Finally, with the actual description of the baby's appearance, the narrator refers to him clinically, as if he is a specimen rather than a human being: "The pendulous lip, the / branching ears, the eyes so wide and wild." This detachment establishes a distance between the reader and the narrative which is erased as the narrator reveals the cold and unfeeling treatment the child eventually faces at home and in the community. Although Lincoln tries desperately to win his parents' affection, "His father could not bear the sight of him," and

> his mother high-piled her pretty dyed hair and
> put him among her hairpins and sweethearts,
> dance slippers, torn paper roses.
> He was not less than these,
> he was not more.
>
> (23)

Rejected by his father, Lincoln receives neither love nor attention from his mother, a flighty, vapidly sentimental, self-absorbed woman with little capacity for maternal affection. To her, Lincoln is another acquisition—hardly a treasured one. But the narrator suggests that even if he had been attractive, he would have been only an object for display, not a child to be loved and nurtured. As the mother of two children whom she reared with unconditional love and support, Brooks, through the narrator, is understandably critical of this mother. For as she has shown in poem after poem—most notably in the sonnet sequence **"Children of the Poor,"** from *A Street in Bronzeville*—mothering entails loving, protecting, and training a child. Viewed in this context, Lincoln's mother is not among those Black women who "create and train their flowers." Lincoln, who is a weed in his parents' sight, experiences continual rejection. The narrator says that "even Christmases and Easters were spoiled" because of him:

> He would be sitting at the
> family feasting table, really
> delighting in the displays of mashed potatoes
> and the rich golden
> fat-crust of the ham or the festive
> fowl, when he would look up and find
> somebody feeling indignant about him.
>
> (24)

This snapshot of the sumptuous feast, the animated child, and the disapproving parents starkly reveals a central point of the poem: that senses can be stirred but not hearts.

As if parental rejection were not enough, the narrator reports that Lincoln's kindergarten teacher showed "a concern for him composed of one / part sympathy and two parts repulsion." Playmates "turned their handsome backs on him" when better-looking children appeared. Conse-

quently, Lincoln "spent much time looking at himself / in mirrors. What could be done? / But there was no / shrinking his head. There was no / binding his ears." An answer arrives unexpectedly while Lincoln and his mother are at the movies. He overhears a comment about himself from a nearby moviegoer, who is whispering to his companion,

> "THERE! That's the kind I've been wanting
> to show you! One of the best examples of the
>   specie. Not like
> those diluted Negroes you see so much of on
> the streets these days, but the
> real thing.
>
> Black, ugly, and odd. You
> can see the savagery. The blunt
> blankness. That is the real
> thing."
>
> (27-28)

Although the mother is outraged, Lincoln, misinterpreting the insult, discovers a new self-image, and whenever he is hurt by others or lonely, the narrator says, he takes comfort in knowing that he is "the real thing."

Brooks's artful narration and vivid language point out the pain that rejected children experience and the necessity for ego-building experiences. Whereas Lincoln, a lovable, good natured child, finds a positive outlet for his pain, other children have resorted to acts of violence against others and themselves. Pioneering Black studies scholar Arthur P. Davis considers this poem a parable (in Wright 103). If so, Lincoln may represent the Black community, whose family members have subverted the negative definition of Blackness imposed by society—"Black, ugly, and odd"— and transformed it into "quality and legitimacy."

The final poem, **"The Boy Died in My Alley"** from *Beckonings* (1975), comments on public and personal indifference to violence among and against children. In the poem, the persona, representing an apathetic community, moves beyond deliberate isolation and indifference to communal responsibility. The opening lines are chilling: "Without my having known. / Policeman said, next morning, / Apparently died alone." The word *Apparently* emphasizes the tragedy of the anonymous boy's death. The end punctuation after the opening phrase highlights the isolation of the persona from the violence surrounding her. To dramatize the point that individuals, however, are not islands unto themselves, Brooks connects the title of the poem and the opening line to form a single statement: "The Boy Died in My Alley Without my having known." This pairing links proximity and emotional distance, calling attention to the fact that the death occurs near the persona, but she is detached emotionally from it. When a police officer asks if she heard the shot, the persona responds:

Shots I hear and Shots I hear.
I never see the dead,
The Shot that killed him yes I heard
As I heard the Thousand shots before;
careening tinnily down the nights
across my years and arteries.

(49-50)

The words "hear," "heard," and "Shot" in conjunction with the onomatopoeic phrase "careening tinnily" emphasize the persona's past indifference to routine violence. The persona recounts, "Policeman pounded on my door [and said] A Boy was dying in your alley. / A Boy is dead, and in your alley. / And have you known this Boy before?" The conspicuous shift in tense—from the past (progressive aspect) "was dying" to the present "is," and to the present (perfect aspect) "have known"—dramatizes the actual death of the boy and suggests, as well, the pervasiveness of the violence. Acknowledging some acquaintance with "this Boy . . . who / ornaments my alley," the persona confesses that "I never saw his face at all." The verb "ornaments" alludes to the red blood and the persona's uncaring attitude toward children who "deal with death." The persona admits, "I have closed my heart-ears late and early." At the end of the poem, however, she recognizes her silent complicity in the boy's death: "I joined the wild and killed him / with knowledgeable unknowing." Remorsefully, the narrator confesses, "I saw where he was going. / I saw him Crossed. And seeing / I did not take him down." The word "Crossed" combined with the statement "I did not take him down" evokes the Crucifixion. Further, "Crossed" means both "placed on a cross" and "betrayed." This complex allusion manifests the persona's guilt and anguish. In street vernacular, "to take someone down" means to kill or to seriously incapacitate that person by violent means. Aware of the fact that children were being "taken down" but ignoring them, the persona feels responsible for their deaths. Brooks employs paradox ("knowledgeable unknowing"), allusion, and ambiguity to reveal the persona's feelings. Finally accepting responsibility and recognizing kinship with these children, the persona states, "The red floor of my alley / is a special speech to me." Likewise, this blood is a special speech to readers who have been pulled into the narrative and forced to look at the pain and destruction around them. Such truth-telling, with Brooks's

"quiet and merciless accuracy" (Johnson 47), leaves readers no hiding place.

The boy in the alley, Lincoln, West, little Laini, Steve Biko, Walter Bradford, Edgar Blakely, the sisters, and the gang girl are creations of a master artist. Although Brooks paints family pictures, the impulse from which they spring embraces all humanity. As Brooks herself has said, "I cite, star, and esteem all that which is of woman—human and hardly human. And I want the people of the world to anticipate ultimate unity, *active* [italics hers] interest in empathy." (**Report from Part Two** 131). The unity to which Brooks subscribes is

a unity of distinct proud pieces. Not a stew. . . . Because each entity is lovely-amazing-*exhilarating* [italics hers] in ubiquity and boldness of clear distinction, good design. I hope that in the world, always, there will be Black, brown, yellow, white, red. (And if time has some surprises let us welcome those too.)

(**Report from Part Two** 131)

The poetry of Gwendolyn Brooks depicts and celebrates the variegated life of one community within the human family. This Black community, with its prismatic family pictures, has inspired, nourished, and sustained her art. Although directed to this community, her canvases of family pictures, like portraits by the Old Masters, hang in full view of the human family for their enrichment, for their illumination, and for their delight.

Note

1. For a discussion of "womanist" and "womanism," see Walker (*In Search of Our Mothers' Gardens,* 1983) and Ogunyemi ("Womanism: The Dynamics of the Contemporary Black Female Novel in English," *Signs: Journal of Women and Culture* 11.1 (Autumn 1985): 63-80). In her essay, Ogunyemi says a womanist "will recognize that, along with her consciousness of sexual issues, she must incorporate racial, cultural, national, economic, and political considerations into her philosophy" (64).

Works Cited

Allan, Tuzylane Jita. *Womanist and Feminist Aesthetics: A Comparative Review.* Athens, OH: Ohio University Press, 1995.

Brooks, Gwendolyn. *Beckonings.* Detroit: Broadside Press, 1981.

———. *Blacks.* Chicago: Third World Press, 1987.

———. *In The Mecca.* New York: Harper and Row, 1968.

———. *To Disembark.* Detroit: Broadside Press, 1981.

———. *Report from Part One.* Detroit: Broadside Press, 1972.

———. *Report from Part Two.* Chicago: Third World Press, 1996.

———. *The World of Gwendolyn Brooks.* New York: Harper and Row, 1971.

Dandridge, Rita, ed. *Black Women's Blues: A Literary Anthology, 1934-1988*. New York: G. K. Hall, 1992.

Davis, Arthur P. "Gwendolyn Brooks." *Dark Tower: Afro-American Writers 1899-1960*. Washington, D.C.: Howard University Press, (1974). Rpt. in *On Gwendolyn Brooks: Reliant Contemplation*. Ed. Stephen Wright, Ann Arbor: University of Michigan Press, 1996: 97-105.

Hansell, William H. "The Poet-Militant and Foreshadowings of a Black Mystique: Poems in the Second Period of Gwendolyn Brooks." *Concerning Poetry* 10 (Fall 1977): 37-45. Rpt. in Mootry and Smith 71-80.

Jaffe, Dan. "Gwendolyn Brooks: An Appreciation from the White Suburbs." *The Black American Writer: Volume 2 Poetry/Drama*. Ed. C. W. E. Bigsby. Deland, FL: Everett/Edwards, 1969: 89-98. Rpt. in Wright 50-59.

Johnson, James N. "Blacklisting Poets." *Ramparts* 7 (1968): 53-56. Rpt. in Wright 45-49.

Melhem, D. H. *Gwendolyn Brooks: Poetry and the Heroic Voice*. Lexington: University of Kentucky Press, 1987.

———. *Heroism in the New Black Poetry: Introductions and Interviews*. Lexington: University of Kentucky Press, 1990.

Mootry, Maria, and Gary Smith. *A Life Distilled*. Urbana, IL: University of Illinois Press, 1987.

Ogunyemi, Chikwenye Okonjo. "Womanism: The Dynamics of the Contemporary Black Female Novel in English." *Signs: Journal of Women and Culture* 11.1 (Autumn 1985): 63-80.

Omolade, Barbara. "Black Women and Feminism." *The Future of Difference*. Ed. Hester Eisenstein and Alice Jardine. Boston: G. K. Hall, 1980: 248-257.

Walker, Alice. *In Search of Our Mothers' Gardens*. New York: Harcourt, Brace, Jovanovich, 1983.

Webster, Harvey Curtis. "Pity the Giants." Review of *The Bean Eaters, Annie Allen*, and *A Street in Bronzeville*, by Gwendolyn Brooks. *The Nation* (1 September 1962). Rpt. in Wright 19-22.

Wright, Stephen, ed. *On Gwendolyn Brooks: Reliant Contemplation*. Ann Arbor, MI: University of Michigan Press, 1996.

TITLE COMMENTARY

Maud Martha

HARRY B. SHAW (ESSAY DATE 1987)

SOURCE: Shaw, Harry B. "*Maud Martha*: The War with Beauty." In *A Life Distilled: Gwendolyn Brooks, Her Poetry and Fiction*, edited by Maria K. Mootry and Gary Smith, pp. 254-70. Urbana: University of Illinois Press, 1987.

In the following essay, Shaw discusses Brooks's treatment of conventional American standards of female beauty in her novel.

Arthur P. Davis's article of December 1962, "The Black-and-Tan Motif in the Poetry of Gwendolyn Brooks," even after twenty years provides a fitting springboard for a discussion of the same motif in Brooks's novel, **Maud Martha**.[1] Davis explores the social theory that among black people the inside color line had tended "to create a problem *within* the group similar to that between colored and white in America."[2] He points out that this color difference within the group caused special problems for the dark girl, who during the early decades of the century was often the object of ridicule among black men.

Davis's social theory is that "as cruel as it was, the whole attitude of ridicule is a natural reaction to the premium which America by law and custom and by its uncivilized institution of segregation had placed on color."[3] To paraphrase and extend Davis's remarks and expand on the literary significance of the social theory, I contend that **Maud Martha** as well as Brooks's poetry makes a sharply ironic commentary on human nature by revealing that in American society rejection is caused less by deep-rooted cultural, religious, or ideological differences than by aesthetic difference, or what we think about body proportions, facial features, skin color, and hair texture. The psychological effect of this familiar and pervasive kind of ridicule and of the standard of beauty in America is explained by psychiatrists William Grier and Price M. Cobbs in "Achieving Womanhood" in *Black Rage*:

> In this country, the standard is the blond, blue-eyed, white-skinned girl with regular features. . . . The girl who is black has no option in the matter of how much she will change herself. Her blackness is the antithesis of a creamy white skin, her lips are thick, her hair is kinky and short. She is, in fact, the antithesis of American beauty. However beautiful she might be in a different setting with different standards, in this country she is ugly.[4]

Brooks's conscious subscription to this social premise is epitomized by Maud's tendency, like the tendency of the mother in "the children of the poor," to shield, to protect her children from the harshness of the environment. For instance, in Brooks's poem "**What shall I give my children? who are poor**," when the children

> . . . have begged me for a brisk contour,
> Crying that they are quasi, contraband
> Because unfinished, graven by a hand
> Less than angelic, admirable or sure

the mother laments her powerlessness:

> My hand is stuffed with mode, design, device,
> But I lack access to my proper stone,
> And plenitude of plan shall not suffice
> Nor grief nor love shall be enough alone

To ratify my little halves who bear
Across an autumn freezing everywhere.[5]

The same frustration and "baffled hate" are expressed by Maud after her daughter, Paulette, has been virtually ignored by Santa Claus in a department store:

Maud Martha wanted to cry.

Keep her that land of blue!

Keep her those fairies, with witches always killed at the end, and Santa every winter's lord, kind, sheer being who never perspires, who never does or says a foolish or ineffective thing, who never looks grotesque, who never has occasion to pull the chain and flush the toilet.
(**WGB** [*The World of Gwendolyn Brooks*], p. 203)

Although Maud Martha herself is accepting and supporting as a parent, she never forgets the mild reinforcement of the American standard of beauty by her family. Closely paralleling Brooks's own depiction, Grier and Cobbs further point out the devastating effect when parents wittingly or unwittingly reinforce the standard: "When the feeling of ugliness is reinforced by the rejection of family and society, the growing girl develops a feeling not only of being undesirable and unwanted but also of being mutilated—of having been fashioned by Nature in an ill-favored manner."[6]

Color and color prejudice are also treated from strikingly similar perspectives in the literature of other black writers, particularly black female writers. In her autobiographical novel, *I Know Why the Caged Bird Sings,* for example, Maya Angelou reveals the debasing effect that the pervasive white standard of beauty has on the self-image of black girls. Aware from an early age of the exclusive nature of the standard, Maya thinks that her "new" Easter dress would make her "look like one of the sweet little white girls who were everybody's dream of what was right with the world."[7] As she continues to fantasize, the extent of the demoralization is evident:

Wouldn't they be surprised when one day I woke out of my black ugly dream, and my real hair, which was long and blonde, would take place of the kinky mass that Momma wouldn't let me straighten? My light-blue eyes were going to hypnotize them. . . . Because I was really white and because a cruel fairy stepmother . . . had turned me into a too-big Negro girl, with nappy black hair, broad feet and a space between her teeth that would hold a number-two pencil.[8]

Maud's own attention to color, features, and hair are paralleled in Brooks's autobiography, *Report from Part One,* and in her poetry.[9] The novel portrays a woman with doubts about herself and where and how she fits into the world. Maud is clearly less concerned with being thought inferior than she is with being perceived as ugly. This concern is filtered through the point of view of an insecure, self-disparaging black woman who feels that she is homely and, therefore, uncherished because she is black and has nappy hair and "Negro features." This perspective leads her to give a disparaging although undue deference to white people and to society's invidious standard of beauty. As I point out in the chapter "Maud Martha" in my introductory study, *Gwendolyn Brooks:*

She measures herself and her work against the standards of the world and feels that she comes out short inevitably—that white or light beauty often triumphs, though somehow unfairly—and that the deprivation of the beholder is to blame. The book is also about the triumph of the lowly. She shows what they go through and exposes the shallowness of the popular, beautiful, white people with "good" hair. One way of looking at the book, then, is as a war with beauty and people's concepts of beauty.[10]

One of the first casualties of the war is Maud's self-assurance about her own image. Self-doubt is an important part of the novel, providing a rather constant backdrop to almost every vignette. However, the situations where doubt is presented are not simple. Rather, in most cases Brooks holds out something positive such as hope, promise, or comfort, which is then assaulted by the American standard of beauty, leaving a condition of doubt and insecurity that itself often gives way to a grudging deference to whites. Occasionally the positive aspects prevail, leaving a sense of small but sweet victories in individual isolated battles in a larger lost war. This dialectic provides the main tension of the novel.

In "Description of Maud Martha" the stage is set for the war with beauty that is waged throughout the novel by Maud's ready identification with the dandelion, her favorite flower. She refers to them as "yellow jewels for everyday," and "she liked their demure prettiness second to their everydayness. . . ." In so describing the dandelion, she is comparing it to herself, "for in that latter quality she thought she saw a picture of herself, and it was comforting to find that what was common could also be a flower." In this description the word "demure" is important, because it fits the shy, weak nature of Maud's image of her own "prettiness." The everyday or common prettiness of the dandelion contrasts with the more exotic or exquisite beauty of rarer flowers even as Maud's own shy prettiness contrasts with white beauty. Although she thinks the dandelion is pretty, she is aware that others consider it plain or ugly—a weed.

The dialectic potential of this vignette extends to Maud's desires, for "to be cherished was the dearest wish of the heart of Maud Martha Brown. . . ." Because the plain, common dandelion could be cherished, Maud had hope that she, too, could be cherished, although plain. The reader, however, is immediately aware of the tenuous nature of this hope, because it lasts only while Maud is looking at the dandelions. Otherwise, she has doubts that the ordinary dandelion is "as easy to love as a thing of heart-catching beauty." Ironically, it is in Maud's own everyday life when she cannot look at the dandelions to boost her morale that she has the greatest doubts about herself:

> And could be cherished! To be cherished was the dearest wish of the heart of Maud Martha Brown, and sometimes when she was not looking at dandelions (for one would not be looking at them all the time, often there were chairs and tables to dust or tomatoes to slice or beds to make or grocery stores to be gone to, and in the colder months there were no dandelions at all), it was hard to believe that a thing of only ordinary allurements—if the allurements of any flower could be said to be ordinary—was as easy to love as a thing of heart-catching beauty.
>
> (*WGB*, p. 128)

Doubt about the ability to be loved is a permeating theme in the novel, affecting Maud's relationship with her friends and family.

The prime example of a familiar relationship affected by Maud's doubt is that with her sister, Helen. From the earliest descriptions of Helen she is presented as the exquisite, "heart-catching" beauty—a foil and frequently an adversary to Maud. "Helen" suggests Helen of Troy, the ideal beauty, to contrast the common plainness of a girl whose very name suggests drabness. Helen was not one of those "graven by a hand / Less than angelic, admirable or sure." The rub, however, is that Helen is "easy to love" simply because she is "a thing of heart-catching beauty." The relationship between beauty as it is perceived in the Western world and being loved or cherished is very positive. To further emphasize the importance of beauty in the formula for being loved, Maud points out that in all other considerations, she and Helen were about equal:

> a thing of heart-catching beauty.
>
> Such as her sister Helen! who was only two years past her own age of seven, and was almost her

own height and weight and thickness. But oh, the long lashes, the grace, the little ways with the hands and feet.

> (*WGB*, pp. 128-29)

These are not terms of endearment.

Helen's natural proximity as a sister facilitates discussion of the efficacy of beauty. One of the numerous instances that helps to convince Maud that being beautiful brings favors as categorically as being ugly brings rejection is Maud's experience of being rejected by Emmanuel for a ride in his wagon while Helen is accepted. Emmanuel, riding his wagon, approaches the two young girls and asks, "How about a ride?" When the shy Maud uncharacteristically responds with, "Hi, handsome!" Emmanuel scowls and says, "I don't mean you, you old black gal. . . . I mean Helen." Helen gets the ride because she is beautiful—not because she otherwise deserves it any more than Maud. This experience visits and revisits Maud many times during her life. Years later the memory hurts as Maud observes that Helen makes $15 a week as a typist while she, Maud, makes $10 a week as a file clerk. She realizes that the basic situation has never changed. "Helen was still the one they wanted in the wagon, still 'the pretty one,' 'the dainty one.' The lovely one."

Helen remains the favored one because of her beauty. Maud makes the efficacy of Helen's beauty clear by removing all of the other variables:

> She did not know what it was. She had tried to find the something that might be there to imitate, that she might imitate it. But she did not know what it was. I wash as much as Helen does, she thought. My hair is longer and thicker, she thought. I'm much smarter. I read books and newspapers and old folks like to talk with me, she thought.
>
> But the kernel of the matter was that, in spite of these things, she was poor, and Helen was still the ranking queen, not only with the Emmanuels of the world, but even with their father—their mother—their brother. She did not blame the family. It was not their fault. She understood. They could not help it. They were enslaved, were fascinated, and they were not at all to blame.
>
> (*WGB*, pp. 160-61)

Maud is more than merely equal to Helen in all other variables. She deserves Harry's loyalty, but Helen gets it. Their father prefers Helen, although Maud really works harder at getting love and respect by doting on her father and sympathizing with him. Even against these odds, however, Helen's beauty triumphs, making Maud the pauper and Helen the "ranking queen."

One result of continually having life's situations assailed by measurement against an alien and artificial standard is not merely to doubt the possibility of positive evaluations, but to develop the inclination to project the likelihood of negative evaluations. Maud Martha begins as a young girl to project toward the portentous rather than the propitious. In observing those around her, she begins to attribute thoughts and motives to them that are not always self-evident from their behavior. For example, as her thoughts dwell on Helen and her advantages, she assumes that she knows her father's thoughts: "It did not please her, either, at the breakfast table, to watch her father drink his coffee and contentedly think (oh, she knew it!), as Helen started on her grapefruit, how daintily she ate, how gracefully she sat in her chair, how pure was her robe and unwrinkled, how neatly she had arranged her hair. Their father preferred Helen's hair to Maud Martha's (Maud Martha knew) . . . (*WGB,* pp. 162-63). Maud's doubts progressively give rise to more elaborate and more depreciative thinking about her physical appearance. Chapter 13, "low yellow," consists almost entirely of her thoughts like the following about Paul Phillips's thoughts about her color, hair, and features:

> I know what he is thinking, thought Maud Martha, as she sat on the porch in the porch swing with Paul Phillips. He is thinking that I am all right. That I am really all right. That I will do. . . .
>
> But I am certainly not what he would call pretty. . . . Pretty would be a little cream-colored thing with curly hair. Or at the very lowest pretty would be a little curly-haired thing the color of cocoa with a lot of milk in it. Whereas, I am the color of cocoa straight, if you can be even that "kind" to me.
>
> He wonders, as we walk in the street, about the thoughts of the people who look at us. Are they thinking that he could do no better than—me? Then he thinks, Well, hmp! Well, huh!—all the little good-lookin' dolls that have wanted *him*—all the little sweet high-yellows that have ambled slowly past *his* front door—What he would like to tell those secretly snickering ones!—That any day out of the week he can do better than this black gal.
>
> (*WGB,* pp. 178-79)

The title of this chapter, "low yellow," accurately and rather bluntly reflects the subject that weighs heavily on Maud's mind for a significant portion of the novel. There are some moderately auspicious projections of Paul's assessment of Maud, such as his thinking that "she will do," or that Maud is "sweet," or that she has "nice ears."

She is also optimistic that she will "hook him" in spite of his predilection for "the gay life, spiffy clothes, beautiful yellow girls, natural hair, smooth cars, jewels, night clubs, cocktail lounges, class." Still, Maud's realization that she embodies the antithesis of Paul's "idea of pretty" does not bode well for her sense of security.

In chapter 19, "if you're light and have long hair," Maud is even less subtle and more pessimistic in her projections. Whereas in "low yellow" she is able to perceive some benefit of the doubt that she feels, in "if you're light" she imputes only the most negative interpretation to Paul's behavior. When Paul is invited to attend what to him is the most important social event imaginable, the Foxy Cats Dawn Ball, Maud is filled with trepidation and doubt about whether he will want to take her. Although they are married at the time, she believes that Paul will take her only grudgingly. She does not feel that she will fit in with the "beautiful girls, or real stylish ones" at the ball. She speculates that he will take her only out of a sense of obligation, and that if he could assemble the right words, he would tell her that he could tolerate the marriage only as long as he was free. She further believes he wants to humor her only because she is pregnant.

In Maud's mind, Paul's behavior at the ball can only mean that he would rather not be with her. When after their second dance he leaves her sitting, "she sat, trying not to show the inferiority she did not feel." Maud is even more concerned when Paul dances closely with Maella, who is "red-haired and curved, and white as a white." A dark man dances with Maud, but she hardly notices him for watching Paul and Maella. The dark dance partner tries to make small talk, and even tells her, "You're a babe. . . . You're a real babe." Again Maud hardly notices, but she does notice Paul and Maella and begins to project: "But it's my color that makes him mad. I try to shut my eyes to that, but it's no good. What I am inside, what is really me, he likes okay. But he keeps looking at my color, which is like a wall. He has to jump over it in order to meet and touch what I've got for him. He has to jump away up high in order to see it. He gets awful tired of all that jumping" (*WGB,* pp. 213-14).

Whether the threat to their marriage is real or generated out of Maud's insecurity, it is clear from the symbolism of the gradual demise of a snowball bush that Maud believes the threat is real. She is escorted to a chair near a rubber plant, where she sits and briefly considers violently attacking

Maella. However, her final thought on the matter suggests that she perceives the problem with Paul's standard of beauty—and consequently with their marriage—to extend far beyond Maella. As she puts it, "But if the root was sour what business did she have up there hacking at a leaf?"

Maud's doubts and her self-deprecating projections attend most of the major events of her life. When her daughter, Paulette, is born, for instance, Maud notices that her mother, Belva Brown, "looked at the newcomer in amazement. 'Well, she's a little beauty, isn't she!' she cried. She had not expected a handsome child." Maud is so sensitive about color and other aspects of appearance that she interprets possibly well-meaning statements as pejorative. Another time Maud imagines that she sees Paul's eye-light take leave of her, and she projects his rejection of her and the life they live together. "She knew that he was tired of his wife, tired of his living quarters, tired of working at Sam's, tired of his two suits." She thinks that Paul's boredom occurs partially because "the baby was getting darker all the time." But that fear could be just as easily attributed to Maud herself, for Maud as mother is very concerned with the war and the battles that Paulette will have to fight as a black girl.

One such battle occurs early in Paulette's life. Maud and Paulette go to a store where there is a Santa Claus. Santa's high enthusiasm for the children suddenly dies when Paulette's turn comes. When Santa is coldly indifferent to Paulette, Maud takes her away. As they leave the store, Paulette wonders why Santa does not like her. Maud finds herself in the same position as the parent in "children of the poor," "holding the bandage ready for your eyes." She lies to Paulette, telling her, "Baby, of course he liked you." Maud views this kind of battle as something peculiar to her. She realizes that neither Helen nor Paul, two people who are very close to her, would have reacted with the same venom with which she reacted. For different reasons neither of them would have had to fight nor to appreciate the same kind of battles that Maud Martha had fought. But the problem for Maud is too real to ignore and too complex to unravel: "She could neither resolve nor dismiss. There were these scraps of baffled hate in her, hate with no eyes, no smile and—this she especially regretted, called her hungriest lack—not much voice" (**WGB**, p. 302).

In spite of the "baffled hate" resulting from fighting and losing many skirmishes in the war with beauty, Maud Martha, being part of the society she fights, ironically subscribes in part to the same standard of beauty that she fights. In spite of herself, she gives a kind of deference to whites and to the society's standard of beauty.

While throughout the novel Maud is overly concerned about other's perceptions of her, she is especially concerned with the perceptions that whites have not only of her, but also of black people in general. That she is aware of and concerned about their perceptions is evident in chapter 5, "you're being so good, so kind," by her hesitancy and fear concerning the visit of Charles, her white schoolmate. She feels that "she was the whole 'colored' race, and Charles was the personalization of the entire Caucasian plan." She defers to him by dashing about straightening up the house and raising all the windows because she is aware that whites often say that "colored people's houses necessarily had a certain heavy, unpleasant smell." Her inordinate concern about the general appearance of her home and the odor in the house is a product of her projecting Charles's thoughts on the situation. When he rings hesitantly, she further ascribes thoughts to Charles that further reveal her doubt that she can be considered favorably, especially by this representative white: "No doubt regretting his impulse already. No doubt regarding, with a rueful contempt, the outside of the house, so badly in need of paint. Those rickety steps" (**WGB**, p. 144). Her deference proceeds to the extent that she is "sickened" to realize that she is grateful for his coming to visit her "as though Charles, in coming, gave her a gift."

Although Maud is sickened at her own fawning behavior during Charles's visit, she makes no comment during David McKemster's soliloquy on the virtues of the good life—"a picture of the English country gentleman"—versus the depravity in the ghetto. This chapter, "second beau," reveals the extent to which one can become unreasonably enamored with a given standard. Beyond his wanting to master the American literary critic, Vernon Paddington, David wishes to adopt white ideals, to emulate the white-middle-class lifestyle.

McKemster's desire in "second beau" to change his style to escape his own heritage (like Satin-Legs Smith) is somewhat comparable to Maud's own desire to change whatever she can to be accepted—to be cherished. The contrast is that although McKemster can effectively affect white styles, Maud will always be plain Maud.

There are times when Maud also engages in the desire to escape her situation. The glitter and shine in Maud's perception of New York in "Maud Martha and New York" is not unlike McKemster's idealized description of the white section east of Cottage Grove. "People were clean," he says, "going somewhere that mattered, not talking unless they had something to say." Maud, meanwhile, sees the material and stylistic splendor of New York as a symbol of what life should be like—jeweled. She, like McKemster, even makes an allusion to the lustrous style of the English as perhaps the accepted pinnacle of style and class. Both McKemster and Maud are products of the ghetto, who dream, realistically or unrealistically, of escaping their situations. It is ironic that in both cases the places and things that they would escape to or through are associated with the very aesthetic that condemns them for being what they are—black Americans. McKemster would shed his black background where his mother had said, "I ain't stud'n you," and his father "hadn't said anything at all," where "he himself had had a paper route. Had washed windows, cleaned basements, sanded furniture, shoveled snow, hauled out trash and garbage for the neighbors." McKemster's dream of changing his life is more materialistic and attainable: "He wanted a dog. A good dog. No mongrel. An apartment—well-furnished, containing a good bookcase, filled with good books in good bindings. He wanted a phonograph, and records. The symphonies. And Yehudi Menuhin. He wanted some good art. These things were not extras. They went to make up a good background. The kind of background those guys had" (*WGB,* p. 172). The fallacy is that one comes with a background. A background is not simply superimposed with the acquisition of certain material things.

Maud's fantasy is more to escape a stultifying mental and aesthetic environment: "What she wanted to dream, and dreamed, was her affair. It pleased her to dwell upon color and soft bready textures and light, on a complex beauty, on gemlike surfaces. What was the matter with that? Besides, who could safely swear that she would never be able to make her dream come true for herself? Not altogether, then!—but slightly?—in some part?" (*WGB,* p. 177). Maud would keep her background, but would have others to evaluate her by a different standard of beauty.

Maud Martha never gets to New York, but David McKemster does take steps toward the fulfillment of his dream. Several years after their first conversation about McKemster's need to acquire a new background, he is ensconced at the University of Chicago. In "an encounter," Maud meets him by chance on the campus. She is hesitant to strike up a conversation because "this was the University world, this was his element. Perhaps he would feel she did not belong here, perhaps he would be cold to her." He is cold to her because she too is part of the black past that he has illusions of shedding. He merely tolerates her company glumly for a few minutes "till they met a young white couple. . . . David's face lit up," and McKemster comes alive with cultured conversation as viewed by Maud Martha: "Had they known about the panel discussion? . . . Tell him, when had they seen Mary, Mary Ehrenburg? Say, he had seen Metzger Freestone tonight. . . . (He lit a cigarette.) Say, he had had dinner with the Beefy Godwins and Jane Wather this evening. Say, what were they doing tomorrow night? . . . (He took excited but carefully sophisticated puffs.). . . . Say, how about going to Power's for a beer?" (*WGB,* p. 255). Maud senses that he wishes to be rid of her. Having completely subscribed to the white values he had idealized earlier, McKemster views Maud as old, excess baggage.

When McKemster offers to have a cup of coffee with Maud and the young white couple, Maud assumes that he is trying to pacify her before "disposing" of her. Maud interprets the young white man's stare as saying, "Well! and what have we here!" Maud Martha's "baffled hates" make her suspect of disparaging, benign, or even friendly gesture alike. It is not easy to be kind to Maud Martha. Maud sees the young white lady as "attractive," suggesting once again that she subscribes to the prevailing standard of beauty even while she fights the effects of it. Maud sees her as bold and confident: "She leaned healthily across the table; her long, lovely dark hair swung at you; her bangs came right out to meet you, and her face and forefinger did too (she emphasized, robustly, some point)" (*WGB,* p. 257).

The references to health and robustness in describing the girl's behavior suggest that Maud would like to be this way. But Maud has not the white face, the "summer-blue eyes. . . . lovely dark hair" nor the confidence (which is itself a testimony to the efficacy of beauty) to do so. She instead describes her own behavior in terms as sharply contrasting as her own physical description would contrast that of the girl. "But herself stayed stuck to the back of her seat, and was shrewd, and 'took in,' and contemplated, not quite warmly, everything" (*WGB,* p. 257). Maud's discomfort is exacerbated by McKemster's attempt to "look down" on her physically as he had been socially, although "when they sat their heights were equal."

Maud's war with beauty, then, is partially internal, for not only does she rail against the standard, but she also grapples with her own ambivalent aesthetic sense in order not to see whites as beautiful and, more critically, in order not to see herself and her daughter, Paulette, as ugly. The crudest application of the standard of beauty is to see whites as beautiful and to see blacks, the antithesis, as ugly. Application of this standard, however, is complicated by the varying degrees to which blacks can approximate the physical attributes that are associated with the standard. Hence, Maud often sees her white or light-skinned rivals as "attractive," "lovely," or "beautiful." In "low yellow," little doubt is left about the deference that Maud and Paul both give to the white standard of beauty. They are contemplating marriage and the kinds of children they would have:

> "I am not a pretty woman," said Maud Martha. "If you married a pretty woman, you could be the father of pretty children. Envied by people. The father of beautiful children."
>
> "But I don't know," said Paul. "Because my features aren't fine. They aren't regular. They're heavy. They're real Negro features. I'm light, or at least I can claim to be a sort of low-toned yellow, and my hair has a teeny crimp. But even so I'm not handsome."
>
> No, there would be little "beauty" getting born out of such a union.
>
> (*WGB*, p. 180)

They both idealize light skin, wavy or straight hair, and fine or regular features. Likewise, it is clear from their conversation that black skin, nappy hair, and "real Negro features" make them less than beautiful in their own eyes.

Well after they are married Maud and Paul continue to show their perhaps unwitting but nonetheless real deference to whites. Being black in a white environment is central in "we're the only colored people here." Maud's only hesitation in asking Paul to go downtown to a movie is that he will object that there are "too many white folks." Once there, they feel conspicuous and alone. They stand in the lobby looking sheepishly about and whispering. Immediately Maud notices the refined "cooked, well cared-for" appearance of the whites and contrasts it favorably to that of the ghetto blacks. At one point Paul is hesitant to approach a white girl at the candy counter to ask about tickets. He is afraid of intruding or even of her coldness. From Maud's point of view she is described as "lovely and blonde and cold-eyed, and her arms were akimbo, and the set of her head

was eloquent." Maud and Paul both defer to her whiteness, her beauty. Maud contrasts the white and black environments almost enviously but certainly qualitatively or valuatively. They attribute an uplifting effect just to being in the theater frequented by whites:

> But you felt good sitting there, yes, good, and as if, when you left it, you would be going home to a sweet-smelling apartment with flowers on little gleaming tables; and wonderful silver on night-blue velvet, in chests; and crackly sheets; and lace spreads on such beds as you saw at Marshall Field's. Instead of back to your kit'n't apt., with the garbage of your floor's families in a big can just outside your door, and the gray sound of little gray feet scratching away from it as you drag up those flights of narrow complaining stairs.
>
> (*WGB*, p. 203)

As they leave the theater, they are very concerned with not making the whites feel intruded upon:

> the Negroes stood up . . . looked about them eagerly. They hoped they would meet no cruel eyes. They hoped no one would look intruded upon. They had enjoyed the picture so, they were so happy, they wanted to laugh, to say warmly to the other outgoers, "Good, huh? Wasn't it swell?"
>
> This, of course, they could not do. But if only no one would look intruded upon. . . .
>
> (*WGB*, p. 204)

This kind of deference is associated closely with their sense of aesthetic worth. Both before and after the movie they are self-conscious and apologetic about the appearance of their color, hair, features, clothes, and even, through extension, their very habitats.

Maud continues to defer to whites in various ways such as continued projection of disparaging thoughts into the minds of white people whom she encounters. One such incident occurs in "Millinery," when Maud visits a shop and attributes the following negative thoughts to the white manager: "Oh, not today would she cater to these nigger women who tried on every hat in her shop, who used no telling what concoctions of smelly grease on the heads that integrity, straightforwardness, courage, would certainly have kept kinky" (*WGB*, p. 281). To Maud, the manager is yet another critic finding only fault.

In encountering the manager in the millinery shop Maud is facing her main adversary—the white woman. Therefore, she determines that she can and will win some small victory in the ongoing war with beauty. In Maud's mind the manager cannot bring herself to say that the hat Maud tries on makes Maud beautiful. "Looks lovely on you," she says. "Makes you—" She stops, perhaps searching for the right word. In her effort to sell the hat to Maud the manager assures her of what a bargain the hat would be at "seven ninety-nine," and that she is doing Maud a favor because "you looked like a lady of taste who could appreciate a good value." At another point when she "looked at Maud Martha, it was as if God looked." Maud starts twice for the door. On both occasions the manager stops her with another pitch. The last ploy is to say that she will "speak to the—to the owner," who "might be willing to make some slight reduction, since you're an old customer." Even when Maud assures the manager that she has never been in the store before, the manager "rushed off as if she had heard nothing." Maud's cynical mind completes the act: "She rushed off to consult with the owner. She rushed off to appeal to the boxes in the back room" (**WGB,** p. 282).

After having the manager go through the difficulty of finally agreeing on the price that Maud has indicated, Maud is delighted to calmly tell her, "I've decided against the hat." She has made a decision—a firm, unflinching decision after the white woman has tried in every way she could to make Maud feel obligated to buy the hat. The terrible frustration of the manager is captured in the final scene:

> "What? Why, you told—But, you said—"
>
> Maud Martha went out, tenderly closed the door.
>
> "Black—oh, black—" said the hat woman to her hats—which, on the slender stands, shone pink and blue and white and lavender, showed off their tassels, their sleek satin ribbons, their veils, their flower coquettes.
>
> (**WGB,** pp. 282-83)

All the while the terrible frustration is contrasted with the peaceful physical background that is unbiased and indifferent, an ironic reflection of that gentle and genteel side of the white woman that her terrible anger and frustration belie.

It is obvious that Maud's reaction is quite different from Sonia Johnson's in "the self-solace." When a young white woman comes into Sonia Johnson's beauty shop to sell lipstick, Sonia listens to her pitch and finally orders some lipstick. Maud, who is in the shop at the time, is furious for several reasons. One is that Sonia did not use the opportunity for a small victory over this young white woman with what Maud thinks of as "beautiful legs." Maud knows that some beauticians, glad to have the white saleswomen at their mercy if only for a few minutes, would make them

crawl. They are sometimes insulting, brusque, and then they "applied the whiplash." "Then they sent the poor creatures off—with no orders. Then they laughed and laughed and laughed, a terrible laughter." A second reason Maud is furious is that the saleswoman sells the order to Sonia, saying that "this new shade . . . is just the thing for your customers. For their dark complexions." Maud wonders if the saleswoman realizes that the "Negro group" included all complexions from those lighter than her own, to "brown, tan, yellow, cream which could not take a dark lipstick and keep their poise." But Maud is primarily furious because the saleswoman has used the word "nigger" and has not been taken to task by Sonia. She has said, "I work like a nigger to make a few pennies." Sonia has an opportunity for a small victory in the continuing war, but she does not take it.

"At the Burns-Coopers" presents Maud with a chance for a small although Pyrrhic victory. Driven by desperation caused by Paul's unemployment and her not being able to find more suitable work, Maud seeks a job as a domestic. Mrs. Burns-Cooper is very superior and authoritative and particularly condescending and unwittingly insulting. Bearing her insults in silence is barely manageable for Maud. Both Mrs. Burns-Cooper and her mother-in-law complain that the potato parings are too thick and proceed to treat Maud like a child: "As though she were a child, a ridiculous one, and one that ought to be given a little shaking, except that shaking was—not quite the thing, would not quite do. One held up one's finger (if one did anything), cocked one's head, was arch. As in the old song, one hinted, 'Tut tut! now now! come come!'" (**WGB,** pp. 288-89).

Maud does not return to the Burns-Coopers'. She says that she cannot explain why to Mrs. Burns-Cooper. Like the millinery shop manager and the lipstick saleswoman, Mrs. Burns-Cooper does not understand that there is a war. As long as they can perceive black women as inferiors who ought to be grateful for the opportunity to work or to buy, they will not even be conscious of the war nor of any casualties on the black side. When there is "retaliation" that amounts only to failure to comply with the wishes of the white women, they are shocked and see Maud and her kind as belligerent and uncooperative. It is hard to fight a war with an enemy who does not know a war is being fought, but who nevertheless has all of the weapons and continues to inflict casualties.

Maud's explanation, which would certainly have escaped Mrs. Burns-Cooper, is simply that she is a human being:

> One walked out from that almost perfect wall, spitting at the firing squad. What difference did it make whether the firing squad understood or did not understand the manner of one's retaliation or why one had to retaliate?
>
> Why, one was a human being. One wore clean nightgowns. One loved one's baby. One drank cocoa by the fire—or the gas range—come the evening, in the wintertime.
>
> (*WGB*, p. 289)

The last vignette of **Maud Martha,** "back from the wars!" provides a fitting final comment on the various kinds of war that rage among people. Because World War II is over and her brother, Harry, has returned, she, like others, exults. She does notice, however, that some wars are continuing. "And the Negro press (on whose front pages beamed the usual representations of womanly Beauty, pale and pompadoured) carried the stories of the latest of the Georgia and Mississippi lynchings . . ." (*WGB*, p. 305). This passage, in addition to suggesting that all the wars are not over, refers to the war of black people for freedom and dignity and to the specific war that black women wage with the standards of beauty (which Brooks capitalizes for emphasis).

In the midst, however, of Maud Martha's concern with lynching and color prejudice, she is optimistic. On a sun-filled spring day her hope lies in the fact that man's foolishness cannot destroy even "the basic equanimity of the least and commonest flower: for would its kind not come up again in the spring? come up, if necessary, among, between, or out of—beastly inconvenient!—the smashed corpses lying in strict composure, in that hush infallible and sincere" (*WGB*, p. 305).

The "commonest flower" is the dandelion with which she identifies in the book's first vignette, "description of Maud Martha." Her war continues against "the usual representation of womanly Beauty, pale and pompadoured."

The image is like that of the Phoenix, rising from its ashes, or like the sun and the children in "spring landscape: detail," who on a gray spring day are "little silver promises somewhere up there, hinting," able to shut out all the world's inhibitions and ridiculousness. These images cause Maud to end on a note of hope and promise:

> And was not this something to be thankful for?
>
> And, in the meantime, while people did live they would be grand, would be glorious and brave, would have nimble hearts that would beat and beat. They would even get up nonsense, through wars, through divorce, through evictions and jiltings and taxes.
>
> And, in the meantime, she was going to have another baby.
>
> The weather was bidding her bon voyage.
>
> (*WGB*, pp. 305-6)

Notes

1. Arthur P. Davis, "The Black-and-Tan Motif in the Poetry of Gwendolyn Brooks," *College Language Association Journal* 6 (Dec. 1962): 90-97.

2. Davis, "The Black-and-Tan Motif," p. 90.

3. Ibid.

4. William Grier and Price Cobbs, *Black Rage* (New York: Basic Books, 1968), pp. 40-41.

5. Gwendolyn Brooks, *The World of Gwendolyn Brooks* (New York: Harper and Row, 1971), p. 100. Hereinafter cited in the text as *WGB*.

6. Grier and Cobbs, *Black Rage*, p. 52.

7. Maya Angelou, *I Know Why the Caged Bird Sings* (New York: Random House, 1969), pp. 1-3.

8. Angelou, *I Know Why*, p. 2.

9. Gwendolyn Brooks, *Report from Part One* (Detroit: Broadside Press, 1972).

10. Harry B. Shaw, *Maud Martha* in *Gwendolyn Brooks* (Boston: Twayne Publishing, 1980), p. 165.

FURTHER READING

Bibliography

Gerry, Thomas M. F. *Contemporary Canadian and U.S. Women of Letters: An Annotated Bibliography.* New York: Garland, 1993, 287 p.

  Bibliographies of various North American women writers.

Loff, Jon N. "Gwendolyn Brooks: A Bibliography." *CLA Journal* 17, no. 1 (September 1973): 21-32.

  Record of Brooks's published works and a listing of reviews and essays on her writings.

Biographies

Kent, George E. *A Life of Gwendolyn Brooks.* Lexington: University Press of Kentucky, 1990, 287 p.

  Biography of Brooks, compiled with her full cooperation, by a long-time admirer of her work.

Melham, D. H. *Gwendolyn Brooks: Poetry and the Heroic Voice.* Lexington: University Press of Kentucky, 1987, 270 p.

  Biography, analysis and bibliographical materials.

Shaw, Harry B. *Gwendolyn Brooks.* Boston: Twayne, 1980, 200 p.

  Comprehensive coverage of Brooks's life with critical essays on her major publications.

Criticism

Burr, Zofia. "Reading Gwendolyn Brooks Across Audiences." In *Of Women, Poetry, and Power: Strategies of Address in Dickinson, Miles, Brooks, Lorde, and Angelou*, pp. 113-51. Urbana: University of Illinois Press, 2002.

Examination of Brooks's relationships with her white editors and the differing responses by black and white readers to her work.

Gayles, Gloria Wade, editor. *Conversations with Gwendolyn Brooks*. Jackson: University Press of Mississippi, 2003, 167 p.

Provides various interviews with Brooks.

Georgoudaki, Ekaterini. "Black and White Women in Poems by Angelou, Brooks, Dove, Giovanni, and Lorde: Complex and Ambivalent Relationships." In *Race, Gender, and Class Perspectives in the Works of Maya Angelou, Gwendolyn Brooks, Rita Dove, Nikki Giovanni, and Audre Lorde*, pp. 143-95. Thessaloniki, Greece: Aristotle University of Thessaloniki, 1991.

Compares the representations of black/white female relationships in the work of five African American poets.

Hubbard, Stacy Carson. "'A Splintery Box': Race and Gender in the Sonnets of Gwendolyn Brooks." *Genre* 25, no. 1 (spring 1992): 47-64.

Examines Brooks's use of the traditional sonnet form to serve a black, female voice.

Hughes, Gertrude Reif. "Making It *Really* New: Hilda Doolittle, Gwendolyn Brooks, and the Feminist Potential of Modern Poetry." In *On Gwendolyn Brooks: Reliant Contemplation*, edited by Stephen Caldwell Wright, pp. 186-212. Ann Arbor: University of Michigan Press, 1996.

Explores the way Brooks and H. D. employed the conventions of modernist poetry to challenge male privilege.

Mullen, Bill V. "Engendering the Cultural Front: Gwendolyn Brooks, Black Women, and Class Struggle in Poetry." In *Popular Fronts: Chicago and African-American Cultural Politics, 1935-46*, pp. 148-80. Urbana: University of Illinois Press, 1999.

Discusses the Chicago setting of Brooks's work and the poet's contributions to the African American community on the city's South Side.

Park, You-Me Gayle Wald. "Native Daughters in the Promised Land: Gender, Race, and the Question of Separate Spheres." In *No More Separate Spheres!*, edited by Cathy N. Davidson and Jessamyn Hatcher, pp. 263-87. Durham, N.C.: Duke University Press, 2002.

Analysis of the boundaries between public and private domains in texts by African American and Asian American writers. Includes a discussion of Brooks's novel Maud Martha.

OTHER SOURCES FROM GALE:

Additional coverage of Brooks's life and career is contained in the following sources published by the Gale Group: *African American Writers*, Eds. 1, 2; *American Writers Supplement*, Vol. 3; *Authors and Artists for Young Adults*, Vol. 20; *Authors in the News*, Vol. 1; *Black Literature Criticism*; *Black Writers*, Eds. 2, 3; *Children's Literature Review*, Vol. 27; *Concise Dictionary of American Literary Biography, 1941-1968*; *Contemporary Authors*, Vols. 1-4R, 190; *Contemporary Authors New Revision Series*, Vols. 1, 27, 52, 75; *Contemporary Literary Criticism*, Vols. 1, 2, 4, 5, 15, 49, 125; *Contemporary Poets*, Ed. 7; *Contemporary Women Poets*; *Dictionary of Literary Biography*, Vol. 5, 76, 165; *DISCovering Authors*; *DISCovering Authors: Canadian Edition*; *DISCovering Authors Modules: Most-Studied Authors, Multicultural*, and *Poets*; *DISCovering Authors 3.0*; *Encyclopedia of World Literature in the 20th Century*, Ed. 3; *Exploring Poetry*; *Literature Resource Center*; *Major 20th-Century Writers*, Eds. 1, 2; *Modern American Women Writers*; *Poetry Criticism*, Vol. 7; *Poetry for Students*, Vols. 1, 2, 4, 6; *Reference Guide to American Literature*, Ed. 4; *Something about the Author*, Vols. 6, 123; *Twayne's United States Authors*; *World Literature Criticism*; and *World Poets*.

WILLA CATHER

(1873 - 1947)

(Full name Willa Sibert Cather) American novelist, short story writer, essayist, critic, and poet.

Cather is regarded as one of the most important American writers of the twentieth century. Identified often as a "regional" writer because of her frequent use of western and midwestern backdrops in her stories, Cather is equally identified with women's issues because her works foreground the experiences of American and immigrant women in the prairies and towns of a burgeoning country.

BIOGRAPHICAL INFORMATION

Cather was born in Virginia and spent the first decade of her life on her family's farm in Back Creek Valley. After a fire destroyed their sheep barn, Cather's father auctioned off his remaining assets and moved the family to the Great Plains, where his parents and brother had already established a homestead. Arriving in 1884, the Cathers joined the ethnically diverse group of settlers in Webster County, Nebraska, but establishing a farm on the prairie proved a more difficult task than Cather's father was willing to undertake, and a year later the family moved to the nearby town of Red Cloud. Once settled there, Cather began to attend school on a regular basis. She rapidly distin-guished herself as a brilliant, though somewhat temperamental, student. Although her primary interest was science, she displayed a talent for act-ing, and she performed plays she had composed for the entertainment of her family, gave recita-tions, and participated in amateur theatricals staged at the Red Cloud opera house. Planning to become a physician, she also accompanied a local doctor on his house calls, and she was eventually allowed to assist him. Sometime shortly before her thirteenth birthday, Cather adopted the outward appearance and manner of a male and began signing her name "William Cather, Jr." or "William Cather M.D." While some commenta-tors suggest that this behavior can be construed simply as one aspect of Cather's blanket rejection of the strictures placed upon women in the nineteenth century, others contend that Cather's masculine persona was an authentic reflection of her identity, citing as proof her consistent use of male narrators and her strong attachments to some female friends, with whom Cather may have had romantic relationships. In either case, Cather was eventually persuaded by friends to return to a more conventional mode of dress, and she later dismissed the episode as juvenile posturing. Although she intended to study medicine when she entered the University of Nebraska, she reconsidered her career choice when an essay she had written for her English class was published in the local newspaper, accompanied by lavish praise from the editor. Thereafter, Cather pursued a humanities curriculum, studying primarily English, French, German, and classical literature. After graduation, Cather moved to Pittsburgh to serve as editor of a short-lived women's magazine called *Home Monthly*. While she continued to write and publish stories, she made her living as a journalist and teacher for the next seventeen years. In 1906 she moved to New York City to assume the managing editorship of the influential *McClure's* magazine. Her association with that publication brought her national recognition, and it was S. S. McClure, the dynamic, iconoclastic publisher of the magazine, who arranged for the release of Cather's first volume of short stories. While on assignment in Boston in 1908, Cather met Sarah Orne Jewett, an author whose work she greatly admired. After reading Cather's fiction, Jewett encouraged her to give up journalism to write fiction full-time. Cather was profoundly influenced by Jewett's opinion, and shortly afterward she relinquished her responsibilities at *McClure's*. After one unsuccessful novel (*Alexander's Bridge*, 1912), Cather found her stride with subject matter drawn from childhood memories of the Nebraska prairie, using them and other incidents from her life to create a series of well-received novels published between her retirement from journalism in 1912 and her death in 1947.

MAJOR WORKS

Although many critics have focused on Cather's American prairie themes, recent criticism has noted Cather's strong interest in women's personal development throughout her most recognized novels. In *O Pioneers!* (1913) Cather featured Alexandra Bergson, the daughter of Swedish immigrants in Nebraska. On his deathbed, her father leaves her the family land and assets. When difficulties set in over the next few years, her brothers want to leave the farm and move on to other pursuits; Alexandra, however, chooses to remain. Struggling against both the surrounding wilderness and conventional female roles upheld by her brothers and the neighboring farmers, Alexandra turns the farm into a success despite the fear and resentment she inspires. In *The Song of the Lark* (1915) Cather turned to a different aspect of women's experience. Her protagonist, Thea Kronborg, is a young Swedish immigrant trying to pursue a career as an opera singer. In her small midwestern town, however, Thea—like Alexandra—encounters different expectations of what she will become. It is made clear to her that she

may sing in the church choir, but pursuing a life as an artist is considered out of the question for a woman. Cather detailed the challenges and prejudices a woman artist faces, and the price she must pay for artistic freedom and success. *My Ántonia* (1918) is widely considered Cather's masterpiece; it is also her most problematic novel for feminist critics. *My Ántonia* begins with an introduction ostensibly narrated by Cather herself, which tells of meeting an old friend, Jim Burden, who has written a memoir of a girl both knew during their childhoods. The narrator of the introduction agrees to read Burden's manuscript, which then forms the body of the novel. In Book I, Burden describes his initial encounter with Ántonia's family, the Shimerdas, his friendship with fourteen-year-old Ántonia, and her father's suicide. Book II follows both Burden and Ántonia in their move to the town of Black Hawk, Ántonia having left her family to work for the Burdens' neighbors, the Harlings. Ántonia is absent from Book III, in which Burden goes to the state university, and she is featured only indirectly in Book IV, with Burden learning of her scandalous love affair and illegitimate child with a neighbor. She reappears only in the final section of the novel, when Burden visits the farm where she and her husband are raising their large family. As straightforward as the plot outline appears, *My Ántonia* presents several difficulties for feminists. First is the fact that Cather chose to tell Ántonia's story with a male narrator, thus disallowing her a voice of her own. Second is the complete absence of mutually satisfying sexual relationships, particularly the asexual relationship between Burden and Ántonia. While admitting that Cather's avowed impatience with the limitations imposed by men upon women in the nineteenth century led to a consistently negative portrayal of male-female relationships in her fiction, many commentators nevertheless consider such portrayals reflections of Cather's more basic and unacknowledged ambivalence toward heterosexuality. Either way, a darkness pervades the novel where sex is concerned. Finally, Ántonia's reappearance at the end of the story is viewed by some scholars as a joyous or affirmative event; but by others as a portrayal of a submissive, defeated, and weary character. While Ántonia survives childhood poverty, her father's suicide, an illicit affair, and the birth of an illegitimate child, she is triumphant mainly in the eyes of Jim Burden. Her appearance has declined dramatically, and the title of the final chapter, "Cuzak's Boys," not only focuses on Ántonia's children's patrimony, thus denying her a significant role in their lives, but also ignores Ántonia's daughters as well.

CRITICAL RECEPTION

Recent critical attention has placed Cather's undocumented lesbianism in the foreground. Whether or not she was in fact a lesbian, most critics agree that Cather's fiction displays a marked discomfort with female sexuality. Cather's frequent use of male narrators to tell the stories of women, as well as her archetypal treatment of the women themselves, has led critics to link her works with her life, particularly her early cross-dressing phase. Despite her apparent difficulties in dealing with sexuality in her writings and her penchant for using male narrators, Cather and her works remain a subject of great interest for feminists into the twenty-first century.

PRINCIPAL WORKS

April Twilights (poetry) 1903

The Troll Garden (short stories) 1905

Alexander's Bridge (novel) 1912

O Pioneers! (novel) 1913

The Song of the Lark (novel) 1915

My Ántonia (novel) 1918

Youth and the Bright Medusa (short stories) 1920

One of Ours (novel) 1922

A Lost Lady (novel) 1923

The Professor's House (novel) 1925

My Mortal Enemy (novel) 1926

Death Comes for the Archbishop (novel) 1927

Shadows on the Rock (novel) 1931

Obscure Destinies (short stories) 1932

Lucy Gayheart (novel) 1935

Not under Forty (essays) 1936

The Novels and Stories of Willa Cather. 13 vols. (novels and short stories) 1937-41

Sapphira and the Slave Girl (novel) 1940

The Old Beauty, and Others (short stories) 1948

On Writing: Critical Studies on Writing as an Art (essays) 1949

WILLA CATHER (ESSAY DATE 1931)

SOURCE: Cather, Willa. "My First Novels [There Were Two]." In *On Writing: Critical Studies on Writing as an Art*, pp. 91-7. New York: Alfred A. Knopf, 1976.

In the following essay, originally published in The Colophon *in 1931, Cather provides background information on the writing and publication of her first two novels.*

My first novel, *Alexander's Bridge*, was very like what painters call a studio picture. It was the result of meeting some interesting people in London. Like most young writers, I thought a book should be made out of "interesting material," and at that time I found the new more exciting than the familiar. The impressions I tried to communicate on paper were genuine, but they were very shallow. I still find people who like that book because it follows the most conventional pattern, and because it is more or less laid in London. London is supposed to be more engaging than, let us say, Gopher Prairie; even if the writer knows Gopher Prairie very well and London very casually. Soon after the book was published I went for six months to Arizona and New Mexico. The longer I stayed in a country I really did care about, and among people who were a part of the country, the more unnecessary and superficial a book like *Alexander's Bridge* seemed to me. I did no writing down there, but I recovered from the conventional editorial point of view.

When I got back to Pittsburgh I began to write a book entirely for myself; a story about some Scandinavians and Bohemians who had been neighbours of ours when I lived on a ranch in Nebraska, when I was eight or nine years old. I found it a much more absorbing occupation than writing *Alexander's Bridge;* a different process altogether. Here there was no arranging or "inventing"; everything was spontaneous and took its own place, right or wrong. This was like taking a ride through a familiar country on a horse that knew the way, on a fine morning when you felt like riding. The other was like riding in a park, with someone not altogether congenial, to whom you had to be talking all the time. Since I wrote this book for myself, I ignored all the situations and accents that were then generally thought to be necessary. The "novel of the soil" had not then come into fashion in this country. The drawing-room was considered the proper setting for a novel, and the only characters worth reading about were smart people or clever people. "O. Henry" had made the short story go into the world of the cheap boarding-house and the shop-girl and the truck-driver. But Henry James and Mrs. Wharton were our most interesting novelists, and most of the younger writers followed their manner, without having their qualifications.

O Pioneers! interested me tremendously, because it had to do with a kind of country I loved, because it was about old neighbours, once very dear, whom I had almost forgotten in the hurry and excitement of growing up and finding out what the world was like and trying to get on in it. But I did not in the least expect that other people would see anything in a slow-moving story, without "action," without "humour," without a "hero"; a story concerned entirely with heavy farming people, with cornfields and pasture lands and pig yards,—set in Nebraska, of all places! As everyone knows, Nebraska is distinctly déclassé as a literary background; its very name throws the delicately attuned critic into a clammy shiver of embarrassment. Kansas is almost as unpromising. Colorado, on the contrary, is considered quite possible. Wyoming really has some class, of its own kind, like well-cut riding breeches. But a New York critic voiced a very general opinion when he said: "I simply don't care a damn what happens in Nebraska, no matter who writes about it."

O Pioneers! was not only about Nebraska farmers; the farmers were Swedes! At that time, 1912, the Swede had never appeared on the printed page in this country except in broadly humorous sketches; and the humour was based on two peculiarities: his physical strength, and his inability to pronounce the letter "j." I had certainly good reasons for supposing that the book I had written for myself would remain faithfully with me, and continue to be exclusively my property. I sent it to Mr. Ferris Greenslet, of Houghton Mifflin, who had published *Alexander's Bridge,* and was truly astonished when he wrote me they would publish it.

I was very much pleased when William Heinemann decided to publish it in England. I had met Mr. Heinemann in London several times, when I was on the editorial staff of *McClure's Magazine,* and I had the highest opinion of his taste and judgment. His personal taste was a thing quite apart from his business, and it was uncompromising. The fact that a second-rate book sold tremendously never made him hedge and insist that there must be something pretty good in it after all. Most publishers, like most writers, are ruined by their successes.

When my third book, *The Song of the Lark,* came along, Heinemann turned it down. I had never heard from him directly that he liked *O Pioneers!* but now I had a short hand-written letter from him, telling me that he admired it very much; that he was declining *The Song of the Lark* because he thought in that book I had taken the wrong road, and that the full-blooded method, which told everything about everybody, was not natural to me and was not the one in which I would ever take satisfaction. "As for myself," he wrote, "I always find the friendly, confidential tone of writing of this sort distressingly familiar, even when the subject matter is very fine."

At that time I did not altogether agree with Mr. Heinemann, nor with Randolph Bourne, in this country, who said in his review almost the same thing. One is always a little on the defensive about one's last book. But when the next book, *My Ántonia,* came along, quite of itself and with no direction from me, it took the road of *O Pioneers!*—not the road of *The Song of the Lark.* Too much detail is apt, like any other form of extravagance, to become slightly vulgar; and it quite destroys in a book a very satisfying element analogous to what painters call "composition."

GENERAL COMMENTARY

SUSAN J. ROSOWSKI (ESSAY DATE AUTUMN 1981)

SOURCE: Rosowski, Susan J. "Willa Cather's Women." *Studies in American Fiction* 9, no. 2 (autumn 1981): 261-75.

In the following essay, Rosowski explores the ways in which Cather portrays her female characters not only as feminine archetypes but also as individual women.

Willa Cather created a gallery of powerful women. It includes the indomitable pioneer Alexandra Bergson, the great artist Thea Kronborg, the Earth Mother Ántonia Shimerda, the artful teacher of civilized standards Marian Forrester, the fiercely individual Myra Driscoll Henshawe. As critics have recognized, each functions as a type, an allegorical figure, of Cather's major themes, as Alexandra and Ántonia are allegorical of the pioneer experience, Thea and Myra Henshawe of the artistic soul, and Mrs. Forrester of the corrupting power of materialism.[1] Yet these critical categories have led readers from similarities among them. All are female, and Cather makes her character's sex central to the characterization of each. Aside from recent studies on sexuality in specific novels, however, the broader question of Cather's treatment of these characters as women has received little attention, as if her insistence that individuals deal with permanent values has diverted readers from the directness with which she treats the economic and social conditions that shape a woman's relationships to those values. Just as Cather's women embody themes concerning the pioneer, artist, and materialism, so they embody themes concerning female experience.

The emotional pattern of two selves that runs through Cather's fiction is especially suited to writing about women's lives. There are two selves in each person, Cather suggests: a personal, worldly self expressed with family and friends, and an otherworldly, imaginative second self expressed in creative work. The ideal human condition, described in Cather's early novels, involves a synthesis of the two, with the outward-moving self rooted in the settled personal self. In society, however, a woman encounters contradictions between the human pattern of two selves and cultural myths that would limit her to only one of them. Cather's later novels present increasingly complex examinations of social roles assigned to women and of the implication of those roles for individuals caught in them.

In her early novels—*O Pioneers!*, *The Song of the Lark,* and *My Ántonia*—Cather presents women who either live or move outside conventional society; their strengths are due in part to this fact. Of the three, *O Pioneers!* offers the purest example of Cather's myth of human greatness. It was, Cather later said, a book she wrote entirely for herself;[2] in it, she abandoned the conventional setting and characterization of her first novel, *Alexander's Bridge,* and turned to Nebraska as her setting and to a woman, Alexandra, as her major character.

Alexandra dominates the book. Assuming mythic dimensions, she is an Earth Mother, a corn goddess, and an epic heroine.[3] But just as Alexandra represents ideal forms of being, so her development presents Cather's ideal growth of the two selves, first by extending her creative self with the land and then by extending her personal self with Carl. This development follows that traditionally associated with a man, who through his work "encounters change and progress" and "senses his extension through time and the universe" then later turns to personal stability, "a home, a fixed location, and an anchorage in the world."[4]

Early scenes of *O Pioneers!* establish Alexandra's independence by contradicting cultural restrictions imposed upon a female character. Alexandra dresses comfortably and practically in a man's long ulster;[5] just as naturally, she assumes conventionally male attitudes, walking "rapidly and resolutely," fixing her gaze "intently on the distance" (p. 6) and "into the future" (p. 14), then "gathering her strength . . . to grasp a situation which, no matter how painful, must be met and dealt with somehow" (p. 10). Throughout, Alexandra moves as a subject rather than an object, a distinction Cather drives home in one brief encounter. When a drummer admires the girl's hair, Alexandra "stabbed him with a glance of Amazonian fierceness," "mercilessly" crushing his "feeble flirtatious instincts" (p. 8).

A cultural pattern of restriction contrasts to this dominant pattern of independence. A foil to Alexandra, Marie Tovesky assumes the traditional role reserved for a female character: she is a "city child" dressed in the "'Kate Greenaway' manner," with "brown curly hair, like a brunette doll's," (p. 11). While Alexandra defiantly rejects the drummer's admiration and, in so doing, romantic conventions that reduce a woman to an object for male attention, Marie becomes such an object in a grotesque parody of courtship. In town, Joe Tovesky's "cronies formed a circle about him, admiring and teasing the little girl. . . . They told her that she must choose one of them for a sweetheart, and each began pressing his suit and offering her bribes; candy, and little pigs, and spotted calves. She looked archly into the big, brown, mustached faces, smelling of spirits and tobacco, then she ran her tiny forefinger delicately over Joe's bristly chin and said, 'Here is my sweetheart'" (p. 12).

It is not enough, of course, to escape limitations; one must develop also the positive qualities that enable growth. Alexandra has little imagination about her personal life (p. 203), "not the least spark of cleverness" (p. 61), and, apparently, no unusual physical strength. Instead, she is distinguished by her capacity for sympathy, for feeling the promise of the land (p. 67) and, on the Divide, achieving union with it, "as if her heart were hiding down there, somewhere, with the quail and the plover" (p. 71). Significantly, Alexandra awakens a female principle of active receptivity in the land. In the description of spring plowing, for example, Cather scarcely mentions the plow or the seed; instead, she describes a receptive land as "the brown earth [that] with such a strong, clean smell, and such a power of growth and fertility in it, yields itself eagerly to the plow" (p. 76).[6]

Once the land has been tamed, Cather turns to Alexandra's "personal life, her own realization of herself" that has remained "almost a subconscious existence" (p. 203). Again, Alexandra's growth is relatively pure, as was her previous outward movement to universal values; and again, Cather contrasts traditional cultural patterns to Alexandra's independence. The community that has come in the intervening sixteen years has brought with it the assumption of male superiority. The clearly defined responsibility delegated to the young Alexandra by her dying father has, with time, been obscured, and Alexandra's brothers, asserting she is overweening in insisting to her right to her own land, declare "'the property of a family really belongs to the men of the family, no matter about the title'" (p. 169). Even in her old friend and future husband, Carl, Alexandra encounters traditional social restrictions. In a reversal of roles, Alexandra proposes to Carl, saying "'what I have is yours, if you care enough about me to take it'"; he, however, stung by criticism of his dependency, leaves for Alaska in a lonely and futile effort to prove himself worthy (p. 182).

In developing Alexandra's personal self, Cather again establishes her character's independence from convention. Alexandra "had never been in love, she had never indulged in sentimental reveries" but, instead, had always looked upon men as "work-fellows" (p. 205). Again, Marie serves as a foil, in her love for Emil following the general romantic pattern by which lovers, seeking transcendence through each other, are doomed. In Cather's novels, such love corrupts; it led to Marie's disastrous marriage to Frank and leads to her tragic love for Emil.

Alexandra's relationship with Carl develops in marked contrast to the Marie-Emil relationship. With her expected marriage to Carl, Alexandra turns from her romantic dream of being carried by a lover who "was like no man she knew; he was much larger and stronger and swifter, and he carried her as easily as if she were a sheaf of wheat" (p. 206). The action reveals, according to one reader, "the pathos of her limitation," for she and Carl "are of different natures—she an earth goddess, he a not very notable tinker."[7] A more accurate distinction might be made between the natures of the experiences. Alexandra seems larger than life—an "earth goddess"—in her reaching toward the land, but she lives her personal life in the human dimension of time. Carl is not an "earth god," and there is little evidence that "for [Alexandra] at least Carl and the vegetation god have become one."[8] Indeed, Alexandra's growth

in the second part of the novel is away from the romantic dream of transcendence through human love and toward the real value of personal stability through love. For Carl offers an anchorage, and "Alexandra and Carl mate not as passionate lovers but more like . . . ongoing companions."[9] Most importantly, Carl recognizes that Alexandra "'belong[s] to the land'" (p. 307), and the happiness that Alexandra predicts for them is defined not by a self-limited passion but by "the great peace . . . and freedom" (p. 307) of that land.

In **O Pioneers!** Cather both presented the two selves she will explore in later novels and sketched the restrictions to those selves that she will later focus upon: social expectations of male superiority, the economic dimension of courtship and marriage, the romantic myth that places the ideal in a love object, and the insistence that women make themselves objects to conform to cultural myths. But these restrictions remain background concerns, scarcely touching Alexandra. Instead, the frontier setting offers "the metaphorical isolation"[10] that enables a pure form of heroism; the early action of Alexandra's father, before his death passing responsibility for the family and farm to Alexandra, makes her authority formal; and the narrative structure, with its omniscient narrator, avoids sexist expectations that Cather will develop in later works.

In her next novel, **The Song of the Lark,** Cather moves her character into society, using "cultural not bucolic"[11] elements. Thea Kronborg is an artist. Through her, Cather presents her most straightforward account of second-self growth: Thea moves from the personal security of her family life in a small Midwestern town to greatness as an opera singer. Remarkably, Cather avoids the stereotypic female artist's attitude toward work noted by critics from Beauvoir to Spacks—narcissism and a resulting view of art as a means to love and power. Instead, Thea acts according to her instinctive allegiance to universal values; her highest moments involve the loss of self in art. Again, the basic metaphor of the novel is both female and active: Thea nurtures her second self through stages of (1) gestation and birth; (2) growth toward active receptivity; and (3) creative reproduction of eternal truths into worldly form.

As an artist, Thea Kronborg lives in a rarified atmosphere by which talent is its own justification and creates its own myths. Around her, secondary characters construct secondary myths: Ray Kennedy, the railway man, sees her as Thee, his ideal love; Doctor Archie as the promise of his own lost youth; her aunt Tillie as the romantic heroine she would be. But just as Thea would not play a part assigned for her for a church play, she refuses to play these parts. In the end, she creates her own myth and returns it to her society. Like Alexandra Bergson, Thea Kronborg acts independently of cultural expectations that a woman exist as an object to a male perspective.

But our cultural myths assign to women the position of objects and restrict women to immanence. In *My Ántonia, A Lost Lady,* and *My Mortal Enemy,* Cather focuses squarely on the implications for women of cultural myths concerning them. In each novel, a distinct narrator represents conventions that are contradicted by a major female character who works out her individual destiny in defiance of the narrator's expectation. Cather perfectly adapts the narrative structure of *My Ántonia* to cultural assumptions of two selves. The male narrator, Jim Burden, assumes the subject position, moves outward, engages in change and progress, and writes about "my Ántonia"; Ántonia, the archetypal woman, provides an anchorage to which Jim can return and serves as the muse for his creative imagination. Through Jim, Cather presents myths of male transcendence—of man as a liberating hero, romantic lover, and creative genius; of a woman to be rescued, loved, and transformed into art.

My Ántonia is Jim Burden's account of all that Ántonia means to him or, more precisely, of his youthful attempt to *make* her "'anything that a woman can be to a man.'"[12] By his account, Ántonia seeks primarily to nurture by giving—to give her ring to the ten-year-old Jim and "to appreciate and admire" (p. 50) his exploits; to give her love to Larry Donovan, and to give "a better chance" than she had to her children (p. 320). As important, she makes no demands upon the world or upon others in it. Even after becoming pregnant, Ántonia did not press Larry Donovan to marry her, for "'I thought if he saw how well I could do for him, he'd want to stay with me'" (p. 313); her husband, Cuzak, affirms "'she is a good wife for a poor man'" because "'she don't ask me no questions'" (pp. 365-66). Ántonia offers unconditional love: both her strength and her weakness is that "'I never could believe harm of anybody I loved'" (p. 344). Through her love, Ántonia, like the orchard she tends, offers "the deepest peace" of escape from worldly demands (p. 341). Finally, Jim presents Ántonia as a well-spring for male activity in the larger world. On a physical level, she bears sons. Jim titles his final chapter "Cuzak's Boys," and he concludes "it was no wonder that her sons stood tall and straight." On a spiritual level, she is a muse to Jim, for she "had that something which fires the imagination" (p. 353). Through Ántonia, Jim comes to realize what his country girls mean: "If there were no girls like them in the world, there would be no poetry" (p. 270).

At the same time that Cather uses Jim to present "the collective myths"[13] about women, she builds tension against his account. There emerges a certain ruthlessness about Jim's affection for Ántonia that belies his stated affection for her. His love, unlike hers, *is* conditional. He is proud of Ántonia when he believes her to be "like Snow-white in the fairy tale" (p. 215); he turns from her when she asserts her individuality. He resents her protecting manner toward him, is angered over her masculine ways when she works the farm, is bitter and unforgiving when she "throws herself away on . . . a cheap sort of fellow" and, once pregnant, falls from social favor.[14] Jim's allegiance is consistently to his dreams and illusions; when they conflict with reality, he denies the reality.

The world and the people in it just as consistently belie the myths Jim attempts to impose upon them. Otto Fuchs is not a Jesse James desperado but a warmhearted ranchhand; Lena Lingard is not a wild seductress but a strong-minded girl who becomes an independent businesswoman; Jim himself is not the adventurer, the lover, or the poet that he pretends to be. By contrasting the boast and the deed, Cather suggests comic, self-serving, and ineffectual dimensions of male gallantry. Picturing himself as a dragon slayer, Jim kills an old, lazy rattlesnake. Forced by his grandmother into service as Ántonia's rescuer, Jim sleeps at the Cutters, saving Ántonia from rape but feeling something close to hatred of her for embarrassing him. Resolving to "'go home and look after Ántonia'" (p. 268), Jim returns to her only twenty years later, after being assured that he will not have to part with his illusions (pp. 327-28). Finally, Ántonia and Lena, the objects of Jim's benevolence, react to his promises with smiles (pp. 322-23) and "frank amusement" (p. 268). They get on with their lives basically independently from men, whether by design, as when Lena resolves that she will never marry and that she will build a house for her mother, for "'the men will never do it'" (p. 241), or by necessity, as when Ántonia, deserted by her lover, proceeds to raise her daughter well and proudly.

Tension against Jim's account increases as his narrative role changes. In the initial sections, Cather presents Ántonia through Jim's perspective. Jim measures Ántonia against his idea of women, approving of her when she assumes a role he expects of her. But in Book IV, "The Pioneer Woman's Story," Cather moves Jim aside, to the position of tale recorder, and makes the midwife who attended Ántonia the tale teller. The Widow Steavens provides a woman's account of a woman's experience and, with it, a significant change in tone toward Ántonia. She relates her story with understanding and sympathy rather than with Jim's shocked and bitter insistence that Ántonia play her part in his myth.

By the fifth section, Jim and Ántonia have reversed roles. Jim began the novel as the story teller in several senses, telling the account he titles *my* Ántonia and also telling it in terms of stories he has read: *The Life of Jesse James, Robinson Crusoe, Camille,* the *Georgics.* But the child Jim grew into a man who followed the most conventional pattern for success: he left the farm to move to town, then attended the university, studied law at Harvard, married well, and joined a large corporation as a lawyer. In the process he seems to have lost his personal identity. Conversely, Ántonia, who began the novel as a character rendered by Jim, in the fifth section breaks through myths Jim had imposed upon her and emerges powerfully as herself. With her children around her, she is the center of "the family legend" (p. 350), to whom her children look "for stories and entertainment" (p. 351). But Ántonia's stories, unlike Jim's, are not from literature. They are instead "about the calf that broke its leg, or how Yulka saved her little turkeys from drowning . . . or about old Christmases and weddings in Bohemia" (p. 176).

As Jim leaves the Cuzak farm in the last paragraphs, Ántonia recedes into the background. One of a group standing "by the windmill," she is "waving her apron" (p. 368). Returning to the larger male world, Jim spends a "disappointing" day in Black Hawk, talking idly with "one of the old lawyers who was still in practice" (p. 369) and, finally, walking outside of town to the unploughed prairie that remained from early times. There Jim's "mind was full of pleasant things," for he intended "to play" with Cuzak's boys and, after the boys are grown, "to tramp along a few miles of lighted streets with Cuzak" (p. 370). But these plans seem curiously empty, irrelevant to the center of life represented by the female world of Ántonia. The early male myths of adventure have led to pointless wandering and lonely exile, and the women, originally assigned roles of passivity, have become the vital subjects who create the myths that Jim can only hope to witness and to record.

In her next novel, *One of Ours,* Cather incorporates many of Jim Burden's characteristics into her central character. Claude Wheeler, a young man in search of "something splendid," passively follows abstract cultural myths (now of pure love and noble war), is frightened by complex human reality, and, when confronted by conflict between the two, sacrifices the reality to the dream. As one reader has suggested, the title, "which labels Claude 'one of ours,' suggests a national malaise, perhaps a cluster of them,"[15] for here, as elsewhere, a male character is imprisoned in simplistic patterns of transcendence. In presenting Claude, Cather also presents with great sensitivity the two women most directly affected by Claude's actions. Claude perceives the two as stereotypic seductress and virgin, yet Cather develops in each a human reality that contradicts the role Claude assigns to her. Furthermore, unlike Claude, a character astonishingly lacking in self knowledge, each knows herself and, if given the opportunity, would choose for herself action appropriate to her nature—Enid Royce the ascetic life of the missionary and Gladys Farmer the more physical life of marriage to Claude.

In *A Lost Lady,* Cather turns again to the narrative structure of *My Ántonia*: the male narrator, Niel Herbert, recounts his memories of a woman, Marian Forrester, and through them, recalls his own growth. But Niel and Jim write about quite different women. Ántonia is a "'natural-born mother,'" creating her own myth independently from society. Marian Forrester is a wife and, as such, a woman defined in *terms* of society, a society provided by her husband's business, money, and interests. Twenty-five years younger than Captain Forrester, she was brought by him as a bride to the small town of Sweet Water, where she became renowned as a great hostess.

As a wife, Mrs. Forrester is a magnificent object to be adorned, admired, and cherished. It gratified Captain Forrester to have men admire his fine stock and his fine wife. She gives him identity: he is remembered as the man "'with the beautiful wife,'"[16] and she provides a means by which he may display his success. The gems she wears represent, for example, her husband's "archaic ideas about jewels. . . . They must be costly; they must show that he was able to buy them, and that she was worthy to wear them" (p. 51-52). Most of all, she gives value to her husband's domain by transforming it, by creating an atmosphere of calm, timelessness, and absolute security. It is an atmosphere that enables those in it to dream.

In *A Lost Lady,* Cather asks what happens to such a woman without the props by which she acts, then presents the paradox of the married woman's situation. Her strength lies in her ability to transform the world so that others may dream, but this apparent strength makes her highly vulnerable. First, her domain is wholly within a context of change. Marian Forrester came to Sweet Water to witness the loss of pioneer values, the railway men's departure, her husband's loss of fortune, and, finally, his decline and death. In these changes, she gradually lost both the friends and the money necessary to her. Second, such a woman is valued because she carefully subordinates her individuality so that others may see her as they wish her to be. The young Niel, for example, initially perceives her as from a magical realm, always lovely, never changing. Consequently, Niel judges her by his own illusion and, inevitably, human reality contradicts the illusion. For Niel, then, Mrs. Forrester's story is initially a story of betrayal. He responds to her in stages, similar to but more clearly defined than those of Jim Burden.[17] Initially, he worships her as "belonging to a different world" (p. 42). Upon discovering her sexual relationship with Frank Ellinger, however, he is disillusioned, charging that she betrayed his "aesthetic ideal" (p.87). Niel's disillusionment deepens when, after Captain Forrester's death, he discovers Marian Forrester's liaison with Ivy Peters. With Ivy Peters, Marian Forrester is guilty, Neil believes, of commonness and lack of discrimination. Throughout this period, there runs the charge that Marian Forrester has betrayed others' values—those of Captain Forrester, of the noble pioneers of the past, and, most of all, of Niel himself.

But in *A Lost Lady,* far more than in her previous novels, Cather pits her character against conventions imposed upon her. First, Marian Forrester clearly contradicts the social conventions of Sweet Water, represented by the Molly Beasleys who forage throughout her house and who see only material objects they reduce to items for barter. Second, and more important, Marian Forrester just as clearly contradicts the aesthetic conventions of Niel, who holds it against her that she did not immolate herself to the past and to his romantic illusion.

By the end of *A Lost Lady,* Niel has reached a third stage in which "he came to be very glad that he had known her, and that she had had a hand in breaking him in to life" (p. 171). Recalling her, he wonders about "the secret of that ardour," of that ability to transform reality and appear "to promise a wild delight that he has not found in life" (p. 171). No longer measuring her by the aesthetic ideal she created for him, he appreciates in her "the power of suggesting things much lovelier than herself, as the perfume of a single flower may call up the whole sweetness of spring" (p. 172). The change is significant, from Niel's viewing Marian Forrester solely as a passive object representing his aesthetic ideal, to recognizing in her the active, willed power of suggesting that ideal. Supporting this change, Cather provides glimpses of the human subject herself: the lines of exhaustion, the smell of spirits, the momentary lowering of the "lively manner" that she kept "between her and all the world" (p. 68). But as with *My Ántonia,* at the end Cather returns to a male world with a sense of loss, having only suggested the woman herself beneath the overwhelming male perspective of the account.

My Ántonia and *A Lost Lady* present major cultural myths about women: *My Ántonia* the woman as archetypal mother and muse, *A Lost Lady* the woman as teacher, bearer of culture. In both, Cather uses male narrators who view women in terms of their own spiritual growth, and in each she gives her female character the strength to break through conventional roles imposed upon them. But convention offers to the woman herself a different route to transcendence from that offered to men, that of romantic love. In *My Mortal Enemy,* Cather focuses squarely on women's perspectives of the romantic love convention. In using Nellie Birdseye to write about Myra Driscoll Henshawe, Cather suggests a sequential relationship between narrator and character: the female narrator in writing about a female subject explores a possible future self; the female subject in speaking to the narrator speaks as if to a younger self. The overall effect is to extend Cather's concern with cultural patterns that restrict individuals from permanent values, for in *My Mortal Enemy,* Cather goes beyond her previous contrast between convention and reality to present the ways in which these patterns are passed from one generation to another.

In *My Mortal Enemy,* the adult narrator, Nellie Birdseye, recalls her life-long knowledge of Myra Driscoll Henshawe; in so doing, she presents tension between the romantic and the human perspective. The romantic, offered by Nellie's Aunt Lydia, Myra's husband Oswald, and by the young girl Nellie once was, dominates the first of the novel. By this perspective, Myra Driscoll is the "brilliant and attractive figure"[18] of family legend who lives on in love stories taught to generation after generation of young girls. Cather suggests the ritualistic transmission of myth when Nellie recalls that her Aunt Lydia "used to take me for a walk . . . around the old Driscoll grounds" and "would tell me again about that thrilling night" (pp. 15-16). The story itself is strikingly conventional: young lovers, denied permission to marry as a result of "a grudge of some sort" between their elders, defy worldly restrictions and elope, though their marriage results in disinheritance. This is the stuff on which girls dream and which, finally, shapes their imaginations.

As Nellie grew older, she not only incorporated the romantic perspective passed to her but elaborated on it, ignoring a Myra and an Oswald she had never known and turning instead to sweeping myths and personifications: "When I was older I used to walk around the Driscoll place alone very often. . . . I thought of the place as being under a spell, like the Sleeping Beauty's palace; it had been in a trance, or lain in its flowers like a beautiful corpse, ever since that winter night when Love went out of the gates and gave the dare to Fate" (p. 17). Nellie's reminiscence distills the timelessness of the romantic love convention, which promises escape from human dimensions of change and decay. But consequently, this same convention requires either that lovers die or that they live happily ever after. Myra Driscoll and Oswald Henshawe, however, live on and are, as it turns out, only "'as happy as most people,'" a conclusion that Nellie finds "disheartening" for "the very point of their story was that they should be much happier than other people" (p. 17).

Nellie's reaction here anticipates the second perspective of the novel, offered by Myra Henshawe herself. Clearly, the forty-five-year-old woman is unlike the romantic heroine immortalized in family legend. When Nellie first meets "the real Myra Henshawe, twenty-five years older than I had always imagined her," she feels disappointed and is tempted to prefer the illusions to the reality. She wonders whether it wasn't "better to get out of the world . . . than to linger on in it . . . getting a double chin" (p. 19). But Nellie, like Cather's other narrators, goes through stages in her view of the woman she writes about.[19] Youthful idealization ends in disillusionment when Nellie glimpses the anger and malice that, along with love and affections, exist in the Henshawe's marriage. And this disillusionment gradually gives way to mature understanding and appreciation. When, after a long separation, she finds Myra, now in ill-health and living with Oswald in

severely reduced circumstances, Nellie is no longer disappointed in the human reality but instead "delighted" that "she was herself, Myra Henshawe!" (p. 62). For what Nellie recognizes in Myra Henshawe is the magnificent complexity of a mature woman who "sat crippled but powerful in her brilliant wrappings. She looked strong and broken, generous and tyrannical, a witty and rather wicked old woman, who hated life for its defeats, and loved it for its absurdities" (p. 65).

The stages of youthful idealization, disillusionment, and mature understanding are familiar: Cather used them for Jim Burden and Niel Herbert. But the rendition of these stages is quite different from that of previous novels. Far more than the women Cather's male narrators wrote about—Ántonia Cuzak and Marian Forrester—Myra Henshawe actively guides Nellie's growth and directly questions the romantic convention by which Nellie perceives her. Initially, Myra warns Nellie in general terms of the "bad luck" that love draws on a woman and of the hell that is likely to follow youthful romantic commitments (pp. 28-31). In her dying days, however, Myra's warnings become painfully personal as she rejects Oswald's sentimental version of their lives and reveals the hell they created for one another. Their lives were not always like "'those days when [they] were young and loved each other,'" and human existence is not so simple as the romantic convention pretends: "'People can be lovers and enemies at the same time, you know. We were. . . . A man and woman draw apart from that long embrace, and see what they have done to each other'" (p. 88).

Through Oswald and Nellie, Cather presents sharply contrasted responses to her central character's attempt to break through the myth that had shaped her. Oswald, faced with the same painful honesty that Myra offers to Nellie, chooses not the woman but instead a romantic figure from the past. Viewing his aging wife as "'the mother of the girl who ran away with me,'" Oswald declares "'nothing ever took that girl from me,'" then charges Nellie, too, to sacrifice the woman to the myth by remembering a young Myra, "'when she was herself, and we were happy'" (pp. 103-04). The "'wild, lovely creature'" Oswald recalls seems curiously detached from reality, presented only through Lydia's stories and Oswald's reminiscences. Clearly, this "creature" is unlike the woman Nellie has come to admire. The change in Nellie is significant: no longer the moon-struck girl who perceived in terms of convention, Nellie has become a woman capable of understanding and respecting the woman Myra Driscoll Henshawe and, in turn, capable of guiding the reader to a similarly enlarged understanding. For Cather has pitted Myra Driscoll Henshawe against her narrator's and her reader's expectations of a female character and, by her character's complex richness, has exposed those expectations as stagnant and self limiting.

In "Old Mrs. Harris," Cather comes full circle in her concern with what it is to be a woman, presenting female characters who neither follow a traditionally male route toward transcendence nor struggle for individuality against male expectations. Instead, Cather presents the most traditional pattern of women's lives within their family and community. On one level, such lives are conventionally limited. The story concerns events during one summer in the daily lives of the Templeton family: a neighbor brings a slice of cake for Mrs. Harris; a family cat dies; fifteen-year-old Vickie wins a college scholarship; her mother, Victoria Templeton, learns she is pregnant; the family attends a church supper; and old Mrs. Harris dies.

But on a second level, Cather reveals that apparently individual events affect the entire family and apparent restricted spheres yield universal values. Cather uses omniscient narration to extend the story beyond the daily lives of its characters to patterns of women's lifetimes. Point of view is almost entirely female, as Cather presents the thoughts of Mrs. Rosen, the Templeton's learned and childless neighbor who is drawn to "a pleasantness in the human relationships"[20] she feels in the Templeton's house, and three generations of women: Vickie, self-absorbed by her own youth and inexperience; her mother, Victoria, self-absorbed by knowledge of yet another pregnancy announcing yet another child to care for in an already crowded house; and Mrs. Harris, Victoria's mother, who lives with her daughter's family and works to keep "the light-heartedness . . . going" in those about her (p. 112). As their names suggest, Vickie will become as Victoria, and both, "when they are old . . . will come closer to Grandma Harris" (p. 190).

Significantly, Cather describes this larger pattern in terms reminiscent of her earliest treatments of women. As Alexandra Bergson and Thea Kronborg were before her, Mrs. Harris is "perfectly happy" in "the realest and truest things" (p. 184). But unlike the earlier characters, who reached a loss of self through the land and art, Mrs. Harris does so through family relationships. When "she heard the children running down the uncarpeted back stairs . . . she ceased to be an individual, an old woman with aching feet; she became part of a group, became a relationship" (pp. 136-37).

In this late work, as elsewhere, Cather presents a character reaching toward permanent values, for "that is happiness; to be dissolved into something complete and great."[21] And this, Cather's concern for permanent values, is the constant that runs throughout her career. Treating this constant, Cather devotes works long recognized as among her most powerful to gradually narrowing the question of what it is to be a woman. She places her female characters within increasingly complex and restrictive contexts. In setting, Cather turns from the natural expanses of Alexandra's frontier to the ever-narrowing circumstances of Marian Forrester, Myra Henshawe, and Mrs. Harris; in convention, Cather turns from women as mythic goddess and earth mother to the more specifically cultural myths of woman as aesthetic ideal and romantic heroine and, finally, to women who live apparently ordinary lives as daughter, mother, and grandmother. But at the same time that she creates increasingly restrictive contexts, Cather gives to her characters increasingly personal and specific strength to defy apparent restrictions placed upon them. She moves from the otherworldly, mythic power of Alexandra to the personal strength of exceptional women to defy convention (Ántonia, Marian Forrester, and Myra Driscoll Henshawe) to, in "Old Mrs. Harris," conventional women living conventional women's lives who, by the fullness of these personal lives, become exceptional.

Notes

1. See, for example, Edward A. Bloom and Lillian D. Bloom, *Willa Cather's Gift of Sympathy* (Carbondale: Southern Illinois Univ. Press, 1962), pp. 13-14, *et. passim.* A version of this paper was presented at the 1979 convention of the Modern Language Association. I am most grateful to Professor Bernice Slote, Univ. of Nebraska-Lincoln, for suggestions during the various stages of this study and to Professor Patrick Morrow, Auburn Univ., for suggestions on the manuscript.

2. "My First Novels [There Were Two]," in *Willa Cather on Writing* (New York: Alfred A. Knopf, 1949), p. 92. Cather uses the phrase "for myself" three times in the six pages of the essay.

3. See, for example, David Daiches, *Willa Cather: A Critical Introduction* (1951; rpt. Westport: Greenwood Press, 1971), p. 28; J. Russell Reaver, "Mythic Motivation in Willa Cather's *O Pioneers!*" *WF,* 27 (1968), 19-25; and David Stouck, *Willa Cather's Imagination* (Lincoln: Univ. of Nebraska Press, 1975), pp. 23-32.

4. Simone de Beauvoir, *The Second Sex,* trans. and ed. H. M. Parshley (1953; Modern Library Edition, New York: Random House, 1968), p. 430.

5. (1913; rpt. Sentry Edition, Boston: Houghton Mifflin Company, 1941), p. 6. Subsequent references to *O Pioneers!* will be to this edition.

6. Other examples of active receptivity, frequently expressed in sexual imagery, occur throughout the novel. Alexandra at times felt "close to the flat, fallow world about her, and felt, as it were, in her own body the joyous germination in the soil" (pp. 203-04), and, similarly, Marie's great talent for "living" is a talent for responding actively, for feeling "as the pond must feel when it held the moon like that; when it encircled and swelled with that image of gold" (p. 250).

7. Maynard Fox, "Symbolic Representation in Willa Cather's *O Pioneers!*," *WAL*, 9 (1974), 196.

8. J. Russell Reaver, "Mythic Motivation in Willa Cather's *O Pioneers!*," *WF*, 27 (1968), 24.

9. Bernice Slote, "Willa Cather: The Secret Web," from *Five Essays on Willa Cather: The Merrimack Symposium*, ed. John J. Murphy (North Andover: Merrimack College, 1974), n.p.

10. Ellen Moers, *Literary Women* (1976; Garden City: Anchor, 1977), p. 350.

11. Elizabeth Shepley Sergeant, *Willa Cather: A Memoir* (1953; reissued with a new foreword and an index as a Bison Book, Lincoln: Univ. of Nebraska Press, 1963), p. 104.

12. (1918; Sentry edition, Boston: Houghton Mifflin, 1961), p. 321. Subsequent references to *My Ántonia* will be to this edition.

13. Beauvoir, *The Second Sex*, pp. 248-49.

14. Significantly, Jim, seeing Ántonia as "'a natural-born mother'" (p. 318), does not admit her sexuality: sexuality involves physicality rather than spirituality, activity rather than passivity, change rather than timelessness. Accordingly, Jim separates sexuality from Ántonia and dreams only of Lena Lingard as a seductress. See Blanche H. Gelfant's discussion, "The Forgotten Reaping-Hook: Sex in *My Ántonia*," *AL*, 43 (1971), 60-82.

15. John J. Murphy, "Willa Cather: The Widening Gyre," in *Five Essays on Willa Cather: The Merrimack Symposium*," n.p.

16. (1923; New York: Alfred A. Knopf, 1963), p. 121. Subsequent references to *A Lost Lady* will be to this edition.

17. For a detailed discussion of these stages, see my essay, "Willa Cather's *A Lost Lady*: The Paradoxes of Change," *Novel*, 11 (1977), 51-62. Other readers have similarly focused upon the discrepancy between Niel's description of Marian Forrester and the character herself: Eugenie Lambert Hamner, "Affirmations in Willa Cather's *A Lost Lady*," *MQ*, 17 (1976), 245-51; and Anneliese H. Smith, "Finding Marian Forrester: A Restorative Reading of Cather's *A Lost Lady*," *CLQ*, 14 (1978), 221-25.

18. (1926; New York: Vintage, 1961). Subsequent references to *My Mortal Enemy* will be to this edition.

19. For a more detailed discussion of these stages, see my essays, "Narrative Technique in Cather's *My Mortal Enemy*," *JNT*, 8 (1978), 141-49; and "The Novel of Awakening," *Genre*, 12 (1979), 313-32.

20. In *Obscure Destinies* (1932; New York: Vintage, 1974), p. 111. Subsequent references to "Old Mrs. Harris" will be to this edition.

21. *My Ántonia*, p. 18.

JOAN ACOCELLA (ESSAY DATE 2000)

SOURCE: Acocella, Joan. "Cather and the Feminists: The Problem." In *Willa Cather and the Politics of Criticism*, pp. 37-43. Lincoln: University of Nebraska Press, 2000.

In the following essay, Acocella discusses the difficulty that Cather's apparent ambivalence about women causes for feminist critics attempting to analyze her work.

An important job for feminist literary critics in the 1970s and 1980s was to assemble a "female canon," a list of first-rate woman-authored books that would demonstrate that women were the equal of men as writers and therefore that their underrepresentation in the approved catalog of great literature—and in allied enterprises, such as publishing and the universities—was the result of politics, not biology. Cather was of course necessary to such a list. But the feminists didn't just need first-rate writers; they needed them to be feminists. Gertrude Stein's declaring the women's movement a bore, George Eliot's writing an essay called "Silly Novels by Lady Novelists"—these things were an embarrassment.[1] Cather's early prairie novels were everything a feminist could have asked for. In *O Pioneers!* Alexandra not only raises up a farm out of the barren plain; she is the head of her household. As for *The Song of the Lark,* it is even better, for it is about a woman becoming an artist.

But as we saw, something changed in Cather after *The Song of the Lark.* Life came to seem to her less a matter of victory than of sorrow and memory and art. And those became the subject of her next novel, *My Ántonia.* In a move that has given more pain to her feminist critics than almost anything else she ever did, she placed a male narrator, Jim Burden, between the reader and Ántonia: men silencing women all over again. Furthermore, *My Ántonia* is really Jim's book. Ántonia drops out of it for a long stretch, and as the title indicates, the subject is not really her, it is Jim's vision of her, and the meditations on memory and art to which that vision prompts him. Finally, Ántonia is not victorious. She has a hard life: poverty, toil, an illegitimate child. Eventually she marries a good man, Anton Cuzak, and we find her at the end of the book in her kitchen, doing the dishes, with her sons and daughters gathered around her. But this is not what most feminists would call a victory. As a culminating insult, the last section of the book is entitled "Cuzak's Boys," not "Ántonia's Children."

That was just the beginning. In Cather's next novel, **One of Ours,** the *main character* was a male, and one who went to war, and liked it. And so on it went, for the rest of Cather's career. Sometimes her protagonists were women, sometimes men, and sometimes they did good, and sometimes evil, but not along sex lines. She seems no longer to have viewed the difference between male and female as crucial. Life was hard for everyone— "Even the wicked get worse than they deserve," as one of her characters says (**One of Ours,** 257)— and the suffering had simply to be borne or, if possible, transcended through memory and art. The principles of life were changeless, and so, consequently, were the themes of art. Hence Jim Burden's description of Ántonia as something out of Virgil or ancient myth, something "universal and true" (342). This, of course, is exactly what feminists did not want to hear. Universals, transcendence—those were the magic words by which women were taught to accept a fate that in fact was not universal, but assigned to only half of humanity, the female half. As for Ántonia, who stays home and stays poor while Jim goes to Harvard to study the Virgilian texts to which he will compare her, the feminists did not see her as the embodiment of a changeless principle. They saw her as an oppressed woman.

It wasn't just Cather's fiction that fell short. Her life did too, from childhood on. She was much closer to her father than to her mother— not good news to feminists who were now stressing the mother-daughter relationship. (Adrienne Rich: "The dutiful daughter of the fathers is only a hack."[2]) At her father's funeral Cather was inconsolable—grief-stricken, panicked. Her mother's funeral she did not attend (though she did help care for Jennie during her final illness). In the list of other adults who nurtured her, the men greatly outnumber the women. The town doctors, who took her on their rounds; Herr Schindelmeisser, the piano teacher, who talked to her about music and Europe; William Ducker, who taught her Greek; the professor who published her Carlyle essay and made her see that she was a writer: men, men.

Then there is the matter of the "William Cather period." Innocent readers might imagine that this is something feminists would sympathize with. It is not. "Male-identified" is a bad word in feminist circles. As one disgruntled feminist, Jean Elshtain, put it recently, "One is either part of the group of those who have found their authentic voices as women or one is a 'male-identified' dupe of the patriarchy."[3] Remember Cather's page in her friend's album. The trait she most admired in men was an original mind; in women, flirting. As long as she was free to develop an original mind, it was okay by her if women had to go on flirting. Indeed, she liked it, just as a man would. Nor did Cather's male identification really end when she grew her hair out again. A journalist who interviewed her in 1924 said that she seemed less like a writer than like the head of "a great law practice or a successful dairy farm."[4] For the times, she was a mannish woman.

She had no high opinion of women, at least as writers. "Sometimes I wonder why God ever trusts [literary] talent in the hands of women, they usually make such an infernal mess of it," she wrote in 1895. "I think He must do it as a sort of ghastly joke" (**The Kingdom of Art,** 408). Female poets were so gushy—"emotional in the extreme, self-centered, self-absorbed" (**The World and the Parish,** 146). As for female novelists, all they could write about was love: "They have a sort of sex consciousness that is abominable" (**The World and the Parish,** 276). She went on to attack various women's novels on this score—for example, Kate Chopin's *The Awakening* (1899), a book sacred to feminists. How could Chopin have devoted her gifts to "so trite and sordid a theme" as adultery (**The World and the Parish,** 697)? And when women writers were not splashing about in their emotions, they were doing other inartistic things, like running after causes. "The feminine mind has a hankering for hobbies and missions": Just look at *Uncle Tom's Cabin,* she said (**The Kingdom of Art,** 406). All in all, women seemed to Cather to *use* art rather than to make it. "Has any woman every really had the art instinct, the art necessity? Is it not with them a substitute, a transferred enthusiasm, an escape valve for what has sought or is seeking another channel?" (**The Kingdom of Art,** 158). This is basically the same complaint that Virginia Woolf later made in *A Room of One's Own,* that women used writing as "self-expression" rather than as art. But Cather made it with uncommon ferocity: "If I see the announcement of a new book by a woman, I—well, I take one by a man instead. . . . I prefer to take no chances when I read" (**The World and the Parish,** 362).

Finally, in a time when feminist critics were trying to show that women inherited their literary tradition not from men but from women—literary "foremothers," often excluded from the established canon—it was not a pleasure to see Cather so clearly take her inspiration from male writers. Apart from Virgil, the Bible, and *Pilgrim's Progress,* the books that left the strongest imprint on her were those of Tolstoy, Flaubert, and Henry James. One woman writer was crucial to her: Sarah Orne Jewett. Jewett, she says, told her to use her "home" material, distilled over a long period, and to "write it as it is, don't try to make it like this or that"—in other words, don't imitate Henry James. Jewett not only gave Cather these rules; with her "local-colorist" tales of her native Maine, she exemplified them. But as Cather's early writings suggest, she already knew before meeting Jewett that she had to turn back to Nebraska. She just needed somebody to push her, and that's what Jewett did. Jewett was more a mentor than a model to Cather.[5]

So Cather, having once looked as though she might advance the cause of feminism, turned out to be a disaster. A number of feminists bit the bullet and condemned her as such. According to Carolyn Heilbrun, in her 1979 book *Reinventing Womanhood,* Cather was one of many female writers who "have been unable to imagine for other women . . . the self they have in fact achieved." In *The Song of the Lark,* Heilbrun claimed, Cather created her "last major woman character with a 'self.'" In her subsequent novels she simply demonstrated the "female urge toward the destruction and denial of female destiny." Another writer, Frances Kaye, published a whole book arguing that Cather's writings were politically dangerous. Because Cather distanced herself from the cause of women in general, awarding victories only to a few, male-identified women, her work discouraged collective action and thus could involve "psychic and social costs" for the unwary reader.[6]

Other feminist critics, however, were sorry to lose Cather from their team, and wondered if something might be done. What if the wrongful attitudes that she expressed were not hers at all, but the attitudes of *men,* the men in her novels? Godfrey St. Peter's disdain for the materialism of his wife and daughters in *The Professor's House;* Jim Burden's intrusion into Ántonia's story and his acquiescence in her hard fate—what if these were acts of irony on Cather's part, her way of criticizing St. Peter and Jim?

Thus was born what can be called the unreliable-narrator school of Cather criticism. A good example is Jean Schwind, who has devoted a number of essays to defending Cather from the charge that she held incorrect views. *The Professor's House,* Schwind argues in a 1993 article, is not a story about the professor's despair, it is a critique of the patriarchy. The professor is an "ungenerous and dishonest" man, basically a sexist pig, who cares only about his work and who,

under the cover of his hypocritical antimaterialism, abuses the excellent women around him. By exposing these facts, Cather is exploring "frame-ups of women in literature." The same goes for *My Ántonia,* Schwind asserts in a 1985 article. Jim Burden is an utterly unreliable narrator— genteel, sexist, indeed racist and imperialist. Furthermore, he reads too much. The Homeric epithets and pastoral conventions that he uses in his narrative show that he imposes on reality a "faulty literary vision," a romantic vision. He is "devoted to ideal 'forms'" that have nothing to do with prairie realities, including Ántonia. Ántonia belongs to the free, true-grit New World, Jim to the hidebound, patriarchal Old World, and Cather subtly celebrates the former and disparages the latter.[7]

This interpretation of *My Ántonia* has since been enlarged upon by others. Elizabeth Ammons, in her 1992 book *Conflicting Stories,* congratulates Cather on her "subtle exposure" of Jim's attempt to "take over and rewrite a strong, threatening woman's story in terms that suit his own image of her." Annette Bennington McElhiney, in a 1993 essay, says that by having Ántonia remain silent and letting Jim's "supposed" narrative drone on and on, Cather "re-creates in her novel circumstances similar to what happened historically in America"—the silencing of women by men.[8] So yes, Cather's fiction contains patriarchal attitudes, but only because she is decrying them. People just didn't notice before.

A number of feminists were apparently uncomfortable with such readings, however. And well they might have been, for the traits that supposedly disqualified Cather's male narrators and protagonists as reliable witnesses were her traits as well. Romantic, elegiac, attached to ideal forms, besotted with Virgil, deeply read in classical literature and given to alluding to it—Cather was all these things, and she believed in them, as her other writings show.[9] Furthermore, if her contemporaries misread her, failing to notice her sustained attack on the patriarchy, why had she never corrected them?

Clearly a subtler reading was needed, something that would both acknowledge Cather's endorsement of unfeminist values and yet show her in conflict with those values. According to some feminists, conflict was endemic to women writers anyway, for they were torn between the need to tell their own, female story and the wish to write something acceptable to the male literary establishment. Consequently, in the words of Elaine Showalter, women's fiction was "a double-voiced discourse, containing a 'dominant' and a 'muted' story," which oscillated back and forth before our eyes.[10] But Cather's prose didn't look oscillatory. Plain and pure, it rose like a cliff wall in the face of the conflict seekers, denying them access, insisting that it really did mean what it said. Something was needed, some stick of dynamite, to blow Cather's world open. As the feminists soon realized, the thing they needed was already there. In a 1975 book called *Lesbian Images,* Jane Rule, a Canadian novelist and critic, had matter-of-factly declared that Cather was homosexual.

Notes

1. Stein's indifference to the women's movement is discussed by Sandra M. Gilbert and Susan Gubar in *No Man's Land,* 2: 242.

2. Rich, *On Lies, Secrets, and Silence,* quoted in Showalter, *The New Feminist Criticism,* 7.

3. Elshtain, in "Race and Racism," 6.

4. Rascoe, "First Meeting with Willa Cather," 63.

5. Cather quoting Jewett in F. H., "Willa Cather Talks of Work," 11. Of the writings which suggest that Cather knew before meeting Jewett the things she later claimed Jewett taught her, the most notable is her 1900 essay "When I Knew Stephen Crane." There she says that Crane told her, "'The detail of a thing has to filter through my blood, and then it comes out like a native product, but it takes forever'" (*The World and the Parish,* 776-777). James Woodress points out (*Willa Cather,* 99) that this describes the slowstarting Willa Cather far better than the precocious Stephen Crane, who produced enough to fill twelve volumes before dying at age twenty-nine. As for her evaluation of Jewett as a writer, Cather, in her preface to the 1925 Mayflower edition of *The Best Short Stories of Sarah Orne Jewett,* compared Jewett's *The Country of the Pointed Firs* to *Huckleberry Finn* and *The Scarlet Letter,* but this exalted compliment was probably an act of loyalty more than of sincerity. (Jewett was much neglected at the time.) When Cather revised and reprinted that essay in 1936, she shrank her praise, saying only that Jewett, like Twain and Hawthorne, possessed that "very personal quality of perception, a vivid and intensely personal experience of life, which make a 'style'" (*Not Under Forty,* 95). But already in 1924, a year before the publication of the Mayflower collection, Cather told an interviewer that Jewett "was a very uneven writer. A good portion of her work is not worth preserving. The rest, a small balance—enough to make two volumes—is important" (quoted in Rascoe, "Willa Cather," 66).

6. Heilbrun, *Reinventing Womanhood,* 79, 81. Kaye, *Isolation and Masquerade,* 187. In their condemnation of Cather on feminist grounds, these writers were preceded by Josephine Lurie Jessup, who in her 1965 book *The Faith of Our Feminists* judged Cather's greatness to be confined to the prairie novels, which "sing of triumph and a woman" (56). "Where no woman dominates the action," Jessup continues, "a novel by Willa Cather tends to fall into the hopelessness of *One of Ours* or of *The Professor's House;* or to become less a

record of human conflict than a series of insubstantial reveries, such as *Death Comes for the Archbishop*" (75). Gilbert and Gubar, in *No Man's Land,* agree that Cather's work is fatally weakened after *The Song of the Lark.* In their view, the falling off is due to Cather's "fatal attraction to a renunciation of passion" (2:205), which, however, is attributable in turn to her gender conflicts and her suppression of lesbian desire.

7. Schwind, "This Is a Frame-Up," 82, 88; Schwind, "The Benda Illustrations to *My Ántonia,*" 59, 61.

8. Ammons, *Conflicting Stories,* 135. McElhiney, "Willa Cather's Use of a Tripartite Narrative Point of View in *My Ántonia,*" 75.

9. Cather was one of the most allusive novelists in Western literature. Tracking down her literary sources was a great part of the task of John March's 846-page *Reader's Companion to the Fiction of Willa Cather* (1993) and of the University of Nebraska Press's scholarly editions of *O Pioneers!* (1992), *My Ántonia* (1994), *A Lost Lady* (1997), *Obscure Destinies* (1998), and *Death Comes for the Archbishop* (1999). The project of decoding Cather's allusions continues today. See, for example, Marilyn Arnold's 1996 essay "The Allusive Cather."

10. Showalter, *The New Feminist Criticism,* 266.

TITLE COMMENTARY

O Pioneers!

C. SUSAN WIESENTHAL (ESSAY DATE JANUARY 1990)

SOURCE: Wiesenthal, C. Susan. "Female Sexuality in Willa Cather's *O Pioneers!* and the Era of Scientific Sexology: A Dialogue between Frontiers." *Ariel* 21, no. 1 (January 1990): 41-63.

In the following essay, Wiesenthal examines parallels between Cather's treatment of female sexuality in O Pioneers! *and late nineteenth- and early twentieth-century scientific preoccupations with "deviant" female sexuality.*

Perhaps the most critical issue which immediately confronts any discussion of Willa Cather's fictional portrayal of sexuality is the nature of the relationship between the author's life and her work, between biography and art. For it is primarily on biographical bases such as Cather's adolescent rejection of femininity—her masquerade as the short-haired, boyishly-dressed 'William Cather Jr.'—and her adult relationships with women such as Louise Pound, Isabelle McClung, and Edith Lewis, that an increasing number of critics have been led to consider her as a 'lesbian writer.' Although no evidence exists to indicate that any of Cather's relationships with women involved an erotic dimension, many scholars agree that, at the very least, her life may be

ABOUT THE AUTHOR

KATHERINE ANNE PORTER ON CATHER'S CHILDHOOD

I have not much interest in anyone's personal history after the tenth year, not even my own. Whatever one was going to be was all prepared for before that. The rest is merely confirmation, extension, development. Childhood is the fiery furnace in which we are melted down to essentials and that essential shaped for good. While I have been reading again Willa Cather's essays and occasional papers, and thinking about her, I remembered a sentence from the diaries of Anne Frank, who died in the concentration camp in Bergen-Belsen just before she was sixteen years old. At less than fifteen, she wrote: "I have had a lot of sorrow, but who hasn't, at my age?"

In Miss Cather's superb little essay on Katherine Mansfield, she speaks of childhood and family life: "I doubt whether any contemporary writer has made one feel more keenly the many kinds of personal relations which exist in an everyday 'happy family' who are merely going on with their daily lives, with no crises or shocks or bewildering complications. . . . Yet every individual in that household (even the children) is clinging passionately to his individual soul, is in terror of losing it in the general family flavor . . . the mere struggle to have anything of one's own, to be oneself at all, creates an element of strain which keeps everybody almost at breaking point.

". . . Even in harmonious families there is this double life . . . the one we can observe in our neighbor's household, and, underneath, another—secret and passionate and intense—which is the real life that stamps the faces and gives character to the voices of our friends. Always in his mind each member is escaping, running away, trying to break the net which circumstances and his own affections have woven about him. One realizes that human relationships are the tragic necessity of human life; that they can never be wholly satisfactory, that every ego is half the time greedily seeking them, and half the time pulling away from them."

This is masterly and water-clear and autobiography enough for me: my mind goes with tenderness to the lonely slow-moving girl who happened to be an artist coming back from reading Latin and Greek with the old storekeeper, helping with the housework, then sitting by the fireplace to talk down an assertive brood of brothers and sisters, practicing her art on them, refusing to be lost among them—the longest-winged one who would fly free at last.

Porter, Katherine Anne. "Reflections on Willa Cather." In *The Collected Essays and Occasional Writings of Katherine Anne Porter*, pp. 29-39. New York: Delacorte Press, 1970.

regarded as 'lesbian' in the sense of Adrienne Rich's extensive definition of the term. Briefly, Rich conceives of a broad "lesbian continuum" which "includes a range . . . of woman-identified experience," embracing any extra-sexual or emotional form of "primary intensity between women," and "not simply the fact that a woman has had or [has] consciously desired genital experience with another woman" (648).

Almost invariably, however, when critics turn to Cather's novels, it is precisely the absence of any 'lesbian' sensibility which they emphasize. Thus, Jane Rule, the first writer to situate Cather specifically within a lesbian literary tradition along with Radclyffe Hall, Gertrude Stein, and others, sharply reproves readers who attempt to find a homoerotic sensibility in Cather's art, claiming that if the author's private "sexual tastes" manifest themselves in the fiction at all, it is only in her "capacity to transcend the conventions of what is masculine and feminine" (87, 80). More recently, Phyllis Robinson has flatly asserted that "the loving relationships with women that were so important in [Cather's] personal life are no where reflected in her fiction" (158). In *Willa Cather: The Emerging Voice*, Sharon O'Brien concurs, stating that "[c]ertainly the most prominent absence and the most unspoken love in her work are the emotional bonds between women that were central to her life" (127). O'Brien does not insist on wholly divorcing author and text, however, and argues instead that Cather's fiction works to both disclose and conceal a lesbian psyche. Nevertheless, in "'The Thing Not Named': Willa Cather as a Lesbian Writer," she concentrates on the latter aspect of her thesis—on those "literary strategies" whereby Cather is able to "disguise" or "camouflage" the "emotional source of her fiction." For O'Brien, Cather's 'lesbian' sensibility represents "the unwritten text" of the novels ("The Thing Not Named" 577, 593-94, 577).

The object of this essay is not to determine whether the authorial sensibility manifest in Cather's fiction is or is not a specifically 'lesbian' one. Rather, it is to reverse the prevailing critical preoccupation with the "absent" and "unwritten," and to explore the possible ways in which an authorial attitude towards a broader concept of 'deviant' female sexuality, in general, does disclose itself in the written text. In the written text of *O Pioneers!,* in particular, this authorial attitude may be perceived to inhere implicitly in the hermaphroditic, heterosexual, and same-sex relationships Cather does portray. In this novel, for example, the heroine, Alexandra Bergson, is depicted as a character who embodies a seemingly hermaphroditic sexual nature which is viewed positively, as a potentially self-fulfilling value, while the more unambiguously heterosexual natures of other characters, on the contrary, are seen to result exclusively in unhappy and debilitating 'love' relationships. This dichotomous portrayal seems to suggest an authorial sensibility, which, while it is not specifically sympathetic to a homosexual nature, is certainly sensitive to the potential gratification which unconventional forms of sexuality may yield.

In order to grasp the full significance of Cather's portrayal of sexuality in *O Pioneers!* it is necessary to consider not only the dialectic between life and art, but the dynamic relationship between text and context as well. For as the "golden age of scientific determinism, Social Darwinism, and eugenics" (Smith-Rosenberg 267), Cather's contemporary milieu represented, in fact, a stridently heterosexual era especially obsessed with what it perceived as the 'unnatural' or 'inverted' (that is, lesbian) nature of virtually all manifestations of female sexuality or eroticism beyond heterosexual marriage (Smith-Rosenberg 53-76, 245-96; Faderman 147-277). The extent to which *O Pioneers!* courageously challenges dominant medical and cultural assumptions about female sexuality can be gauged only when the text

is considered in a dialogic relation to this larger historic discourse. For indeed, Cather's positive delineation of the sexually unorthodox Alexandra, and, conversely, her negative or critical depiction of conventional heterosexuality, actually work together to controvert systematically a number of contemporary tenets about the nature of the sexually 'inverted' woman. In this way, Cather's novel of pioneer life indirectly addresses the issues of the "New Scientific Discourse" (Smith-Rosenberg 265) being promulgated by such influential and widely popularized theorists as Richard von Krafft-Ebing and Havelock Ellis. And in so far as these late nineteenth- and early twentieth-century 'sexologists' also self-consciously beheld themselves as "pioneers" in a hitherto unexplored psychosexual "borderland" (Ellis 2:219), the subtle interplay between text and context may be regarded as a form of dialogue between two disparate sorts of frontiers.[1]

Ultimately, however, the crucial limits of the challenge implicit in Cather's treatment of sexuality in *O Pioneers!* must be also firmly acknowledged. For although she repeatedly re-inverts, as it were, contemporary convictions about the perversity of female 'inversion,' her novel also reflects an element of self-conscious restraint which expresses itself most clearly in her highly circumspect handling of close female friendship—an integral thematic and structural component of the novel, which is deftly and gingerly developed by Cather, only to be rather abruptly abandoned when she is brought to deploy a somewhat disappointing, conventional romance closure, an ending both marked and marred, as one critic suggests, by the purely "token marriage" of the heroine (Bailey 396).[2] Whether this novelistic outcome may be ultimately ascribed, as critics such as Sharon O'Brien would contend, to "the lesbian writer's need to conceal the socially unacceptable" ("The Thing Not Named" 592) must remain, perhaps, a moot point. A close reading of *O Pioneers!,* however, does, at least, appear to substantiate the more general claim that internalized cultural strictures governing the 'socially unacceptable' in the realm of sexuality do indeed exert a profound force upon Cather's artistic impulse, and, consequently, upon the shape of this novel as a whole.

Through a comprehensive examination of contemporary women's diaries and letters, as well as medical literature and fiction, feminist historians such as Lillian Faderman and Carroll Smith-Rosenberg have been able to trace the critical late nineteenth-century shifts in the theoretic conceptualization and social experience of female homosexuality throughout the Western world. Unlike male homosexuality, that is, which had long been perceived as a punishable offence against scriptural and secular order, lesbianism had not only been "generally ignored by the law" until this point, but did not even constitute a conceptual category of deviance until the 1880s and 1890s (Faderman, "The Morbidification of Love" 77, 75; Smith-Rosenberg 266). Indeed, in the earlier decades of the Victorian century, passionate homosocial bonds between women—physically uninhibited as well as emotionally intense relationships—were "casually accepted in American society" as forms of romantic love "both socially acceptable and fully compatible with heterosexual marriage" (Smith-Rosenberg 53, 50).[3] Such 'legitimate' romantic friendships between women, however, came to be stigmatized by medical authorities and educators as 'morbid' and 'unnatural' during the final decades of the century, because it was at this point that such alliances first became an economically feasible alternative to heterosexual marriage for a small, but growing, group of autonomous, college-educated New Women. "For the first time," as Lillian Faderman remarks, "love between women became threatening to the social structure," posing truly portentous consequences, not only for the institutional nucleus of the social fabric, the family, but—as eugenicists and imperialists alike pointed out—for the already "dangerously low" birth-rate of the American Republic as well (Faderman 238).[4]

As steadily increasing numbers of New Women, like Willa Cather herself, began to eschew marriage and motherhood for higher education and professional livelihoods, one form which the simultaneously escalating anti-feminist reaction took was in the widespread expression of fear and repugnance of an 'intermediate sex': an appalling type of "semi-woman" whose behaviour and physical appearance "violated normal gender categories" (Smith-Rosenberg 265, 271). To accommodate such freaks of nature, the leading European neurologist, Richard von Krafft-Ebing, promptly created in his *Psychopathia Sexualis* (1886) the new "medico-sexual category" of the "Mannish Lesbian": a nosological classification in which, as Smith-Rosenberg observes, "women's rejection of traditional gender roles and their demands for social and economic equality" were linked directly to "cross-dressing, sexual perversion, and borderline hermaphroditism" (272). More influential yet in Britain and America, however, were the theories of Havelock Ellis. It

was his 1901 work, *Sexual Inversion,* which most powerfully contributed to the "morbidification" of the formerly innocent "female world of love and intimacy," because in it, Ellis re-defined the close friendships of college-aged and adult New Women "as both actively sexual and as actively perverted" (Smith-Rosenberg 269, 275).[5] Thus, forms of affection between women which had long been regarded with equanimity or indifference suddenly came to be viewed with suspicion and alarm as subversive and abnormal affairs.

If the theories and beliefs of Krafft-Ebing, Ellis, and others were a matter of "common knowledge" by the turn-of-the-century, as Faderman contends (*Surpassing the Love of Men* 238), then by 1910-1920, the decade during which *O Pioneers!* was written, medical tropes of the "Mannish Lesbian" or the 'unsexed' woman had been so pervasively disseminated throughout the cultural imagination—via newspaper caricatures, anti-feminist tracts, and sensational as well as 'high' literature—that they had begun to have a substantial impact upon the marital and educational standards of young women, as statistical evidence of the period clearly shows (Smith-Rosenberg 281).

That Cather herself would have been fully conscious of the contemporary medico-cultural discourse of deviant female sexuality, then, seems almost inevitable on historical bases alone. More specifically, however, biographical details further support this assumption. Cather's work as an editor for *McClure's Magazine,* for example, led her to regularly read the columns of the rival *Ladies' Home Journal,* in which articles admonishing women "against forming exclusive romantic bonds with women" often appeared (O'Brien, *Willa Cather* 133). More importantly, despite the fact that Cather and Edith Lewis destroyed the vast majority of Cather's personal correspondence, some of the letters she wrote during her two-year obsession with Louise Pound—"the most serious romantic attachment of [her] college life"—have indeed survived. Unfortunately, testamentary restrictions prevent scholars and biographers with access to these letters from quoting them directly (Robinson 58).[6] According to Sharon O'Brien, however, Cather states in one of these epistles that "it is so unfair that female friendships should be unnatural," before she goes on to accede that, nevertheless, "they are." As O'Brien suggests, Cather's self-conscious, if grudging, awareness of the fact that female friendships are "unnatural," reflects the extent to which she internalized the sexual norms of her age, and recognized the nature of her intense attachment to Louise as a "special category not sanctioned by the dominant culture" (O'Brien, *Willa Cather* 131-32).[7]

If critics' descriptions of Cather's "turbulent" and "passionate" "love letters" (O'Brien, "The Thing Not Named" 583) are accurate, her college 'crush' on Louise Pound represents precisely the sort of "flame," "rave," or "spoon" relationship which so gravely concerned sexologists and educators of the period. Ellis, for instance, devotes a lengthy appendix in his book to documenting such unsavoury "School-Friendships of Girls," in which he cites the cautionary words of one "American correspondent": "Love of the same sex . . . though [it] is not generally known, is very common; it is not mere friendship; the love is strong, real, and passionate"—sometimes, indeed, as he has been informed, it is "insane, intense love."[8] Speculating on the explosive end of the Cather-Pound alliance, one biographer has even suggested that Pound's older brother may have intervened because he interpreted their relationship apprehensively in this current context:

> Perhaps he called the friendship unnatural and his sister's friend perverse. He may have even used the term 'lesbian' to describe her. We do not know. We do know, however, that losing Louise caused Willa the most intense suffering she had ever known.
>
> (Robinson 60-61)[9]

In any case, whether or not the widespread cultural anxieties of deviant female sexuality, fanned by the 'New Scientific Discourse' of the sexologists, actually affected Cather's personal life with such painful immediacy, it remains plausible to assume, at the very least, that a sharp awareness of such medico-cultural censures must have impinged uncomfortably upon her conscious mind at one time or another.

It is with such biographical and contextual background in mind that one may, perhaps, most fruitfully approach the question of sexuality in *O Pioneers!* For as Annette Kolodny has argued, whether one speaks of critics "reading" texts or writers "reading" the world, one "call[s] attention to interpretive strategies that are learned, historically determined, and thereby necessarily gender-inflected" (47). In this sense, Cather's fictional portrayal of sexuality represents a cultural construct shaped largely by the lived experiences of her gender. And because she experienced and observed, or 'read,' female sexuality in an age in which traditional sexual roles and distinctions were being rapidly erased and eroded, sparking feelings of confusion, fear, and guilt, it is relatively unsurprising that her fictional treatment of the

YOUTH
AND THE BRIGHT MEDUSA
BY
WILLA CATHER

"We must not look at Goblin men,
We must not buy their fruits;
Who knows upon what soil they fed
Their hungry, thirsty roots?"

Goblin Market

NEW YORK
ALFRED · A · KNOPF
MCMXX

Title page from *Youth and the Bright Medusa*, published in 1920.

subject should embody an element of the conflict which marked both her life and her times.

Set on a wild, windswept prairie frontier, *O Pioneers!* initially appears far removed indeed from Cather's controversial modern era. And yet the profound extent to which her novel is informed by the milieu in which it was produced is apparent even in the central character of Alexandra Bergson: a heroine who incorporates many definitive features of the New Woman upon whom the contemporary debate of the 'intermediate sex' centred. In so far as the New Woman of the age "constituted a revolutionary demographic and political phenomenon" (Smith-Rosenberg 245), of course, Alexandra eludes the historical paradigm: unlike Cather herself, she is neither part of a novel, homogeneous group of college-educated women, nor does she self-consciously resist traditional gender roles on intellectual or ideological grounds. Practical circumstances, as she angrily informs her brothers, have dictated the nature of her pioneering career: "Maybe I would never have been very soft, anyhow; but I certainly didn't choose to be the kind of girl I was" (Cather, *O Pioneers!* 171). On the other hand, there are also strong suggestions in the text that the intellectually gifted Alexandra would have made a fine student, and that had she in fact had a choice in the matter, she would not have remained on the outside of the State University's "long iron fence" curiously "looking through," and observing campus life from a distance (287).

At any rate, beyond these few fundamental differences, Cather's heroine embodies the majority of qualities typical of the late nineteenth-century New Woman: she is single, economically autonomous, and quite ready to assert her legal and social equality, defiantly maintaining her right to "do exactly as [she] please[s] with her land" (167). Moreover, with her innovative silos and pig-breeding schemes, Alexandra is the owner of "one of the richest farms on the Divide" (83), and as such, assumes the position of a community leader. In these respects, she corresponds closely to Smith-Rosenberg's description of the quintessential New Woman:

> Eschewing marriage, she fought for professional visibility, espoused innovative, often radical, economic and social reforms, and wielded real political power. At the same time, as a member of the affluent new bourgeoisie, most frequently a child of small-town America, she felt herself part of the grass roots of her country.
>
> (245)

It is also interesting to note that although Alexandra presents a new type of heroine in the tradition of American frontier fiction, she is by no means an anomaly in a historical context; indeed, by the late nineteenth century, many women had begun to take advantage of the Homestead Act to acquire property in the West—some of them single, adventurous New Women who "exploited their claims to earn money for other ventures" like college tuition (Myers 258-59). The conceptual distance between the modern era of the New Woman and that of Cather's farming pioneer, then, is not so great as it may first appear to be.

The affinities between the New Woman of Cather's period and the heroine of *O Pioneers!* extend to the portrayal of Alexandra as a representative of a type of 'intermediate sex': a vaguely intimidating sort of 'mannish' woman who appears to combine certain traditional aspects of masculinity and femininity in one. This trait is immediately apparent in Cather's initial description of Alexandra as "a tall, strong girl" who

walked rapidly and resolutely, as if she knew exactly where she was going and what she was going to do next. She wore a man's long ulster (not as if it were an affliction, but as if it were very comfortable and belonged to her; carried it like a young soldier), and a round plush cap, tied down with a veil. She had a serious, thoughtful face, and her clear, deep blue eyes were fixed intently on the distance.

(6)

Krafft-Ebing, who believed, as Smith-Rosenberg states, that "only the abnormal woman would challenge gender distinctions—and by her dress you would know her" (272)—would have likely recognized his 'Mannish Lesbian' here, on the basis of Alexandra's manly ulster alone. Ellis, too, would have detected an element of perversity in the "comfortable" confidence with which Alexandra "carries" her masculine garb, since he maintained that the "very pronounced tendency among sexually inverted women to adopt male attire when practicable" could be "chiefly" accounted for by the fact that "the wearer feels more at home in them" (245). Moreover, the heroine's rapid and resolute gait and the "Amazonian fierceness" with which she cows the "little drummer" who dares ogle her (8) also reflect the sort of "brusque, energetic movements" and "masculine straightforwardness and sense of honour . . . free from any suggestion of either shyness or audacity," which, according to a "keen observer" like Ellis, betrayed an "underlying psychic abnormality" (250). As a heroine of epic proportions, in fact, Alexandra corresponds strikingly to one sexologist's profile of the typical female 'invert,' whom he held to be

> more full of life, of enterprise, of practical energy, more aggressive, more heroic, more apt for adventure, than either the heterosexual woman or the homosexual man.
>
> (Magnus Hirschfeld, qtd. in Ellis 251)

Endowed with a greatness of stature which dwarfs the "little men" who surround her (181), as well as a "direct[ness]" of manner which often makes men "wince" (121), Alexandra is indeed the most enterprising, energetic, and heroic character in Cather's novel.

Importantly, however, this positive vision of the heroic 'manly woman' appears to constitute the exception rather than the rule in medical literature of the period. For while early nineteenth-century commentators could still gloat contemptuously that "Amazonian" types were "their own executioners" and presented no danger of "perpetuating their race," since they had "unsexed themselves in public estimation,"[10] most of the sexologists of Cather's era were much less confident—for by then it was clear that the ranks of the 'intermediate sex' were indeed continuing to swell. Such women were thus viewed collectively with a good deal of trepidation as the "ultimate symbol of social disorder" (Smith-Rosenberg 181).

This understandable though fallacious perception of the 'deviant' woman as an emblem of social disruption emerges as the first issue implicitly addressed and refuted by Cather in *O Pioneers!* For having once established her heroine as an 'Amazonian' or 'manly woman,' Cather proceeds to depict her not as a harbinger of chaos, but as precisely the opposite: as a pre-eminent symbol of order and a bedrock of stability. Under Alexandra's creative and loving will, for example, the natural world is gradually though steadily transformed from a hostile "wild land" to a productive and geometrically neat farm, noteworthy for its "most unusual trimness and care for detail" (83). Hence, there is an

> order and fine arrangement manifest all over [Alexandra's] great farm; in the fencing and hedging, in the windbreaks and sheds, [and] in the symmetrical pasture ponds.
>
> (84)

"Not unlike a tiny village" (83), Alexandra's farming homestead also represents a contained microcosm of fair but efficient social and domestic order. When she has no "visitors" and dines with "her men," for instance, Cather's heroine sits "at the head of the long table," and the place to her left is routinely reserved for old Ivar, her trusted advisor (85-86). With a democratic spirit, Alexandra "encourage[s] her men to talk" during these meals, to voice their opinions and concerns over the business affairs of the farm, but throughout the novel there is never a doubt that she retains an absolutely firm control over the hierarchical structure she has created. "As long as there is one house there must be one head," John Bergson declares before his death, and it is a maxim by which his "dotter" unswervingly abides (25-26).

Cather's affirmative portrayal of the 'manly woman' also works in a similar fashion to subvert or re-invert the prevailing medical and cultural conception of the sexually inverted woman as a physiologically 'morbid' or diseased, mutant being. For not only were such women of 'intermediate sex' judged to be 'unnatural' in the sense of being quirkily unconventional in dress and behaviour, but, as the "visible symptom[s] of a diseased society," they were also held to be innately sick—organically degenerative and neurotic as well as morally contaminating. Because contemporary authorities habitually transposed social and political evils into physiological terms, medical discourses of the sexually deviant woman abound in metaphors of morbidity and pathology (Smith-Rosenberg 245, 261-62). Krafft-Ebing, for example, believed that lesbianism was the sign of "an inherited diseased condition of the central nervous system," which he referred to as a form of "taint."[11] Similarly, Ellis, although ostensibly aware that "the study of the abnormal is perfectly distinct from the study of the morbid," still claimed that female sexual inversion was a type of "germ" fostered by the feminist movement (319, 262).[12]

The Amazonian Alexandra may assume manly attire, but she is not, as the narrator notes, in any sense "afflicted" by it; quite the contrary, in fact, she is depicted by Cather as the epitome of health and wholesomeness. Her body, so "tall and strong" that "no man on the Divide could have carried it very far," is also a "gleaming white body" (206), consistently associated with images of both vigour and purity. While Cather thus likens her heroine's sun-kissed face to "one of the big double sunflowers" in the garden, she also emphasizes the contrasting "smoothness and whiteness" of the delicate skin beneath her shirt collar and sleeves: it is skin which "none but Swedish women ever possess; skin with the freshness of the snow itself" (88). Just as Jim Burden, in *My Ántonia*, thinks "with pride that Ántonia, like Snow White in the fairy tale, is still the fairest of them all" (215), so in this novel does Carl Lindstrum remember admiringly how the fair Alexandra used to appear at dawn with her milking pails, "looking as if she had walked straight out" of the "milky light" "of the morning itself" (126). Even as an older, successfully established farming businesswoman, the pristine aura of the dairymaid still suffuses Alexandra, who blandly admits that people find her "clean and healthy-looking" appearance pleasant (132).

At once robust and delicate, fusing conventional attributes of male and female within herself, the heroine's healthy, hermaphroditic nature also facilitates a vital, erotically fulfilling relationship with the land—virtually the only salutary relationship offered by Cather in *O Pioneers!* Indeed, the Nebraskan prairie is charged with "the same tonic, puissant quality" characteristic of Alexandra herself (77). Like her tanned face and white body, "the brown earth" is yet so clean and pure that it rolls from the shear of the plow without "even dimming the brightness of the metal" (76). And like Alexandra, too, the land is presented as a hermaphroditic entity. Thus, it both "yield[s] itself eagerly" to her active and yearning "human will" (76, 65), and "stir[s]" beneath her like a giant leviathan, eliciting, in turn, a sensual responsiveness or 'yielding' in the heroine herself:

> Alexandra remembered . . . days when she was close to the flat, fallow world about her, and felt, as it were, in her own body the joyous germination in the soil.
>
> (204)

As a sexually animated presence within the text, however, the land may constitute not so much an autonomous entity in its own right as it does a specular reflection of the heroine's own hermaphroditic nature. For it is, in fact, Alexandra who sublimates her sexual energies into the land—who sets her face "toward it with love and yearning" (65)—and it is also her perception and sense of it that are invariably conveyed to the reader, who sees only the way the land "seem[s]" to her or the way she "remember[s]" it (65, 204).

What Cather actually appears to present, then, is a type of autoerotic, onanistic relationship of the heroine with a part of her hermaphroditic sexual self which has been displaced onto the "Other" of the land. In this respect, her portrayal of sexuality in **O Pioneers!** is comparable to that of Martha Ostenso's in the Canadian prairie novel *Wild Geese* (1925), in which the heroine, Judith, lies upon the "damp ground" nude and feels that "here was something forbiddenly beautiful;" something as "secret as one's own body" (67). Seemingly complete in herself, Cather's heroine may be perhaps best likened, though, to the "single wild duck" she so fondly recalls in her memory: the "solitary bird" which "take[s] its pleasure" quite alone, and which strikes Alexandra as more "beautiful" than any "living thing had ever seemed to [her]" (204-05). A subtle celebration of the hermaphroditic and perhaps even bisexual sensibility, the portrayal of Alexandra's fulfilling erotic life suggests that she may not be as lonely in her unmarried state as the narrator would sometimes have us believe.

By presenting her 'manly woman' as a fresh and vital human being whose hermaphroditic attributes constitute the source of positive erotic gratification, Cather's novel works to break down the contemporary myth of the diseased and degenerative woman of 'intermediate sex.' Significantly, however, her artistic response to the large, pseudo-scientific discourse of sexuality does not end at this point, for Cather also proceeds to challenge her culture's yet more fundamental assumption of the intrinsic desirability and 'normalcy' of

heterosexuality itself. In **O Pioneers!,** indeed, it is not the seemingly 'deviant' but the socially acceptable heterosexual impulse which is portrayed as 'morbid' and unhealthy. Thus, when Alexandra does indulge in one of her rare heterosexual fantasies, she is apt to experience it as a form of profoundly sordid "reverie": literally, an unclean impulse which she immediately attempts to wash away, via a penitential ritual of Spartan ablution, with "buckets of cold well-water" (206). And the one and only time that Alexandra does envisage a heterosexual embrace as a positive desire to be unresisted, it is rather alarmingly associated with the hooded figure of Death, "the mightiest of all lovers" (283).

Similarly, Cather also consistently links the major heterosexual relationship within her novel—the love of Emil and Marie—to images of decay, sickness, and pain. Emil's passion, for example, is compared to a defective grain of corn which will never shoot up "joyfully into the light" but is destined instead to rot and fester in the dark, damp earth (164). The essential morbidity of his relationship with Marie is further conveyed by the nature of the three gifts he drops into the lap of his beloved over the course of the novel: the uncut turquoises are pretty, but must, like the grain of corn, remain concealed in dark secrecy (224-25); the branch full of "sweet, insipid fruit" is already overripe and on the verge of decay (153); and, in stark contrast to Alexandra's sportive and contented solitary duck, the birds associated with the two young lovers are dead and dripping with blood (127-28). Gone for both Emil and Marie are those "germless days" of childhood (216), for their experience of adult heterosexuality is indeed like a type of "affliction," a perverse sort of malaise in the grip of which they "cannot feel that the heart lives at all" unless "its strings can scream to the touch of pain" (226).

Neatly reversing her society's binary equation of deviant sexuality with disease and heterosexuality with health, Cather also continues to turn contemporary medical theory upon its head by attributing to the nature of heterosexuality a number of other specific aberrations which sexologists typically ascribed to the sexual 'invert.' By the early twentieth century, for instance, the notion of 'sexual inversion' was commonly associated not only with physical disease, but with all manner of tragedy, insanity, and criminality as well. "Inverted women," as Ellis asserts in his work, "present a favourable soil for the seeds of passional crime," and to illustrate his point, he promptly proceeds to recount, in gruesome detail, several cases of lesbian homicides and suicides, deeming one particularly sensational 1892 murder of a young Memphis woman by her female lover as quite "typical" (201). The sexual nature of the 'inverted' person, moreover, was thought to "constitute as well a specific atavistic response, a sudden throwback to a primitive bisexuality, a tragic freak of nature" (Smith-Rosenberg 269). "[F]rom a eugenic standpoint" such as Ellis's, therefore, "the tendency to sexual inversion" could be regarded as "merely . . . nature's merciful method of winding up a concern which, from her point of view, has ceased to be profitable" (335).

In Cather's novel, conversely, it is heterosexuality which is presented as the direct cause of such grievous afflictions and processes. While the component of tragedy is, of course, most dramatically evident in the violent and premature deaths of Marie and Emil, almost all of the heterosexual alliances in the text are presented as unhappy or pathetic. Hence, John Bergson is "warped" by his marriage, which is described as a mere "infatuation" on his part: "the despairing folly of a powerful man who [could] not bear to grow old" (23). Similarly, the snug security of Angélique's happy little family is blighted by the sudden death of Amédée; the confused young Signa is afraid of her bullish husband even before he forces her to plod home with the cows on their wedding day; and "young farmers" like Lou betray a measure of embarrassed discomfort in their spousal relations in that they can seldom bring themselves to address their wives by name (111). And, unlike Alexandra's orderly household, the Shabata home is frequently the scene of domestic crises and violence, for Frank is a rash and volatile man whose unleashed temper has "more than once" compelled Marie to struggle with him over a loaded gun (265-66). Uniting themselves in relationships which all too often result in animosity, violence, divorce (148), or death, the majority of heterosexual characters in this novel are to some degree culpable, like Marie, of "spread[ing] ruin around" (304), and as such, they are viewed collectively by the author not only as a tragic lot but, indeed, as the 'ultimate symbol' of what the sexual invert was supposed to represent: utter social and domestic chaos.

It is also Frank Shabata, the most aggressively heterosexual character in the novel, who emerges from Cather's perspective as the "most favourable soil for the seeds of passional crime," as well as madness and degeneration. After his passionate jealousy has resulted in the murders of Emil and Marie, he regresses in prison to an atavistic creature, a grey, unshaven, and stooped figure who appears "not altogether human." Left to ponder his guilt in a wretched cell, the now pathetic Frank depicts a dismal future for himself; as he confesses to Alexandra when she visits him, "I guess I go crazy sure 'nough" (294). The implicit but clear message in Cather's text, then, is that the heterosexual nature, far from embodying an unambiguously 'normal' or healthy appetite, may manifest itself as 'unnatural' and 'morbid' in precisely the same ways as those of 'inverted' or 'deviant' sexual tendencies were thought to. Or, considered from an obverse angle, Cather's novel is one whose sexually unorthodox but sane, vigorous, and prosperous heroine serves as a timely reminder to those, who, like Ellis, tended to forget that what may be perceived as 'abnormal' need not necessarily be 'morbid.'

Through her own process of conceptual 'inversion,' then, Cather may be seen to respond in a creative and challenging way to dominant contemporary theories of sexuality, quietly establishing, in *O Pioneers!*, her own alternate paradigms of human sexuality. And yet it is, perhaps, an authorial consciousness of implicitly engaging—and controverting—this larger medico-cultural ethos which may also be seen to constitute the source of an inhibiting force in Cather's art. In *O Pioneers!*, this aspect of the narrative is best illustrated by Cather's treatment of the relations between women. For indeed, contrary to the pervasive critical over-generalization that Cather "never" deals in her fiction with the homosocial emotions and bonds which filled and fuelled her own life, a very complex and subtle relationship does unfold in this novel between Alexandra and Marie, which, to the best extent of my knowledge, has not been extensively or adequately examined. And it is important that it should be, for it suggests that within this novel of pioneer life, Cather begins to explore a second sort of 'frontier': not a historical and geographical one, but a psychic "frontier between friendship and love" (M. Tarde, qtd. in Ellis 75). This is not to argue that Cather depicts the friendship between her heroine and Marie as one which moves toward incipient lesbianism. Rather, it is to suggest that, along with its nostalgia for the heroic cultural and geographical Nebraskan frontier of the past, Cather's text also quietly but perceptibly mourns the passing of that older world of passionate yet innocent female love, so well documented by Smith-Rosenberg, into a modern era of 'morbidified' relations.

Perhaps because of the disparity of their respective ages, the affection Alexandra feels for Marie clearly manifests itself on one level as a type of maternal love. "Sit down like a good girl, Marie," Alexandra says in her best matronly manner, for example, "and I'll tell you a story" (137). Marie, that "crazy child" who married at eighteen (119), seems in this respect to present a surrogate daughter-figure for Alexandra, just as she thinks of her younger brother, Emil, as her "boy." On the other hand, however, the friendship between the two women is marked by both a degree of intensity and a dimension of sensuality which makes it a far more "romantic" relationship than, in fact, Alexandra's ostensibly 'real' romance with Carl Lindstrum. Indeed, when Cather's heroine reflects on the "pretty lonely life" she has led, the primacy of her bond with the young Bohemian girl is indicated by the order in which she names her two closest companions: "Besides Marie, Carl is the only friend I have ever had" (177). Unlike Carl, who drifts in and out of Alexandra's life between long intervals, Marie is woven closely into the fabric of her daily existence. "It is not often," therefore, that Alexandra "let[s] three days go by without seeing Marie"—and when Carl does reappear at one point, and Alexandra postpones her regular visit, she frets guiltily that her younger friend will think she has "forsaken her" (130). Later, of course, it is Alexandra herself who feels woefully "forsaken" when she learns of Marie's affair with Emil:

> Could you believe that of Marie Tovesky? I would have been cut to pieces, little by little, before I would have betrayed her trust in me!
>
> (303)

Not only is it revealing that Alexandra apparently does not recognize Marie "Tovesky" as Frank Shabata's wife, but her emphatic language and words of "betrayal" and "forsaken" anguish also clearly echo the "romantic rhetoric" of "emotional intensity" which Smith-Rosenberg notes as characteristic of close female friendships before the late nineteenth century (59).

Furthermore, while Alexandra's relationship with Carl remains a fairly dispassionate affair throughout—arrested, in fact, at the stage of hand-holding until a light kiss at the very end of the novel is offered as a prelude to a marriage of "friends" (308-09)—her relationship with Marie allows for a great measure of uninhibited physical contact. At one point, for example, Marie runs up to her friend "panting," throws "her arms about Alexandra," and then gives her arm an affectionate "little squeeze" as they begin to walk together

(134). And Alexandra similarly expresses her sentiments by "pinch[ing] Marie's cheek playfully" when they meet (192). The two women have an acute and joyful sense of each other's physical proximity as well; hence, Alexandra confides that she is "glad" to have Marie living "so near" her, while Marie delights in the delicate scent of rosemary on Alexandra's dress (119, 134).

Like Cather herself, who so ardently admired female beauty that she sometimes strapped herself financially by loaning money to attractive actresses whose plays she reviewed (Woodress 105; O'Brien, *Willa Cather* 134), Alexandra responds to Marie with pleasure and admiration on an aesthetic level. Of course, almost every character in the novel does, for Marie's spectacular "tiger eyes" (11) are irresistibly captivating. Indeed, at the risk of pressing a fine (but in this context, relevant) point too closely, Marie's striking eyes may reflect a subtle authorial allusion to Balzac's sensational lesbian novel, *The Girl With the Golden Eyes*—particularly since that novel is believed to have been inspired by the real-life relationship of George Sand (Cather's avowed role-model) and a woman named Marie Dorval.[13] At any rate, Alexandra is especially drawn by the unique blend of exoticism and innocence in Marie, comparing her to both a "queer foreign kind of doll" and a "little brown rabbit" (192, 133). Carl's observation of Marie's sensuously "full" and "parted" lips, and of the "points of yellow light dancing in her eyes" (135) reinforces Alexandra's perception of her friend as an attractively animated yet vulnerable young woman who is "too young and pretty for this sort of life" (121).

With Marie, Alexandra thus enjoys an emotional and physical intimacy which is a source of innocent pleasure to them both. The crucial point, however, is how others perceive their relationship. Through the perspective of Carl Lindstrum, Cather subtly but deftly probes the perverse interpretations apt to be construed from such close homosocial bonds in the new era of 'scientific' sexology. When Alexandra explains to Carl how "nice" it has felt for her to have "a friend" at "the other end" of the path between the Bergson-Shabata homesteads since he has lived there, for instance, Carl responds with a rueful "smile": "All the same, I hope it hasn't [*sic*] been *quite* the same" (130). It is an odd remark, laden with an innuendo that makes Alexandra look at Carl "with surprise," and respond defensively:

> Why no, of course not. Not the same. She could not very well take your place, if that's what you mean. I'm friendly with all my neighbors, I hope.

But Marie is really a companion, someone I can talk to quite frankly. You wouldn't want me to be more lonely than I have been would you?

(130)

To this, Carl laughs nervously, fusses with his hair, and replies uncertainly:

Of course I don't. I ought to be thankful that this path hasn't been worn by—well, by friends with more pressing errands than your little Bohemian is likely to have.

(131)

Carl realizes that he "ought" to be thankful that Alexandra's female "friend" is not "likely" to pose a serious rival for her affections, but his hesitant manner and doubtful language suggest that his suspicions are obviously not allayed. When he does, therefore, have an opportunity to scrutinize the type of relationship the two women share, he carefully "watch[es]" them from "a little distance" (135). That they make a "pretty picture" together is his first thought, but after observing Marie's intense and delighted absorption in Alexandra for a time, Carl goes on to reflect: "What a waste . . . she ought to be doing all that for a sweetheart. How awkwardly things come about!" (136).

Significantly, it is not long after Carl's reappearance on the Divide that the pleasant state of affairs between Cather's heroine and the attractive young immigrant girl begin to alter. Indeed, the shift in Alexandra and Marie's friendship, the point at which each woman first begins to distance herself warily from the other, occurs as issues of their respective heterosexual relationships begin to impinge upon their lives. When it comes to the subject of Carl and her differences with her brothers over him, for example, Alexandra "instinctive[ly]" feels that "about such things she and Marie would not understand one another" (188). Suddenly, when the topic is Alexandra's relationship with a male, Marie no longer appears to represent the "real" "companion" she "can talk to quite frankly" (130). It is a blind "instinct" which Alexandra follows without testing when she has the opportunity. For when during one of their last intimate moments together, Marie begins to speak "frankly" about her own unhappy union with Frank, Alexandra withdraws guardedly from the conversation, abruptly recalling Marie to the "crochet patterns" for which they have been searching: "no good," she rationalizes, can ever come "from talking about such things" (198).

Immediately after this incident, a reciprocal process of withdrawal takes place on Marie's part. As the narrator observes:

After that day the younger woman seemed to shrink more and more into herself. When she was with Alexandra she was not spontaneous and frank as she used to be. She seemed to be brooding over something, and holding something back.

(200-01)

The pain, confusion, or guilt which each woman experiences over her respective relationship—or relationships—with men is the one thing they cannot share with each other directly, and it is as a stave which wedges them further and further apart. Finally, when Alexandra places her hand tenderly on the arm of a pale and tired-looking Marie, just after Emil has drained the blood from her cheeks with an electrifying kiss, she can feel her young friend "shiver": "Marie stiffened under that kind, calm hand. Alexandra drew back, perplexed and hurt" (226).

Cather's novel thus clearly traces the steady disintegration of a formerly intimate female friendship to the point of physical recoil and abiding resentment. But what happened? Certainly, in so far that the "pretty picture" which consists of Alexandra and Marie becomes "awkward" only when men enter into it, it may be argued that Cather's depiction of a loving female relationship is intended as an illustration of the sad consequences of social pressures which compel women (and men) to erect psychic barriers between one another in an obsessively heterocentric culture—lest their affection, that is, be construed by the Carls of the world as suspiciously 'unnatural.' If this is what Cather attempted, however, she does not wholly accomplish her goal. For although she does begin to critique the contemporary attitude toward, and perception of, innocently romantic female friendships, she eventually abandons this daring impulse in what seems a silent submission to the established sexual prejudices and stereotypes of her day, a submission which sharply reinforces O'Brien's contention that Cather never fully "freed herself from male constructs of femininity" ("The Thing Not Named" 596; *Willa Cather* 124-25). Because indeed, the whole tragic point of the devolution of Alexandra and Marie's relationship is undermined by Cather's ultimate reliance upon the archetypal paradigm of the fallen Eve for Marie, and by her apparently unqualified endorsement of a conventional marriage for Alexandra—an authorial enthusiasm which is nevertheless unconvincing because it purports to applaud a heterosexual alliance which has been portrayed from the beginning as tepid and watery, at best.

Ultimately, then, Cather's careful dissolution and final destruction of the poignant bond first established between her women represent an authorial retreat into literary convention and rather insipid romanticism. It is a retreat which is in itself tragic. For as the character of Carl suggests, Cather was at some point while writing her novel obviously aware of just how "awkwardly" her portrayal of an artless and genuine female friendship might appear to her modern audience. Whether unconsciously or with a painful memory of her own past friendship with Louise Pound, Cather therefore defuses the potentially scandalous subject she has begun to probe, before it becomes too overt an issue within the text. The simple beauty of a loving friendship between women was the one central aspect of the contemporary discourse of sexuality which Cather could not fully address, because it involved not merely an indirect, artistic inversion of her culture's metaphors, myths, and theories, but entailed, rather, a direct and necessarily polemical authorial entry into the heartland of the sexologists' "frontier" territory, that twilight and controversial no-woman's land separating socially acceptable female companionship from illicit same-sex love. And for all the dramatic adolescent rejection of frocks and frills and curls; for all the aggressively outspoken, critical target-shooting of youth; for all the steadfast, personal commitments to other women in her maturity, this was something the adult 'Billy Cather, Jr' was not rebel enough to risk.

Notes

1. Ellis uses terms such as "frontier," "pioneer," and "borderland" quite extensively throughout.

2. For a differing interpretation of the marriage of Carl and Alexandra, see O'Brien, *Willa Cather* 444-46.

3. This chapter of Smith-Rosenberg's book, entitled "The Female World of Love and Ritual: Relations Between Women in Nineteenth Century America," appeared originally in the first issue of *Signs* (1975).

4. Smith-Rosenberg also explores the potentially revolutionary social implications which a strong network of homosocial female bonds posed in the context of the feminist movement, and makes a similar point; see *Disorderly Conduct* 277-82.

5. The term 'morbidification,' however, is taken from Faderman.

6. On Cather's destruction of her letters and the legal provisions of her will, see Robinson 33-34 and 274; Brown xxiii; Woodress xiii-xiv.

7. See 127-37 for the most compelling and comprehensive account, to date, of Cather's complex and contradictory sense of lesbian self-identity.

8. E. G. Lancaster, qtd. in Ellis, *Sexual Inversion* 382. The colloquial terms "flame," "rave," and "spoon" also appear in Ellis's appendix, 368-84 *passim*.

9. It should be noted, however, that subsequent biographers have dismissed Robinson's suggestion as "pure speculation" (Woodress 87).

10. Anon., "Female Orators," *The Mother's Magazine*, VI (1838): 27, qtd. in Faderman, *Surpassing the Love of Men* 235.

11. Krafft-Ebing, qtd. in Faderman, "The Morbidification of Love" 77. Faderman points out that Krafft-Ebing later changed his stance on homosexuality as a disease, but that this was announced only shortly before his death in 1902 and had "minimal" impact "on popular notions regarding homosexuals" (77-78, n. 6).

12. In fairness, it must be noted that Ellis also uses the word "germ" elsewhere in *Sexual Inversion* in a purely organic sense. In language very appropriate to the context of Cather's novel, in fact, he describes human sexuality in terms of a "soil" which at conception is "sown" with an equal amount of masculine and feminine "seeds" or "germs." In bisexuals and homosexuals, he maintains, the "normal" process whereby the "seeds" of one sex come to "kill off" most of those of the other sex has somehow dysfunctioned, a phenomenon, he says, that can only be attributed to an inherent abnormality "in the soil" (309-11).

13. On the relevance of Balzac's novel in the context of late nineteenth-century French aesthetic-decadent literature, see Faderman, *Surpassing the Love of Men* 254, 267. Cather was known to be a fan of such literature, which strengthens the possibility that she had indeed come across Balzac's book; see O'Brien, *Willa Cather* 134-35; Woodress 119; and Brown 98, 103.

Works Cited

Bailey, Jennifer. "The Dangers of Femininity in Willa Cather's Fiction." *Journal of American Studies* 16.3 (1982): 391-406.

Brown, E. K. *Willa Cather: A Critical Biography.* Completed by Leon Edel. New York: Knopf, 1953.

Cather, Willa. *O Pioneers!* 1913. Boston: Houghton, 1941.

——. *My Ántonia.* 1918. Cambridge, Mass.: Riverside P, 1926.

Ellis, Havelock. *Sexual Inversion.* Vol. 2 of *Studies in the Psychology of Sex.* 6 vols., 3rd ed. Philadelphia: Davis, 1918.

Faderman, Lillian. *Surpassing the Love of Men: Romantic Friendship and Love Between Women from the Renaissance to the Present.* New York: William Morrow, 1981.

——. "The Morbidification of Love Between Women by Nineteenth-Century Sexologists." *Journal of Homosexuality* 4.1 (1978): 73-90.

Kolodny, Annette. "A Map for Rereading: Gender and the Interpretation of Literary Texts." *The New Feminist Criticism: Essays on Women, Literature, and Theory.* Ed. Elaine Showalter. New York: Pantheon, 1985. 46-62.

Myers, Sandra L. *Westering Women and the Frontier Experience, 1800-1915.* Albuquerque: U of New Mexico P, 1982.

O'Brien, Sharon. *Willa Cather: The Emerging Voice.* New York: OUP, 1987.

———. "'The Thing Not Named': Willa Cather as a Lesbian Writer." *Signs* 9.4 (1984): 576-99.

Ostenso, Martha. *Wild Geese.* Toronto: McClelland & Stewart, 1925.

Rich, Adrienne. "Compulsive Heterosexuality and Lesbian Existence." *Signs* 5.4 (1980): 631-61.

Robinson, Phyllis. *Willa: The Life of Willa Cather.* Garden City, New York: Doubleday, 1983.

Rule, Jane. *Lesbian Images.* Garden City, New York: Doubleday, 1975.

Smith-Rosenberg, Carroll. *Disorderly Conduct: Visions of Gender in Victorian America.* New York: Knopf, 1985.

Woodress, James. *Willa Cather: A Literary Life.* Lincoln: U of Nebraska P, 1987.

The Song of the Lark

LAURA DUBEK (ESSAY DATE SEPTEMBER 1994)

SOURCE: Dubek, Laura. "Rewriting Male Scripts: Willa Cather and *The Song of the Lark.*" *Women's Studies* 23, no. 4 (September 1994): 293-306.

In the following essay, Dubek argues that Cather may have identified more strongly with her male characters in Song of the Lark *than with her main female character, Thea, because of artificial models of behavior imposed on men.*

Sharon O'Brien's *Willa Cather: The Emerging Voice* has drawn attention to Cather's unique position as a lesbian writer who often employed male characters to explore love relationships between women. Certainly, *The Song of the Lark,* with its emphasis on the divided self, the tension between disclosure and concealment, public masks and erotic desire, qualifies as a novel which may contain a lesbian subtext. At the very least, the novel demonstrates the author's intuitive understanding of "man's" struggle to deny and repress desires that culture deems unnatural or improper. Cather adored the theater because it "gives what the everyday world lacks—strong emotions and experience to warm and uplift, sharpening what custom or caution obliterates" (Slote 66). She must have enjoyed novel-writing for the same reason, creating characters who liberate their second, secret selves and triumph as her heroine in *The Song of the Lark,* Thea Kronborg, finally does. But Cather called this novel her fairy tale, and so Thea's success is only a wish that comes true in fiction. Perhaps precisely because Thea succeeds so thoroughly in fairy-tale fashion, Cather may have invested more sympathy in those destined to live without such happy endings. Although critics consider *The Song of the Lark* her most autobiographical novel, I suspect that Cather's real identification lies not with Thea and her flowering as an artist but with her male characters who suffer from a script imposed on them by a repressive society frightened of desire.

Intent on proving the subservient nature of the male roles and so Cather's reversal of traditional gender convictions, many critics of *The Song of the Lark* remain trapped in dualisms that Cather herself sought to transcend in her novel about discovery, integration, and continuity. Susan Rosowski argues that while Cather gives Thea typically "male qualities," she casts the men "as instruments in the central [female] character's advancement" (63). Others support Rosowski's view that the men play minor roles: Shirley Foster calls them "social or economic units" rather than love interests, men from whom Thea must nevertheless protect *her* inner-self (170) and Linda Huf writes of the men as "teachers and friends" who invest in Thea's future only to have her climb "beyond their reach" (84). Although recognizing that others are drawn to the heroine's "magnetic center," Demaree Peck explores Thea's own emptiness rather than the hunger of her admirers (33). Published in 1968, Giannone's work on Cather's use of music contains the fullest treatment of the male characters in *The Song of the Lark.* Giannone, writing of music's ability to arouse man's higher self, identifies Doctor Archie, Professor Wunsch, Ray Kennedy, and Fred Ottenburg as four of Thea's friends who have musical responses that imply "the higher self which society does not discern and which the friends themselves cannot reach or release on their own" (87). Like other critics, though, Giannone writes mainly of what the men "give" to Thea (money, encouragement, knowledge), evaluating them strictly in terms of their effect on the heroine rather than in their own rights.

Naturally, the criticism on *The Song of the Lark* highlights Thea Kronborg as the opera star who defies tradition and achieves worldly success; virtually everyone who writes about this novel focuses on Thea's dominant "voice" in a world where power, control, and creation are usually reserved for men.[1] Envisioning a world that does not restrict a woman's influence to the private/domestic sphere nor require a complete surrendering of the "female self" for success in the public/male sphere, Cather does indeed attack the notion that femininity perforce implies passivity and subordinate status. By defining Thea in terms of her ability to integrate ostensibly antithetical attributes, however, Cather questions rather than reverses the traditional gender roles which rely on Western civilization's use of dichotomies (male/female, mind/body, dominant/submissive) to maintain the social order. Thea Kronborg embodies the author's idea of the artist as one who "possesses traits conventionally divided between the sexes: intellect, discipline, and control as well as intuition, passion, and self-abandonment" (O'Brien 425). But while Thea frees herself from the confining, fixed gender role prescribed for her by Victorian society and realizes the full integration of feminine and masculine qualities that ensures her success, her male supporters struggle with the images of woman which have hitherto secured their positions but are now, in Thea's case, inadequate. Cather's new definition of womanhood signals the need for a readjustment not just of the options granted to women but of the ways in which men construct and maintain their distinctively masculine identities.

Historically, masculinity has been identified with reason and control. John Shepard traces the beginnings of such an association to Post-Renaissance man, who thought himself into "the entirely mythical position of being separate from the world, of being able analytically to pin down physical, human and social existence as a unidimensional, static display having relevance only for the gaze of the beholder" (58). To protect these feelings of power and control, men have had to separate themselves from their natures (passions and desires), learning to act out of a sense of duty rather than in accordance with their feelings. Culture aids this process by teaching men that they are divided against themselves, (Griffin 140) that their minds/reason must dominate their bodies/passions. Victor Seidler points out a crucial consequence of defining masculine identity in terms of "a disembodied conception of reason"—man's systematic denial of his material and emotional self (96). Men construct their identities, then, by suppressing their need for dependency and connectedness, a negation of sexuality which Freud saw as producing "misery and unhappiness in the name of virtue and morality" (Seidler 100).[2] Divorced from nature by a culture that identifies male identity/sexuality with self-control, men live in constant fear of the revelation of their true natures, their secret selves.

The degree to which four of the major male characters[3] in *The Song of the Lark* succeed in negotiating a compromise between social definitions of masculine identity and their secret, second selves varies. Doctor Howard Archie and Professor Wunsch, both friends from Thea's childhood, desperately cling to the public masks society has provided them (doctor, husband, teacher, substitute-father, drunk) to ensure a strict separation between their minds/reason and bodies/passion. While Archie manages quite successfully to suppress his hidden desires and instead focus on his social obligations, Wunsch reveals his vulnerability prior to a self-imposed exile from Moonstone. Archie and Wunsch each demonstrate the debilitating nature of patriarchal society's script for men, a script that teaches men to fear intimacy and erotic passion because they threaten the sense of independence, rational control, and dominance so closely identified with masculinity. This denial of the need for connectedness fosters the creation of Archie's and Wunsch's secret, second selves—"others" who seek to resolve the conflict between nature and culture, between instinctual desires and socialized life by embracing the engulfment offered by intimate relationships. Andor Harsanyi, Thea's piano instructor in Chicago, fares much better than Archie or Wunsch; he succeeds in liberating his secret self primarily because of his understanding of and appreciation for music. Unlike vision, which emphasizes separation, objectification, and distance, sound stresses what Shepard calls "the integrative and relational"; it reveals the "world of depth surrounding us, approaching us simultaneously from all directions, totally fluid in its evanescence, a world which is active and constantly prodding us for a reaction" (159). So, the voice, as paradigm of sound, has the power to awaken man's secret self, bringing to his consciousness the buried knowledge of his connection to the world of nature. Thea herself consciously realizes music's unique power to recognize and call to the secret selves in her listeners: "How deep they lay, these second persons, and how little one knew about them, except to guard them fiercely. It was to music, more than to anything else, that these hidden things in people responded" (273). Giannone asserts that Cather shows music as revelatory of a previously unshared, buried self that longs for expression (240). Thea's music, her ability to enter "the very skin of another human being," (Sergeant 111) enables Harsanyi to release more fully that buried self. A confidant and artistic equal, Harsanyi shares one aspect of Thea's life—her passion for art—and so finds an expression for his hidden desires that Archie and Wunsch do not. While Harsanyi shares Thea's artistic passion, Fred Ottenburg, the young beer prince, earns her love by completely bridging the gap between inhibition and fulfillment. Cather's "new man," Fred meets the challenge of Thea's voice (inseparable from her self) by merging the worlds of nature and culture and revising the stifling gender role imposed on him by patriarchal society, a role characterized by denial and repression.

Cather symbolically portrays these male secret selves through images of locks and enclosure. The novel opens with Doctor Archie snapping the lock on the cupboard that hides his liquor. O'Brien, quoting Bachelard's *The Poetics of Space,* asserts that a closed box represents the human need for secrecy, for emotional hiding places, and a lock symbolizes a "psychological threshold"; in Cather's early fiction, O'Brien thinks "closed boxes signify both the female body with its sexual secrets and the creative or hidden self" (410). Content and secure alone in his office with his locked cupboard, Archie fears "being discovered and ridiculed" more than anything else. He refuses to divorce his estranged wife because a "divorced man was a disgraced man; at least, he had exhibited his hurt, and made it a matter for common gossip" (107). Physically and mentally confined to Moonstone's ideas of propriety, Archie receives no warmth from his wife and presumably little sex—Mrs. Archie prefers her "house" to be "clean, empty, dark, locked" (42). Lacking "the courage to be an honest thinker," comforting himself "by evasions and compromises" (108), Archie escapes his unsatisfying marriage and personal sense of failure by hiding behind his role as Moonstone physician. His neighbors are friendly and respectful of his position, but because he was "transplanted" from Michigan, Archie never truly belongs. Years later, after his wife has died and he has left the small Colorado town, Archie reflects on his life as the young country doctor and remembers his only comfort:

> [W]herever his life had touched Thea Kronborg's, there was still a little warmth left, a little sparkle . . . *when we look back, the only things we cherish are those which in some way met our original want; the desire which formed in us in early youth, undirected, and of its own accord.*
>
> (488, my italics)

Thea satisfies Archie's "original want," his need to be connected and part of something bigger than himself by offering him a "continuous sort of relationship" (487) and an outlet for the expression of his secret self.

Thea's bout with pneumonia provides Doctor Archie with the opportunity to indulge his secret self and fulfill his need for emotional connected-ness. Archie touches and looks at Thea while she lies practically unconscious. Laura Mulvey describes such looking as "scopophilia," receiving pleasure by gazing at others as objects, usually of sexual stimulation (61). Reflecting on his unhappy marriage, Archie undresses Thea and thinks to himself "what a beautiful thing a girl's body was—like a flower. It was so neatly and delicately fashioned, so soft, and so milky white" (12). The doctor, experiencing a tension between his sense of duty and his desire, objectifies Thea, for in her childhood innocence lies his own memory of a wholeness associated with the knowledge of the body that culture has taught him to forget. Susan Griffin's study of pornography argues that in the child's world, we rediscover eros: "The beauty of the child's body. The child's closeness to the natural world. The child's heart. Her love. Touch never divided from meaning. Her trust. Her ignorance of culture" (254). At the end of the novel, Archie tells Thea, "When I dream about you, I always see you as a little girl" (549). As a ten-year-old girl, Thea represents the part of nature beyond Archie's control, the part of himself that lies hidden, and the "something" that he forever searches for and finds only in his memories of Thea's childhood.

Archie controls his erotic feelings for Thea by playing the white knight to her fairy princess, by turning their relationship into a story-book romance;[4] his mind cannot, however, always control his body, and his hidden desires often surface. When Thea talks with Doctor Archie about her frustrations and her fierce desire to get everything she wants out of life, Archie notices that she has grown up and is "afraid to touch her" (306). Unmistakably a woman, "goaded by desires, ambitions, revulsions that were dark to him," Thea threatens to awaken Archie's secret self by demanding an emotional response. While Thea's heart labors, Archie's mind struggles desperately to control the instinctual drive that seeks expression through his body. When Thea stands over Archie, her dress barely touching him, "she was breathing through her mouth and her throat was throbbing with excitement." Looking up at her, "Archie's hands tightened on the arms of his chair. He had thought he knew Thea Kronborg pretty well, but he did not know the girl who was standing here. She was beautiful, as his little Swede had never been, but she frightened him" (307). Archie had thought he knew *himself* pretty well; his own reaction to Thea frightens him more than anything else because it brings to consciousness his own sexuality. Doctor Archie, then, confronted with Thea's womanhood and his attraction to her "throbbing throat," maintains control by willing his body to be silent. Archie's advice to Thea dramatically illuminates his understanding of his own inability to break the chains of culture as well as his castration anxiety. Feeling the sharp edge of his paper-cutter, Archie murmurs half to himself,

> He either fears his fate too much
>   Or his deserts are small,
> Who dares not put it to the touch
>   To win . . . or lose it all.
>
> (306)

Afraid to "touch" the womanly Thea, Archie loses the chance to merge with something larger than himself. His secret self, his memory of a wholeness before culture separated him from others, remains carefully hidden, and he carries on with the business of denial and repression.

To suppress his sexual attraction to Thea, Archie casts himself in the role of substitute father; playing benefactor provides him with a socially acceptable image to hide behind while he indulges his secret self. Before Thea leaves to study voice in Germany, she writes to Archie for money, advice, and friendship. Archie immediately buys a train ticket to New York, shoving his money "under the grating of the ticket window as if he could not get rid of it fast enough" (435). He realizes that, at forty, he has never traveled farther east than Buffalo and that his pursuit of material wealth has prevented him from satisfying his own, personal interests. Glad "that his first trip had a human interest, that he was going for something, and because he was wanted," Archie thinks "it's worth paying out to be in on it—for a fellow like me. And when it's Thea—oh, I back her!" (436). Unable to completely suppress the part of himself that yearns for human connections, Archie looks forward to rescuing Thea and filling his own emptiness. His natural instincts once again betraying his mind's precarious control over his emotions, Archie rushes to get a new suit because he doesn't want "to look different to her from everybody else there," and he knows his tailor, Wan, will "put him right." Noticing his client's exuberance, Van calls Archie a bridegroom who must have a date in New York; his comment "made [Archie] remember that he wasn't one" (436). Catching him with his public mask off, the tailor makes Archie aware of the secret self that seeks union with Thea.

Archie's need for emotional nurturance and connectedness cannot be openly acknowledged, but it cannot be obliterated either. Years later, when the doctor talks about perhaps going to

Japan or Russia and then blurts out that he wants to go to New York, Fred asks him if he will see Thea, and the older man replies, "'I suspect I am going exactly *to see* her'" (482). Thea represents the "something" Archie wants for himself, the connection to others that he cannot experience because culture denies him access to the emotional selves of others. Offered no acceptable means of expressing his hidden desires, Archie seeks pleasure in watching Thea perform. Overwhelmed first by the largeness of Thea's downtown apartment building and then by the enormous height of the audience room in the Metropolitan Opera House, Archie expects Thea "to appear and sing and reassure him," but when she does enter the stage, "her face was there . . . and he positively could not see it. She was singing, at last, and he positively could not hear her . . . whatever was there, she was not there—for him" (499). Archie was so intent on seeing the Thea who was his fairy princess, that when "Kronborg" the opera star appeared, he could see only "this new woman" who had "devoured his little friend" (500). Unable to integrate culture and nature as Thea has done, Archie remains the spectator firmly entrenched in a society which objectifies, separates, and mystifies human relations. He realizes that "the ocean he could cross, but there was something here he could not cross"—at least not while he lived in this world:

> [P]resently he found that he was sitting quietly in a darkened house, not listening to, but dreaming upon, a river of silver sound. He felt apart from the others, drifting alone on the melody, as if he had been alone with it for a long while and had known it all before . . . he seemed to be looking through an exalted calmness at a beautiful woman from far away, from another sort of life and feeling and understanding than his own, who had in her face something he had known long ago, much brightened and beautified. As a lad he used to believe that the faces of people who died were like that in the next world; the same faces, but shining with the light of a new understanding.
>
> (500)

Rich with images of birth and death, of engulfment and isolation, this passage exposes Archie's unconscious memories of a wholeness associated perhaps first with his mother and later with Thea. In his dreams, Archie remembers, but only in death, when culture releases its grip on his mind, body, and soul, will he embrace the full knowledge of his secret self. During the second act, "the doctor's thoughts were as far away from Moonstone as the singer's doubtless were . . . he [feels] the exhilaration of getting free from personalities, of being released from his own past as well as from

Thea Kronborg's" (501). While he witnesses Thea's theatrical "marriage," Doctor Archie gives his little girl to the world, his mind finally conquering his body and restoring the control that was constantly threatened by his intimate, secret feelings for Thea. Archie joins the others in applauding Kronborg's performance, "but it was the new and wonderful he applauded, not the old and dear. His personal, *proprietary* pride in her was frozen out" (502). Archie's revision of traditional manhood, then, amounts to his public recognition of Thea's identity separate from his fantasies and his private recognition of his own inability to embrace the world of nature.

If Thea's first piano teacher, Professor Wunsch, could have heard the "new and wonderful" Kronborg, his faith in the power of hope might have been restored, for Thea certainly fulfills the dreams Wunsch fears to covet for her when she's his young pupil in Moonstone. Like Archie, Wunsch feels a "natural" attraction to Thea, her "fierceful nature" recalling to him hidden desires and memories of a time when life was "wild with joy" and culture hadn't yet demanded the suppression of his secret self. Wunsch "had been a musician once, long before he wandered into Moonstone, but when Thea awoke his interest there was not much left of him" (219). Walking the wet streets of Moonstone without an overcoat or overshoes, poor, drunk, and starving for nurturance, Wunsch finds little to rejoice about until the Kohlers, a German couple, take him into their home. While Doctor Archie escapes his troubled life by hiding behind his professional mask, Wunsch escapes into the Kohlers' garden. Separated from the rest of Moonstone by the railroad tracks and a deep ravine, the Kohlers' home and garden provide Wunsch with a sanctuary, an enclosure which shields Wunsch from the penetrating light of self-reflection and the burning heat of desire. The Edenic garden stands in marked contrast with the harsh desert, a place Cather thought of as the locus for "celibate withdrawal" as well as "primitive passion," "sensual indulgence," and "spiritual and aesthetic revelation" (O'Brien 407). When Thea, as a child of the desert, enters the Kohlers' garden, she threatens to expose the secret self that Wunsch tries so desperately to silence:

> And there was always the old enemy, more relentless than others. It was long since he had wished anything or desired anything beyond the necessities of the body. Now that he was tempted to hope for another, he felt alarmed and shook his head.
>
> (37)

Like Doctor Archie, Wunsch struggles to maintain a strict separation between his mind and body, silencing the voice of nature within in order to avoid his secret self. Wunsch cannot win this battle, though, because while bodily needs and material wants can, in fact, be satisfied, "a symbolic need of the mind perpetually hungers if in reality that need is to silence the body . . . such insatiability [arising] precisely because the mind contrives against nature" (Griffin 102). Culture forcing him to act out of a sense of duty rather than according to instinctual desires, Wunsch responds coldly to Thea's aversion to the way he has marked the fingering of a particular passage by saying, "'It makes no matter what you think, . . . [t]here is only one right way'" (33). And yet Wunsch's passions, deep and powerful, refuse to be controlled by reason (the one right way) and continually seek expression. Rather than embracing the vitality which Thea rekindles in him, Wunsch represses such emotions, labelling them shameful, deviant, and necessarily sexual in nature because they arouse his hidden, "evil" nature.

Try as he might to suppress them, Wunsch's repressed feelings nevertheless resurface, just as Archie's do. On Thea's thirteenth birthday, Wunsch's struggle with his divided self comes to a climax, leading ultimately to a drunken rampage and his final retreat from Moonstone. After giving Thea her piano lesson, Wunsch leads his pupil out to the garden where they walk hand-in-hand among the flowers and plants. Wunsch has Thea repeat in German a favorite song:

> In the soft-shining summer morning
> I wandered the garden within.
> The flowers they whispered and murmured,
> But I, I wandered dumb.
> The flowers they whisper and murmur,
> And me with compassion they scan:
> 'Oh, be not harsh to our sister,
> Thou sorrowful, death-pale man!'
>
> (96-7)

Associating Thea with the flowers in the garden, Wunsch paces the garden, recalling his past years teaching girls who had nothing inside them compared to Thea, pseudo-musicians unable to elicit any emotional response from him. Breathless and upset, without even saying goodbye, the old teacher storms out of the garden when Thea will not discuss the song's significance to their relationship. Wunsch's sudden outburst represents more than simple frustration over a pupil's refusal to answer a question. If, as Griffin argues, "the body speaks the language of the soul," the body's fevered longing unmasking "a deep desire for that part of the self to come to consciousness [and] be remembered," (88) Wunsch's tantrum reveals his inner-struggle with the secret self which seeks union with others. Since sexual imagery pervades the birthday scene (the prickly-pear blossoms with their thousand stamens, the two symmetrical linden trees standing proud, the purple morning-glories that ran over the bean poles, the wild bees buzzing, the green lizards racing each other), Wunsch undoubtedly associates these longings with eros. After the German's outburst, Thea "felt there was a secret between her and Wunsch. Together they had lifted a lid, pulled out a drawer, and looked at something. They hid it away and never spoke of what they had seen; but neither of them forgot it" (100). O'Brien identifies the hidden drawer Wunsch and Thea look into as either Pandora's box of sexuality or a "container of unexpressed but potential activity" (202). Once he peers inside, Wunsch finds it impossible to deny his emotional starvation and dire need to merge with another and so drinks himself into oblivion.

Unable to continue following society's script for manhood and yet terribly frightened of his secret self, Wunsch decides to destroy both his selves (cultural and secret) and end his torment. Awakening from his drunken coma, Wunsch rises "to avenge himself, to wipe out his shame, to destroy his enemy" (116). Dressed in only his undershirt and drawers, the old German, "his face snarling and savage, his eyes . . . crazy," stumbles to the garden and chops down the dove-house (117). When Wunsch faces humiliation and risks his already questionable reputation in Moonstone, he destroys the false/public/cultural image of himself which requires the denial of desire and dependence. Society, which characterizes such displays of emotion as insane, even criminal, then condemns him to a wanderer's life. Forced to leave Moonstone, Wunsch severs his relationships with the Kohlers and his prized pupil, thereby eliminating the possibility of a further encounter with his secret self. On her next birthday, Thea receives a greeting from her old teacher, a postcard from an obscure mid-western town with "a white dove, perched on a wreath of very blue forget-me-knots (135). Apparently, Wunsch didn't forget the day he looked inside himself and discovered the same "fierceful nature" he recognized in his extraordinary pupil even though he realizes that his desires must remain forever hidden if he is to function at all.

Thea's second piano teacher, Andor Harsanyi, looks forward to his meetings with Thea "for the same reason that poor Wunsch had sometimes dreaded his; because she stirred him more than anything she did could adequately explain" (240). His hour with Thea "took more out of him than half a dozen other lessons . . . [she] set him vibrating" (220-21). Unlike the old, discouraged German who believes that if he hopes for another, disaster will follow, Harsanyi lives for such opportunities. He tells his wife, "'All this drudgery will kill me if once in a while I cannot hope something, for somebody! If I cannot sometimes see a bird fly and wave my hand to it'" (268). A true artist, secure and happy with a wife and children, Harsanyi embraces the world of nature in a way that Wunsch and Archie cannot.

But while Harsanyi finds expression for his secret self in his own artistry, Theas's passion elicits an emotional response from her teacher that, nonetheless, disturbs him because it threatens the delicate balance of mind/body that protects him from confronting his own sexuality. When Harsanyi first hears Thea sing, he sits mesmerized, "looking intently at the toes of his boots, shading his forehead with his long white hand" (235). When she finished, the young Hungarian "sprang from his chair and dropped lightly upon his toes, a kind on *entre-chat* that he sometimes executed when he formed a sudden resolution, *or when he was about to follow a pure intuition, against reason*" (236, my italics). Not afraid to follow his instincts, Harsanyi puts his hands to Thea's throat, feeling it throb and vibrate. Excited over his discovery, Harsanyi entertains the idea "that no one had ever felt this voice vibrate before" (237). Like Archie and Wunsch, Harsanyi experiences a tension between his sense of duty and his desire; he resolves this conflict later when he turns Thea over to a voice specialist, but first he indulges his own fantasies by giving up one-half hour of his own time at the end of her lesson to teach her some songs:

> He found that these *unscientific* singing lessons stimulated him in his own study . . . He had never got so much back for himself from any pupil as he did from Miss Kronborg. From the first she had stimulated him . . . She often wearied him, but she never bored him. Under her crudeness and brusque hardness, he felt there was a nature quite different . . . It was toward this hidden creature that he was trying, for his own pleasure, to find his way. (239-40)

Harsanyi differs from Archie and Wunsch in that he actively, consciously seeks the engulfment that the other men associate with dependency and emasculation. His secret self not nearly as frightened of or starved for intimacy as Archie's or Wunsch's, Harsanyi thrives in his relationship with Thea because her passion *renews* rather than awakens him, though her voice often overwhelms him. For example, when Thea sings 'Die Lorelei,' Harsanyi feels the room so "flooded" that he has to open a window, imploring her to stop singing. Later, he tells his wife, Miss Kronborg "'had my room so reeking of a song this afternoon that I couldn't stay there,'" adding that he's glad "'there are not two of her'" (243). Harsanyi's secret self surfaces in response to Thea's "summons" while his "cultural self" gasps for air in the study which has now become the world of nature devoid of the social conventions which inhibit men from giving in to their hidden desires. Giannone argues that "when she grasps the idea of a river enduring beneath the havoc above it, Thea gives the end of 'Die Lorelei' an 'open flowing' tone to suggest continuity" (91). Thea's interpretation leaves her listener breathless but exhilarated, both his mind and body struggling to embrace the "stream of life" gushing from the singer's vessel/throat. Harsanyi manages to harness such intensity of feeling for his own artistic use before joining Archie and Wunsch in their renunciation of any claim to Thea herself. When Harsanyi sends her away to a new instructor, he "took one of her hands and kissed it lightly upon the back. His salute was one of greeting, not of farewell, and it was for someone he had never seen" (267). Unlike Archie and Wunsch, each frightened and enervated by Thea's womanhood, Harsanyi feels privileged to have witnessed her flowering and shared her passion—what he later calls "an open secret."

Of all her teachers, Thea feels closest to Harsanyi, but of all the men in her life, she wants Fred Ottenburg for a sweetheart: "Certainly she liked Fred better than anyone else in the world. There was Harsanyi, of course—but Harsanyi was always tired" (381). Fred's youth and personality enable him to respond to Thea and her voice in a more open, socially acceptable way even though his secret marriage prevents him from publicly acknowledging his love for her. Like Archie, Wunsch, and Harsanyi, Fred feels a "natural" attraction to Thea because she represents the wholeness that he desperately craves but finds lacking in a patriarchal society whose survival depends on separation, not integration, on reason divorced from desire. Unlike the other men, however, Fred feels so uncomfortable with such notions that he is "always running away" (334) from his work in the Ottenberg brewing business to gratify the secret self that finds expression in his relationship with his mother, his love for sports, parties, and music,

and his affair with Thea. A sensuous man, Fred lives for the moment; Thea likes him because "with Fred she was never becalmed. There was always life in the air, always something coming or going, a rhythm of feeling and action—stronger than the natural accord of youth" (392). Fred, in turn, enjoys Thea's vivacity, "brilliancy of motion," and "direction." Finally, Cather shows a man who does not find Thea's "fierceful nature" threatening, a man secure enough with himself and his own sexuality to welcome the engulfment which to others means loss of control. Although already married, Fred convinces himself that he is the best match for Thea because he will not hold her back to satisfy his own ego or any conventional notions of masculinity:

> He meant to help her, and he could not think of another man who would . . . The clever ones were selfish, the kindly ones were stupid. 'Damn it, if she's going to fall in love with somebody, it had better be me than any of the others—of the sort she'd find. Get her tied up with some conceited ass who'd try to make her over, train her like a puppy!'
>
> (423)

Challenging the idea that a woman must follow the script of a sexist society, Fred later tells Thea, "'You will never sit alone with a pacifier and a novel. You won't subsist on what the old ladies have put into the bottle for you. You will always break through into the realities. That was the first thing that Harsanyi found out about you; that you couldn't be kept on the outside'" (444). Fred wants to be on the inside with Thea; he confides to her, "'I've had a lot of sweethearts, but I've never been so much—engrossed before'" (403). Torn between his social obligation to an estranged wife (he desperately wants a divorce, but she promises a disastrous scandal) and his desire to complete himself by merging with Thea, Fred reveals his secret marriage but doesn't disengage because "nobody could look into her face and draw back, nobody who had any courage" (425). In the Epilogue, we learn that Thea has married Fred after all—not surprising considering Fred's intuitive understanding of and respect for Thea's ambition, independence, and "natural rhythm"—although Cather never explains how Fred was able to free himself from his wife. Because Fred knows that his existence depends not on his ability to control nature or deny his feelings of dependency but on whether he can construct his identity in relation rather than in opposition to others, he represents Cather's alternative to patriarchy's definition of masculinity.

In her article on Katherine Mansfield, Cather remarks that in his mind each member of a social unit constantly escapes, runs away, and tries "to break the net which circumstances and his own affections have woven about him" (136). The male characters in *The Song of the Lark* demonstrate the devastating effects the patriarchal net of repression and denial can have on the individual, perhaps offering their creator a chance to explore her own sexuality while hiding behind the role of novelist.

Notes

1. Much criticism of *The Song of the Lark* focuses on the feminist aspect of the novel. Besides Foster, Huf, and Peck, see Susan Rosowski, "The Pattern of Willa Cather's Novels," *Western American Literature* 15 (1981): 243-63; Linda Panill, "Willa Cather's Artist-Heroines," *Women's Studies* 11 (1984): 223-30; Susan Leonardi, "To Have a Voice: The Politics of the Diva," *Perspectives on Contemporary Literature* 13 (1987): 65-72; and Susan Hallgarth, "The Woman Who Would Be Artist in *The Song of the Lark* and *Lucy Gayheart*," *Willa Cather: Family, Community, and History*, ed. John J. Murphy (Provo: Brigham Young, 1990) 169-173.

2. Besides Seidler's study of masculinity, see Harry Brod, "Pornography and the Alienation of Male Sexuality," *Men, Masculinities & Social Theory*, ed. Jeff Hearn & David Morgan, (London: Unwin Hyman, 1990) 124-39.

3. My study is necessarily limited to only four men in an attempt to provide an in-depth analysis of each rather than a general survey of every male character in the novel. Strong arguments could be made, however, for including Spanish Johnny, Ray Kennedy, Peter Kronborg, and Oliver Landry as males whose relationships with the heroine demonstrate Cather's challenge to traditional definitions of masculinity.

4. Marilyn Berg Callander devotes the first chapter of her book *Willa Cather and the Fairy Tale* (Ann Arbor: UMI Research P, 1989) 7-18, to *The Song of the Lark*. Recognizing Archie's sexual attraction to Thea, Callander labels the older man one of Thea's various "father/Kings" and discusses his and Thea's relationship in terms of the Oedipal complex.

Works Cited

Cather Willa, "Katherine Mansfield." *Not Under forty*. New York: Knopf, 1953. 123-147.

———. *The Song of the Lark*. London: Virago, 1982.

Foster, Shirley. "The Open Cage: Freedom, Marriage, and the Heroine in Early Twentieth-Century American Women's Novels." *Women's Writing: A Challenge to Theory*. Ed. Moire Monteith. Great Britain: Harvester P, 1986. 154-74.

Giannone, Richard. *Music in Willa Cather's fiction*. Lincoln: U of Nebraska P, 1968.

Griffin, Susan. *Pornography and silence: Culture's Revenge Against Nature*. New York: Harper & Row, 1981.

Huf, Linda. *A Portrait of the Artist as a Young Woman*. New York: Frederick Unger, 1983. 81-102.

Mulvey, Laura. "Vision Pleasure and Narrative Cinema." *Feminism and Film Theory*. Ed. Constance Penley. New York: Routledge, Chapman, and Hall, 1988. 57-68.

O'Brien, Sharon. *Willa Cather: The Emerging Voice*. Oxford: Oxford UP, 1987.

Peck, Demaree. "Thea Kronborg's 'Song of Myself': The Artist's Imaginative Inheritance in *The Song of the Lark*." *Western American Literature* 26 (1991): 21-38.

Rosowski, Susan J. "Writing Against Silences: Female Adolescent Development in the Novels of Willa Cather." *Studies in the Novel* 21 (1989): 60-77.

Seidler, Victor J. "Reason, Desire, and Male Sexuality." *The Cultural Construction of Sexuality*. Ed. Pat Caplan. London: Tavistock Publications, 1987. 82-112.

Sergeant, Elizabeth Shepley. *Willa Cather: A Memoir*. Philadelphia: J. B. Lippincott, 1953.

Shepard, John. *Music as Social Text*. Cambridge: Polity P, 1991.

Slote, Bernice. *The Kingdom of Art: Willa Cather's First Principles and Critical Statements 1893-1896*. Lincoln: U of Nebraska P, 1966.

My Ántonia

DEBORAH G. LAMBERT (ESSAY DATE JANUARY 1982)

SOURCE: Lambert, Deborah G. "The Defeat of a Hero: Autonomy and Sexuality in *My Ántonia*." *American Literature* 53, no. 4 (January 1982): 676-90.

In the following essay, Lambert asserts a lack of character development in Cather's My Ántonia *attributable to the author's personal distress about her sexuality at the time she wrote the novel.*

My Ántonia (1918), Willa Cather's celebration of the American frontier experience, is marred by many strange flaws and omissions. It is, for instance, difficult to determine who is the novel's central character. If it is Ántonia, as we might reasonably assume, why does she entirely disappear for two of the novel's five books? If, on the other hand, we decide that Jim Burden, the narrator, is the central figure, we find that the novel explores neither his consciousness nor his development. Similarly, although the narrator overtly claims that the relationship between Ántonia and Jim is the heart of the matter, their friendship actually fades soon after childhood: between these two characters there is only, as E. K. Brown said, "an emptiness where the strongest emotion might have been expected to gather."[1] Other inconsistencies and contradictions pervade the text—Cather's ambivalent treatment of Lena Lingard and Tiny Soderball, for example—and all are in some way related to sex roles and to sexuality.

This emphasis is not surprising: as a writer who was also a woman, Willa Cather faced the difficulties that confronted, and still do confront, accomplished and ambitious women. As a professional writer, Cather began, after a certain point in her career, to see the world and other women, including her own female characters, from a male point of view. Further, Cather was a lesbian who could not, or did not, acknowledge her homosexuality and who, in her fiction, transformed her emotional life and experiences into acceptable, heterosexual forms and guises. In her society it was difficult to be a woman and achieve professionally, and she could certainly not be a woman who loved women; she responded by denying, on the one hand, her womanhood and, on the other, her lesbianism. These painful denials are manifest in her fiction. After certain early work, in which she created strong and achieving women, like herself, she abandoned her female characters to the most conventional and traditional roles; analogously, she began to deny or distort the sexuality of her principal characters. *My Ántonia,* written at a time of great stress in her life, is a crucial and revealing work, for in it we can discern the consequences of Cather's dilemma as a lesbian writer in a patriarchal society.

I

Many, if not all, achieving women face the conflict between the traditional idea of what it is to be a woman and what it is to achieve. Achievement in most fields has been reserved for males; passivity—lack of assertiveness and energy, and consequent loss of possibility of achievement—has been traditionally female. When the unusual girl, or woman, rebels, and overcomes the limitations imposed on women, she suffers from the anxiety produced by conflict. Although such a woman is, and knows she is sexually female, in her professional life she is neither female nor male. Finding herself in no-woman's land, she avoids additional anxiety by not identifying herself professionally as a woman or with other women. Carolyn Heilbrun, who diagnoses and prescribes for a variety of women's dilemmas, writes: "Sensing within themselves, as girls, a longing for accomplishment, they have, at great cost, with great pain, become honorary men, adopting at the same time, the general male attitude towards women."[2]

From childhood, Willa Cather was determined to achieve and she perceived, correctly, that achieving in the world was a male prerogative. When she decided as a child to become a doctor, she also began to sign herself "William Cather, MD," or "Willie Cather, MD," and she pursued

her vocation seriously, making house calls with two Red Cloud physicians, and on one occasion giving chloroform while one of them amputated a boy's leg. She also demonstrated her clear understanding of nineteenth-century sex roles and her preference for "male" activities when she entered in a friend's album two pages of "The Opinion, Tastes and Fancies of Wm. Cather, MD." In a list that might have been completed by Tom Sawyer, she cites "slicing toads" as a favorite summer occupation; doing fancy work as "real misery"; amputating limbs as "perfect happiness"; and dressing in skirts as "the greatest folly of the Nineteenth Century."[3] At college in Lincoln, her appearance in boyishly short hair and starched shirts rather than the customary frilly blouses—like her desire to play only male roles in college dramatic productions—continued to reflect her "male" ambition. James Woodress, Cather's biographer, speaks of a "strong masculine element" in her personality, a phrase that may obscure what she saw clearly from childhood: that womanhood prohibited the achievement she passionately sought.[4]

After some measure of professional success, Cather began to identify with her male professional peers, rather than with women. Her review of Kate Chopin's novel *The Awakening* (1899) is a poignant example of the troubling consequences of this identification. First, Cather describes Edna Pontellier's struggle towards identity as "trite and sordid" and then, comparing Edna to Emma Bovary, adds contemptuously that Edna and Emma "belong to a class, not large, but forever clamoring in our ears, that demands more out of life than God put into it." In a final irony, Cather writes of Chopin that "an author's choice of themes is frequently as inexplicable as his choice of a wife." Like Flaubert and other male authors with whom she identifies, Cather fails to understand, let alone view sympathetically, the anguish that Chopin brilliantly portrays in Edna's life and death.[5]

Nevertheless, in two novels written before *My Ántonia,* she accomplished what few women authors have: the creation of strong, even heroic, women as protagonists. Cather succeeded in this because she could imagine women achieving identity and defining their own purposes. The woman author, whose struggle toward selfhood and achievement is marked by painful conflict, rarely reproduces her struggle in fiction, perhaps finding its recreation too anxiety-producing, or perhaps simply not being able to imagine the forms that a woman's initiation might take. George Eliot and Edith Wharton, to mention only two familiar examples, never created women characters who possess their own intelligence, ambition, or autonomy. Characteristically, women authors transpose their own strivings to their male characters and portray women in conventional roles. (In this case, the roles ascribed to women in fiction are the same as those ascribed to them in society.) The occasional male author—E. M. Forster, James, and Hawthorne are examples—will create an independent, even heroic, female character, perhaps because male progress toward identity, demanded and supported by society, is generally a less anxious process.

Alexandra Bergson in *O Pioneers!* (1913) and Thea Kronberg in *The Song of the Lark* (1915) are female heroes, women not primarily defined by relationship to men, or children, but by commitment to their own destinies and to their own sense of themselves. Alexandra inherits her father's farm lands and grandfather's intelligence:

although her father has two grown sons, he chooses Alexandra to continue his work, because she is the one best-suited by nature to do so. Developing Nebraska farmland becomes Alexandra's mission, and she devotes herself to it unstintingly. She postpones marriage until she is nearly forty years old, and then marries Carl, the gentle and financially unsuccessful friend of her childhood. Ultimately, Alexandra has success, wealthy independence, and a marriage which, unlike passionate unions in Cather's fiction, will be satisfying rather than dangerous. In this portrait of Alexandra, Cather provides a paradigm of the autonomous woman, even while she acknowledges, through the images of Alexandra's fantasy lover, the temptations of self-abnegation and passivity.

Thea Kronberg dedicates herself to music, and her talent defines and directs her life. Born into a large frontier family, she clear-sightedly pursues her goals, selecting as friends those few who support her aspirations. Subordinating personal life to the professional, Thea, like Alexandra, marries late in life, after she has achieved success; and her husband, too, recognizes and accepts her special mission. There is never a question of wooing either of these women away from their destinies to the conventional life of women. Marriage, coming later in life, after identity and achievement, is no threat to the self; moreover, Cather provides her heroes with sensitive, even androgynous, males who are supportive of female ambition. But Alexandra and Thea are unusual, imaginative creations primarily because they embody autonomy and achievement. In these books, Cather does not transpose her struggle for success to male characters, as women authors often have, but instead risks the creation of unusual female protagonists.

What Cather achieved in these two early novels she no longer achieved in her later works. Indeed she stopped portraying strong and successful women and began to depict patriarchal institutions and predominantly male characters. Although she wrote ten more novels, in none of them do we find women like Alexandra and Thea. *Death Comes for the Archbishop* (1927) and *Shadows on the Rock* (1931) are Cather's best-known late novels, and in the former there are virtually no women, while in the latter, women are relegated to minor and entirely traditional roles. Cather's movement toward the past in these novels—toward authority, permanence, and Rome—is also a movement into a world dominated by patriarchy. The writer who could envision an Alexandra and a Thea came to be a celebrant of male activity and institutions.[6]

In this striking transformation, *My Ántonia* is the transitional novel. Given the profound anxieties that beset women authors when they recreate their search for selfhood in female characters, it is not surprising that Cather turned to a male narrative point of view. She rationalized that the omniscient point of view, which she had used in both *O Pioneers!* and *The Song of the Lark,* was not appropriate for her subject matter and continued to ignore the advice of Sarah Orne Jewett, who told her that when a woman tried to write from a man's point of view, she inevitably falsified.[7] Adopting the male persona was, for Cather, as it has been for many other writers, a way out of facing great anxiety. Moreover, it is natural to see the world, and women, from the dominant perspective, when that is what the world reflects and literature records. Thus, in *My Ántonia,* for the first time in her mature work, Cather adopts a male persona, and that change marks her transition to fiction increasingly conventional in its depiction of human experience.[8]

II

Cather was not only a woman struggling with the dilemma of the achieving woman: she was also a lesbian, and that, too, affected the fiction that she wrote. Early in life she had decided never to marry, and in reviews and letters she repeatedly stressed that marriage and the life of the artist were utterly incompatible. She seems always to have loved women: indeed her only passionate and enduring relationships were with women. Her first, and probably greatest, love was Isabel Mc-Clung, whom she met in Pittsburgh in 1898. Moving into the McClung family home, Cather lived there for five years and worked in a small room in the attic. There she wrote most of *April Twilights* (1903), her book of poems; *The Troll Garden* (1905), a short story collection; and major parts of *O Pioneers!* and *The Song of the Lark.* Her affair with McClung continued until 1916, when Mc-Clung suddenly announced that she was going to marry the violinist Jan Hambourg. At this point, Cather's world seems to have collapsed. She was first stunned and then deeply depressed. Her loss of McClung seems to have been the most painful event of her life, and it was six months before she could bring herself to see the couple. After a long visit to Red Cloud, and a shorter one to New Hampshire, she eventually returned to New York.[9] There she took up her life with Edith Lewis, with whom she was to live for forty years in a relation-ship less passionate than that with McClung. But clearly, throughout her life, Cather's deepest affections were given to women. During the troubled period when she felt abandoned by McClung, Cather was writing *My Ántonia*: both her sense of loss and the need to conceal her passion are evident in the text.

Cather never adequately dealt with her homosexuality in her fiction. In two early novels, the question of sexuality is peripheral: *Alexander's Bridge* (1912) and *The Song of the Lark* concern the integration of identity, and the expression of sexuality is limited and unobtrusive. Yet Cather began to approach the issue of homosexuality obliquely in subsequent novels. Many, although not all, of the later novels include homosexual relationships concealed in heterosexual guises. Joanna Russ points out that these disguised relationships are characterized by an irrational, hopeless quality and by the fact that the male member of the couple, who is also the central consciousness of the novel, is unconvincingly male—is, in fact, female and a lesbian.[10] The relationships of Claude and Enid in *One of Ours* (1922) and Niel and Marian Forrester in *A Lost Lady* (1923) are cases in point. In *O Pioneers!,* the novel which preceded *My Ántonia,* the love story of Alexandra's brother Emil and Marie, is also such a transposed relationship: to consider its treatment is to notice, from another perspective, the significant changes that occurred in Cather's writing at the time of *My Ántonia.*[11]

In the subplot of Emil and Marie's love, which unexpectedly dominates the second half of *O Pioneers!,* Cather implies the immense dangers of homosexual love. The deaths of Emil and Marie at the moment of sexual consummation suggest more than a prohibition against adultery: their story expresses both a fantasy of sexual fulfillment and the certainty that death is the retribution for this sort of passion. Seeing the story of Emil and Marie in this way, as the disguised expression of another kind of passion, becomes increasingly plausible when one examines Emil's character and behavior and observes that he is male in name only; moreover, it offers a convincing explanation for the sudden and shocking intrusion of violence in this otherwise uniformly elegiac novel. But what is most important here is that Alexandra, Cather's hero, is not destroyed by the consequences of Emil's passion; instead, passion vicariously satisfied, Alexandra retreats to the safety of heterosexual marriage. Thus the fantasy of homosexuality, and the fear of it, are encapsulated and controlled, only slightly distorting the narrative structure. Three years later, Cather's fear is pervasive and dominates the development of *My Ántonia,* so that the narrative structure itself becomes a defense against erotic expression.

The original of Ántonia was Annie Sadilek Pavelka, a Bohemian woman whom Cather had loved and admired from childhood, and with whom she maintained a lifelong, affectionate friendship. In 1921, after completion of the novel, Cather wrote of her feeling for Annie and her decision to use the male point of view:

> Of the people who interested me most as a child was the Bohemian hired girl of one of our neighbors, who was so good to me. . . . Annie fascinated me and I always had it in mind to write a story about her. . . . Finally, I concluded that I would write from the point of view of the detached observer, because that was what I had always been. Then I noticed that much of what I knew about Annie came from the talks I had with young men. She had a fascination for them, and they used to be with her whenever they could. They had to manage it on the sly, because she was only a hired girl. But they respected her, and she meant a good deal to some of them. So I decided to make my observer a young man.[12]

Here Cather suggests the long genesis of this tale and, significantly, her own replication of the "male" response to Annie, reflected in the language of the passage: "Annie fascinated me"/"She had a fascination for them." The fascination here seems to imply not only a romantic and sexual attraction, but also horror at the attraction. Cather suggests that the young men's response to Ántonia is ambivalent because Annie is forbidden; she is a hired girl, with all of that phrase's various suggestions, and so they see her "on the sly." For Cather that fascination is more complex. Identifying with the young men in their forbidden response to Annie, her impulse is that of the lesbian. Yet, when she wrote the novel and transposed to Jim her own strong attraction to Annie/Ántonia, she also transposed her restrictions on its erotic content. Although she adopts the male persona, she cannot allow him full expression of her feelings. Thus, what would seem to be Jim's legitimate response to Ántonia is prohibited and omitted: its homosexual threat is, evidently, too great, and so we find at the heart of the novel that emptiness noted by Brown.

The avoidance of sexuality (which does not extend beyond the Jim-Ántonia relationship, however) must be seen in connection with McClung's desertion of Cather, which occurred after she had composed the first two or three chapters of *My Ántonia.* During this time of grieving, she seemed not to trust herself to write of her own experience of love and sex. For the Cather persona and the beloved woman are not only separated: both are actually denied sexuality, although sexuality arises in distorted, grotesque forms throughout the novel.

During the writing of *My Ántonia,* Cather's grief coincided with the already great burden of anxiety of the woman who is a writer. After this time, her heroic stance in her fiction could not continue, and she abandons the creation of strong fictional women. In *My Ántonia* she denies Jim's erotic impulses and Ántonia's sexuality as well; and she retreats into the safety of convention by ensconcing Ántonia in marriage and rendering her apotheosis as earth mother. She abandons Ántonia's selfhood along with her sexuality: as Mrs. Cuzak, Ántonia is "a battered woman," and a "rich mine of life, like the founders of early races."[13] Interestingly, critics have recognized the absence of sexuality in Jim, although not in Ántonia, and focus their analyses on the male in the case, as though the novel had been written about a male character by a male author—or, as if the male experience were always central.

The most complex and instructive of the psychological analyses of Jim is by Blanche Gelfant, who sees Jim as a young man whose adolescence "confronts him with the possibility of danger in women."[14] He cannot accept the "nexus of love and death," and so retreats to perpetual boyhood. Noting many of the novel's ambiguous elements, Gelfant assumes that male fragility and male fear of womanhood is the crux of the problem. In her view, Jim is the protagonist and Ántonia is his guide: she is responsible for his failed initiation and, later, for his sexual humiliation and confusion.[15] Gelfant's analysis assumes traditional sex roles as normative: Jim's experience is central and Ántonia's is the subordinate, supporting role in his adventure. Yet, to understand the ambiguity in this, and perhaps in other texts by women writers, requires the reversal of such assumptions. If we assume the centrality of Ántonia and her development in the novel, we can observe the stages by which Cather reduces her to an utterly conventional and asexual character.

III

In childhood, Ántonia is established as the novel's center of energy and vitality. As a girl she is "bright as a new dollar" (p. 4) with skin "a glow of rich, dark colour" and hair that is "curly and wild-looking" (p. 23). She is always in motion: holding out a hand to Jim as she runs up a hill, chattering in Czech and broken English, asking rapid questions, struggling to become at home in a new environment. Wanting to learn everything, Ántonia also has "opinions about everything" (p. 30). Never indolent like Lena Lingard, or passive like her sister Yulka, or stolid like the Bohemian girls, Ántonia is "breathless and excited" (p. 35), generous, interested, and affectionate. By the end of her childhood, however, intimations of her future social roles appear.

When Ántonia reaches puberty, Cather carefully establishes her subordinate status in relation to three males, and these relationships make an interesting comparison with Alexandra's and Thea's. First, Ántonia's brutal brother, Ambrosch, is established as the head of the house and the "important person in the family" (p. 90). Then Jim records his need to relegate Ántonia to secondary status and receive deference, since "I was a boy and she was a girl" (p. 43), and in the farcical, pseudo-sexual snake-killing episode, he believes he accomplishes his goal. In fact, he and Ántonia enact a nearly parodic ritual of male and female behavior: in his fear, he turns on her with anger; she cries and apologizes for her screams, despite the fact that they may have saved his life; and she ultimately placates him with flattery. Forced to leave school, she soon relinquishes all personal goals in favor of serving others. No longer resentful or competitive, she is "fairly panting with eagerness to please" (p. 155) young Charley Harling, the son of her employers: "She loved to put up lunches for him when he went hunting, to mend his ball-gloves and sew buttons on his shooting coat, baked the kind of nut-cake he liked, and fed his setter dog when he was away on trips with his father" (p. 155). Cather's protagonist has been reduced to secondary status, as Alexandra and Thea were not: having challenged our expectations in earlier works, Cather retreats in this novel to the depiction of stereotypical patterns.

The second book of **My Ántonia,** with its insinuative title "The Hired Girls," dramatizes the emergence of Ántonia's intense sexuality and its catastrophic effects on her world. Now a beautiful adolescent woman, Ántonia is "lovely to see, with her eyes shining and her lips always a little parted when she danced. That constant dark colour in her cheeks never changed" (p. 223). Like flies the men begin to circle around her—the iceman, the delivery boys, the young farmers from the divide; and her employer, Mr. Harling, a demanding, intimidating, patriarch insists that she give up the dances where she attracts so much attention. When she refuses, he banishes her from his family. Next becoming the object of her new employ-er's lust, Ántonia loses Jim's affection and, by the end of the summer, has embarked on a disastrous affair with the railroad conductor, Donovan. Ántonia's sexuality is so powerful, in Cather's portrayal, that it destroys her oldest and best friendships and thrusts her entirely out of the social world of the novel.

Jim's intense anger at Ántonia once again reveals his fear, this time a fear of her sexuality that is almost horror. When Cutter attempts to rape her, Jim, the actual victim of the assault, returns battered to his grandmother's house. He then blames Ántonia and her sexuality for Cutter's lust, and recoils from her: "I heard Ántonia sobbing outside my door, but I asked grandmother to send her away. I felt I never wanted to see her again. I hated her almost as much as I hated Cutter. She had let me in for all this disgustingness" (p. 250). This eruption of sexuality marks the climax, almost the end, of the friendship between Ántonia and Jim, and after this, Ántonia is virtually banished from the novel.

At this point, Cather, evidently retreating from the sexual issue, broadens the novel's thematic focus. Jim and Ántonia do not meet again for two years, and all of Book III is devoted to Jim's frivolous, romanticized affair with Lena Lingard, with which he and the reader are diverted. Moreover, the events of Ántonia's life—her affair with Donovan, her pregnancy, her return home, the birth of her daughter—are kept at great narrative distance. Two years after the fact, a neighbor describes these events to Jim as she has seen them, or read about them in letters. Yet, as though banishing Ántonia and distracting Jim were not sufficient, her sexuality is diminished and then, finally, destroyed. After a punitive pregnancy and the requisite abandonment by her lover, she never again appears in sexual bloom. The metaphoric comparisons that surround her become sexually neutral, at best. In one example her neck is compared to "the bole of a tree" (p. 122), and her beauty is cloaked: "After the winter began she wore a man's long overcoat and boots and a man's felt hat with a wide brim" (p. 316). Her father's clothes, like Mr. Harling's ultimatum, seem well designed to keep Ántonia's sexuality under wraps.

After a two-year separation, during which Ántonia returns to her brother's farm, bears her child, and takes up her life of field work, Jim and Ántonia meet briefly. Dream-like and remote, their meeting is replete with nostalgia not readily accounted for by events; as Jim says, "We met like people in the old song, in silence, if not in tears" (p. 319). Inappropriately, though in a speech of great feeling, Ántonia compares her feeling for Jim to her memory of her father, who is lost to her for reasons that the text does provide:

> "... you are going away from us for good. ... But that don't mean I'll lose you. Look at my papa here, he's been dead all these years, and yet he is more real to me than almost anybody else. He never goes out of my life."
>
> (p. 320)

Jim's response expresses similar nostalgia and an amorphous yearning:

> "... since I've been away, I think of you more often than of anyone else in this part of the world. I'd have liked to have you for a sweetheart, or a wife, or my mother, or my grandmother, or my sister—anything that a woman can be to a man. ... You really are a part of me."
>
> (p. 321)

The seductive note of sentiment may blind us as readers to the fact that Jim might offer to marry Ántonia and instead abandons her to a life of hardship on her brother's farm with an empty, and ultimately broken promise to return soon. Cather forcibly separates Jim and Ántonia because of no logic given in the text; we have to assume that her own emotional dilemma affected the narrative and to look for the reasons within Cather herself.

Following this encounter is a twenty-year hiatus: when Jim and Ántonia finally meet again, the tensions that have lain behind the novel are resolved. Ántonia, now devoid of sexual appeal, no longer presents any threat. In addition, she has been reduced to a figure of the greatest conventionality: she has become the stereotypical earth mother. Bearing no resemblance to Cather's early female heroes, she is honored by Jim and celebrated by Cather as the mother of sons. By the novel's conclusion, Cather has capitulated to a version of that syndrome in which the unusual, achieving woman recommends to other women as their privilege and destiny that which she herself avoided. While recognizing the conflict that issues in such self-betrayal, one also notes the irony of Cather's glorification of Ántonia.

Autonomy and unconventional destiny are available only to the subordinate characters, Lena Lingard and Tiny Soderball, two of the hired girls. Lena, having seen too much of marriage, childbearing and poverty, has established a successful dress-making business and, despite her sensuous beauty, refrained from marriage. Her companion, Tiny, made her fortune in the Klondike before settling down in San Francisco. They lived in a mutually beneficial, supportive relationship: "Tiny audits Lena's accounts occasionally and invests her money for her; and Lena, apparently, takes care that Tiny doesn't grow too miserly," Jim tells us (p. 328). Both Lena and Tiny are independent and unconventional; Lena particularly understands and values the single self. In a revealing detail, she instructs her brother to buy handkerchiefs for their mother with an embroidered "B" for her given name, "Berthe," rather than with an "M" for mother. Lena, who describes marriage as "being under somebody's thumb" (p. 229), says, "It will please her for you to think about her name. Nobody ever calls her by it now" (p. 172). Although relegated to subordinate roles, these women are initially presented favorably; but, by the end of the novel, Cather simultaneously praises Ántonia's role as mother and demeans the value of their independent lives.

In her concluding gesture, Cather offers a final obeisance to convention. Her description of Lena and Tiny undercuts their achievement and portrays them as stereotypical "old maids" who have paid for their refusal of their "natural" function. Thus, Tiny has become a "thin, hard-faced woman, very well dressed, very reserved" (p. 301) and something of a miser: she says "frankly that nothing interested her much now but making money" (p. 301). Moreover, Tiny has suffered the "mutilation" of her "pretty little feet" (p. 301)—the price of her unnatural success in the Klondike. Though a little more subtly, Lena is similarly disfigured, physically distorted by her emotional aberration. Jim presents her as crude and overblown in a final snapshot: "A comely woman, a trifle too plump, in a hat a trifle too large ..." (p. 350). So it is, too, with their friendship. Jim's barren account stresses unpleasantness about clothes and money and implies that an edge of bitterness has appeared. So much for female independence and success; so much for bonds between women. Cather, through Jim's account of them, has denigrated Tiny and Lena and their considerable achievement. In betraying these characters, versions of herself, Cather reveals the extent of her self-division.

Equally revealing is the transformation of Ántonia in the concluding segment. Now forty-four, she is the mother of eleven children, a grandmother without her former beauty. So changed is she that Jim at first fails to recognize her. She is "grizzled," "flat-chested," "toothless," and "battered" (pp. 331-32), consumed by her life of childbearing and field work. The archetypal mother, Ántonia now signifies nourishment, protection, fertility, growth, and abundance: energy in service to the patriarchy, producing not "Ántonia's children" but "Cuzak's boys" (despite the fact that five of the children mentioned—Nina, Yulka, Martha, Anna, and Lucie—are girls). Like Cather's chapter title, Jim recognizes only the male children in his fantasy of eternal boyhood adventure, forgetting that in an earlier, less conventional and more androgynous world, his companion had been a girl—Ántonia herself.

Now Ántonia is glorified as a mythic source of life. Not only the progenitor of a large, vigorous family, she is also the source of the fertility and energy that have transformed the barren Nebraska prairie into a rich and fruitful garden. From her fruit cellar cavern pour forth into the light ten tumbling children—and the earth's abundance as well. In the images of this conclusion, she, no longer a woman, becomes Nature, a cornucopia, a "mine of life" (p. 353). Representing for Jim "immemorial human attitudes" which "fire the imagination" (p. 353), she becomes an idea and disappears under a symbolic weight, leaving for his friends and companions her highly individualized male children.

The conclusion of *My Ántonia* has usually been read as a triumph of the pioneer woman: Ántonia has achieved victory over her own hard early life and over the forces of Nature which made an immense struggle of farm life in Nebraska. But in fact, as we have seen, Cather and her narrator celebrate one of our most familiar stereotypes, one that distorts and reduces the lives of women. The image of the earth mother, with its implicit denial of Ántonia's individual identity, mystifies motherhood and nurturing while falsely promising fulfillment. Here Cather has found the means to glorify and dispose of Ántonia simultaneously, and she has done so in a way that is consonant with our stereotypical views and with her own psychological exigencies. The image of Ántonia that Cather gives us at the novel's conclusion is one that satisfies our national longings as well: coming to us from an age which gave us Mother's Day, it is hardly surprising that *My Ántonia* has lived on as a celebration of the pioneer woman's triumph and as a paean to the fecundity of the American woman and American land.

Cather's career illustrates the strain that women writers have endured and to which many besides Cather have succumbed. In order to create independent and heroic women, women who are like herself, the woman writer must avoid male identification, the likelihood of which is enhanced by being a writer who is unmarried, childless, and a lesbian. In the case of *My Ántonia*, Cather had

to contend not only with the anxiety of creating a strong woman character, but also with the fear of a homosexual attraction to Annie/Ántonia. The novel's defensive narrative structure, the absence of thematic and structural unity that readers have noted, these are the results of such anxieties. Yet, because it has been difficult for readers to recognize the betrayal of female independence and female sexuality in fiction—their absence is customary—it has also been difficult to penetrate the ambiguities of *My Ántonia*, a crucial novel in Cather's long writing career.

Notes

1. E. K. Brown and Leon Edel, *Willa Cather: A Critical Biography* (New York: Knopf, 1953), p. 203.

2. *Reinventing Womanhood* (New York: Norton, 1979), pp. 31-32. This essay grew out of a 1979 NEH Summer Seminar entitled "The Woman as Hero: Studies in Female Selfhood in British and American Fiction" directed by Professor Heilbrun.

3. Mildred Bennett, *The World of Willa Cather* (Lincoln: Univ. of Nebraska Press, 1961), pp. 110-14.

4. *Willa Cather: Her Life and Art* (Lincoln: Univ. of Nebraska Press, 1970), pp. 45, 53, 176.

5. Willa Cather, rev. of *The Awakening,* in Kate Chopin, *The Awakening,* ed. Margaret Culley (New York: Norton, 1976), pp. 153-54.

6. Two lesser late novels, *Lucy Gayheart* (1935) and *Sapphira and the Slave Girl* (1940), are devoid of heroes of either gender. Instead they present women, trapped in traditional situations, who are weak or cruel and who end in suicide and paralysis. *Lucy Gayheart* can usefully be compared to *The Song of the Lark,* since it is a weaker and conventional version of similar, if not identical, subject matter.

7. Woodress, *Willa Cather,* p. 132.

8. Heilbrun, *Reinventing Womanhood,* pp. 81-92.

9. Woodress, *Willa Cather,* pp. 172-74, 178-79.

10. "To Write 'Like a Woman': Transformations of Identity in Willa Cather," unpublished paper presented at 1979 MLA meeting; Judith Fetterley argues similarly in "*My Ántonia,* Jim Burden and the Dilemma of the Lesbian Writer," unpublished paper presented at SUNY Conference, "Twentieth Century Women Writers," June 1980 Professors Russ and Fetterley were both kind enough to send me copies of their essays.

11. Referring to McClung's marriage, Leon Edel wrote in *Literary Biography* (London: Rupert Hart Davis, 1957), p. 75, that "it is from this moment that the biographer can date a change in Willa Cather's works."

12. Bennett, *The World of Willa Cather,* pp. 46-47.

13. Willa Cather, *My Ántonia* (Boston: Houghton Mifflin, 1954), p. 4. All references to this edition, and page numbers will be supplied in parentheses in the text.

14. "The Forgotten Reaping Hook: Sex in *My Ántonia,*" *American Literature,* 43 (1971), 61-82.

15. Ibid., pp. 66, 64.

FURTHER READING

Bibliographies

Arnold, Marilyn. *Willa Cather: A Reference Guide* Boston, Mass.: G. K. Hall, 1986., 415 p.

Bibliography of Cather from the "Reference Guide to Literature" series.

Crane, Joan. *Willa Cather: A Bibliography.* Lincoln: University of Nebraska Press, 1982.

Lists secondary sources on Cather.

Lathrup, JoAnna. *Willa Cather: A Checklist of Her Published Writing.* Lincoln: University of Nebraska Press, 1975, 118 p.

Bibliography of Cather and her works.

Biographies

Bohlke, L. Brent and Sharon Hoover. *Willa Cather Remembered,* edited by Sharon Hoover. Lincoln: University of Nebraska Press, 2002, 217 p.

Provides reflections on Cather's life and career.

Lee, Hermione. *Willa Cather: A Life Saved Up.* London: Virago, 1989, 409 p.

Offers an alternative interpretation to what has traditionally been described as Cather's conservatism, examining her life, language, and landscapes.

Sergeant, Elizabeth Shepley. *Willa Cather: A Memoir.* Athens: Ohio University Press, 1992, 312 p.

Biography of Cather, written as a memoir by a friend and admirer.

Stout, Janis P. *Willa Cather: The Writer and Her World.* Charlottesville: University Press of Virginia, 2000, 381 p.

Examination of Cather within the context of her era.

Wagenknecht, Edward. *Willa Cather.* New York: Continuum, 1994, 203 p.

A respected biography accompanied by lengthy analysis of Cather's fiction.

Woodress, James. *Willa Cather: A Literary Life.* Lincoln: University of Nebraska Press, 1987, 583 p.

Utilizes Bernice Stole's noted collection of primary sources, alternating between details of Cather's life and examinations of her writing.

Criticism

Acocella, Joan. *Willa Cather and the Politics of Criticism.* Lincoln: University of Nebraska Press, 2000.

Explores how various branches of literary criticism, including feminist criticism, have at times claimed Cather as their own for political reasons.

Carlin, Deborah. *Cather, Canon, and the Politics of Reading.* Amherst: University of Massachusetts Press, 1992.

Argues that Cather's later works have been ignored due to her unconventional use of fictional forms and unsettling questions raised about sex, power, race, and class.

Gelfant, Blanche H. "The Forgotten Reaping-Hook: Sex in *My Ántonia.*" *American Literature* 43, no. 1 (March 1971): 60-82.

Views Jim Burden as an unreliable narrator in My Ántonia, *arguing for a new reading of the novel that includes discussion of Cather's ambivalence about sex.*

Kaye, Frances W. *Isolation and Masquerade: Willa Cather's Women.* New York: Peter Lang, 1993, 204 p.

Discusses Cather's portrayal of women's experiences with men as mostly negative.

Motley, Warren. "The Unfinished Self: Willa Cather's *O Pioneers!* and the Psychic Cost of a Woman's Success." *Women's Studies* 12 (1986): 149-65.

Argues that Alexandra must become isolated and "psychologically deadened" to achieve success as a female pioneer.

O'Brien, Sharon. "'The Thing Not Named': Willa Cather as a Lesbian Writer." *Signs* 9, no. 4 (1984): 576-99.

Examines evidence of Cather's lesbianism and explores how her need to hide her sexuality affected her fiction writing.

Rosowski, Susan J. "Willa Cather's Women." *Studies in American Fiction* 9, no. 2 (autumn 1981): 261-75.

Explores the ways in which Cather portrays her female characters not only as feminine archetypes, but also as individual women.

——. "Writing against Silences: Female Adolescent Development in the Novels of Willa Cather." *Studies in the Novel* 21, no. 1 (spring 1989): 60-77.

Provides discussion of Cather's treatment of adolescence as a uniquely female experience.

Wasserman, Loretta. "The Lovely Storm: Sexual Initiation in Two Early Willa Cather Novels." *Studies in the Novel* 14, no. 4 (winter 1982): 348-58.

Finds Cather to have been a reticent person but not, as many critics have suggested, devoid of sensual feeling and interest.

Women's Studies 11, no. 3 (1984): 219-372.

Issue devoted to the study of women in Cather's works.

OTHER SOURCES FROM GALE:

Additional coverage of Cather's life and career is contained in the following sources published by the Gale Group: *American Writers; American Writers: The Classics,* Vol. 1; *American Writers Retrospective Supplement,* Vol. 1; *Authors and Artists for Young Adults,* Vol. 24; *Beacham's Encyclopedia of Popular Fiction: Biography & Resources,* Vol. 1; *Concise Dictionary of American Literary Biography, 1865-1917; Contemporary Authors,* Vols. 104, 128; *Dictionary of Literary Biography,* Vols. 9, 54, 78, 256; *Dictionary of Literary Biography Documentary Series,* Vol. 1; *DISCovering Authors; DISCovering Authors: British Edition; DISCovering Authors: Canadian Edition; DISCovering Authors Modules: Most-studied and Novelists; DISCovering Authors 3.0; Encyclopedia of World Literature in the 20th Century,* Ed. 3; *Exploring Novels; Exploring Short Stories; Literature and Its Times,* Vol. 3; *Literature and Its Times Supplement,* Ed. 1; *Literature Resource Center; Major 20th-Century Writers,* Eds. 1, 2; *Modern American Women Writers; Novels for Students,* Vol. 2; *Reference Guide to American Literature,* Ed. 4; *Reference Guide to Short Fiction,* Ed. 2; *Short Stories for Students,* Vols. 2, 7, 16; *Short Story Criticism,* Vols. 2, 50; *Something about the Author,* Vol. 30; *Twayne's United States Authors; Twentieth-Century Literary Criticism,* Vols. 1, 11, 31, 99, 132; *20th Century Romance and Historical Writers; Twentieth-Century Western Writers,* Ed. 2; and *World Literature Criticism.*

SANDRA CISNEROS

(1954 -)

American short story writer, poet, and novelist.

Drawing heavily upon her childhood experiences and ethnic heritage as the daughter of a Mexican father and Mexican American mother, Cisneros addresses poverty, cultural suppression, self-identity, and gender roles in her fiction and poetry. She creates characters who are distinctly Latin and are often isolated from mainstream American culture yet equally unaccepted in traditional Latin American cultures. She is perhaps best known for her award-winning *The House on Mango Street* (1983), a collection of short fiction focusing on adolescent rites of passage and the treatment of women in Chicano communities. Cisneros illuminates the dual predicament of being a Chicana in a white-majority land and a woman in a patriarchal society. Through her poetry and fiction, she emphasizes the need for Chicana women to gain control of their bodies, language, and destinies.

BIOGRAPHICAL INFORMATION

Born in Chicago, Cisneros was the only daughter among seven children. Assuming that she would adopt a traditional female role, her brothers attempted to control her life; as a result, Cisneros has recalled feeling as if she had "seven fathers." Her father's homesickness for his native country and his devotion to his mother who still lived there caused the family to move often between the United States and Mexico. Consequently, Cisneros often felt homeless and displaced. She began to read extensively, finding comfort in such works as Virginia Lee Burton's *The Little House* and Lewis Carroll's *Alice's Adventures in Wonderland*. Cisneros earned a bachelor's degree from Loyola University in 1976. She had written poems and stories throughout her childhood and adolescence, but she did not find her literary voice until attending the University of Iowa's Writers Workshop in 1978, where she completed a master's degree in creative writing. During a discussion of French philosopher Gaston Bachelard's *The Poetics of Space* and his metaphor of a house as a realm of stability, she realized that her experiences as a Chicana woman were unique and outside the realm of dominant American culture. She observed that with "the metaphor of a house—a house, a house, it hit me. What did I know except third-floor flats. Surely my classmates knew nothing about that. That's precisely what I chose to write: about third-floor flats, and fear of rats, and drunk husbands sending rocks through windows, anything as far from the poetic as possible." Shortly after participating in the Iowa Workshop, Cisneros returned to Loyola, where she worked as a college recruiter and counselor for minority and disadvantaged students. Troubled by their problems and haunted by conflicts related to her own upbringing, she began writing seriously as a form of release. Cisneros has worked as an educator of both high school and college students, serving as a creative writing instructor at institutions including the University of California's Berkeley and Irvine campuses and the University of Michigan in Ann Arbor. Cisneros has received a number of awards, including National Endowment for the Arts fellowships in 1982 and 1988, the Before Columbus American Book Award in 1985 and the American Book Award for *The House on Mango Street,* and the 1992 PEN Center West Award for her short story collection *Woman Hollering Creek* (1991).

MAJOR WORKS

Cisneros's short story collections are praised for powerful dialogue, vivid characterizations, and well-crafted prose. Cisneros has stated that her objective in writing short fiction is to create "stories like poems, compact and lyrical and ending with a reverberation." While each story within her collections is complete in itself, it is bound to the others by common themes that focus on Latinas, divided cultural loyalties, feelings of alienation, sexual and cultural oppression, and degradation associated with poverty. *The House on Mango Street* features a semi-autobiographical Chicana adolescent named Esperanza who, humiliated by her family's poverty and dissatisfied with the repressive gender values of her culture, overcomes her situation by writing about her experiences: "I put it down on paper and then the ghost does not ache so much." Esperanza hopes her writing will someday enable her to leave Mango Street but vows to return for the women left behind—"the ones who cannot get out." *Woman Hollering Creek and Other Stories* features twenty-two narratives that involve numerous Mexican American characters living near San Antonio, Texas. This work follows a structural and thematic pattern similar to *The House on Mango Street,* but the female protagonists are more mature and complex. Ranging in length from a few paragraphs to several pages, the stories are first-person narratives of individuals who have been assimilated into American culture but feel a residual loyalty to Mexico. In "Never Marry a Mexican," for example, a young Latina expresses feelings of contempt for her white lover, fueled by her emerging sense of inadequacy and guilt over her inability to speak Spanish. In *Caramelo,* the protagonist, Celaya, struggles to find her identity as the only daughter among six brothers.

The narrative alternates between the present (Ceyala's time) and the past (her grandmother's era). By discovering her grandmother's history, Celaya learns many lessons about her own life and is able to take control of her own destiny. Although Cisneros is noted primarily for her fiction, her poetry has also garnered attention. In *Loose Woman: Poems* (1994), Cisneros offers a portrait of a fiercely proud, independent woman of Mexican heritage. In *My Wicked, Wicked Ways* (1987), a collection of sixty poems, Cisneros writes about her native Chicago, her travels in Europe, and, as reflected in the title, guilt over the conflict between her sexuality and her strict Catholic upbringing.

CRITICAL RECEPTION

Critics of Cisneros's short fiction point out that for several reasons she has yet to be fully embraced by the American literary community. They have argued that because Cisneros's prose combines elements of several genres, it diverges from generally accepted literary patterns in American fiction. Some commentators have also considered Cisneros's dialogue overly simplistic, especially in *The House on Mango Street,* where she often incorporates children's speech and games into her stories. Further, a number of critics have contended that her recurrent portrayal of male violence toward women presents an unflattering view of Hispanic life. Many commentators, however, have lauded these same elements in Cisneros's fiction, asserting that her distinctive literary and innovative techniques have been greatly underappreciated and that her concentration on cultural imperialism and women's issues has universal appeal. According to these critics, it is these aspects, in addition to her skillful prose, striking realism, and dynamic characterizations, that have established Cisneros as an emerging feminist literary figure. While Cisneros's poetry has received little recognition, her *House on Mango Street* and *Woman Hollering Creek* are lauded for illuminating the dual marginality faced by Chicana women: fighting for equal status with both whites and men.

PRINCIPAL WORKS

Bad Boys (poetry) 1980

The House on Mango Street (novel) 1983

The Rodrigo Poems (poetry) 1985

My Wicked, Wicked Ways (poetry) 1987

Woman Hollering Creek and Other Stories (short stories) 1991

Hairs: Pelitos (juvenilia) 1994

Loose Woman: Poems (poetry) 1994

Caramelo (novel) 2002

PRIMARY SOURCES

SANDRA CISNEROS (ESSAY DATE 1996)

SOURCE: Cisneros, Sandra. "Only Daughter." In *Beacon Book of Essays by Contemporary American Women,* edited by Wendy Martin, pp. 10-13. Boston, Mass.: Beacon Press, 1996.

In the following essay, Cisneros describes her struggles to attain self-worth in a patriarchal society and recounts the joy of gaining her father's respect and pride in her accomplishments as a writer.

Once, several years ago, when I was just starting out my writing career, I was asked to write my own contributor's note for an anthology I was part of. I wrote: "I am the only daughter in a family of six sons. *That* explains everything."

Well, I've thought about that ever since, and yes, it explains a lot to me, but for the reader's sake I should have written: "I am the only daughter in a *Mexican* family of six sons." Or even: "I am the only daughter of a Mexican father and a Mexican-American mother." Or: "I am the only daughter of a working-class family of nine." All of these had everything to do with who I am today.

I was/am the only daughter and *only* a daughter. Being an only daughter in a family of six sons forced me by circumstance to spend a lot of time by myself because my brothers felt it beneath them to play with a *girl* in public. But that aloneness, that loneliness, was good for a would-be writer—it allowed me time to think and think, to imagine, to read and prepare myself.

Being only a daughter for my father meant my destiny would lead me to become someone's wife. That's what he believed. But when I was in fifth grade and shared my plans for college with him, I was sure he understood. I remember my father saying, "*Que bueno, mi'ja,* that's good." That meant a lot to me, especially since my brothers thought the idea hilarious. What I didn't realize was that my father thought college was good for girls—for finding a husband. After four years in college and two more in graduate school, and still

no husband, my father shakes his head even now and says I wasted all that education.

In retrospect, I'm lucky my father believed daughters were meant for husbands. It meant it didn't matter if I majored in something silly like English. After all, I'd find a nice professional eventually, right? This allowed me the liberty to putter about embroidering my little poems and stories without my father interrupting with so much as a "What's that you're writing?"

But the truth is, I wanted him to interrupt. I wanted my father to understand what it was I was scribbling, to introduce me as "My only daughter, the writer." Not as "This is my only daughter. She teaches." *El maestra*—teacher. Not even *profesora.*

In a sense, everything I have ever written has been for him, to win his approval even though I know my father can't read English words, even though my father's only reading includes the brown-ink *Esto* sports magazines from Mexico City and the bloody *¡Alarma!* magazines that feature yet another sighting of *La Virgen de Guadalupe* on a tortilla or a wife's revenge on her philandering husband by bashing his skull in with a *molcajete* (a kitchen mortar made of volcanic rock). Or the *fotonovelas,* the little picture paperbacks with tragedy and trauma erupting from the characters' mouths in bubbles.

My father represents, then, the public majority. A public who is disinterested in reading, and yet one whom I am writing about and for, and privately trying to woo.

When we were growing up in Chicago, we moved a lot because of my father. He suffered periodic bouts of nostalgia. Then we'd have to let go our flat, store the furniture with mother's relatives, load the station wagon with baggage and bologna sandwiches, and head south. To Mexico City.

We came back, of course. To yet another Chicago flat, another Chicago neighborhood, another Catholic school. Each time, my father would seek out the parish priest in order to get a tuition break, and complain or boast: "I have seven sons."

He meant *siete hijos,* seven children, but he translated it as "sons." "I have seven sons." To anyone who would listen. The Sears Roebuck employee who sold us the washing machine. The short-order cook where my father ate his ham-and-eggs breakfasts. "I have seven sons." As if he deserved a medal from the state.

My papa. He didn't mean anything by that mistranslation, I'm sure. But somehow I could feel myself being erased. I'd tug my father's sleeve and whisper: "Not seven sons. Six! and *one daughter*."

When my oldest brother graduated from medical school, he fulfilled my father's dream that we study hard and use this—our heads, instead of this—our hands. Even now my father's hands are thick and yellow, stubbed by a history of hammer and nails and twine and coils and springs. "Use this," my father said, tapping his head, "and not this," showing us those hands. He always looked tired when he said it.

Wasn't college an investment? And hadn't I spent all those years in college? And if I didn't marry, what was it all for? Why would anyone go to college and then choose to be poor? Especially someone who had always been poor.

Last year, after ten years of writing professionally, the financial rewards started to trickle in. My second National Endowment for the Arts Fellowship. A guest professorship at the University of California, Berkeley. My book, which sold to a major New York publishing house.

At Christmas, I flew home to Chicago. The house was throbbing, same as always; hot *tamales* and sweet *tamales* hissing in my mother's pressure cooker, and everybody—my mother, six brothers, wives, babies, aunts, cousins—talking too loud and at the same time, like in a Fellini film, because that's just how we are.

I went upstairs to my father's room. One of my stories had just been translated into Spanish and published in an anthology of Chicano writing, and I wanted to show it to him. Ever since he recovered from a stroke two years ago, my father likes to spend his leisure hours horizontally. And that's how I found him, watching a Pedro Infante movie on Galavision and eating rice pudding.

There was a glass filmed with milk on the bedside table. There were several vials of pills and balled Kleenex. And on the floor, one black sock and a plastic urinal that I didn't want to look at but looked at anyway. Pedro Infante was about to burst into song, and my father was laughing.

I'm not sure if it was because my story was translated into Spanish, or because it was published in Mexico, or perhaps because the story dealt with Tepeyac, the *colonia* my father was raised in, but at any rate, my father punched the mute button on his remote control and read my story.

I sat on the bed next to my father and waited. He read it very slowly. As if he were reading each line over and over. He laughed at all the right places and read lines he liked out loud. He pointed and asked questions: "Is this So-and-so?" "Yes," I said. He kept reading.

When he was finally finished, after what seemed like hours, my father looked up and asked: "Where can we get more copies of this for the relatives?"

Of all the wonderful things that happened to me last year, that was the most wonderful.

GENERAL COMMENTARY

DEBORAH L. MADSEN (ESSAY DATE 2000)

SOURCE: Madsen, Deborah L. "Sandra Cisneros." In *Understanding Contemporary Chicana Literature*, edited by Matthew J. Bruccoli, pp. 105-34. Columbia: University of South Carolina Press, 2000.

In the following essay, Madsen explores Cisneros's dual marginality as a Latin female, examines her self-determination and control over the physical, sexual and social aspects of her life, and highlights the autobiographical elements in Cisneros's poetry and fiction.

In a 1990 interview Sandra Cisneros joked that after ten years of writing professionally she had finally earned enough money to buy a second-hand car.[1] Her struggle for recognition as a Chicana writer earned her critical and popular acclaim with the publication of *The House on Mango Street* (1984), the success of which was followed by *Woman Hollering Creek and Other Stories* (1991). Her poetry collection *My Wicked, Wicked Ways* was published by the Berkeley-based Chicana Third Woman Press in 1987, and the outrageous themes of these poems continued in the poems collected in *Loose Woman*, which appeared in 1994. Cisneros's work is characterized by the celebratory breaking of sexual taboos and trespassing across the restrictions that limit the lives and experiences of Chicanas. These themes of trespass, transgression, and joyful abandon feature prominently in her poetry. The narrative techniques of her fiction demonstrate daring technical innovations, especially in her bold experimentation with literary voice and her development of a hybrid form that weaves poetry into prose to create a dense and evocative linguistic texture of symbolism and imagery that is both technically and aesthetically accomplished.

Sandra Cisneros was born in the Puerto Rican district of Chicago on 20 December 1954. Her parents' mixed ethnic background (Spanish-speaking Mexican father and English-speaking Mexican American mother) is reflected in the cultural hybridity that is one of Cisneros's recurring themes. She is the third child and only daughter in a family of seven children, a condition that Cisneros has described as leaving her marginalized as a consequence of her gender.[2] During Cisneros's childhood her father's restless homesickness caused the family to move frequently between Chicago and her paternal grandparents' house in Mexico City, and always she lived in urban neighborhoods. Although her early years were spent in cramped urban apartments, Cisneros recalls her childhood as solitary. Cisneros ascribes to the loneliness of those formative years her impulse to create stories by re-creating in her imagination the dull routine of her life.

She graduated with a B.A. degree from Loyola University in 1976 and completed an M.F.A. in creative writing at the Iowa Writers' Workshop in 1978. It was at Iowa that Cisneros discovered, first, a sense of her own ethnic "otherness" and, second, the unique literary voice that characterizes both her poetry and her fiction. She describes her early writing as inferior imitations of the work of mainstream writers; in the discovery of her difference came a rejection of this attempt to join the American literary orthodoxy. The voice she discovered, the voice she had unconsciously suppressed, is the voice of the barrio.

An ongoing commitment to those who grow up in the barrio has led Cisneros to become involved as a teacher in educational projects designed to assist the urban underprivileged, such as the Latino Youth Alternative High School in Chicago. She has worked variously as a teacher, a counselor, a college recruiter, a poet-in-the-schools, and an arts administrator in order to support her writing. Cisneros has taught creative writing at the University of California at Berkeley, the University of California at Irvine, and the University of Michigan in Ann Arbor. She is the recipient of a National Endowment for the Arts Fellowship; the Before Columbus Foundation's American Book Award; a Lannan Foundation Literary Award; the PEN Center West Award for the best fiction of 1991; the Quality paperback Book Club New Voices Award; a MacArthur Foundation Fellowship; and the Frank Dobie Artists Fellowship, Austin, Texas. Sandra Cisneros moved to the Southwest in 1984; she now lives in San Antonio, Texas, and is currently working on a novel, *Caramelo.*

Cisneros describes writing as something she has done all her life from the time when, as a young girl, she began writing in spiral notebooks poems that only her mother read. Her first published book, **Bad Boys,** appeared as the Chicano Chapbook No. 8 (1980). Her novel *The House on Mango Street* was published by a small regional press in 1984 and the following year was awarded the Before Columbus Foundation's American Book Award. The novel draws heavily upon childhood memories and an unadorned childlike style of expression to depict life in the Chicano community. Issues of racial and sexual oppression, poverty, and violence are explored in a sequence of interconnected vignettes that together form a modified autobiographical structure. ***Woman Hollering Creek and Other Stories*** continues the exploration of ethnic identity within the patriarchal context of Chicano culture. The stories in this volume offer snapshots of Mexican American life: sights and smells recalled in childish memories, stories told by witches who see all of Chicano history from past to future, the hopes and aspirations of grandparents and grandchildren, friends and neighbors, Mexican movies, and "Merican" tourists. Her first volume of poetry, ***My Wicked, Wicked Ways,*** is described by Cherríe Moraga as "a kind of international graffiti, where the poet— bold and insistent—puts her mark on those travelled places on the map and in the heart."[3] ***Loose Woman*** similarly invokes the cultural and the emotional in an intoxicating sequence of outrageously confessional moments. Cisneros has also published essays on writing and her role as a writer, most notably the selections titled **"From a Writer's Notebook. Ghosts and Voices: Writing from Obsession"** and **"Notes to a Young(er) Writer,"** both of which appeared in the *Americas Review* (1987). Her books have been translated into ten languages.

In Cisneros's work the effort to negotiate a cross-cultural identity is complicated by the need to challenge the deeply rooted patriarchal values of both Mexican and American cultures. Cisneros writes, "There's always this balancing act, we've got to define what we think is fine for ourselves instead of what our culture says."[4] Chicana feminism has arisen largely from this need to contest the feminine stereotypes that define machismo, while at the same time identifying and working against the shared class and racial oppression that all Chicanos/as—men, women and children—experience. To adopt models of femininity that are thought of as Anglo is, as Cisneros describes, to be told you're a traitor to your culture. And it's a horrible life to live. We're always straddling two countries, and we're always living in that kind of schizophrenia that I call, being a Mexican woman living in an American society, but not belonging to either culture. In some sense we're not Mexican and in some sense we're not American.[5]

Patriarchal definitions of feminine subjectivity, some Anglo but mostly Mexican, affect all of Cisneros's characters by creating the medium in which they live. The protagonist of **The House on Mango Street**, the girl Esperanza, compares herself with her great-grandmother with whom she shares her name and the coincidence of being born in the Chinese year of the horse,

> which is supposed to be bad luck if you're born female—but I think this is a Chinese lie because the Chinese, like the Mexicans, don't like their women strong.[6]

This fiery ancestor, "a wild horse of a woman, so wild she wouldn't marry" (**Mango Street,** 11), is forcibly taken by Esperanza's great-grandfather, and her spirit broken, she lived out her days staring from her window. The narrator remarks, "I have inherited her name, but I don't want to inherit her place by the window" (11). This woman is the first of many Esperanza encounters who are broken in body and spirit by the patriarchal society that defines the terms by which they live.

The primary effect of these prescriptive definitions is the experience of the self as marginal, as failing to belong in the culture in which one lives. Cisneros challenges marginality but in subtle ways and using the weapons at her disposal as an artist: imagery, symbolism, forms of narrative connectivity that are at odds with rational, discursive logic. Like so many Chicana writers, Sandra Cisneros rejects the logic of the patriarchy in favor of more provisional, personal, emotional, and intuitive forms of narrative. She creates stories, not explanations or analyses or arguments. The stories that comprise **The House on Mango Street** are linked according to a loose and associative logic. In this way the fragmented structure of the text embodies a quest for freedom, a genuine liberation that resolves rather than escapes the conflicts faced by the Chicana subject. María Elena de Valdés describes how Cisneros's narrative technique relates to the theme of feminist resistance:

> The open-ended reflections are the narrator's search for an answer to the enigma: how can she be free of Mango Street and the house that is not hers and yet belong as she must to that house and that street. The open-ended entries come together only slowly as the tapestry takes shape, for each of

the closed figures are also threads of the larger background figure which is the narrator herself.[7]

The threads with which the story is then woven are the complex image patterns Cisneros gradually develops and the imagistic connections she builds among the vignettes. The first story, which describes the houses in which Esperanza has lived, ends with her father's promise that their cramped and shabby house is temporary. The next story, "Hairs," begins with a description of her father's hair and goes on to contrast it with her mother's. The contrast between mother and father is continued and generalized in the third story, "Boys and Girls," which ends with Esperanza's hope that she will one day have the best friend for whom she yearns. The fourth story concerns the meaning of Esperanza's name, "Hope." In this way Cisneros creates vignettes that are self-contained, autonomous, yet link together in an emotionally logical fashion and build to create a picture of life in the barrio, seen through the experiences of the young Esperanza and her developing consciousness of herself as an artist.

The stories collected in **Woman Hollering Creek** are organized according to a similar associative logic. The volume is divided into three named sections: "My Lucy Friend Who Smells Like Corn," "One Holy Night," and "There Was a Man, There Was a Woman." Each section shares a loosely defined theme: the experience of Chicano/a children in **"My Lucy Friend Who Smells Like Corn," "Eleven," "Salvador Early or Late," "Mexican Movies," "Barbie-Q," "Mericans,"** and **"Tepeyac"**; the betrayal of Chicana girl children in the stories **"One Holy Night"** and **"My Tocaya"**; and the limited choice of adult relationships available to women in patriarchal Chicano/a society in **"Woman Hollering Creek," "The Marlboro Man," "La Fabulosa: A Texas Operetta," "Remember the Alamo," "Never Marry a Mexican," "Bread," "Eyes of Zapata," "Anguiano Religious Articles Rosaries Statues . . . ," "Little Miracles, Kept Promises," "Los Boxers," "There Was a Man, There Was a Woman," "Tin Tan Tan,"** and **"Bien Pretty."** Though many of these stories depict the lives of individuals who are comprehensively defeated by the sheer burden of work, worry, and care they are required to bear, in some of them Cisneros creates characters who are able to subvert oppressive definitions of gender identity in favor of marginal, hybrid selves.

The story **"Never Marry a Mexican,"** for example, begins with the disappointment of the narrator's grandparents that their son should have married a United States-born Mexican—a woman who is neither white like an Anglo nor raised properly in the ways of Mexican femininity:

> what could be more ridiculous than a Mexican girl who couldn't even speak Spanish, who didn't know enough to set a separate plate for each course at dinner, nor how to fold cloth napkins, nor how to set the silverware.[8]

The lesson learned by the narrator is **"Never Marry a Mexican,"** which she generalizes into a determination never to marry. Instead she cultivates a hybrid identity, belonging to several socioeconomic classes and yet to none. She describes herself as "amphibious"—capable of surviving in radically different environments. And although she is United States-born, still the native idiom does not come naturally to her. She exclaims, ironically in the very idiom she denies, "I can't ever get the sayings right even though I was born in this country. We didn't say shit like that in our house" (73). This awareness of cross-cultural marginality extends even to the endearments used by her lover; he calls her Malinche, "my courtesan," the native woman taken by Cortés and mother of the hybrid Chicano race. But this woman, Cisneros's narrator, takes her own peculiar revenge upon her adulterous lover: in his wife's absence she plants around the house a trail of sticky sweets, in places only his wife will look—her makeup bag, her nail polish bottles, her diaphragm case. Then she seduces this faithless lover's son, and the significance of the story becomes clear as a confession to this son and an explanation of the relationship in which he has become involved. This vengeance is more than personal; it is revenge upon an Anglo man who believes he can **"Never Marry a Mexican."** This is vengeance sought on behalf of La Malinche for all her Chicana daughters who are good enough to seduce but never good enough to marry. This is vengeance on behalf of all the women who are led to believe that marriage is the only mechanism by which their lives may be validated and if they are not married then they themselves are somehow not valid.

The legacy of La Malinche is the fragmentary subjectivity commonly experienced by Chicanas: women who seek approval on both Anglo and Mexican terms, so that the unitary sense of self is inevitably sacrificed. The Chicana writer perhaps experiences this conflict most intensely:

> the Chicana has had to be a cultural schizophrenic in trying to please both the Chicano and Anglo publishers, not to mention pleasing the readers, who may neutralize her potential to create within her own framework of ideas.[9]

In these words Marcela Christine Lucero-Trujillo describes the experience of cross-cultural identity and alienation that is perhaps the single most common theme in ethnic women's writing. To lose one's sense of self in the effort to satisfy mutually antagonistic sets of cultural values is the danger negotiated by Cisneros's characters. The image of living under occupation, of living in an occupied territory or even of becoming occupied territory, describes the experience of both a woman under Chicano patriarchy and a Chicana under Anglo dominance. This accounts for Cisneros's use of the image of the window in several of the stories in **The House on Mango Street.** Women are depicted sitting by their windows, forbidden or afraid to enter the world represented by the street, literally and physically trapped in their imposed domesticity. Esperanza's friend Sally is beaten by her jealous husband if she so much as speaks to anyone in his absence; Rafaela's husband locks her in their apartment, so she communicates with the world solely through the window; Mamacita refuses to leave her building because she cannot speak English. Such women experience the world in a series of vignettes which permit no unifying structure. They live lives without narrative, without context, but representing a logic of oppression and cruelty too ugly to confront. In her fiction Cisneros tells of living with a double burden imposed by white women and by men of all colors. The complexities of gender, race, and class, which will not remain distinct but instead compound their oppressive effects, form the labyrinth that Cisneros seeks to map.

Fiction is used to expose the many lies that are told to children, especially girl children, in order to regulate their desires, ambitions, and aspirations. The narrator of the story **"One Holy Night"** tells her girl cousins who are curious to know "how it is to have a man": "It's a bad joke. When you find out you'll be sorry" (**Woman Hollering Creek,** 35). But these girl children seem to have no choice other than to "find out," eventually. The juxtaposition of the vignettes in **The House on Mango Street** dramatizes the attempts of the adolescent Esperanza to reconcile her childish naïveté with the realities of adult Chicana life. In the story **"Papa Who Wakes Up Tired in the Dark"** Esperanza makes an important distinction between her own father and other men as she struggles to reconcile her love for her father with the treatment she receives from other men and the patriarchal attitudes that inform their behavior toward her. In the preceding story, **"First Job,"** Es-

CISNEROS

FEMINISM IN LITERATURE: A GALE CRITICAL COMPANION, VOL. 5   259

peranza describes her first experience of sexual harassment, by a man old enough to be her father:

> he said it was his birthday and would I please give him a birthday kiss. I thought I would because he was so old and just as I was about to put my lips on his cheek, he grabs my face with both hands and kisses me hard on the mouth and doesn't let go.
>
> (55)

In one of the pivotal stories of *The House on Mango Street,* "Red Clowns," Esperanza describes her sexual initiation. She is assaulted by a group of Anglo boys while waiting at the fairground for her friend Sally. Esperanza's feelings of helplessness, confusion, and pain are overwhelmed by the sensation of betrayal: betrayal by Sally who was not there when Esperanza needed her but also betrayal by all the women who ever failed to contradict the romantic mythology of love and sex. Esperanza says, "You're a liar. They all lied. Only his dirty fingernails against my skin, only his sour smell again" (100). Esperanza directs her anger and shame not at the perpetrators of this violent act; she does not have the words, the language with which to direct blame at men, and privileged white men at that, and so she internalizes that sense of blame and accuses women instead. As María Herrera-Sobek explains:

> The diatribe is directed not only at Sally the silent interlocutor but at the community of women who keep the truth from the younger generation of women in a conspiracy of silence: silence in not *denouncing* the 'real' facts of life about sex and its negative aspects in violent sexual encounters, and *complicity* in embroidering a fairy-tale-like mist around sex and romanticizing and idealizing unrealistic sexual relations.[10]

In the earlier story **"Beautiful and Cruel"** Esperanza tells of her desire to become like the movie actresses who are beautiful and cruel. The kind of actress Esperanza most wants to be "is the one who drives the men crazy and laughs them all away. Her power is her own. She will not give it away" (**Mango Street,** 89). This image of an empowered woman is quite distinct from the imagery of femininity encountered in popular culture. The character Marin, for example, represents the young victim of patriarchal popular culture. Esperanza recalls that Marin sings popular songs of romantic love, and she tells the younger girls

> how Davey the Baby's sister got pregnant and what cream is best for taking off moustache hair and if you count the white flecks on your fingernails you can know how many boys are thinking of you and lots of other things I can't remember now.
>
> (**Mango Street,** 27)

Marin's ambition is to work in a department store, where she can look beautiful and wear fashionable clothes and meet someone to marry. Romantic love and personal beauty are the ideologies that inform her sense of herself, her worth, and the direction of her life. Esperanza realizes that Marin is waiting for someone, a man, to come along and take control of her life. She refuses to accept responsibility for her life herself; she places that responsibility with the unknown man for whom she is waiting. As Esperanza imagines, Marin is "waiting for a car to stop, a star to fall, someone to change her life" (27). Unlike the movie actress in the story **"Beautiful and Cruel,"** whatever feminine power Marin possesses she gives away.

But in **"Red Clowns,"** Esperanza tells of her discovery that a "Spanish girl" does not possess any power and that whatever is desired of her will be taken from her by force. Ignorance of her own helplessness is what Esperanza most resents: the deliberate falsehoods that lead her to believe she has a power that always has been denied her. The adults into whom children like Esperanza mature are deceived by their culture about who they are and what they can achieve in their lives. Esperanza's mother uses her own life to warn her daughter of the danger of the ideology of personal beauty. She tells how she left school because she had no nice clothes to wear and only when it was too late did she see the mistake she had made. The lives led by her parents represent for Esperanza the discrepancy between the promises made by her culture and the reality of the life that is actually delivered. Her parents believe that hard work will be rewarded in material ways. They live in the expectation that life will become easier and their next house will be bigger and better. Eventually Esperanza stops believing them and the mythology they believe. She refuses to accompany the family on Sunday afternoon drives to admire the houses and gardens of rich Anglo-Americans—the people for whom her parents and neighbors toil. America promises its citizens more than it is willing to deliver; but Chicano culture promises its little girls less than they are capable of achieving—a life of drudgery, servitude, and self-denial.

Cisneros's treatment of sexuality is divided between a celebration of the power of a demythologized feminine sexuality and a powerful awareness of misogyny and the control of women through the control of their sexuality. The control of bodily appearance, how the female body is represented in words and in flesh, is a powerful strategy for the control of women's minds. In the language of patriarchy, femininity is defined closely with the female body. It is because she is a woman that Alicia must rise before dawn to do her dead mother's work before she goes to school. Alicia is told that "a woman's place is sleeping so she can wake up early with the tortilla star" (*Mango Street*, 31) to begin another day of cooking, cleaning, and serving her family. Female identity is inscribed upon the feminine body, as the girls speculate about the true function of women's hips:

> They're good for holding a baby when you're cooking, Rachel says. . . . You need them to dance, says Lucy. . . . You gotta know how to walk with hips, practice you know—like if half of you wanted to go one way and the other half the other.
>
> (*Mango Street*, 49)

It is in terms of feminine usefulness to men—as entertainment (dancing), bearing and raising children, cooking, appearing sexually attractive—that the female body derives its usefulness, not as the representation of individual or feminine subjectivity. So the feminine is defined in objective terms, as women appear to men, rather than the subjective terms of feminine experience.

Many women are trapped within these cultural constructs. They find their femininity represented in a language that serves the interests of men and the masculine view of the world. Consequently, these women are unable to describe, even to themselves, the reasons for their suffering. The title story of *Woman Hollering Creek* tells of the young woman Cleófilas, who is brought to Texas from Mexico by the husband she hopes will transform her life into the kind of romance she knows from magazines, novels, and telenovelas.

> Cleófilas thought her life would have to be like that, like a *telenovela*, only now the episodes got sadder and sadder. And there were no commercials in between for comic relief. And no happy ending in sight.
>
> (52-53)

She discovers instead a life of neglect, abuse, beatings, loneliness. This is until a nurse introduces her to an entirely different kind of woman—someone who will help her leave her violent husband and return to Mexico, someone who suggests that the "hollering" for which the creek is named does not have to signify only sadness or anger but perhaps also defiance, a bold assertion of femininity and the will to self-determination. This woman, Felice, introduces Cleófilas to a whole new perspective on femininity and a range of previously unthinkable possibilities for living her life. Felice fractures the patriarchal narratives of womanhood that have constrained Cleófilas's thinking about herself and her potential.

Cisneros devotes much of her work to this effort of fracturing the powerful narratives of femininity that serve the interests of the patriarchy. Not limited to deconstructing patriarchal gender definitions, Cisneros also devotes her energies to telling about her sexuality but from her own feminine point of view, which is emphatically not a male point of view. This is the significance of Cisneros's "wicked, wicked ways," the title of her 1987 volume of poems. She is "wicked" in that she has reappropriated, taken control of, her own sexuality and the articulation of it—a power forbidden to women under patriarchy. Her wickedness is that of defying a patriarchally constructed boundary separating that which is legitimate for a woman from that which is not. The "loose woman," described in the poem of the same name, assumes mythological proportions as a consequence of her subversive powers: "They say I'm a beast . . . a bitch. / Or witch . . . the woman of myth and bullshit. . . . By all accounts I am / a danger to society. / I'm Pancha Villa" (*Loose Woman*, 112-13, 2.1, 4-5, 24)—come to save the women! This loose woman breaks laws, disregards religion, terrorizes men; "In other words, I'm anarchy" (*Loose Woman*, 114, 1.47).

The poems collected in *Loose Woman* enact a defiant reclamation of feminine sexuality—for example, "I Let Him Take Me," "I Am So in Love I Grow a New Hymen," "Black Lace Bra Kind of Woman," "Down There," "A Man in My Bed Like Cracker Crumbs," and "Loose Woman." Titles such as these are indicative of the boisterous humor, the earthiness, the extrovert energy of these poems. All are short, all set a scene and implicitly tell a tale, and all speak in powerful images that celebrate a demythologized femininity. A "black lace bra kind of woman" is a "loose woman," a woman who defies the polite rules governing feminine behavior, a woman who has "rambled / her '59 Pontiac between the blurred / lines dividing sense from senselessness" (*Loose Woman*, 78, 2.7-9). She is dangerous, the kind every girl's mother warned against: "Ruin your clothes, she will. / Get you home way after hours" (2.10-11). This kind of woman is reckless in her enjoyment of her life, her self, her body, and the poem celebrates this vibrant state of being: "And now the good times are coming. Girl, / I tell you, the good times are here" (2.17-18).

In the poem "Down There" Cisneros creates a vocabulary with which to write poetry about the reality of women's bodies. She does this not only to make of feminine sexuality a legitimate subject for poetry but also to challenge the decorum governing the ways in which the female body has been represented in poetry. The poem begins by administering a shock to poetic decorum: "Your poem thinks it's *bad.* / Because it farts in the bath. / Cracks its knuckles in class. / Grabs its balls in public" (**Loose Woman**, 79, 2.1-4). The poem is characterized initially by a sequence of "bad" macho habits: farting, peeing in the pool, picking one's nose, spitting, and swaggering like a macho John Wayne or Rambo. Then the tone shifts slightly and the poem is likened to objects rather than behaviors: a used condom, testicle skin, a lone pubic hair, a cigarette stub "sent hissing / to the piss pot" (2.59-60), half-finished beer bottles—in short, "the miscellany of maleness" (1.64). In these stanzas the poem is deliberately offensive, the images deliberately shocking, an outrageous violation of poetic decorum. But then comes Cisneros's ironic twist: as she turns to the central (the real) subject of her poem, the language assumes a more serious, decorous, "poetic" tone, yet the subject itself is an outrageous violation of patriarchal poetic decorum—"men-struation": "Yes, / I want to talk at length about Men- / struation. Or my period" (2.88-90). The ironic hyphenation of "men-struation" draws attention to the gendered fashion in which women's and men's bodies enter poetic discourse. Cisneros goes on to describe this feminine blood as the link between sexuality and creativity: "I'd like to dab my fingers / in my inkwell / and write a poem across the wall. / 'A Poem of Womanhood'" (2.120-23). But this poem is not just made of a woman's experience and produced by a woman; it is also for women and of them; it is representative of the commonality of all women: "Words writ in blood. But no, / not blood at all, I told you. / If blood is thicker than water, then / menstruation is thicker than brother- / hood" (2.125-29). It is in the true and authentic representation of feminine experience, including the reality of feminine sexuality, that women will find the solidarity that comes from shared gender experiences. Only by casting off the poetic stereotypes of patriarchal discourse will women overcome the divisive effects of those stereotypes and discover the potential for joy in their own bodies that is denied them.

Cisneros describes the discovery of this potential for joy, this subversive enjoyment of one's own sexuality, as a source of power for women: "Sexyness [*sic*], I think, it's a great feeling of self-empowerment."[11] She has been criticized both by other women and by men for some of the forms taken by this celebration of her sexuality, such as

the highly suggestive photograph of Cisneros as "vamp" that adorns the cover of *My Wicked, Wicked Ways.* Cisneros describes that photography:

> The cover is of a woman appropriating her own sexuality. In some ways, that's also why it's wicked; the scene is trespassing that boundary by saying 'I defy you. I'm going to tell my own story.'[12]

Cisneros goes on to describe her dismay when women failed to perceive the transgressive meaning of her gesture. She reports the following encounter, when

> some feminist asked: 'How could you, a feminist, pose like lewd cheesecake to sell your book?' And that offended me. At first I was hurt, then I thought about it and said: 'Wait a second, where's your sense of humor? And why can't a feminist be sexy?'[13]

The breaking of sexist stereotypes cuts both ways in Cisneros's work, against both the male and female limits that can be placed upon feminine sexuality. The transgression of patriarchal taboos is an important aspect of Cisneros's work as a Chicana writer. Sandra Cisneros is under no illusions about the power of feminine sexuality as a weapon used against women. She recognizes that in the context of the barrio, or any poor neighborhood, feminine sexuality is equated with vulnerability: "I was writing about it [the barrio] in the most real sense I knew, as a person walking those neighborhoods with a vagina," she says in reference to her subject in *The House on Mango Street.*[14]

Cisneros is not coy when it comes to articulating clearly the reasons why women become trapped in situations of extreme oppression. Fear of violence, sexual violence especially, is one of the prime strategies by which women are kept under control. Poverty, illiteracy, inability to speak English—these reinforce and exaggerate the coercive effect of patriarchal violence by limiting the mobility and opportunities of women. In poetry Cisneros carves out a space for these subjects and the words with which to articulate them. In **"Still Life with Potatoes, Pearls, Raw Meat, Rhinestones, Lard, and Horses Hooves,"** for example, she contrasts the myth of genteel poverty with the reality of life in Mexican San Antonio: "poverty's not quaint when it's your house you can't escape from. / Decay's not beautiful to the decayed" (**Loose Woman**, 109, 2.37-38).

Although Cisneros does not flinch from depicting the squalor and deprivation of the life lived by many Chicanos, she does not dwell upon these hardships. Mexican history and mythology offer a rich vocabulary of poetic allusions with which to represent the complexity of a dual cultural heritage. In particular Cisneros addresses the issue of Mexican role models: "We're raised in a Mexican culture that has two role models: La Malinche y la Virgen de Guadalupe. And you know that's hard route to go, one or the other, there's no in-betweens."[15] The virgin and the whore—these categories of "good" versus "bad" women are complicated by the perception, shared by many Chicana feminists, that they risk betrayal of the people if they pursue an alternative construction of femininity that is perceived to be Anglo. In her 1986 essay **"Cactus Flowers: In Search of Tejana Feminist Poetry"** Cisneros questions the playful tone of some Chicana feminist poetry that dares to criticize Chicano men only to a certain point, a point from which the poet can "slip back into the safety zone and say 'just kidding.'"[16] She asks of the poet under discussion, Angela de Hoyos, in her collection *Woman, Woman*:

> Why is de Hoyos afraid to fall out of the graces of the males whom she is obviously angry with? Is she afraid of being labelled a Malinchista by them, corrupted by gringa influences which threaten to splinter her people?[17]

Threats to Chicana self-definition come, then, from *Angla* America as well as from the machismo of Chicano culture.

As a Chicana feminist Cisneros needs to revise aspects of her hybrid culture as a woman: that is, both by using her power as a woman and by challenging those aspects of her double cultural inheritance that prescribe what she as a woman can be. In order to do this Cisneros claims a symbolic vocabulary of Aztec allusions in her poems and in stories such as **"Never Marry a Mexican,"** which is discussed above. For instance, the poem **"You Bring Out the Mexican in Me"** works through a frenetic list of all those things that comprise "Mexicanness." Throughout the poem this notion of Mexicanness has encompassed multitudes, including the most radical opposites (*Loose Woman*, 4-6). From "the filth goddess Tlazolteotl . . . the swallower of sins . . . the lust goddess without guilt" to the Virgin, this poem and the subjectivity it describes aspire toward a kind of unity that can never be unitary, that is always predicated on conflict, the "Aztec love of war," the "pre-Columbian death and destruction," the "rain forest disaster, nuclear threat . . . Mexico City '85 earthquake," extremes

of passion. In poems such as this Cisneros claims her right to the inheritance passed down to her by Aztec women, the conquered women who survived despite the Virgin's people. Catholicism is a powerful legacy, but the pagan legacy is just as potent. In poems such as **"You Bring Out the Mexican in Me"** Cisneros uses this pagan force to resist the gender stereotypes of Catholicism and the guilt with which they are enforced.

Traces of these stereotypes are to be found in every household, in every Chicano/a community. Cisneros's commitment to the *cultura y raza* is represented by the extension of the family to encompass the entire community. In her stories family members are often evaluated for their effectiveness as role models in the ongoing effort to resist oppressive patterns of behavior. This is especially true of female relatives: mother, aunts, comadres, girl cousins, *abuelitas*. The lives that make up the family are subjected to a subtle ideological analysis to reveal the conditions of their entrapment. An ironic commentary on this analytical watchfulness is represented in the story **"Barbie-Q."** The title itself is a pun—signifying both the universal attraction of Barbie dolls for all little girls and also the fact that the dolls our narrator can afford to own are those salvaged from a warehouse fire:

> So what if our Barbies smell like smoke. . . . And if the prettiest doll, Barbie's MOD'ern cousin Francie with real eyelashes, eyelash brush included, has a left foot that's melted a little—so?
> (***Woman Hollering Creek***, 16)

The narrator has absorbed the merchandising rhetoric together with the values represented by the doll. Consequently the vignette is presented in a tone of naive defiance of those socioeconomic pressures that will ensure these little girls never can meet the standard of feminine beauty signified by the doll. The doll is both role model (in terms of body image, at least) and evidence of the exclusion of Chicanas from governing Anglo definitions of femininity.

In ***The House on Mango Street*** Esperanza learns first what she does not want to be and then learns what she has the potential to become. She is named for a great-grandmother who was dominated by her husband and spent her life sitting at her window looking out, thinking of all the things she might have been. There are the characters Marin, the neighbor who has been brought from Puerto Rico to baby-sit her young cousins and look for a husband; Minerva, who writes poetry but is trapped physically in an abusive marriage; Esperanza's mother, who speaks two languages and sings opera but is too scared to go downtown because she cannot speak English; and Sally, who marries to escape her violent father. But then there are the comadres, the three sisters, who tell Esperanza that she must escape in order to come back for those who cannot find a way out themselves; it is for them she must always remember:

> A circle, understand? You will always be Esperanza. You will always be Mango Street. You can't erase what you know. You can't forget who you are.
>
> (**Mango Street**, 105)

And Alicia repeats this lesson: if life on Mango Street is ever to improve, then it will be because people like Esperanza have made it better. In response to Esperanza's insistence that she does not belong and does not want to belong, Alicia insists that not only is Esperanza shaped by the culture of Mango Street, but she will return to change it because, she asks, "Who's going to do it? The mayor? And the thought of the mayor coming to Mango Street makes me laugh out loud" (**Mango Street**, 107). It is as a writer that Esperanza must struggle to make that difference, because politicians will not. No one else will do it.

It is as an artist that Esperanza discovers how she can make a difference to life on Mango Street. But the altruistic aspect of her writing is slow to dawn upon her. This is because the Chicana artist needs to be selfish in order to have the time to write. Cisneros has written of her mother who let her read and study in her room rather than do her chores; later it was her family who provided financial assistance when she needed it.[18] The Chicana writer needs to resist the traditional lifestyles available to Mexican American women: marriage and children would leave no time and no energy for creativity. Cisneros tells how even a regular job can threaten the concentration of energy necessary for writing. "I would like a wife, instead of a husband, because then he could take care of the kids," she jokes.[19] For the woman writer, marriage means a burden of housework with which creative work cannot compete. The solitary time needed for thinking and writing is incompatible with marriage—but this is the traditional lifestyle for the Chicana who is expected to move from the father's house to that of the husband. The private mental space in which the creative process occurs is crucially related to physical space and interpersonal space.

It is no accident, then, that the house provides a controlling metaphor in **The House on Mango Street** and that Esperanza's growing awareness of herself as an artist is tied to her need to discover a space of her own; a place to think her own thoughts and to write them down in an appropriate silence. The characters Aunt Lupe and Minerva in **The House on Mango Street** seek in poetry both a refuge from their oppressive lives and an authentic kind of freedom that resolves rather than simply eludes the conflicts that characterize their experience of subjectivity. But these women have no space to call their own. Esperanza experiences the house in which she lives as a metaphor for her entire sense of self. In the first vignette she describes the shame evoked by a nun's words: "You live there? The way she said it made me feel like nothing. There. I lived there" (**Mango Street**, 5). From this humiliation comes a determination to live in a "real" house. And with this real house will come a firm and stable sense of being, in place of the nothingness evoked by the nun. Esperanza sees an image of herself reflected in the nun's face and in her words; as a poet Esperanza is able to use words to construct both a means of escape and a means to return to the house on Mango Street.

Poetry, writing, becomes in Cisneros's work much more than words on a page. Poetry is the real business of living because the writing process engages the poet in the difficult business of contesting all those cultural pressures that are placed upon the ethnic woman. To live in freedom and to be free to write are complementary aspects of the same effort at self-liberation. As a consequence, Cisneros writes many poems about poetry, poems that deliberately confuse poetry with other passionate engagements. "I Let Him Take Me," for instance, misleads the reader by using the language of romantic love in such a way that the poetic muse is personified as a lover. But we are aware only of the lover—until the final line. Then the love which is sneered at by others, the love at which the poet labors and which she nurtures, and the lover who "never disappointed, / hurt, abandoned" is dramatically identified as "Husband, love, my life— / poem" (**Loose Woman**, 11, 2.15-16, 17-18).

The discovery and protection of a space in which to be alone is one of the threads that unifies the vignettes of **The House on Mango Street**. The narrative sequence develops as a Kunstlerroman—a portrait of the artist as a young Chicana. In their instructive essay "Growing Up Chicano: Tomás Rivera and Sandra Cisneros" Erlinda González-Berry and Tey Diana Rebolledo contrast the characteristics of the male coming-of-age narrative with Cisneros's narrative style in **The House on Mango Street**.[20] Esperanza first learns to see herself as an artist and then realizes how to be an artist by discovering a mission that is defined by what she can do for all the women, not just herself. Her escape from the barrio must be instructive, for then it can be true freedom based on acceptance rather than self-denial. Esperanza wants not simply to escape or transcend her surroundings, for however brief a time; she embraces literature as a potent opportunity to take control over her own life's story. Agency, in the determination of her self and her life, is what writing offers. Speaking as a Chicana, Cisneros explains:

> None of us wants to abandon our culture. We're very Mexican, we're all very Chicanas. Part of being Mexican is that love and affinity we have for our *cultura*. We're very family centered, and that family extends to the whole Raza. We don't want to be exiled from our people.[21]

Though many of her characteristic themes and subjects are shared in both her poetry and fiction, the two forms appear quite distinct to Cisneros—opposed almost:

> Poetry is the art of telling the truth, and fiction is the art of lying. The scariest thing to me is writing poetry, because you're looking at yourself *desnuda*. You're always looking at the part of you that you don't show anybody.[22]

But at the center of that self-scrutiny is the core of truth that Cisneros identifies as the poem itself. In radical contrast fiction is as extroverted as poetry is introverted: "the definition of a story is something that someone wants to listen to. If someone doesn't want to listen to you, then it's not a story."[23] Cisneros's poems do tell stories, but in a compact, economical, and highly imagistic fashion. Her poetry is a kind of storytelling; it can be narrative in this way. But more striking is the highly poetic and evocative quality of Cisneros's fiction.

Several commentators have remarked upon the richly poetic, allusive quality of Cisneros's prose, and she, remarking upon the formal indeterminacy of *The House on Mango Street,* describes how she wanted to create stories that read like compact and lyrical poems, formed into a collection that could be read at any point in the sequence or as a single narrative.[24] The literary structures Cisneros uses are as multifaceted as her cultural identity. In seeking to forge a language that will express but not misrepresent her experiences Cisneros, like many Chicana writers, encounters a number of difficulties. First, there is the question of language and the competing claims of English and Spanish to prominence in her work. Second, many of the canonical literary styles

within the American tradition were created to express the realities of masculine experience. Even those forms suited to feminine expression manifest an Anglo vision of the world. Cisneros, along with many of her Chicana sisters, confronts the twin difficulties of writing as a woman and as a Chicana every time she begins to write. The patriarchal bias of Chicano culture and the Anglo bias of American women's culture represent the twin obstacles of sexism and racism that Chicanas must negotiate in order to write authentically. American English is commonly perceived as a language of duplicity, the language of treaty violation, the voice of the master. English threatens to corrupt Chicana expression just as Anglo-American cultural values corrupt the Mexican American community. Cisneros writes mostly but not exclusively in a hybrid English that is required to accommodate Spanish words and phrases. She describes in a witty bilingual fashion the choice she made to write in English as resulting from her lack of familiarity with the nuances of a Spanish-language culture:

> I never write in Spanish, y no es que no quiero sino que I don't have that same palate in Spanish that I do in English. No tengo esa facilidad. I think the only way you get that palate is by living in a culture where you hear it, where the language is not something in a book or in your dreams. It's on the loaf of bread you buy, it's on the radio jingle, it's on the graffiti you see, it's on your ticket stub. It must be all encompassing.[25]

But Cisneros's command of idiom is most striking. The narrative voice of *The House on Mango Street* captures the nuances of a child's expression, balanced against the demands of the vocabulary of adulthood into which Esperanza is entering. Cisneros favors the first-person mode of address, and it is this quasi-confessional, seemingly autobiographical style that lends her work (in fiction and poetry) such immediacy and such power.

Power is a word that recurs constantly when describing Sandra Cisneros's writing. She has described the Chicana writer as someone who is necessarily an obsessive. By virtue of who she is and the circumstances of her birth, the Chicana writer has no leisure to pursue the aesthetic just for its own sake. She is motivated not so much by inspiration but by the need to articulate pressing issues and to give expression to the ghosts that haunt her.[26] "Night Madness Poem" describes this compulsion to seek relief in the crafting of words. The poem that seeks expression is likened to "A pea under twenty eiderdowns. / A sadness in my heart like stone" (*Loose Woman,* 49, 2.3-4).

As the poem continues, we realize that the words Cisneros wants to speak are to the absent lover she cannot telephone, but these are also the words of her poetry. Frustrated love and frustrated writing merge and are confused, so the poem ends with a challenge: "Choose your weapon. / Mine— the telephone, my tongue" (2.30-31). The struggle for language in which to represent the realities of her experience is the subject of poems such as **"By Way of Explanation,"** in which she uses geography to describe her body: her knees, "devout Moroccans," her hands "twin comedies / from Pago Pago," "The breasts / to your surprise / Gaugin's Papeete" (**Wicked Ways,** 92, 2.23, 24-26, 30-31). Cisneros deliberately includes the physical body in her poetry in order to contest the assumption that bodily existence is not an appropriate subject for poetry and also to challenge the idea that the body and bodily functions ought not to be spoken of.

This silence is a form of ignorance that oppresses women in particular by keeping them from knowledge of the power they can access through their physical femininity and by promoting feelings of shame and guilt about their sexuality. In the essay **"Guadalupe the Sex Goddess"** Cisneros discusses her own inherited ignorance of her body and her sexuality. She exclaims,

> No wonder, then, it was too terrible to think about a doctor—a man!—looking at you down there when you could never bring yourself to look at yourself. *¡Ay, nunca!* How could I acknowledge my sexuality, let alone enjoy sex, with so much guilt? In the guise of modesty my culture locked me in a double chastity belt of ignorance and *vergüenza,* shame.[27]

Many of the poems in **My Wicked, Wicked Ways** address and affirm the poet's transgressive sexuality: in poems about adultery (for example, **"For All Tuesday Travellers"** and **"Amé, Amo, Amaré"**), about sexual obsession (such as **"Drought"**), and about her sensuality and sexual attraction to men (in **"Sensuality Plunging Barefoot into Thorns"**).

The 1992 preface to the reprinted collection is itself a poem that establishes the context for the poems and introduces the primary themes: the difficult choice to become a writer, the transgression of family and cultural expectation: "A woman like me / whose choice was rolling pin or factory / An absurd vice, this wicked wanton / writer's life" (**Wicked Ways,** x). The poem **"His Story"** develops this theme by presenting the father's view of his nonconformist daughter. He searches among family precedents for women who have trespassed across the borders of approved feminine behavior, trying to find an explanation for his sorrow. The poem concludes with the poet's reflection on her father's explorations: "An unlucky fate is mine / to be born woman in a family of men"; and her father's lament: "Six sons, my father groans, / all home. / And one female, / gone" (**Wicked Ways,** 38-39, 2.33-34, 35-38). The poems that follow this preface are then presented as the offspring of her union with the poetic muse: a brood of "colicky kids / who fussed and kept / me up the wicked nights" (**Wicked Ways,** xii). And in poems such as **"The Poet Reflects on Her Solitary Fate,"** Cisneros describes the compulsion to write, the need to express her creativity: "The house is cold. / There is nothing on TV. / She must write poems" (**Wicked Ways,** 37, 2.13-15).

Though this poem, like all of Cisneros's work, is intensely personal she has discovered how to uncover the subtle and intricate web of connections that bind the personal with the cultural. Cisneros begins with personal experiences, feelings, and thoughts and suggests the complex ways in which these attributes of the private self have been shaped, prescribed, and monitored by cultural, racial, political, and economic forces. Her sense of responsibility as a writer is conceived in terms of these social and cultural influences. She explains that she is the first woman in her family to assume a public voice through writing, to take upon herself the power to speak and find that she is heard.[28] This privilege brings with it a responsibility to witness the lives and to register the worlds of those who remain invisible: the powerless, the silent. Cisneros tells of how she admires the poetry of Emily Dickinson and what she took to be Dickinson's ability to live both domestic and artistic lives simultaneously. Then Cisneros discovered Dickinson's housekeeper, the woman who performed the routine chores to keep the household running, freeing Dickinson to pursue her intellectual work. Cisneros describes how Emily Dickinson's housekeeper helped her to recognize the enormous contribution her own mother made to enable the young Sandra to read and write when instead she should have been washing dishes.[29]

In a sense, then, Cisneros's work is dedicated to her mother and to Emily Dickinson's housekeeper, the women who are forgotten but who made possible the lives of other literary women. In her essay **"Cactus Flowers"** Cisneros describes the courage it takes to define oneself as a Chicana writer:

To admit you are a writer takes a great deal of audacity. To admit you are a feminist takes even greater courage. It is admirable then when Chicana writers elect to redefine and reinvent themselves through their writing.[30]

To be a writer is, for Sandra Cisneros, to have the opportunity to do something for the silenced women and for all women by inventing new paradigms, by defining new Chicana voices, and by living as a liberated feminine subject of the story she has written for herself.

Notes

1. Pilar E. Rodríguez Aranda, "On the Solitary Fate of Being Mexican, Female, Wicked and Thirty-three: An Interview with Writer Sandra Cisneros," *Americas Review* 18 (Spring 1990): 64.

2. See Sandra Cisneros, "Ghosts and Voices: Writing from Obsession," *Americas Review* 15:1 (1987): 69-72.

3. Cherríe Moraga, jacket blurb, Sandra Cisneros, *My Wicked, Wicked Ways* (1987); rpt. (New York: Alfred K. Knopf, 1995).

4. Aranda, "Interview," 66.

5. Ibid.

6. Sandra Cisneros, *The House on Mango Street* (1984); rpt. (London: Bloomsbury, 1992), 10. Future page references are given in the text.

7. María Elena de Valdés, "The Critical Reception of Sandra Cisneros's *The House on Mango Street*," in *Gender, Self, and Society Proceedings of IV International Conference on the Hispanic Cultures of the United States,* ed. Renate von Bardelben (Frankfurt, Germany: Peter Lang, 1993), 293.

8. Sandra Cisneros, *Woman Hollering Creek and Other Stories* (1991); rpt. (London: Bloomsbury, 1993), 69. Subsequent page references are given in the text.

9. Marcela Christine Lucero-Trujillo, "The Dilemma of the Modern Chicana Artist and Critic," in *The Third Woman: Minority Women Writers of the United States,* ed. Dexter Fisher (Boston: Houghton Mifflin Co., 1980), 330.

10. María Herrera-Sobek, "The Politics of Rape: Sexual Transgression in Chicana Fiction," in *Chicana Creativity and Criticism: Charting New Frontiers in American Literature,* ed. María Herrera-Sobek and Helena María Viramontes, special issue, *Americas Review* 15, no. 3, 4 (Fall-Winter 1987): 178.

11. Aranda, "Interview," 69.

12. Ibid., 68.

13. Ibid., 69.

14. Ibid.

15. Ibid., 65.

16. Sandra Cisneros, "Cactus Flowers: In Search of Tejana Feminist Poetry," *Third Woman* 3:1,2 (1986): 74.

17. Ibid. 74.

18. Aranda, "Interview," 79.

19. Ibid., 71.

20. Erlinda González-Berry and Tey Diana Rebolledo, "Growing Up Chicano: Tomás Rivera and Sandra Cisneros," *Revista Chicano Requeña* 13.3-4 (1985): 109-19.

21. Aranda, "Interview," 66.

22. Ibid., 75.

23. Ibid., 76.

24. See Sandra Cisneros, "Do You Know Me? I Wrote *The House on Mango Street*," *Americas Review* 15 (Spring 1987): 78.

25. Aranda, "Interview," 74.

26. See Cisneros, "Ghosts and Voices," 73.

27. Sandra Cisneros, "Guadalupe the Sex Goddess," in *Goddess of the Americas: Writings on the Virgin of Guadalupe,* ed. Ana Castillo (New York: Riverhead Books, 1996), 46.

28. See Sandra Cisneros, "Notes to a Young(er) Writer," *Americas Review* 15 (Spring 1987): 76.

29. Ibid., 75.

30. Cisneros, "Cactus Flowers," 79.

Primary Bibliography

Cisneros, Sandra. *Bad Boys*. Chicano Chapbook No. 8. 1980.

———. "Cactus Flowers: In Search of Tejana Feminist Poetry." *Third Woman* 3, nos. 1 and 2 (1986): 73-80.

———. "Do You Know Me? I Wrote *The House on Mango Street*." *Americas Review* 15 (Spring 1987): 77-79.

———. "From a Writer's Notebook. Ghosts and Voices: Writing from Obsession." *Americas Review* 15 (Spring 1987): 69-73.

———. "Ghosts and Voices: Writing from Obsession." *Americas Review* 15, no. 1 (1987): 69-72.

———. "Guadalupe the Sex Goddess." In *Goddess of the Americas: Writings on the Virgin of Guadalupe,* edited by Ana Castillo, 46-51. New York: Riverhead Books, 1996.

———. *The House on Mango Street*. 1984. 2d rev. ed. Houston: Arte Público, 1988.

———. "Living as a Writer: Choice and Circumstance." *Feminist Writers Guild* 10 (February 1987): 8-9.

———. *Loose Woman*. New York: Alfred Knopf, 1994.

———. *My Wicked, Wicked Ways*. Berkeley, Calif.: Third Woman Press, 1987.

———. "Notes to a Young(er) Writer." *Americas Review* 15 (Spring 1987): 74-76.

———. "Only Daughter." In *Máscaras,* edited by Lucha Corpi, 120-23. Berkeley, Calif.: Third Woman Press, 1997.

———. *Woman Hollering Creek and Other Stories*. New York: Vintage, 1991.

———. "A Writer's Voyages." *Texas Observer,* 25 September 1987, pp. 18-19.

TITLE COMMENTARY

The House on Mango Street

ELLEN MCCRACKEN (ESSAY DATE 1989)

SOURCE: McCracken, Ellen. "Sandra Cisneros' *The House on Mango Street*: Community-Oriented Introspection and the Demystification of Patriarchal Violence." In *Breaking Boundaries: Latina Writing and Critical Readings*, edited by Asunción Horno-Delgado, Eliana Ortega, Nina M. Scott, and Nancy Saporta Sternbach, pp. 62-71. Amherst: University of Massachusetts Press, 1989.

In the following essay, McCracken studies the instances of physical, sexual, and mental abuse committed against women in the male-dominated society depicted in The House on Mango Street. *McCracken probes the effects these abuses have on Esperanza, the protagonist, and questions the apparent dearth of positive role models for her.*

Introspection has achieved a privileged status in bourgeois literary production, corresponding to the ideological emphasis on individualism under capitalism, precisely as the personal and political power of many real individuals has steadily deteriorated. In forms as diverse as European Romantic poetry, late nineteenth-century Modernismo in Latin America, the poetry of the Mexican Contemporáneos of the 1930s, the early twentieth-century modernistic prose of a Proust, the French *nouveau roman,* and other avant-garde texts that take pride in an exclusionary hermeticism, the self is frequently accorded exaggerated importance in stark contrast to the actual position of the individual in the writer's historical moment. Critical readers of these texts are, of course, often able to compensate for the writer's omissions, positioning the introspective search within the historical dimension and drawing the text into the very socio-political realm that the writer has tried to avoid. Nonetheless, many of us, at one time or another, are drawn into the glorified individualism of these texts, experiencing voyeuristic and sometimes identificatory pleasure as witnesses of another's search for the self, or congratulating ourselves on the mental acuity we possess to decode such a difficult and avant-garde text.

Literary critics have awarded many of these texts canonical status. As Terry Eagleton has argued, theorists, critics, and teachers are "custodians of a discourse" and select certain texts for inclusion in the canon that are "more amenable to this discourse than others."[1] Based on power, Eagleton suggests metaphorically, literary criticism sometimes tolerates regional dialects of the discourse but not those that sound like another language altogether: "To be on the inside of the discourse itself is to be blind to this power, for what is more natural and non-dominative than to speak one's own tongue?" (203).

The discourse of power to which Eagleton refers here is linked to ideology as well. The regional dialects of criticism that are accepted must be compatible, ideologically as well as semantically, with the dominant discourse. Criticism, for example, that questions the canonical status of the introspective texts mentioned above, or suggests admission to the canon of texts that depart from such individualistic notions of the self, is often labeled pejoratively or excluded from academic institutions and publication avenues.

We can extend Eagleton's metaphor to literary texts as well. How does a book attain the wide exposure that admission to the canon facilitates if it is four times marginalized by its ideology, its language, and its writer's ethnicity and gender? What elements of a text can prevent it from being accepted as a "regional dialect" of the dominant discourse; at what point does it become "another language altogether" (to use Eagleton's analogy), incompatible with canonical discourse?

The specific example to which I refer, Sandra Cisneros' *The House on Mango Street,* was published by a small regional press in 1984 and reprinted in a second edition of 3,000 in 1985.[2] Difficult to find in most libraries and bookstores, it is well known among Chicano critics and scholars, but virtually unheard of in larger academic and critical circles. In May 1985 it won the Before Columbus Foundation's American Book Award,[3] but this prize has not greatly increased the volume's national visibility. Cisneros' book has not been excluded from the canon solely because of its publishing circumstances: major publishing houses are quick to capitalize on a Richard Rodríguez whose widely distributed and reviewed *Hunger of Memory* (1982) does not depart ideologically and semantically from the dominant discourse. They are even willing to market an Anglo writer as a Chicano, as occurred in 1983 with Danny Santiago's *Famous All Over Town.* Rather, Cisneros' text is likely to continue to be excluded from the canon because it "speaks another language altogether," one to which the critics of the literary establishment "remain blind."

Besides the double marginalization that stems from gender and ethnicity, Cisneros transgresses the dominant discourse of canonical standards ideologically and linguistically. In bold contrast to the individualistic introspection of many canonical texts, Cisneros writes a modified autobiographical novel, or *Bildungsroman,* that roots the individual self in the broader socio-political reality of the Chicano community. As we will see, the story of individual development is oriented outwardly here, away from the bourgeois individualism of many standard texts. Cisneros' language also contributes to the text's otherness. In opposition to the complex, hermetic language of many canonical works, *The House on Mango Street* recuperates the simplicity of children's speech, paralleling the autobiographical protagonist's chronological age in the book. Although making the text accessible to people with a wider range of reading abilities, such simple and well-crafted prose is not currently in canonical vogue.

The volume falls between traditional genre distinctions as well. Containing a group of 44 short and interrelated stories, the book has been classified as a novel by some because, as occurs in Tomas Rivera's . . . *y no se lo tragó la tierra,* there is character and plot development throughout the episodes. I prefer to classify Cisneros' text as a collection, a hybrid genre midway between the novel and the short story. Like Sherwood Anderson's *Winesburg, Ohio,* Pedro Juan Soto's *Spiks,* Gloria Naylor's *The Women of Brewster Place,* and Rivera's text,[4] Cisneros' collection represents the writer's attempt to achieve both the intensity of the short story and the discursive length of the novel within a single volume. Unlike the chapters of most novels, each story in the collection could stand on its own if it were to be excerpted but each attains additional important meaning when interacting with the other stories in the volume. A number of structural and thematic elements link the stories of each collection together. Whereas in *Winesburg, Ohio,* one important structuring element is the town itself, in *The House on Mango Street* and . . . *y no se lo tragó la tierra* the image of the house is a central unifying motif.

On the surface the compelling desire for a house of one's own appears individualistic rather than community oriented, but Cisneros socializes the motif of the house, showing it to be a basic human need left unsatisfied for many of the minority population under capitalism. It is precisely the lack of housing stability that motivates the image's centrality in works by writers like Cisneros and Rivera. For the migrant worker who has moved continuously because of job exigencies and who, like many others in the Chicano community, has been deprived of an adequate place to live because of the inequities of income distri-

bution in U.S. society, the desire for a house is not a sign of individualistic acquisitiveness but rather represents the satisfaction of a basic human need. Cisneros begins her narrative with a description of the housing conditions the protagonist's family has experienced:

> We didn't always live on Mango Street. Before that we lived on Loomis on the third floor and before that we lived on Keeler. Before Keeler it was Paulina, and before that I can't remember. But what I remember most is moving a lot . . .

> We had to leave the flat on Loomis quick. The water pipes broke and the landlord wouldn't fix them because the house was too old. . . . We were using the washroom next door and carrying water over in empty milk gallons.

> (P. 7)

Cisneros has socialized the motif of a house of one's own by showing its motivating roots to be the inadequate housing conditions in which she and others in her community lived. We learn that Esperanza, the protagonist Cisneros creates, was subjected to humiliation by her teachers because of her family's living conditions. "You live *there?*" a nun from her school had remarked when seeing Esperanza playing in front of the flat on Loomis. "*There.* I had to look where she pointed—the third floor, the paint peeling, wooden bars Papa had nailed on the windows so we wouldn't fall out.

FROM THE AUTHOR

CISNEROS ON THE EPISODIC, SHORT-STORY FORM OF *THE HOUSE ON MANGO STREET*
I didn't know what I was writing when I wrote *House on Mango Street,* but I knew what I wanted. I didn't know what to call it, but I knew what I was after. It wasn't a naive thing, it wasn't an accident. I wanted to write a series of stories that you could open up at any point. You didn't have to know anything before or after and you would understand each story like a little pearl, or you could look at the whole thing like a necklace.

Cisneros, Sandra. Excerpt from *Writing Women's Lives: An Anthology of Autobiographical Narratives by Twentieth-Century American Women Writers.* New York: Harper Perennial, (1994): 467.

You live *there?* The way she said it made me feel like nothing . . ." (p. 9). Later, after the move to the house on Mango Street that is better but still unsatisfactory, the Sister Superior at her school responds to Esperanza's request to eat lunch in the cafeteria rather than returning home by apparently humiliating the child deliberately: "You don't live far, she says . . . I bet I can see your house from my window. Which one? . . . That one? she said pointing to a row of ugly 3-flats, the ones even the raggedy men are ashamed to go into. Yes, I nodded even though I knew that wasn't my house and started to cry . . ." (p. 43). The Sister Superior is revealing her own prejudices; in effect, she is telling the child, "All you Mexicans must live in such buildings." It is in response to humiliations such as these that the autobiographical protagonist expresses her need for a house of her own. Rather than the mere desire to possess private property, Esperanza's wish for a house represents a positive objectification of the self, the chance to redress humiliation and establish a dignified sense of her own personhood.

Cisneros links this positive objectification that a house of one's own can provide to the process of artistic creation. Early on, the protagonist remarks that the dream of a white house "with trees around it, a great big yard and grass growing without a fence" (p. 8) structured the bedtime stories her mother told them. This early connection of the ideal house to fiction is developed throughout the collection, especially in the final two stories. In **"A House of My Own,"** the protagonist remarks that the desired house would contain "my books and stories" and that such a house is as necessary to the writing process as paper: "Only a house quiet as snow, a space for myself to go, clean as paper before the poem" (p. 100). In **"Mango Says Goodbye Sometimes,"** the Mango Street house, which falls short of the ideal dream house, becomes a symbol of the writer's attainment of her identity through artistic creation. Admitting that she both belonged and did not belong to the "sad red house" on Mango Street, the protagonist comes to terms with the ethnic consciousness that this house represents through the process of fictive creation: "I put it down on paper and then the ghost does not ache so much. I write it down and Mango says goodbye sometimes. She does not hold me with both arms. She sets me free" (p. 101). She is released materially to find a more suitable dwelling that will facilitate her writing; psychologically, she alleviates the ethnic anguish that she has heretofore attempted to repress. It is important, however, that she view

her departure from the Mango Street house to enable her artistic production in social rather than isolationist terms: "They will know I have gone away to come back. For the ones I left behind. For the ones who cannot get out" (p. 102).

Unlike many introspective writers, then, Cisneros links both the process of artistic creation and the dream of a house that will enable this art to social rather than individualistic issues. In **"Bums in the Attic,"** we learn that the protagonist dreams of a house on a hill similar to those where her father works as a gardener. Unlike those who own such houses now, Esperanza assures us that, were she to obtain such a house, she would not forget the people who live below: "One day I'll own my own house, but I won't forget who I am or where I came from. Passing bums will ask, Can I come in? I'll offer them the attic, ask them to stay, because I know how it is to be without a house" (p. 81). She conceives of a house as communal rather than private property; such sharing runs counter to the dominant ideological discourse that strongly affects consciousness in capitalist societies. Cisneros' social motifs undermine rather than support the widespread messages of individualized consumption that facilitate sales of goods and services under consumer capitalism.

Another important reason why Cisneros's text has not been accepted as part of the dominant canonical discourse is its demystificatory presentation of women's issues, especially the problems low-income Chicana women face. Dedicated "A las Mujeres/To the Women" (p. 3), *The House on Mango Street* presents clusters of women characters through the sometimes naive and sometimes wise vision of the adolescent protagonist. There are positive and negative female role models and, in addition, several key incidents that focus the reader's attention on the contradictions of patriarchal social organization. Few mainstream critics consider these the vital, universal issues that constitute great art. When representatives of the critical establishment do accord a text such as Cisneros' a reading, it is often performed with disinterest and defense mechanisms well in place.

Neither does *The House on Mango Street* lend itself to an exoticized reading of the life of Chicana women that sometimes enables a text's canonical acceptance. In **"The Family of Little Feet,"** for example, Esperanza and her friends dress up in cast-off high heels they have been given and play at being adult women. At first revelling in the male attention they receive from the strangers who see them, the girls are ultimately disillusioned after a drunken bum attempts to purchase a kiss for a dollar. While capturing the fleeting sense of self-value that the attention of male surveyors affords women, Cisneros also critically portrays here the danger of competitive feelings among women when one girl's cousins pretend not to see Esperanza and her friends as they walk by. Also portrayed is the corner grocer's attempt to control female sexuality by threatening to call the police to stop the girls from wearing the heels. Cisneros proscribes a romantic or exotic reading of the dress-up episode, focusing instead on the girls' discovery of the threatening nature of male sexual power that is frequently disguised as desirable male attention and positive validation of women, though what is, in fact, sexual reification.

Scenes of patriarchal and sexual violence in the collection also prevent a romantic reading of women's issues in this Chicano community. We see a woman whose husband locks her in the house, a daughter brutally beaten by her father, and Esperanza's own sexual initiation through rape. Like the threatening corner grocer in "**The Family of Little Feet**," the men in these stories control or appropriate female sexuality by adopting one or another form of violence as if it were their innate right. One young woman, Rafaela, "gets locked indoors because her husband is afraid [she] will run away since she is too beautiful to look at" (p. 76). Esperanza and her friends send papaya and coconut juice up to the woman in a paper bag on a clothesline she has lowered; metonymically, Cisneros suggests that the sweet drinks represent the island the woman has left and the dance hall down the street as well, where other women are ostensibly more in control of their own sexual expression and are allowed to open their homes with keys. The young yet wise narrator, however, recognizes that "always there is someone offering sweeter drinks, someone promising to keep [women] on a silver string" (p. 76).

The cycle of stories about Esperanza's friend Sally shows this patriarchal violence in its more overt stages. Like Rafaela, the young teenager Sally is frequently forced to stay in the house because "her father says to be this beautiful is trouble" (p. 77). But even worse, we learn later that Sally's father beats her. Appearing at school with bruises and scars, Sally tells Esperanza that her father sometimes hits her with his hands "just like a dog . . . as if I was an animal. He thinks I'm going to run away like his sisters who made the family ashamed. Just because I'm a daughter . . ." (p. 85). In "**Linoleum Roses**," a later story in the Sally cycle, we learn that she escapes her father's brutal-

ity by marrying a marshmallow salesman "in another state where it's legal to get married before eighth grade" (p. 95). In effect, her father's violent attempts to control her sexuality—here a case of child abuse—cause Sally to exchange one repressive patriarchal prison for another. Dependent on her husband for money, she is forbidden to talk on the telephone, look out the window, or have her friends visit. In one of his fits of anger, her husband kicks the door in. Where Rafaela's husband imprisons her with a key, Sally's locks her in with psychological force: "[Sally] sits home because she is afraid to go outside without his permission" (p. 95).

A role model for Esperanza, Sally has symbolized the process of sexual initiation for her younger friend. Two stories in the cycle reveal Esperanza's growing awareness of the link between sex, male power, and violence in patriarchal society. In "**The Monkey Garden**," Esperanza perceives her friend Sally to be in danger when the older girl agrees to "kiss" a group of boys so that they will return her car keys; ". . . they're making her kiss them" (p. 90), Esperanza reports to the mother of one of the boys. When the mother shows no concern, Esperanza undertakes Sally's defense herself: "Sally needed to be saved. I took three big sticks and a brick and figured this was enough" (p. 90). Sally and the boys tell her to go home and Esperanza feels stupid and ashamed. In postlapsarian anguish, she runs to the other end of the garden and, in what seems to be an especially severe form of self-punishment for this young girl, tries to make herself die by willing her heart to stop beating.

In "**Red Clowns**," the story that follows, Esperanza's first suspicions of the patriarchy's joining of male power, violence, and sex are confirmed beyond a doubt. She had previously used appellation throughout the first story in the Sally cycle to ask her friend to teach her how to dress and apply makeup. Now the appellation to Sally is one of severe disillusionment after Esperanza has been sexually assaulted in an amusement park while waiting for Sally to return from her own sexual liaison:

> Sally, you lied. It wasn't like you said at all . . . Why didn't you hear me when I called? Why didn't you tell them to leave me alone? The one who grabbed me by the arm, he wouldn't let me go. He said I love you, Spanish girl, I love you, and pressed his sour mouth to mine . . . I couldn't make them go away. I couldn't do anything but cry . . . Please don't make me tell it all.
>
> (P. 93)

This scene extends the male violence toward Esperanza, begun on her first day of work, when an apparently nice old man "grabs [her] face with both hands and kisses [her] hard on the mouth and doesn't let go" (p. 52). Together with other instances of male violence in the collection—Rafaela's imprisonment, Sally's beatings, and the details of Minerva's life, another young married woman whose husband beats her and throws a rock through the window—these episodes form a continuum in which sex, patriarchal power, and violence are linked. Earlier, Cisneros had developed this connection in the poem "**South Sangamon**," in which similar elements of male violence predominate: "he punched her belly," "his drunk cussing," "the whole door shakes / like his big foot meant to break it," and "just then / the big rock comes in."[5] *The House on Mango Street* presents this continuum critically, offering an unromanticized, inside view of Esperanza's violent sexual initiation and its links to the oppression of other women in the Chicano community.

Cisneros does not merely delineate women's victimization in this collection, however. Several positive female role models help to guide Esperanza's development. Minerva, for example, although a victim of her husband's violence, makes time to write poetry. "But when the kids are asleep after she's fed them their pancake dinner, she writes poems on little pieces of paper that she folds over and over and holds in her hands a long time, little pieces of paper that smell like a dime. She lets me read her poems. I let her read mine" (p. 80). Minerva's artistic production is reminiscent of Dr. Reefy in *Winesburg, Ohio*'s "Paper Pills," who scribbles words of wisdom on scraps of paper he crumples up, finally sharing them with a patient. It is also similar to the character of Rosendo in Soto's *Spiks,* a barrio artist who can only find space to paint an idyllic scene on the crumbling wall of his tenement bathroom and whose wife, acutely aware of the pressing economic needs of their young children, cannot afford the luxury of appreciating this non-revenue-producing art. Like Dr. Reefy, but unlike Rosendo, Minerva succeeds in communicating through her art; exchanging poems with Esperanza, she contributes to the latter's artistic development while at the same time offering a lesson in women's domestic oppression and how to begin transcending it.

Also supportive of Esperanza's artistic creativity is her invalid aunt, Guadalupe: "She listened to every book, every poem I read her. One day I read her one of my own . . . That's nice. That's very good, she said in her tired voice. You just remember to keep writing, Esperanza. You must keep writing. It will keep you free . . ." (p. 56). Although the aunt lives in squalid, poor surroundings and is dying from a disease that has disfigured her once-beautiful body, she listens to the girl's stories and poems and encourages Esperanza's artistic talent. The story, "**Three Sisters,**" recounts the wake held for the baby sister of Esperanza's friends Lucy and Rachel and is also the theme of Cisneros' earlier poem, "**Velorio,**" in the collection entitled *Bad Boys.* Expanding upon "**Velorio,**" however, this story introduces the figures of "the aunts, the three sisters, *las comadres,*" visitors at the *velorio* who encourage Esperanza to see her artistic production in relation to the community: "When you leave you must remember always to come back . . . for the others. A circle, you understand? You will always be Esperanza. You will always be Mango Street. . . . You can't forget who you are" (p. 98). Although Esperanza doesn't understand the women's message completely, the seeds of her socially conscious art have been planted here through the directives these women give her at the baby's wake.

Alicia, another positive role model who appears in "**Alicia Who Sees Mice**" and "**Alicia and I Talking on Edna's Steps,**" also counsels Esperanza to value Mango Street and return there one day to contribute to its improvement: "Like it or not you are Mango Street and one day you'll come back too." To Esperanza's reply, "Not me. Not until somebody makes it better," Alicia wryly comments "Who's going to do it? The mayor?" (p. 99). Alicia had previously appeared in the collection as a university student who takes "two trains and a bus [to the campus] because she doesn't want to spend her whole life in a factory or behind a rolling pin" (p. 32). Rebelling against her father's expectations of her, that "a woman's place is sleeping so she can wake up early . . . and make the lunchbox tortillas," Alicia "studies all night and sees the mice, the ones her father says do not exist" (p. 32). Fighting what the patriarchy expects of her, Alicia at the same time represents a clear-sighted, non-mystified vision of the barrio. As a role-model and advice-giver to Esperanza, she embodies both the antipatriarchal themes and the social obligation to return to one's ethnic community that are so central to Cisneros' text.

Cisneros touches on several other important women's issues in this volume, including media images of ideal female beauty, the reifying stare of male surveyors of women, and sex roles within the family. In an effort to counter the sexual division of labor in the home, for example, Esperanza refuses one instance of women's work: "I have begun my own quiet war. Simple. Sure. I am the one who leaves the table like a man, without pulling back the chair or picking up the plate" (p. 82). Although this gesture calls critical attention to gender inequities in the family, Cisneros avoids the issue of who, in fact, will end up performing the household labor that Esperanza refuses here. This important and symbolic, yet somewhat adolescent gesture merely touches on the surface of the problem and is likely, in fact, to increase the work for another woman in Esperanza's household.

The majority of stories in **The House on Mango Street,** however, face important social issues head-on. The volume's simple, poetic language, with its insistence that the individual develops within a social community rather than in isolation, distances it from many accepted canonical texts.[6] Its deceptively simple, childlike prose and its emphasis on the unromanticized, non-mainstream issues of patriarchal violence and ethnic poverty, however, should serve precisely to accord it canonical status. We must work toward a broader understanding among literary critics of the importance of such issues to art in order to attain a richer, more diverse canon and to avoid the undervaluation and oversight of such valuable texts as **The House on Mango Street.**

Notes

1. Terry Eagleton, *Literary Theory: An Introduction* (Minneapolis: University of Minnesota Press, 1983), 201 and passim.

2. Sandra Cisneros, *The House on Mango Street* (Houston: Arte Público Press, 1985). Subsequent references will be to this edition and will appear in the text. For the figures on the press run see Pedro Gutiérrez-Revuelta, "Género e ideología en el libro de Sandra Cisneros: *The House on Mango Street,*" *Críticas* 1, no. 3 (1986): 48-59.

3. Gutiérrez-Revuelta, "Género e ideología," 48. This critic also cites nine articles that have appeared to date on Cisneros' text. They consist primarily of reviews in Texas newspapers and articles in Chicano journals. See also Erlinda González-Berry and Tey Diana Rebolledo's "Growing up Chicano: Tomás Rivera and Sandra Cisneros," *Revista Chicano-Riqueña* 13 (1985): 109-19.

4. Sherwood Anderson, *Winesburg, Ohio* (New York: Viking Press, 1964, rpt. 1970); Pedro Juan Soto, *Spiks,* trans. Victoria Ortiz (New York: Monthly Review Press, 1973); Gloria Naylor, *The Women of Brewster Place* (New York: Penguin Books, 1983); and Tomás Rivera, *. . . y no se lo tragó la tierra/And the Earth Did Not Part* (Berkeley: Quinto Sol, 1971). Among the many specific comparisons that might be made, Naylor's "Cora Lee" has much in common with Cisneros' "There Was an Old Woman She Had So Many Children She Didn't Know What to Do."

5. Sandra Cisneros, *Bad Boys* (San Jose, Calif.: Mango Publications, 1980).

6. Other critics have argued that Esperanza's departure from Mango Street is individualistic and escapist, and that the desire for a house of her own away from the barrio represents a belief in the American Dream. See Gutiérrez-Revuelta, "Género e ideología," 52-55 and Juan Rodríguez, "*The House on Mango Street* by Sandra Cisneros," *Austin Chronicle,* 10 Aug. 1984 (cited in Gutiérrez-Revuelta, p. 52). I find that the text itself supports the opposite view, as does the author's choice of employment. Cisneros has returned to a Chicago barrio, teaching creative writing at an alternative high school for drop-outs. See "About Sandra Cisneros," *The House on Mango Street,* 103.

Woman Hollering Creek and Other Stories

SUSAN E. GRIFFIN (ESSAY DATE 1997)

SOURCE: Griffin, Susan E. "Resistance and Reinvention in Sandra Cisneros' *Woman Hollering Creek.*" In *Ethnicity and the American Short Story,* edited by Julie Brown, pp. 85-96. New York: Garland Publishing, Inc., 1997.

In the following essay, Griffin chronicles the steps that the female protagonists in Woman Hollering Creek and Other Stories *must take in order to gain control over their lives and destinies.*

In her prefatory poem to **My Wicked, Wicked Ways,** Sandra Cisneros asks, "What does a woman [like me] inherit that tells her how to go?" (x). This question about the cultural inheritance of Mexican American women and how it shapes their perceptions of the choices available to them is central to Cisneros' work. Throughout her poetry and fiction, she has depicted the material and ideological forces that circumscribe Mexican American women's lives.[1] In her novel **The House on Mango Street,** and in several of the poems in **My Wicked, Wicked Ways,** Cisneros portrays women who are trapped by poverty and controlling, often violent, relationships with men. In her second book of fiction, **Woman Hollering Creek and Other Stories,** she explores the cultural as well as the material limitations of the lives of Mexican American women. Like Cisneros herself, her female characters often must come to terms with a cultural tradition that they love but also view as oppressive because of the limited conception of appropriate behavior for women available within Mexican narratives and culture (Rodríguez Aranda 66). In **Woman Hollering Creek,** the role that Mexican popular culture and traditional

Mexican narratives play in limiting women's sense of identity becomes one of Cisneros' central concerns.

The limitations of traditional Mexican representations of women are embodied in the dichotomy between two of the most influential women in Mexican myth and culture—the Virgin of Guadalupe and Malintzin Temepal, often referred to as Malinche, the translator for and lover of Hernan Cortes, the Spanish conqueror of Mexico. Cisneros describes growing up with these two female figures—the Virgin of Guadalupe and Malinche—as the two primary role models for women in her culture as "a hard route to go"—a position in which she felt she must choose "one or the other, there's no in-between" (Rodríguez Aranda 65). Traditionally, Mary is defined primarily in terms of her role as a mother and is associated with family life and the beliefs of the Catholic Church; because of the story of her appearance to Juan Diego in Teyapec, she is also seen by many Mexicans as the protector of their people, their patron saint. Malinche, in contrast, is associated with lust, selfishness, and the betrayal of her race. In "From a Long Line of Vendidas: Chicanas and Feminism," Cherríe Moraga describes how Malinizin's actions are perceived: "To put it in its most base terms: Malinizin, also called Malinche, fucked the white man who conquered the Indian people of Mexico and destroyed their culture. Ever since, brown men have been accusing her of betraying her race" (175).

In Cisneros' depiction of the cultural influences upon Mexican American women in **Woman Hollering Creek,** it is not only the literal figures of the Virgin and Malinche that influence women's views of identity, however. The women in her stories are also influenced by all the contemporary forms of popular culture, like movies, television, and songs—particularly genres within these media that emphasize romance—which utilize the Virgin/Malinche, good/evil, pure/fallen paradigm and define women primarily in terms of their relationships with men. In stories like **"Woman Hollering Creek,"** television is the primary medium that embodies beliefs about appropriate behavior for women. In this story, Cisneros depicts a world in which television, along with movies and songs, is becoming our common mythology (77).[2] But she portrays these forms of popular culture as reinforcing the same limited roles for women as narratives about Malinche and the Virgin. These limitations are illustrated by the two types of women depicted in the *telenovelas*[3] of **"Woman Hollering Creek"** and **"Bien Pretty,"**

the evil scheming woman and the pure, passive, long-suffering woman who must endure great hardships for love.

Cisneros and other Mexican American women authors and feminist critics have noted that Mexican women who reject traditional familial roles are often perceived by those within their culture as Malinche has been, as traitors to their race. The question that Sandra Cisneros attempts to work out in **Woman Hollering Creek** is how Mexican American women can create new roles for themselves—ones that reject the Virgin/Malinche dichotomy and the definition of women mainly in terms of their relations with men—without wholly rejecting Mexican culture. For Cisneros, this means not abandoning the narratives of her culture but reinventing and revising both traditional myths and the narratives of current popular culture. Through the short stories in this collection, Cisneros is able to illustrate different ways in which women can reject and even rewrite traditional narratives.

Cisneros' title story, **"Woman Hollering Creek,"** is the story in which she most clearly illustrates the negative effects of popular romance genres' portrayal of women, and it is also the story in which she begins to illustrate how women can resist the romance narrative. Within this work, Cleófilas, the story's central character, interprets the events that happen to her in the literal, chronological narrative of the story within the context of another narrative—one she has absorbed from the *telenovelas* she watches and the romance novels she reads. Cleófilas's actions in **"Woman Hollering Creek"** are constructed by—and eventually in resistance to—this type of romance narrative.

Cleófilas, like several of the girls in **The House on Mango Street,** believes in a view of romantic love that is perpetuated through the media and the popular culture of both Mexico and the United States. This view is connected to what she reads in romance novels and sees in the *telenovelas.* Like American soap operas, *telenovelas* focus on women characters and romance, but, because they have endings and include a limited number of characters, they have more in common with romance novels—both the Spanish-language Corín Tellado type, which Cleófilas reads, and the similar English-language Harlequins—than with American soap operas.

Cleófilas accepts the idea promoted by the *telenovelas* that love is the ultimate good, "the most important thing" (44). She daydreams about the characters in the *telenovelas*—handsome men who finally confess their love and devotion to the women who adore them—and she imagines this kind of passion in her own life. What Cleófilas has been waiting for all her life is "passion . . . passion in its purest crystalline essence. The kind the books and songs and *telenovelas* describe when one finds finally the great love of one's life" (44).

The love of the *telenovelas* and romance novels, however, is linked with images of wealth and escape and, at the same time, connected with suffering and self-sacrifice. Like the ideas of the women in **The House on Mango Street**, Cleófilas' ideas about romance and her decision to marry are connected to her desire to be materially better off. The girls on Mango Street are aware of the shabbiness of their shoes and clothes and the houses they live in, and, with the exceptions of Esperanza and Alicia, they believe that marriage is their best opportunity to have better things. This wish for more material wealth is interwined with romantic visions of being rescued by a man who will carry them away from their present lives. What they desire most is a means of escape, so love, distant places, beautiful clothes, jewelry, and houses all become part of the same fantasy. Marín, a friend of Esperanza, the narrator of **The House on Mango Street**, tells Esperanza that the best jobs for girls are downtown because there you "get to wear nice clothes and can meet someone in the subway who might marry you and take you to live in a big house far away" (26). This is the kind of fantasy—a man rescuing a woman from a dreary life and taking her away to a life of love and luxury—toward which romance novels' plots build. As Ann Barr Snitow explains in "Mass Market Romance: Pornography for Women Is Different," romances like Harlequins are based on "a sustaining fantasy of rescue, glamour, and change" that includes descriptions of exotic places and detailed descriptions of consumer items, like furniture, clothes, and gourmet food (248, 250).[4] It is this fantasy of glamour and change that Cleófilas believes in when she marries. After hearing the name of the town where Juan Pedro, the man who has proposed to her, lives, she thinks it has "[a] nice sterling ring to it. The tinkle of money. She would get to wear outfits like the women on the *tele*, like Lucía Mendez. And have a lovely house . . ." (45).

Cleófilas daydreams about the passionate professions of love on the *telenovelas,* but there is a sharp contrast between this romantic passion and her thoughts about her husband with acne scars and a pot-belly "whose whiskers she finds each morning in the sink, whose shoes she must air every evening on the porch, this husband . . . who doesn't care at all for music or *telenovelas* or romance or roses or the moon floating over the *arroyo*" (49). In even greater contrast to the perfect passion of the *telenovelas* is the violence that Cleófilas is a victim of in her own life and is aware of in the world around her. The first time her husband hits her—an incident in which he slaps her "again and again" until her lip splits and bleeds "an orchid of blood" (47)—is only the first of many beatings that begin soon after he and Cleófilas are married and sometimes leave her with black and blue marks all over her body. Cleófilas also notices that the newspapers seem filled with tales of women being beaten and killed:

> This woman found on the side of the interstate. This one's cadaver, this one unconscious, this one beaten blue. Her ex-husband, her lover, her father, her brother, her uncle, her friend, her co-worker. Always. The same grisly news in the pages of the dailies.
>
> (52)

Although the combination of the myths of romantic love and the reality of men's control over and violence against women initially may appear to be antithetical, the romantic myths play a role in perpetuating the cycle of violence in **"Woman Hollering Creek"** because both are dependent upon male action and female passivity. At one point in **"Woman Hollering Creek,"** Juan Pedro throws one of Cleófilas's Spanish romance novels across the room, hitting her and leaving a raised welt on her cheek. In this scene, the language of romance embodied by the book and the reality of violence literally intersect, and the romance novel becomes something that Juan Pedro uses as a weapon against his wife, but *telenovelas* and romance novels also function as destructive forces in more subtle, less literal ways in **"Woman Hollering Creek."** They bring love and sacrifice or love and suffering together. After the *telenovela* episode when Lucía Mendez from *Tú o Nadie* confesses her love, Cleófilas thinks that the sacrifices this character has made and the hardships she has endured are worth the price "because to suffer for love is good, The pain all sweet somehow. In the end" (45). Although Cisneros does not indicate whether this woman from the *telenovela* is suffering physical abuse, one of the ideas that Cleófilas absorbs from the *telenovelas* is that suffering for love is a good thing—immediate sacrifice and suffering lead the women on television to a final happy ending.

This idea that love is the ultimate good and therefore worth suffering for is embedded in the plots of romance novels and *telenovelas*. The romance blends love and suffering because, as Ann Barr Snitow argues, romance novels—and I would extend this to *telenovelas* as well—"Make bridges between contradiction; they soothe ambivalence" (253). In them, love magically converts "a brutal male sexuality" to romance (253); through his relationship with the heroine, the hero softens. Snitow argues that, in romances, cruelty, callousness, and coldness are equated with maleness, and the novels' happy endings offer the "possibility that male coldness, absence, and boredom are not what they seem" (250). In the end, a rational explanation for the male hero's behavior appears, and it becomes apparent that "in spite of his coldness or preoccupation, the hero really loves the heroine and wants to marry her" (250). Before the happy resolution, the heroine may suffer as a result of the hero's indifference or his anger and abuse, but the emphasis is on the happy ending, and the heroine's suffering becomes just part of the plot that leads to this ending. In *Reading the Romance: Women, Patriarchy, and Popular Literature*, Janice Radway describes the message inherent in this process:

> When a romance presents the story of a woman who is misunderstood by the hero, mistreated and manhandled, and then suddenly loved, protected, and cared for by him because he recognizes that he mistook the meaning of her behavior, the novel is informing its readers that minor acts of violence can be similarly reinterpreted as the result of misunderstandings or jealousy born of "true love."
>
> (75)

This view of love allows Cleófilas to see the suffering of the character in the *telenovela* as ". . . all sweet somehow. In the end"; she believes that for "the great love of one's life," a woman does "whatever one can, must do, whatever the cost" (44). For most of **"Woman Hollering Creek,"** her belief in romance allows Cleófilas to retain the hope that, beyond her own suffering, there may be a happy ending.

Because of this belief in happy endings, Cleófilas does not reject the romance plot when her husband begins to beat her as Esperanza does when she is raped in **The House on Mango Street**. After Esperanza's rape, the gap between the romance plot and her own life becomes too great to reconcile, and she feels betrayed by the images of love and sex she has seen in the media. "They all lied," she thinks,"All the books and magazines everything that told it wrong" (100). Even after her husband has begun to beat her regularly, however, Cleófilas clings to the romance plot and

tries to reconcile it with her own life. She begins thinking of her life as a *telenovela* in which "the episodes got sadder and sadder. And there were no commercials in between for comic relief. And no happy ending in sight" (52-53). She imagines romance and happy endings as things that happened to someone with a romantic name and thinks that if she were to change her name to something "more poetic than Cleófilas," her life might be more like the lives of the women in the *telenovelas* (53).

Radway argues that romantic violence arises from an inability to imagine "a situation in which a woman might acquire and use resources that would allow her to withstand male opposition and coercion" (72), and, for most of **"Woman Hollering Creek,"** Cleófilas is in this very position. She is simply unable to imagine rejecting the romance plot and resisting her husband. Along with the violence of Cleófilas's life and the images and language of the *telenovelas,* however, there is a third narrative that emerges in **"Woman Hollering Creek."** The creek itself comes to represent the voices of real women who are silenced by violence and by the myths the *telenovelas* and romance novels perpetuate. After moving to Texas, Cleófilas is always aware of the creek's presence and is fascinated by its name, but it is only when she meets Felice at the end of the story that the creek becomes linked with resistance to the romance plot. When Cleófilas moves to Seguín, she is puzzled by the name of the creek—*La Gritona,* Woman Hollering. "Such a lovely name for a creek," she thinks, "Though no one could say whether the woman hollered from anger or from pain" (46). For most of the story, these are the only two emotions that Cleófilas can imagine as this woman's motivation—anger or pain, rage or suffering—because these are the only explanations her life or the *telenovelas* offer her for a woman's shout. She speculates about whom the creek is named for, imagining it might be *La Llorona,* the weeping woman of Mexican folklore (51).[5] Yet she is unable to come up with an explanation that satisfies her, and the only women she knows in Seguín are unable to or uninterested in helping her. Cleófilas observes that no one in the town "questioned, little less understood" the name Woman Hollering.

Even when she is puzzled by the river, Cleófilas experiences it as "an alive thing, a thing with a voice all its own" (51), and, when she finally seizes an opportunity to leave her husband and return to Mexico, she realizes that the voice of the woman hollering may be a voice of celebration. In the scene in which Cleófilas is leaving Seguín, Cisneros uses a woman's shout, a holler, to represent a voice that resists both male violence and the romance narrative. When Felice, who has promised to give Cleófilas a ride to the Greyhound station, yells as they cross the river, Cleófilas is shocked. Felice yells not out of anger or pain, but because she wants to shout—as a kind of tribute to the woman for whom the river was named and the other women she represents. "Every time I cross the bridge I do that," Felice tells her, "Because of the name, you know. Woman Hollering. *Pues,* I holler" (55). "Did you ever notice," Felice continues, "how nothing around here is named after a woman?" (55). The shout Felice gives is filled with strength, fearlessness, celebration rather than with pain, fear, or pleading—a shout that both Felice and Cleófilas describe as a "a holler like Tarzan" (55-56).

It is appropriate that Felice is the vehicle of such celebration because her emotional and economic self-sufficiency make her unlike any woman Cleófilas has ever met before. When Cleófilas asks if the pickup Felice is driving is her husband's, Felice tells her she does not have a husband; "the pickup was hers. She herself had chosen it. She herself was paying for it" (55). Everything about Felice amazes Cleófilas and helps her begin to imagine alternatives for women beyond either her own life or the lives of love and suffering in the *telenovelas* and Corín Tellado romance novels. By witnessing the power of Felice's shout—a shout that defies the idea of women as silent victims or sufferers—Cleófilas becomes aware of her own voice. After Felice shouts, Cleófilas hears laughter, and her first response to this is to think that Felice must be laughing, but she soon realizes it is not Felice. The sound is "gurgling out of her own throat, a long ribbon of laughter like water" (56). This laughter is a form of expression that cannot be contained or understood within the romance plot that Cleófilas has accepted for most of "**Woman Hollering Creek.**" Like Felice's shout and the creek itself, it represents a voice in opposition to the romance script and implies Cleófilas's potential to reclaim her own life, as well as her voice, by resisting the popular romance narrative.

The ending of "**Woman Hollering Creek,**" however, marks only the first step Cisneros depicts in the rejection of equating women with passivity and suffering. While the final scene of this story demonstrates that Cleófilas is beginning to realize that there are other possibilities for women's lives than the ones she has previously imagined, the story does not reveal how she will use this realization, how it will affect her own self-image and her view of the *telenovelas.* In "**Little Miracles, Kept Promises,**" Cisneros portrays a young woman who is not only able to resist a traditional narrative but is also capable of appropriating and rewriting it. In this story composed of different characters' petitions to various saints, including the Virgin Mary, Chayo, the character whom Cisneros describes at the greatest length, feels alienated from the other women of her culture—both the Virgin and the women of the *telenovelas.* Chayo, who wants to devote herself to painting rather than motherhood, tells the Virgin in her letter, "Though no one else in my family, no other woman, neither friend nor relative, no one I know, not even the heroine in the *telenovelas,* no women, wants to live alone. I do" (127). Chayo even confesses to Mary that she has been unable to accept her, to "let you in my house," because she has associated Mary with her mother and grandmother's silent acceptance of suffering (127). Chayo desires an image not of a woman suffering but of a woman who is strong and powerful. She writes to Mary, "I wanted you bare-breasted, snakes in your hands. I wanted you leaping and somersaulting the backs of bulls. I wanted you swallowing raw hearts and rattling volcanic ash. I wasn't going to be my mother or my grandma. All that self-sacrifice, all that silent suffering" (127).

Chayo is able to accept Mary only by revising or reinventing her image of her. She begins to see her as the spiritual force that is incarnated in images of Aztec deities as well as in portraits of the Virgin. She views her as *Nuestra Senora de Soledad,* Our Lady of the Rosary, Our Lady of Perpetual Sorrow and also as Tonantzín, Coatlaxopeuh, Teteoinnan, Toci, Xochiquetzal, and she addresses her as Mighty Guadalupana Coatlaxopeuh Tonantizín. To Chayo, Mary becomes a figure who embodies both the suffering and endurance of women and their strength and power, and this frees her not only to love Mary but to love herself—to choose not to repeat the lives of her mother and grandmother without feeling like a traitor to her race.

The central character in Cisneros's "**Bien Pretty**" also engages in this process of rewriting or reinventing, both in relation to a traditional Mexican myth and in relation to contemporary romances. Like Chayo, Lupe is an artist. She is a painter who is using her lover, Flavio, as a model for Prince Popocatépetl in her "updated version of the Prince Popocatépetl/Princess Ixtaccíhuatl volcano myth"[6] until her lover leaves her and returns to his wife and children in Mexico (144). After Flavio leaves, Lupe continues her job as an art director for a community cultural center but is unable to paint and begins watching television when she comes home from work—first old Mexican movies and then *telenovelas*—and begins buying Corín Tellado romance novels and magazines with stories about *telenovela* stars.

Her response to the *telenovelas* is different than Cleófilas's, however. Lupe realizes what the attraction of *telenovelas* is, but she also realizes that the images of women in the *telenovelas* reinforce traditional stereotypes of women. After a conversation with a cashier at Centano's Drugstore about one of the latest *telenovelas*, "Si Dios quiere," Lupe thinks:

> *Amar as vivir.* What it comes down to for that woman at Centano's and for me. It was enough to keep us tuning in every day at six-thirty, another episode, another thrill. To relive that living when the universe ran through the blood like river water. Alive. Not the weeks spent writing grant proposals, not the forty hours standing behind a cash register shoving cans of refried beans into plastic sacks.
>
> (163)

But what the *telenovelas* can provide is only a severely limited version of what it means to be alive—living as devising ways to attain the attention and favor of men and, as in **"Woman Hollering Creek,"** romance linked with suffering. Lupe's frustration with these limitations is illustrated in the dreams she begins having about the *telenovelas* she is watching—dreams that express her desire to revise the actions of the *telenovela* characters:

> I started dreaming of these Rosas and Briandas and Luceros. And in my dreams I'm slapping the heroine to her senses, because I want them to be women who make things happen, not women who things happen to. Not loves that are tormentosos. Not men powerful and passionate versus women either volatile and evil or sweet and resigned. But women. Real women. The ones I've loved all my life.
>
> (160)

In **"Bien Pretty,"** Cisneros implies both that women can find a different kind of female figure in some popular culture narratives and that where these models are unavailable they can choose to create their own. Lupe can listen, not to "Lola Beltran sobbing 'Soy infeliz' into her four *cervezas*. But Daniela Romo singing 'Ya no. *Es verdad que te adoro, pero mas me adoro yo.*' I love you, honey, but I love me more" (163). By the end of this short story, Lupe realizes that she must make an effort

to "right the world and live . . . the way lives were meant to be lived" (163)—not the way lives are portrayed in the *telenovelas*. This means living with self-respect, independence, and strength as well as with passion, desire, and pain.

When Lupe returns to her volcano painting to finish it, this need to rewrite the kinds of stories told about women affects her work, and she decides to switch the positions of Prince Popocatépetl and Princess Ixtaccíhuatl because "after all who's to say the sleeping mountain isn't the prince, and the voyeur the princess, right?" (163). What Lupe, like Cleófilas, and Chayo has discovered is a different way of viewing an old story, a process that can be applied both to traditional Mexican and Aztec stories and to popular romance genres in order to yield new narratives.

Notes

1. Cisneros has published three collections of poetry, *Bad Boys* (1980), *My Wicked, Wicked Ways* (1987), and *Loose Woman* (1994); one novel, *The House on Mango Street* (1983), composed of forty-four brief narratives of vignettes; and one collection of short stories, *Woman Hollering Creek and Other Stories* (1991). She was born in 1954 in Chicago and, like Esperanza Cordero, her narrator from *The House on Mango Street,* grew up there. Cisneros is a 1978 graduate of the University of Iowa Writer's Workshop, which she attended after graduating with a BA in English from Loyola University. From 1978 to 1980 she taught creative writing at an alternative high school in Chicago. Since the early 1980s she has received several grants and fellowships, including two from the National Endowment for the Arts.

2. In her interview with Pilar E. Rodríguez Aranda, Cisneros discusses the possibility that "the visual is taking the place of oral myth" and explains that, while she was teaching, she realized she must resort to references to television characters in order to make her points because "that was our common mythology, that's what we had in common, television" (77).

3. Literally translated *telenova* means "a novel transmitted by television" (Rector and Trinta 194). Although in the United States they are often referred to as Spanish-language soap operas, *Telenovelas* differ from American soap operas because they have endings—usually happy ones. A *telenovela* usually runs for several months, and then a new one begins in the same time slot.

4. In her article "The Incorporation of Women: A Comparison of North American and Mexican American Popular Culture," Jean Franco asserts—using the work of Carola Garcia Calderon's *Revistas Femininas, La mujer como objecto de consumo*—that Harlequins and Corín Tellado romance novels are similar but notes that in the Corín Tellado romance novels, the kind of Spanish romance novels Cleófilas reads in "Woman Hollering Creek" and Lupe reads in *"Bien* Pretty," luxury items, expensive clothes, and jewelry are emphasized even more than in Harlequins (Franco 124).

5. Llorona is a mythical apparition of a weeping woman. Many versions of the Llorona legend exist throughout Mexico and the Pacific and Southwestern portions of the United States. Explanations of the reason for Llorona's sorrow vary greatly among the different versions of the story. In several of these variants, she mourns drowned children and is sighted near a river, creek, or other body of water.

6. Popocatépetl and Ixtaccíhuatl are dormant volcanoes in central Mexico named after legendary Aztec lovers, Ixtaccíhuatl, an Aztec emperor's daughter, and Popocatépetl, an Aztec warrior. For a description of the myth, see Frances Toor's *A Treasury of Mexican Folkways*. Mexico, D. F.: Mexico Press, 1947.

References

Cisneros, Sandra. *The House on Mango Street*. New York: Random House, 1989.

——. *My Wicked, Wicked Ways*. New York: Random House, 1992.

——. *Woman Hollering Creek and Other Stories*. New York: Random House, 1991.

Franco, Jean. "The Incorporation of Women: A Comparison of North American and Mexican American Popular Culture." *Studies in Entertainment: Critical Approaches to Mass Culture*. Ed. Tania Modleski. Bloomington: Indiana University Press, 1986. 119-138.

Moraga, Cherríe. "From a Long Line of Vendidas: Chicanas and Feminism." *Feminist Studies/Critical Studies*. Ed. Teresa de Lauretis. Bloomington: Indiana University Press, 1986. 173-190.

Radway, Janice. *Reading the Romance: Women, Patriarchy, and Popular Literature*. Chapel Hill: University of North Carolina Press, 1984.

Rector, Monica, and Aluizio Ramos Trinta. "The Telenovela." *Diogenes* 113-114 (1981): 194-204.

Rodríguez Aranda, Pilar E. "On the Solitary Fate of Being Mexican, Female, Wicked and Thirty-Three: An Interview with Writer Sandra Cisneros." *The Americas Review: A Review of Hispanic Literature and Art of the USA*. 18 (1990): 64-80.

Snitow, Ann Barr. "Mass Market Romance: Pornography for Women Is Different." *Powers of Desire: The Politics of Sexuality*. Eds. Ann Barr Snitow, Christine Stansell, and Sharon Thompson. New York: Monthly Review Press, 1983. 245-263.

Caramelo

CAROL A. CUJEC (REVIEW DATE MARCH 2003)

SOURCE: Cujec, Carol A. "Caramel-Coated Truths and Telenovela Lives: Sandra Cisneros Returns with an Ambitious Novel about the Latino Community." *World & I* 18, no. 3 (March 2003): 228.

In the following review, Cujec compliments Cisneros's storytelling in Caramelo *and studies the novel's portrayal of the choices available to Chicana women past and present, illustrating the importance of decision-making on women's self-determination.*

In her new novel *Caramelo,* Sandra Cisneros bathes our senses in Latino culture as we accompany her characters walking the scorched sands of Acapulco, buying shoes at Chicago's Maxwell Street flea market, listening to a grandmother complain about the mangoes, and eventually finding their destinies and their destinations. *Caramelo* loops and spirals among four generations, traveling from Mexico City to Chicago to Texas and back in eighty-six chapters. Cisneros admits that this is her most ambitious and challenging work, which is why it took her eight years to complete.

Cisneros was the first Chicana writer to emerge on the mainstream literary scene in the 1980s. Her first novel, *The House on Mango Street,* is now a staple of countless high school and college literature classes. Critical praise as well as several prestigious awards, including the Before Columbus American Book Award and a MacArthur "genius" grant, have established her literary prominence. No wonder she faced so much pressure to complete this long-awaited work. As Cisneros explained in a phone interview, "In the past, when I wrote other books, most of the time people had no idea what I was doing, nor did they care. What I felt this time was the pressure of the public waiting for this book. Even my family, this time they were waiting for this book as well."

Mementos, memories

Caramelo, a fictionalized autobiography, is not heavily plot-driven but more a series of vignettes similar to Cisneros' other works of prose. The novel begins with a memento—a photograph taken in Acapulco during a tumultuous family vacation nearly ending in divorce. The Reyes family stands in the photo: Inocencio, his wife, Zoila, and his six sons, along with Inocencio's mother, called "the Awful Grandmother" by the narrator. The only one missing, curiously, is the narrator herself, Inocencio's youngest child and only daughter Celaya (called Lala), who was five at the time. "They've forgotten about me," complains Lala, adding, "It's as if I'm the photographer walking along the beach with the tripod camera on my shoulder asking,—Un recuerdo? A souvenir? A memory?"

In fact, by writing these memories Lala is the photographer, with her vivid words creating snapshots of everyday life and significant moments that make up a true family portrait. In the end, her words become the most enduring memento: "Remembering is the hand of God. I remember you, therefore I make you immortal."

FROM THE AUTHOR

CISNEROS ON THE POWER OF LANGUAGE
There are ways to be a revolutionary without guns or violence. You can be a pacifist revolutionary. My weapon has always been language, and I've always used it, but it has changed. Instead of shaping the words like knives now, I think they're flowers or bridges.

Cisneros, Sandra. Excerpt from "An Interview with Sandra Cisneros," in *Missouri Review* 25, no. 1 (2002): 105.

Lala brings her images into sharp focus with sensory details that transform a collection of static photos into fragrant, sweaty, mouthwatering slices of life. She records a trip across the border into Mexico, for example, as an explosion of the senses: "Churches the color of flan, . . . the smell of diesel exhaust, the smell of somebody roasting coffee, the smell of hot corn tortillas along with the pat-pat of the women's hands making them, the sting of roasting chiles in your throat and in your eyes."

Like the intricate caramel-colored shawl, the *caramelo rebozo,* given to the Awful Grandmother by her own mother, the story is an intricate and incomplete tapestry. The theme of weaving, with the caramelo rebozo as its symbol, is clearly feminine. The rebozo was used at every significant moment in a woman's life, explains Lala. It could be used as a dowry, a burial shroud, to carry or breast-feed a child, cover one's head in church, even communicate silent vows of love. The caramelo rebozo, coming from the mother, is specifically a maternal symbol; the characters find themselves suckling its fringe or draping it around themselves like arms in moments of despair.

The word *caramelo,* meaning caramel, also evokes a sweet, thick syrup running down the throat and the warm brown color of skin, Candelaria's skin. Candelaria, whom Lala calls Cande (candy), is the daughter of her grandmother's washerwoman. Immediately, young Lala is entranced by her color: "Smooth as peanut butter, deep as burnt-milk candy . . . A color so sweet, it hurts to even look at her." Lala sees Candelaria as beautiful, although others look down on her for her indigenous roots and poverty. "How can you let that Indian play with you . . . she's dirty. She doesn't even wear underwear," complains Aunty Light-Skin. At her young age, Lala isn't aware that dark skin is considered ugly. Through this snapshot and numerous other references to skin color, Cisneros shows the cruel and absurd racial and class discrimination that dark-skinned Latinos face from those with lighter skins. In the end, Lala learns that this girl she met in her youth was actually her half sister.

Soledad

How the Awful Grandmother earned her nickname is no mystery. In the first part of the novel, when the family visits her in Mexico City, she treats everyone like dirt—except for her first son, Inocencio, her only passion. She makes life miserable for Zoila, a Chicana and therefore beneath her son. She considers her grandchildren barbarians who can't even speak proper Spanish. Her most vicious act: revealing Inocencio's illegitimate daughter Candelaria to his wife in an attempt to break up the marriage. "You're better off without her kind," she tells her son. "Wives come and go, but mothers, you have only one!"

Though this portrait is as flat as an old photograph, Cisneros takes us back in time to tell the Awful Grandmother's girlhood story in part 2 of the novel, adding dimension and humanity to this woman. Before becoming powerful, she was powerless. Before becoming intolerable, she was invisible. Before becoming the Awful Grandmother, she was Soledad. Like Cinderella without the fairy godmother, Soledad lost her mother at an early age, and her father remarried a woman who cared little for her. Her only memento of her mother, famous for her intricate weaving of rebozo fringe, was the unfinished caramelo rebozo: "No soft hair across her cheek, only the soft fringe of the unfinished shawl."

Soledad's father sent her away to live with his cousin, who couldn't even keep track of how many children she had, and an uncle who would try to lift Soledad's skirt while she slept. Soledad— her name means loneliness—toiled for several years in this filthy household that smelled of "the scorched-potato-skin scent of starched cloth," "the sour circles of cottage cheese stains on the shoulder from burping babies," "the foggy seaside tang of urine."

With fairy-tale notions of being saved by love, at one decisive moment she declared that she would marry the next man who walked down the street. This person was Narciso Reyes. Draped in her caramelo rebozo, Soledad sobbed out her story to him; taking pity, Narciso asked his parents to hire her as a servant. Narciso provided her a means of escape and even seemed to be a protective, fatherly figure. Yet naively, Soledad continued to romanticize this meeting as a romance of destiny, envisioning herself as a star-crossed character in a *telenovela,* a Mexican soap opera.

So starved was Soledad for affection that she welcomed Narciso's lustful advances, even confusing them with parental love ("She had not felt this well loved except perhaps when she was still inside her mother's belly, or had sat on her father's lap"). In contrast, Narciso selfishly regarded her compliance as just another household duty: "was it not part of her job to serve the young man of the house?" Even after becoming pregnant and marrying Narciso, Soledad remained emotionally isolated, especially after his potent affair with the bewitching Exaltacion Henestrosa, from which he would never recover. Soledad suffered from this discovery because she loved fiercely, "the way Mexicans love." "We love like we hate," describes Cisneros. Turning to a wisewoman selling tamales outside the church, Soledad asked for advice to end her pain. The only cure was to fall in love again, which is exactly what happened the day that Inocencio was born. This one satisfying bond of love, a mother's love, filled a great canyon in her heart. For the rest of her life, her love for Inocencio was strong enough to fill the void of lost parental and romantic love.

Destiny and destination

Before Lala becomes the insightful, impassioned narrator of her family story, she is a confused adolescent struggling to create an identity in the face of conflicting cultural and gender expectations. Cisneros herself, who has proudly stated that she is "nobody's wife, nobody's mother," struggled with stepping out of the traditional roles expected of a Latina. "I think that growing up Mexican and feminist is almost a contradiction in terms," she explained. "Your culture tells you that if you step out of line, if you break these norms, you are becoming anglicized, you're becoming the malinche," she told one interviewer. Thus, much of her work deals with straddling two cultures in an attempt to redefine what it means to be Latina. This is Lala's struggle in the final part of the novel.

Lala finds herself depressed, yet unsure of what she wants: "A bathroom where I can soak in the tub and not have to come out when some-body's banging on the door. A lock on my door. A door. A room . . . Somebody to tell my troubles to . . . To be in love." She contemplates both a liberated and traditional life for herself. She's not training for the traditional Latina role of housewife. At the same time, she faces cultural restrictions. "If you leave your father's house without a husband you are worse than a dog . . . If you leave alone you leave . . . como una prostituta," warns her father. When her brother Toto enlists, her father boasts that it will make a man out of him. "But what's available to make a woman a woman?" wonders Lala.

Sharing the naive, fairy-tale notions held by Soledad, she dreams of being rescued by true love. When she finds her first boyfriend, Ernesto, she pushes him toward marriage, despite the warnings of the Awful Grandmother's spirit. "It's you, Celaya, who's haunting me," the spirit insists. "Why do you insist on repeating my life? . . . There's no sin in falling in love with your heart and with your body, but wait till you're old enough to love yourself first." Lala finally realizes that she can take charge of her destiny: "You're the author of the telenovela of your life. Comedy or tragedy? Choose." Playing on the double meaning of destino, Lala declares, "Ernesto. He was my destiny, but not my destination."

The spirit of the Awful Grandmother, trapped in limbo as penance for her unkindness, begs Lala to tell her story so that she may be understood and finally forgiven. Weaving stories and in the process healing old family wounds becomes Lala's new destiny: "Maybe it's my job to separate the strands and knot the words together for everyone who can't say them, and make it all right in the end." Cisneros has also declared this her own mission as a writer—to be a voice to the voiceless.

Healthy lies

Cisneros begins *Caramelo* with this disclaimer: "The truth, these stories are nothing but story. . . . I have invented what I do not know and exaggerated what I do to continue the family tradition of telling healthy lies." Yet this is the most autobiographical work Cisneros has written. She began it when her father was ill, and it is dedicated to him. *Caramelo* chronicles the history of his family, describes her own struggles within the family, and portrays her father's unending devotion to her with the sentimentality of a daughter looking back fondly rather than a young girl struggling to be free from his overprotectiveness.

Cisneros begins with these kernels of truth, weaving them with fiction to create a work that is as authentic as it is fantastic. In this way, she is examining the very nature of storytelling. What is a storyteller? "Liar/Gossip/Troublemaker, Big-Mouth," she writes in one chapter title. The fictional author Lala freely admits having to make up details to fill in gaps. Cisneros uses an inventive and humorous technique to elucidate the creative process; in part 2, the spirit of the Awful Grandmother repeatedly interrupts the narrator to interject or condemn her for exaggerating, lying, or (more likely) telling too much of the ugly truth. "I have to exaggerate," insists Lala. "I need details. You never tell me anything." At other times, Lala defends the truth of her story, reminding her listeners that life is more outrageous than any telenovela: "I know this sounds as if I am making it up, but the facts are so unbelievable they can only be true." Cisneros even purposely tells different versions of the same stories to show the fluidity of memory and how the truth changes according to the storyteller.

Cisneros compares the art of storytelling to weaving. Like life, the novel is not neat and complete; it is complex and sometimes tangled, with many loose threads. "Because a life contains a multitude of stories and not a single strand explains precisely the who of who one is, we have to examine the complicated loops," explains the narrator. The effect borders on overwhelming at times, as we are introduced to numerous minor characters in footnotes and even footnotes to footnotes. This gives a sense of the vastness of experience connected to one family. We are not told a complete story; rather, we are allowed to examine the various interlocking threads of a small patch: "Pull one string and the whole thing comes undone." Cisneros admits that at first she did not know how all these stories would fit together: "As a reader, you will think that I planned all of the loops and the double backs and the repetition, but I didn't. It was something that just occurred and gave me a confirmation in the idea of divine providence because I really was writing this just by following my heart."

Caramelo contains not only a personal, emotional tale but, as in her other works, a clear political message as well. "I was writing it on behalf of the immigrant community and hoping to get to people like President Bush, policy makers, citizens that might feel frightened of people unlike themselves, communities in Germany, Finland, Japan," says Cisneros. "I really was thinking by the time the book ended that maybe this was something I was writing for the state that the globe is in right now." Her goal: to create empathy for all those considered "other." This goal is best accomplished through her vibrant, authentic characterization.

An element of nonfiction has been added to the novel by incorporating numerous footnotes and a chronology intended to educate readers on Latino history and culture. Cisneros explains that these notes are intended for everyone—even readers within the Latino community: "I feel as if so many children who are of Mexican descent don't know their own history. I'm especially talking about Mexicans on this side of the border. I saw those footnotes being for the sake of everyone." The cultural footnotes are light: descriptions of music, movies, well-known Latino entertainers. The historical footnotes are more overtly political; for example, a biting list of U.S. anti-immigrant policies is contrasted with examples of the honorable role Latinos have played in American wars. Given the complexity of the story, these educational tidbits weigh down the text at times and give the impression that perhaps the author wants to accomplish too much.

All in all, this is a stunning, creative novel that shows sparks of genius in its use of language: poetic, authentic, and deliciously spiced with Spanish. Should you look for *Caramelo* at a theater near you anytime soon? Realizing its cinematic quality, Cisneros has thought about adapting it for the big screen; however, she worries about what would have to be eliminated from this complex family album by changing the medium. "I realized the book was huge with so many stories, and the idea of what would be left out bothered me," she explained. Her solution—to turn it into a telenovela. "I finally realized that the form that could contain so many stories wouldn't be a two-hour film but something like a telenovela. That's what I think would be perfect for this book."

As for her next project, Cisneros plans on writing vignettes, which she describes as "small and jewel-like and very beautiful." The subject: erotica. The title: *Infinito*. Let us hope that another eight years do not pass before she once again cloaks us in her colorful tapestry of words.

FURTHER READING

Biography

Cisneros, Sandra, Feroza Jussawalla, and Reed Way Dasenbrock. "Sandra Cisneros." In *Writing Women's Lives: An Anthology of Autobiographical Narratives by Twentieth-*

Century American Women Writers, edited by Susan Cahill, pp. 459-68. New York: Harper Perennial, 1994.

Cisneros discusses political, economic, and social concerns, racial issues, and her literary influences.

Criticism

Brunk, Beth L. "En otras voces: Multiple Voices in Sandra Cisneros' *The House on Mango Street.*" *Hispanófila*, no. 133 (September 2001): 137-50.

Analyzes Cisneros's narrative style in The House on Mango Street *and the underlying reasons behind these narrative techniques.*

Cisneros, Sandra, and Gayle Elliot. "An Interview with Sandra Cisneros." *Missouri Review* 25, no. 1 (2002): 95-109.

Cisneros explains her political and social motivations, her use of short story and full novel forms, and the importance and power of language.

Curiel, Barbara Brinson. "The General's Pants: A Chicana Feminist (re)Vision of the Mexican Revolution in Sandra Cisneros's 'Eyes of Zapata'." *Western American Literature* 35, no. 4 (winter 2001): 403-27.

Examines Cisneros's demythologizing of Emiliano Zapata by retelling history through the eyes of Ines, his lover. Through this retelling, Cisneros provides a voice to the many voiceless and almost anonymous women throughout history.

————. "Sandra Cisneros, *Woman Hollering Creek and Other Stories.*" In *Reading U.S. Latina Writers: Remapping American Literature*, edited by Alvina E. Quitana, pp. 51-60. New York: Palgrave Macmillan, 2003.

Discusses the major themes in the stories in Woman Hollering Creek and Other Stories, *and analyzes Cisneros's dual role as feminist writer and Latina/o culturist.*

Doyle, Jacqueline. "More Room of Her Own: Sandra Cisneros's *The House on Mango Street.*" *MELUS* 19, no. 4 (winter 1994): 5-53.

Evaluates the differences between majority, white feminism and the feminism of minorities by studying differences between Virginia Woolf's A Room of One's Own *and Cisneros's* The House on Mango Street. *Also analyzes feminist ideas of claiming language and space as tools for empowerment.*

————. "Haunting the Borderlands: La Llorona in Sandra Cisneros's 'Woman Hollering Creek'." *Frontiers: A Journal of Women Studies* 16, no. 1 (15 May 1996): 53-70.

Chronicles the struggles of Cleofilas, the protagonist in the short story "Woman Hollering Creek." Cleofilas attempts to control her destiny in a male-dominated society; she is haunted by and grateful to the women in history who shaped her life and have fought within and against the patriarchal system.

Ganz, Robin. "Sandra Cisneros: Border Crossings and Beyond." *MELUS* 19, no. 1 (spring 1994): 19-29.

Provides biographical information about Cisneros and examines her body of work, noting its poetic prose, medley of narrative voices, and representation of marginalized and silenced people.

González, Myrna-Yamil. "Female Voices in Sandra Cisneros' *The House on Mango Street.*" In *U.S. Latino Literature: A Critical Guide for Students and Teachers*, edited by Harold

Augenbraum and Margarite Fernández Olmos, pp. 101-11. Westport, Conn.: Greenwood Press, 2000.

Provides discussion of Esperanza's feminist empowerment in The House on Mango Street, *examining her taking control of language, home, and her body in the book.*

Herrera, Andrea O'Reilly. "'Chambers of Consciousness': Sandra Cisneros and the Development of the Self in the BIG House on Mango Street." In *Having Our Way: Woman Rewriting Tradition in Twentieth-Century America (Bucknell Review Series, Vol. 39, No. 1)*, edited by Harriet Pollack, pp. 191-204. Lewisburg, Pa.: Bucknell University Press, 1995.

Explores the symbolic aspects of space, room, and home in Cisneros's The House on Mango Street.

Herrera-Sobek, Maria. "The Politics of Rape: Sexual Transgression in Chicana Fiction." *Americas Review* 15, no. 3-4 (fall-winter 1987): 171-81.

Details the use of rape scenes in contemporary Chicana literature as a theme that reinforces the lack of power women experience in a male-dominated society.

Randall, Margaret. "Weaving a Spell." *Women's Review of Books* 20, no. 1 (October 2002): 1-3.

Provides a positive assessment of Caramelo.

Rangil, Viviana. "Pro-Claiming a Space: The Poetry of Sandra Cisneros and Judith Ortiz Cofer." *MultiCultural Review* 9, no. 3 (September 2000): 48-51.

Analyzes the dual marginality of Latinas, and uses examples of poetry by Cisneros and Ortiz Cofer to highlight the difficulties faced by women who must fight for both cultural and sexual identity.

Rojas, Maythee G. "Cisneros's 'Terrible' Women: Recuperating the Erotic as a Feminist Source in 'Never Marry a Mexican' and 'Eyes of Zapata'." *Frontiers: A Journal of Women Studies* 20, no. 3 (1999): 135-57.

Studies Cisneros's female protagonists' physical and sexual journeys from male receptacles and possessed objects to self-directed, non-subordinate bodies, and explores the mental and spiritual changes that accompany these efforts.

Saldivar-Hull, Sonia. "Mujeres en Lucha/Mujeres de Fuerza: Women in Struggle/Women of Strength in Sandra Cisneros's Border Narratives." In *Feminism on the Border: Chicana Gender Politics and Literature*, pp. 81-123. Berkeley: University of California Press, 2000.

Illuminates the many borders that appear in Cisneros's poems and short stories, such as physical boundaries, economical chasms, and gender-based demarcations—and her protagonists' attempts to not only cross, but erase these borders.

Szadziuk, Maria. "Culture as Transition: Becoming a Woman in Bi-ethnic Space." *Mosaic* 32, no. 3 (September 1999): 109-29.

Examines the works of Cisneros, Esmeralda Santiago, and Cherríe Moraga, and explores the authors' similar themes of displacement, their characters' quests for identity, and women's interrelationships.

de Valdes, Maria Elena. "In Search of Identity in Cisneros's *The House on Mango Street.*" *Canadian Review of American Studies* 23, no. 1 (fall 1992): 55-72.

Examines the connecting themes that run throughout the stories in The House on Mango Street, *demonstrates the poetic quality of Cisneros's writing, and chronicles the protagonist's development toward self-possession.*

Wyatt, Jean. "On Not Being La Malinche: Border Negotiations of Gender in Sandra Cisneros's 'Never Marry a Mexican' and 'Woman Hollering Creek'." *Tulsa Studies in Women's Literature* 14, no. 2 (fall 1995): 243-71.

Stresses Cisneros's protagonists' efforts to break away from the traditional stereotypical portraits of Mexican woman—typically either as mother/wife or manipulator/ whore. Wyatt asserts that the characters attempt to claim sexuality, freedom, and personal space without being labeled or defined by men.

Yarbo-Bejarano, Yvonne. "Chicana Literature from a Chicana Feminist Perspective." *Americas Review* 15, no. 3-4 (fall-winter 1987): 139-45.

Illustrates the importance of writing as an instrument for liberation for Chicanas, providing a voice for previously silenced and marginalized women.

OTHER SOURCES FROM GALE:

Additional coverage of Cisneros's life and career is contained in the following sources published by the Gale Group: *American Writers Supplement*, Vol. 7; *Authors and Artists for Young Adults*, Vols. 9, 53; *Contemporary Authors*, Vol. 131; *Contemporary Authors New Revision Series*, Vols. 64, 118; *Contemporary Literary Criticism*, Vols. 69, 118; *Contemporary Women Poets*; *Dictionary of Literary Biography*, Vols. 122, 152; *DISCovering Authors Modules: Multicultural*; *DISCovering Authors 3.0*; *Encyclopedia of World Literature in the 20th Century*, Ed. 3; *Exploring Novels*; *Feminist Writers*; *Hispanic Literature Criticism*; *Hispanic Writers*, Eds. 1, 2; *Latino and Latina Writers*, Vol. 1; *Literature and Its Times*, Vol. 5; *Literature and Its Times Supplement*, Ed. 1; *Literature Resource Center*; *Major Authors and Illustrators for Children and Young Adults*, Ed. 2; *Major 20th-Century Writers*, Ed. 2; *Novels for Students*, Vol. 2; *Poetry Criticism*, Vol. 52; *Reference Guide to American Literature*, Ed. 4; *Reference Guide to Short Fiction*, Ed. 2; *St. James Guide to Young Adult Writers*; *Short Stories for Students*, Vols. 3, 13; *Short Story Criticism*, Vol. 32; and *World Literature and Its Times*, Vol. 1.

HÉLÈNE CIXOUS

(1937 -)

Algerian-born French novelist, short-story writer, essayist, nonfiction writer, playwright, and screenwriter.

A major figure in contemporary feminist critical theory, Cixous is known for works that analyze and attempt to counter Western culture's traditional concepts of male and female. Cixous is best known for her essay collaboration with Catherine Clément, *La jeune née* (1975; *The Newly Born Woman*) and her essay "Le rire de la Méduse" (1975; "The Laugh of the Medusa"). Both texts are recognized as being markedly influenced by the writings of Jacques Derrida, the French philosopher and founder of the critical method known as deconstructionism; Michel Foucault, the French philosopher and historian who rejected the theory of human nature and was a proponent of the notion of an ever-changing self; Jacques Lacan, the French psychoanalyst and philosopher who proposed a linguistic theory of the unconscious; and Sigmund Freud, the originator of psychoanalysis. A proponent of écriture féminine, or feminine writing, Cixous strives in all of her works to establish a uniquely feminine perspective, both to correct what she and many feminist theorists view as the traditionally masculine character of Western discourse and as a methodology with which to critique that discourse.

BIOGRAPHICAL INFORMATION

Cixous was born in Oran, Algeria, to a French-colonial father and Austro-German mother. Members of her family were Sephardic Jews, and Cixous grew up with a sense of kinship with persecuted groups. Her father, a physician, died when she was eleven, an event some critics suggest informs her writing. In her teens, Cixous read myths, the German Romantics (including Heinrich von Kleist), and English literature, especially the writings of William Shakespeare. Cixous moved to France in her late teens, where she earned an *agrégation d'anglais* degree in 1959 and became a *docteur des lettres* in 1968. She also founded, with Gérard Genette and Tzvetan Todorov, the prestigious literary and critical journal *Poétique* in 1968. She was a founder of the University of Paris-Vincennes (also known as Paris VIII), a liberal school offering an alternative to traditional education, and the Centre de Recherches en Etudes Feminines in 1974. Also that year, she established Europe's first doctoral program for women's studies. Cixous has taught at various universities in France, including the University of Paris, the Sorbonne, and the University of Bordeaux; she has also been a visiting professor at such institutions as Yale University, Columbia University, and Dartmouth College.

MAJOR WORKS

Cixous's first published work of criticism was her doctoral thesis, *L'exil de James Joyce ou l'art du remplacement* (1968; *The Exile of James Joyce or the Art of Replacement*). In this work she examines Joyce's experimental literary techniques and the ways in which they express his belief in the mutually influential relationship between linguistic and mental structures. She criticizes Joyce, however, for emphasizing a connection between guilt and death; she argues that this leads to the unnecessary paradox, detectable in all of his works, that one must "lose" in order to "gain," kill in order to live. In *Prénoms de personne* (1974), a collection of essays, Cixous presents psychoanalytic analyses of literary texts by Freud, August Heinrich Hoffman, Kleist, Edgar Allan Poe, and Joyce. These essays deal with the concept of the "unified subject," or the individual's sense of being or "possessing" a distinct, whole personality. In 1975, Cixous published "The Laugh of the Medusa", a well-known essay that examines Freud's concept of castration anxiety. Freud argued that this anxiety stems from a fear of female genitalia, perceived by males at a subconscious level as the result of castration—the female body understood subconsciously as "lacking" a phallus. Freud suggested that the mythical story of Medusa, in which people turn to stone when they look at the snake-covered head of the Gorgon, could be read as addressing this psychoanalytic fear. In "The Laugh of the Medusa" Cixous argues, following many theorists, that this masculine view of women as "lacking" has broad social and political implications and manifestations. *The Newly Born Woman* consists of three parts: Catherine Clément's essay "The Guilty One," Cixous's "Sorties," and "Exchange," a dialogue between the two authors in which they discuss the similarities and differences in their views on women and writing. Through their readings of various historical, literary, and psychoanalytical texts, the two explore the role played by language in determining women's secondary place in society. They go on to propose that Western culture's repressive language must be replaced with a language of liberation. *La venue à l'écriture* (1977), co-authored with Annie Leclerc and Madeleine Gagnon, further evinces Cixous's preoccupations with language, psychoanalysis, and feminine pleasure. In her novel *Illa* (1980) Cixous restructures the story of Persephone and Demeter. The Greek goddess Persephone, according to legend, was the daughter of Zeus and Demeter (the Roman goddess Ceres, goddess of crops and fertility). She was abducted and raped by Hades and forced to be his wife. Demeter searched for Persephone and, grieving over her disappearance, decided that the land would be infertile until she was reunited with her daughter. Zeus brokered a deal that would allow Persephone to reside with her mother for two-thirds of the year; for the other third she would be imprisoned in Hell with Hades. Greek mythology uses this myth to explain the earth's barren condition during the winter months. In *Illa*, Cixous highlights the male-dominated, colonizing aspects of this tale and changes the story to reflect a more self-determined, feminist text. In *Illa*, she celebrates camaraderie among women, underscores women's link with nature, and highlights the feminine goals of love and nonviolence. *Entre l'écriture* (1986; "Coming to Writing," and Other Essays) collects translations of a number of Cixous's critical works written after 1976, including "Clarice Lispector: An Approach," "Trancredi Continues," and the title essay.

CRITICAL RECEPTION

Reaction to Cixous's critical works has been mixed. Many critics have praised her attempts to revolutionize traditional beliefs about women and writing. Others, however, have castigated what they consider the contradictory nature of her work and her intentional resistance to analysis. Her penchant for using both feminine and masculine writing techniques within feminine literature has confused some commentators, yet many find that writers need to claim both the male and female identity to present a whole self. Some reviewers also suggest that Cixous's attempts to redefine gender differences reduce women to what one critic has called an "anatomical essence," and that her works are, in fact, antifeminist. Others argue that Cixous's work is expansive rather than reductive. Most critics, however, praise Cixous's belief that the creation of a new language of discourse is essential for feminine expression and women's search for identity.

PRINCIPAL WORKS

Le prénom de Dieu (short stories) 1967

L'exil de James Joyce ou l'art du remplacement [*The Exile of James Joyce or the Art of Replacement*] (doctoral thesis) 1968

Dedans [*Inside*] (novel) 1969

Le troisième corps [*The Third Body*] (novel) 1970

Neutre (novel) 1972

Portrait du soleil (novel) 1974

Prénoms de personne (essays) 1974

La jeune née [*The Newly Born Woman*] (essays) 1975

Portrait de Dora [*Portrait of Dora*] (play) 1975

"Le rire de la Méduse" ["The Laugh of the Medusa"] (essay) 1975

Souffles (novel) 1975

LA (novel) 1976

Partie (play) 1976

Angst (novel) 1977

La venue à l'écriture [with Annie Leclerc and Madeleine Gagnon] (nonfiction) 1977

Vivre l'orange/To Live the Orange (novel) 1979

Illa (novel) 1980

With ou l'art de l'innocence (novel) 1981

Limonade tout était si infini (novel) 1982

Entre l'écriture ["Coming to Writing" and Other Stories] (essays) 1986

Hélène Cixous, Photos de racines [*Hélène Cixous, Rootprints: Memory and Life Writing*] (interviews) 1994

Les Rêveries de la femme sauvage (nonfiction) 2000

PRIMARY SOURCES

HÉLÈNE CIXOUS (ESSAY DATE 1975)

SOURCE: Cixous, Hélène. "The Laugh of the Medusa," translated by Keith and Paula Cohen. In *New French Feminisms: An Anthology*, edited by Elaine Marks and Isabelle de Courtivron, pp. 245-47. New York: Schocken Books, 1981.

In the following excerpt from "The Laugh of the Medusa," originally published in 1975, Cixous calls for all women to write and claim language and literature in order to liberate themselves from male oppression.

I shall speak about women's writing: about *what it will do.* Woman must write her self: must write about women and bring women to writing, from which they have been driven away as violently as from their bodies—for the same reasons, by the same law, with the same fatal goal. Woman must put herself into the text—as into the world and into history—by her own movement.

The future must no longer be determined by the past. I do not deny that the effects of the past are still with us. But I refuse to strengthen them by repeating them, to confer upon them an irremovability the equivalent of destiny, to confuse the biological and the cultural. Anticipation is imperative.

Since these reflections are taking shape in an area just on the point of being discovered, they necessarily bear the mark of our time—a time during which the new breaks away from the old, and, more precisely, the (feminine) new from the old (*la nouvelle de l'ancien*). Thus, as there are no grounds for establishing a discourse, but rather an arid millennial ground to break, what I say has at least two sides and two aims: to break up, to destroy; and to foresee the unforeseeable, to project.

I write this as a woman, toward women. When I say "woman," I'm speaking of woman in her inevitable struggle against conventional man; and of a universal woman subject who must bring women to their senses and to their meaning in history. But first it must be said that in spite of the enormity of the repression that has kept them in the "dark"—that dark which people have been trying to make them accept as their attribute—there is, at this time, no general woman, no one typical woman. What they have *in common* I will say. But what strikes me is the infinite richness of their individual constitutions: you can't talk about *a* female sexuality, uniform, homogeneous, classifiable into codes—any more than you can talk about one unconscious resembling another. Women's imaginary is inexhaustible, like music, painting, writing: their stream of phantasms is incredible.

I have been amazed more than once by a description a woman gave me of a world all her own which she had been secretly haunting since early childhood. A world of searching, the elaboration of a knowledge, on the basis of a systematic experimentation with the bodily functions, a passionate and precise interrogation of her erotogeneity. This practice, extraordinarily rich and inventive, in particular as concerns masturbation, is prolonged or accompanied by a production of forms, a veritable aesthetic activity, each stage of rapture inscribing a resonant vision, a composition, something beautiful. Beauty will no longer be forbidden.

I wished that that woman would write and proclaim this unique empire so that other women, other unacknowledged sovereigns, might exclaim: I, too, overflow; my desires have invented new desires, my body knows unheard-of songs. Time and again I, too, have felt so full of luminous torrents that I could burst—burst with forms much more beautiful than those which are put up in frames and sold for a stinking fortune. And I, too, said nothing, showed nothing; I didn't open my mouth, I didn't repaint my half of the world. I was ashamed. I was afraid, and I swallowed my shame and my fear. I said to myself: You are mad! What's the meaning of these waves, these floods, these outbursts? Where is the ebullient, infinite woman who, immersed as she was in her naiveté, kept in the dark about herself, led into self-disdain by the great arm of parental-conjugal phallocentrism, hasn't been ashamed of her strength? Who, surprised and horrified by the fantastic tumult of her drives (for she was made to believe that a well-adjusted normal woman has a . . . divine composure), hasn't accused herself of being a monster? Who, feeling a funny desire stirring inside her (to sing, to write, to dare to speak, in short, to bring out something new), hasn't thought she was sick? Well, her shameful sickness is that she resists death, that she makes trouble.

And why don't you write? Write! Writing is for you, you are for you; your body is yours, take it. I know why you haven't written. (And why I didn't write before the age of twenty-seven.) Because writing is at once too high, too great for you, it's reserved for the great—that is for "great men"; and it's "silly." Besides, you've written a little, but in secret. And it wasn't good, because it was in secret, and because you punished yourself for writing, because you didn't go all the way, or because you wrote, irresistibly, as when we would masturbate in secret, not to go further, but to attenuate the tension a bit, just enough to take the edge off. And then as soon as we come, we go and make ourselves feel guilty—so as to be forgiven; or to forget, to bury it until the next time.

Write, let no one hold you back, let nothing stop you: not man; not the imbecilic capitalist machinery, in which publishing houses are the crafty, obsequious relayers of imperatives handed down by an economy that works against us and off our backs; and not *yourself*. Smug-faced readers, managing editors, and big bosses don't like the true texts of women—female-sexed tests. That kind scares them.

I write woman: woman must write woman. And man, man. So only an oblique consideration will be found here of man; it's up to him to say where his masculinity and femininity are at: this will concern us once men have opened their eyes and seen themselves clearly.[1]

Now women return from afar, from always: from "without," from the heath where witches are kept alive; from below, from beyond "culture"; from their childhood which men have been trying desperately to make them forget, condemning it to "eternal rest." The little girls and their "ill-mannered" bodies immured, well-preserved, intact unto themselves, in the mirror. Frigidified. But are they ever seething underneath! What an effort it takes—there's no end to it—for the sex cops to bar their threatening return. Such a display of forces on both sides that the struggle has for centuries been immobilized in the trembling equilibrium of a deadlock.

Note

1. Men still have everything to say about their sexuality, and everything to write. For what they have said so far, for the most part, stems from the opposition activity/passivity from the power relation between a fantasized obligatory virility meant to invade, to colonize, and the consequential phantasm of woman as a "dark continent" to penetrate and to "pacify." (We know what "pacify" means in terms of scotomizing the other and misrecognizing the self.) Conquering her, they've made haste to depart from her borders to get out of sight, out of body. The way man has of getting out of himself and into her whom he takes not for the other but for his own, deprives him, he knows, of his own bodily territory. One can understand how man, confusing himself with his penis and rushing in for the attack, might feel resentment and fear of being "taken" by the woman, of being lost in her, absorbed or alone.

GENERAL COMMENTARY

VERENA ANDERMATT CONLEY (ESSAY DATE 1984)

SOURCE: Conley, Verena Andermatt. "Textual Strategies." In *Hélène Cixous: Writing the Feminine*, pp. 3-13. Lincoln: University of Nebraska Press, 1984.

In the following essay, Conley addresses Cixous's theories of feminine discourse and illustrates the author's opinions of the femininity and masculinity of texts and writing.

May 1968: student-worker uprisings, the occupation of the Sorbonne—a stronghold of outworn pedagogical traditions. Intellectuals cast aside their differences and march in the streets. Their demands: new universities; improved curricula; access to schools for everyone, not just for the privileged few. The political ferment is paralleled by an intellectual ferment with the advent of the human sciences, and readings in philosophy, psychoanalysis, anthropology, linguistics. It is a period of belief in the revolutionary power of language and of hopes for a shattering of millenary oppressive structures. Women want their share. They rally behind the banner of "liberation" in teaching, criticism, writing. Twenty years after the publication of Simone de Beauvoir's *Second Sex,* women in search of a new feminism continue their readings of Freud and Marx, to whom they add others. They read new theoretical works in and about major discourses governing society in an effort to determine how and where women have been excluded and how to question and undo that exclusion.

It is not my intention here to establish a historical determinism, or to link such a historical "event" to such a cultural "event." I simply want to read some of Cixous's writings, published roughly since the May uprisings in 1968, the period of the founding of Vincennes, the founding of the *Centre de recherches en études féminines* in 1974, and her temporary involvement with the MLF,[1] followed by a new departure, away from an official political affiliation. In these fifteen years, a writing of enthusiasm and effusive energy appears almost mensually. It is here, during that time and in those rhythms, that I situate the pages to follow.

Subversion through Poetry

Cixous comes to writing via fiction. A collection of short stories, *Le Prénom de dieu,* is published in 1967. In 1969, *Dedans,* a fictional autobiography about her entrapment in an Oedipal scene, is awarded the Prix Médicis and catapults her to the fore of the Parisian literary scene, which she has occupied ever since. She publishes her 900-page doctoral thesis, *The Exile of James Joyce,* in 1968. Her radicalism spills over the boundaries of a narrowly defined feminism. As an Algerian, Jew, and woman, she finds herself thrice culturally and historically marked and vows to fight on all fronts against any form of oppression. One of the founders of France's furthest left university, Paris-Vincennes (Paris VIII)—now moved for political reasons to the suburb of Saint-Denis—she was been conducting seminars on writing, femininity, and sexuality over the last decade. Though there is a shift in her work from a covert to an overt "feminism," Cixous has always been interested in the inscription of the feminine in text and society.

A longstanding French tradition believes that art is necessarily "to the left," on the side of subversion of existing "bourgeois" values. In the wake of the rise of human sciences, moreover, Cixous asserts that social structures cannot be dissociated from linguistic structures. Language, far from being an atemporal tool, is inextricably linked to history and society. Its structures define and constitute the subject. There are no absolute, immutable values beyond words or the grammar and syntax that order them. To change existing social structures, the linguistic clichés that purvey them and make them appear as transparent, immutable truths must be detected, re-marked, displaced. Hence Cixous's interest in language and its use in artistic practices.

First and foremost a writer, Cixous considers poetry—defined not in opposition to prose but as the subversion of coded, clichéd, ordinary language—necessary to social transformation. For Cixous as well as for many other writers, poetry condenses, renders opaque, carries greater psychic density. It is opposed to discourse that flattens, systematizes.

Most important for her definition of the feminine is the fact that Cixous does not proceed on a purely conceptual level, though she dialogues with concepts of philosophy and psychoanalysis. While her texts alternately emphasize one over the other, Cixous, like other modernists, questions the distinction between theory and practice. Her poetic texts are more a theoretical praxis; her critical and her pedagogical readings at Paris VIII emphasize the theoretical. As a result of her own resistance, little of her theoretical work has been published except for *Prénoms de personne,* "Sorties" in *La Jeune Née, La Venue à l'ecriture,* and a number of articles in *Poétique, New Literary History, Signs.*

As a writer, Cixous engages by definition in a solitary, narcissistic (selfish) activity. Writing keeps the other out, physically, and presupposes leisure time as well as an income. An individualistic activity, writing may nevertheless bring about some changes in others' perceptions of the world. One should not, therefore, confuse levels nor let oneself be indicted by tribunals where one does not belong. A writer is not a lawyer or a guerrilla-woman. In a collective endeavor, each fights in her own way, with her own medium, according to her talents and a freedom of choice dictated to some degree by economics and geography. Cixous's concerns are political, but textually political, and she states the premises (and limits) of her enterprise: to read and write texts in order to displace the operating concepts of femininity in major discourses governing (Western) society. In this she is close to other "feminists"—Julia Kristeva, Luce Irigaray, Sarah Kofman—as well as male thinkers: Jacques Lacan, Gilles Deleuze, but mainly Jacques Derrida, with whom Cixous from her specifically (*féminine*) literary border, maintains an ongoing dialogue.

The Loss of the Self

The French attempt at a feminine writing has its equivalent in the United States, where women advocating the expression of a self abound. Writers like Adrienne Rich praise feminine experience in poetry and prose, while critics like Kate Millett expose its exclusion through (male) sexual politics in criticism and fiction. But whereas the former work is based on the importance of an experience lived and felt, on the expression of a self, the latter proposes a loss of subjectivity and ego, a plural self always already other, as well as an erasure of the division between life and text, between before and after. This is not to say that there is no experience; quite the contrary. But there is no experience prior to its enunciation in and through language. This is most important for Cixous, who, following psychoanalysis, believes in speech that enables her to do the economy of her desire, to "traverse" an experience. There is always room for something to be desired, yet this desire is not based on lack. The insistence is on movement, not stasis. Speech is never all rational, scientific. Always becoming, it never becomes the system, the recipe to be applied. Conflating poetry and politics, reading and writing, from what she calls a feminine border, Cixous has been the major proponent of a writing of the feminine or a feminine writing.

Like that of other feminists, Cixous's writing attempts to break away from cultural stereotypes, essentializing concepts and their attributes such as man/woman, masculine/feminine, active/passive. She tries to displace the conceptual opposition in the couple man/woman through the very notion of writing and bring about a new inscription of the feminine. Simone de Beauvoir had written from the vantage point of an existentialist humanist: "*On ne naît pas femme, on le devient*" (one is not born woman, one becomes woman). Similarly, though less humanistically, Cixous questions the traditional concept "woman" defined by its predicate *passive* and shows how what appeared as an immutable concept was part of a historical moment, that of logocentric (Western) thinking, privileging the concept, presence, truth, and making possible our idea of paternity, the father/son relation, and the repression of woman.

Philosophy with Psychoanalysis

In her classes at Paris VIII, Cixous insists on what is of importance in all her writings, as in anybody's writings. She does this via a quotation from Derrida's *Dissemination*:

> A text is not a text unless it hides from the first comer, from the first glance, the law of its composition and the rules of its game. A text remains, moreover, forever imperceptible. Its laws and its rules are not, however, harbored in the inaccessibility of a secret; it is simply that they can never be booked in the *present,* into anything that could rigorously be called a perception.
>
> And hence, perpetually and essentially, they run the risk of being definitely lost. Who will ever know of such disappearances?
>
> The dissimulation of the woven texture can in any case take centuries to undo its web: a web that envelops a web, undoing the web for centuries; reconstituting it too as an organism, indefinitely regenerating its own tissue behind the cutting trace, the decision of each reading.[2]

In Derrida's remark "a text remains imperceptible," one must listen to the etymology of imper-cept-ible, from *captio,* to capture, to take, the very *cept* of the con-*cept*. The imperceptible of the text is that which cannot be arrested, which remains elusive. There is no hidden secret to be revealed, no truth to be extorted, but there is always that part of the text, the imperceptible, the writerly, the unconscious dimension that escapes the writer, the reader. Even an attempt to reconstitute what an author "really meant" (*vouloir dire*) comes back to saying only "what I meant when my reading crossed this text, on this day, at a certain hour."

Reading then is writing, in an endless movement of giving and receiving: each reading reinscribes something of a text; each reading reconstitutes the web it tries to decipher, but by adding another web. One must read in a text not only that which is visible and present but also the *nontext* of the text, the parentheses, the silences. Silence is needed in order to speak, to write. One phoneme differs from another phoneme, and in speaking, a voice traces, spaces, writes. There is no true beginning; writing is *always already* there, as Derrida said, adopting and making famous a Heideggerian expression. This critique of the origin, of the paternal capitalization, of the castratory gesture of an *à partir de,* a "from there, from then on," is essential. It questions authority (of the father). It opens onto *differance*—not a concept, not even a word, but the movement of something deferred or of something that differs, escaping an assignation, a definition. *Differance* does not have a punctual simplicity, that of the *point,* the period, of the *sujet un,* identical to itself, an author-head-god. What passes from one language to another, from one sex to another, in translation, is always a question of *differance*. Sexual *differance* replaces difference; movement supersedes stasis and Hegelian differences recuperable into dialectics. Derrida insists on the differential between masculine and feminine as both, neither one nor the other, where one signifier always defers the other. He undoes paternal authority, in Cixous's words, from a "masculine border," yet does not broach the possibility of a maternal, a matrical. This is where *her* work "begins."

Such a philosophical reading and writing already questions and displaces the truth of its genre through recourse to psychoanalysis. Yet the real analytical contribution comes from Lacan. Freud, notes Cixous, had recourse to literature, but his readings differ from ours. Freud thought of the text as a product of the author, as a verification of the writer's neuroses, as a process of identification. Freud was interested in the signified. The work of art had a hidden message to be deciphered. Cixous praises Lacan, who was able to show through a double contribution by contemporary linguists, Ferdinand de Saussure and Roman Jakobson, how a signifier always refers to another signifier in an endless chain. With help from Freud's *Interpretation of Dreams* and Jakobson's theory of language, Lacan was led to establish the two poles in language: that of condensation, substitution, metaphor, or symptom, and that of concatenation, metonymy, or desire. Combined with Saussure's readings of the anagrams in Latin poems where the name of a general is reinscribed through letters and phonemes, this opened the way to a different analytic reading practice, away from themes and signification. In her classes Cixous stresses what her texts perform, a philosophical *and* analytical reading, one that combines both dimensions but without attempting to enclose the world in its discourse, as a kind of total analysis. To this must be added a reading on the semantic level, a graphico-phonic reading, which listens to silences, looks at graphic tracings.

Cixous reads and writes at the interstices of Lacan's theory of language—that of the chain of signifiers and not that of the phallus—and Derrida's *differance*. She focuses on reading and writing from a feminine border, not from the between, which for her is too much of a masculine position. She attempts to displace further Derrida's "masculine" displacement toward what she will come to call a feminine economy.

Until now, the majority of writing has fallen under the phantasm of castration, a masculine phantasm which some women under pressure have interiorized. Writing has always been done in the name of the father, and the question must be asked, how do women write? What are the effects in artistic productions of the inscription of their desire?

For Cixous, the terms "masculine" and "feminine" do not refer to "man" and "woman" in an exclusive way. A clean opposition into man and woman would be nothing but a correct repression of drives imposed by society. Cixous writes (of) sexual *differance* from her feminine poetic border in dialogue with a certain philosophy and a certain psychoanalysis. She searches poetically for operating concepts of femininity and economies of sexual difference(s) that would not come back to unity and sameness.

Cixous carries out her call to writing, and her production is abundant. Aware of the violence of our gesture, of the *coup de dé,* the dice throw of our *de*cision, we *de*cided to "begin" reading her ongoing questioning of femininity around different strategic moments, where text and biography engender each other, flow into each other:

1. Cixous's dialectics of excess, an exuberant practice for the limitless as social liberation, based on readings by Georges Bataille, Nietzsche, Hegel; critical articles collected in **Prénoms de personne;** an article on character in fiction; the writing of the limitless in **Le Troisième Corps, Commencements, Neutre**; a questioning of the law (of the father) and a re-traversing of her North African origin in **Portrait du soleil**; a rewriting of one's name in a neo-Joycean work, **Partie.** Cixous meditates on the possibility of social changes through writing and, like other new novelists, on the transformation of narrative.

2. **La Jeune Née, La Venue à l'ecriture, LA, Souffles.** Cixous calls on women to break their silence, to write themselves, to explore their unconscious. She develops the notion of a "bisexual" writing around Freud's Dora. **Angst** marks the passage toward a writing to and from the woman.

3. **Vivre l'orange, Illa, With ou l'art de l'innocence, Limonade tout était si infini.** Cixous's (belated) discovery of a Brazilian woman writer, Clarice Lispector. From the insistence on a rewriting of the Hegelian desire of recognition, the emphasis shifts toward a Heideggerian problematic of the approach of the other and the calling of the other. Though not advocating separatism, Cixous writes more from and toward the woman. This move is accompanied by a temporary

shift from established publishing houses like Grasset and Gallimard to Des Femmes. Cixous discards the notion of bisexual writing and develops her theory of libidinal economies.

The Question of the Canon

Cixous, like other French writers, does not limit her critique of logocentrism to an a priori gender distinction but, on the contrary, reads male authors who exceed dialectics, who are "singers of spending and waste," who transgress limits and inscribe feminine libidinal effects. There are women who write on the masculine side and men who do not repress their femininity. We should note that in France, feminist readings are not equivalent, as much as in the United States, to "opening the canon." Feminist readings all question a certain type of logocentric or phallogocentric discourse that may be used by men and women alike. It has been used predominantly by men because of historical and cultural circumstances. The "canon" as it exists in American English departments does not have its exact equivalent in France, where reading and writing do not necessarily go through university channels and where an academic affiliation is not a prerequisite to intellectual success. Rather, the question of the canon is linked to social classes. There has always been a conflictual coexistence of several literatures and literary histories, Communist, Catholic, and maybe an official academic one. Throughout the century, iconoclasts—dadaists, surrealists, existentialists, and new novelists—have been busy questioning what they referred to as "bourgeois tradition." In a French tradition, letters and politics are seldom separated, and letters are usually thought to be on the side of subversion—at least since the French revolution.

French writers have been wanting to shock the bourgeoisie (to which they also belong) since that class came into power. Recently, Sartre's existential literature has not observed the rules of "le beau," of aestheticism or decorum; adepts of the new novel dehumanized what they called the traditional novel—anthropomorphic, ethnocentric—by "decentering" man and putting him within objects. Cixous's writings are part of a long chain which, from nineteenth-century poets to new novelists, attempts to question the values of bourgeois art. Cixous, like many others, defies the very language on which these values are founded. As an institution, literature reinforces the values of the dominant class. The literary establishment serves a class interest under the guise of moral and aesthetic values. Literary discourse must mar-

ginalize itself not through socialist-realist techniques but through the questioning of language. Cixous does not address the question of bringing literature to the masses, presupposing that anyone can read anything at all times and that accusations of hermeticism usually come from educated readers. She does, however, following May 1968, question the connection between literary establishments and pedagogy, and it has to be noted that many of the participants in her seminar are working women and foreign students.

Cixous writes at the interstices of fiction, criticism, psychoanalysis, and philosophy without enclosing herself in any of them. Mocking a certain academic approach to "literature" as a "rite of passage" into culture, a rite through which a ruling social class integrates itself into a symbolic mode, she urges a different literary reading/ writing. Writing is not the simple notation on the page; life-and-fiction, life-as-fiction is one of unending *texte* (or *sexte*). Cixous does not privilege an economy of death, which she sees inevitably linked to conservatism and unity of self. She emphasizes an affirmation of life, movement, exuberance.

Absolute knowledge represses the senses, effaces signifiers and the body in order to accede to an idealized signified and the spirit; textuality based on originary repression eroticizes writing, questions the sign and its binary structure. In Cixous's writing of the feminine, subversive practices intervene on multiple levels: on a material level (phonemes and graphemes), on a conceptual level (questioning of the concept), and in an ongoing reflection on writing. The real she wants to transform is never a natural real, is never separated from language. Such a writing, we have said, calls for different reading practices. Reading and writing are not separate activities. A text is always guilty, in an Althusserian sense. A text is a rereading, not only because we must reread in order not to consume but also because it has already been read. We approach it with the memory of other texts, and there is no innocent reading as there is no innocent writing.

For Cixous, all writing is necessarily "autobiographical," and in each text there are unconscious dimensions. "Consciously," from *Dedans* to *Limonade tout était si infini,* Cixous writes texts of transformation and addresses the problem of writing as a woman, from a writing of the feminine to a feminine writing. In the pages to follow, it will be a question of reading Cixous's texts from the angle of sexual *differance,* in their movement, in their *cheminement.* The insistence of recurrent motifs grouped around woman, body, law, writing, is evident. We chose not to group these motifs but to read them in an ongoing (re)writing of the scene of sexual *differance*. We decided to read the texts around certain strategic moments of writing the feminine, in its play with other feminines, other masculines, and ask in turn questions of textual economy. This leads at times to extensive quoting, a repetition which is not a duplication. The necessity of quoting also derives from the urgency to "present" many of the texts unavailable to the English-speaking reader in an effort to give breadth to Cixous's *oeuvre* beyond "**The Laugh of the Medusa**" and *La Jeune Née*.

Notes

1. MLF is the acronym of the *Mouvement de libération des femmes* (Women's Liberation Movement). In an interview with Catherine Clément in *La Matin* (July 16, 1980), Antoinette Fouque, one of its founders, explains the genesis of the movement, which grew out of the political scene of May 1968. Women noticed that political contradiction did not deal with sexual contradiction and grouped themselves around a movement called *Psyche et po* (Psychoanalysis and Politics). At Paris VIII-Vincennes they studied the only discourse that dealt with sexual difference, psychoanalysis. Reading Freud, Marx, and Lacan, they first had to overcome the resistance from the Sartrian camp. The acronym MLF started to circulate in the early seventies. At the end of 1973, Antoinette Fouque and some other women founded the publishing house Des Femmes. Underlining that their enemy is not *man* but phallocracy, she states that their aim is "to transform women's condition into one not of emancipation but of independence." Discussing the danger of disintegration the movement faces with the progressive institutionalization of woman (laws on abortion, laws on rape, laws on homosexuality, an office of the condition of woman), she explains how the MLF, after establishing a publishing house and founding a monthly and a weekly paper, felt the necessity to create a *legal* movement in 1979.

2. Jacques Derrida, "La Double Séance," in *La Dissémination* (Paris: Seuil, 1972), 71.

MORAG SHIACH (ESSAY DATE 1991)

SOURCE: Shiach, Morag. Introduction to *Helene Cixous: A Politics of Writing*, pp. 1-5. London: Routledge, 1991.

In the following essay, Shiach appraises both the feminine form and feminist content of Cixous's writings and highlights the relationships between politics, sexuality, philosophy, and literature in Cixous's works.

Hélène Cixous is a contemporary French writer, critic, and theorist, whose works span a number of genres and address a wide range of problems which have preoccupied the disciplines of English and French Studies over the last twenty

FROM THE AUTHOR

CIXOUS ON THE ELEMENT OF SONG IN WOMEN

In feminine speech, as in writing, there never stops reverberating something that, having once passed through us, having imperceptibly and deeply touched us, still has the power to affect us—song, the first music of the voice of love, which every woman keeps alive.

The Voice sings from a time before law, before the Symbolic took one's breath away and reappropriated it into a language under its authority of separation. The Deepest, the oldest, the loveliest Visitation. Within each woman the first, nameless love is singing.

Cixous, Hélène. Excerpt from "Sorties: Out and Out: Attacks/Ways Out/Forays." In *The Logic of the Gift*, p. 165. New York: Routledge, 1997.

years. In France she is best known as the author of a large number of avant-garde fictions and theatrical texts. Her early work has been placed in relation to the *nouveau roman*, with its investigation of the materiality of writing, of the complexity of subjectivity, and of the transgressive potential of the literary text. In the 1970s she became increasingly identified with a literary and philosophical project that aimed to explore the relations between sexuality and writing: a project that might also be seen as involving theorists such as Irigaray, Kristeva, Derrida, and Barthes, as well as writers like Jean Genet and Marguerite Duras. More recently, her work has focused on the relations between ethical, linguistic, and historical structures, through explorations of a variety of moments of historical change and crisis.

In English Studies, however, the role of Cixous's writings has been quite specific, and relatively distinct from this complex and continuing project. Her incorporation into the critical language of English Studies has been almost entirely at the level of 'theory'. A small number of her texts has been translated, and these texts have repeatedly been mobilized in support of, or as ammunition against, a reading of the relations between gender and writing. "**The Laugh of the Medusa**" and "**Sorties**", two essays dating from the mid-

CIXOUS

1970s where Cixous discusses the transgressive potential of writing and the relations between sexuality and textuality, have been continually worked over, are frequently cited, and have come to mark the parameters of a long-running debate about 'feminine writing'.

The main aim of this book is to try to put these two different versions of Cixous into some more active relation. Much of the argument about Cixous's 'theoretical' texts has suffered from inadequate attention to the context of their writing and to their relations to other elements of Cixous's work. Equally, much of the discussion of her work in France seems reluctant to take on the transformations in her writing as it has developed over the last twenty years, choosing instead either to place her definitively in the 1970s and within the problematic of 'writing the body', or to talk about her most recent work, with little attention to earlier texts and earlier literary and political commitments. To some extent, this problem is likely to arise in the discussion of any contemporary writer: critical categorization tends to replace complexity, and the urgency of her immediate writing tends to reshape understanding of her earlier texts. In Cixous's case, however, such partial accounts are particularly unhelpful, since it is precisely the modifications of her writing that allow us to assess the validity of her theoretical and critical claims, and to understand the shaping of her work in response to changing historical conditions.

Cixous's writing as a whole raises questions about the relations between politics and writing, the dimensions and implications of sexual difference, the possible interactions between philosophy and literature, and the tenability of an identity based on ethical, textual, and political difference from dominant social relations. It cannot be reduced to one 'position', or summed up by reference to one or two of her texts. Instead, it is important to examine the development of her critical and political ideas, as well as her writing practice, paying attention both to what is developed and what is discarded, in order to assess the significance and viability of her project as a whole.

Despite this commitment to seeing Cixous's work as a whole, however, it is with the better-known 'theoretical' Cixous that this book begins. Partly, the reason for this is strategic: a clarification of my readings of the texts with which readers are likely to be familiar may render my subsequent considerations of Cixous's critical, fictional, and dramatic texts more accessible. Secondly, although Cixous's theoretical writings exhibit many of the allusive, intertextual, and metaphoric qualities of her fiction, they are clearly written both for and within a recognizable set of theoretical debates. The meta-discursive illusion implicit in criticism is thus easier to sustain in relation to these texts: an illusion that seems important in an 'introductory' book. My reading of these theoretical writings aims to establish the parameters of Cixous's writing project, to establish the arguments she is making about writing and sexual difference, and to follow through the texture of these arguments in her discussions of literary and philosophical texts.

In the second chapter I look at Cixous as critic, analysing her readings of a range of writers, from James Joyce to Clarice Lispector. Although Cixous has been assimilated in both Britain and the USA as 'theorist', many of her theoretical positions are in fact developed from the close reading of a wide range of mostly European literary texts. A number of philosophers and theorists, particularly Freud and Derrida, have shaped her writing, but the most important source of her critical and theoretical positions seems to lie in the work of what amounts to an alternative canon of literary writers who challenge the dominant order of representation and of ethical values. Even when engaging explicitly with Freud, or Derrida, or Heidegger, she prefers to do so through the medium of literary texts, whose ambiguity and scandalousness she clearly values. In her readings of the works of Joyce, Hoffmann, Kleist, or Lispector, we can follow the development of her interests from a deconstructive commitment to the materiality of the signifier, through an exploration of subjectivity and sexuality, and towards the development of an alternative textual, political, and ethical economy which she describes as 'feminine'.

With the framework provided by her theoretical and critical writings, Cixous's fictional texts become more accessible. Equally, however, an exploration of her fictional writings clarifies much that she discusses in her theoretical and critical texts: particularly the priority of voice, the importance of lightness and 'flight', and the necessity of combining deconstructive and reconstructive techniques of writing. The sheer volume of Cixous's fictional writings precludes the possibility of any exhaustive treatment: a chronological gallop through her texts would, anyway, prove less than enlightening. Instead, I have focused on a relatively small number of her fictional texts, which seem to illuminate her writing project as it develops.[1] The non-availability of most of these texts in translation raises particular problems for the discussion of a writer who is so committed to the materiality of the signifier, and whose writing frequently plays on rhythms, verbal echoes, and puns, which are hard to render into English. My discussion of these texts has thus been forced towards a level of abstraction that does not always do justice to their linguistic specificity—a defect which I have tried to signal whenever it seems helpful to do so.

Cixous's fictional texts involve the intense working-over, and reworking, of a series of philosophical and textual problems, the constant exploitation of an intertext that includes, but exceeds, many of the works discussed by her in critical mode, a pushing of the limits of intelligibility to arrive at a style that is both dense and deceptively simple, a painful progression from an exploration of a violent and divided unconscious towards the assertion of an alternative form of subjectivity, and an interest in the intersubjective relations that underlie historical change. This move from exploration of the unconscious, towards an understanding of historical process which exceeds but does not exclude individual consciousness, is echoed in Cixous's work for the theatre.

The last chapter examines Cixous's theatrical texts, which have formed a major element of her writing in recent years. Here my aim is to explore the appeal of theatre as a form for Cixous, in a way that relates her dramatic writings to the rest of her work. Also, given that Cixous's identity in English Studies is so closely bound to her role as a theorist of 'feminine writing', I explore the implications of her move away from the exploration of individual feminine subjectivity, and towards an understanding of history as a struggle between competing economies, described as 'masculine' and 'feminine'. The movement of her writing towards the exploration of collective identities, and her extension of the theory of libidinal economies towards a model of social change, developments which have taken place in the context of the collective working practices of the Théâtre du Soleil, represent an exciting challenge to the narrowness of dominant versions of the 'literary', and offer the potential for a much more extensive use of her critical and theoretical ideas.

Overall, this book aims neither to praise Cixous nor to blame her. Instead, it recognizes the importance of her work for many of the issues that dominate contemporary literary and cultural studies, and attempts to put the ideas, techniques, and images found in her texts in their historical and philosophical contexts. If it also provokes in

the reader a desire to explore more of her texts than the small number that have so far entered into theoretical debates, it will have served its purpose.

TITLE COMMENTARY

"The Laugh of the Medusa"

MARGRET BRÜGMANN (ESSAY DATE 1993)

SOURCE: Brügmann, Margret. "Between the Lines: On the Essayistic Experiments of Hélène Cixous in 'The Laugh of the Medusa,'" translated by Debbi Long. In *The Politics of the Essay: Feminist Perspectives*, edited by Ruth-Ellen Boetcher Joeres and Elizabeth Mittman, pp. 73-84. Bloomington: Indiana University Press, 1993.

In the following essay, Brügmann analyzes each section of Cixous's "The Laugh of the Medusa," noting parallels between each of the seven sections and the biblical account of the seven days of creation.

Mirror Games

When I was small, I knew a magic place. When I was alone, I would go into my parents' bedroom and stand in front of my mother's dressing table. It was a familiar piece of furniture which aroused associations with the hall of mirrors at the fair and an altar in the church. Comb, brush, perfume, manicure set were all carefully laid out on the glass tabletop. I used these forbidden objects to experiment with who I was, what I could be, to see what variations on the theme of "me" were possible. I turned to the mirror to see the results. The mirror had side wings you could adjust so you could see every angle of yourself. The most wonderful sensation of the mirror game occurred when I placed the mirrors so that I could see unending reflections of myself and the area around me. When I moved the side wings, I was engulfed in an infinity of dancing girls stretching into endless space.

This image returns to me as I read Hélène Cixous' masterly, witty essay "**The Laugh of the Medusa.**" As with Cixous' other works, this piece survives many rereadings for me, each reading opening new panoramas of insight. And yet at the same time, it leaves me disturbed, with mixed feelings about what it is that Cixous is presenting us with. Her articulation of how game and reality are interwoven is exquisite. In "**The Laugh of the Medusa,**" she writes on the one hand of the historic, mythical, and social situation of women, and on the other she leads us through her utopian vision of possibilities that can and must be imagined and developed. Cixous blends these two sides in all her work. It is hardly surprising that she so often chooses the novel or play as her medium; in both aesthetic forms she is free to use unscientific, nonempirical methods to describe the so-called truth of women's lives. Although many texts have grown out of Cixous' readings and lectures, she has produced relatively few essays.

It could be that this is not coincidental but rather indicates an extremely delicate balance and "delicate difference" in the way that women express themselves publicly in their speaking and writing and the way in which femininity is valued in our society. Let us begin with a historic dilemma: In past centuries when women were openly involved in intellectual debate, it was mainly through letter-writing or in hosting a literary or political salon. The female voice was mainly placed and kept within the private sphere, as the advisor, the listener, or the inspirational muse, being regarded in all cases as subjective. Although subjectivity was linked with women, men could also legitimately express their subjectivity. Within mainstream literature the essay form developed as a subjective form of expression relatively free from the constraints of academic argument. In traditional classification systems, poetic language was (and is) associated with femininity. In the course of the nineteenth century, elements of "the feminine" were annexed by art, in the so-called "decadence" and later the avant-garde. Forms of spontaneous creativity (and not academic commentary) that until then were attributed to women, found their place in the essay and are surely a reason for its popularity in the dominant discourse.

As always, when women have the chance to be published and enter into the intellectual debate, they express an ambivalence towards the dominant tradition. On the one hand, we find women who use their academic space to write weighty tomes laden with a surplus of footnotes aimed at reinforcing their academic validity. On the other hand, we find women who make use of the existing, dominant models of recalcitrance, such as the essay, to express their strength and vision. It is a balancing act, this use of existing forms in an attempt to create new meanings. In my opinion, Cixous is one of this latter group of writers.

When I try to place Cixous' writing, I think of the theoretician Theodor W. Adorno. Adorno, a rebellious spirit and an outsider (as a Jewish intel-

lectual in Germany), saw the essay as political dynamite in the academic world. Before I go further into Cixous' particular use of the essay form, I would like to comment on the special form and the possibilities of this genre. I draw largely on Theodor W. Adorno's inspiring writings on the essay. I will then use this theoretical perspective to examine Cixous' **"The Laugh of the Medusa."**

The Musical Logic of the Essay

In "Der Essay als Form" ("The Essay as Form") Adorno champions the distinctive mixture of media he defines as the essay. According to him, scientists distrust the essay form because the essay can choose to approach the whole mountain of knowledge from whichever angle it chooses, beginning and ending wherever it pleases. This goes against the "rules of the game" of disciplines which like to see themselves as scientific or scholarly. The essay can speak with several voices at one time and in that way is reminiscent of a work of art, which can present a number of different—sometimes even contradictory—statements. In this way, the essay is surely a superior medium to an academic discipline that presumes to pigeonhole reality into easily controlled concepts and ordered definitions. Rather than proceeding from definitions of axiomatic assumptions, the essay uses existing concepts as they are without necessarily redefining them. In an essay, concepts are given new and original meanings through the contexts in which they are placed and the connections made by the author. In this way, the essay can present new possibilities for existing concepts that are currently unexpressed and/or hidden. Adorno contends that the essay plays with concepts, in what he describes as a "systematically unsystematic method." It is not scientific definitions or dictionaries that help our understanding when we read an essay. "When the reader reads the same word in a variety of contexts thirty times, they will understand the meanings better than if they had looked up the different meanings in a dictionary, because they are often, in context, either too narrow or too vague" [21].

The essay is, then, not an analytical construction but a movement of interweaving concepts that demand neither origin nor end, completeness nor continuity. The essay recognizes that there is no single reality but rather realities that are discontinuous and brittle, and that people are not 'lords and masters' of creation. The essay frequently employs parody to emphasize this. The more the essay offers a critique of an essentialist concept, the more clearly we can see that some concepts seen as natural are in fact cultural constructions. The essay addresses the relationship between culture and nature by playing with apparently unshakeable convictions. This playing and the very enjoyment of the game lead "serious" scholars to brand the essay form as flippant. This joy of thinking, and the imagination of the new, the utopian, are given room to move in this medium. Cross-connections can be brought to light precisely because it is not necessary to argue within an accepted scientific paradigm. This goes against Cartesian thought. "Wherever a word has more than one meaning, the various meanings are never completely different from each other, but sometimes show how deeply hidden some connections between things are" [32]. Adorno concludes that the essay can be seen as a sort of heresy within the sciences, because it brings to the surface issues that science and philosophy are blind to, and that traditional concepts fail to recognize.

In his analysis of the essay, Adorno describes the possibility of breaking through the prevailing academic discourse to generate new meanings. For me, the attractiveness of the essay as Adorno describes it lies in the flexibility he gives it: it gives us the possibility of introducing new meanings and ways of thinking without necessarily having to be prescriptive. Unfortunately, Adorno did not further examine the implications of a text's subject matter for contextual meaning.

Women's Writing: A Never-Ending Essay?

If we apply Adorno's comments on the essay to feminine aesthetics and women's writing a number of observations can be made, particularly when we look at *écriture féminine*. Like the essay, this way of writing can be criticized as elitist and hermetic. If the writers of *écriture féminine* come from the academic world, and this is expressed unhesitatingly in their work, the label elitist certainly applies. These texts also often exhibit an unwillingness to explain concepts in lay terms and to make their political standpoints and directives explicit. The use of terminology and concepts from psychoanalysis and French postmodernism adds to the difficulties of translating the meaning of these works directly into feminist politics. The writers' standpoints are not always unambiguous. They employ concepts and definitions from psychoanalysis and literary criticism of male theoreticians at the same time as they criticize them or present their work parodically or ironically. The "I" in the text, which is so often in the

foreground in the essay as the manifest opinion of the author, is frequently withdrawn into such a maze of varying textual styles and voices that the reader is left not knowing where she or he stands. The text plays with the reader: to join in the game readers often must be prepared to let go of their traditional manner of reading. This is not always easy: many of us are used to choosing texts that comply with our way of thinking, that are supple in fitting themselves to our reading needs.

Such a master/servant relationship does not apply to the reader and some texts, Cixous' among them. These texts demand to be approached with care, and without too many prejudices. They require time if one wants to get to know them; the reader must become acquainted with them calmly and gently, often through more than one meeting. The reader must "travel light"—these texts cannot be approached with literary or intellectual baggage. Moreover, it is not important whether you begin in the middle or at the beginning. **"The Laugh of the Medusa,"** for example, is comprised of many small, independent pieces that can each stand on their own. But it is only when you can see the text in its entirety that you discover that the game of the never-ending mirrors is being played, where each new reading offers new perspectives and meanings.

This way of reading is made possible by the flexible form of the essay. And this flexibility suits the needs of the woman who writes about, for, and through women. The "I" of the author mirrors itself in the existing theories, myths, and clichés about women, turns these around, places them in shifting contexts, permits a normally unpermissible mingling of discourse levels, so that the text buzzes and sings in the reader's ears. The essay is constantly assailed by feminine identities, which explode and multiply in the text until the reader loses her way in this maze of identities. By "playing" with the inadequacies of concepts and definitions of femininity, Cixous creates the thought-space necessary to realize new possibilities.

This inherent possibility of the essay as described by Adorno, which is generated from the subversion and splintering of concepts and thought structures, has much to offer feminist criticism. At the same time, in my opinion, it can be quite risky. The deconstructionist style that precludes redefinition and limits us to playing with the existing discourse cannot offer us an answer to the question of feminine identity or address the socio-political concept of societal change. If a woman writer strictly follows Adorno's form of the essay, her voice and her "I" will be splintered, and she will be in danger of rendering herself dumb, without her own melody, when she herself comes to speak. It is clear that if a woman writer wishes to avoid the trap of essentialism (false definition) and the pitfall of identity-crushing deconstruction (losing all self-relativity), she must bend and mold the enticing medium of the essay, draw it to herself, and fit it to her own needs. In **"The Laugh of the Medusa,"** Hélène Cixous risks this experiment.

The Future Must No Longer Be Determined by the Past

In a series of seven sequences, Cixous leads us at a furious pace through woman's history and future, her shortcomings and possibilities. The overriding imperative of the essay is: "Woman, write!" But it also demands of us that we live—live out our own lives, determine our own history. "Write" is used in its original meaning of *inscribere*—she challenges us to make a notch, make our mark on the traditional culture. Woman is continually addressed, even accosted, as a principal actor in this process. Cixous sees that this meaning-giving process has to follow a ruptured, circuitous route.

In the first sequence, Cixous addresses herself intimately to all women readers: "I write this as a woman, toward women. When I say 'women,' I'm speaking of woman in her inevitable struggle against conventional man, and of a universal woman subject who must bring women to their senses and to their meaning in history . . . there is, at this time, no general woman, no one typical woman" [875-76]. She shows us immediately that woman and women cannot simply be lumped together in one convenient category. On the one hand, she examines the concrete, everyday struggle against traditional man. She links this to woman's need for a subject construction different from that of man. Cixous concedes that there is no symbolic, autonomous, female subject existing in our culture. She searches for the reason for this absence and sees it in the fact that from the time she is a small girl, woman is deprived of her sexuality, her energy, her imagination. If a girl is deprived of her potential for sexual pleasure, she is deprived of her joy of discovery, her own writing, her own eloquence. "The little girls and their 'ill-mannered' bodies immured, well-preserved, intact unto themselves, in the mirror. Frigidified. But are they ever-seething underneath! What an effort it takes—there's no end to it—for the sex cops to bar their threatening return" [877]. We

find this text movement returning throughout the entire essay, a form of militant analysis coupled with an encouragement that anticipates the future.

It is hardly surprising to find that the second sequence begins by ascertaining the continuing presence of women. "Here they are returning, arriving over and over again, because the unconscious is impregnable" [877]. Cixous does not identify woman with the unconscious, as is often done in postmodernism. Rather, she sees that everything that has to do with her own life, everything coupled with the lives of others, is supplanted by self-hate: self-hate generated by the fact that she is not a man. Cixous briefly mentions the link between Freud's metaphor of women as "the dark continent" and the struggle of blacks against oppression by whites. According to Cixous both have been pacified and made silent by white men. She contends that because of this oppression, there is still no real women's writing. Women who have written have "obscure[d] women or reproduce[d] the classical representations of women [as sensitive-intuitive-dreamy etc]" [878]. Cixous deliberately labels this masculine writing and claims that the dominant libidinal and cultural economy works hand in hand with women's oppression.

In the third sequence, Cixous links "factual" history with the history of writing, presenting both as being thoroughly permeated with phallocentric thought. She makes some minor exceptions: a few—very few—male poets have shown a glimpse of the feminine in their work (Heinrich v. Kleist, E. T. A. Hoffmann, Jean Genet) in that they broke with social codes and structures that deny women. It is precisely this step that Cixous demands of woman. She has to step out of man's shadow, out of her passive, servile role, and actively speak out. Cixous does not deny the difficulties involved. Often the only female voices that are heard are those that speak in a traditionally acceptable manner. But women must be able to withdraw from and reject the disconnected discourse of so-called logicians. We must be able to go further than merely mastering the discourse for its own sake. We must mix, mingle, interweave levels of discourse in order to create new levels of understanding.

Cixous asks that women include the primary experience of contact with the mother in "male causal symbolism." In contrast to Western cultural thinking that denies and/or abhors the many variations of early bonding with the mother, Cixous sees this as a chance to reestablish an unsublimated, unrepressed enjoyment of the body and to regain the music, sound, and language that are connected with this. "Even if phallic mystification has generally contaminated good relationships, a woman is never far from 'mother' (I mean outside her role functions: the 'mother' as nonname and as source of goods). There is always within her at least a little of that good mother's milk. She writes in white ink" [881]. This deeply poetic and highly suggestive passage concludes with the women writing in "white ink."

It is always dangerous to write about women in terms of anatomical metaphors—we are still fighting to free ourselves from the dualistic association of women as purely physical beings with no connection with the intellectual, the spiritual, the non-physical. But Cixous chooses this direction to emphasize that it is not the role of the mother that she means but the experience of an intense and loving physical enjoyment that is presented to us both as reclaimed memory and future possibility. Taking the metaphor of the "white ink" further, we can associate it with secrets or a secret code (writing in milk). In each instance the image is diametrically opposed to what is visibly written. Maybe we can see it as the space between the letters that is free for anyone to fill in at their own discretion according to their own imagination—"writing between the lines."

Cixous spins out the mother metaphor further in her fourth sequence. She recalls for us the bodily contact linked with mothering (and being mothered), the caresses, rhythms, songs, joys, and passions of the phase where you are being encouraged to come "out of your heart into language." Cixous sees this motherly affection and encouragement as an economy of unselfish distribution, in contrast to the classic economy of giving only to receive. As this female economy becomes more significant in social and political terms, traditional structures and codes will undergo fundamental changes. "As subject for history, woman always occurs simultaneously in several places. Woman un-thinks (*dépense*) the unifying, regulating history that homogenizes and channels forces, herding contradictions into a single battlefield. . . . As a militant, she is an integral part of all liberations" [822]. This militant position will lead to a changing, rather than a changed writing form, a female form that is neither definable nor theorizable. "[I]t does and will take place in areas other than those subordinated to philosophico-theoretical domination. It will be conceived of only by subjects who are breakers of automatisms, by peripheral figures that no authority can ever subjugate" [882]. Here

Cixous broadens the concept of women in an interesting way. She begins with woman as a subject from history and gives her a revolutionary function in all historical change. Finally, she equates the feminine in writing with anti-authoritarianism and the nomadic situation of marginal figures in general. In this way she shows us that it could be possible for men also to articulate the feminine.

From this position, Cixous continues her ideas on writing in her fifth sequence. She differentiates two economies of writing: an open, revealing, feminine style, and a conservative, phallic, masculine one. Cixous rages against the classic constellation, whereby under the primacy of the masculine symbolic and libidinal economy, the feminine as other is appropriated. (Think of male artists who claim to "give birth to" their works of art.) Cixous' vision is of another type of difference, another type of "bisexuality": ". . . that is, each one's location in self (*repérage en soi*) of the presence—variously manifest and insistent according to each person, male or female—of both sexes, nonexclusion either of the difference or of one sex, and from this 'self-permission,' multiplication of the effects of the inscription of desire, over all parts of my body and the other body" [884]. Although Cixous frequently disparages psychoanalysis, in the passage quoted she cites Freud's theory that every person is in principle bisexual, and it is only through cultural conditioning that one of the sexes is closed out or repressed. Cixous sees the theoretical constructions of Freud's castration complex and penis envy and Lacan's "lack" as ways to present and reinforce the feminine as the negative, the dead, the inadequate in our culture. With a hint of the Medusa myth and an idiosyncratic interpretation, Cixous refuses to negate the feminine as lack. She pleads with us to embrace the masculine and the feminine in each person, so that both poles can be present and active, each attractive in their differences. This gives us a starting point to deal with other aspects of multisexuality. This circulation of desire should also have its effect on texts. Cixous suggests that under this libidinal economy genres will become interwoven, linear logicians undermined. An unending, circular text production will begin.

In the sixth sequence, the disturbance of order within syntax and culture is further spun out and radicalized. Cixous refers to the strength of the protest of the hysterics. She calls Freud's Dora the Signifier's mistress (a sophisticated word play): Dora, papa's little darling, whom he misuses as a pawn in the adults' sexual game-playing. With her self-confident appearance and her precocious background, Dora is Freud's teacher in hysteria analysis. Dora, who masters the discourse, remains closed throughout Freud's analysis, breaks off the analysis, and refuses to be molded into the traditional female role. We see here how many layers one sentence, one metaphor, can generate. How, connected with other sentences and passages, it can say everything that the text can accommodate. We see it romping, cavorting, playing in and with the white ink!

Cixous creates for us another of her favorite metaphors in this passage. She use the verb *voler* in its double meaning of flying and stealing to show the ways in which women relate to the Law, to the cultural order. Cixous compares the woman to a bird and a thief. Thieves take what they want, and disturb the order of the house. Birds fly overhead, flying away from where they don't want to be, flying to where they do want to be. Because woman has learned not to be scared of anonymity—she so easily loses her titles (as spouse) or her property (of her spouse)—she will, like a thief, throw the property relationship between the sexes into confusion. This "lightness of being" means she can flit swiftly from one place to another; Cixous calls her an "airborne swimmer, in flight, she does not cling to herself" [889-90].

In the seventh sequence, Cixous returns to earth with her extremely personal flight through many aspects of meanings and meaningful elements. She summons women not to preclude themselves nor to allow themselves to be precluded from any single thing that they want to do, even when it comes to the precarious area of motherhood. Earlier in her text, she emphasizes that she is not talking about motherhood as a social role, yet here that is exactly what she means. She places motherhood in opposition to psychoanalysis, where a child represents a surrogate penis. She thunders against the "necessity" of seeing the mother-child relationship in terms of family structures. She encourages the pregnant woman to go on with her pregnancy as with her life—to "live" her passions, her language, and her intellectual and spiritual autonomy. Pregnant women are always suspect—their bulging bellies irrefutable evidence of the sexuality, the base physicality of women. But they are also unique here—giving birth means neither an increase nor a decrease in their body—they do not fit into the masculine economy. This sequence ends in increasingly shorter emotional statements on the importance of writing and the longing for the other. It tells us of the renouncing and yet the

simultaneous use of symbolic meanings to radiate an image of love. A love that constantly experiences the similarities and differences of the other, that even surpasses all expectations, a love that, in this text, does not differentiate between text, erotic, self, other, meaning, and subconscious, and that withdraws from articulation: "This is an economy that doesn't have to be put in economic terms" [893]. But then, why should it? The starting point was always: "The future must no longer be determined by the past" [875].

Who is Still Laughing?

If we start with the assumption that the form of the essay is not fixed, that it offers the author complete freedom, then it can be difficult to define what is innovative or experimental. Everything is permissible in terms of style and theme, even if it is only a small, recalcitrant work of art. Yet I want to return to what it is that makes the aesthetic form of Cixous' essay so exciting.

Cixous tends towards an openness that is at home in the essay; she moves from a personal statement and expands it into generalizations—one of the major elements of the essay. Now and then she broadens her considerations in directions which include men. Here Cixous deviates from the usual essay that assumes a male author/narrator who is placed against a self-evidently male-dominated cultural background. This, however, does not automatically make Cixous' essay more experimental than many other essays. What makes Cixous' essay special is that she positions herself clearly as a female author writing for a female public, with only some of her assertions being valid for men as well. She deviates from the standard essay form that addresses a public that is automatically coded as masculine.

It is worthwhile examining some of Cixous' structural elements of style. Cixous divides her text into seven sequences; in the first, she presents us with her paradigm that the future must be anticipated. At the end of the final sequence, she leaves us with "In the beginning are our differences" [873]. With this structure, and this final passage, Cixous parodies the seven days of the Creation. She re-creates the universe out of the chaos of male disorder. She brings into being a new, renewed, and renewing female creation. Her often hymnal tone, her utopian encouragement, her prophetic visions blend with her critical-historical analysis to emphasize this image. Her heretical amendment of the first line of the Creation is feminist and provocative. Here again, Cixous challenges us to test the intertextual connections. My reading of the essay takes the following line: Cixous places the proclamation "In the beginning are our differences" at the end of the seventh sequence—metaphorically speaking, on the seventh day. This is the biblical day of rest, when God admired his creation with satisfaction, Adam and Eve were already created, the Creation was in complete harmony, and God was the Father-by-projection to whom the world owed its existence.

Cixous revises the Creation. She begins on her first "day" of creation by telling us that we must not allow ourselves to be restrained and blinkered by what has been when we set ourselves the task of imagining what could be. She calls up the world—she is a second creator of a universe that partly supersedes the present one and is partly still being elaborated. She plows relentlessly through the universe with open, searching eyes, both admonishing and encouraging us. Then comes her seventh—one of the oldest sacred numbers—text fragment, which is both the most personal and the most utopian. It could, at the same time, be read as the first fragment, as the beginning. In the beginning there is not the Word (as in the Bible) or the Deed (as in Goethe's *Faust*), but the Differences, our differences. The basic premise of Cixous' re-Creation is humanity as it exists, with no ontologically defined essential characteristics. There are only Differences. People are different from each other, and we also change from one moment to the next, becoming "different from ourselves" as we were.

This fundamental supposition of the Creation à la Cixous implies that all ordering must be rethought and that no one has any prior claim to any particular form of existence by virtue of their sex or status. This means, too, that all symbolic systems are both provisional and flexible because nothing can be invoked on the basis of concrete, unchanging attributes. The primacy of difference will always modify symbolic forms. Above all, this means that all existing stories, canonized theories, and myths exist by the grace of the Denial of Difference. Cixous once again uses fragments of myth in her essay (and her literary work) to show us that this masculine story-telling tradition has generated a world that is very different from the one that would come into being through feminine myth-making.

A female retelling would be another story: it would consist of other stories, with different aspects of the tale honored and valued. The collected stories that have sprung from the resistance to male fear and female self-hate, and vice versa,

stories of death, love, conquest, would, in another economy, lead to other myths. Cixous uses the image of Ariadne's thread to show another way of handling myths. She builds no cathedrals, no symbolic buildings with matriarchal precursors. Rather, she spins her yarn, teasing language into new and unfamiliar chains of association. The Word is not, in the figurative sense, used as a metaphor; rather, the metaphor is taken literally and returned to its original image. Here *prendre la parole* is no symbolic deed—it is spun out through the sound, the music, the orality, the mouth, the body that speaks, she who speaks, she who is spoken to, what it is that speaks, what she speaks about, what she could speak about, why she stays mute. A word, a thought, chases other thoughts in an interior monologue that is orchestrated so that the reader can insert her own part. This spontaneous concert may well seem chaotic from the outside. But there is a melody line, and that is the theme "woman," in all her many and varied synonyms, in all of her resonances, assonances, fugues, codas, and echoes.

We return finally to the beginning that is no beginning. We return to the story of creation—one of the finest myths there is, the myth that functions, as Northrop Frye put it, as the "Great Code" of western society. Cixous is bantering with this code, all the while taking a position as a speaking "I" in the text that is reminiscent of the Creator, here recreated in female form. Cixous loves her creation and her creatures, most certainly those of the female variety. What sort of guiding light do we have before us? Who is this seductress who is raging and wild, magnetic and compelling? In other words, I must ask the question: Where do you stand, Hélène Cixous, in your own Creation?

Jane Gallop tells us, with considerable irony, that Irigaray never actually comes to grips with the question of the daughter who seeks affection and understanding from the father. And Gallop finds that Kristeva's brilliance and authoritarian voice demand the position of the phallic mother. So where should we situate Cixous? Two pieces from Cixous' text haunt me. At the end she says "I want it all." This is a valid wish, and in itself is not extraordinary. But if it is linked with her vehement plea of a fundamental bisexuality, and her statement that no woman has essentially broken her tie with her childhood, which is supported by her almost mystical veneration of the mother, then I receive the impression that she places woman in her most original stage in this childhood, after which cultural patterning robs her of

FROM THE AUTHOR

CIXOUS ON HER LITERARY AND EMOTIONAL EVOLUTION

I think that what is inscribed in what I have written is a certain story, a certain history, which is mine and, I believe, that of every woman. I think it is quite exemplary. Besides, it is truly a history insofar as it has a development in time, because I absolutely do believe in experience. I think we traverse in time moments which, little by little, allow us to advance and to learn to live. One does not know how to live; one learns to live.

Cixous, Hélène. Excerpt from *Hélène Cixous: Writing the Feminine*, p. 161. Lincoln: University of Nebraska Press, 1984.

her originality. In this phase of life, children play with and try on for size all the roles and rituals that they are offered, not critically, but acceptingly, so that they can find their place in their environment and deal emotionally with events in their lives. This "child's play" is often played in deadly earnest and is not wanting for aesthetic beauty. Children do not yet reflect their history—or a history. They are working on finding a place for themselves in history.

Adults look indulgently upon children's games. The innocence ascribed to children comes from the fact that they don't yet have their "place" in history. This cultural attitude is reflected in the New Testament; people must enter the kingdom of heaven as if they were children. I am inclined to think that Cixous sees this naïveté as either an imitation, or a source of, female creativity. This would explain her avoidance of "political statements," and why, when she does make strategic feminist statements, she takes refuge in poetic, mythical, ageless description. Perhaps these distractions are consciously laid out by the author to preclude a new theory or concept of femininity from being distilled from her text. The result is a curious paradox: on the one hand, her "I" in the text continually encourages her readers, obstinately and unequivocally, to realize—in both senses of the word—an existence in language, culture, and history. On the other hand, just when

the reader wishes to take up the challenge and seeks a concrete directive, a solid standpoint, the subject of the text withdraws itself as a leading or advisory figure. It would be sufficient if the challenges the author so enthusiastically presents were linked with an occasional personal experience, even assuming that such challenges could not be representative of all women. Cixous' writing style creates an enormous distance between herself and the reader, even though she speaks constantly of closeness, intimacy, giving, of the physical. It throws suspicion on whether her postulation of the unselfish giving of the feminine economy is perhaps merely a noncommittal postmodern mannerism, or whether it can only be realized in the hereafter. In her argument, Cixous combines the promise of an experienced friend, of a mother, with the experimenting fury of a small child. The one looks at the other over her shoulder in the three-sided mirror. Perhaps because of that, she has forgotten that there are other rooms in the house. In reading Cixous' "**The Laugh of the Medusa**," that leaves me with no inclination to laugh.

Nevertheless, Cixous' text remains an interesting experiment with the essay form. Cixous mixes different discourse forms to illustrate the complexity of the concept of femininity, without insisting on a new definition. In this way she works within the style of the essay as Adorno describes it. Still, she alters the form in two ways. First, she pours her associative style into the relatively strict structure of seven sequences in an analogy of the creation myth. This evokes associations with a play or a mythical story-telling and gives a solidity usually missing in the essay, at least according to Adorno.

Secondly, in her narrative perspective, Cixous brings out the position of the subject of the text as problematic. Cixous refuses to recognize the masculine subject/narrator as taken for granted. Sometimes she is dominantly present, and sometimes she disappears behind her descriptions of historical impediments or her visions of the future. This can be irritating to the reader, yet this subject position can also be read as an indicator of the place that the female voice takes in the intellectual, masculine domain. Her voice rings out as she analyzes the historical position of women. She sounds hopeful and strong as she encourages change, but the female voice becomes uncertain when it comes to describing her visions of possible futures. With this change of tone, Cixous shows us the difference that exists between the taken-for-granted male critical voice in the essay and a new and critical female perspective that is trying to articulate itself. This is not a one-dimensional endeavor; it is happening in different ways and on different levels at the same time. And it lies with us, her readers, to develop this further, on the multitude of levels offered to us. The essay is but one of these levels.

Works Cited

Adorno, Theodor W. "Der Essay als Form." *Noten zur Literatur.* Frankfurt am Main: Suhrkamp Verlag, 1974. 9-34.

Cixous, Hélène. "The Laugh of the Medusa." Trans. Keith and Paula Cohen. *Signs* 1, 4 (Summer 1976): 875-93.

Frye, Northrop. *The Great Code: The Bible and Literature,* New York: Harcourt Brace Jovanovich, 1981.

Gallop, Jane. *Feminism and Psychoanalysis: The Daughter's Seduction.* London/Basinstoke: MacMillan, 1982.

Illa

MARTINE MOTARD-NOAR (ESSAY DATE 1994)

SOURCE: Motard-Noar, Martine. "From Persephone to Demeter: A Feminist Experience in Cixous's Fiction." In *Images of Persephone: Feminist Readings in Western Literature,* edited by Elizabeth T. Hayes, pp. 153-69. Gainesville: University Press of Florida, 1994.

In the following essay, Motard-Noar studies Cixous's reclaiming of history and myths in her novel Illa *through the deconstruction of male-based myths that relegate women to roles of passivity.*

Hélène Cixous is one of the most controversial thinkers and writers in France. Despite her unwillingness to be labeled a "feminist"—a reductive categorization, according to her, just another "ism"-ending word[1]—she is considered a representative of one of the major creative and critical drives in the New French Feminist movement. She has developed her avant-garde practice of writing in numerous genres and forms, such as the bilingual novel *To Live the Orange* (Cixous 1979), and the play *Portrait of Dora* (Cixous 1979), her revision of Freud. Her most significant theoretical essays include the now classic manifesto "**The Laugh of the Medusa,**" and collaborative projects such as *The Newly Born Woman* (Cixous and Clément 1986).

In 1980, Cixous published *Illa,* which works precisely on this central concept in her works—the newly born woman. In *Illa,* Cixous paradoxically introduces a story apparently opposed to the idea of a newly born woman—the ancient myth of Demeter, goddess of the earth and fecundity, who roams the earth in search of her daughter

Persephone (or Kore) throughout the text. The paradox is, however, explained by the narrator's insistence that women must work their way through myths again to situate themselves in the past and present and to examine enigmatic accounts about their own sisters, past and present. In fact, in an interview, Cixous clearly explained why her exploration of the feminine must privilege myths in general: "I am passionately interested in myths, because they are always . . . outside the law, like the unconscious" (Andermatt Conley 1984, 155-56). It is not surprising that images of Persephone/Demeter are present in *Illa,* especially because Persephone represents one of the greatest Greek goddesses. In actuality, the goddess soon disappears as a specific historical figure, to be metamorphosed into a general figure of women that will then freely circulate in the text. As one of the many narrators in *Illa* admits, "There is nothing left in me that is not impregnated with her" [Il ne reste rien de moi qui ne soit imprégné d'elle].[2] It is in such a broad context that the inclusion of the myth of Persephone in *Illa,* a fictional work, can be understood. Nowhere is there a reference to or even a particular historical definition of the Persephone myth, which has known widely different interpretations, as documented, for instance, by Barbara Walker (1983, 786-87). This free adaptation of the myth by Cixous cannot surprise, for it is consistent with the general pattern in her writing, which the author has explained in interviews and essays. For her, the issue at stake is both political and ideological—Cixous's "feminist" writing will not accept any canonical form or any mythological story/ "his"tory determined by a particular variation of the myth. She has already formulated a clear critical theory about the necessity of such disruption and recreation: "One never questions enough the traditions of interpretation of myth, and all myths have been referred to a masculine interpretation. If we women read them, we read them otherwise" (Cixous 1984, 156.) On the contrary, in all of the identities given to her in variations of the myth, Persephone often lives, in the overall image of the Woman, an unwilling participant in the constitution of her own myths. Following Michel Foucault's theory that "the real political task in a society such as ours is to criticize the working of institutions which appear to be both neutral and independent; to criticize them in such a manner that the political violence which has always exercised itself obscurely through them will be unmasked, so that one can fight them" (1992, 1). Cixous decides to "discover and create our [women's] myths in the process of a-mazing tales that are phallic" (Daly 1978, 129). In that way, the character of Persephone belongs to a global corpus of myths about women. But Cixous finds her specificity in the fact that her central figure binds them all together in the image of the Mother.

In fact, the accent is immediately put on Demeter's identity as Mother at the beginning of the fiction, because she is defined, when entering the narrative scene, as a mother searching for Kore, her daughter. For that reason, she "runs along the earth, the sea. . . . Roams outside of herself" [Court au bord de la terre, la mer. . . . Erre hors d'elle] (7). Although there is no mention of a cult surrounding "Illa" ("that woman"), it is interesting that Cixous first develops the figure of Demeter in relation to the earlier cults, where Demeter defined the feminine in both its sexual and reproductive aspects, in much the same way as patriarchy has defined the feminine. The text accumulates symbols relating Demeter to images of fertility (wheat) and bluntly affirms Demeter's figurative role: "the mother who comes back" [la mère qui revient] (12-13). The allusion to the maternal relationship in the myth is even more direct farther on: "GODDESS DECIDES NO LONGER BE DIVINE UNTIL RETURN HER DAUGHTER, HER DIVINITY." [DEESSE DECIDE NE PLUS ETRE DIVINE JUSQU'A RETOUR SA FILLE, SA DIVINITE.] (17). Demeter's presence can thus be immediately identified as the tale of the search for a daughter by her mother in the first few pages of the novel. Cixous, unlike most French feminist writers except for Chantal Chawaf, has always recognized and in some way glorified the figure of the mother and maternity, which French feminist writers like Monique Wittig have tried to escape or deny, keeping away from the dangers of heterosexual and patriarchal discourses. Cixous, however, both for personal and political reasons, has written along bisexual lines to express a multiple discourse that encompasses both lesbian desire and the acknowledgment of the need for "mater-renelle" (1981, 9) language, a French portmanteau word bringing together the concept of mother and of earth to the heart of her quest.

Beyond any easy categorization, Cixous sets an example of what other figures can accomplish as well in terms of allowing mothers and daughters to create a relationship of their own: "One And becomes real and opens up each time that a woman gives birth back to one of her mothers. And each time that a woman asks to receive the light from another woman" [Un Et devient réel et s'ouvre chaque fois qu'une femme rend naissance à une de ses mères. Et chaque fois qu'une femme

demande à recevoir la lumière d'une autre femme] (202). It has become, indeed, a movement back and forth between mothers, women of the origin, and daughters, who stand also as the images of the narrator. Demeter being the traditional image of the mother and even more specifically, of the mother of daughters, it is now the daughter's/narrator's duty to recreate her for the sake of self-knowledge and better understanding of women's oppression by men, as well as for a possible elucidation of feminist struggle. Reverence for women's "Ur-story" is present in a tale-like narrative in which women are compared to potatoes, an image obviously related to that of roots, origins, and earth. The potato stands as the "metaphor for Cixous's persistent search for feminine identity" (Shiach 1991, 93). Therefore, what could be seen as a humorous or at the very least ironic comparison is actually a serious attempt on her part to deconstruct the biblical story of Woman and the apple, or *pomme* in French, and reconstruct it under the sign of the potato/earth apple (*pomme de terre*) or concept of germination, and even better, self-germination from potato/woman to another, that is to say rebirth, despite its/her burial. In fact, Cixous gives the following definition to her reconstitution of women's epic:

> Different from other vegetables, the potato is not a plant, it is an expression from the earth as original matter. . . . Like Cretan civilization, potatoes are the most refined and repressed fruit. Potatoes in culture as in the cult are closely linked to the love-life association which make up for the first First Woman and her daughter the second and third. They are sometimes called Demeter and Persephone, often simply called "the Goddesses" or the potatoes. The potatoes are worth venerating: thus we do not disdain them, but we often make it so we can send them back into that dark oblivion in which they can stay quietly for thousands of years. The story of the potatoes constitutes the tender and crumbly matter, veiled with very fine, brown scrapings, of the central myth hidden in the heart of the universally known legend which tells of the origin of women, and the metamorphosis of potatoes.
>
> [À la différence des autres légumes, la pomme de terre n'est pas une plante, c'est une expression de la terre en tant que matière originaire. . . . Comme la civilisation crètoise, les pommes de terre sont les fruits les plus raffinés et les plus refoulés. Les pommes de terre dans la culture comme dans le culte sont étroitement unies au couple amour-vie que forment la première Première et sa fille la deuxième et troisième, parfois appelées Déméter et Perséphone, souvent simplement appelées "les Déesses" ou les pommes. Les pommes de terre sont vénérables: nous ne les méprisons donc pas, mais nous nous arrangeons fréquem-

ment pour les renvoyer à l'enfouissement dans lequel elles peuvent se tenir coites des millénaires. L'histoire des pommes de terre constitue la matière tendre, friable, voilée par de très fines pelures brunes, du mythe central caché au sein de la légende universellement répandue qui raconte l'origine des femmes, et la métamorphose des pommes de terre.]

(203)

Demeter and Persephone carry out the chant of oppression as its archetypes. Nonetheless, several other "potatoes" join them in the narrative, as if Cixous felt the need to exemplify her theoretical proposal. This may explain the presence of a character like Cordelia, a clear allusion to Shakespeare's Cordelia, one of King Lear's daughters, who decided to "Love, and be silent" (1961, 983) when faced with the lies blinding her father's love. The fiction also opens with a direct quotation from Virgil's *Georgics* that alludes to Eurydice's lost chance to leave Hades, after Orpheus looks back at her.[3] These characters, although they introduce a male variant to the mother/daughter story, all converge toward an implicit accusation of male dominance, the power to throw women into oblivion. Women's love-giving (whether it comes from a mother like Demeter, a daughter like Cordelia, or a wife like Eurydice) ends up being buried deeply.

Illa ends up accusing all caught in such social conditioning, apparently both men and women, of repressing women's instinctive drives. And women's feeling of unity throughout the myths and the ages paradoxically grows out of the story of their oppression: "We too, in a way, are potatoes together. The goddesses came like us from the southern hemisphere. They lived happy among the other earth nymphs, far from any concept of marriage, until the primitive abduction whose grave and sorrowful consequences for us are still perceptible all along the paths in this text" [Nous aussi nous sommes d'une certaine manière pommes de terre ensemble. Les déesses étaient originaires comme nous de l'hémisphère sud. Elles vivaient heureuses parmi les autres nymphes de terre, loin de toute idée de mariage, jusqu'à l'enlèvement primitif dont les conséquences endeuillantes pour nous sont encore perceptibles tout le long des chemins de ce texte] (203). Despite the presence of other potato stories, the particular choice of the Persephone/Demeter pair in *Illa* indeed raises the question of the ultimate act of male oppression of women—ravishment or rape. Demeter's wrath ("dies illa dies irae" [52]) becomes that of the narrator and of all women in the face of Persephone's brutal abduction by Hades into

the chasm as she was gathering flowers. Although the narrator is using the particular myth of Persephone/Demeter, her wrath is globally targeted at most myths, created by men for men in their unconscious need to reveal their perverse desires against women, and young women in particular. Exasperation spreads over Demeter's rage:

The whole series of grotesque appearances under which the old perverse saw themselves forced to be in order to abduct the vigilant virgins, with a sharp shuttle she represents the gang of those insect-like reduced to their true aspect, as in themselves the rape drive changes them forever, with the entire zoo they put together, here they are, underneath their hair, leather, scales, as they are revealed in dreams, in the horror of their nature, with a look able to disgust leda, demeter, kore, melantho, ariadne, asterie, medusa, theophane, you my friend, angela, or you deo, or you, memory, my sister, or illa, as well as all the women who find no charm in being bitten, torn apart, stabbed in the back, caressed with ram's and bull's horns, and snakes' and eagles' claws, hooves and beaks, and have no libidinal interest in being unveiled by a satyr.

[Toute la série des grotesques apparences sous lesquelles les vieux pervers se sont vus contraints de se présenter dérobés pour enlever les vierges vigilantes, d'une navette aiguë elle figure la bande des insectueux réduits à leur véritable aspect, tels qu'en eux-mêmes la pulsion de viol les change pour l'éternité, leur zoo entier tout craché, les voilà rendus, sous poil, sous cuir, sous écailles, tels qu'en rêve ils sont révélés, horreur nature, avec leur aspect propre, à dégoûter léda, démèter, koré, mélantho, ariane, astérié, méduse, théophané, toi mon amie, angela, ou toi déo, ou toi, mémoire, ma soeur, ou illa, ainsi que toutes les femmes qui ne trouvent aucun charme à se faire mordre, déchirer, poignarder dans le dos, caresser à coups de cornes de bélier, de boeuf, de serres de serpents, d'aigles, de sabots, de becs, et aucun intérêt libidinal à se faire connaître par un satyre.]

(71)

The narrator's interest in the Persephone/Demeter pair exemplifies a general need to strike all myths. Because it is impossible to cancel the past, Cixous's political goal is to stress at least the feminine component in each myth to undercut the male violence and perverse sexuality expressed in mythological deeds. In fact, neither Hades nor Zeus, Persephone's father, who tacitly consented to her abduction, appears in *Illa.* They are now finally made impotent in the fiction written by a woman. Bitterness and sorrow now follow in close parallel with Demeter's own reaction: "We no longer love the titans who used to hold the main roles in our passions, the gods we loved. . . . They are keeping away a lost child, about whom we keep thinking with loving sorrow, with sad and peaceful tenderness, a child who leads an unknown existence in our unconscious" [Nous n'aimons plus les titans qui détenaient les rôles principaux dans nos passions, les dieux que nous avons aimés. . . . Ils ont la garde d'un enfant perdu, auquel nous pensons avec une tristesse aimante, avec une tendresse triste et paisible, et qui mène parmi nos inconscients une existence inconnue] (120). Thus, Demeter's wrath finds a more positive outlet, beyond aggression, death, and revenge, for Cixous has started to put together a new poetics of women, a new mythical body characterized by a drive for life. In a direct allusion to *Prometheus Unbound* and an open feminization of Shelley's canonical test, Cixous explains the reasons for Demeter's final restraint in a chapter entitled "Illa unbound": "Because a woman does not surrender to death unless she has forgotten the secret of her strength; . . . because there is in every woman a great passion which does not surrender" (84). Wrath is then replaced by a specific sense of communion with the feminine victims, to whom Cixous obviously belongs. The feminine anger characterized by Cixous's use of the myth can be found and reaffirmed in another work, published one year after *Illa*, **With ou l'art de l'innocence,** which has not yet been translated into English. In a continuing search for the presymbolic wealth represented by ancient Greek mythology, Cixous uses the story of Eurydice in a presentation that parallels that of Persephone and Demeter quite remarkably and is alluded to in *Illa* in the Latin quotation from Virgil's *Georgics*. In **With,** however, she might be considered as going further than in *Illa,* as there is no mention whatsoever of the male figure, Orpheus. Somewhere between indifference and accusation, the many women narrators of the fiction appear to have expelled or "decentered" the masculine as the eternal culprit in the Eurydice story. To make her point even clearer, Cixous has Amina, a character and one of the women narrators in the book, successfully rescue Eurydice from Hades. The path from the masculine to the feminine in Cixous's works resounds with bitterness, love, and, in the end, hope for radical change.

Persephone and, by extension, Demeter thus become the representation of love and innocence still present in women's hearts, according to Cixous. Fiction, rewriting of the myth, and/or memory actually attempt to make up for the abduction of the maiden. Therefore, the dynamic principle of the text is an absence/presence dichotomy, Persephone's presence being found in her very absence, one that keeps accusing her oppressor. Cixous, unlike other writers (such as Monique Wittig), finds a feminist tune of reparation that does not entail forgiveness but rather a personal search for the maiden in each woman, while conjuring up in the background the father/male figure, who is also faced with an absence/presence dichotomy.

One of Cixous's narrative talents in *Illa,* and in many of her other fictions as well, is to weave traditional Greek mythology into her own invented mythology. As a French feminist writer, she is not the only one to do so. Her interest in Greek mythology and her gestures away from its determinism reminds one of Monique Wittig, who, in her very personal version of a woman's dictionary, attempts to recapture women's history in a partially fictional manner. In this work, culture, mythologies, oral tradition, personal imagination, and projection are gathered to constitute a purely feminine and lesbian domain, which women have been indirectly prohibited from defining. These motives explain why the subconscious and the imaginary in both Cixous's and Wittig's texts participate in the identification and fictional representation of women's realm. Wittig also stresses the importance of the female couple in the following entry from her dictionary: "DEMETER AND PERSEPHONE—Famous ancient goddesses, companions and lovers from Pelasgia. One was born from the other. When Persephone had to part from her, Demeter would show her sorrow by destroying everything alive on the surface of the earth until Persephone returned. From this come the winter and the autumn, it is said" (Wittig and Zeig 1979, 42). The violence and impact of female love—a representation typical of Wittig's writing—do not appear in Cixous as images of external destruction but rather of self-destruction. Nevertheless, for both Cixous and Wittig, the female couple evokes a privileged topos and a possibility for mythical re-creation.

As for the possibility of self-destruction, it is depicted in *Illa* in a passage written with a semi-autobiographical overtone. The narrator, drawing a parallel between herself and Cixous's identity as a Jewish woman, reaffirms the concept of loss and rapture, this time in modern terms, although in very similar fashion to the Persephone/Demeter situation. In a somewhat nightmarish scene, the narrator evokes having to leave abruptly to be taken to a concentration camp. Just like Persephone, she is a wanted woman, a "Jewoman" (*juifemme*)—as Cixous likes to write in many texts. This time, it is the mother who is forced to leave her daughter, in an exchange of female roles. The mother says, "I am afraid, I hurt, I didn't say good-bye, I didn't have time to think intelligently, I didn't tell my mother to take my children to England, I didn't call my love to say 'I love you' before I die, I didn't ask you who is not a jewoman to give my life to my daughter" [J'ai peur, j'ai mal, je n'ai pas fait mes adieux, je n'ai pas eu le temps de penser intelligemment, je n'ai pas dit à ma mère d'emmener mes enfants en Angleterre, je n'ai pas téléphoné à mon amour pour lui dire qu'avant de mourir je l'aime, je n'ai pas demandé à toi qui n'es pas juifemme de transmettre ma vie à ma fille] (166).

At this point of the fiction, the narrator manages to encompass both roles—that of mother and that of daughter—in a gesture of indifference toward the traditional notion of specific roles and characters. For Cixous's fiction strips the notion of character from its capitalist economy, from all its usual attributes, in favor of a notion of characters' free exchange.[4] She is both Demeter and Persephone in a movement of appropriation of total existential anguish, as conveyed in the Persephone/Demeter myth. And again possible self-destruction (caused by the Jewish woman's inability to act before leaving for a concentration camp) is the result of outside oppression. The narrator, just like Persephone, is taken away, in danger of losing her own self, together with the self known to those who love her; the danger of self-destruction is therefore extended to the narrator's daughter and to Demeter herself. The precarious condition in which women find themselves, and their paradoxical feeling of guilt when faced with their own victimization, are here reintroduced by Cixous in a personal light, using a modern background to the tragic myth. The account is nonetheless to be taken in the broad ideological context defined earlier, as the account of a particular woman's condition echoing in its own way the general condition of women as witnessed in Persephone and Demeter.

The question of forced separation in *Illa* has been so obvious to critics that they have discerned a desire for revenge, but only in Cixous's choice of words. Verena Andermatt Conley notes that Cixous's use of the name of Koré for Persephone has separatist undertones: "Cixous changes the Greek name Persephone, which had been used by male theoreticians to allude to problems of voice (*phonè*), to the more material Koré (*corps-ai*), substituting the masculine letter K for the more commonly used C" (1984, 107). There exists an undeniable interest on Cixous's part to undermine any traditional acceptance of the myth and to distort all clichés about Persephone's fragility as a female object. Becoming Koré, Persephone seems and literally sounds as if she is finally able to struggle on even ground, since Koré sounds like *corps-ai* or "body-[I] have." The glorification of women in the Persephone myth in Cixous cannot therefore be conflated with the cult of femininity, a potentially controversial matter, because the concept of femininity is transformed in her use of the myth. For, in the end Koré, by her name alone, can announce her presence and deny her symbolic oppression.

Despite the change in spelling from C to K and the revelation of her strong identity, Koré cannot prevent Persephone from being present in the text in allusions to problems of voice. A whole syncretism is in process in *Illa*, relating the voice to, in the end, the Female: "The voice is the uterus. The voice contracts and gives birth, gives birth, and for each new joy, breaks into laughter, and gives a name" [La voix est l'utérus. La voix se contracte et met au monde, met au monde, et à chaque nouvelle joie, éclate de rire, et met un nom] (168). Persephone loses her voice by being abducted, yet she is still alive in the underworld. It is now Demeter's grief that speaks of her daughter and speaks for her daughter. In this way, Persephone's voice is immortal as it runs through women, her mother, and then others who give birth to it. As for Demeter, she is allowed to hope for the strength of a female voice of iron, which the narrator conveys in a direct quotation from Virgil, "*Non, mihi si linguae centum oraque centum*" (Cixous 1980, 8; the quotation is from Virgil 1990, 2:43), which is followed in Virgil by an allusion to the possibility of having a voice of iron in addition to one hundred tongues and one hundred mouths. There is hope therefore for "Illa," the third person, the narrator, who roams the earth, like Demeter, in search of herself and all women—she too, as a woman, is given a voice in the fiction. Another source of hope resides in the meaningful sounds made by the actual name used by Cixous to allude to Persephone, as Andermatt Conley suggests. Koré, alias Persephone, is definitely not lost; her absence-presence is voiced by many women, for those who in turn pronounce the word *corps-ai* actualize themselves in the discovery of a body they now themselves own. Similarly, Persephone's body is given back to her in the shape of Koré through *Illa*.

Ultimately the Persephone/Demeter question and that of a/the narrative voice are one and the same, for writing is directly related to the earth and the voice in the sensual quality of their fertility, their creation. For that reason, "the daughter unable to get help from her mother any more stays away from her own life, resembles a writing without a feather in its hands" [la fille n'ayant plus le secours de sa mère reste en deçà de sa propre vie, ressemble à une écriture qui n'a pas de plume entre les mains] (196), and, similarly for Demeter, "who has not seen the moment when her daughter was stolen—she resembles a mouth without a tongue" [qui n'a pas vu l'instant où sa fille a été volée: elle ressemble à une bouche qui n'a pas de langue] (196). It is then easy for the narrative figure, which is, by definition, a writing figure, to assimilate herself as a woman with Persephone/Koré ravished away from the mother tongue, from the only possibility to speak out and give form (corps) to words: "May I remember how I came from a first woman, may I remember just once at least one mother, just once an all-giving mother with an absolutely faithful and natural voice from birth, please!" [Puissé-je garder en mémoire comment je suis venue d'une première, puissé-je une seule fois ne pas oublier une seule mère, rappeler une seule fois toute donnante d'une voix absolument fidèle et natale et naturelle, puissé-je!] (196). The loss of the daughter's voice, leading to all women's loss of voice(s), causes the mother's wrath as well as the impossibility of her living as a mother, woman, daughter herself, and goddess. The dissolution of her being is stressed in a telegram-style passage: "GODDESS DECIDES NO LONGER BE DIVINE UNTIL RETURN HER DAUGHTER, HER DIVINITY. NO LONGER LIVE. SEARCH. SURVIVE. DEMETER." [DEESSE DECIDE NE PLUS ETRE DIVINE JUSQU'A RETOUR SA FILLE, SA DIVINITE. PLUS VIVRE. CHERCHER. SURVIVRE. DEMETER.] (18).

Demeter's despair and love are, in the end, the only feminine response that can pressure the (masculine) world into Persephone's release. Women's alliance, although multivoiced, still remains powerless and only serves as an intermediary phase. Demeter's direct power over events is limited to the identity given to her by her very name: pronounced in French, Demeter is homonymic of d'aimer terre, or "to love the earth," a play on words used by Cixous in *Illa* (18). Demeter chooses not to love the earth, with the result that she threatens the world and, at the same time, is threatened in her own power to love, which Cixous stresses in the description of Demeter's desperate wandering.

Demeter's wandering, however, leaves no room for any dispersion or disintegration of the self. Her wandering soon becomes a method, an account of and a search for love with no specifically targeted objective, contrary to what is commonly involved with a heterosexual relationship, according to Cixous. The wandering becomes a fictional experience in the plural, as the title of the book underlines. *Illa,* a singular and plural Latin demonstrative pronoun used here in the feminine, evokes a concept for which there is no word in French or in English. *Illa,* meaning "that woman *or/and* those women," announces the core principle of the text, encompassing the singular *and* the plural under woman's/women's general history. Moreover, this pronoun is often used in Latin in a positive and emphatic way, which seems perfectly to fit with the intention of the text.

On the other hand, the pronoun may convey as well a notion of distance both in time and space, like a finger pointing at a third person, probably the woman narrator: "Who? Am? The third woman. . . . Whos? Am we? Who? I? We? Wanders out of herself. *Illa.* A young person. The third woman [my italics]." [Qui? Suis? La troisième. . . . Quis? Suis nous? Qui? Je? Nous? Erre hors d'elle. Illa. Une jeune personne. La troisième] (7). The narrator of *Illa* thus opens the book declining the pronoun from the feminine singular to the feminine plural, from "Who? Am?" to "Whos? Am *we?"* [my italics] and soon after, into a general feminine gender crying out for a solidarity found in the distancing enforced upon it by male discourse. *Illa* thus represents women's position parallel to that of Persephone.

The quality of patriarchal discourse represented by the word *illa* as expressing women's unwilling marginality has also been recognized by writers other than Cixous, particularly feminist psychoanalytic critics. Jane Gallop notes that, in Freudian discourse, woman becomes a third person, the Other, about whom men speak, used as an object of analysis and experimentation; woman is *Illa* for Freud according to Gallop's analysis of one of his speeches: "Although Freud begins his lecture 'Ladies and Gentlemen,' a few pages later he says, 'Nor will *you* have escaped worrying over this problem because *you* are men; as for the *women among you* this will not apply, *they* are themselves this riddle' [my italics]. When he explicitly addresses the audience as sexed beings, he reserves the second-person pronoun for men and refers to women with the third-person pronoun. Freud talks *to* men *about* women" (1985, 38).

Illa, character(s) and title, struggle against the same ambiguity—closeness and distancing. *Illa* represents the closeness among women and, at the same time, women's separation, which paradoxically allows them to gather together under the identity of the persecuted. To counteract any attempt to keep Persephone/women in exile, however, *Illa,* as a fiction, tries to stay close to any movement, transformation, or sensation of women in its narration. The narrator even initiates a conversation about a third person: "Her or me? Me or oneself? Illa?" [Elle ou moi? Moi ou soi? Illa?] (79). The chiasmus playfully points to a tension between women ("her" as opposed to "me"), to be resolved in another entity, that of "Illa." By extension, in this search for "oneself" (*soi*), which could also be translated as "herself," the narrator reestablishes a distance that, in the image of Persephone's condition, appears to be the only historical and chronological path toward a possible feminine reunion. Within this framework, the myth of Persephone can be understood in *Illa* as both a thematic and narrative construction.

Cixous, however, could not totally build her text on such a dual pattern. As a binary movement, it would disqualify her previous theoretical stance against all binary constructs in our patriarchal society. In *The Newly Born Woman,* Cixous questions precisely the dual opposition upon which our society has been based: "Dual, hierarchical oppositions. Superior/Inferior. Myths, legends, books. Philosophical systems. Everywhere (where) ordering intervenes, where a law organizes what is thinkable by oppositions (dual, irreconcilable; or sublatable, dialectical). And all these pairs of oppositions are *couples.* Does that mean something? Is the fact that Logocentrism subjects thought—all concepts, codes and values—to a binary system, related to 'the' couple, man/woman?" (Cixous and Clément 1986, 64). After accusing logocentrism and phallocentrism, she allows herself to dream of a way out of the masculine order and, most importantly, out of the masculine order of dreaming and writing: "If some fine day it suddenly came out that the logocentric plan had always, inadmissibly, been to create a foundation for (to found and fund) phallocentrism, to guarantee the masculine order a rationale equal to history itself. . . . When they [women] wake up from among the dead, from among words, from among laws" (Cixous and Clément 1986, 65).

Cixous's fiction indeed discovers a path leading out of such alienating dichotomy. *Illa* may in fact point to this third pronoun as a third element in a trinity that escapes traditional religious boundaries. This third party accounts for a newly found serenity in the text after the rage expressed immediately following the tale of Koré/Demeter

at the beginning of the fiction and even after the quiet disdain and resolution of female rebirth. The real revelation arrives with an *illa*—"the Clarice-voice" [la voix-Clarice] (131). Clarice, who stands for the Brazilian fiction writer Clarice Lispector, whose fiction Cixous read in the late 70s and immediately fell in love with, opens up a new "calm school of approaches" [Calme école d'approches] (134).

Illa-Clarice not only provides for a possibility out of the binary situation in which the book is placed; it/she also actually heals the world of women. Exaltation explodes throughout the very end of the book. Clarice embodies Demeter's attributes—creation, nature—and is therefore able to return the earth back to its original condition, before Persephone's abduction and rape and before Demeter's wrath and need for revenge: "Then the day goes by. But leaves behind a symphony, and sometimes a new species of flowers, and a promised future" [Puis le jour passe. Mais laisse en partant une symphonie, et parfois une nouvelle espèce de fleurs; et un futur promis] (181). *Illa* is thus a piece of "remembrement" (195), a neologism with a double meaning—the action of putting all parts of the body back together, and the English meaning of remembering. In fact, the book claims to be reinventing none other than Demeter by being *livres-terres* ("books-earths") (186), as opposed to *démet-terres* ("undoes-earths"), another homonym of Demeter.

Cixous finds a way past the binary structure that encompasses proximity and distance toward Woman and the Other thanks to the renewed sanctity she gives to the number three, which was sacred in ancient pre-patriarchal worship of the Goddess. She entitles the last section of *Illa* "The new beginning begins by three . . ." [Le recommencement commence par trois . . .] (198). These words might be considered an allusion to a concept that Cixous has always advocated—bisexuality instead of homosexuality. Another possibility would be that the number three, standing for mother-daughter-woman friend, is more restrictive, and thus this movement could be criticized as a reduction to a unitary world. Yet *Illa* is probably to be taken as a preliminary step toward a new beginning, as mentioned in the above quotation. Thus, a triplicity that would hide sexual limitations can be seen as a springboard toward the liberation of feminine libidinal economy. Besides, it is also important to note that Cixous never characterizes the feminine by women and the masculine by men, knowing that the masculine economy can be assumed by women and that, in some cases, men can do the opposite. Therefore, the number three may symbolize a variety of gender choices in hope for reparation.

It is then clear that the use of the myth of Persephone in **Illa** could summarize much of Cixous's writing as well as much of the attitude taken in the last twenty years by feminist writers and critics. They seem to show a chronological evolution from the formal study of ancient myths to freer and more directly contemporary allusions. Both ends of the spectrum demonstrate women's slavery and, at the same time, challenge of slavery throughout the centuries, starting with representative figures such as Persephone/Koré and Demeter. As the depiction of the unconscious, however, the myth of Persephone and Demeter stands as the first recognized set of ideas on which to build an interpretation. Cixous's interpretation, which often uses poetic language for subversive reasons, "proposes [a] mythic construct as a possibility—and even the only possibility—for all women" (Sankovitch 1988, 146). For Cixous and many other feminists, interpretation has recently led to a more global quasi-prophetic understanding of feminism. Women's "remembrance" in no way constitutes an inward movement; it extends to all women in the world for all times, the way it extends to the Brazilian writer Clarice Lispector who comes to rescue Persephone and Demeter. In that sense, euphoria can exist again in women's minds and bodies—in the belief in the possibility of a renewal for women, and in general for the feminine, of creative, expanding (as opposed to binary) relationships in the image of Demeter and Persephone/Koré.

Notes

1. Cixous, like several other French women writers, has always denied being a feminist. Her hostility to the term seems to result from semantics (feminism would be defined as the exclusion of men and the replacement of their power by another tyranny—that of women) and from her desire to distance herself from any specific political group or agenda. The words *feminism* and *feminist* will still be used in this chapter for the same practical reasons as those mentioned by Marks and Courtivron in *New French Feminisms:* "There is as yet no better word to account for the phenomenon" (1981, x). My definition of feminism, much broader than Cixous's, is closer to Marks and Courtivron's: "An awareness of women's oppression-repression that initiates both analyses of the dimension of this oppression-repression and stategies for liberation" (1981, x).

2. Cixous 1980, 37. Subsequent page numbers in parentheses refer to this edition. Unless otherwise specified, all English translations of Cixous's texts in this article are mine. The original French text will follow the

translation to convey the richness and complexity of the original, which my translation may simplify.

3. "Illa: 'Quis et me' inquit 'miseram et te perdidit, o tu, quis tantus furor?'" (7). The quotation is from Virgil 1990, 4:494-95.

4. For a good analysis of this phenomenon in Cixous's work, see Sankovitch 1988, 140-41.

Bibliography

Andermatt Conley, Verena. *Hélène Cixous: Writing the Feminine.* Lincoln: Univ. of Nebraska Press, 1984.

Cixous, Hélène. *Portrait of Dora.* Translated by Anita Barrows. London: Calder, 1979.

———. *Vivre l'orange/To Live the Orange.* Paris: Ed. des femmes, 1979.

———. *Illa.* Paris: Ed. des femmes, 1980.

———. *With ou l'art de l'innocence.* Paris: Ed. des femmes, 1981.

———. "Appendix." In *Hélène Cixous: Writing the Feminine,* edited by Verena Andermatt Conley. Lincoln: Univ. of Nebraska Press, 1984.

Cixous, Hélène, and Catherine Clément. *The Newly Born Woman.* Translated by Betsy Wing. Minneapolis: Univ. of Minnesota Press, 1986.

Daly, Mary. *Gyn/Ecology: The Metaethics of Radical Feminism.* Boston: Beacon Press, 1978.

Foucault, Michel. Quoted in Laurie Finke, *Feminist Theory, Women's Writing.* Ithaca, N.Y.: Cornell Univ. Press, 1992.

Gallop, Jane. *The (M)other Tongue: Essays in Feminist Psychoanalytic Interpretation.* Ithaca, N.Y.: Cornell Univ. Press, 1985.

Marks, Elaine, and Isabelle de Courtivron, eds. *New French Feminisms.* New York: Schocken Books, 1981.

Motard-Noar, Martine. *Les fictions d'Hélène Cixous: une nouvelle langue de femme.* Lexington, Ky.: French Forum, 1991.

Sankovitch, Tilde. *French Women Writers and the Book: Myths of Access and Desire.* Syracuse, N.Y.: Syracuse Univ. Press, 1988.

Shakespeare, William. *The Complete Works of Shakespeare.* Edited by Hardin Craig. Glenview, Ill.: Scott, Foresman, 1961.

Shiach, Morag. *Hélène Cixous: A Politics of Writing.* London: Routledge, 1991.

Virgil. *Georgics.* Edited by R. A. B. Mynors. Oxford: Clarendon, 1990.

Walker, Barbara. *The Women's Encyclopedia of Myths and Secrets.* San Francisco: Harper and Row, 1983.

Wittig, Monique, and Sande Zeig. *Lesbian Peoples.* New York: Avon, 1979.

FURTHER READING

Bibliography

Nordquist, Joan. *French Feminist Theory. III, Luce Irigaray and Hélène Cixous: A Bibliography.* Santa Cruz, Calif.: Reference and Research Services, 1996, 72 p.

Bibliography of French writers Cixous and Luce Irigaray.

Criticism

Arens, Katherine. "From Caillois to 'The Laugh of the Medusa': Vectors of a Diagonal Science." *Textual Practice* 12, no. 2 (1998): 225-50.

Compares Jacques Derrida's, Michel Foucault's, and Jacques Lacan's theories with those of Cixous and examines Cixous's social and philosophical contributions to modern French thought.

Brown, Erella. "The Lake of Seduction: Body, Acting, and the Voice in Helene Cixous's *Portrait de Dora*." *Modern Drama* 39, no. 4 (winter 1996): 626-49.

Provides a detailed study of the subversive qualities that Portrait of Dora *displays toward Freudian, male-centered psychoanalysis.*

Cixous, Helene. "Sorties: Out and Out: Attacks/Ways Out/ Forays," translated by Betsy Wing. In *The Logic of the Gift*, edited by Alan D. Schrift, pp. 148-73. New York: Routledge, 1997.

Discusses the theory of self-definition in social and literary endeavors by journeying toward the Other and embracing the Other, yet keeping one's own identity-working within the parameters of a system to change the system.

Davis, Robert Con. "Woman as Oppositional Reader: Cixous on Discourse." *Papers on Language & Literature* 24, no. 3 (summer 1988): 265-82.

Examines Cixous's role as an oppositional writer in "The Laugh of the Medusa," "Castration or Decapitation?" and "Sorties," investigating Cixous's theories of feminine/ masculine discourse and analyzing supporting and contrasting opinions from feminist scholars.

Dykstra Hayes, Ned. "Whole 'Altarity': Toward a Feminist A/Theology." In *Divine Aporia: Postmodern Conversations about the Other*, edited by John C. Hawley, pp. 172-89. Cranbury, N.J.: Bucknell University Press, 2000.

Analyzes Julia Kristeva's theory of abjection, Mark C. Taylor's idea of altarity, male/female differences, using texts by Ntozake Shange, Lucille Clifton, and Cixous.

Penrod, Lynn. *Hélène Cixous*. New York: Twayne Publishers, 1996, 176 p.

Examines Cixous's life and career and provides bibliographical material.

Sellers, Susan. *Hélène Cixous: Authorship, Autobiography, and Love*. Madison, N.J.: Fairleigh Dickinson University Press, 1999, 191 p.

Studies Cixous's work and contains a bibliographical guide.

van der Poel, Ieme and Sophie Bertho, eds. *Traveling Theory: France and the United States*. Madison, N.J.: Fairleigh Dickinson University Press, 1999, 177 p.

Contains a bibliographical guide along with a chapter titled "Hélène Cixous Across the Atlantic: The Medusa as Projection?"

Wilson, Emma. "Helene Cixous: An Erotics of the Feminine." In *French Erotic Fiction: Women's Desiring Writing, 1880-1990*, edited by Alex Hughes and Kate Ince, pp. 121-45. Oxford, England: Berg, 1996.

Underscores the sexuality of Cixous's writings. Wilson believes that Cixous's lesbian and bi-sexual themes are often overlooked in current criticism.

OTHER SOURCES FROM GALE:

Additional coverage of Cixous's life and career is contained in the following sources published by the Gale Group: *Contemporary Authors*, Vol. 126; *Contemporary Authors New Revision Series*, Vols. 55, 123; *Contemporary Literary Criticism*, Vol. 92; *Contemporary World Writers*, Ed. 2; *Dictionary of Literary Biography*, Vols. 83, 242; *Encyclopedia of World Literature in the 20th Century*, Ed. 3; *Feminist Writers; Gay & Lesbian Literature*, Ed. 2; *Literature Resource Center; Major 20th-Century Writers*, Eds. 1, 2; and *Twayne's World Authors*.

H. D.

(1886 - 1961)

(Full name Hilda Doolittle; also wrote under the pseudonym John Helforth) American poet, novelist, playwright, translator, memoirist, and editor.

H. D. is best known as an exemplar of Imagism, the first important movement in twentieth-century poetry and a precursor of literary Modernism. As formulated by Ezra Pound, Imagism rejected conventional verse forms and upheld the image as the primary source of poetic expression. While H. D. gradually abandoned the movement's principles to accommodate her interest in mythology, occultism, and psychoanalysis, critical attention during her lifetime remained focused on her Imagist works and their revelations concerning her association with such prominent intellectuals as Pound, Richard Aldington, D. H. Lawrence, and Sigmund Freud. In recent years, however, scholars have more fully explored H. D.'s quest to define herself as an artist and to create in her later works a female mythology based on classical sources.

BIOGRAPHICAL INFORMATION

Hilda Doolittle was born in Bethlehem, Pennsylvania, to an academic family with ties to the Moravian and Puritan faiths. She attended Bryn Mawr College for two years, during which time she became friends with the poets Marianne Moore and William Carlos Williams. In 1907 H. D. became engaged to Ezra Pound, whom she had met at the age of fifteen. Although they did not marry, their intermittent relationship drew H. D. to London, where Pound had settled in 1908. She actively participated in the city's literary scene, associating with D. H. Lawrence, May Sinclair, W. B. Yeats, and Richard Aldington, whom she married in 1913. That same year Pound arranged for the publication of several of H. D.'s poems in *Poetry* magazine. Submitted under the name "H. D., Imagiste," the poems "Hermes of the Ways," "Priapus," and "Epigram" embodied Pound's concept of Imagism, which incorporated elements from classical Greek lyrics, Japanese haiku, and French symbolism. Following the appearance of these poems, which were hailed as revolutionary by reviewers, H. D. assumed a leading role in the Imagist movement. During World War I she replaced Aldington as the literary editor of the *Egoist,* a forum for Imagist writers, and was a major contributor to *Des Imagistes: An Anthology,* a collection of Imagist poetry edited by Pound and published in 1915. When Pound abandoned Imagism following the publication of this volume, H. D. and Aldington, in conjunction with Amy Lowell, led and further developed the movement, arranging the publication of three succeeding Imagist anthologies.

In 1918 H. D. separated from Aldington and began living with the novelist Winifred Ellerman, who wrote under the pseudonym Bryher. They traveled extensively after the birth of H. D.'s daughter in 1919, visiting Italy, Greece, and Egypt before settling in Switzerland. In 1933 and 1934 H. D. underwent psychoanalysis with Sigmund Freud, a process that proved pivotal in her artistic development. She resolved many of her feelings concerning her bisexuality and her difficulties with writer's block. Psychoanalysis also prompted her to view her personal experiences as part of a universal pattern that linked her to women throughout the ages and to regard her poetry as the key to understanding that pattern. In 1956 she published her recollections of this period in *Tribute to Freud*, which Vincent Quinn characterized as essentially "a self-portrait brought into focus by her confrontation with Freud." H. D. later developed an interest in mysticism and esoteric religions, particularly those which emphasize the strength and independence of matriarchal figures. The poems she wrote during World War II while residing in Great Britain reflect these concerns. After the war she returned to Switzerland, where she wrote her third major work of fiction, *Bid Me to Live (A Madrigal)* (1960), a semi-autobiographical account of her life in London in the 1920s. In 1960 she became the first woman to receive the Award of Merit Medal from the American Academy of Arts and Letters. She died in 1961.

MAJOR WORKS

During the 1920s H. D. established herself as an important Imagist poet with the publication of the collections *Hymen* (1921) and *Heliodora, and Other Poems* (1924) and began to experiment more widely with different genres and techniques. For example, *Palimpsest* (1926) and *Hedylus* (1928), nominally considered novels though they defy easy categorization, evince H. D.'s development of her narrative voice, particularly her use of flashbacks and stream-of-consciousness monologues. H. D.'s verse, especially that collected in *Sea Garden* (1916), *Hymen*, and *Heliodora*, epitomized the practices of Imagism, which included the use of concrete, sensual images, common speech, concision, and the creation of new rhythms, intended to produce, according to the Imagist credo, "poetry that is hard and clear, never blurred nor

indefinite." Her poems of this era, including "Oread" and "Garden," have been widely anthologized, and the publication of her *Collected Poems* in 1925 inextricably linked H. D. with the Imagist movement. H. D., however, once observed: "One writes the kind of poetry one likes. Other people put labels on it. Imagism was something that was important for poets learning their craft early in this century. But after learning his craft, the poet will find his true direction."

H. D.'s experimentation beyond the tenets of Imagism has drawn increasing attention from critics, particularly feminist scholars. In the verse following *Collected Poems,* she employed increasingly complex rhymes and rhythms and ultimately rejected the predominantly visual imagery characteristic of her early work in favor of phonetic and rhythmic effects to recreate moods and objects. Her "war trilogy," which includes the volumes *The Walls Do Not Fall* (1944), *Tribute to the Angels* (1945), and *The Flowering of the Rod* (1946), was inspired by the realities of living in war-torn London during World War II and presents the "Goddess," or mother-symbol, as a means of transcending the horrors of war and attaining spiritual wholeness and self-realization. H. D.'s last major work, *Helen in Egypt* (1961), is a book-length combination of poetry and prose that embodies the philosophical and aesthetic concerns that dominated her later work. Rejecting the traditional male focus of such epics as *The Iliad* and *The Odyssey,* H. D. concentrated on Helen of Troy and her efforts as an exile in Egypt to come to terms with her past and to forge an independent self-identity. Many commentators contend that this work and those that followed the *Collected Poems* are her best, although a few maintain that she broadened her range at the expense of the clarity and conciseness that had been her trademark as the quintessential Imagist poet.

CRITICAL RECEPTION

H. D. has been recognized as a leading figure in the movement of Imagism and an important influence on modern poetry. Yet despite her prominent position in modern letters, several feminist critics have asserted that the critical neglect of her work is due to her gender and the fact that she wrote poetry about the struggles and concerns of women. Such scholars have praised her efforts to rescue women's stories from a masculine literary tradition, her questioning of masculine definitions of women, and her challenging of established gender roles. Commentators have also lauded her exploration of her own identity as a woman and author and her attempts to redefine literary traditions with a women's voice. In recent years, there has been increasing critical attention to H. D.'s oeuvre, particularly from feminist commentators. She has earned praise for her technical achievements, her poignant portrayals of her personal struggles, and the beauty of her work. H. D. has often been referred to as "the perfect Imagist" and is viewed as one of the major poets of the twentieth century.

PRINCIPAL WORKS

Sea Garden (poetry) 1916

Hymen (poetry) 1921

Heliodora and Other Poems (poetry) 1924

Collected Poems of H. D. (poetry) 1925

Palimpsest (novel) 1926

Hedylus (novel) 1928

Red Roses for Bronze (poetry) 1931

Kora and Ka (novel) 1934

The Walls Do Not Fall (poetry) 1944

Tribute to the Angels (poetry) 1945

The Flowering of the Rod (poetry) 1946

By Avon River (poetry and prose) 1949

Tribute to Freud (memoir) 1956

Selected Poems of H. D. (poetry) 1957

Bid Me to Live (A Madrigal) (novel) 1960

Helen in Egypt (poetry and prose) 1961

*Hermetic Definition (poetry) 1972

Trilogy: The Walls Do Not Fall, Tribute to Angels, The Flowering of the Rod (poetry) 1973

†End to Torment: A Memoir of Ezra Pound (memoir) 1979

HERmione (memoir) 1981

The Gift (memoir) 1982

*   This work includes the long poems *Winter Love, Sagesse,* and *Vale Ave.*

†   This work includes "Hilda's Book," a collection of poems by Ezra Pound.

PRIMARY SOURCES

HILDA DOOLITTLE (NOVEL DATE 1981)

SOURCE: Doolittle, Hilda. "Chapter One." In *HERmione,* pp. 3-8. New York: New Directions Publishing, 1981.

In the following excerpt from HERmione, a posthumously published novel, Doolittle opens the autobiographical work with a detailed inner portrait describing the mindset and torturous feelings experienced by protagonist Her (Hermione) Gart.

I

ONE

Her Gart went round in circles. "I am Her," she said to herself; she repeated, "Her, Her, Her," Her Gart tried to hold on to something; drowning she gasped, she caught at a smooth surface, her fingers slipped, she cried in her dementia. "I am Her, Her, Her," Her Gart had no word for her dementia, it was predictable by star, by star-sign, by year.

But Her Gart was then no prophet. She could not predict later common usage of uncommon syllogisms; "failure complex," "compensation reflex," and that conniving phrase "arrested development" had opened no door to her. Her development, forced along slippery lines of exact definition, marked supernorm, marked subnorm on some sort of chart or soul-barometer. She could not distinguish the supernorm, dragging her up from the subnorm, letting her down. She could not see the way out of marsh and bog. She said, "I am Hermione Gart precisely."

She said, "I am Hermione Gart," but Her Gart was not that. She was nebulous, gazing into branches of liriodendron, into network of oak and deflowered dogwood. She looked up into larch that was now dark, its moss-flame already one colour with the deciduous oak leaves. The green that, each spring, renewed her sort of ecstasy, this year had let Her down. She knew that this year was peculiarly blighted. She could not predict the future but she could statistically accept the present. Her mind had been too early sharpened.

She could not know the reason for failure of a somewhat exaggeratedly-planned "education," was possibly due to subterranean causes. She had not then dipped dust-draggled, intellectual plumes into the more modern science that posts signs over emotional bog and intellectual lagoon ("failure complex," "compensation reflex") to show us where we may or where we may not stand. Carl Gart, her father, had been wont to shrug away psychology as a "science." Hermione Gart could not then know that her precise reflection, her entire failure to conform to expectations was perhaps some subtle form of courage.

It was summer. She wasn't now any good for anything. Her Gart looked up into liriodendron branches and flat tree leaf became, to her, lily pad on green pool. She was drowned now. She could no longer struggle. Clutching out toward some definition of herself, she found that "I am Her Gart" didn't let her hold on. Her fingers slipped off; she was no longer anything. Gart, Gart, Gart, and the Gart theorum of mathematical biological intention dropped out Hermione. She was not Gart, she was not Hermione, she was not any more Her Gart, what was she?

TWO

Her Gart stood. Her mind still trod its round. I am Her Gart, my name is Her Gart. I am Hermione Gart. I am going round and round in circles. Her Gart went on. Her feet went on. Her feet had automatically started, so automatically she continued, then stumbled as a bird whirred its bird oblivion into heavy trees above her. Her Gart. I am Her Gart. Nothing held her, she was nothing holding to this thing: I am Hermione Gart, a failure.

Her eyes peered up into the branches. The tulip tree made thick pad, separate leaves were outstanding, separate bright leaf-discs, in shadow. Her Gart peered far, adjusting, so to speak, some psychic lens, to follow that bird. She lost the bird, tried to concentrate on one frayed disc of green, pool or mirror that would refract image. She was nothing. She must have an image no matter how fluid, how inchoate. She tried to drag in personal infantile reflection. She said, "I'm too pretty. I'm not pretty enough." She dragged things down to the banality. "People don't want to marry me. People want to marry me. I don't want to marry people." She concluded. "One has to do something."

The woods parted to show a space of lawn, running level with branches that, in early summer, were white with flower. Dogwood blossom. Pennsylvania. Names are in people, people are in names. Sylvania. I was born here. People ought to think before they call a place Sylvania.

Pennsylvania. I am part of Sylvania. Trees. Trees. Trees. Dogwood, liriodendron with its green-yellow tulip blossoms. Trees are in people. People are in trees. Pennsylvania.

THREE

Pennsylvania had her. She would never get away from Pennsylvania. She knew, standing now frozen on the wood-path, that she would never get away from Pennsylvania. Pennsylvania whirled round her in cones of concentric colour, cones . . . concentric . . . comic sections was the final test she failed in. Conic sections would whirl forever round her for she had grappled with the biological definition, transferred to mathematics, found the whole thing untenable. She had found the theorem tenable until she came to comic sections and then Dr. Barton-Furness had failed her, failed her . . . they had all failed her. Science, as Bertram Gart knew it, failed her . . . and she was good for nothing.

Music made conic sections that whirled round in circles but she was no good for music and in Pennsylvania it had never occurred to people to paint green on green, one slice in a corner that made a triangle out of another different dimension. Such painting, it was evident to Her Gart (static, frozen in early summer on a woodpath) must lead to certifiable insanity.

Seeing in a head that had been pushed too far toward a biological-mathematical definition of the universe, a world known to her as Pennsylvania go round and form words within worlds (all green) Her Gart said, "I am certifiable or soon will be." She realised precisely that people can paint nor put such things to music, and science, as she saw it, had eluded her perception. Science as Carl Gart, as Bertrand Gart defined it, had eluded her perception. Her Gart went on. "I must hurry with the letters."

She flung herself down, the letters flung down with her. Pennsylvania contained a serviceable river, more rivers than one dreamt of, torrents of white water running through deep forests. A river and white streams held nothing . . . nothing . . . she wanted sand under bare heels, a dog, her own, some sort of Nordic wolfhound; a dog that would race ahead of her while breakers drew up, drew back; she wanted a dog, nothing else, no one else. She wanted to be alone on some stretch of sand with dunes rising at the back and behind sand dunes, stretches of fibrous marsh grass, Indian paintbrush and the flat, coloured water lilies.

Another country called her, the only thing that would heal, that would blot out this concentric gelatinous substance that was her perception of trees grown closer, grown near and near, grown translucent like celluloid. The circles of the trees were tree-green; she wanted the inner lining of an Atlantic breaker. There was one creature that could save her, a hound, one of her own choosing, such a hound as she had often dreamt of, and one country . . . a long sea-shelf. Pennsylvania could be routed only by another; New Jersey with its flatlands and the reed grass and the salt creeks where a canoe brushed Indian paintbrush.

She felt herself go out, out into this water substance, Water was transparent, nor translucent like this celluloid treestuff. She wanted to see through reaches of sea-wall, push on through transparencies. She wanted to get away, yet to be merged eventually with the thing she so loathed. She did not struggle toward escape of the essential. She did not sigh as people did in those days, "Well, I'll some day get to Europe." Europe existed as static little pictures, the green and mosaic of several coloured prints of Venice and Venice by moonlight. Paul Potter's Bull and the lithographic prints to ruin Turner's victory. Pictures were conclusive things and Her Gart was not conclusive. Europe would be like that. She had felt no rise of emotion at the turn of speech that led "faculty ladies" in their several manners to coo, "Pollaiuolo at Vicenza, no it was Crivelli, don't you remember, at Verona?" Verona, Vicenza, Venice even, were so many boxes of coloured beads to be strung or to be discarded. Her Gart wanted a nobler affinity. She did not know what it was she wanted.

She wanted the Point. She wanted to get to Point Pleasant. She wanted the canoe, she wanted a mythical wolfhound. She wanted to climb through walls of no visible dimension. Tree walls were visible, were to be extended to know reach of universe. Trees, no matter how elusive, in the end, walled one in. Trees were suffocation. "Claustrophobia" was a word that Her Gart had not yet assimilated.

"Agoraphobia" rang some bell when Mrs. de Raub said, "I have agoraphobia, fear of the market place you know." Yet though a distant bell rang somewhere, it followed with no wide door opening. Her Gart had no a, b, c Esperanto of world expression. She was not of the world, she was not in the world, unhappily she was not out of the world. She wanted to be out, get out but even as her mind filmed over with grey-gelatinous substance of some sort of nonthinking, of some sort of nonbeing or of nonentity, she felt psychic claw unsheathe somewhere, she felt herself clutch toward something that had no name yet.

She clung to small trivial vestiges, not knowing why she so clung. Like a psychic magpie she gathered little unearthed treasures, things she did not want, yet clung to. She said, "What made me think of that slipper pincushion with Maria Frederick embroidered in pinheads on it?" She opened eyes that snapped wide open like metallic open-and-shut doll eyes. The eyes were glass now, not filmed with psychic terror. She saw trees now as trees. She said, "How funny . . . I thought I had got at something and I remembered the green blue ribbon pincushion cut out like a slipper, with Maria Frederick on it."

GENERAL COMMENTARY

SUSAN FRIEDMAN (ESSAY DATE MARCH 1975)

SOURCE: Friedman, Susan. "Who Buried H. D.?: A Poet, Her Critics, and Her Place in 'The Literary Tradition.'" *College English* 36, no. 7 (March 1975): 801-14.

In the following essay, Friedman contends that "as a woman writing about women, H. D. explored the untold half of the human story, and by that act she set herself outside of the established tradition."

H. D. is a major twentieth-century poet who all too often receives the response "H. D.?—who's he?" When people are reminded that "H. D." was the pen name for Hilda Doolittle, it is generally remembered that she was one of those imagist poets back in the beginning of the century who changed the course of modern poetry with their development of the "image" and free verse. Her early poems, like **"Oread"** or **"Heat,"** still appear regularly in modern poetry anthologies, but the more difficult epic poetry she went on to write is seldom studied or taught. The canon of her major, largely unread work is considerable: *The Walls Do Not Fall* (1944), *Tribute to the Angels* (1945), and *The Flowering of the Rod* (1946) are the three long poems of her war *Trilogy*, which has recently been reissued; *Helen in Egypt* (1961) is the work she called her own "Cantos"; the newly published volume *Hermetic Definition* (1972) contains three more long poems, the title poem, *Winter Love*, and *Sagesse*; and *Vale Ave* is another, as-yet-unpublished epic poem. While poetry was undoubtedly the genre giving fullest expression to her creative energies, she also published numerous translations, acted in a movie whose script she wrote ("Borderline," with Paul Robeson, 1930), experimented with drama (*Hippolytus Temporizes,* 1927), and wrote several novels

(*Hedylus,* 1928; *Palimpsest,* 1926; *Bid Me to Live (A Madrigal),* 1960; and the largely unpublished *The Gift*), interesting at the very least for her own style of rendering stream of consciousness. Her memoir of Freud, *Tribute to Freud* (1956), is both an impressionistic record of their sessions together and a serious reevaluation of his impact on the twentieth century; it too has been recently reissued in expanded form. Caged in a literary movement that lasted all of six or seven years, the magnificent poet of these epics and the writer who experimented in a wide variety of genres is like the captured white-faced Scops owl in her poem *Sagesse.* While the onlookers at the zoo chatter about his comical whiskers and baggy trousers, the owl who is both the embodiment of divinity and the personification of the poet is "a captive and in prison":

> You look at me, a hut or cage contains
> your fantasy, your frantic stare;
>
> . . . . .
>
> May those who file before you feel
> something of what you are . . .
>
> . . . . .
>
> they will laugh and linger and some child may
>   shudder,
> touched by the majesty, the lifted wings,
> the white mask and the eyes that seem to see,
> like God, everything and like God, see nothing.[1]

As Hugh Kenner wrote in his review of *Hermetic Definition,* to identify H. D. as an imagist poet is "as though five of the shortest pieces in 'Harmonium' were to stand for the life's work of Wallace Stevens" (*New York Times Book Review,* December 10, 1972). But if H. D. is not already buried in a single moment of literary history, she is rapidly becoming so.

Why is her poetry not read? H. D. is part of the same literary tradition that produced the mature work of the "established" artists—T. S. Eliot, Ezra Pound, William Carlos Williams, D. H. Lawrence. She in fact knew these artists well; she had known and almost married Pound while the two were students in Philadelphia (H. D.'s intensely absorbing recreation of their lifetime friendship, *End to Torment,* is being prepared for publication); her friendship with Williams goes back to those student days; but most important, she was an active member of the London literary circle that spun out the dazzling succession of artistic "isms"—imagism, dadaism, vorticism, futurism—before the catastrophe of the First World War smashed this coterie into the confusion of a spiritual wasteland. Like these artists, H. D. began writing in the aestheticism and fascination for pure form characteristic of the imagists;

and like them, she turned to epic form and to myth, religious tradition, and the dream as a way of giving meaning to the cataclysms and fragmentation of the twentieth century. Her epic poetry should be compared to the *Cantos, Paterson,* the *Four Quartets,* and *The Bridge,* for like these poems, her work is the kind of "cosmic poetry" the imagists swore they would never write.

The pattern of her poetic development not only paralleled that of more famous artists, but it was also permeated by major intellectual currents of the century. In 1933 and 1934 she was psychoanalyzed by Freud, an exploration deep within her own unconscious that ultimately linked for her the personal with the universal, the private myth with the "tribal" myths. At the same time that she studied with Freud, the convinced materialist, she was a student of comparative religion, of esoteric tradition, and, like Yeats, of the occult. The forces perpetually at work to bring a directionless century to war were a constant preoccupation in her work. Consciously rejecting the mechanistic, materialist conceptions of reality that formed the faith of the empirical modern age, H. D. affirmed a "spiritual realism" and the relevance of a quest for intangible meanings. Her growth into a poet exploring the psyche or soul of humanity and reaching out to confront the questions of history, tradition, and myth places her squarely in the mainstream of "established" modern literature. But still, outside of a few poets like Denise Levertov, who wrote "An Appreciation" of H. D., Robert Duncan, and the afficionados who circulate a pirated edition of *Hermetic Definition,* few people read her poetry. Once again, why?

Is her poetry just plain "bad," however serious the philosophic and human issues she embodies in image and epic narration? For me, the answer is obvious—her poems captivate, enchant, and enlighten me. From my single, necessarily subjective perspective, there is no doubt that her poetry is magnificent. But I have no intention here of raising the thorny questions of what makes literature "great," who determines the standards for greatness, or even whether the literary reputation of an author has much of anything to do with genuine genius. I do insist, however, that H. D. was a serious prolific poet exploring the same questions as her famous counterparts and thus inviting comparison with them. It is something of an understatement, I think, to say that in our profession artists do not have to wear the badge of greatness in order to have articles and books written about them. The simple relevance of her work to the issues and experiments of modern poetry demands that it be studied. And so I am still asking why H. D.'s work is buried under a scattered knowledge of "**Oread**" or "**Heat**."

The answer is simple enough, I think. It lies biographically and factually right in front of our critical noses—too close perhaps to be seen easily. It lies in what makes H. D. and her work different from a long string of more studied poets like Eliot, Pound, Crane, Williams, and Yeats. And it lies in the response of her critics. She was a woman, she wrote about women, and all the ever-questioning, artistic, intellectual heroes of her epic poetry and novels were women. In the quest poetry and fiction of the established literary tradition (particularly the poetic tradition), women as active, thinking, individual human beings rarely exist. They are instead the apocalyptic Pocahontas and the demonic prostitute of *The Bridge,* the goddess in the park sought by the poet Paterson, the superficial women walking to and fro talking of Michelangelo. They are the static, symbolic objects of quest, not the questors; they are "feminine principles," both threatening and life-giving, and not particularized human beings. Women are dehumanized, while the quest of the male poet is presented and understood as the anguished journey of the prophet-seer for the absolute on behalf of all humankind. For "mankind" they may be the spokesmen, but for "womenkind" they are not. As a woman writing about women, H. D. explored the untold half of the human story, and by that act she set herself outside of the established tradition. She became a "woman poet" in a world in which the word "poet" actually means male poet and the word "mankind" too often includes only men. From this perspective there are poets, and then there are the lady poets, or poetesses; there are people, and then there are women.

If her sex and her women subjects were not enough to exile her from the roster of the literary establishment, the response of many critics to her epic poetry completed the process. Her critics have rarely forgotten that she was a woman writing poetry. And I don't think they should have forgotten that fundamental fact. But her appearance in criticism as "woman poet" is never positive as it should be; it becomes instead the subtle ground on which she can be ultimately ignored. Elaborate intellectual scaffolds resting on the fact of her sex have been constructed by some of her critics whose net effect has been to dismiss her.

I will be concrete. In 1969 a special issue of *Contemporary Literature* was devoted to H. D. after years of critical silence about her work. It was the hope of L. S. Dembo, *Contemporary Literature's* edi-tor, who had recently published a serious chapter introducing her late poetry, that this special issue would spark renewed interest in her work. It did not. Aside from two fine reviews of her new publications (in *The Hudson Review,* XXVII [Summer 1974], 309-11; *Poetry,* CXXIV [June 1974], 162-67), no articles or books have followed. Her later poetry is rarely studied in the universities; and she is not even appearing in the wonderfully useful bibliographies of forgotten literature written by women and the new anthologies of redis-covered women writers (Florence Howe's *No More Masks!* is an exception).

Looking at the first two articles in *Contemporary Literature's* special issue—and they are both long, serious, thoroughly researched articles by well-known scholars, Joseph N. Riddel and Norman N. Holland—I am not surprised that it produced more critical silence instead of new studies. Riddel in his "H. D. and the Poetics of 'Spiritual Realism'" and Holland in his "H. D. and the 'Blameless Physician'" take as their starting point H. D.'s psychoanalysis with Freud and her book about that experience. Holland and Riddel are absolutely correct in pointing to that experience as the key to her poetry. But in their hands this valuable key ends up locking the doors to our understanding instead of opening them as it can do.

Although Holland and Riddel dutifully quote some of her careful statements in **Tribute to Freud**—and they are as careful as Thoreau's in *Walden*—about why she went to talk with Freud, their basic analysis (particularly Riddel's) ignores what she said about how she went to Freud as his "student," his "disciple," about how she saw psychoanalysis as a medium of quest in a drifting century, about how she found with his guidance the way to link her personal past with that of people in all places, at all times. Refusing to take seriously H. D.'s own comments about the impact of Freud on her artistic identity, Riddel and Holland dissect her with all the Freudian terminology they can muster—as if she were a neurotic woman, a "patient" instead of the artist who warned her readers that "in our talks together he [Freud] rarely used any of the now rather overworked technical terms, invented by himself and elaborated on by the growing body of doctors, psychologists and nerve specialists." And, we might add, literary critics. Holland explicitly and Riddel implicitly start with Freud's statement that a woman's "strongest motive in coming for treatment was the hope that, after all, she might still obtain a male organ, the lack of which was so painful to her" (Holland,

p. 485). For these critics, a central issue of H. D.'s psychoanalysis is "penis envy"—in Riddel's article, it is *the* central issue; in Holland's essay, penis envy shares the stage with the longing to fuse with her mother, a carryover from the oral phase. But even more destructively, in their discussion of her psyche as the generating source in her art, H. D.'s supposedly self-evident longing for a penis (don't all women want one?) becomes the focus for their discussion of her artistic identity and poetry.

Riddel, like Freud, reduces the psychology of women to a physiological level, seeing the woman's genitals as the fundamental metaphor of what *he* calls "feminine incompleteness," "inwardness," "subjectivity," and "softness" and measuring her anatomy against a male standard of power and sufficiency, the penis.[2] Just as Freud refers in his own voice to a girl's clitoris as a "stunted penis," Riddel writes about H. D. as "phallus-less," having an "ontological deprivation." "Suffocating" from her "feminine inwardness," Riddel concludes, H. D. turned to the hard, male objectivity of myth, poetic form, and symbolic objects (Riddel's subjective assumption that poetic form and art objects are male is not even Freudian; it contradicts what many Freudians argue: that artistic "forms" are "vessels" and represent the artists' oral wish to reunite with the mother).

While Holland is more likely than Riddel to use the careful language of H. D.'s perceptions ("again, we seem to be coming to the theme of overcompensating for what *she feels* is the inferior quality of her feminine body," my italics), his basic thesis is still that H. D.'s creative expressions are evidence for her perpetual search for the "masculinity" which was "lost" or "missing" in the first place.[3] At the same time that she sought through therapy to "close the gap" between herself and her mother (oral stage), she transferred to Freud all the "phallic power" she had attributed to her father and her brother (phallic and oedipal stages). In the transference H. D. was able to absorb some of Freud's masculine power ("Fusion with a man insures against deficiency: thus H. D. found it easy to project into and identify with Freud"). Her poetry, with its reliance on "hard" "signs," completed the process she had begun with Freud of closing up the gaps in her body as well as her consciousness.

Both critics conclude that H. D.'s infantile wishes were resolved in therapy as Freud succeeded in rooting out her penis envy, in teaching her to accept her "feminine incompleteness," in giving her "the ability to live in her wingless self" and to discover her "woman's role." Ignoring H.

D.'s own interpretation of the "wingless Niké"—wingless in myth so that Victory can never fly away from Athens, a positive symbol of hope for H. D.—the critics change it into the phallusless, powerless woman. Freud's gift to H. D. was to resign her to the fact of her winglessness, her femininity.

Yet once having argued that Freud successfully convinced H. D. that she was a woman, both critics somewhat inconsistently conclude that H. D.'s poetry was a product of her unresolved penis envy. Holland writes finally that her poems are the legacy of her continuing search for those "missing things." He generously concludes:

> I feel sadness for a woman who had to become a royal and mythic sign [he refers to her use of her initials as a pen name and her portrayal of her women heroes as "hieroglyphs"] to make up for all those missing things. But I honor the poet. She did indeed close up the gap with signs and, in doing so, left to us a body of poems for which we can be grateful.
>
> (Holland, p. 501)

Riddel stresses the inherent difficulty all women have in creating an artistic identity:

> The identity of the creative self as woman is threatened not only by the incompleteness of the female but by the insubstantiality of subjectivity. . . . In terms of the self-consciousness that forces her to contemplate her ambiguous role as woman poet, she seeks the completeness of the subject in the object. She must turn herself into a poem.

And since the poem is designated objective and "male" in Riddel's scheme of things, he argues implicitly that H. D. must abandon her identity as a woman if she is to develop as a poet. For Riddel, not only are poems masculine, but myths, symbols, and cult objects are linked with the "phallus . . . the signifier, the giver of meaning" (Riddel, p. 462). By what yardstick Riddel measures things like words or myths as penis-connected or masculine, he never says. But identify the tools of an artist's trade and the kind of images H. D. chose with all that's masculine, Riddel definitely does do. He comes as close as any critic to affirming that the province of the poet is entirely masculine and the woman poet who succeeds in writing poetry must overcome, destroy, or transcend her femininity and write like a man.

For all that the general tone of his essay appears to be detached, scholarly, and objective, Riddel's assumptions about women and women poets color and often distort his discussion of her epic poetry. Her impulse to write poetry—to handle words, to create images—originates in his perspective in her recognition of the inferiority of women and the superiority of men, in short, in penis envy. And the epic poetry of her later years which shows a turning to myth and the imagery of sacred cult objects—poetry that Riddel discusses brilliantly if his psychoanalytic framework is ignored—emerges out of her anguished search for masculine objectivity. Riddel has reduced the creative urge and poetic vision of H. D. to her desire to have what any ordinary man, poet or not, possesses from birth.

Is it any wonder that Riddel's and Holland's descriptions of H. D.'s quest for the phallus have not stimulated renewed interest in her work? Why should anyone bother reading a poet in search of "masculine hardness" when you can take your pick from among any number of "hard" male poets?

Although the work of these two critics has angered me greatly, both as a woman and as a person who sees H. D.'s poetry unjustly treated, my point is not to attack the criticism of individuals. I am far more concerned with the general issue of what impact the male-oriented criticism of modern scholarship has had on the literary reputations of women writers like H. D. I am interested in Riddel's and Holland's articles for their blatant documentation of the fact that criticism is written from a subjective male point of view; that, no matter how scholarly and well-researched such articles may be, they are not value-free.

While Riddel tends to present himself as an objective scholar, Holland himself would not disagree that all criticism is subjective. In fact, the central argument of his newest book, *Poems in Persons*,[4] is that *all* literary experiences—including the logical, careful, internally coherent work of literary critics—are necessarily subjective. But what he means by "subjectivity" (the recreation of a literary work within the terms of an individual reader's "ego identity," his or her uniquely woven pattern of childhood psychosexual fantasy) is not at all what I mean. His own "subjective" viewpoint which colors so much of what he writes about H. D. is instead a misogynist set of psychoanalytic presuppositions about the infantile wishes of young girls which he takes to be "objective" truth. This type of political and cultural subjectivity that so pervades Holland's and Riddel's work is symptomatic of the prejudiced inadequacies of much literary criticism, non-psychoanalytic as well as that heavily influenced by Freud.

I can hear voices objecting to my generalization—you are making a mountain out of a mole hill; Riddel and Holland are only two men; dismiss them as male critics and get back to the business of criticism. It is true that by themselves they are only two men; but if they are pushed to the side as exceptions—rather than seen as examples of a hidden pattern set in bold relief—the main body of criticism can continue to put forth its mask of scholarly objectivity. In their criticism of H. D.'s works they are not simply exceptions to a generally fair rule; perhaps because of their psychoanalytic interests, their work is a more explicit version of the double standard in criticism. Vincent Quinn, for example, wrote a generally useful book on H. D., *Hilda Doolittle* (1967), that focuses mainly on her imagist poetry. But a subtler form of male perspective is evident in his discussion of her epic poetry. He provides a good introduction to the religious, prophetic vision of the war *Trilogy*—he has understood what her work is about—but he is entirely uncomfortable with it. It is too abstract, too philosophical; its theology, based on a belief in the essential oneness of divinity throughout all cultures, is confusing. As a writer of short, lyric, emotional poems about nature, love, and beauty, H. D. was at her best, in Quinn's opinion. But a double standard of judgment for men and women writers may have something to do with Quinn's evaluation of H. D.'s poetry. H. D.'s compatriots, Eliot, Williams, and Pound, left the imagist poem to write epics permeated with mythological and religious allusions and with complex philosophical abstractions; yet they are praised for the profundity of their poetic thought and not accused of abstraction. In fact, none of her late work, which always has a highly personal as well as a mythic dimension, is as abstract as a poem like the *Four Quartets*. But subtle enough so that even Quinn might not have been aware of his own assumptions may be the feeling that H. D.'s work was too abstract for a woman to write. The short, passionate lyric has conventionally been thought appropriate for women poets if they insist on writing, while the longer, more philosophic epic belongs to the real (male) poet. Perhaps it is this presupposition about women writers that has caused so many of H. D.'s critics (see Douglas Bush and Thomas Swann, for example) to label her interest in mythology "escapist." Even Linda Welshimer Wagner (women, too, can analyze from the male perspective—that has been, after all, our training), who has some interesting comments to make on the "feminine" in *Helen in Egypt*, saw H. D.'s fascination with myth as a search for "solace" and escape.⁵ When Eliot, Pound, Williams, and Yeats show that same rejection of materialist conceptions of reality, they are praised for their struggle to deal with the ultimate questions of human existence. It is a kind of double talk emerging out of a hidden bias that makes Eliot deeply religious, Pound profound, Crane prophetic, Williams archetypal, and Yeats visionary while the same phenomenon in H. D. is "escapist." If there is to be any growth in the understanding of literature by women, or by any other group not accepted within the recognized literary tradition, or even by the established artists, these hidden biases and the necessarily subjective nature of all criticism (as all art) must be confronted.

H. D.'s poetry itself brings into bold relief the assumptions of her critics that have been so damaging to her reputation. Her own explorations of women's experience and the dilemma of women writers correct, more eloquently than I can, the mistaken prejudices of her critics and the distorting lens of a double standard for men and women writers. Riddel's and Holland's Freudian conception of a woman torn with desire to possess the penis—or at any rate something "hard"—is nowhere demonstrated in the "woman's epic" that H. D. writes. Missing also are various other critical assumptions they make: that H. D. found her fulfillment as a woman by resignation to "winglessness"; that the "phallic" and the "masculine" are associated with power, myth, poetry, objectivity, and meaning in opposition to the "feminine" qualities of weakness, softness, insubstantiality, subjectivity; and so forth. The more diffused, less psychoanalytic, description of the mature poet as a fragile naiad escaping into the still world of an imaginary Greece bears no relationship to the H. D. who used myth to confront the most contemporary and timeless problems in women's lives. Even less do H. D.'s women heroes fit the stereotypes of women in the kitchens of the world or in the poetry of male poets.

Winter Love (Espérance), a newly published poem of H. D.'s (continuing in twenty-eight sections the quest of Helen in ***Helen in Egypt***), demonstrates forcefully how distant the stereotypes and conventions of literature and the complementary distortions of criticism often are from the reality of a woman's perspective. Helen of Troy, that symbol of dangerous love and beauty in so many poems by male poets, is in H. D.'s poem not a distant symbol, nor some soft creature seeking to fuse with some male hero, nor a reflec-

tion of H. D.'s willingness to accept her "ontological deprivation." Listen instead to the woman's anguish in the final section of ***Winter Love*** as Helen gives birth to her child Espérance and recalls the succession of lovers who have come in and gone out of her life:

28

I am delirious now and mean to be,
the whole earth shudders with my ecstacy,
take Espérance away;

cruel, cruel *Sage-Femme,*
to place him in my arms,
cruel, cruel *Grande Dame,*

to pull my tunic down,
so Odysseus sought my breast
with savage kiss;

cruel, cruel midwife,
so secretly to steal my phantom self,
my invisibility, my hopelessness, my fate

the guilt, the blame, the desolation,
Paris slain to rise again
and find Oenone and mortality,

Achilles' flight to Thetis
and the Sea (deserting *Leuké*),
Menelaus with his trophies in the palace,

Odysseus—take the Child away,
cruel, cruel is Hope,
terrible the weight of honey and of milk,

Cruel, cruel, the thought of Love,
while Helen's breasts swell, painful
with the ambrosial sap, *Amrita*

that must be given;
I die in agony whether I give or do not give;
cruel, cruel *Sage-Femme,*

wiser than all the regents of God's throne,
why do you torture me?
come, come O *Espérance,*

Espérance, O golden bee,
take life afresh and if you must,
so slay me.

(***H. D.***, pp. 116-17)

In this moment of delirium, when the aging Helen sees the lovers of her life pass before her—Paris at Troy, Achilles in Egypt and Leuké, Menelaus back in Sparta, and finally Odysseus, the father of Espérance—she is left with "my phantom self, / my invisibility, my hopelessness, my fate, / the guilt, the blame, the desolation." She is a woman used—sought in violence by Odysseus; abandoned finally by Paris, who returns to his first love Oenone; and Achilles, who deserts Helen for his mother Thetis (Menelaus is something of a bore with his trophies and stale stories). And is the child Espérance consolation for the emptiness of life that has left her clinging to the only identity she has—"my phantom self, / my invisibility?" Is he, in Freudian terms, the satisfying sublimation for penis envy? "The whole earth shudders with my ecstasy;" Helen cannot help but feel joy in the overwhelming experience of the birth, but mixed with this "ecstasy" is great pain, for the Child, with the added irony of his name, Hope, brings a special agony. Helen sees him as linked to the older men who took from her and fled: "cruel, cruel, *Grande Dame,* / to pull my tunic down, / so Odysseus sought my breast / with savage kiss." For, like a lover, the Child demands and she must give. She is not even to be left in peace with her "phantom self," a kind of death itself (see section 27 of **Winter Love**), but at least her own. To the Child she must give milk—"while Helen's breasts swell, painful / and the ambrosial sap, *Amrita* / that must be given"; to deny the baby is torture, to give all he demands is agony: "I die in agony whether I give or do not give." The Child, in taking milk and love from his mother, is bringing a kind of death upon her: "Espérance, O golden bee, / take life afresh and if you must, / so slay me." The special cruelty is that the birth of this child should be, as his name suggests, a woman's hope, but the Child's all-encompassing demands mean death for Helen because once again she will have to give and give and give, only to be left by the grown child in the end: "take the Child away, / cruel, cruel, is Hope / . . . / cruel, cruel the thought of Love." Yet, as with her lovers, she finally puts the Child's needs before her own; Helen's cry in the middle of the poem to "take the Child away, / cruel, cruel, is Hope," becomes by the end "come, come, O Espérance" as she welcomes the newborn to her breast.

Rather than suggesting consoling escape from reality, rather than representing the acquisition of "phallic objectivity," the mythic dimension of the poem adds cruel irony to the agony of this woman, to this poetic version of postpartum depression. From the time of Homer to the twentieth century Helen has been the symbol of woman in her most perfect form. Yet this poem with Helen as the subjective voice instead of the object of some poet's glazed eyes reveals desperate unhappiness. The "Sage-Femme" (literally "midwife" in French), the "Grande Dame," who brings the child safely to term and into the world is not worshipped here by Helen as the Great Earth Mother—she is "cruel," all the more so because she and Helen are both women, sisters. And

capitalization of "Child" makes explicit the parallel between Helen-Espérance and Mary-Jesus, Isis-Horus, and all the other mother figures in mythology and art. Yet instead of reveling in this mythic parallel, instead of celebrating her fulfillment as a woman, Helen cries out in agony as she once again witnesses the death of her individual self. H. D. is not writing about Helen of Troy, however; we shouldn't let the poem's ancient speaker and this whole mythic dimension interfere with the direct, contemporary, universal voice of the poem—the agony of a middle-aged woman who has given and cannot stop giving to her lovers and her children. H. D.'s poem is all about women who are driven to fulfill others' demands only to find themselves left with a "phantom self," an "invisibility," a "hopelessness."

The woman in **Winter Love** is lamenting "missing things," but not the missing penis of Holland's analysis. Throughout all the sections of the poem, as in many of H. D.'s epics, she searches for the missing identity, for a direction and purpose which is so often denied to women. Caught within the Freudian or even more generally male-oriented categories of her critics, this theme of missing identity or "invisibility" in the midst of love and birth could easily be twisted into evidence for the persistence of H. D.'s unresolved phallic stage, for her desire to flee "feminine inwardness," or for her attempt to acquire power by merging with a man and with the "phallic signifiers" of knowledge. But such readings would be a total distortion of what H. D. is saying—about how that "phallic power" has presented Helen with a lifetime of demands, only to desert the drained phantom in the end; about how the ecstasy of birth is mingled with the recognition of a death of the individual self. Freed from the confines of a critical cage, this poem clearly contradicts the kinds of assumptions H. D.'s critics have made as they approach her work.

Perhaps, however, my reading of one small section of only one poem by H. D. is too limited an example upon which to rest my case that a male-oriented bias has had dire consequences in the understanding of H. D.'s poetry. What about the whole sweep of her epic quests? Do they bear out my contention that H. D. has set herself outside the established literary tradition by her exploration of human experience from a woman's perspective and that conventional male categories of literary criticism must be abandoned if her work is to be understood? The thematic thrust and "arguments" of her major poems do indeed reveal how misleading some of her critics have been. In the war *Trilogy,* written as the German bombs created a crucible of fire out of her home, and in *Helen in Egypt,* written a few years later in quiet reflection on a war-torn century, H. D. expresses a vision in total opposition to envy for the male world. Both epics are poetic arguments for a belief similar to Carolyn Heilbrun's in *Towards a Recognition of Androgyny*: the dominance of masculine values has brought destruction and suffering, like the catastrophe of the two world wars. The "phallus" and its weaponed manifestations are never the "signifiers" of meaning as Riddel rather self-importantly suggests; they have been instead the destroyers of human potentiality.

In *Helen in Egypt* Achilles represents the "Whirlwind of War" as the leader of the "warrior cults" of the "purely masculine iron-ring." It is *he* who must learn from Helen how his sword "has blighted that peace" embodied in the Goddess and how he can become the "new Mortal" by recapturing the feminine values of union and creation represented in his past by his mother Thetis and in the present by Helen herself. Even more explicitly in the war *Trilogy,* H. D. resurrects the powerful ancient deities of the matriarchies whom she associates with the positive values of love, peace, regeneration, and synthesis as the poet tranforms degraded "venery" into "veneration" for Venus, Aphrodite, Isis—the Lady or female principle in general. In both epics these active, powerful forces of birth and reintegration are scarcely similar to the placid, fecund goddesses awaiting some lance-carrying hero for fulfillment that abound in the patriarchal mythologies and literature. And they bear little resemblance to Riddel's portrayal of "soft," "weak" femininity seeking escape into the strength of whatever he happens to label "masculine." In fact both epics attempt to transcend the divisions into male and female as they reach for a vision of individual identity, society, and religion based on an androgynous union of the strongest and most creative aspects of the traditionally "masculine" and "feminine." In so doing they reveal a writer who believes that to rectify the understanding of women's experience and matriarchal values leads the poet-prophet to confront universal questions of history, time, and humanity.

The last poem the aging, ailing poet wrote, the recently published *Hermetic Definition,* sharply focuses the broader issues explored in the earlier epics to a highly personal account of the dilemma faced by the woman poet. As she tries to combine the woman in love and the woman at work into a single artistic identity, her difficulties are great, as Holland and Riddel suggested they would be. But totally inconsistent with her final resolution are both Holland's description of the "ego theme" by which she writes poetry to acquire the power she associated with a whole string of male figures since childhood, and Riddel's contention that H. D. had to transcend her femininity to write like a man. The poem is first of all an implicit rejection of a Freudian tenet that infuses both Holland's and Riddel's work and our culture in general. Freud saw an unbridgeable chasm separating the "masculine" woman—the active, competitive woman whose early development was "arrested" in penis envy and its consequent sublimation into all sorts of "male" activities, and the "feminine" woman—the passive, weak woman who had passed beyond penis envy into an acceptance of her domestic role.[6] In Freud's eyes and within the perspective of the generally acceptable attitudes which Freud's "science" did so much to legitimize, a woman is simply not expected to be capable of both the joys of love and motherhood and the rigors of work beyond the home. Yet H. D. in the poem, as in so much of her work, portrays a woman poet simultaneously passionate in her love for a man and in her commitment to write poetry.

The poet's search is not for a man to fuse with or be like—it is precisely the opposite: the process of the poem's quest is how to escape from the influence of two men in order to find her own vision and direction. One man is Lionel Durand, who represents for H. D. the Lover and the Son and whom she actually met when he came to interview her for a *Newsweek* review of her novel *Bid Me To Live.* At age seventy H. D. fell electrically in love with Durand, and was in fact obsessed with this love for the nine months it took her to write the poem, as her diary of the period reflects. But both in her life and in the poem Durand rejected H. D., as a woman and as a poet. His personal letters to her were polite and distant; her work, he wrote, was "fascinating if you can stand its preciousness" (*H. D.,* p. 7). To deny his condemnation of her work she listens to the voice of her guide, her Muse—once again the powerful female deity and patron of the mysteries, not any representative of the "phallus" or "masculine" objectivity: Isis "draws the veil aside, / unbinds my eyes, / commands / write, write or die" (*H. D.,* p. 7). In contrast to Riddel's description of the ambivalence of her role as a woman writer, H. D. writes about the problem of many women writers—the ridicule they receive from their critics and reviewers.

Rejection by Durand leads H. D. into an intense study of the hermetic poetry of St.-John Perse. As she is entranced with Perse's philosophic, esoteric vision and his acceptance of her as a poet, she gradually comes to realize that she must pass beyond the poetry of Perse to find her own way, one which will "recover the human equation," the human experience of her love for Durand, a dimension which is missing from Perse's more abstract, more "formal and external" (**H. D.,** p. 51) poetry. She cannot rely on any man to be her voice. To insure herself against "deficiency," to echo Holland, she must speak for herself and avoid fusion with a man, lover, or fellow poet. Her symbolic expression of her successful independence is this poem itself, whose writing she images as a pregnancy and a final painful birth. Such a metaphor for poetic creation has been somewhat conventional in poetry by men, but coming from a woman poet it has a special power since the woman can in fact give birth to both human life and poetry. Isis, the mother-goddess-Muse, commands, directs, protects, and infuses the growing artistic identity of the woman poet throughout the poem. The resolution is no easy one: the difficulties of being a writer are somehow part of the necessary process of writing. But as she closes the poem the voices of her critics must quiet their talk of phallic power and female insubstantiality so that they can hear the woman's voice and strength which closes H. D.'s poetic career:

> Rain falls or snow, I don't know,
> only I must stumble along, grope along,
> find my way; but believe me,
>
> I have much to sustain me.
>
> (**H. D.** p. 53)

Once again, however, the central issue at stake is not the mistaken theories of individual critics. What the chasm between H. D.'s poetry and the readings of some of her critics demonstrates is how distortions in this one case are part of a more general pattern in criticism by which the work of women writers is misread. Let no one argue at this point that as long as all reading is subjective one person's theories are as valid as another's. It must be recognized that distortions of a literary work which result from prejudiced political and cultural categories do have real consequences for the reputations of many writers—those of different races, nationalities, classes, and political persuasions, as well as of sex. These distortions play a central part in what literature is admitted to the informal roster of the established tradition, what literature is regularly studied and taught. Criticism is a link of the broad cultural chain that in this country, especially now that once excluded students are sitting in university classrooms, does not exist for a privileged elite alone. Consequently, criticism does not exist in a polite vacuum in which one person's views are as good as another's, in a gentlemanly sort of way. It can perpetuate the slow burying process that is suffered by writers whose vision and experience are somehow out of the more privileged mainstream. And with this burial comes the alienation of readers who cannot find their own experience reflected in what they study in college.

The growth of Women's Studies—like Afro-American Studies, Puerto Rican Studies, Chicano Studies, Asian Studies, Native American Studies—has been a necessary answer to the closed curriculums of the established literary tradition. There should be no doubt that poems like *Hermetic Definition* and *Winter Love* can be studied in a course on women and literature. H. D. was a woman writer who faced the peculiar difficulties imposed on women writers by the society at large and the established literary tradition with its retinue of critics in particular. Although she never wrote her own *A Room of One's Own,* many of her novels and poems center around the problems of women artists and intellectuals. In addition, her heroes are always women; and as individuals in quest instead of abstract symbols, the women in her work are strikingly different from those in the poetry written by her male counterparts. What H. D. and poets like her have to say about women's experience and potential is as much a legitimate focus for a course as any thematic or chronological breakdown in a college curriculum. If literature and politics of the thirties, or frontier literature, or the angry young men in Britain, or the absurd in modern fiction, are all valid subjects for study, then surely women and literature must also be.

But having separate courses on women and literature is not enough; in fact this kind of separation by itself fosters the continuation of the idea that there are poets and then women poets, artists and then black artists, literature and then radical propaganda. To say that "lost" literatures by women, blacks, and other minority groups belong in separate niches all to themselves is to claim a kind of universality for literature by white males that it does not have. The poetry of H. D., along with that of other women and minority writers, should be as much a part of the training of a graduate student in modern poetry as the work of Eliot, Yeats, Williams, Crane, Stevens, Pound, and any other of the numerous male poets whose works are required reading in the universities. H. D. is a part of modern poetry—that she was a woman writing about women should not exclude her from "The Literary Tradition." What she has to say about women and men in her poetry should be as much a part of any class as what Pound or Eliot have to say about men and women. If the elite of acceptable literature will have explored the experience of only half the human race (at best), with this incompleteness, this subjectivity, it will have lost a profound understanding of its own humanity. For when men see women in terms of stereotypes, they also understand themselves inadequately.

Notes

1. *Sagesse,* in *Hermetic Definition* (New York: New Directions, 1972), p. 59. This volume will hereafter be referred to in the text as *H. D.* I am grateful to Norman Pearson, H. D.'s literary executor, for the suggestion that the caged owl of the poem is the aging poet herself.

2. For Riddel's references to the inferior anatomy of women and the spiritual or psychological consequences, see his "H. D. and the Poetics of 'Spiritual Realism,'" *Contemporary Literature,* X (Autumn 1969), 448, 453-54, 455, 456, 459.

3. For Holland's references to genitals as representations of physical and psychical inadequacies, see his "H. D. and the 'Blameless Physician,'" *Contemporary Literature,* X (Autumn 1969), 476, 482, 483, 485, 486, 490-91, 493, 497, 499-500, 501, 502.

4. Norman Holland, *Poems in Persons: An Introduction to Psychoanalysis and Literature* (New York: Norton, 1973). Two thirds of this book uses H. D. as a case study for his broader argument concerning psychoanalytic criticism as a general method. His *Contemporary Literature* article appears with few changes as Chapter One where his argument is more clearly seen as a method of tackling any writer, male or female. Many of the stylistic changes are eliminations of Freudian terminology ("anal," "phallic," "oral," etc.); some of the "penis envy" language has been softened or diffused. But his argument that H. D.'s childhood "phallic stage" left within the adult poet a sense of longing for the penis her mother and father never gave her is as much present as ever in spite of the "gentler" language.

5. Wagner's article, *"Helen in Egypt*: A Culmination," is in *Contemporary Literature,* X (Autumn 1969), 523-36. See also Thomas Swann's *The Classical World of H. D.* (Lincoln: Univ. of Nebraska Press, 1962) and Douglas Bush's *Mythology and the Romantic Tradition in English Poetry* (Cambridge: Harvard Univ. Press, 1937), pp. 497 ff.

6. See Sigmund Freud, "Femininity," in *New Introductory Lectures,* trans. James Strachey (New York: Norton, 1964), pp. 112-35; Freud, *An Outline of Psychoanalysis,* trans. James Strachey (New York: Norton, 1949), pp. 80-99.

DIANA COLLECOTT (ESSAY DATE SPRING 1985)

SOURCE: Collecott, Diana. "Remembering Oneself: The Reputation and Later Poetry of H. D." *Critical Quarterly* 27, no. 1 (spring 1985): 7-22.

In the following essay, Collecott investigates the critical neglect of H. D's work and the poet's recent rediscovery by female writers and critics.

Not to forget the forenames of presence. Labour: Clarice. The labour of un-forgetting, of un-silencing, of un-earthing, of un-blinding and un-deafening oneself . . .

　　　　　　—Hélène Cixous, *Vivre l'Orange* (1979)

I

For half a century there has been an absence among the poets of Anglo-American modernism. Its dominant voices have been those of men: T. S. Eliot, Ezra Pound, William Carlos Williams. H. D. (Hilda Doolittle Aldington, 1886-1961) belongs to this generation of writers and her career was closely associated with theirs, but in their company she has been forgotten, silenced. This silence was in part imposed from without, in part self-imposed.[1] Until women writers and critics began the work of unearthing H. D.'s life and writings, she could be heard only faintly, through the texts of the men named above, seen distortedly through the partial accounts of some male critics.

Now an 'un-forgetting' is taking place. H. D.'s voice can be heard at last in the *Collected Poems, 1912-1944,* meticulously edited by Louis Martz of Yale University and published in Britain by the Carcanet Press. Martz's notes place certain poems in the context of H. D.'s life, acknowledging for instance her lasting relationship with Winifred Ellerman (the British novelist Bryher). A biography by the poet Barbara Guest, *Herself Defined,* is now available; it offers an account of H. D.'s external world to complement those of her internal world given by Susan Stanford Friedman in *Psyche Reborn* and (less convincingly) by Janice S. Robinson in *H. D.,* but it fails to discuss the content or circumstances of H. D.'s writing with anything like the thoroughness accorded the men of her generation in recent literary biographies.[2]

Yet, for the first time ever, almost all of H. D.'s poetry is in print. The *Collected Poems* includes everything she published up to the end of the Second War, including the *Trilogy,* which should be read alongside Eliot's *Four Quartets* and Pound's *Pisan Cantos.* However, H. D. went on to compose major poetic works after 1944. The last of these, another trilogy, was completed in the year of her death and published posthumously as *Hermetic Definition.* The book-length *Helen in Egypt,* written in the early 1950s, appeared in 1961; it will soon be available in a British edition. Still missing is **'Good Frend'**, written just after the Second War and all but ignored along with the *Trilogy.*

Before we discuss these later volumes, it is worth reviewing the distorted image of H. D. that has resulted from the tardy and partial publication of her work on both sides of the Atlantic. H. D. is as much a British as an American poet. She left the United States in 1911 at the age of twenty-four and lived in Europe for fifty years. She spent the war years 1914-18 and 1939-44 in London and returned there continually in the intervening period. Her exile as well as her sex helped to marginalise her as a writer. If H. D. has been known at all in Britain in the past half-century, it was in a context she had already outgrown in 1931 when she was identified as 'The perfect imagist'. As Hugh Kenner has pointed out, this was 'as though five of the shortest pieces in *Harmonium* were to stand for the life-work of Wallace Stevens'.[3]

In the absence of a full understanding of H. D.'s life and post-Imagist work, critics who should know better constructed a myth of her personality, hinting at 'a series of self-destructions', at 'her withdrawal into the past'.[4] The authors of the only book-length studies of H. D. hitherto available construed her use of Greek myth as escapism, and she was said by another defender to have shown no concern with 'the public preoccupations of the age'.[5] All the evidence, both internal and external, contradicts these mis-readings of her work. Two early poems, **'Eurydice'** and **'The tribute'**, show her using Greek myth to confront feminine experience, and to express it in direct opposition to the predominant masculine ideology—an ideology that oppressed women and promoted war (*CP* 51-5 and 59-68). In 1916-17, when these poems are published in the *Egoist,* both feminism and pacifism were subversive and had to be internalised (little wonder that the same defender of H. D. comments that 'her struggles were all inward'). H. D.'s concern with both, and with the reconciliation of 'masculine' and 'feminine' principles that offers a creative alternative to personal and political destruction, continued powerfully in her *Trilogy,* which is directly concerned with the war, and in *Helen in Egypt.* Both works involve the remembering and re-interpretation of myths from Greece and elsewhere, as part of their project for recovering the positive values of love and creativity that H. D. identifies with female divinities, to offset the negative values of hatred and aggression that dominate heroic legend. If these positive values are not 'public preoccupations of the age' then the age stands to destroy itself.

Until quite recently, women writers who, by virtue of their art, made their preoccupations public, exposed themselves to patronisation as *poetesses* or even *poetettes.*[6] They are still subject to stereotyping based on attenuated notions of femininity. 'In her essence H. D. is a slight, extremely feminine figure' writes C. H. Sisson, taking an attitude to her writing similar to that of Henry James when he referred to female subjects in the novel as 'these slimnesses'.[7] Grace, elegance, wit, precision, neatness of finish are especially valued in poetry written by women: very rarely is it praised in terms of the energy, largeness and power which have been assumed to be the physical and intellectual attributes of men. (Marianne Moore—a colleague of H. D.'s at Bryn Mawr—made herself room to manoeuvre in the feminine mould, and thus out-witted her admirers; Laura Riding became, because of it, a true Fugitive.) Comparable assumptions about the vocal capacity of men and women have traditionally reserved the major key of epic poetry for the one and the minor key of lyric verse for the other. It may well be due to interference of this kind that H. D.'s later longer poems have been unheard, and listeners have had ears only for her earliest shorter work, though both have their own music.

The men in the avant-garde of American modernism in the 1920s were sometimes generous in their praise of female poets, but this praise is rarely free from the old stereotypes. Smallness is treated as a specifically feminine quality, hence Marsden Hartley praised three women, Emily Dickinson, Adelaide Crapsey and H. D., for their 'brevity': '"H. D." is another woman who understands the beauty of compactness . . . Singular that these three artists, so gifted in brevity, were women.'[8] Brevity suggests artistic control, but also limitation. Formalism or minimalism has in our era found adepts among women whose gender is experienced both by themselves and by their male colleagues as a limitation. Since literature is public language, and the public world was still a male domain, intelligent women were reticent in print: this reticence translated private inhibitions about their right to speak and be heard.

In the history of modern poetry, reticence, brevity, were aspects of the hygiene Ezra Pound prescribed for a literature dedicated to 'Tennysonianness of speech'. Hence H. D.'s minimalist poems were selected—from her more expansive writings—to launch the Imagist movement. Pound's letters to Harriet Monroe, persuading her to publish them in *Poetry,* equates modernism with laconicism: '. . . am sending you some *modern* stuff by an American, I say modern, for it is in the laconic speech of the Imagistes, even if the subject is classic' and 'This is the sort of American stuff that I can show here and in Paris without its being ridiculed . . . It's straight talk, straight as the Greek!' Thus brevity is valued at a critical moment for modern poetry, together with the precision and objectivity that H. D. exemplified and Pound prized. When he praises H. D. for her 'Hellenic hardness', or Marianne Moore and Mina Loy for their lack of emotion, he is also promoting in Europe a certain idea of the modern American woman: smart, hard-hearted, clear-sighted, *desabusée.* In the early work of Moore and Loy he finds 'The arid clarity, not without its own beauty, of *le tempérament de l'américaine*'; yet while he claims *kudos* for the cosmopolitan modernity of his taste in women, he can also patronise 'these girls' for having written 'a distinctly national product'.[9]

Pound, who had known H. D. intimately since his postgraduate days in Pennsylvania where he wrote her the poems in 'Hilda's Book', knew also that there were other sides to H. D. These sides filter through his idealisation of Hilda Doolittle as a child-like 'Is-hilda' or 'Ysolt' in his earliest verse and as the 'Dryad' of Canto 83. Her memoir of him, *End to Torment,* leaves us in no doubt that their mutual appreciation was founded on a sharing of the finest levels of perception. Yet, as he commented on the manuscript, 'Torment title excellent, but optimistic'.

In a recent book on D. H. Lawrence, Paul Delany addressed himself in passing to the tormented or submerged aspect of H. D.'s character. 'One need hardly stress' he said, on no apparent evidence, 'the pitfalls that awaited anyone who became intimate with H. D.' The very casualness of this remark implies complicity with the reader in a shared male assumption about the threat to men constituted by women who are not subject to fathers or husbands. In a letter of 1917 Lawrence showed, in his idiosyncratic way, a truer recognition of H. D.'s reality: '. . . my "women", Esther Andrews, Hilda Aldington, etc. represent,

in an impure and unproud, subservient cringing, bad fashion, I admit—but represent none the less the threshold of a new world, or underworld, of knowledge and being.'[10] There is a world of difference between Delany's 'pitfalls' and Lawrence's 'underworld'. It is from this submerged, forgotten and neglected world that Lawrence has the H. D.-like priestess of Isis speak in his story 'The man who died'; it is from there that the female deities are disinterred in H. D.'s later work, and that Helen (in Egypt now, not in Greece or Troy) is finally allowed to speak.

In her lectures to women in Cambridge, published as *A Room of One's Own,* Virginia Woolf considered 'What would have happened had Shakespeare had a wonderfully gifted sister . . .' and concluded that she would have 'killed herself one winter's night and lie buried at some crossroads'. Suicide is a form of self-destruction chosen by too many women writers, a way of silencing oneself. H. D. chose instead to struggle out of silence into speech. The nature of that struggle, that 'labour' as Hélène Cixous calls it, is identified by Denise Levertov:

> The poet is in labour. She has been told that it will not hurt but it has hurt so much that pain and struggle seem, just now, the only reality. But at the very moment when she feels she will die, or that she is already in hell, she hears the doctor saying, 'Those are the shoulders you are feeling now'—and she knows the head is out then, and the child is pushing and sliding out of her, insistent, a poem.[11]

This is the reality of H. D.'s late poetic utterance. *Winter Love,* composed in 1959, is a kind of coda to *Helen in Egypt.* In the final sections Helen is heard as she brings to painful birth her Child Espérance (inspite of the struggle, His name means Hope):

> Grandam, midwife, *Sage-Femme,*
> let me rest, let me rest,
> I can't struggle any more;
> far, far, let them beget their children
> in the wastes or palaces; what is their happiness,
> their bliss to this accomplishment?
> . . . . .
>
> grandam, midwife, *Sage-Femme,*
> I pray you, as with his last breath,
> a man might pray, keep *Espérance,*
>
> our darling from my sight,
> for bliss so great,
> the thought of that soft touch,
>
> would drag me back to life
> and I would rest;
> grandam, great *Grande Dame,*

midwife and *Sage-Femme,*
you brought Him forth in darkness,
while I slept.

(HD 115)

The most powerful presence in this passage is that of the grandmother/mid-wife; indeed with the mother and the divine Child she completes a sort of matriarchal trinity. For as the play on 'grandam . . . *Grande Dame'* suggests, she too is divine—possibly Artemis, who as moon-goddess presided over childbirth. Biographers have identified the figure of the midwife with Bryher, who cared for H. D. through the birth of her only surviving child in 1919. Bryher was a devotee of the goddess, as the title of her memoir *The Heart to Artemis* implies. But the elision and assonance of '*Grande Dame . . . Sage Femme'* indicates a mobile, composite entity here, much like those we see in dreams. In **Hermetic Definition,** with which **Winter Love** was eventually published, the speaker invokes the mother-goddess in her aspect of preceptor: a stern muse who 'unbinds my eyes, / commands, / write, write or die' (**HD** 7). As in Cixous, vision and utterance are once again linked; in **Winter Love,** Espérance is a forebears among the writers who had preceded her. Nearly a century later, is dying and would rest. Thus, almost at the point of death, H. D. is writing as 'the poet in labour'.

The presence at the birth of a grandmother signifies hindsight as well as foresight. 'I look everywhere for grandmothers and see none!' was the cry of the Victorian 'poetess' Elizabeth Barrett Browning as she sought for female forebears among the writes who had preceded her. Nearly a century later, Virginia Woolf looked forward to a time when 'drawing her life from the lives of the unknown who were her forerunners, as her brother did before her' some 'Shakespeare's sister' could be born. H. D. suffered also from the sense of isolation that is the fate of a woman writer in the absence of a continuous literary tradition. In 1959, while typing 'Winter love', the seventy-three-year-old poet expressed her own sense of difference from the men in whose company she had learned her craft and whose work was studied in the universities while hers was ignored: 'I can't think' she confessed, 'that I *must* be POUND-ELIOT'.[12]

One of the first people to perceive that H. D. was not 'Pound-Eliot', but a poet 'in her own write' was Robert Duncan whose 'H. D. Book', published piecemeal in little magazines, was to the 1960s what Pound's 'Hilda's Book' was to a few people in the 1900s. Duncan's own mytho-poeic sympathies alerted him to the inner meanings of H. D.'s work. He and Denise Levertov met H. D. when she visited New York to receive the poetry award of the American Academy of Arts and Letters a year before her death. They were H. D.'s lifeline to the younger generation of American poets. Levertov remembers her own discovery or recovery of H. D. in a short essay of 1962: 'The early poems seemed final, the end of some road not mine; and I was looking for doors, ways in, tunnels through. When I came to her later work . . . what I found was precisely doors, ways in, tunnels through . . .' She celebrates a poem of the 1930s which, as she puts it, 'ends with [a] sense of beginning':

perceiving the other-side of everything,
mullein-leaf, dog-wood leaf, moth-wing
and dandelion-seed under the ground.

(CP [Collected Poems] 413)

Levertov concludes: 'She showed a way to penetrate mystery; . . . to *enter into* darkness, mystery, so that it is experienced. And by *darkness* I don't mean *evil,* not evil but the Other Side, the Hiddenness before which man must shed his arrogance; Sea out of which the first creeping thing and Aphrodite emerge; Cosmos in which the little speck of the earth whirls, and in the earth "the dandelion seed".' In echoing and capitalising the 'Other Side', Levertov is conscious that in Jewish mystical tradition this term refers to the forces of evil or impurity—the world of Lilith rather than of Eve. In a one-sided orthodoxy such energies are suppressed, obscured and perceived only in their destructive phase: Lawrence glimpsed both their destructive and constructive possibilities. As women unafraid of their own creativity, Denise Levertov and Adrienne Rich (in her essay of 1971, 'When we dead awaken: writing as re-vision') began the labour of bringing this other side into the light.[13] These women writers, in their search for 'grand-mothers' have both found H. D. and recovered forgotten parts of themselves. They have helped to inspire the re-membering of H. D.'s work and the re-writing of her life that is currently in process.

II

Remembering is also a vital feature of H. D.'s art. We are now aware that H. D. was a prolific writer of prose as well as a poet. Throughout the 1920s, 1930s and 1940s, much of her creative energy went into the writing of autobiography. In a series of fictions and memoirs, H. D. composed her story, recovering experience that had been repressed or forgotten and repeatedly naming and re-naming herself. With the exception of **Bid Me to Live,** which appeared as a *roman à clef* in 1960, all of these texts remained unpublished for many years after H. D.'s death. Several are still in typescript; two prose-poems of her childhood and young womanhood are now in print. In reverse order, these are **Her** (1927), and **The Gift** (1941-3), which is available only in a heavily edited version[14].

In both of these texts, remembrance involves the writer's recognition of her love for women. **The Gift** is dedicated to her self-effacing mother, Helen Wolle; hence it is a work of 'un-forgetting', of burrowing beneath memories of her brilliant and influential father. In **Her,** H. D. unearths from recollections of the time of her engagement to Ezra Pound, her 'concentric intimacy' with Frances Gregg, who was the recipient of her earliest translations from Theocritus. In both texts, too, H. D. is present as character and as author, the 'forenames of presence' (in Cixous' phrase) being 'the child Hilda' in **The Gift** and, in **Her,** the girl Hermione whose nickname gives the text its title. These names meant much to H. D., providing her female figures with genealogies that reached into literature and legend. Thus Hermione is both mother and daughter, a doubly female *persona*: her name recalls the silenced wife and banished mother of Perdita in Shakespeare's *The Winter's Tale;* she is also, in Greek myth, the daughter of Helen of Troy. Hilda Doolittle named her own daughter Perdita and was herself daughter to Helen. This recognition of Helen as a fore-mother prepared H. D. for the writing of **Helen in Egypt.** She remarked: 'The Mother is the Muse, the Creator, and in my case especially as my mother's name was Helen' (**ET** [**End to Torment**] 41). Ultimately, 'Helen-Hermione' become one in the poetry of **Winter Love.**

In **Her,** H. D.'s remembered sense of identity with another woman is also a re-membering of herself: 'I know her. Her. I am Her. She is Her. Knowing her, I know Her . . . I am a sort of mother, a sort of sister to her.' This wordplay, in which the same homophone is the direct object ('I know her'), the subject complement ('I am Her') and the speaking subject ('Her'), does more than imitate the reciprocity of the relationship between the two women. It also negotiates the speaker's difficulty with presenting herself as subject and object of her own experience—a difficulty reinforced, in literature as in life, by women's object-status in relation to men. As other writers have pointed out, the heroine's nickname 'signals a fusion, one that gives birth to two selves,

subject and object indistinct'.[15] All the evidence suggests that this fusion created a matrix for H. D.'s later poetry.

In her late poetic sequence **Helen in Egypt** (1952-4), this kind of recall is vital to the plot, and to the conception of the work as a whole. H. D. had long been drawn to the Helen of Homeric legend whose name her own mother bore. However, her perception of Helen differs profoundly from the image presented in the legend itself and persistently re-used by male poets. H. D. was familiar with the figure Helen cut in English literature, from the classicism of Marlowe's 'Was this the face that launched a thousand ships?' to the late romanticism of Yeats's 'girl . . . that had red mournful lips'. They all rhymed with a masculine ideal of feminine beauty and a male sense of female evil. In an early poem H. D. presents another view of Helen as an object of hatred, not of love:[16]

> All Greece reviles
> the wan face when she smiles,
> hating it deeper still
> when it grows wan & white,
> remembering past enchantments
> and past ills.

As a symbol of evil memory, Helen is best dead, reduced to nothingness:

> Greece sees unmoved,
> God's daughter, born of love,
> the beauty of cool feet
> and slenderest knees,
> could love indeed the maid,
> only if she were laid,
> white ash amid funeral cypresses.
>
> (**CP** 154-5)

In the same way, the legendary Helen has been effectively stereotyped out of existence. H. D. set herself to recover those aspects of Helen which had been marginalised in myth and history: her girlhood, motherhood, old age; aspects which made up her whole as a woman, but were extraneous to the image of her as a lover of men. H. D.'s recovery of Helen is thus derived from her own knowledge of life, but also depends on her scholarly work on Greek texts. She is indebted to what Horace Gregory, in his introduction, calls 'half-forgotten, pre-Homeric sources', in particular to the only surviving fragment of the writings of Stesichorus of Sicily, who lived in the sixth century before Christ. His *Pallinode,* like Euripides' little-known **Helen in Egypt** is, H. D. tells us, 'a defence, explanation or apology'. Her commentary continues: '*According to the* Pallinode, *Helen was never in Troy. She had been transposed or translated from Greece into Egypt. Helen of Troy was a* *phantom, substituted for the real Helen, by jealous deities. The Greeks and the Trojans alike fought for an illusion'* (**HE** [**Helen in Egypt**]1). H. D.'s poem seeks to present 'the real Helen', the substance behind the 'phantom' of Homeric legend; but to re-construct her she must deconstruct the traditional texts. Her first move, is the 'translation' of Helen from Greece and Troy to Egypt, and she does this in full awareness that translation is a cultural as well as a linguistic process. Yet, as Gregory points out, 'H. D.'s **Helen in Egypt** is no translation (of Stesichorus), but a re-creation in her own terms of the Helen-Achilles myth'; she referred to the work as her '*Cantos*'. Just as Helen is perceived by H. D. through the texts of Homer, Stesichorus and Euripides, so she begins to perceive herself through the versions of her made by the men she has loved: Menelaus, Paris, Achilles, Helenus, and also Theseus who had abducted her as a child from Sparta.

Theseus has a crucial part in this process of self-remembering. He seeks her again in Egypt, and assumes the role that Freud assumed in H. D.'s life. Theseus finds Helen silenced, numb, entranced by her own dreams of the past, and begins 'to remember the story' (**HE** 172). In doing so, he places her name among those of the other Trojan women 'all sacrificed in one way or another': Polyxena, Hecuba's daughter, Chryseis, Briseis, Deidamia, Clytaemnestra, and these connect in the text with the names of other women who were destroyed or ignored when men went to war: Iphigenia, Cassandra. Yet as H. D. comments in her argument to the poem, Theseus's remembrance 'is another story'; she adds: 'He seems deliberately to have stepped out of the stream of our and of Helen's consciousness' (this explicit relationship of writer and reader with the poem's *persona* should not be ignored). Helen's consciousness returns to the text when she interrupts Theseus to correct his version of the story—precisely when it touches on her own family relationships:

> Pyrrhus, his son, married your daughter;
> 'Hermione? never, it was Orestes loved her,
> the son of Clytaemnestra, my sister';
>
> how do you know that?
> can you read the past
> like a scroll?

(**HE** 173)

Theseus's challenge to Helen's knowledge of the past is what summons her to speak, finally, in her own defence. Precisely, she does not 'read the past / like a scroll'; it is within her, she is it, and to remember it is to re-member herself:

> It comes to me, lying here,
> it comes to me, Helena;
> do you see the cloth move,
>
> or the folds, to my breathing?
> no, I breathe quietly,
> I lie quietly as the snow,
>
> drifted outside; how did I find
> the threshold? marble and snow
> were one; is this a snow-palace?
>
> does the ember glow
> in the heart of the snow?
> yes—I drifted here,
>
> blown (you asked) by what winter-sorrow?
> but it is not sorrow;
> draw near, draw nearer;
>
> do you hear me? do I whisper?
> there is a voice within me,
> listen—let it speak for me.

(**HE** 174-5)

The 'white ash' of the early Helen poem is transposed to drifted snow: a whiteness that connects her silence with the blank space on the unwritten page, and recalls that she has survived as a person only in the margins of men's texts. But Helen is now at the 'threshold' of speaking for herself, and when she does so, H. D. comments, 'It is an heroic voice, the voice of Helen of Sparta'. In other words, Helen has recovered her lost self and at the same time a capacity for utterance traditionally denied to women.

H. D. discovered in **Helen in Egypt** a form of writing in verse and prose whose creative possibilities should be compared with those of Eliot's *Waste Land* or Joyce's *Ulysses* or Williams's *Paterson*. Her presentation of Helen also bears comparison with the uses to which Pound and Eliot put the dramatic mask or *persona*. H. D. might well echo, concerning her own relationship with the Helen of the text, Pound's comment that 'I'm no more Mauberley than Eliot is Prufrock'. Yet there is a difference in their positions. In those early poems both Pound and Eliot used *personae* to mask their own concerns, to give an impression of impersonality, to separate 'the man who suffers and the mind which creates'. H. D., however, in her admission of a connection between 'our and . . . Helen's consciousness' is owning not disowning her female speaker, and she is willing to admit her share of Helen's suffering. More directly than Pound's *Personae*, **Helen in Egypt** is a 'search for the real' and Helen is a closer 'mask of the self' than many of Pound's translations. Eliot's comment on Pound would be apt if we were to transpose it from the masculine to the feminine gender:

'. . . good translation like this is not merely translation, for the translator is giving the original through himself, and himself through the original.'[17]

The early critical reception of **Helen in Egypt** indicates the pressing need for translations of this kind and for readers who are prepared to make the transposition of gender necessary for a true hearing of the poem. Although Rex Warner reviewed the book favourably in 1961, Vincent Quinn could not recognise the substantial reality of H. D.'s Helen; he saw only the 'insubstantiality of the theme', adding: 'H. D. wished to present the entire poem from a supra-mundane level of consciousness, but she succeeded only in making everything unreal'. However, he must be given credit for admitting his difficulty as a (male) reader with a (female) text: 'The reader feels that H. D. brings a lifetime of passionate involvement with classical antiquity to every detail in the poem, but he cannot be sure that his response is in tune with her passion. He fears that Helen's remarks sometimes carry overtones that he either fails to hear or misunderstands.'[18] It is this failure to hear on the part of willing male readers that is responsible for their silence about aspects of H. D. that female readers have begun to perceive: to cite her involvement in 'classical antiquity' is to miss the *presence* of personal passion in her work.

To be un-heard is to be reluctant to speak, as Helen was when she began to 'whisper' her reality. As *she* re-crossed the threshold into poetry after the partial silence of the 1930s, H. D. expressed her concern with the relationship between silence and the female voice in other poetic *personae*. Almost lost among these poems is 'Good Frend', which takes its title from Shakespeare's epitaph in the parish church of Stratford-upon-Avon, through which the poet silenced by death speaks to the friend who survives him. The poem was published with a prose meditation on Shakespeare and other writers of the English renaissance in *By Avon River*. This essay poignantly celebrates a literary tradition from which H. D. felt excluded, as an American and as woman, but of which she was a natural inheritor.[19] In it H. D. notes that 'Queen Elizabeth is commonly the only woman listed among the more than one hundred Elizabethan lyrists'. Yet she perceives the other royal women behind some of the texts: Eleanor of Aquitaine for her association with troubadour poetry and Elizabeth of Bohemia for whose marriage celebration *The Tempest* was written, and

whose later title 'The winter queen' may have suggested to H. D. Helen's 'winter sorrow' and her own **Winter Love.**

'Good Frend' takes its cue from Shakespeare's late play, *The Tempest,* which lends its title to the first section of the poem:

> We know little of *the king's fair daughter*
> *Claribel*; her father was Alonso,
> King of Naples, her brother, Ferdinand,
> And we read later, *in one voyage*
> *Did Claribel her husband find at Tunis:*
>
> Claribel was outside all of this,
> *The Tempest* came after they left her;
> Read for yourself, *Dramatis Personae.*

Only the name marks her presence in Shakespeare's text, a forename denoting absence and resonating in silence:

> Read through again, *Dramatis Personae*;
> She is not there at all, but Claribel,
> Claribel, the birds shrill, Claribel,
> Claribel echoes from this rainbow-shell,
> I stooped just now to gather from the sand . . .
>   (*BAR* [*By Avon River*] 5-6)

H. D.'s project in this poem is to recover Claribel, as she recovered Helen and gave her voice and presence. She has Claribel come home from Tunis, and seek herself. She does not find herself among Shakespeare's heroines, but through remembrance. The second section of the poem bears the herb's name and the girl's name, Rosemary, following Ophelia's 'There's rosemary, that's for remembrance' in *Hamlet*. H. D. translates this into Latin (*ros maris*—sea rose) to evoke the sea of memory from which her Claribel recovers the self that was drowned in *The Tempest*:

> What rose of memory,
> *Ros maris,*
> From what sea of bliss!
>   . . . . .
>
> Full fathom five
>   and under
> The sea-surge
>   thunder,
>   Rosalind and Rosaline
>   With Juliet and Julia
>   Join hands with Maria,
>   Mariana and Marina,
>   Katherine and Katherina
>   And with many other bright
>   Spirits;
>   Iras,
>   Iris,
>   Isabel,
>   Helen, Helena; Helenus
>   With other princes leads the host
>   From Arden, Navarre and Illyria,
>   Venice, Verona and Sicilia;

Knowing these and others well,
Seeing these whom I have loved,
Hearing these—why did I choose
The invisible, voiceless Claribel?

(*BAR* 13-14)

H. D.'s choice of Claribel from all the *personae* in the plays of Shakespeare alluded to in these lines is inspired by the perception that she too is a potential 'bright spirit'. Claribel herself is unable to perceive this since her own identity is obscured: she does not know her own name! Her return to Europe is a pilgrimage in search of meaning: the meaning of existence and in it the meaning of herself. The third section of the poem is entitled 'Claribel's way to God'. On the way her first encounter is with a daughter of St Francis, a 'Poor Clare'; she recognises another self in this sister whose name chimes with her own: 'I, too, was Clare but Clare-the-fair, / Claribel, not a Poor Clare'. To overcome this difference, she changes the robes of a queen for a nun's habit; but still her inner self is hidden from her. Finally, caring for the sick, she encounters a dying knight; he is a Templar returned from the Crusades, and his insight helps her to discover the meaning within her name:

Consolamentum here and now,
I heard as my lips touched his brow;
To him alone I told my secret,
Sir, I am nothing but a name,

Claribel; Brightly-fair, he said,
O clearly beautiful, thou Spirit;
So he alone among them all
Knew I was other than I seemed,

Nor nursing-sister nor a queen,
And he it was that broke the spell . . .

(*BAR* 23-4)

Her 'secret' is in a sense her silence, her lack of presence in the human drama. Her name is both 'nothing' and all she has; the knight's knowledge allows her to turn this nothing into something, and teaches her the reality which Claribel names: the beauty and clarity of the spirit shining through the body. It is to be questioned whether this spiritual teaching, which allows Claribel to ignore her physical presence as a woman, is more appropriate to her selfhood than Freud's psychological teaching was to H. D.: whether it provides either the poet or her *persona* with true solace or merely consolation.

'Claribel', which chimes with Hélène Cixous' 'Clarice', thus takes its place among the names behind which Hilda Doolittle's own identity was hidden: Is-hilda, Dryad, Helen, Hermione, 'H. D.' Her anonymity, her absence from the *dramatis personae* of Anglo-American literature, is such that she is still to be sought in most indices under the name of the husband from whom she parted in 1918: H. D. Aldington. Likewise her daughter Perdita is lost under a married name, so that a recent writer presented her, without intentional irony, as 'a friend of Pound's daughter': that is, at two removes from a great *man*, rather than as the daughter of another major modern poet who was also a woman.[20]

Notes

1. The testimony of H. D.'s former husband, Richard Aldington, in a letter of 1959, that 'Ezra and Eliot pushed her aside ruthlessly', needs to be corroborated; see *Literary Lifelines: the Richard Aldington—Lawrence Durrell Correspondence,* ed. Ian S. MacNiven and Harry T. Moore (Boston: Faber & Faber, 1980), p. 110. H. D.'s contemporary, Virginia Woolf, said of women writers: 'Anonymity runs in their blood. The desire to be veiled still possesses them' (*A Room of One's Own* (Harmondsworth: Penguin, 1945) p. 52).

2. Guest, *Herself Defined: the Poet H. D. and her World* (New York: Doubleday, 1984), British edition due from Harvill Press/Collins in 1985; Friedman, *Psyche Reborn: the Emergence of H. D.* (Bloomington: Indiana U.P., 1981); Robinson, *H. D.: the Life and Work of an American Poet* (Boston: Houghton Mifflin, 1982).

3. See Glenn Hughes, *Imagism and the Imagists* (New York: Biblo & Tannen, 1972), chapter VI, first publ. 1931; Kenner, review of *Hermetic Definition, New York Review of Books* (10 Dec. 1972), p. 55.

4. See Hugh Kenner, *The Pound Era* (London: Faber & Faber, 1972), p. 175; Peter Jones, introduction to *Imagist Poetry* (Harmondsworth: Penguin, 1972), p. 164.

5. See Vincent Quinn, *Hilda Doolittle (H. D.)* (New York: Twayne, 1967) and T. B. Swann, *The Classical World of H. D.* (Lincoln, Neb.: Nebraska U.P., 1962); Douglas Bush was equally dismissive in *Mythology and the Romantic Imagination* (Cambridge, Mass.: Harvard U.P., 1937). The defender is C. H. Sisson in 'H. D.: an appreciation' (1975), repr. in *The Avoidance of Literature* ed. Michael Schmidt (Manchester: Carcanet, 1978), p. 487.

6. *Poetèsses:* the term still implies severe limitation, viz. 'Most of the new poets it [*Poetry*] was printing were nonentities—there was a large number of poetesses among them . . .' (K. L. Goodwin, *The Influence of Ezra Pound* (London: Oxford U.P., 1966), p. 52). *Poetettes:* this patronising diminutive was contemporary with, perhaps inspired by, 'suffragettes'; Pound used it in a letter of 1913: *The Letters of Ezra Pound, 1907-1941* ed. D. D. Paige (London: Faber & Faber, 1951), p. 63.

7. See note 5 on Sisson. James, preface to *The Portrait of a Lady* (Harmondsworth: Penguin, 1966), p. xii, first publ. 1908.

8. Hartley, *Adventures in the Arts* (New York: Hacker, 1972), p. 214; first publ. 1921.

9. Pound, letters of 1915 and 1912 respectively, *Letters,* pp. 91 and 45; 'A List of Books' (1918), repr. in *Selected Prose, 1909-1965* ed. William Cookson (London: Faber & Faber, 1973), p. 394.

10. Delany, *D. H. Lawrence's Nightmare: the Writer and his World in the Years of the Great War* (Hassocks: Harvester, 1979), p. 330; Lawrence, *Collected Letters* ed. Harry T. Moore (London: Heinemann, 1962), p. 532: names supplied from Ms. by Delany.

11. Levertov, *The Poet in the World* (New York: New Directions, 1973), p. 107.

12. H. D., unpublished letter, cited by Norman Holmes Pearson in his introduction to *Hermetic Definition*.

13. Levertov, 'H. D.: an appreciation', *The Poet in the World*, pp. 244-8; Rich's essay is reprinted in *On Lies, Secrets and Silence: Selected Prose, 1966-1978* (London: Virago, 1980), pp. 33-49.

14. The typescripts of these and other autobiographical works by H. D.—including *Paint it Today* (1921), *The Sword Went Out to Sea* (1947) and *Magic Mirror* (1955)— are in the Collection of American Literature, Beinecke Rare Book and Manuscript Library, Yale University.

15. Susan Stanford Friedman and Rachel Blau DuPlessis, '"I had two loves separate": the sexualities of H. D.'s *Her*', *Montemora* 8 (1981), pp. 7-30.

16. 'Helen' was first published in 1923; Friedman identifies a dialogue of the 1930s, 'Calypso' (*CP*, 388-96), as a 'pivotal poem' between the mute Helen of the early poem and the central *persona* of *Helen in Egypt*: see *Psyche Reborn*, pp. 236-43.

17. See, respectively: Pound, *Letters*, p. 248; Eliot, 'Tradition and the individual talent' (1919) in *Selected Prose* ed. Frank Kermode (London: Faber & Faber, 1975), p. 41; Pound, *Gaudier-Brzeska: a memoir* (New York: New Directions, 1970), p. 85, first publ. 1916; Eliot, introduction to *The Selected Poems of Ezra Pound* (London: Faber & Faber, 1928), p. 13.

18. Quinn, *Hilda Doolittle (H. D.)*, pp. 132, 145. For revised feminist readings, see Susan Stanford Friedman, 'Creating a woman's mythology: H. D.'s *Helen in Egypt*', *Women's Studies* V, 1 (1977), pp. 163-98, and 'Psyche reborn: tradition, re-vision and the goddess as mother-symbol in H. D.'s epic poetry', *Women's Studies* VI, 2 (1979), pp. 147-60.

19. See Susan Stanford Friedman, '"Remembering Shakespeare always, but remembering him differently": H. D.'s *By Avon River*', *Sagetrieb* II, 2 (1983), pp. 45-70.

20. See Peter Ackroyd, *Ezra Pound and His World* (London: Thames & Hudson, 1980), p. 105. The irony arises from the fact that Ackroyd's source must be Perdita Schaffner's 'Merano, 1962' in *Paideuma* IV, 2 & 3 (1975) in which she describes her meeting with Mary de Rachewiltz, 'Truly *ma semblable, ma soeur*', and remarks: 'Had they [H. D. and E. P.] married, their child would have been some other child, not me . . .'; in *End to Torment* (p. 30) H. D. recalls Pound's complaint that her daughter was not his child.

ERIKA ROHRBACH (ESSAY DATE 1996)

SOURCE: Rohrbach, Erika. "H. D. and Sappho: 'A Precious Inch of Palimpsest.'" In *Re-Reading Sappho: Reception and Transmission*, edited by Ellen Greene, pp. 184-98. Berkeley and Los Angeles: University of California Press, 1996.

In the following essay, Rohrbach examines H. D.'s identification with the classical female poet Sappho.

Like all deeply famous figures, Sappho keeps her anonymity. I do not mean this in the sense that Sappho is no one; rather, she could be anyone. Having borne witness to the 1890s' boom of interest in her, modernists were well aware of the interpretative leeway that Sappho's ambiguous biography and minced verse grant readers. They saw in her a woman whose life had been erased, her poetry fragmented and written over, and yet whose style had been canonized. We think of modernist writers like H. D. and Richard Aldington, for whom the classical era represented the keystone of their own aesthetic, as attempting to rescue Sappho from centuries of scholarly misinterpretation and bad translation. But even though they set themselves up to be the archaeological Red Cross, these modernists knew that the "real" Sappho was an unrecoverable ideal. Hence, they explored the one aspect of study open to them: Sappho's transmission through the ages.

I want to argue that H. D.'s identification with Sappho is primarily a poetic one, and furthermore, that the layers of interpretation insulating Sappho's fragments provided H. D. with as much of a stylistic model as did the fragments themselves. For a number of modernists, much was at stake in the reading of Sappho, but particularly fascinating about H. D. is the way in which she turned this palimpsestic reading relationship into a writing style. In her own fragment poems H. D. used Sappho to expand her poetic relation to imagism, while encoding her personal relationship with Aldington. Aldington too had masked feelings for H. D. in his "Letters to Unknown Women," and capitalized on Sappho and other classical figures to promote his own aesthetic of antiacademism. His presence, then, is an important inclusion in any consideration of H. D.'s relation with Sappho, for it enlarges and complicates the accepted belief that H. D. mostly sought refuge in Sappho's lesbianism as a poetic escape from real heterosexual trauma.[1] Like Aldington, whose classicism was enmeshed in his reaction to classicism, and Virginia Woolf, whose intellectual pursuit of Sappho was aggravated by the sexism of her male peers, H. D. used Sappho as a projection of her life, not as she wished it to be, but as it was.

The Egoist provided Aldington the forum to engage the same kind of life projection through classical writers that H. D. would accomplish with Sappho. By late 1915, he had been married to H. D. for two years, and, with her help, was editing *The Egoist*'s Poets' Translation Series. The Translation Series was Aldington's brainchild and amounted to six pamphlets published between

1915 and 1916. At Aldington's provocation, the second pamphlet in the series, published in 1915, consisted of Edward Storer's *Poems and Fragments of Sappho*.[2] Storer's introduction to his translation had a strong impact on Aldington and H. D., and was most likely read by Ezra Pound, Marianne Moore, James Joyce, Amy Lowell, F. S. Flint, Harriet Shaw Weaver, Dora Marsden, and T. S. Eliot, who were also frequent *Egoist* contributors.

> Sappho was born in the island of Lesbos about 612 B.C. Her name in her own language is "Psappha." She was a contemporary of Alkaios and Stesichoros. At some period of her life she was exiled from Lesbos. An inscription in the Parian Chronicle says: "When Aristokles reigned over the Athenians Sappho fled from Mitylene and sailed to Sicily." But it is through her own poems that we see most clearly into the beauty and tragedy of her life. She is there revealed to us as a woman of ardent nature, noble, delicate-minded, and fond of pleasure. That her poems were chiefly love-poems, and love-poems written to women, is clear even from the mutilated fragments which remain. Any other explanation destroys at once their art and their reality. Yet sedulous hypocrites are to be found to-day who will wilfully mistranslate and misconstrue in order to envelope the manners of antiquity in a retrospective and most absurd respectability.[3]

Storer's portrait of Sappho is significant on a number of counts. First, he presents us with the poet in exile, which must have struck a familiar chord in the modernist vein. Then he asks us to join him in reading Sappho's life "most clearly" through her poems. If we then follow him and read her life through her poems, we discover it not only in fragments but *"mutilated* fragments." Having thus collapsed Sappho's body into her work, Storer finally rebukes those contemporary, "sedulous hypocrites" for attempting to envelope her lesbian "manners of antiquity" in the "most absurd" cloak of modern heterosexual "respectability."

Under the guise of rescuing Sappho from Victorian misconstruction, Storer turns her "mutilated fragments" into the muted body of Philomela. His portrayal of Sappho as a woman whose artistic work ultimately saves her from isolation and violation focuses our attention on the poetry and the process by which it becomes fragmented. It also places Storer (or any translator) in Procne's position as the lone reader capable of restoring to Sappho "the beauty and tragedy" of her life. For modernist poets who identified with Sappho's queerness, fragmentation, ambiguity, and alienation—as well as her artistry—this was the most important aspect of the Sapphic reading relationship. Whatever form of textual harassment they

ON THE SUBJECT OF...

THE FEMINIST INTEREST IN H. D.'S WORK

The explosion of feminist criticism in the 1970s combined with the revival sparked by *Contemporary Literature* to produce the kind of extended, serious critical examination that H. D.'s modernist work demands. Feminist critics in particular have created a body of theoretical and practical criticism that illuminates the anomalous position of the woman writer in the largely male literary tradition, the thematic and formalist aspects of the female literary tradition, and the androcentric lens of established critical traditions that has led to the undervaluation of many important women writers. The revival of interest in women writers accomplished by feminist criticism led to renewed attention to H. D.'s entire oeuvre among readers and scholars of widely varying perspectives.

Friedman, Susan Stanford. An excerpt from "Hilda Doolittle." *Dictionary of Literary Biography, Volume 45: American Poets, 1880-1945, First Series*. A Bruccoli Clark Layman Book. Edited by Peter Quartermain. Gale Group, 1986.

chose to address, for modernists, rescuing Sappho meant reading modernly: that is, with one eye on the text in hand and the other on whose hand the text is in. On the one hand, Sappho as Philomela mandates attention to the history of the fragments' transmission; on the other, it warrants the modernists' preoccupation with their unique position as readers.

For these reasons, Aldington (and H. D.) embraced Storer's reading. In the first of his "Letters to Unknown Women," which appeared in *The Dial*, 14 March 1918, Aldington describes the lengths one must go to in addressing these "unknown," Philomela-like figures:

> Helen the queen and Sappho the poet are "unknown" to us because their legends have been altered and overlaid by so many men of different personalities that we have difficulty in deciphering the true character from the additions. Like all very great people they have become what we wished them to be, and those who seek the truth about them must search for it among a thousand lies.

(226)

Aldington's point here of course is not that these women are "unknown" to us like strangers we pass on the street, but that they have been made unknowable by centuries of "men's," read here scholarly, mishandling. If we wish to learn the "truth" about them, *we* must seek it out; Sappho and Helen alone can tell us nothing. This is an important point driven home in Aldington's second "letter," published 9 May 1918 in *The Dial*:

> To Sappho of Mitylene:
>
> Like so many notorious characters in history you have become an enigma, as ambiguous as an oracle.
>
> (430)

Here, as in Storer's portrait, is the second half of the Philomela story. If Sappho has been "mutilated" to the extent that only her work can reveal her suffering, this forces on subsequent readers Procne's burden of privileged reading; if Sappho is "as ambiguous as an oracle," she is that much in need of interpretation and a qualified interpreter.

Enter Aldington with the Poets' Translation Series, assembled by his handpicked coterie of poet-translators. The statement of objectives for the series embodies familiar imagist tenets, as Caroline Zilboorg observes; more importantly, it stresses the backgrounds of the translators:

> The object of the editors of this series is to present a number of translations of Greek and Latin poetry and prose, especially of those authors who are less frequently given in English. This literature has too long been the property of pedagogues, philologists, and professors. Its human qualities have been obscured by the wranglings of grammarians, who love it principally because to them it is so safe and so dead.
>
> But to many of us it is not dead. It is more alive, more essential, more human than anything we can find in contemporary English literature. The publication of such classics, in the way that we propose, may help to create a higher standard of appreciation of the writers of antiquity, who have suffered too long at the hands of clumsy metrists. . . .
>
> These translations will be done by poets whose interest in their authors will be neither conventional nor frigid. The translators will take no concern with glosses, or notes or any of the apparatus with which learning smothers beauty.[4]

Note the emphasis on these translators being warm-blooded, bohemian poets set apart from the cold, convention-bound set of "pedagogues, philologists, and professors." Zilboorg argues that Aldington's objectives stem from his belief in there being "an audience to whom one was linguistically and morally responsible,"[5] but if

anything, his views merely reflect a wish to salvage the integrity of the classical source. Crucially, the audience is left out of this aesthetic imperative. Remember, Procne and Philomela were sisters. Aldington clearly believes that only footnote-free contemporary poets and authors can resuscitate their muted classical counterparts.

This strike against academia should not, however, be read as any sort of attempt to take the classics to the people. Largely because he was never afforded easy access to the classics, Aldington concerned himself mainly with the modern translator or reader of Greek, as opposed to the translator's audience. In a letter dated 22 December 1918, he listed his motives for wanting to rejuvenate the translation series: "I want it first to establish a canon of taste, *our* taste, against a mob of clergymen and schoolmasters and professional critics; that will give us a point d'appui for defense of our own work. Then I want it also for the pleasure of doing that work and getting a number of people to work on it. If my plan is properly carried out the series will be an important contribution to modern English culture."[6] Thus the series offers Aldington, whose family's slim means deprived him of an Oxbridge education, and his renegade band of poets both the authorization and the means to plunder the stores of what Jane Marcus has called the "intellectual aristocracy."[7]

The sexism to which Marcus notes Virginia Woolf and the women of her circle were subjected by their male Oxbridge peers for wanting to know Greek carries with it the overriding academic classism that so galled Aldington and his troupe. Much as Woolf and company make Sappho the object of study for the formation of their own insular female "society,"[8] Aldington and his modernist translators choose Sappho and other maligned classical figures to subvert the influence of the intellectual aristocracy and ratify their own outlaw status as poets. Perhaps more than any other classical figure, Sappho authorized these modernist arbiters of taste to be what they were.

In this light we are now ready to deal with H. D., who, like Aldington, Storer, and others, adopted Sappho as a persona and not as an alternative to her life. She wrote five poems that take their epigraphs from Sappho: "**Fragment 113**," published in *Hymen* (1921), and "**Fragment Thirty-six**," "**Fragment Forty**," "**Fragment Forty-one**," and "**Fragment Sixty-eight**," published in *Heliodora* (1924); she also wrote an essay entitled "**The Wise Sappho**" between 1918 and 1920. Like Aldington, she was an accomplished translator of Greek and was familiar with other contemporary

Sappho translations.[9] Susan Gubar has suggested that H. D. sought in Sappho a motherly precursor, and that the incorporation of Sappho into her verse is an homage to the lesbian relationship she began in 1918:

> While Sappho's lyrical evocation of Aphrodite triumphs over the pain and confusion of mortal love, H. D.'s lyrical invocation of Sappho testifies to her own artistic survival, which was in large measure due to the companion who took her to the Hellas she associated with Helen, her mother. Indeed, just as H. D. is empowered to find the strength and integrity to create poetry out of the pain of abandonment by turning to the intensity she associates with Sappho, in her life she survived male rejection by returning to Bryher, a woman who quite literally shared her visions.[10]

But H. D. wrote three of the fragment poems two years before she had even met Bryher. The poems in question, "**Fragment Forty**," "**Fragment Forty-one**," and "**Fragment Sixty-eight**," were originally composed under the titles "**Amaranth**," "**Eros**," and "**Envy**" at Corfe Castle in 1916. They did not appear with the epigraphs until 1924, shuffled, retitled, and purged of direct male references.[11] Given that some of H. D.'s Sapphic allusions precede both Bryher's arrival by two years and the later addition of the epigraphs, it would seem that something other than the neat recuperation of Sappho in Bryher's image is at stake here.

While 1916 reveals nothing relating to Bryher, it marks a significant moment in H. D.'s relationship with Aldington. In late May, Aldington and his friend Carl Fallas enlisted as infantry privates in the Eleventh Battalion of the Devonshire Regiment, and by June, Aldington wrote to F. S. Flint that he had twice consummated the erotic attraction (which had sprung up in March) between him and Flo Fallas, Carl's wife. H. D. knew of the affair, and initially did not find it particularly threatening, as both she and Aldington believed in and, at various times, practiced "free love." By the fall, however, H. D. was "fearful that perhaps it was a more serious relationship, although there was little evidence for this conclusion."[12] So if we are to interpret H. D.'s fragment poems via her life, we should read with the Aldington rift and not the Bryher refuge in mind.

Remembering that H. D. sat on those three soon-to-be fragment poems for eight years, during which time she composed "**The Wise Sappho**" and the remaining two "fragments," and during which she also rather permanently broke with Aldington and took up with Bryher, one might argue that Bryher's devotion prompts her to overtly summon Sappho and omit the obviously male-

directed sections in the revised works. When compared with only one identification H. D. offers in "**The Wise Sappho**," this reading becomes nearly irresistible. She states:

> True, Sappho has become for us a name, an abstraction as well as a pseudonym for poignant human feeling, she is indeed rocks set in a blue sea, she is the sea itself, breaking and tortured and torturing, but never broken. She is the island of artistic perfection where the lover of ancient beauty (shipwrecked in the modern world) may yet find foothold and take breath and gain courage for new adventures and dream of yet unexplored continents and realms of future artistic achievement. She is the wise Sappho.[13]

Could it be one pseudonym (H. D.) molding Sappho as such to represent another—Bryher? Possibly. Given that this Sappho embodies both a feeling and a place where H. D. "may yet find foothold," one must note that in "**The Islands**" (published in 1920, and to which the "Amaranth-Eros-Envy" triad is linked), "beauty" cannot connect with it.

> But beauty is set apart,
> beauty is cast by the sea,
> a barren rock,
> beauty is set about
> with wrecks of ships,
> upon our coast, death keeps
> the shallows—death waits
> clutching toward us
> from the deeps.
>
> Beauty is set apart;
> the winds that slash its beach,
> swirl the coarse sand
> upward toward the rocks.
>
> Beauty is set apart
> from the islands
> and from Greece.
>
> (section V, 126-27)

Obviously if Sappho or Bryher is the island, that could not be who is setting "beauty" or H. D. apart from it, and here I divorce my interpretation of H. D.'s poetic Sappho of any references to Bryher, for they produce an unreasonably inconsistent Sappho. Turning instead to "**Amaranth**"'s final two sections, which H. D. did not include in her revision of the poem as "**Fragment Forty-one**," we witness the speaker's rage at her lover's leaving her for another.

> But I,
> how I hate you for this,
> how I despise and hate,
> was my beauty so slight a gift,
> so soon forgot?
>
> I hate you for this,
> and now your fault be less,

I would cry, turn back,
lest she the shameless and radiant
slay you for neglect.

Neglect of finest beauty upon earth
my limbs, my body and feet,
beauty that men gasp
wondering that life
could rest in so burnt a face,
so scarred with her touch,
so fire-eaten, so intense.

(from section V, 314)

While these lines sizzle in bursts of Sapphic imagery and condensation, they address a man as Sappho's do not. H. D.'s lover, "Atthis," who leaves her for Andromeda, is not Sappho's female Atthis mentioned in section II of the poem, but a play on the male fertility god "Attis," who was driven mad by the goddess Cybele to castrate himself, and whose story was immortalized by Catullus.[14] Just the hint of Catullus here makes me think that quite possibly H. D. was using "Atthis," a name by which Aldington actually referred to himself,[15] in the same fashion in which Catullus employed the pseudonym "Lesbia" in his poems to mask the identity of his great love.

In **"Fragment Forty-one"** H. D. removes all readily identifiable evidence of the poem's original male address and direct mention of Atthis, going so far as to further fragment the Sappho epigraph by printing only ". . . *thou flittest to Andromeda,"* and not "But to thee, Atthis, the thought of me is hateful; thou flittest to Andromeda."[16] In this version, H. D. restores Aphrodite as the goddess addressed throughout, and hints that her flitting lover is a man only in the last stanza.

I offer more than the lad
singing at your steps,
praise of himself,
his mirror his friend's face,
more than any girl,
I offer you this:
(grant only strength
that I withdraw not my gift,)
I give you my praise and this:
the love of my lover
for his mistress.

("Fragment Forty-one" 184)

In **"Amaranth,"** the third last line of this stanza reads, "I give you my praise for this"—a distanced, passive release of the speaker's lover; whereas in the revised "I give you my praise *and* this," the speaker actively offers two gifts, her praise and her lover's love, ostensibly to the goddess Aphrodite. Here, applying to the line a sound bit of advice from Adalaide Morris, who says that in reading H. D., "to listen well is to listen loosely,"[17] we not only hear "and this," but "At-

this." I read this as an echo of Attis that anticipates the surprising "his" in the poem's last line, and reinforces the placement of a heterosexual fissure at the core of the work.

After witnessing a similar scattering and spackling of personal trauma involving Aldington from **"Eros"** to **"Fragment Forty"** and **"Envy"** to **"Fragment Sixty-eight,"** we cannot help but wonder: why Sappho? Had H. D. somewhat randomly slapped on the epigraphs and revised the poems to fit them, one could claim that she applies the Sapphic Band-Aid to protect a deep heterosexual wound, while simultaneously airing her revised, lesbian lifestyle. But while these epigraphs do not introduce the texts of **"Amaranth,"** **"Eros,"** and **"Envy,"** we can readily identify their presence, and that of other Sapphic fragments, within these poems. And then what do we do with **"Fragment 113"** and **"Fragment Thirty-six"**? I suggest we return to **"The Wise Sappho."**

"Little, but all roses," is how H. D. begins this lyric essay (57). Not her words, nor even Sappho's, but the tribute of Meleager—"late Alexandrian, half Jew, half Grecian poet" (67). Starting with the color of those roses, she then reads down through rock, island, country, and planet, to arrive at a world of emotion imaginable only "by the greatest of her own countrymen in the greatest period of that country's glamour, who themselves confessed her beyond their reach, beyond their song, not a woman, not a goddess even, but a song or the spirit of a song. A song, a white star that moves across the heaven to mark the end of a world epoch or to presage some coming glory" (58-59).

The song without a throat to sing it, the shooting star that must be seen and interpreted—these images set up the same kind of oracular reading relationship as Storer's and Aldington's view of Sappho. H. D. devotes a few pages to romanticizing Sappho but finally extols her, like Plato, for her wisdom.

> Wisdom—this is all we know of the girl, that though she stood in the heavy Graeco-Asiatic sunlight, the wind from Asia, heavy with ardent myrrh and Persian spices, was yet tempered with a Western gale, bearing in its strength and its salt sting, the image of another, tall, with eyes shadowed by the helmet rim, the goddess, indomitable.

> This is her strength—Sappho of Mitylene was a Greek. And in all her ecstasies, her burnings, her Asiatic riot of colour, her cry to that Phoenician deity, "Adonis, Adonis—" her phrases, so simple yet in any but her hands in danger of overpowering sensuousness, her touches of Oriental realism,

"purple napkins" and "soft cushions" are yet tempered, moderated by a craft never surpassed in literature. The beauty of Aphrodite it is true is the constant, reiterated subject of her singing. But she is called by a late scholiast who knew more of her than we can hope to learn from these brief fragments, "The Wise Sappho."

(63)

H. D.'s Sappho is blessed by not only the radiantly tressed Aphrodite but also the helmeted, crafty Athena, goddess of wisdom. Like Aldington and other modernists, H. D. is fascinated by her unsurpassed craft, as well as its transmission through the ages. She writes: "Legend upon legend has grown up, adding curious documents to each previous fragment; the history of the preservation of each line is in itself a most fascinating and bewildering romance" (68).

I believe that there are two roots to H. D.'s "bewildering romance" with Sappho; one is to be found in the archival history surrounding each fragment. H. D. reaches back to her chosen epigraphs as much for emotional content and superior craft as for historical context. Each of H. D.'s epigraphs survives in a classical source, all of which are books on writing. "Fragment 113" appears in Tryphon's *Figures of Speech*; "Fragment Thirty-six" in Chrysippus's *Negatives*; "Fragment Forty" and "Fragment Forty-one" may have been consecutive in Hephaestion's *Handbook on Meters*; and "Fragment Sixty-eight" is found in Stobaeus's *Anthology* (on folly).[18] Viewing the fragment poems from this perspective grants us and H. D., a poet obsessed with palimpsest, access to Sappho only through another writer's personal history. And here we must not overlook the titles of the fragment poems, taken from random numbers assigned by a modern scholar, as opposed to directly from Sappho or as one of H. D.'s interpretative gestures.

The other root to H.D's Sapphic "romance" is buried in her bewildering relationship with Aldington. The palimpsestic layering of personalities inherent in any reading of Sappho sets the stage for the rhetorical encoding of H. D. and Aldington's own relationship. As we saw hints of Catullus's castrated Attis running around in "Amaranth," in "Fragment Sixty-eight," with its epigraph ". . . *even in the house of Hades*," H. D. subtly uses Sappho to cut down Aldington. Read in conjunction with the abandoned section from "Envy," one could view this poem as H. D.'s somewhat hyperbolic jealousy of Aldington's increased chances of dying a soldier's noble death,

while she molders away at home, abandoned by him as lover and friend. The omitted section reads:

> Could I have known
> you were more male than the sun-god,
> more hot, more intense,
> could I have known?
> for your glance all-enfolding,
> sympathetic, was selfless
> as a girl's glance.
>
> Could I have known?
> I whose heart,
> being rent, cared nothing,
> was unspeakably indifferent.
>
> ("**Envy**," section III, 321)

H. D. concludes both versions of the poem, "Do not pity me, spare that, / but how I envy you / your chance of death," leading us to think that the speaker too wishes to die, as well as conjuring up the Swinburnean image of a cliff-diving Sappho. But if we examine the remainder of the fragment from which H. D. excerpts "**Fragment Sixty-eight**"'s epigraph, we find that its ending foretells a much less dismal conclusion: "*But thou shalt lie dead, nor shall there ever be any remembrance of thee then or thereafter, for thou hast not of the roses of Pieria; but thou shalt wander obscure even in the house of Hades, flitting among the shadowy dead.*"[19] In this fragment Sappho not only envisions a salon rival's death but directs her to Hades. Rayor interprets it as "an invective against someone who does not share the Muses' gift of poetry. She was a nonentity in life and once she has died, she will remain unknown among the obscure dead."[20] This epigraph suggests that H. D. is really telling Aldington to go to hell, that he will die an obscure poet, and that the woman he is involved with is as talentless and "selfless" as he. Here H. D. uses Sappho's classical pen to open a modern vein.

On a less personal stylistic level, she does the same in "**Fragment 113**." H. D. chooses for an epigraph perhaps Sappho's most famous line, "*Neither honey nor bee for me*," which Campbell tells us comes down from Tryphon's *Figures of Speech* and is referred to in Diogenian's *Proverbs* as "used of those who are not willing to take the bad with the good."[21] I read "**Fragment 113**," the lone fragment poem published in *Hymen* in 1921, as basically H. D.'s attempt to work out the Sapphic style. Here H. D. adopts the Greek priamel, imitating the repetition of negation and recurrent images to recapture its melodic line. Particularly Sapphic is the final stanza.

> not iris—old desire—old passion—
> old forgetfulness—old pain—

not this, nor any flower,
but if you turn again,
seek strength of arm and throat,
touch as the god;
neglect the lyre-note;
knowing that you shall feel,
about the frame,
no trembling of the string
but heat, more passionate
of bone and the white shell
and fiery tempered steel.

(131-32)

The speaker moves away from past desire in what seems to me an echo of the *Homeric Hymn to Demeter,* with the withdrawal from the lushness of both honey and fruit tree, the fertility of the bee, and association with the iris. Here too I think we find H. D. turning away from imagism, and it is important to keep in mind how her stylistic proximity to Sappho enabled H. D. to make this move. Many of the imagist tenets we find so exquisitely enacted in H. D.'s verse are equally applicable to Sappho's: for example, direct treatment of subject, as few adjectives as possible, individuality of rhythm, and the exact word.[22]

Of all the fragment poems, **"Fragment Thirty-six"** best reflects imagism, Sappho, and H. D.'s wrestling to expand her relation to both. This intricately woven poem begins with the most generative of the epigraphs: *"I know not what to do. / my mind is divided."* Rayor translates the fragment, "I don't know what I should do— / I'm of two minds," noting that "what I should do" could mean "'what I should set down,' in regard to composing poetry."[23] John Winkler further suggests that the speaker's dilemma might hinge upon the revelation of some women-only secrets, offering "I am not sure which things to set down and which to keep among ourselves, my mind is divided," as a possible meaning.[24] Undoubtedly H. D. plays upon this double entendre in the poem's first stanza:

I know not what to do,
my mind is reft:
is song's gift best?
is love's gift loveliest?
I know not what to do,
now sleep has pressed
weight on your eyelids.

(165-66)

This is the only poem in which H. D. actively debates her recuperation of Sappho—will it be through song or love? Is it a poetic gift that enables her to craft the Lesbian song, or lesbian perspective that empowers H. D. to read Sappho? Does H. D. dare break her meter to translate Sappho into her own imagist language?

Shall I break your rest,
devouring, eager?
is love's gift best?
nay, song's the loveliest:
yet were you lost,
what rapture
could I take from song?
what song were left?

(stanza 2, 166)

Notice the crossing here—"love's gift" becomes "best" and "song's the loveliest." The two blend, "each strives with each," and she fears privileging one over the other. Should the poet transmit her passion through Sappho and risk disturbing her icy perfection?

I know not what to do:
to turn and slake
the rage that burns,
with my breath burn
and trouble your cool breath?
so shall I turn and take
snow in my arms?
(is love's gift best?)
yet flake on flake
of snow were comfortless,
did you lie wondering,
wakened yet unawake.

(stanza 3, 166)

Were H. D. to adopt Sappho's cool control, taking "snow" in her arms, would it stir her; is the remedy to "slake / all the wild longing [. . .] as two white wrestlers / standing for a match" (stanza 4-5, 166-67)? Throughout the poem, waves of sound and phrase surge over one another, forcing the speaker's doubled mind to hesitate above passion and song, waiting for one to "fall" into the other.

I know not what to do:
will the sound break,
rending the night
with rift on rift of rose
and scattered light?
will the sound break at last
as the wave hesitant,
or will the whole night pass
and I lie listening awake?

(final stanzas [8-9], 167-68)

The poem ends as it began with the poet's reft mind now waiting to see if sound will split the night "with rift on rift of rose / and scattered light." And suddenly we are back to roses and **"The Wise Sappho,"** yet no nearer either poet than before. H. D. leaves us in these poems to find her wise Sappho, "a great power, roses, but many, many roses, each fragment witness to the love of some scholar or hectic antiquary searching to find a precious inch of palimpsest among the funereal glories of the sand-strewn Pharaohs" (69).

The intimate rose, with its lesbian and Sapphic resonances, and the dusty palimpsest, the measure of centuries of scholastic interest, represent the twofold reading relationship that H. D. sees in Sappho and then reproduces in her own work. Part of the reason the fragment poems are such successful artistic ventures is because they move away from the impersonal object-dependence of imagism without ever moving back toward the poet. H. D.'s fragments, like Sappho's, are extremely potent and invite the direct attention of the reader—saying, "I hate," or rendering her speaker's touch "so fire-eaten, so intense"—yet like Sappho's, they too have been alternately fragmented and written over. Like Aldington, H. D. notes the presence of complex relationships surrounding the fragments and writes her own Atthis into the poems; then she takes that knowledge one step further by writing him out. It is important to see that the fragment poems' later revisions were prompted not by the love of Bryher, nor even by a need to kill Aldington, but by H. D.'s desire to emulate Sappho: queerness, craft, fragmentation, and all. The fragment poems then testify not only to H. D.'s skill as a modern poet, but to the depth and nature of her understanding as a modernist reader.

Notes

1. Susan Gubar popularized this view in "Sapphistries." She argues that H. D. and Renée Vivien wished to form a "fantastic collaboration" (203) with Sappho as a poet, and importantly as a fellow lesbian poet. Gubar's reading is plausible, but her basis for this claim—that H. D.'s fragment poems are a tribute to Bryher (Winifred Ellerman)—is, as I will show, unfounded.

2. See also his article in *The Egoist*, "Poems and Fragments of Sappho." Storer (1880-1944) produced two volumes of poetry, *Inclinations* (1907) and *Mirrors of Illusion* (1908), which contain rather ineffective experiments with free verse. According to Zilboorg, he dropped out of the modernist poetry scene after 1908, and Pound writes to Flint in 1915 that imagism was "most emphatically NOT the poetry of friend Storer" (qtd. in Harmer, *Victory in Limbo* 45). For more on his relationship with Aldington, see Zilboorg, *Richard Aldington and H. D.*

3. Storer, "Poems and Fragments" 153.

4. Aldington, trans., *The Poems of Anyte of Tegea* 7-8, cited in Zilboorg, "Joint Venture" 90. Zilboorg's thorough studies of Aldington and H. D. have proven instrumental to my understanding of their roles as modernists and of Sappho's meaning to them.

5. Zilboorg, "Joint Venture" 90.

6. Cited ibid., 82. The letter is addressed to Bryher, H. D.'s companion after Aldington; she was also a young writer with strong classical leanings.

7. Marcus, *Virginia Woolf and the Languages of Patriarchy* 92.

8. Woolf, "A Society" (1921).

9. Two translations H. D. consulted were H. T. Wharton's *Sappho* (1885) and Renée Vivien's *Sapho* (1903). Storer's introduction recommends Wharton's as the best English translation ("Poems and Fragments" 153), and in a letter from Aldington, dated 13 December 1918, in which he outlines his plans for the second Poets' Translation Series—among them, making H. D. Greek editor—Aldington tells H. D.: "Any foreign books you may need, whether Greek or French—any of Renée Vivien for example—you may need; order from David Nutt . . ." (qtd. in Zilboorg, *Richard Aldington and H. D.* 167). H. D.'s own numbering of the fragments follows Wharton's, which is based on that of the standard Greek edition at the time, Bergk's *Poetae Lyrici Graeci*.

10. Gubar, "Sapphistries" 212.

11. I am indebted to Louis L. Martz, whose introduction and notes to the *Collected Poems* lucidly detail the composition and revisionary history of the fragment poems. See H. D., *Collected Poems*, esp. xiv-xix, 613, 616, 617-18. All citations of H. D.'s poetry are to this edition. Martz relates that the original triad of poems was "preserved in a carefully bound typescript containing only these poems and bearing on the flyleaf the inscription in H. D.'s hand, 'Corfe Castle—Dorset—summer 1917—from poems of *The Islands* series—' The date should probably be 1916, for that was the summer she spent at Corfe Castle, while Richard Aldington was beginning his military training nearby" (xiv).

12. Zilboorg, *Richard Aldington and H. D.* 23. Zilboorg derived this information from H. D.'s letters to John Cournos during this period.

13. H. D., "The Wise Sappho" 67. Further citations will be given in parentheses in the text.

14. H. D. also transforms another Sapphic fragment in "Amaranth"'s first section, by setting "Andromeda, shameless and radiant" in place of Sappho's "Aphrodite, shameless and radiant." By deifying Andromeda, H. D. makes Atthis's attraction toward her somehow more comprehensible to speaker and reader, while at the same time commenting on the unreality of such a tryst and the dangerous frivolity of the caprice.

15. In a letter to H. D. dated 12 June 1918 Aldington wrote: "Pardons à ton vieux amant tous ses torts et tous ses petitesses et ne te souviens que de cette partie de lui que tu as aimé autrefois—Atthis" [trans. by Zilboorg] "Let's pardon your old lover all his faults and all his pettiness and remember only that part of him that you used to love—Atthis" (qtd. in Zilboorg, *Richard Aldington and H. D.* 65-67).

16. Three translations have been indispensable to this study, only one of which could have been consulted by H. D.: Wharton's *Sappho*, which houses the exact translations of the epigraphs she chose. The second is Campbell's new Loeb edition, *Greek Lyric* vol. 1, and the third is Rayor, *Sappho's Lyre*. I have used Wharton's translation of the fragment both he and H. D. number 41.

17. Remark made during "An H. D. Retrospective" at Poet's House, New York, 14 November 1991.

18. See Campbell, *Greek Lyric* 1:159, 97, 147, 149, 99.

19. Wharton, trans., *Sappho* 90.

20. Rayor, *Sappho's Lyre* 165.

21. Campbell, *Greek Lyric* 1:159.

22. I take these characteristics from Aldington's review of *Des Imagistes*, which appeared in *The Egoist*, 1 June 1914, and included a list of the imagists' "fundamental doctrines" (202).

23. Rayor, *Sappho's Lyre* 80, 169.

24. Winkler makes the compelling argument that it is the "many-mindedness" of the varying perspectives offered in Sappho's poetry itself that encourages a diversity of readings. See "Double Consciousness," esp. 166-67.

TITLE COMMENTARY

Trilogy

JOYCE LORRAINE BECK (ESSAY DATE SPRING 1982)

SOURCE: Beck, Joyce Lorraine. "Dea, Awakening: A Reading of H. D.'s *Trilogy*." *San Jose Studies* 8, no. 2 (spring 1982): 59-70.

In the following essay, Beck finds Trilogy *to be a noteworthy feminist work because it exhibits an emerging spiritual consciousness and awareness embodied and symbolized in a central female figure, the Awakening Dea.*

H. D., Hilda Doolittle Aldington, is best known as the co-founder—with T. E. Hulme, Ezra Pound, and others—of the pre-World War I English Imagist movement in poetry. However, while it has long been acknowledged that Pound, Eliot, and Williams moved beyond Imagism to more comprehensive and meaningful visions in *Four Quartets*, the *Cantos*, and *Patterson*, the longer and later "major works" of their female contemporary and colleague, H. D., have until recently gone largely unpraised, uncriticized, and unrecognized. Rachel Blau DuPlessis' essay "Romantic Thralldom in H. D.," which appeared in *Contemporary Literature* in the Spring of 1979, remains a convincing demonstration of how H. D.'s *Helen in Egypt* helps lead to a reconstructionist view of personal and human integrity, wholeness, or holiness which is relevant to, and present in, twentieth-century women, as well as men. Other significant studies of this poem are those by Susan Friedman "Creating a Woman's Mythology: H. D.'s *Helen in Egypt*" in *Women's Studies* (Winter 1977) and Chapter 2 of L. S. Dembo's *Conceptions of Reality in Modern American Poetry* (Berkeley, 1966).

Susan Gubar in "The Echoing Spell of H. D.'s *Trilogy*" (*Contemporary Literature*, Spring 1978)

views H. D. as a poet who contributed not only "distinct images" but a total and coherent spiritual vision and a "creative stasis" at once immediate and authentic for contemporary women and men. In this essay Gubar sums up H. D.'s "re-invocation" or "re-creation" of male myths, patriarchal culture, and religious thought in her female epic, the *Trilogy*, so as to include those women whose names have not been in the book. In the first of the three sections, *The Walls Do Not Fall*, says Gubar, H. D. "demonstrates the need for imagistic and lexical redefinition, an activity closely associated with the recovery of female myths, especially the story of Isis." In the second and third books, however, the poet moves beyond both imagism and classical mythology to a substantial re-vision or re-creation of Western patriarchal religious thought and tradition. In *Tribute to the Angels*, she "actually begins transforming certain words, even as she revises Apocalyptic myth." Finally, in *The Flowering of the Rod*, H. D. "translates the story of the New Testament," "feminizing a male mythology as she celebrates the female or 'feminine' Word made flesh."[1]

H. D. is important, then, not only as an imagist poet but as a visionary poet who contributed substantially to the discovery of an archetypal identity for contemporary woman. Not only is her concluding masterpiece *Helen in Egypt* a search for and recognition of archetypal, or prototypal, integrity and wholeness, her *Trilogy* presents an emerging spiritual consciousness and awareness embodied and symbolized in an important central female figure. H. D.'s Awakening Dea, who appears in her *Tribute to the Angels*, stands at the poetic center of the *Trilogy*.

Fascinating as this Goddess may be, she is, within the compass of the poem, still in process of appearing—or of emerging into H. D.'s and our own, spiritual consciousness. *Tribute to the Angels*, says Norman Holmes Pearson, describes new life springing from the ruins of a city and of a human soul.[2] The city is London in 1945, and the human soul is H. D.'s. But whose, we might ask, is the "new Life?" The poet calls us to attention in her wartime hymn and asks that we see—that we behold—this "new Life" as it is placed before us. The life which emerges or springs forth is, indeed, "new," a surprise as well as an expectation even to the soul who conceives it. H. D. had thought only to recall Gabriel, the Angel of Annunciation. How could "she imagine," the poet asks, that the one he is announcing would "come instead:"

We see her visible and actual, . . .

we asked for no sign
but she gave a sign unto us; . . .

she set a charred tree before us,
burnt and stricken to the heart. . . .

Invisible, indivisible Spirit,
how is it you come so near![3]

Neither the poet nor we can say exactly who this archetypal figure is yet, or is to be, but we catch gleaming glimpses.

She appears in the fullness of time to the sound of music from the "other world," the realm of "no need of the moon to shine in it," says the poet:

I was talking casually
with friends in the other room,

when we saw the outer hall
grow lighter—then we saw where the door was,

there was no door
(this was a dream of course),

and she was standing there,
actually, at the turn of the stair.

(*TA* [*Tribute to the Angels*] 25)

However, H. D. as Mother of Dea does not always have unfailing eyesight or vision. While the Dea struggles to be seen and recognized, or to emerge, so does her poetic Mother, H. D., struggle to give poetic birth:

This is no rune nor riddle
it is happening everywhere;

what I mean is—it is so simple
yet no trick of the pen or brush

could capture that impression;
music could do nothing with it,

nothing whatever; what I mean is—
but you have seen for yourself

that burnt-out wood crumbling . . .
you have seen for yourself.

(*TA* 21)

Often doubt is expressed, qualifications suggested, prayers offered, comparisons affirmed or denied, truths sorted through and out, figures explored—as the poet continues to evoke Gabriel, and the Mercurial flame which might purify love or through interpretation translate vision into revelation, as dross to golden light:

O swiftly, re-light the flame . . .

Hermes . . . poet,

take what the old-church
found in Mithra's tomb,

candle and script and bell,
take what the new-church spat upon

and broke and shattered;
collect the fragments of the splintered glass

and of your fire and breath,
melt down and integrate,

re-invoke, re-create
opal, onyx, obsidian,

now scattered in the shards
men tread upon.

(*TA* 11, 1)

There are a few conclusions the poet tentatively arrives at concerning the awakening Dea. She is the "Presence" announced by "Spirit" during a time of crisis. The Dea first appears to H. D. at a time of desolation, when World War II recalls the war experience and post-war collapse of the twenties, which had coincided with the poet's own crisis and mental breakdown. Now, the forties have become, once again, a time of crisis, a time when "Spirit announces the Presence":

the shrine lies open to the sky
the rain falls, here, there
sand drifts; eternity endures:

rain everywhere, yet as the fallen roof
leaves the sealed room
open to the air,

so through our desolation,
thoughts stir, inspiration stalks us
through gloom:

unaware, Spirit announces the Presence;
shivering overtakes us,
as of old. . . .

(*WDNF* [*The Walls Do Not Fall*] 1)

The Dea is announced by the poet-prophets, who, miraculously, have withstood the ordeal. Now, as before, the bards or poets, "companions of the flame," have endured: "the bone-frame was made for / no such shock knit within terror, / . . . yet the frame held: / we passed the flame: we wonder / what saved us? what for?" "Never / in Rome," says the poet, "so many martyrs fell; / not in Jerusalem / never in Thebes, so many stood and watched" as "the lightning shattered earth and splintered sky," nor did those who endured flee to hide in caves:

but with unbroken will,
with unbowed head, watched
and though unaware, worshipped

and knew not that they worshipped
and that they were

that which they worshipped,
had they known the fire

of strength, endurance, anger
in their hearts,

was part of that same fire
that in a candle or on a candle-stick

or in a star
is known as . . .

judgement and will of God,
God's very breath.

                              (*TA* 6)

Also, as before, the poet-prophets must suffer for the awakening Dea's sake and outlast persecution if they are to succeed in their mission of annunciation. Once again the poets, "authentic relic / bearers of the secret wisdom, / living remnant of the inner band / of sanctuaries initiate" are called "useless" creators of "intellectual adornment." This, says H. D., is the "new heresy:"

but if you do not even understand what words
    say,

how can you expect to pass judgement
on what words conceal?

yet the ancient rubrics reveal that
we are back at the beginning:

you have a long way to go
walk carefully, speak politely.

                              (*WDNF* 8)

It is the poet-prophet who, by challenging critics and outlasting those who insult or ignore her, has fought for breath and won new life: ". . . the stylus / the palette, the pen, the quill endure, / though our books are a floor / of smouldering ash under our feet; / we fight, . . . they say, for breath." When asked, "so what good are your scribblings?" the poet answers, "this—we take them with us / beyond death." (*WDNF* 10)

The scribes or poets who announce the Dea are true to themselves and to their craft or art; they are loyal to the god Mercury, or to the angel Gabriel. H. D. identifies herself as one of these poet-apostles, one of the "living remnant of the inner band / of sanctuaries initiate." She is herself one of the "companions of the flame:"

(I speak of myself individually
but I was surrounded by companions

in this mystery);
do you wonder we are proud,

aloof,
indifferent to your good and evil?

peril, strangely encountered, strangely endured,
marks us;

we know each other
by secret symbols,

though, remote, speechless,
we pass each other on the pavement,

at the turn of the stair;
though no word pass between us,

there is subtle appraisement;
even if we snarl a brief greeting

or do not speak at all,
we know our Name,

we nameless initiates
born of one mother,

companions
of the flame.

                              (*WDNF* 13)

To remain true to her quest of annunciation requires great virtue, authenticity, and courage of the poet. Indeed, her task seems almost impossible. However, even when her psychoanalyst, Freud, and contemporary medicine and technology are not sufficiently moved, enlightened, or impressed by her interpreted visions or disciplined dreaming, H. D., courageously, does not abandon her vocation to see, to say, and to make known. She remains the castilian soul who is "unintimidated by multiplicity of magnified beauty;" who is characteristically "persistent:"

In me (the worm) clearly
is no righteousness, but this—

persistence; I escaped spider-snare,
bird-claw, scavenger bird-beak, . . .

I escaped, I explored
rose-thorn forest,

. . . I know how the Lord God
is about to manifest, when I,

the industrious worm,
spin my own shroud.

                              (*WDNF* 6)

The "persistent" poet arrives, tentatively, at a few conclusions concerning the nature and person of the awakening Dea who is "about to manifest." She resembles many medieval visions but seems not to be identical with any of these:

the painters did very well by her;
it is true, they missed never a line

of the suave turn of the head
or subtle shade of lowered eye-lid

or eye-lids half-raised; you find
her everywhere (or did find),

in cathedral, museum, cloister,
at the turn of the palace stair. . . .

But none of these, none of these
suggest her as I saw her, . . .

In **Tribute to the Angels,** says Pearson, "H. D. was moving forward and backward in spiritual realities." All that the poets have written or artists have painted of the Dea over the centuries is "implicit;" but, "all that *and* much more:"

Ah (you say), this is Holy Wisdom
Santa Sophia, the SS of Sanctus Spiritus

so by facile reasoning logically
the incarnate symbol of the Holy Ghost; . . .

I see her as you project her, . . .

all you say is implicit,
all that and much more; . . .

the same—different—the same attributes,
different yet the same as before.

(*TA* 36-39)

She comes as she is "sensed over the centuries in the differing dreams of artists," from "the green-white of the blossoms as in a dreamed epiphany." In a letter about the **Trilogy,** dated 1943, H. D. expresses her belief that "protection of the scribe" seems to be the "leitmotif" of the work, along with the "feeling of assurance back of it of the presence of the God of the Scribe—Thoth, Hermes, Ancient of Days." The place of the scribe or poet in the "mysteries of all-time," she sees as "the keeping track of the 'treasures' which contain *for every scribe which is instructed,* things new and old." The scribes to whom "our Lady Universally" has appeared over the centuries Pearson calls "scribes with the brush;" and, he concludes, "Now, to H. D., she had emerged once more."[4]

Another characteristic of the awakening Dea is that she loves and actively encourages artists and poets. H. D. is, perhaps, led on in the rediscovery and interpretation of old mysteries through her own intelligence and persistence. But she is also encouraged through the appearance of the awakening Dea Herself, who receives the poems gratefully, as gifts. She is respectful of the poet who gives her birth, of the self-actualized and perfected soul who is "hallowed" by "other standards" than pompous fanfare of brittle fame: "strange texture, a wing covered us, and though

there was whirr and roar in the high air / there was a Voice louder, / though its speech was lower / than a whisper." (*WDNF* 12) It is the writers, the "companions of the flame," whom the annointed Dea loves and salutes. She knows those who know her:

So she must have been pleased with us,
who did not forgo our heritage

at the grave-edge;
she must have been pleased

with the straggling company of the brush and
    quill
who did not deny their birthright;

she must have been pleased with us,
for she looked so kindly at us

under her drift of veils,
and she carried a book.

(*TA* 35)

For John Peck, writing in *Parnassus*, "the focus of H. D.'s poems is dream-vision," and her Queen is *eidolon,* a "dialectical image that returns our look." The poet's perception of the Goddess' aura or wholeness frees the Dea to respond; she in turn frees the poet by returning her look, thus overcoming or "verifying" enchantment and restoring aura to fact. He quotes Walter Benjamin's citation of Valery: "In dreams, however, there is an equation. The things I see, see me just as much as I see them." H. D.'s awakening Dea, likewise, sees and responds to the poet who sees her. Peck finds in H. D.'s *eidolon* of mutual creating and receiving a "suggestive token of healing."[5] DuPlessis also views H. D.'s *"glorie"* as "spiritual vision, which sees the aura of objects." The spiritual quest for this "special realm of consciousness," she contends, "occurs above and beyond the cultural institutions of heterosexuality. The Biblical echo ('neither marriage nor giving in marriage') signifies that H. D. was trying to construct some perspective that avoided the constant subordination of the woman to the man in normal sexual and cultural life. In her view, men and women are equals in the spiritual realm, not seeking the distinctions of fixed sex roles, but rather a mutual suffusion of insight and wisdom. The spiritual dimension termed *glorie* is the inner radiance set forth by an object or experience, substance beyond dualism."[6] It would seem that H. D. bears with her as her own that "glorious faculty" which marks her as one of those "higher minds" who "from their native selves / can send abroad /

Kindred mutations; for themselves create / A like existence; and, whene'er it dawns / Created for them, catch it"—or be caught "by its inevitable mastery."

Finally, the awakened Dea appears at the center of H. D.'s *Tribute to the Angels* as a fully developed archetypal presence. When she is seen, she is recognized by the apostle-poet as the beatific Queen of Heaven, as the Redeemer of the Angels, or as Sanctus Spiritus. Her "drift of veils" is a nimbus or starlit galaxy, and her book contains the testaments of new life and of future glory:

> she carries over the cult
> of the *Bona Dea,*
>
> she carries a book but it is not
> the tome of the ancient wisdom,
>
> the pages, I imagine, are the blank pages
> of the unwritten volume of the new.
>
> (*TA* 38)

Her book, which is "our book," says the poet, is still being written; it is "the same," yet "different"—"different yet the same as before." The Angels of Revelation whom H. D. evokes pay tribute to, or celebrate with, the Dea as H. D. pays tribute to them:

> So we hail them together,
> One to contrast the other, . . .
>
> And the point in the spectrum
> where all lights become one,
>
> is white and white is not no-colour, . . .
>
> but all-colour;
> where the flames mingle
>
> and the wings meet, when we gain
> the arc of perfection,
>
> we are satisfied, we are happy,
> we begin again.
>
> (*TA* 43)

As a Goddess of new beginnings, of Alpha and Omega, the awakening Dea is associated with Spring, "a season more bountiful . . . more beautiful, richer in leaf and colour; . . . the may flowering mulberry and rose-purple." (*TA* 17) But, perhaps most importantly, H. D.'s Dea is symbolized in the flowering of the rood. This is her gift to the poet as the poem is the poet's gift to her:

> . . . my eyes saw
> it was not a dream

> yet it was vision,
> it was a sign,
>
> it was the *Angel which redeemed me,*
> it was the Holy Ghost—
>
> a half-burnt-out apple-tree
> blossoming;
>
> this is the flowering of the rood,
> this is the flowering of the wood.
>
> (*TA* 23)

When the "jewel / melts in the crucible / we find not ashes, not ash-of-rose, . . . not *vas spirituale,* not *vas mystica* even, but a cluster of garden pinks / or a face like a Christmas-rose." (*TA* 43) In H. D.'s *Trilogy,* as in W. B. Yeats' "The Rose of the World" or the Anglo-Saxon "Dream of the Rood," Eternal Beauty, or Holy Wisdom, suffers with humanity and redeems passion through pervading love. The stricken rood becomes the tree of life and glory.

The annointed Dea of H. D.'s *Trilogy* also is associated with epiphany or consummation. Much as the "great leaves" of Yeats' "inviolate Rose" "enfold / the ancient beards, the helms of ruby and gold / Of the crown Magi;" so does H. D.'s Dea reveal her "shining loveliness" to the scribe-poets of the *Trilogy,* in or through the symbol of the flowering rood or Christmas rose. The Epiphany becomes the theme of the third part of the poem, *The Flowering of the Rod.* Pearson sees the gift of the Magi in this work linked with the scribe's gift or offering of the poem: "We recognize the Magi not as Kings of the Orient but as the intellectually elite in the worship of Zoroaster and Mithra, possessing, as Gilbert Vezin puts it in his *L'Adoration et Le Cycle des Mages* (1950), the sum knowledge of their age: astrology, astronomy, medicine, mathematics and occult science. The Magi were Wise Men; they were Scribes. Their offering was 'like the offering of a poem.'"[7]

If the symbol of H. D.'s Dea of beatitude is the flowering rood, her part, or action, is redemption: ". . . she brings the Book of Life, obviously." The Dea is a Goddess of new life, or resurrection; and resurrection is discovered beyond the "geometry of perfection," or "the smouldering cities," beyond even "duty or pity:"

> now having given all, let us leave all;
> above all, let us leave pity
>
> and mount higher
> to love—resurrection. . . .

In resurrection, there is confusion
if we start to argue; if we stand and stare, . . .
in resurrection, there is simple affirmation, . . .

seeking what we once knew,
we know ultimately we will find
happiness . . . in Paradise.

(*FR* [*The Flowering of the Rod*] 1)

However, H. D.'s Goddess in Glory is human and visible as well as divine. Her colors are still red and white as well as gold:

what I wanted to indicate was
a new phase, a new distinction of colour;

she was not impalpable like a ghost,
she was not awe-inspiring like a Spirit,

she was not even over-whelming
like an Angel.

(*TA* 40)

The poet's archetypal figure is not arrogant; nor is she discovered apart and alien, although she has dignity; "she wasn't hieratic, she wasn't frozen, she wasn't very tall." (*TA* 38) She is us, with us, or "one of us": "She carried a book, either to imply / she was one of us, with us / or to suggest she was satisfied / with our purpose." Yet neither is she a simple symbol of dead pieties:

she is the counter-coin-side
of primitive terror;

she is not-fear, she is not-war
but she is no symbolic figure

of peace, charity, chastity, goodness,
faith, hope, reward;

she is not Justice with eyes
blindfolded like Love's;

I grant you the dove's symbolic purity
I grant you her face was innocent. . . .

her attention is undivided . . .
her book is our book.

(*TA* 38)

In a letter dated December, 1944, H. D. links her figure with Santa Sophia, Holy Wisdom, and with "the SS of Sanctus Spiritus;" but the poet's Dea also signals resurrection, new life, and new beginnings: "we were there or not-there / we saw the tree flowering; then it was an ordinary tree in an old garden square." (*TA* 20) She is a bringer of light and life. The apostrophe concludes **Tribute to the Angels**. "This is the flowering of the rod," says Pearson, [which] "was to re-blossom in the presence of . . . Christ,—that is, in Life." Here

"Golgotha gives way to love and resurrection.[8]" H. D. places her Dea of resurrection before us and asks that we see, that we "behold" Her. "We see her visible and actual." Her pages reveal "a tale of a Fisherman," and she is associated with "purple as with purple spread upon an altar." The annointed Dea is visible, tangible, and communal New Life:

We are part of it;
we admit the transubstantiation,

not God merely in bread
But God in the other-half of the tree . . .

this is the flowering of the rood,
this is the flowering of the wood

where . . . we pause to give
thanks that we rise again from death and live.

(*TA* 23)

The **Trilogy** and **Helen in Egypt** are H. D.'s poetic masterpieces; as such, they are her discovery of an authentic, heroic, and sacred destiny for the woman poet, artist, creator. If H. D.'s poetry receives the attention it deserves, she may yet take her rightful place alongside Ezra Pound, Richard Aldington, D. H. Lawrence, James Joyce, T. S. Eliot, and other friends, companions, and fellow writers. Hilda Doolittle Aldington should be recognized as a poet who contributed not only "distinct images" but a total, coherent, spiritual vision and a perception of religious experience and holiness meaningful, relevant, and authentic for twentieth-century women and men.

Notes

1. Susan Gubar, "The Echoing Spell of H. D.'s *Trilogy*," *Contemporary Literature*, 19, No. 2 (Spring 1978), 196-218. The essay is reprinted in *Shakespeare's Sisters: Feminist Essays on Women Poets*, ed. Sandra M. Gilbert and Susan Gubar (Bloomington: Indiana Univ. Press, 1979), pp. 200-218.

2. Norman Holmes Pearson, "Foreword" to the *Trilogy* (New York: New Directions, 1973), p. v.

3. H. D., *Tribute to the Angels* in *Trilogy* (New York: New Directions, 1973), 19, p. 82. Copyright 1945 by Oxford University Press. Subsequent references will be from the Pearson edition and will be noted in the text by the capitalized initials of *The Walls Do Not Fall* (WDNF), *Tribute to the Angels* (TA), or *The Flowering of the Rod* (FR) and the number of the poem.

4. Pearson, p. viii.

5. John Peck, "Passio Perpetuae H. D.," *Parnassus: Poetry in Review*, 3, No. 2 (Spring-Summer, 1975), p. 45.

6. Rachel Blau DuPlessis, "Romantic Thralldom in H. D.," *Contemporary Literature*, 20, No. 2 (Spring 1979), 186-187.

7. Pearson, pp. viii-ix.

8. Pearson, p. xi.

Helen of Troy

ALBERT GELPI (ESSAY DATE APRIL 1982)

SOURCE: Gelpi, Albert. "Hilda in Egypt." *Southern Review* 18, no. 2 (April 1982): 233-50.

In the following essay, Gelpi describes H. D.'s Helen in Egypt *as "a final and climactic efflorescence of creative energy."*

H. D. always wrote her own personal and psychological dilemma against and within the political turmoil of the twentieth century, the toils of love enmeshed in the convulsions of war. Her marriage to and separation from Richard Aldington turn on World War I, and that concatenation of private and public trauma stands behind the poems of *Sea Garden,* which sum up the Imagist concision of her first phase. The sequences of *Trilogy,* written through the London blitzes of World War II, usher in the longer, multivalent and more associative poems of her later years. The travail of aging and illness in her last years did not issue in the stoic silence which made Pound leave incomplete his life's work in the *Cantos,* but instead, as with William Carlos Williams, made for a final and climactic efflorescence of creative energy. The results were *Helen in Egypt,* published in 1961 almost concurrently with her death, and *Hermetic Definition,* published posthumously in 1972.

Even the reviewers who shied away from dealing with *Helen in Egypt* as a poem by detaching particular lyrics from the whole for dutiful praise (as though they were still Imagist pieces) recognized dimly that *Helen* was the culmination of a life in poetry. But it is an event even more culturally signal than that: it is the most ambitious and successful long poem ever written by a woman poet, certainly in English. It is so often observed as to take on a kind of fatality that no woman has ever written an epic, that women poets seem constrained to the minor note and the confabulations of the heart. H. D. confounds that complacent dictum by assuming and redefining the grounds of the epic. Early on the poem asks:

> Is Fate inexorable?
> does Zeus decree that, forever,
> Love should be born of War?

The *Iliad* showed War born of Love, but H. D. repossessed the Trojan materials that have inspired the Western epic from Homer to Pound and converted them into an anti-epic centered not on heroes like Achilles and Hector but on a heroine, none other than the woman who, male poets have told us, roused men to Love, and so to War.

Many of the masterworks of American writing—*Walden* and *Moby-Dick* and *Absalom, Absalom!, Leaves of Grass* and *The Cantos, Four Quartets* and *Paterson*—are *sui generis.* They make their idiosyncratic statement in their own unique form. So *Helen in Egypt* draws Greek and Egyptian myths, epic and psychoanalysis and occult gnosticism into an "odyssey" of consciousness enacted as a series of lyrics written in irregular free-verse tercets of varying length and linked by prose commentaries sometimes longer than the lyrics. The poem is divided into books, eight lyrics to a sequence, and there are seven books to Part I, "Pallinode," and Part II, "Leuké," and six to the concluding part, "Eidolon." "Pallinode" was written at Lugano in the summer of 1952; "Leuké," the next year at the Klinik Brunner in Küsnacht near Zurich, H. D.'s home after 1953; and "Eidolon," again at Lugano during the summer of 1954. The speakers in "Pallinode," which takes place in an Egyptian temple near the coast after the War, are Helen, who was rumored to have spent the War there rather than at Troy, and Achilles, the Trojan nemesis now apparently dead and shipwrecked in Egypt; the speakers in Part II are Helen and her old lover Paris on Leuké, *l'isle blanche,* and then Helen and Theseus, her old benefactor and counselor in Athens; the speakers in "Eidolon" are Helen and Paris and Achilles. Helen's is, of course, not only the point of view but the subsuming consciousness. The action transpires in no time and no place, and so in any time and place: in Helen's psyche, where the dead are quick and where the past is present, pregnant with fatality.

And Helen is, of course, H. D.'s persona as she writes her epic of consciousness. If this strategy seems more archly literary and aesthetically distanced than Whitman's stance in "Song of Myself," we need only remember that the "I" who spoke in *Leaves of Grass* as "Walt Whitman, a kosmos," is a fiction in some ways more deceptive than "Helen" because it pretends not to be a fiction. Moreover, in *Helen in Egypt* the configuration of the three male figures around Helen's central consciousness presents H. D. re-creating mythicized and fantasized versions of Richard Aldington in Achilles, of Freud in Theseus, and, in the figure of Paris, a recapitulation of her romantic passions from Ezra Pound to Dr. Erich Heydt, the analyst and doctor at the Klinik Brunner.

A notebook entry from an unpublished journal entitled *Compassionate Friendship* in 1955 observed: "I had found myself, I had found my alter-ego or my double—and that my mother's name was Helen has no doubt something to do with it." As for Achilles, he begins the poem in the aggressive male posture adopted by Aldington during World War I and dramatized by H. D. as Rafe in *Bid Me to Live*: the swaggeringly blunt warrior used to using his women. Like Freud, who served H. D. during the thirties as wise old man, surrounded in his office by ancient Greek figurines, and applying his reason to help her sort out the confusion of her life and feelings, Theseus is for Helen the wise man and paternal authority who offers his couch to her for rest and an analytic rehearsal of her amatory embroilments.

The associations with Paris are more complicated and more inclusive; they span all H. D.'s adult life up to the time of her writing of the poem. In a notebook she confessed that her involvement with Dr. Heydt, which almost immediately passed into the personal and romantic despite the fact that she was decades older than he, gave rise to the second part of the poem and specifically to the introduction of Paris. But behind Heydt stood Pound, who wrote his famous poem "A Tree" to and about the young Hilda at the peak of their passionate affair, just as Paris calls Helen his "Dendritis, . . . Helena of the trees." In the same notebook H. D. rehearsed "the sequence of my initiators" throughout her life: Pound; Aldington; from the London days of World War I John Cournos and D. H. Lawrence and Cecil Gray ("Lawrence in the middle"); Bryher's second husband Kenneth MacPherson "as a later double, as it were of Gray"; Walter Schmideberg, her analyst as well as close friend during the years of the final divorce decree from Aldington in 1938; and now Eric Heydt as the "inheritor" of the male line.

Paris, then, summed up all the men in her life, from Pound to Heydt, including Aldington, but Heydt was specifically connected with Pound in her mind from the first. When Heydt gave her an injection at perhaps their initial encounter at the Klinik, he transfixed her with the question "You know Ezra Pound, don't you?" "This was a shock coming from a stranger," she told her journal. "Perhaps he injected me or re-injected me with Ezra."[1] The sexual image is appropriate enough; Heydt persisted in pressing her about her relationship with her first lover, and once even asked her—to her distaste—whether the relationship had been sexual. The Pound memoir, *End to Torment*, H. D. wrote in 1958 only after repeated urging from Heydt that she recover her memories of the young man whom she almost married and who confirmed her a poet. Testimony that Pound was a living presence in her mind extends beyond *End to Torment* to the separate Helen sequence "Winter Love," written in 1959 and published in *Hermetic Definition*, in which Helen/Hilda relives her early love for "Odysseus." So too she incorporated into the Paris of her *Helen* an imaginative presence or medium who stood behind Heydt and was associated with "the history of poor Ezra and my connection with him."

The point of these autobiographical connections is not that the characters portray real people accurately, as *Bid Me to Live* intended, but rather that they are psychological fantasies or fictions which represent areas of psychological experience of the masculine on which H. D.'s selfhood turned. Where in her previous poetry she had sought to project her autobiography into myth, here at the end she sought to assimilate and validate myth within herself. "Is Fate inexorable? / does Zeus decree that, forever, / Love should be born of War?" The poem finally answers *yes*: divine decree requires that we submit ourselves to Life, for all the war wounds and deathblows, so that, providentially, in comprehending the train of temporal events, we can accept and transcend them in an earned identity through participation in the design ordained for time. *Helen in Egypt* is, then, H. D.'s death song which is at once a capitulation to and a reconstitution of life.

If the warrior Achilles suggests the Aldington H. D. lost in life, the Achilles who comes to Helen in death presents another possibility. In fact, Helen's union with Achilles is posited from the start. She tells his lost companions:

> God for his own purpose
> wills it so, that I
>
> stricken, forsaken draw to me,
> through magic greater than the trial of arms,
> your own invincible, unchallenged Sire. . . .

Paris and Theseus will play their parts; but everything contributes, however unwittingly, to the foreordained syzygy of Helen and Achilles, and God's emissary and instigator is the mother-goddess of the sea Thetis. It was Thetis who had unintentionally precipitated the war; she failed to invite Eris (Strife) along with the other gods to the banquet celebrating her marriage to Peleus. In retaliation Eris sowed the discord which ended in the Trojan conflict, which in turn would kill Achilles, son of Thetis and Peleus. Eris was devious in her revenge; she tossed a golden apple marked "for the fairest" into the banquet hall and when Hera, Athene, and Aphrodite began to wrangle for it, Zeus ordered that the quarrel be settled by the judgment of Paris, the youthful shepherd-son of the Trojan King. Aphrodite won the apple by promising Paris the most beautiful woman in the world, who turned out to be Helen, Menelaus' Queen. Thetis had counter-schemes to thwart Eris' vengeance and save her son from the war that was to follow the elopement of the Trojan prince and the Greek queen: she sought immortality for her son by dipping him into the river Styx, she charged Chiron with tutoring him in peaceful pursuits, she settled him into a safe, remote marriage with the daughter of the King of Scyros. But all in vain: Achilles left that haven with Patroclus to fight before the walls of Troy and to take various women as his sexual prize—until with Greek victory at hand under Achilles, Paris avenged Hector's death and the sack of Troy by slaying Achilles with Apollo's arrow shot into the heel Thetis had held when the waters of the Styx rendered him otherwise invulnerable.

All this background is sketched in early as flashbacks and memories, but the poem begins with the dramatic encounter between Helen and Achilles, which, we can now see as Homer could not, was the upshot and outcome of the war. Stesichorus' "Pallinode," uniting Helen and Achilles, provides the point of departure for H. D.'s archetypal fantasy. Dead and past the "fire of battle" and the "fire of desire," he is ferried to Egypt, an alien shore where he does not recognize as the dread Helen the woman brooding on the hieroglyphs in the temple of Amen. From the time when Helen's glance from the Trojan ramparts had locked with his below on the plains, they had moved—fated but unknowing—to this meeting, and Thetis is the link and catalyst: "How did we know each other? / was it the sea-enchantment in his eyes of Thetis his sea-mother?" When Achilles grieves with a boy's petulant outrage at suffering the mortal fate of a mere man, Helen prays to comfort him like a mother:

> let me love him, as Thetis, his mother,
> for I knew him, I saw in his eyes
> the sea-enchantment, but he
>
> knew not yet, Helen of Sparta,
> knew not Helen of Troy,
> knew not Helen, hated of Greece.

When he does recognize her, he "clutched my throat / with his fingers' remorseless steel," but

Helen's plea to Thetis relaxed his grip. The last book of "Pallinode" presents Thetis speaking now "in complete harmony with Helen." For Thetis becomes Helen's mother too—her surrogate mother, adopted by the mutually consenting love of "mother" and "daughter," and so the transformation and apotheosis of Hilda's mother Helen, whose presence Hilda had always felt as an absence. From that Helen, Hilda felt that she drew her poetic and religious capabilities, her affinity with the power of the word and the Word, but from that Helen, Hilda received no word of instruction or blessing; she seemed—understandably, Hilda admitted painfully—to prefer her brother. But in the poem Hilda assumes her mother's name and speaks, and the word she is given to speak to Achilles by Thetis is her own name, the mother-name. In this decisive meeting between Helen and Achilles, therefore, Thetis folds Helen into her care along with her son, in fact yokes the two in a single destiny.

So complete is the mother's harmony with the filial Helen at the climax of "Pallinode" that she acts as psychopomp revealing Helen's selfhood, to be achieved under her aegis. Thetis' runic lyric inaugurates Helen's imitation into arcane female mysteries drawn from the deeps of nature and of the psyche:

> A woman's wiles are a net;
> they would take the stars
> or a grasshopper in its mesh;
>
> they would sweep the sea
> for a bubble's iridescence
> or a flying-fish;
>
> they would plunge beneath the surface,
> without fear of the treacherous deep
> or a monstrous octopus;
>
> what unexpected treasure,
> what talisman or magic ring
> may the net find?
>
> frailer than spider spins,
> or a worm for its bier,
> deep as a lion or a fox
>
> or a panther's lair,
> leaf upon leaf, hair upon hair
> as a bird's nest,
>
> Phoenix
> has vanquished
> that ancient enemy, Sphinx.

Thetis' unriddling of the temple hieroglyphs reveals Helen's name rising from the rubble of war:

The Lords have passed a decree,
the Lords of the Hierarchy,
that Helen be worshipped,

be offered incense
upon the altars of Greece,
with her brothers, the Dioscuri;

from Argos, from distant Scythia,
from Delos, from Arcady,
the harp-strings will answer

the chant, the rhythm, the metre,
the syllables H-E-L-E-N-A;
Helena, reads the decree,

shall be shrined forever;
in Melos, in Thessaly,
they shall honour the name of Love,

begot of the Ships and of War;
one indestructible name,
to inspire the Scribe and refute

the doubts of the dissolute;
this is the Law,
this, the Mandate:

let no man strive against Fate,
Helena has withstood
the rancour of time and of hate.

Thetis goes on to distinguish Helen's fate from that of her twin sister Clytemnestra. For Clytemnestra's relation to the masculine has been destructive and self-destructive. As Helen's "shadow" she has obscured her sister's quest for identity, but now Thetis directs Helen to self-discovery through a creative connection with the masculine. Helen shall be immortalized with her twin brothers the Dioscuri. The decree of Amen-Thoth, "Nameless-of-many-Names," is

that *Helena* shall remain
one name, inseparable
from the names of the Dioscuri,

who are not two but many,
as you read the writing, the script,
the thousand-petalled lily.

And the union with the brothers is concurrent with, or consequent to, the divine decree that "Helena / be joined to Achilles." The hieroglyphs have sealed Helen's name with dim intuitions of providential fate, but the periplum to Achilles is a circle-round: a journey first to Paris on the white isle of Leuké and then to Theseus in Athens to find the future by sorting out the past. The journey of Part II draws unconscious mystery and transconscious wisdom further into conscious verbal denomination.

Why Leuké, *l'îsle blanche*? "Because," the prose commentary says, "here, Achilles is said to have married Helen who bore him a son, Euphorion." The import of this remark will come later, but at the present it seems misleading since the first three books of "**Leuké**" narrate the re-encounter between Paris and his "*Dendritis, . . .* Helena of the trees." Paris calls them "Adonis and Cytheraea," associating Helen with his goddess Aphrodite, and seeks to rouse her from Egyptian secrets and Greek intellection to rekindled sexual passion: "O Helena, tangled in thought, / be Rhodes' Helena, *Dendritis, /* why remember Achilles?"; "I say he never loved you." Paris harkens back to a life of passion on the old terms, now to Helen past feeling and past recall. ***End to Torment*** recounts an ecstatic moment of passion shared by Pound and his "Dryad" in a tree in the Doolittles' back yard; in 1958 H. D. still feels, but with poignancy, that emotion: "Why had I ever come down out of that tree?" Out of that paradisal garden-love into a world torn by Love and War, Eros and Thanatos. The love poems of "Hilda's Book," inscribed and bound for her by Pound and only recently reprinted with ***End to Torment***, celebrate her as Hilda of the trees: "My Lady is tall and fair to see / She swayeth as a poplar tree . . ."; "Thou that art sweeter than all orchard's breath"; "She hath some tree-born spirit of the wood / About her . . ."; and, most glowingly, "The Tree," which survived the juvenilia of "Hilda's Book" into *A Lume Spento* and *Personae* ": I stood still and was a tree amid the wood / Knowing the truth of things unseen before / Of Daphne and the laurel bow. . . ." Now in the late years of their lives Pound was again in touch with his Dryad.

But after Thetis, Helen knows that she cannot go back to old loves and old lovers. She flees Paris' importuning for the sage counsel of the aged Theseus, who wraps her in the security of warm blankets on his couch, like a swaddled baby or cocooned butterfly. Theseus counters her recoil from "Paris as Eros-Adonis" with Athenian reasonableness, urging happiness with Paris and denouncing Achilles as a choice of death over life: "even a Spirit loves laughter, / did you laugh with Achilles? No"; "you found life here with Paris. . . ." Why should she choose to "flame out, incandescent" in death with Achilles, who has exploited women all his life? But Helen is no longer Dendritis, and Achilles may not be his old self either. In any case, Paris seems too fevered and puerile to be the one she seeks.

Theseus comes to see that she longs for a new and perfect Lover "beyond Trojan and Greek"; she

ON THE SUBJECT OF...

H. D.'S *HELEN OF TROY*

Although the *Trilogy, Tribute to Freud, Winter Love* and *Hermetic Definition* are all crucial to understanding H. D.'s canon within the context of her total contribution to the female poetic tradition, *Helen in Egypt* brings into sharp focus her place within that tradition. Her choice of a mythological persona through which to explore contemporary realities is the first clue to H. D.'s understanding of the conditions of quest for the woman hero. H. D.'s hero is the Greek Helen, symbol throughout centuries of mythology and literature of the twin images of woman—beauty and evil. Helen in the patriarchal tale is a Greek Eve. Tempted by the delights of the flesh, she leaves her husband Menelaus, King of Sparta, and goes to Troy with Paris. Because of her (and the goddess of sexual love, Aphrodite, who directs her), Troy and Greece are doomed, victors as well as victims. To write an epic of genuinely female quest, H. D. goes directly to the heart of the patriarchal mythology of woman's nature—woman as representative of the flesh who tempts mankind to evil and death though her sexuality. This woman becomes the center of consciousness in an epic aimed at revising both mythology and the concept of woman's selfhood.

Friedman, Susan. An excerpt from "Creating a Women's Mythology: H. D.'s *Helen in Egypt.*" *Women's Studies: An Interdisciplinary Journal* 5, no. 1 (1977): p. 166.

is the Phoenix ready to rise from the ashes, the butterfly cracking the chrysalis and "wavering / like a Psyche / with half-dried wings." Nonetheless, for all that he comprehends, Theseus does his own importuning. Even his touching and tender suggestion that for the nonce he might serve as someone "half-way" to that Lover is beside the point. As with Freud and H. D., Theseus becomes Helen's "god-father" by bringing her to a wisdom which essentially differs from his own. He has prepared her to leave him as well as Paris behind to seek out Achilles, more aware now of her goal.

As for old transgressions, Achilles and she are "past caring"; the future need not be blocked by the past, life can only lead us to afterlife.

Part II reaches a sustained climax in the final exchange between Theseus and the departing Helen, suddenly displaying a new maturity. Paris' compulsive eroticism makes him seem her adolescent child, perhaps Achilles' son—in fact, "incarnate / Helen-Achilles," so that, in an inversion of chronological time, "he, my first lover, was created by my last. . . ." On one level this line may recall again the special connection between Pound and Heydt in the sequence of male initiators, and the reappearance of Pound as a potent psychological presence during these late years largely through the agency of Heydt. But a more relevant reading of the line would see Helen as setting aside as outdated and outgrown all the lovers and initiators of her previous life for a new kind of love to be found with Achilles. When the prose commentary informed us at the beginning of Part II that on Leuké "Achilles is said to have married Helen who bore him a son," the statement seemed erroneous or misleading, for Helen met not Achilles but Paris. But, as it turns out, her refusal to turn back the life-cycle makes Paris seem, regressively, a child to her. Her past becomes hers in her reclaiming it; she reconstitutes herself a new person by possessing it as mother. And so by a kind of backwards illogic the recognition of Paris as child confirms Achilles as husband-father in her new dimension of consciousness.

For in this poem Achilles and Paris matter only in relation to and in definition of Helen. The central insight which opens the resolution of the poem is the realization that she is the Phoenix, the Psyche self-born. Though Theseus favored Paris, he also recognizes:

> beyond all other, the Child,
> the child in the father,
> the child in the mother,
>
> the child-mother, yourself. . . .

Helen enwombs the entire process; the "child-mother" bears herself. When Helen asks, in the next lyric, how the masculine dualities—her twin brothers Castor and Pollux, Achilles and Theseus—can be reconciled, the wise old man answers that the polarities meet in herself. Theseus' reply is hallucinative, the sound-echoes and rhythms of the words rocking the lines to a resolution beyond words. The incantation is direct in statement and indirect in signification; the language is at once limpid and opaque, veiling the revelation in the act of revealing the veiled secret.

Thus, thus, thus,
as day, night,
as wrong, right,

as dark, light,
as water, fire,
as earth, air,

as storm, calm,
as fruit, flower,
as life, death,

as death, life;
the rose deflowered,
the rose re-born;

Helen in Egypt,
Helen at home,
Helen in Hellas forever.

The prose commentary informs us that "Helen understands, though we do not know exactly what it is that she understands," but the interplay of opposites in a transcendent pattern (which Emerson called the cosmic law of Compensation) is now to her "very simple." Reconciled "to Hellas forever," she sets out to return to Achilles in Egypt for the long-appointed union; Theseus has no choice but to bless her voyage to "Dis, Hades, Achilles." Her fate is not her dead life with Paris, but renewal with the dead Achilles; her myth is not Venus and Adonis, as Paris urged, but Persephone and Hades. And the hierogamy will be personal and psychological: "I will encompass the infinite / in time, in the crystal, / in my thought here."

Early in Part III, "**Eidolon**," Paris abandons his recriminations against Pluto-Achilles ("his is a death-cult") and accepts him as father with Helen replacing Hecuba as mother. Now the poem circles back with deeper comprehension to the meeting with which it began, when Achilles, raging against his mortality, attacks Helen, until his mother's— Helen's god-mother's—intervention relaxes his death-grip into an embrace. Achilles had forsaken his mother when he went to war; only after ten years on the Trojan plains did he promise to return to her if she helped him seize victory. But with victory in his grasp, he suffered his human destiny. Paris' arrow found Achilles' heel, and he returned to his mother in a strange land, finding her in the eyes and person of Helen. And, with Paris reclaimed as son, Helen reaches her apotheosis as mother. The single word "Thetis" which she gasped to Achilles in his strangle-grasp metamorphoses her in his eyes into a sea-goddess. For that mother-name

would weld him to her
who spoke it, who thought it,

who stared through the fire,
who stood as if to withstand
the onslaught of fury and battle,

who stood unwavering but made
as if to dive down, unbroken,
undefeated in the tempest roar

and thunder, inviting mountains
of snow-clad foam-tipped
green walls of sea-water

to rise like ramparts about her,
walls to protect yet walls to dive under,
dive through and dive over; . . .

The two "will always" for that "eternal moment" comprise a syzygy of L'Amour, La Mort: "this is Love, this is Death, / this is my last Lover." The offspring of that syzygy is not just Paris, nor the mysterious Euphorion, but themselves restored: Achilles "the child in Chiron's care," Helen the maiden at Theseus' knee. In their end is their beginning, and in their beginning is their end. But the mythic psychological status which Helen attains in the poem is not merely that of daughter-maiden; she becomes mother before daughter, encompassing the whole feminine archetype: Demeter-Persephone-Kore in one. In writing her own Helen-text, H. D. arrived at a reading of identity which resumed and surpassed the past. That moment—between time and eternity and participating in both—is the "final illumination" of the poem, and it is the moment of death. Through the mother-goddess she has conceived and come full term, dying and rising to herself. That metamorphosis, spelled out in the poem, has sealed her life cycle in the eternal pattern. "Sealed" in several senses: it brings her life to fulfillment and conclusion, it impresses on that life its distinctive signet (or sign or hieroglyph, as H. D. would say), and it affirms that life with irrevocable authority. Helen had said: "to me, the wheel is a seal . . . / the wheel is still." Under the name of Helen, H. D. spelled out her hermetic definition. Though *Helen in Egypt* is a death-hymn, H. D. told her journal: "I am alive in the *Helen* sequence" because "there I had found myself"; those poems "gave me everything."

Early in the poem Helen asks: "is it only the true immortals / who partake of mortality?" The poem's response inverts the proposition: true partakers of mortality achieve immortality. The moment of death is the moment of gnosis, in which life and consciousness conclude and transcend themselves; Helen becomes, with Achilles, a "New Mortal"—L'Amour/La Mort in a higher configuration. This is what the last lyric of the poem postulates in lines whose declarative simplicity does not designate the mystery they bespeak:

> Paris before Egypt, Paris after,
> is Eros, even as Thetis,
> the sea-mother, is Paphos;
>
> so the dart of Love
> is the dart of Death,
> and the secret is no secret;
>
> the simple path
> refutes at last
> the threat of the Labyrinth,
>
> the Sphinx is seen,
> the Beast is slain
> and the Phoenix-nest
>
> reveals the innermost
> key or the clue to the rest
> of the mystery;
>
> there is no before and no after,
> there is one finite moment
> that no infinite joy can disperse
>
> or thought of past happiness
> tempt from or dissipate;
> now I know the best and the worst;
>
> the seasons revolve around
> a pause in the infinite rhythm
> of the heart and of heaven.

To many readers the "final illumination" to which **Helen in Egypt** builds is at best impenetrably gnomic and at worst hypnotic nonsense, and this explication of the poem admittedly leaves many matters unaddressed and many questions unanswered. But the vision of the eternal moment, with time concentered individually and cosmically in eternity, is H. D.'s occult version of Eliot's Christian "still point of the turning world." In fact, the conclusion of **Helen in Egypt** deserves to be set beside such exalted moments in poems of old age as Eliot's in the *Quartets*, when "the fire and the rose are one."[2] Or Frost's arrival in "Directive" back at the spring-source which is his watering place ("Drink and be whole again").[3] Or Williams' declaration through his dead "Sparrow": "This was I, / a sparrow. I did my best; / farewell."[4] Or Pound's conclusion to *The Cantos*: "Do not move. / Let the wind speak. / That is Paradise"; or his version of Herakles' expiring words:[5]

> what
>
> SPLENDOUR,
>
> IT ALL COHERES.

Different in tone and perspective as these moments are, the reader either is or is not already there with the poet. By this point, in the particular poem and in the evolution of the poet's life's work, evocation has become invocation; image and symbol, bare statement. Further demonstration is out of the question.

Where Frost's final sense of life remained skeptical and Williams' naturalistic, H. D.'s was like Eliot's religious, and like Pound's heterodoxly so. No resumé or excerpting of passages can indicate how subtly the images and leitmotifs of **Helen in Egypt** are woven into the design. Some reviewers found the prose passages distracting intrusions among the lyrics, but H. D. wanted, like the other poets I have cited, a counterpoint of lyric expression and reflective commentary. In identification with the mother-goddess, assimilating Greek and Egyptian, Christian and gnostic wisdom, H. D. came to read the scribble of her life as hieroglyph. Nothing need be forgotten; nothing could be denied; everything was caught up in the resolution.

The summons of Thetis the sea-mother which closes Part I, "Helen—come home," and initiates a refrain that echoes throughout the poem, receives a gloss in her notebook entry: "We say (old-fashioned people used to say) when someone dies, he or she has *gone home*. I was looking for home, I think. But a sort of heaven-is-my-home. . . ." The recovery of the human mother as goddess, the discovery of the mother in herself and herself in the mother constituted "heaven-is-my-home." The coda which succeeds the final lyric concludes the poem with a return to the mother-sea:

> *But what could Paris know of the sea,*
> *its beat and long reverberation,*
> *its booming and delicate echo,*
>
> *its ripple that spells a charm*
> *on the sand, the rock-lichen,*
> *the sea-moss, the sand,*
>
> *and again and again, the sand;*
> *what does Paris know of the hill and hollow*
> *of billows, the sea-road?*
>
> *what could he know of the ships*
> *from his Idaean home,*
> *the crash and spray of the foam,*
>
> *the wind, the shoal, the broken shale,*
> *the infinite loneliness*
> *when one is never alone?*
>
> *only Achilles could break his heart*
> *and the world for a token,*
> *a memory forgotten.*

The poem links Helen's recovery of the mother with a shift in her relation to the masculine, dramatized by the progression from Paris as sexual lover to Achilles as filial-fraternal partner, and the shift signals a re-imagining of woman's unhappy lot, which has been the theme of H. D.'s fiction and verse. As we know, Richard Aldington's succeeding Pound as "initiator" and lover ended in marriage in 1913, and the rupture of the marriage in the years during and immediately after the war set the course of her life, and of her relations with men.

But all along she sought the reconciliation that would heal the psychic wounds. Despite the pain she was introduced with Aldington from time to time during the twenties. Her correspondence with John Cournos, a member of their London circle, shows her intense concern about Aldington before, during, and after the separation. As late as February, 1929, she wanted to scotch any rumor Cournos had heard of a "final quarrel" with Aldington, and in July she sent Cournos this excited word:

> . . . without any intervention R. wrote me and I have been in close touch with him ever since. . . . We saw one another much in Paris and write constantly. We are very, very close to one another intellectually and spiritually. There may be some definite separation later, but if there is, it will be because of FRIENDLINESS and nothing else. There is no question of R. and self ever becoming in any way 'intimate' again and that is why this other relationship is so exquisite and sustaining.[6]

In fact, as she might well have known, she was never to reach "this other relationship"—intellectual and spiritual without the compulsions and vulnerabilities of the physical—with Aldington, but even their divorce in 1938 did not break off communications between them. They went their separate, and often stormy, ways; but during the years at Klinik Brunner they were still corresponding, and Dr. Heydt was as curious about Aldington as he was about Pound. But it is clear that after she fell from the innocence of that first love with Pound in the tree into the betrayals and counter-betrayals of sexual relationships, she often asked herself "Why had I ever come down out of that tree?" and sought the sort of "exquisite and sustaining" relationship she could never establish in life.

And so by the time that Achilles succeeds Paris at the end of *Helen,* those male characters have assimilated their initial biographical associations with Aldington and Pound into higher archetypal functions within the design of female consciousness which the poem formulates. H. D. saw the whole succession of initiators, including Dr. Heydt, behind Pound, and she also saw Achilles, as she told her notebook, as the "héros fatale" who had failed her repeatedly—from Pound and Aldington down to the "Lord Howell" of the unpublished World War II novels and now Heydt at the Klinik. And yet since the "héros fatale" held the key to her self-fulfillment, she must dream of Helen marrying Achilles. But an Achilles who had undergone a sea-change: the Aldington she lost early in her marriage, imagined and possessed once and for all in the "exquisite and sustaining" consanguinity of the mother. The mother gave her the word, and the word was her own name—and Helen's poem. Helen the daughter becomes Helen the mother. Achilles is her "Achilles" now, within the psyche and the poem, and together they consign themselves to the mother-sea in the last words of the poem.

The union of Helen and Achilles, attainable psychologically and imaginatively in the poem as it is not in external circumstance, is therefore a death marriage, as in the "marriage" poems of Emily Dickinson. But, also as with Dickinson, a mythic and mystic marriage within the psyche. And if Dickinson's "love" poetry seems to remain more indirect and inhibited than *Helen in Egypt,* the cause may lie in part in Dickinson's attachment to her stern father: a bonding so strong that it kept her from experience of the mother and allowed her to experience the masculine only as the virgin-daughter—Kore and not Demeter, Diana and not Thetis. H. D.'s Helen would not be daughter to Theseus nor hetaera to Paris; through Thetis she made Achilles her own. Helen Doolittle was the source of Hilda's visionary power over the word, and in her Helen-poem Hilda formulated her hermetic definition.

The scope of that vision also made for another notable difference between *Helen in Egypt* and Dickinson's love poems. Wrenching and exhilarating as they are, Dickinson's love poems remain a collection of individual pieces at cross purposes, recording ambivalences that kept her, almost all the time, the father's virgin-daughter. In the long, tortuous, fragmented history of women writing about their womanhood, the supreme distinction of *Helen in Egypt,* with all its idiosyncrasies, is that it transforms the male epic into the woman's lyric sustained at a peak of intensity for an epic's length, and the woman's myth it evolves posits the supremacy of the mother: Helen self-born in Thetis, Hilda self-born in Helen.

Notes

1. *End to Torment: A Memoir of Ezra Pound, with the Poems from "Hilda's Book" by Ezra Pound* (New York: New Directions, 1979), p. 11.

2. *Collected Poems 1909-1962* (New York: Harcourt, Brace & World, 1963), pp. 177, 209.

3. *The Poetry of Robert Frost*, ed. Edward Connery Latham (New York: Holt, Rinehart & Winston, 1969), p. 379.

4. *Pictures from Breughel and Other Poems* (New York: New Directions, 1962), p. 132.

5. *The Cantos* (New York: New Directions, 1972), p. 803; *Women of Trachis* (New York: New Directions, 1957), pp. 49-50.

6. H. D.'s letters to Cournos are at the Houghton Library, Harvard; the journal quotations, cited earlier, come from *Compassionate Friendship* in the Beinecke Library, Yale.

FURTHER READING

Bibliography

Boughn, Michael. *H. D.: A Bibliography, 1905-1990.* Charlottesville: Bibliographical Society of the University of Virginia, 1993, 229 p.

Essential primary and secondary bibliography.

Biography

Guest, Barbara. *Herself Defined: The Poet H. D. and Her World.* Garden City, N.Y.: Doubleday, 1984, 360 p.

Seeks to define the enigmatic life and work of H. D., providing a view into her lifelong search for self.

Criticism

Buck, Claire. *H. D. and Freud: Bisexuality and a Feminine Discourse.* New York: Harvester Wheatsheaf, 1991, 195 p.

Thematic study of the links between sexuality and language in H. D.'s works.

Burnett, Gary. *H. D. Between Image and Epic: The Mysteries of Her Poetics.* Ann Arbor, Mich.: UMI Research Press, 1990, 198 p.

Examines the poetry H. D. wrote between the World Wars.

Contemporary Literature 10, no. 4 (autumn 1969).

Special issue devoted to H. D.'s works.

DiPace Fritz, Angela. *Thought and Vision: A Critical Reading of H. D.'s Poetry.* Washington, D.C.: Catholic University of America Press, 1988, 231 p.

Full-length critical study of H. D.'s poetry.

DuPlessis, Rachel Blau. "Romantic Thralldom in H. D." *Contemporary Literature* 20, no. 2 (spring 1979): 178-203.

Explores the issue of submissiveness in romantic relationships as portrayed in H. D.'s prose and poetry.

——. *H. D.: The Career of That Struggle.* Bloomington: Indiana University Press, 1986, 168 p.

Overview of H. D.'s literary career written from a feminist perspective.

Edmunds, Susan. "'I Read the Writing When He Seized My Throat': Hysteria and Revolution in H. D.'s *Helen in Egypt.*" *Contemporary Literature* 32, no. 4 (winter 1991): 471-95.

Examines H. D.'s thematic treatment of repressed memories in Helen in Egypt, *concluding that the work's "interest for feminists lies in H. D.'s ability to render the acute tension between her strongly articulated desire to reform the patriarchal family and her resilient nostalgia for it, with complexity and force."*

Freibert, L. M. "From Semblance to Selfhood: The Evolution of Woman in H. D. Neo-Epic *Helen in Egypt.*" *Arizona Quarterly* 36, no. 2 (summer 1980): 165-75.

Argues that Helen in Egypt *is "the epic of woman evolving from the traditional passive image into the contemporary active person."*

——. "Creating a Women's Mythology: H. D.'s *Helen in Egypt.*" *Women's Studies* 5, no. 1 (1977): 163-97.

Discusses Helen in Egypt *as an "epic aimed at revising both mythology and the concept of woman's selfhood."*

Friedman, Susan Stanford. *Psyche Reborn: The Emergence of H. D.* Bloomington: Indiana University Press, 1981, 332 p.

Explores H. D.'s involvement in psychoanalysis and esoteric religions.

——. "'Remembering Shakespeare Always, but Remembering Him Differently': H. D.'s *By Avon River.*" *Sagetrieb* 2, no. 2 (summer-fall 1983): 45-70.

Maintains that By Avon River *"deserves to be better known not only for its poetic achievement and what it reveals about H. D.'s development, but also for its fascinating revelation of the process by which a woman poet transforms the man many consider the greatest English writer of all times from a male threat into a male ally."*

——. *Penelope's Web: Gender, Modernity, H. D.'s Fiction.* Cambridge, Mass.: Cambridge University Press, 1990, 451 p.

Analyzes H. D.'s published and unpublished prose works.

——. and Rachel Blau DuPlessis, eds. *Signets: Reading H. D.* Madison: University of Wisconsin Press, 1990, 489 p.

Collection of critical essays.

Hollenberg, Donna Krolik. *H. D.: The Poetics of Childbirth and Creativity.* Boston: Northeastern University Press, 1991, 285 p.

Investigates the relationship between H. D.'s maternal experiences and the development of her poetic vision.

King, Michael, ed. *H. D.: Woman and Poet.* Orono, Maine: National Poetry Foundation, 1986, 522 p.

Collection of critical essays from several prominent critics.

Kloepfer, Deborah Kelly. *The Unspeakable Mother: Forbidden Discourse in Jean Rhys and H. D.* Ithaca, N.Y.: Cornell University Press, 1989, 191 p.

Argues against Freudian theories concerning mother-child relations through an examination of the mother-daughter dyad in the works of Jean Rhys and H. D.

Newlin, Margaret. "'Unhelpful Hymen!: Marianne Moore and Hilda Doolittle." *Essays in Criticism* 27, no. 3 (July 1977): 216-30.

Compares the views of Moore and H. D. on "the special problem of marriage for artistic and intellectual women."

Ostriker, Alicia. "The Poet as Heroine: Learning to Read H. D." In *Writing Like a Woman*, pp. 7-41. Ann Arbor: University of Michigan Press, 1983.

Describes H. D. as a visionary poet and outlines three main phases in her career.

Quinn, Vincent. *Hilda Doolittle (H. D.).* New York: Twayne, 1967, 160 p.

Critical overview including a chronology of H. D.'s life and selected primary and secondary bibliographies.

Robinson, Janice S. *H. D.: The Life and Work of an American Poet.* Boston, Mass.: Houghton Mifflin, 1982, 490 p.

Biographical and critical study.

OTHER SOURCES FROM GALE:

Additional coverage of H. D.'s life and career is contained in the following sources published by the Gale Group: *American Writers Supplement,* Vol. 1; *Contemporary Authors,* Vols. 97-100; *Contemporary Authors New Revision Series,* Vol. 35; *Contemporary Literary Criticism,* Vols. 3, 8, 14, 31, 34, 73; *Dictionary of Literary Biography,* Vols. 4, 45; *DISCovering Authors; DISCovering Authors: Canadian Edition; DISCovering Authors Modules: Most-studied Authors* and *Poets; Encyclopedia of World Literature in the 20th Century,* Ed. 3; *Feminist Writers; Gay & Lesbian Literature,* Ed. 1; *Literary Movements for Students,* Vol. 2; *Literature Resource Center; Major 20th-Century Writers,* Eds. 1, 2; *Modern American Women Writers; Poetry Criticism,* Vol. 5; *Poetry for Students,* Vol. 6; *Reference Guide to American Literature,* Ed. 4; and *World Literature Criticism.*

MARGUERITE DURAS

(1914 - 1996)

(Born Marguerite Donnadieu) French novelist, playwright, screenwriter, short story writer, and essayist.

Duras was one of France's most important and most prolific writers in the twentieth century. During her long writing career, she produced a large number of texts in a wide variety of genres. She is best known for her prize-winning autobiographical novel *L'amant* (1984) and the screenplay for Alan Resnais's 1959 film *Hiroshima mon amour*.

BIOGRAPHICAL INFORMATION

Duras was born Marguerite Donnadieu on April 4, 1914, in a small town near Saigon, French Indochina (now Vietnam). Her parents, Henri Donnadieu and Marie Legrand Donnadieu, were teachers, originally from the northern part of France. Although her father's death in 1918 and her mother's purchase of worthless land from the corrupt colonial government left the family in financial distress, Duras nonetheless was able to attend the Lycée de Saigon where she studied both French and Vietnamese. In 1931, she left Indochina to study at the Sorbonne, where she completed a degree in law and political science four years later. From 1935 to 1941 Duras worked as a secretary for the Colonial Ministry, where she met the author Robert Antelme. They married in

1939; both were active members of the Communist Party. During World War II, Antelme was imprisoned for a year in a German concentration camp while Duras worked with the French Resistance and began writing fiction. She published her first novel, *Les impudents,* in 1943. When Antelme was released after the war, Duras nursed him back to health although the couple had already agreed to divorce. She later married Dionys Mascolo, a philosopher and fellow Communist, with whom she had a son, Jean. In 1950, Duras and a number of other French intellectuals were expelled from the Communist Party. In 1984, while recovering from alcoholism in a treatment center, she produced *L'amant,* her most celebrated and most commercially successful effort. Her lifelong battle with alcoholism led to serious health problems which resulted in her death on March 3, 1996.

MAJOR WORKS

Duras's writing career spanned more than four decades during which she produced more than seventy novels, plays, screenplays, and adaptations. Her experiences in life often surfaced in her fiction: her novel *Un Barrage contre le Pacifique* (1950; *The Sea Wall*) contains one of many representations of her mother's struggle against the corrupt colonial government in Indochina; *La Douleur* (1985; *The War*) includes a narrator who nurses her husband back to health after his release from a prisoner-of-war camp; and both *Hiroshima mon amour* and *Moderato Cantabile* (1958), among others, feature characters plagued by the alcoholism that destroyed Duras's own health. Many of her early works are based on her experiences in French Indochina and reflect her fascination with colonial culture and her concern with issues of social justice. Her novels from the 1950s, such as *Le marin de Gibraltar* (1952; *The Sailor from Gibraltar*) and *Les petits chevaux de Tarquinia* (1953; *The Little Horses of Tarquinia*), are less linear and more ironic, and feature fewer, more individual, characters. The works she produced in the 1960s, including *Le ravissement de Lol V. Stein* (1964; *The Ravishing of Lol V. Stein*) and *Le vice-consul* (1966; *The Vice-Consul*), employ minimalist techniques and are often referred to as antinovels. The eclectic group of texts she wrote during the 1980s is characterized by isolation and the self-destruction associated with the inability to love. These works include *La maladie de la mort* (1982; *The Malady of Death*) and *Emily L.* (1987). Also during this period, Duras produced her most celebrated work at the age of seventy. *L'Amant* was awarded the prestigious Prix Goncourt in 1984, and Barbara Bray's English translation of the work, *The Lover*, won the 1986 Ritz Paris Hemingway Award. The work recalls Duras's experiences as a child in Indochina and her relationships with her domineering mother, her lazy and philandering older brother, and her beloved younger brother.

In addition to her novels and short stories, Duras wrote a number of plays in the late 1950s and 1960s, among them the murder mystery *Les viaducs de la Seine-et-Oise* (1959; *The Viaducts of Seine and Oise*) and *Des journées entières dans les arbres* (1968; *Whole Days in the Trees*), an adaptation of the title piece from her 1954 short story collection. During this time, Duras established an international reputation as a screenwriter with her first screenplay, *Hiroshima mon amour*. Her other original screenplays include *Nathalie Granger* (1972) and *Le camion* (1977). Most of her other films were adaptations of her plays and novels, such as *Moderato cantabile* (1964), based on her 1958 novel, and *India Song* (1974), based on her play of the same name.

CRITICAL RECEPTION

Although Duras's work was critically acclaimed, it was considered inaccessible to the general public until the appearance of her enormously popular autobiographical novel *L'Amant*, which renewed overall interest in her career.

While the work won the 1984 Prix Goncourt, Duras believed she should have won the award in 1950 for *Un Barrage contre le Pacifique*. As a woman and a dissident Communist, she considered herself the victim of both sexism and political discrimination. Her novels from the 1950s, more minimalist than her earlier work, were often categorized by critics as part of the *Nouveau Roman* school associated with Alain Robbe-Grillet. Duras, however, rejected the label and claimed she had no affiliation with the movement. She did, however, acknowledge an affinity with literary surrealism, which privileged poetry as the highest form of writing. Several critics have noted that Duras often blurred the distinction between prose and poetry in her work, particularly in her later writing.

Duras's position as a feminist is ambiguous. Although she espoused feminist views in interviews and in articles for *Sorcières,* a French periodical, she was not consistently active in the French feminist movement nor were her representations of women consistently progressive. She has, nonetheless, been embraced by some feminist critics who believe she created a space for the female desiring subject, as opposed to the female object of male desire. However, she has been rejected by other feminist scholars who contend that her work reinforces traditional gender roles and that her advocacy of a specifically feminine writing style is essentialist. Sharon A. Willis acknowledges that Duras's essentialist approach may account for her "antagonistic stance" to some feminist theory. Willis maintains, however, that Duras's "interest for and influence upon overtly feminist literary, critical, and theoretical enterprises is powerful."

PRINCIPAL WORKS

Les impudents (novel) 1943

La vie tranquille (novel) 1944

Un barrage contre le Pacifique [*The Sea Wall*] (novel) 1950

Le marin de Gibraltar [*The Sailor from Gibraltar*] (novel) 1952

Les petits chevaux de Tarquinia [*The Little Horses of Tarquinia*] (novel) 1953

Des journées entières dans les arbres [*Whole Days in the Trees and Other Stories*] (short stories) 1954

Le Square [*The Square*] (novel) 1955

Moderato cantabile (novel) 1958

Hiroshima mon amour (screenplay) 1959

Les viaducs de la Seine-et-Oise [*The Viaducts of Seine and Oise*] (play) 1959

Dix heures et demie du soir en été [*Ten-Thirty on a Summer Night*] (novel) 1960

Une aussi longue absence [with Gérard Jarlot] (screenplay) 1961

L'après-midi de Monsieur Andesmas [*The Afternoon of Monsieur Andesmas*] (novel) 1962

Moderato cantabile (screenplay) 1964

Le ravissement de Lol V. Stein [*The Ravishing of Lol V. Stein*] (novel) 1964

Théâtre I: Les eaux et forêts; Le square; La musica [*The Rivers in the Forests; The Square*] (plays) 1965

La musica (screenplay) 1966

Le vice-consul [*The Vice-Consul*] (novel) 1966

L'amante anglaise (novel) 1967

L'amante anglaise (play) 1968

Théâtre II: Suzanna Andler; Des journées entières dans les arbres; "Yes," peut-être; Le shaga; Un homme est venu me voir [*Suzanna Andler; Whole Days in the Trees*] (plays) 1968

Détruire, dit-elle [*Destroy, She Said*] (novel) 1969

Abahn Sabana David (novel) 1970

L'amour (novel) 1971

Jaune le soleil (screenplay) 1971

Nathalie Granger (screenplay) 1972

India Song (screenplay) 1973

Les parleuses [*Woman to Woman*] (interviews) 1974

Baxter, Vera Baxter (screenplay) 1976

Son nom de Venise dans Calcutta désert (screenplay) 1976

Des journées entières dans les arbres (screenplay) 1976

Le camion (screenplay) 1977

L'eden cinéma (play) 1977

Le navire night (screenplay) 1978

Aurélia Steiner, dite Aurélia Melbourne (screenplay) 1979

Aurélia Steiner, dite Aurélia Vancouver (screenplay) 1979

Césarée (screenplay) 1979

Les mains négatives (screenplay) 1979

L'homme assis dans le couloir [*The Seated Man in the Passage*] (novel) 1980

Agatha (novel) 1981

Agatha ou les lectures illimitées (screenplay) 1981

L'homme Atlantique (screenplay) 1981

Outside (essays) 1981

Dialogue de Rome (screenplay) 1982

L'homme Atlantique (novel) 1982

La maladie de la mort [*The Malady of Death*] (novel) 1982

L'amant [*The Lover*] (novel) 1984

La douleur [*The War: A Memoir*] (novel) 1985

Les enfants (screenplay) 1985

Les yeux bleus, cheveux noirs [*Blue Eyes, Black Hair*] (novel) 1986

Emily L. (novel) 1987

Le vie materielle [*Practicalities: Marguerite Duras Speaks to Jérôme Beaujour*] (conversations) 1987

La pluie d'été [*Summer Rain*] (novel) 1990

L'Amant de la Chine du nord [*The North China Lover*] (novel) 1991

Le monde exterieur (essays) 1993

C'est tout [*That's All*] (essays) 1995

La Mer écrite (essays) 1996

PRIMARY SOURCES

MARGUERITE DURAS AND ALICE A. JARDINE (INTERVIEW DATE 1988)

SOURCE: Duras, Marguerite, and Alice A. Jardine. "Marguerite Duras," translated by Katherine Ann Jensen. In *Shifting Scenes: Interviews on Women, Writing, and Politics in Post-68 France*, edited by Alice A. Jardine and Anne M. Menke, pp. 71-8. New York: Columbia University Press, 1991.

In the following interview, Duras discusses her ideas on writing as a woman and on misogyny in both France and America.

[*Jardine*]: *Question 1: What does it mean to you to write at the end of the twentieth century?*

[Duras:]—Writing . . . I've never asked myself to be aware of what time period I was living in. I have asked myself this question in relation to my child and his future activities, or in wondering what would become of the working class—you see, in relation to political considerations or issues. But not as concerns writing. I believe writing is beyond all . . . contingency.

Question 2: Is it valid/of value to write as a woman, and is it part of your writing today?

—I have several opinions about that, several things to say. Perhaps I should give a personal example. I don't have any major problems anymore in terms of the reception of my books, but the way men in society respond to me hasn't changed.

—That hasn't changed at all?

—No, each time I see critics who are . . . Misogyny is still at the forefront.

—Only in France or . . .

—I haven't read the foreign papers. **The Lover,** you know, has been translated in twenty-nine countries. There have been thousands and millions of copies sold. I don't think that in America there's been as much [misogyny] . . . because a lot of women write articles [on my work]. I don't think there's been any misogyny, strictly speaking, aimed at me in America.

—I have the same impression.

—No, actually, there is someone at the *New York Times* who doesn't like me at all, because I was once rather nasty to him. It was after a showing of **India Song**. The auditorium was full, I remember that, and at the end the students were really pleased and gave me a big ovation. The audience was asked to speak; I was there to answer. So this guy got up, you know, from the *Times*, very classic, old. He began, "Madame Duras, I really got bored with your . . ."

—He said that?! in public?

—Yes, it was a public thing. So I said: "Listen, I'm really sorry, but it's hardly my fault. There must be something wrong with you." He just looked at me. (Usually this works well.) "Please excuse me, but I can't do anything for you." It was really terrible. Since then, people tell me, "I can't invite you anymore because he'll never forgive you." It doesn't matter to me. I'm very happy.

—I have the impression that misogyny, in the most classic sense of the term, exists in France much more than in the United States. Even if it's on the tip of American men's tongues or the tip of their pens, they stop themselves now because there's been so much . . . They swallow their words because they know what will happen afterward if they don't; whereas here in France, it seems to me that they get away with it. No one says anything. And that's why, for me, to write as a woman in France begins to have a very different meaning. . . .

—But I have safety valves. That is, from time to time, I write articles about critical theory, and that scares the critics.

—I can imagine.

—But . . . it scares women too. It has to do with *écriture féminine*. There are a lot of women who align themselves with men. Recently, a guy did a whole page in a journal about me to say that I don't exist, that I'm . . . I don't remember what. So in that instance, I said that he was the victim of great pain at the thought of my existence. And I can't do anything about that.

—It's not worth the energy.

—No. It's not a question of energy. It's just that in France, if you don't pay attention, you can get eaten up.

—As a woman or as a writer generally?

—As a woman writer. There are two potential attacks: those from homosexuals and those from heteros.

—And they're different?

—At first, no; but in the end they each think that they do such different things, although it's not true at all. They do the same things. It's about jealousy, envy . . . a desire to supplant women. It's a strange phenomenon. I write quite a lot about homosexuality . . . because I live with a man who's homosexual . . . as everyone knows . . . but I write outside all polemic. You see, **Blue Eyes, Black Hair** is outside any polemic. Homosexuals are often not interested in their experiences, they think they've said everything there is to say. That's a limitation. They're not interested in knowing what a woman can get from that experience. What interests them is knowing what people think about homosexuality, whether you're for or against it, that's all.

—You have been describing men's reactions to your work as a woman writer. I too have been intrigued by the question of how men respond to woman and women. My latest book, Men in Feminism,[1] *coedited with Paul Smith, is a collection of articles addressing the complicated relationship men have to feminism, and women have to feminist men. My book* Gynesis[2] *intervenes in this debate by examining how the metaphor of woman operates in several key French texts by men from the last twenty-odd years, for example, those by Blanchot, Deleuze, Derrida, and Lacan.*

—You know, even before those writers, there was Beauvoir. She didn't change women's way of thinking. Nor did Sartre, for that matter. He didn't change anything at all. Is *Gynesis* coming out in France?

—*Yes. One of the interesting problems that has come up with my translator is how to find an expression for the term "man writer." In the United States, you see, we're trying to deuniversalize: we say woman writer. We try to give terms genders. But in French, it doesn't work at all. If my translator uses "man writer," everyone will say it's horrible.*

—It's too late.

—*Yes, it's too late. But I can't just put the gender of the writer in the footnotes either. When I say "writer," I mean "man writer" because that's how the universal returns.*

—Because "writer" historically means male, is that it?

—*Yes, the universal.*

—But even when they were making distinctions between men and women writers twenty-five years ago, in newspaper headlines, there were no women writers or men writers. There were "novels by women," "novels by men," and books by women or books by men. But that was always a minor distinction, always in a footnote.

—*It's odd, in French you can get woman out of the universal, but not man (you can say woman writer [femme écrivain] but not man writer [homme écrivain]).*

Question 3: Many women writing today find themselves, for the first time in history, at the center of such institutions as the university or psychoanalysis. In your opinion, will this new placement of women help them to enter the twentieth-century canon, and if so will they be at the heart of this corpus or (still) in the footnotes?

—I think that the women who can get beyond the feeling of having to correct history will save a lot of time.

—*Please explain.*

—I think that the women who are correcting history, who are trying to correct the injustice of which they're victims, of which they always were and still are victims—because nothing's changed, we have to really get that: in men's heads everything's still the same. . . .

—*You really think so?*

—I'm sure, yes. The women who are trying to correct man's nature, or what has become his nature—call it whatever you want—they're wasting their time.

—*What you're saying is really depressing.*

—I think that if a woman is free, alone, she will go ahead that way, without barriers; that is how I think she'll create fruitful work.

—*All alone?*

—Yes. I don't care about men. I've given up on them, personally. It's not a question of age, it's a question of intellectuality, if you like, of one's mental attitude. I've given up on trying to . . . to put them on a logical track. Completely given up.

—*It's true that in the United States, after so many years, especially in the university, after so much effort to change what and how we read, what and how we interpret, etc., the new generations may be feeling a sort of exhaustion and boredom with that struggle.*

—That's what I think.

—*Yes, but it's really complicated . . . this desire not to be always criticizing, always in negation.*

—Yes, it's an impasse.

—*I have always believed in the importance of this struggle, but I recognize more and more why young women can say that the struggle isn't for them.*

—I'm certainly not leading it.

—*But you did lead it at a certain period, didn't you?*

—No. Maybe you're thinking about a woman from the women's movement who interviewed me.[3] I don't remember anymore. I said there was a women's writing, didn't I?

—*Yes.*

—I don't think so anymore. From the position I have today, a definitive one, the most important writer from the standpoint of a women's writing is Woolf. It's not Beauvoir.

—*Yes, but for me, there's more of a schizophrenia to it, because when I think of my intellectual, institutional, political life, Beauvoir is the one who plays the part of the phantasmatic mother . . . I must do everything, read everything, see everything . . . but in my desire for writing, it's Woolf. They go together.*

—Yes, exactly. It's not all of Woolf. *A Room of One's Own* is the Bible.

—*And in my imaginary, Marguerite Duras, you are there with Woolf.*

—Yes, well, still. You know, when I was young, I was very free. I was part of the Resistance during the Algerian War. I took a lot of risks, I risked . . .

even with Algeria, I ran the risk of being imprisoned. Maybe it's in that sense that I'm still free.

—*That is, because you've already taken risks.*

—Because I haven't written on women. Or very little. I see women as having pulled themselves through. That is, they've taken the biggest step. They're on the other side now. All the successful books today are by women, the important films are by women. The difference is fabulous.

—*So perhaps, according to you, we have to turn away somewhat from the reactive struggle and move instead toward creativity.*

—Yes, that's what I think.

—*Do you think this is going to happen by itself? I'd like to believe it, but I'm not sure.*

—I believe that a book like **The Lover**—which was a slap in the face for everyone, for men—is a great leap forward for women, which is much more important. For a woman to claim international attention makes men sick. It just makes them sick.

—*I didn't see it like that from the United States.*

—That's how it was. I don't know how it was for Americans because I got an important American prize . . . and six Americans voted for me. You see, there were 700 voters, then 500, then 300, and finally 70 and then less—you know at different stages of the competition. In the end, there were nine voters. The six Americans all voted for me. The three Frenchmen (France has never had a prize in America) all voted *against* me.

—*You're kidding?*

—Some papers, and probably they were right . . . said that they didn't want a writer from the Left to have the first American prize. But that's not it. It's because I was a *woman* writer. Of course, we must recognize that those three people were on the Right. I think that women on the Left are less alienated; whereas on the Right, so many women with government responsibilities are just followers. It's striking how visible that is.

Question 4: Today we are seeing women produce literary, philosophical, and psychoanalytical theory of recognized importance, and parallel to this, we are seeing a new fluidity in the borderlines among disciplines and genres of writing. Will this parallelism lead only to women being welcomed alongside men, or to a definitive blurring of these categories?

—I don't know, it's dangerous. Because men's criteria have been tested a long time, and men manipulate them astutely and diplomatically. Men aren't politicians, they're diplomats, and that's a degree lower.

Question 5: Given the problematic and the politics of the categories of the canon, and given the questions we've been dealing with here, do you think your oeuvre will be included in the twentieth-century canon, and if so, how will it be presented? In your opinion, what will be the content of the canon?

—*This is an indiscreet question. . . .*

—No it isn't. I don't know what it will be, I don't know, how can I say this, who will be deciding. The only thing that reassures me is that, now, I've become a little bit of an international phenomenon—even a pretty big one. And what France won't do, other countries will. So I'm safe. But those are the terms that I have to use. I'm not safe in France. I'm still very threatened.

—*You think so really?*

—Yes, I'm sure, I know, I'm sure.

—*For me though, coming from the outside, that's incredible, incomprehensible even.*

—But they never attacked Simone de Beauvoir.

—*What do you mean?*

—They never attack Simone de Beauvoir. They never attack Sarraute. But in my case, I've been involved in men's things. First, I was involved in politics. I was in the Communist Party. I did things that are considered in bad taste for a woman. That's the line England took for a long time. In England, they said that Marguerite Duras could never be a novelist because she was too political. Now, my literary oeuvre, my literary work has never gotten mixed up with politics. It never moves to rhetoric. Never. Even something like **The Sea Wall** remains a story. And that's what has saved me. There's not a term, not a trace of dialectic in my fiction. Well, there might be some in **The Square,** perhaps, a kind of theory of needs from Marx that was figured in the little girl, the maid who did everything, who was good for everything, but that was the only time, I think.

—*But still, your book **Les Parleuses** has come out from Nebraska press with a great deal of success.*

—How was that translated?

—**Woman to Woman.**

—Isn't that a little outmoded now, **Les Parleuses?**

—*Not in the United States. Here maybe. No, not even here; people recognize that there are really beautiful things in it.*

—The speaking women, that is?

—*Yes, the image of two women engaged in speaking to each other.*

—You know, when I gave that title to my publisher, he was afraid it would have a negative effect. But I said I wanted it because others would say that women just gossip.

—*Right. . . .*

Question 6: And a last question just for you: we are asking you these questions about the future destiny of the work of contemporary women, when, in fact, your work seems to have been canonized already. Actually, you are one of the few people who has been able not only to see her work emerge from an unfair obscurity into the limelight but who has seen it attain worldwide recognition. How has becoming a celebrity influenced a vision that was intentionally critical and other?

—You know, **The Lover** came late in my life. And even its fame wasn't something new for me. I had already had two things make it on the worldwide scene, and so I was used to that phenomenon—of something operating totally independently of you. It happens like an epiphenomenon, it takes place in inaccessible regions. You can't know why a book works, when it works that well. First, it was **Hiroshima, mon amour,**[4] which was seen all over the world. And then I had **Moderato cantabile,** which must have had the same effect as **The Lover,** for it was translated everywhere. Such a small book that was a worldwide hit, it's strange. Well, I was no young girl in the face of those events. As for the end of your question, "a vision that was intentionally critical and other"—that doesn't have anything to do with it. I understand the implication in your question that being famous somehow intimidates, inhibits. No, no, on the contrary. . . .

—*But there's a mythology that says that being famous is a defeat in mass culture.*

—Yes, I know that. . . . That reminds me of what Robbe-Grillet told me one day. He said, "When you and I have sold 500,000 copies, that will mean we don't have anything else to say." Well, so I don't have anything else to say—and he has another book.

Notes

1. *Men in Feminism* (New York: Methuen, 1987).

2. *Gynesis: Configurations of Woman and Modernity* (Ithaca: Cornell University Press, 1985).

3. Duras is referring to Xavière Gauthier's interview with her, published as *Les Parleuses.*

4. Screenplay and dialogue by Marguerite Duras, directed by Alain Resnais.

GENERAL COMMENTARY

TRISTA SELOUS (ESSAY DATE 1988)

SOURCE: Selous, Trista. "Order, Chaos and Subversive Details." In *The Other Woman: Feminism and Femininity in the Work of Marguerite Duras,* pp. 233-52. New Haven: Yale University Press, 1988.

In the following essay, Selous claims that Duras's writing provides a space for the feminine desiring subject as opposed to the stereotypical representation of woman as the object of male desire.

Although Duras's novels are works of fiction, in both the structural place they give to women, and the way in which they portray 'what women want', they resemble the writings of theorists using the Lacanian theoretical framework to look at women's sexuality such as, in addition to Lacan himself, Montrelay, Marini, Irigaray, Lemoine-Luccioni, and many more. In the work of these writers, most of whom are women, women's desire, sexuality and relation to language are seen as difficult or impossible to define. Apart from Irigaray, the Lacanian women say little about their own way of writing, but one assumes they have adopted what is in their own terms the masculine position. Certainly they write about women as being different, as objects of investigation. Marini says that Duras writes from 'a place which is radically other, that of the feminine',[1] but does not gender her own place of departure. Irigaray writes of the 'other language'[2] which has yet to emerge and which, according to Marini, can now only manifest itself as silence, whilst Lemoine-Luccioni, Montrelay and Lacan all see 'the feminine' as excluded from 'the nature of things which is the nature of words', although both women allow their sisters access to a masculine Symbolic order via secondary psychic formations, and only Lacan is adamant that Woman does not know what she is talking about.

With the exception of Irigaray, all these writers see women in the context of heterosexual relations as objects of the desire of the male subject, or else in relation to their mothers. It is not surprising that their work should be linked with that of Duras, since the underlying assumptions and range of concerns of the latter are similar. Certainly this is true in her writing following and including **Moderato cantabile,** which is that which is most often discussed in the context of psychoanalysis. In these later novels Duras writes about 'beings of desire and fear'[3] portrayed as figures in the context of familial or (hetero) sexual relations, but other social relations between them are, if mentioned, not explored. Feminist claims for both Duras's writing and that of Lacanian psychoanalysis are that they acknowledge the existence of and explore (where possible) the regions of 'unrepresentable' femininity, showing up masculinist domination for what it is: the suppression of difference and denial of the Other. The idea is that, whether or not 'femininity', or 'women's desire' is constructed through the workings of 'feminine drives' or as the result of the respective positions of women and men in relation to desire (positions which are at present inevitably fixed according to gender), women's desire has always been denied expression. The way to remedy this situation is then seen as being to demonstrate that such is the case so that women and men will realise a) that the feminine position exists and b) that women's desire as it springs from that position, which is the position of object of desire, has never been recognised. This, runs the argument, is what Duras's writing does:

> The spaces built into the very heart of the language-inheritance through Marguerite Duras's writing practice define the place in which a new signifier can arise. Out of this we can suggest the following hypothesis: the subject—whether it be masculine or feminine—is no longer born simply out of the binary play of a single signifier qualified by plus and minus, the phallus, but out of the space made by the play between two different signifiers.[4]

Venet in her article suggests similarly:

> M Duras's writing could be defined as feminine writing which is disconcerting because it does not conform to logical masculine discourse; ambiguous in that it inevitably has recourse to the masculine language of society to speak the feminine; and creative in that it says something else, beyond literal meaning . . .[5]

As I have indicated above, whilst I think that the view that women have a specific 'feminine' relation to language grounded in a psychic organisation produced by 'feminine drives' has a rather shaky theoretical basis, I do think it is valid to describe Duras's writing as giving a place to femininity, where this is defined as a position within a relation of (sexual) desire and not as an effect of fixed meanings attached to anatomical

makeup. And as I have tried to show, some of the women she portrays in this position are constructed as the subjects of more or less unutterable, but nevertheless present, desires. But having said this, I cannot agree with the feminist argument that has been put forward in relation to Duras's work for it relies on the assumption that representations of woman-as-object-of-desire usually represent the woman as being without desire herself. However, I would argue that, on the contrary, it is basic to the construction of a woman as object of desire that she be seen also as subject of desire. The important factor which either facilitates or precludes her construction into the position of object of desire is the kind of desire of which she is seen as being the subject.

As I have discussed above in relation to fetishism, representations of women as objects of desire do also portray them as subjects of desire as well. Duras herself shows a clear understanding of this in her portrayal of herself as an object of desire in **L'Amant:** 'It wasn't a question of attracting desire. It was present in she who aroused it, or it did not exist.'[6] And the desire of 'she who aroused it' is principally narcissistic, constructing her always as an object for someone else: 'As I want to appear, so I appear. Beautiful too, if that's what people want me to be, or pretty; pretty, for example, for the family, for the family, no more, I can become everything that people want from me. And believe in it . . .'[7]

It is intrinsic to the portrayal of the adolescent in **L'Amant** that she should have this powerful narcissism, which manifests itself in the ability to make herself into an object of desire, principally for 'the man from Cholon'.

In representations of a woman as an object of desire, an element of her own sexual desire, either potential or already present, is always built in. Whether it is solely narcissistic, or produced in relation to other (male) subjects, inviting their desire (as Lemoine-Luccioni suggested), the focus is always on this sexual desire, whilst other areas in which the woman's desire might be produced are either excluded or given lesser importance. Generally speaking, representations of women as objects of desire do not show them immersed in their work or artistic creativity: women who are used to advertise cars are never shown driving them, but rather draped over them, narcissistically inviting the gaze of the spectator. The myth and mystery surrounding Marilyn Monroe constructs her not as the fine actress she clearly was, for whom making a film was work, but simply as a 'sexy' woman—vulnerable too, perhaps to reduce the threat her powerful image might otherwise pose. Representations of women as objects of desire construct them as desiring to be desired—by men. Perhaps 'the enigma of Woman', the mysteriousness of the beautiful object, arises out of this narcissism—a part of the woman's desire is always directed towards herself.

The other area in which a woman's desire may traditionally be represented in a positive light is that of the family. However, this area and that of sexual desire are also traditionally mutually exclusive. A mother may be represented as a subject of sexual desire but not, without stigma, in front of the children. By the same token, representations portraying mothers as objects of desire, that is, as inviting the desire of men, are also usually condemnatory of the woman. Perhaps the roots of this mutual exclusivity lie in the child's distress at discovering the existence of the mother's desire as well as in the patriarchal Law which requires that a woman restrict her sexual relations to one man to guarantee his paternity. Whatever its motivations, it is certainly one which Duras's texts uphold.

Beyond the realms of the sexual or the familial, women's desire is often either simply not represented, or else shown as dependent on or subordinate to the two more conventionally recognised forms. Aspects of a woman's personality or behaviour at work are far more often attributed to the repression, sublimation, or deviation of her heterosexual 'sex-drive' than is the case with men, particularly if the woman in question seems more involved with her work than in sexual relationships or with children. In men such a balance is traditionally acceptable and is unlikely to lead to the same level of comment and speculation on their sexuality. Perhaps we owe a debt to psychoanalysis insofar as it indicates that the popular wisdom concerning women can also be extended to men, giving a primacy to the sexual in the psychic workings of individuals of both sexes.

Unfortunately, however, psychoanalytic theory has done little to extend the general recognition of women's desires as they arise in areas other than those of sexuality and the family. Indeed, concepts such as penis-envy or the masculinity complex may be used against a woman who seems too determined to overstep the boundaries traditionally confining her desires. Changes so far made in the ways women are represented, the inroads into areas traditionally reserved for men, such as representations of workers, thinkers, politicians, athletes and other sublimators, are due more to a gradual movement of which psycho-analysis is quite possibly symptomatic, but which it has not necessarily facilitated, that is, the changing position of woman in many societies, including our own.

Seen in this light, the construction of women's desire in Duras's work is quite similar to other, more obviously conventional representations of women. Almost all of Duras's women figures are either mothers or lovers or both and very few of them are portrayed in any other context. The exceptions, the eponymous heroine of **Madame Dodin**, or the servant of **Le Square**, disappear from the later work. And as objects of desire Duras's women are almost clichés: innocence and the awakening of (narcissistic) desire are crystallised in Valérie Andesmas and suggested in the portrayal of the childlike Alissa, perhaps also in Lol V. Stein, who has remained 'unhealthily young'. Certainly the latter has the mysterious quality which is a familiar attribute of the *femme fatale,* coupled with a determination to get what she wants, the exact nature of which is not clear, but which requires the participation of a lover. Anne-Marie Stretter is an example of the rich and gracious lady of leisure who fills her empty life with lovers and has the wisdom of her mature years, a beautiful and mysterious haven of intuitive understanding, whilst Tatiana Karl is the woman whose narcissism is lacking in self-sufficiency, whose sexual desire is too easily visible and comprehensible for her to be enigmatic, and who is portrayed as abject, an 'admirable whore'.

Almost clichés, but not. Duras's women do not have the banal familiarity of the cliché. The reader who accepts the place of the narratee will not be struck with the humdrum familiarity of Anne-Marie Stretter or Valérie. The secret of this lies largely in Duras's style, in the 'blanks' which compel the reader/narratee to participate in the telling of the story by interpreting what seems to be missing and by investing her/his own desire in the figures and in the text as a whole. What Duras has done, and often with consummate skill, is to hone down the scope of her texts so as to allow the maximum power to accrue to the image of the central woman figure. She has eschewed those aspects of realist novels which are productive of 'character', the likes, dislikes, habits, moods or particular ways of speaking of any given figure which differentiates her or him from another. Thus, she does away with all the manifestations of that figure's desires as they exceed the specifically sexual or familial, as well as the ways in which any figure's desires within sexual or family relations manifest themselves in particular and individual ways.

Novels of psychological realism tend to use such devices in an attempt to mirror reality, since the desires of extra-textual human beings are in evidence in all kinds of areas besides the sexual and the familial. Such details construct a particular figure as an individual, distinct in her/his specificity from other figures and from the narratee. However, since such novels also most often portray women in the context of either sexual or family relations, it is possible not to include such details of character without breaking down the basic structure around which many realist texts are built. The structural status of a character does not depend on her/his personal idiosyncrasies.

In Duras's later work the figures are whittled down to a point where they almost lose their capacity to appear as 'beings like us', their desire being constructed entirely in the context of the structural relations around which the text is built, usually a sexual relation. The reader is asked to adopt the position of the narratee and to concentrate all her/his attention on this structural relation, within which the woman is constructed as the object of desire whose own desires manifest themselves just enough in the required area—that of the sexual relation—for her to be produced as a desirable object, and not too much for her to lose her mystery and power. At least this is a balance which I think Duras strikes with the greatest success in the most acclaimed of her novels. There are exceptions, as always, to the format I have just outlined: the early novels of course, the structure of *Le Square*, the role of Maria in *Dix heures et demie du soir en été*, that of Claire Lannes in *L'Amante anglaise*, source of death rather than love, or that of Sabana in *Abahn Sabana David*, where again it is Thanatos rather than Eros who is at work. However, when women figures are portrayed as subjects of desire, Maria or the maid in *Le Square*, their desires are contained within the areas of sexual or family relations.

So Duras's novels give refined and crystallised versions of a particular way of representing women, which is widespread in our culture. This form is the one which constructs an individual image of a woman as a particular instance of Woman, source and object of (men's) desire. The reference points of Duras's work have been discussed by other critics, for example Marini, whose words I shall borrow here:

> [Marguerite Duras] starts, for example, with the stereotyped schemas of romantic, psychological or popular novels—the domain to which they try to restrict women, writers or readers—, stories all ultimately built to the same pattern—adultery, consuming passion, crimes of passion, family duties, elementary conflicts, whose basic givens, unfolding and resolutions are all known in advance.[8]

I think the most obvious intertextual links of Duras's work are those with 'romantic' fiction, which is, as Marini points out, precisely a domain traditionally reserved for women writers and readers. However, I part company with Marini after this, for according to her, 'It is all these models whose messages Marguerite Duras subverts by dislocating them',[9] whereas I would argue on the other hand that what Duras does is precisely the opposite. Rather than dislocate the model, she strips it down to the skeleton, a skeleton which will only permit the flesh to be laid on its bones in a specific way—by the narratee. It is her particular skill that she is then able to draw the reader to take up that position and to concentrate on the process of reconstruction of that which the text only suggests. This she does by her use of very clear, simple and yet evocative language, describing in many cases only the visible, with undisturbed authority and a complete concentration on the matter in hand: the story of desire and/or death. Not much happens in most of Duras's novels, most could be retold as very basic love stories. What gives them their particular quality is that the process of reconstruction is never completed. The crucial element which would make the reader's inference into certainty is constructed as beyond the scope of the text, an irretrievable 'blank.' Duras is not inviting her readers to learn something, to understand 'what happened' and to think about it as they will; she is inviting them to feel something through an act of identification in the place of the narratee. She is inviting them to lend their own desires to flesh out her portrayal of the workings of desire between two (or more) figures.

Herein lies the immediacy and power of Duras's work, arising from the reader's participation in the text. However, I think it is misleading to suggest that by this process the text subverts the models to which it refers. For after and including *Moderato cantabile*, almost all Duras's novels demand that the reader/narratee draw on all the intertextual references to (for example) 'romantic' fiction at her/his disposal, whilst also banishing them from consciousness whilst reading. 'How,' asks Marini, 'can one read the work of Marguerite Duras without creating silence and emptiness at the threshhold of the reading room?'[10] My interpretation of this question would be that in order to get the most out of reading Duras, the reader must temporarily suspend all her/his own preoccupations and identifications which might get in the way of her/his adoption of the place of the narratee. S/he must draw unconsciously on the intertextual references of, say, 'romantic' fiction and other representations of women as objects of men's desire to carry her/him across the 'blanks'.

If **Moderato cantabile,** for example, permitted a reading where it was possible for the reader to 'understand' a precise meaning in what is related and the enigma of Anne's desire were solved, then s/he could compare it with other texts, other representations, in terms of the meanings it produces and how it does so, as s/he was reading, or at least on reaching the end. But the end of **Moderato cantabile** leaves a 'blank'. S/he can of course, as I am doing here, think about the meaning(s) that the novel produces, but the text itself has an alibi in that the solution to its problem is beyond its scope and it can never be pinned down. Furthermore, to try to do so spoils the pleasure, and feels ungrateful, running contrary to the role of the reader/narratee. All the same, meanings are produced in, for example **Moderato cantabile** or **Le Vice-consul,** even if the reader is invited not to dwell on them too much and to concentrate on the pleasure of fascination involved in their production.

The effects of this are twofold. Firstly, by inferring unstated meanings which are not allowed to become fully conscious, the reader is led tacitly to reinforce them, at least while s/he is reading. This process can be seen at work elsewhere in the way in which jokes reinforce and reproduce certain traditional meanings, for example, the way in which in England the word 'Irish' is used to mean 'illogical' as well as 'coming from Ireland'. The projection of undesirable qualities on to the inhabitants of another place with which one's own home has close historical and linguistic links is common to many cultures and no doubt serves a function in the construction and perpetuation of a group identity. But the idea that Irish people are illogical is not expounded in serious theoretical works in England. Indeed, if it were it would no doubt have far less currency, for it is propagated highly effectively through jokes and unstated assumptions.

In order to laugh at the joke or to understand the story, the addressee must understand the idea that the Irish are illogical, s/he must assume it as a basic given and from that position can prepare for and understand the punch-line. The idea itself is not brought out and examined, but each time the link between 'Irish' and 'illogical' is made, and the pleasure at repetition of the old idea in a new configuration produces a laugh, or just a smile, it is reaffirmed, even though, if asked to discuss the matter seriously, none of the individuals participating in the joke-telling say that they really believe in the innate illogicality of the Irish. The idea remains unconscious and may be retrieved to surface in contexts other than that of ritual joke-telling if required. *The Sun* newspaper used the power of the unconscious assumption to strengthen meanings at a time when Mrs Thatcher and the rest of the EEC leaders appeared to be at odds, by featuring anti-French jokes, a tactic which aims to generate support for the 'British' (i.e., Mrs Thatcher's) position against 'the French', without necessitating a detailed exposition of the arguments, which might bore the paper's readers, confuse them, or even turn them against the position that the paper wished them to espouse.

In Duras's work unstated assumptions are similarly reinforced by the very necessity of their remaining unstated. In fact the reader's desire to 'understand' gives those meanings which have apparently been suppressed more credence because it is in the 'blanks' of the texts that the answers to the questions they ask apparently lie. The 'suppressed' meanings, the unstated assumptions may not be explicitly present in the text, but the reader will already have learnt to read and understand stories of sexual desire elsewhere for they are all around us and our own desires and ways of thinking about sex and love are formed in the context of these other representations. For the woman reader, Duras is restaging the old problem that women face of confrontation with representations of Woman as the signifier of the presence of (masculine) desire. She offers her readers the place of the male subject in reading her novels, from which to see women as more or less compelling manifestations of 'the absolute object of desire'.

In our culture all women have to find ways of identifying themselves in relation to archetypal images of Woman. Amongst feminists, responses vary. Some have rejected identification with her altogether, along with all her outward trappings of makeup, dresses etc., and others have not; some enjoy watching other women perform as an object of desire, others do not. But whatever our individual responses, the images are still there and they retain their power. We have to deal with them. I do not think Duras's later writing facilitates this process, although undoubtedly it harnesses the power of images of Woman, the power of the archetypal feminine as our culture defines it. For the reader/narratee is held by a kind of fascination, a hinting at veiled knowledge, but cannot move from that fascination through to understanding and on from there. The demands of the text are absolute.

The effect created is reminiscent of Lemoine-Luccioni's description of the fascination and mutual mirroring of mother and daughter, or the Imaginary fascination of Lacan's mirror phase, both of which need to be broken for the subject to move on. The reader cannot maintain a grip on her/his separate identity while reading and s/he who reads thinking 'Yes, but . . .' will miss both the pleasure and the point. So my dispute with claims that Duras's writing carries feminist meanings is on the grounds that it concentrates exclusively on and repeats traditional images of women as manifestations of Woman the Other and does not allow for interaction and difference between women. Some feminists might take the view that any representation of a woman as powerful has implicitly feminist effects, no matter what form that power takes. However, this is not a view I share, since I think that finding a way of relating to the power of Woman the Other actually gives individual women a lot of trouble.

However, the fact that women, whether feminists or not, have found Duras's work fascinating and have felt touched by it seems to me to have implications for feminism. It is clearly not sufficient to decide that certain ways of representing women are 'male-defined' (even in the case of Duras's work, where almost all women are seen through implicitly or explicitly masculine eyes) and to reject them on those grounds. They appeal to women too and will not cease to do so because some feminists find them restricting. I cannot see what purposes will be served by those of us who enjoy her work denying ourselves the pleasure on grounds of ideological purity.

On the other hand, I do not think that we should try to justify that pleasure by upholding the power of the Woman-as-phallus as the means to women's liberation. It is quite possibly as old as patriarchy itself and has not helped us a great deal yet. My own view is that the main problem with such representations is that they are culturally dominant. If other kinds of representations of women, in relation to each other and each other's desires, in different relations to men, were more frequent, the power that now accrues to women as incarnations of Woman might become more diffused through these other manifestations. After all, men must also identify themselves in relation to archetypal Man—and they don't all find it so easy, but they seem to have more variations to play with. So I would argue for equality of diversity, rather than greater restriction, in the ways that women are portrayed, a diversity which already exists in a rather embryonic form, although not, it should be said, within the work of Duras.

It is not just in their representations of women that Duras's novels reinforce traditional and familiar meanings. *Moderato cantabile* for example restages the myth of the free-flowing sexuality of the working-class man, which releases the frustrated middle-class woman's pent-up desires, where her repressed husband has failed. My own thoughts turn to D H Lawrence and Wilhelm Reich as earlier purveyors of this myth of the working man's uninhibited sexual potency, but it is sufficiently widespread for examples not to be needed. In another area of myth, *Le Vice-consul* offers an image of India as the great ungraspable country of starving millions, seen from the rather unsettled viewpoint of the ruling whites. E M Forster produced a fine example of this particular way of representing India in *A Passage to India* (complete with a woman with an unutterable secret), but the undifferentiated starving of the 'Third World' looks out at us daily from charity posters and television programmes and the exotic decadence and cultural poverty of colonial rulers as viewed by their compatriots in Europe is also familiar enough. *Le Vice-consul* constructs India as the great unknowable Other and Indians as individuals do not figure at all, unless it be as examples of suffering humanity—*les lépreux*. Ninette Bailey encapsulates the view of India and the Indians as it is produced in *Le Vice-consul* in her article in *La Chouette* no 6. Speaking of the vice-consul's act of smashing mirrors and shooting lepers she says: '. . . the sound of gunshots, the smashing of broken mirrors and cries, that is, another form of language, language returned to a primitive state and thus meeting the primitive needs of the Indian masses: hunger.'[11]

Bailey's formulation is, I think, very apt in relation to *Le Vice-consul*. The novel portrays, in some detail, a few white figures who are disturbed, even horrified beyond the bounds of sanity by an undifferentiated, inarticulate mass, presented as products of the white figures' imagination and represented by the beggar-woman and her 'primitive needs'. Nothing here contradicts the kind of assumptions common amongst peoples of imperialist nations that the conquered nation is at a lower stage of civilisation than their own and that, rather than living in a society run on complex rules and reflecting distinct and ancient cultures, its people have remained at the level of 'primitive needs'. There are, of course, many other representations of India circulating in Europe. India the land of spirituality, of riches, of natural beauty, of bizarre customs. None of these is really in evidence in *Le Vice-consul* and none of them intrudes into the myth of India the Incomprehensible which the novel upholds and which is the way India must be constructed by the reader in order to make sense of the text, whatever s/he may or may not think about the country otherwise.

This brings me to the second effect of the importance given to the actual process of inference in Duras's novels as opposed to any possible 'message' or meanings produced in them. The later novels construct representations in terms of a binary system of presence or absence of meaning, where apparently expressive and transparent language is opposed to silence or 'oblivion'. However, these texts do not allow for the simultaneous presence of conflicting meanings. The meanings offered to the reader have been very carefully constructed so as to be as uncontradictory as possible. This effect is perceptible both at the level of the language of the novels and also at the level of the political or ideological meanings they produce.

To look at the language first, the binary effect of presence and absence of meaning is fostered by the bare style Duras uses, without rhetorical devices, which allows the illusion of one-to-one correspondence of the word with its referent to go unimpeded, producing as nearly as possible the illusion of fixed and unitary meaning. Any specific 'subjectivity' of the narrator disappears into what appears to be a narration of the visible, of things present, from a point of view which is that of *l'objectif*.[12] Even in sections where, as in *Le Ravissement de Lol V. Stein*, the narrator is also a figure in the novel who 'invents' what is described, or, as in *Le Vice-consul,* the narration apparently enters into the thoughts of one of the figures, the language still maintains its apparent uncontradictory 'clarity'. This produces for the reader an effect of certain knowledge perforated with 'blanks', the latter being not points of conflict in the discourse, but rather absences of meaning. That the reader draws on intertextual references to make sense of the text is not acknowledged by the text itself, other than at points of obvious reference to other works by Duras. This form of reference within the context of Duras's work, coupled with the bare but highly literary style and the

sparsely described and clearly fictitious location of the closed 'durassian universe' tends to have the effect of lifting her writing out of its intertextual context. The reader does not think about other texts or images whilst reading. The result is that Duras's texts set up oppositions: between that which can be described and understood, usually constructed as that which is visible, and that which cannot; and between meaningful language, which fixes and describes, and the 'blanks', which appear as instances of the inarticulable and unknowable.

On the ideological level, an analogous opposition is discernible. This is between the social status quo as constructed in the novels and its rejection in favour of the absence of any social structure. No other possibilities are offered. The 'transparent' language Duras uses appears to describe simply what is, but does so in a manner which implicitly denies the specificity of its own ideological context and connotations. This is not to deny that Duras's work is critical on an ideological level. It is, but from a position which, by producing one order of things as the only thinkable order, can oppose to it only the end of all order.

This opposition can be seen for example in the dinner-party scene in *Moderato cantabile,* which is clearly critical of the manner in which the meal takes place:

> The salmon passes from one to the other following a ritual which nothing disturbs, unless it be the hidden fear of each that so much perfection might suddenly be broken or stained with a too obvious absurdity. Outside, in the gardens, the magnolias are developing their funereal flowering in the black night of emerging spring.[13]

This paragraph taxes with absurdity the ritual of eating the salmon, that is to say, it refuses to accept the rules of the dinner-party as a framework for understanding what is happening, but rather steps outside them, opposing the artifice of the ceremony of the passing of the salmon with, not only nature in the form of the magnolias and the 'emerging spring', but also with death and 'the black night'. The order of a bourgeois dinner is criticised and its ceremony denied its significatory function, reduced to the absurd. But this is not ostensibly from the point of view of some different order or orders of things, a different set of meanings, but in the name of a refusal of ritual or order and a 'return' to a 'natural' world of death and unutterable desire.

The opening paragraphs of Chapter VII, of which the above is one, establish a hierarchy of 'truth' or 'authenticity'. The world of the dinner-party is produced as one of ritual, of invented rules or conventions in terms of which the ritual has meaning, and of fear of the breaking-down of those rules. The reader is given a certain amount of interpretation or explanation of events, implying that s/he might not instantly understand the meaning of the proceedings and also undercutting any effect of self-evidence that the ritual might have. In contrast, the descriptions of the world of flowers, desire and death give no interpretations. The reader is required to interpret unaided, to recall the meanings which have accrued to the magnolia flower, to be aware of all the connotations of these descriptions. In this way the dinner-party is portrayed as a constructed ritual, productive of 'artificial' meaning, liable to collapse into absurdity, whilst the description of the world outside, which carries no interpretations, no acknowledgment of the existence of a framework or frameworks in the context of which it has meaning, enables its meanings to appear 'natural', beyond the grasp of language.

The symbolic resonances of the natural world, magnolia flower, night, the wind and spring, acquire this appearance of 'naturalness' and of being more 'real' because the reader is required to infer them without being told how to, aided by a vast number of inter- and intra-textual references which must remain, for the most part, unconscious. The effect produced is thus one of an immediacy of understanding without words. The reader, if s/he is to enjoy the fascination exerted by the text, must take up the position of the narratee and read as if the resonances of meanings attached to the description of the magnolia flowers are both coming from her/his own psyche and are at the same time universal, the point where the pre- or extra-linguistic fundamentals of human existence meet her/his specific individuality, via the specific experiences of Anne Desbaresdes and Chauvin. S/he may, however, as I do, wish to investigate the 'invisible' conventions which give meaning to Duras's magnolia flowers, which are no more or less 'artificial' or constructed than those governing a dinner-party. For here, as throughout most of her work, Duras's narrative style renders the conventions on which it rests as unobtrusive as possible, and is selective in what it interprets. Both are necessary in order to create the effect of an objective style interrupted by 'blanks', of order undermined.

The opposition of 'artificial' oppressive order and a kind of primaeval, inarticulate chaos which breaks into and appears to undermine that order can be identified in all of Duras's work, but

particularly in the later novels. Bailey discusses this oppositional structure as it operates in *Le vice-consul*'s portrayal of colonial society. She points to many different instances of opposition in the text, which she links to an opposition of whites and 'natives' which 'underlies the entire text'.[14] As in *Moderato cantabile*, there is an opposition between an unstable structure of social meanings and an inarticulate chaos upon which that structure has been erected, with the white figures representing those who have a place in the world of meaning and the Indians and the beggar-woman being those who remain in chaos. Bailey makes this point in her study of a passage from *Le Vice-consul* which describes Anne-Marie Stretter, Michael Richard and Charles Rossett driving to the Prince of Wales hotel through the paddy fields:

> So present together for the one and only time, apart from the Indian servants, are Whites on the one hand, who have left the protective enclosure of the Residency, and natives on the other. In the rest of the novel the 'suffering hordes of Calcutta' only exist within the discourse of the text, evoked in the indistinctness of a common, inarticulate voice: 'Again Calcutta cries out softly' (p 158)— 'Muffled howlings again, along by the Ganges' (p 154). 'Here, although it is still anonymous and dumb, the crowd can be counted, is countless moreover, next to the three Whites'.[15]

In *Le Vice-consul*, the white figures, who have names and other attributes, stand in marked contrast to the 'native crowd'. Or perhaps I should say it is the 'native crowd' which stands in marked contrast, as irredeemably Other, to the white figures from whose point of view the text is narrated. Theirs are the eyes through which the reader is invited to look upon the 'suffering of India'. Nevertheless, as in *Moderato cantabile* the text constructs the same somewhat paradoxical hierarchy, which makes of the 'blank' which is India the ultimate reality which the whites (*les Blancs*) try to make sense of in their artificial way. Thus they attempt to recreate structures of meaning which were possible in Europe (although liable to be overthrown, as suggested by the vice-consul's 'joyful happiness at Montfort') and erect them on the vast and shifting foundations of the enigmatic East, which stands, in the novel, for Reality in all its excess. Bailey makes a similar point in her analysis:

> The car drives though a fluvial landscape: 'black junks advancing through the waterways, between the paddy-fields with their black water. Here and there there are patches newly sown, brilliant, soft green spaces, painted silk' (ibid). This time there is a contrast between the elements that make up the landscape, the double black of black junks and

black water, which connote, as is right, the native, whilst the occasional touches of colour, green connoting the home country of the Whites, are rendered unreal by the substance of cloth and the optical illusion of painting: *'painted silk'*. There is an opposition to be read here: the black reality of the native context, the brilliant unreality of the notations linked to the Whites.[16]

One might wish to argue that Bailey is making assumptions in her analysis that the 'black' of junks and water must connote 'native', whilst the bright splashes of colour like painted silk connote Europe. However, I think that such an opposition of 'black reality' and 'brilliant unreality' is most certainly encouraged in *Le Vice-consul* by the opposition of 'artificial' European civilisation and the countless millions of unheard Indians with their needs which may be portrayed as 'primitive', but which are also implicitly all the more 'real' for all that. Elsewhere, Bailey reiterates the point:

> . . . insignificant words of the guests at the embassy, repetitive and stereotyped, the lies of the vice-consul's interminable speeches at the Circle. Talking to say nothing: to these empty words the text opposes the dumbness of the beggar-woman, the silences of the ambassador's wife, but above all the cry. A whole range of sound is associated with the vice-consul: detonations, the smashing of broken mirrors, cries. An inarticulate language, which the text valorizes above that which is articulate language *par excellence,* literary discourse.[17]

Whilst I would be unwilling to confer the name 'language' upon bangs and crashes which, although they no doubt signify something, do so less by reference to each other, as linguistic elements do, than by reference to the action which produced them, I agree with Bailey's basic thesis that *Le Vice-consul,* presenting the reader with a choice between 'empty words' and 'silence', suggests that the latter is preferable, more 'real'. However, Bailey and other writers have seen this opposition in Duras's work as a subversion of dominant ideological positions, and this is a view I cannot share, for reasons similar to those I have discussed in relation to claims that Duras's work is feminist.

For *Le Vice-consul,* or any other of Duras's novels, can only be seen as subverting language, representations of society, or anything else if one accepts the binary vision they propose, which opposes language/rules/meanings to silence/screams/chaos. Duras's texts portray figures who have apparently stepped out of any specific position within different social relations, leaving them only the general categories of woman/object and man/subject in which to place themselves. All the varia-

tions of discourse which mark differences of position in such relations, and which produce meanings which may be at variance with one another, are reduced to the most simple literary language. In the novels following *Moderato cantabile,* all Duras's figures speak a very literary French, be they workers, Laotian beggars, rich and idle housewives or murderers. The differences that might therefore be perceptible between them via the language they use are thus removed, as are the social contexts of those who do not fit into the category of the rich. As the literary French they speak is also the language traditionally used in narration, it does not appear marked with the specificity of its usage when used in a literary work as Duras has done, but becomes apparently transparent; at least in the kind of unselfconscious reading which her work requires of the reader/narratee.

Nevertheless, this literary style has connotations of social class—the educated bourgeoisie—into which all the figures, no matter what their declared social status, are thus spirited. (This implicit social positioning may facilitate the reader's willingness to believe in their lack of concern with the details and problems of everyday life, concerns traditionally associated with the poor, although no doubt the rich suffer from them as well.) Such undifferentiated style allows the construction of the figures as undifferentiated human beings, stripped of the differences societies construct. Their speech does not mask them as different from each other. Instead the emphasis is on its constant failure to express the fundamentals of love and death, which are perceived as present in screams and in silence. Bailey has pointed to this lack of differentiation in *Le Vice-consul,* where she finds not only a 'form of writing that does away with demarcations by use of the pronoun *'on'* ('one')',[18] but also an abolition of difference via the collapse of language: 'So it is through the cry, in the absence of articulate language, that the indifferenciation of human beings is postulated.'[19]

So Duras's novels offer a vision of the world in which certain human beings—almost always white, Gentile men—construct artificial meaning upon a fundamental chaos to which women, children, Indians, Jews and some white Gentile men have access. Duras's concern is not with the conflict between the different constructions which might be produced from different positions, but with the relation of particular, and in Western Europe ideologically dominant constructions to their absence or collapse. I do not think that this really undermines those ideologically dominant constructions. Indeed, if anything it shores them up, since the texts rely, in order to be able to produce the effect of 'blanks', upon implacability and lack of contradiction. This lack of contradiction can be seen both in the way that the workings of the world are portrayed in the texts and in the language which is used to portray them.

In the schema proposed by Duras, meanings and their absence are like yin and yang, or two sides of the same coin. The irony of the 'subversion' operated by the 'blanks' in Duras's work is that it relies on the reader's ability to draw on, understand and accept, at least for the duration of her/his reading, precisely those ideological elements it is supposed to be subverting: traditional representations of heterosexual desire, of decadent white colonials faced with the seething black masses, or of the grandeur and ceremony of a bourgeois dinner in contrast to the animality of the working man. No alternative visions are offered to counter these representations, which we are asked to use to fuel our journey through Duras's novels. No ripples suggestive of a different way of seeing or of understanding the vision come to trouble the smooth surface of the images she produces for us, unless, that is, we the readers make them ourselves, in which case the texts become impossible to read with the same pleasure of fascination. The only option Duras offers to escape the confines of the social and linguistic structures which she presents as being so fixed is that of 'capital destruction', through (sexual) desire, death or madness.

This fits very well with the views expressed by Duras in 1974 on effective political action, which she saw in terms of refusal.

> But the people who are denouncing a whole load of things are calling for political action, when the first thing to do should be to refuse to do things. They should be telling people first of all, before all the programmes: 'Don't pay your telephone bill, go shoplifting, don't buy any more cars, don't vote, don't pay your tax.' There'd have to be millions of us doing it.[20]

There are obvious problems with such a strategy. Duras is ignoring two basic points here. The first is that shops, cars and taxes are bound together in intricate variations of social structures rather than being simply aspects of the same monolith which can be rejected in its entirety. The second is that we human beings are characterised by our construction, wherever we are, of complex social structures—of meanings. The axiom 'nature abhors a vacuum' applies also to the human psyche. We cannot just do away with Meaning, but we can change meanings and the structures in which they are produced.

The difference between Meaning, seen as a structured process of production, and meanings, which are what is produced in the workings of the process, is a crucial one. Duras sees the process as the problem. Her answer is to posit the end of Meaning as the way forward: 'Let the world run to rack and ruin, to rack and ruin, that's the only politics possible.'[21]

Because she presents a vision of the world in which language can only tell lies, the truth of human existence being inarticulate, she does not explore the different ways in which different people use the same language. Because she presents language as a maker of 'artificial' order, or as a babble, she does not investigate the details of the contradictions, conflicts and excesses of meaning which it can produce and which themselves generate new meanings, and by apparently lifting the utterances of her figures out of the specificity of social context (beyond the literary), she also suppresses the political dimension of language itself.

In her concentration on Meaning rather than specific meanings and the relations between them, Duras's approach resembles that of psychoanalysis [. . . .] and in this sense, her work has particular similarities with that of Lacan, who also deals in general psychic structures and does not go in for lengthy discussion of individual manifestations of his general laws. Freud fills his pages with examples, which not only prove his point about, for example, the general rules governing the workings of the unconscious, but also testify to the differences of meanings and positions in relation to those meanings which are unconsciously produced, and their specificity to the individual and context in which they occur. Lacan's writings on the other hand are mainly presented as extracts from a monolithic, all-embracing theory, which claims to account for every manifestation of desire, every production of meaning, within the general structure it elaborates, without concerning itself with the investigation of individual cases, the few exceptions being most often allusions to Freud's patients.

I think it is reasonable, although perhaps a little ironic, to say that both Lacan and Duras are producers of monoliths: the former attempts to encompass the structure of the human psyche, whilst the latter constructs a vision in which all ordering processes are part of the same restrictive structuring of primordial chaos. Both are concerned with the opposition of the monolithic structure they have constructed and the absence or lack upon which it is built and both seem to deny the possibility of real change and the importance of history by denying the production of difference and by refusing to look at detail. Thus both reinforce dominant representations, especially those of relations between the sexes. Lacan's 'Woman' is an abstraction, a particular position in a theory of relations of desire which owes, I suspect, as much to conventional representations of heterosexual relations as it does to analyses of individual men and women that Lacan may have undertaken. In the same way, Duras's 'ravaged beings' are the result of a refinement of novelistic conventions concerning the creation of 'character' which, by eschewing any 'irrelevant' detail, produces figures who are only a little more than points in a narrative structure. Perhaps the symbiotic relationship of their writings is symptomatic of this similarity.

Duras's writing has been called subversive because it shows up women's silence, constructing it as more 'true' or 'real' than the meaning produced in language, perforating and disturbing the dominating chatter of men. However, dominant meanings and representations that women (and/or men) might wish to change cannot just simply be abolished, others must be produced to combat, and eventually to supercede them. Indeed, they already exist. As I have discussed above, the kind of representation of woman-as-object that Duras produces are distillations of a particular aspect of the way in which women are generally represented in Western cultures. But there are other types of representation which could be drawn on. Even the most traditionally portrayed wives, girlfriends and mothers are often provided with quirks of character to make them 'individuals', different from other women as well as just examples of Woman the object of desire, and which allow them to be also, albeit in a small way, portrayed as subjects of desire.

These are the very details that Duras eschews and yet I think it is precisely by looking at and concentrating upon those details of women's difference from one another in terms of our desires and actions that we can escape from the constraints of being always either seen as manifestations of Womanhood or honorary men. The dominant picture within society at the moment is one in which men, the subjects, the unmarked sex, are always primarily examples of Womanhood. If this division is to change and become more balanced, no doubt the manhood of men, the fact that they are not just human beings, but specifically male human beings, will require more emphasis, so that women can gain a greater measure of individuality. Dominant representations of subject and object positions in the context of heterosexual relations will have to be disturbed. But of course, there are other representations, even now, and it should be stressed that those positions have never been immutably fixed.

In this light, then, I would not hold up Duras's work as a landmark in the journey towards the end of women's oppression. However, there is one important aspect I have ignored thus far in my analysis of the feminist implications of her work, and that is the impact of Duras herself as a writer. She is now widely acknowledged to be one of France's great contemporary writers, particularly since she was awarded the Goncourt prize in 1984 for *L'Amant*. For however far her work may, in itself, reinforce traditional representations and divisions of the sexes, the fact that it is a woman's work also affects the way that women are regarded generally. Duras is an immensely skillful and highly individual writer, and, though her own portrayal of herself in *L'Amant* is chiefly as an object of men's desire, it is as an innovative and powerful writer and film-maker that she has deservedly found wide acclaim. When her readers contemplate Anne-Marie Stretter, or Lol V. Stein, those obscure objects of desire, they will also remember that these fictional figures have been fashioned from the desires of an impressively authoritative subject, who makes words do just what she wants them to do: a very particular woman, Marguerite Duras.

Notes

1. Marini, op cit, p 62.

2. Irigaray, *Ce sexe qui n'en est pas un*, p 77.

3. Blanchot, 'Détruire', p 141.

4. Marini, op cit, pp 47-8.

5. Venet, op cit, p 6.

6. *L'Amant*, p 28.

7. ibid, p 26.

8. Marini, op cit, p 54.

9. ibid, p 55.

10. ibid.

11. Ninette Bailey, 'Une écriture de la subversion: Lecture narratologique du *Vice-consul* de Marguerite Duras', in *La Chouette* no 6, p 52.

12. *L'objectif* can be translated either as 'the camera lens' or 'objectivity'.

13. *Moderato cantabile* pp 91-2.

14. Bailey, 'Discours social: Lecture socio-critique du *Vice-consul* de M Duras', in *Literature and Society—Studies in Nineteenth and Twentieth Century French Literature*, presented to R J North, C A Burns ed, Birmingham University, 1980, p 5.

15. ibid, p 4.

16. ibid.

17. ibid, p 52.

18. ibid, p 50.

19. ibid, p 52.

20. *Les Parleuses,* p 108.

21. *Le Camion,* Paris, Gallimard, 1977, p 74.

22. The distinction between novels and *récits* is one made in many bibliographies, including that published by Minuit. It has not been formally established by Duras herself to my knowledge, some of her texts bear the designation *roman* on the title page, but *récit* is never used in such a way. However, I have used the two terms as the distinction seems to me to be a valid one.

Bibliography

I Works by Marguerite Duras

NOVELS AND RÉCITS[22]

Le Square, Paris, Gallimard, 1955.

Translated as *The Square* by S P Rivers, London, Calder.

Also in: *Three Novels,* London, Calder, 1977 and in *Four Novels,* translated by Richard Seaver et al, New York, Grove, 1965.

Moderato Cantabile, Paris, Minuit, 1958.

Translated as *Moderato Cantabile* by Richard Seaver, New York, Grove and London, Calder, 1966.

Dix heures et demie du soir en été, Paris, Gallimard, 1960.

Translated as *Ten-thirty on a Summer Night* in *Four Novels,* New York, Grove, 1965, and in *Three Novels,* London, Calder, 1977.

Le Ravissement de Lol V. Stein, Paris, Gallimard, 1964.

Translated as *The Ravishing of Lol V. Stein* by Richard Seaver, New York, Pantheon, 1986.

Le Vice-consul, Paris, Gallimard, 1965.

L'Amante Anglaise, Paris, Gallimard, 1967.

Translated as *L'Amante Anglaise* with *Suzanna Andler* and *La Musica* by B Bray, London, Calder, 1975.

Détruire, dit-elle, Paris, Minuit, 1969.

Translated as *Destroy, she said* by Barbara Bray, New York, Grove, 1986.

Abahn Sabana David, Paris, Gallimard, 1970.

L'Amant, Paris, Minuit, 1984.

Translated as *The Lover* by Barbara Bray, London, Collins and New York, Pantheon, 1985.

FILMS AND SCREENPLAYS

Le Camion (film), 1977.

Le Camion (screenplay), followed by *Entretien avec Michelle Porte,* Paris, Minuit, 1977.

MISCELLANEOUS

Les Parleuses with Xavière Gauthier, Paris, Minuit, 1974.

Translated as *Woman to Woman* by Katerine Jensen, University of Nebraska Press.

II Critical Work on Marguerite Duras

BOOKS

Marcelle Marini, *Territoires du féminin avec Marguerite Duras,* Paris, Minuit, 1977.

Madeleine Renouard and Ninette Bailey (eds), *La Chouette* no 6 (special issue on Duras), French Department, Birkbeck College, University of London, September 1981.

ARTICLES

Ninette Bailey, 'Discours social: Lecture socio-critique du *Vice-Consul* de Marguerite Duras', in *Literature and Society—Studies in Nineteenth and Twentieth Century French Literature,* presented to R J North, C A Burns (ed), Birmingham University, 1980.

III Feminist Theory and Literary Criticism

Luce Irigaray, *Ce Sexe qui n'en est pas Un,* Paris, Minuit, 1977.

Translated as *This Sex which is not One* by Catherine Porter and Carolyn Burke, New York, Cornell University Press, 1985.

LISA F. SIGNORI (ESSAY DATE 2001)

SOURCE: Signori, Lisa F. Introduction to *The Feminization of Surrealism: The Road to Surreal Silence in Selected Works of Marguerite Duras,* pp. 1-24. New York: Peter Lang, 2001.

In the following essay, Signori explores Duras's transformation of surrealist poetics into a feminist literary practice.

Mais comment réunir le tout d'un écrivain?: livres, articles de revues, commentaires, critiques, interviews, interventions de toutes sortes dans les journaux ou ailleurs . . . bref, tout ce qui, de près ou de loin, fait texte—prétexte à ma propre recherche. A tout cela, à tous ces écrits, majeurs ou mineurs selon le cas, mais tous aussi signifiants quels qu'ils soient, il s'agit de donner cohérence et forme, unité et sens ultime, tâche impossible, en réalité (car comment réunifier le sujet d'une écriture?).

—Gabrielle Frémont[1]

In the above comments, Gabrielle Frémont astutely summarizes my own struggle as I face the task of trying to come to terms with the essence of the enigmatic work of Marguerite Duras. Her corpus is extraordinarily complex, not to mention varied, and large in scope, but I take comfort in the knowledge that I am obviously not alone in my dilemma, for, as Aliette Armel implies in her article "J'ai vécu le réel comme un mythe," "malgré l'ampleur de son retentissement et la variété des domaines que Duras englobe: roman, théâtre, cinéma et même journalisme—elle a suscité un certain nombre de thèses mais pas encore de véritable synthèse." In fact, the difficulty created by the task to appraise her corpus seems insurmountable, although numerous attempts by various critics have been made. As Bertrand Poirot-Delpech writes in an article appearing in *Le Monde* on March 5, 1996, two days after Duras's death, "pourquoi la mort, qui n'apprend rien permettrait-elle tout à coup de classer un artiste, d'augmenter la postérité? Marguerite Duras s'est tue, voilà la seule certitude, énorme." What Duras leaves behind after her death, then, is a vast corpus that spans more than five decades and crosses the boundaries of genre classification. Her writings eliminate all genre distinctions, for her novels become film scenarios, her cinema is played out on stage, and all becomes poetry. The poetic quality in Duras's work is evident given the intuitive, emotional intensity her work evokes in the reader. As Christiane Makward states, "there is a strangeness, an otherness to Duras's style which . . . may function more attractively for readers of experimental texts who are not desperately clinging to a respectable but unrealistic need to make perfect sense of every message, i.e., to readers of contemporary poetry." So how is it possible to take into account the richness and complexity of the literary universe (sixty-three fictional works, twenty films, and approximately twenty-five plays and theatrical adaptations according to Robert Harvey and Hélène Volat)—and let us not forget the countless interviews and journalistic pieces written for various newspapers and journals as well—that this enigmatic writer has been creating since she began publishing in 1943, and whose final work, **La Mer écrite,** was published 12 days after her death in her Rue Saint-Benoît apartment in Paris on March 3rd, 1996? To the present moment, critics have used many different approaches in an attempt to analyse Duras's literary universe: feminism, autobiography, the theme of silence or destruction, alienation or absence, the body, love and desire, as well as the "legacy of mourning" to name a few.[2] Yet Duras's work eludes categorization, which reinforced her own disdain for the practice of literary criticism. Her abhorrence of the "isms" that dominate the literary world was evident when she expressed the desire in *Le Camion* "que tous les 'isms' aillent à leur perte." Thus when reading and discussing Duras, the reader must above all heed Alain Vircondelet's suggestion to "se laisser porter par ces mots, ces phrases, au coeur desquelles l'on devrait se loger, ne pas tenter de s'en éloigner sous peine de ne plus comprendre, ou de revenir à une banalité vulgaire et dérisoire" (*Pour Duras* 11).

I take heed of Vircondelet's comments, but think it is nonetheless important to situate Marguerite Duras's place in literary history. Amid much controversy, Marguerite Duras earned a place among France's most noteworthy female writers of the 20th century. She has come to share the limelight with Colette, Simone de Beauvoir, Nathalie Sarraute, and Marguerite Yourcenar. Yet Duras believed her writing was different from that of these other female writers, an opinion she expressed in an interview with Alice Jardine in *Shifting Scenes*. Duras explained to Jardine that her works had been singled out by French critics, but not in order to give them favorable reviews. "They never attacked Simone de Beauvoir. They never attacked Sarraute," she said, "But in my case, I've been involved in men's things. First, I was involved in the Communist Party. I did things that are considered in bad taste for women."[3] This study focuses precisely on Duras's involvement in "men's things." In fact, her involvement in "men's things," in particular, her relationship to the male dominated literary domain of Surrealism, greatly influenced her fiction. Moreover, this approach will ultimately allow a greater understanding of her work, and broaden the realm of surrealist aesthetics as well.

As Jane Winston suggests, Duras's earliest French critics knew a great deal about her personal life and political persuasions, and this in turn led to their less than favorable comments on her life and works.[4] Marilyn Schuster points out, moreover, that there is an abundance of material available on Duras's life; yet it is difficult to know her as a woman, for no two biographies are the same. Marguerite Duras, *née* Donnadieu, was born April 4th, 1914 to Emile and Marie Donnadieu in Gia Dinh, Cochinchina, then French Indochina and now part of Vietnam. Her parents were both teachers; her father taught mathematics until an illness forced him to return to France where he died in 1918. Sometime after her father's death, Marie Donnadieu took her family back to the father's house in southwestern France for two years to settle his estate before returning to

Cambodia in 1920. Duras chose her pseudonym after the name of the town where her father died, *Duras* in the *Lot-et-Garonne* region of France. As a widow, her mother continued to teach in Indochina, first appointed to Phnom Penh, then Vinh-long, and finally to Sadec. Marguerite spent her childhood and adolescence in a milieu of poverty, colonial exploitation, and social injustice. She had two older brothers, Paul and Pierre (Marguerite spent much time with the younger brother, nicknamed Paulo), as well as two step brothers from her father's previous marriage to Alice Rivière who had died in Hanoi 20 years earlier. The family was more closely tied to the local population than to the other French colonists, and spoke Vietnamese fluently. As a result, Duras chose to write her *baccalauréat* examination in Vietnamese. In 1930 she enrolled in high school in Saigon, where she met the Chinaman who was to become her lover when she was not yet 16 years old.

In 1932, Duras left for France to finish her studies. She moved to Paris where she studied mathematics, law, and political science. In 1935 she was employed by the *Ministère des Colonies* in Paris in the *Service intercolonial de l'information et de la documentation.* Duras wrote (still as Marguerite Donnadieu), along with Philippe Roques, one of her friends from the *Ecole coloniale,* *L'Empire français.* In this text, which was published in 1940, she and Roques attempt to justify French colonialism and all that the French thought to bring to the *indigènes:* equal opportunity for education, scholarships and travel, and improved health care are a few examples that she and Roques give in this apology of imperialism. In the troubled period in France before the second World War, Duras and Roques wrote propaganda to spread the message of the grandeur and strength of France. Now, from our twenty-first century perspective, it is hard to understand why Duras collaborated in the writing of such a work that suppressed her own life experience of colonialism. According to Frédérique Lebelley, Duras, in this work, "a tout occulté: images, souvenirs, sentiments. Elle les a livrés à ce texte imbécile, momifiés. Elle voulait enterrer ce passé tyrannique de peur qu'il ne l'empêche d'exister. Elle l'a neutralisé" (113). Nonetheless, this work represented the first opportunity for Marguerite to come into contact with "la chose écrite, le premier pas vers le livre" (Lebelley 108).[5]

In 1930, Marguerite married Robert Antelme, a left-wing writer under whose influence she began to write. During the Occupation, Duras worked for the *Cercle de la librairie* at *L'Edition française* as secretary for the *Commission du contrôle du papier.* In this role, she took writer's requests for paper and determined whether or not their manuscripts were worthy of the paper to be printed on. Thus, she was continuously surrounded by writers and their ideas. Duras, too, finally discovered her literary calling in her desire to discover herself and her place in France amidst the turmoil of the second World War. Lebelley thinks that Duras's new found compulsion to write came from her desire to "s'enraciner dans le sol de France" (118). So, she began to write in her newly adopted country. Her first manuscript, *La Famille Taneran,* originally entitled *Les Complices,* was refused by Gallimard in 1942.[6] During the same year, her younger brother died suddenly, a loss which greatly affected her, especially since it followed the death of her first child at birth. At this time, she also met Dionys Mascolo who was working as a reader for Gallimard.[7] They would eventually have a son together in 1947.

In 1943, Duras became a member of the *Mouvement national des prisonniers de guerre* along with Robert Antelme and Dionys Mascolo. All three then participated in the Resistance movement during the German Occupation. In the midst of her political involvements, Duras did not give up writing. She diligently reworked her first novel, *La Famille Taneran,* into **Les Impudents,** which was published by Plon with the encouragement of Raymond Queneau, who saw in her the promise of a great writer. The following year, Robert Antelme was arrested and deported to Dachau, while her second novel, **La Vie tranquille,** was accepted by Gallimard. During this time, Duras, motivated by her own personal interest in trying to get information on her husband, created a research service that published the journal *Libres.* This journal listed information about those emprisoned and deported by the Germans. Apparently, this experience, and her experience of waiting for the return of her husband, led to the writing of a collection of texts entitled **La Douleur.** The first text in the collection, also entitled **La Douleur,** recounts Duras's anxious vigil awaiting the return of her husband from a German concentration camp. Interestingly enough, Duras suppressed the publication of this text, and proclaimed to have forgotten all about it until she came across the manuscript many years later. Though the writings date from the second World War, the collection was not published until 1985. Several of the other texts in the work describe Duras's involvement with a resistance group led by former President

Mitterand under the name of François Morland. These writings, however, are far from being a coherent text with a structured plot and chronology. Instead, all the anxieties and suppressed emotions Duras felt during the absence of her husband surface in **La Douleur**. As Leslie Hill puts it, this work, which begins as a diary, "is less a series of events than stages in the experience of fear, grief, and loss" ("Marguerite Duras and the Limits of Fiction" 7).

Duras was a member of the French Communist Party from 1944 until 1950, at which time she was forced to leave the party due to ideological differences. According to Jane Winston, Duras also had earned a reputation for "amorous meanderings" by the late 1940's. Winston argues that many people were upset about the unusual trio she formed with her husband Robert Antelme (until their divorce in 1946) and her lover (from 1942) Dionys Mascolo and the sociosexual norms that they together transgressed (469). Thus, the early critical reception of her work was clearly influenced by her controversial personal life and political dealings. Duras herself believed that she was not awarded the 1950 *Prix Goncourt* for **Un Barrage contre le Pacifique** because "she was a woman and a dissident communist to boot, and that the Academy's ubiquitous sexism had penalized her for both of those transgressions."[8] Duras spent the next two decades writing at a furious pace. By the end of the 1960's, when the events of May 1968 broke out, she had published 19 works of various genres—novels, plays and film scenarios. Primed by her earlier political involvements, Duras's militant spirit was revived during the student revolution in 1968 when she joined the students in their *défilés* and protests, appeared alongside them on the barricades, signed their petitions, and was even arrested. She adopted their motto as her own: "brûler le passé pour tout recommencer" (Lebelley 223). As a member of the *Comité des intellectuels contre la poursuite de la guerre d'Algérie,* she had already spoken out virulently against De Gaulle; and, as a founding member of the *Comité d'action étudiants-écrivains,* she wrote a manifesto for the committee that was rejected. During these turbulent times, Duras demonstrated a sense of political engagement and a desire to transgress the status quo, for, as Winston indicates, she sheltered such student leaders as Henri Weber and Daniel Bensaïd in her Saint-German-des-Près apartment.[9]

After 1950, Duras's style changed and her texts became more minimalist. When asked by Xavière Gauthier in **Les Parleuses** why her style had

changed, Duras explained that it was due to an extremely traumatic, even violent love affair. Though Duras does not name the other party, Françoise Lebelley thinks that Duras was referring to her tragic love affair with Gérard Jarlot. In **Les Parleuses,** Duras suggests that **Moderato cantabile** is based upon a comparable destructive affair, and that this "expérience érotique, très, très, très violente" also led to a "crise suicidaire qu'elle raconte dans **Moderato cantabile.**" Duras said that "cette femme qui veut être tuée, je l'ai vécu . . . et à partir de là les livres ont changé" (59). The self-avowed influence that this love affair had on Duras's life and writing is a living example of surrealist André Breton's belief in the power of love to transform an individual.

Several critics, noting the change in her writing style, chose to classify Duras with the writers grouped together as the school of the *Nouveau Roman,* although Duras denied adherence to any movement or group whatsoever. As Duras herself stated in an interview with Thérèse de Saint-Phalle, she rebelled against any and all labels: "Le Nouveau Roman est perclus de consignes, alors que la seule consigne d'un écrivain serait de n'en avoir aucune. Aucune autre que la sienne" ("Le Monde" 20 janvier 1962). In 1963 she added that "je ne crois pas à ce mouvement littéraire qui est un rewrite plus ou moins adroit de la littérature américano-surréaliste" ("Paris-Théâtre" n. 198 s.d.1963), an interesting comment in light of the topic of this study. Regardless of her involvement, Duras had always scorned being involved with any movement, literary or otherwise. But given that various critics choose to include her in the New Novel, it is necessary to examine her "noninvolvement." According to one critic, Mireille Calle-Gruber, the *Nouveau Roman* only existed from 1971-1974, which is not the accepted idea about the existence of the *Nouveau Roman.* For Calle-Gruber, the group officially began in 1971 when Jean Ricardeau and Françoise Van Rossum-Guyon organized a colloquium at Cerisy to "institutionalize" the movement. Duras was invited to the meeting, but chose not to attend. Her refusal indicates an unwillingness to be associated with the "group." In 1974, the colloquium that served to mark the demise of the group dealt with the work of Alain Robbe-Grillet, and also took place at Cerisy (Calle-Gruber 14). Although Duras was not included on Ricardou's definitive honorary list of *nouveaux romanciers* in his 1973 work entitled *Le Nouveau Roman,* Robbe-Grillet nonetheless insisted on including her in the *Nouveau Roman.* Robbe-Grillet stated that her refusal not to attend the colloquium was not pertinent since "elle ne supporte pas d'être mélangée à quoi que ce soit. Mais il n'en reste pas moins que c'est du *Nouveau Roman*. Au sens large. . . ." (Calle-Gruber 13). In 1971, Duras again emphatically denied any and all involvement with the Nouveau Roman when she said "Non. Je ne fais pas partie de ce groupe" ("The French" Review n. 4 mars 1971). In a 1990 interview with Alain Veinstein for France Culture, Duras once more refused her inclusion: "Je n'en fais pas partie. . . . C'est Robbe-Grillet qui m'a fait croire ça un jour. J'ai rigolé."

It is revealing that even in light of her refusal to be associated with the *Nouveau roman*, many critics have included her. For example, Raylene L. Ramsay's article links Duras and Robbe-Grillet together in a discussion "The Power of the Erotic and the Eroticization of Power in the works of Marguerite Duras and Alain Robbe-Grillet." According to Calle-Gruber, what she does share with the new novelists is the refusal of "quelque chose à dire préexistant à l'écriture" (15). Like the *nouveaux romanciers*, Duras did not sit down to write with the artifice of subject or plot in mind to dictate the text. But unlike the members of the New Novel, her works are emotionally charged examples of surrealist *écriture automatique*. Duras herself insisted that "ce qui vous arrive dessus, dans l'écrit, c'est sans doute tout simplement la masse du vécu" (*Les Parleuses* 99), and because "on est hanté par son vécu, il faut le laisser faire."[10] Her emphasis, then, on the "lived" experience replete with its emotional overflow as the building block of the text differentiates her from most of the *nouveaux romancers*.

Duras's critics eventually acknowledged the intertwining of Duras's life and writing. However, it was not until after 1984, with the publication of *L'Amant* and its reception of the Prix Goncourt, that critics finally heeded Duras's cry, "je suis le livre." With this autobiographical work, critics had begun to introduce Duras's biography into the interpretation of her works. As Jane Winston observes from a feminist viewpoint, a contextual reading of Duras's life could offer further insight into the origins of Duras's writing and would "anchor her writings in the concrete and provide a means for moving beyond conservative images of a patriarchally feminine Marguerite Duras."[11] From the standpoint of autobiography, Christiane Blot-Labarrère believes that Duras's "oeuvre et vie sont les deux visages d'une unique aventure" (7). With Surrealism in mind, such a statement inevitably recalls Breton's cry that one should "vivre la poésie." For Breton, existence and poetry were one

and the same, and when Duras wrote that "l'argument de mon livre, c'est l'écriture. L'écriture c'est moi. Donc, je suis le livre," she echoes Breton's belief in the continuity between existence and the search for revelation through writing. Often Duras wrote about the act of writing, but she claimed to have lived the process as well, so much so, in fact, that each work she wrote drained a bit of life out of her. "Je vois le livre," said Duras, "comme une soustraction du corps, comme un dépeuplement du corps." The completion of each work was generally followed by illness and even coma. For example, after the completion of her 1987 work, ***Emily L.***, Duras fell into a coma that lasted several months. Duras's companion, Yann, writes about her coma and recovery in his 1983 work entitled *M.D.* In *Cet Amour-là*, Yann's 1999 love-letter written more than three years after her death, he writes to Duras that each work "chaque fois il vous laisse comme morte, anéantie, et votre main et votre esprit" (195). The act of writing for Duras is necessarily physical and painful: "Ce qui est douloureux, la douleur—le danger—c'est la mise en oeuvre, la mise en page, de cette douleur, c'est crever cette ombre noire afin qu'elle se répande sur le blanc du papier, mettre dehors ce qui est de nature intérieure" ("Entretien avec Michelle Porte" 83-136 in Duras ***Le Camion***). In brief, Duras's life and work are, admittedly, inexorably intertwined, and this connection allows the argument that Duras heeded Breton's cry that one should "live poetry." In fact, Duras created a new literary realm that extends beyond poetry, one that is in line with Breton's surrealist aesthetic, "porté par le souffle poétique et l'envol de l'imaginaire, où l'écriture et la vie sont intimement liées. . . ." (Armel "Le Jeu autobiographique" 31).

In accordance with Duras's involvement with *men's things*, Jane Winston astutely points out, along with Alain Vircondelet, that the origin of Duras's writing lies in her involvement with men, and, specifically, that her inspiration came from her ex-husband Robert Antelme. Antelme chronicled his experience in concentration camps during World War II (478) in *L'Espèce humaine*. In his 1991 *Duras biographie*, Alain Vircondelet claims that Antelme ultimately gives birth to Duras's writing, and that her characteristic silences, holes, and repetitions stem from his influence. If we accept Vircondelet's explanation, then we might say that the blanks and silences in Duras's work represent her fear, grief, and anguish at her husband's sufferings. It seems that her husband internalized her silences as his own, for, as

Frédérique Lebelley states, upon completion of *L'Espèce humaine,* Antelme "choisit de se taire. Il ne reparle plus. On ne l'entendra plus jamais prononcer ces mots. Jamais plus. Pas même le titre de son livre" (146). According to Vircondelet's analysis, Maurice Blanchot had a hand in forming Duras's literary style as well. He believes that Blanchot intuitively showed Duras the path to follow in her writing and that her work was "nourished" in his own *Espace littéraire* (*Duras biographie*).

To the two "male" influences briefly alluded to here, I am going to add the literary practice of Surrealism. When Vircondelet comments that "plus Duras avança dans l'oeuvre, plus elle accorda d'importance aux accrocs du langage, *au surgissement des images, à l'inattendu,* à ce qui vient, brut et barbare" (*Pour Duras* 83), his references to the sudden appearance of images, and of the unexpected, confirm my belief that, in order to understand fully Marguerite Duras, we must look for the parallels to surrealist aesthetics. I agree with Vircondelet when he says he is not surprised that "le surréalisme fut une de ses influences avouées" (*Pour Duras* 83). In spite of her rejection of what she labeled as the *américano-surréaliste* literature of the New Novel, on at least two occasions, as Christiane Blot-Labarrère points out, Duras herself acknowledged direct surrealist influence on her work. In an interview with Pierre Hahn, published in *Paris-Théâtre* Duras said: "j'ai vécu dans le bain existential. J'ai respiré l'air de cette philosophie. . . . Et il en va de même pour le surréalisme." Then, in a 1967 piece that appeared in *Le Monde,* Duras affirmed to Jacqueline Piatier, in reference to her writing syle that: "le surréalisme, je ne suis pas allée à lui, mais maintenant il vient à moi et j'en suis très heureuse" (29 mars 1967). In this interview, Duras explained that she did not strive to master a certain, preconceived and desired form of writing, but that the creative impulse for her is more like an outpouring of emotion during the moment of writing. Her outpouring of emotion is, as I shall demonstrate, her own form of *écriture automatique.*

It is not surprising, then, that in a number of articles and footnotes, other scholars have noted Duras's affiliation with Surrealism. In the most hyperbolic claim, Jean Decottignies traces "tout un champ de la littérature contemporaine" back to the tenets of Surrealism, including "entre autres, l'oeuvre entière de Marguerite Duras" (95). Madeleine Cottenet-Hage finds other indirect signs of kinship between Surrealism and Duras, and among these, Duras's book-length interview with Xavière Gauthier in **Les Parleuses.** In 1972,

Gauthier wrote an important work entitled *Surréalisme et surréalité,* a stringent critique of Surrealism that nonetheless links her to the surrealist movement. And her interest in Duras would suggest that Gauthier, too, according to Cottenet-Hage, found Duras to be a kindred surreal spirit. Another critic, Susan Rubin Suleiman, uncovers surrealist ties in Duras's work in an article entitled "Nadja, Dora, Lol V. Stein: Women, Madness and Narrative." Suleiman thus makes the connection between André Breton's *Nadja* (1928) and Duras's **Le Ravissement de Lol V. Stein** (1964) through the mediation of madness. Of even more importance is Duras's interview entitled "le surréalisme en octobre 1967" with Jean Schuster (a critic for the surrealist review, *L'Archibras*). In this interview, Duras's notion of *ombre interne* appeared for the first time. According to Aliette Armel in her article "La Force magique de l'ombre interne," Duras was implicitly referring to the surrealists when she remarked as early as 1966 that "la nature même de l'ombre interne . . . est donnée commune, qu'elle dépasse très largement l'histoire individuelle, tout en conservant le pouvoir de porter l'homme hors de soi" (12).

In the realm of Duras's biography, more links to Surrealism appear. Jacques Lacan, who proclaimed himself one of Duras's greatest admirers in his article entitled "Hommage fait à Marguerite Duras," was at one time closely linked to the surrealist group (Cottenet-Hage 541). Duras's involvement with Dionys Mascolo led her to direct contact with André Breton and other surrealists. In an interview with Aliette Armel, Mascolo explained that in 1955 *le groupe de la rue Saint-Benoît* founded *le Comité des Intellectuels contre la poursuite de la guerre en Algérie,* and, as Mascolo suggested, the political ideals they shared permitted "un rapprochement entre notre groupe et le groupe surréaliste" ("Un Itinéraire politique" 39). According to Mascolo, "Breton s'est déclaré immédiatement d'accord. Il a même déclaré . . . que ce comité a permis aux surréalistes de sortir de l'isolement politique où ils étaient confinés depuis la Libération" (39-40). Then, when de Gaulle came into power in 1958, Mascolo founded an antigaulliste review entitled *Le 14 juillet* with surrealist Jean Schuster. The third volume of the journal, appearing in April of 1959, contained a questionnaire written by Maurice Blanchot and André Breton which was "un appel à la résistance contre le nouveau régime de la part des intellectuels" ("Un Itinéraire politique" 40). Another link to Surrealism is Duras's acquaintance with Michel Leiris, who in the 1960's, was a frequent visitor to the rue Saint-Benoît apartment. Duras, Mascolo, and Antelme's involvement in May 1968 events, whose "surrealist inspiration was attested to by graffiti, mottoes, posters" (Cottenet-Hage 540), also allows a connection to Surrealism.

It may seem somewhat contradictory to draw close parallels between Duras, a woman writer, and Surrealism, given Surrealism's blatant and desired occultation of women as objects. The surrealist's conception of women as objects seems to contrast with Duras's concern in her works with women as subjectivities, and the conditions and oppressive attitudes and conventions under which they live. Rudolf E. Kuenzli emphasizes that surrealist works are addressed to men; in their function as erotic object or muse, women serve only as a means of inspiration for surrealist art and poetry (18). Many contemporary feminists criticize the emphasis that the male surrealists place on imagery of the female body. And, in a more damning critique, critic Gwen Raabert suggests that the marginal roles that women held in society were reproduced in the male surrealists' works. In her opinion, these works represent a "male subject seeking transformation through a female representational object" (8). The images of the female body offered a path to the desired realm of surreality. Duras also denounced Surrealism's position toward women in the following statement. "Whatever form this veneration of women takes," Duras said, ". . . be it religious or surrealist . . . it is still racism." This comment leads me to ponder her seemingly contradictory affinity for Surrealism.[12] How is it possible to link her work with a literary movement that virtually excluded women?

To begin to answer this question, it is first necessary to examine, in greater detail, Surrealism. The surrealist movement was officially founded in 1924 with the publication of André Breton's *Manifeste du surréalisme*. The first issue of the official review of the movement, "La Révolution surréaliste," also appeared that year and continued through 1929. In 1930, due to the polemic surrounding the surrealists's relationship to Communism, a new journal "Le Surréalisme au service de la révolution" replaced "La Révolution surréaliste." This new journal was published through 1933 when it folded and the movement was left without an official review. Meanwhile, the movement endured numerous defections and exclusions at the same time it constantly acquired new members. For example, Louis Aragon, one of the founding members and most visible participants, left the group in 1932. As a genuine avant-garde movement, Surrealism died around 1935 (though

Breton did not share this opinion). According to Maurice Nadeau, one historian of the movement, Surrealism continued to maintain itself as a movement and organize collective exhibits in the late 1930's and throughout the war, when many of its members were in New York. Even today, as certain critics believe, Surrealism has become an integral part of our consciousness. For example, as Alain Virmaux points out, "il en reste trace jusque dans le bagage linguistique moyen de l'homme aujourd'hui" (9), since, as he says, Surrealism now refers to anything that qualifies as bizarre, unexpected or upsetting. The movement was officially dispersed in 1969, three years after Breton's death, but, as Susan Suleiman notes, "for a long time by then, it had been no more than a surviving remnant" (168).

Historically, between 1924 and 1933, during the most dynamic period of Surrealism, it is revealing that no women were listed as official members of the movement and that their signatures were absent from the manifestoes. But that does not mean that there were no women present behind the scenes, or in the margins, so to speak. Though women were not active participants in Surrealism, they were obviously important as muse in their roles as wives and lovers to the male surrealists. For example, the artist Leonora Carrington was the partner of Max Ernst. Like Leonora Carrington, these women were, at the same time, artists and writers in their own right, though this was not "officially" recognized by the early surrealist movement. In "A Double Margin: Reflections on Women Writers and the Avant-garde in France," Susan Suleiman examines the difficulties one encounters when one examines Surrealism as a "men's club" with regard to women. She refers to Xavière Gauthier's 1971 pioneering work *Surréalisme et sexualité,* in which Gauthier examines surrealist poetry and painting to illustrate and explain, in psychoanalytical terms, the misogynous nature of many of the male surrealists. Though the male surrealists were somewhat supportive of several women writers and artists (Breton's promotion of Joyce Mansour, for example), they generally failed to acknowledge their female counterparts. The roles they had assigned to women in surrealist poetics, those of muse and object of desire, blocked the surrealist's ability to see women as "independent, active subjects" (Raabert 2). The "women behind the scenes" of Surrealism were, as Raaberg states, on average younger than the male surrealists, and thus they "often produced their most mature work after their relationships with the male Surrealists and the movement had ended" (2). As Raaberg also acknowledges, the women associated with the movement belong more properly to a "second generation of surrealists" (2).

One might argue that the Surrealism of the works of these women was finally officially recognized in the 1977 review *Obliques*. This surrealist journal was devoted to *La Femme surréaliste*. This issue of *Obliques* represented the first catalog of "surrealist women" in alphabetical order, complete with photographs and bibliographies. However, J. H. Matthews did include Joyce Mansour in his 1969 collection of surrealist poets entitled *Surrealist Poetry in France*. Suleiman also mentions Lea Vergine's 1980 work *L'Autre moitié de l'avant-garde*, which "sought to document the lives and work of women artists associated with all the major European avant-garde movements between 1910 and 1940, and which included eighteen women under the heading *Surréalisme*" (Suleiman 157). More recent efforts include *Surrealism and Women*, edited by Mary Anne Caws et al. (MIT Press, 1991), Whitney Chadwick's *Women Artists and the Surrealist Movement* (Boston: Little, Brown, 1985), and Jacqueline Chénieux-Gendron's *Le Surréalisme et le roman* (Lausanne: L'Age d'Homme, 1983). There was a "hidden" association of women artists and writers behind the surrealist movement, and one can understand that Marguerite Duras, too, fell under Surrealism's spell, and that, as a result, she might, in her own writing, expand our conception of this male movement to include the feminine viewpoint. Duras thus renders the movement feminine, in what I will call her feminization of Surrealism.

Both André Breton, our representative surrealist, and Marguerite Duras seem to have had similar agendas in mind in many respects: both sought the subversion of existing order and the freeing of individual desire (Cottenet-Hage 541). As Cottenet-Hage points out, love is the seminal, if not the unique, theme of Duras's work. When asked to describe her writing, she labels herself "un écrivain du désir." Breton, too, believed in the power of erotic desire to transform one's life by projecting one into the realm of the marvelous. For Duras, writing necessarily has a sexual role, since, as she said in *La Vie matérielle*, writers are "des objects sexuels par excellence" (77). In Surrealism, too, writing, sexuality and desire are all interrelated. For the surrealists, poetry and love "represent the overthrow of restraint, and the affirmation of total liberty" (Matthews *Surrealist Poetry* 8). Thus, the surrealists, believing in the revolutionary and transformational powers of

erotic desire wanted to use poetry as the locus where they could give free reign to desire. In their quest for an absolute and unique love, they placed woman at the center of their activities. As Whitney Chadwick notes, "no artistic movement since Romanticism has elevated the image of woman to as significant a role in the creative life of man as Surrealism did; no group or movement has ever defined such a revolutionary role for her" (7). Chadwick is essentially interpreting what Breton said in his *Manifestes*. In a note in his 1929 *Manifeste du surréalisme*, Breton writes that "le problème de la femme est, au monde, tout ce qu'il y a de merveilleux et de trouble" (129). Breton and the surrealists believed in the power of erotic desire in their attempt to flee the temporal and spatial limits of society as they knew it. Woman opened the pathway to a new conception of the world.

With the projection of love and desire in surrealist poetry, the surrealists wanted to create the conditions necessary for an epiphany of new forms of meaning. For the surrealists, love has the power to reveal a side of the real which had been previously hidden by conventions of habit (Matthews *Surrealist Poetry* 112). As Susan Suleiman suggests:

> There has existed since Surrealism a strong and almost continuous current in French literary and artistic practice and thought, based on the double exigency to "be absolutely modern" and to change, if not the world, at least—as a first step—the way we think about the world. This recurrent tendency has expressed itself with remarkable consistency, privileging certain concepts (heterogeneity, play, marginality, transgression, the unconscious, eroticism, excess), and mounting heavy attacks on others (representation, the unitary subject, unitary meaning, linear narrative, the realist novel, paternal authority).[13]

Both writers in question indeed privilege the concepts of marginality, transgression, and eroticism. They try to liberate the imaginary through an exploration of the unconscious. To this end, Duras and Breton each seek to destroy linear narrative, unitary meaning, representation, and the realist novel in the process. But in Surrealism, the language of love is a male language, its object woman. The surrealists define her image in terms of male desires (Chadwick 103). We have seen that there are female artists associated with the surrealist movement, yet:

> a woman surrealist cannot simply assume a subject position and take over a stock of images elaborated by the male imagery; in order to innovate, she has to invent her own position as subject and elaborate her own set of images—different from, yet as empowering as the image of the exposed

female body, with its endless potential for manipulation, disarticulation and rearticulation, fantasizing and projection, is for her male colleagues.

("A Double Margin" 164)

The male surrealists chose to forget that "not all spectators of art are heterosexual males," so if "women are to be part of an avant-garde movement, they will do well to found it themselves" (Suleiman 158). And this is what Duras does: I want to argue that Duras, in her feminization of Surrealism, creates her own feminine realm of the marvelous.

As I have already suggested, for Breton, the novel and poetry as genres, are diametrically opposed. Actually, in opposition to Breton, Duras wrote novels, and only progressively did they become poetic in nature. In Duras's most recent, and final, work, *C'est tout,* she seems to blend the two genres together, and in doing so, frees literature from strict genre constraints. Duras seems to illustrate, as the title of Jacqueline Chénieux-Gendron's article suggests, this critic's comment that there are many "versants et versions du surréalisme français,"[14] for Duras's feminization of Surrealism culminates in *C'est tout.*

When *C'est tout* was published in 1995, many critics, as David Coward states, dismissed it as a "tasteless exercise in deathbed exploitation" ("Light from a Dying Star" TLS May 21 1999). I, however, find that this work serves as a point of departure that calls for a reexamination of Duras's corpus. *C'est tout* consists of a series of writings from November 20th, 1994 to August 1st, 1995, and reads much like a *journal intime* in which Duras expresses her fears of imminent death, and comments on the process of her writing. In this text, she also demonstrates her love and desire for Yann Andréa, a young homosexual man with whom she lived from 1980 until her death in 1996. But more importantly, this work is poetic in nature, and the words are arranged on the pages like lines of poetry. Much in the way Breton and the surrealists combine and manipulate words in novel ways in their poetry in an attempt to liberate the marvelous occasionally resulting from the interaction of contradictory meanings, "the elliptic fragments of Duras's discourse produce *poetic écarts.*"[15] When asked about the poetic nature of her work in the phone interview with Susan Detlefsen, Duras quipped: "S'il y a un élément poétique dans mon oeuvre, j'en suis tout à fait inconsciente. D'ailleurs, les questions de style ne m'ont jamais beaucoup intéressé" (61). Duras elsewhere refers to the poetic quality of her own work, in a blatant contradiction that is common to Duras,

when she calls her work, *Moderato cantabile,* a poem as opposed to a novel in an interview with Bettina L. Knapp. Duras describes the written word as "un poème par le mot. Le mot jouant tous les rôles. . . . Le mot étant jeté" (Vircondelet *Marguerite Duras ou le temps de détruire* 162). Duras's conception of the written word again links her to the surrealists who privilege poetry over all other forms of writing.

Thus Duras's later writing increasingly fuses prose with poetry. For example, the short diary *C'est tout* is reminiscent of the surrealist poetry of Paul Eluard, for whom the love of and desire for a woman is the source of all inspiration and revelation. Yet, Duras reverses the surrealist role of women, when, often, the female becomes the desiring subject, and the male becomes the object of desire. This is the springboard by which Duras transforms and feminizes the literary practice of Surrealism. In a reversal of surrealist poetics, Duras indicates that "sans homme il n'y aura plus rien" (36), and she dedicates *C'est tout* to Yann: "Pour Yann mon amant de la nuit. Signé Marguerite, l'amante de cet amant adoré, le 20 novembre 1994, Paris, rue Saint-Benoît" (7).

In the surreal and poetic tradition of the *troubadours,* Yann, as her muse, served as the inspiration for her writings: "Tu es l'auteur de tout" (41) she says, and "Tout a été écrit par toi, par ce corps que tu as" (42). In fact, Yann is the anonymous hero to whom Duras dedicated the series of works I refer to as the "Yann cycle:" *Les Yeux bleus cheveux noirs, Emily L., L'Homme atlantique, Yann Andréa Steiner, L'Eté 80, La Maladie de la mort,* as well as *La Pute de la côte Normande, L'Homme assis dans le couloir,* and *C'est tout.* In *C'est tout,* the "entry-poem" of July 24th in particular reads as a surrealist ode to man, which emphasizes Duras's feminization of Surrealism.

Venez m'aimer.
Venez.
Viens dans ce papier blanc.
Avec moi.

Je te donne ma peau.
Viens.
Vite.

Dis-moi au revoir.
C'est tout.
Je ne sais plus rien de toi.

Je m'en vais avec les algues.
Viens avec moi.

(53)

Here, the reader can envision Duras lying on a bed made up of white sheets ("Viens dans ce papier blanc"), as she calls to her companion to join her in her longing for a surreal fusion with his being ("Je te donne ma peau"). This entry poem recalls, to press my analogy, the opening lines of Breton's "Sur la route de San Romano," in which "La poésie se fait dans un lit comme l'amour / Ses draps défaits sont l'aurore des choses" (Signe ascendant. Gallimard, *Poésie.* 1968. 122). For Duras, as for the surrealists, all boundary limitations between the real and the unreal are blurred, as the above example illustrates. Duras renders these surreal images feminine when she becomes the desiring subject. Her skin envelops Yann as he becomes one with her in the bed made up of white sheets. The white sheets also suggest a sheet of white paper as it, too, envelops and covers that which is underneath. Duras says of her writing: "que du moment que ce n'est pas, toutes choses confondues . . . écrire ce n'est rien. Que du moment que ce n'est pas, chaque fois, toutes choses confondues en une seule par essence inqualifiable, écrire ce n'est rient que publicité" (*Amant* 14-15), which I translate to mean that for Duras, the act of writing is not a worthwhile endeavor unless it surpasses all boundary limitations.

Duras's conception of the act of writing itself is analogous to the surrealist practice of *écriture automatique*. The goal of Surrealism is to liberate the unconscious freed from all control of reason. In 1924, André Breton defined Surrealism as the "automatisme psychique pur par lequel on ne propose d'exprimer, soit verbalement, soit par écrit, soit de toute autre manière, le fonctionnement réel de la pensée. Dictée de la pensée, en l'absence de tout contrôle exercé par la raison" (*Manifestes du surréalisme* 36). The narrator of Duras's **Emily L.** gives an analogous definition of *écriture automatique* in the following passage: "il fallait écrire sans correction, pas forcément vite, à tout allure, non, mais selon soi et selon le moment qu'on traverse, soi, à ce moment-là . . . ne rien élever de sa masse inutile, rien, la laisser entière avec le reste, ne rien assagir, ni vitesse ni lenteur, laisser tout dans l'état de l'apparition" (153-154). Duras said herself that to write is to "laisser le mot venir quand il vient, l'attraper comme il vient, à sa place de départ, ou ailleurs, quand il passe. Et vite, vite écrire" (qtd. in Armel "J'ai vécu le mythe" 20). And Duras often seems to practice automatic writing, for, as she explains, "le livre s'inventait, se faisait à son insu: Tout se fait sans contrôle, dans un ordre qui échappe à soi et même au monde . . . Il s'agit d'attraper vite les mots qui s'échappent de la tête (cette passoire), et de les inscrire sur le papier." And for Duras, the creative process is necessarily

the fruit of chance when she states: "C'est ainsi que tout se fait; étrange histoire de la création . . . issue du hasard." Breton and the surrealists heeded the impulse of chance when they, too, committed their automatic, spontaneous thoughts to paper.

The surrealists label these spontaneous thoughts *le hasard objectif,* which, according to Michel Carrouges, "serait l'ensemble des prémonitions, des rencontres insolites et des coïncidences stupéfiantes, qui se manifestent de temps à autre dans la vie humaine."[16] In her writing, Duras mentioned two such coincidences which she recounted to Michelle Porte in *Les Lieux de Marguerite Duras.* When asked about the place name *S. Thala* that she used in her work **Le Ravissement de Lol V. Stein,** Duras acknowledged that "c'est très tard que je me suis aperçue que ce n'était pas S. Thala, mais Thalassa" (85). Michelle Porte asked Duras if she intended to write *Thalassa* in her work, to which Duras replied "no." For the surrealists, this is a revelatory coincidence [. . . .] In the same interview Duras referred to a second incidence of discovery that was not consciously controlled nor intended when she made the film **Hiroshima mon amour**: "j'ai fait **Hiroshima,** il y a seize ans maintenant et je me suis aperçue il y a deux ans peut-être que Nevers c'était *never* (jamais) en anglais. Je me jouie des tours comme ça, souvent, c'est bizarre" (85). Duras went on to say that: "ça me fait plaisir quand je découvre ça, les choses que je n'ai pas voulues, ces accidents, si vous voulez" (85). For Breton, the coincidences that arrive from moments of chance are revelatory, and he delights in their lack of intentionality. Such moments are revelatory because they link together two similar, yet separate events that occurred at different times. The first event, already forgotten, is thus mysteriously called back to the present. For example, in *L'Amour fou,* Breton recounted one day that in 1934, he bought a spoon with a little shoe (slipper) worked into the handle while walking in a flea market with Alberto Giacometti. After his purchase, he recalled that a few months earlier he had tried to convince Giacometti to make an ash tray that Breton called a *cendrier Cendrillon,* whose inspiration stems from a phrase Breton had imagined when he was not yet fully awake (Chénieux-Gendron 114). Thus, this incident of coincidence was revelatory for Breton since the spoon recalled to him his earlier idea for a Cinderella slipper ash tray. In this case, chance, knocking on his unconscious, somehow urged Breton to purchase the spoon. After his purchase, he then was able to link the two episodes together.

In his *Premier manifeste du surréalisme* Breton lists several "secrets de l'art magique surréaliste," and among these is the recommendation to "écrire vite sans sujet préconçu" (41). Duras's conception of writing fiction is analogous of Breton's imperative to "capter la coulée d'un autre sens" (Picon 23) by using the technique of *écriture courante* which is analogous to *écriture automatique.* Like the flow of running water, Duras, too, would begin the writing process without regard for a preestablished or mapped out story line. She told Michelle Porte that: "Je me méfie, d'une histoire faite, toute faite, voyez, déjà avant d'écrire, avec un commencement, un milieu, une fin, des péripéties, . . . Je ne comprends pas comment on peut écrire une histoire déjà explorée, inventoriée, recensée" (*Les Lieux de Marguerite Duras* 37). For Duras, the term *écriture courante* replaces the surrealist *écriture automatique,* and implies a transformation of this concept. Duras coined the expression *écriture courante* in her novel *L'Amant* in the passage where she explains that she can write about her mother now that she no longer remembers the color of her eyes or the perfume she wore. "C'est fini," Duras says, "je ne me souviens plus. C'est pourquoi j'en écris si facile d'elle maintenant, si long, si étiré, elle est devenue *écriture courante*" (38). In French, the *adjectif courant* means, among other things, "quotidian" or "common;" and the emphasis on "daily" parallels the way the surrealists attempted to capture sparks of the marvelous in everyday occurrences.

Duras used what she called *écriture courante* for the first time in *Eté 80,* which is a collection of essays dealing with daily events first published in *La Libération.* Aliette Armel describes this work by saying that it is "la première mise en oeuvre de ce que Duras appelle *l'écriture courante,* où les événements de Gdansk en Pologne se mêlent au récit très intime de ses rêves de vacances et de l'arrivée d'un homme dans sa vie" ("Le Jeu autobiographique" 31). In 1987, in *La Vie matérielle,* Duras referred to her writing as "l'écriture flottante" (9). And as many critics have pointed out, *courant* in French also refers to the movement of water—i.e. running water—and this image is appropriate because, in the Durassian universe, bodies of water abound in images of the *mer, delta,* and *fleuves.* Water serves as the foreground to much of Duras's work, which leaves the reader with the impression that there is no stable ground on which the discourse is fixed, there is only the fluid passage of water "in which scenarios, situations, persons are never arrested, jelled, but emigrate and fuse with each other."[17] In Marie-Paule Ha's analysis, Duras's writing thus became a kind of *mer-écriture* where "the movement of writing itself which like the lines traced by the Pacific tides, erases itself no sooner has it been formed. Constantly on the move, the Durassian text is never fixed" (318).

In addition to the practice of writing, Duras shared the surrealist goal to reject the fixity of language in their search for the transformation of consciousness. With explicably political designs in **Les Parleuses,** Duras allowed Xavière Gauthier to call her works revolutionary: "je crois que ce sont des livres entièrement révolutionnaires, entièrement d'avant-garde, et d'un point de vue habituel révolutionnaire et d'un point de vue de femme . . ." (61). Surrealist works in general are also considered revolutionary because they looked to previously unexplored realms to find an absolute. Dreams, madness, and the unconscious were their realms, and they purposefully played with language in hopes of producing the spark that would open for them the domain of an absolute reality. In this sense, they heeded Baudelaire's revolutionary cry: "Au fond de l'inconnu pour trouver du nouveau." As a feminist revolutionary, Duras, too, delves into her feminine unconscious, as she takes Surrealism's rejection of the fixity of "normal" language one step farther by totally rejecting, in dadaistic fashion, language. For her, meaningful communication will take place outside the realm of language, and is a revolutionary act. As Roland Barthes suggests, "déplacer la parole, c'est faire une revolution."[18] And though Duras does not consciously seek to follow Breton's imperative, she seemingly adopts the culminating cry of the *Premier manifeste du surréalisme* that "l'existence est ailleurs" (60) when she displaces the writing in her works into silence. In line with surrealist goals, Duras, too, is in search of a new form of writing, one that, according to Noëlle Carruggi, "laisse transparaître toute la dimension de l'impalpable, de l'insaisissable ou de l'irréprésentable" (*Marguerite Duras* 3). Carruggi astutely observes that ignorance is "la seule vraie connaissance" (3) in the Durassian universe, which ultimately leads Duras down the road to silence. As Verena Andermatt Conley suggests, Duras writes of "meaning that is about to merge but also to disappear."[19]

For Duras, emptiness and silence become the basis for a feminine aesthetic that equals the surrealist ideal of the marvelous that is revealed in "the repeated transformation of the individual subject through the fusion with others" (Hirsch 84). Marianne Hirsch explains that Duras's feminine aesthetic "lies in the affirmation of death and destruction, not as an end of life, but as a means to other lives which emerge after silence and emptiness have been reached, which emerge through emptiness and silence, through fiction and beyond it."[20] Duras believes that women have, "in response to centuries of silence and oppression imposed on them, turned in on themselves and become attuned to silence" (Murphy *Alienation and Absence* 26). But whereas Murphy claims that it is the emergence from silence that Duras aims to portray in her works (as manifested in the female protagonists in her texts when they break out of their mold of lethargy and inaction), I would say that the emergence from silence is only implied and hoped for at the end of her literary career. Duras's last work, **C'est tout,** a postscriptum if you will, ends in silence, for by then Duras has exhausted all possibility of expression, written or spoken. As Alain Vircondelet suggests, "chacun des textes de sa bibliographie est une trace de plus dans la comprehension générale de Marguerite Duras, dont on ne saura l'ampleur et l'importance qu'après sa mort, quand elle aura cessé d'écrire" (*Pour Duras* 75). If we heed Vircondelet's suggestion, Duras's final work is revealing and serves as a starting point from which to evaluate her entire corpus.

For Duras, the end was always a beginning, and the ultimate silence at which her work aimed was hinted at from the beginning. With her final text (*C'est tout*) in mind, I suggest a re-evaluation of the Durassian corpus based on a comparison of the ultimate silence of her texts to the surrealist ideal of the marvelous. For Duras, silence is the only solution possible to "l'immense tristesse du monde" that she talks about in her first published novel (**Les Impudents** 233). This idea, as Carol Murphy puts it, "lays the thematic and stylistic groundwork for future texts" (*Alienation and Absence* 27). Like the surrealists, Duras, too, was looking for a solution to a world gone bad. It is through writing that Duras transforms "le monde pourri en lendemain nouveau" (Vircondelet *Marguerite Duras* 1972 8). But, as Duras herself suggests, the reader must interpret the silences, for these gaps leave space for sentences to come: "Parfois c'est la place d'une phrase à venir qui se propose. Parfois rien, à peine une place, une forme, ouverte, à prendre. Mais tout doit être lu, la place vide aussi" (**Les Yeux verts** 49). Thus for Duras, the feminine locus for a surreal revelation is the space language leaves behind when it disappears into the whiteness of the page.

Due to Duras's emphasis on the void, on silence, her fiction has been labeled, on the one

hand, experimental and, on the other hand, interpreted as representative of feminist writing. Hélène Cixous gives praise to Marguerite Duras, whose writing, she believes, is the best representation of *écriture feminine*. Hélène Cixous believes that the act of women writing is necessarily revolutionary, which goes hand in hand with the surrealist concept that writing represents the very possibility of change. Cixous's concept of *écriture feminine* closely resembles the surrealist practice of *écriture automatique,* for it is a type of writing that emanates from the body, and allows the unconscious to speak. This type of spontaneous writing challenges normal "male" language because it "disrupts the text down to the level of sentences and word usage. In so doing language is being decentered and liberated."[21] But Duras liberates language more than the surrealists with her use of breaks and blanks in her writing; she does more than decenter it; she displaces language into silence, and in doing so, she adds a feminine dimension to surrealist aesthetics.

In **Les Parleuses,** Xavière Gauthier questioned Duras about "feminine writing," about the blanks and holes specifically in **L'Amour,** and suggested that only a woman could write such a work. Duras in turn replied "qui sait," but then went on to explain that the appearance of such blanks is not due to a conscious effort on her part: "C'est des blancs, si vous voulez, qui s'imposent. Ça se passé comme ça: je vous dis comment ça se passé, c'est des blancs qui apparaissent, peut-être sous le coup d'un rejet violent de la syntaxe . . ." (12). The incorporation of silences in her works challenges phallocentric discourse and linear narrative. But more importantly, "the silences of course, demonstrate the failure of language to accommodate female experience" (Wiedermann 106). Bernard Alazet, in his discussion of *Le Navire night,* evokes the image of the white page, referring to the text as a "territoire aveuglé de lumière qu'est la page blanche" (38). The white page could also refer to the empty page, in that the writing on the page is obliterated by the intense light until nothing remains. If one accepts the traditional view that light is typically associated with the masculine—in Greek mythology Helios is a sun god—and dark with that which is feminine, then one could say the feminine is being oppressed, subverted by the masculine. The introduction of silences (blanks) represents the *leitmotiv durassien,* that of "l'impossibilité de dire, le dire et ne pas dire, le dire indicible."[22] The Durassian paradox is that as a writer, Duras nonetheless uses language, in writing, to express that which cannot be expressed:

"ces pages vides à force d'être pleines, illisibles à force d'être écrites, d'être pleines d'écritures."

To conclude this introduction, Duras's writing is analogous to the surrealist endeavor in the areas of convergence mentioned above. Yet, up to the present time, no in-depth study exists that explores Duras's affiliation with Surrealism. Several brief but significant articles, footnotes, and references to Surrealism in her works have set the groundwork for such a study. I have already referred to Cottenet-Hage's groundbreaking article "Magnetic Fields II," and mentioned Jean Decottignie's suggestive footnote in the "Le Poète et la stature," as well as relevant remarks made by Duras herself and those of her critics such as Alain Vircondelet and Christiane Blot-Labarrère. Susan Rubin Suleiman explores similarities between Duras and Surrealism in "Nadja, Dora, Lol V. Stein," and Micheline Tison-Braun compares Breton and Duras's concept of fidelity in her 1985 work entitled *Marguerite Duras*. More recently, in her 1998 biography, *Marguerite Duras*, Laure Adler expresses the opinion that Duras's writing is "profondément influencée par le surréalisme" (440) in the sense that Duras is interested in all that which lies outside the limits of "un réel qu'elle trouve bien pauvre et trop plat" (440). Building on these articles and books, I propose here a more detailed analysis of the relation between Surrealism and Duras's work. There are many areas of convergence to explore, as Madeleine Cottenet-Hage would put it. Duras and the surrealists share a similar quest for the universal or absolute. In each case, the desired effect of writing evokes a strong emotional reaction (whether positive or negative) on the part of the reader. They both appeal to the depths of the unconscious, and they equally privilege the significance of *l'attente* for love. And of course, *la folie* is prevalent in the Durassian universe and in surrealist aesthetics as well. Madness ultimately leads us to the surrealist concept of *l'amour fou,* a type of love that expresses desires that defy the control of social norms or reason. In her literary universe, Marguerite Duras expands the surrealist notion of *amour fou* by replacing the male language used to express feminine sexuality. She celebrates the feminine. To study this, it is necessary to examine the degree to which, in selected works, Duras expands or transforms surrealist principles and creates a new realm that translates the female experience. Madeleine Cottenet-Hage states that if "Surrealism can be credited with having facilitated the shameless expression of Man's erotic impulses, Duras can be credited with having endowed woman's eroticism with a direct

language" (546). Though, as this study will show, the "direct language" ultimately becomes the non-language of silence. Duras's work shows that it is possible for women to find meaning within the masculine literary practice of Surrealism by breaking down the barrier to what is traditionally considered a male domain. In my opinion, a surrealist sensuality infuses the Durassian corpus from beginning to end and serves as a "conceptual thread" that allows the reader a fresh approach in understanding, evaluating, and appreciating *Durasie.*[23]

Notes

1. Gabrielle Frémont, "Madeleine Gagnon: Du politique à l'intime," *Voix et Images* 8.1 (1982): 23.

2. I quote part of the title of Michelle Beauclair's innovative work entitled *Albert Camus, Marguerite Duras and the Legacy of Mourning* (New York: Peter Lang, 1998).

3. Alice J. Jardine and Anne M. Menke, *Shifting Scenes: Interviews on Women, Writings, and Politics in Post-68 France* (New York: Columbia University Press, 1991): 77.

4. See Jane Winston, "Forever Feminine: Marguerite Duras and Her French Critics," *New Literary History* 24.2 (1993).

5. Interestingly enough, Marguerite Duras brought a suit against Frédérique Lebelley for her work *Duras ou le poids d'une plume,* referred to here as a "biographie romancée," according to her son Jean Mascolo in an interview with Danielle Laurin for *Courrier International* 364 (23-29 octobre 1997) 22.

6. Germaine Brée refers to this novel as *La Famille Thanakya,* and states that it was rejected in 1941 by Gallimard ("A Singular Adventure: The Writings of Marguerite Duras." *L'Esprit créateur* 30.1 (1990): 8-14.).

7. Dionys Mascolo, father of Jean Mascolo, died August 20, 1997.

8. Winston quotes Alain Vircondelet, *Duras: biographie* (Paris: François Bourin, 1991) 469.

9. See Alain Vircondelet, *Duras: biographie* (Paris: François Bourin, 1991) 304-305.

10. Alain Vircondelet, *Pour Duras* (Mesnil-sur-l'Estrée: Editions Calmann-Lévy, 1995) 85.

11. Winston 480.

12. From an interview in *La Création étouffée,* Horay, 1973, quoted in Elaine Marks and Isabelle de Courtivron, eds., *New French Feminisms* (Amherst: The University of Massachusetts Press, 1980): 112.

13. Susan Suleiman, "A Double Margin: Reflections on Women Writers and the Avant-garde in France," *Yale French Studies* 75 (1988): 149.

14. Jacqueline Chénieux-Gendron, "Versants et versions du surréalisme français," *Revue des Sciences Humaines* 56.184 (1981): 11-31.

15. Susan Detlefsen, "A Rethinking of Genre and Gender Through a Reading of *Yes peut-être*," *Journal of Durassian Studies* 1 (1989): 66.

16. Michel Carrouges, "Le hasard objectif," *Entretiens sur le surréalisme,* Ed. Ferdinand Alquié (Paris: Mouton & Co., 1968): 271.

17. Germaine Brée, "A Singular Adventure: The Writing of Marguerite Duras," *L'Esprit Créateur* 3.1 (1990): 10.

18. Quoted in Bénédicte Mauguière, "Critique littéraire féministe et écriture des femmes au Québec (1970-80)," *The French Review* 63.4 (1990): 632.

19. Verena Andermatt Conley, "Signs of Love: Duras's Minimal Ways," *L'Esprit Créateur* 29.3 (1989): 107.

20. Mariane Hirsch, "Gender, Reading, and Desire in *Moderato Cantabile,*" *Twentieth Century Literature* 28.1 (1982): 84.

21. Barbara Wiedeman, "The Search for an Authentic Voice: Hélène Cixous and Marguerite Duras," *Journal of Durassian Studies* 1 (1980): 103.

22. Mareille Calle-Gruber, "L'Amour fou, femme fatale: Marguerite Duras," *Le Nouveau Roman en Questions,* Ed. Robert-Michel Allemand (Paris: Lettres Modernes, 1992): 19.

23. The term is coined by Claude Roy in "Duras tout entière à la langue attachée" in *Le Nouvel Observateur* 31 août 1984.

TITLE COMMENTARY

The Malady of Death

SHARON A. WILLIS (ESSAY DATE 1989)

SOURCE: Willis, Sharon A. "Staging Sexual Difference: Reading, Recitation, and Repetition in Duras' *Malady of Death.*" In *Feminine Focus: The New Women Playwrights,* edited by Enoch Brater, pp. 109-25. New York: Oxford University Press, 1989.

In the following essay, Willis examines Duras's treatment of sexual difference as a site of resistance within her novel Malady of Death.

Duras is hardly a "new" woman playwright. She first published in 1943; her accelerated output in recent years has roughly coincided with her first widespread popular reception in the United States as well as in France. Nor is she primarily known for her dramatic productions, at least in the English-speaking world. Rather, her theater has tended to arise as a consequence of her other literary work, in critical reformulations that change the stress of problems and scenes already presented in narrative form. Further, some of the earlier plays are more widely known in the form of published scripts that prolong them after they are no longer theatrically produced. Most recently, however, Duras' texts have appeared under a rubric which blends genres, as in *texte-théâtre-film* or, simply, *récit,* a term which has no exact English equivalent but is used in textual studies to convey the sense of "story" as opposed to "discourse": what is told, what is narrated. It is this mixing of textual categories, this refusal of boundaries, that may be Duras' point of insertion in postmodern textual and reading formations, a grounding she may share with "new" woman playwrights.

As complicated as Duras' relation to textual boundaries is, her relation to constructions of "Woman" and to recent theoretical discourses surrounding women's literary production is even more complex. While she contends that there is a specificity to feminine writing, for her this specificity is an essential one. This essentialist position may be the basis of her antagonistic stance with respect to feminist theoretical discourses and their political implications. Nevertheless, her interest for and influence upon overtly feminist literary, critical, and theoretical enterprises is powerful. It resides in her compelling and often disturbing textual work on sexual difference, upon its figurations as a site of textual conflict and resistance. This site of resistance, then, is the focus of this essay.

Duras' texts always remember. Disjunctive and repetitive, they insist on reproducing uncannily accurate, though fragmentary, memories drawn from previous texts; these "remembered" fragments from somewhere else produce the choppiness and hesitancy in the narratives. To read them one must sift through layers of interference; one must reconstruct the narrative in more than one register. Recalling other occurrences of the repeated scenes and figures that interweave her texts, our readings both reconstruct past texts and build another narrative of this memory; there is a story *between* the texts.[1] On the other hand, our reading process also segments the narrative according to its interferences, moments of repetition, similarity, and recall; that is, the narrative's memory dis-members the text. Reading, then, both dis-members and re-members.[2] It would be possible to say that a reading of more than one of Duras' texts necessarily entails this double labor of recognition and distinction, of reconstructing, or reproducing and separating, keeping apart.

In a sense Duras' texts are always based in an irretrievable absence, another space beyond their boundaries—a previous text partially recalled, another genre or form, or the scene of reading itself—a scene the writing can never fully embody, articulate, or occupy. At the same time, her texts tend to *thematize* this absence as loss or violent separation and to do so on a particular ground, that of sexual difference. In their obsession to figure the absence and the loss in which they are "grounded," Duras' texts of the eighties operate performatively to stage absence and disappearance. They produce particularly compelling intersections of "sexual difference" with "remembering" and "reading," since all three terms are staged as both delirious repetitions and obsessive efforts to differentiate. Meanwhile, these recent works steadfastly erode the integrity of genre. As novel, *récit* (this is the most recent designation which appears on the title pages), film, or theater, each text *appeals* to another scene of representation, another genre, often mixing one in with another. That is, each text exhibits a fundamental dependence on an outside against which it defines itself, while refusing consolidation within a particular genre. Consequently, the instability of differentiations and borders is reproduced at the textual boundary itself.

The Malady of Death, presented as a novel written in the second person, opens with the line, "You wouldn't have known her, you'd have seen her everywhere at once" (p. 7). This narrative recounts nothing but the sexual interactions of a woman character and a man character, "you," who pays her to spend a set number of nights with him. The text ends with a kind of "post-face" in which Duras provides some suggestions about staging this text as a play.

> ***The Malady of Death*** could be staged in the theater. . . . Only the woman would speak her lines from memory. The man never would. He would read his text, either standing still, or walking about around the woman.
>
> The man the story is about would never be represented. Even when he speaks to the young woman, he does so through the man who reads his story.
>
> Acting here is replaced by reading. I always think that nothing can replace the reading of a text, that no acting can ever equal the effect of a text not memorized.
>
> (p. 56)
>
> Je crois toujours que rien ne remplace la lecture d'un texte, que rien ne remplace le manque de mémoire du texte, rien, aucun jeu.
>
> (***La Maladie de la mort**, p. 59)

As Duras envisions it staged, this play would be split between theatrical performance and reading—the young woman's part would be acted while the man's story would be read by an actor whose very act of reading, in its literalness, would figure the absence of that character. So reading and acting would coexist, split the stage, constituting two mutually interfering registers. Reading

and acting would both support and resist each other. On the level of the two bodies before us onstage, however, a question arises: what is the status of the actors? Which one would call attention more compellingly to the art of acting? And how would we calculate or stabilize the space between acting and reading? How would we describe the difference?

Yet there is another equally fascinating question involving memory and reading. Careful attention to the English and French versions of the text yields a slight but powerful difference of sense here. The French could be translated as "I still think that nothing replaces the reading of a text, nothing replaces the text's lack of memory, nothing, no acting." On this reading the text is taken to replace acting's memorized recitation. But as a substitute for memory in the form of memorization, the text here is a memory with no memory of itself; that is, it is memory only when actualized, figured in the literal reading that is staged. On this level the staged event would be organized as a coexistence and conflict between two kinds of spoken text, recitation and reading, and between two kinds of memory, memorization and writing.[3]

At the extreme, memorization might be opposed to writing in the following way. Memorization would imply a prior reading internalized, now independent of the text, which it reproduces entirely in the mental images it stores for repeated restoration in oral performance. Writing, meanwhile, would look like an externalized form of memory, replacing "natural" recall. However, memorization itself remains a technique with a long history (as in the classical opposition between writing and oratory). As examined by Ellen Burt in "Poetic Conceit: The Self-Portrait and Mirrors of Ink," it constitutes a metonymic displacement on the level of the signifier:

> An orator who wants to remember a speech memorizes neither the words, nor yet the argument. Instead, by means of an elaborate and apparently uneconomical process, he recodes the words or *res* (things or subjects of his speech) in a series of images. . . . These images, like dream images, are formed as rebuses, as riddles, to be read off. . . . The images themselves get their content by a process of semanticization of the signifier. . . . The displacement of meaning away from the signified, and the subsequent construction of an image from the signifier, is what allows each image to be read so easily.
>
> (pp. 23-24)

Considered this way, memorization would be itself a work of writing, inscription, as well as perpetual rereading. The coexistence of writing and memorization in Duras' text, then, figures a memory autonomous of the subject's recollection, autonomous of a relation to the past. It thus maintains the simultaneity of memory and the event or discourse it recalls. Within this conjunction it is impossible to distinguish original from copy, production from reproduction. Furthermore, Duras insists that "the two actors should speak as if they were reading in separate rooms, isolated from one another. The text would be completely nullified if it were spoken theatrically" (p. 57). In other words, the dialogue read and recited would be staged as autonomous monologues. There is no exchange between these levels of reading/ acting; there is only separation and interference. This radical separation of competing "interpretations" (in the sense of an actor's interpretation of a role), or readings, is staged on the axis of sexual difference, by a woman and a man.

But if this text is designed to stage radical separation and interference effects, it also stages absence. "You" is never onstage. He is replaced by a partial stand-in, another man who reads the story for him. Or is it *to* him, since "you" necessarily evokes the sense of direct address, posing as the addressee of the speech? This unseen protagonist also figures a whole set of absences: the absence of memory from the text, the actor's necessary absence from the scene in which he is cast as a reader, the actress' absence from his reading, the characters' absence from themselves. Finally, there is the written text's absence to itself at the moment it is staged. It is never entirely *there* where it is read and performed simultaneously; indeed, it is this simultaneity that renders both versions of it partial and supplementary.

We might find the same "absenting" effects in the conditional mode that opens the text and continues to haunt Duras' concluding intervention, as well as my own writing here. How, we might well ask, could one stage the conditional mode? Isn't this mode profoundly alien to theatrical representation? Is the stage perhaps even hostile to the conditional, on the level of its representation, if not its dialogue? The conditional, it seems to me, can be spoken onstage but never *acted,* owing to the resistant presence of the actor before us.

This text's highly unstable figuration would be founded on two unfigurable elements. Hovering between two nonsituations—as the future of the past and the mode of wish, hypothesis, and desire—the conditional mood destabilizes the temporality of both stage and reading. Similarly,

the sheer resistance of the stubbornly nontheatrical reader, the *literal* reader onstage, signals an unfigurable absence. But these instabilities call up others: the reader/spectator's position is disrupted by several competing appeals. "You," to whom the reading addresses itself, is absent, just as we are. How can we avoid slipping into the posture of the addressee from time to time? On the other hand, how can we coincide with that position, particularly if we remember our own gendered bodies and if we are female? How can we determine the space and the temporality of our absence from this scene when one actor performs exactly as we have performed or are performing—as readers?

Such destabilization of reader/spectator position is coherent with and implicated in this text's shifting and contradictory framing effects. These range from the splitting of the stage between reading and recitation, to the unanchored direct address, to two contradictory, mutually exclusive positions, and to the intervention of the author's discourse which prolongs the text's work beyond its ending, both by repeating its conditional mode and by reframing it as a play. Thus, the text we have just read as a novel demands an immediate rereading that casts it in another frame altogether.

This kind of intervention is an effect repeated and transposed in most of Duras' recent work. *Savannah Bay,* a play organized around a conversation between two women, questions one character's inability to remember and opens with a brief author's preface written in direct address to "you." Madeleine, an elderly actress, remembers almost nothing; memories of her life have been replaced by the memorized scripts she has played, and even these are only partially recalled. The other character is an unnamed young woman whose role consists in trying to restore Madeleine's story. She recites bits of the *récit* of Madeleine's life, telling the story as, we presume, Madeleine had once told it to her. Memory, then, comes back to the actress not as proper to her or continuous with her lived life but from elsewhere, from outside, as already "told," read, and memorized by another.

But here the conjunctions and distinctions between repetition of a story and its recitation are impossible to establish. We never know if the story that is being told is that of the "life" or of a "role." The "originary" moment already seems to be representation and performance. Further, because Madeleine was originally played by Madeleine Renaud, the actress as *acted* became overly coincident with the actress acting. The "Madeleines" were both too close together and too far apart.

The character was too close to the historically bound actress who played her. Meanwhile, the speech of the real, historical actress betrayed the figure she played; her *good* memory was essential to this staging of theater's nightmare, the failure of memory. Oblivion seemed to have a memory, one that was quite explicitly supplied through an elsewhere, beyond the stage, which nonetheless constantly invaded the scene.

Invasion is also the text's point of departure since, before any staging, there is the author's discourse about it, posed in direct address.

> Tu ne sais plus qui tu es, qui tu as été, tu sais que tu as joué, tu ne sais plus ce que tu as joué, ce que tu joues, tu joues, tu sais que tu dois jouer, tu ne sais plus quoi, tu joues.
>
> [You no longer know who you are, who you have been, you know that you have played, you no longer know what you've played, what you play, you play, you know you must play, you no longer know what, you play.]
>
> (p. 7)[4]

This play opens with a description addressed to the main character/actress concerning the inability to distinguish between the playing and the role. She is told she cannot remember *what* she plays, only *that* she plays it. But then the status of acting is as unstable as the distinction between the two Madeleines; for to play a role demands a differentiation (between one's private memory and the script, between the acting subject and the subject acted) as well as a recognition of that difference, which is the space of interpretation.

Here we are confronted with a text whose frame is ruptured by this authorial intervention, one that simultaneously reframes, preinterprets the text, and produces interferences which constitute a space of interpretation. And where are we in the space of interpretation? Once again, direct address is split between us, the real actress Madeleine Renaud, and the actress staged. At the same time, this preface becomes a sort of memory that will haunt the play, a memory whose recall will persist within *our* interpretation. Our reading, then, occupies the space of interpretation opening into the text. Because it is disturbed by reframing, by a discourse that is both inside and outside it, the scene of representation is dependent upon and conditioned by a voice from elsewhere, by another scene. Similarly, our reading is haunted by this voice, by a direct-address "you" that is aimed elsewhere, and by its own construction as the play's absent space—an outside incorporated.

When framing effects focus on the incorporation of an absent outside space, that absence evacuates interiority, dissolves a stable border separating inside and outside. Such a gesture conditions *L'Homme atlantique,* a novel that narrates the making of a film in the future, future anterior, conditional, and past tenses. Not only is the film's temporality distorted, destablized, but its character is addressed only as "you" and is unequivocally designated as a man. The opening lines inscribe absence and forgetting as future events, but in a future tense that can also be read as injunction: "Vous ne regarderez pas la caméra. . . . Vous oublierez. . . . Que c'est vous, vous l'oublierez. . . . Vous oublierez aussi que c'est la caméra" ("You will not look at the camera. . . . You'll forget. . . . That it's you, you will forget. . . . You'll also forget that it's the camera" [p. 7]).

The scene to be filmed is nothing but the process of forgetting—the self-forgetfulness of the subject viewed. "Vous regarderez ce que vous voyez. . . . Vous essaierez de regarder jusqu'à l'extinction de votre regard" ("You will look at what you see. You will try to look as far as the extinction of your gaze" [p. 8]). Here the text splits its address in a radical disjunction. "You" is the subject framed, but it is also the potential spectator who is invited into a split look: one that is looking both at what she/he sees and at the gaze itself. This splitting produces stunning coincidences: "Vous êtes le seul à tenir lieu de vous-même auprès de moi dans ce moment-là du film qui se fait" ("You are the only one to take the place of yourself for me in that moment of the film that is being made" [p. 10]). Here the text's insistence on the unity and specificity of the "you" only serves to underline its impossibility. "You" is divided by the process of taking the place of itself as its own stand-in and by its coincidence with an ambient, anonymous, floating addressee constructed through the direct address and the unsituated phrase "that moment of the film."

Our implication emerges fully at a slightly later point in the text: "Vous êtes sorti du champs de la caméra. Vous êtes absent. Avec votre départ votre absence est survenue, elle a été photographiée comme tout à l'heure votre présence" ("You have left the camera's field. With your departure, your absence has occurred, it has been photographed as your presence just was" [p. 15]). We are indeed outside the frame, held beyond it, but pulled into it, as the text speaks of a film that might be/might have been—a film of passage outside the frame. It is impossible to situate our own relation to the frame, to refuse fully or to occupy fully the "you," determined textually as a male lover. Here again the text depends upon the absences it perpetually evokes. First, it stresses the absence of a visual level—the work is characterized as a *récit;* it is a purely imaginary film, a blind film. It also obsessively recalls the subject's absence from the visual field. But *who* is the subject? The character "you" or the spectator "you"? It is impossible to separate or distinguish our absence from his.[5] The spectator position, then, is split, ruptured, contradictory, caught between two appeals in the lure of an impossible sight—our own look. At the same time, the film inscribes the passage of a subject and a look beyond its frame.

If *L'Homme atlantique* thematizes a passage beyond the frame, a passage which then reverberates on the performative level through this disconcerting plurality of the lure posed by "you," *The Malady of Death* performs its "passages" in quite another way. The primary textual event, breaking the repetitive series of the indistinguishable nights, is the young woman's departure. Previously the text has repeated the fragmented dialogue, the man's explorative looking at the woman, his demands, and their lovemaking in such similar terms that we can only punctuate the flow of erotic exchanges through the text's long silences. Duras writes in her post-face: "There should be great silences between the different paid nights, silences in which nothing happens except the passage of time" (p. 58). Consequently, we must endure the passage, the loss of voice, where our desire is suspended in an anxiety structured around these repeated, premonitory losses, each of which might prove to be final. The differentiation between nights is produced as absence, loss, a break in the theatrical passage which burdens us with the passage of our own time as well.

The final loss, the one event of the text, is told as follows: "One day she isn't there anymore. You wake and she isn't there. She has gone during the night. The mark of her body is still there on the sheets" (p. 51). It is to be performed, according to Duras' suggestions, in such a way that we as readers/spectators experience the same abrupt break as the man does, the same sudden loss: "The young woman's departure isn't seen. There should be a blackout when she disappears, and when the light comes up again there is nothing left but the white sheets in the middle of the stage and the sound of the sea" (pp. 59-60). Like the man, we miss the moment of her passage off-scene, the passage that changes everything. As Duras envisions it, the young woman should be lying on the same white sheets as when the play opens: "The stage should be low, almost at floor level, so that the

young woman's body is completely visible to the audience" (p. 56). We have been placed, then, at the man's level, investigating this body before us. As we have shared the privilege of sight with him, we now share its loss.

The exchanges between these two figures are now organized around the question of love and death. The man hires the woman to pass these nights with him because "he cannot love," because he has never been with a woman, and, he implies, he wants to see if he can love. What he discovers instead is his malady. Rather than produce love in him, the woman will produce only the recognition of his illness, his death, and his difference.

Death and difference are inextricably bound here, but in a curious way. "You stop looking. Stop looking at anything. You shut your eyes so as to get back into your difference, your death. . . . You don't love anything or anyone, you don't even love the difference you think you embody" (pp. 32-33). While death might be constructed as what is most alien to, most utterly, radically different from life, it is also bound to the indifferentiation of death and life—too much or too little difference. But the complexity of this problem lies elsewhere as well. Death and difference share a trait; neither can ever be embodied. The malady of death that the woman first sees in the man without naming it, and which she later names, continually circulates in discourse, as if it exceeded character boundaries. It is in her look that he sees his own death, in his look that she sees his death, and, finally, in her body that he sees death inscribed. Which is to say that death *is* nowhere but is bound to the look of the other, bound into the gaze upon the other.

There is more to the malady, however. "You ask: 'why is the malady of death fatal?' She answers: 'Because whoever has it doesn't know he's a carrier, of death. And also because he's likely to die without any life to die to, and without even knowing that's what he's doing'" (p. 19). It is as if death were separated from its own fatality, at the same time that it can not be fully separated from life. Thus, the text arrives at an unresolvable problem: how can these terms be differentiated?[6] Can one fix their difference in representation?

When the woman is gone, "the difference between her and you is confirmed by her sudden absence" (p. 52). *A* difference, then, only gets established by an absent term, in and through representation. This loss generates a story, but one we do not hear, told in a bar the following day.

Only its telling is described; the story is never told. "At first you tell it as if it were possible to do so. Then you tell it laughing, as if it were impossible for it to have happened" (p. 53). Indeed, this whole text is founded on the impossibility of telling: telling the story, telling the difference, telling a death.

Love, difference, and death, all unsituated, seem to emerge only as passages through a space that confuses "before" and "after," in which no punctual event can occur, no narrative is possible. "Even so, you have managed to live that love in the only way possible for you. Losing it before it happened" (p. 55). This whole text is founded on the reading and recitation of what cannot be narrated or even held in view, held in frame, since the text is reframed immediately in the post-face.

The impossibility of love, which would depend on a sufficient or stable difference between these two figures, is replicated in our inability to attain a stable differentiation from the "you." But how, within this space of indifferentiations, are we to account for the sexual difference that organizes the whole textual scene—the exchange between the man and the woman? How are we to account for the weight of sexual difference as it imposes itself in our reading? In a text which demonstrates that neither death nor difference can be punctually or permanently embodied, the body nevertheless remains in the resistant presence of actors' bodies and in the site of reading itself. The "identificatory" lure of the direct-address "you" meets resistance or interruption when it is occupied by the gendered body of the reader, who might find her body interfering here. Or, should she separate her reading from her body, she does so only through a gesture that then forces her to recognize a division within reading—either she reads from and through a gendered body or her reading is disembodied.

Finally, there is another crucial difference to be accounted for: that of the actor reading the text and of the silent, unseen man whose story is told. Since his place onstage is occupied by a stand-in, the man is also split, utterly noncoincident with himself. He is both the central figure and an absent third. But the spectator is also an absent third: the absent, abstracted addressee and voyeur exploring the woman's body staged for our look and for the man's story read alongside it. But this problem of differentiation is contagious on the larger textual level, for this sexual scene is repeated in several other texts. This drama of failed exchange between a man and a woman, where the man dominates a nearly silent, abandoned woman, first appears in a short text, *L'Homme assis dans le couloir* (written in the late fifties or early sixties and later rewritten and published in 1980). At that time, Duras writes, she made a number of discoveries about her text. That is, the new text is a completely redone version based on what she read in the old text. "Then I found out that the lovers were not isolated, but seen, doubtless by me, and that this seeing ought to be mentioned, integrated into the action" (Lydon, p. 269).

Here again is a third term, another subject whose ambiguous voyeurism haunts the text. This text is a short narrative of a sadistic sexual scene in which the woman performs fellatio on the man, who then urinates on her, steps on her, kicks her, makes love to her, and finally, at her request, beats her. During the first sequence of events, the narrator makes her only intervention in the scene: "I speak to her and tell her what the man is doing. I tell her what is happening to her. What I want is for her to see" (Lydon, p. 270). We are made aware that our view of this scene is focalized by an "I," who is a woman ("I see that other people are watching, other women" [Lydon, p. 275]). But the relation of this woman narrator to the scene observed is impossible. Her voyeuristic distance is undermined by the movement of narrated discourse. Yet even here, entering the scene, she only does so to narrate, to tell the woman what we already know—what is happening to her. The relation between knowing and seeing is rendered ambiguous. At the end she says, "I see nothing of her except her motionlessness. I haven't a clue; I don't know a thing; I don't know whether she is sleeping" (Lydon, p. 275). In this discourse that inverts and destroys the equation of seeing with knowing, what is the place of the partially absent third for whom the scene is staged? What is our place as readers?

This question has gained a particular urgency, given that the text has been disturbing to many feminist readers because it figures a fantasy of a woman voyeur watching the beating of another woman. Consequently, it operates on a split feminine identification. But even this split identification is unstable, since the text implies a circulation of positions akin to that of the fantasy structure Freud examines in "A Child Is Being Beaten." In this regard, Mary Lydon's contention that *L'Homme assis* produces a "linguistic subversion of sexual identity," where "the 'pure' sexual difference, the difference between the sexes that the narrative of *L'Homme assis dans le couloir* might be thought to impose is contaminated, subverted at the textual level, the level of the signifier," is crucial to a reading that would be equal to the text's complexities (Lydon, 264 and 265, respectively). Not only are the referentially gender-bound words used in the text undermined by their linguistic genders in French, but the text's recapitulation of Freudian fantasy structure indicates that position and gender do not remain fixed or coherent with each other.[7]

A reading of Freud's essay on the sadistic fantasy, "A Child Is Being Beaten," reveals a circulation of positions through grammatical structures of pronouns whereby the subject of the fantasy is not fully inside it, not fully outside, not permanently located in active or passive position, and not bound to gender position. (Freud's remarks reveal that the girls' fantasies about a child being beaten are composed of several phrases between which subject and object are transformed. Genders are conferred upon them in the following sequence: a child is being beaten; my father is beating the child, who is a boy; I am being beaten by my father). What is crucial in this reading of fantasy structure is that gender is circulating, constructed in the telling or representation. It cannot be anchored to activity or passivity, since even these are seen to be positions, postures established in relation to each other.

L'Homme assis is conditioned by a structure whose circulating positional effects are reproduced in *The Malady of Death*, a text than can be read as its reenactment, its rereading of *L'Homme assis*. *The Malady* displaces these positions to locate a third term offstage as the central one, while playing on a structure of voyeurism whose mediation through reading is literalized here.

This reenactment itself becomes a grounding, a kind of original trauma repeated in a later text, *Les Yeux bleus cheveux noirs,* which once again stages a series of paid nights between a man and a woman. Again there is an absent third male, but this time he is the lover the man has lost—and, as the text will later reveal, the one the woman has lost also. The discursive exchanges of these nightly encounters are organized around repeated *récits* and descriptions of this missing lover as well as of another man the woman sees during the daytime. What the "lovers" in question exchange, then, is stories about departed lovers. Again the woman is nude, this time veiling her face in black silk; again the man hits her. Again the figures are brought together and held apart by a story exchange.

The reenactment that has been so central a feature of Duras' work strikes a resonance with Freudian psychoanalytic studies of recollection and repetition, specifically, as detailed in "Further Recommendations in the Technique of Psychoanalysis: Recollection, Repetition, Working Through." In Freud's later work on therapeutic technique, he recognizes that what the analysand cannot recollect will be acted out in repetition which does not know itself as such; that is, in repetition which replaces remembrance. In the analytic situation the goal of "working through" is achieved through the construction of an artificial repetition, the transference of the forgotten past onto the current analytic scene.

Repetition, then, is reframed when it is inserted into the analytic situation. Within this frame the analysand can *read* his own memory, lost to him, in the unconscious reproduction or replaying which has replaced it. Ideally, then, one remembers by reading one's own performance in the analytic situation. It is the reproduction which is supposed to revive memory—that is, the reproduction generates the "original" memory as its own production. Thus, the scene of psychoanalytic interpretation is also a stage. The analytic situation is the theater in which the subject's drama of repetition is reframed, set off from life, so that it may be read and analyzed. Transference effects, then, include the transfer of repetitions of the unremembered past into the analytic space as well as the performance of past conflicts upon the relation with the analyst, as in transference love and hate. Transference is a matter of performance, reading, and interpretation.

Duras' works ask us to consider the metaphoric and metonymic relays of transference which may be at work in our reading and interpretation of the reading and performance that they stage. Grounded in the fundamental imbrication of production and reproduction, where reproduction/repetition is posed as the "originary" moment, Duras' work confuses internal and external textual boundaries. It dissolves the borders between repetition as memory and repetition as forgetting, between reading as interpretation and reading as performance. Within the performative space itself, it rejects a division between the performance on the stage and the spectator/reader's performance.

Les Yeux bleus cheveux noirs textually actualizes the problem of confused borders between narration and performance. This text begins and ends with a discourse attributed to *l'acteur,* "the actor," someone whose situation in (or in relation to) the text and its story is never specified. He operates as a kind of internal gaze from elsewhere, an incorporated frame. "'Une soirée d'été,' dit l'acteur, serait au coeur de l'histoire" (p. 9). This is the first line of the text, which will end with several passages spoken by the actor:

C'est la dernière nuit, dit l'acteur. Les spectateurs s'immobilisent et regardent dans la direction du silence, celle des héros. L'acteur les désigne du regard. . . . Leur regard est effrayé . . . toujours coupable d'avoir été l'objet de l'attention générale, celle des actuers sur la scène et celle des spectateurs dans la salle.

[It's the last night, says the actor. The spectators are immobilized and look in the direction of the silence, that of the heroes. The actor indicates them by a look. . . . Their gaze is frightened . . . still guilty of having been the object of general attention, that of the actors on stage and of the spectators in the house.]

(pp. 159-60)

In this continuous undifferentiated look, shared by spectators and actors, it is impossible to separate the house from the stage. Such indifferentiation is reproduced in the continual reenactment of the text's performance:

La salle serait dans le noir, dirait l'acteur. La pièce commencerait sans cesse. A chaque phrase, à chaque mot.

Les acteurs pourraient ne pas être nécessairement des acteurs du théâtre. Ils devraient toujours lire à voix haute et claire, se tenir de toutes leurs forces exempts de toute mémoire de l'avoir jamais lu, dans la conviction de n'en connaître rien, et cela chaque soir.

[The house would be in the dark, the actor would say. The play would begin continually. At each phrase, at each word.

The actors might not necessarily be stage actors. They should always read loudly and clearly, making every effort to remain free of all memory of having read it, with the conviction of not knowing anything about it, and this, each evening.]

(p. 49)

This theatrical reading asserts a radical separation between repetitions that do not know themselves as such, and which is articulated as a separation of staged reading from knowledge and memory. The status of reading here is always in question and under transformation, as is evident in the final indifferentiation, established in several registers: those of the reading, the performance, and the gaze surrounding this scene:

L'écoute de la lecture du livre, dit l'acteur, devrait toujours être égale. Dès qu'entre les silences la lecture du texte se produirait, les acteurs devraient être suspendus à elle et, au souffle près, en être immobilisés . . .

Les acteurs regarderaient l'homme de l'histoire, quelquefois ils regarderaient le public.

Des événements qui seraient survenus entre l'homme et la femme, rien ne serait montré, rien ne serait joué. La lecture du texte se proposerait donc comme le théâtre de l'histoire.

[Listening to the reading of the book, says the actor, should always be the same. When, in between the silences, the reading happens, the actors should be suspended upon it, and except for their breathing, completely still . . .

The actors would look at the man of the story, sometimes they would look at the audience.

Of the events which would have occurred between the man and the woman, nothing would be shown, nothing would be acted out. The reading of the text would offer itself, then, as the story's theater.]

(p. 38)

This maneuver supports the overall textual strategy, which inverts conventional relations of reading to script, where the script is conceived as outside of and prior to theatrical performance. Here the narrative is the theater of its own performance; it is thus split by the intrusion of an elsewhere. Its destabilized boundaries are replaced by perpetual reframings which produce a mobility of address that entails continual reconstruction of the spectator/reader position.

In their obsessive restaging of a scene of sexual desire and violent separations, Duras' recent works suggest that sexual difference is never stable nor in place; indeed, they suggest that it has no place. Rather, it is perpetually staged and restaged, read, reread, and constructed, just as it is constructed on the sites of reading mapped by these textual performances.

Notes

1. Indifferentiation is contagious. It is obliquely connected to critical issues surrounding these texts. It would be fair to say, I think, that Duras' critics frequently suffer from an inability to separate their discourse from that of the texts. This inability is expressed through meditations on her texts which mimic their style, which reproduce, in an attenuated form, the textual gestures they attempt to analyze. As such, Duras' texts threaten to leave us speechless or reduced to the "already said."

2. I want to express my appreciation to my colleague David Pollack for reminding me, in reference to a different subject, of the possibilities in the pair remembering/dismembering. He suggests this might provide an interesting opposition from which to consider structures of the gaze, particularly as it is organized around sexual difference.

3. Such conflict between levels and modes of discourse has long been thematized within Duras' work. More recently, however, these resistances have been increas-

ingly produced on the performative level. One of the earlier emergences of such a struggle appears in *Le Camion* (Paris: Minuit, 1977), a film-text which stages a conversation between a long-distance truck driver and a woman passenger as they follow his highway route. In this case the actors are never photographed in the truck. Rather, we see shots of a truck rolling down a highway, crosscut with scenes of the two actors, Duras herself and Gérard Depardieu, as they sit in her house and read their lines from scripts. The film itself is framed by Duras' discourse about it, a discourse which often enters the diegesis and which is cast in the conditional.

4. Unless otherwise stated, all translations are my own. Here I have tried to maintain the repetitive minimalism of the passage by using only one verb, however awkward, for acting. *"Jouer"* and "to play" are roughly correspondent in that they are both more normally connected to the noun "role," as "to play a role."

5. I have considered these issues and some of these texts in somewhat sketchier detail and within a different framework in the last chapter of *Marguerite Duras: Writing on the Body* (Urbana and Chicago: University of Illinois Press, 1987).

6. See Jacques Derrida, *La Carte postale* (Paris: Flammarion, 1980), for an explanation of Freud's writing on the repetition compulsion in *Beyond the Pleasure Principle,* where the theoretical enterprise dedicated to distinguishing and mapping the interactions of the pleasure principle and the death drive founders on its own discovery that these two principles keep turning into each other. They remain inextricable from one another, an imbrication which is replicated in the relation of representation to the unrepresentable.

7. The comments which follow were inspired by Mary Lydon in a conversation following a reading of her translation of *L'Homme assis* and of a critical analysis of the text. It was she, I believe, who originally suggested that I look at "A Child Is Being Beaten" in relation to this text.

Bibliography

Burt, E. S. "Poetic Conceit: The Self-Portrait and Mirrors of Ink." *Diacritics* 2, no. 4 (1982), 17-38.

Duras, Marguerite. *L'Homme atlantique.* Paris: Minuit, 1982.

———. *La Maladie de la mort.* Paris: Minuit, 1982.

———. *The Malady of Death.* Translated by Barbara Bray. New York: Grove Press, 1986.

———. *Savannah Bay.* Paris: Minuit, 1983.

———. *Les Yeux bleus cheveux noirs.* Paris: Minuit, 1986.

Freud, Sigmund. "A Child Is Being Beaten." In *Sexuality and the Psychology of Love,* edited by Philip Rieff, pp. 107-32. New York: Macmillan, 1963.

———. "Further Recommendations in the Technique of Psychoanalysis: Recollection, Repetition, Working Through." In *Therapy and Technique,* edited by Philip Rieff, pp. 157-66. New York: Macmillan, 1963.

Lydon, Mary. "Translating Duras: *The Seated Man in the Passage.*" *Contemporary Literature* 24 (1983), 259-75.

Hiroshima mon amour

DEBORAH LESKO BAKER (ESSAY DATE 1998)

SOURCE: Baker, Deborah Lesko. "Memory, Love, and Inaccessibility in *Hiroshima mon amour.*" In *Marguerite Duras Lives On,* edited by Janine Ricouart, pp. 27-37. Lanham, Md.: University Press of America, 1998.

In the following essay, Baker reviews Duras's representation of forbidden love in her screenplay Hiroshima mon amour *and its relationship to the Tristan story.*

The classic French film, **Hiroshima mon amour** (dir. Alain Resnais, 1959), explores several critical obsessions that traverse the life and literary career of screenwriter Marguerite Duras as she has risen to the stature of one of France's most eminent female writers. As the psychoanalytic investigations of critics like Julia Kristeva and Sharon Willis have suggested, these obsessions involve densely-layered and richly-connected notions of inaccessible love, of mourning, and of individual memory.[1] What I want to outline here is how these issues relate to several aspects of the mytho-literary tradition concerning forbidden erotic passion—specifically the Tristan story—in the particular context of the heroine's personal history. In Part V of the screenplay, for example, during an interior monologue before a bathroom mirror in the hotel room to which she has returned alone after telling her story to the Japanese lover, the French woman utters these words: "Quatorze ans que je n'avais pas retrouvé . . . le goût d'un *amour impossible*" (90) ["For fourteen years I hadn't found . . . the taste of an *impossible love* again" (73); my italics].[2] The impossible love evoked here and rendered more powerful by its dual repetition within the woman's psychic itinerary is a fundamental figuring of the Tristan myth, whose complex configuration of erotic passion dominates so much of Western love aesthetics from the Middle Ages to our own time. Certain tropes connected with this myth in fact operate in both the thematic and structural composition of **Hiroshima mon amour.** The most blatant and yet ultimately, perhaps, the most complicated of these tropes is that of unattainability itself, which translates psychically into the dissociation of desire and possession, such that the perpetuation of desire is fueled and intensified by interdiction and separation.

The unattainability trope is reflected in the text and film in a series of obvious obstacles impeding the intertwined love relationships of the French woman and the Japanese man and, previously, the French woman and her German lover. On the social and moral plain, both relationships exist outside of marriage, with the force of the prohibition coming on one hand from the adulterous interracial love affair of the Hiroshima couple and on the other hand from the societally-prohibited love affair of the Nevers couple. Yet, if the fourteen-year time span since the war somewhat attenuates the cultural or political taboo vis-à-vis the Hiroshima couple, this taboo nevertheless subsists, and is implicitly marked by the obstacle of their imminent and definitive geographical separation.

In the film, the presence of obstacles which feed the inaccessibility crisis of the two couples is highlighted symbolically by a series of striking visual and auditory images. For example, as the conversation of the French woman and the Japanese man moves toward emotionally intimate territory before they part in front of the hotel the morning after their first tryst, their dialogue is drowned out by traffic noise. Later that afternoon, as they leave Peace Square to be together once again, they are physically pulled apart in the crowd at the parade being filmed for the movie which has brought the heroine to Hiroshima in the first place. In the middle of that same night, after the climactic confessional scene in the café and just hours before her departure to France, he follows her down a darkened boulevard, but with slackening steps which gradually lengthen the distance between them. Finally, in flashback scenes portraying the Nevers love story, the French girl is seen stumbling over obstacles on the terrain as she hurries to meet her German lover. The obstacle marking definitive separation in the Nevers sequence, of course, is the German lover's death, an obstacle in itself constituting a key figure in the Tristan myth which is centrally problematized and exploited in the film.

A second crucial trope of the Tristan myth is the characterization of love itself as a profoundly ambivalent and paradoxical experience. The source of this contradictory impulse is found in the word *passion* itself, where the connotation of intense (and pleasurable) erotic love coincides with the etymological sense of intense suffering (Lt. patior, pati, *passus sum*), the limit of which is death, as in the passion of Christ. The passion of the lovers in the Tristan myth is thus oxymoronically defined as "l'âpre joie et l'angoisse sans fin, et la mort" (Bédier 51) ["bitter joy and anguish without end, and death" my translation]—that is, a perpetual overlap of conflicting emotions whose only authentic resolution lies in death. However, the positive and negative poles of each feeling are experienced as an interim series of figurative deaths and rebirths within the lovers, such that actual death, following the model of Christ, is differed and elevated as a means to attain an ultimate transcendance of suffering.

Like the rhetoric of the Tristan myth, the text and film of *Hiroshima mon amour* are structured according to the paradoxical juxtaposition of seemingly contradictory words, concepts, and images referring to love, death, and rebirth. Nowhere is this paradoxical rhetoric more apparent than in the title, in which the seemingly de-individualized place name and historical referent of Hiroshima, calling forth an image of global destruction and death, is juxtaposed to a purposefully vague yet intimate invocation of love attributed to a privatized "I." Moreover, the title insists not only on the brutal conjunction of love and death, but on the profound *ambiguity* of that relationship, since, semantically, love might refer either to the affective concept or to an erotic object and since, grammatically, as Sharon Willis has pointed out, "mon amour" may be taken either as a vocative or as an appositional structure of uncertain reference (34). Julia Kristeva reads the duality of the title in two ways, suggesting these possible paraphrases: "Mon amour est un Hiroshima" ["My love is a Hiroshima"] or "J'aime Hiroshima car sa douleur est mon eros" ["I love Hiroshima, for its pain is my eros"] (240-41). The first of these might be interpreted as metaphorizing a tragic love experience as massive trauma inflicting unimaginable suffering and loss; the second, rather, might be seen as ironically valorizing the pain of the trauma as the paradoxical catalyst for a rebirth or reperpetuation of eros—where eros is associated not so much with erotic pleasure, but instead with the impeded and therefore intensified desire alluded to earlier. The female protagonist participates in both these scenarios; psychically, she lives this unchangeable ambiguity inherent in the paradoxical unity of love and death.

The images as well as the language of the film reproduce and expand the apparent contradiction and the ambiguities of its title. As Kristeva reminds us, the initial image we see on the screen is that of an as-yet unidentified, intertwined couple whose ash-covered bodies at first strangely appear to figure the agonizing throes of a nuclear death before passing through a kind of renewing liquification that illuminates their movements as love-making (239). This passage from the couple's embrace of death to a regrasping of life through the agency of desire is doubled in the subsequent opening images of Hiroshima itself projected on the screen and described by the French woman. These images juxtapose the most graphic evidences of human destruction and deformation after the bomb to the amazing resurgence of nature observed, for example, in the re-emergence of flowers which the heroine says "renaissaient des cendres avec une extraordinaire vigueur" (21) ["rose again from the ashes with an extraordinary vigor" (19)]. We see a kind of mirroring of this persistent organic rebirth after destruction in the flashbacks to Nevers, where inevitably the longer light of spring enters the dark cellar in which the French girl is sometimes banished and where her own metaphorically cataclysmic deformation—her shaved-off hair—uncontrollably grows back to decent length: "Mes cheveux repoussent. A ma main, chaque jour, je le sens. Ça m'est égal. Mais quand même, mes cheveux repoussent" (76) ["My hair is growing back. I can feel it every day, with my hand. I don't care. But nevertheless my hair is growing back" (61)].[3] Likewise, a sense of cyclic repetition and renewal is captured affectingly across the entire spectrum of the film in the movement between the Loire River, whose beautiful light emerges from the heroine's long-blocked childhood memory but on whose quay her German lover died, and the River Ota, whose daily drainings and refillings she invokes in her incantatory opening description of Hiroshima and next to whose banks in the café dialogue her past in Nevers is reborn.[4]

But this inexorable renascence of the natural—the continuation of life after trauma and destruction—further complicates the ambiguities of the love-death paradox. For the French woman, the pull away from death, from loss, and from disfigurement entails an accompanying increase in the difficulty of accessing that center of pain from which erotic love and desire can be re-experienced in its most intense form. It is the fear of this sort of detachment that makes the young heroine cling to the disfigurement constituted by her head-shaving and by the self-imposed scraping and bloodying of her fingers against the cellar wall. In telling her Nevers story she says, "Je ne suis attentive qu'au bruit des ciseaux sur ma tête. Ça me soulage un tout petit peu . . . de . . . ta mort . . . comme . . . comme, ah! tiens, je ne peux pas mieux te dire, comme pour les ongles, les murs" (77) ["All I hear is the sound of the scissors on my head. It makes me feel a little better about . . . your death . . . like . . . like, oh, I can't give you a better example, like my nails, the walls"

(62)]. However, at the same time, the revelation of natural renewal through cyclic repetition becomes powerfully linked with the reiteration of the impossible love experience through the Japanese man, a reiteration which allows her to re-seize her psychic pain, thereby catalyzing the rediscovery of her past and its necessary and heretofore unaccomplished mourning.

It is, finally, this entire complex of ambiguities and contradictions engaged by the love-death duality that emerges in the haunting paradoxical language of the French woman's first, recitative-like interior monologue:

> Je te rencontre.
> Je me souviens de toi.
> Qui es-tu?
> Tu me tues.
> Tu me fais du bien . . .
> Déforme-moi jusqu'à la laideur.
>
> (27)

> [I meet you.
> I remember you.
> Who are you?
> You destroy me.
> You're so good for me . . .
> Deform me, make me ugly.
>
> (24-25)]

Here, in the barest yet most provocative form, we perceive the power of repetition, the simultaneous annihilation and affective renewal engendered by erotic trauma, and the demand to reinscribe the disfiguring marks of suffering. These three phenomena define the dynamic of the "I" and the "You" from the psychic vantage point of the desiring female subject, in the face of an already blurred and doubled erotic object.

The French woman's declaration of "Je me souviens de toi" ["I remember you"] in the monologue excerpt just quoted serves to introduce the other rhetorical duality that dominates the depiction of love as paradoxical and ambivalent experience in **Hiroshima mon amour**—that of memory and forgetting. The compelling juxtaposition of these two notions dominates the dialogic itinerary of the Hiroshima couple as well as the internal battle of the French woman to assimilate and preserve her own history. Memory and forgetting are first thematized, like their rhetorical counterparts of rebirth and destruction, in terms of the Hiroshima disaster. As the Japanese man at first almost cynically refutes her self-proclaimed knowledge of what remembering and forgetting truly mean in respect to a trauma of Hiroshima's magnitude, the French woman cryptically betrays their absolute centrality to her own analogous, but thus far unrevealed traumatic experience:

Comme toi, moi aussi, j'ai essayé de lutter de toutes mes forces contre l'oubli. Comme toi, j'ai oublié. Comme toi, j'ai désiré avoir *une inconsolable mémoire,* une mémoire d'ombres et de pierres. *J'ai lutté* pour mon compte, de toutes mes forces, chaque jour, contre l'horreur de ne plus comprendre du tout le pourquoi de se souvenir. Comme toi, j'ai oublié. . . . Pourquoi nier l'évidente nécessité de la mémoire?

(24-25; my italics)

[Like you, I too have tried with all my might not to forget. Like you, I forgot. Like you, I wanted to have *an inconsolable memory,* a memory of shadows and stone. For my part I *struggled* with all my might, every day, against the horror of no longer understanding at all the reason for remembering. Like you, I forgot. . . . Why deny the obvious necessity for memory?

(23; my italics)]

Especially starting from the key moment the morning after these words are spoken, when she observes her sleeping lover's trembling hands and has an involuntary flashback to the twitching hands of the dying German soldier, the role of the Japanese man will be to lead the heroine back through the multiple layers of forgetting and to build a bridge back to her "inconsolable memory" of brutal death, of irretrievable loss. During the central café scene in which he symbolically takes on the identity of the German lover through a role-playing process resembling psychoanalytic transference, the French woman is finally able to verbalize her traumatic personal history and so to begin the active mourning that the silencing imposed by her social and familial stigmatization did not allow her to undertake.[5] One partial effect of this social silencing which becomes a defining mark of her grief and a fascinating element of her story is how the actual Nevers crisis of separation and death is almost immediately doubled by a parallel crisis of memory: an obsessive desire to remember and an obsessive fear of forgetting the love, the pain, and the death to which she could not give voice.[6] This crisis of memory is revealed at a number of junctures in her story and further illuminates her embrace of her own disfigurement, since it is her only weapon against the terror of oblivion. When talking about bloodying her own hands against the cellar walls, she cries: "C'est tout ce qu'on peut trouver à faire pour se faire du bien . . . et aussi pour *se rappeler*" (72) ["That's all you can find to do, to make you feel better . . . and also to *remember*" (55) my italics]). Later, when she recalls emerging from her madness, she laments: "Ah! C'est horrible. Je commence à moins bien *me souvenir* de toi . . . Je commence à t'*oublier.* Je tremble d'avoir *oublié* tant d'amour" (78-79) ["Oh! It's horrible. I'm beginning to re-

member you less clearly . . . I'm beginning to *forget* you. I tremble at the thought of having *forgotten* so much love" (64) my italics]. These statements function as a kind of insistent metatext which suggests that in one sense the most powerful image left by the resurrected memory of Nevers is that of how excruciatingly difficult it is to *remember,* and thus, truly to mourn.

Indeed, not surprisingly, it is this memory of the failure of memory that remains with her when she re-emerges from her almost trance-like visitation of the past. Movingly, she unravels the layers of the process of forgetting across the fourteen years that separate her from her lover's death in Nevers: "Même *des mains* je me souviens mal . . . De *la douleur,* je me souviens encore un peu . . . Oui, ce soir je m'en souviens. Mais un jour je ne m'en souviendrai plus. Du tout. *De rien*" (81-82) ["I don't even remember *his hands* very well . . . *The pain,* I still remember the pain a little . . . Yes tonight, I remember. But one day I won't remember it anymore. Not at all. *Nothing*" (67) my italics]. This passage from the disappearance of visual imagination of the Other, to the disappearance of affective feeling within the self, to the disappearance of everything, is construed, finally, not only as the ultimate fate of the past, but the ultimate fate of the future, since it will prospectively contaminate the current love affair in Hiroshima. When the French woman has finished her story, the Japanese man responds to it precisely in terms of his own projected loss of her identity over time; in this vision the woman herself will be forgotten, and the act of recall for him, as for her this night in the café, will paradoxically turn around the remembering of forgetting: "Dans quelques années, quand je t'aurais *oubliée,* et que d'autres histoires comme celle-là, par la force encore de l'habitude, arriveront encore, je *me souviendrai* de toi comme de *l'oubli* de l'amour même. Je penserai à cette histoire comme à l'horreur de *l'oubli*" (83) ["In a few years, when I'll have *forgotten* you, and when other such adventures, from sheer habit, will happen to me, I'll *remember* you as the symbol of love's *forgetfulness.* I'll think of this adventure as of the horror of *oblivion*" (68) my italics]. And, at last, in a culminating act of textual closure, the heroine moves through a series of interior monologues beginning with a reinvocation of the "I meet you, I *remember* you" recitative that we have discussed, but relentlessly replacing both past memory and present experience with a discourse of anticipated forgetting and an actual conferring of both loves to an oblivion seen as total and inevitable:

Petite tondue de Nevers je te donne à l'oubli . . .
Comme pour lui, l'oubli commencera par tes
     yeux. . . .
Puis, comme pour lui, l'oubli gagnera ta
     voix. . . .
Puis, comme pour lui, il triomphera de toi tout
     entier, peu à peu.

                                        (37)

[Little girl with shaven head, I bequeathe you to
     oblivion . . .
As it was for him, oblivion will begin with your
     eyes. . . .
Then, as it was for him, it will encompass your
     voice. . . .
Then, as it was for him, it will encompass you
     completely, little by little.

                                        (80)]

I would like to close by expanding my discussion of the duality of memory and forgetting in the context of the paradoxical depiction of love that I have suggested is a fundamental trope of the Tristan myth taken up in **Hiroshima mon amour.** The interplay between remembering and forgetting in the text and film is all the more crucial, I would argue, because of its striking metaphorical relationship to the contradictory impulses of death and rebirth that sustain the tension of unattainable love. Indeed, in the psychic drama of the French woman in **Hiroshima** both memory and forgetting are paradoxically double phenomena, because each of them is a metaphor for a certain kind of renascence and a certain kind of death. For the heroine, oblivion is an obvious analogue of real death, since it figures a disappearance or an *effacement* of impossible love from the mind and renders the sought-after intensity of both desire and suffering inaccessible to conscious experience. Nevertheless, although the rebirth it effectuates is a sterile one, forgetting is connected with the resumption of a so-called "normal" life and a deliverance from the exquisite pitch of anguish and longing that is incompatible with regular daily existence.

The act of remembering that constitutes the central focus of the film has a similarly oxymoronic force. For the heroine, it, too, is a death not because it effaces, but because it reinscribes, however briefly, the images of the actual death of her German lover and of her own figural death—that is, the madness, the loss of self which his murder provoked. Additionally, it reactivates both the desire and pain of inaccessibility and motivates a *wish for death* as the only authentic vehicle of transcendence. Yet memory does conquer one kind of death—that of oblivion, and it does catalyze a rebirth, although what it resurrects here is nothing other than the profound human experience of death in love. In allowing the French woman to go back and confront momentarily that intolerable, unresolvable experience, the act of remembering engenders a renascence of the loss that *defines* her as a person, that which, to paraphrase the words of her Japanese lover, has made her begin to be what she is today ("C'est là, il me semble l'avoir compris, que tu as dû commencer à être comme aujourd'hui tu es encore" 64). To be able to *know* and *define* the self through suffering in love is Tristan's legacy of unattainable passion; and in the space between the lived forgetfulness of the past and the inevitable oblivion of the future, the heroine arrives at a glimpse of this knowledge.[7]

Notes

1. For these two important critical discussions of the screenplay and film, see Julia Kristeva's "La maladie de la douleur: Duras" in *Soleil noir* and Sharon Willis's "*Hiroshima mon amour:* Screen Memories" in *Marguerite Duras: Writing on the Body.* Translations of quotations from Kristeva are my own.

2. All French quotations from Duras's screenplay are from the original edition, *Hiroshima mon amour* (Paris: Gallimard, 1960). Translations from the English edition are by Richard Seaver (New York: Grove P, 1961).

3. Duras emphasizes the remarkable destructive proportion of the heroine's head-shaving in her synopsis statement accompanying the screenplay text: "Tondre une fille parce qu'elle a aimé d'amour un ennemi officiel de son pays, est *un absolu* et d'horreur et de bêtise" (7) ["To shave a girl's head because she has loved—really loved—an official enemy of her country, is *the ultimate* of horror and stupidity" (12); my italics].

4. The musical score also accentuates the river's evocation with its haunting "Ota theme."

5. As Freud says of transference in the *Introductory Lectures on Psychoanalysis:* "In this way we oblige him (the patient) to transform his repetition into a *memory*" (444; my italics).

6. The obsessive character of the French woman's quest to unearth her past experience through this psychic repetition is of course enhanced by the act of drinking in the café. In *Crack Wars,* her book exploring addictions and their relationship to patterns of obsessive, repetitive behavior in literary texts, Avital Ronell imagines Marguerite Duras herself discussing the café scenes which stimulate the addictive propensities and psychic crises of her characters: ". . . I'd saturate my couples, watch them dissolve in cafés. Yes, maybe they would know fusional desire but without all that operatic noise. You know what I mean? I like to alcoholize my texts, turn down the volume and let them murmur across endless boundaries and miniscule epiphanies" (155). The catalytic role of drinking in Duras' screenplay is not without relationship to the topos of the *philtre* in the Tristan myth.

7. This fundamental idea of self-knowledge accrued through the experience of inaccessible love is part of the thesis of Denis de Rougemont's classic work on

the Tristan myth in the Western literary and cultural tradition, *L'amour et l'occident* (trans. *Love in the Western World*):

> Passion veut dire souffrance, chose subie, prépondérance du destin sur la personne libre et responsable. Aimer l'amour plus que l'objet d'amour, aimer la passion elle-même . . . c'est aimer et chercher la souffrance . . . Pourquoi l'homme d'Occident veut-il subir cette passion qui le blesse et que toute sa raison condamne? Pourquoi veut-il cet amour dont l'éclat ne peut être que son suicide? C'est qu'il *se connaît* et *s'éprouve* sous le coup de menaces vitales, dans la souffrance et au seuil de la mort.
>
> (41; my italics)

> [Passion means suffering, something undergone, the mastery of fate over a free and responsible person. To love love more than the object of love, to love passion for its own sake . . . has been to love to suffer . . . Why does Western man wish to suffer this passion which lacerates him and which all his common sense rejects? Why does he yearn after this particular kind of love notwithstanding that its effulgence must coincide with his self-destruction? The answer is that he reaches self-awareness and tests himself only by risking his life—in suffering and on the verge of death.
>
> (50-51); my italics]

Works Cited

Bédier, Joseph. *Le Roman de Tristan et Iseut.* Paris: Union Générale d'Editions, 1981.

De Rougemont, Denis. *L'Amour et l'occident.* Paris: Plon, 1939. Trans. as *Love in the Western World* by Montgomery Belgian. New York: Harper & Row, 1956.

Duras, Marguerite. *Hiroshima mon amour.* Paris: Gallimard, 1960. Transl. by Richard Seaver. New York: Grove P, 1961.

Freud, Sigmund. *Introductory Lectures on Psychoanalysis.* Ed. and trans. by James Strachey. New York: Norton, 1977.

Kristeva, Julia. *Soleil noir: dépression et mélancolie.* Paris: Gallimard (Folio), 1987.

Ronell, Avital. *Crack Wars: Literature, Addiction, Mania.* Lincoln: U of Nebraska P, 1992.

Willis, Sharon. *Marguerite Duras: Writing on the Body.* Urbana: U of Illinois P, 1987.

FURTHER READING

Bibliography

Harvey, Robert Hélène Volat. *Marguerite Duras: A Bio-Bibliography.* Westport, Conn.: Greenwood Press, 1997, 273 p.

Reference guide to Duras's life and works.

Biographies

Adler, Laure. *Marguerite Duras: A Life,* translated by Anne-Marie Glasheen. London: Victor Gollancz, 1998, 424 p.

Biography that seeks to circumvent Duras's deliberate attempts to hide the facts associated with certain areas of her life.

Vircondelet, Alain. *Duras: A Biography.* Translated by Thomas Buckley. Normal, Ill.: Dalkey Archive Press, 1994, 378 p.

Celebrated biography whose author acknowledges the difficulty of accurately capturing the story of Duras's complicated, unconventional life.

Criticism

Baker, Deborah Lesko. "A Rethinking of Genre and Gender through a Reading of *Yes peut-être*." In *Marguerite Duras Lives On,* edited by Janine Ricouart, pp. 11-25. Lanham, Md.: University Press of America, 1998.

Maintains that Duras's text blurs the distinction between prose and poetry and at the same time collapses the distinction between masculine and feminine.

Cismaru, Alfred. *Marguerite Duras.* New York: Twayne Publishers, 1971. 171 p.

Provides interviews with Duras.

——. *Marguerite Duras.* New York: Palgrave, 2002. 146 p.

Contains bibliographical section.

Cohen, Susan D. *Women and Discourse in the Fiction of Marguerite Duras: Love, Legends, Language.* Amherst: University of Massachusetts Press, 1993, 239 p.

Employs theories of feminism, Marxism, and postmodernism in an examination of Duras's fiction.

Crowley, Martin. "Writing and Sex." In *Duras, Writing, and the Ethical: Making the Broken Whole,* pp. 185-232. Oxford: Clarendon Press, 2000.

Discussion of Duras's unrelenting questioning of sexual difference and heterosexual relationships in her writing.

Duras, Marguerite Xavière Gauthier. "First Interview." In *Woman to Woman,* translated by Katharine A. Jensen, pp. 1-32. Lincoln: University of Nebraska Press, 1987.

Discussion of Duras's ideas on language and gender issues.

Etienne, Marie-France. "Loss, Abandonment, and Love: The Ego in Exile." In *In Language and In Love: Marguerite Duras: The Unspeakable,* edited by Mechthild Cranston, pp. 66-88. Potomac, Md.: Scripta Humanistica, 1992.

Examines Duras's treatment of absence and death throughout her work.

Gross, Janice Berkowitz. "Writing Across Purposes: The Theatre of Marguerite Duras and Nathalie Sarraute." *Modern Drama* 32, no. 1 (March 1989): 39-47.

Examination of the similarities between the dramatic works of Duras and Sarraute.

Günther, Renate. *Alienation and Absence in the Novels of Marguerite Duras.* Lexington, Ky.: French Forum, 1982, 172 p.

Focuses on Duras's life and career with bibliographical material.

——. "Gender and Sexuality." In *Marguerite Duras,* pp. 96-133. Manchester, England: Manchester University Press, 2002.

Analyzes Duras's preoccupation with gender issues in her screenplays.

Ha, Marie-Paule. "Durasie: Women, Natives, and Other." In *Revisioning Duras: Film, Race, Sex,* edited by James S. Williams and Janet Sayers, pp. 95-111. Liverpool, Eng.: Liverpool University Press, 2000.

Contrasts Duras's fictional representations of white women with those of the colonized women of Asia.

Lamont, Rosette C. "The Off-Center Spatiality of Women's Discourse." In *Theory and Practice of Feminist Literary Criticism,* edited by Gabriela Mora and Karen S. Van Hooft, pp. 138-55. Ypsilanti, Mich.: Bilingual Press, 1982.

Maintains that Duras and Elizabeth Hardwick have attempted in their writing to formulate an "aesthetic of marginality."

Rava, Susan. "Marguerite Duras: Women's Language in Men's Cities." In *Women Writers and the City: Essays in Feminist Literary Criticism,* edited by Susan Merrill Squier, pp. 35-44. Knoxville: University of Tennessee Press, 1984.

Discussion of Duras's urban fiction and her attempts to articulate, through her female characters, a distinctively female voice within a predominantly male discourse.

Schuster, Marilyn R. *Marguerite Duras Revisited.* New York: Twayne Publishers, 1993, 185 p.

Critical analysis of Duras supplemented with bibliographical section.

Waters, Julia. "'La lutte des sexes est le moteur de l'histoire': Overview and Context." In *Intersexual Rivalry: A 'Reading in Pairs' of Marguerite Duras and Alain Robbe-Grillet,* pp. 27-51. Bern, Switzerland: Peter Lang, 2000.

Examines the fifty-year professional competition between Duras and Alain Robbe-Grillet, the most prominent member of the Nouveau Roman *movement.*

Willis, Sharon. "Preliminary Mappings." In *Marguerite Duras: Writing on the Body,* pp. 11-32. Urbana: University of Illinois Press, 1987.

Explores Duras's treatment of desire, representation, and gender in her novels, plays and screenplays.

OTHER SOURCES FROM GALE:

Additional coverage of Duras's life and career is contained in the following sources published by the Gale Group: *Beacham's Encyclopedia of Popular Fiction: Biography & Resources,* Vol. 1; *Contemporary Authors,* Vols. 25-28R, 151; *Contemporary Authors Autobiography Series,* Vol. 21; *Contemporary Authors New Revision Series,* Vol. 50; *Contemporary Literary Criticism,* Vols. 3, 6, 11, 20, 34, 40, 68, 100; *Contemporary World Writers,* Ed. 2; *Dictionary of Literary Biography,* Vol. 83; *Encyclopedia of World Literature in the 20th Century,* Ed. 3; *Guide to French Literature,* 1789-Present; *The International Dictionary of Films and Filmmakers: Writers and Production Artists,* Ed. 4; *Literature Resource Center; Major 20th-Century Writers; Reference Guide to World Literature,* Eds. 2, 3; *Short Story Criticism,* Vol. 40; and *Twayne's World Authors.*

ANDREA DWORKIN

(1946 -)

American nonfiction writer, novelist, essayist, short story writer, and poet.

A highly controversial author and activist, Dworkin is a leading radical feminist and member of the contemporary women's movement. Her provocative investigations into the cultural origins of misogyny and sexual violence have generated contentious debate among feminists, academics, politicians, and free speech advocates. A forceful spokesperson against pornography, Dworkin calls attention to the sexual myths that perpetuate the role of women as degraded objects of male gratification and exploitation. Alternately revered and reviled for her firebrand polemics and castigation of mainstream feminists, Dworkin has exerted an important influence on public discourse surrounding the modes, extent, and human cost of male-dominated sexuality and female oppression.

BIOGRAPHICAL INFORMATION

Born in Camden, New Jersey, Dworkin was raised in a liberal Jewish home. While still in grade school, Dworkin expressed her desire to effect social change as a writer or lawyer. Her early literary interests were shaped by the writings of Arthur Rimbaud and Fyodor Dostoyevsky, and later Virginia Woolf, the Brontës, George Eliot, and revolutionary Che Guevara. Politically active by age eighteen, Dworkin was arrested at an antiwar rally in New York City in 1964. While jailed at the Women's House of Detention, she was sexually assaulted during an invasive body search, prompting her to lead a public demonstration upon her release. Dworkin attended Bennington College in Vermont, where she earned a bachelor's degree in 1968 after a one-year leave of absence in Greece. Dworkin's writing first appeared in the privately printed volumes *Child* (1966), a book of poetry produced in Crete, and *Morning Hair* (1968), a collection of poetry and prose. Disillusioned by American involvement in Vietnam, Dworkin moved to the Netherlands for a five-year period after graduating from Bennington. During this time she endured a physically and emotionally abusive marriage to a Dutch man, whom she escaped in 1971 with the help of intervening feminists. Returning to the United States in 1972, Dworkin supported herself as a waitress, receptionist, secretary, salesperson, factory worker, and prostitute, and was periodically homeless. She was eventually hired as an assistant to poet Muriel Rukeyser while working on her first book, *Woman Hating* (1974), which she began in Amsterdam. Dworkin was also active in feminist demonstrations and established herself as a powerful speaker at the National Organization for Women's Conference on Sexuality in 1974.

During the 1980s, Dworkin joined forces with Catharine A. MacKinnon, a law professor at the University of Michigan, to campaign for anti-pornography legislation. Together they authored an important civil rights ordinance in Minneapolis that recognized pornography as a form of sexual discrimination. The ordinance was passed in 1983 and became a model for similar legislation in other American cities and Canada. Dworkin also appeared before the Attorney General's Commission on Pornography in 1986. Her research and lobbying resulted in *Pornography: Men Possessing Women* (1981) and *Pornography and Civil Rights* (1988), a collaborative volume with MacKinnon. A frequent lecturer at feminist gatherings and contributor to numerous periodicals, Dworkin also published the book-length studies *Right-Wing Women* (1983) and *Intercourse* (1987), the nonfiction collections *Letters from a War Zone* (1988) and *Life and Death* (1997), the novels *Ice and Fire* (1986) and *Mercy* (1990), and the autobiographical *Heartbreak* (2002).

MAJOR WORKS

The primary subjects of Dworkin's critical studies and fiction—sexual abuse, pornography, and female subordination—are introduced in her first book, *Woman Hating*. In this work, Dworkin examines the socialization of gender roles and misogyny through analysis of fairy tales and pornographic writings. Such cultural artifacts, according to Dworkin, represent a continuum through which hierarchical heterosexual relationships are prescribed from childhood through adulthood. Her examination of sources ranging from "Snow White" to Pauline Réage's *The Story of O* demonstrates that women are consistently portrayed as weak, submissive, and despised. These themes are expanded upon in *Pornography* and *Intercourse*. In *Pornography*, Dworkin examines the content, social context, and effects of pornography as a tool of male domination over women. Dismissing claims that pornographic writings and images fall under the protected category of free expression, Dworkin asserts that pornography is an exploitative medium of mass propaganda by which the ideology of male supremacy is transmitted. Drawing attention to the victimization of real women who perform in pornographic films, Dworkin contends that the creation of pornography is inseparable from the degradation of women it falsely portrays as fantasy; thus the production of pornography embodies its harmful effect. In *Intercourse*, Dworkin discusses the physical act of

heterosexual intercourse as the quintessential manifestation of male hegemony and female inequality. According to Dworkin, male penetration during copulation signifies possession of the woman, rendering impossible the notion of female liberation or selfhood, as she is compelled to submit to male desire as occupation. Incorporating analysis of religious and legal strictures governing female sexuality and texts by Leo Tolstoy, Kobo Abe, James Baldwin, Tennessee Williams, Isaac Bashevis Singer, and Gustave Flaubert, Dworkin maintains that—for women—the manipulative, demeaning experience of sexual intercourse precludes mutual respect or integrity.

Dworkin's semi-autobiographical novels, *Ice and Fire* and *Mercy*, give vivid expression to the conclusions in her nonfiction. *Ice and Fire* relates the experiences of an unnamed young feminist from Camden, New Jersey. She grows up in a working-class Jewish neighborhood, goes to college, marries an abusive husband, and eventually settles in New York City where she lives in squalor, prostitutes herself, and is brutalized by various men while attempting to write a book. After much difficulty locating a publisher, the protagonist finally gets her book into print, though it flounders due to its spiteful publisher and poor sales. Dworkin's alter ego in *Mercy*, also a young woman from Camden, is named Andrea. The first-person narrative documents a long history of horrific sexual abuse inflicted upon its protagonist, beginning with her molestation in a movie theater at age nine. Andrea is sexually assaulted by sadistic prison doctors, raped and mutilated by her husband, and repeatedly violated while living a bohemian existence in New York City. Her rage finally gives way to retributive violence, leading her to firebomb sex shops and assault homeless men while envisioning an international guerilla war on men. The narrative action is framed by a prologue and epilogue, both entitled "Not Andrea," in which Dworkin parodies her liberal feminist and academic detractors. Dworkin's views on the political, cultural, and physical subjugation of women are further elaborated in the essays, columns, and speeches collected in *Our Blood* (1976), *Letters from a War Zone*, and *Life and Death*. In the nonfiction work *Right-Wing Women*, written during the early years of the Reagan administration, Dworkin attempts to explain the appeal of the Republican Party for women, despite its opposition to the Equal Rights Amendment and other legislation to enhance the well-being of women. According to Dworkin, fear of male violence compels many conservative women to relinquish their autonomy for the security of traditional sex roles that demand passivity and subservience. The book was in part an attempt by Dworkin to distance herself from the anti-pornography advocacy of anti-feminist, religious, and conservative groups such as the Moral Majority.

CRITICAL RECEPTION

Dworkin's compelling examination of sexual politics and pornography is the subject of divisive controversy in academic, political, and feminist circles. Though praised by some for her insightful, groundbreaking analysis of cultural misogyny and sexual exploitation, her detractors typically object to her abrasive presentation. Critics frequently complain that Dworkin's bombastic rhetoric distorts and sensationalizes the substance of her findings while alienating much of her audience. Critics also condemn Dworkin's interchangeable use of literal and metaphorical statements and her tendency to construct sweeping generalizations based on overstated or anecdotal evidence. Dworkin's vigilant condemnation of pornography has also been censured by feminist activists, especially those reluctant to challenge First Amendment rights. However, Dworkin's focus on pornography as a Fourteenth Amendment infringement—instead of an obscenity issue, a strategy formulated with MacKinnon—is considered an important legal maneuver for anti-pornography advocacy. Dworkin is less appreciated as a novelist. While some reviewers commend her visceral evocation of sexual violence, most fault her for simplistic prose, undeveloped characters, an overt feminist agenda, and graphic sexuality that some reviewers assert resembles the pornography she decries. Eschewing theoretical abstractions and the insular ideological battles of academic feminists, Dworkin has won many supporters for her willingness to address distasteful and often overlooked aspects of sexual abuse. A formidable independent thinker and activist, Dworkin is regarded as an influential contemporary feminist.

PRINCIPAL WORKS

Child (poetry) 1966

Morning Hair (poetry and prose) 1968

Woman Hating (nonfiction) 1974

Our Blood: Prophecies and Discourses on Sexual Politics (essays and speeches) 1976

The New Woman's Broken Heart (short stories) 1980

Pornography: Men Possessing Women (nonfiction) 1981

Right-Wing Women: The Politics of Domesticated Females (nonfiction) 1983

Ice and Fire (novel) 1986

Intercourse (nonfiction) 1987

Pornography and Civil Rights: A New Day for Women's Equality [with Catharine A. MacKinnon] (nonfiction) 1988

*Letters from a War Zone: Writings 1976-1987 (essays) 1988

Mercy (novel) 1990

Life and Death: Unapologetic Writings on the Continuing War against Women (nonfiction) 1997

In Harm's Way: The Pornography Civil Rights Hearings [editor; with MacKinnon] (nonfiction) 1997

Scapegoat: The Jews, Israel, and Women's Liberation (nonfiction) 2000

Heartbreak: The Political Memoir of a Feminist Militant (memoir) 2002

*   Republished as *Letters from a War Zone: Writings 1976-1989* in 1989.

PRIMARY SOURCES

ANDREA DWORKIN (ESSAY DATE 1978)

SOURCE: Dworkin, Andrea. "Pornography and Grief." In *Letters from a War Zone: Writings 1976-1989*, pp. 19-23. New York: E. P. Dutton, 1988.

In the following excerpt, originally written as a speech for a "Take Back the Night" march in 1978, Dworkin argues that pornography "functions to perpetuate male supremacy and crimes of violence against women because it conditions, trains, educates, and inspires men to despise women, to use women, to hurt women."

I searched for something to say here today quite different from what I am going to say. I wanted to come here militant and proud and angry as hell. But more and more, I find that anger is a pale shadow next to the grief I feel. If a woman has any sense of her own intrinsic worth, seeing pornography in small bits and pieces can bring her to a useful rage. Studying pornography in quantity and depth, as I have been doing for more months than I care to remember, will turn that same woman into a mourner.

The pornography itself is vile. To characterize it any other way would be to lie. No plague of male intellectualisms and sophistries can change or hide that simple fact. Georges Bataille, a philosopher of pornography (which he calls "eroticism"), puts it clearly: "In essence, the domain of eroticism is the domain of violence, of violation."[1] Mr Bataille, unlike so many of his peers, is good enough to make explicit that the whole idea is to violate the female. Using the language of grand euphemism so popular with male intellectuals who write on the subject of pornography, Bataille informs us that "[t]he passive, female side is essentially the one that is dissolved as a separate entity."[2] To be "dissolved"—by any means necessary—is the role of women in pornography. The great male scientists and philosophers of sexuality, including Kinsey, Havelock Ellis, Wilhelm Reich, and Freud, uphold this view of our purpose and destiny. The great male writers use language more or less beautifully to create us in self-serving fragments, half-"dissolved" as it were, and then proceed to "dissolve" us all the way, by any means necessary. The biographers of the great male artists celebrate the real life atrocities those men have committed against us, as if those atrocities are central to the making of art. And in history, as men have lived it, they have "dissolved" us—by any means necessary. The slicing of our skins and the rattling of our bones are the energizing sources of male-defined art and science, as they are the essential content of pornography. The visceral experience of a hatred of women that literally knows no bounds has put me beyond anger and beyond tears; I can only speak to you from grief.

We all expected the world to be different than it is, didn't we? No matter what material or emotional deprivation we have experienced as children or as adults, no matter what we understood from history or from the testimonies of living persons about how people suffer and why, we all believed, however privately, in human possibility. Some of us believed in art, or literature, or music, or religion, or revolution; or in children, or in the redeeming potential of eroticism or affection. No matter what we knew of cruelty, we all believed in kindness; and no matter what we knew of hatred, we all believed in friendship or love. Not one of us could have imagined or would have believed the simple facts of life as we have come to know them: the rapacity of male greed for dominance; the malignancy of male supremacy; the virulent contempt for women that is the very foundation of the culture in which we live. The Women's Movement has forced us all to face the facts, but no matter how brave and clear-sighted we are, no matter how far we are willing to go or are forced to go in viewing reality without romance or illusion, we are simply overwhelmed by the male hatred of our kind, its morbidity, its compulsiveness, its obsessiveness, its celebration of itself in every detail of life and culture. We think that we have grasped this hatred once and for all, seen it in its spectacular cruelty, learned its every secret, got used to it or risen above it or organized against it so as to be protected from its worst excesses. We think that we know all there is to know about what men do to women, even if we cannot imagine why they do what they do, when something happens that simply drives us mad, out of our minds, so that we are again imprisoned like caged animals in the numbing reality of male control, male revenge against no one knows what, male hatred of our very being.

One can know everything and still not imagine snuff films. One can know everything and still be shocked and terrified when a man who attempted to make snuff films is released, despite the testimony of the women undercover agents whom he wanted to torture, murder, and, of course, film. One can know everything and still be stunned and paralyzed when one meets a child who is being continuously raped by her father or some close male relative. One can know everything and still be reduced to sputtering like an idiot when a woman is prosecuted for attempting to abort herself with knitting needles, or when a woman is imprisoned for killing a man who has raped or tortured her, or is raping or torturing her. One can know everything and still want to kill and be dead simultaneously when one sees a celebratory picture of a woman being ground up in a meat grinder on the cover of a national magazine, no matter how putrid the magazine. One can know everything and still somewhere inside refuse to believe that the personal, social, culturally sanctioned violence against women is unlimited, unpredictable, pervasive, constant, ruthless, and happily and unselfconsciously sadistic. One can know everything and still be unable to accept the fact that sex and murder are fused in the male consciousness, so that the one without the imminent possibility of the other is unthinkable and impossible. One can know everything and still, at bottom, refuse to accept that the annihilation of women is the source of meaning and identity for men. One can know everything and still want desperately to know nothing because to face what we know is to question whether life is worth anything at all.

The pornographers, modern and ancient, visual and literary, vulgar and aristocratic, put forth one consistent proposition: erotic pleasure for men is derived from and predicated on the savage destruction of women. As the world's most honored pornographer, the Marquis de Sade (called by male scholars "The Divine Marquis"), wrote in one of his more restrained and civil moments: "There's not a woman on earth who'd ever have had cause to complain of my services if I'd been sure of being able to kill her afterward."[3] The eroticization of murder is the essence of pornography, as it is the essence of life. The torturer may be a policeman tearing the fingernails off a victim in a prison cell or a so-called normal man engaged in the project of attempting to fuck a woman to death. The fact is that the process of killing—and both rape and battery are steps in that process—is the prime sexual act for men in reality and/or in imagination. Women as a class must remain in bondage, subject to the sexual will of men, because the knowledge of an imperial right to kill, whether exercised to the fullest extent or just part way, is necessary to fuel sexual appetite and behavior. Without women as potential or actual victims, men are, in the current sanitized jargon, "sexually dysfunctional." This same motif also operates among male homosexuals, where force and/or convention designate some males as female or feminized. The plethora of leather and chains among male homosexuals, and the newly fashionable defenses of organized rings of boy prostitution by supposedly radical gay men, are testimony to the fixedness of the male compulsion to dominate and destroy that is the source of sexual pleasure for men.

The most terrible thing about pornography is that it tells male truth. The most insidious thing about pornography is that it tells male truth as if it were universal truth. Those depictions of women in chains being tortured are supposed to represent our deepest erotic aspirations. And some of us believe it, don't we? The most important thing about pornography is that the values in it are the common values of men. This is the crucial fact that both the male Right and the male Left, in their differing but mutually reinforcing ways, want to keep hidden from women. The male Right wants to hide the pornography, and the male Left wants to hide its meaning. Both want access to pornography so that men can be encouraged and energized by it. The Right wants secret access; the Left wants public access. But whether we see the pornography or not, the values expressed in it are the values expressed in the acts of rape and wife-beating, in the legal system, in religion, in art and in literature, in systematic economic discrimination against women, in the moribund academies, and by the good and wise and kind and enlightened in all of these fields and areas. Pornography is not a genre of expression separate and different from the rest of life; it is a genre of expression fully in harmony with any culture in which it flourishes. This is so whether it is legal or illegal. And, in either case, pornography functions to perpetuate male supremacy and crimes of violence against women because it conditions, trains, educates, and inspires men to despise women, to use women, to hurt women. Pornography exists because men despise women, and men despise women in part because pornography exists.

Notes

1. Georges Bataille, *Death and Sensuality* (New York: Ballantine Books, Inc., 1969), p. 10.

2. Bataille, *Death and Sensuality*, p. 11.

3. Donatien-Alphonse-François de Sade, *Juliette*, trans. Austryn Wainhouse (New York: Grove Press, Inc., 1976), p. 404.

GENERAL COMMENTARY

ERICA JONG (ESSAY DATE JUNE 1988)

SOURCE: Jong, Erica. "Changing My Mind about Andrea Dworkin." *Ms.* (June 1988): 60-4.

In the following essay, Jong discusses her reassessment of Dworkin's work, concluding that Dworkin's feminist writings are gripping and raise important questions.

If we judge a society's freedom by how it treats the nonconformist, then by this rather Thoreauvian measure, America's treatment of Andrea Dworkin has not been a credit to our sense of liberty. Since 1971 we have had in our midst a passionately committed feminist philosopher, activist, and author whose seriousness is beyond dispute. We have largely attacked her, silenced her, condemned her without reading her.

What opprobrium her books have garnered! Here is a relatively typical example, written by a woman reviewer:

Time to restock the aspirin: Andrea Dworkin, the demagogue's ideologue, has two new books out— one a lamebrained appeal for universal chastity, the other a surprisingly pornographic fiction that's so dreary in style and feeble in plot and character it hardly qualifies as a novel. . . . Dworkin has built her reputation on taking man-hating further than even the most doctrinaire lesbian separatists. Defining sex categorically as a male activity, she denies the very existence of personal freedom for women.

One would think Dworkin's books were nuclear fallout, acid rain, germ warfare. They are—merely—books, books published (when they are published at all) in very small editions, read by few. It is a rule of thumb with me that the more outrage something generates, the more the author is likely to be on to some unacknowledged hypocrisy in our culture. We tend to like our satirists in white suits, with good party manners, like Tom Wolfe. We do not like them when they undermine the whole structure without even paying lip service to its vanities.

Andrea Dworkin is a child of the 1960s (Bennington '68 to be exact): uncompromising, unkempt, unfashionable. She looks as if she walked off the streets of the Latin Quarter circa 1968; or Amsterdam or Greece, where she did, in fact, live. In the Age of Reagan/Thatcher yuppieism, she is an anomaly, a risk-taker in a world of bet-hedgers, impoverished in a world that only wants to read Rich Writers, a serious woman of letters in a world that has rediscovered "The New Bimbo." Her appearance is an insult to McLuhanist medium-as-message principles—and her rare combination of brilliance, bravado, and empathy is not what the age demands. She does not wear new clothes and she reads not the times but the eternities.

I would never have gotten to know Andrea Dworkin were it not for Phil Donahue.

Last spring, in the midst of a book tour for my fifth novel, *Serenissima: A Novel of Venice*, I was asked if I would appear on *Donahue* with Andrea Dworkin, who had just published *Intercourse*. Knowing all too well the habit talk shows have of pitting one woman against the other in a staged cat fight, I didn't want to play that game. I had read enough of Andrea Dworkin's work to know that I violently disagreed with many of her positions—and that she was a serious and committed writer and champion of women's rights. I believed (then as now) that dissent within the Women's Movement (or any movement) was a sign of life and while *I* knew that I could disagree with Dworkin yet still honor her as a colleague, I wasn't sure that the subtlety of my position would come across on *Donahue*—or any talk show.

The trouble with television is that, in reducing all discourse to four-and-a-half-minute "segs," interrupted by commercials, it tends to degrade subtle philosophical argument to the level of comic strips.

POW. BANG. SPLAT. Jong and Dworkin face off about *Intercourse*. I did not want to attack other feminists. The Women's Movement was in enough trouble without women attacking women. I conveyed my doubts to the producers at *Donahue*, who assured me that Andrea Dworkin and I would not be set up as antagonists. Reluctantly, I accepted the gig.

Then I began to prepare by reading Dworkin.

Years ago, I had tried to read Dworkin's first (mainstream) book, **Woman Hating**, and had been turned off by its rhetoric, its 1960s cant, and by what I took then to be its crude overstatement of woman's lot. But I was a lot younger and more innocent then, and as Gloria Steinem says: women are the sex that grows more radical with age.

So I read *Intercourse* and I was—to use a sixties locution—blown away. Here was a book that had collected the most ghastly reviews, and I was finding it thrilling in a way I had not found a book about men and women thrilling since *The Second Sex* by Simone de Beauvoir or *The Female Eunuch* by Germaine Greer.

I do not mean to say that I agreed with every assertion in *Intercourse.* I only mean to say that anyone taking the argument of the book—that the act of sex *itself* preconditions female inferiority and male dominance—intellectually rather than personally has to acknowledge that this book raises questions that desperately need raising.

Why has the Women's Movement arisen in every modern era—from the 17th century to the 20th—only to be pushed back by a tide of reaction? Why do women collude in their own oppression? Why do women side with their fathers, husbands, brothers, and sons against their daughters, mothers, and their own self-interest? Does "sexual freedom" further oppress women or does it put them in touch with their sense of liberty? Is patriarchy innate in the human species or is it socially conditioned? Is chastity an option for women who wish to be intellectually free or is it the last refuge of female paranoia?

Reading Andrea Dworkin's **Intercourse** as an intellectual work rather than a battle cry, one is dazzled by the profundity of the questions it raises about men and women. The chapter on Joan of Arc ("Virginity") is worth the price of the book.

We suddenly understand why *La Pucelle* had to wear men's clothes and be a militant virgin to lead her army into battle—and understand why all the male interpretations of her behavior make no sense.

> Her virginity was a self-conscious and militant repudiation of the common lot of the female with its intrinsic low status, which, then as now, appeared to have something to do with being fucked. . . . Unlike the feminine virgins who accepted the social subordination while exempting themselves from the sex on which it was premised, Joan rejected the status and the sex as one thing—empirical synonyms: low civil status and being fucked as indistinguishable one from the other.

Dworkin is a real writer. She burns with a determination to change the world. She really believes books matter, that they are *actions*. She is not cynical about this—using a book as a stepping-stone to personal power like so many. She believes that the word matters and that the word can change the world. This, after all, is the girl who started out to be a rabbi.

We met in Donahue's green room in Rockefeller Center; our seconds were our publishers' publicity chiefs. We exchanged books and shook hands warmly. I realized that Andrea was trembling. She was terrified.

Once on the air the show went swimmingly. Andrea stated her position passionately without for a moment offering disrespect for mine. She argued that the act of intercourse itself in patriarchal culture both defined and conditioned female inferiority. I argued that the act of intercourse can be nurturing, nourishing, loving—even as it can be intrusive and violent—and that the act itself does not have a fixed nature but reflects the feelings of the people engaging in it. Andrea continued to assert that the personal is political and that sex, for most women, is both travesty and sham.

In general, women in the audience seemed to see themselves as self-determining and free creatures whose personal experience *was* personal, not political. They did not really grasp the notion that their most intimate behavior was conditioned by cultural norms. Still, for television, it was as subtle a rendering as one could expect. Andrea spoke for all the oppressed, beaten, battered women of the world; I outlined a vision of a more humane and feminized society in which women's values, women's sexual needs, and women's nurturance would become norms rather than exceptions in our culture. What was remarkable about the show was how supportive two women authors were of each other—even though they did not agree.

FROM THE AUTHOR

DWORKIN ON THE FEMALE COLONIZED MIND

Feminists are now threatened in every area of activity because men are trying to recolonize our minds—minds that have been trying to be free of male control. Everywhere, women are confronted by the urgency of male demands, all of which are supposed to supersede in importance the demands which women must make toward our own integrity. This story is so old that it should be tired and dead, but it is not. Feminists tell the tales over and over: how women contributed to this and that revolution and were sold out in the end, sent packing back to the house to clean it up after the revolutionary dust had settled, pregnant and poor; how women contributed to this and that movement for social change and were raped and exploited and abused, and then sent back to clean the house, pregnant and poor. But the colonized mind cannot remember. The colonized mind does not have the pride or militancy of memory. The colonized mind refuses to politicize anger or bitterness. The colonized mind must meet the demands of the colonizer: devotion and good behavior, clean thoughts and no ugly wrath.

Dworkin, Andrea. Excerpt from *Letters from a War Zone: Writings 1976-1989.* New York: E. P. Dutton, 1988, p. 128.

What was also remarkable was how different Andrea Dworkin and I *looked* on television. If the medium is both the message *and* the massage, then I was a masseuse and Andrea a picador. Andrea wore overalls, no makeup, frizzy hair. And I was coiffed, dressed, shod, and made up in a way that entirely reflects my pleasure in being female.

I watched the videotape before beginning this piece and again marveled at the visual impact we make together. Andrea dresses to keep men and the world at bay; I not only to attract but also for my own delight in costume and color. What does this reflect in terms of our psychologies and our ideas? Andrea Dworkin would say that any "femininity" is both an outward sign of capitulation and a clear signal indicating that I have bought into the male definition of woman: I am here to be dominated. I dispute that, finding in femininity something pleasing in itself—apart from male definition. But perhaps I am self-deluded. As Dworkin says:

> "No one can bear to live a meaningless life. Women fight for meaning just as women fight for survival: by attaching themselves to men and the values honored by men."

Most articles are written either by antagonists or proponents. This is one article being written by a respectful dissenter. The fact that women can be both respectful to each other *and* dissent is new to the world. I see it as one sign of the progress the Women's Movement has wrought—despite all the other discouraging signs. It is my hope that in showing respect and tolerance for each other women are creating a new paradigm of political discourse—a paradigm that does not institutionalize conflict and dualism, but rather sees a web of relationships between people as life-sustaining, nurturing. Such a paradigm is one of the things women can bring to the world once they reject the patriarchal, male system with its dualisms, conflicts, and wars.

Andrea and I have this in common: we both began writing seriously during sojourns in Europe. I in Heidelberg, Germany—married to a Chinese-American psychiatrist (whose last name became my nom de plume); she in Greece during a leave of absence from Bennington College and later in Amsterdam, where she lived with her Dutch husband—who turned out to be a batterer and a violent man.

"Why do American writers often start writing in Europe?" I asked Dworkin.

> "For me it had to do with getting away from this country which, number one, has no respect for writers; number two, has no respect for . . . activists. . . . For me also, though, it was that I was enraged with this country's policies on Vietnam [and] the racism here was deeply distressing to me. . . . There was no women's movement, so there was no support for me pretty much anywhere."

For Andrea Dworkin, as for many other rebellious young Americans, Europe was a place to find one's self both politically and literarily.

> "What I most want is to be a great writer and to leave a legacy of real change. Books and social justice for me are inseparable. You can't pull them apart . . . and of course there is nothing in this country that honors that tradition of writing, or that tradition of politics."

I also believe that books and social justice are inseparable, but I have a different notion of the way the written word affects the general culture. There is no question that the written word still underlies every cultural phenomenon and still has the capacity to change attitudes enormously, but it does so in the way that irrigation transforms desert into arable land—under the surface of visible things. The changes wrought by books happen in a subterranean field and they extend everywhere.

Books, by their nature, work slowly. And our whole instant-media culture is beginning today to erode the power of the book in a way uncontemplated even 15 years ago. The short shelf life of serious books in bookstores is a problem, as is the short attention span of an audience that has no time to read. We have the freest country in the world intellectually, we have the greatest choice of reading material, and yet our most successful people have the least time of any to read. The very terms in which we define success—constant busyness, frantic social life, constant ego-massage by underlings—leave no time for the slow, centered, solitary pleasure of reading books and absorbing ideas. We want our information in four-and-a-half-minute "segs"—as if that were more efficient.

But reading is important not only because of the *ideas* it imparts, but because the mental state it creates allows participation in a way that other media do not. Reading is relaxing, contemplative, nurturing; other media are often merely numbing. Reading allows space for the play of the reader's mind.

On the subject of her love relationships, Andrea Dworkin is maddeningly general. She doesn't want to discuss her marriage, her relationships with women, or her relationship with the friend she lives with, John Stoltenberg. "We love each other" is all she will say.

I understand and empathize with her obtuseness. Any woman who is a public figure is driven nearly insane by the scrutiny directed at her personal life and the harshness with which any deviation from the norm—whatever *that* is—is judged.

"In your writings, you have declared yourself a lesbian," I say. "How do you regard lesbianism?"

"Exactly as I regard being Jewish: as a badge of pride."

"A sort of proud tribal identity?" I ask.

"That's a beautiful way to put it," she says.

Other things one should know about Andrea Dworkin that seem important: she is a Libra, born September 26, 1946, and she regards herself as typically Libran and says most Librans are "fair, detached, promiscuous." She tells me that Librans' detachment drives other members of the zodiac mad. But in my extensive talks with her, I have not found her particularly detached. I would say she is driven by an intense sense of fairness, a burning outrage about injustice, and a continuing anger about the limitations of being female.

Before a recent trip to Europe to promote one of her books and enjoy a writing vacation, she shared with me her distress about being a woman alone in Europe and how limiting femaleness can still be. These are feelings I have written about, but they have not troubled me in my daily life. I know that women all over the world are often in physical danger of rape and battery, but do not personally focus on this fear. Wherever I am in the world, I feel relatively safe because I feel strong in myself.

Andrea Dworkin is concerned about rape and violence to a degree that I cannot completely understand from my talks with her. When one hears her talk about rape and battery, or reads her autobiographical fiction, it's clear that this is a woman who has been severely abused at various times in her life and who trembles awaiting the next incidence of abuse. Talking with her, I feel I must have led the most sheltered of lives and I wonder whose experience is more typical, Andrea's or mine?

Reading her work, I have wondered about her terror of the male world. It seems more than just empathy with the plight of oppressed women. It seems to have a dimension of paranoia to it. It certainly leaves out the experience of women who enjoy sex, have had loving lovers, have enjoyed pregnancy and their children. I count myself among these fortunate women—but that is *not* the point. It is irrelevant that some women seem to lead charmed lives. "If one woman were to tell the truth about her life, the world would split open," said Muriel Rukeyser, one of Andrea Dworkin's and my mentors, and a great and unappreciated woman poet. We are often afraid to tell the truth publicly because our view of the world has been invalidated by patriarchy and our very interpretation of our condition and the language in which to phrase it has been taken from us.

Andrea Dworkin is a lesbian. I am not. I know that women can be militantly pro-women without being lesbians but I also know it is easier for a lesbian to criticize patriarchal society because she is an outsider, owing no sexual allegiance to a man. I myself find that I am more inclined to be free in criticizing society when I am not worrying, even subliminally, about pleasing some lover or husband. Perhaps the lesbian, cut off as she already is from the world of male protection and privilege, is freer to disclose the hypocrisies of the patriarchal system. I cannot commit my sexual life to my own sex, however convenient that might be for my writing and general peace of mind. But I have enough imagination to understand the intellectual freedom that may come with lesbianism.

One of the most complicated, difficult, and challenging tasks for a woman artist is to live with and among men, and yet still retain her intellectual integrity. It necessitates a very strong center, an ego that can keep its boundaries while still allowing love to enter, to nurture, and to be returned. Our divorce rate bears witness to its difficulty, and the general unhappiness of both sexes in our culture bears witness to its frequent failure. For we are living in a time of unprecedented sexual discontent in which men and women regard each other testily at best. We are in the midst of an incomplete social revolution; women are unhappy, but men are equally perplexed and troubled. The question is what to do about it—and how?

Andrea Dworkin's position—articulated in all her books and in the antipornography legislation she coauthored with Catharine A. MacKinnon for the city of Minneapolis—is that the whole patriarchal system must be eradicated from the ground up. And replaced with—what? This she does not say. Dworkin makes a stunning case for the harm that pornography does. She shows that far from being a "victimless crime" it does, in fact, destroy the lives of millions of women and children who are abused as participants or abused as a result of men having been inflamed by it. But as much as I share Andrea Dworkin's outrage about the way violence against women and children is condoned in our pop-and-porno culture, I fear even more than its proliferation the hand of the state censor. I remain a strict free-speech advocate even though I know that in a materialistic culture all freedom is conditioned by economic access.

What paradigm of human interaction do Andrea Dworkin's books participate in and create? Andrea Dworkin comes out of the old left of the sixties, and she brilliantly describes in *Right-wing Women* the situation of women in the old left, their outrage and despair when they realized that the rights of man did not apply to them. Out of this outraged recognition that the male paradigm had not changed in the antiwar movement, women created the so-called Second Wave of the feminist movement, which utterly transformed our culture.

Many phenomena we now take for granted were the work of this second wave—from the recognition of wife-battering as a crime, to the prominence of women in publishing, television, and film, to the new woman executive in her dress-for-success suit. The revolution is still partial, but it is a revolution compared to the world we knew in 1960—and many younger women who do not even realize it are indebted to the feminists of the sixties-turning-seventies for their jobs, their lives, their increased options.

But the second wave of the feminist movement was the sister of the old left and participated, willy-nilly, in *its* paradigms. It saw politics in terms of left and right, visualizing the political dialectic in a dualistic way that basically began with the French and American revolutions and has remained unchanged until this day. That was its strength in the sixties. But that also accounts for its obsolescence today—and for the deadened, despairing feeling we get reading Andrea Dworkin's books, searching for hope and finding none.

For the next phase of movement for women and for children and all humanity cannot come out of these old paradigms, which, in their very language and concepts, institutionalize struggle and dualism. Even the phrases—"war between the sexes," "Women's Movement," "feminism"—fill many people with despair because they suspect that society will not be changed by dualistic thinking. They are right.

In *When Society Becomes an Addict,* Anne Wilson Schaef brilliantly analyzes what has gone wrong with male patriarchal society and why it has become diseased, prone to addictions, and indeed follows an addictive model. We live in a society of materialism run riot in which people relate to things rather than to each other. Even in our love lives we objectify—and pornography institutionalizes this objectification. But a society in which parents have less and less time to relate to their children except by giving them *things* creates and perpetuates just such an addictive model. In the old patriarchal world men pursued things, and women took care of human relationships—including children. In the post-second-wave world, both women and children have frenziedly followed the male addictive model.

What women can bring to the world in terms of a *true* counterculture, a counterculture of the future, is a new paradigm for society in which relationships are more important than things and addiction as a model of behavior becomes obsolescent. It's a tall order, but nothing less will save us.

I believe that childbirth is a profoundly radicalizing act for women, opening them up to their humanity and interdependence in ways often denied to men and giving them a new model for the web of relationships between people. If this model could permeate our society, it would have the effect of humanizing it. It is this hope that keeps me writing. I do not think it is a vain hope, though I do not underestimate the difficulty of changing institutions.

In a sense the answer lies more with men and with a new men's movement than it does with women. Unless men give up their denial that the society they have created is deeply diseased, most women have no choice but to be either semi-slaves colluding in their own oppression, or militant separatists à la Dworkin. How to get past male denial when most men have so much to gain by denying the existence of female pain? Privileged groups seldom give up their privilege without bloody revolution. And it is unthinkable that women will take up arms against their own sons, brothers, husbands. However violent our dreams, we are tied by ties of love and loyalty. Men have always known this and abused it.

The only hope for creating a new society lies in the privileged male elite finally coming to realize that its *own* survival is doomed unless society begins to change. That takes insight, self-questioning, and self-criticism. Many individual men are capable of this, but men in groups usually are not. Women have been Cassandras all along—pointing to the fault lines due for slippage and warning the other sex of the damage we are doing to the planet and our own future as a species.

Another paradigm exists, and New Age philosophers are beginning to explore it. The only way to solve the male/female dilemma is to stop thinking of the sexes as discrete and opposed entities and start thinking of them as two parts of a whole organism. If man and woman begin to cultivate their oneness, their interdependence as one organism, if they reject the war paradigm, and see themselves in a new light, perhaps the planet and the race have a future after all.

I would like to propose that we have other alternatives—if only men, the sex still in control, will see them and the necessity for change. Andrea Dworkin does not believe that change is possible without militancy. I do. I believe we can change attitudes about women and what is acceptable, civilized behavior without killing each other. As Niels Bohr says, "The opposite of a fact is a falsehood, but the opposite of one profound truth may very well be another profound truth."

TITLE COMMENTARY

Intercourse

JOANNE GLASGOW (REVIEW DATE SEPTEMBER-OCTOBER 1987)

SOURCE: Glasgow, Joanne. "Dworkin Critiques Relations between the Sexes." *New Directions for Women* (September-October 1987): 18-19.

In the following review, Glasgow praises Intercourse *as a groundbreaking book, one that "should be read, discussed, argued about passionately."*

For more than two months, I have been waiting to read a decent, fair discussion of Andrea Dworkin's newest book, *Intercourse.* I would have settled for an honest pan, provided the reviewer had been willing to wrestle with the ideas in the book.

But in review after review, and in talk show after talk show, all I have seen are distortions at best and, far more often, savage personal attacks on Dworkin. Instead of discussing the book, people have focused on her outspoken anti-pornography stand. Or they have attacked her recent novel *Ice and Fire* as a pornographic book. Or they have isolated a controversial line or two, as *The New York Times* review did. Or they have tried to pin a derogatory label on her, as Erica Jong did on *The Donahue Show* (In that instance, Jong simplistically reduced Dworkin's position to a discredited form of old-fashioned biological determinism.)

When, in all this shameful public wrangling, is anyone going to discuss what to me seems the most important critique of male/female bonds since Adrienne Rich's *Of Woman Born?*

Like Rich, Dworkin has taken on one of the most "sacred" of institutions. Rich examined the institution of motherhood and concluded that the experience individual mothers have is systematically buried beneath layers of misogyny, patriarchal control and symbolic interpretation that

denies the existence of women's witness. Women's truth is not even examined or disputed. It is simply erased.

That, argues Dworkin, is precisely what happens to women's witness when intercourse is institutionalized, as it has been in this country and indeed all over the world.

Although she does not refer to Rich, nor do I think she intended the parallel, Dworkin shows in chapter after harrowing chapter just what the act of intercourse has meant in men's eyes. It is the instrument of misogyny for men like Tolstoy, of patriarchal control for men like Isaac Bashevis Singer, of symbolic warfare against other men for men like James Baldwin.

And for women? Dworkin examines two responses: the no of the marriage resisters, for whom Joan of Arc is the exemplar, and the lie of the collaborators, for whom all the anonymous respondents in Shere Hite's *Report* are the representatives (that is, 70 percent of all women). This lie of the collaborators is perhaps the sticking point for many readers. As Dworkin says, "*Intercourse* is a loyalty test for women." In a man-made world intercourse has to occur, has to be central and has to be centrally valued.

Prior to modern reproductive technology, intercourse had indeed been necessary for human procreation. It is still the method of choice for most people, even in advanced technological societies like ours. But is it central? And for whom, Freud and Lacan notwithstanding, is it central? Evidently, according to Dworkin, not for women. If statistics are accurate, most women do not find intercourse centrally satisfying, despite enormous pressure to do so. But they must not say so. Their silence must be won. They must fake orgasm, pretend they want nothing more or simply (perhaps preferably) know nothing else.

I think this is the part of her book that most feminists who live with men find hardest to accept. Indeed, if Dworkin's analysis is correct, their reluctance is proof of the argument. And they may, justifiably, find the argument loaded. But that is no reason to distort Dworkin's views and certainly no justification for ignoring the argument completely in favor of cheap shots and irrelevant commentary. Instead, the book should be read, discussed, argued about passionately. Silence, too, distorts.

Sex Laws

In the final section of the book Dworkin argues for a reexamination of the ways men have

DWORKIN

erected laws to protect the centrality of intercourse. Of all her analyses, the most compelling to my mind is the manipulation of language and categories. Men have for centuries passed laws that forbid many acts of sexual intimacy. But as Dworkin says, "Folks keep getting it wrong, and wanting to put the wrong thing in the wrong place at the wrong time." And so the powers of coercion called law step in to regulate such behavior. And these laws are justified by the label "natural." What a piece of circular reasoning it is! Dworkin's analysis should finally lay to rest the claim many antagonists have made that she is secretly in league with (some have said in bed with) the New Right. Hardly!

But whatever individual readers think about it, this is at least what the book is about—the symbolic meaning attached to intercourse in a man-made world and our individual and sometimes collective struggles with that meaning. It is a work of imaginative power. It is controversial. It is sometimes maddening. But it is truly important. It is the most important book I have read in ten years. Readers should give it a chance.

FURTHER READING

Criticism

Assiter, Alison. *Pornography, Feminism, and the Individual.* Winchester, Mass.: Pluto Press, 1989. 166 p.

Critical examination with bibliographical references.

Eberly, Rosa A. *Citizen Critics: Literary Public Spheres.* Urbana: University of Illinois Press, 2000. 199 p.

Contains reference material following a critical article titled "Andrea Dworkin's Mercy: Pain and Silence in the "War Zone."

Jenefsky, Cindy Ann Russo. *Without Apology: Andrea Dworkin's Art and Politics.* Boulder, Colo.: Westview Press, 1998, 163 p.

Full-length study of Dworkin's feminist ideology.

Maitland, Sara. "Inside Out." *New Statesman* 113, no. 2935 (26 June 1987): 31.

Presents objections to Dworkin's assertions in Intercourse.

Mullarkey, Maureen. "Hard Cop, Soft Cop." *Nation* (30 May 1987): 720-26.

Negative assessment of Intercourse.

Nussbaum, Martha C. "Rage and Reason." *New Republic* 217, nos. 6-7 (August 11-18 1997): 36-42.

Exploration of Dworkin's feminist ideas, particularly her controversial theories on physical violence against women found in Life and Death.

Russo, Ann, and Lourdes Torres. "Beyond the 'Porn Wars': Why Feminists Should Read Andrea Dworkin." *Sojourner: The Women's Forum* 15, no. 10 (June 1990): 16-17.

Examination of the defining characteristics of Dworkin's feminist politics and writings.

Wolfe, Alan. "Dirt and Democracy." *The New Republic* (19 February 1990): 27-31.

Discusses Dworkin's objections to pornography as delineated in Pornography.

OTHER SOURCES FROM GALE:

Additional coverage of Dworkin's life and career is contained in the following sources published by the Gale Group: *Contemporary Authors,* Vols. 77-80; *Contemporary Authors Autobiography Series,* Vol. 21; *Contemporary Authors New Revision Series,* Vols. 16, 39, 76, 96; *Contemporary Literary Criticism,* Vols. 43, 123; *Feminist Writers; Gay and Lesbian Literature,* Ed. 1; *Literature Resource Center;* and *Major 20th-Century Writers.*

BUCHI EMECHETA

(1944 -)

(Full name Florence Onye Buchi Emecheta) Nigerian novelist, autobiographer, and author of children's books.

A Nigerian-born author who has resided in England since 1962, Emecheta is best known for her novels that address the difficulties facing modern African women forced into traditional and subservient roles. Emecheta's heroines often challenge the restrictive customs imposed on them and aspire to economic and social independence. Although some critics have categorized Emecheta's works as feminist in nature, Emecheta rejects the label, stating, "I have not committed myself to the cause of African women only. I write about Africa as a whole."

BIOGRAPHICAL INFORMATION

Emecheta was born in 1944 in Yaba, a small village near Lagos, Nigeria. Her parents, both from eastern Nigeria, died when she was a child. Emecheta was taken in by foster parents who mistreated her. She grew up listening to the women around her telling stories, but in her culture women were not expected to be writers. She attended a missionary high school in Lagos until she was sixteen and then married a man to whom she had been promised since age eleven. At nineteen, Emecheta followed her husband to

London. She had two children at the time and was pregnant with her third; she eventually became a mother of five. During this time in London Emecheta began to write. Her husband was so upset over her intention to become a writer that he burned her first novel, and after this, Emecheta decided to leave him. She later rewrote the novel and published it as *The Bride Price* (1976). While struggling to become a writer, she worked part-time jobs to support her family and earned a degree in sociology at the University of London. Emecheta's early writing efforts initially met with repeated rejections from publishers. Her break came when the *New Statesman* accepted several of her essays about her life in London; these eventually became her first published work, the novel *In the Ditch* (1972).

MAJOR WORKS

Three of Emecheta's works focus on events in her life. Her first two novels, *In the Ditch* and *Second-Class Citizen* (1975), are loosely based on her own experiences as a single parent and are regarded as her most accomplished works. Both books revolve around a young Nigerian woman named Adah and her search for a better quality of life. In the first book, Emecheta depicts Adah's struggle to raise five small children while depending on welfare payments, attending college, and attempting to complete her first novel. The second book recounts Adah's immigration to England and her marriage to a domineering man who attempts to thwart her educational and professional aspirations. Their marriage dissolves as Adah, influenced by the women's liberation movement, begins to assert her individuality. *Head above Water* (1986) is a nonfiction work detailing Emecheta's childhood in a small Nigerian village, her career as a social worker in London, and the problems she encountered in securing a publisher for her writings.

Three of Emecheta's novels dramatize the problems that African women typically encounter in a traditional, male-oriented society: *The Bride Price, The Slave Girl* (1977), and *The Joys of Motherhood* (1979). *The Bride Price* centers on a young woman who defies tribal custom by marrying a man outside her social class. After her husband fails to pay her dowry, or bride price, she dies in childbirth, as prophesied by tribal myth. *The Slave Girl*, which accuses the patriarchal social system of treating females as commodities, focuses upon the coming of age of an orphan girl whose older brother sells her to a distant relative. *The Joys of Motherhood* relates the story of a young Ibo woman named Nnu Ego who feels inferior when she is unable to give her husband a child. She flees her village to the city of Lagos and begins a new life with a new husband. She becomes a mother several times over, but the joy of fulfilling her dream is tempered by the reality of having to feed a large family with little income. After her children grow up and move away, Nnu Ego dies alone on the side of the road.

CRITICAL RECEPTION

Critics have lauded Emecheta for convincing characterizations and amusing yet poignant evocations of her heroines' tribulations. Many critics have asserted that she provides a thorough presentation of social themes in her novels, but some reviewers have argued that Emecheta has either ignored or shied away from certain larger social issues in her works. For example, several scholars claim that she did not address sexual discrimination in England in *Second-Class Citizen*. Commentators have disagreed over Emecheta's relationship to feminism and to traditional African culture. Much of this commentary has focused on *The Joys of Motherhood*. Some critics have asserted that Emecheta created Nnu Ego as the representative African woman, while others hold that Emecheta had neither the authority, nor the

intention to speak for all African women. Salome C. Nnoromele (see Further Reading) has argued that "*The Joys of Motherhood* is not a construction of the universal African woman. . . . [It] is simply the story of a woman who makes devastating choices and sacrifices her health and selfhood in the pursuit of failed traditions, capsulated in the idea of motherhood." Critics have also argued that the novels set in Africa, including *The Joys of Motherhood*, represent a feminist indictment of African patriarchal culture, and have lauded Emecheta for her portrayal of the effects of this culture on African women. Certain critics contend that Nnu Ego is not a victim of patriarchal oppression, but rather a victim of the clash between traditional African society and the culture of the colonizers. Critics generally agree, however, that Emecheta provides a needed feminine perspective on the lives and culture of African women. Katherine Frank (see Further Reading) concluded, "Emecheta's novels compose the most exhaustive and moving portrayal extant of the African woman, an unparalleled portrayal in African fiction and with few equals in other literatures as well."

PRINCIPAL WORKS

In the Ditch (novel) 1972

Second-Class Citizen (novel) 1974

The Bride Price (novel) 1976

The Slave Girl (novel) 1977

The Joys of Motherhood (novel) 1979

Titch the Cat (juvenile fiction) 1979

The Moonlight Bride (juvenile fiction) 1980

Nowhere to Play (juvenile fiction) 1980

The Wrestling Match (juvenile fiction) 1980

Destination Biafra (novel) 1982

Naira Power (novella) 1982

Adah's Story (novel) 1983

The Rape of Shavi (novel) 1983

Head above Water (autobiography) 1984

A Kind of Marriage (novella) 1986

Gwendolen (novel) 1989

Kehinde (novel) 1994

PRIMARY SOURCES

BUCHI EMECHETA (ESSAY DATE 1988)

SOURCE: Buchi Emecheta, "Feminism with a Small 'f'!" In *Criticism and Ideology: Second African Writers' Conference*, edited by Kirsten Holst Petersen. Scandinavian Institute of African Studies, 1988, pp. 173-85.

In the following essay, Emecheta discusses her artistic concerns and feminist perspective. As Emecheta illustrates, African feminism differs significantly from Western feminism due to the distinct cultural values and sexual identity of African women.

I am just an ordinary writer, an ordinary writer who has to write, because if I didn't write I think I would have to be put in an asylum. Some people have to communicate, and I happen to be one of them. I have tried several times to take university appointments and work as a critic, but each time I have packed up and left without giving notice. I found that I could not bring myself to criticize other people's work. When my husband burned my first book, I said to him 'If you can burn my book, you can just as well burn my child, because my books are like my children, and I cannot criticize my children'. When I had my babies they were very, very ugly; they had big heads, like their father and their bodies looked like mine. But if anybody looked into the pram and said 'What an ugly baby', I would never talk to that person again. And I know that I am not the only writer who finds it hard to accept criticism. One critic asked me 'You have so much anger in you, how can you bear it?' 'Well', I said, 'I can't bear it, so I have to let it out on paper'. I started writing in 1972, and a few weeks ago I handed in my sixteenth novel. In order to make you understand how I work I will tell you about my background.

I was born in Lagos, Nigeria, and was raised partly there and partly in my village, Ibuza, and this explains my wish to tell stories when I was a child. My parents both came from Ibuza and moved to Lagos in search of work. As both of them were partly educated they embraced the C.M.S (Church Missionary Society) way of life. But being of the old Ibo kingdom they made sure that my brother and myself never lost sight of home, of life in Ibuza.

We worked at home during the rains, to help on the farm and to learn our ways. If I lived in Lagos I could start to have loose morals and speak Yoruba all the time. So my parents wanted me to learn the rigorous Ibo life. You can see that even in Nigeria we still discriminate against each other.

It was at home that I came across real story tellers. I had seen some Yoruba ones telling their stories and songs and beating their drums whilst we children followed them—Pied Piper like—from street to street. But the Ibo story teller was different. She was always one's mother. My Big Mother was my aunt. A child belonged to many mothers. Not just one's biological one. We would sit for hours at her feet mesmerized by her trance like voice. Through such stories she could tell the heroic deeds of her ancestors, all our mores and all our customs. She used to tell them in such a way, in such a sing-song way that until I was about fourteen I used to think that these women were inspired by some spirits. It was a result of those visits to Ibuza, coupled with the enjoyment and information those stories used to give us, that I determined when grew older that I was going to be a story teller, like my Big Mother.

I learned to my dismay at school in Lagos that if I wanted to tell stories to people from many places I would have to use a language that was not my first—neither was it my second, or third, but my fourth language. This made my stories lose a great deal of their colour, but I learned to get by. My English must have been very bad because when I first told my English teacher, who came from the Lake District, and who was crazy about Wordsworth that I was going to write like her favourite poet, she ordered me to go to the school chapel and pray for forgiveness, because she said: 'Pride goeth before a fall'. I did not go to the chapel to pray because even then I knew that God would have much more important things to do than to listen to my dreams. Dreams which for me, coming both from the exotic so-called Ibo bush culture and the historic Yoruba one, were not unattainable.

Some of these early missionaries did not really penetrate the African mind. That incident confirmed what I had always suspected as a child, that the art of communication, be it in pictures, in music, writing or in oral folklore is vital to the human.

I never learn from my experiences. My first attempt to write a book, called The Bride Price was resented by my husband. He too, like my English teacher, told me that 'Pride goeth before a fall'. I left him and I found myself at twenty-two, husbandless with five young children. I thought I would wait to be as old as Big Mother with a string of degrees before writing. But I had to earn my living and the only thing I could do was write.

Whilst looking after my fast-growing family I decided to read for a degree that would help me master the English language and help me write about my society for the rest of the world. I chose sociology and continued writing. I had enough rejection slips to paper a room. But in 1972 the New Statesman started serializing my work and those recollections later appeared as my first book, In the Ditch.

I have been writing ever since, and I am now living entirely on my writing. Those babies of mine are now beginning to leave home. One of them has started to write as well, so perhaps writing runs in the family. I am not doing anything particularly clever. I am simply doing what my Big Mother was doing for free about thirty years ago. The only difference is that she told her stories in the moonlight, while I have to bang away at a typewriter I picked up from Woolworths in London. I am not good at reading, and sometimes when I write I can't even read my writing. Writing is a very lonely profession. One is there at one's desk, thinking of ideas and reasoning them out and putting them into works of fiction or stories, and if one is not careful, one will start living the life of the characters in the book. Conferences like this one save some of us from becoming strange.

Writers are often asked 'Who are you writing for?'. How am I supposed to know who is going to pick up my works from the library shelf? I wonder sometimes if people ask painters, when they are doing their paintings, who they are painting them for. The painter can control the picture while he is still painting it, but can we expect him to foretell who is going to love looking at it? A book is akin to a child on his mother's back. The mother knows she is carrying a baby on her back but the child can use its hands to lift anything that passes by, without the mother knowing. I find this question sometimes rather patronizing. In fact it is sometimes healthier not to think of one's readers at all. Writers are communicators. We chronicle everyday happenings, weave them into novels, poetry, documentary fiction, articles etc. The writer has the freedom to control, to imagine and to chronicle. I write for everybody.

The writer also has a crucial control over the subject s/he writes about. For myself, I don't deal with great ideological issues. I write about the little happenings of everyday life. Being a woman, and African born, I see things through an African woman's eyes. I chronicle the little happenings in the lives of the African women I know. I did not know that by doing so I was going to be called a

feminist. But if I am now a feminist then I am an African feminist with a small f. In my books I write about families because I still believe in families. I write about women who try very hard to hold their family together until it becomes absolutely impossible. I have no sympathy for a woman who deserts her children, neither do I have sympathy for a woman who insists on staying in a marriage with a brute of a man, simply to be respectable. I want very much to further the education of women in Africa, because I know that education really helps the women. It helps them to read and it helps them to rear a generation. It is true that if one educates a woman, one educates a community, whereas if one educates a man, one educates a man. I do occasionally write about wars and the nuclear holocaust but again in such books I turn to write about the life and experiences of women living under such conditions.

Maybe all this makes me an ordinary writer. But that is what I want to be. An ordinary writer. I will read to you two pieces from my own observations. The style is simple but that is my way. I am a simple and unsophisticated person and cultural people really make me nervous. First I want to read a short piece about polygamy. People think that polygamy is oppression, and it is in certain cases. But I realize, now that I have visited Nigeria often, that some women now make polygamy work for them. What I am about to relate happened only a few weeks ago. I was in my bedroom in Ibuza listening to a conversation. It was cool and damp and I was debating whether to get up from my bed or not. I knew it was about six in the morning. I did not have to look at the clock. I just knew because I could hear the songs of the morning, children on their way to fetch water, a cock crowing here and there. Then the penetrating voice of Nwango, the senior wife of Obike came into my thoughts. 'Go away you stinking beast. Why will you not let me sleep? I have a full day ahead of me and you come harassing me so early in the morning. You are shameless. You don't even care that the children sleep next-door. You beast. Why don't you go to your new wife.' Now the man: 'All I have from you is your loud mouth. You are never around to cook for me, and when I come to your bed, you send me away. What did I pay the bride-price for?' The voice of Obike was slow and full of righteous anger. 'Go to your wife.' 'She is pregnant', said Obike. 'So what, get another woman. I need my energy for my farm and my trading, and today is the market-day', Nwango insisted. I was sorry to miss the end of the quarrel because my mother-in-law came in and told me not to mind them. 'They are always like that, these men. They are shameless. They think we women are here just to be their partners at night. He can marry another girl. But again which girl in her right senses will take him? He is too lazy to go regularly to his farm.' My mother-in-law should know. She had thirteen children. They lived in the capital, Lagos, and her husband did not have room to bring home another wife, so she had to do everything. If they had spent their life in the village it would have been different.

I know this is a situation which our Western sisters will find difficult to understand. Sex is important to us. But we do not make it the centre of our being, as women do here. In fact most of the Nigerian women who are promiscuous are so for economic reasons. The Yorubas have a saying that a woman must never allow a man to sleep with her if, at the end of the day she is going to be in debt. Few of our women go after sex per se. If they are with their husbands they feel they are giving something out of duty, love, or in order to have children. A young woman might dream of romantic love, but as soon as they start having children their loyalty is very much to them, and they will do everything in their power to make life easier for them. In the villages the woman will seek the company of her age-mates, her friends, and the women in the market, and for advice she goes either to her mother or to her mother-in-law. Another woman in the family will help share the housework, like Nwango cited earlier. The day her husband wanted her was an Eke day, a big market day. She had to be up early to be at the market. She had to contribute her twenty naira which is almost ten pounds, to the savings fund of the market women. That is the way we raise capital for our business without having to go to the bank, because most banks will not lend money to a woman. So she had to contribute her twenty naira and later on in the evening, she had to put on her otuogu and she had to be at the Agbalani group, as they were going to dance at the second burial of the grandmother of one of their members. For that dance they had to tie the otuogu with the Akangwose style; all of which took them three years to save up for. They had to wear a navy-blue head-tie and carry a navy-blue Japanese fan and wear black flat shoes or slippers. None of these items was bought by their husbands. Nwango worked on her cassava farm four days of the week—we have a five-day week—and sold the garri made from the cassava on the fifth day, Eke market day. She gave twenty naira esusu of her profit to the collector who was one of the women in her group. It is from this esusu forced saving that she is sending her son to college, and she spends the rest exactly as she likes. At the funeral dance the group will give the bereaved lady a thousand naira (about five hundred pounds), from their fund to help out. And the dance will go on till very late. At about eight p.m. one will hear these women going home, singing their heads off. They drink anything from whisky, beer, gin, brandy, you name it, and no man dares tell them not to. Cooking for the husband, fiddle sticks! Get another woman to do it. Especially if the other woman is still a young seventeen- or eighteen-year old with her head full of romantic love. By the time she is twenty-five she will become wiser too. Nwango's husband is almost a stud. Not a nice word, but that is the way most village women feel.

Sex is part of life. It is not THE life. Listen to the Western feminists' claim about enjoying sex, they make me laugh. African feminism is free of the shackles of Western romantic illusions and tends to be much more pragmatic. We believe that we are here for many, many things, not just to cultivate ourselves, and make ourselves pretty for men. The beauty in sisterhood is when women reach the age of about forty. The women who cultivated sisters either through marriage or through the village age-group start reaping their reward. In England for example I belong to the war-babies. They call us 'the saltless babies'. That means we were born in Nigeria when they didn't have salt because of the war. So in our village we were called 'the Saltless Women'. There are about sixteen of my age-mates in London, and we have our own group here too. Last year a member of our group was in hospital and she said that other patients called her the Princess of Africa. On visiting days the nurses and doctors invariably shooed us away. She was there for three weeks, and the two days I went to visit her I had to wait over fifteen minutes before it came to my turn. I live in North London, a long way from her house, but those members who lived near her made sure she had visitors every night as well as her seven children. Her husband left her over three years ago to do some business in Nigeria, but we all know that he lives with another woman over there. Did our group member care? No. She is too busy to care. If he returns, good, if not, better still. She is training to be a hairdresser, now that all her children are at school. She is converting her large house into flats so that she and her older daughter can start a bed-and-breakfast business. And when she is ready she is going to come to our group and take an interest-free loan from our funds. If her husband had been around he would probably have been a help, just by being there, since he had no job anyway, but he could also be in the way of our member's self-realization. Looking after a man for sexual rewards does take a lot of time. I assure you.

In the West many women hurry to get married again after a divorce or a bereavement. Our women are slower. And many who have children don't even bother, because a new life opens for them. A new life among other women and friends. Women are very quarrelsome and jealous. We always make it up, especially after we have had a few brandies and consumed, I don't know how many chicken legs. This is because we realize that what we gain by forgiving one another is better than what we gain by being alone in order to avoid jealousy. In my book Joys of Motherhood I describe a family in which the women went on strike and refused to take the housekeeping money, because they knew that the husband was drinking the greater part of his income. I also describe a life of another woman who was so busy being a good mother and wife that she didn't cultivate her women friends. She died by the wayside, hungry and alone. In the same book I describe how jealous she was, when her husband brought home a new wife. Instead of going to sleep on the first night she stayed awake listening to the noise made by her husband and the new wife in love-making. She learned only a few days later that it would be better and to their mutual advantage, if she and the new wife became friends, rather than quarrel over their shared husband. They soon became so busy in their everyday life that sexuality was pushed into the background.

In many cases polygamy can be liberating to the woman, rather than inhibiting her, especially if she is educated. The husband has no reason for stopping her from attending international conferences like this one, from going back to University and updating her career or even getting another degree. Polygamy encourages her to value herself as a person and look outside her family for friends. It gives her freedom from having to worry about her husband most of the time and each time he comes to her, he has to be sure that he is in a good mood and that he is washed, and clean and ready for the wife, because the wife has now become so sophisticated herself that she has no time for a dirty, moody husband. And this in a strange way, makes them enjoy each other.

The small son of one of our group-members in London told his teacher that he had two Mum-

mies. 'My Mummy number one is working. Mummy number two will come and collect me.' The teacher did not understand until she realized that his solicitor father had two wives, and the little child enjoys being loved and looked after by two women, his mother and the senior wife. What a good way to start one's life. In Ibuza it is the same. Once a woman starts making money she stops having children regularly. This is because women who are lucky to find the work which they love and which they are good at derive the same kind of enjoyment from it as from sex. Many female writers, many English female writers I have spoken to claimed that they find their work, not only sexually satisfactory but sometimes masturbatory. I certainly find my work satisfying. Sex is part of our life—it shouldn't be THE life.

In this next section I will give you a quick overview of some issues concerning black women. In many parts of Africa only one's enemies will go out of their way to pray for a pregnant woman to have a girl-child. Most people want a man-child. The prayers will go: 'You will be safely delivered of a bouncing baby boy, a real man-child that we can and make jolly with whisky and beer.' The pregnant woman will not protest at this prayer because in her heart, she too would like to have a man-child, who will not be married away, but will stay in the family home and look after his mother when she becomes weak and old. In most African societies the birth of a son enhances a woman's authority in the family. Male children are very, very important. Yet, this girl-child that was not desired originally comes into her own at a very early age. From childhood she is conditioned into thinking that being the girl she must do all the housework, she must help her mother to cook, clean, fetch water and look after her younger brothers and sisters. If she moans or shows signs of not wanting to do any of this, she will be sharply reminded by her mother. 'But you are a girl! Going to be a woman.'

It is our work to bring the next generation into the world, nurture them until they are grown old enough to fly from the nest and then start their own life. It is hard. It could be boring and could sometimes in some places be a thankless job. But is it a mean job? I had my photograph taken once in my office where I do my writing. The photojournalist was a staunch feminist, and she was so angry that my office was in my kitchen and a package of cereal was in the background. I was letting the woman's movement down by allowing such a photograph to be taken, she cried. But that was where I worked. Because it was warmer and more convenient for me to see my family while I put my typewriter to one side. I tried to tell her in vain that in my kitchen I felt I was doing more for the peace of the world than the nuclear scientist. In our kitchens we raise all Reagans, all Nkrumahs, all Jesuses. In our kitchens we cook for them, we send them away from home to be grown men and women, and in our kitchens they learn to love and to hate. What greater job is there? I asked. A mother with a family is an economist, a nurse, a painter, a diplomat and more. And we women do all that, and we form, we are told, over half of the world's population. And yet we are on the lowest rung. Men did not put us there, my sisters, I think sometimes we put ourselves there. How often do you hear colleagues say; 'Oh, I don't know anything I am only a housewife'?

There should be more choices for women, certainly women who wish to be like Geraldine Ferraro should be allowed to be so. We need more of her type, especially among the black women. We need more Golda Meirs, we need more Indira Gandhis, we even need more Margaret Thatchers. But those who wish to control and influence the future by giving birth and nurturing the young should not be looked down upon. It is not a degrading job. If I had my way, it would be the highest paid job in the world. We should train our people, both men and women to do house-work. A few privileged African women are now breaking bonds. They live at home and work outside. Most of these women were lucky enough to come from families where the girls were al-lowed to go to school and to stay there long enough to acquire knowledge to equip them to live away from their families and to rub shoulders with men. Black women are succeeding in various fields along these lines.

This we must remember is not new to the black woman, because her kind has always worked. In the agrarian setting women do petty-trading. Usually, they have small children with them. They trade in anything from a few loaves of bread to a few packages of matches. The lucky ones have stalls or sheds. Others not so fortunate use the front of their house as their stall. Many Nigerian women live in the cities, collect their es-usu profits and bank it when they think it is big enough. I have a great number of friends who have built up their families this way. This means that the others who were trained to do the lower-middle-class jobs of, for example, teaching have invariably given up their work in order to take up trading.

Being successful in whatever we undertake is not new to the women of Africa. The Aba riot is a case in point. This was a riot that spread from Ow-erri in Eastern Nigeria to Calabar among women who did not even speak the same language, and it included all the towns in the area to Onitsha by the river Niger and went further across the river to include women from the Asaba area. Although the white male chroniclers called it a riot, it was a real war. It was a marvel that women at that time were able to organize themselves; remember, there were no telephones, no letters, only bushtracks and dangerous rivers. The whole area was equiva-lent to the distance from London to Edinburgh. The actual war was organized with women from different groups wearing various headgears and all using their household utensils as weapons. The war, which took place in 1929 was in answer to British demands that women should pay taxes. The black women of that war were praised by all their menfolk. They received admiration not rebuke. And in desperation, the British administra-tors jailed all men whose wives took an active part in the war. They could not acknowledge that women, especially barbaric women, could orga-nize themselves to achieve such a feat.

Working and achieving to great heights is nothing new to the woman of Africa, but there are still many obstacles in her way. Her family still prefers to educate the boy, while she stays at home to do the important jobs called 'women's duties'. And we accept the tag, knowing full well that the boy, however clever he is, would not be where he is today without the sacrifices made by his mother, his sweetheart, his wife or even his sister. The African woman has always been a woman who achieves. This does not necessarily mean that she becomes a successful international lawyer, a writer or a doctor, although African women in these professions are doing very well, and there are quite a few of us. But for the majority of women of Africa, real achievement—as I see it—is to make her immediate environment as happy as is pos-sible under the circumstances, by tending the crops or giving comfort. But she still will have higher aspirations and achieve more when those cleverly structured artificial barriers are removed, when education is free and available to every child, male or female, when the male-dominated media does not give exposure to a black woman simply because she is a beautiful entertainer, thereby undermining our brain power, and when we ourselves have the confidence to value our contribution to the world. It is about time we start singing about our own heroic deeds.

TITLE COMMENTARY

The Joys of Motherhood

TERESA DERRICKSON (ESSAY DATE 2002)

SOURCE: Derrickson, Teresa. "Class, Culture, and the Colonial Context: The Status of Women in Buchi Emecheta's *The Joys of Motherhood.*" *International Fiction Review* 29, nos. 1 & 2 (2002): 40-51.

In the following essay, Derrickson explores the theory that the women in Emecheta's The Joys of Motherhood *suffer from a clash between the traditions and values of Ibo culture and the values of British colonizers, instead of being victims of an oppressive patriarchal culture.*

Much of the written scholarship on Buchi Emecheta's *The Joys of Motherhood* (1979) focuses on the novel's critique of traditional Ibo society.[1] Specifically, such articles read Emecheta's text as a denunciation of the reproductive practices of the Ibo people, practices that do harm to women by promoting (and indeed institutionalizing) the idea that a proper wife should seek only to beget and care for her offspring.[2] As critical texts that recognize Emecheta's attempt to expose the gender politics operating within indigenous Africa, these readings are important. They collectively validate *The Joys of Motherhood* as a work of sociohistorical import, as a novel that fills noticeable gaps in the historical record of African women's experiences. Nevertheless, the scholarly consensus that valorizes this work obscures other thematic threads that are equally important in the recovery of African women's history. As S. Jay Kleinberg discusses in his introduction to *Retrieving Women's History*, the effort to rectify women's erasure in history entails not only an analysis of their work and their role in the family, but also an analysis of "both formal and informal political movements and . . . their impact upon women, women's participation in them and the ways in which they shape male-female interactions and men's and women's roles in society."[3]

Kleinberg's call for an analysis of the way in which women's experiences are impacted by local politics encourages us to return to Emecheta's text to analyze a question that most critics of this book raise but do not fully explore: to what extent does colonialism impinge upon the lives of Ibo women? One compelling answer to this question is introduced by Rolf Solberg, who suggests that the lives of the Ibo women in *The Joys of Motherhood* are determined by the tensions of a "culture collision" between the institutions of traditional Ibo society and the institutions of western Europe.[4] The focus

of this paper will be to develop this suggestion and to argue its validity. In particular, I will demonstrate that the hardships endured by the women of Emecheta's novel do not emanate from an oppressive cultural practice regarding women's role in Ibo villages, but from a historical moment of political and economic transition, a historical moment in which the values and priorities of British culture clash destructively with the values and priorities of indigenous Africa.[5]

The Joys of Motherhood bears out the fact that this transitional period was particularly disadvantageous for African women. As the plight of the novel's key character reveals, colonialism was a costly reality for those who were forced to walk a fine line between that which was demanded of them by their village communities and that which was demanded of them by the rules of a European political regime. This paper will demonstrate that the Ibo women of Emecheta's novel find themselves in this very predicament: specifically, they are subjected to new forms of exploitation as they are asked to assume traditional duties and responsibilities under a newly imported economic system that—unlike their native system—fails to validate or reward them for such work. In essence, this paper traces the destructive influence of Western capitalism and its associated ideologies on the relative power and autonomy of Ibo women. Colonialism, I hope to show, was a far greater threat to their collective well-being than the strictures of village patriarchy.

Set in the British colony of Nigeria in the 1930s and 1940s, *The Joys of Motherhood* details the life story of an Ibo woman named Nnu Ego who escapes the ignominy of a childless first marriage by fleeing to the distant city of Lagos to start anew with a second husband. Nnu Ego's simple dream of becoming a mother—a dream rooted in the cultural values of Ibo society, where motherhood is the primary source of a woman's self-esteem and public status—is happily realized several times over in this new setting. The pleasures associated with motherhood that the protagonist so eagerly anticipates, however, are ultimately negated by the difficult economic conditions of her new urban environment. In short, there are so few job opportunities for her husband to pursue (and so little ambition on his part to pursue them) that Nnu Ego spends her entire life alternately birthing children and working day in and day out as a cigarette peddler to stave off the hunger and poverty that invariably haunt her household. The novel focuses on this grueling battle, a battle that ends in a loss for Nnu

Ego, as she witnesses her beloved sons grow up and leave Nigeria for good and her daughters marry and move away. Nnu Ego's hopes of living out her final years in the company of her grand-children disappear before she turns forty, and she dies at the side of a country road, alone and un-noticed.

The title of Emecheta's novel is patently ironic, for it would seem that there are few joys associated with motherhood after all. And yet while that reality is certainly one message the novel imparts, there is far more to the text than a critique of motherhood. The fact that Emecheta's novel moves beyond this critique to explore the costs of colonialism for women in urban Nigeria is summarized in a crucial passage midway through the novel in which Nnu Ego pauses to as-sess the injustices of her life in Lagos: "It was not fair, she felt, the way men cleverly used a woman's sense of responsibility to actually enslave her. . . . [H]ere in Lagos, where she was faced with the harsh reality of making ends meet on a pittance, was it right for her husband to refer to her respon-sibility? It seemed that all she had inherited from her agrarian background was the responsibility and none of the booty."[6] This excerpt is key in locating the source of Nnu Ego's anguish not in her position as a mother per se, but in her posi-tion as a woman who is asked to assume the same obligations of her "agrarian background" within a new cultural setting that confers "none of the booty" normally associated with such labor. Nnu Ego is able to interpret the inequity of this ex-change as something that "enslaves" and "impris-ons" her. She is also able to identify, at least on some level, the political economy of colonial La-gos as the Western construct of "the new" that proves to be unaccommodating of her traditional role as wife and mother: she notes, for example, that it is the "harsh reality of making ends meet on a pittance" that secures her thralldom.

Before discussing in further detail the political dynamics underwriting this thralldom, it might be useful to review the role women played in Ibo society before the widespread influence of British rule. As Kamene Okonjo points out, the popular belief that African women were impotent and/or trivial in the male-dominated communities of Ibo culture is a gross misconception.[7] While men's labor was widely considered to be more prestigious than women's labor, and while the practice of polygamy and patrilocal domicile (married women dwelling in their husbands' villages rather than in their own) secured men's power over women in general,[8] Ibo women still wielded

considerable influence both within their marriages and within the larger community. Women, for example, were a major force in the society's agrar-ian economy: they planted their own crops, sold their crop surplus (as well as that of their husbands), and exerted exclusive control over the operation and management of the village market, the site where all local commerce took place.[9] In addition, women were active participants in the dual-sex political system of Ibo society, a system in which Ibo men and Ibo women governed themselves separately, both sexes selecting their own set of leaders and cabinet members to legis-late issues relevant to the members of their respec-tive constituencies.[10]

Women's formidable presence in the eco-nomic and political realms of the village gave them significant say in how the village was run and ensured that their needs would not be ig-nored. Surprisingly, the practice of polygamy worked in subtle ways to contribute to this out-come. While polygamy was not a perfect marital arrangement, it was well-suited to the agrarian lif-estyle of the Ibo people and contained several built-in mechanisms that allowed women to bet-ter cope with the burdens of that type of lifestyle. As Janet Pool observes, polygamy allowed co-wives, for example, to "form a power-bloc within the family," a power-bloc that was notoriously ef-fective in coercing an otherwise stubborn husband to behave in ways congenial to his wives.[11] Polygamy also eased the workload of Ibo women by making it a common practice for women of the same union to share domestic chores, such as cooking and babysitting. This benefit was particu-larly advantageous in the context of Ibo society, for Ibo women were encouraged to have numer-ous children—far more children than they were probably able to manage on their own.[12] Finally, in addition to the cultural prestige conferred upon those associated with such a union, polygamy protected the economic interests of women by ensuring that a given family had enough mem-bers, that is, sufficient manual labor to produce and harvest a bountiful crop.[13]

It would be incorrect to assert, even in light of the foregoing facts, that the status of women in precolonial Ibo society matched the status of men, for this was simply not the case. However, as Leith Mullings argues, although women of African agrarian societies did not enjoy the same roles and privileges as men, they were equal to men in all the ways that counted: they had equal access to resources and to means of production.[14] As Mull-ings goes on to explain, the shift of indigenous

Africa from subsistence-based societies to money-based societies (a shift precipitated by British colonialism) upset this power balance by introducing a new type of production called cash-cropping. Planting crops for cash (as opposed to planting crops for food or exchange) was a form of labor that was quickly taken up and dominated by African men. Cash-cropping proved so superior to other forms of productive labor within the context of the new capitalist economy that it immediately undercut the value of women's work (which was not aimed at producing cash) and rendered such work practically superfluous.[15]

These facts are crucial to understand the hardships experienced by the female protagonist of Buchi Emecheta's novel. As the novel makes evident, Nnu Ego is a victim of this newly imported capitalist society, a society in which African women are required to continue performing traditional duties and responsibilities in an economic setting where that labor is no longer of any market value. In other words, Nigeria's transition from a tribal culture and a tribal moral value system to a Western capitalist system with all its benefits and pitfalls has occurred at the expense of women like Nnu Ego, who have exchanged one form of patriarchy with another, while being stripped of former privileges and denied the right to new ones.

Ketu Katrak's analysis of the effects of the colonial capitalist system on women's sociopolitical situation in Nigeria confirms that the local economy was indeed a major force in contributing to the subjugation of women like Nnu Ego.[16] Katrak explains, for example, that while African men were allowed to enter the formal economy of colonial Nigeria by acquiring jobs that paid standard wages, African women were excluded from this sphere and were edged instead into the informal and highly unstable economy of street-side peddling: "Women were forcibly kept outside of the wage market dominated by men in this Nigeria of the 1930s and 1940s."[17]

The gender bias inscribed in the new, dominant capitalist system proves to be devastating for Nnu Ego, who is pressured to maintain her role as a traditional wife and mother regardless of the fact that this new system works against the success of that role. Nnu Ego's barred access from reliable modes of production confines her to levels of poverty that make it nearly impossible for her to feed, clothe, and educate her eight children. This would not have been the situation in her tribal village of Ibuza, where Nnu Ego's crop yield would have sustained her large family, and where

Nnu Ego and the other women of the community would have controlled key sectors of the local economy through the production and exchange of household goods and services. Women's influence over the economic affairs of their community gave them significant political leverage and allowed them to participate in village-wide decisions that affected their well-being as women.

Nnu Ego's life in colonial Lagos not only lacks this measure of security, but it also entails a life of self-abnegation that is never mitigated by the kinds of dividends—both abstract and concrete—that Nnu Ego has come to expect in return for the fulfillment of her maternal role. Her largest payoff, for example, never materializes. From the very onset of the text, Nnu Ego anticipates the rewards she will reap as a result of her motherhood, dreaming that "her old age [will] be happy [and] that when she die[s] there [will] be somebody left behind to refer to her as 'mother'" (54). This reward, however, remains elusive, a fact that Nnu Ego begins to realize long before her eldest son's move to the States exposes the presumption of such an expectation. In a moment of clarity she reflects, "I was born alone, and I shall die alone. What have I gained from all this? Yes, I have many children, but what do I have to feed them on? On my life. I have to work myself to the bone to look after them, I have to give them my all. And if I am lucky enough to die in peace, I even have to give them my soul" (186). This interior monologue interrogates the gross discrepancy between the struggles and rewards of motherhood, a discrepancy staged by a new capitalist economy that not only promotes Western values of individualism over familial responsibility, but also no longer awards security and status solely on the basis of one's offspring. Nnu Ego is forced to adhere to the rules of her indigenous culture even though she realizes, on some level, that those rules are no longer the ones that govern what is of value in the colonial context.

The absence of appropriate returns in exchange for Nnu Ego's self-sacrifice is apparent in other situations in the novel as well. At one notable point, for example, Nnu Ego tries to comfort herself with the fact of her privation, recalling that in Ibo society, "part of the pride of motherhood was to look a little unfashionable and be able to drawl with joy: 'I can't afford another outfit, because I am nursing [my child], so you see I can't go anywhere to sell anything'" (80). This reminder of the former esteem of hardship, however, fails to console Nnu Ego. As the passage suggests, the kind of poverty associated with motherhood in Ibo society was not a burden or an embarrassment, but a point of pride. In Ibo society having children was the primary index of a woman's worth, and therefore the straitened circumstances brought about by childbearing were of little consequence, for they were far outweighed by the symbolic value of being a mother. Although Nnu Ego's own penury is a result, in part, of the children she has borne, she nevertheless is unable to take comfort in that fact. Her situation is shaped by a harsher economic setting, a setting where poverty is not alleviated by the "blessing" of children because children are too much of a material liability in a place of such limited resources and because there is no longer a communal setting or a community forum where the "flaunting" of one's maternal success can occur. Thus, while Nnu Ego is obliged to accept cheerfully the fact that "money and children don't go together" (80), she is denied the maternal pride and recognition that once would have made it acceptable for her to endure the kind of poverty associated with childbearing. She is, in this way, injured by the new political economy of Lagos, injured by a social setting where the tribal glorification of motherhood is still espoused in the face of cultural and economic forces that no longer reward women for their role as mothers.

Similar to the cultural "privilege" of poverty, the accolades of the title "senior wife"[18] are also undermined in the colonial context and no longer offer the same material and psychological benefits for the Ibo women it describes. This shift does not go unnoticed by Nnu Ego, who on more than one occasion questions the motives of a patriarchy that insists on using such a title despite its irrelevance outside the tribal sphere. After a scolding by her husband for engaging in a cooking strike, for example, Nnu Ego lashes back, charging, "Whenever it comes to sacrifice then everyone reminds me about being the senior wife, but if there is something to gain, I am told to be quiet because wanting a good thing does not befit my situation. I can understand the value of being a senior wife in Ibuza; not here [in Lagos], Nnaife. It doesn't mean a thing" (134). In a later passage, Nnu Ego makes a similar reflection: "Men [are] so clever. By admonishing [me] and advising [me] to live up to [my] status as senior wife, they made it sound such an enviable position, worth any woman's while to fight for" (167). These passages underscore the fact that Nnu Ego's standing as senior wife requires her to engage in "sacrifice" and self-restraint, and yet, once again, the gains that would presumably compensate for such

sacrifice are notably absent. Nnu Ego mentions these benefits elsewhere, observing that "[a]t home in Ibuza [I] would have had [my] own hut and would at least have been treated as befitting [my] position" (137). In urban Nigeria, however, where financial hardship places space at a premium and where the newly imported capitalist ideology of the nuclear family enforces cohabitation of spouses,[19] Nnu Ego is left without these rewards. Her predicament as a woman is exacerbated, therefore, by the fact that the capitalist system she now lives under still requires her to play the role of the responsible senior wife without offering her the small privileges and benefits that once accompanied that role under the former tribal system.

The overall effect of this cultural confrontation between Ibo traditions and morals and Western traditions and morals is registered most profoundly in the decline of women's political agency within the domestic sphere. This shift of power can once again be traced to broader economic structures within urban Nigeria, where the lack of formal employment opportunities for women altered their position in the home by forcing them to become materially dependent on their husbands. Indeed, as Maria Mies argues, the very structure of imported Western capitalism arranges for this dependency by insisting on a separate domain for women, one that removes them from spaces of public production and exchange and secures them in the role of the housewife, making them financially reliant on their husbands.[20]

The fluctuating levels of poverty that define Nnu Ego's situation throughout the novel illustrate this new dependency. When Nnaife works, Nnu Ego and her children are schooled and fed, but when Nnaife stays at home or when his paychecks fail to make it back to Lagos in a timely manner, Nnu Ego and the children face starvation. Such a situation would not have been the case in the agrarian economy of Ibuza. As Nnu Ego herself admits as she prepares to return to her village for the last time, "at least there would be no rent to pay and, if it came to the worst, [I] could always plant . . . food at the back of [my] hut" (219).

The city setting of Lagos does not offer these alternatives, and hence Nnu Ego's life there is characterized by a material dependency on her husband. The resounding failure of the novel's infamous cooking strike demonstrates that her new role as a trapped housewife divests her of virtually all political power within the home. In a rare show of solidarity, both Nnu Ego and Adaku (Nnaife's second wife) agree to stop preparing meals for their husband until Nnaife increases their housekeeping allowance. Their dependence on him is so great, however, that his blanket refusal to raise the amount forces Nnu Ego to end the strike for her children's sake. Her prompt capitulation underscores her new predicament as an African woman in Lagos: neither she nor Adaku are in any position to make demands as to how their home will be run. Their shared political impotency is inscribed in Nnu Ego's pathetic groveling: "[She] went on pleading till morning, and when Nnaife was setting out for work she ran after him and begged him again. . . . 'Please help, Nnaife, please!'" (137).

Judith Van Allen's comparative analysis of the political power exercised by Igbo women both before and after colonialism suggests a second loss encoded in this incident that is inextricably connected to the loss of domestic authority experienced by both wives as a result of their dependency on Nnaife. Such a loss entails a forfeiture of the powerful gender alliance that unites Nnu Ego and Adaku as women of common interests.[21] Van Allen's historical review of precolonial indigenous power structures affirms that African women, as a unit of solidarity, exercised considerable influence over village affairs and were notoriously effective at using boycotts, strikes, and a process called "sitting on a man"[22] to legislate the politics of both their private lives and their communities.[23] The effectiveness of such collective maneuvering was, as Van Allen observes, not in question: "where individually [Igbo] women couldn't compete with men, collectively they could often hold their own."[24]

Thus the cooking strike of the text illustrates not only the new marginalization of African women within the home but also the way in which colonialism dismantles the collective power of women by requiring them to place their own needs over the needs of other women. An explanation for this shift resides, according to Johnson, in the fact that precolonial alliances between women were forged on the basis of their shared roles in the agrarian economy and on the mutual class standing that such roles arranged.[25] By forcing women out of these formal sectors of exchange and by introducing a class system of advanced social stratification, the adoption of a Western capitalist system not only destroyed the basis on which African women's coalitions were formed, but it also relegated women to the ranks of such destitution that collective action was no longer a

possible means of organization: survival became a competitive game that was best played on one's own.

Nnu Ego has no choice, then, but to think of her own children and to arrange a separate truce with Nnaife. She tries to explain her actions to Adaku, arguing, "we can't carry on this way and let the children starve. . . . I'm not going to play strike with my children's stomachs" (138). However, this explanation does little to appease Adaku, whose similarly precarious situation in terms of money and provisions leads her to question Nnu Ego's motivations. Adaku, for example, assumes that Nnu Ego ended the strike in order to curry favor with Nnaife, in order to ensure that she—Nnu Ego—might be seen as the more favorable wife, as the wife most deserving of money and support. Tensions mount between the two as their shared needs lead them to act in increasingly selfish and divisive ways.

According to Susan Andrade, the hostility between Nnu Ego and Adaku is due primarily to their struggle over "limited resources in the urban colonial context."[26] The novel confirms this conclusion by revealing Nnu Ego's feelings toward Adaku as the two wives meet for the first time: "Jealousy, fear and anger seized Nnu Ego in turns. She hated this type of woman, who would flatter a man, depend on him, need him" (118). As this passage suggests, Nnu Ego hates Adaku not so much because Nnu Ego feels personally threatened by her or inferior to her, but because Adaku is "needy" and "dependent." Nnu Ego realizes that her own well-being and the well-being of her children are jeopardized by this new woman who will undoubtedly make demands on the family's scarce resources. Any possible alliance between Nnu Ego and Adaku is thus spoiled from the beginning by the grim financial conditions of their shared situation, conditions caused by a colonial economy which denies women the opportunity to obtain positions as wage laborers and thus the chance to support themselves.

The rivalry between both women becomes so intense that it ultimately drives them apart, and their paths do not cross again until the end of the novel. The physical separation characterizing their relationship is not only suggestive of their loss of political power within the home, but it also signifies the loss of a collective support system within African society. Village life was characterized by an informal system in which women worked together and interacted with each other throughout the course of each day. Such interaction was crucial, for it enabled women to deal with the dual demands of marriage and motherhood in ways that took less of a physical and psychological toll on each person.

Nnu Ego's return to her village home of Ibuza after the death of her father underscores the importance of female affiliation by demonstrating the way in which African women express solidarity through shared tasks and other meaningful encounters. It is notably a girl who first greets Nnu Ego and her family as they arrive on the outskirts of Ibuza. The girl "came tearing into the motor park, hugged each of the children and said she was going home straight away to fetch the young men to help them. Noting Nnu Ego's pregnancy, she instructed her not to move an inch until the men arrived. She left her bowls of groundnuts for the children, then dashed into the market to bring them some salted *ukwa* bean cake" (151). This passage illustrates the nature of the informal support structures that bind African women together. Several scenes describe how efficiently women work together and provide emotional support for each other. As Nnu Ego enters her village, she is immediately welcomed by another woman, who instantly takes it upon herself to lighten the older woman's load by volunteering to summon the help of the village men. This errand is carried out, however, only after the girl orders Nnu Ego to rest and takes over Nnu Ego's responsibilities as a mother, feeding her children and rushing off to secure even more provisions for them. Another passage involves a group of women working collaboratively to assist Nnu Ego as she bathes her children (152). Shortly thereafter, we see women helping Nnu Ego prepare her father's widows for mourning (154). Later on we learn that a trusted female friend is caring for Nnu Ego's latest child (156-57). These scenes all situate Nnu Ego as the recipient of female compassion and assistance. The pattern they construct establishes an important contrast between traditional Igbo society and colonial Lagos. While the female collective of the village succeeds in mitigating the burdens of motherhood, the female collective of Lagos is all but inaccessible to Nnu Ego and thus does little to ameliorate her situation.

At first, Emecheta obscures this discrepancy, highlighting the philanthropy of an urban-based women's group that lends Nnu Ego both the money and the know-how with which to start her own business (52). Emecheta also equips Nnu Ego with a friend, an Owerri woman named Cordelia who responds to Nnu Ego's unspoken appeal for companionship with an appropriately charitable response: "'We are like sisters on a pilgrimage. Why should we not help one another?'" (53). This spirited invocation of sisterhood, not unlike the sympathetic intervention of the urban women's group, suggests the presence of an extensive female support system that binds and unifies the indigenous women of Lagos. And yet, in reality, these passages serve only to underscore that which is generally not accessible to African women in urban areas. Nnu Ego's forays into the business of petty trading, made necessary by the increasing demands of her children, render her a slave to cheap labor and prevent her from maintaining contact with the women who originally helped her. The loss of such companionship is acutely felt (cf. 72; 81).

The impetus behind women's isolation is both colonialism's new capitalist economy and the pressures that such an economy places on lower-income families. It is the need to earn money that keeps Nnu Ego on the streets. It is the need to earn money that bars her from attending church services and women's meetings (171). And it is the need to make money that prevents her from feeling part of a larger community in Lagos. Nnu Ego has internalized the script of a modern housewife, accepting the home as her proper domain and her position therein as subordinate. The economic strictures of a male-controlled economy and Nnu Ego's own attempt to play according to the rules of her newly westernized setting (81) enslave her in a role in which she is prevented from forming useful relationships with the women around her.

The loss of such companionship and of any meaningful connection with the public sphere are explicitly inscribed in one of the most pervasive visual images of the text: the encroaching walls and cramped spaces of Nnu Ego's one-room flat. Nnu Ego's isolation within the confines of this space prevents her from accessing opportunities that almost certainly would have made her job as a mother of eight more bearable. The image gives definition to the person Nnu Ego becomes and also reflects the experiences of the other women in Lagos who share similar circumstances. That their lives are imprinted by the profit motive of capitalism and by other social forces that extend beyond the material fact of gender is a conclusion that is both readily apparent and highly problematic. It is only after a life of want and struggle that Nnu Ego finally realizes the value of female companionship, admitting that she "would have been better off had she had time to cultivate those women who had offered her hands of friendship" (219). At the same time, however, she concedes that her forced situation as both a mother and a household provider does not afford her the luxury of accessing the friendships available to her. Pressured to be a model African mother, but stripped of the means and incentives to fulfill that role successfully, Nnu Ego becomes a casualty of a conflict between the old and the new, a casualty of a colonial system whose modern values and modern economic configurations are fundamentally irreconcilable with the traditional social structures of indigenous Africa. That Nnu Ego finally comes to recognize her predicament as such by the end of the novel is somewhat auspicious, and yet Emecheta ultimately offers no real solution as to what it means to be an African woman who is contained neither by the confines of the old patriarchy nor by the confines of the new. Nnu Ego's final role as a vengeful spirit who denies the blessing of children to other Ibo women seems to locate one solution in a shift toward Westernization, and yet cultural homogenization can hardly be the answer. Adaku, who chooses that path, finds herself rejected by her own people. Nnu Ego, who chooses the opposite, dies destitute and alone. In the end, each path is condemned as unacceptable for African women, a fact that remains both the point of Emecheta's novel and the problem it cannot solve.

Notes

1. The Igbo are a society of African peoples who dwell primarily in southeastern Nigeria. They constitute one of West Africa's many diverse ethnolinguistic groups. Although the preferred name for these people is "Igbo" rather than "Ibo," I have used the latter spelling to be consistent with the version used in Emecheta's novel. See Victor C. Uchendu, *The Igbo of Southeast Nigeria* (New York: Holt, Rinehart and Winston, 1965) for an engaging look at Ibo culture and society.

2. See Marie A. Umeh, "*The Joys of Motherhood*: Myth or Reality?" *Colby Library Quarterly* 18.1 (1982): 39-46 and Nancy Topping Bazin, "Venturing into Feminist Consciousness: Two Protagonists from the Fiction of Buchi Emecheta and Bessie Head," *Emerging Perspectives on Buchi Emecheta,* ed. Marie Umeh (Trenton, NJ: Africa World Press, 1996) 141-54.

3. S. Jay Kleinberg, introduction, *Retrieving Women's History: Changing Perceptions of the Role of Women in Politics and Society,* ed. S. Jay Kleinberg (Paris: Unesco Press, 1988) ix.

4. Rolf Solberg, "The Woman of Black Africa, Buchi Emecheta: The Woman's Voice in the New Nigerian Novel," *English Studies* 63 (1983): 250.

5. The historical moment in question refers to the period of colonization that brought present-day Nigeria under the control of the British Empire. The British had been in West Africa since the mid-seventeenth century, initially to steal a piece of the lucrative African slave trade, and then to wrest control over the sale of Africa's natural resources. Lagos, the capital of Nigeria, became a British colony in 1861, but it wasn't until 1906 that the entire country was formally brought under the control of the British government. The setting of *The Joys of Motherhood* takes place in the 1930s and 1940s, a time when many parts of Nigeria were still adjusting to the changes imposed by foreign rulers. See Helen Chapin Metz, ed., *Nigeria: A Country Study* (Washington. DC: Federal Research Division, Library of Congress, 1992).

6. Buchi Emecheta, *The Joys of Motherhood* (New York: George Braziller, 1979) 137. All subsequent references are to this edition and are cited in the text in parentheses.

7. Kamene Okonjo, "The Dual-Sex Political System in Operation: Igbo Women and Community Politics in Midwestern Nigeria," *Women in Africa: Studies in Social and Economic Change,* ed. Nancy J. Hafkin and Edna G. Bay (Stanford: Stanford University Press, 1976) 45.

8. Robert A. LeVine, "Sex Roles and Economic Change in Africa," *Ethnology: An International Journal of Cultural and Social Anthropology* 5.2 (1966): 187.

9. Uchendu 24-25, 27 and Okonjo 48-49.

10. Okonjo 45-55.

11. Janet E. Pool, "A Cross-Comparative Study of Aspects of Conjugal Behavior among Women of Three West African Countries," *Canadian Journal of African Studies* 6.2 (1972): 252.

12. According to Pool's study (255), a "small" family among West African women, even after years of European influence, meant a woman having four to seven children.

13. Pool 249, 252.

14. Leith Mullings, "Women and Economic Change in Africa," *Women in Africa: Studies in Social and Economic Change,* ed. Nancy J. Hafkin and Edna G. Bay (Stanford: Stanford University Press, 1976) 240-44.

15. Mullings 247-49.

16. Ketu H. Katrak, "Womanhood/Motherhood: Variations on a Theme in Selected Novels of Buchi Emecheta," *Journal of Commonwealth Literature* 22.1 (1987): 159.

17. Katrak 167.

18. In a polygamous marriage, the co-wives of a common husband are ranked according to their seniority. The first wife, generally referred to as the "senior wife," is assigned special privileges and responsibilities associated with her status as the primary wife.

19. Maria Mies, "Colonization and Housewifization," *Materialist Feminism: A Reader in Class, Difference, and Women's Lives,* ed. Rosemary Hennessy and Chrys Ingraham (New York: Routledge, 1997) 182-83.

20. Mies 175-85.

21. Judith Van Allen, "'Sitting on a Man': Colonialism and the Lost Political Institutions of Igbo Women," *Canadian Journal of African Studies* 6.2 (1972): 177-78.

22. According to Judith Van Allen, "'Aba Riots' or Igbo 'Women's War'? Ideology, Stratification, and the Invisibility of Women," *Women in Africa: Studies in Social*

and Economic Change, ed. Nancy J. Hafkin and Edna G. Bay (Stanford: Stanford University Press, 1976) 61, to "sit on a man" describes a practice in which the women of a given village collaborate to punish a man who has in some way offended one or more of them. The village women exact their punishment by meeting at the man's hut and "dancing, singing scurrilous songs detailing the women's grievances . . . banging on [the man's] hut with the pestles used for pounding yams, and, in extreme cases, tearing up his hut." The women generally refuse to leave the man alone until he expresses contrition for his wrong-doing and promises to mend his ways.

23. Van Allen, "'Sitting on a Man'" 169-71.

24. Van Allen, "'Sitting on a Man'" 170.

25. Cheryl Johnson, "Class and Gender: A Consideration of Yoruba Women during the Colonial Period," Women and Class in Africa, ed. Claire Robertson and Iris Berger (New York: Holmes & Meier, 1986) 238.

26. Susan Z. Andrade, "Rewriting History, Motherhood, and Rebellion: Naming an African Women's Literary Tradition," Research in African Literatures 21.2 (1990): 103.

FURTHER READING

Criticism

Allan, Tuzyline Jita. "The Joys of Motherhood: A Study of a Problematic Womanist Aesthetic." In Womanist and Feminist Aesthetics, pp. 95-117. Athens: Ohio University Press, 1995.

Examines Emecheta's themes in comparison to Alice Walker's womanist aesthetic presented in her work The Joys of Motherhood.

Davis, Christina. "Mother and Writer: Means of Empowerment in the Work of Buchi Emecheta." Commonwealth: Essays and Studies, no. 13 (autumn 1990): 13-21.

Discusses how Emecheta empowers her female protagonists in her fiction.

Ebeogu, Afam. "Enter the Iconoclast: Buchi Emecheta and the Igbo Culture." Commonwealth: Essays and Studies 7, no. 2 (1985): 83-94.

Analyzes Emecheta's relationship to the Igbo culture and her portrayal of it in her fiction.

Emenyonu, Ernest N. "Technique and Language in Buchi Emecheta's The Bride Price, The Slave Girl, and The Joys of Motherhood." Journal of Commonwealth Literature 23, no. 1 (1988): 130-41.

Traces the development of Emecheta's technique and her use of language through The Bride Price, The Slave Girl, and The Joys of Motherhood.

Ezenwa-Ohaeto. "Tropes of Survival: Protest and Affirmation in Buchi Emecheta's Autobiography, Head above Water." In Emerging Perspectives on Buchi Emecheta, by Marie Umeh, pp. 349-66. Trenton, N.J.: Africa World Press, Inc., 1996.

Highlights Emecheta's instinct for survival and penchant for protest that emerge throughout her autobiography Head above Water.

Frank, Katherine. "The Death of the Slave Girl: African Womanhood in the Novels of Buchi Emecheta." World Literature Written in English 21, no. 3 (autumn 1982): 476-97.

Asserts that feminist themes are present in Emecheta's novels and contends that her works portray a broad spectrum of the lives of African women.

Hunter, Eva. "'What Exactly Is Civilisation?' 'Africa', 'The West' and Gender in Buchi Emecheta's The Rape of Shavi." English Studies in Africa 37, no. 1 (1994): 47-59.

Discusses critics' differing interpretations of Emecheta as an African or feminist writer and traces her portrayal of African and colonial cultures in The Rape of Shavi.

Iyer, Lisa H. "The Second Sex Three Times Oppressed: Cultural Colonialism and Coll(i)(u)sion in Buchi Emecheta's Women." In Writing the Nation: Self and Country. The Post-Colonial Imagination, by John C. Hawley. Amsterdam: Rodopi, 1996.

Analyzes different types of oppression from which Emecheta's heroines suffer.

Katrak, Ketu H. "Womanhood/Motherhood: Variations on a Theme in Selected Novels of Buchi Emecheta." Journal of Commonwealth Literature 22, no. 1 (1987): 159-70.

Discusses Emecheta's demystification of African motherhood in her novels.

Mezu, Rose Ure. "Buchi Emecheta's The Bride Price and The Slave Girl: A Schizoanalytic Perspective." Ariel 28, no. 1 (January 1997): 131-46.

Applies Gilles Deleuze's and Felix Guattari's theory of schizoanalysis to Buchi Emecheta's The Bride Price and The Slave Girl.

Nnoromele, Salome C. "Representing the African Woman: Subjectivity and Self in The Joys of Motherhood." Critique 43, no. 2 (winter 2002): 178-90.

Contends that many of the feminist readings of Emecheta's The Joys of Motherhood actually reinforce stereotypes of African women and offers a differing viewpoint to Nnu Ego's experience in the novel.

Oha, Obododimma. "Language and Gender Conflict in Buchi Emecheta's Second-Class Citizen." In Emerging Perspectives on Buchi Emecheta, edited by Marie Umeh, pp. 289-308. Trenton, N.J.: Africa World Press, 1996.

Analyzes the role that language plays in the gender conflict in Second-Class Citizen and Emecheta's use of rhetoric.

Solberg, Rolf. "The Woman of Black Africa, Buchi Emecheta: The Woman's Voice in the New Nigerian Novel." English Studies 64, no. 3 (June 1983): 247-62.

Examines Emecheta's conflicted feminist perspective and her representation of African women and contemporary social themes, asserting that her harsh criticism of male chauvinism is tempered by a respect for traditional African culture.

Sougou, Omar. "The Experience of an African Woman in Britain: A Reading of Buchi Emecheta's Second-Class Citizen." In Crisis and Creativity in the New Literatures in English, by Geoffrey V. Davis and Hena Maes-Jelinek, pp. 511-21. Amsterdam: Rodopi, 1990.

Asserts that Emecheta's Second-Class Citizen examines issues beyond female oppression and explores the racial discrimination the narrator faces in England.

Uraizee, Joya. "Buchi Emecheta and the Politics of Gender." In *Black Women Writers across Cultures,* by Valentine Udoh James, James S. Etim, Melanie Marshall James, and Ambe J. Njoh, pp. 171-203. Lanham, Md.: International Scholars Publications, 2000.

Asserts that the focus of Emecheta's writing is on African patriarchal systems and how they oppress women of all classes and races.

Ward, Cynthia. "What They Told Buchi Emecheta: Oral Subjectivity and the Joys of 'Otherhood.'" *Publications of the Modern Language Association of America* 105, no. 1 (1990): 83-97.

Discusses the oral subjectivity in Emecheta's work.

OTHER SOURCES FROM GALE:

Additional coverage of Emecheta's life and career is contained in the following sources published by the Gale Group: *African Writers; Black Literature Criticism Supplement; Black Writers,* Vols. 2, 3; *Concise Dictionary of World Literary Biography,* Vol. 3; *Contemporary Authors,* Vols. 81-84; *Contemporary Authors New Revision Series,* Vols. 27, 81; *Contemporary Literary Criticism,* Vols. 14, 48, 128; *Contemporary Novelists,* Vol. 7; *Dictionary of Literary Biography,* Vol. 117; *DISCovering Authors Modules: Multicultural; DISCovering Authors 3.0; Encyclopedia of World Literature in the Twentieth Century,* Vol. 3; *Literature Resource Center; Major Twentieth-Century Writers,* Eds. 1, 2; *Novels for Students,* Vols. 12, 14; *St. James Guide to Children's Writers,* Vol. 5; *Something about the Author,* Vol. 66; and *World Literature and Its Times,* Vol. 2.

LOUISE ERDRICH

(1954 -)

American novelist, poet, essayist, short story writer, and author of children's books.

In her fiction and poetry, Erdrich draws upon her Chippewa heritage to examine complex familial and sexual relationships among midwestern Native Americans, along with their conflicts with white communities.

BIOGRAPHICAL INFORMATION

Erdrich was born June 7, 1954, in Little Falls, Minnesota, and grew up near the Turtle Mountain Chippewa Reservation in North Dakota, the setting for her first novel *Love Medicine* (1984). Both her parents—her father was German-born and her mother French Ojibwe—worked for the Bureau of Indian Affairs, and Erdrich often visited her maternal grandparents on the Chippewa Reservation, where her grandfather was the tribal chairman.

In 1972, while attending Dartmouth College, Erdrich met her future husband and literary collaborator, anthropologist Michael Dorris, who is also part Indian and who heads the Native American studies program at Dartmouth. After graduation in 1976, Erdrich returned to North Dakota and held a variety of jobs. She soon returned to

school to study creative writing, earning her master's degree from Johns Hopkins University in 1979. She went on to become a writer-in-residence at Dartmouth, and married Dorris in 1981. Dorris had three children from a previous relationship, and he and Erdrich have since had three children of their own. The couple collaborated on many of their works. They separated in 1995, and Dorris committed suicide in 1997. Erdrich lives in Minneapolis, Minnesota, where she owns a bookstore.

MAJOR WORKS

Erdrich's first published volume, *Jacklight* (1984), is a collection of poetry that garnered praise for infusing ordinary American westerners and everyday situations with mythic qualities. Her first novel *Love Medicine* (1984), for which Erdrich won the National Book Critics Circle Award, gathers fourteen interconnected stories that are related by seven different members of the Kashpaw and Lamartine families of the Turtle Mountain Chippewa community.

In *The Beet Queen* (1986) Erdrich continued her portrait of the Turtle Mountain Chippewa but shifted her focus to the community outside the reservation. In this novel a woman orphaned in childhood settles into middle-age in the small fictional town of Argus, North Dakota, while her brother, a traveling salesman, repeats the familial pattern of manipulation and abandonment before fathering Dot, a character in *Love Medicine*.

In Erdrich's third novel, *Tracks* (1988), a Chippewa elder and an abusive young woman of white and Indian heritage relate the exploits of Fleur Pillager, a destructive yet magical woman who is an ancestor of several characters from *Love Medicine*. *The Bingo Palace* (1994) is set in a reservation bingo hall and again concerns the conflicted identities of women on the reservation. *The Antelope Wife* (1998), published shortly after Michael Dorris's suicide, features a mysterious woman known as the Antelope Wife. Set in contemporary Minneapolis, the novel is deeply mythic yet maintains its roots in real, everyday life. *The Last Report on the Miracles at Little No Horse* (2001) tells the story of Father Damien Modeste, a priest who has served the people of the remote reservation Little No Horse for fifty years and who is, in fact, a woman.

The Master Butchers Singing Club (2003) again includes characters from Erdrich's earlier novels, but primarily concerns Fidelis Waldvogel, a German soldier who returns from World War I to marry his best friend's pregnant widow, Eva. The couple move to Argus, North Dakota to set up a butcher shop. The locals they befriend there become the center of the story, including Delphine Watzka and her traveling vaudeville act.

In addition to her novels and poetry, Erdrich has published, among other works, *The Blue Jay's Dance: A Birth Year* (1995), a nonfiction account of the birth and first year of one of her children; and two novels for children, *The Birchbark House* (1999) and *The Range Eternal* (2002).

CRITICAL RECEPTION

Erdrich's evocation of a particular American region through multiple narrative voices and striking imagery has prompted comparison to William Faulkner's creation of Yoknapatawpha County, Mississippi. While her work is sometimes faulted for seeming contrived, most critics find her storytelling compelling and her narration lyrical. Of particular interest to feminist studies is Erdrich's use of Native American mythology in creating her female characters, who are seen as complex and mysterious yet believable.

PRINCIPAL WORKS

Imagination (textbook) 1980

Jacklight (poetry) 1984

Love Medicine (novel) 1984; expanded edition, 1993

The Beet Queen (novel) 1986

Tracks (novel) 1988

Baptism of Desire (poetry) 1989

The Crown of Columbus [with Michael Dorris] (novel) 1991

The Bingo Palace (novel) 1994

The Falcon: A Narrative of the Captivity and Adventures of John Tanner (nonfiction) 1994

The Blue Jay's Dance: A Birth Year (memoir) 1995

Grandmother's Pigeon (children's book) 1996

Tales of Burning Love (novel) 1996

The Antelope Wife (novel) 1998

The Birchbark House (juvenile novel) 1999

The Last Report on the Miracles at Little No Horse (novel) 2001

The Range Eternal (juvenile novel) 2002

The Master Butchers Singing Club (novel) 2003

Four Souls (novel) 2004

PRIMARY SOURCES

LOUISE ERDRICH (ESSAY DATE 1995)

SOURCE: Erdrich, Louise. "Women's Work." In *The Blue Jay's Dance: A Birth Year*, pp. 42-7. New York: Harper Perennial, 1995.

In the following essay, originally published in Harper's *magazine, Erdrich describes the experience of labor and birth.*

Rocking, breathing, groaning, mouthing circles of distress, laughing, whistling, pounding, wavering, digging, pulling, pushing—labor is the most involuntary work we do. My body gallops to these rhythms. I'm along for the ride, at times in some control and at others dragged along as if foot-caught in a stirrup. I don't have much to do at first but breathe, accept ice chips, make jokes—in fear and pain my family makes jokes, that's how we deal with what we can't change, how we show our courage.

Even though I am a writer and have practiced my craft for years, and have experienced two natural childbirths and an epidural-assisted childbirth, I find women's labor extremely difficult to describe. In the first place, there are all sorts of labor and no "correct" way to do it. I bow to the power and grandeur of those who insist on natural childbirth, but I find the pieties that often attend the process irritating. I am all for pain relief or caesareans when women want and need these procedures. Enduring pain in itself doesn't make one a better person, though if your mind is prepared, pain of this sort—a meaningful and determined pain based on ardor and potential joy—can be deeply instructive, can change your life.

Perhaps there is no adequate description for something that happens with such full-on physical force, but the problem inherent to birth narratives is also historical—women haven't had a voice or education, or have been overwhelmed, unconscious, stifled, just plain worn out or worse, ill to the death. Although every birth is a story, there are only so many outcomes possible. Birth is dictated to the consciousness by the conscious body. There are certain frustrations in approaching such an event, a drama in which the body stars and not the fiction-making mind. In a certain way, I'm jealous. I want to control the tale. I can't—therein lies the conflict that drives this plot in the first place. I have to trust this body—a thing inherently bound to betray me, an unreliable conveyance, a passion-driven cab that tries its best to let me off in bad neighborhoods, an adolescent that rebels against my better self, that eats erratically and sleeps too much, that grows another human with my grudging admiration, a sensation grabber, unpenitent, remorseless, amoral.

Birth is intensely spiritual and physical all at once. The contractions do not stop. There is no giving up this physical prayer. The person who experiences birth with the closest degree of awareness is the mother—but not only am I physically programmed to forget the experience to some degree (our brains "extinct" fear, we are all programmed to forget pain over time, and hormones seem to assist), I am overwhelmed by what is happening to me. I certainly can't take notes, jot down my sensations, or even have them with any perspective after a while. And then, once our baby is actually born, the experience of labor, even at its most intense, is eclipsed by the presence of an infant.

The problem of narrative involves, too, more than just embarrassment about a physical process. We're taught to suppress its importance over time, to devalue and belittle an experience in which we are bound up in the circular drama of human fate, in a state of heightened awareness and receptivity, at a crux where we intuit connections and, for a moment, unlock time's hold like a brace, even step from our bodies. Labor often becomes both paradigm and parable. The story of the body becomes a touchstone, a predictor. A mother or a father, in describing their labor, relates the personality of the child to some piece of the event, makes the story into a frame, an introduction, a prelude to the child's life, molds the labor into the story that is no longer a woman's story or a man's story, but the story of a child.

The first part of labor feels, to me anyway, like dance exercises—slow stretches that become only slightly painful as a muscle is pulled to its limit. After each contraction, the feeling subsides. The contractions move in longer waves, one after another, closer and closer together until a sea of physical sensation washes and then crashes over. In the beginning I breathe in concentration, watching Michael's eyes. I feel myself slip beneath the waves as they roar over, cresting just above my head. I duck every time the contraction peaks. As the hours pass and one wave builds on another there are times the undertow grabs me. I struggle, slammed to the bottom, unable to gather the force of nerve for the next. Thrown down, I rely on animal fierceness, swim back, surface, breathe, and try to stay open, willing. Staying *open and willing* is difficult. Very often in labor one must fight the instinct to resist pain and instead embrace it, move toward it, work with what hurts the most.

The waves come faster. Charlotte asks me to keep breathing *yes, yes*. To say yes instead of shuddering in refusal. Whether I am standing on the earth or not, whether I am moored to the dock, whether I remember who I am, whether I am mentally prepared, whether I am going to float beneath or ride above, the waves pound in. At shorter intervals, crazy now, electric, in storms, they wash. Sometimes I'm gone. I've poured myself into some deeper fissure below the sea only to be dragged forth, hair streaming. During transition, as the baby is ready to be pushed out into life, the waves are no longer made of water, but neons so brilliant I gasp in shock and flourish my arms, letting the colors explode from my fingertips in banners, in ribbons, in iridescent trails—of pain, it is true, unendurable sometimes, and yet we do endure.

Every birth is profoundly original and yet plotted a billion times, too many times. We move into the narrative with medical advice and technological assistance and frail human hopes, and yet we often find ourselves inadequately shaped by culture, by family, by each other for the scope of the work. The task requires mystical tools and helpers. For religions to make sense to women, there should be a birth ritual that flexes and exercises the most powerful aspects of the personality in preparation. Organized Christian religion is more often about denying the body when what we profoundly need are rituals that take into regard the blood, the shock, the heat, the shit, the anguish, the irritation, the glory, the earnestness of the female body.

Some push once, some don't push at all, some push in pleasure, some not and some, like me, for hours. We wreak havoc, make animal faces, ugly bare-toothed faces, go red, go darker, whiter, stranger, turn to bears. We choke spouses, beat nurses, beg them, beg doctors, weep and focus. It is our work, our body's work that is involved in its own goodness. For, even though it wants at times to lie down and quit, the body is an honest hard-working marvel that gives everything to this one task.

GENERAL COMMENTARY

JULIE THARP (ESSAY DATE 1993)

SOURCE: Tharp, Julie. "Women's Community and Survival in the Novels of Louise Erdrich." In *Communication and Women's Friendships: Parallels and Intersections in Literature and Life*, edited by Janet Doubler Ward and JoAnna Stephens Mink, pp. 165-80. Bowling Green, Ohio: Bowling Green State University Popular Press, 1993.

In the following essay, Tharp explores the effects of Native American cultural corrosion on women's interpersonal relationships in Erdrich's novels.

. . . The old women sit patiently in a circle, not speaking. Each set of eyes stares sharply into the air or the fire. Occasionally, a sigh is let loose from an open mouth. A Grandmother has a twitch in the corner of her eye. She rubs her nose, then smooths her hair.

The coffee is ready. Cups are brought from a wooden cupboard. Each woman is given the steaming brew. They blow on the swirling liquid, then slurp the drink into hungry mouths. It tastes good. Hot, dark, strong. A little bitter, but that is all to the good.

The women begin talking among themselves. They are together to perform a ceremony. Rituals of old women take time. There is no hurry.

(Brant 15)

This excerpt from Beth Brant's *Mohawk Trail* sheds light on the traditional women's community of her Native origins. Within the old traditions of the Longhouse, Brant finds a spirituality grounded within the Grandmothers' gathering to honor life, to honor one another as sources of life and healing. The women speak very little, but smile, laugh and sing, kiss and hug one another during the ritual. They need few words because

the significance of their gathering is understood. She ends "Native Origin" with this: "The Grandmothers gather inside the Longhouse. They tend the fire" (17). Female community signifies the life of the people, their survival in spirit as well as in body.

In *Mohawk Trail* this kind of community seems almost wholly a way of the past; Brant offers only one notable example of contemporary women's friendship, within a lesbian bar in Detroit, Michigan. The women there cling to one another as family because of legal and social difficulties in creating or maintaining other kinds of families. And, indeed, throughout Native American women's literature, the lack of women's gatherings like that depicted in Brant's "Native Origin" is conspicuous. Within the novels of Louise Erdrich, friendships between women are rare, much less formalized or ritualized. In *Love Medicine* the two powerful grandmothers, Lulu Nanapush Lamartine and Marie Lazarre Kashpaw, are intense rivals throughout most of the novel. In *Tracks* Pauline and Fleur are divided by their contrasting loyalties to assimilation and tradition. *The Beet Queen,* alternatively, narrates the friendship between Mary Adare and Celestine James, a friendship that can, however, only exist because of the women's particular circumstances. As Erdrich carefully points out in all of her novels, the circumstances that made life felicitous for her ancestors have been disrupted and distorted in contemporary Native culture. There are clear historical reasons for the shift from the powerful women's groups depicted in Brant's story to the isolated women in Erdrich's novels.

Paula Gunn Allen connects the dispersal and dissolution of women's communal power to the waning of Native power, saying:

. . . the shift from gynecentric-egalitarian and ritual-based systems to phallocentric, hierarchical systems is not accomplished in only one dimension. As LeJeune understood, the assault on the system of woman power requires the replacing of a peaceful, nonpunitive, nonauthoritarian social system wherein women wield power by making social life easy and gentle with one based on child terrorization, male dominance, and submission of women to male authority.

(40-41)

Allen locates four sites of change in the historical acculturation efforts of the federal government and of early missionaries: a change in religion that replaces female deities like White Buffalo Woman and Grandmother Spider with a male creator; a movement from egalitarian tribal government to hierarchical, male centered government; economic conversion from self-sufficiency to government dependency; and a shift from the clan system to the nuclear family system. The first change alters inner identity, cutting the individual loose from spiritual grounding within a matrifocal system and replacing that with the abstract notions of patriarchal dominance; individuals cease to recognize the "Grandmother powers that uphold and energize the universe" (Allen 203). The movement from tribal to hierarchical government discredits women's political alliances in favor of one representative who needs to be male to interact with the federal government. The spiritual basis for tribal government is erased.

Converting from familial self-sufficiency to wage labor further increases the perceived power of the men, since they frequently earn the money to support the family, while women remain at home with the children. This movement intersects with the breakup of clan units (often matrilocal) and the subsequent isolation within nuclear families which Nancy Bonvillain argues "results in the isolation of women within small households, exacerbated by their husbands' absence from home. Work which previously had been shared between spouses today falls exclusively to women" (11), and, Allen would add, to lone women rather than to groups of women laboring together. Marie Kashpaw, Lulu Lamartine and Zelda Kashpaw, for instance, all from *Love Medicine,* are depicted almost exclusively in their homes, often in their kitchens, husbands absent. Both the nuclear family household and wage labor isolate women from one another.

Acculturation to Anglo-American gender typing seems inevitable within these shifts. Citing both Patricia Albers and Paula Gunn Allen, Rebecca Tsosie argues that traditional Native gender roles were flexible and adaptive: "the ideal relationship between male and female [was] complementary and based on principles of individual autonomy and voluntary sharing. Because of this ethic, Albers claims that the concept of male 'dominance' was meaningless for the traditional Sioux" (Tsosie 5). Molding the man into patriarch, however, and further dividing chores more strictly between men and women, replicates Anglo notions of gender as differential and hierarchical, notions that have, further, bred institutionalized control of women. Allen notes that battered wives and "women who have been raped by Indian men" are no longer rare (Allen 50). Bonvillain's research concurs in this assessment and Er-

drich illustrates it in *The Beet Queen* when Isabel Pillager marries a Sioux and moves to South Dakota:

> We hear she has died of beating, or in a car wreck, some way that's violent. But nothing else. We hear nothing from her husband, and if she had any children we never hear from them. Russell goes down there that weekend, but the funeral is long past. He comes home, telling me it's like she fell off the earth. There is no trace of her, no word.
>
> (*BQ* 100)

Although Isabel is a powerful woman, niece of Fleur Pillager and foster mother to her siblings after the death of their mother, she too can be swallowed up by domestic violence and utterly forgotten within a culture that once honored strong women. King Kashpaw of *Love Medicine* beats his wife with astounding regularity, emulating mainstream Anglo notions of male gender, as Nora Barry and Mary Prescott point out in their article on Native American gender identity.

Because of reservation land allotments, women have been and often are geographically distant from one another. Rather than living in closely knit villages with an interdependent network of kin and friends, people live miles apart and gather occasionally. The very struggle to keep land often tore families and friends apart. Erdrich dramatizes this in *Tracks* when Margaret and Nector Kashpaw use all of the money saved to pay for Fleur Pillager's land allotment to instead pay for their own. Once close friends, Margaret and Fleur are wedged apart over the struggle for newly limited resources.

Within all three of Erdrich's novels heterosexuality either threatens to or does divide women. Pauline's sexual jealousy of Fleur keeps the women wary of one another and creates a vindictive streak within Pauline. Marie and Lulu cannot speak to one another as long as Nector lives. In *The Beet Queen* Erdrich deconstructs the heterosexual unions that disrupt female community. Neither Mary Adare nor Celestine James fits the stereotypical gender notions formulated within American popular culture and they, therefore, have a difficult time attracting men (not that they seem to care much). Mary at one point considers a relationship with Russell Kashpaw. She invites him to dinner with less than lustrous results:

> He looked at me for the first time that night. I'd drawn my eyebrows on for the evening in brown pencil. I'd carefully pinned my braids up and worn

a black chiffon scarf to set off my one remarkable feature, yellow cat eyes, which did their best to coax him. But I don't know coaxing from a box lunch.

(65)

When Russell lets her know that he would be interested in Sita Kozka (blond, thin and pretty), if anyone, and then later makes a joke of her touching him, Mary concludes: "I was cured, as though a fever had burned off. One thought was clear. I would never go out of my way for romance again. Romance would have to go out of its way for me" (68). Because the experience is humiliating, from that point on Mary concentrates instead on her relationship with Celestine, one which affirms her "as is."

Celestine more obviously deconstructs the romantic ideology that influences both women when Karl Adare seduces her. It is quite possibly Celestine's non-stereotypical female beauty that attracts the bisexual Karl to her in the first place. She is taller than he and stronger; her face is "not pretty" (114). Celestine evaluates the encounter through reference to the romance magazines she has read. (She "never had a mother to tell [her] what came next" [115].) When Karl gives her a knife demonstration after their love-making, she ponders her expectations: "So, I think, this is what happens after the burning kiss, when the music roars. Imagine. The lovers are trapped together in a deserted mansion. His lips descend. She touches his magnificent thews. 'Cut anything,' he says . . ." (117). In a capitalist society the lover is ultimately a vendor looking for a quick sale. Karl does leave quickly, but he returns and this time Celestine asks him to leave: "In the love magazines when passion holds sway, men don't fall down and roll on the floor and lay there like dead. But Karl does that" (121). Rather than boldly declaring his love and ravishing Celestine in the true fashion of the male hero, Karl passes out. Celestine's worldly assessment reveals both self-irony for having read the "love magazines" and a cynicism about popular culture versions of reality.

Months later she thinks, "Something in this all has made me realize that Karl has read as many books as I, and that his fantasies have always stopped before the woman came home worn out from cutting beef into steaks with an electric saw" (122). Clearly the reason his fantasies and hers stopped short is because this reality defies the conventions of gender roles and romance. No heroine should be working as a butcher, and no hero should lie around the house all day. Celestine finds that heterosexual love does not live up to its reputation. It makes her feel like a "big, stupid heifer" (123). It is further made unattractive to her because it comes between her and Mary, who "talks around [her], delivers messages through others. I even hear through one of the men that she says I've turned against her" (122). Almost immediately after getting rid of Karl, Celestine calls to tell Mary.

When both women repudiate the expectations of romance and its attendant gender roles, they return with perhaps greater loyalty to their friendship and ultimately to themselves. In an interview with Joseph Bruchac, Erdrich speaks of writing for her daughters and sisters: "I have an urgent reason for thinking about women attuned to their power and their honest nature, not the socialized nature and the embarrassed nature and the nature that says, 'I can't possibly accomplish this'" (Bruchac 82). Neither obstinate, eccentric Mary nor fierce Celestine could be said to give up one ounce of their own power, except in their catering to Dot.

When Celestine gives birth to Dot, the two women find a mutual fixation. Mary continually tries to insinuate herself as a co-parent, although Celestine guards the right to herself. In the baby, Celestine finds a passion "even stronger than with Karl. She stole time to be with Dot as if they were lovers" (157). For Mary, Dot is a small version of herself. The two women quarrel over parenting issues, even behave as jealous rivals, but ultimately act as co-parents to the child. They create a family. Toward the end of the novel when they are both aging, they behave like an old married couple, sleeping together at Sita's house, conspiring together, griping at each other and even reading each other's thoughts.

The two women can also be close to one another because of their economic self-sufficiency. Mary owns and runs the "House of Meats" and Celestine works there, enabling them to set their own timetables and living arrangements. They need not depend on men for money. Instead they hire men. They also work very hard, however, perhaps resembling Celestine's grandmothers in their butchering of animals and preparation of foods. The infant Dot is propped in a shopping cart instead of a cradleboard. Their work literally feeds the community.

Their kinship network, while geographically apart, is interdependent—Sita Kozka, Russell Kashpaw, Wallace Pfeff, Karl Adare, Mary, Celestine and Dot all comprise a clan of sorts that is notable in its tenuous connection to larger communities like the town of Argus or Turtle Mountain Reservation. Karl—a drifter—has no family whatsoever beyond this group. Sita would like to claim the beau monde of the Midwest (if that's not oxymoronic), as her community, but even a Minneapolis department store clerk snubs her. Wallace, entrepreneurial spirit of Argus, is marginalized by his sexuality. His bogus deceased fiancee is a secret that forever thwarts genuine interaction with the other townspeople. Russell, though canonized by the local museum for his war exploits, would not be welcome within one of the local families. He only returns to the reservation permanently as an invalid. These characters cannot or will not conform to community expectations of gender, ethnicity or sexuality. Within this marginalized group, the two female parents and their child form a core, a familial center from which to grow. Their dual mothering is attractive to the many characters who lack a mother themselves. The lone child of the many adults is their "dot" of hope for the future.

Erdrich, in the interview with Bruchac, poses a question shortly after her comment about women's power that provides a useful entry into this dilemma and that has everything to do with women's community within her three novels. She says, "There's a quest for one's own background in a lot of this work . . . All of our searches involve trying to discover where we are from" (83). Although Erdrich does not specify here, background almost inevitably signifies "mother" for her characters. While many characters of *Love Medicine* and *Tracks* have lost their mothers through hardship or acculturation (I will say more on this later), the mothers of *The Beet Queen* are denied or renounced.

Both Karl and Mary renounce their mother for having left them stranded at the fairgrounds. Mary goes so far as to send word to her mother that her children starved to death. For Mary this solution seems plausible since she so readily plants herself within the new home in Argus. Karl, however, becomes completely unbalanced, helplessly relying upon any woman who will mother him as Fleur does when she finds him on the side of the railroad track and as Celestine does when she takes him in. He has no roots, only the branch he tears off the tree in Argus. Sita too renounces her own mother, identifying instead with her elusive aunt.

Mary and Celestine in fact first cement their friendship around their lack of parents. Asked about her mother and father, Mary responds, "They're dead," and Celestine answers, "Mine are

dead too" (30). Sita observes that suddenly the two girls seemed very much alike, with "a common sort of fierceness" (30). The fierceness would seem to arise out of their motherless status. Forced to rely upon themselves, they develop an aggressive edge. In a sense, the two are grounded in their lack of a mother, perhaps the only coping strategy available to them and certainly better than Karl's strategy. Nonetheless, the ruling element of the novel is air, suggesting just how disconnected these characters are. Paula Gunn Allen develops the concept of grounding:

> Among the Keres, "context" and "matrix" are equivalent terms, and both refer to approximately the same thing as knowing your derivation and place. Failure to know your mother, that is, your position and its attendant traditions, history, and place in the scheme of things, is failure to remember your significance, your reality, your right relationship to earth and society. It is the same as being lost . . . not confined to Keres Indians; all American Indian Nations place great value on traditionalism.
>
> (210)

Failure to know one's actual mother within Erdrich's novels is a metaphor for failure to grasp one's own significance within tribal traditions, within history. For women in particular, who lose all status within Anglo patriarchal traditions, it is a failure to embrace your own power. Celestine and Mary do not simply deny their mothers, however; they also create themselves in their own images of mother. Because Celestine did not know her mother well enough to carry on her traditions, and actually finds that her mother's heterosexual lifestyle does not suit her in any event, she becomes the mother she wanted. Mary rejects her distant self-centered mother and becomes an overprotective, indulgent mother. Both women are creating, from scratch, a family that can survive the harshness and sterility of Argus, North Dakota. Nevertheless, their lack of a women's tradition, of clan wisdom, leads to many mistakes in their mothering as Wallace Pfeff points out and as Celestine surmises.

In an article entitled "Adoptive Mothers and Thrown-Away Children in the Novels of Louise Erdrich," Hertha D. Wong describes in great detail the manner in which Erdrich develops complex mother/child relationships to dramatize the destruction of traditional family identities and the present need for maternal nurturance. That nurturance would not have been provided only by women in the past but rather by the entire tribe. Wong concludes that:

Erdrich's novels, then, transcend easy categories of gender and ethnicity, reflect both Native American and Euroamerican influences, and extend Western notions of mothering. Mothering can indeed be a painful process of separation; it might be the necessarily insufficient dispensation of grace. But mothering can also be a communal responsibility for creating and maintaining personal identity.

(191)

Whatever Celestine and Mary's faults, they maintain Dot's identity, try to mother Sita and create a familial context for the men in their kinship network, men who are otherwise isolated. They take on the responsibility of mothering that the other characters either ignored or lost. Without each other, however, it is doubtful if the two women could even sustain that.

As Wong points out, Nanapush, in *Tracks,* is a nurturing figure in the tribal tradition of communal parenting, but his nurturing is put to harsh tests when he loses his entire family one by one, his land and ultimately his way of life. Although both lyrical novels, *Tracks* and *Love Medicine* are firmly situated within historical events. Julie Maristuen-Rodakowski confirms the historical accuracy of Erdrich's depiction of the Turtle Mountain Reservation in North Dakota and their rapid assimilation to American culture. Maristuen-Rodakowski notes in particular the strong bicultural nature of this reservation, bred as it is from both Ojibwa and French trapper/traders. She also maps out a genealogical chart of the characters, illustrating how central family is within these works, that the reader should even be capable of drawing a detailed chart, and suggesting that such a chart is necessary for comprehension of the families' complex interrelationships (Wong's article contains a less detailed genealogical chart). The almost obsessive concern with family origins within *Love Medicine* and *Tracks* seems in part to arise from the characterization and status accorded to each family—largely the Kashpaws, Nanapushes and Pillagers on the clearly Chippewa side and the Lamartines, Lazarres and Morrisseys on the more French, mixed blood side, the latter holding far less worth in most characters' eyes.[1]

Another factor in this obsession is the mystery surrounding the parentage of many characters. Pauline, for example, hides her identity as Marie's mother after her liaisons with Napoleon Morissey result in the child's birth. Fleur is raped by three men, so literally does not know which man fathered Lulu. The destruction of Fleur's family leaves her orphaned; the removal of Lulu to a government boarding school divides her from her mother; because of Pauline's entrance into the Catholic order she leaves Marie with Sophie Lazarre. In *The Beet Queen* Adelaide Adare hides her children's father's identity until his death. For her, sexual license is not so much a choice made out of desire but rather one made out of economic necessity; her economic desperation leads to her abandonment of the children. Throughout all three novels families are both created and torn apart by economic, spiritual and social upheaval. Those same changes separate the women, who, together, could and eventually do resist their force.

The mothers of the two families most extensively portrayed within *Love Medicine* both obscure origin in their own ways, I would argue, because their own origins are problematic for them. Marie Lazarre Kashpaw raises, in addition to her own children, many stray and orphaned babies on the reservation, June Morrissey and Lipsha Morrissey to name two; to Lipsha she says only that his mother would have "drowned him in the slough" if she had not taken him in, a patent falsehood, as he learns later in the novel. Lulu Nanapush gives birth to eight sons and one daughter, all of different fathers and none fathered by the man she was married to the longest and whose name several bear. Both women redefine notions of the nuclear family. Marie's elastic household forms a kind of clan unit. In Lulu's many partners lies a deconstruction of the patriarchal family and Christian monogamy.

Nora Barry and Mary Prescott, in discussing the holistic vision of gender in *Love Medicine,* imply that Marie and Lulu act as facilitators to that holistic vision, Marie because she is "a blending of two complementary gender based traditions. Her life includes risk, transformation, householding, and medicine, as well as an integration of past and present" (127). Speaking of Lulu, they write that she is "a worthy adversary because she is as effective at complementarity as Marie is. The two characters mirror one another in their role as mother, in their ability to take risks, in their way of blending past and present, and in their wielding of power in old age" (129). Clearly it is because they resist gender bifurcation and emulate gender complementarity that they can become powerful in their old age, speaking as Grandmothers of their clans. Still, while separate, they are unable to create an empowering matrix for these children.

In the role of Grandmother they are able to mediate various Anglo institutions. Marie rejects the "deadliness of the convent" in favor of life (Barry 128) and Lulu remains mindful of the "conflict between old values and the influences of the white standard of economic success" (129). One mother serves as a mediator between her people and white religious ideology, answering a call to the convent and just as quickly rejecting it when she confronts the violence of Sister Leopolda. The other mother mediates commodity culture, calling the "tomahawk" factory proposed to be built on the site of her house "dreamstuff."

Marie and Lulu also unite the two family groupings—Chippewa and French—the historical discord between which has eased Anglo appropriation of land. Marie seeks to deny the French/Catholic side and embrace traditional Native culture. Even so, her healing powers are associated with Catholicism. She is truly a sister of mercy in caring for orphaned children and in attending to Lulu. Even though that power is not exclusive of Native identity by any means, here it carries Catholic overtones. Lulu seeks to deny her Native/traditionalist mother and ignore her Nanapush/father's teachings and marries the French Lamartine. Ironically she is only a good Catholic in her fecundity. The fact that her boys all have different fathers reveals her innate attachment to her rebellious mother.

These two women, however, who have so much in common and could become powerful allies, can only come together after Nector dies, suggesting that heterosexuality as it has been influenced by Anglo culture takes priority over women's community and therefore divides women and dissipates tribal strength.[2] Once the women have become fast friends Lipsha reports to Gerry Nanapush that Lulu had "started running things along with Grandma Kashpaw. I told him how she'd even testified for Chippewa claims and that people were starting to talk, now, about her knowledge as an old-time traditional" (268). Women's friendship here signifies tradition and resistance to acculturation, but Lulu and Marie's friendship also reunites the characters with their own pasts, with their mothers, ultimately with their tribal past.

Tracks takes up the subject of displaced origins from early in the novel when Fleur conceives Lulu. The complexity is well expressed in Nanapush's decision to give Fleur Pillager's daughter his and his deceased daughter's names, not knowing what to tell Father Damien since the father was unknown:

> There were so many tales, so many possibilities, so many lies. The waters were so muddy I thought I'd give them another stir. "Nanapush," I said. "And her name is Lulu."
>
> (61)

The muddy waters originate with speculation, particularly about Fleur's relationship to the water monster in Lake Matchimanito. Like her mother, Lulu is stigmatized for her unconventional sexuality, but they both see through the hypocrisy of others. When the townspeople jeer Lulu at a town meeting, she offers to enlighten everyone as to the fathers of her children, an offer the people decline.

Lulu's "wild and secret ways" are an obvious legacy from her mother Fleur Pillager, one of the last two surviving Pillagers, a wild and powerful family living far back in the bush. The Pillagers know the ways to "cure and kill." Lulu rejects her mother—Nanapush's narrative is in part his attempt to explain Fleur's actions to Lulu—but in fact Lulu greatly resembles her mother in her ability to stand up to the current notions of "progress" and in her steadfast defense of erotic integrity in the face of community opposition. That Lulu should come to be in her old age a bearer of the old traditions marks at least a symbolic reconciliation with her mother.

The young mixed-blood Pauline Puyat, who seeks to punish her body in any way imaginable in the effort to drive out the devil, also seeks sexual experience before becoming a nun. Her rendezvous with Napoleon Morrissey results in an unwanted pregnancy. Pauline's efforts to keep the child from being born in order to kill both her and the infant force the midwife, Bernadette, to tie Pauline down and remove the baby with iron spoons used as forceps. The dual surprise of the novel is that Pauline becomes, at the end of the novel, Sister Leopolda; and the girl she gives birth to and names Marie is eventually raised by the soft-witted Sophie Lazarre. Rather than the offspring of a "drunken woman" and a "dirty Lazarre," Marie is the child of Pauline and Napoleon Morrissey. Marie obviously has no clue to Sister Leopolda's identity in *Love Medicine*, but Leopolda recognizes Marie at least up to the end of *Tracks*. Marie and Sister Leopolda's mutual obsession, which leads to Leopolda's sponsoring Marie at the convent, is ostensibly religious and caring. That Leopolda should lock Marie in closets, scald her with hot water, brain her with an iron pole and skewer her hand with a meat fork suggests that, like Lulu, Marie has a difficult relationship with her mother. In retaliation for the scalding, Marie attempts to push Leopolda into a huge oven. Nonetheless, from her experience with Sister Leopolda, Marie learns pity, a gift that enables her to help her husband back to her side and that leads her to reconcile with Lulu. (Marie's compulsion to visit the dying nun many years later ironically leads to a battle over the iron spoon that Leopolda habitually bangs on her metal bedstead.)

Lulu's mother is deeply harmed in obviously material ways by Anglo encroachment—her parents and siblings are decimated by disease, her land is lost and her forest leveled, she and her family are starved, killing her second child. Still Fleur Pillager maintains her will to fight, crushing the wagons of the loggers when they come to throw her off her land. To keep Lulu safe from these circumstances Fleur has sent her to a boarding school, an act for which Lulu cannot forgive Fleur. Pauline/Leopolda is deeply harmed in more obviously psychological ways. An odd person from the outset, Pauline desires to move with the times, assimilating rather than "living in the old ways" as Fleur does. One critic describes Pauline as a trickster figure, but Nanapush, himself a trickster, confesses to being completely baffled by the girl. In several places Erdrich seems to suggest that it is Pauline's unattractiveness that drives her outside of the community. She cannot marry and so must find an occupation. In a community that has accepted Anglo definitions of use, value and gender roles, a woman like Pauline can find no recourse.

Marie and Lulu's friendship closes the circle as the daughters of Pauline—who rejects mothering from a distorted allegiance to Anglo culture—and Fleur—who gives up mothering the child upon whom she dotes in order to fight for Native culture—come together in the effort to nurture one another. In putting "the tears in [Lulu's] eyes," Marie helps Lulu to finally feel pity for her mother. Together the women have reconciled their own and their mothers' dilemmas, Marie by taking the good from Leopolda's venom and Lulu by claiming her mother's protective spirit. In that relationship lies the potential for community transformation that Lipsha notes. Wong writes, "It remains for those left behind, the adoptive mothers and thrown-away youngsters, to reweave the broken strands of family, totem, and community into a harmonious wholeness" (191).

The reconciliation takes place when Marie volunteers to help Lulu recover from cataract surgery. In the scene there is little dialogue and long periods in which the two women simply drink coffee and listen to music on the radio. Lulu thinks that "Too much might start the floodgates flowing and our moment would be lost. It was enough just to sit there without words" (236). The women understand that with a gulf as wide as the one they must cross, words will only divide them

further. The benign music on the radio, the "music" of Marie's voice, and the soft touch of her hand provide the healing communication necessary to their alliance.

For Lulu this meeting provides a revelation: "For the first time I saw exactly how another woman felt, and it gave me deep comfort, surprising. It gave me the knowledge that whatever had happened the night before, and in the past, would finally be over once my bandages came off" (236). Marie indeed helps Lulu to "get [her] vision" as Lipsha testifies in the next chapter (235): "Insight. It was as though Lulu knew by looking at you what was the true bare-bones elements of your life. It wasn't like that before she had the operation on her eyes, but once the bandages came off she saw. She saw too clear for comfort" (241). Having seen "how another woman felt" Lulu is now capable of seeing into everyone; she is given a "near-divine" power of vision. Through imagery, however, Erdrich reveals that this connection is not simply one of friendship. Lulu imagines Marie, caring for her eyes, swaying "down like a dim mountain, huge and blurred, the way a mother must look to her just born child" (236).

In its coffee, contemplation and vision-seeking, this scene resembles the old women's ritual described at the outset and also depicted within Linda Hogan's short story "Meeting" about a contemporary women's ceremony:

> Mom was boiling coffee on the fire and serving it up. The women sipped it and warmed their palms over the fire. They were quiet but the lines of their faces spoke in the firelight, telling about stars that fell at night, the horses that died in the drought of 1930, and the pure and holy terror of gunshots fired into our houses. . . . Exhaustion had covered up all the mystery and beauty the women held inside. . . . I met myself that night and I walked in myself. I heard my own blood. I learned all secrets lie beneath even the straggliest of hair, and that in the long run of things dry skin and stiff backs don't mean as much as we give them credit for.
>
> (280)

In the meeting between Marie and Lulu rest the seeds for a return to powerful female political alliances, for necessary friendship that will signify not just caring, but survival, and not just survival, but prosperity. Significantly, it is in the nursing home, a communal dwelling place that ends the women's previous geographical isolation, that Marie and Lulu come together. Neither is their friendship strained, however, by familial or spousal demands.

Clearly the community can never again be what it was previous to the events of *Tracks,* but its very survival is at stake with the outside forces of capitalism and Anglo-American social, governmental and religious systems tearing at its fabric. That survival cannot take place without some kind of cohesive resistance. Since the traditionalist male figures—Old Man Pillager and Eli Kashpaw—have retreated into the bush and silence, it is left to the women in the novels to somehow save the children. Even though for some of those children the mothers may only be a shadowy presence, Lulu's sons idolize her and Marie's clan quickly materializes en masse for family gatherings. The two women's mutual grandson, Lipsha, as an old people's child and a caregiver to the old ones on the reservation, holds forth promise for a more powerful male presence. Although the desperation of some Turtle Mountain Reservation characters depicted in *Tracks* and *Love Medicine* may seem greater than of those characters living in Argus, the reservation also offers a portal to empowering traditions. Argus counts communal and personal strength only in dollar amounts.

Allen writes that in response to the "inhuman changes" wrought by Anglo colonization Indian women are trying to "reclaim their lives. Their power, their sense of direction and of self will soon be visible. It is the force of women who speak and work and write, and it is formidable" (50). Female friendship enables the women in Erdrich's novels to recreate an empowering matrix that was frequently lost or disrupted through colonization and acculturation. In turn the women are strengthened in their capacity to act as leaders for ensuing generations.

Notes

1. Robert Silberman reads *Love Medicine* as largely a meditation on home, beginning as it does with June going "home" in a fatal blizzard. He writes: "Clearly, home in *Love Medicine* is an embattled concept, as ambiguous as June Kashpaw's motives in attempting her return" (108). The characters' loss of a satisfying home, while always functioning on a personal and familial level, surely carries echoes of their literal loss of homeland.

2. Carolyn Neithammer argues that sexual jealously in traditional Ojibwa communities could be intense: "Great shame was felt by any Ojibwa woman whose husband took another wife, and her wounded self-esteem was only aggravated by the talk of the rest of the villagers, who openly speculated on just what qualities the woman lacked that forced her husband to take another wife" (94). This underscores Marie's forgiveness of Nector and Lulu. The other community members, however, side with Marie and brand Lulu a Jezebel, calling her "the Lamartine." The aspersion may reflect French Catholic ideology.

Works Cited

Allen, Paula Gunn. *The Sacred Hoop.* Boston: Beacon, 1986.

Barry, Nora, and Mary Prescott. "The Triumph of the Brave: *Love Medicine*'s Holistic Vision." *Critique* 30.2 (1989).

Bonvillain, Nancy. "Gender Relations in Native North America." *American Indian Culture and Research Journal* 13.2 (1989).

Brant, Beth. *Mohawk Trail.* New York: Firebrand Books, 1985.

Bruchac, Joseph. "Whatever is Really Yours: An Interview with Louise Erdrich." *Survival This Way: Interviews with American Indian Poets.* Tucson: U of Arizona P, 1987.

Erdrich, Louise. *Tracks.* New York: Harper, 1988.

———. *The Beet Queen.* 1986. Rpt. New York: Bantam Books, 1987.

———. *Love Medicine.* New York: Bantam Books, 1984.

Hogan, Linda. "Meeting." *The Stories We Hold Secret.* Eds. Carol Bruchac, Linda Hogan and Judith McDaniel. New York: Greenfield Review P, 1986.

Maristuen-Rodakowski, Julie. "The Turtle Mountain Reservation in North Dakota: Its History as Depicted in Louise Erdrich's *Love Medicine* and *The Beet Queen.*" *American Indian Culture and Research Journal* 12.3 (1988).

Neithammer, Carolyn. *Daughters of the Earth: The Lives and Legends of American Indian Women.* New York: Macmillan, 1977.

Silberman, Robert. "Opening the Text: *Love Medicine* and the Return of the Native American Woman." *Narrative Chance.* Ed. Gerald Vizenor. Albuquerque: U of New Mexico P, 1989.

Tsosie, Rebecca. "Changing Women: The Cross-Currents of American Indian Feminine Identity." *American Indian Culture and Research Journal* 12.1 (1988).

Wong, Hertha D. "Adoptive Mothers and Thrown-Away Children in the Novels of Louise Erdrich." *Narrating Mothers: Theorizing Maternal Subjectivities.* Eds. Brenda O. Daly and Maureen T. Reddy. Knoxville: U of Tennessee P, 1991.

ANNETTE VAN DYKE (ESSAY DATE 1999)

SOURCE: Van Dyke, Annette. "Of Vision Quests and Spirit Guardians: Female Power in the Novels of Louise Erdrich." In *The Chippewa Landscape of Louise Erdrich,* edited by Allan Chavkin, pp. 130-43. Tuscaloosa: University of Alabama Press, 1999.

In the following essay, Van Dyke assesses female power in Erdrich's novels, specifically in terms of Chippewa tradition.

When Native American women are thought of at all, and in the annals of American history that is seldom, two images come to mind: that of the exotic princess, guide and benefactor of white men—a good Indian—and that of squaw—a kind of savage beast of burden, subject to the whims of her mate, the befeathered Indian chief—a bad

Indian. In both of these stereotypes Native American women are defined by their relationship to men and are not seen as powerful in their own right. However, as Paula Gunn Allen demonstrates in *Sacred Hoop,* and as early chronicles from American history show, Native American women were seen by their own people as "powerful, socially, physically, and metaphysically" (48), nothing like the common idea of the weaker sex applied to upper-class white women. Allen says of Native American women today: "Most Indian women I know are in the same bicultural bind: we vacillate between being dependent and strong, self-reliant and powerless, strongly motivated and hopelessly insecure," trying to deal "with two hopelessly opposed cultural definitions of women" (49).

As a Native American writer, Louise Erdrich is concerned with countering these stereotypical images and the cultural bifurcation of Native American women. By virtue of being female, her independent and feisty women characters exemplify a kind of power central to life on the reservation— what Erdrich calls "transformational power." In contrast, the males must seek to find their power and place. For example, in *Tracks,* Nanapush toys with the idea of representing his tribe to the United States government, but it is Fleur on whom the hopes of the tribe are pinned to transform or arrest the encroaching white civilization. In *Love Medicine* and in *Bingo Palace,* Marie and Lulu become the real power on the reservation, despite the outward show of control by the tribal government official, Lyman Lamartine. In *Bingo Palace,* Marie's daughter, Zelda, has also become a powerful force on the reservation. This essay explores the power of women as seen in two sets of mothers and daughters, Fleur/Lulu and Marie/Zelda— power which comes from the Chippewa vision quest and spirit guardian and which often takes on a peculiarly sexual form for Chippewa women.

In an interview, Erdrich makes clear that the bifurcation of Native American women's roles and status is of major importance to her. She says: "We are taught to present a demure face to the world and yet there is a kind of wild energy behind it in many women that *is* a transformational energy, and not only transforming to them but to other people" (Bruchac 82). Because of her three daughters and sisters, she has "an urgent reason for thinking about women attuned to their power and their honest nature, not the socialized nature and their embarrassed nature and the nature that says, 'I can't possibly accomplish this'" (Bruchac 82).

In the encounters between Erdrich's male and female characters, this transformational power is often sexual. In discussing her poem "**Jacklight**," Erdrich notes that "[j]acklighting and hunting are both strong metaphors for me of sexual and love relations between men and women. In the male tradition, men are the hunters and women are their prey"[1] (George 243). However, Erdrich believes that instead "[t]here must be an exchange, a transformation, a power shared between them. . . . [I]t is this transformation where we arrive at a different stage of power" (George 243). Further, some of Erdrich's characters use their "sexuality in the same way that the men in the poems are using the jacklight, to attract in an animal way, to paralyze and fascinate. The difference is that [they are] . . . defiant because . . . men are still in control" (George 244). This defiant use of sexuality is illustrated in the poem, "**The Lady in the Pink Mustang**," in which the lady, "whose bare lap is floodlit from under the dash," lures truckers into her power: "She owns them, not one will admit what they cannot / come close to must own them. She takes them along . . ." (*Jacklight* 17).

Explaining the transformational power, Erdrich also says: "When, in some of the poems, it takes the form of becoming an animal, that I feel is a symbolic transformation, the moment a woman allows herself to act out of her own power" (Bruchac 82). An example of this appears in the poem, "**The Strange People**," in which an antelope woman defies the hunter who thinks he has killed her, and yet she still waits for one with whom she could share the transformational power:

> Safely shut in the garage,
> when he sharpens his knife
> and thinks to have me, like that,
> I come toward him,
> a lean gray witch,
> through the bullets that enter and dissolve.
>
> I sit in his house
> drinking coffee till dawn,
> and leave as frost reddens on hubcaps,
> crawling back into my shadowy body.
> All day, asleep in clean grasses,
> I dream of the one who could really wound me."
> (*Jacklight* 68-69)

In her novels, Erdrich has used the concept of the transformational power in developing the characters of Fleur, Lulu, Marie, and Zelda, among others. Traditionally, the Chippewa went on vision quests and had spirit guardians whose animal characteristics the recipient often took on.[2] Consequently, the transformational power also has a particularly Chippewa spiritual character which lessens as it is affected by Euro-American culture. Throughout the novels *Tracks, Love Medicine,* and *Bingo Palace,* the water spirit man, Misshepeshu, plays a prominent role lending his animal characteristics to Fleur, her daughter Lulu, Moses, and Lipsha—all in the Pillager line.[3] He is also featured on Nector's pipe bag handed down to Lipsha and Zelda.

In *Tracks* Fleur is described as having a good deal of transformational power illustrated in her animal characteristics which she takes on from her spirit guardian, Misshepeshu. She is described as having: "shoulders . . . broad and curved as a yoke, her hips fishlike, slippery, narrow. An old green dress clung to her waist, worn then where she sat. Her glossy braids were like the tails of animals, and swung against her when she moved, deliberately, slowly in her work, held in and half-tamed" (*T* 18). She also has "sly, brown eyes and . . . teeth, strong, sharp and very white" (*T* 18) which seem to be wolf-like Pillager characteristics.

Fleur exudes sexual power. She is always the hunter and never the prey, although some of the male characters attempt to be the aggressor. Eli follows the trail of a wounded deer he has shot to Fleur at her cabin near the lake and tries to claim the deer she is skinning. She denies his claim to it, and finally, he helps her skin it and gives the meat to her. After that he is obsessed with her and goes to the elder Nanapush for instruction. Nanapush tries to warn him away because Fleur is dangerous. She is "so impossible and yet available at the same time, that even the dried-out and bent ones around the store could see enough to light a slow fuse in their dreams" (*T* 55). She is "a woman gone wild, striking down whatever got into her path" (*T* 45). When Eli leaves to return to Fleur, Nanapush likens her to a bear: "It's like you're a log in a stream. Along comes this bear. She jumps on. Don't let her dig in her claws" (*T* 46).

Erdrich presents Fleur as firmly in control of the relationship between her and Eli. After Eli has a relationship with Sophie, Fleur uses her sexual power to punish him by ignoring him. According to Nanapush,

> After three days of Fleur's avoidance, he longed for her with the vigor of their first encounters, when . . . those two had coupled outdoors, against trees, down on pine-needle couches or out in the bare yard. After a week, he needed her with twice the force of their first meetings, and after two he was in desperate pain. His blood pounded at the rustle of her skirts. If she brushed him by accident his skin felt scorched. The fire spread. He even strained for her like a flame toward air.
>
> (*T* 106-7)

The descriptions of Fleur in *Tracks* are almost always animal-like; she is Erdrich's character who acts the most out of her own transformational power or who, we might say, is most herself. For instance, Eli believes that Fleur is mating with her spirit guardian Misshepeshu in the frozen lake at night. Eli describes her as moving, "[s]tealthily, smooth as an otter sliding from a log" (*T* 106). She stays under the frozen crust of the lake longer than a human could stand. When he wakes in the night, her hair is "a damp braid tossed against [him] . . . and once, from along her neck, [he] . . . picked a curl of black weed from the bottom of the lake" (*T* 107).

Fleur's powers are formidable and in *Bingo Palace,* the reader sees her win back her land once again using her gambling skills—this time from the Indian Agent. She returns to the reservation from the Twin Cities with a innocent-looking boy and a white Pierce-Arrow as her bait. Her hair hangs in long braids down her back, "bound together with a red strip of cloth" like the old-time warriors used to wear their hair "to meet an enemy" (*BP* 139). She is the woman acting out of her own power: "[S]he'd always acted as though she owned everything and nothing: sky, earth, those who crossed her path, road, and Pillager land. It was because she owned herself" (*BP* 140).

However, times change, and in *Love Medicine* the female characters are less themselves, having lost knowledge of the old ways and having been affected by Euro-American culture and Catholicism, forcing them to take on the bicultural split between strength and weakness. In spite of this, Lulu, Fleur's daughter, acts as a bridge character. Although she was sent to boarding school, which had the effect for most of erasing the Native culture, Lulu has a potent legacy from her mother. It is almost as if Lulu cannot help but be herself—be in her power. Erdrich's addition of the section "The Island" to the "new and expanded version" of *Love Medicine* illustrates this. This section shows Lulu's vision quest; before its addition, the reader did not see her seeking and coming into her transformatory power. Lulu has inherited her mother's sexual powers. She has become "a Pillager kind of woman with a sudden body, fierce outright wishes, a surprising heart" (*LMN* 71), but she has no guidance for her power since her mother is not around.

Like her mother, she sees herself in control of any relationships with men. Nector Kashpaw has indicated his interest in her, and she has returned that interest. However, when Nector is suddenly caught by Marie (to be discussed later), she says Nector would have been hers if she'd "jumped" for him, but since she doesn't "jump for men," he was apparently lost. She had thought of "maybe stepping high" for him when she discovered his attachment to Marie. She had wanted to meet Nector halfway, neither being the pursued nor pursuer—to share power.

However, in her anger at the situation and to irritate Nector's mother, Margaret Rushes Bear Kashpaw, she decides to seek out her very strange cousin, Moses Pillager, who survived the illness that killed the rest of her mother's relatives. Moses lives on an island in the middle of the lake with his cats, becoming cat-like himself and following his spirit guardian, Misshepeshu, who is alternately described as the big cat and as the horned lynx who lives in the lake.

Lulu is at puberty, the traditional age for a vision quest. She practices for Moses by kissing her arm. She notices "how the eyes of grown men stuck to" her at the store (*LMN* 75). Seeking she knows not what, Lulu goes to the island to charm Moses and to test her powers. The trip to the island is her vision quest, and Moses is no ordinary man:

> He was surprising, so beautiful to look at that I couldn't tell his age. His heavy hair coursed all the way down his back, looped around his belt. His face was closely fit, the angles measured and almost too perfect. My mother's face was like that too—too handsome to be real, constructed by the Manitous.
>
> (*LMN* 77)

Lulu uses her sexual powers to ensnare Moses, who is really old enough to be her father but who has remained animal-like and innocent. "I had dusted him, chilled him in the shape of my shadow when I stood against the sun. I had loosened the air, stolen the strings from his hands and legs, bent him like a stem of grass marking my trail" (*LMN* 80). He tries to leave, but she holds him and pulls him to her: "My black eyes opened wide, my *windigo* stare caught him, and I let him see the sharp flash of my teeth. He followed both of his hands as they flew forward and stroked me" (*LMN* 80). But something happens and Lulu loses control; she doesn't know if she is "acting from [her] . . . own intentions" or not. He comes to her cat-like—licking her and exploring her curiously until they share transforming power: "Suddenly his breath went deep and ragged in my ear. There was no more light from the fire, and I couldn't feel where he ended or began. He was made of darkness—weightless, fragile, lifting and falling around me with each breath" (*LMN* 81).

Moses is brought back from the invisible state in which he hid from the spirits in the time of disease. He gains his voice; he says his name "which harbored his life" (*LMN* 82) and which had not been said in fear of death. He becomes more human.

Lulu's quest fills her with the desire for more of the transformational union. It is as if she can never get enough, and how often can one expect such mystical transport? She says:

> To this day, I still hurt. I must have rolled in the beds of wild rose, for the tiny thorns—small, yellow—pierced my skin. Their poison is desire and it dissolved in my blood. The cats made me one of them—sleek and without mercy, avid, falling hungry upon the defenseless body. I want to grind men's bones to drink in my night tea. I want to enter them the way their hot shadows fold into their bodies in full sunlight. I want to be their food, their harmful drink, to taste men like stilled jam at the back of my tongue.
>
> (*LMN* 82)

Lulu's vision quest has other results. She finds her mother in her understanding of the power she has been given, and she again hears her mother's voice keeping her from harm. As a result of her liaison with Moses, she gives birth to Gerry Nanapush, the magical trickster whom no jail can hold. Through her exuberant animal-like sexuality she has eight children, all by different fathers, some of them married to her and some not. She feels no remorse and says she is "in love with the whole world and all that lived in its rainy arms." She would "open . . . and let everything inside" (*LMN* 276) so that after a while she "would be full" (*LMN* 277). She continues to be known for her catlike characteristics: "loving no one, only purring to get what she wants" (*LMN* 276).

As a respected elder, Lulu causes plenty of trouble. In another new chapter in *Love Medicine,* she allies herself with her rival Marie, and together they change the plans for the tomahawk factory into making "'museum-quality' artifacts" (*LMN* 303). Later, they quarrel and the whole factory is destroyed. The factory manager, Lyman says of his aging mother, Lulu, that "[s]he has no fear, and that's what's wrong with her" (*LMN* 302)— Lulu is always herself.

Lulu also uses her Pillager power to delay the hunt for her escaped-convict son Gerry Nanapush.

She dresses herself perfectly as if for a powwow and leads her questioners on for hours. Then when they take her off to jail, she "dances the old-lady traditional, a simple step, but complex in its quiet balance, striking. She dances with a tucked-in wildness, exactly like an old-time Pillager" and before they can take her away in the federal car, she gives "the old-lady trill, the victory yell that runs up our necks" (**BP** 265) before the news cameras. The reservation joins her, "[d]rawing deep breaths, hearts shaking" (**BP** 265), and she has created a unifying act.

Of course, if one wished, the character of Lulu could be used to reinforce the stereotype of Native American women being promiscuous. However, with the addition of "The Island" section that appears more difficult, for it puts her sexuality into the realm of the spiritual if the reader is paying attention at all. The new material may be, in fact, a reaction to the propensity that some reviewers have for seeing novels as anthropological documents and in reading the characters as racial stereotypes as happened in several reviews of **Love Medicine**.[4] One reviewer saw only stereotypes in Erdrich's female characters: "Meanwhile the women, with the exception of the stalwart Marie, are likely to take up with any man who comes along" (Towers 36).

Another reviewer also using sexual and racial stereotypes saw the scene in the "Wild Geese" section between Nector and Marie as a rape (Portales 6). However, perhaps to counter such interpretation, Erdrich has rewritten this scene so that even the most recalcitrant reader has to deal with Marie's sexual power. Marie is a mixed-blood girl of fourteen, the right age for a vision quest. She is from a marginal reservation family when she enters the convent. She wants to become a saint to rectify her position. There she meets Sister Leopolda, whom she does not know is her biological mother. Partly a result of Leopolda's physical mistreatment of her, she has a vision in which she takes on the characteristics of the water spirit man who "casts a shell necklace at your feet, weeps gleaming chips that harden into mica on your breasts. . . . He's made of gold" (**T** 11). Marie is "rippling gold." Her "nipples flashed and winked. Diamonds tipped them" (**LMN** 54).

When Marie descends from the convent, she has come into her power. She seizes her chance to improve herself by ensnaring Nector Kashpaw, who is from a well-thought-of family on the reservation. Nector thinks she is "a skinny white girl" (**LMN** 64) making off with the nuns' valu-

ables, perhaps with a chalice hidden under her skirt. What he finds is the "chalice" of her sexual power:

> Her breasts graze my chest, soft and pointed. I cannot help but lower myself the slightest bit to feel them better. And then I am caught. I give way. I cannot help myself, because, to my everlasting wonder, Marie is all tight plush acceptance, graceful movements, little jabs that lead me underneath her skirt where she is slick, warm, silk. I touch her with one hand and in that one touch I lose myself. . . . [S]omehow I have been beaten at what I started on this hill.
>
> (**LMN** 65)

After their physical encounter, Marie says, "I've had better." However, Nector thinks, "I know that isn't true because we haven't done anything yet. She doesn't know what comes next" (**LMN** 65). This time Erdrich has not left to chance that the reader will misunderstand that Marie is exerting her transformational power. Erdrich reinforces her intention that Marie is in control of her sexual power by deleting a line in the chapter "**Flesh and Blood**" in which Marie and her daughter, Zelda, go up the hill to see the dying Sister Leopolda. In the original version, when she points out to Zelda as they walk the place where she met Nector, Marie thinks: "For all I knew it was the place we made Gordon as well, but I never exactly said that" (**LM** 114). This line is deleted in the revised version.

In the scene in which Marie encounters Nector, she is also described in both animal and nature terms, another clue that she is acting "out of her own power" (Bruchac 82). She has "brown eyes" that "glaze over like a wounded mink's, hurt but still fighting vicious" (**LMN**). She is "rail-tough and pale as birch . . . the kind of tree that doubles back and springs up, whips, singing" (**LMN** 63-64). She has eyes, "tense and wild, animal eyes" that send "chills" up his neck. She "makes an odd rapsfile noise, cawing like a crow" (**LMN** 64).

Nector's response to Marie finally is as if she is a wounded animal, but still she does not release him from her power. Sometimes he

> find[s] a wounded animal that hasn't died well, or, worse it's still living, so that I have to put it out of its misery. . . . I touch the suffering bodies like they were killed saints I should handle with a gentle reverence. . . . This is how I hold her wounded hand in my hand. . . . Her hand grows thick and fevered, heavy in my own, and I don't want her, but I want her, and I cannot let go.
>
> (**LMN** 66-67)

Marie turns her considerable powers to making her husband Nector one of the most respected men on the reservation—the tribal chairman—and to keeping his drinking under control. She mothers her own children and those discarded by others such as June and Lipsha. As a respected elder on the reservation, she returns to "the old language, falling back through time to the words that Lazarres had used among themselves, shucking off the Kashpaw pride, yet holding to the old strengths Rushes Bear had taught her" (*LMN* 263). Her mother-in-law Margaret Rushes Bear Kashpaw had given Marie and subsequently, Zelda, the strength to be attuned to their own powers as women and to reject the Euro-American image of women as weak and helpless and herself as marginal—a dirty Lazarre.

She is not able to extend that transformational power to all, however. Despite her mothering of June, June's childhood is so horrendous—being raped by her mother's boyfriend—that she never comes fully into her own power and she eventually chooses death by walking into a blizzard. June's considerable sexual power traps Marie's son Gordie, but it is the power of the jacklight, used to hunt and kill in defiance for what has been done to her and not shared power. Gordie's life is devastated by his marriage to June, and Marie must deal with her son's decline. In another new chapter added to *Love Medicine,* Marie gathers her strength and refuses to allow Gordie to leave the cabin again in search of alcohol. She thinks: "There was no question in her mind that if she let him go he would get himself killed. She would almost rather have killed him herself" (*LMN* 275). Gordie dies after drinking Lysol with Marie sitting at the cabin door with her axe.

June's harm extends to her own son, Lipsha, who she tries to drown as an infant. Lipsha is saved by the water spirit man, and therefore given his gift of touch and connected firmly to the Pillagers, Fleur, and Moses, who also have the water man as a spirit guardian. Lipsha remembers it as:

> Darkened and drenched, coming toward me from the other side of drowning—it presses its mouth on mine and holds me with its fins and horns and rocks me with its long and shining plant arms. Its face is lion-jawed, a thing of beach foam, resembling the jack of clubs. Its face has the shock of the unburied goodness, the saving tones. . . . I am rocked and saved and cradled.
>
> (*BP* 218)

When Lipsha seeks out his great grandmother Fleur for some love medicine, their connection is reaffirmed. Later Fleur performs her last transforming act—she trades her life for Lipsha's: "Outdoors,

into a deep cold brilliance that often succeeds a long disruptive blizzard, she went thinking of the boy out there. Annoyed, she took his place" (*BP* 272).

For Marie's daughter, Zelda, the vision quest, which sets an adolescent on her adult path, comes late. At sixteen she "did not know what she wanted yet" (*LMN* 148). Like her mother and her biological grandmother Pauline (Sister Leopolda), she thinks of going up the hill to join the nuns in the convent, but she has not chosen any particular path. It is after she and her mother visit the dying Sister Leopolda that the incident which shapes her life occurs. Zelda's vision takes the form of her father's infidelity with Lulu Lamartine. She finds his farewell letter to her mother and goes to bring him back. Her father, Nector, sees her as a vision of Marie and instead of animal characteristics, common to women coming into their own power, she has the characteristics of an avenging angel:

> I see Marie standing in the bush. She is fourteen and slim again. I can do nothing but stare, rooted to the ground. She stands tall, straight and stern as an angel. She watches me. Red flames from the burning house glare and flicker in her eyes. Her skin sheds light. We are face to face, and then she begins to lift on waves of heat. Her breast is a glowing shield. Her arm is a white-hot spear. When she raises it the bush behind her spreads, blazing open like wings.
>
> (*LMN* 145)

In acting for her mother, Zelda aborts her natural self. She decides that she wants a white man who "would take . . . [her] away from the reservation to the Twin Cities, where . . . [she'd] planned her life all out from catalogs and magazines" (*BP* 46). Unlike her father, Nector, she would never be subject to love; she would never share her transformational power with a man. Instead she uses her sexual power to thwart the love of Xavier Toose:

> She was capable of hovering in a blanket, in a room where her own breath rose and fell, a plume of longing, all night. She could exist in the dark cell of her body. She was capable of denying herself everything tender, unspoken, sweet, generous, and desperate. She could do it because she willed it. She could live in the shell of her quilt as the cold night lengthened, and she could let a man's fires flash and burn, flash and burn, until they disappeared.
>
> (*BP* 244)

Nevertheless, despite Zelda's refusal of Xavier, she uses her power to control events on the reservation. As Lipsha says of her,

When women age into their power, no wind can upset them, no hand turn aside their knowledge; no fact can deflect their point of view. . . . My aunt knows all there is to know. She has a deep instinct for running things. She should have more children or at least a small nation to control. Instead, forced narrow, her talents run to getting people to do things they don't want to do for other people they don't like. Zelda is the author of grit-jawed charity on the reservation, the instigator of good works that always get chalked up to her credit.

(*BP* 13-14)

Zelda has raven-like hair "which still sweeps its fierce wing down the middle of her back," and she wears the legacy from her paternal grandmother, Margaret Rushes Bear Kashpaw, a skinning knife in a beaded sheath "at her strong hip" (*BP* 15). Despite her marriage to her white man, the "morose" Swede (*BP* 23), she named her daughter "Albertine" after her first love, Xavier Albert Toose, her denial of his love affecting her all of her life. Zelda is visited with a vision which accompanies the return of her father's ceremonial pipe—the pipe which was "Earth and heaven, connecting, the fire between that burned in everything alive" (*BP* 245). The pipe also had a "horned man radiating wavering lines of power . . . beaded into the other end" (*LMN* 259). In a series of painful visions connected to heart attacks, she sees that she has denied her own nature, her love for Xavier Toose. When she thinks of him, her heart "yawned open like a greedy young bird, ready to be fed" (*BP* 246). Finally, she stands before him, "new as if naked, but she had no shame" (*BP* 247). So, even though Zelda has denied her own nature and only accepted it as a mature woman, still she is not weak; she is transformed. She meets Xavier half way: "Light dashed itself upon Zelda, but she wasn't shaken. Her hands floated off the steering wheel and gestured, but she wasn't helpless" (*BP* 247).

Fleur, Lulu, Marie, and Zelda all exemplify Erdrich's transformational sexual power when women are most themselves. Erdrich counters the stereotypes of Native American women as weak by using the traditional Chippewa concepts of the vision quest and the spirit guardian, most often the water spirit man. Her characters are shown as taking on the animal characteristics of their spirit guardians and acting out of their own power. With the revisions in *Love Medicine,* and through *The Bingo Palace,* Erdrich brings these concepts firmly onto the contemporary reservation—offering images of strong, self-reliant, powerful Chippewa women.

Notes

1. The *Random House Dictionary of the English Language,* 2nd edition, defines jacklight as: "a portable cresset, or oil-burning lantern, or electric light used as a lure in hunting or fishing at night."

2. See Vecsey 121-43 for discussions of puberty and the vision quest.

3. See Van Dyke for a discussion of the role of the water spirit man in Erdrich's work.

4. See McKenzie 53-55 for a discussion of stereotypes in reviews of *Love Medicine.*

Works Cited

Allen, Paula Gunn. *The Sacred Hoop: Recovering the Feminine in American Indian Traditions.* Boston: Beacon Press, 1986.

Bruchac, Joseph, ed. "Whatever Is Really Yours: An Interview with Louise Erdrich." *Survival This Way: Interviews with American Indian Poets.* Tucson: U of Arizona P, 1987. 73-86.

Erdrich, Louise. *Jacklight.* New York: Holt, 1984.

George, Jan. "Interview with Louise Erdrich." *North Dakota Quarterly* 53 (1985): 240-46.

McKenzie, James. "Lipsha's Good Road Home: The Revival of Chippewa Culture in *Love Medicine.*" *American Indian Culture and Research Journal* 10.3 (1986): 53-63.

Portales, Marco. "People with Holes in Their Lives." Rev. of *Love Medicine,* by Louise Erdrich. *New York Times Book Review* 23 December 1984: 6.

Towers, Robert. "Uprooted." Rev. of *Love Medicine,* by Louise Erdrich. *New York Review of Books* 11 April 1985: 36.

Van Dyke, Annette. "Questions of the Spirit: Bloodlines in Louise Erdrich's Chippewa Landscape." *Studies in American Indian Literatures* 4.1 (1992): 15-27.

Vecsey, Christopher. *Traditional Ojibwa Religion and Its Historical Changes.* Philadelphia: American Philosophical Society, 1983.

TITLE COMMENTARY

Tracks

LAURA E. TANNER (ESSAY DATE 1994)

SOURCE: Tanner, Laura E. "'Known in the Brain and Known in the Flesh': Gender, Race, and the Vulnerable Body in *Tracks.*" In *Intimate Violence: Reading Rape and Torture in Twentieth-Century Fiction,* pp. 115-41. Bloomington: Indiana University Press, 1994.

In the following essay, Tanner discusses the double implications of gender and race in Erdrich's portrayal of rape in her novel Tracks.

Rape begins, like many other forms of violence, with the painful confrontation of two bodies; more importantly, however, its dynamics originate out of two opposing experiences of embodiment. For the male violator, embodiment emerges as a source of strength rather than vulnerability. Often imaged as solid, fixed, powerful, the body of the rapist is capable not only of asserting his presence but of appropriating, reshaping, and violating the female body so that it conforms to the dictates of his pleasures. The male body, then, functions as a tool that extends the power of subjectivity out into a larger universe that the violator can remake within the configurations of his own desire.

For the rape victim, on the other hand, embodiment is a source of vulnerability rather than power. Fixed within her body, the woman is unable to shield herself from the force of the violator as he pins her within the confines of a form over which he assumes control. Beneath the violator's hand, the rape victim's body becomes a text on which *his* will is inscribed, a form that bears the mark of his subjectivity even as she cannot divorce it from her own. Within such a scenario, the entanglement of subject and body allows the violator to assume control of both and the victim to assert power over neither. The image of bodily penetration is thus bound up with an assault on subjectivity in which the victim is annihilated from both inside and outside; the woman's body continues to allow the violator access to her subjectivity even as the power of agency is stripped away from her, imprisoning her in a material form over which she as subject has no control.

The dynamics of rape are further complicated when the victim of sexual violence is a woman of color for whom the experience of embodiment cannot be separated from the experience of oppression. In such a case, the rapist's physical appropriation of the female body as the object of his desire may exaggerate a sense of powerlessness that the victim experiences daily within a hegemonic culture that defines her body as the source of her Otherness. The increased statistical vulnerability of women of color to the violence of rape is a daily and constant threat to personal autonomy that intensifies an already difficult struggle to claim the power of subjectivity. In the literature of African American, Hispanic, and Native American women, then, the dynamics of rape often become intertwined with the dynamics of oppression.

In *I Know Why the Caged Bird Sings*, Maya Angelou describes her own childhood experience of rape by observing, "The act of rape on an eight-year old body is a matter of the needle giving because the camel can't. The child gives, because the body can, and the mind of the violator cannot" (65). In such a case, the victim's body becomes the imprint on which the rapist's identity is forcibly inscribed, her own being the mark of his desperate claim to power. In raping, the violator not only assaults his victim but turns her presence into an absence that she may be unable to reclaim. The destructive power of such an assault is heightened when its victim already experiences her claim to her own body and subjectivity as tenuous. The twelve-year-old rape victim in Cherrie Moraga's *Giving Up the Ghost* describes the rapist's attempt to penetrate her young body as a literal and figurative process of transforming her into a hole: "there was no hole / he had to make it / 'n' I see myself down there like a face / with no opening / a face with no features. . . . HE MADE ME A HOLE!" (42-43). In Moraga's representation, the subjectivity of the young victim is effaced by a rapist who not only violates her physically but makes her *see herself* as a featureless absence, a hole. The apparent intimacy of physical closeness and the absolute denial of the victim's subjectivity converge to lend the rapist an awful power that the torturer/protagonist of Maria Irene Fornes's *The Conduct of Life* describes by saying, "It is a desire to destroy and to see things destroyed and to see the inside of them" (*Plays*, 82).

That assault from the inside defines not only the anatomy of the rape experience but the invisible operation of a hegemonic culture that constructs the woman of color, like the rape victim, as a featureless absence. In "Poem about My Rights," June Jordan links the experience of rape with the self-destructive act of internalizing the values of a dominant culture: "I am the wrong / sex the wrong age the wrong skin. . . . / I am the history of rape / I am the history of the rejection of who I am / I am the history of the terrorized incarceration of / my self . . ." (*Passion*, 86, 88). As an act in which physical and emotional violation converge, in which the external force of the violator is necessarily contained within the most intimate space of the victim, rape is an assault often imaged as self-destruction, an experience defined by the literal violation of the boundaries of anatomy *and* autonomy. Such an experience of fragmentation, as Jordan observes here, is also the fundamental experience of a woman attempting to claim an identity in a culture that defines her as the weakness against which to measure its own strength or the absence that serves only to mark its presence.

The attempt to unveil the oppressive mechanisms of a dominant culture that governs through sign and metaphor leads many women writers of color not merely to metaphorize rape but to trace the way in which its material dynamics are experienced, interpreted, or appropriated by both victim and violator. In this chapter, I will explore the vulnerable body as it emerges within the dynamics of rape and oppression in Louise Erdrich's *Tracks*. *Tracks* not only investigates the psychological effects of rape as an act that can "terrorize and incarcerate" women within their own bodies; it also explores the way in which that experience of vulnerable embodiment is exaggerated by the victim's internalization of essentialist assumptions about race and gender.

Although the rape that takes place early in Louise Erdrich's *Tracks* is perpetrated against Fleur Pillager, the "strong and daring" Native American heroine of the novel, the reader's access to that rape is mediated through the perspective of Pauline, the young mixed-blood Native American woman who both witnesses and narrates the crime.[1] The psychological consequences of Fleur's rape—either for the victim or the violators—are never fully addressed in the novel; Fleur's rapists die shortly after they attack her, while Fleur herself never articulates her pain or acknowledges that the rape took place. It is, then, only in Pauline's imagination that the act of violation remains present in the novel.[2] Its impact on *her* character surfaces not only in her recounting (or, according to other characters in the novel, fabrication) of the incident but in the images of sexual violation that permeate the psychological landscapes through which Pauline moves both as character and as narrator. Although critics of Erdrich's novel have largely ignored the rape, it is impossible to disentangle Pauline's understanding of race, gender, and power from her response to Fleur's violation.

The intersection of issues of race and gender complicates any discussion of the sexual violence represented within Erdrich's novel. In exploring the ideological function of criticism that takes gender as its starting point, recent feminist critics have pointed to the danger of using feminist theory to reinforce the values of a dominant race and class system.[3] Reading rape in the context of Erdrich's text makes visible dynamics that often operate invisibly in texts by white authors. The body, as *Tracks* reveals, is marked not only by sex but by race, and the dynamics of intimate violence may be written within narratives highlighting both. In the case of Erdrich's novel, however, critics have focused almost exclusively on the issue of race.[4] Because it is structured as a series of chapters narrated alternately by Nanapush and Pauline—the elder tribesman and the young mixed-blood woman aspiring to whiteness—Erdrich's novel is often read as a struggle between traditional Native American life and the dangerous lure of white acculturation. The tensions that emerge in *Tracks*, however, stem from differences of gender *and* race, as the prominent place of Fleur's rape early in the novel demonstrates. The challenge that Erdrich's novel poses to the critic is the challenge to avoid privileging one category of difference over another. In order to claim herself as subject, Pauline must negotiate her identities as both woman and mixed-blood Native American; the division of those identities can be effected only artificially, in intellectual rather than practical terms. My discussion of Erdrich's novel, insofar as it makes use of categories of race and gender, tends to separate in theory what cannot be divorced in practice, to isolate in the very act of articulating connection. My attempt, nonetheless, is to gesture toward the points of intersection that cannot properly be named by exploring in dialogic rather than dualistic terms the rape that constitutes one center of Erdrich's novel.

In the figure of Pauline, Erdrich offers us a character suffering from both racial and gender disempowerment. As a woman whose body is not marked by the conventions of femininity and a "half-breed" caught between her white and Native American backgrounds, Pauline is trapped in the margins of cultural definition. *Tracks* traces her attempt to reclaim a subjectivity that has been appropriated by others by turning against a body that she defines as the source of her Otherness. Pauline images her own vulnerability—as a woman and a Native American—with a vocabulary of violation that grows out of her experience of listening, against her will, as Fleur is raped. A discussion of the dynamics of rape in the novel begins to unveil the way in which Pauline's understanding of herself as subject is caught up in essentialist notions of the body that lead, ultimately, to her literal and figurative self-destruction.

The issue of how Pauline's body is read by others surfaces immediately in the novel as she travels to Argus to live with her aunt and work in the

ON THE SUBJECT OF...

ERDRICH'S MYTHIC WOMEN
In fashioning Fleur, Antelope Wife, and Windigo Dog, Erdrich becomes a mythmaker like her characters who stand as symbols of the possibility that the unknown spirit world can still assert itself in the lives of her contemporary Chippewa people. When Fleur brings the great powers of the spirit bear and Misshepeshu into the lives of her people, she exemplifies the possibility of living in right relationship to the spirits. Chippewa people regularly used to seek access to manito powers through the Midéwewin ceremonies, and this relationship remains available, even in modern times, to those willing to seek it. [. . . .] The possibility and probability of a continued relationship with the manitos exist through several community members by the end of the North Dakota novels: Shawnee Ray knows how to talk sweetly to the spirits, and her uncle Xavier Toose serves as an intermediary to the spirits by directing traditional sweat lodges. Lipsha bumbles along being granted visions he does not understand and powers he does not know how to use, but he is beginning to understand the role he is destined to fill in the community. The urban Indians, likewise, still have access to animal helpers if only they live in respect and right relation with them. [. . . .] In her novels, Erdrich creates female characters who embody or are recipients of manito power still aiding her Indian people. Fleur's story and Cally's story are Erdrich's tribute to an enduring spiritual dimension in Chippewa life, and the myth Erdrich creates around Fleur and Antelope Wife positions Erdrich as a secondary hero, one who passes on traditional stories in contemporary form. Erdrich through her novels sustains the mythic tradition of a people who, having survived for at least a millennium, enter the twenty-first century attended by the presence of their ancestral spirits.

Jacobs, Connie A. An excerpt from "'Power Travels in the Bloodlines, Handed Out before Birth': Louise Erdrich's Female Mythic Characters." *The Novels of Louise Erdrich. Stories of Her People*, pp. 173-74. New York: Peter Lang, 2001.

butcher shop there. Because the men who surround her in the shop fail to read the conventional signs of "femaleness" on her skinny teenaged form, Pauline's body seems to disappear before their gaze:

> I was fifteen, alone, and so poor-looking I was invisible to most customers and to the men in the shop. Until they needed me, I blended into the stained brown walls, a skinny big-nosed girl with staring eyes. . . . Because I could fade into a corner or squeeze beneath a shelf I knew everything: how much cash there was in the till, what the men joked about when no one was around, and what they did to Fleur.
>
> (15-16)

Gendered neither male nor female, Pauline's body ceases to exist in the men's world; unmarked by the signs of gender difference, it "blends" and "fades" into a landscape controlled and interpreted by men. Her subjectivity also remains unacknowledged as, caught in the space between the cultural labels of male and female, Pauline becomes "no one." In a patriarchal society, as Mary Ann Doane observes, "to desexualize the female body is ultimately to deny its very existence" (79). Seemingly bodiless, Pauline does not interact with the men around her but becomes instead the observer, the witness, the watcher.

In racial as well as gender terms, Pauline's subjectivity is consistently denied. She responds to the powerlessness of her position as a Native American in a white world not by questioning the values of the dominant culture but by internalizing those values to see herself through the mediation of the white gaze. "I wanted to be like my mother, who showed her half-white . . . ," she remarks early in the novel. "I saw through the eyes of the world outside us. I would not speak our language" (14). As the words of Pauline's disavowal reveal, her claim to white identity is effected only at the cost of self-alienation. The split implied in separating her white being from her Native American self is revealed as she simultaneously claims and disavows her native language: "I would not speak *our* language." Similarly, her decision to appropriate "the eyes of the world outside *us*" implies the internalization of a vision that necessarily redefines *us* as *Other*. In Pauline's case, to see herself through the eyes of the world, to define herself through the images of a dominant culture, is a form of self-violation that perpetuates the white culture's negation and destruction of the Native American Other. Her own assumptions of a fundamental Otherness bind her to a destructive vision of herself as not-white that parallels and exaggerates the powerlessness of her presence beneath a male gaze that defines her as "no one."

Fleur's rape unsettles the dominance of a patriarchal, white gaze in the text by challenging the notion of Pauline's bodily invisibility and exposing the dynamics of self-violation that underlie her disavowal of the racial self. Until the point at which Fleur is raped, Pauline's occupation of the space between female and male, Native American and white, seems to lend her a perverse kind of power; the looker but never the seen, her gaze does not seem to originate out of a body that circumscribes perspective. Unattached to any single form or subject position, Pauline seems to possess a kind of liberating fluidity emphasized by descriptions of her body. The novel's early representations emphasize the insubstantiality of Pauline's "skinny" form; as she describes herself as a "moving shadow" (22), only her "staring eyes" locate her in the novel's early scenes (16).

Not surprisingly, then, Pauline's response to Fleur's rape is to close her eyes to the act she witnesses, almost as if the loss of vision will bring about the complete erasure of a body already imaged as invisible. As the men whom Fleur has humiliated at cards corner her inside the smokehouse and rape her in punishment, Pauline is paralyzed by the recognition of a vulnerability she shares with Fleur, and responds by attempting to escape from her own body:

> The men saw, yelled, and chased [Fleur] at a dead run to the smokehouse. . . . That is when I should have gone to Fleur, saved her, thrown myself on Dutch the way Russell did. . . . He stuck to his stepfather's leg as if he'd been flung there. Dutch dragged him for a few steps, his leg a branch, then cuffed Russell off and left him shouting and bawling in the sticky weeds. I closed my eyes and put my hands on my ears, so there is nothing more to describe but what I couldn't block out: those yells from Russell, Fleur's hoarse breath, so loud it filled me, her cry in the old language and our names repeated over and over among the words.
>
> (26)

Despite Pauline's decision not to speak the language in which Fleur cries out, Fleur's articulation of pain remains intelligible to her; Pauline's disavowal of her Native American identity cannot undo her connection to the "old language." Similarly, Pauline's attempt to move outside the body that not only makes her vulnerable to rape but links her in sensory terms to Fleur's painful experience proves ineffectual as well. Pauline's futile efforts to block out awareness of Fleur's

violation only call attention to her physical presence as witness; as Fleur's body disappears from this representation of rape, the image of Pauline closing her eyes and putting her hands over her ears directs the reader's focus toward the very body that Pauline would erase.

The reader's attempt to access the details of Fleur's rape, then, is frustrated not only by the mediating force of Pauline's narration but by its emphasis on *Pauline's* experience of her body during the rape rather than Fleur's. When the reader finally "witnesses" Fleur's violation many pages later, the materiality of violence is once again obscured as Pauline recalls not the rape itself but her dreams about it. Erdrich's interpolation of such dreams into the plot of her novel in part reflects her appropriation of Native American traditions based on a mythic or symbolic epistemology.[5] As a character caught between Native American and white religions, experiences, and conventions, Pauline authors a narrative that foregrounds questions of interpretation as it moves between "imaginary" and "real" events; that narrative, as Catherine Rainwater argues, "vexes the reader's effort to decide upon an unambiguous, epistemologically consistent interpretive framework" (407). Although Rainwater does not address Pauline's narrative of the rape, it most clearly exposes the implications of the reader's suspension between opposing interpretive frameworks:

> I relived the whole thing over and over, that moment so clear before the storm. Every night when my arms lowered the beam, it was my will that bore the weight, let it drop into place—not Russell's and not Fleur's. For that reason, at the Judgment, it would be my soul sacrificed, my poor body turned on the devil's wheel. And yet, despite that future, I was condemned to suffer in this life also. Every night I was witness when the men slapped Fleur's mouth, beat her, entered and rode her. I felt all. My shrieks poured from her mouth and my blood from her wounds.
>
> (66)

Despite Pauline's apparent revelation of the details of the rape—"the men slapped Fleur's mouth, beat her, entered and rode her"—the reader remains dislocated in a scene of violence that offers him or her few points of material reference. The origin of these images in Pauline's dreams exaggerates the already blurred line between the experiential and the imagined, just as Pauline's rendering effaces the boundaries between her body and Fleur's. The reader's attempt to assign cause and effect or to place the location of victim, violator, or observer is frustrated by Pauline's confusion of material and immaterial categories. Despite Pauline's physical distance from the rape, for example, she renders its impact on her in material terms as she describes her shrieks and her blood pouring from Fleur's body. Although Pauline covers her "staring eyes" during the rape, she cannot escape from the scene in either body or mind, and her obsessive reenactments of the crime force her into the position of a voyeur who witnesses the violation of a body that dissolves into her own form.

The reader's attempt to access the materiality of violence in this representation is thus frustrated by a narrative that moves the reader away from the empirical dynamics of violation into a semiotic universe in which it is impossible to disentangle mind from body, imagination from materiality. As these categories become blurred within the text, the narrative propels the reader away from the immediacy of the rape which it represents and discourages the reader from connecting Fleur's violation to the empirical dynamics of rape. As I have argued in my introduction, the act of reading a representation of violation is defined by the reader's suspension between the semiotic and the real, between a representation and the material dynamics of violence which it evokes, reflects, or transforms. "Semiotics," as Teresa de Lauretis observes, "specifies the mutual overdetermination of meaning, perception, and experience, a complex nexus of reciprocally constitutive effects between the subject and social reality, which, in the subject, entail a continual modification of consciousness; that consciousness in turn being the condition of social change" (*Alice Doesn't*, 184). Representations of violence locate the readerly subject at the "nexus of reciprocally constitutive effects" that may ultimately result in a transformation of attitudes about empirical as well as textual reality. Because the language of fiction is by definition never simply referential, however, fictional representations of violence that disorient the reader by manipulating experiential conventions may obscure any connection to empirical violence.

Such readerly disorientation may account for the glaring absence of a discussion of Fleur's rape in the criticism of Erdrich's novel. Even the most current analysis of *Tracks,* which focuses on gender issues as they affect the construction of Pauline's subjectivity, lacks a single reference to the incident of sexual violence with which Pauline's narrative begins.[6] Such an omission can be explained only by exploring the way in which both Pauline and the reader of *Tracks* interpret the presence of the vulnerable body. As Pauline

conflates the materiality of her body with the hegemonic culture's semiotic construction of it, the reader engages with a series of representations that obscure the materiality of the body in favor of its semiotic construction. Both Pauline and the reader, then, negotiate between empirical and semiotic realities; as Pauline reduces the semiotic to its material counterpart, the reader is pushed toward enacting the opposite process.

As Pauline's narrative dissolves the representational boundaries between body and mind, it magnifies the immaterial dynamics of the reading process to heighten the reader's experience of the text and the violence represented within it as imaginative constructs. The reader, whose access to the materiality of violence is always problematized by the operation of representation, encounters an absence of referentiality even at the level of plot. Even as Pauline struggles to deal with an act of violence that remains urgently present in her mind, the events of the rape are continually displaced for the reader by Pauline's reflections about them. In her initial description of Russell's attempt to lock the rapists into the meat lockers, for example, Pauline states, "He strained and shoved. . . . Sometimes, thinking back, I see my arms lift, my hands grasp, see myself dropping the beam into the metal grip. At other times, that moment is erased" (27). Even this simple bodily act becomes an issue of interpretation as the reader comes to access Pauline's experience only through the mediating force of an imagination capable of creating and erasing realities.

Pauline's vexed relationship with her body thus intrudes upon the reader's experience of the text through the force of a narrative that represents without transition empirical and imaginary events. In Pauline's dream recollection of the rape quoted above, Russell is able to respond to the horror of the rape physically while Pauline "bears the weight" of the beam on the freezer door imaginatively; it is her "will" that drops the latch and not her body. The confusion of mind/body categories evident in Pauline's narrative thus operates not only to deny the reader material reference but to mark Pauline's double vulnerability; Pauline experiences not only the pain of a rape that she resists imaginatively but the guilt of complicity in a crime in which she appears not to intervene physically. As the boundary between body and imagination dissolves, Pauline suffers the consequences of a seeming disembodiment that implicates her as passive witness to Fleur's suffering but does not protect her from imaginative vulnerability to Fleur's pain.

After the rape, Pauline's reflections on the gaze reveal her attempt to renegotiate the position of powerlessness into which the rape forces her. If her own body enforces her reluctant perception of Fleur's violation yet offers no physical medium through which to resist the rape, Pauline envisions an alternative body that resists rather than invites vulnerability:

> Power travels in the bloodlines, handed out before birth. It comes down through the hands, which in the Pillagers are strong and knotted, big, spidery and rough, with sensitive fingertips good at dealing cards. It comes through the eyes, too, belligerent, darkest brown, the eyes of those in the bear clan, impolite as they gaze directly at a person.
>
> In my dreams, I look straight back at Fleur, at the men. I am no longer the watcher on the dark sill, the skinny girl.
>
> (31)

Pauline's focus on the physical texture of these powerful hands, which are "strong and knotted, big, spidery and rough, with sensitive fingertips," renders the body that she ascribes collectively to the Pillager family surprisingly tactile and immediate in contrast to the vague abstraction of Pauline's individual form. As the "watcher" whose skinny body blends into darkness and the mixed-blood Native American who sees herself only as not-white, Pauline lacks the substantiality of the Pillagers. Even her gaze is seemingly sourceless, its trajectory indirect; originating out of no concrete form, it is capable of "looking straight back" at the other only in Pauline's dreams. Unlike Pauline, who sees "through the eyes of the world outside us," the Pillagers possess a "direct" and unmediated gaze imaged in part by the physical presence of eyes that assert their owners' embodiment *and* subjectivity. Both "darkest brown" and "belligerent," these eyes provide an anchor for the penetrating gaze that issues from them; their claim to materiality is also a claim to subjectivity that Pauline implicitly contrasts with her own inability to affirm her presence in either category.

The interpenetration of body and subject in Pauline's imaging of the gaze reflects in part her own struggle with the notion of biological determinism and racial identity. The power implicit in the Pillager form travels, in Pauline's analysis, "in the bloodlines, handed out before birth"; the body, in such a view, carries the mark of identity and determines not only the physical configuration of an individual but the power and variety of subject positions available to him or her. If their pure "bloodlines" lend power and solidity to the Pillager gaze, Pauline's own family status as a mixed-blood Native American seems to deny her access to that power, as her description of the Puyats reveals:

> During the time I stayed with them, I hardly saw Dutch or Regina look each other in the eye or talk. Perhaps it was because . . . the Puyats were known as a quiet family with little to say. We were mixed-bloods, skinners in the clan for which the name was lost.
>
> (14)

Located biologically in the space between Native American and white, defined by the mixing of two racial bloodlines, the Puyats lack a stable base from which to affirm their presence. The quiet demeanor of Pauline's relatives and their inability to "look each other in the eye" contrasts sharply with the strong hands and belligerent gazes of the Pillagers. The fear of Pauline's father that she will change if sent to the white town—"'You'll fade out there,' he said, reminding me that I was lighter than my sisters. 'You won't be an Indian once you return.'" (14)—is imaged in bodily terms, as the white world's assault on an Indian identity marked so weakly on Pauline's body that she is in danger of dissolving into the whiteness that her father defines as nothingness.

In racial as well as gender terms, then, Pauline's body threatens to fade into invisibility. Because the novel constructs Pauline's marginality within a framework that is self-consciously racial, criticism has tended to focus exclusively on her role as a half-breed whose perspective has been coopted by the dominant white culture. As Trinh T. Minh-ha theorizes, however, any such isolationist reading can be said to reinscribe the very Euro-American dynamics that critics of *Tracks* attempt to unveil. Minh-ha states, "The idea of two illusorily separated identities, one ethnic, the other woman (or more precisely female), again, partakes in the Euro-American system of dualistic reasoning and its age-old divide-and-conquer tactics" (104). Only by restoring the link between Pauline's racial and gender identities is it possible to explore the full implications of the rape scene with which Pauline's narrative begins and to which it continually alludes.

Within the deterministic frame that Pauline posits, Fleur's status as a Pillager dictates that her hands be marked by strength and her gaze defined by its penetrating stare. As the rape makes clear, however, Fleur's body is not merely a racial text, the strength of her Native American name not the only signifier of her power or powerlessness. Fleur's cultural heritage is imaged throughout the novel as a source of a mystical strength; more than once, she survives her own drowning, manipulates the lives and deaths of others, and moves into and out of different physical forms. Fleur's inability to escape the female form that makes her vulnerable to rape is thus all the more shocking. Within the context of sexual violence, Fleur's strength is overwhelmed by males and her body transformed from the source of the penetrating gaze to the object of penetration. Although Pauline frames the rape with references to Fleur's mystical powers, culminating in the tornado that eventually results in the death of the rapists, the experience to which Pauline returns again and again is the moment of violation itself, a moment in which Fleur is defined not by racial empowerment but by gender powerlessness.

Both in imaging Fleur's rape and in reenacting it in different forms, Pauline attempts to come to terms with her own vulnerability to violation. Like her attempt to respond to racial otherness by denying her Native American identity, however, Pauline's effort to escape the vulnerability she experiences as a woman by destroying the body that is the most visible manifestation of that vulnerability only succeeds in reinscribing the dynamics of violation that she fears. Although the novel begins with Pauline's rejection of the Native American self that she defines as Other, the rape propels her to view the marks of her gender as signs of her powerlessness as well; after Fleur's violation, the gaze that she comes to adopt as she sees "through the eyes of the world outside us" is not only white but male. Pauline's attempt to appropriate the vision of the empowered only results in the continued reinscription of her identity as Other; her borrowed eyes are anchored in a body that intrudes again and again to reinforce her vision of her own insignificance: "Clarence was the one I should have tried for, I saw that, but I also saw what he saw—the pole-thin young woman others did, the hair pulled back and woven into a single braid, the small and staring eyes that did not blink . . ." (74). Pauline's representation of her body reinscribes its object status even as she attributes the process of objectification to the male gaze: "I also saw what he saw." Having internalized the gaze of the oppressor, Pauline images her own eyes as static; her wooden, motionless look defines her not as subject but as object. Even as she attempts to appropriate the power of the gaze, Pauline becomes overpowered by it; as long as she defines herself according to what she is not—white, Pillager, male—Pauline remains uncomfortable in her own body.

That discomfort is revealed again as Pauline images the power of men in the same way she imaged the power of the Pillagers: in the strength and solidity of their hands. Describing her failed encounter with a potential lover, Pauline claims, "I hadn't liked the weight of Napoleon's hands, their hardened palms. I hadn't liked seeing myself naked, plucked and skinned" (74). This passage renders the female form both transparent and malleable; assigning weight and solidity to the male body, Pauline contrasts Napoleon's "hardened palms" with her own vulnerable nakedness. Although Pauline consents to the sexual interchange that she describes here, she images the physical act that is not rape as a form of psychic violation. In "forcing" her to see herself "naked, plucked and skinned," Napoleon metaphorically strips away the layer of protection that would allow Pauline to claim autonomy as both body and subject. Ironically, of course, it is Pauline who is the subject of her own violation as she reduces herself to the object of a gaze that originates in her consciousness rather than in Napoleon's eyes.

Pauline's horror at being "skinned" beneath the force of Napoleon's gaze reflects her notion of the body as a kind of container which houses the subject within; the skin, then, becomes the boundary between body and subject, the protective layer that is the final physical barrier to a self vulnerable to intimate violence. "Naked, plucked and skinned," the female form becomes a permeable structure invaded by a masculine body that Pauline images as hard, substantial, anchored: "With my clothes gone, I saw all the bones pushing at my flesh. I tried to shut my eyes, but couldn't keep them closed, feeling that if I did not hold his gaze he could look at me any way he wanted" (73). Pauline's fear of violation is not merely a fear of physical assault; it is a fear that her body itself will dissolve, her skin melt away, to unveil to the masculine eye the very bones that support her frame. The male gaze, it seems, contains the power not only to see those bones but, in isolating them, to reconstruct them into a form of its own making. Lacking a sense of herself as stable subject, Pauline collapses into a body that serves not as the shield she desires but as a passageway into the self. The subject "contained" by those bones, it becomes clear, exists only incidentally as it is created by others. In looking at her "any way he wanted," Napoleon possesses the power to make her anything he wants, and although she seems determined to hold his gaze to keep him from doing so, Pauline's internalization of his perspective guarantees that she will continue to construct herself as an absence in the shadow of his presence.

Pauline's response to such vulnerability is to disavow the physical form through which others gain access to her as subject. "Plucked and skinned" beneath the male gaze, Pauline can assert her identity as desiring subject rather than victim only by abandoning her body. She succeeds in enacting her desire for her cousin Eli only by attaching herself to another body in the text, a body that she images as opaque and invulnerable:

> With the dim light cloaking us together, I could almost feel what it was like to be inside Sophie's form, not hunched in mine, not blending into the walls, but careless and fledgling, throwing the starved glances of men off like the surface of a pond, reflecting sky so you could never see the shallow bottom.
>
> (78)

"Hunched" in her own form, Pauline sees her body as a kind of prison; its boundaries constrict her even as they remain permeable to others. Pauline's extreme self-consciousness pushes her to attribute to the male gaze the power of penetrating her flesh to the bones. The "careless and fledgling" Sophie, on the other hand, deflects that gaze; Pauline images Sophie's body as a barrier that refuses penetration by "throwing off" the male look.

"Cloaked together" with Sophie, Pauline gains imaginative access to a form that she associates with strength rather than vulnerability. In the scenes that follow, Pauline appears to gain pleasure without exposure; she does so by thrusting Sophie's body between Eli's and her own so that her own form becomes invisible: "Eli stared after her [Sophie] and saw through me, still as the iron wedge I sat on, dark in a cool place. He could not see into the shadow" (81). Using Sophie's body to deflect attention away from her own, Pauline seems to achieve the kind of invisibility that she associates with invulnerability after Fleur's rape. In the scenes that follow, Sophie and Eli come together in a passionate encounter that Pauline claims to have orchestrated herself.

As the encounter proceeds, however, the dynamics of rape from which Pauline attempts to escape reassert themselves:

> And then, as I crouched in the cove of leaves, I turned my thoughts on the girl and entered her and made her do what she could never dream of herself. I stood her in the broken straws and she stepped over Eli, one leg on either side of his chest. Standing there, she slowly hiked her skirt. . . .

> She shivered and I dug my fingers through the tough claws of sumac, through the wood-sod, clutched bark, shrank backward into her pleasure. . . . He lifted her and brought her to the water. She stood rooted, dazed, not alert enough to strip off her dress. . . . She waited in shallow mud, then waded in, obedient. . . . He ran his mouth over her face, bit her shoulder through the cloth, held her head back by the pale brown strands and licked her throat. He pulled her hips against him, her skirt floating like a flower. Sophie shuddered, her eyes rolled to the whites. . . .
>
> (83-84)

Although Sophie participates in this encounter physically as she straddles Eli, hikes her skirt, and wades into the water, the absence of any sense of will or volition on her part exaggerates Eli's violent manipulations of her pliable body; as he bites her shoulder, holds her head back by the hair and pulls her hips against him, Sophie not only fails to "throw off" his glance but loses the power of her own vision; "her eyes rolled to the whites," Sophie's presence in the scene is reduced to that of a mechanical puppet or a frightened animal.

Although it is Eli who physically manipulates Sophie's body, Pauline casts herself as the orchestrator of this scene of violation. Physically distanced from the scene, Pauline emerges not only as its observer but as its author; in her representation of the event she, rather than Sophie, remains the subject of an encounter that Sophie "could never dream of herself." The powerlessness that Pauline experiences during Fleur's rape results in her attempt to sever the subject/body connection that makes her vulnerable to male manipulation. As her mind is "cloaked together" with Sophie's body in this scene, however, the result is not an escape from the dynamics of rape but a reinscription of them. Detached from her own body, Pauline uses her imagination to violate Sophie—"I turned my thoughts on the girl and entered her." Having "entered" Sophie, "stood" her on the straw, and made her behave in ways she cannot understand, Pauline strips Sophie of her presence and reduces the body that she appropriated for its strength to the form of a lifeless puppet: "They [Sophie and Eli] were not allowed to stop. . . . I was pitiless. They were mechanical things, toys, dolls wound past their limits" (84). By robbing Sophie of her subjectivity and making her assume the postures of another's will, Pauline serves as the orchestrator of yet another rape. As long as she is unable to imagine sexual intercourse without violation, Pauline can achieve pleasure only by placing someone else in the position of experiencing pain. By the conclusion of this scene,

Sophie's "careless and fledgling" form becomes weakened and physically vulnerable, her body the object of Pauline's physical as well as imaginative manipulation: "she [Sophie] sank to her knees in the sour mud, hung her mouth open and went limp so I had to drag her" (84).

In the attempt to escape from the vulnerability of her own body, Pauline not only recreates the dynamics of rape and reduces Sophie to the role of powerless victim but offers herself no lasting access to invulnerability. As long as she remains attached imaginatively to Sophie's body, Pauline cannot sever her connection to Sophie's pain. After Sophie returns home, Pauline relates, "I heard [Bernadette] laying into Sophie with a strap, and I felt it, too, the way I'd absorbed the pleasure at the slough, the way I felt everything that happened to Fleur" (86). Ultimately, the kind of detachment that Pauline longs for escapes her; her attempt to liberate herself from her own body by attaching herself to another form fails. As Sophie and Eli come together before her eyes, the woman who envisioned herself as "hunched" in her body remains "crouched in the cove of leaves," the cramped posture of her body asserting its uncomfortable material presence even in the midst of a scene over which Pauline claims imaginative control.

For the reader, then, Pauline's body emerges as the one stable presence in a scene that propels the reader toward what Catherine Rainwater describes in another context as "an hermeneutical impasse" (410). Because the reader's access to the bodies of Eli and Sophie is only through the path of Pauline's mind, it is impossible to disentangle the material dynamics of their encounter from her imaginative rendering of it; the reader is suspended between a natural and supernatural interpretation of the scene. If, as Pauline claims, she has a mystical control over Sophie's mind, then an imaginative form of rape occurs: "I turned my thoughts on the girl and entered her." If Pauline simply projects her obsessions on two lovers, as the text sometimes seems to suggest, issues of violence and consent associated with any sexual encounter between an adult and a minor still haunt the scene and are unearthed by Pauline's portrayal. The reader of Fleur's rape cannot know if an act of violence occurred; the reader of Sophie and Eli's encounter cannot know whether the act that occurred was violence. As in the portrayal of Fleur's rape, interpretive issues so encircle this portrayal that the process of representation becomes foregrounded and the material dynamics of violation obscured.

Pauline's attempt to escape the dynamics of violation underlies not only her sexual manipulation of Sophie and Eli but her decision to reject her cultural heritage and embrace the tenets of Catholicism. In responding to a statue of the Virgin Mary, Pauline recontextualizes Christian myth by situating Mary's experience within the paradigms of sexual violation rather than religious epiphany:

> Perhaps, I thought, at first, the Virgin shed tears . . . because She herself had never . . . been touched, never known the shackling heat of flesh. Then later, after Napoleon and I met again and again, after I came to him in ignorance, after I could not resist more than a night without his body, which was hard, pitiless, but so warm slipping out of me that tears always formed in my eyes, I knew that the opposite was true.

> The sympathy of Her knowledge had caused Her response. In God's spiritual embrace She experienced a loss more ruthless than we can imagine. She wept, pinned full-weight to the earth, known in the brain and known in the flesh and planted like dirt. She did not want Him, or was thoughtless like Sophie, and young, frightened at the touch of His great hand upon Her mind.

(95)

Pauline's appropriation of the vocabulary of sexual violation rather than religious symbolism highlights Mary's experience as "the Virgin" and rewrites "God's spiritual embrace" as a form of rape. Tracing the loss the Virgin experiences at the hand of God to the connection between body and subject, Pauline reveals the extent to which the physical violation of rape is inextricably tied to the violator's assault on female subjectivity. The blurring of material and psychological categories in Pauline's description of the Virgin's rape reveals the double empowerment of the male violator and the consequently heightened vulnerability of his female victim. Like Napoleon, God seems to possess a physical solidity that marks his body as an extension of his power; imaged here in material as well as spiritual terms, God enacts his wishes by touching his frightened victim with "His great hand."

The strength of materiality that the male violator displays here, however, is not attended by the consequent limitations of spatial and physical boundaries. "[F]rightened at the touch of His great hand upon Her mind," the young Virgin is the victim of an assault that seems to acknowledge no proper division of surface or category. The male God is capable of penetrating the Virgin Mary's mind as well as her body; it is the double-edged aspect of this rape that makes the loss she experiences "more ruthless" than can be imagined. In an inversion of the violator's position, the victim is bound by the limitations of a materiality which controls her but over which she has no control: "She wept, pinned full-weight to the earth, known in the brain and known in the flesh and planted like dirt." Never directly imaged, the Virgin's body exists only as a negative presence that restricts, defines, and fixes her. "Pinned" and "planted" to her physical form, she is attached to a body over which she is denied autonomy. Her "flesh" becomes an extended surface through which the violator can access her vulnerable subjectivity, but not a means of extending her own will into space.

Napoleon's ability to penetrate Pauline's skin with his gaze, to dissolve what she images as the boundary between body and subject, is reenacted here as the Virgin Mary is "known in the brain and known in the flesh." In playing on the biblical connotations of the verb "to know," this passage forges a connection between the rapist's assault on the body and the corresponding assault on subjectivity figured here as knowledge of the victim's brain. Both forms of intimacy involve a penetration of boundaries that the subject uses to define herself, a cooptation of being that dissolves the autonomous self as it erases the physical space between violator and victim. As the physiological penetration of the victim's body allows the violator literally to come inside her, rape is experienced as a form of self-destruction marked by the subject's seeming complicity in her own violation.

Pauline's response to her own body during and after Fleur's rape can best be understood as a response to the dynamics of rape revealed through her representation of the Virgin Mary. Pauline's attempt to make her body invisible during the rape results from her panicked recognition of its visibility and her resulting vulnerability. Describing herself as "hunched" in her form, Pauline reveals imagistically the tension she experiences between her body and the subject "contained" within it; the parameters of her body seem not only to constrain the presentation of herself as subject but to fix her in a hostile space and prevent her from dissolving into nonbeing. It is through her body that Pauline, like the Virgin, is "pinned full-weight to the earth," reduced to an object that can be seen and known not only in the flesh but in the brain. Her wariness of her own body, then, results in part from the fact that it exists as a text that she never authors but through which others are free to read into her subjectivity as well as her materiality.[7]

As the novel continues, Pauline devises other strategies to escape her vulnerability, each of which results in an equally destructive conclusion. In her desire to avoid being defined, fixed, either as woman or as Native American, Pauline attempts to disavow the body which bears traces that others can use to construct her identity. Rather than asserting authorship of a body that has been misread and manipulated, Pauline attempts to liberate herself by destroying the physical form that others view as text. Such a desperate claim to empowerment, however, perpetuates the very dynamics that it seeks to overturn; having internalized a hegemonic system of interpretation, Pauline engages in numerous acts of self-violation that merely reinforce the dominant culture's reading of a body over which she is unable to claim the power of signification.

Because it is not merely physical but emotional assault that she fears, not merely the violation of the body but a corresponding violation of the mind, Pauline attempts to preserve some semblance of autonomy by defining herself as the agent of her own assault. Unsuccessful in her attempt to sever the connection between herself as subject and her physical form, she attempts instead to define and control that connection. By willing the destruction of a body she is incapable of rendering invulnerable to violation, she attempts to use that body to reassert the power of a subjectivity equally threatened. In doing so, Pauline turns to the Christian ideology of self-sacrifice as rationale for embracing the role of self-violator:

> At the convent my hands cracked. The knuckles were tight and scabbed. . . . At night, I did not allow myself to toss or turn for comfort, but only to sleep on my back, arms crossed on my breasts in the same position as the Virgin received the attentions of our Lord. . . . I put burrs in the armpits of my dress and screwgrass in my stockings and nettles in my neckband. . . . I let my toenails grow until it ached to walk. . . .
>
> (151-52)

By willingly embracing her status as victim of physical pain, Pauline attempts to reduce violation to its material origin and preempt any corresponding assault on her subjectivity. Having figured the Virgin Mary's impregnation as a type of rape, Pauline casts herself in the Virgin's role not mentally but physically; her literalist attempt to recreate the physical configurations of the assault—she sleeps on her back with arms crossed on her breasts "in the same position as the Virgin"—functions as a means of deflecting the real horror of a violation the physical consequences of which are but one small component. Pauline's efforts to manipulate, mark, and assault her body represent a negative form of empowerment through which she attempts to preempt the force of a violation she sees as inevitable.

Whereas the Christian mode of sacrifice that Pauline appropriates as her model is aimed at destroying individual subjectivity to effect a greater union with God, Pauline's self-destructive actions function as an attempt to reclaim the power of her own subjectivity from the domination of others. In choosing to suffer at her own hand, Pauline removes her body from beneath the hands of the violator, be he man or God. Embracing a physical pain that she sees as in some sense inevitable, Pauline uses suffering to affirm her presence and reconstitute herself as subject:

> That night in the convent bed, I knew God had no foothold or sway in this land, or no mercy for the just, or that perhaps, for all my suffering and faith, I was still insignificant. Which seemed impossible.
>
> I knew there never was a martyr like me.
>
> I was hollow unless pain filled me, empty but for pain. . . .
>
> (192)

In the context of Pauline's earlier fear that the male gaze would strip away her skin to reveal the hollowness within, her body continually threatened to open up into a revelation of absence. Here, she reveals the strategy by which she has seemingly reclaimed that body as a tool to affirm her presence. Pauline invokes the self-abnegating vocabulary of Christianity only to undercut it; the pain that she has embraced functions not to erase her presence as subject but to reveal the impossibility that she is "still insignificant." If earlier in the novel she as subject was reduced to an object constructed by the male gaze, here her fundamental emptiness is filled only by the pain that she embraces.

Pauline's fear of being "skinned" beneath the male gaze results from a sense of her own insubstantiality as subject; even the bones that "push" at her flesh are defined by motion rather than constancy, contributing to the image of Pauline's form as malleable material unrestricted by a defining structure, be it the parameters of a subject position or the constraints of a skeleton (73). Instead of choosing to use such elasticity to construct herself as subject, however, Pauline burns away the physical flexibility that marks, in her mind, a malleability of self. Despite excruciating pain, she deliberately submerges her hands in boiling water, literally skinning herself so that others will be unable to skin her:

> Later, when the binding was excruciatingly changed, I shed a skin with the dirty wrapping. Every few days I shed another, yet another, and I drank or ate whatever my Sisters brought, I fattened in bed, took on subtle heft. . . . New flesh grew upon my hands, smooth and pink as a baby's, only tighter, with no give to it, a stiff and shrunken fabric, so that my fingers webbed and doubled over like a hatchling's claws.
>
> (195-96)

Unable to free herself of the skin that in her mind marks the margin between subject and body, Pauline attempts to limit others' ability to access her through it. The "new flesh" that results from her act of self-violation is no longer flexible skin that can be made or remade into many different configurations. This skin is defining, taut, a "stiff and shrunken fabric" that cripples the movement and autonomy of the subject who wears it, but resists the manipulation of others. Pauline has remade her own body in such a way that it cannot be taken from her; in doing so, however, she sacrifices its ability to enact her will or desire. The price of her invulnerability is the loss of the nerves that link the subject with the physical world. Her hands encased in scar tissue, Pauline locks herself within her body even as she locks others out.

Only by burning away her skin is Pauline able to create for herself a body that speaks the kind of invulnerability she associates with whiteness as well as maleness. Pauline describes the members of her family as "mixed-bloods, skinners in the clan for which the name was lost" (14). The slang term "skinners" suggests both Pauline's sense of entrapment within a skin that can be identified as half-white by Native Americans and half-Indian by whites, and her fear of being "plucked and skinned," having the self beneath the skin revealed to the world.

Just as the models through which Pauline attempts to liberate herself from the vulnerable female body are inexorably structured around the dynamics of rape, so the models she chooses to liberate herself from the racial body are structured around and lead toward racial oppression. Having chosen the Virgin Mary and Christian mysticism as her models, Pauline is forced to embrace a hegemonic logic that leads racially to genocide just as it leads physically to self-mutilation. Directed by Christ to "fetch more" Indian souls for his heaven, Pauline states that that "is what I intended by going out among them with the net of my knowledge. He gave me the mission to name and baptize, to gather souls. Only I must give myself away in return, I must dissolve. I did so eagerly" (141). With her "net of knowledge," Pauline intends to gather the spirits of dead Indians, pulling their souls away from their bodies to a foreign yet more powerful culture where they will be met by the figure of Christ "dressed in glowing white" (140). In gathering up the souls of her community and collecting them for a white God, Pauline "gives herself away" even as she snatches up the souls of others. Her eagerness to distance herself from the racial identity that in her own mind defines her is reflected in the verb that she chooses to describe the process of losing herself; Pauline literally wants to "dissolve," to break down her body so thoroughly that it can be reconstituted in a form of her own making.

Having mutilated and destroyed the body that marks her as Other, however, Pauline is still unable to distance herself sufficiently from her Native American identity. In the effort to eliminate every trace of her connection, she makes one last trip to a homeland that she now describes as "the kingdom of the damned":

> I had told Superior this would be my one last visit to Matchimanito before the day of my entrance as novice, after which I would repudiate my former life. I knew I would not see Pillagers, Kashpaws, or old Nanapush again after that. . . . They could starve and fornicate . . . worship the bones of animals. . . . I would have none of it. I would be chosen, His own, wiped clean of Fleur's cool even hand on my brow, purged of the slide of Napoleon's thighs. . . .
>
> (196)

In her eagerness to "repudiate [her] former life," Pauline translates the haunting attachments that she cannot escape psychologically into physical images that render them visible and manipulable. Pauline's desire to be "wiped clean" or "purged" of Fleur's hand and Napoleon's thigh is really a desire to escape the sense of vulnerability that the presence of each elicits in her; once again, the body emerges as the material surface on which Pauline projects conflicts of the mind. Having inflicted violence upon her own body, she uses that "purged" form to engage in a physical battle with the Indians, a battle that serves as the culmination of her war with her own racial and gendered self.

As she leaves the convent to pilot herself into the midst of the lake with her scarred hands, Pauline for the first time defines her body by its strength rather than vulnerability: "naked in my own flesh . . . I tumbled forward when the boat slammed on shore, scrambled upright on the balls of my feet, ready and strong as a young man" (201). No longer experiencing her body as an object created by the male gaze, Pauline likens herself to a young man and asserts her nakedness as a strength rather than a weakness. Her probing gaze now penetrates the bodies of others to unveil their fragility and randomness; looking to the shore, she describes the bodies of the people she sees: "They were such small foolish sticks strung together with cloth that in the heat of my sudden hilarity I nearly tumbled over the side . . ." (197). For the first time in the novel, other bodies seem contingent to Pauline while her own appears essential; beneath her gaze, individual subjects fragment into images of "small foolish sticks" connected not of necessity or reason but "strung together" haphazardly. Although Pauline's shrunken hands pin her within her body in much the same way that the "great hand" of God pins Mary to the earth, she experiences this self-inflicted limitation as liberation. Pauline's response to her physical mutilation cannot be understood outside the dynamics of rape revealed in her discussion of the Virgin Mary; the inviolability she associates with masculine power is an experience of mind as well as body. "This," she claims, "was how God felt: beyond hindrance or reach" (197-98).

Having boiled away the skin that would lend others access to the subject she sees "contained" within it, Pauline now experiences herself as invulnerable to the manipulation of others; she proclaims her own strength by asserting Fleur's weakness: "I was important, beyond their reach, even Fleur's though she must have been hiding in the cabin, weakened by my act, for I caught no glimpse of her" (198). Pauline's hostility toward Fleur may be traced to her identification with her; in order to assert her own strength, Pauline must obliterate her connection to Fleur. Her attempt to do so, however, is as unsuccessful as her attempt to render herself inviolable by destroying her own body. With the newfound strength of a body she images as masculine, Pauline turns against Fleur only to emerge as the victim of her own assault:

> I screamed at her, but the wind flattened out my words.
>
> Her figure swelled into relief, as if the force of my yell enlarged her. Her hair was covered by a scarf white and brilliant as the moon rising. . . . But the rest of her was planted tight. Her heavy black clothes, her shawl, the way she held herself so rigid, suggested a door into blackness.
>
> I stood before it and then she turned, so slowly I heard the hinges creak. A moment and I was inside where I could not breathe and water filled me, cold and black water of the drowned, a currentless blanket. I thought I would be shut there, but she turned again and off she walked, a black

slot into the air, a passage into herself. A crushing sadness. I was glad when night approached.

(200)

In its allusions to a vocabulary of rape present throughout the text, this passage appears at first to reinforce Pauline's notion of her own empowerment by defining her voice as the "force" that swells Fleur's figure. As Fleur's body appears to enlarge in response to Pauline's words, it loses its solidity to become a flexible form shaped by the violence of Pauline's will. Fleur's malleability is accompanied by an entrapment within the confines of the physical; like Sophie and the Virgin Mary, Fleur too emerges as "planted," pinned in one place by her physical form. Defined by the confines of a physicality that simultaneously restricts her motion but allows others to access her, Fleur's body becomes both a "black slot" defined by emptiness and a "passage into herself" through which others can manipulate her subjectivity, or the emptiness that emerges in its place.

In order to appropriate the violator's power to effect such manipulation, however, Pauline must detach herself from Fleur to claim a psychological as well as a physical distance from the victim's subjectivity. Although Fleur's figure seems to swell in response to the "force" of Pauline's yell, that force turns against Pauline. Unable to overcome her identification with the victim, Pauline herself is imaged as swollen, "filled" with the "cold and black water of the drowned" in the same way that she was "filled" with Fleur's cries of pain during the rape (26). Pauline's self-conscious repudiation of her female body, like her rejection of her racial self, barely masks a knowledge of her own vulnerability that turns her every act of violence into a form of self-violation. Because she continues to define herself as Other even as she projects that Otherness onto an external force that she attempts to destroy, it is not only Fleur but Pauline who is "weakened by [Pauline's] act." Although Pauline gratefully embraces the coming of the night, then, its darkness will fail to obscure distinctions that emerge not from the visible configurations of bodies but from the constructed notions of identity that Pauline cannot escape.

The futility of Pauline's attempt to render herself invulnerable by repositioning herself within the dynamics of violation rather than rejecting them becomes most apparent in her attack on Napoleon. Pauline's murder of Napoleon enacts in visible terms the violence of her attempt to "repudiate" her Native American self; in her increasingly desperate effort to destroy her connection with her Native American background,

she mutilates and murders the Indian "devil" who would defy her white God. The carefully mapped racial and religious symbolism of this scene may overwhelm the reader's understanding of its gender dynamics. Pauline's newfound confidence in her body not only leads her to image herself as male but to image her murder of Napoleon as a rape in which she is cast in the role of violator rather than victim:

> There was an odd pleasure to the tiny stinging blows and in the words, which tightened me from nape to heels. . . . I felt his breath, a thin stream that swept along my collarbone and my throat as we crushed close. And then I seized him and forced myself upon him, grew around him like the earth around a root, held him still.
>
> . . . He began to pound beneath me like a driving wind and I went dizzy with the effort of holding on, light and dry as a fistful of matches. He rose, shoved me against a scoured log, rubbed me up and down until I struck. I screamed once and then my tongue flapped loose, yelled profane curses. I stuffed the end of the blanket in his mouth, pushed him down into the sand and then fell upon him and devoured him, scattered myself in all directions, stupefied my own brain in the process so thoroughly that the only things left of intelligence were my doubled-over hands.
>
> What I told them to do, then, they accomplished. My fingers closed like hasps of iron, locked on the strong rosary chain, wrenched and twisted the beads close about his neck until his face darkened and he lunged away. I hung on while he bucked and gagged and finally fell, his long tongue dragging down my thighs.
>
> I kicked and kicked away the husk, drove it before me with the blows of my feet.

(202)

This act, like Pauline's initial juxtaposition of her own strength with Fleur's weakness, seems to reflect Pauline's newfound empowerment. Pauline's representation evokes the vocabulary of sexual violence to image a scene in which two bodies, "crushed close," are described as "tightening," "pounding," and "driving" against one another. The rape that plagues Pauline throughout most of the novel is reenacted in this final scene. This time, however, Pauline emerges as the violator rather than the helpless observer; "I seized him," she proclaims, "and forced myself upon him." The assault on subjectivity that is part of rape is also recreated here; as Pauline the character forces herself upon Napoleon, Pauline the narrator delays even the acknowledgment of her victim's identity until after she has murdered him.

In recasting her role within the rape scenario rather than rejecting the dynamics of rape, however, Pauline moves once again into the domain of self-violation. When she attacks Napoleon, the imagery of Pauline's narrative suggests that the violation is double-edged. For most of the representation Pauline, while the aggressor, emerges not as the actor but as the individual being acted upon. Napoleon's motions are described with direct action verbs: he pounds, shoves, and rubs her. When Pauline "strikes," on the other hand, her action emerges only as a reaction to Napoleon's physical manipulation: "He rose, shoved me against a scoured log, rubbed me up and down until I struck." Pauline's actions seem only to reinforce the solidity and stability of Napoleon's body. When she says that she "forced [herself] upon him, grew around him like the earth around a root," her body is the one being transformed. The word "force" does not suggest one form imprinting itself upon another, but a form molding itself to another; even as Pauline "rapes" Napoleon, she is unable to escape the malleability that defines the victim's experience of violence. Although Pauline goes on to "devour" Napoleon, he does not dissolve; rather, Pauline herself fragments as her interior is bruised and broken outward: "I pushed him down into the sand and then fell upon him and devoured him, scattered myself in all directions, stupefied my own brain in the process." In this representation, "devouring" emerges as a form of self-violation, just as "force" emerges as a form of weakness; Pauline's categories of identity have become so self-destructive that her very means of expression has inverted.

Even as Pauline casts herself as rapist, then, her experience seems closer to that of the rape victim. The character who lamented Mary's pain as she was "known in the brain and known in the flesh" becomes the agent of a similarly double-edged assault against herself; as Pauline attacks Napoleon, she also attacks herself, not only damaging her body but "stupefying" her "own brain." Throughout the book Pauline has sought to break the intimate connection between body and subject, hoping to achieve the violator's status of physical power and emotional inviolability. Having envisioned the body as the physical locus of a subjectivity always vulnerable to assault, Pauline effects her liberation only by becoming the victim of a "rape" that she herself initiates. Whereas Fleur's body serves as "a passage into herself," Pauline's body now appears to bear no trace of her existence as subject. Having "scattered [her]self in all directions," Pauline can no longer be located in or through her body: "the only things left of intelligence," she claims, "were my doubled-over hands." Whereas before she violated

her body to forestall the possibility of others' violation, here she assaults the very connection between mind and body, "stupefying" the synapses that register physical pain and psychological violation just as she burned the nerves from her hands. Pauline's hands—like the hands of men, of God, of the Pillagers—now appear to serve as an extension of her power rather than a sign of her vulnerability. "What I told them to do, then," she observes, "they accomplished. My fingers closed like hasps of iron . . ." (202). Her body, no longer a passageway to the self, is imaged here as a tool that she controls as if from a distance.

Pauline's newfound distance from her body allows her to finger her own wounds with a kind of detached bemusement. Having seemingly forestalled any assault on her subjectivity, she now views her body as a surface on which the marks of physical violation are inscribed in imagistic patterns: "I had committed no sin. . . . I could certainly prove that over doubt, for I was marked here and there, pocked as if we'd rolled through embers, stamped by his molten scales in odd reddened circles, in bruises of moons and stars" (203). Pauline's detachment from her body culminates in her aesthetic rendering of the marks of her own violation. Citing her wounded body as evidence of Napoleon's assault, Pauline claims the bruises and abrasions on her body as a register of the legitimacy of her violence but not a register of her own pain. Pauline's strategic assertion of her connection to this wounded body is a tactic for further empowerment; having severed the essential link between body and subject, she appears to reclaim that bond at will even as she continues to reject the vulnerability coincident with it. For perhaps the first time, Pauline reads her body as a text the signification of which she controls.

The motion away from materiality and into textuality also defines the reader's initial experience of Pauline's assault on Napoleon. The mythic tone and surrealistic imagery of Pauline's representation intensify the reader's confusion about agency and materiality in the text. While this assault is represented, unlike Fleur's rape, the representation invokes so many imaginative and literary conventions, so unsettles the line between mind and body and victim and violator, that the reader is distanced from its material dynamics. The physically exhausted and mentally unstable Pauline begins her assault on Misshepeshu by dropping a rock from the boat, and seeing it wake the monster "in [her] mind" (197). Encountering the monster on land she is blinded by the fire and sees "double, or not at all in the flickering glow"

(202). In the representation that follows, the reader also seems to see double or not at all, never knowing quite how the bodies represented are making contact, and whether these bodies operate by material laws or by some supernatural dynamism.

Although at times the representation seems to push toward a revelation of material bodies, the reader cannot assume that physical effects will follow from physical causes. Physical wounds are not enumerated; the violence instead batters Pauline's "self" and "brain." Material forms are replaced by images of roots, wind, matches, and logs, and even words become "black lake pebbles." As the categories of mind and body that separate dream from reality and words from objects are lost, the reader experiences the representation as a dynamic but primarily semiotic experience in which the empirical dynamics of violence emerge only in a murky, confusing light. Catherine Rainwater discusses the way in which the reader's experience of Pauline's narrative is complicated by the intersection of conflicting Christian and Native American religious codes.[8] That experience, I would argue, is complicated here by the way in which the narrative unsettles epistemological and hermeneutic distinctions encoded in Western conventions of reading. As Pauline's narrative moves freely from material to immaterial categories, the reader searches for a single interpretive frame that will reconcile a representation that is neither realistic nor fantastical.

When, at the end of the portrayal, the fantastical Misshepeshu emerges as the very real and very dead Napoleon Morrissey, however, the reader is suddenly propelled toward recognition of the material consequences of Pauline's act:

> I kicked and kicked away the husk, drove it before me with the blows of my feet. A light began to open in the sky and the thing grew a human shape, one that I recognized in gradual stages. Eventually, it took on the physical form of Napoleon Morrissey.
>
> As the dawn broadened, as the fire shrank and smoldered, I examined each feature and confirmed it for the truth. . . .
>
> There was hard work to do, then. I dragged him by the suspenders down a crooked path, into the woods, and left him in high weeds.
>
> (202-203)

As the "husk" that Pauline kicks before her is transformed into the heavy materiality of Napoleon's "physical form," the reader is forced to revise his or her perception of Pauline's assault on Misshepeshu.[9] Pauline continues to insist that Napoleon's body may or may not be present: "How could I have known what body the devil would assume?" (203). For the reader, however, the revelation of the violated body also reveals how far toward a purely semiotic conception of violence the reader has been pushed by Pauline's confusion of material and immaterial categories. As Pauline recognizes the need to drag Napoleon's body into the woods, her description of that act as "hard work" exposes not only the material weightiness of Napoleon's body but the contrast between the difficult task of hauling that body away and the apparent ease with which she almost magically murdered her victim. As the reader is propelled toward an acknowledgment of the empirical dynamics of violation, what seemed a symbolic reenactment of a possibly imaginary rape emerges as a representation of murder.

The reader's awareness of the material, victimized body in the text thus undercuts Pauline's subsequent, and apparently victorious, attempts to efface her own materiality by literally reconstructing her physical form:

> . . . then I realized I was still naked, with no covering. I rolled in slough mud until my arms and breasts, every part of me was coated. . . . I was a poor and noble creature now, dressed in earth like Christ, in furs like Moses Pillager, draped in snow or simple air. . . . I rolled in dead leaves, in moss, in defecation of animals. I plastered myself with dry leaves and the feathers of a torn bird . . . so that by the time I came to the convent . . . I was nothing human, nothing victorious, nothing like myself. I was no more than a piece of the woods.
>
> (203-204)

Even as it displays Pauline's apparent liberation from the confines of her bodily form, this passage reveals her inability to escape completely from the assumptions of biological determinism. Although she seems to claim the power of resignification that allows her to make her body speak for her, Pauline is able to do so only after she obliterates all trace of her actual physical form. As she undertakes to remake herself as subject, the lengths to which she goes to obscure her body reveal her fear of its betrayal. Only when "every part of [her]" is "coated" with mud—the breasts that define her as woman, the dark skin that marks her as Indian—is Pauline able to reclaim her body as the ground from which to assert herself as subject. After rolling in slough mud, Pauline images herself not as a woman covered with grime but as a being "draped in snow or simple air." Such rhetoric moves toward a myth of origin, a rhetoric of purity and simplicity through which Pauline recasts herself as a "poor and noble creature" freshly created. Pauline's every effort to create herself anew as subject, however, is hampered by her need to destroy a self that she sees inscribed on her body each time she looks in a mirror or into the eyes of another.

Here, as earlier in the novel, Pauline's claim to subjectivity is deeply entangled with her attitude toward a body that she must destroy or obscure before she can make it speak for her. Pauline's essentialist assumptions about the body dictate that even the most self-conscious manipulations of her physical form emerge in the shadow of a body that speaks the powerlessness of race and gender. Because the body that she images as "draped in snow" will continue to bear the traces of the dominant story that she has whited out, Pauline's every act of assertion must be accompanied by an act of erasure. As long as she continues to read the inscriptions of a hegemonic culture on her form, Pauline's claim to the power of signification remains a purely negative one; "I was," she asserts at the end of this scene, "nothing human, nothing victorious, nothing like myself" (204).

Pauline's long struggle to remove herself from the disempowered, easily violated position of an embodied Native American woman in a white patriarchal culture seems to her to have succeeded. The reader is aware, however, that the mechanisms Pauline chooses to avoid violation simply victimize her again. Pauline falls prey to the fact that her subjectivity can be constructed by others, but at the same time she has imbibed the notion that the body determines the self. Rather than trying to resignify the socially constructed self, Pauline accepts these social constructions; the only way she sees to live with her body is to sever body, which bears the marks of race and gender, from self. Pauline undertakes the severing process with the only models available to her: rape of physically vulnerable women by men, Christian mortification of the flesh, and the destruction of Native American spiritual culture through white cultural imperialism. The book records the crossing and recrossing of these modes of oppression and self-violation, and the transitional points in Pauline's life—Fleur's rape, her vision of the Virgin Mary, her murder of Napoleon, and her final induction into the convent—all involve such nexuses.

This is not to say that in the book rape serves as a metaphor for racism, or vice versa, or even that the two are mutually reflexive symbols. Erdrich offers us a character suffering from both racial and gender disempowerment who manages to combine them into a single set of symbols, and allows us to witness how racial and gender op-

pression can work together in a dynamic of psychological self-violation. Rather than simply despising Pauline for the absurd lengths to which her denial of identity takes her, Erdrich asks us to understand how the fear of rape, arising out of physical embodiment, can interact with the sense of disempowerment and bodily self-consciousness promulgated by racism.

Pauline's efforts to create a new subject, an "I," that is "nothing like [her]self" culminate in her return to the convent and her decision to take the veil.[10] Such a decision involves not only a denial of her culture and a rejection of her past but a literal veiling of her body and redefinition of her identity. For Pauline, whose deterministic assumptions about race, gender, and the body have consistently undercut her efforts to create herself anew, the Catholic church seems to offer a ready-made identity that extends even to the level of a new name. Having donned the "camphor-smelling robes" of the nun, Pauline goes forward to draw a name from the Mother Superior's hand:

> I prayed before I spread the scrap of paper in air. I asked for the grace to accept, to leave Pauline behind, to remember that my name, any name was no more than a crumbling skin.
>
> *Leopolda.* I tried out the unfamiliar syllables. They fit. They cracked in my ears like a fist through ice. (205)

In this passage, Pauline reveals her essentialist assumptions even as she attempts to deny them. While the insubstantiality of the scrap of paper and the arbitrary process of selection point to the social constructedness of identity, Pauline's description of the ritual points the reader back toward an essential link between name and subject or body and subject. She does not ask for the grace to "leave the name 'Pauline' behind" but simply to "leave Pauline behind"; the signifier of her name blends in the reader's mind with the person that it identifies, suggesting that she could not abandon the name without abandoning the person.

Even Pauline's assertion that a name is "no more than a crumbling skin" dissolves into its opposite as the terms of Pauline's metaphor jar uneasily with the reader's experience of the novel. Paralleling the name with the body, Pauline asserts that neither is capable of determining identity. Her description of the body's insubstantiality, however, is belied by the violence of her earlier efforts to destroy her physical form; the words "crumbling skin" strike a reader who has witnessed Pauline's brutal attempts to contain, cover, and burn away her own skin as eerily passive.

Racial and gender issues meet at the nexus of violence because, Erdrich shows us, essentialist assumptions about the relationship between body and self generate violence from within and from without. The violent oppression of the Native Americans justified by the essentialism of white culture is paralleled and exaggerated by Pauline's more subtle and intimate form of essentialist violence. Pauline's story emerges as a perverted *bildungsroman,* the tale of a young woman who overcomes the disadvantages of her birth to access a position of some power in the dominant culture; given Pauline's assumption of an essential link between body and subject as well as the pervasive racism and sexism of her society, however, such success can only come through violence perpetrated against the body to which inhere the disadvantages of birth. Pauline succeeds at overcoming her Native American identity and her female vulnerability only through a form of self-violation that ultimately reinscribes rather than reverses her powerlessness. To have done otherwise would have involved a level of self-consciousness about the social construction of identity and power not available to a young Native American woman who continues to see, in her own words, "through the eyes of the world outside us."

The body in *Tracks,* then, emerges as a material presence on which Pauline projects her essentialist notions of race and gender and a narrative absence seldom acknowledged in the reader's semiotic construction of the novel's violence. Pauline's narrative points to a definition of intimate violence that acknowledges its material and immaterial consequences; "known in the brain and known in the flesh," the victim of violence is assaulted not only as body but as subject. Pauline's attempt to preserve her subjectivity by manipulating the materiality of her body represents one response to these dynamics; because she fails to acknowledge the way in which that body's significance is constructed by the interpretation of a hegemonic culture, however, Pauline's material manipulations of her form fail to lend her the inviolability that she seeks. The reader ignores the materiality of the vulnerable body to focus on the way in which it is constructed in the act of representation; the reader's concentration on Fleur's rape as a literary or symbolic phenomenon may blind him or her to the dynamics of violation that the text naturalizes. As Pauline fails to recognize the textuality of the body, then, the reader may fail to acknowledge the materiality of the text. Critical analyses of the novel that ignore

its representations of intimate violence in favor of a symbolic recasting of the material dynamics of violation accept the narrative's semiotic invitation without recognizing its potentially radical unsettling of the very process of semiosis. Caught between the materiality of violence and its semiotic construction, the reader who charts the dangers of Pauline's essentialist response to the violability of the body must also be wary of completely dematerializing a violence the dynamics of which return us, not only as victims but as readers, to the urgent presence of the vulnerable body.

Notes

1. Pauline's narration, of course, represents only one of two narrative perspectives in the novel; for a discussion of the way in which Nanapush's narrative "masters" Pauline, see Daniel Cornell, "Woman Looking."

2. Although Fleur is the actual victim of rape, its effects are registered only through Pauline's presence in the novel. Fleur remains seemingly intact and emerges as a kind of romance figure whose mysterious presence in the novel lends her an aura of invulnerability to the material dynamics of rape. Pauline can thus be seen as Fleur's surrogate, the character who exposes the consequences of a rape written out of the romance world associated with Fleur in the novel. In the argument that follows, I will focus on Pauline's function in the novel, addressing Fleur's presence only as it relates to Pauline's experience. (My thanks to Andy Von Hendy for his discussion of Fleur.)

3. As Lorraine Gamman and Margaret Marshment point out, for example, psychoanalytic criticism's emphasis on gender as "the category which structures perspective" ignores other forms of power relations which also underlie processes of identification and objectification in narrative fictions (7). See also Jane Gaines, "White Privilege and Looking Relations."

4. See Catherine Rainwater, "Reading between Worlds"; James Flavin, "The Novel as Performance"; Victoria Walker, "A Note on Perspective in *Tracks.*" The most recent critical essay on *Tracks* is the first to focus extensively on gender as well as race; see Daniel Cornell, "Woman Looking."

5. For a useful discussion of the symbolic imagination in Native American culture, see Paula Gunn Allen, *The Sacred Hoop.* Allen argues that "Symbols in American Indian systems . . . articulate . . . that reality where thought and feeling are one, where objective and subjective are one, where speaker and listener are one . . ." (71).

6. See Daniel Cornell, "Woman Looking." This absence is particularly interesting given the title of Cornell's article; the rape is not only the one event that Pauline is unable to "look" at but, I would argue, the single most important event underlying her attempts to revise her subject position.

7. The comparison between Mary and Sophie with which this passage ends points to the way in which Pauline's efforts to escape her own body have implicated her in

the dynamics of violation that she here attempts to unveil. Like the Virgin Mary, who is "planted like dirt," her mind as well as her body assaulted by a male God, Sophie is stripped of her will and planted in shallow mud through Pauline's machinations; once there, "She stood rooted, dazed, not alert enough to strip off her dress" (83). In her attempt to disavow her vulnerability as victim, Pauline lays claim to Sophie's brain as well as her flesh; if Sophie is "thoughtless," as Pauline describes her here, she is so because Pauline has stripped her of autonomy, "rooted" her in a body that Pauline—and not Sophie—controls.

8. See Rainwater, "Reading between Worlds," pp. 407-13.

9. The transformation of an insubstantial "husk" into Napoleon's body represents a motion toward acknowledging the human consequences of violence, a motion that reverses the reader's experience of Fleur's rape. In the earlier scene, Lily's attack on Fleur is prefigured by his violent encounter with the sow:

> The sow screamed as his body smacked over hers. She rolled, striking out with her knife-sharp hooves and Lily gathered himself upon her, took her foot-long face by the ears, and scraped her snout and cheeks against the trestles of the pen. . . . She reared, shrieked, and then he squeezed her . . . his arms swung and flailed. She sank her black fangs into his shoulders, clasping him, dancing him forward and backward through the pen.
>
> (25)

Although this representation moves toward aestheticization by imaging the interaction between Lily and the sow as a dance, it acknowledges the painful force of the assault on the animal's body with an immediacy that is absent in the novel's representation of the rape that follows. The horror of Fleur's suffering is, in a sense, deflected onto the representation of the pig's struggle with Lily. By contrast, the assault on Fleur that occurs shortly thereafter in the novel renders the material consequences of violence almost invisible. The Napoleon scene reverses this motion by unveiling the supernatural creature or inhuman "husk" that Pauline manipulates as a human being whose body bears the consequences of her violence. (My thanks to Anne Fleche for our conversations on the function of the sow.)

10. Pauline, of course, emerges as the sadistic Leopolda of *Love Medicine*; her actions in that novel are rendered more intelligible in light of her experiences as Pauline in *Tracks*.

FURTHER READING

Criticism

Castillo, Susan. "Women Aging into Power: Fictional Representations of Power and Authority in Louise Erdrich's Female Characters." *Studies in American Indian Literatures* 8, no. 4 (winter 1996): 13-20.

Examines Erdrich's portrayal of powerful women in her characters Marie and Zelda.

Cornell, Daniel. "Woman Looking: Revis(ion)ing Pauline's Subject Position in Louise Erdrich's *Tracks*." *Studies in American Indian Literatures* 4, no. 1 (spring 1992): 49-64.

Understands the character Pauline's "experience of feminine desire" to be "mastered through a discourse of insanity" in the novel Tracks.

Flavin, Louise. "Gender Construction Amid Family Dissolution in Louise Erdrich's *The Beet Queen*." *Studies in American Indian Literatures* 7, no. 2 (summer 1995): 17-24.

Discusses Erdrich's creation of a nonconventional family at the end of The Beet Queen.

Silberman, Robert. "Opening the Text: *Love Medicine* and the Return of the Native American Woman." In *Narrative Chance: Postmodern Discourse on Native American Indian Literatures,* edited by Gerald Vizenor, pp. 101-20. Albuquerque: University of New Mexico Press, 1989.

Examines the ways in which Love Medicine *differs from other contemporary Native American narratives due largely to its female central character.*

Stookey, Lorena L. *Louise Erdrich: A Critical Companion.* Westport, Conn.: Greenwood Press, 1999, 184 p.

Discusses Erdrich's novels from Love Medicine *to* The Antelope Wife, *and includes a biography and bibliography.*

Tanrisal, Meldan. "Mother and Child Relationships in the Novels of Louise Erdrich." *American Studies International* 35, no. 3 (October 1997): 67-79.

Discusses the effects of Erdrich's nonchronological narratives on her portrayal of mother-child relationships.

OTHER SOURCES FROM GALE:

Additional coverage of Erdrich's life and career is contained in the following sources published by the Gale Group: *American Writers Supplement* Vol. 4; *Authors and Artists for Young Adults,* Vols. 10, 47; *Beacham's Encyclopedia of Popular Fiction: Biography & Resources,* Vol. 1; *Bestsellers,* Vol. 89:1; *Concise Dictionary of American Literary Biography Supplement; Contemporary Authors,* Vol. 114; *Contemporary Authors New Revision Series,* Vols. 41, 62, 118; *Contemporary Literary Criticism,* Vols. 39, 54, 120, 176; *Contemporary Novelists,* Ed. 7; *Contemporary Poets* Ed. 7; *Contemporary Popular Writers; Contemporary Women Poets; Dictionary of Literary Biography,* Vols. 152, 175, 206; *DISCovering Authors Modules: Multicultural, Novelists* and *Popular Writers; DISCovering Authors 3.0; Encyclopedia of World Literature in the 20th Century,* Ed. 3; *Exploring Poetry; Literature and Its Times,* Vol. 5; *Literature and Its Times Supplement,* Ed. 1; *Literature Resource Center; Major 20th-Century Writers,* Ed. 1; *Native North American Literature; Novels for Students,* Vol. 5; *Poetry Criticism,* Vol. 52; *Poetry for Students,* Vol. 14; *Reference Guide to American Literature,* Ed. 4; *Short Stories for Students,* Vol. 14; *Something about the Author,* Vols. 94, 141; and *Twentieth-Century Western Writers,* Ed. 2.

MARILYN FRENCH

(1929 -)

(Born Marilyn Edwards; has also written under the pseudonym Mara Solwoska) American novelist, critic, essayist, memoirist, historian, and nonfiction writer.

Best known for her first novel, the highly popular *The Women's Room* (1977), French is an author of controversial works that provoke both enthusiastic and antagonistic responses from critical audiences. A former homemaker whose academic aspirations led her to Harvard University during the politically turbulent 1960s, French draws upon her experiences with motherhood, divorce, academia, and political activism to evoke the concerns of women who rebel against domesticity, sexual submission, and discrimination in the workplace. While some critics denounce French's ideological fiction and nonfiction as polemical, her works are widely read and often examined in women's studies courses.

BIOGRAPHICAL INFORMATION

French was born November 21, 1929, in New York City, to a poor family of Polish descent. She received a bachelor's degree from Hofstra College (now Hofstra University) in Long Island in 1951. French married Robert M. French Jr., with whom she has two children. French returned to Hofstra to earn her master's degree in 1964, while also

teaching English at the college from 1964 to 1968. In 1967 French divorced her husband and enrolled in the English graduate program at Harvard University, receiving her Ph.D. in 1972. French used her personal experiences as the basis for the central character of Mira in *The Women's Room*; Mira also divorced her husband and enrolled at Harvard in the same year.

From 1972 to 1976 French taught English at the College of the Holy Cross in Worcester, Massachusetts. She also served as the Mellon fellow in English at Harvard from 1976 to 1977 and as artist in residence at the Aspen Institute for Humanistic Study in 1972. Aside from her novels and nonfiction works, French has contributed essays and articles to such journals as *Soundings* and *Ohio Review,* often under the pseudonym Mara Solwoska. In 1992 French was diagnosed with metastasized esophageal cancer. She recovered from the illness and the experience later became the basis for *A Season in Hell: A Memoir* (1998).

MAJOR WORKS

One year after French published her first work—*The Book as World: James Joyce's "Ulysses"* (1976), a critical reexamination of Joyce's novel—she published *The Women's Room*, which is generally considered one of the most influential novels of the modern feminist movement. The novel follows the evolution of Mira, a repressed and submissive woman, who is trapped in an unsatisfying marriage. Mira eventually divorces her neglectful husband, returns to college, and joins a group of feminist activists. Ranging from the stultifying suburban milieu of the 1950s to the male-dominated counter-culture of the 1960s, *The Women's Room* depicts sexism in America as a pervasive and pernicious social force that acts to advance the oppression and exploitation of women. Through the various female characters in Mira's group, French illustrates the psychological and physical abuses frequently inflicted on women and recreates the consciousness-raising dialogues of the era that inspired many women to take up political activism. Extending French's discussion of moderate feminism is a more radical orientation represented by Val, an eloquent member of the group who becomes militant after her daughter is sexually assaulted. When the rape trial becomes more of an indictment of the young woman than of the rapist, Val joins a women's separatist colony that advocates the violent overthrow of patriarchal American society.

French continued her commentary on gender relations in her second novel, *The Bleeding Heart* (1980), a chronicle of a love affair between Dolores, a divorced feminist writer seeking an egalitarian relationship, and Victor, a married executive with traditional values. To cultivate a healthy relationship, each confronts past tragedies and failures in their marriages and parenthood, and Dolores persuades Victor to reassess his assumptions about gender roles.

French examines the origins of societal male dominance in *Shakespeare's Division of Experience* (1981), a collection of broadly theoretical essays. The work asserts that the woman's capacity to bear children has historically aligned her with nature and, consequently, has left her vulnerable to man's compulsion to exercise power over nature.

French again combines her interest in political doctrine and scholarly pursuits in *Beyond Power: On Women, Men, and Morals* (1985), which reinterprets world history through a feminist perspective. Often compared to the metahistorical essays of Jean-Jacques Rousseau and Michel Foucault, *Beyond Power* surveys such diverse disciplines as anthropology, medicine, political science, philosophy, astronomy, zoology, and law in its argument against patriarchal domination. According to French, early egalitarian, mother-centered societies were overthrown by a conspiracy of men

obsessed with a desire for control over women and nature. With the pursuit of power as its impetus, patriarchal culture enslaved women and devised social structures emphasizing male-centered religion, property rights, and the division of labor. As a result, French argues, women have suffered in every human society from ancient Greece to modern China.

In *Her Mother's Daughter* (1987), French examines emotional and familial bonds among four generations of American women, beginning in the early 1900s. Frances, a widowed Polish immigrant who is forced by poverty to send three of her four children to orphanages, consigns her bitterness to her only remaining child, Isabelle. In turn, Isabelle's overprotective nurturing prompts her rebellious daughter to achieve success in a competitive male world, while ultimately neglecting her own children. French invests her narrative with myriad domestic details to demonstrate the sobering effects of unwanted pregnancies, abusive husbands, and tedious household responsibilities.

French's *The War against Women* (1992) surveys the oppression of women on a global scale. Considering such activities as ritualized female genital mutilation in Africa and the burning of brides in India, along with economic disparities between women and men, French argues that women have become disempowered and overwhelmed by patriarchal societies.

French's novel *Our Father* (1994) depicts a troubled family reunion that occurs after a wealthy man, Stephen Upton, suffers a stroke, inspiring a visit from his four estranged daughters—all of whom have different mothers. Each hoping to gain either money or acknowledgment from her father, the women initially compete and argue among themselves. The daughters' discovery that they have all been the victims of incest during their childhood, however, becomes a source of bonding and mutual support.

My Summer with George (1996) follows Hermione Beldame, a successful, sixty-year-old romance novelist, who meets a handsome newspaper editor named George Johnson one summer at Columbia University. Hermione spends the next few months creating a romanticized vision of her relationship and future with George, only to become disappointed after she realizes that George is not the man she imagined him to be.

A Season in Hell: A Memoir recounts French's personal battle with and eventual triumph over metastasized esophageal cancer. French discusses her various medical treatments and the resulting effects of her aggressive chemotherapy, including brittle bones, kidney problems, and diabetes. The work focuses on the experience of being a patient, with French asserting that many doctors, regardless of gender, are insensitive and aloof to the pain experienced by the people under their care.

In 2002 French released the first volume of the three-volume series *From Eve to Dawn: A History of Women*. Bringing together scholarly and academic information, the series offers a careful critical examination of issues pertaining to the history of women throughout the world since the dawn of time. The first volume, *Origins* (2002), examines the roles of women from the advent of recorded history to the Middle Ages. The second volume, *The Masculine Mystique* (2002), follows women's history from the feudal era to the French Revolution. The final volume, *Paradises and Infernos* (2003), covers the nineteenth century to the modern era.

CRITICAL RECEPTION

Critical assessment of French's oeuvre has been sharply divided, inspiring numerous debates over the validity of her fiction and nonfiction. Although many feminist critics have praised French as a groundbreaking pioneer in the field of women's studies, other critics have charged that French's works are belligerent, artless, and ideologically clumsy. Detractors of *The Women's Room* have criticized French for her sympathetic portrayal of the violently militant Val and have argued that the novel is virulently anti-male and grim. However, several scholars have noted that the novel's immense popularity confirms its integrity, and they have continued to regard the novel as one of the most important works in the feminist canon. Many reviewers have praised French's candid illustrations of mid-life anxiety and her examination of sexual stereotypes in *The Bleeding Heart*, though some have argued that the novel is overly rhetorical and unconvincing. Critical reaction to the essays in *Beyond Power* has been diverse and emphatic, with a number of commentators faulting French's arguments as fallacious and inane, while others have defended the collection as innovative and erudite. Despite some assertions that her work holds a militant and uncompromising bias, French has remained a major figure in modern feminist studies.

PRINCIPAL WORKS

The Book as World: James Joyce's "Ulysses" (criticism) 1976

The Women's Room (novel) 1977

The Bleeding Heart (novel) 1980

Shakespeare's Division of Experience (essays and criticism) 1981

Beyond Power: On Women, Men, and Morals (essays and criticism) 1985

Her Mother's Daughter (novel) 1987

The War against Women (nonfiction) 1992

Our Father (novel) 1994

My Summer with George (novel) 1996

A Season in Hell: A Memoir (memoir) 1998

From Eve to Dawn: A History of Women, Volume I: Origins (history and criticism) 2002

From Eve to Dawn: A History of Women, Volume II: The Masculine Mystique (history and criticism) 2002

From Eve to Dawn: A History of Women, Volume III: Paradises and Infernos (history and criticism) 2003

PRIMARY SOURCES

MARILYN FRENCH (ESSAY DATE 1990)

SOURCE: French, Marilyn. "Is There a Feminist Aesthetic?" In *Aesthetics in Feminist Perspective*, edited by Hilde Hein and Carolyn Korsmeyer, pp. 68-76. Indianapolis: Indiana University Press, 1993.

In the following essay, originally published in 1990, French discusses defining "feminist" works of art and the characteristics she feels necessary to judge a piece of literature as feminist.

Literary art that is identifiably feminist approaches reality from a feminist perspective and endorses female experience. A feminist perspective demystifies patriarchal assumptions about the nature of human beings, their relation to nature, and the relation of physical and moral qualities to each other. To endorse female experience, the artist must defy or stretch traditional literary conventions, which often means offending or alienating readers. Traditional literary conventions are rooted in philosophical assumptions several thousand years old and still widely current. A third principle of feminist art—which not all feminists subscribe to—is accessibility. When feminist art is difficult, the reason usually lies not in purposeful obfuscation, but in the poverty of our language of feeling, and the difficulty of rendering feeling.

It is questionable whether the terms and issues of traditional aesthetics are applicable to feminist art. Some critics claim traditional aesthetic principles are universal, and that art is "above" sex, or at least, that sex is irrelevant to it. There is an art which is specifically feminist: that much is clear. Some, by virtue of its feminism, would deny it the title *art,* arguing that its political interest violates aesthetic standards. An aesthetics like Susanne Langer's, which defines what art creates and is indeed universal, fits feminist art as well as any other (Langer 1953). But most aesthetics are more prescriptive, and therefore more political: feminism has taught us that all critical approaches imply political standards, however tacitly. Before we can evaluate feminist art by any aesthetic principles, we need a definition of the art. In what follows, I will discuss the characteristics of feminist art as I understand them. For the sake of brevity, I will limit myself to the art I know best, literature; but the principles have parallels in the other arts.

The clearest proof of the existence of a feminist aesthetics is the distaste or rage feminists feel on encountering works that violate it. Sometimes a negative response seems to refer to subject matter—for example, I loathe lingering loving descriptions of mutilations of female bodies; yet when a writer like Andrea Dworkin treats such a theme, I feel it to be not offensive, but only unpleasant—it falls within the boundaries of "taste." So it is less subject-matter (content) than treatment (style) that is at issue (I will not here address the identity of style and content). Perhaps all a prescriptive aesthetic can be is a set of principles describing a particular style, a taste.

There are two fundamental, related principles that mark a work of art as feminist: first, it approaches reality from a feminist perspective; second, it endorses female experience. Each principle has several ramifications, so is more complicated than it sounds.

In a work with a feminist perspective, the narrational point of view, the point of view lying behind the characters and events, penetrates, demystifies, or challenges patriarchal ideologies. So much has been written about patriarchy in the last two decades that one tends to assume readers understand the term; yet I have met highly educated people who do not understand the feminist use of the term, so I'll explain it briefly. Patriarchy is a way of thinking, a set of assumptions that has been translated into various structures or ideologies. The assumptions are, first: males are superior to females. Their superiority may be granted by a deity or by nature, but it is absolute in conferring on men authority over women. Second: males have individual destinies; they are promised domination, a surrogate godhead, transcendence over the natural world through power in heroism, sainthood, or some form of transcendent paternity—founding a dynasty, an institution, a religion, or a state, or creating an enduring work of art or technology. Third: the form taken by patriarchy is hierarchy, a structure designed to maintain and transmit power from spiritual father to spiritual son. This form absolutely excludes females unless they "make themselves male" (the requirement Jesus places on women entering "the Life" in the gnostic Gospel of Thomas) (1977). Women control biological transmission, the ability to bring forth young passed from mother to daughter. Having this power, they must be excluded from institutional power—which was modeled on the biological sort—if they are not to overwhelm men. Females have only a "natural" destiny; interchangeable parts of nature's cycles, they are maids (in both senses), who become mothers, and finally widows (or hags), in which avatar they are expendable.

Finally, domination is divine, so to pursue it is noble, heroic, glorious. The material to be dominated is, essentially, nature—all women; the body and emotions; "bestial" men; and natural processes, the flux and transitoriness of time, material decay, life itself. Patriarchal works focus on individual males who pursue glory; lonely, self-made and self-defeating, men are isolated from community and exiled forever from the "female" fate of happiness.

Since almost all modern worlds are patriarchal, feminist literature necessarily depicts patriarchy. But it does not underwrite its standards. Feminist literature may show patriarchal attitudes destroying a character or a world, but the narrative does not approve the destruction. When, in *The Faerie Queene,* Guyon destroys the luscious female world called The Bower of Bliss, Spenser, who has used his highest imaginative skills to create the Bower, judiciously approves its ruin. This is true also of Vergil in *The Aeneid.* The poet sighs about the tears of things (*lacrimae rerum*), regretting that beauty and feeling (Dido and sexual love for instance) are destroyed in the pursuit of glory, yet approves Aeneas's desertion of Dido, and his slaughter of those who oppose his domination. Aeneas's destiny is to found Rome; it overrides humanitarian or emotional concerns. Clearly, despite their feelings, both poets uphold patriarchy.

It is less clear where Tolstoy stands in *Anna Karenina*, or Austen in *Pride and Prejudice*. Both authors accept the patriarchal societies in which they live. Yet the pity Tolstoy lavishes on Anna, and the acute irony with which Austen pricks upper-class pretention and the unctuous ambition of the middle-classes, subvert patriarchal standards. This sympathy is not in the eye of the reader; it is built-in. Tolstoy's novel induces readers to feel the world lessened by Anna's death, rather than to feel that it was necessary, like Dido's, to a greater purpose. Austen's heroines maintain self-respect and integrity (wholeness) even as they triumph within a patriarchal structure. Many works of the past three centuries stretch patriarchal standards in this way; they are not feminist, but do not wholly support patriarchy either.

The feminist perspective is partly a reversal of patriarchal views. Feminism sees women as at least equal to men, humanly if not politically or economically; it considers transcendence illusory or factitious and pursuit of power a fatally doomed enterprise, since it cannot ever be satisfied, and usually or always involves the destruction of vital qualities and even life itself. Domination is not divine but lethal to dominator and dominated. It harms the dominator by cutting him off from trust and mutuality, the foundations of friendship and love, the two primary values; it harms the dominated by forcing them into dependency, which precludes truth in relationships. Domination creates false forms of friendship (society) and love (conventional marriage) which mask power relations. And feminist art focuses on people as wholes; the human is made up of body and emotion as well as mind and spirit; she is also part of a community, connected to others; and—on the broadest level—to nature in both positive and negative aspects.

The second principle is equally complicated. To endorse women's experience, feminist art must present it honestly, wholly. This is difficult because literature, like all art, is made up of conventions which are particularly marked in the area of gender. Just as it would be startling to observe a painting of a male nude reclining seductively à la Maja, or Olympe, or of a clothed female Picasso contemplating a naked male with emphatic genitals, literary shifts in presentation of gender startle, distracting attention from *what* is being shown to *the fact* that it is shown. A work's political impact obliterates its other features. This means that either considerable time—decades or even centuries—must elapse before readers can concentrate on what is being shown, or the work will be forgotten without this ever happening. And conventions governing female characters in literature are extraordinarily powerful and tenacious.

One convention holds women's work trivial, insignificant, uninteresting. Indeed, even men's work was considered an inappropriate subject for literature until recently. Yet work fills our lives; domestic work *is* most women's entire life and takes up considerable time even for women who also work outside the home. What such work means to one's sense of self, of the larger world; how it affects a woman's relation to her children, mates, lovers, friends; its pleasures, pains, the personal and political consequences of endless work for which one is not paid: these experiences remain relatively unexplored because of convention.

Conventionally, women's stories had happy endings, usually marriage to a prince and living happily ever after—unless the heroine is guilty of a sexual transgression, in which case she is required to die. This convention has stretched to allow sexual women to survive, but readers still complain when a "good" woman does not live happily ever after. The assumption behind this convention seems to be that the world is ruled by a male bar of justice. All female characters come up before this bar, and males, being just, grant the good ones happiness—a female, not a male condition (male heroes almost never live happily ever after). If the author does not grant a virtuous female character eternal felicity, either she doesn't deserve it or the male bar is not just. Since in a patriarchal world the latter is unthinkable, her virtue must be deceptive. So male critics pore over Shakespeare's Cordelia searching for the hidden flaw that explains her fate and alter Edith Wharton's perception of her heroines (who *are* flawed), making them responsible for their own unhappiness.

If the definition of a "good" woman no longer involves chastity, heroines are still required to be sweet, vulnerable, *likeable*. Readers do not expect sweetness or honesty of male protagonists: they don't even have to be likeable: consider the heroes of *Under the Volcano, Notes from Underground, Look Back in Anger*. Authoritative, angry, rebellious heroines make most readers impatient; they tend to blame the character for not finding a way to be happy. I think about Andrea Dworkin's *Ice and Fire*, which could not at first find an American publisher, or my own *The Bleeding Heart*, which female and male reviewers (if not readers) uniformly condemned. Actual women, we ourselves, may walk around in a constant state of rage and yet reject heroines like us. The most lethal combination is authority and sexuality; it is almost impossible to depict a woman with both except as a villain.

I am very conscious of this because I am planning a novel with an authoritative, sexual woman character, who lives in rage and despair, and who may not be likeable—but who has real grounds for her feelings, and lives in pain, and is in some ways admirable. Someone like, say, Ivan Karamazov. I already know how she will be received, and I dread it. There should be room for every kind of female experience, even the inability to live happily ever after. There should be room for depictions of women who are monstrous. Again, difficulties occur in distinguishing portrayals of monstrous women from portraits drawn by woman-haters. Woman-hating nestles deep at the root of patriarchy; all of us, women and men, are probably infected by it to some degree. Women's own woman-hatred needs exploration in feminist art.

In portraying female experience, feminist art also portrays men, showing them as they impinge upon women or as they appear to women to be. There are no heroes who save women: not because men would not like to do this, but because it can't be done. This is not to say there is no heroism, male and female, in life; only that there are no princes. What men are in themselves or for other men may contradict what they are for women; women's dreams and hopes about men may be mere wishfulness; women may be complicit in male monstrousness. Feminist portraits of males must examine these realities, but there are serious dangers in doing so. Although women (and even men) offer blanket condemnation of male treatment of females in conversation, such condemnation on a printed page is tantamount to mutiny (so wives' disobedience of husbands, in Shakespeare's era, was called "revolution") and leads to the work being dismissed.

These principles may sound limiting, as if feminist work could deal only and always with the middle ground, the mundane, the probable, eschewing flights of fancy, excessive characters, extremes of good and evil. This is not at all the case, although precisely that middle ground needs examination. Consider that for the 2,500-plus years of its existence, Western philosophy has looked at life strictly from a male perspective, and strictly as if men were constituted only of intellect, ambition, and political concern; as if they

never had to deal with upset stomachs, irritation at their children, emotional dependency, hunger, or distress at growing bald. As Nietzsche pointed out, philosophy has ignored and dismissed the life of the body and the emotions, and—I would add—social involvement with women and children. It has been able to show men transcending only by pretending that the mundane does not exist and that other people do not matter.

In addition, for millennia, at least since fifth century BCE Athens, male thinking has divided human experience into two unequal categories. These may be mind/body, reason/sense, spirit/flesh (sexual desire), or intellect/emotion, but the two are always opposed like enemies, and one is always ascribed moral superiority—in the righteous man, mind (or reason, spirit, intellect) will triumph. By dividing experience this way, men have been able to build a world they claim is based on mind, reason, spirit, intellect, a culture which controls and belittles body, senses, desire, emotion; and have felt legitimate in using ruthless means to suppress people associated with what is disparaged. Valuing only certain talents and ignoring or denigrating others, certain men have created a science-based industrial-technological environment without giving a single moment of thought to its effect on living, feeling, and desire; and have disparaged, debased, and killed women of all sorts and men of discredited colors, religions, cultures, or backgrounds.

It is essential for the healing of a sick world that this division be mended. To begin with, it is false. Humans are of a piece, made up of thousands of intricate interconnections, mind body spirit sex sense intellect being only points in an indescribable continuum. Bodymind swirls around in us, without us; we contain it, it contains us. We can try to understand the processes by which we function, but we cannot control them. Every step at control is counteracted by the power of what is hidden; too many steps and we fall ill, off-balance.

Not only is each of us a complex network whose working we barely understand, but each of us is connected to other people and ideas and things in equally complex ways. There is no such thing as a self-made man—or woman. Scientists are discovering more fully each decade that *nothing dominates*. No planet dominates the cosmos, no part of a cell dominates it, no single person, not even the boss, dominates any situation. The drive to control that informs patriarchy is an unremitting, relentless drive to an invulnerability, impregnability (consider the root of this word), that does not exist on earth. People spend their lives trying to reach a pinnacle of power from which they can affect others without being affected in return—one definition of god. But even a Stalin, who arguably controlled more, in terms of people and territory, than any other human in our century, lived within prison walls, with a taster to try his food, without the possibility of trust, without which both friendship and love are impossible. And bosses are afraid in direct proportion to the degree of control they possess—of those beneath them as well as those above. And are affected by them, in all kinds of ways. Power is a moment, a temporary station on a telephone line; tomorrow, the powerful man may be forced out even if he is president, chairman, Shah.

We have not yet created a language to describe interconnection: our language is based on fabricated dichotomies, and trying to speak about mind/body/senses all at once makes one feel she has a mouthful of marbles. But in whatever ways the genius of the artist can devise, feminist art suggests that things are connected as well as divided, that a person is not always at war with herself or her world, that in fact people seek to live harmoniously with themselves and their world *even though they can't control either*. Feminist work often focuses on groups, community, people as part of a context, and helps to remind us of a reality alternative to the Western tradition of individualistic, alienated man, lonely in a hostile, aggressive world.

So, a third kind of endorsement of female experience is showing a pluralistic reality made up of connection, flow, interrelation, and therefore equality—for when nothing dominates, all parts are equally necessary, and require equal attention. In the workings of the human being or of cosmic space, the puffing up of one part with claims of superiority leads to catastrophe for all parts. Human superiority is not a possibility, no matter how many have claimed it. Shakespeare may endow his kings and lords with social and political superiority, but he also regularly shows their underlings—a simple clown, a powerless girl—to be superior to them in common sense, morality, and understanding.

Works of art that assume the existence of human superiority are invariably anti-woman. I have been paying attention now for many years: works that presume that some people are and ought to be "better" than others betray contempt for those others on grounds of their identity—in Western literature, usually blacks or Jews. And when you find the one, you find the other: where there is contempt for any identity, there is also contempt

for femaleness or things associated with femaleness—body, sex, desire, need—even in works written by women. Although writers of the late twentieth-century United States are inhibited from expressing anti-Semitism or racism, many, especially television writers, allow themselves the complacency of moral superiority in their literary treatment of prostitutes, who are not shown as people but as attractive subhumans, unworthy of humane consideration.

A third feminist principle, to which I myself am committed, is accessibility, language and style that aim at comprehensibility. I mention this separately because unlike the two principles already discussed, it is not a necessary condition of feminist art. It is, however, a standard about which I feel strongly.

For thousands of years, women were locked out of high culture. For example, sometime between 200 BCE and 550 CE, Hindu women were forbidden to learn Sanskrit, the language in which all the great Hindu religious and literary documents were composed. The rationale for this was that women were not capable of *moksha*, salvation, and so did not need to read about religion. But the prohibition kept women from learning the religious, mythic, and poetic backgrounds of their culture.

In the fifth century, Japan imported Chinese culture, philosophy, and language; at this time, Japanese women were still powerful. In later centuries, they were degraded and diminished, and male authorities forbade them to learn Chinese, by then the prestige language of Japan, the language of philosophy, government, and "high" literature. Ironically, in the eleventh century, while learned men trotted out tedious pretentious Chinese imitations, literary women writing in the vernacular produced some of Japan's greatest literature, including its masterpiece, the *Tale of Genji*, by Murasaki Shikibu.

Some societies refused to teach females how to read and write. But even if some women were literate, once a particular language became exalted, became the language of scholarship, poetry, diplomacy, or law, theology, and medicine, women were forbidden to learn it. When humanism swept Europe after the fourteenth century, and it became essential to cultivated discourse to know Latin and Greek, women were excluded from schools that taught Latin and Greek. As more lower-class men learned classical languages, a new literary form emerged: allegory, intended to separate the low from the high mind. The medieval allegorist prided himself on concealing spiritual meaning under a sensuous surface. Of course, this also permitted him to write splendid sensuous poetry, filled with sexual and chivalric exploits, while claiming to offer a more severe and exalted "kernel" of hidden significance to the truly learned. Often, poets were also offering serious moral instruction, usually about power, in this coded language.

In our own time, in our own country, our own language, English, is the prestige tongue, the one in which advanced scientific, social, philosophical, and technological documents are written. But these documents are rarely written in an English all of us can comprehend. Rather, each discipline has created a special language, a jargon accessible only to those who have been trained in the field. Women now learn these languages, and use them with it seems to me special pleasure, as if they knew they were using tools formerly sacrosanct, kept in the part of the temple forbidden to females. Some degree of specialist language is necessary; feminists who must use special languages can develop a critique of those languages, and acknowledge and renounce, even as they use them, the patriarchal assumptions implanted in their codes.

What I find non-feminist is intentional obfuscation, the kind of writing that purposes to impress the reader with the writer's knowledge or intellect or high style or "inness," the kind that makes a point of excluding all but the chosen few. With reservations, I love the work of James Joyce, T. S. Eliot, and Ezra Pound, writers who make frequent use of allusion, quoting fragments of poetry, namedropping, and otherwise referring to great poets and thinkers of the past. By this they accomplish several things: they add depth to their work, texturing, enriching it with allusions to a literary tradition. They also parade their learning, placing themselves above the perhaps less-learned reader, presenting themselves as distant and superior. And they legitimate themselves. Western poetry traditionally *required* citation of authority. By bringing in Homer, Cavalcante, Dante, Shakespeare, these men suggest that they are writing in the same tradition as the great men of the past; that they are the equals of these forebears; and that they deserve the same reverence.

Few women use such devices. In the first place, there are few female authorities and women do not seem to feel that males can legitimate them. Second, the device is itself patriarchal: patriarchy is about the transmission of power, the mantle handed from father to nonbiological son, a tradition excluding women. But most important,

women seem to feel legitimated not by power and authority, as men do, but by experience itself. And experience is made up of feeling. Women seek legitimacy by finding ways to express what it feels like to live their particular reality. When women's writing is opaque, or what some might call inaccessible, it is because there is no language of expression of a context of emotion: each woman has to create a language for herself. So, some might find inaccessible Monique Wittig's *Les Guérillères* or Susan Griffin's *The Roaring inside Her*, or Luce Irigaray's *And the One Doesn't Stir without the Other*, or Lois Gould's *A Sea-Change* and *Subject to Change*, or Christa Wolf's *Cassandra* or *No Place on Earth*: but whatever inaccessibility exists in these works emerges not from pretention but from the difficulty of rendering the life of the emotions.

My own style is based on my decision, made after almost twenty years of (unpublished) writing in a different mode, to address the reader like a friend talking across a kitchen table, over coffee: I see the reader as an equal, who will out of friendship try as hard to understand the narrator's reality as she to express it. I believe that a healthy literature, one that attempts to create a healthy culture, is inclusive—of everyone—implicitly or explicitly. It is directed at an entire society, and considers everyone in it a member of that society. Choosing to write in such a style necessarily involves some loss and therefore some anguish. But any style requires sacrificing others.

Finally, there may be a distinction between patriarchal and feminist forms. In *Feeling and Form*, Susanne Langer describes the form of tragedy as expressing the rhythms of individual life as the hero realizes his potential and exhausts it, comparing it with comedy, the form of which celebrates vital continuity. In **Shakespeare's Division of Experience**, I draw on Langer's definitions to describe Shakespeare's tragedy and comedy as masculine and feminine forms respectively: tragedy focuses on an individual male, is linear, and leads to a destiny which must be death but suggests transcendence; comedy focuses less intensely on a female, is circular, communal, and leads to harmony and integration of an entire society (although in Shakespeare, the most seriously disruptive element may be excluded from the happy conclusion) (French 1981). Twentieth-century literature, patriarchal or feminist, rarely fits the categories of either traditional tragedy or comedy; yet I think a study of form in any art would yield similar conclusions.

The art I describe in these principles is a different entity from the art described by traditional aesthetics. Itself transcendent, embodying universal aesthetic principles, singular and useless except to move the sensibility exquisite enough to apprehend it, art as traditionally seen is the delicate flower expressing the spirit of a culture. But for feminists, as Lily Tomlin's baglady Trudy tries to work it out (in Jane Wagner's words, with Andy Warhol's image of cans of Campbell's soup), art is soup (Wagner 1986, 29). Art nourishes a society, feeds it; sturdy, not delicate, it arises from the life of a people like food from the ground, teaching us what we do not know, reminding us of what we tend to forget, emphasizing what is important, grieving over pain, celebrating vitality. It is useful and beautiful and moral—not moralistic.

The standards I hold for a feminist art are thus, as you have probably guessed, my standards in life. And that is what I believe an art, any art, ought to be: an expression of a vision that is at once a belief and a faith—belief in humanity and faith in its future. I have always accepted the Horatian definition of the purpose of art—to teach and to delight—and I believe feminist art can make us better, just as I think a feminist world would make us better. But art is not just a moral act. There is a last principle which is not feminist but truly universal: vitality. Art must create the illusion of "felt life," as Henry James suggested. Without it, the best-intentioned piece of work is mere words, a dead shell. And that is a quality for which no one can write prescriptions.

References

French, Marilyn. 1981. *Shakespeare's division of experience.* New York: Summit Books.

The gospel of Thomas. 1977. In *The Nag Hammadi Library in English.* J. M. Robinson, ed. New York: Harper & Row.

Langer, Susanne. 1953. *Feeling and form.* New York: Scribner's.

Wagner, Jane. 1986. *The search for signs of intelligent life in the universe.* New York: Harper & Row.

TITLE COMMENTARY

The Women's Room

AMANDA LOHREY (ESSAY DATE 1979)

SOURCE: Lohrey, Amanda. "The Liberated Heroine: New Varieties of Defeat?" *Meanjin* 38, no. 3 (1979): 294-304.

In the following excerpt, Lohrey examines the plot and themes of The Women's Room, *and comments on Diana Trilling's assertion that feminist works should avoid "existential despair."*

As Patricia Meyer Spacks has noted, novels by women writers are an area where we have not had time to develop aesthetic distance, and any collection of them will often do no more than exemplify the eclecticism of modern fiction. This is true if one is surveying the full range (Murdoch, Lessing, Spark, Oates *et al*) but within that wide spectrum the last decade has seen the emergence of a clearly recognisable *genre* of American women's fiction—the biographical novel of the single heroic female self. This is most often a rambling episodic ego-portrait with no revealing structure that moves on the one unvarying pulse of feeling through to an indifferent or 'liberating' end. The best of these is probably Lisa Alther's *Kinflicks*; notable among the rest are the Canadian Margaret Atwood's *Lady Oracle,* Erica Jong's *How To Save Your Own Life,* Francine du Plessix Gray's *Lovers and Tyrants* and Alix Kates Shulman's *Memoirs of An Ex-Prom Queen.*

Almost all the novels within the *genre* owe something to *The Bell Jar.* Like Plath's Esther Greenwood, the heroines grow up acutely aware of being different; they want to succeed by passive pleasing but are troubled by the perversion of self involved in the effort. Like Esther they exhibit a certain craziness in the process of escaping their female conditioning but significantly, a craziness which is seen in retrospect to be a form of 'real' sanity—Plath without the pathology. For contemporary women writers, if not armed with a polemical feminist ideology, are at the very least informed by a neo-feminist consciousness, one which enables them to externalise their rebellion in terms of breaking out rather than internalise it self-destructively by caving in. Despite this, the end result is often much the same for the modern heroine as for Dorothea Brooke or Isabel Archer, namely some form of defeat. The former may achieve an increase in her economic and psychological independence, but at a cost often of being placed beyond society and embracing the fate of a rootless eccentric (the fate that would presumably have settled upon Isabel Archer had she not decided to sublimate her sense of destiny in the guardianship of her stepdaughter). The limitations of the new writers, whether wry and comic like Alther or precious and narcissistic like Gray, are the limitations of self-knowledge. Very few offer more than the crudest social critique, and almost all lack a political vision: a narrowness of focus is reinforced by the general reliance on individualism as a philosophy and psychology as a method.

This is reflected in the current pre-occupation of feminist literary criticism with endings. The new consciousness, while it may dissolve barriers,

ON THE SUBJECT OF...

THE WOMEN'S ROOM

Marilyn French's **The Women's Room** is the most fully realized of various attempts to work through the conflicts created by cultural expectations for women, and as in most feminist novels, feminism is a positive possibility within otherwise annihilating choices. French follows her protagonist Mira through girlhood, adolescence, marriage, life as a suburban housewife and mother, divorce, graduate school, and ultimately—and not optimistically—to a lonely existence as a junior-college instructor of English literature in a town isolated on the coast of Maine. This is not a happy ending, but Mira is introspective and intact at the novel's conclusion, no mean feat considering the extent to which her ostensibly "normal" and certainly conventional life experiences are represented in terms of their ability to inflict psychic and even physical damage, despite Mira's reasonably protected status as an open-minded, intelligent, middle-class, well-educated white woman.

Dever, Carolyn. "The Feminist Abject: Death and the Constitution of Theory." *Studies in the Novel* 32, no. 2 (summer 2000): 185-206.

does not of itself engender solutions. To critics in the liberal tradition, like the Trillings, neo-feminism does not in itself offer sufficient moral baggage to engage the ethical dilemmas which are the proper sphere of the novel. In her recent essay on 'The Liberated Heroine',[1] Diana Trilling points to what she regards as the common failure of women writers to address themselves 'with courage' to the 'outcome of the heroine's choice'. In other words, self-knowledge for what? The goal of liberation is eventually reached, but what comes after? A survey in this article of the fates that recent writers bestow on their heroines suggests that the neo-feminist position tends to work itself out within one of four categories: existential pessimism; emotional optimism; stoic resignation or moral impasse.

The latest of the novels by American women writers to be published in Australia makes some attempt to confront the problem of 'what happens after?' before collapsing into the first of these categories, namely existential pessimism. **The Women's Room** by Marilyn French[2] is a novel in two parts: the second part is a liberationist version of *The Group*, Harvard Class of '68; a chronicle of Val, campus activist and radical feminist; Isolde, lesbian scholar; Kyla, post-grad student married to MCP nuclear physicist; Clarissa, rich girl, and Mira, the author's surrogate who arrives at Harvard in middle-age via a tortuous route that occupies the first two-thirds of a very long book.

The first part is a slice-of-women's-life-in-suburbia treatment. It begins with Mira overdoing the flirting in the local soda-parlour, experiencing a near gang-bang and marrying the dour Norm, a medical student, out of fright. Two quick children follow on agonies of poverty and failed contraception, and Mira discovers mother love. When Norm graduates they move to a lower-middle-class neighbourhood and eventually to a more affluent one. Each change of scene brings a new group of friends, all of whose marital pains are relentlessly and pedestrianly catalogued. When each group has been 'done', we move onto the next in an unending parade of Harrys and Sandras and Toms and Geraldines in what begins to read like a long-running feminist soap-opera; a saga of domestic violence, childbirth and divorce, with every now and then a perfunctory political reference dropped (Joe McCarthy, Kennedy assassinations, My Lai) to remind us of our location in time and space. But the focus of real concern rarely strays from the domestic hearth with disaster piling on disaster, until the middle of the book where Mira and her best friend have what could be reasonably described as an exchange of attempted suicides. Such literary *chutzpah* is breathtaking.

Eventually the eminently undesirable and flatly characterised Norm leaves the withdrawn Mira for another woman, and she takes herself off to State College where she wins a scholarship to Harvard and Adele and Sandra are replaced by Val and Co. At Harvard Mira meets Ben, a research fellow, has satisfying sex for the first time, discovers she loves him but declines to follow him to Africa and have the child he wants. Her self-assertion and refusal to fall into old traps are not altogether rewarded. The bottom drops out of the academic market, and Mira ends up a teacher in a 'third-rate community college', a lonely and eccentric figure much given to walks along the beach and existential despair: '. . . in a way it doesn't matter whether you open doors or close them, you still end up in a box.'

The Women's Room has a readability and earnestness that qualify it as prime consciousness-raising material: as the blurb says 'This novel changes lives'. It's an easy book to lampoon in soap-opera terms—French herself refers to her characters as 'paper dolls'—but the whole adds up to a formidable moral polemic. Of moral subtlety it has little and of emotional resonance less. None of the men exists other than as a cardboard cut-out, while the women are divided into doomed victims and opportunistic survivors. Moreover the madness, infidelity, child-bashing and wife-baiting are too routinely presented as if to say: let's not over-dramatise this; it happens every day; this is what it's really like in the kitchen, one damned horrific statistic after another. In her desire to spare us nothing French produces an effect of overkill: she presents too much too thinly, and the plight of any particular character is about as affecting as a statistical profile.

The interest of the novel lies in its ending. Mira is a character of great honesty, and this honesty exemplifies itself in the resolution of her fate: the world does *not* ignite because Mira asserts her independence, and in her walks on the beach and in her dreams there are hints of psychological terrors yet to come, reminding us of Lionel Trilling's injunction that the writer who writes on behalf of liberal values does his/her best work 'not in confirming liberalism in its sense of general righteousness' but in making clear that 'to act against social injustice is right and noble but to choose to do so does not settle all problems, but on the contrary generates new ones of an especially difficult sort.' The High Priestess of this point of view is of course Mary McCarthy, in whose novels there is only one moral virtue beyond sceptical appraisal and that is doubt itself—doubt and the absence of self-delusion. But Diana Trilling has presumably lost patience with this relatively modest requirement. Trilling complains that the novels of feminist writers are not 'life-giving' enough, end in too much existential despair and are in danger of 'adding to the dismays of the world we live in'. She scolds writers like Lessing and Alther (and by implication Didion and French) for becoming the new 'imperialists of the self', over-absorbed in 'the quest for freedom instead of rights within society', leaving us with heroines 'vagrant, without boundaries or purchase in life'. It is no longer sufficient to confront the

pitfalls attendant on any change in moral position—it is incumbent upon the heroine to make the most of it.

Notes

1. Diana Trilling, 'The Liberated Heroine', *Times Literary Supplement*, 13 October 1978.

2. Marilyn French, *The Women's Room* (Harcourt-Brace Jovanovich, New York, 1978).

The Bleeding Heart

KAREN ALKALAY-GUT (REVIEW DATE FALL 1983)

SOURCE: Alkalay-Gut, Karen. "The 'Stirring Conversation': American Literature and *The Bleeding Heart*." *Atlantis: A Women's Studies Journal* 9, no. 1 (fall 1983): 129-31.

In the following review, Alkalay-Gut examines the plot, structure, and characters in The Bleeding Heart, *concluding that French's examination of gender roles in the novel is a "step in the right direction."*

When Marilyn French's ***The Bleeding Heart*** was first reviewed, the major criticism levelled against it was that there was too much talking about issues. "Overly polemical," says Julia Klein of *The New Republic*.[1] ". . . It is hard to believe it is her incessant rhetoric that instructs either her lover or her reader," says Rosellen Brown in *The New York Times Book Review*.[2] Yet R. Z. Sheppard notes, at the conclusion of her review, "paradoxically much of the dialogue works . . . attentive male readers will discover why so many women are now saying 'Yes, yes' when there's 'No, no' in their eyes."[3] And this is precisely the point of the endless conversations.

Conversations between men and women are rare and usually stilted in American Literature. When they exist, the point of the conversation is not to communicate information but to win a kind of power game. Hemingway's Lady Brett does not finish her sentences and thus forces others to interpret her intentions. Daisy Buchanan whispers so that men will have to lean toward her to hear her. Women win, not by convincing, but by using the situation of conversation to wield power.

But the game of power has lost its fascination to the man and woman in ***The Bleeding Heart***. They have both learned that simply to win the battle of the sexes is to lose something more vital. Dolores Durer has "won" her freedom by leaving her weak, terrorizing husband, Anthony, and manipulating him into granting her a divorce. But she has lost because his subsequent suicide remains with her, and the children, marked by her ex-husband, are a constant memory and source of guilt. Victor Morrissey has won a passive wife. His infidelities drive her to smash her car into a wall and lose her legs. The plastic surgeons redo her maimed face, and his mistress points out:

> Oh, how nice. You have what you always wanted! A woman with a child's face and a child's dependency. You don't have to worry about her running around because she's numb, and you don't have to worry about her running away because she has no legs! She's utterly housebound, utterly subject, and utterly passive. Just what you wanted! How nice to get what you want. Just what you deserve![4]

Although he belongs to a society in which victory is success, the highest value, he has of course not won: the passive-aggressive situation of guilt his wife inflicts upon him for causing her accident controls him even though he is now free to be a bachelor in form and a married man in name.

Dolores is caught in her suffering and Victor in his victory. This use of symbolic names, criticized by reviewers as a "heavy handed reminder"[5] is quite deliberate: the characters are caught in the stereotypes of their self-images. And they need each other to begin to break out of these stereotypes. Gradually, over the year granted to them in the book, Victor and Dolores reveal themselves, through intensive discussions, in the full horror of the stereotypes they have fulfilled. Both learn about themselves and the other as they allow themselves to react and mirror past tragedies. Having lost the game of power, they both come to realize that the stereotypes of their names—the woman as long suffering, the man as ruler—have to be changed before a more fruitful conception of human relationships can be conceived.

These roles cannot merely be rejected: Dolores tells her daughter Elspeth she has quit as a mother, but when Elspeth kills herself almost immediately after this scene, perhaps partly as a result of her mother's rejection (not of Elspeth, but of motherhood), Dolores discovers she still has the role of mother in her, even though her daughter is dead. And it is this role of mother that is the most deeply engrained and the most painful of all. These roles cannot be denied or rejected, but they may be able to be transformed.

Throughout the endless conversations there is a constant attempt on both sides to see and enable to see the stereotyped roles for what they are, and perhaps, to transcend them through mutual understanding. For the couple does not reject each other for having committed such atrocities on people who are not unlike themselves. Dolores understands Edith, Victor's wife, and identifies with her. Victor can help to explain Anthony, Dolores' ex-husband, in a way she has not conceived because she could not have understood the pressures of being a husband, a man, a father. So both are victims in the other's story of suffering. Had they married twenty years ago, they would have done similar things to each other as they had done to their spouses. When they come to understand the extent to which both of them are locked into their social stereotypes, these crimes are almost forgivable.

Victor wants to leave his wife and go with Dolores at the end. But, she feels, only by "breaking her legs," by curbing her personality, can he succeed. Still locked in his masculine personality, he does not ask her, but tells her:

> I've decided . . . I'm going to leave Edith . . . I know you insist on keeping a place of your own. I won't try to move in with you. I can't anyway, I have to be in New York. But it's only a forty-five minute plane ride between cities, and we can spend weekends together. . . .
>
> (p. 364)

She rejects this offer because he has simply not gone far enough. He maintains the position of the conquering male, even while his decision is a dependent one—dependent on Dolores. Although Dolores has learned to incorporate both masculine and feminine understanding, Victor has remained primarily masculine. "What I want, Victor," she tells him, "is to change the world, what do you think? To make it a place . . . where maybe even men will join the women because they will see that woman's way of thinking is more decent, more humane, and in the long run, Victor, more likely to preserve the human race." (p. 309) The author agrees. In an interview, Marilyn French states:

> I don't want to be like men. Women still are full of the old, traditional female virtues. They cook you a pot of soup. They do the serving. They try to make you feel better. They create the felicities of life. These things are important, *essential,* and I don't want women to give them up. I want men to learn them. I want to feminize the world.[6]

And yet, although Dolores rejects Victor, and refuses to commit herself to any relationship that is not entirely free on both sides, the connection between the two does not end. The book concludes with the feeling of joy Dolores feels in Victor's presence, and the hope, faint but real, that this year of true conversation has had enormous benefits, and that some solution may be found.

> All of us, round plump children, long skinny children, brown and yellow and pale and pink and red and chocolate, all born with the cancer inside, tearing around from clinic to clinic, seeking diagnosis, cure.
>
> (p. 374)

A review of *The Bleeding Heart* in *Ms.* complains that women today want some kind of guideline for modern heterosexual relationships, ". . . how (and how much, and when, and why) to relate to the sort of man one might describe as *Duke* Charming."[7] While a plea to learn how to live life from literature is absurd, it is clear that—for literature, at least—a cure, or a progressive diagnosis, is here in *The Bleeding Heart*. Certainly the attempt to break out of the standard forms of human relationships in literature is a step in the right direction.

Notes

1. (April 5, 1980).

2. (March 16, 1980), p. 9.

3. "Anguish Artist," *Time* (March 17, 1980), p. 92.

4. Marilyn French, *The Bleeding Heart* (New York: Summit Books, 1980), p. 243. All succeeding quotations from this work refer to this text.

5. *Time* (March 17, 1980), p. 92.

6. *New York Times Book Review* (March 16, 1980), p. 9.

7. Lindsey Van Gelder, "Romance Reconsidered," *Ms.* (May, 1980), p. 28.

Her Mother's Daughter

KATHERINE PAYANT (REVIEW DATE 1992)

SOURCE: Payant, Katherine. "Mothers and Daughters in Recent Fiction by Women." *Philological Papers* 38 (1992): 212-25.

In the following excerpt, Payant discusses the plot and characterizations in Her Mother's Daughter, *noting differences between this book and* The Women's Room.

In the 1970s the new feminist movement affected women's novels in a number of ways, but perhaps the most obvious influence was the predominance of the bildungsroman—the novel of development tracing a protagonist struggling for individuation in patriarchy. These novels, written by white middle-class women who came of age in the 1940s and 1950s, recounted the hero-

ine's oppression in childhood, adolescence, marriage, and motherhood. They dealt with restrictions on women in all areas of American life—the double standard, stereotyping of women in the media, limitations on women's reproductive freedom, educational and career barriers faced by women, and above all, the mistreatment of women by men in love and marriage.

Although generalizations are often risky, these novels seemed to closely fit this description. Examples include Erica Jong's *Fear of Flying* (1973), Lisa Alther's *Kinflicks* (1975), Francine du Plessix Gray's *Lovers and Tyrants* (1976), Marge Piercy's *Small Changes* (1972), and perhaps the angriest of all, Marilyn French's *The Women's Room* (1977). Though these feminist novels differed in the amount of overt politics and tone (some were satiric and others somber), in each the author protested societal restrictions faced by women. Reading such a novel was a crash course in consciousness raising, and the writer's anger could generate anger in the reader against patriarchy in general and the men in her life in particular.

In their content "First Wave" feminist novels seemed to reflect the general thrust and tone of the women's movement during these years. These were the years of "naming the oppressor," of tracing misogyny in male literature, of documenting examples of oppression of women in the workplace and throughout American history, and of debunking Freudian thought, which said that women's primary function is to bear and nurture the next generation. So, it was natural that fiction writers, whether they were political activists or only influenced by feminist ideas, would concentrate on "naming the oppressor"[1] as well.

In the 1980s, however, though women writers have continued to reflect feminist themes, those themes have changed, one obvious difference being a turning away from women's oppression in patriarchy. Instead, writers have reflected cultural feminist attitudes, an approach stressing the strengths and values of female culture, what women can offer patriarchal society and each other, with the ultimate goal of ending patriarchy.[2] Favorite topics have been themes such as female friendship—the gifts women give each other—thus the enormous popularity of Alice Walker's *The Color Purple* in the 1980s. Though this novel certainly portrayed the oppression of women the dominant theme was the love and support women offer other women.

One popular subject in 1980s fiction unexplored in earlier decades is the experience of motherhood and the relationship of mothers to their children, especially their daughters. Often these two related themes can be found within the same novel. Novels dealing with motherhood reflect maternalist feminist attitudes, a school of thought exploring and elevating woman's maternal function. Essentially, the maternalists, who include a founding mother of American feminism, Elizabeth Cady Stanton, and Adrienne Rich in our own times, believe that motherhood makes women better people. Through nurturing small children the mother, unlike the father, is forced to extend herself beyond her own ego and thus develops compassion and skill in relating to those outside herself.[3]

In the 1980s Marilyn French has explored the effects of motherhood and mother-daughter relations in **Her Mother's Daughter** (1987). In this story of three generations of American women, the protagonist is Anastasia, a liberated woman photographer of the eighties who, in her fifties, is still seeking approval and a closer relationship with her mother Belle. Belle is the daughter of Polish immigrant Frances, a poor and abused wife of a tyrannical husband. Upon her husband's death, Frances had to relinquish several of her children to foster care, and because of guilt, sorrow, and overwork is never able to nurture Belle enough.

Raised in poverty, Belle vows to give Anastasia everything she never had—music lessons, a comfortable home, and beautiful clothes. But, because of her own starved heart, she never shows her daughter the love and approval the child and woman desperately longs for. A bitter, unhappy woman, Belle sacrifices herself physically for her children's comfort but neglects their emotional nurturing. French uses the metaphor of the "midge mother," an insect whose body is sucked dry by her offspring (12). By the time her children are grown, Belle has indeed been sucked dry, but her children have not really been nourished. In this treatment of the effects of the lack of nurturing, French demonstrates the daunting power of a mother in a nuclear family, held responsible by society, herself, and her children themselves for their psychological security.

Throughout the novel, French emphasizes the primal power of the mother bond. For example, Anastasia watches her sleeping children:

> Arden with her eyes open just a crack, so you couldn't be sure she was sleeping, and Billy with his thumb in his mouth—clear through until he was ten years old. They would be pink and sweet-

smelling from their baths and their sweat, and warm with sleep, and my heart would roll over as I looked at them and often I'd kneel down by the side of the bed and lay my face on their cheeks. . . .[4]

Although she is powerfully drawn to her children, Anastasia realizes this primal tie can be women's ruin if they allow themselves to be consumed by it, as society has said they should. On the other hand, it is women's greatest source of strength, perhaps, as the maternalists say, what makes women morally superior to men. Says Anastasia, "women are more sensitive, more fun— all the things you have to be to raise kids . . ." (565).

Though Anastasia acknowledges the pleasures and power of motherhood, she vows never to be a "midge mother" like Belle. She will have a career, a life of her own, and she does, an exciting career as a free-lance photographer that takes her all over the world. As a result, her own daughter Arden resents Anastasia's career because she does not stay home like the other fifties moms and provide milk and cookies after school. For a time in the 1960s, vowing she will be a better mother than Anastasia, Arden joins a primitive commune where women do traditional work. However, by the end of the novel, Arden and Anastasia are moving toward a closer relationship; frustrated by a life of full-time child care, Arden is beginning to understand Anastasia's need for her own life, and Anastasia understands Arden's temporary need to take the opposite tack. Sadly, this rapprochement seems impossible for Belle and Anastasia. French suggests that closeness is very difficult between the pre-feminist mothers and their post-feminist daughters.

Like other 1980s novelists, French frankly acknowledges women's occasional anger at their children for restricting their lives. The bitter Belle has almost totally repressed this anger, but the feminist Anastasia recognizes it:

> Mother love. There is supposed to be no room in it for coldness of heart, for a private cell for oneself, with doors that sometimes clank shut. And the more you love your children, the more shocked they are to discover that you possess a single strand of ambivalent—or negative—feeling.
>
> Insatiable for this love we expect to be absolute, we cannot forgive its mere humanness.
>
> (71-72)

The fact is that women do not always love their own children, and can even feel a murderous rage against them that can translate into abuse. Other feminist writers treating this subject include Mary Gordon, who in several of her novels discusses the new mother's resentment against this tiny creature who demands her whole existence, and Toni Morrison, who compassionately deals with child abuse in *Tar Baby* (1980). Morrison does not excuse such abuse but traces its roots to the mother's feeling of lack of control brought about by the child's intrusion into her life.

A number of feminist novelists in the 1980s suggested that woman's function of caregiver and nurturer, though sometimes dangerously limiting, can provide both gifts for the society by humanizing it, and for the woman as well. While the authors of the bildungsroman of the 1970s saw marriage and motherhood as bondage restricting female individuation, writers in the 1980s were more likely to view such relationships as vehicles for growth. In **Her Mother's Daughter** Anastasia explains:

> I believed freedom was independence, needing no one, having your work and doing what you damn well wanted to do. And that this was what the heroic man—or woman—did, this was how they lived. And if you ended up lonely, then you lived with that. Because being with people was a compromise, a deference, a dependency. . . . . That's what I felt. Until very recently.
>
> (674)

In other words, we find ourselves in relationship. Near the end of the novel when Arden asks if she should stay with her husband with whom she is having problems, Anastasia replies, "I can only tell you what I know" (675). In recounting what she learned from her own marital troubles, Anastasia gives Arden the gift of her own experience and suggests that some dependency and compromise for those we love can be a source of a woman's meaning and strength. The difficult thing is not to end up like Belle, "a midge mother." This conclusion to **Her Mother's Daughter** seems markedly different from that of **The Women's Room,** whose heroine Mira refused to compromise, lived a heroic life, but ended up lonely and neurotic. . . .

The women's movement of the last twenty years has had profound effects on fiction by women, effects which are continuing to evolve. If the 1970s was the era of "naming the oppressor" and exploring male-female power struggles, the 1980s must be seen as the era of women together. Women writers have moved ever deeper into women's experience, telling painful and joyful truths about aspects of that experience which twenty years ago we might have considered insignificant. The most exciting part of this writing is the unfolding insights it continues to give women readers about themselves. Women writers are not only naming the oppressor, they are naming themselves, and as it has done since ancient times, this act of naming confers knowledge and power.

Notes

1. Carol Ruth Berkin, "Clio in Search of Her Daughters/ Women in Search of Their Past," in *Major Problems in American Women's History,* ed. Mary Beth Norton (Lexington, MA: Heath, 1989) 11.

2. Josephine Donovan gives a good explanation of cultural feminism in ch. 2 of her book *Feminist Theory: The Intellectual Traditions of American Feminism* (New York: Ungar, 1985).

3. Gerda Lerner, *The Creation of Patriarchy* (New York: Oxford UP, 1986) 26-28.

4. (New York: Summit, 1987) 92.

FURTHER READING

Criticism

Dunlap, Lauren Glen. Review of *The War against Women,* by Marilyn French. *Belles Lettres* 8, no. 1 (fall 1992): 20-1.

Praises French's focus on the injustices suffered by women in The War against Women.

French, Marilyn. "Women in Language." *Soundings* 59, no. 3 (fall 1976): 329-44.

Examination of the semantic differences among such words as "man," "lady," and "gentleman," focusing on the ways words change in context and their impact on defining gender.

———. "Muzzled Women." *College Literature* 14, no. 3 (1987): 219-29.

Discusses several prominent women authors, ironically noting that female characters are seldom portrayed by women writers as having fulfilling, complete, rewarding lives.

McDaniel, Maude. "Sisters and Other Strangers." *Chicago Tribune Books* (2 January 1994): section 14, p. 5.

Compliments French's prose in Our Father, *commenting that the work is the most balanced of French's novels.*

Peat, Irene M. Review of *A Season in Hell,* by Marilyn French. *British Medical Journal* 318, no. 7179 (30 January 1999): 336.

Lauds French's insightful and meticulously detailed account of her battle with cancer in A Season in Hell.

Selway, Jennifer. "Dad's the Word." *Observer* (1 May 1994): 23.

Offers a mixed assessment of Our Father, *noting that the novel's central themes remain "elusive."*

Wagner, Linda W. "The French Definition." *Arizona Quarterly* 38, no. 4 (winter 1982): 293-302.

Evaluation of the plot and structure of The Women's Room *and* The Bleeding Heart, *contending that French's desire to define terms and language in her narratives slows her storytelling but makes the importance of language clear.*

Wilson, Anna. *Persuasive Fictions: Feminist Narrative and Critical Myth,* Lewisburg, Pa.: Bucknell University Press, 2001, 161 p.

Includes the essay "The Women's Room and the Fiction of Consciousness," as well as bibliographical information.

OTHER SOURCES FROM GALE:

Additional coverage of French's life and career is contained in the following sources published by the Gale Group: *Beacham's Encyclopedia of Popular Fiction: Biography & Resources,* Vol. 1; *Contemporary Authors,* Vols. 69-72; *Contemporary Authors New Revision Series,* Vols. 3, 31; *Contemporary Literary Criticism,* Vols. 10, 18, 60, 177; *Contemporary Novelists,* Ed. 7; *Contemporary Popular Writers; DISCovering Author Modules: Dramatists, Novelists* and *Popular Fiction and Genre Authors; Feminist Writers; Literature Resource Center;* and *Major 20th-Century Writers,* Eds. 1, 2.

CHARLOTTE PERKINS GILMAN

(1860 - 1935)

American short story writer, essayist, novelist, poet, and autobiographer.

A distinguished social reformer and feminist, Gilman produced several works of nonfiction devoted to her social and economic theories, as well as fictional texts embodying those principles. Her most famous works are *The Yellow Wallpaper* (1892), depicting a young mother's descent into madness, and the utopian fantasy *Herland* (1915).

BIOGRAPHICAL INFORMATION

Born July 3, 1860, in Hartford, Connecticut, Gilman was the daughter of Frederick Beecher Perkins, a librarian and magazine editor, and Mary Fitch Wescott Perkins. She was the grandniece of the abolitionist Harriet Beecher Stowe, the feminist Catherine Beecher, and the suffragist Isabella Beecher Hooker. Gilman's father, known for his volatile temper, had difficulty measuring up to the standards of the Beecher family; he tried several professions before finally devoting himself to literature. He served as assistant director of the Boston Public Library, and in 1880 became director of the San Francisco Public Library. He left the family shortly after Gilman was born and provided only meager financial support on an irregular basis until 1873, when Mary Perkins filed for divorce. Plagued by financial difficulties, Gilman, her mother, and Gilman's older brother Thomas moved frequently and occasionally stayed with relatives. Gilman was thus exposed to the independence and social activism of her great aunts.

When she was fourteen, aided by an inheritance, Gilman began attending a private school. Within two years she was teaching art and working as a commercial artist. At the age of nineteen, Gilman began studying art at the Rhode Island School of Design, where she met her first husband, artist Walter Stetson. They were married in 1884 and a year later had a daughter, Katherine Beecher Stetson. Following Katherine's birth, Gilman began suffering from depression and traveled to California for an extended stay with her good friend, Grace Channing. When she returned, she began writing articles and poetry which were published in *People*, a weekly newspaper in Providence, and *Women's Journal*, a publication of the American Woman Suffrage Association. Her depression soon returned, however, and she consulted S. Weir Mitchell, the famous Philadelphia neurologist noted for his "rest cure." The prescribed treatment—complete inactivity and isolation—brought Gilman, in her own words, "perilously close to losing my mind." It was an experience that would later form the basis for *The Yellow Wallpaper*.

In 1887 the Stetsons separated, and mother and daughter moved to Pasadena, California, where Gilman took up life as a writer and activist. She lectured throughout the United States and England on labor reform and women's issues, and began publishing her nonfiction theoretical works. In 1891 she moved to Oakland and became active in a number of reform movements, including the Nationalist Party, a socialist group devoted to the program of social reform outlined in Edward Bellamy's novel *Looking Backward: 2000-1887*. In 1900 Gilman married George Houghton Gilman, who proved very supportive of her work as an activist. From 1909 to 1916 she served as writer and editor of *The Forerunner*, a monthly journal devoted to social reform, which featured Gilman's essays, poems, short stories, and sketches. In 1932 she was diagnosed with inoperable breast cancer; two years later her husband George died, and the following year Gilman took her own life to escape the pain and inevitability of a slow death from her condition. She died August 17, 1935.

MAJOR WORKS

During her lifetime, Gilman's most influential work was the theoretical piece *Women and Economics* (1898), in which she outlined the consequences of women's economic dependence, both for individual women and for society as a whole. Her other major theoretical writings include *Concerning Children* (1900), containing her thoughts on educating and disciplining children; *The Home: Its Work and Influence* (1903), dedicated to dispelling the common myths surrounding the sanctity of the home and describing the price women pay for lives of domestic service; and *Human Work* (1904), a discussion of the social and civic functions of labor, considered by Gilman her most important work.

Much of Gilman's literary output was published in her monthly magazine *The Forerunner*, which she published from 1909 to 1916, serving as both its editor and sole contributor. The magazine contained short stories and plays, poetry, essays, reviews of current books and articles, and an advice column called "Personal Problems." Some of her works, both fiction and nonfiction, were originally serialized in *The Forerunner*; one such work was *The Man-Made World; or, Our Androcentric Culture*, which appeared in the magazine in 1909 and was published in book form two years later. Gilman's fictional contributions to the magazine were normally devoted to the themes

and concerns raised in her works of social and political theory. Many of her stories involved the wrongs inflicted on women by men, including extramarital affairs, venereal diseases, and physical abuse.

Gilman is best known for her novella *The Yellow Wallpaper*, originally published in *New England Magazine* and reprinted in William Dean Howell's collection *The Great Modern American Stories* (1920). The work has been variously interpreted as a gothic horror story, a feminist polemic, and an autobiographical tale of the author's own experience with the popular medical treatment of Dr. S. Weir Mitchell. *The Yellow Wallpaper*, along with Gilman's feminist utopian novel *Herland*, were rediscovered by feminist scholars in the 1970s, after many decades of critical neglect. *Herland* originally appeared in serial form in *The Forerunner* (1915) and depicts an all-female world where men are unnecessary, even for reproduction. Three males from the outside world enter Herland and, along with three of its inhabitants, engage in an extended dialogue that points out the differences between their respective cultures. Both *The Yellow Wallpaper* and *Herland* were reissued in the 1970s and remain among the most-studied works in women's studies courses.

CRITICAL RECEPTION

Gilman's reputation during her lifetime was based on the vast body of nonfiction work she produced on social and political issues. Her contemporaries praised *Women and Economics*, her most celebrated work, and compared it to John Stuart Mill's *The Subjection of Women*. Such social reformers as Jane Addams and Florence Kelly contributed to the book's positive reception. However, *Women and Economics*, like most of Gilman's writings, entered a long period of critical neglect until feminist scholars in the 1970s led a revival of interest in her fiction. A reassessment of her nonfiction works began later, with her treatise on women's economic dependence on men gaining recognition as an important work in the field of economics as well as in the area of women's studies.

Although scholars generally agree that Gilman was a pioneer in analyzing social and economic relationships based on gender, many modern critics fault the narrowness of her reformist vision. According to Ann J. Lane (see Further Reading), Gilman "seriously neglected issues of class, race, and ethnicity and their complex interaction with gender. She believed in laws of racial development, which today are read, usually correctly, as racist and ethnocentric." Similarly, Shelley Fisher Fishkin acknowledges that some of Gilman's theories "do not wear well" today, among them "her racism, her ethnocentrism, her anti-Semitism, her homophobia, her xenophobia, and her simplistic faith in evolutionary progress." However, many of Gilman's ideas on gender relations seem as relevant to contemporary students as they were in Gilman's own time, and Fishkin reports the widespread use of Gilman's texts in American college courses, ranging from literature and women's studies to economics and American studies.

Most prominent of the Gilman texts used in the classroom today is *The Yellow Wallpaper.* Catherine Golden reports that not only was the work virtually unknown until the early 1970s, Gilman originally had great difficulty getting the story published. Golden reprints a rejection letter from the editor of the *Atlantic Monthly,* who was so disturbed by the piece that he claimed he could not make his readers as miserable as he had made himself by reading it. In the twenty-first century, the work frequently appears in anthologies and has established "a firm place in the feminist literary canon," according to Golden, and criticism of the story has reached a point of such complexity that "critics openly debate central aspects of the story with each other," and are "as actively engaged in reading and responding to each other's interpretations of 'The Yellow Wallpaper' as they are in reading the story itself." Golden attributes this debate to the open-ended quality of the text, which "seems to raise more questions than it answers."

PRINCIPAL WORKS

"The Yellow Wallpaper" (novella) 1892; published in book form as *The Yellow Wallpaper* 1899

In This Our World (poetry) 1893

"The Rocking Chair" (short story) 1893

Women and Economics: A Study of the Economic Relation between Men and Women as a Factor in Social Evolution (nonfiction) 1898

Concerning Children (essay) 1900

The Home: Its Work and Influence (essay) 1903

Human Work (essay) 1904

The Punishment That Educates (essay) 1907

Women and Social Service (essay) 1907

"The Cottagette" (short story) 1910

What Diantha Did (novel) 1910

The Crux (novel) 1911

Something to Vote For (play) 1911

"Making a Change" (short story) 1911

The Man-Made World; or, Our Androcentric Culture (essay) 1911

Moving the Mountain (novel) 1911

"Turned" (short story) 1911

Benigna Machiavelli (novel) 1914

Herland (novel) 1915

With Her in Ourland (novel) 1916

His Religion and Hers: A Study of the Faith of Our Fathers and the Work of Our Mothers (essay) 1923

The Living of Charlotte Perkins Gilman (autobiography) 1935

The Charlotte Perkins Gilman Reader (short stories and novel fragments) 1980

Charlotte Perkins Gilman: A Nonfiction Reader (nonfiction) 1991

The Diaries of Charlotte Perkins Gilman (diary) 1994

A Journey from Within: The Love Letters of Charlotte Perkins Gilman, 1897-1935 (letters) 1995

The Dress of Women: A Critical Introduction to the Symbolism and Sociology of Clothing (nonfiction) 2002

PRIMARY SOURCES

CHARLOTTE PERKINS GILMAN (ESSAY DATE 1898)

SOURCE: Gilman, Charlotte Perkins. "Women and Economics." In *The American Reader: Words That Moved a Nation,* edited by Diane Ravitch, pp. 205-06. New York: HarperCollins Publishers, 1990.

In the following excerpt from her 1898 book Women and Economics, *Gilman discusses the cost of the restrictions placed upon women in America—to individuals and to society as a whole.*

What we do modifies us more than what is done to us. The freedom of expression has been more restricted in women than the freedom of impression, if that be possible. Something of the world she lived in she has seen from her barred windows. Some air has come through the purdah's folds, some knowledge has filtered to her eager ears from the talk of men. Desdemona learned somewhat of Othello. Had she known more, she might have lived longer. But in the ever-growing human impulse to create, the power and will to make, to do, to express one's new spirit in new forms,—here she has been utterly debarred. She might work as she had worked from the beginning,—at the primitive labors of the household; but in the inevitable expansion of even those industries to professional levels we have striven to hold her back. To work with her own hands, for nothing, in direct body-service to her own family,—this has been permitted,—yes, compelled. But to be and to do anything further from this she has been forbidden. Her labor has not been limited in kind, but in degree. Whatever she has been allowed to do must be done in private and alone, the first-hand industries of savage times. . . .

It is painfully interesting to trace the gradual cumulative effect of these conditions upon women: first, the action of large natural laws, acting on her as they would act on any other animal; then the evolution of social customs and laws (with her position as the active cause), following the direction of mere physical forces, and adding heavily to them; then, with increasing civilization, the unbroken accumulation of precedent, burnt into each generation by the growing force of education, made lovely by art, holy by religion, desirable by habit; and, steadily acting from beneath, the unswerving pressure of economic necessity upon which the whole structure rested. These are strong modifying conditions, indeed.

The process would have been even more effective and far less painful but for one important circumstance. Heredity has no Salic law. Each girl child inherits from her father a certain increasing percentage of human development, human power, human tendency; and each boy as well inherits from his mother the increasing percentage of sex-development, sex-power, sex-tendency. The action of heredity has been to equalize what every tendency of environment and education made to differ. This has saved us from such a female as the gypsy moth. It has held up the woman, and held down the man. It has set iron bounds to our absurd effort to make a race with one sex a million years behind the other. But it has added terribly to the pain and difficulty of human life,—a difficulty and a pain that should have taught us long since that we were living on wrong lines. Each woman born, re-humanized by the current of race activity carried on by her father and

re-womanized by her traditional position, has had to live over again in her own person the same process of restriction, repression, denial; the smothering "no" which crushed down all her human desires to create, to discover, to learn, to express, to advance. . . .

To the young man confronting life the world lies wide. Such powers as he has he may use, must use. If he chooses wrong at first, he may choose again, and yet again. Not effective or successful in one channel, he may do better in another. The growing, varied needs of all mankind call on him for the varied service in which he finds his growth. What he wants to be, he may strive to get. What he wants to get, he may strive to get. Wealth, power, social distinction, fame,—what he wants he can try for.

To the young woman confronting life there is the same world beyond, there are the same human energies and human desires and ambition within. But all that she may wish to have, all that she may wish to do, must come through a single channel and a single choice. Wealth, power, social distinction, fame,—not only these, but home and happiness, reputation, ease and pleasure, her bread and butter,—all, must come to her through a small gold ring. This is a heavy pressure. It has accumulated behind her through heredity, and continued about her through environment. It has been subtly trained into her through education, till she herself has come to think it a right condition, and pours its influence upon her daughter with increasing impetus. Is it any wonder that women are oversexed? But for the constant inheritance from the more human male, we should have been queen bees, indeed, long before this. But the daughter of the soldier and the sailor, of the artist, the inventor, the great merchant, has inherited in body and brain her share of his development in each generation, and so stayed somewhat human for all her femininity. . . .

GENERAL COMMENTARY

MARY A. HILL (ESSAY DATE 1980)

SOURCE: Hill, Mary A. "Charlotte Perkins Gilman: A Feminist's Struggle with Womanhood." In *Charlotte Perkins Gilman: The Woman and Her Work*, edited by Sheryl L. Meyering, pp. 31-50. Ann Arbor, Mich.: UMI Research Press, 1989.

In the following essay, originally published in 1980, Hill discusses the development of Gilman's feminism within the confines of her prescribed roles as wife and mother.

In a letter written from Belmont, New Hampshire, September 2, 1897, Charlotte Perkins Stetson exclaimed, "Thirty-five hundred words I wrote this morning, in three hours!" A book's chapter in one sitting; a successive six-week dizzy pace of morning writing; elaborate consultations with her closest critic, Houghton Gilman, soon to be her second husband; and thus was ***Women and Economics*** dashed into print. Jane Addams, already emerging as one of America's foremost social reformers, expressed her gratitude to Charlotte, her "pleasure and satisfaction," her "greatest admiration" for the "Masterpiece." Florence Kelly, another pioneer of social settlement reform viewed it as "the first real, substantial contribution made by a woman to the science of economics." According to *The Nation*, "Since John Stuart Mill's essays on *The Subjection of Women*, there has been no book dealing with the whole position of women to approach it in originality of conception and brilliancy of exposition."[1]

Charlotte Gilman quite naturally felt increasingly elated as positive reviews rolled in, despite the societal distortions her book both reflected and described. A flamboyant speaker, a writer with a penetrating wit, she was rapidly emerging as a major theorist and popularizer for the woman's movement in turn-of-the-century America. Publicly she attempted to analyze and expose the ubiquitous effects of sex-based inequalities and the sources of female strength; and privately she acknowledged that many of her perceptions emerged as well from agonizing conflicts of her life. "We ourselves," she publicly and sweepingly asserted, "have preserved in our own character the confusion and contradiction which is our greatest difficulty in life."[2] And privately she acknowledged the war between contending factions in herself. To Houghton Gilman she described a major challenge of her life: "To prove that a woman can love and work too. To resist this dragging weight of the old swollen woman-heart, and force it into place—the world's Life first—my own life next. Work first—love next. Perhaps this is simply the burden of our common womanhood which is weighing on me so."[3]

The seeds of Charlotte's radical feminism were rooted in an early struggle for independence, self-assertion, and self-respect. Raised primarily within a female kinship network necessitated by her father's absence, and deprived from early infancy of the motherly affection for which she yearned, Charlotte nonetheless disclosed in her diaries and notebooks a growing strength of character, a playful, lively, independent personality. Rebellious

against the model of repressive discipline her unhappy mother, Mary Perkins, attempted to impose, she was active in physical fitness programs, lecture clubs, and language classes. Armed with books and reading lists provided by her librarian father, Frederick Perkins, Charlotte was well-read in contemporary philosophical, historical, and anthropological thought. She delighted in her physical as well as her mental agility; her effort to control her body was maintained within her larger program to control her life. By the age of 21, she was self-supporting, busy from 6 A.M. to 10 P.M., and thriving in the process.

Despite the limitations imposed in her mother's prudish discipline, Charlotte constantly had calls, visitors, and stimulating friendships with males as well as females. She enjoyed hiking, sleighing, rowing, playing whist, and was exhilarated in her triumphs at the chess board. She enjoyed inspiring evening talks with Ada Blake and Augusta Gladding, and many long walks with Grace Channing, who became her lifelong friend. Also, she developed an intimate relationship with Martha Luther, a relationship of mutual trust and shared interests. They delighted in each other's company. "With Martha I knew perfect happiness," she later wrote. "Four years of satisfying happiness with Martha, then she married and moved away."[4]

Charlotte's friendship with Martha provided the kind of support, encouragement, and mutual affection historians currently believe was central to the experience of most nineteenth-century women. The reality of Charlotte's love was quite apparent, her grief at the impending separation was intense and disruptive. In 1881, Charlotte noted that "some swain" was threatening her relationship with Martha, that because of marriage she might lose her "most intimate friend." On November 5th she wrote: "Pleasant, to ring at the door where you've always been greeted with gladness; to be met by the smile that you value all other above—to see that smile flicker and vanish and change into sadness because she was met by *your* presence instead of her love." On November 16th she noted, "Walk in the dark streets for an hour or so in dumb misery." In December, she summarized: "A year of steady work. A quiet year, and a hard one. . . . A year in which I knew the sweetness of perfect friendship, and have lost it forever."[5] After a typical self-scourging, she became more stoic, striving to submerge her grief by helping others. But the vacuum left by Martha's absence heightened Charlotte's longings for affection, and may have paved the way for her acceptance of the comforting protection of a man.

On January 12, 1882, Charlotte met an aspiring artist, Walter Stetson. Within seventeen days of their first meeting he proposed. Her diary entry reads: "I have this day been asked the one great question in a womans [sic] life and have refused." Two days later she wrote:

Now that my head is cool and clear, now before I give myself any sense to another; let me write down my Reasons for living single.

In the first place, I am fonder of freedom than anything else—. . . .

I like to be *able* and *free* to help any and everyone, as I never could be if my time and thoughts were taken up by that extended self—a family. . . .

I am cool, fearless, and strong. . . .

For reasons many and good, reasons of slow growth and careful consideration, more reasons that I now can remember; I decide to Live—Alone.

God help me![6]

For a time at least, Charlotte remained committed to her rationale for spinsterhood: "if I were to try the path you open to me I could never try my own," she wrote. "I know of course that the time would come when I must choose between two lives, but never did I dream that it would come so soon, and that the struggle would be so terrible." It was, as she put it directly to Walter, "a trial which in very truth *does* try me like fire."[7]

Despite her misgivings, Charlotte began to express increasing affection for Walter—"I am beginning to wonder how I ever lived through this winter, before you—; . . . You want to give me something! You are giving me back myself." By 1883, she was engaged to Walter and began to accept his sympathy, his comforting, his advice, even when it was constricting. For example, when a close friend gave her a new copy of Walt Whitman's *Leaves of Grass* she noted, "I am obliged to decline, as I had promised Walter I would not read it." She now resolved, first and foremost, to be "*Absolutely unselfish* . . . To find my happiness in the pleasurable sensations of others rather than in my own. To consider others, think of others, think first 'will he or she like it?' rather than shall I."[8]

As Charlotte's expressions of affection and self-sacrifice intensified, so also did her gloom. She experienced a loss of strength, discipline, and courage which she had worked so consciously to acquire. In December, 1883, she wrote: "Let me not forget to be grateful for what I have. Some strength, some purpose, some design, some pro-

gress, some esteem, respect—and affection. And some Love. Which I can neither feel, see, nor believe in when the darkness comes." She continued: "I mean this year to try hard for somewhat of my former poise and courage. As I remember it was got by practice." Nonetheless, a severe depression began to take its toll:

I would more gladly die than ever yet; saving
    for the bitter agony I should leave in the
    heart
of him who loves me. And mother's pain.
    But O! God knows I am tired, tired, tired of
    life!
    If I could only know that I was doing right.[9]

Charlotte's expressed attitudes toward marriage and motherhood were fiercely ambivalent. Rationally aware of possible conflicts between self-development and love, she was largely unprepared to meet the complex unconscious as well as deliberate patterns of socialization which forced most women to accept self-sacrificing love as natural, inevitable, and right. Drawing from conflicting signals of her mother, Mary Perkins, Charlotte knew that women could achieve a modicum of independence, but always at a price. Mary Perkins was a divorced and eventually self-supporting woman, nourished and sustained by a female network of friends and relatives; her nonconformity strengthened Charlotte's capacity for independence. But suffering from the stigma of divorce, from economic hardship, from the guilt and emotional insecurity of her single lifestyle caused her, Mary quickened Charlotte's fear of spinsterhood. Both parents had also unwittingly encouraged Charlotte's independence by withholding their affection. Mary Perkins had denied caresses to her daughter: "I used to put away your little hand from my cheek when you were a nursing baby," Mary told Charlotte in her later years. "I did not want you to suffer as I had suffered." Likewise her librarian father, Frederick Perkins, kept his distance: "the word Father, in the sense of love, care, one to go to in trouble, means nothing to me," Charlotte wrote, "save indeed in advice about books and the care of them—which seems more the librarian than the father."[10]

A contemporary psychologist, Alexandra Symonds, discussed symptoms in her recent patients quite similar to those that Charlotte was beginning to exhibit. The women Symonds treated were active, vital, and self-assured before their marriages. Yet they were also often women who had to "grow up in a hurry." Denied experiences of warmth in childhood, they were encouraged to control their feelings and give the impression of strength and self-sufficiency. Symonds suggests a frequent pattern: "They repressed their healthy needs to be taken care of and repressed the child in them as well." Perhaps Charlotte's difficulties were rooted in the discipline and loneliness of youth, the loss of her friend Martha Luther serving only to exacerbate her thirst for love. Perhaps, as Symonds puts it, she desired "to put down a tremendous burden which she had been carrying all her life, and be the dependent little girl she had never been before."[11]

On May 2, 1884 Charles Walter Stetson and Charlotte Anna Perkins were married in Providence, Rhode Island. "O my God! I thank thee for this heavenly happiness!" she wrote in her diary the evening of the wedding.[12]

There were commonly expected roles of men and women in marriage that both Charlotte and Walter accepted. As a man, Walter was expected to provide for his family. He did not have to choose between marriage and his work. In fact, marriage lent further purpose to his artistic growth and creative efforts. Charlotte, by contrast, felt a momentous change occurring in her life. Formerly self-supporting, independent, and career-oriented, she found herself involved with time-consuming domestic chores which conflicted with the work she loved—painting and writing. Within a week, some spontaneous rebellion seemed to be occurring. She wrote in her diary, "I suggest he [Walter] pay me for my services; and he much dislikes the idea. I am grieved at offending him; mutual misery. Bed and cry." She was beginning to experience firsthand what later she would depict to trenchantly: "the home which is so far from beautiful, so wearing to the nerves and dulling to the heart, the home life that means care and labour and disappointment, the quiet, unnoticed whirlpool that sucks down youth and beauty and enthusiasm, man's long labour and woman's longer love."[13]

Although the personal dynamics of Charlotte's relationship with Walter remain elusive, sexual experiences may have contributed to her growing discontent. At times Charlotte viewed sexuality with traditional Victorian prudery: "Purity," she wrote in 1883, "is that state in which no evil impulse, no base thought can come in; or if forced in dies of shame in the white light. Purity may be gained by persistent and long continued refusal to entertain low ideas." Yet it is also clear that she was by no means always cold or unapproachable in early marriage. On June 15, 1884, she noted: "Am sad: last night and this morning. Because I find myself too—affectionately expressive. I must keep more to myself and be asked—not borne with." And on June 25 the same year she wrote, "Get miserable over my old woe—conviction of being too outwardly expressive of affection."[14]

Soon Charlotte was pregnant, a condition which lessened her physical and emotional stamina. Even after the birth of Katharine Stetson in 1885, Charlotte wrote in her diary, "Every morning the same hopeless waking . . . same weary drag." She appreciated her home, her healthy baby, the services of her mother and a competent domestic servant, yet was helpless and despondent: "and I lay all day on the lounge and cried."[15] A failure in her own eyes, she looked to Walter for protective love, and increasingly for pity. She was assuming what Carroll Smith-Rosenberg has referred to as those "character traits assigned to women in Victorian society and the characteristic symptoms of nineteenth-century hysteric: dependency, fragility, emotionality, narcissism."[16] Charlotte did not as yet attack the religion of maternity, the assumption that all mothers are "saintly givers." Instead, she resigned herself to misery. She wrote, Walter "would do everything in the world for me; but he cannot see how irrevocably bound I am, for life, for life. No, unless he die and the baby die, or he change or I change, there is no way out." She described her "hysteria" as follows:

> I could not read nor write nor paint nor sew nor talk nor listen to talking, nor anything. I lay on that lounge and wept all day. The tears ran down into my ears on either side. I went to bed crying, woke in the night crying, sat on the edge of the bed in the morning and cried—from sheet continuous pain. . . .
>
> I made a rag baby, hung it on a doorknob and played with it. I would crawl into remote closets and under beds—to hide from the grinding pressure of that profound distress. . . .[17]

In writing her autobiography, Charlotte described her "mental illness" as a disease beyond her understanding, an accidental misfortune. Suffering from recurrent depressions, she continued to believe that causes for her suffering lay not in the personal or political conflicts of her life, but in idiosyncratic weaknesses within herself. The price she paid for nonconformity was guilt, despite the fact that almost all of her feminist writings were inextricably related to her life, and despite the fact as well that her short story, **The Yellow Wallpaper**" was itself a feminist-oriented autobiographical portrayal of insanity.

In "**The Yellow Wallpaper**," an "hysterical woman," overprotected by a loving husband, is taken to a summer home to recover from nervousness, and told to rest and sleep and try to use her "will and self-control" to overcome her miseries. The room her husband John assigns to her is covered with a yellow-patterned wallpaper. "The color is repellent, almost revolting; a smouldering unclean yellow, strangely faded by the slow-turning sunlight." Although the woman is quite ill, her husband, a physician, tells her that there is "no reason" for her suffering; she must dismiss those "silly fantasies." Of course, "it is only nervousness," she decides. But "it does weigh on me so not to do my duty in any way! . . . [and] such a dear baby! And yet I *cannot* be with him, it makes me so nervous." She tries to rest and do as she is told, but suffers doubly since her husband will not believe that she is ill. He "does not know how much I really suffer. He knows there is no *reason* to suffer, and that satisfies him." She thinks she should appreciate the protective love he offers. "He takes all care from me, and I feel so basely ungrateful not to value it more. . . . He took me in his arms and called me a blessed little goose." And yet it is impossible to talk to him "because he is so wise, and because he loves me so." Efforts to discuss the matter only bring a "stern reproachful look" and send her back to bed in shame.

John offers tender love, but enforces the inactivity which deepens her despair. I "am absolutely forbidden to 'work' until I am well again." Here he comes, "I must put this away—he hates to have me write a word." Rest is what her physician husband says is right, so "he started the habit by making me lie down for an hour after each meal."

The first stage of the breakdown is one of self-blame. The woman follows the doctor's orders and tries to stop the fantasies that people tell her are unreal. When a physician of "high standing" assures "friends and relatives that there is really nothing the matter with one but temporary nervous depression—a slight hysterical tendency—what is one to do?" Gradually, however, the woman starts to believe in her fantasies. "There are things in that [wall-]paper that nobody knows but me, or ever will. Behind that outside pattern the dim shapes get clearer every day. . . . I didn't realize for a long time what the thing was that showed behind that dim sub-pattern, but now I am quite sure it is a woman." Dramatically she trusts her perceptions and acts wildly but assertively. "I wasn't alone a bit! As soon as it was moonlight and that poor thing began to crawl and shake the pattern, I got up and ran to help her. I pulled and she shook, I shook and she

pulled, and before morning we had peeled off yards of that paper." The protagonist begins to creep and crawl within her madness. She separates herself from the perception of others, and when in a climactic scene her husband faints, she crawls over his body and says, "I've got out at last . . . in spite of you!"[18]

"The Yellow Wallpaper" stands in dramatic contrast to Charlotte's autobiography, ***The Living of Charlotte Perkins Gilman***. There, the separation from Walter Stetson is portrayed as resulting from her individual weaknesses, or equally simplistically, from a mismatched marriage. She was not inclined publicly or explicitly to indict loved ones in her life. Yet in **"The Yellow Wallpaper,"** she presented insanity as a form of rebellion, a crucial turning point toward independence. Only in a fictional version of her illness would she publicly express her anger: "I've got out at last . . . in spite of you." Anger is also apparent in her diary. On April 18, 1887, she wrote:

I am very sick with nervous prostration, and I think some brain disease as well. No one can ever know what I have suffered in these last five years. Pain pain pain, til my mind has given way. . . . You found me—you remember what I leave you—O remember what, and learn to doubt your judgment before it seeks to mould another life as it has mine.

I asked you a few days only before our marriage if you would take the responsibility entirely on yourself. You said yes. Bear it then.[19]

Although Charlotte often faced uncontrollable depressions during the bleak years of 1884-87, fortunately a determination to trust her own abilities remained. In part, she benefited from a visit in California with Grace Channing and her family in the winter of 1885-1886. In this supportive atmosphere she regained a measure of her former self-confidence. She felt more well, of gayer disposition, when she was separated from her family, a primary source of her guilt-induced anxiety. Moreover, the diaries indicate an emerging feminist consciousness during these same years; her reading, lecturing, and writing on women's issues predated and possibly contributed to her separation from Walter in 1888. For example, in 1883 she argued with a close friend, Jim Simmons, "till 11:45 nearly talking about Woman's Rights." He was a "man far from broad," she noted. In 1884 she read John Stuart Mill's *The Subjection of Women* (she also read it to her mother), and then began to lecture and to write on women's issues. She attended her first Woman's Suffrage Convention in 1886. In January 1887, she read Margaret Fuller's *Woman in the Nineteenth Century* and "started a course of reading about women," although as she noted in her diary she stopped it temporarily to "oblige" Walter. By February she had accepted an offer from Alice Stone Blackwell to manage a suffrage column for a Providence weekly newspaper, *The People*.[20]

Many days Charlotte complained of weakness and exhaustion from domestic obligations yet found strength when she worked on articles or verse. Incensed by the situation of other women, she was depressed when she reflected on her own. On February 20, 1887 she had a "good talk" with a neighbor, Mrs. Smythe, who was "another victim" with a "sickly child" and an ignorant husband who was "using his marital rights at her vital expense." And a month later: "Getting back to the edge of insanity again . . . feel desperate. Write my 'column' though." She also returned to her physical fitness program. For example, on February 7, after getting "discouraged by Walter," she delighted in her "jolly time at the gym in the evening. I seem to slip into my old position of inspirer very easily. And the girls like it."[21]

What is most striking about Charlotte's life, particularly from 1884-1887, is that she had the energy to pursue any of the activities she found most satisfying. She was "ill," yet stubbornly ignored the admonitions of her family, refused their well-intentioned offers of "security," and proceeded to develop an independent plan of action. She rejected the advice of a nerve specialist, Dr. S. Weir Mitchell: "Live as domestic a life as possible. Have your child with you all the time. . . . And never touch pen, brush or pencil as long as you live."[22] Instead, she decided to try new alternatives. She believed that self-assertion, in her case the need to read, write, exercise, and enjoy the companionship of other women was crucial to her mental health. Lacking the support, or even the understanding of friends and relatives in Providence, Rhode Island, and with no income or well-defined plans for work, she determined to move herself and child to California in the fall of 1888. There, in Pasadena, the Channing family provided a brief respite of economic and emotional security.

Gradually, Charlotte began to meet other women like herself who were alone, without means of satisfying work, or without adequate income. Still personally distraught, she nonetheless moved toward a tactical involvement in the burgeoning feminist movement, began more seriously to analyze common problems women faced, and encouraged organizational and individual attacks on what she saw as pervasive social ills. Well-

read in contemporary intellectual theory, and most particularly influenced by the writings of Lester Ward and Edward Bellamy, she became active in the lecture-writing circuit of the then highly politicized and often radical reform movements of the 1890s. Her expanding reputation brought her into close contact with socialist, nationalist, and Fabian thought. As a social theorist, she was eclectic rather than original. But in her partial adoption of socialist theory and in her continuing identification with oppressed groups, she was able to expand her feminist analysis beyond that of many of her contemporaries and to ground it in a broadly-based political perspective.

Turning now to the feminist analysis itself, I suggest that there were four major forces which Charlotte Gilman isolated as having created and perpetuated female inequality, or the "artificial" feminine personality. The underlying premise of her environmentalist analysis was the innate similarity of human potentials of males and females. As she put it:

> That is masculine which belongs to the male sex as such; to any and all males *without regard to species*. . . . That is feminine which belongs to the female sex, as such, *without regard to species*. . . . That is human which belongs to the human species, as such, *without regard to sex*. . . . Every step of social development, every art, craft, and science . . . these have to do with humanity, as such, and have nothing to do with sex.[23]

The first of the major factors impinging on the lives of women, she perceived, was their economic dependence on men. Women had become in effect property of men. Women's work, she argued, had a use value but not an exchange value. She wrote, "whatever the economic value of the domestic industry of women is, they do not get it. The women who do the most work get the least money, and the women who have the most money do the least work." She insisted that economic dependence, wherever it occurred, necessarily resulted in a loss of integrity and self-respect. Encouraging women to view the political dimensions of their situation, she declared, "We have not as a class awakened to the fact that we have no money of our own."[24]

Charlotte Gilman's economic struggles as a separated and subsequently divorced woman, and earlier the child of a divorced woman, made her especially sensitive to woman's economic plight. She knew from experience that economic security in the home was a mirage, that if deprived of the support of a male protector, women would invariably confront extremely limited work opportunities, and often tragic impoverishment. Yet she recognized that it was the family itself, as a social and economic institution, which perpetuated female enslavement and denied women opportunity for economic independence. Consequently, she differed from many feminists who believed that no "fundamental economic change would be necessary in home relationships for women to achieve equality."[25] For Charlotte Gilman, women's most essential goal was the building of an economic power base.

The second significant factor leading to "artificial" femininity, Gilman believed, was nonvoluntary alienating domestic servitude. She argued that inequality of women resulted from a division of labor along sex lines, further evidence of a causative relationship between the institution of the family and women's low level of achievement. Cooking, sewing, nursing, washing, caring for children—"not only do we undertake to have all these labors performed in one house, but by one person." Just consider, she wrote, "what any human business would be in which there was no faintest possibility of choice, of exceptional ability, of division of labor." She decried the fact that domestic industry had become a "sex function, . . . supposed to pertain to women by nature."[26]

Third, Gilman examined the effects of women's psychological dependence on men. An eclectic popularizer as well as a theorist, she reiterated and reshaped the theoretical arguments of her predecessors, Mary Wollstonecraft and John Stuart Mill, for example; but in the process she also anticipated the direction of some of the most recent and perceptive feminist theorists: the concentration on the politics of the family, for example, the recognition that the personal is political, the understanding that only by examining the daily lives of women and their experiences of submission to the demands of family life could an explanation of female "difference" ultimately be found.[27] Viewing women's powerlessness and dependence on men as both psychological and political phenomena, she argued that the female personality had become a slave personality. She wrote, "The position of women, after their long degradation is in many ways analogous to that of the freed slave. He is refused justice on account of his inferiority. To reply that inferiority is largely due to previous injustice does not alter the fact."[28] The female personality was likewise conditioned to submission. "Of women especially have been required the convenient virtues of a subject class: obedience, patience, endurance, contentment,

humility, resignation, temperance, prudence, industry, kindness, cheerfulness, modesty, gratitude, thrift, and unselfishness."[29] Although the conditions of women's lives had important variations, Gilman believed there existed a common institutional experience—the home—which affected women whether rich or poor. The politics of the family crossed class lines.

Fourth, finally, and least persuasively, Gilman ventured beyond many of her socialist contemporaries in exploring the unique effects of sexual oppression on women. She believed that the sexual relationship had become an economic relationship, marriage very often itself being merely a legally enshrined version of prostitution. Forced to emphasize sexuality at the expense of humanity, woman had necessarily to give the impression of weakness, frailty, timidity, and passivity—in short to prove her capacity for submission, the male's for dominance and control. Gilman wrote:

We have been told so long that

"Love is of man's life a thing apart,
Tis woman's whole existence"

that we have believed it. . . . [O]ur whole existence was carefully limited to this field; we were dressed and educated to grace it; we were bloomed out into a brief and glorious career while under inspection and selection before our final surrender, and then we pursued the rest of our lives with varying devotion and satisfaction in this one department of life.[30]

She advocated the distribution of information on birth control and sex-related matters, the development of physical fitness programs for women, and an end to man-made fashion dictates. She called for human fulfillment, for women's full control of their bodies as well as their lives.[31]

However, Gilman's understanding of the causes for sexual oppression was far more impressive than her theoretical projections. In short, she could *attack* the "feminine" woman, but not *envision* an alternative of equal womanhood. Her life and writings were always inextricably related. Where she had achieved certain of her feminist goals—economic independence, physical fitness, and considerable psychological strength as well, she believed in woman's capacity for excellence. But because she could not interpret the conflicting loyalties which seemed to occur, both within herself and other independent women when they entered love relationships with men (and wavering herself between both strength and deference, self-righteousness, and self-sacrifice), Charlotte perhaps understandably concluded that certain stereotypes of "femininity" must somehow be innate.

The personal roots of Charlotte's theoretical contradictions are apparent in her early living, in her struggles with guilt as she faced her separation and divorce from Walter Stetson, and in her love relationship with Houghton Gilman, whom she married in 1900.[32] She wrote letters of passionate intensity to Gilman, but she seemed to fear him as a threat to her marginally established independence. A sensuous woman, she was also a well-trained warrior in the feminist campaign. Unintentionally and tragically, she created sexual and psychological barriers against an intimate male-female relationship.

Charlotte had known Houghton as a child, as an affectionate first cousin eight years her junior, whose companionship she very much enjoyed. After a hiatus of some seventeen years, Charlotte visited Houghton in his law office to obtain legal advice concerning royalties on a publication. Erroneously, she assumed the relationship was "safe" from "complications" because of kinship, though she expressed her preference for even safer grounds than that: "I only wish I was your grandma or great aunt or I have it! an invalid sister that you simply *had* to have around you all the time!!!" She was delighted with his friendship: "You seem very near somehow—a background to most of my thinking when I'm not at work." Or again, "It's astonishing how many times a day I incline to write you."[33] And write she did—twenty- or thirty-page letters, two or more times a week.

Nonetheless, expressions of increasing fondness for Houghton were interspersed with apologetic declarations of resistance:

> To most people . . . I can behave nicely. . . . But as soon as any one comes near me and takes hold, I wobble awfully. Now as you may have seen I am getting exceedingly fond of you. . . . And I don't like it. It makes me unreasonable. It makes me feel—where I don't want to feel; and think—where I don't want to think. It sort of wakes me up where I'm dead, or where, if I'm not dead I ought to be.
>
> Now I can't afford to be fond of anybody in that sort of way—man, woman, or child. I can't afford to want things. . . . But [your] being here . . . and being, to your sorrow—my "entire family"—why it brings out all that is worst and weakest in me, instead of what is strongest and best. It makes me unreasonable—sensitive—disagreeable—absurd. It makes me want to be petted and cared for—me! And then all this makes me very mad; and I say "go to! I'll get out of this in short order!"[34]

Charlotte seemed to vacillate wildly between feelings of strength and insecurity. She was "rich in the tricks and shifts of an old campaigner weather-beaten and coarsened by long exposure." But also, she felt "bitterly depressed, often defeated, lonely, imprisoned, scared and wounded beyond recognition but not crippled past all usefulness. . . ." She seemed to need to ask for pity. She felt a "compelling desire . . . to complain and explain, to whimper . . . and seek for sympathy which don't do me any good if I get it." She extended her growing trust in Houghton with a "childish femininity":[35]

> I temporarily cuddle down and clutch you remorselessly. Later on I shall flop and wobble again. Later still soar off no doubt. But just for a little time—and with excellent reason that I can't help—behold me as it were a sleepy Newfoundland puppy in your overcoat pocket.[36]

Thus did a public advocate of woman's full equality privately reveal the anguish of her personal ambivalence. She wrote:

> I wish I could make a picture of the thing [herself] as I see it—sulky, frightened, discouraged, "rattled" to a degree; one foot forward and the other back; ready to rush forward in tumultuous devotion one minute, and run away shrieking the next—fingers in ears.[37]

However tentatively and indecisively, Charlotte began to break the barriers of her self-imposed lonely isolation. Insecurities sometimes reemerged in the form of uncontrollable depressions, the "grey fog" she had faced since 1884. But increasingly she felt a passionate happy love for Houghton which, characteristically, she had to formulate in writing. She left, therefore, abundant documentation of her sensuous yearnings, as well as of her apprehensions:

> I went to sleep with a smile on my lips and woke only to think again of the dear comfort that you are to me—of your unfailing loving kindness, your quiet strength, your patience and wisdom—and your tenderness. O it *does* feel so good! To have some one care for me enough to—well—to kiss me.[38]

She continued in December: "Everything is so different. I have a home now—in your heart." In February, 1898 she wrote: "Surely you can read it in my eyes—hear it in my voice, feel it in my arms about your neck—taste it on my lips that lean to you. You make me happy—so happy my darling. I love you—love you—love you!" And even more passionately for a supposedly "Victorian" lady, she wrote to him in May: "Sweetheart! You shall kiss me anywhere you want to and all you want to as soon as ever there is a chance. I will wait till you are exhausted and then begin operations on my own account."[39]

Despite such passionate declarations, Charlotte also delighted in the image of herself as cared-for child: "And it will be the wholesomest thing in the world to . . . settle down to the definite and particular feeling of being your little girl."[40] Continuously she seemed to need protective reassurance; and when Houghton did not sufficiently comply, she responded angrily. So vulnerable did she feel, so intense was her level of hurt, that on one occasion in 1899, she threatened to break off the relationship entirely. She wrote: "When I think of what manner of letters I have written to you—of course I want to call them all back and burn them . . . and never think of love again lest I die of shame."[41] She insisted that Houghton be strong and more assertive, and that she, as woman, should wait more passively:

> If you don't love me more than to make dutiful responses to my advances it won't do to marry on. . . .
> It is a woman's business to wait, not a man's.
> It is for a woman to be patient and still—not a man.
> If you are truly lover and husband—show it. If not—God bless you and good bye.[42]

Charlotte's outbursts were frequent but short-lived, her contests with self-hatred a recurring pattern of her life. She recovered from her anger, only to be tormented once again by uncontrollable anxiety. Back and forth she went: "I don't wholly like to be held—and yet I do!" She wanted protective love, yet despised herself for needing it. "Makes me kind of angry too," she later wrote. "Seems a weakness. To be so tangled up in another person."[43] Torn between her feminist convictions and her feelings, she expressed discontent with what she thought she had become—a non-womanly woman:

> Don't you see dear how much at a disadvantage I am beside you? Try and feel like a woman for a moment—put yourself in their place. You know what a woman wants to bring a man—a boundless whole-souled love, absolutely and primarily his own—all his own.
>
> I haven't that . . . I can only give you a divided love—I love God—the world—my work as I love you. I have so little to offer—so pathetically little. . . .
>
> O my dear—do you not see what poignant grief and shame it is to a woman to have no woman's gifts to give![44]

Charlotte apologized for having achieved many of her goals: "I'm sorry," she wrote Hough-

ton, "that I can't add my life to yours—woman fashion . . . the usual style of immersion of the wife in the husband." Theoretically and practically she insisted on the right to satisfying work; emotionally she felt she should give it up to him. Come to my lectures, she had pleaded with Houghton in 1899. "Then you'd know—know me, know why I have felt as I do about marrying and all that. Why I so seriously fear lest the housekeeping part of it [marriage] should prove an injury to my health and a hindrance to my work." But hardly consistently for a radical feminist, she continued, "You see I am so afraid of my own long . . . instincts getting the better of me—and that, in my love for you and natural wish to make you comfortable I shall 'settle' too firmly."[45]

Ambiguities expressed in Charlotte's letters to Houghton were also apparent in her public writings. An advocate of women's full equality, she inconsistently, ironically, contrasted masculine work-instincts with "feminine" instincts of nurturance and service, male adult-like strength and courage with female childlike insecurity and fear. Thus this "militant madonna" portrayed woman's "natural" yearning for a male's protective love.

If to a degree the "instincts" argument served to undermine Gilman's environmentalist analysis of the origins of sexual inequality, it also provided crucial leverage in her fight for female self-respect. Perhaps defensively, Gilman attempted to reverse traditionally negative connotations of "femininity" by emphasizing the virtues of womanhood instead. Like most of her feminist contemporaries, proudly she proclaimed the primacy of womanhood: Woman's archetypal innocence was concomitant to her moral virtue; gentle kindness was a means of power, an antidote to assertive male combativeness. Woman's uniqueness was thus her strength and glory, her mother-love a countervailing force within the baneful androcentric culture.

The most explicit statement of Gilman's admiration and love for women was expressed in the novel *Herland* (1915). Utopia, she told her readers, was a land inhabited only by women and girl children, procreation occurring through parthenogenesis. Faithfully worshipping the "Goddess of mother love," and interacting cooperatively, respectfully, and affectionately, women demonstrated their capacity to build Utopia. Because they were not confined within the isolation of the private selfish home, women could use their nurturant capacities for social and community service. Trusting childcare only to the "highest artists," they developed the *true* "womanly" virtues: "Beauty, Health, Strength, Intellect,

Goodness. . . ." In *Herland,* the "essential distinction of motherhood was the dominant note of their whole culture." Motherhood was the "great, tender, limitless uplifting force."[46]

Theoretically as well as fictionally, Gilman asserted the natural superiority of the female sex. Enthusiastically endorsing the "scientifically based" Gynaecocentric Theory of the sociologist Lester Ward, she elaborated extensively on the civilizing capacities of women, the destructive combativeness of men. She wrote: "The innate underlying difference [between the sexes] is one of principle. On the one hand, the principle of struggle, conflict, and competition. . . . On the other, the principle of growth, of culture, of applying services and nourishment in order to produce improvement."[47] Woman did not want to fight, to take, to oppress. Instead she exhibited "the growing altruism of work, founded in mother love, in the antiselfish instinct of reproduction."[48] Fundamental to the evolutionary process was woman's inherent responsibility for the preservation of the race, the selection of a mate, and the nurturance of children.

Charlotte Gilman presents us with a paradox. Having developed a multidimensional feminist theory based on the idea of the natural equality of the sexes, having challenged patriarchal norms dividing males and females into their respective public-private spheres, she also enthusiastically maintained that women were the saintly givers, men the warring beasts. When she glorified female "instincts" of love and service, her radical theory of feminism dissolved into a sometimes sentimental worship of the status quo. Compromising her environmentalist analysis, she alternately emphasized not female powerlessness, but woman's natural passivity; not artificially imposed dependence, but an innate desire to love and serve; not cowardice, but peacefulness and cooperation; not the oppressive restrictions of motherhood roles, but the glories of mother love. By proclaiming women's natural differences, Charlotte Gilman, like many of her contemporaries, "put to a test the entire ideology upon which arguments for the liberation of women had been based in the United States."[49]

Yet while claims to female nurturant superiority were ultimately dysfunctional, they were nonetheless, historically, a viable response to women's need for expanded decision-making power. A vital struggle for political autonomy lay beneath the mother-worship proclamations. Moreover, "suffragists were not blushing Victorians but seasoned politicians who had learned how to beat the male at his own game."[50] Charlotte Gilman refused to treat women purely as the victims—incompetents within the world of men. Instead, she urged women to develop self-respect on their own terms, not those exclusively defined by men. Thus, when she emphasized woman's role as "the moral redeemer and culture bearer," she was acclaiming a philosophy which "actually permitted women to enhance their self-image as individuals and as a group and, ultimately to organize for action."[51] Whether tactically or ideologically, she seems to have understood that women might necessarily, if temporarily, expand their power by celebrating differences.

While Charlotte's dichotomous theories were in part an outgrowth of the intellectual and socioeconomic forces of her era, my purpose here has been to illustrate instead some private sources for her feminist perspectives. The existence of contradiction in her theories, her fiction, and her living by no means lessens the significance of her historical contribution. Her theoretical analyses were themselves impressive, but so also was her constant testing of those theories in the experimental laboratory of her life. Since she kept voluminous accounts of her private struggles, she unintentionally preserved in the panorama of her eccentricity and genius, a wealth of historical data which will enrich our understanding of the underlying dynamics of feminist theory and practice at the turn of the century.[52]

Notes

1. Quotations from private letters are made with the permission of The Arthur and Elizabeth Schlesinger Library on the History of Women in America, Radcliffe College, Cambridge, Massachusetts. Letters from Charlotte Stetson to Houghton Gilman, September 2, 1897; letter from Jane Addams to Charlotte Stetson, July 19, 1898; letter from Florence Kelley to Charlotte Stetson, July 26, 1898; *The Nation,* June 8, 1899.

2. Charlotte Perkins Gilman, *Women and Economics: A Study of the Economic Relation Between Men and Women as a Factor in Social Evolution* (New York: Harper ed., 1966), p. 331.

3. Letter from Charlotte Stetson to Houghton Gilman, July 26, 1899. My focus here is on the relationships and experiences most richly documented in the Charlotte Perkins Gilman collection, particularly the relationships with Walter Stetson and Houghton Gilman. Charlotte's relationships with her parents, with female friends, and with many significant others will receive further attention in a forthcoming biography—*Charlotte Perkins Gilman: The Birth of a Radical Feminist, 1860-1896.* For an interim biographical and theoretical analysis of the life and writings of Charlotte Gilman see Mary A. Porter (Hill-Peters), "Charlotte Perkins Gilman: A Feminist Paradox" (Ph.D. dissertation, McGill University, 1975).

4. Charlotte Gilman, *The Living of Charlotte Perkins Gilman* (New York: Appleton-Century Company, 1935), pp. 78, 80. Diaries, 1879-1883.

5. See particularly diary entries for October 12, October 30, November 5, November 16, December 16, 1881. Charlotte had many very close relationships with women during her lifetime, with Grace Channing, Adeline Knapp, Martha Luther, and Helen Campbell, for example. The data richly supports Carroll Smith-Rosenberg's suggestion that "women's sphere had an essential integrity and dignity that grew out of women's shared experiences and mutual affection." Carroll Smith-Rosenberg, "The Female World of Love and Ritual: Relations Between Women in Nineteenth-Century America." *Signs* 1:1 (Autumn, 1975), 9-10. As historians increasingly appreciate the significance of female networks of support and companionship, we need also to consider the often painful feeling of rejection close female friends experienced with one another. Among Charlotte's most difficult emotional crises were the departure of Martha Luther and the disruption of the relationship with Adeline Knapp ("Dora" in *Living*, pp. 133, 141-44). See diary entries, 1892-1893.

6. "An Anchor to Windward," Diary, January 31, 1882.

7. Letters from Charlotte Perkins to Walter Stetson, February 20 and 21, 1882. According to the pre-1881 reading lists which Charlotte kept in her diaries, she was apparently unfamiliar with the rich feminist literature she might have drawn on. Moreover, it is striking that she did not mention her two successful great-aunts, Catharine Beecher and Harriet Beecher Stowe, as she described to Walter the seemingly irreconcilable conflict between marriage and career (letter to Walter Stetson, February 20, 1882):

> I am beset by my childhood's conscientiousness . . . the voice of all the ages sounds in my ears, saying that this [marriage] is noble, natural, and right; that no woman yet has ever attempted to stand alone as I intend but that she had to submit or else. . . .

> I have nothing to answer but the meek assertion that I am different from if not better than all these, and that my life is mine in spite of myriad lost sisters before me.

8. Letter to Walter Stetson, March 6, 1882; Diary, April 5, 1883; "Thoughts and Fingerings," November 3, 1883. Charlotte's acceptance in 1883 of Walter's authority contrasts strikingly with her self-confident assertions of February 13, 1882: "You are the first man I have met whom I recognize as an equal; and that is saying a good deal for me. I would call you grandly superior, but that I am fighting just now against a heart-touched woman's passion of abnegation." Letter to Walter Stetson, February 13, 1882.

9. Diary, December 31, 1883.

10. *Living*, pp. 10, 5.

11. "Phobias" emerge, according to the Symonds thesis, from a denial of self-expression that women often felt must be the price of love. "Marriage then becomes their 'declaration of dependence'. . . . [T]hey tend to become the paragons of Victorian femininity—helpless, housebound, and ineffectual." See Alexandra Symonds, M.D., "Phobias after Marriage: Women's Declaration of Dependence," in *Psychoanalysis and Women*, edited by Jean Baker Miller, M.D. (Middlesex, England: Penguin Books, 1973), pp. 288-303.

12. Diary, May 2, 1884.

13. Diary, May 9, 1884. Charlotte Gilman, *The Home: Its Work and Influence* (New York: McClure, Phillips and Company, 1903), p. 12.

14. "Thoughts and Fingerings," November 3, 1883; Diary, June 15, June 25, 1884.

15. Diary, August 30, 1885; *Living*, p. 89.

16. Carroll Smith-Rosenberg, "The Hysterical Woman: Sex Roles and Role Conflict in 19th-Century America," *Social Research* 39:4 (Winter, 1972), p. 671.

17. Diary, August 30, 1885; *Living*, pp. 91, 96.

18. Charlotte Perkins Gilman, "The Yellow Wallpaper," *New England Magazine* 5 (January, 1892), pp 647-56. I am taking the liberty of using "The Yellow Wallpaper" quite literally as autobiographical material. The names are different, and the fantasies symbolic; but when asked to what extent "The Yellow Wallpaper" was based on fact, Charlotte replied, "I had been as far as one could go and get back." *Living*, p. 121.

19. Diary, April 18, 1887.

20. See diary entries November 16, 1883; February 24, October 6, 1886; January 5, January 19, February 5, 1887.

21. Diary entries, February 20, March 20, February 7, 1887.

22. *Living*, p. 96.

23. Charlotte Gilman, "Masculine, Feminine, and Human," *Woman's Journal* 35 (January 16, 1904), 18.

24. *The Home*, p. 22; *Women and Economics*, p. 14-15; Gilman, "Her Own Money: Is a Wife Entitled to the Money She Earns?" *Mother's Magazine* 7 (February 1912), 7.

25. Aileen Kraditor, *Ideas of the Women's Suffrage Movement* (New York: Columbia University Press, 1965), p. 121.

26. Gilman, "Domestic Economy," *Independent* 56 (June 16, 1904), 1359-60; Gilman, "The Normal Social Group Today," *The Forerunner* 4 (July 1913), 175; Gilman, *Women and Economics*, p. 226.

27. See particularly Simone de Beauvoir, *The Second Sex*. Juliet Mitchell *Woman's Estate* (Vintage ed.; New York: Random House, 1973). Juliet Mitchell, *Psychoanalysis and Feminism* (New York: Pantheon, 1974). Kate Millet, *Sexual Politics* (New York: Doubleday and Company, 1970). Shulamith Firestone, *The Dialectic of Sex: The Case for Feminist Revolution* (Bantam ed.; New York: William Morrow, 1970). Sheila Rowbotham, *Women, Resistance, and Revolution* (Vintage ed.; New York: Random House, 1974). Sheila Rowbotham, *Woman's Consciousness* (Middlesex, England: Penguin Books, Ltd., 1973). Maria Della Costa, *The Power of Women and the Subversion of the Community* (2nd ed.; Bristol, England: Falling Wall Press, Ltd., 1973).

28. Gilman, "Educated Bodies," *Woman's Journal* 35 (June 1904), p. 178.

29. Gilman, *His Religion and Hers: A Study of the Faith of Our Fathers and the Work of Our Mothers* (New York: The Century Company, 1923), p. 134.

30. Gilman, "Love Stories and Life Stories." *Woman's Journal* 35 (May 7, 1904), p. 146.

31. Charlotte Gilman's support of Margaret Sanger's work in the birth control movement began roughly in 1915. Adopting the racist and ethnocentric attitudes all too common to her generation, however, Charlotte viewed birth control as an issue not only of personal importance for women; she also maintained that it could be used as a protection against the pressures of population expansion, particularly of the "unfit." See Gilman, "Birth Control, Religion, and the Unfit," *Nation*, 134 (January 27, 1932), p. 109; Gilman, "Birth Control," *The Forerunner*, 6 (July 1915), pp. 177-80.

32. This discussion is limited to Charlotte's attitude toward Houghton Gilman between 1897 and 1900 and is not intended as an interpretation of their marriage relationship from 1900 to 1934.

33. Letter from Charlotte Stetson to Houghton Gilman, September 11, September 2, September 5, 1897.

34. Ibid., October 3, 1897.

35. Ibid., October 1, October 3, 1897; undated letter, October, 1897.

36. Ibid., November 4, 1897.

37. Ibid., November 7, 1897.

38. Ibid.

39. Ibid., February 20, May 6, 1898. On a number of occasions Charlotte mentioned her desire to have a child with Houghton, but when she thought that she might be unable, she expressed delight: "Happy thought—take no precautions—take no treatment—all runs smoothly and nothing happens!!! There's an easy way out of the difficulty!!!" Sex without fears of pregnancy seemed a grand relief. Letter from Charlotte Stetson to Houghton Gilman, May 16, 1900.

Carl Degler argues that many nineteenth-century women may not have been so fearful of or opposed to the sexual experience as was formerly assumed. Historians have too frequently relied on prescriptive data, he maintains, thus distorting the actual attitudes and experiences of women themselves. See Carl Degler, "What Ought to be and What Was: Women's Sexuality in the Nineteenth Century," *American Historical Review* 79 (December 1974), pp. 1467-90. See also Charles E. Rosenberg, "Sexuality, Class, and Role in Nineteenth Century America," *American Quarterly* 25 (May 1973), pp. 131-53.

40. Letter from Charlotte Stetson to Houghton Gilman, January 9, 1898. Also referring to a letter he had written, she responded, "This is the letter that says I'm your darling little girl, which remark I have kissed many times." Ibid., November 14, 1899.

41. Ibid., January 22, 1899.

42. Ibid., January 25, 1899.

43. Ibid., June 2, November 6, 1898.

44. Ibid., November 14, 1899.

45. Ibid., March 14, 1900; February 28, 1899. On December 28, 1898 she wrote: "I quite envy those good women who really feel that the husband is their whole range of duty—it must be so sweet to have no call away from that dear love." In March she wrote, "Dear, it isn't fair! You ought to have a *whole* wife to give herself all to you." Although by November she more confidently asserted, "I want to carry out what I think is perfectly possible—a kind of married life that has both love and freedom. I see no need for the 'yoke.'" See letters, December 28, 1898; March 5, November 14, 1899.

46. Gilman, *Herland*, in *The Forerunner* 6 (May 1915), pp. 127-29; Ibid., *Forerunner* 6 (July 1915), p. 186.

47. Gilman, *His Religion and Hers: A Study of the Faith of Our Fathers and the Work of Our Mothers* (New York: The Century Company, 1923), p. 271. Lester Ward projected a theory of sexual differentiation which he claimed proved "that in the economy of organic nature the female sex is the primary, and the male a secondary element." Clearly Darwinism could not be used as a justification for the subjection of the female sex, he argued, because in fact it was the female who was responsible for the preservation of the species. Since the first function of the male was simply to enable the female to reproduce, it was she who was the source of life and therefore of superior importance. Lester Ward, "Our Better Halves," *Forum* 6 (November 1888), p. 266. See also Lester Ward, *Dynamic Sociology* (New York: D. Appleton, 1883); Lester Ward, *Pure Sociology* (New York: Macmillan Co., 1903); Samuel Chugerman, Lester F. Ward, *The American Aristotle: A Summary and Interpretation of His Sociology* (Durham, N.C.: Duke University Press, 1939). Of Ward's Gynaecocentric Theory, Charlotte Gilman wrote, "nothing so important to humanity has been advanced since the Theory of Evolution, and nothing so important to women has ever been given to the world." Gilman, *The Man-Made World: Our Androcentric Culture* (New York: Charlton Company, 1911), Dedication.

Charlotte Gilman's support of the woman-as-superior argument, side-by-side with her environmentalist feminist position can also be interpreted as yet another manifestation of Social Darwinist and Lamarckian thought. Characteristically, turn-of-the-century thinkers blurred the distinction between inherited and acquired characteristics. Again, however, the emphasis of this paper is on the personal more than the philosophical roots of Charlotte Gilman's feminist paradox.

48. Gilman, *Human Work* (New York: McClure, Phillips and Company, 1903), pp. 211, 207.

49. Jill Conway, "The Woman's Peace Party and the First World War," *War and Society in North America*, ed. J. L. Granatstein and R. D. Cuff (Toronto: Thomas Nelson and Sons, 1971), p. 52. See also Jill Conway, "Women Reformers and American Culture, 1870-1930," *Journal of Social History*, 5 (Winter 1971-72), pp. 164-77; Susan Hartman, "The Paradox of Women's Progress: 1820-1920" (St. Charles, Missouri: Forum Press); Mary Ryan, *Womanhood in America* (New York: Franklin Watts, Inc., 1975), pp. 139-248.

50. Mary Ryan, *Womanhood in America*, p. 246.

51. Barbara Sicherman, "American History: Review Essay," *Signs* 1:2 (Winter 1975), p. 470. Anthropologist Michelle Zimbalist Rosaldo argues "that the very symbolic and social conceptions that appear to set women apart and to circumscribe their activities may be used by women as a basis for female solidarity and worth." Michelle Zimbalist Rosaldo, "Woman, Culture, and Society: A Theoretical Overview," in *Woman, Culture, and Society*, p. 39.

52. Because of the complexities of Gilman's private correspondence, and also because of the rich body of feminist materials that have become available in recent years, I am currently in the process if revising my perspectives on the implications of Gilman's private correspondence with Houghton Gilman. My two earlier volumes (*Charlotte Perkins Gilman: The Making of a Radical Feminist, 1860-1896* (1980) and *Endure: The Diaries of Walter Stetson* (1985) cover the early origins of Gilman's feminist convictions. My forthcoming volume, however, will offer new interpretations of the rich correspondence with Houghton Gilman (1896-1900). It will not only show the depth of Gilman's anti-woman feelings but will also show her long-term struggle to attain a more positive affirmation of her womanhood. (*Charlotte Perkins Gilman: A Journey From Within*, Temple University Press, forthcoming.)

SHELLEY FISHER FISHKIN (ESSAY DATE 2000)

SOURCE: Fishkin, Shelley Fisher. "Reading Gilman in the Twenty-First Century." In *The Mixed Legacy of Charlotte Perkins Gilman*, edited by Catherine J. Golden and Joanna Schneider Zangrando, pp. 209-22. Newark: University of Delaware Press, 2000.

In the following essay, Fishkin discusses Gilman's ideas and writings she deems relevant to contemporary students, and speculates on Gilman's potential reaction to the current condition of women.

When Constance Coiner took a job as an assistant professor at SUNY-Binghamton, she tells us that she

went immediately to the public elementary school, where the principal told me that the kindergarten Ana would attend ended at 10:30 A.M. Having had my expectations affected by 16 years in what *Sixty Minutes* dubbed the People's Republic of Santa Monica, California, I asked, "And what provisions are made for children after 10:30?" "Oh, their mothers come and pick them up," he offered with a shrug. "What about *parents* who work outside the home?" I said, emphasizing "parents" through gritted teeth. "Oh, they get babysitters," he replied.[1]

It was much more than a purely "academic" exercise, then, when Constance required her students that semester—most of whom were pre-law or pre-med or pre-graduate school—to read, as a companion piece to Charlotte Perkins Gilman's **"The Yellow Wall-Paper,"** the epilogue to Sylvia Ann Hewlett's *A Lesser Life: The Myth of Women's Liberation in America*. Coiner writes that

The epilogue describes a reunion that Hewlett organized in 1984 for the female students she had known as a teacher at Barnard from 1974 to 1981. "The first topic the women gravitated toward," Hewlett reports, "was how to combine careers with children." These economically privileged, highly educated, and professionally successful women, who "at eighteen and twenty . . . truly felt the world was at their feet," expressed despair in the face of overwhelming family-work conflict.

Depending on their gender, my students respond to the epilogue in dramatically different ways: the females—many struck for the first time that combining their career aspirations with parenting might be at best difficult, at worst impossible— echo the anxiety expressed by the women at the reunion. But almost unanimously, males consider this a "women's issue."[2]

For Constance Coiner, as for Charlotte Perkins Gilman, these issues were human issues—not women's issues. And nothing less than the fate of society lay in the balance.

These passages come from Constance Coiner's essay titled "Silent Parenting in the Academy" that appears in the book *Listening to Silences*. Constance Coiner lost her life on TWA Flight 800 in the summer of 1996, as did her daughter Ana. Many of us mourn the loss of a friend. All of us are poorer for the loss of an eloquent and imaginative feminist voice—a voice which gave us, most recently, the remarkable book, *Writing Red: The Writing and Resistance of Tillie Olsen and Meridel LeSueur*. My remarks honor both the passion and the wry sense of humor that Constance brought to everything she did. The passion and the humor she brought to her work—and the passion with which she addressed the challenge of both doing meaningful world-work, as Gilman would have put it, and raising a child—continue to inspire and empower those who knew her.

* * *

How will our students read Gilman in the next millennium? Will they read her at all? Will she strike them as hopelessly dated, a curious memento of a bygone era? Or will she strike them as having things to say to them that they need to hear? What, in short, will last? Perhaps that question might best be approached by a quick look at what will not last.

A generation reared under Title IX is one likely to take working out as an entitlement. Gilman's pioneering campaign to give women access to a gym will interest them—since it will underline how relatively recently such access could not be taken for granted—but it will not impress them. Neither will they be impressed by Gilman's arguments in favor of suffrage: they were born, after all, with the right to vote. Gilman's assertion, in **"The Humanness of Women,"** that "the functions of democratic government may be wisely and safely shared between men and women" will produce a yawn.[3] Votes for women, like physical fitness for women, no longer sparks controversy. Equally dated will be Gilman's idea that world-work could be rewarding for women as well as men. The steady move of women into higher education and the work force has made this idea, as well, incontrovertible—although managing the demands of home and work remain highly challenging, as Arlie Hochschild's newest book, *The Time Bind: When Work Becomes Home and Home Becomes Work* painfully demonstrates.[4] Some of Gilman's improvised anthropology and social theory do not wear well; neither do her racism, her ethnocentrism, her anti-Semitism, her homophobia, her xenophobia, and her simplistic faith in evolutionary progress. And no young women of this generation or the next would consider for a moment eating food that had been kept hot in asbestos-lined containers!

Nonetheless, as Ann Lane comments in *To Herland and Beyond*, Gilman

> offered perspectives on major issues of gender with which we still grapple: the origins of women's subjugation, the struggle to achieve both autonomy and intimacy in human relationships; the central role of work as a definition of self; new strategies for rearing and educating future generations to create a humane and nurturing environment.[5]

Since 1973 when Elaine Hedges first drew our attention to the gender issues it illuminated, **The Yellow Wall-Paper** has come into its own in the American literature classroom and the American studies classroom, as well as in the women's studies classroom, and in scholarly journals. I believe that as long as the social structures for running homes and raising children continue to be improvised and often chaotic, as long as every woman must invent her own strategies for meeting the challenge of melding motherhood and work, then it is likely that students will be able to relate to a pattern that is "dull enough to confuse the eye in following, pronounced enough constantly to irritate and provoke study."[6] And I believe that as long as double standards continue to confine women's horizons of expectations and achievement in the world, they will see the patterns shaping too many of their lives reflected in the yellow wallpaper's "lame uncertain curves [that] . . . plunge off at outrageous angles, [and] destroy themselves in unheard-of contradictions" (13). This small masterpiece is likely to continue to spark stimulating discussions in the years to come.

Women and Economics also continues to be taught in American studies, women's studies, and sociology classrooms and still prompts impas-

sioned debates in academic journals like the *Review of Social Economy*. And if a recent thread of discussion on H-AMSTDY, the American studies electronic discussion group on the Internet, is any indication, **Herland** is likely to remain in classrooms as well as in courses in feminist theory, women's studies, and utopian visions, despite the fact that in December 1996 the publication *Christianity Today* declared that it was "neither a good book nor an influential one." But some less familiar works, as well, engage today's and probably tomorrow's students in surprising and powerful ways.

Gilman's list of **"Reasonable Resolutions"** published in a *Forerunner* issue of January 1910 never fails to surprise my students. "Let us collectively resolve," Gilman wrote,

> That we will stop wasting our soil and our forests and our labor!
>
> That we will stop poisoning and clogging our rivers and harbors.
>
> That we will stop building combustible houses.
>
> That we will now—this year—begin in good earnest to prevent all preventable diseases.
>
> That we will do our duty by our children and young people, as a wise Society should, and cut off the crop of criminals by not making them.[7]

My students often observe that these ideas are as reasonable today as they were eighty-eight years ago—and as honored in their breach.

What of Gilman's analysis of "Masculine Literature" in **"Our Androcentric Culture"**? Gilman writes that while men can do all sorts of things in fiction, women are relegated to "the Love Story",

> the story of the pre-marital struggle. It is the Adventures of Him in Pursuit of Her—and it stops when he gets her![8]

Gilman's own stories, of course, broke this mold; but is it still the norm? Other plots seem to be available to women today, my students note. But a few choice excerpts from Joanna Russ's hilarious experiment in gender reversals, "What Can a Heroine Do?" quickly set off not only peals of laughter but clicks of recognition: maybe, they realize, things haven't changed that much after all. Can a woman heroine star in a made-for-TV movie without a love interest? Several students try to come up with examples. Others point out the man waiting in wings, an actual or potential love interest—a minor character, perhaps, in some cases, but one whose presence reinscribes Gilman's archetypal female plot.

What about Gilman's comments on dress? Consider Molly Mathewson's paean to *pockets* in Gilman's story, **"If I Were a Man"**:

> These pockets came as a revelation. Of course she had known they were there, had counted them, made fun of them, mended them, even envied them; but she never had dreamed of how it *felt* to have pockets.[9]

Will the unisex dressing of today's teenagers make Molly Mathewson's elation incomprehensible to them? Maybe not. Whenever I teach this story, I conduct my annual "pocket survey." I ask each student to count the pockets in his or her clothing (excluding coats and jackets) and have a census taker record the number in two columns, male and female. Even in classrooms where virtually everyone is dressed in jeans, the differences are striking. The average number of pockets the men have is always significantly higher than the average number of pockets the women have. Women students chime in about fake pockets and half pockets and women's suit jackets having none of the hidden real pockets mens' jackets have. Some even confess to buying their clothes in the men's department just for the pockets. Men are puzzled by the disparity. But eventually an underlying principle becomes apparent: the design of women's clothing—even sportswear—still puts form over function, silhouette over utility, while men's clothing puts utility first. The discussion inevitably broadens—as Gilman no doubt hoped it would—to the resonances of these gendered differences and where those differences come from. The number of women who have had their purses snatched always dwarfs the number of men who have had their pockets picked, providing, if you will, a gender-based index of vulnerability that is as thought-provoking as Gilman's story itself.

Gilman may not be generally known for her press criticism. But at least one sagacious column she wrote entitled **"Do We Get The News?"** has earned her my respect in this field, and the respect of my students. Here Gilman wrote,

> These clamorous papers, justifying all sins by their mission as press-vendors, give us from day to day great masses of "facts" in no sense news, and other masses of "facts," new indeed, but of no earthly importance. Meanwhile, the vital incidents of the day—the era-making events, are sometimes passed over and sometimes so buried in unimportant details as to command no attention.[10]

This rather lacerating picture of newspapers of her day—filled with "great masses of 'facts' in no sense news, and other masses of 'facts,' new

indeed, but of no earthly importance"—strikes my students as no less true of the papers of our day than of hers. What era-making events are today's paper missing? they ask. What kinds of massive, incremental changes pass below the radar of contemporary newsbeats and editorial strategies? A couple of years ago the editor of the *Daily Texan* turned up in my seminar. He was so impressed by the challenge Gilman posed to the press that he made **"Do We Get The News?"** required reading for his entire editorial board.

As for a piece by Gilman that works in the upper elementary school classroom and that might remain of interest to children in the future, I nominate **"The Unnatural Mother."** I taught it a few years ago to an enrichment class for fifth graders, and they understood the story and its implications about as well as my college students have.

Might there be approaches to Gilman and her work that are not yet salient but that may be useful to students and teachers in the near future? Let me briefly suggest three such contexts.

First, Gilman's views on architecture are likely to be reexamined with interest by contemporary advocates of co-housing, an increasingly popular strategy for building and structuring communities. [I always tell my students that if I hadn't lived in housing much like that which Gilman describes, my first book would have come out years after it did: I was a resident fellow in a Yale College during the first twelve years of my marriage, and my husband and children and I ate many pleasant meals in the college dining hall. The book got written in large part during the hours I would have spent shopping for, preparing, and cooking food.]

Second, Gilman's life and writings may well come to play a larger role in our growing understanding of the contours of romantic friendships among women in the nineteenth century. Her relationships with women including Martha Luther, Adeline Knapp, and others might help illuminate the spectrum of attachments between women that we are just beginning to explore as scholars. Might it be possible that some future scholar might read **"The Yellow Wall-Paper"** as a parable of thwarted lesbian desire? Will this scholar read it as an expressionistic fable about one woman's separation from another, a reading reinforced by Gilman's traumatic separation from Martha Luther by the latter's marriage?

Third, Gilman may have value to future generations of scholars interested in the challenge of how someone who is progressive and enlightened on issues of gender can be so myopic and unenlightened on issues of race and ethnicity. How these blind spots endure—how someone can decry discrimination against one group while tolerating it, even engaging in it, against another—is something we need to understand more fully in the present as well as the past. Unfortunately, Gilman can be "exhibit A" in our investigations of the phenomenon.

In a *Forerunner* piece entitled "**Mind Cleaning**," Gilman writes,

> When we are housecleaning we should clear out and destroy, give or sell if we can, bury in the wholesome earth or consume with clean fire, as much old stuff as possible. Old papers, old bottles, old rags, old junk of all sorts—out it must go, if we are to have a clean house.
>
> When we are mind-cleaning we should clear out and cast away the moldy heaps of old ideas, still to be found in the dark corners of the mind . . . [11]

We might as well face it: some of Gilman's own ideas belong in those moldy heaps we need to discard. But others—indeed, others like the very notion of tossing out worn and useless ideas as readily as we toss out a threadbare garment—are likely to remain fresh and vital for generations to come.

How would Gilman read "us" in 1997? What would this writer who fashioned herself as the consummate archeologist of the present say if she took a stroll to the newsstand today and perused such publications as *Teen, Woman's World, Mc-Calls, Glamour, Cosmopolitan, Vogue, Seventeen, Self, Ebony, Essence, New Woman,* and *Ladies Home Journal,* among others?[12]

The Gilman who wrote, "For the health and beauty of the body it must have full exercise"[13] would be pleased by the focus on women's fitness in these magazines—by a sportswear ad, for example, featuring a stunning, muscular woman athlete. The headline, "Sports Are Giving Women a Strong, Sexy, Smart, Female Bravado" would please the Gilman who wrote, "Men have filled the world with games and sports, from the noble contests of the Olympic plain to the brain and body training sports of to-day, good, bad, and indifferent. Through all the ages the men have played; and the women have looked on, when they were asked."[14] She would be intrigued by an article entitled "How I Got Stronger—and Happier" about one woman's participation in a study of whether women were capable of physical tasks traditionally thought to be beyond them. An ad for clothes that "move the way you do" and

another for comfortable shoes would please the author of "**If I Were a Man**." The "shocking answer" promised in an article on "How Different Are Men from Women" would not shock Gilman at all. The article's conclusions—that "The scientific evidence on sex differences is really quite paltry," and that "barriers between the sexes are more prejudiced than reasoned"—are things that Gilman knew all along. It's about time, she might sniff. She would probably approve of an article challenging teenage girls to judge whether they were thinking about boys too much ("Do You Have Boys on the Brain?"). And she would be pleased by articles entitled, "Why It's Better Not to Be Perfect," "Protect Your Family from Food Poisoning," and "Are You Too Good a Wife?" Ads and articles featuring women doing work in the world as entrepreneurs and professionals would please her, too, as would a story in *Teen* about a girl named Molly who is a whiz in shop.

But Gilman's pleasure in Molly's story would be offset a bit by other aspects of the June 1997 *Teen Magazine* that undercut this image of strong, competent American girlhood. In 1894 under the heading, "**Woman's Exchange**," Gilman wrote in *The Impress*:

> It was asked of the editor, eagerly, if *The Impress* could be written to about matters of special interest of women and women's clubs; if it was to be a medium for exchange of thought on such subjects. That is one of the things *The Impress* is for. Letters should be short, very short, and only those dealing with matters of real importance will be answered.
>
> No inquiries as to what is good to remove freckles, and whether a lady should take a gentleman's arm or he hers, or what color goes with what kind of dress you want to make over will be answered here.[15]

What would the Gilman who refused to answer inquiries about what is good to remove freckles make of the pressing questions considered here: "What's the hottest look for toenails this summer?" and "What's the best way to remove glitter nail polish?" Or how would she read a similar column in a magazine pitched to the teenager's mother that deals with how to conceal a beauty mark? And what would she make of the cover of *Teen Magazine,* which features, alongside an article on "How to Show Your Hair Who's Boss," a "true story" titled, "My Mom Killed Herself"? Or of an ad featuring a girl who changes her nail polish every time she calls a boy and hangs up?

Gilman's pleasure in ads for clothes that move as you do and comfortable women's shoes would be diluted by the opposing images of what women should wear that appear alongside them. Omnipresent ads for spike heels would prompt her to repeat a comment she made in her essay, **"Why Women Do Not Reform Their Dress"**: "The present style of dress means, with varying limits, backache, sideache, headache, and many other aches; corns, lame, tender or swollen feet, weak, clumsy and useless compared to what they should be; . . . with a thousand attendant . . . restrictions and unnatural distortions amounting to hideousness."[16] As she wrote in a poem entitled **"The Cripple,"** "There are such things as hoofs, sub-human hoofs, / High-heeled sharp anomalies; / Small and pinching, hard and black, / Shiny as a beetle's back, / Cloven, clattering on the track, / These are hoofs, sub-human hoofs . . ."[17] Some of the more *outré* concoctions in the fashion pages might prompt her to repeat the observation that women tend to put upon their bodies "without criticism or objection every excess, distortion, discord, and contradiction that can be sewed together" (**The Home** 55). And she would be disheartened by the piece entitled "Guy Spy" featuring a young man who opines that comfortable shoes and clothing look "ridiculous" on a girl.

The Gilman who wrote—probably with things liked cinched waists in mind—that "physical suffering has so been so long considered an integral part of a woman's nature, and is still so generally borne, that a little more or less is no great matter"[18] might, nonetheless, be shocked at the physical suffering today's women voluntarily undergo in the name of beauty (not that Gilman was against reconstructive plastic surgery for accident victims, as her novel **Unpunished** demonstrates).

Regarding the vibrant young women enjoying themselves ecstatically in the ubiquitous cigarette ads that target women, Gilman would likely repeat a comment she had made in a letter to Katharine: "The mass of women are the same old fools they always were. . . . I have small patience with them—painted, powdered, high-heeled, cigarette-smoking idiot. To deliberately take up an extra vice—or bad habit—just to show off—imbecile."[19]

In these magazines, ads for romance novel book clubs, provocative, steamy ads for perfume, and ads for china sculptures featuring Clark Gable scooping Scarlet O'Hara up in his arms would give Gilman ample reason to assume that the "love story" plot was no less prevalent in our day than in hers.

An ad for crystal candles and porcelain collectibles which asks, "What do women want?" and answers, "Beautiful things," would leave Gilman muttering to herself,

> To consume food, to consume clothes, to consume houses and furniture and decorations and ornaments and amusements, to take and take and take forever,—from one man if they are virtuous, from many if they are vicious, but always to take and never to think of giving anything in return except their womanhood—this is the enforced condition of the mothers of the race.
>
> (**Women and Economics** 118-19)

Gilman would sigh at the level of meaningless consumption of an ad that urged women to change the sheets on their beds every night.

She would be intrigued by the labor-saving devices for the home that she would see advertised in these magazines—washing machines and dishwashers that would revolutionize housework. But Gilman would soon recognize that these machines were being marketed for private kitchens in private homes, and her old anger would rise.

> We have to pay severally for all these stoves and dishes, tools and utensils, which, if properly supplied in one proper place instead of twenty, would cost far less to begin with; and, in the hands of skilled professionals, would not be under the tremendous charge for breakage and ruinous misuse which now weighs heavily on the householder. Then there is the waste in fuel for these nineteen unnecessary kitchens, and lastly the largest of any item except labour, the waste in food.
>
> First the waste in purchasing in the smallest retail quantities; then the waste involved in separate catering, the "left overs" which the ingenious housewife spends her life in trying to "use up"; and also the waste caused by carelessness and ignorance in a great majority of cases. . . .
>
> Count as you will, there could hardly be devised a more wasteful way of doing necessary work than this domestic way.
>
> (**The Home** 118-19)

A washing machine ad that asserted, "Washing clothes is a job with no end in sight. But now it can be a cleaner, quicker, easier job with no end in sight," would make it clear to Gilman that not that much had changed. She would fume,

> The bottled discord of the woman's daily occupations is quite sufficient to account for the explosions of discord on her wall and floors. She continually has to do utterly inharmonious things, she lives in incessant effort to perform all at once and in the same place the most irreconcilable processes.
>
> She has to adjust, disadjust, and readjust her mental focus a thousand times a day; not only to things, but to actions; not only to actions, but to

persons; and so, to live at all, she must develop a kind of mind that *does not object to discord.* Unity, harmony, simplicity, truth, restraint—these are not applicable in a patchwork life, however hallowed by high devotion and tender love.

(*The Home* 151-52)

But what in the array of publications on the newsstands today would *really* ignite Gilman's ire? And what figure on the publishing scene today would make her sputter with frustration and rage? Her *bette noire,* I suggest, the "Darth Vader" against whom she would willingly do battle, would be none other than the self-anointed queen of the home herself, Martha Stewart.

Gilman anatomized the isolation of the single-family home, the psychic pain that that isolation inflicted on the wife and mother, and the waste of human energy and fossil fuel in its maintenance; she devoted much of her life to trying to transform it. Gilman would be appalled by Martha Stewart's efforts to make that home even *more* demanding and more time-consuming than it already was. "The free woman," Gilman wrote,

having room for full individual expression in her economic activities and in her social relations, will not be forced to pour out her soul in tidies and photograph holders. The home will be her place of rest, not of uneasy activity; and she will learn to love simplicity at last.

(*Women and Economics* 257)

While Gilman bemoaned the hours women felt obligated to spend fashioning useless antimacassars, Stewart would have us stitch our own upholstery. While Gilman urged families to abandon the single-family kitchen for more efficient communal dining, Stewart would have the housewife become adept in the fine art of crafting crystallized sugar flowers. "'Fancy cookery,'" Gilman writes, is "a thing as far removed from true artistic development as a swinging ice-pitcher from a Greek vase . . . neither pure food nor pleasure, but an artificial performance, to be appreciated only by the virtuoso" (*Women and Economics* 232). Gilman might be impressed by the multiplicity of media through which Martha Stewart pushes her message—magazines, cookbooks, decorating books, television programs, even a line of household paints. But she would mince no words about what is wrong with the ideals Stewart is projecting and glorifying:

For each man to have one whole woman to cook for and wait upon him is a poor education for democracy. The boy with a servile mother, the man with a servile wife, cannot reach the sense of equal rights we need today. Too constant consideration of the master's tastes make the master self-

ish; and the assault upon his heart direct, or through that proverbial side-avenue, the stomach, which the dependent woman needs must make when she wants anything, is bad for the man, as well as for her."[20]

The "kitchen mind," Gilman wrote,

focused continually upon close personal concerns, limited in time, in means, in capacity, and in mechanical convenience, can consider only; a, what the family likes; b, what the family can afford; and c, what the cook can accomplish.

("**Kitchen-Mindedness**" 10)

What gets neglected, in Gilman's view, is "matters of real importance" with which women, as well as men, need to concern themselves not just for their own good, but for the good of the world.

Gilman also wrote,

What sort of citizens do we need for the best city—the best state—the best country—the best world? We need men and women who are sufficiently large-minded to see and feel a common need, to work for a common good, to rejoice in the advance of all, and to know as the merest platitude that their private advantage is to be assured *only* by the common weal. That kind of mind is not bred in the kitchen.

(*The Home* 318)

"The home," Gilman wrote,

is one thing, the family another; and when the home takes all one's time, the family gets little. So we find both husband and wife overtaxed and worried in keeping up the institution according to tradition; both father and mother too much occupied in home-making to do much toward child-training, man-making!

(*The Home* 71)

In her tour of today's magazines for women, then, Gilman would find the same perplexing mixed messages that we ourselves encounter daily: be strong and athletic, but make sure you know the right way to make crystallized sugar flowers; seek out comfortable clothes that move as you do, but also be prepared to torture your feet in the time-honored tradition of spike heels; go out into the world as a professional, but welcome the romance plot lurking in the wings, be sure you consume your quota of beautiful things, and if you feel like being creative and productive, go for it: wrap your wine bottle in five festive ways.

Gilman would take a deep breath. Then she would sigh. Then maybe—just maybe—she would smile and recall the old saying that the good part of working for social change is that at least you know you've got steady work.

For better or worse, much of Gilman's writing is nowhere close to being obsolete. There is still much cultural work left for her to do.

Who else, after all, has the guts to take on Martha Stewart where she lives?

Notes

1. Constance Coiner, "Silent Parenting in the Academy," in *Listening to Silences: New Essays in Feminist Criticism,* ed. Elaine Hedges and Shelley Fisher Fishkin (New York: Oxford University Press, 1994), 198.

2. Ibid., 218.

3. Charlotte Perkins Gilman, "The Humanness of Women," *Forerunner* 1 (January 1910): 13.

4. See also Arlie R. Hochschild, "A Work Issue That Won't Go Away," *The New York Times,* 7 September 1998, A17.

5. Ann J. Lane, *To Herland and Beyond: The Life and Work of Charlotte Perkins Gilman* (New York: Pantheon, 1990), 3-4.

6. Charlotte Perkins Gilman, *The Yellow Wall-paper,* ed. with afterword by Elaine Hedges (New York: The Feminist Press, 1973). 13.

7. Charlotte Perkins Gilman, "Reasonable Resolutions," *Forerunner* 1 (January 1910): 1.

8. Charlotte Perkins Gilman, "Masculine Literature" [part 5 of serialized version of "Our Androcentric Culture: or, The Man-Made World"] *Forerunner* 1 (March 1910): 18.

9. Charlotte Perkins Gilman, "If I Were a Man," in *Charlotte Perkins Gilman Reader,* ed. Ann J. Lane (New York: Pantheon, 1980), 33.

10. Charlotte Perkins Gilman, "Do We Get 'The News'?" *Impress,* 20 October 1894, 2.

11. Charlotte Perkins Gilman, "Mind Cleaning" *Forerunner* 3 (January 1910): 5-6.

12. All of the advertisements cited here appeared in the May or June 1997 issues of *Teen, Woman's World, McCalls, Glamour, Cosmopolitan, Vogue, Seventeen, Self, Ebony, Essence, New Woman,* and *Ladies Home Journal.* The ads were part of national advertising campaigns, running in multiple publications. When this essay was originally presented as the closing plenary talk of the Second International Charlotte Perkins Gilman Conference at Skidmore College in June 1997, it was accompanied by slides of all the advertisements and articles from *Teen, Woman's World, McCalls, Glamour, Cosmopolitan, Vogue, Seventeen, Self, Ebony, Essence, New Woman,* and *Ladies Home Journal.*

13. Charlotte Perkins Gilman, *The Home, Its Work and Influence* (Urbana: University of Illinois Press, 1972), 261.

14. Charlotte Perkins Gilman, *Women and Economics* (New York: Harper & Row, 1966), 308.

15. "The Woman's Exchange," *Impress,* 6 October 1894, 4.

16. Charlotte Perkins Gilman, "Why Women Do Not Reform Their Dress," *Woman's Journal,* (23 October 1886): 338.

17. Charlotte Perkins Gilman, "The Cripple," *Forerunner* 1 (March 1910): 26.

18. Charlotte Perkins Gilman, "Why Women," 338.

19. Gilman's letter to Katharine quoted in Lane, *To Herland and Beyond,* 342.

20. Gilman, "Kitchen-Mindedness," *Forerunner* 1 (February 1910): 9.

Select Bibliography by Charlotte Perkins Gilman

Benigna Machiavelli. Serialized in *Forerunner* 5 (1914). Reprint, Santa Barbara: Bandanna Books, 1993.

Charlotte Perkins Gilman Papers, Schlesinger Library, Radcliffe College, Cambridge, MA.

Charlotte Perkins Gilman Reader. Edited with an introduction by Ann J. Lane, New York: Pantheon, 1990.

Concerning Children. Boston: Small, Maynard & Co., 1900.

The Diaries of Charlotte Perkins Gilman. 2 vols. Edited with an introduction by Denise D. Knight, Charlottesville: University Press of Virginia, 1994.

Forerunner. Vols. 1-7 (1909-16). Reprint, with an introduction by Madeleine B. Stern, New York: Greenwood, 1968.

Herland. Serialized in *Forerunner* 6 (1915). Reprint, with an introduction by Ann J. Lane, New York: Pantheon, 1979.

His Religion and Hers: A Study of the Faith of Our Fathers and the Work of Our Mothers. New York and London: Century Co., 1923. Reprint, London: T. Fisher Unwin, 1924. Reprint Westport, Conn.: Hyperion Press, 1976.

The Home: Its Work and Influence. New York: McClure, Philips & Co., 1903. Reprint, New York: Source Book Press, 1970.

In This Our World. Oakland: McCombs & Vaughn, 1893, 3d. ed. Boston: Small, Maynard & Co., 1898. Reprint, New York: Arno, 1974.

"Kitchen-Mindedness." *Forerunner* 1 (February 1910): 7-11.

The Later Poetry of Charlotte Perkins Gilman. Edited with an introduction by Denise D. Knight, Newark: University of Delaware Press, 1996.

The Living of Charlotte Perkins Gilman: An Autobiography. Foreword by Zona Gale. New York: Appleton-Century, 1935. Reprint, with an introduction by Ann J. Lane, Madison: University of Wisconsin Press, 1990.

The Man-Made World or, Our Androcentric Culture. Serialized in *Forerunner* 1 (1909-10). Reprint, New York: Charlton Co., 1911.

"Mind Cleaning." *Forerunner* 3 (January 1912): 5-6.

"Moving the Mountain." Serialized in *Forerunner* 2 (1911). Reprint, New York: Charlton Co., 1911.

"The New Motherhood." *Forerunner* 1 (December 1910): 17-18.

"The New Mothers of a New World." *Forerunner* 4 (June 1913): 145-49.

Unpunished. Edited with an afterword by Catherine J. Golden and Denise D. Knight. New York: The Feminist Press, 1997.

What Diantha Did. Serialized in *Forerunner* 1 (1909-10). Reprint, New York: Charlton Co., 1910.

With Her in Ourland. Serialized in *Forerunner* 7 (1914).

Women and Economics: A Study of the Economic Relation Between Men and Women as a Factor in Social Evolution. Boston: Small, Maynard & Co., 1898. Reprint, edited with introduction by Carl N. Degler, New York: Harper & Row, 1966.

"The Yellow Wall-Paper." *New England Magazine* (January 1892): 647-56. Reprint, with an afterword by Elaine R. Hedges, Old Westbury: The Feminist Press, 1973. Revised ed. 1996.

The Yellow Wallpaper. Boston: Small, Maynard & Co., 1899.

"The Yellow Wall-Paper" and Selected Stories of Charlotte Perkins Gilman. Edited with an introduction by Denise D. Knight. Newark: University of Delaware Press, 1994.

Secondary Readings

Ceplair, Larry, ed. *Charlotte Perkins Gilman: A Nonfiction Reader.* New York: Columbia University Press, 1992.

Golden, Catherine, ed. *The Captive Imagination: A Casebook on "The Yellow Wallpaper."* New York: The Feminist Press, 1992.

Hill, Mary. *Charlotte Perkins Gilman: The Emergence of a Radical Feminist, 1860-1896.* Philadelphia: Temple University Press, 1980.

——. *The Journey from Within: The Love Letters of Charlotte Perkins Gilman, 1897-1900.* Lewisburg, PA: Bucknell University Press, 1995.

Karpinski, Joanne, ed. *Critical Essays on Charlotte Perkins Gilman.* New York: G. K. Hall, 1992. (Includes critical essays by Catherine Golden, Elaine Hedges, Mary Hill, Shelley Fisher Fishkin, Joanne Karpinski, and Gary Scharnhorst.)

Kessler, Carol Farley. *Charlotte Perkins Gilman: Her Progress Toward Utopia, with Selected Writings.* Syracuse: University of Syracuse Press, 1995.

Knight, Denise D. *Charlotte Perkins Gilman: A Study of the Short Fiction.* New York: Twayne Publishers, 1997.

Kolmerten, Carol A. "Texts and Contexts: American Women Envision Utopia, 1890-1920." In *Utopians and Science Fiction by Women,* edited by Jane A. Donawerth and Carol A. Kolmerten. Syracuse: Syracuse University Press, 1994.

Lane, Ann J. *To "Herland" and Beyond: The Life and Work of Charlotte Perkins Gilman.* New York: Pantheon, 1990.

Lanser, Susan. "Feminist Criticism, 'The Yellow Wallpaper,' and the Politics of Color in America." *Feminist Studies* 15, no. 3 (Fall 1989): 415-41.

Meyering, Sheryl L., ed. *Charlotte Perkins Gilman: The Woman and Her Work.* Ann Arbor, MI: University Microfilms International, 1989.

Robinson, Lillian S. "Killing Patriarchy: Charlotte Perkins Gilman, the Murder Mystery, and Post-Feminist Propaganda." *Tulsa Studies in Women's Literature* 10, no. 2 (Fall 1991): 273-85.

Rudd, Jill and Val Gough, eds. *Charlotte Perkins Gilman: Optimist Reformer.* Iowa City: University of Iowa Press, 1999. Forthcoming.

——. *Charlotte Perkins Gilman: A Very Different Story.* Liverpool: University of Liverpool Press, 1998.

Scharnhorst, Gary. *Charlotte Perkins Gilman.* Boston: Twayne Publishers, 1985.

TITLE COMMENTARY

The Yellow Wallpaper

CATHERINE GOLDEN (ESSAY DATE 1992)

SOURCE: Golden, Catherine. "One Hundred Years of Reading 'The Yellow Wallpaper.'" In *The Captive Imagination: A Casebook on "The Yellow Wallpaper,"* edited by Catherine Golden, pp. 1-23. New York: The Feminist Press, 1992.

In the following essay, Golden offers a comprehensive overview of criticism on The Yellow Wallpaper.

The redefinition of the literary canon has directed attention to a number of overlooked works by late nineteenth- and early twentieth-century women writers. Prominent among this group is Charlotte Perkins Gilman's **"The Yellow Wallpaper."** From its first publication in the January 1892 issue of *New England Magazine*[1] until the early 1970s, **"The Yellow Wallpaper"** was virtually unknown; it found its way into only a few collections of short fiction between 1892 and 1972.[2] A cursory glance at the chronologically arranged Table of Contents and Bibliography of this book reveals the critical attention this complex and controversial story has received since it was republished in 1973. Along with *Herland*, **"The Yellow Wallpaper"** has gained distinction among the fiction produced by Gilman, a leading turn-of-the-century feminist lecturer and writer;[3] her fictional account of a psychological breakdown offers a chilling Poe-esque plot, a well-crafted and powerful style, and a feminist perspective on the sociocultural situation confronting women in the late nineteenth century. It has now been incorporated into the contemporary canon of American literature and hailed in the feminist canon.

The selections included in the Backgrounds and Criticism sections demonstrate multiple ways of looking at **"The Yellow Wallpaper"** and, specifically, of reading the dominant symbol of the wallpaper and understanding the story's protagonist. The essays within this critical edition represent the breadth of theoretical perspectives that scholars have used to approach **"The Yellow Wallpaper"**—principally reader response, biographical, psychological (for example, Lacanian, Freudian, Adlerian), feminist, and linguistic.

FROM THE AUTHOR

WHY I WROTE "THE YELLOW WALLPAPER"
Many and many a reader has asked that. When the story first came out, in the *New England Magazine* about 1891, a Boston physician made protest in *The Transcript*. Such a story ought not to be written, he said; it was enough to drive anyone mad to read it.

Another physician, in Kansas I think, wrote to say that it was the best description of incipient insanity he had ever seen, and—begging my pardon—had I been there?

Now the story of the story is this:

For many years I suffered from a severe and continuous nervous breakdown tending to melancholia—and beyond. During about the third year of this trouble I went, in devout faith and some faint stir of hope, to a noted specialist in nervous diseases, the best known in the country. This wise man put me to bed and applied the rest cure, to which a still good physique responded so promptly that he concluded there was nothing much the matter with me, and sent me home with solemn advice to "live as domestic a life as far as possible," to "have but two hours' intellectual life a day," and "never to touch pen, brush or pencil again as long as I lived." This was in 1887.

I went home and obeyed those directions for some three months, and came so near the border line of utter mental ruin that I could see over.

Then, using the remnants of intelligence that remained, and helped by a wise friend, I cast the noted specialist's advice to the winds and went to work again—work, the normal life of every human being; work, in which is joy and growth and service, without which one is a pauper and a parasite; ultimately recovering some measure of power.

Being naturally moved to rejoicing by this narrow escape, I wrote *The Yellow Wallpaper*, with its embellishments and additions to carry out the ideal (I never had hallucinations or objections to my mural decorations) and sent a copy to the physician who so nearly drove me mad. He never acknowledged it.

The little book is valued by alienists and as a good specimen of one kind of literature. It has to my knowledge saved one woman from a similar fate—so terrifying her family that they let her out into normal activity and she recovered.

But the best result is this. Many years later I was told that the great specialist had admitted to friends of his that he had altered his treatment of neurasthenia since reading *The Yellow Wallpaper*.

It was not intended to drive people crazy, but to save people from being driven crazy, and it worked.

Gilman, Charlotte Perkins. "Why I Wrote 'The Yellow Wallpaper'" (1913). In *The Captive Imagination: A Casebook on "The Yellow Wallpaper,"* edited by Catherine Golden, pp. 52-3. New York: The Feminist Press, 1992.

Although much of the criticism is feminist in its orientation, selections from the Backgrounds section convey the original response to the story as a horror tale, and several essays from the Criticism section suggest the need to extend the feminist perspective.[4]

Overlap occurs between essays, particularly those that read **"The Yellow Wallpaper"** through a given critical lens. However, critics often approach the story from a combination of theoretical perspectives and typically take notice of different dimensions of the story within their essays. In fact, the experience of following all the criticism of **"The Yellow Wallpaper"** begins to mimic that of the fictional narrator as she struggles to read the everchanging text of the wallpaper and follow it to some sort of conclusion: the story evolves before our eyes and gains new definition.

Interpretations from scholars representing different disciplines and articulating distinct and, at times, dissimilar points of view have increased the recognition of Gilman and her story. The now privileged status of "**The Yellow Wallpaper**" conflicts with the reception it received in the 1890s as well as the conclusion Gilman realistically reached about her literary career following the publication of "**The Yellow Wallpaper**" and numerous poems: "All these literary efforts providing but little, it was well indeed that another avenue of work [lecturing] opened up to me at this time" (*Living* 65).[5] Within this critical edition, scholars frequently make reference to the autobiographical roots of the story because of the striking parallels between the narrator's and Gilman's creative life. Revisiting the climate and situation that the author confronted in 1890 through 1892 continues to serve as a reminder of the distance the story has traveled over the past one hundred years.

To recall the apt title of one of Gilman's own poems, it took the overcoming of "**An Obstacle**"[6] for "**The Yellow Wallpaper**" to achieve recognition. Editors and readers were not ready to receive "**The Yellow Wallpaper**" when Charlotte Perkins Gilman (then Stetson)[7] sent it to the well-established novelist, critic, and editor William Dean Howells in 1890. Gilman records in her autobiography, *The Living of Charlotte Perkins Gilman,* that Howells had earlier initiated a correspondence; his "unforgettable letter" made her feel "like a 'real' author at last" (D. Appleton-Century, 113). In this letter dated June 9, 1890, Howells praised two of her poems, "**Similar Cases**" and "**Women of To-day**," and concluded of both: "It ["**Women of To-day**"] is as good almost as the other ["**Similar Cases**"], and dreadfully true" (1935; 113). Thus, it is not surprising that in an effort to publish another work that was also "dreadfully true," Gilman sent Howells, the major proponent of American realism, her consciously autobiographical "**The Yellow Wallpaper**."[8]

Gilman's difficulty in getting her now acclaimed story published is not unique in literary history. But the reaction to her landmark story informs its long-lasting and virtual neglect. Howells, a former editor of the prestigious *Atlantic Monthly,* recommended the story to his friend Horace Scudder, then serving as editor. Scudder's often quoted reply bears repeating:

Dear Madam,

Mr. Howells has handed me this story.

I could not forgive myself if I made others as miserable as I have made myself!

Sincerely yours,
H. E. Scudder.

Gilman concluded of her rejection: "I suppose he would have sent back one of Poe's on the same ground" (*Living* 64). In appraising why Scudder rejected the story, Gilman draws a salient parallel between her fiction and Edgar Allan Poe's that has illuminated the original responses to her story as a horror tale. Many have considered Gilman's tale of a woman's descent into madness a continuation of a genre made popular by Poe. Gilman's first husband, Walter Stetson, found the story more disturbing than Poe's tales of horror.[9] As recently as 1973, horror writer H. P. Lovecraft included it as a "classic example in subtly delineating the madness which crawls over a woman dwelling in the hideously papered room"[10] in a collection titled *Supernatural Horror in Literature.* Nonetheless, the climate of Victorian America and its expectations for literature suggest that Scudder might well have accepted one of Poe's tales of madness yet rejected "**The Yellow Wallpaper**"—on different grounds. Of consequence, the story did not offer the kind of uplifting ending to which *Atlantic Monthly* stories typically adhered. More provocatively, the protagonist who descends into madness is a middle-class wife and mother. As Annette Kolodny has noted: "Those fond of Poe could not easily transfer their sense of mental derangement to the mind of a comfortable middle-class wife and mother; and those for whom the woman in the home was a familiar literary character were hard-pressed to comprehend so extreme an anatomy of the psychic price she paid" (154-5). No doubt Gilman's uncomfortable depiction of a familiar literary figure succumbing to madness within the sacrosanct Victorian domestic circle made Scudder "miserable." He may well have rejected the story in an attempt to protect his late nineteenth-century readers from the story's attack on the appropriate sphere for dutiful women: husband, child, and home.

"**The Yellow Wallpaper**" eventually found a literary residence if not a home in 1892. Gilman employed Henry Austin, a literary agent, who placed it in *New England Magazine,* a relatively conservative periodical offering a range of nonfiction (travel, history, and biographical spotlights), stories, and poems accompanied by photographs and black-and-white illustrations.[11] The story appeared with three illustrations and a decorative pictorial capital designed by Jo H. Hatfield, a staff illustrator for the magazine. Gilman never received any payment for the initial publication of the story although the editor of *New England Magazine* claimed that he paid Austin forty dollars for it. Nonetheless, she did receive ample compensation in reader response, which proved opinionated and mixed. One antagonistic review entitled "Perilous Stuff" (1892), appearing in the Boston *Transcript,* called it: "a sad story of a young wife passing the gradations from slight mental derangement to raving lunacy" (*Living* 64). This protester, an anonymous male physician, argued to censure the story of "deadly peril";[12] but he betrayed his own curiosity when he fearfully admitted that it held the reader "in morbid fascination to the end" (*Living* 64). While the story made this doctor as miserable as the editor of the *Atlantic Monthly,* it evoked praise from another doctor, Brummel Jones, who in 1892 sent Gilman a congratulatory letter. Jones complimented the story's authentic depiction of mental derangement and argued in a self-congratulatory tone: "From a doctor's standpoint, and I am a doctor, you have made a success. So far as I know, and I am fairly well up in literature, there has been no detailed account of incipient insanity" (*Living* 65).

When I read **"The Yellow Wallpaper"** in the original periodical, I was surprised to discover how the illustrations, along with Poe's literary influence, encouraged the original responses to the story as a horror tale of a wife and mother's mental derangement. Heretofore no critic has discussed the illustrations accompanying the story in *New England Magazine.* It was customary to illustrate both fiction and nonfiction pieces printed in *New England Magazine,* and Hatfield's pen-and-ink drawings are realistic, typical of the style of illustration the late century tended to produce.[13] However, these illustrations, corresponding to specific lines of the story, deserve attention because they draw out, to use Brummel Jones's words, a "detailed account of incipient insanity."

Below the first illustration appears the caption "I am sitting by the Window in this Atrocious Nursery," a paraphrase of a line from the early pages of Gilman's diary-like story written from the point of view of a first-person narrative. Prominently placed as a headpiece, this illustration shows the narrator as a respectable-looking Victorian woman engaged in writing. Although the narrator writes only in secret and hides her journal when she senses John's entry, in this illustration Hatfield captures the narrator in an act that directly confronts the opinion of those who prescribe her rest cure: her physician-husband, John, who "hates to have [her] write a word" (26); S. Weir Mitchell, the foremost specialist in nervous diseases for women; and even John's sister Jennie, an "enthusiastic housekeeper" who "thinks it is the writing which made [her] sick" (30). Pen in

hand and inkwell by her side, she is drawn acting deceitfully but not looking so. Seated in a decorative rocking chair by the window,[14] dressed demurely, and hair swept back in a neat bun, she looks like the narrator describes John: "practical" (24). Smiling contentedly, she truly believes that "congenial work, with excitement and change, would do [her] good" (25).

The narrator's facial expression appears not contented but composed and almost rigid in the second, marginal let-in illustration whose caption reads "She didn't know I was in the Room." This illustration responds to the narrator's discussion of how Jennie (and earlier John) suspects her obsession with the paper and is puzzled by it. Less effective than the first illustration, this drawing realizes Jennie's look of alarm and confusion as well as the narrator's consciously "restrained manner" (35) as she asks Jennie to explain why she is inspecting the wallpaper. Hatfield also lightly indicates the sprouting and flamboyant curves and "sprawling outlines" (31) of the yellow wallpaper in the portion of the paper framing Jennie. No major changes occur in the narrator's dress or hairstyle although a peculiar expression clouds her too-tight composure and conveys the very beginning of her hallucinatory state—well established at this point in the story.

The final illustration, dynamically positioned as an endpiece, appears below the line it illustrates: "I had to creep over him every time."[15] The dramatic shift in the portrayal of the narrator between the first two drawings and the third suggests that the narrator succumbs to full-blown madness at an alarming rate and passes through "the gradations from slight mental derangement to raving lunacy," much as the anonymous Boston reviewer describes. The illustration captures the narrator in an act very different than covert writing: creeping on the floor in front of and over John. Conveying a decrepit eeriness, her long and wild dark hair has been freed from the constraints of its late Victorian-style coiffure to accentuate her madness.[16] Although there are no indications of a change in the narrator's appearance in the text (or discussion of her appearance in the text at all for that matter), Hatfield's depiction responds to the traditional conception of the long- and wild-haired madwoman in literature, *Jane Eyre*'s Bertha Mason a prime example.

The narrator's thick and slightly frizzled mane now masks the demure details of her high-necked, long-sleeved Victorian gown. Her hair drapes down her back, in front of her shoulder, and over John, who lies prostrate underneath her in a dead faint. Alongside him lie the tattered strips of the wallpaper that the narrator has torn from the wall. John's three-quarter pose allows the reader-viewer to see the extent of his swoon, leaving his face blank, his hands limp, and his body in a fetal position. The narrator's hands, placed directly on top of John's head and back, facilitate her crawling over her husband. These graphic depictions of John in a position of extreme vulnerability as well as of the narrator in a state of total madness create a visual climax that may have encouraged the traditional response that this tale of "incipient insanity" was of "deadly peril." Totally self-absorbed in her actions, the narrator conveys disregard for and detachment from "that man" (41), who, to recall Gilman's own poem, is reduced to "**An Obstacle**" across her path: "And I walked directly through him / As if he wasn't there."

Anthologizing the story without the illustrations nearly thirty years later, Howells continued this line of interpretation of the story's chilling portrayal of insanity in "A Reminiscent Introduction" to his 1920 collection of *The Great Modern American Stories*: "It wanted at least two generations to freeze our young blood with Mrs. Perkins Gilman's story of 'The Yellow Wall Paper'" (55).[17] Howells was well aware of the polemical intent permeating Gilman's fiction and her feminist principles; in fact, in the Biography and Bibliography section at the end of his collection, he emphasized the latter when he said of Gilman: "She is deeply interested in labor problems and the advance of women."[18] However, Howells did not remark in his very brief introduction that "**The Yellow Wallpaper**" also "wanted [more than] two generations" for its feminist thrust or its polemical intent to be appreciated. Gilman emphasized the latter in her discussions of the story appearing in the *Forerunner* (1909-16) as well as in her autobiography.

In *The Living of Charlotte Perkins Gilman,* Gilman records that when Howells asked her if he might include the story in his collection, she replied, "I was more than willing, but assured him that it was no more 'literature' than my other stuff, being definitely written 'with a purpose'" (65). Her purpose for writing this story has led some critics to call it a polemic against Mitchell's treatment:[19] "the real purpose of the story was to reach Dr. S. Weir Mitchell, and convince him of the error of his ways" (*Living* 65). In 1887 Silas Weir Mitchell treated Gilman at his Philadelphia sanitarium with his well-known rest cure of enforced passivity and confinement, a treatment which is presented by Mitchell, Gilman, and critic

Ann Douglas Wood in the Backgrounds section. A leading nineteenth-century neurologist[20] and specialist in women's nervous disorders, Mitchell diagnosed Gilman's condition as "nervous prostration" or "neurasthenia," a breakdown of the nervous system, in her case brought on by a postpartum depression. Overwhelmed by the demands of marriage and motherhood, she willingly entered into the rest cure treatment, but Mitchell's methods and his therapeutic advice at the close of her treatment proved disastrous.

Gilman—who gave way to tremors and weeping when caring for her infant daughter—attempted to follow Mitchell's prescription: "Live as domestic a life as possible. Have your child with you all the time" (*Living* 62). She made a rag doll baby that she hung on a doorknob and began to crawl into dark corners in a state of mental despair. As Jeffrey Berman notes, "In contrast to Mitchell's dictum to return to her husband and presumably expand her family, Gilman chose the only form of pregnancy she could imagine—literary creation" (229). After nearly losing her mind by rigidly following his remaining injunction "never [to] touch pen, brush or pencil as long as you live" (*Living* 62, Gilman, a commercial artist and writer, defied Mitchell and transformed him into a minor but memorable character in her fiction. In describing the nature of her story, Gilman records: "It is a description of a case of nervous breakdown beginning something as mine did, and treated as Dr. S. Weir Mitchell treated me with what I considered the inevitable result, progressive insanity" (*Living* 63) No doubt to advance her "purpose" as well as to establish medical authenticity, Gilman directly implicated Mitchell by naming the doctor in one salient reference in which the nameless narrator, undergoing a three-month rest cure for a postpartum depression, protests about her physician/husband, "John says if I don't pick up faster he shall send me to Weir Mitchell in the fall. But I don't want to go there at all. I had a friend who was in his hands once, and she says he is just like John and my brother, only more so!" (30). The narrator's "friend" serves as a shadowed reference to the author herself and further exposes the autobiographical roots of the story.

"**The Yellow Wallpaper**" reveals the consequences of following Mitchell's treatment and his therapeutic advice, which Gilman rigidly did for three months. The nameless narrator, like Gilman herself, initially defies the rest cure by writing, much as Hatfield's opening illustration depicts her. Once submissive, the protagonist pursues her ambition to find out the pattern of the wallpaper and to tear the wallpaper to free the woman trapped behind the pattern. She gains a forceful sense of self only as she acts out of madness. As she creeps on the floor, her actions move beyond the realm of sanity where Gilman had also found herself moving before defying her cure; in her words, "I had been as far as one could go and get back" (*Living* 65). Gilman managed not only to "get back" but to turn her sickness into a creative work of art that exposed Mitchell. She sent her doctor a copy of "**The Yellow Wallpaper**" to urge him to rethink his treatment of nervous prostration. Learning second-hand that Mitchell changed his methods upon reading her story, she proudly remarked: "If that is a fact, I have not lived in vain" (*Living* 65).

Gilman conceived of her work only as a story with a mission, a point that many of the critics within this book also note. Although "**The Yellow Wallpaper**" remains compatible with her other fiction in its attention to women's issues and women's problems, it appears distinctive from her oeuvre of fiction, which even Gilman enthusiasts consider too didactic, too ideological, and often hastily crafted. "**The Yellow Wallpaper**" has been singled out as the best of Gilman's creative writing. It is read today, to quote Ann Lane, as "a genuine literary piece."[21] This representative selection from scholarship over the past two decades examines Gilman's rich and complex short story as a work of art. Critics illuminate the sociocultural, psychological, and linguistic dimensions of Gilman's literary piece as well as explore its place within the literary tradition.

The sociocultural importance of the story took nearly eight generations of readers to be appreciated; until the 1970s, as Elaine Hedges notes, "No one seems to have made the connection between insanity and the sex, or sexual role, of the victim, no one explored the story's implications of male-female relationships in the nineteenth century" (125). In her 1973 Afterword to the Feminist Press edition, Hedges reintroduced the story as "one of the rare pieces of literature we have by a nineteenth-century woman which directly confronts the sexual politics of the male-female, husband-wife relationship" (124). Connecting "**The Yellow Wallpaper**" to Kate Chopin's *The Awakening* (1899) for its frank presentation of the submission of the middle-class wife, she links the destruction of both heroines to the climate of their times. Gail Parker initiated this sociocultural line of argument in her 1972 Introduction to *The Oven Birds: American Women on Womanhood, 1820-*

1920. This anthology includes Gilman's "**The Yellow Wallpaper**" as well as poetry and excerpts from *The Home* and her autobiography, alongside letters, diary excerpts, memoirs, and fiction and nonfiction writings by leading feminist thinkers, notably Elizabeth Cady Stanton, Jane Addams, Sarah Orne Jewett, and Gilman's famous Beecher relatives, her great aunts Catharine Beecher and Harriet Beecher Stowe. In her historical anthology, Parker aimed to connect the history of American feminism and literary history; the inclusion of "**The Yellow Wallpaper**" in Parker's collection placed this work of fiction firmly within the context of the history of American feminism. Although Parker's discussion of the story is brief and largely autobiographical, she cast "**The Yellow Wallpaper**" in a feminist context in suggesting that it forces the reader to "recognize what happens to a woman who is denied the right to be an adult" (85). Through Parker's and Hedges's feminist readings, the story became not simply a Poe-esque horror story of mental derangement "chilling" to the blood but a fictional arena in which Gilman voiced and questioned the submissive role prescribed to women.

"**The Yellow Wallpaper**" does not provide an alternative, feasible female model to guide women readers of future generations as Gilman's fiction typically does. Rather, through her depiction of a rest cure, it plays out the extreme restrictions and limitations confronting women in their society in order to accentuate the fatal consequences of making a woman totally dependent on her male protectors and returning her to an infantile state. The narrator's progressive descent into madness further comments upon the doubly authoritative role of the male protagonist in this late Victorian climate: husband and doctor of "high standing" (24). In contrast, the woman trapped behind the barred pattern of the yellow wallpaper with whom the nameless narrator attempts to identify has been read not only as her literary double but as a symbol of the woman's social condition. The story touches on sensitive questions and worries that haunted Gilman and the women of her time, many of which are also raised in the selections included in the Backgrounds section by Barbara Ehrenreich and Deirdre English, Ann Douglas Wood, Jill Conway, and Gail Parker. The story encourages us to ponder: might a woman feel confined in the home and constricted by her male protector much as the narrator does by her paternalistic husband who, despite his well-meaning intentions, drives her into madness in administering a Mitchell-like rest cure? Might the unending demands of caring for a husband and a child she desperately loves drive a woman to a nervous breakdown, especially if she has an imaginative mind and also desires meaningful work, as the narrator does in **"The Yellow Wallpaper"**? The questions Gilman's story raises about the limited sphere for women in the nineteenth century readily engage audiences today as equally as they baffled or bothered Gilman's contemporary readers who, as Kolodny argues, either lacked an awareness of the conventions of women's writing or were unprepared for the uncomfortable depiction of the middle-class housewife it revealed; the narrator's problems were presented as sociocultural rather than idiosyncratic, as was customary in the tales of Poe. More consciously autobiographical than any of her other fictional works, the story expresses Gilman's deep sadness over the lost opportunities for women not allowed to fulfill their own purpose in life.

Although Gilman's own mental illness and personal indictment of S. Weir Mitchell have often been read into **"The Yellow Wallpaper,"** the story's psychological importance apart from Gilman's own life has not gone undetected. The yellow wallpaper lining the walls of the former nursery whose color is "hideous" and "unreliable" and whose pattern is "torturing" (34) functions as the primary symbol of the story. The wallpaper filled with "flamboyant patterns committing every artistic sin" (26) soon becomes "an interminable string of toadstools, budding and sprouting in endless convolutions" (34). Her hallucinations evoke nightmare images revealing of the narrator's own distraught mental state. At any given moment in the story the narrator looks at the paper in disparate ways: "Looked at in one way" (31), the narrator tells us, the principle design appears as a "'debased Romanesque' with delirium tremens . . . But, on the other hand, they connect diagonally, and the sprawling outlines run off in great slanting waves of optic horror, like a lot of wallowing seaweeds in full chase" (31). As the story unfolds, the wallpaper continues to evolve from "delirium tremens" to "wallowing seaweed" into a human form as it gains a personality, odor, and movement.

These changes have provoked a plethora of psychological readings interpreting the changes in the once abhorrent and then obsessively mesmerizing wallpaper as a psychological indicator of the narrator's mental state. Beate Schöpp-Schilling applies the psychoanalytical principles of Alfred Adler to **"The Yellow Wallpaper"** to appreciate the narrator's situation at the end of the story as

well as Gilman's grasp of psychological processes. In her reading, the narrator's mental deterioration manifested through an excessive preoccupation with wallpaper importantly demonstrates the active characteristics of mental illness, "a perverted attempt of a human being to overcome his feelings of inferiority" (143). Jeffrey Berman interprets the changing patterns of the budding, sprouting paper as a reflection of the narrator's own fragmented state and calls it "a projection screen or Rorschach test of the narrator's growing fright" (232), particularly of her morbid fears of marriage, procreation, and motherhood.[22] The dominant/ muted pattern of the paper has led critics such as Judith Fetterley to read the wallpaper as a "palimpsest." The longer the narrator looks at the paper, the more definition she sees in both parts of the paper—a front pattern of bars and a muted back pattern that first looks "like" a woman (33) and then "is" a woman (34). The wallpaper becomes more than personified. As the woman behind the wallpaper becomes the narrator's sole preoccupation, she also becomes the narrator's state of mind, in Loralee MacPike's psychological interpretation. To MacPike the wallpaper, like the narrator, is "itself imprisoned in the nursery, with the humanoid heads, behind their intangible bars, denied the sexuality of bodies" (139). Not only trapped like the narrator, the wallpaper embodies contradictions and so mirrors the narrator as well as the larger social condition for women in which such contradiction remains inherent. Her identification with the formless figure, born of an hallucination, leads the narrator to free the woman and that part of herself trapped by the restrictive pattern of her own society.

Examining the psychology of the wallpaper reveals that its meaning cannot simply be fixed. Likewise, the form and language of the text lead the reader deep into the complex psyche of the narrator and invite a multiplicity of readings. The story is comprised of ten diary-like entries and written in the first person, thus giving the impression that the narrator is writing her own story in which she is also the protagonist. Critics have not typically distinguished the narrator/journalist from the protagonist who stops writing, a point of contradiction which Paula Treichler and Richard Feldstein have raised and explored. As Feldstein poses: "If the protagonist stops writing, how do we explain the completion of her journal?" (315). Answering this question invites a range of disparate interpretations and importantly maintains the multiple meanings of this richly ambiguous story that defies one reductive explanation. Has the narrator written the final entry after the fact? Has she done so consciously to prove her recovery? Both of these interpretations deny any disjunction between the narrator/narrated. But perhaps Gilman wanted to direct our attention to this very disjunction. Gilman may have called upon modernist techniques purposefully to show the narrator to be both fused with and distinct from the narrated much as she consciously shows the narrator to be separate from and joined with the woman trapped behind the wallpaper.

Particularly, the pronoun usage in the opening of the tenth entry suggests the narrator's temporary fusion of identity with the woman behind the wallpaper, which Kolodny and I note in our respective essays: "I pulled and she shook, I shook and she pulled, and before morning we had peeled off yards of that paper" (39). Following this dramatic liberation of the woman behind the paper, the narrator emerges independent and resumes writing in the first person singular. Focusing on the narrator's linguistic struggle to defy the physician's "sentence" that condemns her to silence, Treichler argues that the narrator becomes an involved language user who authors her own sentences in a defiant, "impertinent" language. Nonetheless, the narrator who speaks defiantly remains trapped in a room, creeping.

Revising the way she reads the wallpaper, the narrator, although mad, writes in a way that no longer matches her thoughts and actions or conveys one consistent characterization of an oppressed figure who is fearful and fanciful. Interpreting the entire story as well as its main symbol of the wallpaper as a "palimpsest" allows for further examination of the linguistic features of the story. As I argue in my essay, the thoughts and actions of the narrator logically comprise its dominant text, but the writing through which the narrator expresses them (assuming the narrator/narrated is one) comprises a second, muted text informing the narrator's final characterization. Precisely at the point when she dramatically creeps on the floor, tears the wallpaper, and seemingly condemns herself to madness, the narrator increasingly uses and prominently places the nominative case pronoun in the defiant sentences she authors. Nonetheless, the forcefulness of her language, which both Treichler and I recognize, permits her only a dubious victory over patriarchal control. These discussions of the relationship between the mental and social condition of the narrator and language continue to open the multiplicity of meanings in the text and to invite

further systematic examination of the style and syntax of the narrator as a language user.

Whether "The Yellow Wallpaper" should be regarded a short story or a novella also remains in dispute. While many critics consider it a short story, others call it a novella, a term that some might think increases its literary stature but that also conflicts with its brevity. Echoing the ambiguity surrounding all aspects of the text, the title shifted from being placed in quotation marks when it first appeared as a "short story" in *New England Magazine* in 1892 to being underlined when it was reissued as a single volume "novella" edition first in 1899 by Small, Maynard and again in 1973 by The Feminist Press. While its treatment as a single volume edition has increased attention to "The Yellow Wallpaper" as a work of fiction in its own right, its first inclusion in Howells's anthology, *The Great Modern American Stories,* importantly placed Gilman's landmark story alongside the short fiction of her noted female and male American contemporaries, Sarah Orne Jewett, Edith Wharton, Mark Twain, and Henry James. The story's inclusion in Howells's collection also paved the way for its acceptance in the contemporary American literary canon.

Conrad Shumaker discusses "The Yellow Wallpaper" in relation to central concerns of nineteenth-century American literature, particularly the work of Nathaniel Hawthorne. Shumaker compares Gilman's John to Hawthorne's Aylmer in "The Birthmark," and he argues that Gilman explores an issue central to American literature and culture when she reveals how the imagination becomes destroyed by a world view that leaves no room for anything that is not useful. John embodies this world view on the opening page of the story when the narrator confides: "John is practical to the extreme. He has no patience with faith, an intense horror of superstition, and he scoffs openly at any talk of things not to be felt and seen and put down in figures" (24). The narrator, in contrast, has a strong imagination leading her to invent stories about things that cannot really be "felt and seen." John urges her to check this inclination by exerting self-control. John does not believe his wife is sick, treats her fancy as a "defect," and represses her imaginative nature, as Shumaker notes, "only to find he has destroyed her in the process" (246). The woman's more poetic world view presented through Gilman's narrator conflicts with the extremely "practical" approach of her sensible physician/husband John, who misreads her much as Henry James's Winterbourne crucially misreads Daisy in "Daisy Miller."

Although Shumaker finds the feminist readings of **"The Yellow Wallpaper"** instructive, he raises a concern that such approaches isolate **"The Yellow Wallpaper"** from what he considers to be the "dominant tradition" of Hawthorne, James, Twain, and Wharton, of which it is a part. But in her feminist interpretation Fetterley focuses on the theme of reading about reading, a central concern of the "classics" of American literature, and she reads **"The Yellow Wallpaper"** alongside Susan Glaspell's "A Jury of Her Peers" and Edgar Allan Poe's "The Murders in Rue Morgue." Building upon Kolodny's work, Jean Kennard has argued that the rise of literary conventions of women's writing not available to readers of the 1890s has allowed a feminist reading of the story to be voiced and accepted. The plethora of such feminist readings published between 1973 and 1980 has brought the story its acclaim and has led to its inclusion in the contemporary canons of both American literature and feminist literature. Collectively the work of Hedges, Kennard, Kolodny, Sandra Gilbert and Susan Gubar, and Fetterley helped the text to achieve a privileged status among literature by women. In *The Madwoman in the Attic* (1979), Gilbert and Gubar call **"The Yellow Wallpaper"** "a striking story of female confinement and escape, a paradigmatic tale which (like *Jane Eyre*) seems to tell *the* story that all literary women would tell if they could speak their 'speechless woe'" (145). Through this context, **"The Yellow Wallpaper"** came to be included among those long-neglected works of nineteenth-century women writers which these authors resurrected and reinterpreted.

Along with other overlooked late nineteenth-century works of fiction such as Kate Chopin's *The Awakening*, **"The Yellow Wallpaper"** has been reprinted in numerous mainstream fiction anthologies as well as anthologies of women writers, such as the *Norton Anthology of Literature By Women* (1985), edited by Gilbert and Gubar. Its widespread inclusion in anthologies today demonstrates that the story has become a literary staple in courses in fiction and particularly in those with an emphasis on women's literature. The way in which the story is introduced within these anthologies has also changed. Unlike Howells, who praised the tale for its chilling qualities without reference to its feminist appeal, Gilbert and Gubar connect it to this context in their introduction: "Charlotte Perkins Gilman's story *The Yellow Wallpaper* (1892)

analyzed female madness in terms of women's ambivalent attitudes toward men and maternity."[23]

The now frequent appearance of the story in anthologies is but one indication of its firm place in the feminist literary canon, a point that has not gone without reproach. Janice Haney-Peritz reconsiders the influential feminist criticism of the story by Hedges, Gilbert and Gubar, Kolodny, and Kennard. She raises some of the troubling implications of this criticism in which "Gilman's short story has assumed monumental proportions" (262) and "functions as a feminist monument" (262). Mary Jacobus, also reviewing the work of feminist critics Kolodny and Kennard, points out that their feminist thematic readings importantly contradict the tendency to see women as unstable or hysterical. However, she questions whether such feminist readings may prove too "rationalist" (simply positing that confinement drives the woman mad) and suggests a need to consider dimensions of the story that feminist readings had heretofore barely explored: signs pointing to an "irrationalist, Gothic" reading (the wallpaper drives the narrator mad),[24] the importance of the yellow color of the wallpaper (a color of sickness and decay), and the uncanny creepiness of Gilman's story. In her own essay in feminist criticism, she illuminates the uncanny and reads the disturbing color and odor of the yellow wallpaper as a symbol of the narrator's repressed sexuality, a point that Berman also makes in his more traditionally Freudian psychoanalysis, published just prior to Jacobus's.[25]

Critics continue to debate the ambiguous and controversial ending, particularly the narrator's fate. The ending of the story defies a reductive explanation, no doubt as Gilman intended. Opinions range along a spectrum marked by extremes: liberation versus entrapment, triumph versus defeat. The pioneering studies appearing in the 1970s similarly read **"The Yellow Wallpaper"** as a story of a woman attempting to free herself from her restrictive, patriarchal nineteenth-century society. But these early complementary and sympathetic interpretations disagree somewhat about the degree of triumph and liberation the narrator achieves at the end of the tale. Most optimistic are the readings of Gilbert and Gubar, Kennard, and Schöpp-Shilling. Gilbert and Gubar argue that the narrator, "a supposedly 'mad' woman has been sentenced to imprisonment in the 'infected' house of her own body" (148); however, through identification with the double trapped on the other side of the wallpaper, the woman—whom society perceives as mad—escapes from her textual and architectural confinement into "the open space of [her] own authority" (147). Through Kennard's eyes, the narrator's madness can be seen even more optimistically as "a form of higher sanity, as an indication of a capacity to see truths other than those available to the logical mind" (180). Furthermore, to Kennard the narrator's discomfort in ancestral halls becomes a healthy expression of a desire for freedom and space, and her descent into madness a spiritual quest "if we agree to read madness as sanity" (182). In Schöpp-Schilling's positive reading, the narrator defies her husband, who forbids her to write, by turning to another form of paper—the wallpaper. The heroine's final descent into madness becomes a supreme defiance, "which ultimately enables her to creep triumphantly over her husband" (143). Of these early readings, Hedges and Kolodny, in contrast, emphasize the limitations of the narrator's situation at the end of the story. Through Hedges's lens, the narrator achieves temporary insight but "is destroyed" (132), completely mad. Kolodny similarly interprets the narrator's situation as a liberation into madness only "for in decoding her own projections onto the paper, the protagonist has managed to reencode them once more, and now more firmly than ever, within" (158).

Swinging across this spectrum, the narrator is allowed a partial victory by some critics of the mid-1980s, who place her between the extremes of finding meaning or self-definition in her state of madness to retreating into an inhuman or inanimate state. To Fetterley, the narrator achieves a "temporary sanity"; although this state enables her to express feelings that John represses, these emotions inevitably energize her to act out her madness rather than merely imagine it. Although Fetterley argues that the narrator does not escape the patriarchal text when she "got out at last" (41), she allows that the narrator's choice of literal madness may be preferable to John's confining prescription for sanity. Placing the narrator midway along the spectrum of entrapment versus liberation, Treichler concludes that "the story only hints at possibilities for change. Woman is both passive and active, subject and object, sane and mad" (207). She argues that the social conditions must change before the narrator and other women can truly be free. Writing in the late 1980s, I similarly permit the narrator a "dubious victory" because "Only at the point at which she acts out of madness does she find a place within the patriarchal language she uses, although not yet within her larger social reality" (304).

Not all critics perceive the narrator in limbo between madness and sanity or on the road to victory as some of the pioneering studies do. Marking a turning point in the literary criticism of "The Yellow Wallpaper," the mid-1980s favored a darker reading of the story and a more pessimistic view of the narrator's fate. In opposition to Gilbert and Gubar, Haney-Peritz asserts that "the narrator does not move out into open country; instead, she turns an ancestral hall into a haunted house and then encrypts herself therein as a fantasy figure" (271). Considering the story a "memento mori that signifies the death of (a) woman rather than as a memorial that encloses the body essential to a viable feminist criticism" (271), she suggests that a "memento mori" invokes sympathy for what may happen when a repressed woman can express herself only by encasing herself within an imaginary realm.

Emphasizing the narrator's animalness rather than her inanimateness, Jacobus describes how "The narrator of 'The Yellow Wallpaper' enacts her abject state first by timorousness and stealth (her acquiescence in her own 'treatment,' and her secret writing), then by creeping, and finally by going on all fours over the supine body of her husband" (286). She expands upon the animalhood of the hysterical narrator by likening her to Brontë's madwoman in the attic of Thornfield Hall, an association with *Jane Eyre* far different than Gilbert and Gubar's. To Jacobus, "The woman on all fours is like Bertha Mason, an embodiment of the animality of woman unredeemed by (masculine) reason" (287-8). Whereas the act of crawling becomes a condition of animalhood through Jacobus's 1986 reading, the same act serves as the triumphant overcoming of John (the narrator creeps over him) in Kennard's 1981 essay, or as a purposeful exertion of self-control—a means to shock John into a faint—in Feldstein's more recent 1989 reading. John's fainting has become a subject for discussion, some critics pointing to it as a sign that the narrator has outwitted John and others arguing that he will recover and commit his wife in the end. Feldstein also proposes that the narrator's action of crawling be seen as a form of self-expression: "Prohibited from writing in her journal, the narrator embodies herself as a stylus writing the line, her body being written in the process" (313) or, one might argue, giving birth to itself. The evolution in the way the narrator and the story itself have been read continues to defy a reductive pattern as does the story itself. Moving from the pioneering studies that appeared in the 1970s to the new historicist and cultural studies readings of the late 1980s, Hedges, in her concluding essay, explores the ways critics within and beyond this collection have looked at the story over the last two decades. Returning to examine the criticism following her Afterword accompanying the story's 1973 republication, she provocatively notes what aspects of "The Yellow Wallpaper" subsequent readings have highlighted or shadowed and points out the implications of some of the most recent criticism.

The gathering of many of these essays into a single book foregrounds the discussion among critics who have read "The Yellow Wallpaper" over the past two decades, a conversation that becomes increasingly more complex as critics openly debate central aspects of the story with each other. This aspect of literary criticism is not exclusive to "The Yellow Wallpaper." However, the increasingly dialogic quality of the literary criticism about Gilman's story, however, reveals that scholars are as actively engaged in reading and responding to each other's interpretations of "The Yellow Wallpaper" as they are in reading the story itself. For example, Schöpp-Schilling begins her psychological approach to the story by criticizing the work of feminist scholars Wood, Parker, and Hedges who, in her opinion, read Gilman's biography and personal motivations into the story and so fall prey to the biographical fallacy. In presenting her own feminist interpretation of the story as a woman's quest for identity within an oppressive patriarchy, Kennard draws upon three previously published feminist readings by Hedges, Kolodny, and Gilbert and Gubar. In an explanatory note, Fetterley acknowledges the influence of Kolodny's and Kennard's interpretations on her own feminist reading of the gender dynamics of the story. Although Shumaker finds the feminist approaches of Kolodny and Kennard persuasive, he attempts to broaden discussion of the story by reading it in relation to central concerns of American literature. The critical exchange becomes most striking in the debate occurring among three feminist critics that appeared in *Tulsa Studies in Women's Literature* in 1984 and 1985. Carol Neely and Karen Ford responded to Treichler's essay "Escaping the Sentence: Diagnosis and Discourse in 'The Yellow Wallpaper'" (included in this book), and Treichler, in turn, wrote a rejoinder to both critics printed alongside their pieces.[26]

As the essays in this book show, "The Yellow Wallpaper" continues to prompt an interactive and productive exchange of opinion because it seems to raise more questions than it answers. The nature of the story, the meaning of the wallpaper, the narrator's fate, her act of crawling, and whether or not the narrator has outwitted John and "got out at last" (41) emerge as some of the salient issues critics debate, often in conversation with each other. This critical edition serves as a reminder of the ways Gilman's story has been read but also as an invitation for new readings of it. The essays that follow also encourage teachers, students, and Gilman specialists to respond actively to the work of critics who read "The Yellow Wallpaper" and to entertain the questions that this complex and richly ambiguous story poses.

Notes

1. Although the story first appeared in volume 5, no. 5 (January 1892) of *New England Magazine* (New Series) under the name of Charlotte Perkins Stetson, critics have variously noted the story's original date of publication as May 1891, January 1892, and May 1892. Critics within this collection list the date of the story's first publication most often as May 1892. The confusion surrounding the date no doubt stems from the way in which journals were bound at that time. While today we bind volumes by year, *New England Magazine* at the turn of the century did not. Volume 5 contains six volumes, beginning with September 1891 through February 1892. Had the magazine bound issues by year of publication, volume 5, no. 5 would have been May 1892. Compounding this confusion, Gilman in her autobiography reprints a letter written to *New England Magazine* that suggests that the publication date was May 1891 (*The Living of Charlotte Perkins Gilman* [New York: D. Appleton-Century Co., 1935], p. 119). (All further references will be taken from the reprint here, unless otherwise indicated, and cited in the text.) Gilman does have other inaccuracies in her autobiography. For example, she lists the year she founded a gymnasium for women as 1891 instead of 1881 (D. Appleton-Century, p. 66) and notes that the title of Howells's anthology that reprinted her story was *Masterpieces in American Fiction* instead of *Great Modern American Stories* (p. 65).

2. Small, Maynard reprinted the story as a single-volume edition in 1899. The following anthologies published between 1892 and 1972 reprint the story: William Dean Howells, ed. *The Great Modern American Stories* (New York: Boni & Liveright, 1920); Leslie Y. Rabkin, ed. *Psychopathology and Literature* (San Francisco: Chandler Publications, 1966); Elaine Gottlieb Hemley and Jack Mathews, eds. *The Writer's Signature: Idea in Story and Essay* (Glenview, Ill.: Scott, Foresman & Co., 1972); Seon Manley and Gogo Lewis, eds. *Ladies of Horror: Two Centuries of Supernatural Stories by the Gentle Sex* (New York: Lothrop, Lee, & Shepard, 1971); Gail Parker, ed., *The Oven Birds: American Women on Womanhood, 1820-1920* (Garden City, N.Y.: Anchor Books, 1972).

3. In her essay "'Out at Last'? 'The Yellow Wallpaper' after Two Decades of Feminist Criticism" (in this volume), Elaine Hedges provides useful statistics on the story's widespread republication and recognition. She notes that nearly two decades since its 1973 reissue, "The Yellow Wallpaper" has been reprinted in

England, Iceland, the Netherlands, Spain, Sweden, and Germany. Gilman's landmark story has also inspired several film versions, plays, an opera, and a "Masterpiece Theatre" adaptation, resulting in wider public recognition of Gilman and this important work.

4. The texts of essays included in this volume are reprinted as they appeared originally. Thus, references to editions of "The Yellow Wallpaper" vary as does spelling of the title. For discussion of these and other variations within criticism of the story, see "Reader, Text, and Ambiguous Referentiality in 'The Yellow Wallpaper'" by Richard Feldstein in this volume.

5. For further discussion of Gilman's literary frustrations see the autobiography.

6. This poem is reprinted as an epigram to the critical edition. It also appears in Zona Gale's Foreword to *Living*, pp. xxxiii-xxxiv.

7. Gilman was then Charlotte Perkins Stetson. She also published "The Yellow Wallpaper" under that name. For consistency, I refer to her as Gilman throughout the Introduction.

8. Thus, many critics argue that to read "The Yellow Wallpaper" requires biographical background. Within this book, see, for example, essays by Hedges (her Afterword) and Berman.

9. See Mary A. Hill, *Charlotte Perkins Gilman: The Making of a Radical Feminist 1860-1896* (Philadelphia: Temple University Press, 1980), p. 186 for Gilman's account of Stetson's reaction to "The Yellow Wallpaper."

10. H. P. Lovecraft, "The Weird Tradition in America," *Supernatural Horror in Literature* (New York: Dover Books, 1973), p. 72. Lovecraft goes on to assert that the room confined a former madwoman. Jacobus also raises this idea in her essay in this volume. In the text, Gilman reveals that the room, rather, was a former nursery, then a playroom and gymnasium.

11. The other selections in the January 1892 issue are, in order: "Phillips Brooks," by Julius H. Ward; "The Master of Raven's Woe," a poem by Arthur L. Salmon; "Mice at Eavesdropping," by A. Rodent; "Purification," a poem by George Edgar Montgomery; "The City of St. Louis," by Prof. C. M. Woodward; "Deposed," a poem by Florence E. Pratt; "George William Curtis," a poem by John W. Chadwick; "Salem Witch," a story by Edith Mary Norris; "Author of Old Oaken Bucket," by George M. Young; "Christmas Eve," a poem by Agnes Maule Machar; "Stories of Salem Witchcraft," by Winfield S. Nevins; "Abraham Lincoln," by Phillips Brooks; "'Tis Better To Have Loved And Lost," a poem by Philip Bourke Marston. The periodical concluded with two regular features: "Omnibus," including short one or two stanza poems by a number of male and female authors; "Editor's Table." Of the stories included in the six issues of volume 5, "Dr. Cabot's Two Brains," by Jeanette B. Perry, also illustrated by Jo H. Hatfield (pp. 344-54), comes the closest to Gilman's in its portrayal of a patronizing male physician who has "a very poor opinion of the mental ability of women" (p. 347).

12. The anonymous male physician writes: "To others, whose lives have become a struggle against an heredity of mental derangement, such literature contains deadly peril. Should such stories be allowed to pass without severest censure?" The latter is reprinted on p. 64.

13. A black-and-white decorative square motif surrounds the letter "I." Although it appears that this motif was commonly used in pictorial capital designs for *New England Magazine,* the pictorial capital introducing "The Yellow Wallpaper" proves interesting in relation to the story. The top triangle is of a dark pattern, reminiscent of the designs of the yellow wallpaper, while the bottom triangle remains white. This part of the design appears almost as a Yin-Yang symbol suggesting other dichotomies in the story and its writing. For other examples of Hatfield's capitals, see, for instance, two stories illustrated by Hatfield: "Dr. Cabot's Two Brains," by Jeanette B. Perry, *New England Magazine* 5:344-54; "The Squire's Niece Maria," by Mary F. Haynes, *New England Magazine* 6:461-71.

14. On close examination of the illustration, the lines on the windows look like bars.

15. The caption does not appear in the actual story, but it is listed in the Table of Contents.

16. In the 1989 "Masterpiece Theatre" PBS presentation of "The Yellow Wallpaper," introduced by Alistair Cooke, the narrator in the final scene is similarly shown to be a madwoman with long and mangy hair as she creeps on the floor and crawls over her husband.

17. For further discussion of Howells's brief but informative response to the story, see the Header in the Backgrounds section.

18. William Dean Howells, *Great Modern American Stories* (New York: Boni & Liveright, 1920), p. 427. In these brief biographical entries, Howells also notes Gilman's family background, specifically that she descended from Lyman Beecher and twice married. At the end of the entry he offers a list of Gilman's fiction and nonfiction.

19. In *The Female Malady: Women, Madness, and English Culture 1830-1980* (New York: Pantheon Books, 1985), Elaine Showalter writes, "Her story is a powerful polemic against Mitchell's methods" (p. 141).

20. Mitchell was trained as a neurologist, as was Sigmund Freud. Medical practice of his time considered nerves to be the link between body and mind. Mitchell explored the relationship between psychology and physiology and believed that by healing the body he was also healing the mind. For more thorough discussion, see the Headnote to the selections from Mitchell's *Fat and Blood: And How to Make Them* in the Backgrounds section.

21. Ann J. Lane, ed., "The Fictional World of Charlotte Perkins Gilman." *Charlotte Perkins Gilman Reader* (New York: Pantheon Books, 1980), p. xviii. Lane discusses the limitations of Gilman's writing style in her introduction.

22. For a similar interpretation, see Julian Evans Fleenor, "The Gothic Prism: Charlotte Perkins Gilman's Gothic Stories and Her Autobiography," *The Female Gothic,* ed. Julian Evans Fleenor (Montreal: Eden, 1983).

23. Sandra M. Gilbert and Susan Gubar, eds., *Norton Anthology of Literature By Women: The Tradition in English* (New York: W. W. Norton & Co., 1985), p. 966.

24. For a feminist Gothic reading of "The Yellow Wallpaper," see a 1990 article by Michelle A. Masse appearing in *Signs: Journal of Women in Culture and Society* 15, no. 4: 679-709, entitled "Gothic Repetition: Husbands, Horrors, and Things That Bump in the Night."

25. In a recent essay appearing in *Feminist Studies*, Susan Lanser discusses the relationship between the color of the wallpaper and racism in turn-of-the-century America and also makes an original case regarding the reproduction and repression of racism in "The Yellow Wallpaper." See, "Feminist Criticism, 'The Yellow Wallpaper,' and the Politics of Color in America," *Feminist Studies* 15, no. 3 (1989): 415-41.

26. Whereas Treichler sets her initial discussion of "women's discourse" in the context of medical diagnosis, Neely situates hers in the discourse of midwifery and childbirth, and Ford places hers in the context of female literary narratives. Neely begins her response, entitled "Alternative Women's Discourse," by openly disagreeing with Treichler's argument that the narrator escapes the patriarchal sentence to become an involved language user who authors her own sentences; however, she concludes that "'women's discourse' proves difficult to define because it remains so intertwined with the patriarchal discourse it tries to displace that it is difficult to be sure such a female discourse is really there. Hence Paula Treichler's interpretation of the yellow wallpaper and mine are not, perhaps, as antithetical as they might first appear to be" (*Tulsa Studies* 4, no. 2 [1985]: 321). In "'The Yellow Wallpaper' and Women's Discourse," Ford pursues the apparent difficulties which Treichler's analysis raises. For example, she argues that the narrator does not escape male diagnosis as Treichler suggests but becomes more of a victim of it as she involves herself more actively in the wallpaper and begins "creeping on all fours like the child John has accused her of being" (*Tulsa Studies* 4, no. 2 [1985]: 310). Tearing down the wallpaper signals a retreat from discourse and a recognition that discourse is controlled by patriarchy. Treichler concedes to the logic and persuasiveness of both interpretations in her 1985 rejoinder, entitled "The Wall Behind the Yellow Wallpaper: Response to Carol Neely and Karen Ford," (*Tulsa Studies* 4, no. 2 [1985]: 323-30). Like Neely, she does not find their views incompatible with her own and builds from their dialogue on women's discourse. Specifically, Treichler uses their comments to clarify further her thinking about language and feminist literary analysis, the problems inherent in the terms "women's discourse" and "alternative discourse," and the difficulty of defining the metaphor of the yellow wallpaper. In summarizing this entire debate between Treichler, Neely, and Ford in the introduction to his own 1989 essay, Feldstein foregrounds this earlier dialogue and keeps it ongoing.

RUTH ROBBINS (ESSAY DATE 2000)

SOURCE: Robbins, Ruth. "Reading the Writing on the Wall: Charlotte Perkins Gilman's 'The Yellow Wallpaper.'" *Literary Feminisms*, pp. 242-58. New York: St. Martin's Press, 2000.

In the following essay, Robbins explores how Gilman's The Yellow Wallpaper *may have been viewed at the time of its writing, and provides interpretations of the story from social, psychological, and feminist perspectives.*

A few years ago, Mr. Howells asked leave to include this story in a collection he was arranging . . . I was more than willing, but assured him that it was no more 'literature' than my other stuff, be-

ing definitely written 'with a purpose.' In my judgement it is a pretty poor thing to write, to talk without a purpose.

Charlotte Perkins Gilman, *The Living of Charlotte Perkins Gilman*

Much—perhaps too much—has been written about Charlotte Perkins Gilman's 1892 story, '**The Yellow Wall-paper**'. Since it resurfaced as a feminist text in the feminist context of a single volume edition published by the Feminist Press of New York in 1973, it has become a paradigmatic text of feminist criticism and for feminist theory. There are many reasons for its importance. Its republication in 1973 exemplified the feminist scholarship, the recuperation and rereading of a female literary tradition, that Elaine Showalter had described in her 1979 essay, 'Towards a Feminist Poetics', when she suggested that 'the manuscript and archival sources' for a gynocritical tradition were 'both abundant and untouched' (in Showalter 1986, 132), and that it was the task of feminist criticism to uncover them. It has attracted feminist critics because it draws on the autobiographical experiences of the author, because those experiences speak to our stereotyped ideas of Victorian femininity and because it has an easily recovered historicist basis. It has therefore been a 'useful' text for historical and contextual literary studies of the material conditions of women's lives. It enabled critics to establish literary-historical methodologies which went against the grain of practical criticism's insistence on the text itself, and made contexts (a woman's experience, a woman writer's experience, the discourses of medicine and proper femininity) a legitimate part of the reading experience in the academy. Moreover, it is a very short, short story, its brevity being one of its virtues for the purposes of student readings where length is a notorious inhibitor of commentary.

The earliest readers of the story, however, had not read it this way at all. As Gilman herself narrates in her autobiography, *The Living of Charlotte Perkins Gilman* (1935), she at first struggled to find a publisher for it, despite the recommendations of William Dean Howells (1837-1920, American journalist, critic, editor and novelist). The first editor to whom she sent it rejected it with the comment that it had disturbed him so much that he 'could not forgive myself if I made others as miserable as I have made myself' by publishing it (Gilman 1990, 119). And when it was published, a letter appeared in a rival magazine that deplored it as 'Perilous Stuff', written in a 'somewhat sensational style', holding the reader in 'morbid fascination'. The letter-writer wondered if such texts were really fit to be printed (121). As Annette Kolodny suggests, 1890s' readers, though well-versed in the American Gothic tradition inaugurated by Edgar Allan Poe, could not connect Gilman's story to the Gothic because its narrator/protagonist is a white middle-class wife and mother who belongs in the tame space of domestic fiction, not the monstrous domain of the horror story. Their disgust arose from the story's transgression of the limits of proper femininity, and it was dismissed as an unreadable story that should not have been written (Kolodny in Golden 1992, 153-5).

The story arose from Gilman's experience of what we would probably now describe as postnatal depression, following the birth of her daughter in the late 1880s. Her mental suffering was devastating, particularly as it became clear that her mental health improved as soon as she was away from her husband and child, and that it immediately deteriorated on her return. Her depression, that is, was a function of the conditions of proper femininity, the domesticity of wifedom and motherhood. Her madness was caused by the very aspects of her life that were supposed to codify her as a proper woman. Following a break away in California with friends, Gilman returned to her husband and daughter feeling much better, but 'within a month I was as low as before leaving . . . This was a worse horror than before, for now I saw the stark fact—that I was well while away and sick while at home' (Gilman 1990, 95, ellipsis in original). In order to try to recover from her mental discomfort, she submitted herself to the treatment of Silas Weir Mitchell, the leading 'nerve' specialist. Mitchell's treatment was that of the 'rest cure', and is described in his medical treatise, *Fat and Blood: And How to Make Them* (1877).

Mitchell differentiated between mental disorders in male and female patients. He suggested that male patients (always white, always middle class and wealthy in his expensive practice), had come to sickness through overwork, and needed rest. His middle-class female patients, on the other hand, had generally become ill from the pursuit of too active a social life, too many visits and parties. There were alternative cases where female patients were suffering from the stress of the long-term nursing of a sick relative, but mostly the women were sick from too much frivolous pleasure. This did not, however, mean that Mitchell believed in 'work' as a cure for women as 'rest' was a cure for men. Rest was the answer to nervous conditions in both sexes, despite their different

pathologies. His treatment consisted of isolating his patients from their families in his sanatorium. He then insisted that they go to bed for periods between six weeks and two months. During this time they were fed a bland diet of fattening food (sickness was indicated by pallor and thinness—hence the need to manufacture 'fat and blood'), and they were allowed to do nothing for themselves:

> At first . . . I do not permit the patient to sit up or to sew or write or read. The only action allowed is that needed to clean the teeth. In some instances, I have not permitted the patient to turn over without aid . . . because sometimes the moral influence of absolute repose is of use. In such cases I arrange to have the bowels and water passed while lying down, and the patient is lifted onto a lounge at bedtime and sponged, and then lifted back again into the newly-made bed. In all cases of weakness, treated by rest, I insist on the patient being fed by the nurse, and, when well enough to sit up in bed, I insist that the meats shall be cut up, so as to make it easier for the patient to feed herself.
>
> (Weir Mitchell in Golden 1992, 49)

In other words, the patient was returned to a state of infantile dependency, with the result, according to the doctor, that, having been obliged to lie still for a month or more, 'rest becomes . . . a rather bitter medicine, and they are glad enough to accept the order to rise and go about' when the doctor so orders (48). The infantilisation of the female patient (notice Mitchell's use of the feminine pronoun) is retold in the story, in which the narrator is isolated from her family and friends in an ancestral mansion, confined there to a room like a nursery, allowed no company, no stimulus, no reading, no writing and not even the supremely feminine activity of sewing. Every aspect of her existence is controlled, just as the existence of the helpless infant is controlled by the adults around it.[1]

This is precisely the treatment that Gilman received. 'I was put to bed and kept there. I was fed, bathed, rubbed, and responded with the vigorous body of twenty-six,' she wrote in her autobiography. After a month she felt better, and was sent home with Mitchell's advice ringing in her ears:

> 'Live as domestic a life as possible. Have your child with you all the time. . . . Lie down an hour after each meal. Have but two hours' intellectual life a day. And never touch pen, brush or pencil as long as you live.' I went home, followed those directions, and came perilously near to losing my mind.
>
> (Gilman 1990, 96)

Mitchell's prescription, that is, is a medicalised version of the cultural judgement that 'women can't paint, women can't write' that so hurts Lily Briscoe in Woolf's *To the Lighthouse* (Woolf 1992, 94). It gives the authority of science to the cultural judgements about women's intellectual capacities. Intellectual activity is diagnosed by patriarchal discourses as harmful to the female mind and body. Gilman's story presents a continuum of medical discourse that shades into literary writing. It is also a continuation of the infantilisation of the treatment proper in which every aspect associated with adulthood from physical autonomy to self-expression was denied to the patient, which might also be read as a metaphor for the infantilised position of women in general.

Gilman insists that her breakdown and its treatment left her permanently incapacitated, especially for systematic intellectual work. After a month or two at home, her distress returned, and eventually she and her husband agreed to divorce, and she took up a career as a public speaker and writer on feminist issues. The breakthrough to mental health came only when she decided to disobey doctor's orders, having recognised that it was precisely her domestic life that was making her sick in the first place. The story of '**The Yellow Wall-paper**' is a response to insanity and its treatment, written, says Gilman with a purpose (Gilman 1990, 119). When she had completed the story, she sent it to Mitchell, and though he never acknowledged it, she later heard that he had modified his treatment of nervous ailments in his female patients (20). For her this was success. Her purpose had been fulfilled. Her refusal of the category of 'literariness' for her writing, however, is one of the things that contemporary feminist criticism challenges in its insistence that the aesthetic is also a political category. Politics and poetics are not so easily separated.

The quasi-autobiographical content and the historical context have laid the story open most obviously to materialist feminist criticism. The story and the autobiography, the individual's fiction and her history, alongside the evidence of Mitchell's own writings on the treatment of neurasthenia, are read as a metaphor for the collective experience of women in general, and of women writers in particular. For Gilbert and Gubar, for example, with their interest in the material and cultural obstacles placed in the way of the nineteenth-century woman writer, and their insistence on seeing women's writing as multiple instances of covert and overt protest against these conditions, Gilman's story 'seems to tell *the* story that all literary women would tell if they could speak their "speechless woe"' (Gilbert and Gubar 1979, 89). Like *Jane Eyre,* it is the story of a madwoman in the attic, a tale of the dis-ease as well as the disease at the heart of the family home. It is a disease that renders that home unhomely—Freud's word is uncanny—and the story of this disease is told through the conventions of Gothic fiction, with an unreliable narrator, incipient insanity and the reader's uncertainty about the status of what she reads. Under patriarchy, madwomen is what all women are, or risk becoming since their being is so radically 'other' to the dominant discourses that organise social and psychological life. In this context, the period of the 'sexual anarchy' (Showalter 1991) of the late nineteenth century, the social dissatisfaction of women with their limited horizons was read as a pathological disease; the smallest claims of feminism for female autonomy became the feminine condition of hysteria.

There are, however, problems with this view, not least the class and race blindness that sees Gilman's narrator's plight as the plight of *all* women, and *her* story as *the* story. There is a contextual specificity to this woman's distress which depends on her class position; it is absolutely a privileged white woman's problem. And this is one of the dangers of the insistent reading and rereading of '**The Yellow Wall-paper**', and its establishment as the paradigmatic feminist text. Whilst materialist privilege clearly does not do away with psychic pain, we should be very wary of any assumption that lack of material privilege and the existence of physical pain does away with psychological difficulties. Hunger, torture and exhaustion all take a mental toll as well as having physical effects. Gilman herself wrote that she would prefer any kind of physical pain, including childbirth, to the mental distress she suffered during her breakdown (Gilman 1990, 91), and it's difficult to doubt her sincerity, but it is a metaphysical comparison. The articulacy of the story's protest should not blind the reader to those other women whose woe is rather more 'speechless', since they have neither the materials to write it down (education, pen and paper), nor an audience prepared to listen.

Materialist contexts and the content of the text, however, are not the only aspects of '**The Yellow Wall-paper**' that have been considered during its insistent reappearance as *the* text about which to write. Just as feminist criticism in general has moved away from purely materialist concerns, and towards psychoanalytic and post-structuralist concerns with language, the criticism of the story has changed as well. For it is, of course, primarily a story about a woman who writes—a woman writer—a woman who is also going mad. That fact, along with its insistent references to and re-writings of the conventions of gothic fiction placed alongside the theme of writing in its content, has tended to make it a fruitful text for readings through the various lenses of psychoanalytic feminisms. In her autobiography, Gilman comments: 'In those days a new disease had dawned on the medical horizon. It was called "nervous prostration". No one knew much about it, and there were many who openly scoffed, saying it was only a new name for laziness. To be recognisably ill, one must be confined to one's bed, and preferably in pain' (90). She is writing of the late 1880s, and nervous prostration or neurasthenia can quite legitimately be seen as the forerunners of the Freudian diseases of neurosis and hysteria in which physical symptoms were traced to unconscious mental causes, as opposed to having an organic pathology rooted in the body.

As Barbara Ehrenreich and Deirdre English argued as early as 1973, the psychoanalytic intervention in medical discourse is also a historical moment. Psychoanalysis is often criticised for ahistoricity, but that does not mean that it has no history of its own. Whilst, on the one hand, Freud's separation of mental disease from physical causes represented a break with the past and the insistence that hysteria arose from the anatomy of the womb, on the other, his theories still made biological anatomy into social destiny: 'the female personality was still inherently defective, this time due to the absence of a penis, rather than the presence of the domineering uterus' (Ehrenreich and English in Golden 1992, 109). They read hysteria as a protest against confining social roles; but they also see it as a kind of dead end, firstly because it was an individualised protest which brought about no political changes, since hysterics do not unite to fight their common enemies, and second, because it confirmed patriarchal prejudices that judged women as 'irrational, unpredictable and diseased' (107). And, moreover, as Paula Treichler has suggested, laying the (female) body open to the discourses of medical diagnosis which are associated with masculinity permits the male doctor immense power over the existential rights of the female patient: once a diagnosis is pronounced, it 'not only names reality, but also has considerable power over what that reality is now to be' (Treichler in Golden 1992, 196). Thus, whilst the story expresses an absolute social dissatisfaction and articulates the mental pain that is its result, it

also emphasises the trap of femininity from which there is no escape. The narrator is either repressed out of existence, or she expresses an insane self, which is in turn 'read back' onto her body and its symptoms: whatever choice she makes, she will eventually be silenced.

Psychoanalysis can be a materialist discourse, connecting social oppression and repression with mental aberration, which is, I think, its ideal position. In addition, one of the sources of the importance of psychoanalysis for feminist *literary* theory is that it pays close attention to the textuality of the text. A reading that recovers what Gilman saw as the story's purpose—a political protest against medical discourse—without recuperating its poetics, its literary qualities (which Gilman suggested it did not have), is missing something that even the author missed. Psychoanalysis looks at manner as well as content, how as well as what, poetics as well as politics.

The story tells of the steady mental decline of a unnamed female narrator. It opens with the narrator's feeling that there is something 'queer' (uncanny, unfamiliar, unhomely) about the colonial mansion that she and her husband, along with her sister-in-law and narrator's small baby, have rented for the summer. The house has been taken for her benefit, though there are several logical inconsistencies here. On the one hand, husband John, 'does not believe that I am sick' (Gilman, 1990, 3). Yet despite his disbelief, he has 'diagnosed' her 'condition' as 'temporary nervous depression—a slight hysterical tendency' (4) and prescribed 'phospates or phosphites . . . and tonics, and air, and exercise, and journeys' and has forbidden his wife to work (which appears to mean, 'to write') until she is well again. John is clearly a supreme realist, an absolute believer in rationality. He will not stomach his wife's feeling that there is something 'queer' about the house, and laughs at her when she talks of anything 'not to be felt and seen and put down in figures' (3). He refuses to see her as sick, and yet his every action proclaims that he does not see her as well. What space can his wife have for an identity between these binary oppositions of health and disease?

The space the story offers her is a room at the top of the house—a room of her own since she is often alone in it, but also a kind of prison. The room was once used as a nursery, with bars at the windows, presumably to stop the children from falling out, though other readings of the bars, apart from this 'common-sense' realistic reading, are also possible. The furniture doesn't match. The bed is nailed to the floor. Except for one thing, it is a pleasant room, big and airy and filled with sunshine. Unfortunately, the walls are covered with a disgusting yellow wallpaper, torn off in patches; it is a sulphurous colour, and has an unfathomable pattern. As the tenancy of the colonial mansion continues, the narrator becomes increasingly obsessed by the paper; at first angered and repulsed by its ugliness, she eventually begins to see a female figure trapped behind the bars of the paper. With no other stimulus, it takes over her entire existence and she becomes determined to make sense of the pattern, and then to 'free' the woman she has 'seen' (or perhaps hallucinated) trapped behind its bars. She studies the wallpaper, and then begins to tear it from the walls. The story ends with her creeping around the walls, having removed all the paper. When her husband observes her state, he faints; but the narrator continues to creep, and creeps over his prostrated form at every rotation.

Plot summaries never tell enough of a text's effects which is why the manner of the telling is as important as the story itself. How we read the story depends on how we read the wallpaper. Jeffrey Berman, for example, sees the wallpaper as 'projection screen or Rorschach test of the narrator's growing fright'. Its inconsistent pattern represents the inconsistencies of her own life, her need for security and love opposing her will towards independence, her contradictory impulses towards conventional feminine duty and unconventional feminist protest (Berman in Golden 1992, 232). This is an interesting insight, but it is more complicated than Berman's content-based psychoanalysis presents it as being, since the inconsistencies of the narrator's life are not symptoms of an idiosyncratic pathology: it's not just *her* problem, but goes wider than that. One can see also the gaps and fissures, the holes in the argument, as it were, of the discourses that oppress her. Hence my emphasis above on John's insistence that she is not sick, but that she nonetheless needs treatment. When the voice of reason is so illogical, no wonder the narrator has problems. The concentration on the female figure of the text and on her pathology and problems displaces the need to read the male other of the text, and authorises his version of reality as a seamless whole that is not open to criticism. Children are told not to 'answer back' meaning that they must resist being impertinent and insolent to the adult version of the world. But telling a child not to answer back is usually the response of an adult whose arguments or reason-

ing are a bit shaky. The story shows a woman being treated like a child. One way of reading the story, then, is to see it as a 'reading back' and a 'writing back', an insolent, improper version, which shakes up a particular version of the real, just as, eventually, the narrator's imaginary double shakes the pattern of the wallpaper (Gilman 1990, 11). Part of its subversive effect comes from the manner of the writing, which should not be simply ignored in favour of the story's content.

When one sees **'The Yellow Wall-paper'** on the page, one becomes immediately aware of the staccato effect of the prose. The paragraphs are very short, often consisting of no more than one short sentence. The style is paratactic—that is, connection is made by juxtaposition (placing of ideas in space) rather than by the logic of grammatical subordination. Disconnected ideas are placed side by side as if they have a connection: the connection is spatial, rather than logical, as in the sentence: 'John laughs at me, of course, but one expects that' (3). This sentence is written in the context of two pieces of information, first the narrator's feeling that the house might be haunted, and second, the 'practical' nature of her husband. That simple sentence is, however, very loaded. Its three parts, John's laughter, the narrator's 'of course', and her generalised expectation that John will continue to laugh at her, beg a lot of questions. Why is it 'of course' that a husband laughs at his wife? Why is it expected? It seems stylistically very simple, like a child's narrative, but appearances are deceptive. If there is a power relationship implicit in the way that John reads his wife, there's an answering back insolence in her writing of him in which the tone is very uncertain. Do all husbands laugh at their wives, or just this one? What are we being asked to accept as 'of course'?

The parataxis of the style is an act of political, personal and aesthetic resistance to the totalising narratives of cause and effect (narrated in long sentences, long paragraphs, and, indeed, long novels as well as in the discourses of science and medicine) that usually go by the name of Realism. This is the discourse through which John, who believes in fact, the narrator's brother, who agrees with him, and Silas Weir Mitchell define the world. Medical diagnosis is precisely a realist discourse: a cause produces a symptom (effect); a diagnosis is a reading of that effect; a pre*scription* (which is a kind of writing that comes from the reading) supposedly effects a cure. The story is over, and there are no loose ends. Or, at least, that is the way that the story is supposed to go, as Weir Mitchell's *Fat and Blood* suggests.

Only this isn't really the whole story no matter how totalising Realism attempts to be. Like the pattern in the paper, this story is multiple rather than singular. It does not simply say that the narrator's version of the world is right, and that John's is wrong. The paratactic style, engagingly and disarmingly simple as it is, undoes the distance of perspective required by Realist discourses to make their allegedly objective judgements. It undoes the pretence of objective interpretation. Its performance of naivety and innocence is also therefore a performance of cunning—its textual gestures collapse the structures by which we are used to judge. The style draws the reader into complicity with the narrator, requesting our sympathy and identification with the poor, put-upon writer whose story we are reading. We get too close and suspend our judgement. The reader's conventional position of dispassionate interpretation is interfered with. Mary Jacobus argues that we must never forget the creepiness of the story, the way it makes skins crawl (Jacobus 1986, 234-5): the uncanny effect is played out on the reader—the reader of either sex. If we identify with the narrator, we identify with madness. If we identify with John's realist perspective, we identify with the forces of a highly unattractive oppression. There is no solid ground here. The inconsistencies of the text undermine any reading position.

So, for example, the voices of authority (the brother and husband who are both doctors) are represented in the narrator's text. The brother and the husband say 'the same thing' (Gilman 1990, 4), tell the same story, read the same symptoms and come up with the same diagnosis and treatment. But because their narratives are displaced from the centre of the narrative, retold from a different perspective, their certainties are undermined. The narrator comments:

> Personally, I disagree with their ideas.
>
> Personally, I believe that congenial work, with excitement and change, would do me good.
>
> But what is one to do?
>
> I did write for a while in spite of them; but it *does* exhaust me a good deal—having to be so sly about it, or else meet with heavy opposition.
>
> I sometimes fancy that in my condition, if I had less opposition and more society and stimulus—but John says the very worst thing I can do is think about my condition, and I confess it always makes me feel bad.
>
> So I will let it alone and talk about the house.
>
> (4)

The structures and juxtapositions of sentences here are very tightly put together. Seemingly random ideas do, in fact, have a very close logic. The assertions the narrator makes of her disagreements, for example, do double service. They are at once insistently self-expressive: this is what *I* think; and they are also idiosyncratic—personal opinion is set in opposition to the expert voices of the doctors. Who is to say which discourse is right? Moreover, she expresses what she thinks only to the 'dead paper' on which she writes, not to the men whose pronouncements her writings at once challenge ('I disagree') and endorse ('it *does* exhaust me'). Her writing about her 'condition' is unfinished. She has no language to imagine an alternative because John's reported authoritative voice interrupts her sentence, and sets her off on another track—she will 'talk about the house' instead. Since the house is the only thing that she has to talk about, the house becomes the site of her 'condition', as well as its emblem. It is a beautiful place, with a '*delicious* garden'; but it is also uncared for, derelict and damaged. Which might just be a description of the narrator herself—trapped by a domesticity she does not desire, which, indeed, repulses her, she too becomes derelict and damaged, uncared for despite all the care that is being taken, because it is the wrong kind of care.

Increasingly, therefore, because the text unsettles the totalising and naturalising narratives of Realism, it has been read with a post-structuralist bent; the wallpaper becomes the projection of a female/feminine writing effect. Treichler sees the wallpaper as 'women's discourse' (Treichler in Golden 1992, 195). More recently, Julian Wolfreys has read it as exemplifying the Cixousian notion of *écriture féminine*, a writing of excess and defiance, which resists the closures of definition and telos (Wolfreys 1997, 83). It destabilises any sense that meaning might be 'there' just to be grasped, which in turn destabilises the reading positions that we 'outside' the text might adopt.

I placed the word 'outside' in inverted commas to signal the provisionality of the reading positions that **'The Yellow Wall-paper'** dramatises. Jacques Derrida has written that there is nothing outside the text, no outside text—there is no position outside textuality, no metalanguage in which interpretation is concretised and authorised, nothing outside the languages which we inscribe and by which we are inscribed. Although she uses language differently from the linguistic structures of her husband, for example, the narrator of the story remains implicated in the same language, unable to escape from its hold on her—

the ways in which it inscribes her, describes her, prescribes for her and proscribes her: these are all words to do with writing, deriving from the Latin verb *scripere,* to write. In Lacanian terms, one might say, language speaks her even as she speaks language. Treichler's insight that the wallpaper is 'women's discourse', or Wolfreys's sense that it is a mode of *écriture féminine,* both speak of an entrapment in a language that the narrator has not made or chosen, yet to which she must appeal in order to express anything at all.

The wallpaper, then, is an emblem of many things. Attached to the walls of the house, it is a marker of the kind of domestic space the house is: this is a house that is not quite a home, a domestic space that has been neglected and untenanted, not a home-from-home, rather an unhomely or uncanny space, though we have only the narrator's word for it. It has been rented for three months, so that there is no point in John undertaking repairs or redecoration, for they will not be there long enough. Before their tenancy, 'the place has been empty for years' (Gilman 1990, 4), following legal troubles amongst the heirs. The logical explanation of its emptiness does not, however, quite exorcise its ghostliness: the narrator remains determined to express her feeling that 'there is something strange about the house', something 'queer', a ghostliness and a haunted quality that seems to her the 'height of romantic felicity' despite her husband's insistence on draughts as the sole explanation of its strangeness, and his exhortations to self-control and away from fancy. The Gothic and the realist narrative compete.

The wallpaper signifies the neglect of the house. Even before the narrator arrives, someone—she surmises that it was the children, the previous tenants of the attic—has already started to pull the paper from the walls. The narrator is not surprised because the paper is so very bad:

> One of those sprawling, flamboyant patterns committing every artistic sin. It is dull enough to confuse the eye in following, pronounced enough constantly to irritate and provoke study, and when you follow the lame uncertain curves for a little distance they suddenly commit suicide—plunge off at outrageous angles, destroy themselves in unheard-of contradictions.
>
> (5)

The point about patterns is their regularity. A pattern is supposed to be a repeating structure which has its own coherence, and which might even be thought of as restful so long as it retains its equilibrium. But this wallpaper, although the different lengths repeat, has no other source of repetition. If it is a pattern, it is idiosyncratic. The paper has no balance. And in the absence of other

stimuli, the narrator begins to study it, and to see things in it. She feels the pattern has a vicious influence, and that there is a suppressed violence in it that disturbs her, as she sees 'a broken neck and two bulbous eyes' staring at her hundreds of times in the room, an image of strangulation or stifling which invites us to read it as the metaphor of the narrator's own condition. Even the regularity which, at first, she sought in the pattern has become a source of potential horror, since the reiteration of the pattern, reproduced throughout the room becomes, with constant study, endless and uncanny:

> I get positively angry with the impertinence of it and the everlastingness. Up and down and sideways they crawl, and those absurd unblinking eyes are everywhere. . . . I never saw so much expression in an inanimate thing before, and we all know how much expression they have! I used to lie awake as a child and get more entertainment and terror out of blank walls and plain furniture than most children could find in a toy-store.
>
> (7)

The reference to childhood here is important because the room is a nursery, and the patient has been deprived of her position as an adult in charge of her own destiny. The childlike games of imagination that she plays hark back to an age of innocence, but also speak of regression and loss of adult identity. Moreover, where for a child endowing inanimate objects with human powers is a harmless game, for an adult it is a less innocent pursuit. It is a dangerous lapse into fancy, a refusal of the real. Thus, eventually, the wallpaper obtrudes itself into every thought. The narrator might be thinking about the countryside and the wallpaper enters her mind. She sees different things in different lights so that the idea of seeing and knowing (or seeing and believing) is belied by her narrative. The meaning of the wallpaper is not just a single meaning, and it is not just 'there' to be grasped. It is full of spectral traces—but there's nothing you can put your finger on, even in language—nothing you see and feel and put down in figures (3). In daylight, for example, a second sub-pattern becomes discernible, a subtext for the main pattern. This subtext is only visible at certain times of day, when 'the sun is just so': seeing is no guarantor of knowledge here. Then the narrator can see 'a strange, provoking, formless sort of figure that seems to skulk about behind that silly and conspicuous front design' (8). As Wolfreys suggests, a formless figure is an oxymoron, a contradiction in terms (Wolfreys 1997, 79-80), much like the Kristevan *chora.* Furthermore, none of the adjectives, none of the description as a whole gives a concrete depiction of what the narrator sees. If the wallpaper is dangerously suggestive to her, her descriptions are suggestive too, rather than obvious.

Suggestive of what? Excess, perhaps. It breaks artistic laws (Gilman 1990, 9) and commits every artistic sin. It operates by no design principle of which the narrator has ever heard. Rather it is monstrous, because it is overflowing and excessive: it has 'bloated curves and flourishes' and it 'waddles' rather than progressing regularly (according to the rules of design—regularity is a term derived from the Latin word for 'rules'). The diagonal pattern is an 'optic horror, like a lot of wallowing seaweeds in full chase' (9). Suggestive images indeed, but still no obvious answer as to what they suggest. A vulgar Freudian answer might suggest the terror of the female body, and in particular what Cixous sees as the last taboo, the *pregnant* female body. Those bloated curves, that waddling movement, the entrapping motion of the wallowing seaweed which is at once like entrails (the obscenity of the body when it transgresses its own limits) and the head of the Medusa. Conventionally, according to the *laws* of design, the paper is highly improper. According to the laws of representation, there are some things that should never be represented. And after all, the narrator has just given birth to a baby that she cannot bear to be with, so parturition and the limits (of the body, of representation, the limits imposed by motherhood on ambition and independence) are probably on her mind. The wallpaper speaks of a physical body it represents as grotesque, of artistic representation and its laws, and of sociological context: female nature, feminine culture, sociological observation of a mind going mad. For Gilman and her readers, it is indeed an ugly story.

Reading the wallpaper is a question of multiplying perspectives, and none of the perspectives is valorised over the others. Like the paper, the text proliferates possible meanings, rather than settling on one version. The hidden activity of the paper—its subtexts—come to mirror the subterfuges and evasions of the narrator, who increasingly withdraws even from the limited human contact of her husband and sister-in-law, refusing to discuss the paper with them as the story goes on. This leaves her free to see all its possibilities, 'the things in that wallpaper that nobody knows about but me, or ever will' (11). What she sees is a 'dim shape' that gets clearer with passing time: the clarity is presumably illusory, since what she sees is 'like a woman stooping down and creeping about behind that pattern'—the image gives the narrator the creeps, makes her feel 'creepy' in a terrifying verbal prefiguring of the story's final actions, but there is no escape from it since her husband will not take her away. What the narrator seeks is mastery over the paper (12), since she has mastery nowhere else in her life. But the attempt to take control of the paper, to comprehend it, results in violence: 'You think you have mastered it, but just as you get well under way in following, it turns a back-somersault and there you are. It slaps you in the face, knocks you down, and tramples upon you. It is like a bad dream' (12). The organic images of seaweed and toadstools in florid arabesques (12) are seen by daylight: by night, they solidify into bars, and the sub-pattern resolves itself into a woman behind the bars. The creeping figure of the woman (or sometimes, many women) is trying to escape the paper, but cannot because of the florid bars of the top pattern, which 'strangles them off and turns them upside down, and makes their eyes white!' (15). This horrifying image is placed in the context of John's increasing concern for his wife, as if her madness is becoming more discernible. But by now it is clear that the narrator associates his solicitude with the entrapment of the woman in the paper—his fear of madness traps her—and she has become overtly afraid of him, wishing he would leave her alone, and that she could spend the night alone. With the loss of realist perspective the narrator *becomes* the creeping woman she has 'seen'.

When the opportunity arises, she locks herself into the room—an act of assertion that implies that she is choosing her own status as prisoner—and peels the paper off the walls. By now, she is quite mad: she believes herself to be the figure in the wallpaper, fears being put back behind the bars, and tears the paper down to prevent herself from being trapped again. Like Bertha Mason before her, she considers burning the house to effect her escape from the wallpaper's pervasive influence; and she thinks for a moment of jumping through the window, both of which are Bertha's actions. Her behaviour is that of the caged animal, a relentless, repeated, pathological motion of creeping around the room. The claim she has made for autonomous selfhood has finally robbed her of any semblance of a sane identity; she is no longer a wife and mother: indeed, she has even lost her humanity. When John comes home and sees her state, as well as the state of the room which is a sign of her state, he faints. She crawls over him, in an endless repetition.

The story resists the closure of defining what will happen next. The final image of the creeping woman is creepy precisely because it refuses us a resolution of the problems the text has raised—social, economic, biological, cultural, psychic problems: none is resolved. All that has happened is that the self-styled voice of reason has collapsed in a dead faint in the face of creeping unreason. One system has toppled. But nothing has been erected in its place. There is a blank space for new writing, new patterns on the wall, a space that Gilman has left empty.

Critics have read the narrator's last moments as a scene of temporary triumph over patriarchy. I'm not sure that the story invites any kind of even qualified optimism for our particular protagonist. The problems it enacts are presented as the diagnosis of a disease: the lack of closure implies that there is no prescription, no cure, as yet. There are hints as to what a cure might be: a more varied life, more stimulus, more work for the narrator, and for women like her—though not necessarily for all women. But this is not finally a therapeutic text. D. H. Lawrence spoke of shedding sickness in books, of writing away pain and distress. A feminist text, however, is not necessarily one that makes its readers feel better. For Gilman, the feminism of this text was bound up with its purpose: for her, it was meant to be a transitive text, a story that acted on the world, that made a difference. Inasmuch as Mitchell hinted that reading it had modified his clinical practice—changed his discourse, altered the stories he told—it was a success in Gilman's terms. For contemporary readers, that fact remains important. But the story itself leaves us with an image of pain, not of recovery. And if this is *the* paradigmatic story of feminist literary theory, the story that all women might tell, the theory, like the narrator, remains trapped in a very grim world. Perhaps it is time to imagine, to write, and to read, some of the other possible stories in the blank space of the bare wall. . . . That is, after all, what Gilman's text itself invites us to do in its radical refusals of monolithic points of view, and its proliferation of alternative meanings and possible interpretations. We've had the diagnosis that women are sick because they are oppressed and repressed, and because they lack the means of self-expression. But that is not the end, the sole aim, of feminist theories. There are more spaces to conquer than attic rooms.

Note

1. A version of Weir Mitchell's rest cure was the treatment received by Virginia Woolf during her periodic bouts of mental distress. She hated the treatment, and satirised the doctors who provided it in her 1924 novel *Mrs. Dalloway*. As Elaine Showalter has noted (in *The Female Malady*, London: Virago, 1987), the effects of the treatment were to infantilise the patient into a state of complete dependency; infantilisation and feminisation go together, which is what helps to constitute insanity as the 'the female malady'.

Bibliography

Berman, Jeffrey. 'The Unrestful Cure: Charlotte Perkins Gilman and "The Yellow Wall-paper"'. *The Captive Imagination: A Casebook on The Yellow Wall-paper*. Ed. Catherine Golden. New York: The Feminist Press at CUNY, 1992, 211-41.

Ehrenreich, Barbara and Deirdre English. 'The "Sick" Woman of the Upper Classes'. *The Captive Imagination: A Casebook on The Yellow Wall-paper*. Ed. Catherine Golden. New York: The Feminist Press at CUNY, 1992, 90-109.

Gilbert, Sandra M. and Susan Gubar. *The Madwoman in the Attic: The Woman Writer and the Nineteenth-Century Literary Imagination*. New Haven and London: Yale University Press, 1979.

Gilman, Charlotte Perkins. *The Yellow Wall-paper* in *The Charlotte Perkins Gilman Reader*. London: The Women's Press, 1980.

Golden, Catherine, ed. *The Captive Imagination: A Casebook on The Yellow Wall-paper*. New York: The Feminist Press, 1992.

Jacobus, Mary. *Reading Woman: Essays in Feminist Criticism*. New York: Columbia University Press, 1986.

Kolodny, Annette. 'A Map for Re-reading: Or, gender and the interpretation of literary texts', *The Captive Imagination: A Casebook on The Yellow Wall-paper*. Ed. Catherine Golden. New York: The Feminist Press at CUNY, 1992, 149-67.

Kristeva, Julia. *Desire in Language: A Semiotic Approach to Literature and Art*. Ed. Leon S. Roudiez. Trans Thomas Gora, Alice Jardine and Leon S. Roudiez. Oxford: Basil Blackwell, [1977] 1980.

——. *Revolution in Poetic Language*. Trans. Margaret Waller. New York: Columbia University Press, [1974] 1984.

——. *Polylogue*. Paris: Seuil, 1977.

——. *The Kristeva Reader*. Ed. Toril Moi, Oxford: Blackwell, 1986.

——. *Tales of Love*. Trans. Leon S. Roudiez. New York: Columbia University Press, [1983] 1987.

——. 'Talking about *Polylogue*'. *French Feminist Thought: A Reader*. Ed. Toril Moi. Oxford: Blackwell, 1987, 110-17.

Lawrence, D. H. *Women in Love*. Harmondsworth: Penguin, [1920] 1982.

——. *The Complete Poems*. Eds. Vivian de Sola Pinto and Warren Roberts. Harmondsworth: Penguin, 1977.

Mitchell, Silas Weir. 'From *Fat and Blood: And How to Make Them*' [1877]. *The Captive Imagination: A Casebook on the Yellow Wall-paper*. Ed. Catherine Golden. New York: The Feminist Press, 1992, pp. 45-50.

Showalter, Elaine. *A Literature of their Own: British Women Novelists from Brontë to Lessing*. London: Virago [1977], 1978.

———. ed. *The New Feminist Criticism: Essays on Women, Literature and Theory.* London: Virago, 1986.

———. 'Towards a Feminist Poetics' [1979]. *The New Feminist Criticism: Essays on Women, Literature and Theory.* Ed. Elaine Showalter. London: Virago, 1986. 125-43.

———.'Feminist Criticism in the Wilderness' [1981]. *The New Feminist Criticism: Essays on Women, Literature and Theory.* Ed. Elaine Showalter. London: Virago, 1986. 243-70.

———. *Sexual Anarchy: Gender and Culture at the Fin de Siècle.* London: Bloomsbury, 1991.

Treichler, Paula. 'Escaping the Sentence: Diagnosis and Discourse in "The Yellow Wall-paper"'. *The Captive Imagination: A Casebook on the Yellow Wall-paper.* Ed. Catherine Golden. New York: The Feminist Press, 1992, pp. 191-210.

Wolfreys, Julian. *The Rhetoric of Affirmative Resistance: Dissonant Identities from Carroll to Derrida.* London: Macmillan, 1997.

FURTHER READING

Bibliography

Scharnhorst, Gary. *Charlotte Perkins Gilman: A Bibliography.* Metuchen, N.J.: Scarecrow Press, 1985, 203 p.

Comprehensive bibliography of Gilman's works and biographical sources, and a brief selection of criticism devoted to her work.

Biographies

Kessler, Carol Farley. *Charlotte Perkins Gilman: Her Progress Toward Utopia with Selected Writings* New York: Syracuse University Press, 1995, 316 p.

Offers a biography of Gilman and a critical bibliography.

Lane, Ann J. *To "Herland" and Beyond: The Life and Work of Charlotte Perkins Gilman.* New York: Pantheon Books, 1990, 432 p.

Comprehensive biography covering the hardships and difficulties Gilman faced and the relationship between her life and her work.

Criticism

Allen, Polly Wynn. *Building Domestic Liberty: Charlotte Perkins Gilman's Architectural Feminism.* Amherst: University of Massachusetts Press, 1988, 195 p.

Examination of Gilman's architectural designs for feminist domestic spaces, landscapes, and neighborhoods.

Beer, Janet. "The Means and Ends of Genre in the Short Fiction of Charlotte Perkins Gilman." In *Kate Chopin, Edith Wharton and Charlotte Perkins Gilman: Studies in Short Fiction,* pp. 147-73. Houndmills, England: Macmillan, 1997.

Discusses how Gilman employs a variety of literary genres to deliver her feminist message to readers.

Colatrella, Carol. "Work for Women: Recuperating Charlotte Perkins Gilman's Reform Fiction." In *Research in Science and Technology Studies: Gender and Work,* edited by Shirley Gorenstein, pp. 53-76. Stamford, Conn.: JAI Press, 2000.

Studies Gilman's reform fiction, overlooked by most critics, as the embodiment of the social and economic theories found in her nonfiction prose.

Golden, Catherine J. and Joanna Schneider Zangrando, eds. *The Mixed Legacy of Charlotte Perkins Gilman.* Newark, Del.: University of Delaware Press, 2000, 235 p.

Provides a series of critical and biographical essays about Gilman with bibliographical resources.

Hausman, Bernice L. "Sex Before Gender: Charlotte Perkins Gilman and the Evolutionary Paradigm of Utopia." *Feminist Studies* 24, no. 3 (fall 1998): 488-510.

Encourages an analysis of Gilman's Herland *by means of the category of "sex," as it was defined in Gilman's time—that is, prior to the development of the modern distinction between sex and gender.*

Hill, Mary Armfield. *Charlotte Perkins Gilman: The Making of a Radical Feminist, 1860-1896.* Philadelphia: Temple University Press, 1980, 376 p.

Study of Gilman's public and private writings outlining Gilman's evolution as a feminist.

Hume, Beverly A. "Managing Madness in Gilman's *The Yellow Wallpaper.*" *Studies in American Fiction* 30, no. 1 (spring 2002): 3-20.

Maintains that Gilman's tale of madness should be read less in relation to the events of her life and more in conjunction with the horror tales of Edgar Allan Poe.

Lane, Ann J. "Charlotte Perkins Gilman and the Rights of Women: Her Legacy for the 1990s." In *Charlotte Perkins Gilman: Optimist Reformer,* edited by Jill Rudd and Val Gough, pp. 3-15. Iowa City: University of Iowa Press, 1999.

Assesses Gilman's critical reputation in the late-twentieth century, concluding that her analyses are as relevant today as they were during Gilman's lifetime.

McGowan, Todd. "Dispossessing the Self: 'The Yellow Wallpaper' and the Renunciation of Property." In *The Feminine "No!": Psychoanalysis and the New Canon,* pp. 31-46. Albany: State University of New York Press, 2001.

Addresses recent historicist criticism of The Yellow Wallpaper *that displaces earlier feminist readings of the text.*

Meyering, Sheryl L., ed. *Charlotte Perkins Gilman: The Woman and Her Work.* Ann Arbor, Mich.: UMI Research Press, 1989, 211 p.

Contains biographical and critical essays on Gilman by Mary A. Hill, Susan Gubar, and others with bibliographical index.

OTHER SOURCES FROM GALE:

Additional coverage of Gilman's life and career is contained in the following sources published by the Gale Group: *American Writers Supplement,* Vol. 11; *Beacham's Guide to Literature for Young Adults,* Vol. 11; *Contemporary Authors,* Vols. 106, 150; *Dictionary of Literary Biography,* Vol. 221; *Exploring Short Stories; Feminist Writers; Literature and Its Times,* Vol. 2; *Literature Resource Center; Major 20th-Century Writers,* Ed. 1; *Modern American Women Writers; Reference Guide to American Literature,* Ed. 4; *Reference Guide to Short Fiction,* Ed. 2; *St. James Guide to Horror, Ghost & Gothic Writers; St. James Guide to Science Fiction Writers,* Ed. 4; *Short Stories for Students,* Vols. 1, 18; *Short Story Criticism,* Vols. 13, 62; and *Twentieth-Century Literary Criticism,* Vols. 9, 37, 117.

INDEXES

The main reference

Austen, Jane 1775-1817 **1**: 122, 125, 220; **2**: 104, 196, **333-384**

lists the featured author's entry in volumes 1, 2, 3, 5, or 6 of Feminism in Literature; *it also lists commentary on the featured author in other volumes of the set, which include topics associated with* Feminism in Literature. *Page references to substantial discussions of the author appear in boldface.*

The cross-references

See also AAYA 19; BRW 4; BRWC 1; BRWR 2; BYA 3; CD-BLB 1789-1832; DA; DA3; DAB; DAC; DAM MST, NOV; DLB 116; EXPN; LAIT 2; LATS 1; LMFS 1; NCLC 1, 13, 19, 33, 51, 81, 95, 119; NFS 1, 14, 18; TEA; WLC; WLIT 3; WYAS 1

list entries on the author in the following Gale biographical and literary sources:

AAL: Asian American Literature

AAYA: Authors & Artists for Young Adults

AFAW: African American Writers

AFW: African Writers

AITN: Authors in the News

AMW: American Writers

AMWR: American Writers Retrospective Supplement

AMWS: American Writers Supplement

ANW: American Nature Writers

AW: Ancient Writers

BEST: Bestsellers (quarterly, citations appear as Year: Issue number)

BG: The Beat Generation: A Gale Critical Companion

BLC: Black Literature Criticism

BLCS: Black Literature Criticism Supplement

BPFB: Beacham's Encyclopedia of Popular Fiction: Biography and Resources

BRW: British Writers

BRWS: British Writers Supplement

BW: Black Writers

BYA: Beacham's Guide to Literature for Young Adults

CA: Contemporary Authors

CAAS: Contemporary Authors Autobiography Series

CABS: Contemporary Authors Bibliographical Series

CAD: Contemporary American Dramatists

CANR: Contemporary Authors New Revision Series

CAP: Contemporary Authors Permanent Series

CBD: Contemporary British Dramatists

CCA: Contemporary Canadian Authors

CD: Contemporary Dramatists

CDALB: Concise Dictionary of American Literary Biography

CDALBS: Concise Dictionary of American Literary Biography Supplement

CDBLB: Concise Dictionary of British Literary Biography

CLC: Contemporary Literary Criticism

CLR: Children's Literature Review

CMLC: Classical and Medieval Literature Criticism

CMW: St. James Guide to Crime & Mystery Writers

CN: Contemporary Novelists

CP: Contemporary Poets

CPW: Contemporary Popular Writers

CSW: Contemporary Southern Writers

CWD: Contemporary Women Dramatists

CWP: Contemporary Women Poets

CWRI: St. James Guide to Children's Writers

CWW: Contemporary World Writers

DA: DISCovering Authors

DA3: DISCovering Authors 3.0

DAB: DISCovering Authors: British Edition

DAC: DISCovering Authors: Canadian Edition

DAM: DISCovering Authors: Modules

> *DRAM:* Dramatists Module; *MST:* Most-Studied Authors Module;
>
> *MULT:* Multicultural Authors Module; *NOV:* Novelists Module;
>
> *POET:* Poets Module; *POP:* Popular Fiction and Genre Authors Module

DC: Drama Criticism

DFS: Drama for Students

DLB: Dictionary of Literary Biography

DLBD: Dictionary of Literary Biography Documentary Series

DLBY: Dictionary of Literary Biography Yearbook

DNFS: Literature of Developing Nations for Students

EFS: Epics for Students

EXPN: Exploring Novels

EXPP: Exploring Poetry

EXPS: Exploring Short Stories

EW: European Writers

FANT: St. James Guide to Fantasy Writers

FW: Feminist Writers

The Author Index lists all of the authors featured in the Feminism in Literature *set. It includes references to the main author entries in volumes 1, 2, 3, 5, and 6; it also lists commentary on the featured author in other author entries and in other volumes of the set, which include topics associated with* Feminism in Literature. *Page references to author entries appear in boldface. The Author Index also includes birth and death dates, cross references between pseudonyms or name variants and actual names, and cross references to other Gale series in which the authors have appeared. A complete list of these sources is found facing the first page of the Author Index.*

A

Akhmatova, Anna 1888-1966 **5: 1–38**
  See also CA 19-20; 25-28R; CANR 35; CAP 1; CLC 11, 25, 64, 126; DA3; DAM POET; DLB 295; EW 10; EWL 3; MTCW 1, 2; PC 2, 55; RGWL 2, 3

Alcott, Louisa May 1832-1888 **2: 78, 147, 297–332**
  See also AAYA 20; AMWS 1; BPFB 1; BYA 2; CDALB 1865-1917; CLR 1, 38; DA; DA3; DAB; DAC; DAM MST, NOV; DLB 1, 42, 79, 223, 239, 242; DLBD 14; FW; JRDA; LAIT 2; MAICYA 1, 2; NCLC 6, 58, 83; NFS 12; RGAL 4; SATA 100; SSC 27; TUS; WCH; WLCWYA; YABC 1; YAW

Allende, Isabel 1942- **5: 39–64**
  See also AAYA 18; CA 125; 130; CANR 51, 74, 129; CDWLB 3; CLC 39, 57, 97, 170; CWW 2; DA3; DAM MULT, NOV; DLB 145; DNFS 1; EWL 3; FW; HLC 1; HW 1, 2; INT CA-130; LAIT 5; LAWS 1; LMFS 2; MTCW 1, 2; NCFS 1; NFS 6, 18; RGSF 2; RGWL 3; SSC 65; SSFS 11, 16; WLCS; WLIT 1

Angelou, Maya 1928- **5: 65–92**
  See also AAYA 7, 20; AMWS 4; BLC 1; BPFB 1; BW 2, 3; BYA 2; CA 65-68; CANR 19, 42, 65, 111; CDALBS; CLC 12, 35, 64, 77, 155; CLR 53; CP 7; CPW; CSW; CWP; DA; DA3; DAB; DAC; DAM MST, MULT, POET, POP; DLB 38; EWL 3; EXPN; EXPP; LAIT 4; MAICYA 2; MAICYAS 1; MAWW; MTCW 1, 2; NCFS 2; NFS 2; PC 32; PFS 2, 3; RGAL 4; SATA 49, 136; WLCS; WYA; YAW

Atwood, Margaret (Eleanor) 1939- **5: 93–124**
  See also AAYA 12, 47; AMWS 13; BEST 89:2; BPFB 1; CA 49-52; CANR 3, 24, 33, 59, 95; CLC 2, 3, 4, 8, 13, 15, 25, 44, 84, 135; CN 7; CP 7; CPW; CWP; DA; DA3; DAB; DAC; DAM MST, NOV, POET; DLB 53, 251; EWL 3; EXPN; FW; INT CANR-24; LAIT 5; MTCW 1, 2; NFS 4, 12, 13, 14; PC 8; PFS 7; RGSF 2; SATA 50; SSC 2, 46; SSFS 3, 13; TWA; WLC; WWE 1; YAW

Austen, Jane 1775-1817 **1: 122, 125, 220; 2: 104, 196, 333–384**
  See also AAYA 19; BRW 4; BRWC 1; BRWR 2; BYA 3; CDBLB 1789-1832; DA; DA3; DAB; DAC; DAM MST, NOV; DLB 116; EXPN; LAIT 2; LATS 1; LMFS 1; NCLC 1, 13, 19, 33, 51, 81, 95, 119; NFS 1, 14, 18; TEA; WLC; WLIT 3; WYAS 1

B

Beauvoir, Simone (Lucie Ernestine Marie Bertrand) de 1908-1986 **5: 125–174**
  See also BPFB 1; CA 9-12R; 118; CANR 28, 61; CLC 1, 2, 4, 8,

F

French, Marilyn 1929- **5: 469–484**
See also BPFB 1; CA 69-72;
CANR 3, 31; CLC 10, 18, 60,
177; CN 7; CPW; DAM DRAM,
NOV, POP; FW; INT CANR-31;
MTCW 1, 2

Fuller, Margaret 1810-1850 **3:
167–198**
See also AMWS 2; CDALB 1640-
1865; DLB 1, 59, 73, 183, 223,
239; FW; LMFS 1; NCLC 5, 50;
SATA 25

G

Gilman, Charlotte (Anna) Perkins
(Stetson) 1860-1935 **1: 3–5, 314,
325, 462–463; 5: 485–528**
See also AMWS 11; BYA 11; CA
106; 150; DLB 221; EXPS; FW;
HGG; LAIT 2; MAWW; MTCW
1; RGAL 4; RGSF 2; SFW 4;
SSC 13, 62; SSFS 1, 18; TCLC
9, 37, 117

H

Hansberry, Lorraine (Vivian)
1930-1965 **6: 1–30**
See also AAYA 25; AFAW 1, 2;
AMWS 4; BLC 2; BW 1, 3; CA
109; 25-28R; CABS 3; CAD;
CANR 58; CDALB 1941-1968;
CLC 17, 62; CWD; DA; DA3;
DAB; DAC; DAM DRAM, MST,
MULT; DC 2; DFS 2; DLB 7,
38; EWL 3; FW; LAIT 4;
MTCW 1, 2; RGAL 4; TUS

Head, Bessie 1937-1986 **6: 31–62**
See also AFW; BLC 2; BW 2, 3;
CA 29-32R; 119; CANR 25, 82;
CDWLB 3; CLC 25, 67; DA3;
DAM MULT; DLB 117, 225;
EWL 3; EXPS; FW; MTCW 1,
2; RGSF 2; SSC 52; SSFS 5, 13;
WLIT 2; WWE 1

Hellman, Lillian (Florence)
1906-1984 **6: 63–88**
See also AAYA 47; AITN 1, 2;
AMWS 1; CA 13-16R; 112;
CAD; CANR 33; CLC 2, 4, 8,
14, 18, 34, 44, 52; CWD; DA3;
DAM DRAM; DC 1; DFS 1, 3,
14; DLB 7, 228; DLBY 1984;
EWL 3; FW; LAIT 3; MAWW;
MTCW 1, 2; RGAL 4; TCLC
119; TUS

Holley, Marietta 1836(?)-1926 **3:
199–220**
See also CA 118; DLB 11; TCLC
99

Hurston, Zora Neale 1891-1960 **4:
31–32, 249–251, 485–492; 6:
89–126**
See also AAYA 15; AFAW 1, 2;
AMWS 6; BLC 2; BW 1, 3; BYA
12; CA 85-88; CANR 61;
CDALBS; CLC 7, 30, 61; DA;
DA3; DAC; DAM MST, MULT,
NOV; DC 12; DFS 6; DLB 51,
86; EWL 3; EXPN; EXPS; FW;
HR 2; LAIT 3; LATS 1; LMFS 2;
MAWW; MTCW 1, 2; NFS 3;
RGAL 4; RGSF 2; SSC 4; SSFS
1, 6, 11, 19; TCLC 121, 131;
TUS; WLCS; YAW

J

Jacobs, Harriet A(nn) 1813(?)-1897
3: 221–242
See also AFAW 1, 2; DLB 239;
FW; LAIT 2; NCLC 67; RGAL 4

Jewett, (Theodora) Sarah Orne
1849-1909 **3: 243–274**
See also AMW; AMWC 2;
AMWR 2; CA 108; 127; CANR
71; DLB 12, 74, 221; EXPS;
FW; MAWW; NFS 15; RGAL 4;
RGSF 2; SATA 15; SSC 6, 44;
SSFS 4; TCLC 1, 22

Juana Inés de la Cruz, Sor
1651(?)-1695 **1: 321–358**
See also FW; HLCS 1; LAW; LC
5; PC 24; RGWL 2, 3; WLIT 1

K

Kempe, Margery 1373(?)-1440(?) **1:
87, 193, 222, 359–392**
See also DLB 146; LC 6, 56;
RGEL 2

Kingston, Maxine (Ting Ting)
Hong 1940- **4: 493–496; 6:
127–150**
See also AAL; AAYA 8, 55;
AMWS 5; BPFB 2; CA 69-72;
CANR 13, 38, 74, 87, 128;
CDALBS; CLC 12, 19, 58, 121;
CN 7; DA3; DAM MULT, NOV;
DLB 173, 212; DLBY 1980;
EWL 3; FW; INT CANR-13;
LAIT 5; MAWW; MTCW 1, 2;
NFS 6; RGAL 4; SATA 53; SSFS
3; WLCS

L

Lessing, Doris (May) 1919- **4: 272,
291, 294, 299; 6: 151–178**
See also AFW; BRWS 1; CA
9-12R; CAAS 14; CANR 33, 54,
76, 122; CD 5; CDBLB 1960 to
Present; CLC 1, 2, 3, 6, 10, 15,
22, 40, 94, 170; CN 7; DA;
DA3; DAB; DAC; DAM MST,
NOV; DLB 15, 139; DLBY
1985; EWL 3; EXPS; FW; LAIT
4; MTCW 1, 2; RGEL 2; RGSF
2; SFW 4; SSC 6, 61; SSFS 1,
12; TEA; WLCS; WLIT 2, 4

M

Millay, Edna St. Vincent 1892-1950
4: 245, 259; 6: 179–200
See also AMW; CA 104; 130;
CDALB 1917-1929; DA; DA3;
DAB; DAC; DAM MST, POET;
DLB 45, 249; EWL 3; EXPP;
MAWW; MTCW 1, 2; PAB; PC
6; PFS 3, 17; RGAL 4; TCLC 4,
49; TUS; WLCS; WP

Montagu, Mary (Pierrepont)
Wortley 1689-1762 **1: 116,
118–119, 122, 193, 219–220,
225–226, 393–422; 2: 504, 506**
See also DLB 95, 101; LC 9, 57;
PC 16; RGEL 2

Moore, Marianne (Craig)
1887-1972 **4: 244; 6: 201–232**
See also AMW; CA 1-4R; 33-36R;
CANR 3, 61; CDALB 1929-
1941; CLC 1, 2, 4, 8, 10, 13,
19, 47; DA; DA3; DAB; DAC;
DAM MST, POET; DLB 45;
DLBD 7; EWL 3; EXPP;
MAWW; MTCW 1, 2; PAB; PC
4, 49; PFS 14, 17; RGAL 4;
SATA 20; TUS; WLCS; WP

Morrison, Toni 1931- **4: 349–353;
6: 233–266**
See also AAYA 1, 22; AFAW 1, 2;
AMWC 1; AMWS 3; BLC 3;
BPFB 2; BW 2, 3; CA 29-32R;
CANR 27, 42, 67, 113, 124;
CDALB 1968-1988; CLC 4, 10,
22, 55, 81, 87, 173; CN 7;
CPW; DA; DA3; DAB; DAC;
DAM MST, MULT, NOV, POP;
DLB 6, 33, 143; DLBY 1981;
EWL 3; EXPN; FW; LAIT 2, 4;
LATS 1; LMFS 2; MAWW;
MTCW 1, 2; NFS 1, 6, 8, 14;
RGAL 4; RHW; SATA 57, 144;
SSFS 5; TUS; YAW

The Title Index alphabetically lists the titles of works written by the authors featured in volumes 1, 2, 3, 5, and 6 of Feminism in Literature and provides page numbers or page ranges where commentary on these titles can be found. English translations of foreign titles and variations of titles are cross referenced to the title under which a work was originally published. Titles of novels, dramas, nonfiction books, and poetry, short story, or essay collections are printed in italics; individual poems, short stories, and essays are printed in body type within quotation marks; page references to illustrations appear in italic.

A

Abahn Sabana David (Duras) **5**: 368

"The Abortion" (Sexton) **6**: 352, 365

The Absentee (Edgeworth) **3**: 99, 110–111, 125

Ada (Stein) **6**: 406

Adam Bede (Eliot) **3**: 130–132, *158*

"The Addict" (Sexton) **6**: 352

"Address: First Women's Rights Convention" (Stanton) **3**: 428–430

"Address to the Atheist" (Wheatley) **1**: 477

"An Address to the Deist" (Wheatley) **1**: 519

Adieux: A Farewell to Sartre (Beauvoir)
   See Le cérémonie des adieus: Suivi de entretiens avac Jean-Paul Sartre

"Advancing Luna—and Ida B. Wells" (Walker) **6**: 475–476, 480–481

"African Images" (Walker) **6**: 473

"After Death" (Rossetti) **3**: 276, 282–288

The Age of Innocence (Wharton) **6**: 495–497, 506–507, 509, *520*

Agnes of Sorrento (Stowe) **3**: 456–457

Alexander's Bridge (Cather) **5**: 213–215, 247

Alias Grace (Atwood) **5**: 101–103, 105–107

"Alicia and I Talking on Edna's Steps" (Cisneros) **5**: 272

"Alicia Who Sees Mice" (Cisneros) **5**: 272

"All God's Children Need Radios" (Sexton) **6**: 353–357

All God's Children Need Traveling Shoes (Angelou) **5**: 66–76

All My Pretty Ones (Sexton) **6**: 352, 365, 367, 369, 370

"All My Pretty Ones" (Sexton) **6**: 352, 368

All Said and Done (Beauvoir)
   See Tout compte fait

"A Allegory on Wimmen's Rights" (Holley) (sidebar) **3**: 212

De l'Allemagne (de Staël) **3**: 405–406, 423; **4**: 403–404

"Am I a Snob?" (Woolf) **6**: 567

L'amant (Duras) **3**: 362; **5**: 359–360, 364–366, 375

L'amante anglaise (Duras) **5**: 368

"Amaranth" (H. D.) **1**: 438; **5**: 336–339

"Amé, Amo, Amaré" (Cisneros) **5**: 266

"America" (Angelou) **5**: 66

American Appetites (Oates) **6**: 275–277, 279

"Amnesiac" (Plath) **6**: 312

André (Sand) **3**: 312

"The Angel at the Grave" (Wharton) **6**: 507

"Angel of Beach Houses and Picnics" (Sexton) **6**: 384

"Angel of Fire and Genitals" (Sexton) **6**: 384

"Angels of the Love Affair" (Sexton) **6**: 383–384

"Anguiano Religious Articles Rosaries Statues . . ." (Cisneros) **5**: 258

"Anna Who Was Mad" (Sexton) **6**: 364

Anne Sexton: A Self-Portrait in Letters (Sexton) **6**: 377

The Subject Index includes the authors and titles that appear in the Author Index and the Title Index as well as the names of other authors and figures that are discussed in the Feminism in Literature *set. The Subject Index also lists literary terms and topics covered in the criticism, as well as in sidebars. The index provides page numbers or page ranges where subjects are discussed and is fully cross referenced. Page references to significant discussions of authors, titles, or subjects appear in boldface; page references to illustrations appear in italic.*

Pulitzer Prize **5**: 66
rape **5**: 450
sexuality **5**: 89
"Angels of the Love Affair"
(Sexton) **6**: 383–384
"Anguiano Religious Articles
Rosaries Statues . . ." (Cisneros)
5: 258
"Anna Who Was Mad" (Sexton)
6: 364
Annan, Noël **6**: 543
*Anne Sexton: A Self-Portrait in
Letters* (Sexton) **6**: 377
"The Anniad" (Brooks) **4**: 288; **5**:
180, 184
Annie Allen (Brooks) **5**: 176, 180,
191–192
Anno Domini MCMXXI
(Akhmatova) **5**: 4, 5, 10
Annulla, An Autobiography (Mann)
4: 480
Another Part of the Forest
(Hellman) **6**: 64, 69–70, 79
"Another Song Exciting to
Spiritual Mirth" (Collins) **1**: 248
"An Answer to a Love-Letter"
(Montagu) **1**: 405
"Answer to the Letter from a
Gentleman to His Friend, Upon
the Birth of a Daughter"
(Edgeworth) **3**: 95–98
Antebellum period **2**: 59–65,
149–151, 172
See also Civil War
Antelme, Robert **5**: 378–379,
380–381
The Antelope Wife (Erdrich) **5**: 434
Anthologies **5**: 511, 515
Anthony, Susan B. **2**: 226–229;
(sidebar) **2**: 227; **2**: *284*; **4**:
130–131, 200
arrest of **2**: 245–246, 264
Gage, Matilda Joslyn and **2**:
290–292
Holley, Marietta and **3**: 209
National American Woman
Suffrage Association and **2**:
235, 253
National Woman Suffrage As-
sociation and **2**: 227, 254
Revolution **2**: 251–252
Seneca Falls Woman's Rights
Convention **2**: 285
Sixteenth Amendment and **2**:
274
Stanton, Elizabeth Cady and
(sidebar) **3**: 441; **3**: 449–450
temperance and **2**: 227
Woodhull, Victoria and **3**: 6
"The Anti-Feminist Woman"
(Rich) **6**: 346
Antinomianism **1**: 147
Antipater of Sidon **1**: 464
The Antiphon (Barnes) **4**: 295
Anti-Semitism **4**: 297–299; **6**: 427

Antislavery. *See* Abolitionist
movement
Anti-Slavery Advocate **3**: 226
Anti-Suffrage League **4**: 140–141
Antoinette, Marie **3**: 414–419
Anton, Charles **3**: 81
Antonie (Herbert) **1**: 202–203
Apartheid **6**: 31–32, 50
Aphrodite **3**: 14–26
Apollinaire, Guillaume **4**: 89–90
*The Apparitional Lesbian: Female
Homosexuality and Modern
Culture* (Castle) **4**: 530–531
"Appeal to the U. S. Senate to
Submit the Federal Amendment
for Woman Suffrage" (Wilson) **4**:
134–135
*An Appeal to the Women of the
United States* (National Woman
Suffrage and Educational
Committee) **2**: 223–226
"The Applicant" (Plath) **6**: 303,
304
April Twilights (Cather) **5**: 247
Aquinas, Thomas **1**: 57–58
Arcana, Judith **6**: 445
Arce, Dr. **1**: 324–325
Arden, Jane **1**: 540–543
Arenal, Electa **1**: 337–349
Aria de Capo (Millay) **6**: 189–191
Ariel (Plath) **6**: 294, 297–298, 311
"Ariel" (Plath) **6**: 295, 299,
316–318
Ariès, Philippe **3**: 303–304
"Arion" (Eliot) **3**: 159
Aristocracy. *See* Elite
Aristotle
on gender **1**: 65
on rape **1**: 67
on sexual reproduction **1**: 20,
66
"Armgart" (Eliot) **3**: 159
Armstrong, Nancy **3**: 120, 126,
473
Arndt, Walter **5**: 12–21
Arnow, Harriet **4**: 294–295
*Around 1981: Academic Feminist
Literary Theory* (Gallop) **1**: 569;
4: 526
*Around the World with Josiah
Allen's Wife* (Holley) **3**: 199–200
Art
in 19th-century France **2**:
79–82
20th century **4**: 85–94
for art's sake **4**: 331–332
female experience in **5**: 473–
474
feminist aesthetics **5**: 471–477
feminist perspective **5**: 472–
473
in medieval period **1**: 56-63
propaganda as **4**: 331
as reflection of gender roles **2**:
77–85

Rookwood School of Pottery **2**:
84
women's incapability to
contribute **2**: 178–186
World's Columbian Exposi-
tion, Women's Building **2**:
84–85
See also Visual arts; specific
artists and movements
Art Nouveau **5**: 15–17
"Artemis" (Broumas) **4**: 516
Arts and Crafts Movement **2**:
82–84
*Arts of the Possible: Essays and
Conversations* (Rich) **6**: 330
"As a Wife Has a Cow: A
Love-Story" (Stein) **6**: 430
Asceticism **1**: 56–57
Ascher, Carol (sidebar) **5**: 151
Ashbridge, Elizabeth **1**: 148–149,
251, 261–266
Asian American women
20th-century writers **4**: 493–
497
cultural identity **6**: 437–442
myths of origin **6**: 455
Sui Sin Far **4**: 339–342
"Asparagus" (Stein) **6**: 419
The Assassins (Oates) **6**: 268
Assimilation **5**: 194–195; **6**: 16–17
Astell, Mary (sidebar) **1**: 409; **1**:
413
"At Chênière Caminada"
(Chopin) **3**: 10
At Fault (Chopin) **3**: 2, 9
At Mrs. Lippincote's (Taylor) **4**:
267–269
"At the 'Cadian Ball" (Chopin) **3**:
10
At the Foot of the Mountain
(theater) **4**: 478–479
Athenaeum **2**: 475, 498; **3**: 276
"Athenaïse" (Chopin) **3**: 10
Athletics **4**: 420
Atkinson, Ti-Grace **4**: 523–524
Atkinson v. Atkinson (1980) **4**: 420
Atlantic Monthly **2**: 147; **3**: 243,
457; **5**: 509
An Atlas of the Difficult World
(Rich) **6**: 330
Atwood, Margaret **5**: *93*, **93–123**
autobiographies **5**: 108–112
food imagery in works
(sidebar) **5**: 114
on male stereotypes (sidebar)
5: 102
principal works **5**: 94
protagonists of **5**: 100–107
"Aubade" (Lowell) **4**: 255
Auden, W. H. (sidebar) **6**: 208
Augustus **1**: 45–47
"Aunt Jennifer's Tigers" (Rich) **6**:
333–334

H

Gwathmey, Gwendolyn B. 3: 208–218
"Gwendolyn Brooks" (Mullaney) (sidebar) 5: 188

H. D. 3: *313*; 4: 287, 291–293; 5: **313–357**
   Aldington, Richard and 5: 334–335, 337, 339
   autobiographies 5: 315–317, 329–330, 348–356
   Award of Merit Medal 5: 314
   Bryher and 5: 337
   compared to Dickinson, Emily 5: 355
   in *Contemporary Literature* 5: 319–322
   critical neglect of 5: 317–333
   Durand, Lionel and 5: 324–325
   feminist theory and (sidebar) 5: 335
   Freud, Sigmund and 5: 319–320
   Heydt, Erich and 5: 349
   Imagism 5: 313–314, 318, 328, 342
   lesbianism 5: 337
   Levertov, Denise and 5: 329
   male literary criticism of 5: 317–326
   masochism 4: 291–294
   mythology and 5: 322–323, 327, 330–332, 347–356
   penis envy and 5: 320, 323
   Pound, Ezra and 5: 313, 318, 328, 349, 351
   principal works 5: 315
   psychoanalysis and 5: 314, 319–321
   Sappho and (sidebar) 1: 433; 1: 436–439; 5: 334–341
"H. D. and Sappho: 'A Precious Inch of Palimpsest'" (Rohrbach) 5: 334–342
"H. D. and the 'Blameless Physician'" (Holland) 5: 319–321
"H. D. and the Poetics of 'Spiritual Realism'" (Riddel) 5: 319–321
Hacker, Marilyn 6: 185
Hagen, Lyman B. 5: 87–91
Haggard, H. Rider 3: 9
Hagiography 1: 304–307
Hagood, Margaret Jarman 3: 32–33
Haight, Amanda (sidebar) 5: 23
"Hairs" (Cisneros) 5: 258
Hakluyt, Richard 6: 553–554

Halifax, George Savile, Marquis of 1: 108–109, 141–142
Halkett, Anne 1: 230
Hall, James 2: 161
Hallett, Judith P. 1: 44–48
Hamelton, Mary 2: 10
Hamilton, Catherine J. 2: 181
Hamilton, Cecily 4: 137–138, 140
Hammett, Dashiell 6: 63–64
Hammon, Jupiter (sidebar) 1: 510
"A Handfull of Holesome (though Homelie) Hearbs" (Wheathill) 1: 104–108
The Handmaid's Tale (Atwood) 5: 93–94, 101, 105–107, 108
Haney-Peritz, Janice 5: 515
Hankins, Liz Porter (sidebar) 6: 381
Hansberry, Lorraine 6: *1*, **1–30**
   chronology of life 6: 8–9
   Du Bois, W. E. B. and 6: 15–16
   feminist movement and 6: 10–14
   Nemiroff, Robert and 6: 1, 2, 9
   New York Drama Critics Circle Award 6: 1, 2, 8–9
   political activism of 6: 11–14
   principal works 6: 3
   on race issue 6: 11–13
   radicalism and 6: 11
   social change and 6: 12–14
   socialism and 6: 13
   Theatre of the Absurd 6: 9–10
Hanson, Elizabeth 1: 257–261
Happersett, Minor v. (1875) 2: 246–247
"Happy Women" (Alcott) (sidebar) 2: 310
Hardy, Thomas 2: 132–133
Harlem 4: 31–32
Harlem Renaissance 4: 30–32
   African American playwrights 4: 331–337
   women writers 4: 248–251
   See also names of writers
Harmonium (H. D.) 5: 327
Harper, Frances Ellen Watkins (sidebar) 2: 13
   American Woman Suffrage Association and 2: 268–269
   on slavery 2: 49–50
   on suffrage 2: 251
   themes in poetry 2: 143–146
   on women in politics 2: 12–15
Harper, Ida Husted 4: 129
Harper's Bazaar 4: 125
The Harp-Weaver and Other Poems (Millay) 6: 179–180, 189, 192–193
"Harriet Beecher Stowe's Christian Feminism in *The Minister's Wooing*: A Precedent for Emily Dickinson" (Ramirez) 3: 480–490

"Harriet Beecher Stowe's Interest in Sojourner Truth, Black Feminist" (Lebeden) (sidebar) 3: 466
"Harriet Jacobs' *Incidents in the Life of a Slave Girl*: The Re-Definition of the Slave Narrative Genre" (Braxton) 3: 224–228
Harris, Susan K. 2: 120–129; 3: 487
Harris v. McRae (1976) 4: 419
Harrison, Jane 6: 332
Hatton, Bessie 4: 137–138
Haunted (Oates) 6: 268
"The Haunted Chamber" (Chopin) 3: 6–7
The Haunted Marsh (Sand). *See La mare au diable*
Hause, Steven C. 2: 50–53
Hawaii 4: 423
Haworth Village 2: *417*
Hawthorne, Nathaniel 4: 339; 5: 514–515
Haywood, Eliza 1: 120, 126
Hazards of Helen (Edison Company) 4: 112–114
He and She (Crothers) 4: 305–306, 320–322
"He fumbles at your Soul" (Dickinson) 3: 54, 73
"He Wrote the History Book" (Moore) 6: 212
Head above Water (Emecheta) 5: 418
Head, Bessie 6: *31*, **31–61**
   apartheid 6: 31–32, 50
   autobiographies 6: 32
   "great man" and 6: 55–56
   patriarchy 6: 53–55
   presence of evil (sidebar) 6: 37
   principal works 6: 32
   on South African feminism 6: 38–59
   storytelling 6: 51–53
   on women writers (sidebar) 6: 49
Healey, Dorothy Ray 4: 45
Heape, Walter 4: 76, 80
Heard, Josephine 2: 144, 145, 146
"The Heart Knoweth its Own Bitterness" (Rossetti) 3: 295
The Heart of a Woman (Angelou) 5: 66, 67–76, 83–91
Heartbreak (Dworkin) 5: 406
"Heat" (H. D.) 5: 317, 319
The Heat of the Day (Bowen) 4: 279
"Heaven is not Closed" (Head) 6: 52
Heaven Realiz'd (Davy) 1: 253
"Heavy Women" (Plath) 6: 310
Hecate 3: 85–89
Hedges, Elaine 5: 512
Hedrick, Joan D. 3: 482–483, 487

SUBJECT INDEX

Scoundrel Time (Hellman) **6:** 63–64, 80

Scudéry, Madeleine de (sidebar) **1:** 200

Sculpture **4:** 92

SDS (Students for a Democratic Society) **4:** 388

Sea Garden (H. D.) **5:** 314, 348

The Sea Wall (Duras). *See Un barrage contre le Pacifique*

The Searching Wind (Hellman) **6:** 64, 80

Sears, Albert C. **2:** 187–194

A Season in Hell: A Memoir (French) **5:** 469, 470–471

Second April (Millay) **6:** 180, 187, 195

"The Second Coming of Aphrodite: Kate Chopin's Fantasy of Desire" (Gilbert and Gubar) **3:** 5–30

The Second Common Reader (Woolf, V.) **6:** 567

The Second Sex (Beauvoir). *See Le deuxième sex*

"The Second Wave: A Multiplicity of Concerns" (Burke) **4:** 467–483

Second-Class Citizen (Emecheta) **5:** 417–418

"A Secret" (Plath) **6:** 300–301, 303

"A Secret and Swift Messenger" (Edgeworth) **3:** 104

Secretary's Bill of Rights **4:** 415

Sedgwick, Catharine Maria **3:** *333*, 333–362

Sedgwick, Eve Kosofsky **4:** 529–533

Sedgwick, Pamela Dwight **3:** 340–341

Seek and Find (Rossetti) **3:** 276, 278

The Selected Letters of Marianne Moore (Moore) **6:** 202–207

Selected Poems (Akhmatova) **5:** 5

Selected Poems (Millay) **6:** 185

Selected Poems (Moore) **6:** 221

Selections from George Eliot's Letters (Eliot) **3:** 158

Selfhood
  African American women's struggle **3:** 229–235
  in *The Bell Jar* **6:** 318–326
  in *Eighty Years and More (1815-1897): Reminiscences of Elizabeth Cady Stanton* **3:** 432–435
  in "Everyday Use" **6:** 484
  in "Fever 103°" **6:** 299–300
  Walker, Alice and **6:** 470–473
  in *The Woman Warrior* **6:** 143–148

Self-identity
  in *China Men* **6:** 131–139
  in "The Dilettante" **6:** 515–516

female characters of Cisneros, Sandra **5:** 257–278

films and **4:** 108–114

Kingston, Maxine Hong **6:** 139–143
  in *Maud Martha* **5:** 200–208
  in *Song of Solomon* **6:** 246
  in *Their Eyes Were Watching God* **6:** 102–107
  in *The Woman Warrior* **6:** 131–139

Selous, Trista **5:** 365–376

Seneca Falls Woman's Rights Convention, 1888 **2:** 285; **4:** 312–313
  Anthony, Susan B. and **2:** 285
  Declaration of Sentiments **2:** 59–60, 209–211
  feminist movement **2:** 59–60, 207
  revolutionary event **2:** 236–239
  Stanton, Elizabeth Cady and **2:** 7–9, 209–212, 285; **3:** 428–430

Senf, Carol A. **2:** 413–420, 448–457

"Señor: para responderos" (Cruz) **1:** 342–343

Sense and Sensibility (Austen) **2:** 334, 347–348

"Sensuality Plunging Barefoot into Thorns" (Cisneros) **5:** 266

Sentimental Modernism: Women Writers and the Revolution of the Word (Clark) **6:** 185

Sentimental novels **2:** 121–129; **3:** 209–211

"Separate But Unequal: Woman's Sphere and the New Art" (Chadwick) **2:** 77–86

Separate spheres. *See* Ideology of women, in Victorian era

"The Separative Self in Sylvia Plath's *The Bell Jar*" (Bonds) **6:** 318–327

Seraph on the Suwanee (Hurston) **6:** 90, 100, 118–124

The Seraphim, and Other Poems (Browning, E.) **2:** 467, 468

"Serenade: Any Man to Any Woman" (Sitwell) **4:** 279

Serialization
  19-century literature **2:** 194–204
  films **4:** 101–102

Sermons of John Calvin, Npon the Songe that Ezechias made after he had bene sicke (Lok) **1:** 153–154

Sermons to Young Women (Fordyce) **1:** 142–143

Serowe: Village of the Rain Wind (Head) **6:** 32, 51–52

"712" (Dickinson) **3:** 50–51, 80–89

"754" (Dickinson) **3:** 58

"781" (Dickinson) **3:** 484

"786" (Dickinson) **3:** 60

"The Seventh Book of Questions" (Birgitta of Sweden) **1:** 12

Sex Antagonism (Heape) **4:** 76, 80

Sex in Education: or A Fair Chance for the Girls (Clarke, E.) **2:** 311

Sexism **4:** 429; **5:** 379
  See also Feminism

Sexism and God-Talk: Toward a Feminist Theology (Ruether) **1:** 89

Sexton, Anne **6:** *351*, 351–387, *380*
  awards **6:** 352, 370
  Christian iconography in poetry **6:** 382–385
  confessional poetry **6:** 368–370
  criticism of **6:** 365–366
  Dickey, James and **6:** 385
  Gray, Mary and **6:** 374–377
  imagery **6:** 382–385
  Kumin, Maxine and **6:** 357–372, 379
  Lowell, Robert and **6:** 383
  mental illness of **6:** 371
  Middlebrook, Diane on (sidebar) **6:** 371
  Neruda, Pablo and **6:** 383
  Oedipus and **6:** 381–382
  Paris Review interview **6:** 372–375
  poems as reflection of poet (sidebar) **6:** 381
  principal works **6:** 353
  psychotherapy and **6:** 374
  Pulitzer Prize **6:** 352, 358, 370, 372
  Shelley Award **6:** 352
  suicide of **6:** 366–367, 371, 372–373
  writing workshops **6:** 359–362, 367–368, 373

Sexton, Joy Ladd **6:** *380*

Sexton, Linda Gray **6:** *380*

Sexual abuse **6:** 404
  See also Rape

Sexual differentiation. *See* Gender

Sexual discrimination
  in education **4:** 413–414
  Newsweek and **4:** 413
  in Virginia **4:** 422

Sexual harassment
  California Sanitary Canning Company strike **4:** 45
  Talihook Association **4:** 363
  Thomas, Clarence of Anita Hill **4:** 362–363; **6:** 238–243

Sexual intercourse **5:** 406, 411, 415

Sexual Politics (Millett) (sidebar) **4:** 80

"The Sexual Politics of Sickness" (Ehrenreich and English) **2:** 67–71